1994

Mobil
Travel
Guide®

Southeast

Alabama

Florida

Georgia

Kentucky

Mississippi

Tennessee

Prentice Hall Travel

This series of regional guides is published by Prentice Hall Travel in collaboration with Mobil Corporation, which has sponsored the books since 1958. The aim of the *Mobil Travel Guide* is to provide the most comprehensive, up-to-date, and useful regional guides at the lowest possible price. All properties listed are inspected by trained, experienced field representatives. There is no charge to any establishment for inclusion in these guides, and only establishments that meet *Mobil Travel Guide* criteria are listed.

Every effort has been made to select a variety of all types of lodging and dining establishments available in a given locale. However, space limitations make it impossible to include every fine establishment, and the fact that some omissions occur does not imply adverse criticism or inferiority to listed establishments.

Information in the *Mobil Travel Guide* is revised and updated yearly. Ratings are reviewed annually on the basis of reports from our field representatives, opinions of many local and regional consultants and careful analysis of all available relevant material, including more than 100,000 opinions from users of the *Mobil Travel Guide*. All ratings are impartial and every effort is made to rate fairly and consistently.

At the time of inspection, all establishments were clean, well-managed and met *Mobil Travel Guide* standards. Occasionally an establishment may go out of business or change ownership after date of publication. By calling ahead readers can avoid the disappointment of a closed or changed establishment.

By revising our listings yearly, we hope to make a contribution to maintaining and raising the standards of restaurants and accommodations available to travelers across the country. We are most interested in hearing from our readers about their experiences at the establishments we list, as well as any other comments about the quality and usefulness of *Mobil Travel Guide*. Every communication from our readers is carefully studied with the object of making the *Mobil Travel Guide* better. Please address suggestions or comments about attractions, accommodations, or restaurants to *Mobil Travel Guide*, Prentice Hall Travel, 108 Wilmot Road, Suite 450, Deerfield, IL 60015.

THE EDITORS

Guide Staff

Managing Director and Editor-in-Chief
Alice M. Wisel

Editorial Manager
Janet Y. Arthur

Inspection Manager
Denni Hosch

Production Coordinator
Diane E. Connolly

Staff Assistant
Margaret Bolton

Editors
Thomas Grant   Ann Mendes   Peter Uremovic
Michael Warnecke

Acknowledgements

We gratefully acknowledge the help of our 100 field representatives for their efficient and perceptive inspection of every hotel, motel, motor hotel, inn, resort and restaurant listed; the proprietors of these establishments for their cooperation in showing their facilities and providing information about them; our many friends and users of previous editions of *Mobil Travel Guide;* and the thousands of Chambers of Commerce, Convention and Visitors' Bureaus, city, state and provincial tourism offices and government agencies for their time and information.

Mobil

Published in 1994 by Prentice Hall General Reference and Travel A Division of Simon & Schuster Inc.
15 Columbus Circle
New York, NY 10023

ISBN 0-671-874438
ISSN 0076-9843

Manufactured in the United States of America
10 9 8 7 6 5 4 3 2 1

MAP SYMBOLS

ROAD CLASSIFICATIONS

CONTROLLED ACCESS HIGHWAYS
(Entrance and Exit only at Interchanges)   Interchanges

TOLL HIGHWAYS

OTHER DIVIDED HIGHWAYS

PRINCIPAL THROUGH HIGHWAYS   Paved   Gravel

OTHER THROUGH HIGHWAYS   Paved   Gravel   Dirt

CONNECTING HIGHWAYS   Paved   Gravel   Dirt

HIGHWAY MARKERS

INTERSTATE 80   UNITED STATES 40   STATE AND PROVINCIAL 34

TRANS-CANADA   QUEBEC AUTOROUTE 15   MEXICO FEDERAL 2

SPECIAL SYMBOLS

STATE AND PROVINCIAL PARKS
With Campsites   Without Campsites

RECREATION AREAS
With Campsites   Without Campsites

POINTS OF INTEREST

SCHEDULED AIRLINE STOPS

MILITARY AIRPORTS

PORTS OF ENTRY ●
Open 24 Hours   Inquire Locally

MILEAGES

TIME ZONE BOUNDARIES

MOUNTAIN PASSES
Usually closed in Winter
Usually open in Winter

SPECIAL FEATURES

NATIONAL PARKS, MONUMENTS AND RECREATION AREAS

NATIONAL FORESTS

INDIAN RESERVATIONS

MILITARY RESERVATIONS

POPULATION SYMBOLS

Capital Cities   10,000 to 25,000   100,000 to 500,000

Under 5,000   25,000 to 50,000   500,000 and over

5,000 to 10,000   50,000 to 100,000

*All persons (American citizens and aliens) are required under penalty of law to report for customs inspection when entering the United States. All persons departing from the United States are advised to contact customs officials regarding re-entry.

Contents

Southeast

Introduction

Maps

A map of each state covered in this volume precedes the introduction. Larger, more detailed maps are available in the *Mobil Road Atlas* in bookstores and at many Mobil service stations.

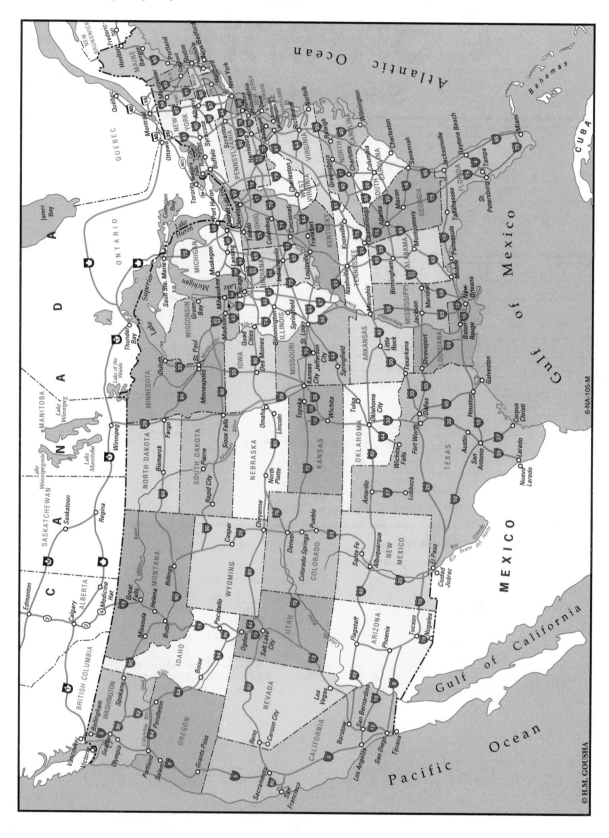

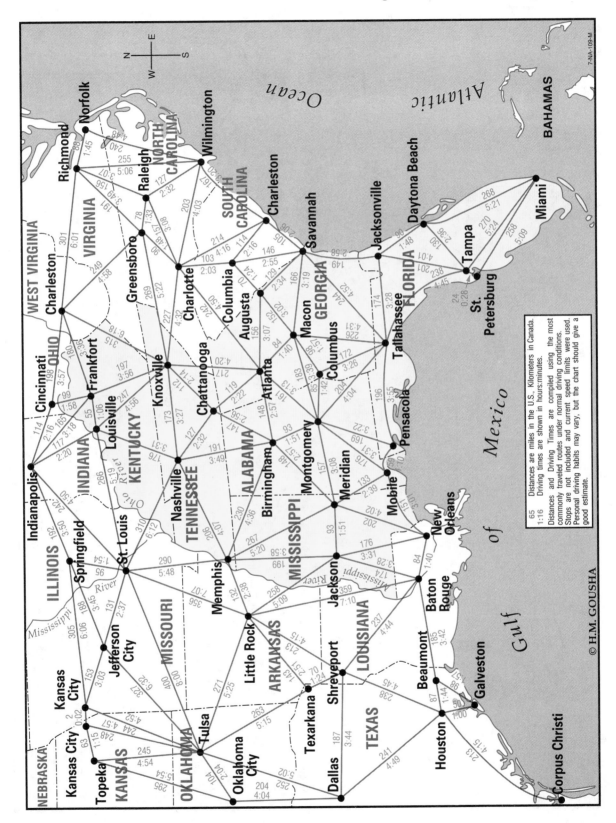

Distances are miles in the U.S. Kilometers in Canada.
Driving times are shown in hours:minutes.

Distances and Driving Times are compiled using the most commonly traveled routes under normal driving conditions. Stops are not included and current speed limits were used. Personal driving habits may vary, but the chart should give a good estimate.

© H.M. GOUSHA

FLORIDA

MILES
:KILOMETERS

GEORGIA

ALA.

WESTERN FLORIDA

GULF OF MEXICO

ATLANTIC OCEAN

FLORIDA KEYS

© H.M. GOUSHA

M-11-UH-1085-S

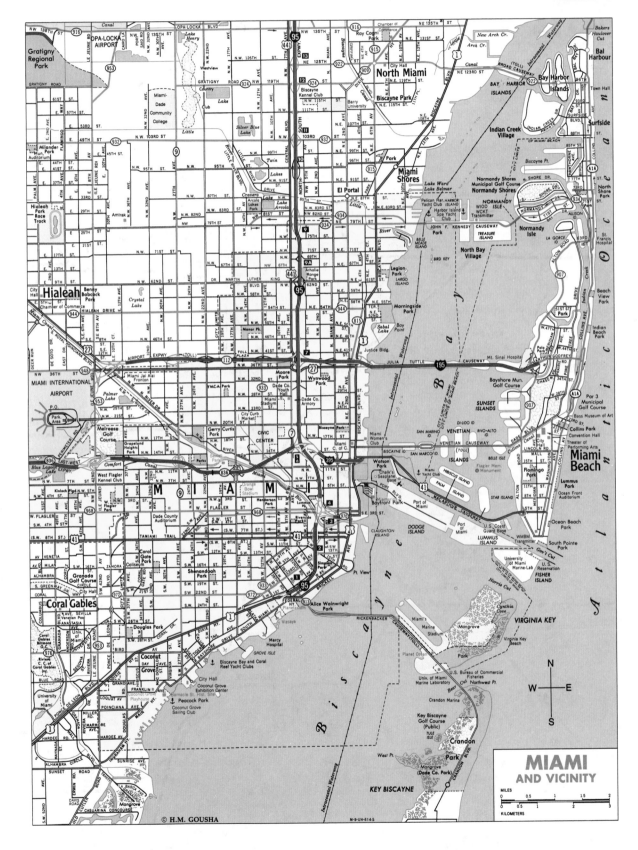

MIAMI
AND VICINITY

MILES
KILOMETERS

© H.M. GOUSHA

M-9-UH-614-5

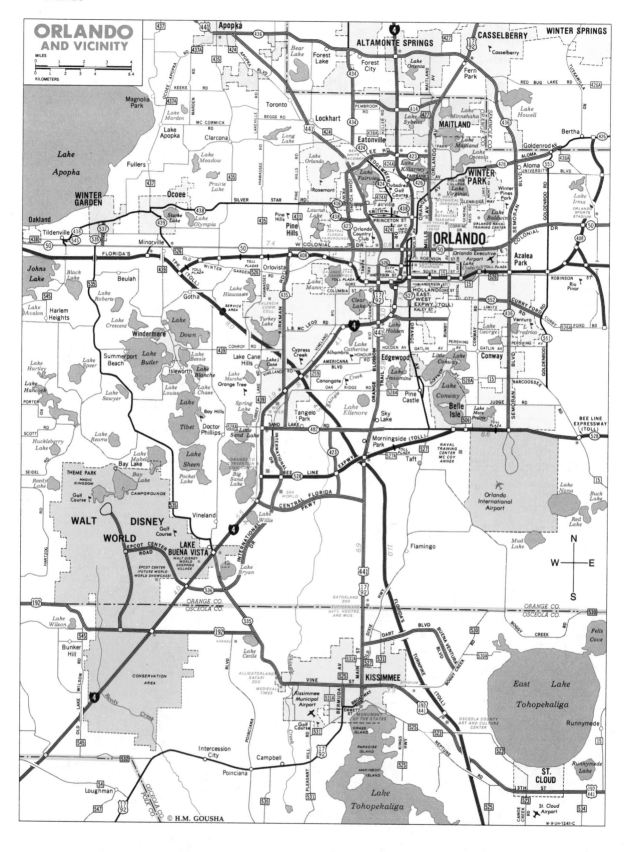

ORLANDO
AND VICINITY

© H.M. GOUSHA

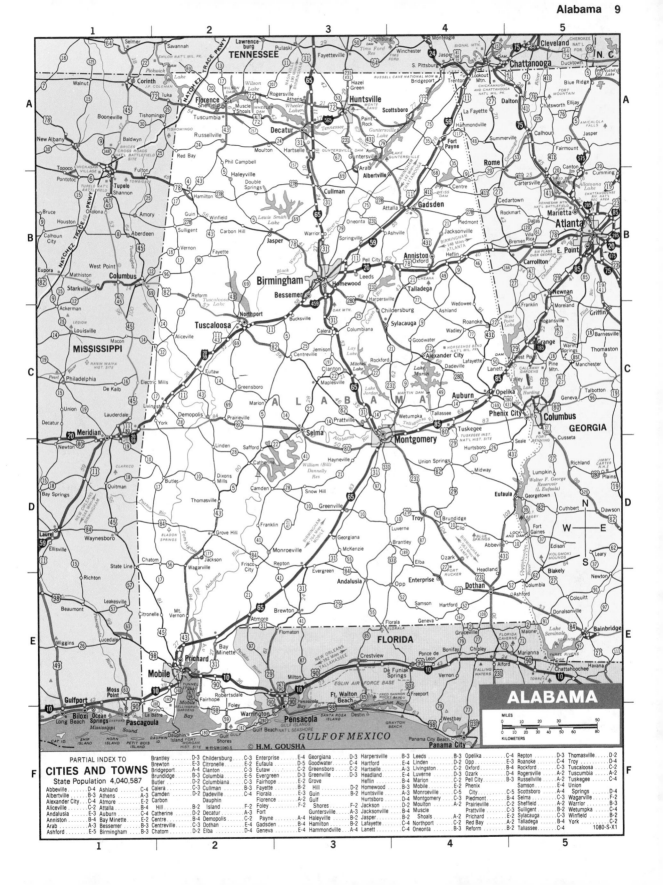

© H.M. GOUSHA

1080-S-X1

M-11-UH-1080-5

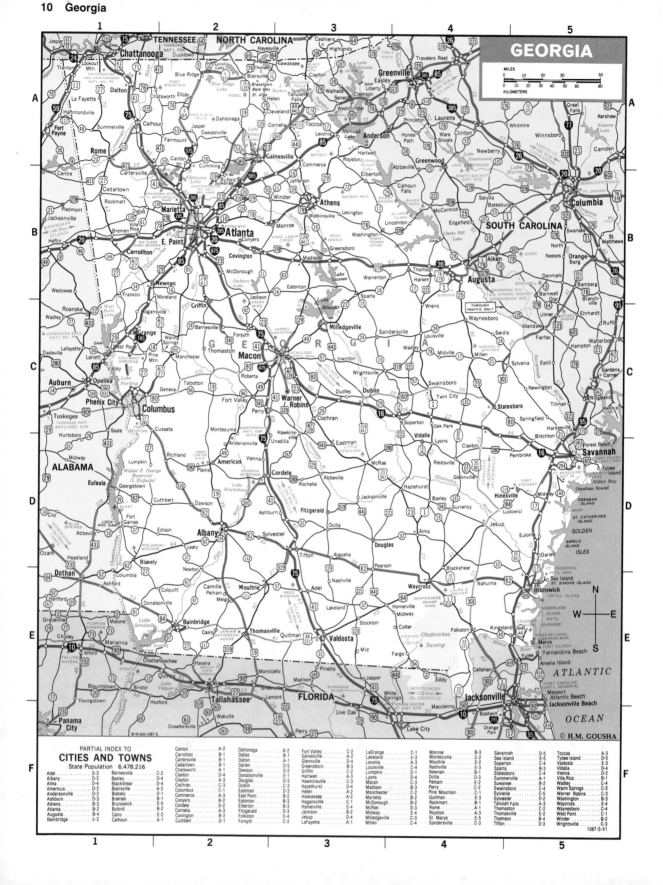

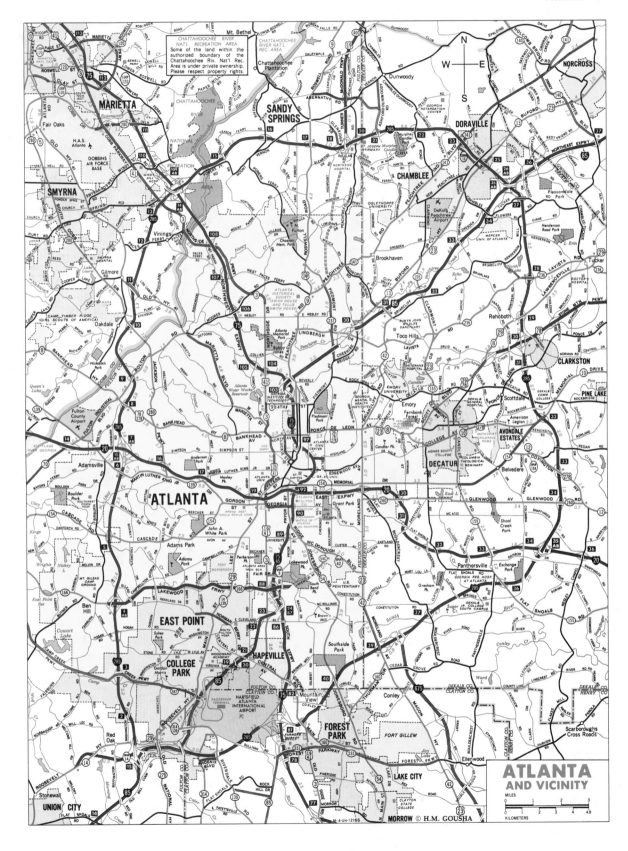

ATLANTA
AND VICINITY

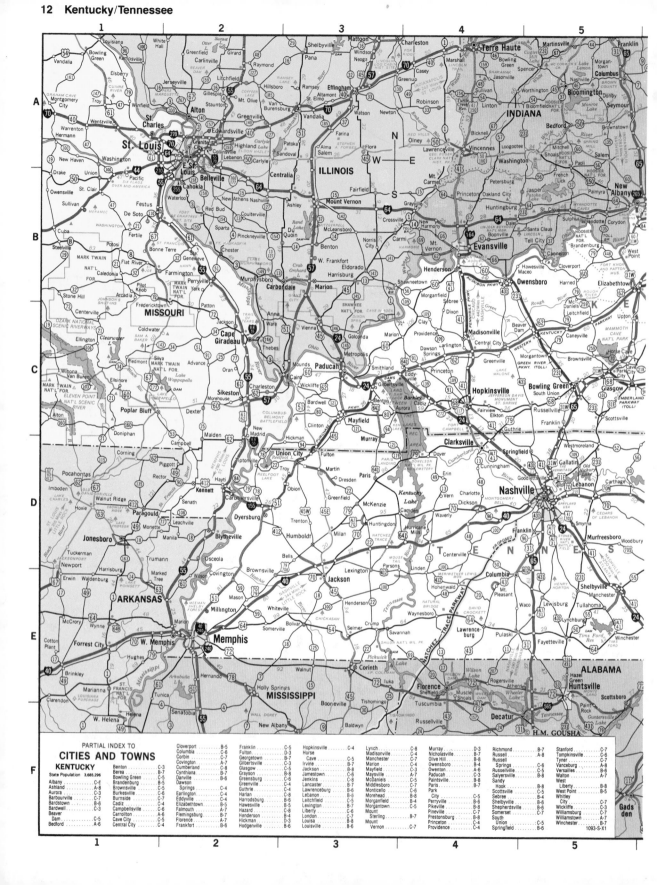

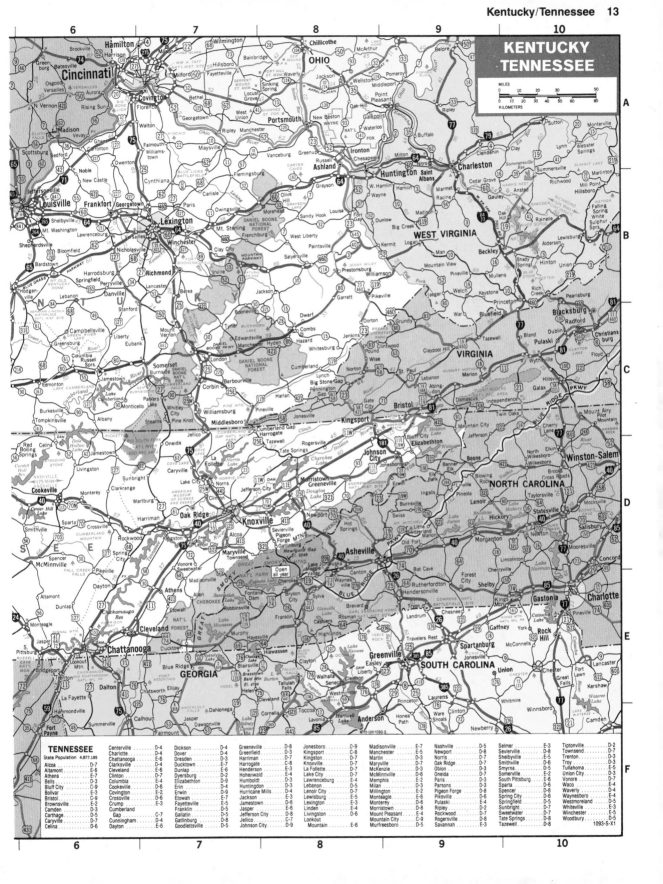

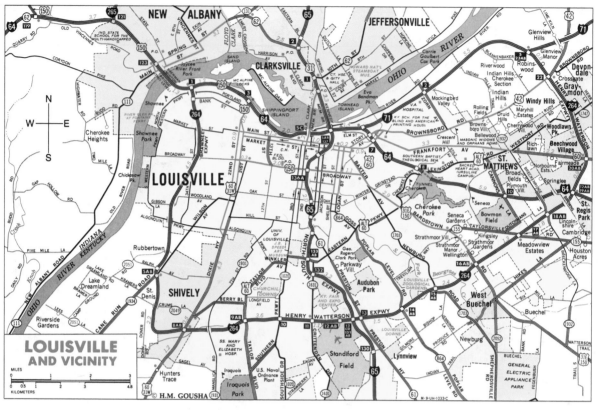

LOUISVILLE
AND VICINITY

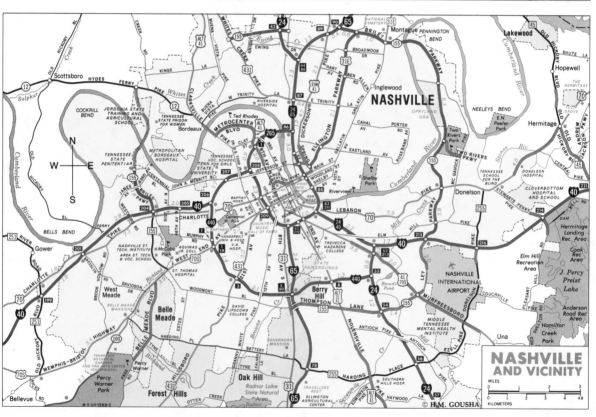

NASHVILLE
AND VICINITY

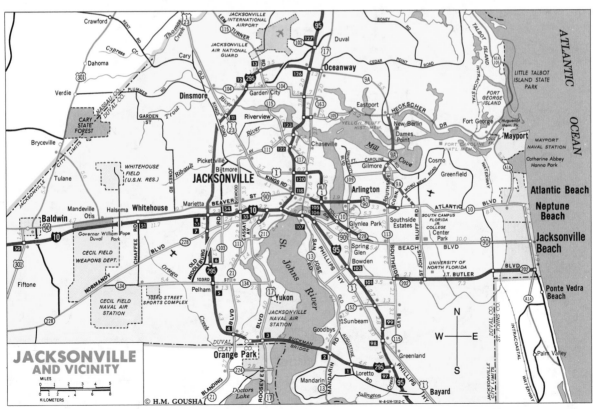

MISSISSIPPI

© H.M. Gousha

M-11-UH-1099-S

YOU CAN HELP MAKE *MOBIL TRAVEL GUIDE* MORE ACCURATE AND USEFUL

ALL INFORMATION WILL BE KEPT CONFIDENTIAL

Your Name _____
(Please Print)

Street _____

City, State _____

Were Children with you on trip? ☐ Yes ☐ No

No. people in your party _____

Your occupation _____

1.

Establishment name _____

Hotel ☐ Resort ☐ Cafeteria ☐
Motel ☐ Inn ☐ Restaurant ☐

Street _____ City _____ State _____

Do you agree with our description? ☐ Yes ☐ No If not, give reason _____

Please give us your opinion of the following:

ROOM DECOR	CLEANLINESS	SERVICE	FOOD
☐ Excellent	☐ Spotless	☐ Excellent	☐ Excellent
☐ Good	☐ Clean	☐ Good	☐ Good
☐ Fair	☐ Unclean	☐ Fair	☐ Fair
☐ Poor	☐ Dirty	☐ Poor	☐ Poor

1994 *GUIDE* RATING _____ ★
CHECK YOUR SUGGESTED RATING BELOW:
☐ ★ good, satisfactory ☐ ★★★★ outstanding
☐ ★★ very good ☐ ★★★★★ one of best
☐ ★★★ excellent in country
☐ ✓ unusually good value

Comments: _____
_____

Date of visit _____

First visit ☐ Yes ☐ No

2.

Establishment name _____

Hotel ☐ Resort ☐ Cafeteria ☐
Motel ☐ Inn ☐ Restaurant ☐

Street _____ City _____ State _____

Do you agree with our description? ☐ Yes ☐ No If not, give reason _____

Please give us your opinion of the following:

ROOM DECOR	CLEANLINESS	SERVICE	FOOD
☐ Excellent	☐ Spotless	☐ Excellent	☐ Excellent
☐ Good	☐ Clean	☐ Good	☐ Good
☐ Fair	☐ Unclean	☐ Fair	☐ Fair
☐ Poor	☐ Dirty	☐ Poor	☐ Poor

1994 *GUIDE* RATING _____ ★
CHECK YOUR SUGGESTED RATING BELOW:
☐ ★ good, satisfactory ☐ ★★★★ outstanding
☐ ★★ very good ☐ ★★★★★ one of best
☐ ★★★ excellent in country
☐ ✓ unusually good value

Comments: _____
_____

Date of visit _____

First visit ☐ Yes ☐ No

1994   WHAT TO SEE AND DO—ATTRACTIONS/EVENTS

3.

Name of Attraction/Event _____

Listed in _____ Date of visit _____
City   State

Do you agree with our description? _____ Yes _____ No

Please give your opinion of the attraction/event:
_____ Excellent _____ Good _____ Fair _____ Poor

Comments: _____
_____
_____
_____

FOLD IN THIRDS AND TAPE (OR SEAL) FOR MAILING—DO NOT STAPLE

CUT ALONG DOTTED LINE

Revised editions are now being prepared for publication next year:

Northeastern States: Connecticut, Maine, Massachusetts, New Hampshire, New York, Rhode Island, Vermont, Eastern Canada.

Middle Atlantic States: Delaware, District of Columbia, Maryland, New Jersey, North Carolina, Pennsylvania, South Carolina, Virginia, West Virginia.

Southeastern States: Alabama, Florida, Georgia, Kentucky, Mississippi, Tennessee.

Great Lakes States: Illinois, Indiana, Michigan, Ohio, Wisconsin; Ontario, Canada.

Northwestern States: Idaho, Iowa, Minnesota, Montana, Nebraska, North Dakota, Oregon, South Dakota, Washington, Wyoming; Western Canada.

Southwestern States: Arkansas, Colorado, Kansas, Louisiana, Missouri, New Mexico, Oklahoma, Texas.

Frequent Travelers' Guide to Major Cities: Detailed coverage of 46 Major Cities, plus airport and street maps.

Mobil Travel Guides are available at Mobil Service Stations, bookstores, or by mail from Mobil Travel Guides, P.O. Box 493, Mt. Morris, IL 61054.

HOW CAN WE IMPROVE *MOBIL TRAVEL GUIDE?*

Mobil Travel Guide is constantly revising and improving. All attractions are updated and all listings are revised and evaluated annually. You can contribute to the accuracy and usefulness of the *Guide* by sending us your reactions to the places you have visited. Your suggestions for improvement of the *Guide* are also welcome. Just complete this prepaid mailing form or address letters to: *Mobil Travel Guide,* Prentice Hall Press, Suite 450, 108 Wilmot Road, Deerfield, IL 60015. The editors of the *Mobil Travel Guide* appreciate your useful comments.

Have you sent us one of these forms before?   ☐ Yes   ☐ No

Please make any general comment here. Thanks! _____

_____

_____

_____

Introduction

The *Mobil Travel Guide* offers complete travel planning information for recreational and business travelers alike. Whether you are planning an extended trip, getting away for the weekend or dining close to home, you will find the current detailed information you need to know in this *Guide*. By selecting and confirming your destination in advance and driving the most direct route, you can save time and money. Use your *Guide* to plan activities in advance so that when you arrive you won't waste valuable time deciding what to do.

An outstanding feature of the *Mobil Travel Guide* is its valuable quality ratings and information on more than 20,000 lodgings and restaurants. **There is no charge to an establishment for inclusion in *Mobil Travel Guide* publications.**

During the inspection of establishments, field representatives identify fire protection equipment in lodgings. The inspection does not extend to every room nor does it determine whether the equipment is working properly. The ⓢ symbol appearing at the end of a lodging listing indicates the presence of smoke detectors and/or sprinkler systems. This symbol does not appear in our restaurant listings because the presence of this equipment is assumed. Travelers wishing to gain more information on fire protection systems at properties should contact the establishment directly to verify the installation and working condition of their systems.

The Ⓓ symbol appearing at the end of a lodging or restaurant listing indicates compliance with the *Mobil Travel Guide* Disabled Criteria. Details on the standards required for a property to receive this symbol are given in the section entitled "Disabled Traveler Information" in this Introduction.

The *Mobil Travel Guide* Disabled Criteria are unique to our publication and were designed to meet the standards developed by our editorial staff. Please do not confuse them with the universal handicap symbol requirements. Travelers wishing to gain more information on facilities and services for the disabled should contact the establishments directly.

The 7 regional editions of the *Mobil Travel Guide* cover the 48 contiguous states and selected cities in 8 Canadian provinces. In each book the information is organized in the same easy-to-follow format. The states are arranged alphabetically and begin with a general introduction covering vital statistics, historical and geographical data, hunting, fishing, and seat belt regulations, visitor centers, and listings of state recreational areas, national forests, National Park Service Areas, interstate highways and ski areas (where applicable).

Cities are arranged alphabetically within each state. Next to city names are map coordinates, for example Boston (B-4), that refer to the appropriate color state map in the front of the *Guide*. Under the bold rule you will find population figures taken from the most recent census of the Bureau of Census, Department of Commerce. The text of larger cities also includes street maps and airport maps. Following city names are brief descriptions of the city, a "What To See and Do" section and listings of annual and seasonal events. Some 16,000 attractions and more than 5,500 events are highlighted. A mailing address and phone number for the local chamber of commerce or office of tourism is given whenever possible, as are cross-references, for example (See Havana, Petersburg), to nearby towns and cities with either additional things to see and do or with accommodations and/or restaurants. The Quality-Rated listings of lodgings and restaurants follow this information.

This Introduction section explains the features of the *Guide* in more detail and provides useful travel advice.

Discount Coupons

The *Mobil Travel Guide* is pleased to offer discounts from major companies for products and services. These coupons can be found at the back of this book.

The *Mobil Travel Guide* and Prentice Hall may not be held responsible for the failure of any participating company to honor these discounts.

Rating System

Pegasus, the Flying Red Horse, is a trademark of Mobil Oil Corporation. This symbol next to a town name indicates the presence of one or more Mobil service stations in the area.

The star symbols and check marks are used in rating hotels, motor hotels, lodges, motels, inns, resorts, and restaurants:

    ★   **Good, better than average**
   ★★   **Very good**
  ★★★   **Excellent**
 ★★★★   **Outstanding—worth a special trip**
★★★★★   **One of the best in the country**
    ✔   **In addition, an unusually good value, relatively inexpensive**

Listing Symbols

Ⓓ   Disabled facilities available

  Pets allowed

  Fishing on property

  Horseback riding on premises

⛷	Snow skiing nearby
🏌	Golf, 9-hole minimum on premises or privileges within 10 miles
🎾	Tennis court(s) on premises or privileges within 5 miles
🏊	Swimming on premises
🏋	Exercise equipment or room on premises
🏃	Jogging on premises
✈	Airport access within 2 miles of premises
🚭	Nonsmoking rooms
⏱	Smoke detector and/or sprinkler system
SC	Senior Citizen rates

Attraction Symbols

Each attraction has a fee code that translates as follows:

Free	=	no charge
¢	=	up to $2
¢¢	=	$2.01 to $5
¢¢¢	=	$5.01 to $10
¢¢¢¢	=	$10.01 to $15
¢¢¢¢¢	=	over $15

Credit Cards

The major credit cards honored by each establishment are indicated by initials at the end of the listing. When credit cards are not accepted, the listing will indicate this information. Please remember that Mobil Corporation credit cards cannot be used for payment of meals and room charges. Be sure the credit cards you plan to use in your travels are current and will not expire before your trip is over. If you should lose one, report the loss immediately

The following letters indicate credit cards that are accepted by the listed establishments:

> A-American Express
> C-Carte Blanche
> D-Diners Club
> DS-Discover
> ER-En Route
> MC-MasterCard
> V-Visa
> JCB-Japanese Credit Bureau

How to Read the Lodging & Restaurant Listings

Each listing of a motel, lodge, motor hotel, hotel, inn and resort gives the quality rating, name, address, directions (when there is no street address), phone number (local and 800), room rates, seasons open (if not year-round) and number and type of rooms available. Facsimile (FAX) numbers appear immediately following an establishment's phone number for properties offering this service to all of their guests. Major cities listings, lodgings and restaurants, include the neighborhood and/or directions from downtown as an aid to finding your way around the city. Maps showing these neighborhoods can be found immediately following the city map. Geographic descriptions of the neighborhoods are given under the "City Neighborhoods" heading, followed by a table of restaurants arranged by neighborhood, in alphabetical order. The listings also include information on recreational and dining facilities on or adjacent to the establishment and credit card information. Some hotels and motor hotels offer **LUXURY LEVELS,** and you will find specific information on these special accommodations within the listing.

Restaurant listings give the quality rating, name, address, directions (when there is no street address), phone number, hours and days of operation, price range for each meal served and cuisine specialties. Additionally, special features such as chef ownership, ambience, entertainment, and credit card information are noted.

When a listing is located in a town that does not have its own city heading, it will appear under the city nearest to its location. In these cases, the address and town appear in parenthesis immediately following the name of the establishment.

When looking for a specific establishment, use the index located at the back of this *Guide.* You will find the establishment name, city and state under which it is listed, as well as the page number.

The ✈ symbol at the end of a lodging listing indicates that the establishment is within two miles of access to a major, commercial airport. Listings located within 5 miles of major, commercial airports appear under the "Airport" heading, following the city listings.

The 🐾 symbol at the end of a lodging listing indicates pets allowed. Further information on restrictions and fees can be found in the listing or by contacting the lodging directly.

You will find that many lodgings and restaurants have a check mark (✔) before the quality rating. This denotes "an unusually good value, relatively inexpensive." The criteria for this designation are found in the section entitled "Explaining the Ratings," under the heading "Good Value Check Mark."

Mobil Travel Guide makes every effort to select a variety of lodging and dining establishments in a given locale. Occasionally, an establishment may go out of business or change ownership just after our publication deadline. By calling ahead for reservations you can avoid the disappointment of discovering a closed or changed establishment. Space limitations necessitate the omission of many fine places; however, no adverse criticism is implied or should be inferred.

Neither Prentice Hall nor Mobil Corporation can be held responsible for changes in prices, name, management or deterioration in services. There is no contractual agreement between management and the *Mobil Travel Guide* to guarantee prices or services. **There is no charge to an establishment for inclusion in *Mobil Travel Guide* publications.**

Motels and Lodges

Motels and lodges provide accommodations in low-rise structures with rooms easily accessible to parking areas. They have outdoor room entry and small, functional lobbies. Shops and businesses will be found only in the higher-rated properties.

Service is often limited and dining may not be offered in lower-rated motels and lodges. However, higher-rated properties will offer such services as bellmen, room service and restaurants serving three meals daily.

Lodges differ from motels primarily in their emphasis on outdoor recreational activities and in location. They are often found in resort and rural areas rather than major cities and along highways.

Motor Hotels

Motor hotels offer the convenience of motels as well as many of the services of hotels. They range from low-rise structures offering limited services to multi-storied buildings with a wide range of services and facilities. Dual building entry, elevators, inside hallways and parking areas near access doors are some of the features of a motor hotel.

Lobbies offer sitting areas, 24 hour desk and switchboard services. Often bellman and valet services are found in motor hotels as well as restaurants serving three meals a day. Expanded recreational facilities and more than one restaurant will be available in higher-rated properties. Because the following features and services apply to most establishments, they are not shown in the listing of motels and motor hotels:

- Year-round operation with a single rate structure
- European plan (meals not included in room rate)
- Bathroom with tub and/or shower in each room
- Air-conditioned/heated, often with individual room control
- Cots
- Daily maid service
- Free parking
- Phones in rooms
- Elevators

The distinction between motor hotels and hotels in metropolitan areas is minor.

Hotels

To be categorized as a hotel, the establishment must have most of the following facilities and services: multiple floors, a restaurant and/or coffee shop, elevators, room service, bellhops, valet services, spacious lobby and some recreational facilities.

A hotel offers its guests a broad spectrum of lodging experiences. Because the following features and services apply to most establishments, they are not shown in the listing:

- Year-round operation with a single rate structure
- European plan (meals not included in room rate)
- Bathroom with tub and/or shower in each room
- Air-conditioned/heated, often with individual room control
- Daily maid service
- Valet service (one-day laundry/cleaning service)
- Room service during hours restaurant is open
- Elevator
- Phones in rooms
- Bellhops
- Oversize beds available

LUXURY LEVEL: Many hotels offer their guests increased luxury accommodations on floors or towers that operate as a separate unit from the main establishment.

A boldface title, **LUXURY LEVEL(S)**, follows the principal hotel listing with information pertinent to that level. There is no separate rating for this listing; the rating given applies to the overall hotel.

The criteria used to determine the qualifications for this distinctive listing are:

1. A minimum of one entire floor of the total structure must be devoted to the luxury level.

2. Management must provide no less than three of these four services:

- Separate check-in and check-out services
- Concierge services
- Private lounge
- Private elevator service (key access)

Complimentary breakfast and snacks are commonly offered on these floors as well as upscale amenities and services.

Resorts

Resorts are establishments specializing in stays of three days or more. They usually offer American Plan and/or housekeeping accommodations, with an emphasis on recreational facilities, often providing the services of a social director.

Food services are of primary importance at a resort. Guests must be able to obtain three meals a day on the premises or be provided with grocery stores to enable them to obtain food for meal preparation without leaving the premises.

When horseback riding is indicated, phone ahead to inquire about English saddle availability; Western style is assumed.

Inns

Frequently thought of as a small hotel, an inn is a place of homelike comfort and warm hospitality. It is often a structure of historic significance, located in an equally interesting environmental setting.

Meals are at a special time at an inn, and frequently tea and sherry are served in the late afternoon. Rooms are usually individually decorated, featuring antiques or furnishings representative of the locale. Phones and bathrooms may not be available in every room.

Guest Ranches

Like resorts, guest ranches specialize in stays of three days or more. Guest ranches also offer meal plans and extensive outdoor activities such as horseback riding. Stables and trails exist on the ranch; daily, expert instruction is part of the program. Ranging from casual to rustic, many guest ranches are working ranches, and guests are encouraged to participate in various aspects of ranch life. Eating is often family style and may also include cookouts as part of morning, midday or evening trail rides. Phone ahead to inquire about English saddle availability; Western style is assumed.

Cottage Colonies

Cottage colonies are housekeeping cottages and cabins that are usually found in recreational areas. When dining or recreational facilities are available on the premises, you will find it noted in the listing.

Restaurants

Unless otherwise specified, restaurants listed:

- Are open daily, year-round
- Offer chiefly American cooking

An *a la carte* menu provides entree prices covering the main dish only. *Semi-a la carte* indicates vegetable, salad, soup, appetizer or other accompaniments to the main dish. *Table d'hôte* means a full meal for a stated price, with no *a la carte* selections available. *Prix fixe* indicates a fixed price for any meal on the menu.

Since restaurant listings include detailed information, by carefully reading the listing and comparing prices you can easily determine whether the restaurant is formal and elegant or informal and comfortable for families. When children's meals are offered you will find it noted in the listing.

Unrated Dining Spots

Chosen for their unique atmosphere, specialized menu and local flavor, restaurants listed under the Unrated Dining Spots category appear without a *Mobil Travel Guide* rating. However, they have been inspected by our team of field representatives and meet our high standards of cleanliness and maintenance.

These establishments feature a wide range of dining, from pizza, ice cream, sandwiches and health food to cafeterias and English tea service in fine hotels. They often offer extraordinary values, quick service and regional flavor and are worth a visit when traveling to a city offering these special listings.

Unrated Dining Spots can be found after restaurant listings in many cities.

Prices and Taxes

All prices quoted in *Mobil Travel Guide* publications are expected to be in effect at the time of publication and during the entire year; however, prices cannot be guaranteed.

In some localities there may be short-term price variations because of special events or holidays. Whenever possible, these price changes are noted. Certain resorts have complicated rate structures that vary with the time of year; it's a good idea to contact the management to confirm specific rates.

State and city sales taxes as well as special room taxes can bring your room rates up as high as 25% per day. We are unable to bring this specific information into the listings, but strongly urge that you ask about these taxes when placing reservations with establishments. Another charge that is often overlooked by travelers is that of telephone usage. Frequently, hotels charge a service fee for unanswered phone calls and credit card calls as well as long distance calls. It is advised that you read the information offered by the establishment before placing phone calls from your room. It is not unusual for a hotel to send bills for telephone calls to your home after you have checked out. Be certain to take the time to read your bill carefully before checking out. You will not be expected to pay for charges that were not explained in the printed matter given to you at the time of check-in. The use of public telephones in hotel lobbies should not be overlooked since the financial benefits may outweigh the inconvenience.

Explaining the Ratings

The *Mobil Travel Guide* has been rating motels, lodges, motor hotels, hotels, inns, resorts and restaurants since the first edition was published in 1958. For years it was the only guidebook to provide such ratings on a national basis, and *Mobil Travel Guide* remains one of the few guidebooks to rate restaurants across the country.

The rating categories, ★ through ★★★★★, apply nationally. The principal areas of evaluation are quality of physical structure, furnishings, maintenance, housekeeping, overall service and food service. Climate, historic, cultural and artistic variations representative of regional differences are major factors in each rating. No rating is ever final and, since each is subject to annual review, each establishment must continue to earn its rating and has a chance to improve it as well.

Every establishment listed in *Mobil Travel Guide* publications is inspected by experienced field representatives who submit detailed reports to the editorial offices. From these reports, the editors extract information for listings and acertain that establishments to be recommended are clean, well-maintained, well-managed and above average.

Ratings are based upon the inspection reports, written evaluations of staff members who stay and dine anonymously at establishments throughout the year, and an extensive review of guest comments received by the *Mobil Travel Guide*.

Every effort is made to assure that ratings are fair and accurate; the designated ratings are published to serve as an aid to travelers and should not be used for any other purpose.

A further rating designation exists and that is Unrated. When major changes have occurred during the one-year period prior to publication, there will be no star rating. These changes may be in management, ownership, general manager and master chef. If an establishment is undergoing major renovation/refurbishment or has been in operation less than one year, it will also appear unrated. The decision to list an establishment "unrated" is the responsibility of the Rating Committee.

The rating for each establishment—motel, lodge, motor hotel, hotel, inn, resort, guest ranch, or restaurant—is measured against others of the same type. The criteria for rating accommodations are related to the number and quality of facilities, guest services, luxury of appointments and attitude and professionalism of staff and management. Restaurant evaluations emphasize quality of food, preparation, presentation, freshness of ingredients, quality of service, attitude and professionalism of staff/management. Because each type of establishment is viewed also in terms of its own style, unique characteristics, decor and ambience, these additional qualities are also considered in determining a rating.

Good Value Check Mark

The check mark (✔) designation appearing in front of the star rating of an establishment listing indicates "an unusually good value, relatively inexpensive." It will appear with the listing in the following manner:

✔ ★ PRENTICE MOTOR INN

Lodging establishments rated with a good value check mark have been determined to be clean and well-maintained, offering some appointments such as room phones, free television, pools and breakfast on or adjacent to the premises, at economical prices. Restaurant establishments rated with a good value check mark have been determined to be clean and well-maintained, offering good food at economical prices.

Due to the fact that prevailing rates vary regionally, we are able to be more selective in our good value rated establishments in some areas than in others. However, you will find a wide range of these properties to visit in all locales.

In major cities and resort areas prices tend to be higher than in outlying areas, therefore the criteria for the good value check mark have two distinct variations. The following price range has been used to determine those properties awarded the good value check mark:

Major City and Resort Area Listings

Lodging—single, average $75-$85 per night
double, average $85-$100 per night

Restaurants—lunch, average $17, complete meal
dinner, exclusive of beverages and gratuities, average $25, complete meal

Local Area Listing

Lodging—single, average $45-$50 per night
double, average $55-$65 per night

Restaurants—lunch, average $9, complete meal
dinner, exclusive of beverages and gratuities, average $17, complete meal

Terms and Abbreviations

The following terms and abbreviations are used consistently throughout the listings.

AP Indicates American plan (lodging plus all meals)
Bar Liquor, wine and beer are served at a bar or in a cocktail lounge and usually with meals unless otherwise indicated (e.g., "wine, beer")
Ck-in; ck-out Check-in time; check-out time
Coin lndry Self-service laundry
Complete meal Indicates soup and/or salad, entree, dessert and non-alcoholic beverage
Continental bkfst Usually coffee and a roll or doughnut
Cover "Cover" is a sum in addition to the actual cost of food and drink in restaurants
D Followed by a price; indicates room rate for two persons in one room (one or two beds; charge may be higher if two double beds are offered)
Each addl Extra charge for each additional person beyond the stated number of persons for a given price
Early In referring to season openings or closings, approximately the first third of a month (May 1 to May 10); check with management for exact date
Early-bird dinner A meal served at specified hours, at a reduced price
EP Indicates European plan (lodging only)
Exc Except
Exercise equipt Two or more pieces of exercise equipment on the premises
Exercise rm When an instructor is on the premises, this term is used to indicate both exercise equipment and room
FAX Facsimile machines available to all guests
Golf privileges Privileges at a course within 10 miles
Hols Holidays
In-rm movies Video cassette player available for use with video tapes
Kit. or kits. A kitchen or kitchenette with stove or microwave, sink, and refrigerator that is either part of the room or a separate room. If the kitchen is not fully equipped, the listing will indicate "no equipt" or "some equipt"
Late In referring to season openings or closings, approximately the last third of a month (May 21 to May 31); check with management for exact date

MAP   Indicates modified American plan (lodging plus two meals)

Mid   In referring to season openings or closings, approximately the middle third of a month (May 11 to May 20); check with management for exact date

No elvtr   In a hotel with more than two stories, it is assumed there is an elevator, so it is not noted; only its absence is noted

No phones   Only the absence of phones is noted

Parking   Indicates that there is a parking lot on the premises

Private club   A cocktail lounge or bar available to members and their guests (in Motels and Hotels where these clubs exist, registered guests can usually use the club as guests of the management; frequently the same is true of restaurants)

Prix fixe   A full meal for a stated price; usually one price quoted

Res   Reservations

S   Followed by a price; indicates room rate for one person

Serv bar   Where drinks are prepared for dining patrons only

Serv charge   Service charge is the amount added to restaurant check in lieu of tip

Snow skiing downhill/x-country   Downhill and/or cross-country skiing within 20 miles of property

Table d'hôte   A full meal for a stated price dependent upon entree selection

Tennis privileges   Privileges at tennis courts within 5 miles

TV   Indicates color television; B/W indicates black-and-white television

Under 18 free   Children under a specific age not charged if staying in room with one or both parents

Valet parking   Indicates that an attendant is available to park and retrieve a car

Disabled Traveler Information

The *Mobil Travel Guide* disabled symbol Ⓓ shown in accommodations and restaurants is intended to serve travelers with limited handicaps, temporary impairments or the semi-ambulatory. In attractions, facilities providing for the needs of the disabled are noted in the description of the attraction.

The *Mobil Travel Guide* Disabled Criteria are unique to our publication and were designed to meet the standards developed by our editorial staff. Please do not confuse them with the universal handicap symbol requirements. Travelers wishing to gain more information on facilities and services for the disabled should contact the establishments directly.

When the Ⓓ symbol appears following a listing, the establishment is equipped with facilities to accommodate persons in wheelchairs, on crutches or the aged in need of easy access to doorways and restroom facilities. Severely handicapped persons, as well as the hearing and visually impaired, should not assume establishments bearing our symbol will offer facilities to meet their needs. We suggest these persons phone an establishment before their visit to ascertain if their particular needs will be met.

The following facilities must be available at all lodging properties bearing our disabled symbol:

Public Areas

- Handicapped parking near access ramps
- Ramps at entryways to buildings
- Swinging entryway doors minimum 3'-0"
- Restrooms on main level with room to operate a wheelchair; handrails at commode areas
- Elevators equipped with grab bars; lowered control buttons
- Restaurants, easy-access doorways; restrooms with room to operate wheelchair; handrails at commode areas

Rooms

- Minimum 3'-0" width entryway to rooms
- Low-pile carpet
- Telephone at bedside and in bathroom
- Bed placed at wheelchair height
- Minimum 3'-0" width doorway to bathroom
- Bath, open sink—no cabinet; room to operate wheelchair
- Handrails at commode areas; tub handrails
- "Peep" hole in room entry door, wheelchair accessible
- Closet rods and shelves, wheelchair accessible

Restaurants

The following facilities must be available at all free-standing restaurants bearing our disabled symbol:

- Handicapped parking beside access ramps
- Ramps at entryways to building (front entry)
- Tables to accommodate wheelchairs
- Main-floor restrooms; minimum 3'-0" width entryway
- Restrooms with room to operate wheelchair; handrails at commode areas

Tips for Travel

The passage of the Americans with Disabilities Act (ADA) of 1990 means that all hotels and motels in the US have to make their facilities and services accessible to all guests. Although this law went into effect early in 1992, it will take some time for the more than 40,000 hotels and motels to implement the renovation programs to make their facilities totally accessible to every guest.

Any facility opened after January 26, 1993, must be designed and built totally in accordance with ADA Accessibility Guidelines. This means that a certain percentage of the rooms must be accessible to guests who have mobility, vision, hearing or speech impairments. In addition, all public spaces must be accessible to all guests to use and enjoy.

While all existing hotels and motels will not be totally accessible, you can expect all properties to be aware of the

ADA and to make efforts to accommodate the special needs of any guest who has a physical disability.

To get the kind of service you need and have a right to expect, do not hesitate when making a reservation to:

- ask about the availability of accessbile rooms, parking, entrance, restaurant, lounge or any other facilities that are important to you.
- inquire about any special accommodations, transportation, hearing impaired equipment or services you may need.
- ask about the accessibility of the room. For example, do both the room entry and bathroom doors have 32″ of clear width? Is there a 5′ diameter turning space in the bedroom and bathroom?

When your stay is over, fill out the guest comment card and let the management know about the facilities, equipment and services that worked for you and those that need to be improved.

Additional Publications

The most complete listing of published material on traveling with disabilities is readily available from *The Disability Bookshop,* Twin Peaks Press, PO Box 129, Vancouver, Washington 98666; phone 206/694-2462 or 800/638-2256.

Access America Series, an Atlas & Guide to the National Parks for Visitors with Disabilities is published by Northern Cartographic, Inc., PO Box 133, Burlington, Vermont 05402, $8.95, and is subdivided into regional publications. Contact *The Disability Bookshop* for current regional titles and costs. A smaller, but still comprehensive, guidebook to the national parks is a 1992 publication, *Easy Access to National Parks: the Sierra Club Guide for People with Disabilities;* Sierra Club, distributed by Random, May 1992, $16 (paperback). Local public libraries should have relevant books on travel for people with disabilities. Individuals should contact the reference librarian at their public library for assistance.

The Reference Section of the National Library Service for the Blind and Physically Handicapped (NLS), Library of Congress, provides information and resources on blindness and physical disabilities, as well as information about the NLS talking-book program. For further information contact: Reference Section, National Library Service for the Blind and Physically Handicapped, Library of Congress, Washington, DC 20542; phone 202/707-9275 or 202/707-5100.

Travel Tips

Lodging

Many hotels in major metropolitan areas have special weekend package plans. These plans offer considerable savings on rooms and often include breakfast, cocktails and some meal discounts as well. Information on specific pricing for these specials is not available because prices change frequently throughout the year. We suggest you phone to obtain such information prior to your trip.

LUXURY LEVEL accommodations, which appear within some hotel and motor hotel listings, frequently offer a good value because many of them provide breakfast, cocktails, newspapers and upgraded amenities which are included in the price of the room.

Dining

Reservations are important at most major city restaurants. Many restaurants will ask you to confirm your reservation by calling back the day you are to dine. Should you fail to do so, your reservation will not be held for you.

In fine restaurants the pace is leisurely, the service is very professional and the prices are above average. Most of the dishes are cooked to order, and patrons' requests for special preparation are handled graciously.

Four-Star and Five-Star establishments are usually quite expensive because they offer higher food quality, superior service and distinctive decor. Read the listing and see if they are open for lunch. While the lunch prices are considerably higher than those at other restaurants, you may still enjoy the ambience, service and cuisine of a famous establishment for about half the cost of a dinner.

''Early bird'' dinners are popular in many parts of the country, and they offer considerable savings on dinner prices. Information on the availability of these dinners has been given to us by restaurant management, but we suggest you phone ahead and ask if they still offer this special plan.

Tipping

Lodgings: Doormen in major city hotels are usually given $1 for getting you into a cab. Bellmen expect $1 per bag, but never less than a $2 tip if you have only one bag. Concierges are tipped according to the service they perform. Suggestions on sightseeing or restaurants, as well as making reservations for dining, are standard services often requiring no tip. However, when reservations are obtained at restaurants known to be difficult to get into, a gratuity of $5 should be considered. If theater or sporting event tickets are obtained, a tip is expected, often $5 to $10. Maids, often overlooked by guests, may be tipped $1 to $2 per each day of your stay.

Restaurants: Coffee shop and counter service wait staff are usually given 8 to 10 percent of the bill. In full service restaurants, 15 percent of the bill, before sales tax, is suggested. In fine dining restaurants, where the staff is large and share the gratuity, 18 to 20 percent is recommended. The number of restaurants adding service charges to the bill is increasing. Carefully review your bill to make certain an automatic gratuity was not charged.

Airports: Curbside luggage handlers expect $1 per bag. Car rental shuttle drivers who help with your luggage appreciate a $1 or $2 tip. **Remember, tipping is an expression of**

appreciation for good service. You need not tip if service is poor—tipping is discretionary.

10 Tips for Worry-Free Travel

1. Be sure to notify local police and leave a phone number where you can be contacted in case of emergency.

2. Lock doors and windows, but leave shades up and lights on (or on an automatic timer).

3. Stop newspaper deliveries and discontinue garbage pickups.

4. Remove food and defrost refrigerator; store valuables in a safe place; disconnect electrical appliances; turn off gas jets, including hot water heater; turn off water faucets and drain pipes in severe weather.

5. Remember to pack personal medicines and duplicate prescriptions; spare eyeglasses or the prescription; sunglasses; suntan lotion; First Aid kit; insect spray; towels and tissues; writing materials.

6. Make sure that proof of car insurance is in your glove compartment; also take along your driver's license and those of other passengers (check expiration dates); car registration; copies of birth certificates (if driving outside U.S.); traveler's checks. Be sure you have a duplicate set of car keys.

7. Check to see that you have a jack, spare tire, repair kit, emergency tools, flashlights, tire chains, spare fan belt, windshield scraper, auto fuses, lug wrench and work gloves. A pre-trip tune-up won't hurt—and, of course, be sure to "fill up" before you start out.

8. Also check vehicle's battery, oil and air filters, cooling system, brakes and lights.

9. Remember "extras" like hunting/fishing licenses and equipment; camera and film; bathing suits, beach accessories, sports equipment; portable radio and/or TV; picnic accessories.

10. Buckle up your seat belt, and have a nice trip!

Maps and Map Coordinates

There is a map of each state and selected cities in the front of the *Mobil Travel Guide*. As you read through the *Guide*, you will find a map coordinate following each town heading. There is a corresponding coordinate on the appropriate state map.

Street and airport maps are included in the text of selected larger cities.

What To See and Do

This section appears at the beginning of each city and town listing and provides concise descriptions of notable attractions

in the area—museums, art galleries, amusement parks, universities, historic sites and houses, plantations, churches, state parks, ski areas and so on. Municipal parks, tennis courts, swimming pools, golf courses, and small educational institutions are generally excluded, since these are common to most towns. *Mobil Travel Guide* editors strive for a balance of recreational, athletic, cultural, historical and educational interests.

Every effort has been made to ensure that the information in this publication was accurate at the time it was printed. Neither Prentice Hall nor Mobil Corporation can be held responsible for changes that occurred after publication. We regret any inconvenience you may incur due to improper information being listed.

Following the name of the attraction is the street address or location. Directions are given from the center of the town under which the attraction is listed; please note that this may not be the town in which the attraction is located. For instance, directions for an attraction listed under Springfield may state "225 W Hawthorne, 12 mi N off US 42 in Zionsville." Area codes are not provided for each attraction if the code is the same as that shown in the city statistics. Similarly, zip codes are given only if they differ from the one listed in the city statistics. Next comes a brief description of the attraction, the months and days it is open, handicapped facilities (if any) and phone number. Each attraction has a fee code that translates as follows:

Free	=	no charge
¢	=	up to $2
¢¢	=	$2.01 to $5
¢¢¢	=	$5.01 to $10
¢¢¢¢	=	$10.01 to $15
¢¢¢¢¢	=	over $15

Events

Immediately following the "What To See and Do" section is the name, address and phone number of the local chamber of commerce or tourist bureau you may contact for further information. Following this are listings of annual, seasonal, and special events. An annual event is one that is held every year for a period of usually no longer than a week to 10 days. A seasonal event is one that may or may not be annual and that is held for a number of weeks or months in the year, such as horse racing, summer theater, concert or opera seasons, professional sports. Special event listings occur infrequently and mark a certain date or event, such as a centennial or commemorative celebration.

Additional Visitor Information

For larger cities, this is where you will find the chamber of commerce name, address and phone number. In addition, you are given the names of magazines or guides to the city, location of visitor centers, information on public transportation, and other helpful information.

Special Travel Features

Federal Recreation Areas

While many national parks and recreation areas may be entered and used free of charge, others require an entrance fee (ranging from $1 to $4/person to $3 to $10/carload) and/or a "use fee" for special services and facilities. Those travelers who plan to make several visits to federal recreation areas will be dollars ahead if they investigate several money-saving programs coordinated by the National Park Service, US Department of the Interior.

Park Pass. An annual entrance permit to a specific park, monument, historic site or recreation area in the National Park System that charges entrance fees, the Park Pass costs $10 or $15, depending upon the area, and is neither refundable nor transferable.

The Pass admits the permit holder and any accompanying passengers in a private noncommercial vehicle or, in the case of walk-in facilities, the holder's spouse, children and parents. It is valid for entrance fees only and does not cover use fees, such as those for cave tours, camping or parking.

A Park Pass may be purchased in person or by mail from the National Park Sevice unit at which the pass will be honored.

Golden Eagle Passport. Issued to persons 17 to 61 years of age is good for one calendar year and costs $25. The Golden Eagle Passport entitles the purchaser and up to 6 people accompanying him or her in a private noncommercial vehicle to enter any federal outdoor recreation area that charges an entrance fee. These include national parks, monuments, historic and memorial parks and seashores. The passport will also admit the purchaser and family to most walk-in admission fee areas such as historical houses, buildings and museums in federal areas. However, it does not cover "use fees," such as fees for camping, boat-launching equipment, parking, or cave tours.

The Golden Eagle Passport may be purchased in person or by mail from: the National Park Service, Office of Public Inquiries, Room 1013, US Department of the Interior, 18th and C Streets NW, Washington, DC 20240, or phone 202/208-4747; at any of the 10 regional offices throughout the country; and at any area of the National Park System. The Golden Eagle Passport is not transferable, nor is the $25 refundable if the passport is not used, stolen or lost.

Golden Age Passport. Issued to citizens and permanent residents of the United States 62 years or older, this passport is a free lifetime entrance permit to fee-charging recreation areas. The fee exemption extends to those accompanying the permit holder in a private noncommercial vehicle or, in the case of walk-in facilities, to the holder's spouse and children. The passport entitles the holder to a 50% discount on "use fees" charged in park areas, but not to fees charged by concessionaires.

Golden Age Passports must be obtained in person; mail requests will not be honored. The applicant must show proof of age, i.e., a driver's license, a birth certificate or a signed affidavit attesting to one's age (Medicare cards are not acceptable proof). Passports are available at most federally operated recreation areas where they are used. They may be obtained at the National Park Service Headquarters in Washington, DC (see preceding Golden Eagle Passport section), at any of the park system's regional offices, at National Forest Supervisors' offices and at most Ranger Station offices (for location see NATIONAL PARK SERVICE AREAS AND NATIONAL FORESTS in the state introductory section of the *Guide*).

Golden Access Passport. Issued to citizens and permanent residents of the United States who are physically disabled or visually impaired, this passport is a free lifetime entrance permit to fee-charging federal recreation areas. The fee exception extends to those accompanying the permit holder in a private noncommercial vehicle or, in the case of walk-in facilities, to the holder's spouse, children and parents. The passport entitles the holder to a 50% discount on "use fees" charged in park areas, but not to fees charged by concessionaires.

Golden Access Passports must be obtained in person; mail requests will not be honored. Proof of eligbility to receive federal benefits is required (under programs such as Disability Retirement, Compensation for Military Service-Connnected Disability, Coal Mine Safety and Health Act, etc.), or an affidavit must be signed attesting to eligibility. These passports are available at the same outlets as Golden Age Passports.

Savings for Seniors

Mobil Travel Guide publications note senior citizen rates in lodgings, restaurants and attractions. Always call ahead to confirm that the discount is being offered. Carry proof of age, such as a passport, birth certificate or driver's license. Medicare cards are often accepted as proof. Contact the following organizations for additional information:

1. American Association of Retired Persons (AARP)
   Special Services Dept
   601 E Street NW
   Washington, DC 20049
   Phone 202/434-2277

2. National Council of Senior Citizens
   1331 F Street NW
   Washington, DC 20004
   Phone 202/347-8800

The mature traveler on a limited budget should look for the senior citizen discount symbol in Lodging and Restaurant listings. Also, pay special attention to all listings in the Guide highlighted by a check mark (✔). (See Federal Recreation Areas for Golden Age Passport information.)

Border Crossing Regulations (Canada)

Citizens of the United States do not need visas to enter Canada, but proof of citizenship is required. Proof of citizenship includes a passport, birth certificate or voter's registration card. A driver's license is not acceptable. Naturalized citizens should carry their naturalization certificates or their US passport, as these documents will be necessary for a return to the United States. Young people under 18 years of age who are traveling on their own should carry a letter from parents or guardian giving them permission to travel in Canada.

Travelers entering Canada in automobiles licensed in the United States may tour the provinces for up to three months without fee. Any necessary permits are issued at port of entry. Drivers are advised to carry their motor vehicle registration card and, if the car is not registered in the driver's name, a letter from the registered owner authorizing use of the vehicle.

If the car is rented, carry a copy of the rental contract stipulating use in Canada. For your protection, ask your car insurer for a Canadian Non-resident Interprovince Motor Vehicle Liability Insurance Card. This card ensures that your insurance company observes the minimum of financial responsibility in Canada.

The use of seat belts by drivers and passengers is compulsory in some provinces. For additional information, see individual provinces. A permit is required for the use of citizens' band radios. Rabies vaccination certificates are required for dogs or cats.

No handguns may be brought into Canada. If you plan to hunt, sporting rifles and shotguns, plus 200 rounds of ammunition per person, will be admitted duty-free. Hunting and fishing licenses must be obtained from the appropriate province. Each province has its own regulations concerning the transportation of firearms.

The Canadian dollar's rate of exchange with the US dollar varies. For specific information on rate of exchange, contact the nearest bank. Since customs regulations can change, the *Guide* recommends that you contact the Canadian consulate or embassy in your area. Offices are located in Atlanta, Boston, Buffalo, Chicago, Cleveland, Dallas, Detroit, Los Angeles, Minneapolis, New York City, Philadelphia, San Francisco, Seattle and Washington, DC. For the most current and detailed listing of regulations and sources, ask for the annually revised brochure "Canada: Travel Information," which is available upon request.

Border Crossing Regulations (Mexico)

Proof of citizenship is required for travel into Mexico; a passport or certified birth certificate are acceptable. Aliens must carry their alien registration cards. Naturalized citizens should carry their certificates. If you take your car, you may find it more convenient to unload all baggage before crossing than to go through a thorough customs inspection upon your return. Your automobile insurance is not valid in Mexico; get a one-day

policy before crossing. US currency is accepted in all border cities.

You will not be permitted to bring any plants, fruits or vegetables into the United States.

Federal regulations permit each US citizen, 21 years of age or older, to bring back one quart of alcoholic beverage, duty-free. However, state regulations vary and may be more strict; check locally before entering Mexico. New regulations may be issued at any time, so be sure to check further if you have any questions. Mexico does not observe Daylight Saving Time.

If you are planning to stay more than 24 hours or if you are a naturalized citizen or resident alien, get a copy of current border regulations from the nearest Mexican consulate or Tourism Office before crossing and make sure you understand them. A helpful booklet, "Know Before You Go," may be obtained free of charge from the nearest office of the US Customs Service.

Car Care

Familiarize yourself with the owner's manual for your car. It provides valuable advice for service and maintenance. Get a lubrication and oil change, an inspection of tires, fan belts and cooling system, and a check of engine performance, lights and brakes. Any other regular services recommended by the car manufacturer should be performed as well.

Once your car is ready for the road, make certain your insurance is paid up—and don't forget your registration certificate, insurance information, driver's license and an extra set of keys.

Keep your seat belt and harness fastened. Watch your instrument panel closely—your panel gauges or indicators will alert you to potential problems. If a problem arises, get to a service station as soon as possible.

A world of convenience is yours with a Mobil credit card. Mobil's gasoline, oil and tires, as well as many other products and services may be charged at Mobil dealers in the U.S. as well as at certain other dealers throughout Canada.

Road Emergencies

The best insurance against an emergency is proper maintenance of your car. Despite care, however, the unexpected can happen. Here are a few tips for handling emergencies:

Accidents. If you should have an accident, observe the following:

- Do not leave accident scene
- Help the injured but don't move them unless necessary
- Call police—ask for medical help if needed
- Get names, addresses, license numbers and insurance company of persons involved
- Get names and addresses of at least two witnesses

- Get description and registration number of cars involved
- Report accident to your insurance company
- Diagram the accident showing cars involved

Breakdowns. If your car breaks down, get out of traffic as soon as possible, pulling off the road if you can. Turn on your emergency flashers and raise the hood. If you have no flashers, tie a white cloth to the roadside door handle or antenna. Stay near your car but off the road. Carry and use flares or reflectors to keep your car from being hit.

Blowout. Do not overreact if you have a tire blowout. Hold the wheel steady—do not jerk it. Gradually let up on the gas pedal, steer straight and coast to a stop. If you have to brake, do so very gently.

Collision. "If a collision is imminent, you will need to make these split-second decisions," advises the National Safety Council's Defensive Driving Course. "Drive right, away from the oncoming vehicle. Drive with control, don't skid off the road. If you are forced to drive off the road, look for either something soft, like bushes or small trees, or something fixed, like a break-away pole or a fence to break your impact. A fixed object has no momentum, and the crash will be less intense than if you had hit the oncoming vehicle. If you are unable to ride off the road, try to collide with the oncoming vehicle at an angle. A glancing blow is less dangerous than hitting a vehicle head on."

Flat tire. Drive off the road, even if you risk ruining your tire. Set the parking brake firmly, but remember it may not hold if a rear wheel is off the ground. Put wooden blocks, bricks or stones tightly against the front and rear of the tire diagonally opposite the flat. After removing the hubcap, loosen each wheel nut about one-half turn. Position the jack exactly as the instruc-tions indicate, then raise the car an inch or two to determine how the jack fits. (If it appears to be about to slip, stop and wait for help.)

Jack the car until the flat is about three inches off the ground, remove the wheel nuts and put them in the hubcap. Keep your body away from the car. Handle the tire from the sides; never put your hand above or underneath the tire.

Slide the spare tire into place, using the wrench as a lever. You may have to raise the jack a little farther. Screw the nuts on firmly, and jack the car down, standing at the side, not in front of the car. Finally, fully tighten the wheel nuts and leave the hubcap off as a reminder to have the flat fixed.

Skids. When your car skids, let up on the gas gently, keeping some power going to the wheels. Steer into the direction of the skid, and brake only after you have the car under complete control.

Stuck wheels. If you get stuck in the mud or snow, don't spin the wheels. Rock the car by gently accelerating ahead and back in rhythm with the car's natural tendency.

Equipment. The following checklist describes the necessary equipment to carry at all times:

- ☐ Spare tire; tool kit; first aid kit; flashlight
- ☐ Road flares; jumper cables; gloves
- ☐ Container of motor oil; a can opener
- ☐ Empty one-gallon container (Note: Check local laws governing type of container to use for gasoline.)
- ☐ Spare parts, fan belt and fuses
- ☐ In winter: chains, ice scraper, de-icer in spray can, shovel, "liquid chain" or a bag of sand
- ☐ Major credit card and auto club identification

HOW TO SURVIVE A HOTEL FIRE

The chances are quite slim that you will ever encounter a hotel or motel fire. In addition, should you hear an alarm or see smoke, the danger is almost always less than you think it to be. But in the event you do encounter a fire, **ENSURE YOUR SURVIVAL WITH BASIC PREPARATION AND CALM ACTION.**

PREPARATION IS QUICK AND EASY

WHEN YOU CHECK INTO YOUR ROOM, DO THE FOLLOWING SAFETY CHECK:
- *Where are the fire exits?* Walk to at least two, counting the doors along the way in case you need to find the exit in the dark.
- *Where are the fire extinguishers and alarms?* Walk to them quickly.
- *Where is the "off switch" on your room's air conditioner?* In case of fire, turn off the air conditioner to prevent smoke from being sucked into your room.
- *Where is your room key?* Keep your key with you so you may reenter your room.

IF THERE'S A FIRE . . . STAY CALM

Keep in mind that smoke, poisonous gases, and panic are the greatest threats. The fresh air you need to breathe is at or near the floor. Get on your hands and knees; stay low, keep calm and react as follows:

If you find a fire,
- pull the nearest fire alarm;
- then use a fire extinguisher *if the fire is small;*
- leave the building through the fire exit.

   Never enter an elevator when fire is threatening.

If you hear an alarm from your room,
- take your room key;
- check the door for heat, but *do not open a hot door;*
- crack the door open if it is cool;
- use the fire exit if the hall is clear of thick smoke, but *slam the door shut if the hall is smoky.*

If your exit is blocked,
- try another exit;
- or if all exits are smoky, go back to your room—it's the safest place;
- and if you cannot get to your room, go to the roof.

If you must stay in your room because thick smoke blocks the fire exits,
- turn off the air conditioner;
- stuff wet towels under the door and in air vents to keep smoke out;
- fill your bathtub with water and keep wastebaskets or ice buckets nearby to remoisten the cloths or toss water on heating walls;
- phone your location to the front desk or directly to the fire department;
- *stay low, below smoke and poisonous gases, and await assistance.*
- A wet towel tied around your nose and mouth is an effective filter.

Hotel/Motel Toll-Free '800' Numbers

This selected list is a handy guide for hotel/motel toll-free reservation numbers. You can save time and money by using them in the continental United States and Canada; Alaska and Hawaii are not included. Although these '800' numbers were in effect at press time, the *Mobil Travel Guide* cannot be responsible should any of them change. Many establishments do not have toll-free reservation numbers. Consult your local telephone directory for regional listings. The toll-free numbers designated 'TDD' are answered by a telecommunications service for the deaf. *Don't forget to dial "1" before each number.*

Best Western International, Inc.
800-528-1234 Cont'l USA & Canada
800-528-2222 TDD

Budgetel Inns
800-4-BUDGET Cont'l USA

Budget Host
800-BUD-HOST

Canadian Pacific/Doubletree Hotels
800-258-0444 Cont'l USA

Clarion Hotels
800-CLARION

Comfort Inns
800-228-5150 Cont'l USA

Courtyard by Marriott
800-321-2211 Cont'l USA

Days Inn
800-325-2525 Cont'l USA

Drury Inns
800-325-8300 Cont'l USA

Econo Lodges of America
800-446-6900 Cont'l USA & Canada

Embassy Suites
800-362-2779 Cont'l USA

Exel Inns of America
800-356-8013 Cont'l USA

Fairfield Inn by Marriott
800-228-2800

Fairmont Hotels
800-527-4727 Cont'l USA

Four Seasons Hotels
800-332-3442 Cont'l USA & Canada

Friendship Inns of America Int'l
800-453-4511 Cont'l USA

Guest Quarters
800-424-2900 Cont'l USA
800-PICKETT

Hampton Inn
800-HAMPTON Cont'l USA

Hilton Hotels Corp
800-HILTONS Cont'l USA
800-368-1133 TDD

Holiday Inns
800-HOLIDAY Cont'l USA & Canada
800-238-5544 TDD

Howard Johnson
800-654-2000 Cont'l USA & Canada
800-654-8442 TDD

Hyatt Corp
800-228-9000 Cont'l USA & Canada

Inns of America
800-826-0778 USA

Inter-Continental Hotels
800-327-0200 Cont'l USA, HI & Canada

La Quinta Motor Inns, Inc.
800-531-5900 Cont'l USA
800-426-3101 TDD

Loews Hotels
800-223-0888 Cont'l USA exc NY

Marriott Hotels
800-228-9290 Cont'l USA

Master Hosts Inns (Hospitality)
800-251-1962 Cont'l USA & Canada

Omni Hotels
800-843-6664 Cont'l USA & Canada

Park Inns Int'l
800-437-PARK

Quality Inns
800-228-5151 Cont'l USA & Canada

Radisson Hotel Corp
800-333-3333 Cont'l USA & Canada

Ramada Inns
800-2-RAMADA Cont'l USA
800-228-3232 TDD

Red Carpet/Scottish Inns (Hospitality)
800-251-1962 Cont'l USA & Canada

Red Lion-Thunderbird
800-547-8010 Cont'l USA & Canada

Red Roof Inns
800-843-7663 Cont'l USA & Canada

Residence Inn By Marriott
800-331-3131

Ritz-Carlton
800-241-3333 Cont'l USA

Rodeway Inns International
800-228-2000 Cont'l USA

Sheraton Hotels & Inns
800-325-3535 Cont'l USA & Canada

Shilo Inns
800-222-2244

Signature Inns
800-822-5252

Stouffer Hotels and Resorts
800-HOTELS-1 Cont'l USA & Canada

Super 8 Motels
800-843-1991 Cont'l USA & Canada
800-800-8000 Cont'l USA & Canada

Susse Chalet Motor Lodges & Inns
800-258-1980 Cont'l USA & Canada

Travelodge International Inc./Viscount Hotels
800-255-3050 Cont'l USA & Canada

Trusthouse Forte Hotels
800-225-5843 Cont'l USA & Canada

Vagabond Hotels Inc.
800-522-1555 Cont'l USA
800-468-2251 Canada

Westin Hotels
800-228-3000 Cont'l USA & Canada

Wyndham Hotels
800-822-4200

Car Rental Toll-Free '800' Numbers

Advantage Rent A Car
800-777-5500 Cont'l USA

Agency Rent-A-Car
800-321-1972 Cont'l USA

Airways Rent A Car
800-952-9200

Alamo Rent-A-Car
800-327-9633 Cont'l USA,
Canada

Allstate Rent-A-Car
800-634-6186 Cont'l USA

Avis-Reservations Center
800-331-1212 Cont'l USA,
Canada

Budget Rent-A-Car
800-527-0700 Cont'l USA,
Canada

Dollar Rent-A-Car
800-800-4000 Cont'l USA,
Canada

Enterprise Rent-A-Car
800-325-8007 Cont'l USA

Hertz Corporation
800-654-3131 Cont'l USA
800-654-3001 Canada

National Car Rental
800-CAR-RENT Cont'l USA,
Canada

Payless Rent-A-Car Inc
800-237-2804 Cont'l USA

Sears Rent-A-Car
800-527-0770 Cont'l USA

Thrifty Rent-A-Car
800-367-2277 Cont'l USA,
Canada

USA Rent-A-Car System, Inc.
800-USA-CARS

U-Save Auto Rental of America
800-272-USAV

Value Rent-A-Car
800-327-2501 Cont'l USA,
Canada

Airline Toll-Free '800' Numbers

American Airlines, Inc. (AA)
800-433-7300

Canadian Airlines Intl, LTD
800-426-7000

Continental Airlines (CO)
800-525-0280

Delta Air Lines, Inc. (DL)
800-221-1212

Northwest Airlines, Inc. (NW)
800-225-2525

Southwest Airlines (WN)
800-435-9792

Trans World Airlines, Inc. (TW)
800-221-2000

United Air Lines, Inc. (UA)
800-241-6522

USAir (US)
800-428-4322

Alabama

Population: 4,040,587

Land area: 51,998 square miles

Elevation: 0–2,407 feet

Highest point: Cheaha Mountain (Cleburne County)

Entered Union: December 14, 1819 (22nd state)

Capital: Montgomery

Motto: We Dare Defend Our Rights

Nickname: Heart of Dixie

State flower: Camellia

State bird: Yellowhammer

State tree: Southern pine

State fair: Early or mid-October, 1994, in Birmingham

Time zone: Central

From the Confederacy's first capital at Montgomery to America's first "space capital" at Huntsville, Alabama has successfully spanned a century that began in sectional conflict but is ending in a dedication to man's quest to bridge the universe. The drive from the business center of Birmingham to the heart of the Cotton Kingdom surrounding Montgomery and Selma is less than 100 miles, but these miles mark one of the transitions between the 19th and 20th centuries.

Harnessing the Tennessee River made it possible to control floods and turn the eroded soil into bountiful crop land. The river became the South's most important waterway, and giant Tennessee Valley Authority (TVA) dams brought electric power and industrialization to once-bypassed cities. They also gave northern Alabama nationally renowned water recreation areas.

Cotton, the traditional wealth of Alabama's rich Black Belt, fed the busy port of Mobile until the 1870s, when Birmingham grew into an industrial center. TVA brought the other great shift in the 1930s, culminating in new hydroelectric and steam-plant power production in the 1960s.

Cotton and river waterways were the combination on which the Old South was built. Alabama, the Cotton State supreme by the 1850s, built river towns like Selma, the old capital of "Cahawba," and Montgomery, the new capital and "cradle of the Confederacy." The red iron ore in the northern mountains was neglected, except for isolated forges operated by individuals, until just before the Civil War.

On January 11, 1861, Alabama became the fourth state to secede from the Union. Jefferson Davis was inaugurated as president of the Confederacy in Montgomery the following month and on April 12, he ordered General P.G.T. Beauregard to fire on Fort Sumter. The Confederate capital was moved to Richmond on May 21, 1861.

Alabama's troops fought with every active Southern force, the state contributing between 65,000 and 100,000 men from a white population of 500,000. At least 2,500 white soldiers and 10,000 black soldiers went north to support the Union. When Huntsville, Decatur and Tuscumbia fell to Union forces in 1862, every male from 16 to 60 was ordered to the state's defense. Little fighting took place on Alabama's soil and water again until Admiral Farragut's Union fleet won the Battle of Mobile Bay in 1864, though the city of Mobile did not fall. Full-scale invasions by Wilson's Raiders occupied several important cities in the spring of 1865.

Reconstruction days were made bitter by carpetbaggers who supported the Republican Party. The state refused to ratify the Fourteenth Amendment, and military law was reinstated. But by the 1880s, recovery was beginning. Birmingham had weathered the national panic of 1873 successfully and was producing steel in earnest.

Historic attractions are plentiful. There is the birthplace of Helen Keller at Tuscumbia (see SHEFFIELD); the unusual Ave Maria Grotto in Cullman (see), an inspiring work of faith by one Benedictine monk who built scores of miniature religious buildings; and the museum and laboratory of the great black educator and scientist George Washington Carver at the Tuskegee Institute (see TUSKEGEE).

On Alabama's Gulf Coast, the port city of Mobile makes a splendid entry to the whole Gulf strip between Florida and New Orleans. Mobile is famous for the Bellingrath Gardens and Home, the annual Azalea Trail and Festival and its own Mardi Gras celebration.

National Park Service Areas

Part of the Natchez Trace Parkway (see under MISSISSIPPI) crosses the northwest corner of the state. Other national parks within Alabama are Horseshoe Bend National Military Park (see); Russell Cave National Monument (see); and Tuskegee Institute National Historic Site (see TUSKEGEE).

National Forests

The following is an alphabetical listing of National Forests and towns they are listed under.

Bankhead National Forest (see CULLMAN): Forest Supervisor in Montgomery; Ranger office in Double Springs*.

Conecuh National Forest (see EVERGREEN): Forest Supervisor in Montgomery; Ranger office in Andalusia*.

Talladega National Forest (see TALLADEGA): Forest Supervisor in Montgomery; Ranger offices in Brent*, Heflin*, Talladega.

Tuskegee National Forest (see TUSKEGEE): Forest Supervisor in Montgomery; Ranger office in Tuskegee.

*Not described in text

State Recreation Areas

The following towns list state recreation areas in their vicinity under What to See and Do; refer to the individual town for directions and park information.

Listed under **Alexander City:** see Wind Creek State Park.

Listed under **Athens:** see Elk River State Park.

Listed under **Atmore:** see Claude D. Kelley State Park.

Listed under **Auburn:** see Chewacla State Park.

Listed under **Bessemer:** see Tannehill Historical State Park.

Listed under **Birmingham:** see Oak Mountain and Rickwood Caverns state parks.

Listed under **Eufaula:** see Lakepoint Resort State Park.

Listed under **Florence:** see Joe Wheeler State Park (Elk River, First Creek and Wheeler Dam units).

Listed under **Fort Payne:** see DeSoto State Park.

Listed under **Gulf Shores:** see Gulf State Park.

Listed under **Guntersville:** see Buck's Pocket and Lake Guntersville state parks.

Listed under **Huntsville:** see Monte Sano State Park.

Listed under **Ozark:** see Blue Springs State Park.

Listed under **Selma:** see Paul M. Grist State Park.

Listed under **Talladega:** see Cheaha State Park.

Listed under **Tuscaloosa:** see Lake Lurleen State Park.

Water-related activities, hiking, riding, various sports, picnicking, camping and visitor centers are available in many of these areas. Nominal entrance fees are collected at some parks. The state parks accept telephone reservations for motel rooms, cabins and improved campsites; primitive campsites are on a no-reservation basis. Fees for improved campsites are $8–$20/site/night. No pets at motels and cabins; pets on leash only at campgrounds. There are many state park fishing lakes and 12 parks that offer boat rentals and water-recreational equipment. Bait, tackle and freshwater fishing permits are $2/day; under 13, 75¢/day. Contact the Alabama Department of Conservation and Natural Resources, Alabama State Parks Division, 64 N Union St, Montgomery 36130; 205/242-3334 for details. For reservations phone 800/252-7275 or 205/242-3333.

Fishing & Hunting

More than 35,000 small ponds and lakes, including 22 public lakes and more than one-half million acres of public impounded waters, provide ample freshwater fishing. Crappie, striped and white bass, bluegill and redear sunfish can be caught statewide. State and national forests and state parks cater to anglers. White sandy beaches of the Gulf Coast are good for surf casting; trolling farther out in Gulf waters can net tarpon, snapper, king mackerel and other game fish. Largemouth bass abound from the Tennessee River to Mobile Bay. The Lewis Smith and Martin reservoirs have both largemouth and spotted bass; the Wilson and Wheeler Dam tailwaters have smallmouth bass; the East Central Alabama streams have redeye bass. Alabama has no closed season on freshwater game fish. Sport fishing licenses, nonresident: annual, $16; 7-day, $8 (includes issuance fee). The fees for reciprocal licenses for the residents of adjoining states and Louisiana vary. For information about fishing licenses phone 205/242-3467.

Waterfowl, small game, turkey and deer are found in the state, with state-managed and national forest wildlife areas providing hunting in season. Deer and turkey hunting require an all-game hunting license. Federal and State Waterfowl Stamps are required in addition to a regular hunting license, when hunting waterfowl. Because nearly all lands in Alabama are under private ownership and state law requires written permission from the owner prior to hunting, persons desiring to hunt should make arrangements accordingly. Hunting licenses, nonresident: annual all-game, $177; annual small game, $17; 7-day all-game, $52; 7-day small game, $16. Management Area Deer and Turkey licenses ($4) are required in the management areas in addition to the regular hunting license. A reciprocal agreement among Alabama and the states of Florida and Georgia may alter the license fees charged residents of those states. License costs for nonresident hunting licenses includes a $2 issuance fee. For detailed information on seasons and other regulations, contact Alabama Dept of Conservation and Natural Resources, Game and Fish Division, 64 N Union St, Montgomery 36130; 205/242-3467.

Skiing

Listed under **Fort Payne:** see Cloudmont Ski Resort.

Safety Belt Information

All passengers in front seat must wear a safety belt. Children under 6 years must be in an approved passenger restraint anywhere in vehicle: ages 4 and 5 may use a regulation safety belt; age 3 and under must use an approved safety seat. For further information phone 205/242-4445.

Interstate Highway System

The following alphabetical listing of Alabama towns in *Mobil Travel Guide* shows that these cities are within 10 miles of the indicated Interstate highways. A highway map should, however, be checked for the nearest exit.

INTERSTATE 10: Mobile.

INTERSTATE 20: Anniston, Bessemer, Birmingham, Tuscaloosa.

INTERSTATE 59: Bessemer, Birmingham, Fort Payne, Gadsden, Tuscaloosa.

INTERSTATE 65: Athens, Atmore, Birmingham, Clanton, Cullman, Decatur, Evergreen, Greenville, Mobile, Montgomery.

INTERSTATE 85: Auburn, Montgomery, Opelika, Tuskegee.

Additional Visitor Information

Travel and vacation information is offered toll free, phone 800/ALABAMA (Mon–Fri, 8 am–5 pm). Travelers also may contact the Alabama Bureau of Tourism & Travel, 401 Adams Ave, PO Box 4309, Montgomery 36103-4309; 205/242-4169 for additional information.

There are eight welcome centers in Alabama; there visitors will find information and brochures that will help plan stops at points of interest: Alabama (I-59S), Ardmore (I-65S), Baldwin (I-10W), Grand Bay (I-10E), Hardy (I-20W, near Heflin), Houston (US 231N), Lanett (I-85S) and Sumter (I-59N); inquire locally for further information on these centers.

Alexander City (C-4)

Settled: 1836 **Pop:** 14,917 **Elev:** 707 ft **Area code:** 205 **Zip:** 35010

Martin Dam at Cherokee Bluffs not only supplies power for the city's industries, but also creates Lake Martin on the Tallapoosa River. Lake Martin, with a 760-mile shoreline, was the largest of its kind when it was formed in 1926. Today, it is one of the South's finest inland recreation areas.

What to See and Do

1. **Wind Creek State Park.** 7 mi SE off AL 63. A 1,445-acre wooded park on Lake Martin. Swimming beach, bathhouses, waterskiing; fishing; boating (marina, ramps). Hiking, bicycling. Picnic area, concessions. Improved campsites. Observation tower. Park open all yr. Standard fees. Phone 329-0845.

2. **Horseshoe Bend National Military Park** (see). 13 mi NE on AL 22 to New Site, then S on AL 49.

(For further information contact the Chamber of Commerce, 100 Tallapoosa St, Box 926; 234-3461.)

(See Sylacauga)

Motels

★**HORSESHOE BEND.** *(Box 343) US 280 at AL 22. 205/234-6311; FAX 205/234-6314.* 90 rms. S $34–$44; D $37–$50; each addl $5. TV; cable. Pool. Restaurant opp open 24 hrs. Bar 4–10 pm, closed Sun. Ck-out 11 am. Meeting rms. Cr cds: A, C, D, DS, MC, V.

🅳 ⤢ 🚭 ◎ SC

✔ ★**SUPER 8.** *1104 US 280 Bypass. 205/329-8858; FAX 205/329-8858, ext 403.* 44 units, 3 story. No elvtr. S $34.99; D $41.99; each addl $4; under 12 free; wkly rates. Crib free. TV; cable. Complimentary coffee in lobby. Restaurant adj 6 am–10 pm. Ck-out 11 am. Cr cds: A, C, D, DS, MC, V.

🅳 🚭 ◎ SC

Restaurant

✔ ★★**CECIL'S PUBLIC HOUSE.** *405 Green St. 205/329-0732.* Hrs: 11 am–2 pm, 5–9 pm; Sat from 5 pm. Closed Sun; most major hols. Bar 5 pm–midnight. Semi-a la carte: lunch $5.50–$6.95, dinner $5.50–$17.95. Child's meals. Specializes in seafood, steak. Parking. Old house (1902); antique plate collection; stained-glass windows. Cr cds: A, MC, V.

🅳

Anniston (B-4)

Settled: 1872 **Pop:** 26,623 **Elev:** 710 ft **Area code:** 205 **Zip:** 36201

Anniston was founded by Samuel Noble, an Englishman who headed the ironworks in Rome, Georgia, and Daniel Tyler, a Connecticut capitalist. They established textile mills and blast furnaces designed to help launch the South into the industrial revolution after the devastation of the Civil War. In 1879, the owners hired accomplished Eastern architects, including the renowned Stanford White, to design and build a modern company town. The town was named after Mrs. Anne Scott Taylor (Annie's Town), wife of one of the local iron magnates. Anniston remained a private company town until 1883 when it was opened to the public. Today, Anniston retains many historic structures and much of its original character.

What to See and Do

1. **The Church of St Michael and All Angels** (Episcopal) (1888). W 18th St & Cobb Ave. Gothic church, parish house, assembly room and bell tower of native stone are connected by cloisters. Twelve-foot Carrara marble altar with alabaster reredos surmounted by seven statues of angels. Stained-glass memorial windows. Lithographs of Christian history are in assembly room. (Daily) Phone 237-4011.

2. **Anniston Museum of Natural History.** 800 Museum Dr, Lagarde Park. Museum featuring Regar-Werner bird exhibit with 600 specimens including many endangered and extinct birds; reconstruction of pteranodon, a 30-foot flying dinosaur; large African animal exhibit featuring large bull elephant; Egyptian mummies; North American mammals; live reptiles; giant termite mound; replica of an Alabama cave; and changing exhibition gallery. Situated in 187-acre John B. Lagarde Environmental Interpretive Center; nature trails, picnic facilities. (Daily exc Mon; closed most major hols) Tours (by appt only, 2 wks advance notice). Phone 237-6766. ¢¢

3. **Fort McClellan.** On AL 21, 6 mi N of I-20 exit 185. Established in 1917, the fort houses the US Army Chemical School, US Army Military Police School and DOD Polygraph Institute. It also serves as a center for basic combat training. Includes three museums (Mon–Fri; wkends by appt; closed hols). **Free.** US Army Chemical Corps Museum, phone 848-3355; US Army Military Police Corps Musuem, phone 848-3522. Also here is

Women's Army Corps Museum. Approx 8 mi N via AL 21 at N edge of Fort McClellan; enter at Galloway Gate. Museum presents the story of women in the Army and the heritage of the WACS, established in 1942. Exhibits, displays and films illuminate the role of women, from private to major general, in war and in peace. (Mon–Fri; closed hols) Phone 848-3512. **Free.**

4. **Dr J.C. Francis Medical Museum and Apothecary** (1850). 310 Church Ave SE, 12 mi N, off AL 21 in Jacksonville. Unusual one-story Greek-revival building served as doctor's office until 1888; medical artifacts, period furnishings. Tours by appt only. Phone 435-5091. **Free.**

5. **Coldwater Covered Bridge.** 3 mi S via US 431, 5 mi W on US 78 in Coldwater at Oxford Lake and Civic Center. Built prior to 1850; one of 13 restored covered bridges in Alabama.

(For further information, including brochures describing local historic tours, contact the Convention & Visitors Bureau, 14th St and Quintard Ave, PO Box 1087, 36202; 237-3536.)

(See Gadsden, Talladega)

Motels

(Higher rates Talladega race weekends)

★★**BEST WESTERN RIVERSIDE INN.** *(Rte 1, Box 1310, Pell City 35125) I-20 exit 162 & US 78. 205/338-3381; FAX 205/338-3183.* 70 rms, 2 story. S $35–$40; D $45–$55; each addl $6; under 12 free; race wkends 4-day min. Crib $2. TV. Pool; wading pool. Restaurant 6 am–2 pm, 5–9 pm. Ck-out 11 am. Coin lndry. Meeting rms. Boating; waterskiing. Pier. On Logan-Martin Lake. Cr cds: A, C, D, DS, MC, V.

🅳 ⬦ 🐟 ⤢ 🚭 ◎ SC

✔ ★★**HAMPTON INN.** *(1600 AL 21 S, Oxford 36203) 2 mi S via AL 21 S. 205/835-1492; FAX 205/835-0636.* 129 rms, 2 story. S $39; D $48; each addl $6; under 18 free; 3-day min Talladega Races. Crib free. TV; cable, in-rm movies. Pool. Complimentary continental bkfst. Restaurant opp open 24 hrs. Ck-out noon. Meeting rms. Cr cds: A, C, D, DS, MC, V.

🅳 ⤢ 🚭 ◎ SC

★★**HOLIDAY INN.** *(Box 3308, Oxford 36203) Jct I-20, AL 21 S, near Municipal Airport. 205/831-3410; FAX 205/831-9560.* 237 rms, 2 story. S, D $48–$66; each addl $6; suites $54–$95; under 19 free; wkend rates. Crib free. TV; cable. Pool; whirlpool. Playground. Coffee in rms. Restaurant 6 am–2 pm, 5–10 pm. Rm serv. Bar 11 am–11 pm; dancing exc Sun. Ck-out noon. Coin lndry. Meeting rms. Bellhops. Valet serv.

Airport transportation. Game rm. Refrigerators avail. Picnic tables, grills. Cr cds: A, C, D, DS, MC, V, JCB.

[D] [symbols]

Inns

★★**NOBLE-McCAA-BUTLER HOUSE.** *1025 Fairmont St, at 11th.* 205/236-1791; FAX 205/237-5997. 6 rms, 2 story. S, D $85–$115; each addl $10. TV; cable. Complimentary full bkfst. Ck-out 11 am, ck-in 1 pm. Antiques. Library/sitting rm. Built 1887; spiral staircase, Oriental rugs. Totally nonsmoking. Cr cds: A, C, D, MC, V.

[symbols]

★★★**VICTORIA.** *(Box 2213) 1604 Quintard Ave.* 205/236-0503; FAX 205/236-1138. 48 units, 3 bldgs, 3 story. S $54; D $64; each addl $10; suites $75–$140; under 13 free. Crib $10. TV; cable. Pool. Dining rm 7 am–9 pm. Rm serv. Ck-out noon, ck-in 3 pm. Concierge. Some bathrm phones. Some rms in historic house (1888). Cr cds: A, C, D, DS, MC, V.

[D] [symbols]

Restaurants

★★**ANNISTONIAN.** *1709 Noble.* 205/236-5156. Hrs: 4–10 pm. Closed Sun, Mon; Dec 25; also wk of July 4. Res accepted Fri, Sat. German, Amer menu. Bar. Semi-a la carte: dinner $8.95–$24.95. Child's meals. Specializes in steak, seafood. Parking. Cr cds: A, C, D, DS, MC, V.

[D]

✔★**TOP O' THE RIVER.** *3220 McClellan Blvd.* 205/238-0097. Hrs: 5–9 pm; Thurs to 9:30 pm; Fri to 10 pm; Sat 4:30–10 pm; Sun noon–9 pm. Closed some major hols. Res accepted Sun–Thurs. Serv bar. Complete meals: lunch, dinner $6.95–$14.95. Child's meals. Specializes in catfish, seafood. Parking. Historic photos on display. Cr cds: A, C, D, DS, MC, V.

[D] [SC]

Unrated Dining Spot

MORRISON'S CAFETERIA. *(700 S Quintard Ave, Oxford) In Quintard Mall.* 205/831-7470. Hrs: 11 am–8 pm; Sun to 7 pm. Avg ck: lunch $5, dinner $5.50. Specializes in vegetables, roast beef, strawberry shortcake. Own desserts. Cr cds: A, MC, V.

Athens (A-3)

Founded: 1818 **Pop:** 16,901 **Elev:** 720 ft **Area code:** 205 **Zip:** 35611

The quiet, tree-lined streets and Greek-revival houses lend an air of the old antebellum South to Athens. This was the first major Alabama town to be occupied by Union troops in the Civil War (1862). It was also the first Alabama city to get electricity (1934) from the Tennessee Valley Authority. Electrification soon spread to the surrounding area, aiding in the development of light manufacturing.

What to See and Do

1. **Athens State College** (1822). (3,200 students) Beaty & Pryor Sts. On campus is Founders Hall (1843), as well as many examples of Greek-revival architecture. On the second floor of Founders Hall is the Pi Tau Chi Chapel, housing a hand-carved altar depicting scenes from New Testament. Tours of campus (academic yr, Mon–Fri). Phone 233-8100.
2. **Houston Memorial Library and Museum.** Market & Houston Sts. Built in 1835, this house was once owned by George S. Houston,

governor of Alabama and US senator. It is now maintained by the city of Athens. Meeting rooms display Houston coat of arms, family portraits and drawing-room furniture. (Mon–Fri, also Sat mornings; closed most hols) Phone 233-8770. **Free.**

3. **Elk River State Park** (part of Joe Wheeler State Park). 15 mi W on US 72. On Elk River north of Wheeler Lake. This 85-acre park offers fishing, fishing supplies; boating (launch, rentals). Picnicking, concession. Group lodge. Phone 729-8228.

(For further information contact Athens-Limestone County Chamber of Commerce, PO Box 150; 232-2600.)

Annual Events

Musical Explosion. Athens Bible School. All types of music exc rock. Two wkends late Mar. Phone 232-3525.

Homespun. Craft show featuring woodworking, quilting, basketmaking; also buggy rides. Phone 232-3525. Early May.

Tennessee Valley Old Time Fiddlers Convention. Athens State College. A weekend of traditional American music. Fiddle, mandolin, guitar, banjo and old-time singing; also buck dancing. National and international musicians perform; ends with the naming of the Tennessee Valley Fiddle King. Phone 233-8100. Fri & Sat of 1st full wk Oct.

(See Decatur, Huntsville)

Motels

★**BEST WESTERN.** *(PO Box 816) 2 mi E via I-65, at US 72 exit 351.* 205/233-4030; FAX 205/233-4551. 88 rms, 2 story. S $34; D $42; each addl $4; under 12 free. Crib free. Pet accepted, some restrictions. TV; cable. Pool. Complimentary continental bkfst, coffee. Restaurant opp 6 am–midnight. Ck-out noon. Picnic tables. Cr cds: A, C, D, DS, MC, V.

[D] [symbols] [SC]

✔★**TRAVELODGE.** *1325 US 72E, 1 mi E of jct US 72 & I-65 exit 351.* 205/233-1446; FAX 205/233-1454. 60 rms, most rms with shower only, 2 story. S $30–$35; D $40–$45; each addl $4; suites, kit. units $45; under 15 free. TV; cable. Complimentary continental bkfst. Complimentary coffee in rms. Restaurant opp open 24 hrs. Ck-out noon. Coin lndry. Some refrigerators. Cr cds: A, C, D, DS, ER, MC, V, JCB.

[D] [symbols] [SC]

★★**WELCOME INN.** *(Box 1125) 1 mi S on US 31 at jct US 72.* 205/232-6944; res: 800/824-6834; FAX 205/232-8019. 80 rms, 1–2 story. S $34–$35; D $37–$41; each addl $5; under 12 free. Crib free. Pet accepted. TV; cable. Pool. Restaurant 6 am–9 pm; Sun to 2 pm. Rm serv. Ck-out noon. Meeting rms. Valet serv. Sundries. Cr cds: A, C, D, DS, ER, MC, V, JCB.

[D] [symbols] [SC]

Atmore (E-2)

Pop: 8,046 **Elev:** 287 ft **Area code:** 205 **Zip:** 36502

What to See and Do

Claude D. Kelley State Park. 12 mi N of I-65, on AL 21 at Atmore exit. A 25-acre lake is located beneath the towering pines of this 960-acre park. Swimming; fishing; boating (ramps, rentals). Picnicking. Primitive camping, RV hookups, cabins. Standard fees. Contact Rte 2, Box 77; 862-2511.

(For further information contact the Chamber of Commerce, 501 S Pensacola Ave; 368-3305.)

(For accommodations see Mobile)

Auburn (C-4)

Settled: 1836 **Pop:** 33,830 **Elev:** 709 ft **Area code:** 205 **Zip:** 36830

Located on the southeastern slope of the Piedmont plateau, this trading and university community is graced with Greek-revival, Victorian and early 20th-century architecture.

What to See and Do

1. **Auburn University** (1856). (21,500 students) SW section of town on I-85, US 29, AL 14, 147. One of the nation's earliest land-grant colleges and the first four-year educational institution in Alabama to admit women on an equal basis with men. A golden eagle, the university mascot, is housed on campus. Tours of campus. Phone 844-4000.

2. **Chewacla State Park.** 4 mi S off US 29; 2 mi off I-85 exit 51. This 696-acre park, on the fall line separating the Piedmont plateau from the coastal plain, includes a 26-acre lake. Swimming, bathhouse (fee); lifeguards; fishing; boating (rentals). Hiking, nature and mountain bike trails. Picnicking, playground, concession. Improved camping, cabins. Standard fees. Phone 887-5621.

(For further information contact the Chamber of Commerce, 714 E Glenn Ave, PO Box 1370; 887-7011.)

(See Opelika, Tuskegee; also see Columbus, GA)

Motel

 **AUBURN CONFERENCE CENTER & MOTOR LODGE.** *(Box 3467)* 1577 S College St, I-85 exit 51. 205/821-7001. 122 rms, 3 story. S $36–$41; D $42–$47; each addl $6; suites $54–$59; under 12 free; higher rates Auburn Univ football games (2-day min). Crib free. TV; cable. Pool. Restaurant 6:30 am–1:30 pm; Sat & Sun to 10 am. Bar 4 pm–1 am. Ck-out 11 am. Meeting rms. Sundries. Gift shop. Free airport transportation. Game rm. Cr cds: A, C, D, DS, MC, V.

Hotel

★★★**AUBURN UNIVERSITY HOTEL & CONFERENCE CENTER.** 241 S College St. 205/821-8200; res: 800/228-2876; FAX 205/826-8755. 248 rms, 6 story. S, D $59–$85; each addl $10; suites $165–$250; under 18 free; higher rates football games. Crib free. Pet accepted. TV; cable. Pool. Restaurant 7 am–9 pm; wkends to 10 pm. Bar 11:30 am–11 pm. Ck-out noon. Convention facilities. Gift shop. Exercise equipt; weights, bicycles. Located on eastern edge of campus opp Samford Hall, university library. Cr cds: A, C, D, DS, MC, V.

Restaurant

 ★★**DENARO'S.** 103 N College St. 205/821-0349. Hrs: 5–10 pm. Closed Sun; Thanksgiving, Dec 24–25. Res accepted. Italian, Amer menu. Bar 4 pm–2 am. Semi-a la carte: dinner $5–$24. Specializes in seafood, baked lasagne, steak. Cr cds: A, C, D, MC, V.

Unrated Dining Spot

MORRISON'S CAFETERIA. 1627 Opelika Rd, in Village Mall. 205/821-3200. Hrs: 10:45 am–8:30 pm. Avg ck: lunch, dinner $5. Specializes in roast beef, seafood, strawberry shortcake. Cr cds: A, DS, MC, V.

Bessemer (B-3)

Founded: 1887 **Pop:** 33,497 **Elev:** 513 ft **Area code:** 205

The city of Bessemer was founded on April 12, 1887 by Henry F. DeBardeleben. It was, however, named after Sir Henry Bessemer, inventor of the steel-making process that bears his name. As additional furnaces were built in Bessemer, the population grew. By the 1930s, the town ranked second only to Birmingham as a state center for heavy industry. The factories turned out iron and steel, cast-iron pipe, steel railway cars, explosives, fertilizer and building materials. Today service industries dominate Bessemer's economy; the medical community is among the city's largest employers.

What to See and Do

1. **Hall of History Museum.** In Southern Railway Depot, 1905 Alabama Ave. Displays of pioneer life in Jefferson County, Mound Indians, prehistoric life, the Civil War and Bessemer city history. (Tues–Sat; closed hols) Phone 426-1633. **Free.**

2. **Tannehill Historical State Park.** 12 mi SW off I-59, exit 100 at Bucksville. Restored ironworks that once produced 20 tons of pig iron a day for the Confederacy. Iron & Steel Museum (daily). Park features bathhouses; fishing. Nature trails. Picnicking, concession. Camping (hookups, dump station; fee); bathhouses. Park (daily). Phone 477-5711. Day use ¢

3. **Tannehill Opry.** 8 mi SW on I-59, Bucksville exit, Tannehill Pkwy in McCalla. Music hall created to preserve and promote country-western, bluegrass and gospel music. Local and guest bands featured. (Sat nights) For further information contact the Chamber of Commerce. **Free.**

(For further information contact the Bessemer Area Chamber of Commerce Center, PO Box 648, 35021; phone 425-3253.)

Annual Event

Christmas Heritage Tour. Usually 1st Sun Dec.

(See Birmingham, Tuscaloosa)

Motels

✔ ★★**BEST WESTERN BESSEMER INN.** *(Box 629, 35021)* 1098 9th Ave SW. 205/424-0880. 114 rms, 2 story. S $35.95–$43; D $38–$48; each addl $6; suites $85; under 12 free. Crib $2. TV; cable. Pool. Coffee in rms. Restaurant 6–9 am, 5–9 pm; closed Sun evening. Rm serv 7–9 am, 6–9 pm. Bar 3 pm–2 am; entertainment, dancing exc Sun. Ck-out noon. Meeting rms. Valet serv. Cr cds: A, C, D, DS, ER, MC, V, JCB.

★★**ECONO LODGE.** 1021 9th Ave SW (35020), on US 11 at jct I-20, I-59. 205/424-9780; FAX 205/424-9780, ext 191. 154 rms, 2 story. S $34–$39; D $39–$45; each addl $5; under 12 free. Crib free. TV; cable, in-rm movies avail. Pool; wading pool. Restaurant 6–9 am, 4 pm–midnight. Rm serv 7 am–9 pm. Bar 4 pm–2 am; entertainment, dancing exc Sun. Ck-out noon. Coin lndry. Meeting rms. Valet serv. Some refrigerators. Cr cds: A, C, D, DS, MC, V.

Restaurants

★★**BRIGHT STAR.** 304 19th St N. 205/424-9444. Hrs: 11 am–10 pm. Closed major hols. Res accepted. Greek, Amer menu. Bar. Semi-a la carte: lunch $4–$6, dinner $9.95–$21.95. Child's meals. Specializes in Greek broiled red snapper, steak. Parking. Cr cds: A, C, D, MC, V.

✔ ★**FURNACE MASTERS.** *22851 Eastern Valley Rd.* 205/477-6102. Hrs: 11 am–9 pm; Sat, Sun from 7 am. Closed Mon; major hols. Semi-a la carte: bkfst $3.25–$5.95, lunch $4–$6, dinner $5–$13. Buffet: bkfst (Sat, Sun) $4.95. Seafood buffet: dinner (Fri, Sat) $11.95. Child's meals. Specialties: Bessemer fried chicken, country ham steak. Parking. Rustic setting. No cr cds accepted.

Unrated Dining Spot

BOB SYKES BAR-B-QUE. *1724 9th Ave.* 205/426-1400. Hrs: 10 am–10 pm; Fri, Sat to 11 pm. Closed Sun; Jan 1, Thanksgiving, Dec 25. Semi-a la carte: lunch, dinner $2.50–$8. Specializes in open pit barbecued pork, homemade pies. Parking. Family-owned. Cr cds: MC, V.

Birmingham (B-3)

Founded: 1870 **Pop:** 265,968 **Elev:** 601 ft **Area code:** 205

A city of great industrial strength, Birmingham once proudly called itself the "Pittsburgh of the South." Today, Birmingham is equally proud of its reputation as an international medical center. Advances in medical science through research at the University of Alabama medical complex attract patients worldwide.

At the turn of the 19th century, Native Americans who painted their faces and weapons red were known by early settlers as "Red Sticks." Even when the red paint was found to be hematite iron ore, it was still considered worthless, and many years passed before Red Mountain ore became the foundation for Birmingham's steel industry. The Confederacy's lack of iron in 1863 led to the building of a small blast furnace, which produced cannonballs and rifles until Wilson's Raiders destroyed it in 1865.

Birmingham was born in 1870 when two railroads intersected. A year later, the Elyton Land Company had sold most of its 4,150 acres at fabulous prices. (It had bought the land for $25 an acre.) But, in 1873 a double disaster struck. First, cholera drove hundreds from the new city; then, the nationwide financial panic nearly doomed Birmingham to extinction. Refusing to give in, Charles Linn, a former Civil War blockade runner who had opened a small bank in 1871, built a grand three-story brick bank for the huge (at that time) sum of $36,000. He then sent out 500 invitations to a "Calico Ball," as he called it, to celebrate its opening. Guests came from all over the state; women in ball gowns and men in formal dress all cut from calico. "Linn's folly" paid off—Birmingham was saved.

Today, Birmingham is a modern, progressive city—one of culture as well as steel, and of education as well as the social life that began with the Calico Ball. To visitors, it offers much in recreational and sightseeing opportunities. Birmingham Green, a major renaissance of the downtown area, added walkways, plantings, benches and the DART trolley. "Five Points South," featuring clubs with many styles of quality entertainment, plays a major role in Birminghams's nightlife. This is indeed the heart of the New South.

Transportation

Birmingham Municipal Airport: Information 599-0533; lost and found 599-0519; weather 945-7000; club lounge, Crown Room (Delta).

Car Rental Agencies: See toll-free numbers under Introduction.

Public Transportation: Buses (Birmingham/Jefferson County Transit Authority), phone 322-7701.

Rail Passenger Service: Amtrak 800/872-7245.

What to See and Do

1. **Vulcan** (1904). On Valley View Dr off US 31 at top of Red Mountain in Vulcan Park. The figure of Vulcan, designed for the Louisiana Purchase Exposition in St Louis, is one of the largest iron figures ever cast, standing 55 feet tall and weighing 60 tons. It surveys the city from a pedestal 124 feet high. Made of Birmingham iron and cast locally, Vulcan, Roman god of fire and forge, legendary inventor of smithing and metalworking, stands as a monument to the city's iron industry. A glass-enclosed elevator takes passengers to observation deck. Park (daily). Phone 328-6198 or -2863. ¢

2. **Arlington** (ca 1850). 331 Cotton Ave SW. Birmingham's last remaining antebellum house in the Greek-revival style features a diverse collection of 19th-century American decorative art. Located on a sloping hill in Elyton, the house is surrounded by shady lawns, oak and magnolia trees and seasonal plantings. (Daily exc Mon; closed major hols) Phone 780-5656. ¢¢

3. **Birmingham Museum of Art.** 2000 8th Ave N, across from Linn Park. Features collections of Renaissance, Asian and American art, including Remington bronzes; 20th-century collection; 17th–19th-century American and European paintings and decorative arts. Also featured are pre-Columbian art and artifacts, art of the Native American and the largest collection of Wedgwood outside of England. Changing exhibits. Multi-level sculpture garden with 2 reflecting pools and a waterfall. (Daily exc Mon; closed major hols) Phone 254-2565. **Free.**

4. **Birmingham/Jefferson Civic Center.** Between 9th and 11th Aves N, 19th and 21st Sts. The entire complex covers four square blocks. The center contains a 120,000-square-foot exhibition hall; 3,000-seat concert hall; 1,000-seat theater; 18,000-seat coliseum. For event information phone 458-8400.

5. **Alabama Sports Hall of Fame Museum.** Civic Center Blvd & 22nd St N. Showcase for memorabilia of Alabama sports figures; sound-sensored displays; theater. (Mon–Sat, also Sun afternoons; closed some major hols) Sr citizen rate. Phone 323-6665. ¢¢

6. **The Discovery Place.** 1320 22nd St S. Museum directed toward children, with hands-on exhibits; science and technology; arts and humanities. Natural science, energy, career and communications exhibits. (Daily exc Mon; closed some major hols, also Sept) Phone 939-1176. Combination ticket with Red Mountain Museum (see #10) is available. Phone 939-1176. ¢

7. **Birmingham Civil Rights Institute.** 520 16th St N. Exhibits portray struggle for civil rights in Birmingham and across the nation from the 1920s to the present; multimedia presentations. For further information phone 323-2276.

8. **Sloss Furnaces National Historic Landmark.** 20 32nd St. An industrial museum and site for concerts and downtown festivals. (Daily exc Mon) For event and further information phone 324-1911. **Free.**

9. **Birmingham Botanical Gardens.** 2612 Lane Park Rd. Includes orchids, lilies, dogwood, wildflowers, azaleas; 26-foot floral clock, conservatory and arboretum of rare plants, shrubs and trees. (Daily) Restaurant on grounds. Phone 879-1227. **Free.** Includes

Japanese Gardens. Gardens landscaped with Oriental plants, waterfalls. Also here is a bonsai complex, Oriental statuary and a Zen garden. Gravel paths. (Daily) **Free.**

10. **Red Mountain Museum.** 1421 22nd St S. Natural history museum located on slopes of Red Mountain. Extensive collection of fossils includes a 14-foot mosasaur (extinct marine lizard); geologic history displays and exhibits. Walkway carved into the face of the mountain above expressway. More than 150 million years of geologic history are exposed for one-third of a mile. Picnicking. (Daily exc Mon; closed hols) Combination ticket with Discovery Place (see #6) is available. Phone 933-4104. ¢

11. **Ruffner Mountain Nature Center.** 1214 81st St S. 538 acres of the last undeveloped section of this area's Appalachian Mountains. Displays focus on Ruffner Mountain's biology, geology and history. Wildlife refuge with nature trails. Fee for special programs.

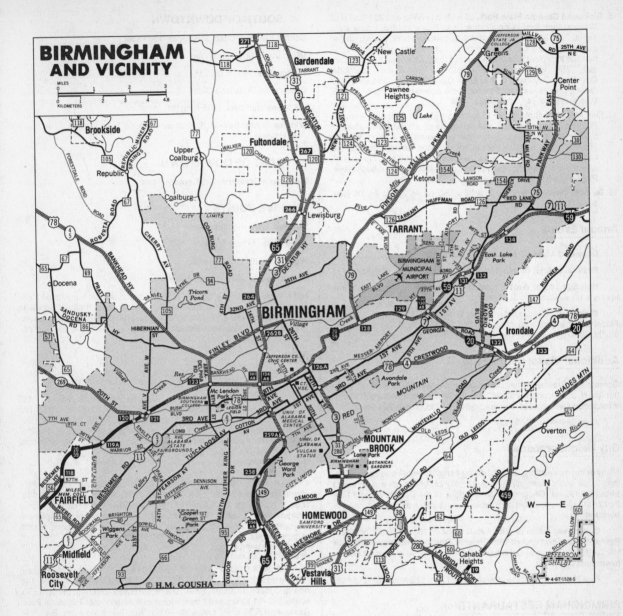

BIRMINGHAM AND VICINITY

© H.M. GOUSHA

(Daily exc Mon; closed most major hols, also Dec 24) Phone 833-8112. **Free.**

12. University of Alabama at Birmingham. (16,500 students) 70-square-block area on S edge of downtown. **Reynolds Historical Library** in the Lister Hill Library of the Health Sciences, 1700 University Blvd, 6 blks west of US 31 and US 280, has collections of ivory anatomical manikins, original manuscripts and rare medical and scientific books; **Alabama Museum of Health Sciences** has memorabilia of Alabama doctors, surgeons, optometrists and other medical practitioners; reproductions of doctor and dentist turn-of-the-century offices. (Mon–Fri) Phone 934-4475. **Free.**

13. Birmingham-Southern College (1856). (1,900 students) Arkadelphia Rd. A 200-acre campus on wooded rolling hills. Here is the state's first planetarium (for schedule, reservations, phone 226-4770; fee). Tours of campus. Phone 226-4600.

14. Samford University (1841). (4,300 students) 800 Lakeshore Dr in Shades Mt section. A 172-acre campus with brick Georgian-colonial buildings. The Samford Murals on view in Rotunda, Dwight and Lucille Beeson Center for the Healing Arts. Concerts on 60-bell Rushton Memorial Carillon (summer, wkdays; schedule varies, phone 870-2921). Tours of campus. Phone 870-2011.

15. Miles College (1905). (700 students) 5500 Myron Massey Blvd in Fairfield. Extensive collection of Afro-American literature; exhibits of African art forms. Two historic landmark buildings. Tours. Phone 923-2771.

16. **Rickwood Caverns State Park.** 20 mi N on I-65 to exit 284 (just N of Warrior) then 4 mi W on Skyline Dr to Rickwood Rd, follow state signs. This 380-acre park offers swimming pools; hiking; carpet golf; miniature train ride. Picnicking, concession, gift shop. Primitive and improved camping (standard fees). One-hour tours of cave with 260 million-year-old limestone formations (Memorial Day–Labor Day, daily; rest of Sept–Oct & Mar–Apr, wkends). Park (all yr); pool (seasonal). Fee for some activities. Phone 647-9692. Park entrance ¢; Cave tour ¢¢¢

17. **Oak Mountain State Park.** 15 mi S on I-65, exit 246, near Pelham. Peavine Falls and Gorge and two lakes sit amidst 9,940 acres of the state's most rugged mountains. Swimming; fishing; boating (marina, ramp, rentals). Hiking, backpacking, bridle trails; golf (18 holes; fee), tennis. Picnicking (shelters, barbecue pits, fireplaces), concession. Camping, cabins. Demonstration farm. Standard fees. Phone 663-6771.

18. **De Soto Caverns Park.** Approx 38 mi SE via AL 280 to AL 76. (See SYLACAUGA)

Annual Events

Dogwood Azalea Trail. Late Mar–early Apr.

Festival of Arts. Different country featured each yr. Mid-Apr.

Heritage Tours. West Jefferson pioneer-style homes open some spring & fall wkends and at Christmas.

State Fair. Fairgrounds. W on Bessemer Rd, US 11. Contact Alabama State Fair Authority, PO Box 3800-B, 2331 Bessemer Rd, 35208; 787-2641. Early or mid-Oct.

Additional Visitor Information

Contact the Greater Birmingham Convention & Visitors Bureau, 2200 9th Ave N, 35203, phone 252-9825; or the Birmingham/Jefferson Visitor Information Center, 1201 University Blvd, 35233, phone 254-1654.

(See Bessemer, Cullman)

City Neighborhoods

Many of the restaurants, unrated dining establishments and some lodgings listed under Birmingham include neighborhoods as well as exact street addresses. Geographic descriptions of the Downtown and Five Points are given, followed by a table of restaurants arranged by neighborhood.

Downtown: South of 10th Ave N, west of 26th St, north of L & N Railroad tracks and east of 15th Street N. **North of Downtown:** North of US 20/US 59. **South of Downtown:** South of First Ave. **East of Downtown:** East of 26th St.

Five Points: Area at the intersection of 20th St S and Highland Ave.

BIRMINGHAM RESTAURANTS BY NEIGHBORHOOD AREAS

(For full description, see alphabetical listings under Restaurants)

DOWNTOWN

Christian's (Tutwiler Hotel). Park Place at 21st St N

La Paree. 2013 5th Ave N

Leo's Cafeteria. 401 18th St S

Michael's Sirloin Room. 431 S 20th St

NORTH OF DOWNTOWN

Niki's West. 233 Finlay Ave W

SOUTH OF DOWNTOWN

Connie Kanakis' Cafe. 3423 Colonade Pkwy

GG in the Park. 3625 8th Ave S

Golden City. 4647K US 280

Grady's. 3470 Galleria Circle

L & N Seafood Grill. 1765 Ring Rd

Winston's (Wynfrey at Riverchase Galleria Hotel). 1000 Riverchase Galleria

EAST OF DOWNTOWN

Morrison's Cafeteria. 236 Century Plaza

FIVE POINTS

Bottega. 2240 Highland Ave

Cobb Lane. 1 Cobb Lane

Highlands. 2011 11th Ave S

Merritt House. 2220 Highland Ave

Note: When a listing is located in a town that does not have its own city heading, it will appear under the city nearest to its location. In these cases, the address and town appear in parenthesis immediately following the name of the establishment.

Motels

(Rates are generally higher during race & football seasons)

★**BUDGETEL INN.** 513 Cahaba Park Circle (35242), I-459 and US 280, south of downtown. 205/995-9990; FAX 205/995-0563. 102 rms, 3 story. S $35.95; D $38.95; each addl $7; suites $44.95–$51.95; under 18 free. Crib free. Pet accepted, some restrictions. TV; cable. Complimentary continental bkfst. Ck-out noon. Meeting rms. Cr cds: A, C, D, DS, MC, V.

D 🐾 🚫 😊 ⊛

✔ ★ ★**COMFORT INN.** 4627 US 280 (35242), at I-459, south of downtown. 205/991-9977; FAX 205/995-0570. 102 rms, 3 story. S $48; D $53; each addl $5; under 18 free. Crib free. Pet accepted, some restrictions. TV; cable. Pool; whirlpool, sauna, steam rm. Complimentary continental bkfst. Coffee in rms. Ck-out 11 am. Meeting rms. Health club privileges. Cr cds: A, C, D, DS, ER, MC, V, JCB.

D 🐾 ⚓ 🚫 😊 SC

★ ★**COURTYARD BY MARRIOTT.** (500 Shades Creek Pkwy, Homewood 35209) S via I-65. 205/879-0400; FAX 205/879-6324. 140 rms, 1–3 story, 14 suites. S $70; D $79; each addl (after 4th person) $10; suites $90–$100; under 12 free; wkend plans. Crib free. TV; cable. Pool. Restaurant 6:30 am–1 pm, 6:30–10 pm; Sat, Sun from 7 am. Bar 4–11 pm. Meeting rms. Guest laundry. Valet serv. Exercise equipt; weight machines, bicycles, whirlpool. Private patios, balconies. Cr cds: A, C, D, DS, MC, V.

D ⚓ 🏋 🚫 😊 SC

★ ★**DAYS INN.** 5101 Airport Blvd (35212), I-20/I-59 Airport exit, near Municipal Airport, east of downtown. 205/592-6110; FAX 205/591-5623. 144 rms, 5 story. S $45–$55; D $51–$61; each addl $5; under 12 free, 13–18, $1. Pet accepted, some restrictions; $5. TV; cable. Pool. Playground. Continental bkfst. Ck-out noon. Meeting rms. Airport transportation. Cr cds: A, C, D, DS, MC, V.

D 🐾 ⚓ ✗ 🚫 😊 SC

✔ ★**ECONO LODGE.** 103 Green Springs Hwy (35209), south of downtown. 205/942-1263; FAX 205/942-1219. 48 rms, 2 story. S $37; D $43–$47; each addl $5; under 12 free. Pet accepted, some restrictions. TV; cable. Complimentary continental bkfst. Restaurant nearby. Ck-out 11 am. Cr cds: A, DS, MC, V.

★★**FAIRFIELD INN BY MARRIOTT.** *(155 Vulcan Rd, Homewood 35209) 3 mi S on I-65 exit 256.* 205/945-9600. 132 rms, 3 story. S $43.95; D $48.95–$58.95; under 18 free. Crib free. TV; cable. Complimentary bkfst in lobby. Ck-out noon. Cr cds: A, C, D, DS, MC, V.

✓★★**HAMPTON INN.** *(2731 US 280, Mountain Brook 35223) S on I-65, NE on Oxmoor Rd to US 280.* 205/870-7822; FAX 205/871-7610. 131 rms, 5 story. S $50; D $56–$60; under 18 free. Crib free. Pet accepted, some restrictions. TV; cable. Pool. Complimentary continental bkfst, coffee. Restaurant adj 6 am–11 pm. Ck-out noon. Meeting rm. Cr cds: A, C, D, DS, MC, V.

★★**LA QUINTA MOTOR INN.** *905 11th Court W (35204), near jct I-20, US 78, north of downtown.* 205/324-4510; FAX 205/252-7972. 106 rms, 3 story. S $49–$65; D $57–$71; each addl $6; under 18 free. Crib free. Pet accepted, some restrictions. TV; cable. Pool. Complimentary continental bkfst, coffee. Restaurant adj open 24 hrs. Ck-out noon. Meeting rms. Cr cds: A, C, D, DS, MC, V.

✓★★**MOTEL BIRMINGHAM.** *7905 Crestwood Blvd (35210), I-20 Montevallo Rd exit, east of downtown.* 205/956-4440; res: 800/338-9275; FAX 205/956-3011. 242 rms, 1–2 story, 18 kits. (no equipt). S $45–$60; D, kit. units $55–$65; suites $75–$90; under 16 free. Crib free. Pet accepted, some restrictions; $10. TV; cable, in-rm movies avail. Pool. Playground. Complimentary continental bkfst. Restaurant adj open 24 hrs. Bar from 4 pm. Ck-out noon. Valet serv. Health club privileges. Cr cds: A, C, D, DS, MC, V.

★★**RESIDENCE INN BY MARRIOTT.** *3 Greenhill Pkwy (35242), at US 280, south of downtown.* 205/991-8686; FAX 205/991-8729. 128 kit. suites, 2 story. Kit. suites $95–$125; wkly, monthly rates. Crib free. TV; cable, in-rm movies avail. Pool; whirlpool. Complimentary continental bkfst. Ck-out noon. Coin lndry. Meeting rms. Valet serv. Sport court. Gas grills. Cr cds: A, C, D, DS, MC, V, JCB.

★★**RIVERCHASE INN GALLERIA.** *1800 Riverchase Dr (35244), 12 mi S off US 31, exit AL 150, south of downtown.* 205/985-7500; res: 800/239-2401; FAX 205/733-8122. 138 rms, 2 story, 6 kits. (no equipt). S, D $48–$53; each addl $5; under 17 free. Crib free. TV; cable. Pool. Complimentary continental bkfst, coffee. Restaurant nearby. Ck-out noon. Meeting rm. Free local transportation. Cr cds: A, D, DS, MC, V.

Motor Hotels

★★**HOLIDAY INN-GALLERIA SOUTH.** *1548 Montgomery Hwy (35216), south of downtown.* 205/822-4350; FAX 205/822-0350. 166 rms, 3 story. S, D $62; each addl $10; under 19 free; higher rates special events. Crib free. TV; cable, in-rm movies avail. Pool; whirlpool. Playground. Restaurant 6 am–2 pm, 5–9 pm. Rm serv. Bar 3 pm–2 am; dancing exc Sun. Ck-out noon. Coin lndry. Meeting rms. Bellhops. Valet serv. Health club privileges. Picnic tables, grills. On 4½-acre stocked lake. Cr cds: A, C, D, DS, MC, V, JCB.

✓★★**HOWARD JOHNSON.** *1485 Montgomery Hwy (35216), I-65 exit 252, south of downtown.* 205/823-4300; FAX 205/823-4300, ext 260. 160 rms, 6 story. S, D $42–$65; each addl $5; suites $60–$70; under 18 free. Crib free. Pet accepted, some restrictions. TV; cable. Pool; wading pool. Complimentary continental bkfst. Restaurant 11 am–midnight. Rm serv. Bar. Ck-out noon. Meeting rms. Bellhops. Lighted tennis. Cr cds: A, C, D, DS, ER, MC, V, JCB.

★★**RAMADA INN-AIRPORT.** *5216 Airport Hwy (35212), I-20/I-59, Airport exit, near Municipal Airport, east of downtown.* 205/591-7900; FAX 205/592-6476. 192 rms, 4 story. S $59–$67; D $63–$71; each addl $8; suites $125. Crib free. Pet accepted, some restrictions. TV; cable. Pool. Playground. Restaurant 6 am–10 pm; Sat–Sun from 7 am. Rm serv from 7 am. Bar 2 pm–2 am; entertainment, dancing exc Sun. Ck-out noon. Meeting rms. Bellhops. Valet serv. Free airport transportation. Exercise equipt; weight machine, bicycle. Cr cds: A, C, D, DS, MC, V.

★★★**RIME GARDEN SUITES.** *5320 Beacon Dr (35210), east of downtown.* 205/951-1200; res: 800/772-7463; FAX 205/951-1692. 290 suites, 3 story. 1-bedrm $70; 2-bedrm $120; each addl $10; under 12 free; wkend, wkly, monthly rates. Crib free. TV; cable. Pool; whirlpool. Complimentary continental bkfst. Restaurant 6:30–9:30 am, 11 am–1:30 pm, 5–10 pm; wkends hrs vary. Rm serv. Bar 5–11 pm. Ck-out noon. Meeting rms. Valet serv. Airport transportation. Tennis privileges. Private patios, balconies. Antiques, paintings. Cr cds: A, C, D, DS, MC, V.

✓★★**UAB UNIVERSITY INN.** *951 S 18th St at 10th Ave S (35205), at Medical Center, south of downtown.* 205/933-7700; res: 800/888-5673; FAX 205/930-0192. 170 rms, 2–7 story. S, D $48–$52; each addl $5; suites $115–$140; under 16 free. Crib free. TV; cable. Pool. Restaurant 6:30 am–8 pm; Sat, Sun from 7 am. Bar from 4 pm, closed Sun. Ck-out noon. Meeting rms. Bellhops. Valet serv. Free airport transportation. Cr cds: A, C, D, DS, MC, V.

Hotels

★★★**CROWN STERLING SUITES.** *2300 Woodcrest Place (35209), south of downtown.* 205/879-7400; FAX 205/870-4523. 243 units, 8 story. S, D $89–$125; each addl $10; under 12 free; wkend rates. Crib free. TV; cable, in-rm movies. Indoor pool; whirlpool, sauna. Complimentary full bkfst. Restaurant 11 am–10 pm. Bar to midnight. Ck-out noon. Meeting rms. Gift shop. Free airport transportation. Health club privileges. Refrigerators. All rms open onto atrium. Cr cds: A, C, D, DS, MC, V.

★★★**MOUNTAIN BROOK INN.** *2800 US 280 S (35223), south of downtown.* 205/870-3100; res: 800/523-7771. 162 rms, 8 story. S $75; D $85; each addl $10; suites $125–$140; under 18 free; wkend rates. Crib $10. TV; cable. Pool. Restaurant 6 am–11 pm. Bar 4 pm–2 am; entertainment, dancing exc Sun. Ck-out noon. Meeting rms. Free airport transportation. Health club privileges. Bathrm phones; wet bar in some suites. Cr cds: A, C, D, DS, MC, V.

★★★**PICKWICK.** *1023 20th St S (35205), downtown.* 205/933-9555; res: 800/255-7304; FAX 205/933-6918. 63 rms, 28 suites. S, D $109; each addl $10; suites $119; under 12 free; wkend plans. Crib free. Pet accepted, some restrictions; $50 refundable. TV. Complimentary continental bkfst. Bar 5–9 pm; closed Sun. Ck-out noon. Shopping arcade. Drugstore. Barber, beauty shop. Free covered parking. Health club privileges. Some refrigerators. In historical area. Art deco decor. Cr cds: A, C, D, MC, V.

★★**RADISSON.** *808 S 20th St (35205), at University Blvd, opp Medical Center, south of downtown.* 205/933-9000; FAX 205/933-0920. 298 rms, 14 story. S, D $89–$99; each addl $10; suites $135–$500; family rates; some wkend rates. TV; cable. Pool; sauna. Restaurant 6:30 am–10 pm. Bars 11–2 am; Sat to midnight. Ck-out noon. Convention facilities. Gift shop. Barber, beauty shop. Free covered parking. Airport, hospital transportation. Health club privileges. Wet bar in suites. Cr cds: A, C, D, DS, MC, V.

★ ★ ★ SHERATON-CIVIC CENTER. 2101 Civic Center Blvd (35203), downtown. 205/324-5000; FAX 205/307-3045. 770 rms, 17 story. S $95; D $105; each addl $10; suites $195; under 16 free; some lower rates. Crib $10. TV; cable. Indoor pool; whirlpool, sauna, steam rm. Restaurant 6 am–11 pm. Bar 11–2 am; entertainment, dancing. Ck-out noon. Coin lndry. Convention facilities. Concierge. Gift shop. Valet parking. Free airport, RR station, bus depot transportation. Minibars. Balconies. Cr cds: A, C, D, DS, MC, V, JCB.

D 🏊 🚭 ⊙ SC

★ ★ ★ SHERATON-PERIMETER PARK SOUTH. 8 Perimeter Dr (35243), south of downtown. 205/967-2700; FAX 205/972-8603. 204 rms, 8 story. S $79–$82; D $87–$92; each addl $10; suites $150–$280; under 18 free; wknd rates. Crib free. Pet accepted, some restrictions. TV; cable. Pool. Complimentary coffee in rms. Restaurant 6:30 am–10 pm. Bar 10–1 am. Ck-out noon. Meeting rms. Gift shop. Free airport, RR station transportation. Health club privileges. Refrigerator in suites. Cr cds: A, D, DS, MC, V.

D 🏌 🏊 🚭 ⊙ SC

★ ★ ★ ★ TUTWILER. Park Place at 21st St N (35203), downtown. 205/322-2100; res: 800/845-1787 (exc AL); FAX 205/325-1183. 147 rms, 8 story, 52 suites. S $112–$118; D $127–$139; each addl $15; suites $144–$169; under 12 free; wkend rates. Crib free. TV; cable. Restaurant (see CHRISTIAN'S). Rm serv 24 hrs. Bar 11 am–midnight; entertainment. Ck-out noon. Meeting rms. Concierge. Free valet parking. Free airport, RR station, bus depot transportation. Some bathrm phones; refrigerators avail. Balconies. Furnished with antique reproductions. Old World atmosphere; combines turn-of-the-century surroundings with modern services. *LUXURY LEVEL:* **THE PRESIDENTIAL FLOOR.** 21 rms, 6 suites. S, D $128–$158; suites $178–$188. Concierge. Private lounge. Complimentary continental bkfst, refreshments. Cr cds: A, D, DS, ER, MC, V.

D 🚭 ⊙ SC

★ ★ ★ ★ WYNFREY AT RIVERCHASE GALLERIA. 1000 Riverchase Galleria (35244), south of downtown. 205/987-1600; res: 800/476-7006; FAX 205/988-4597. 329 rms, 16 story. S, D $98–$160; suites $200–$650; under 12 free; wkend rates. Crib free. Valet parking $3. TV; cable. Pool; poolside serv. Restaurant 6 am–midnight (also see WINSTON'S). Piano bar; dancing Thurs–Sat noon–1:30 am. Ck-out 11 am. Convention facilities. Concierge. Courtesy car; airport transportation. Lighted tennis, golf privileges 10 mi. Exercise equipt; weights, bicycles, steam rm. Bathrm phone, refrigerator in suites. Luxury hotel; marble, brass, paintings. English Chippendale or French Regency furnishings. Framing the hotel is the Riverchase Galleria, one of the largest malls in the southeast. *LUXURY LEVEL:* **CHANCELLOR'S CLUB.** 35 rms, 4 bi-level suites, 2 floors. S $150; D $165; suites $200–$650. Private bi-level lounge. Wet bar in suites. Deluxe toiletry amenities. Complimentary continental bkfst, refreshments, newspaper. Cr cds: A, C, D, DS, MC, V.

D 🚴 🏊 🎾 🚭 ⊙ SC

Restaurants

✔ ★ ★ BOTTEGA. 2240 Highland Ave, at Five Points. 205/939-1000. Hrs: 11 am–11 pm; Sat from noon. Closed some major hols. Italian, Amer menu. Bar. Complete meals: lunch $2.25–$10. Semi-a la carte: dinner $5–$20. Child's meals. Specializes in veal, homemade ravioli, chicken scaloppini. Valet parking. Outdoor dining. Lunch in casual cafe-style surroundings; dinner in more formal atmosphere. Cr cds: A, MC, V.

D

★ ★ ★ CHRISTIAN'S (formerly Tutwiler). (See Tutwiler Hotel) 205/323-9822. Hrs: 6–10 am, 11:30 am–2 pm, 5:30–10 pm; Sat from 5:30 pm; Sun brunch 11 am–2 pm. Closed most major hols. Bar 11 am–midnight. Wine cellar. Semi-a la carte: bkfst $3.95–$9.95, lunch $5.95–$12.95, dinner $15.95–$23.95. Sun brunch $17.95. Specializes in

seafood, beef, veal. Pianist evenings. Valet parking. Cr cds: A, C, D, MC, V.

D SC

★ ★ COBB LANE. 1 Cobb Lane, at Five Points. 205/933-0462. Hrs: 11 am–2:30 pm; Thurs–Sat also 6–10 pm. Res accepted. Bar. A la carte entrees: lunch $5.95–$12, dinner $5.95–$16. Specializes in she-crab soup, Southern cuisine, chocolate roulage. Parking. Outdoor dining. In historic district. Cr cds: A, MC, V.

★ ★ CONNIE KANAKIS' CAFE. 3423 Colonade Pkwy, in shopping center, south of downtown. 205/967-5775. Hrs: 11 am–2:30 pm, 5–10 pm; Fri to 11 pm; Sat 5–11 pm. Closed Sun; major hols. Res accepted. Italian, Amer menu. Bar. Semi-a la carte: lunch $4–$9.50, dinner $6.95–$24.95. Child's meals. Specializes in snapper, steak. Outdoor dining. Cr cds: A, C, D, MC, V.

D

★ FORMOSA. (2109 Lorne Ridge Lane, Hoover) S on I-65 to Hoover exit, then 1 mi W to Lorna Ridge Lane. 205/979-6684. Hrs: 11 am–2:30 pm, 5–10 pm; Fri & Sat to 11 pm. Closed July 4, Thanksgiving, Dec 25. Res accepted. Chinese menu. Bar. Semi-a la carte: lunch $4–$5, dinner $5.25–$25. Specializes in egg rolls, Mongolian beef, sesame chicken. Parking. Chinese decor. View of flower garden. Cr cds: A, DS, MC, V.

D

★ ★ GG IN THE PARK. 3625 8th Ave S, south of downtown. 205/254-3506. Hrs: 4–10:30 pm. Closed most major hols. Res accepted. Bar. Semi-a la carte: dinner $9.95–$19.95. Child's meals. Specializes in char-broiled steak, live Maine lobster. Parking. Family-owned. Cr cds: A, C, D, DS, MC, V.

D

★ GOLDEN CITY. 4647K US 280, in Riverhills Shopping Center, south of downtown. 205/991-3197. Hrs: 11 am–2 pm, 5–10 pm. Closed most major hols. Res accepted. Chinese menu. Bar. A la carte entrees: lunch $3.99–$5.46, dinner $6.40–$18. Specializes in Mongolian beef, chicken with vegetables. Oriental decor. Cr cds: A, MC, V.

D

✔ ★ ★ GRADY'S. 3470 Galleria Circle, adj to Galleria Mall, south of downtown. 205/985-4663. Hrs: 11 am–11 pm; Fri, Sat to midnight. Closed Thanksgiving, Dec 25. Bar. Semi-a la carte: lunch $4–$8, dinner $5–$15. Child's meals. Specializes in prime rib, seafood, mesquite-grilled chicken. Cr cds: A, D, DS, MC, V.

D

★ ★ ★ HIGHLANDS. 2011 11th Ave S, at Five Points. 205/939-1400. Hrs: 11 am–2 pm, 6–10 pm; Fri to 10:30 pm; Sat 6–10:30 pm. Closed Sun, Mon; major hols. Res accepted. Bar to 1 am. Wine list. A la carte entrees: lunch $5.95–$12, dinner $16–$20. Specializes in seafood, grain-fed beef. Own pastries, desserts, ice cream. Valet parking. Cr cds: A, MC, V.

D

✔ ★ L & N SEAFOOD GRILL. 1765 Ring Rd, south of downtown. 205/987-2616. Hrs: 11:30 am–10 pm; Fri, Sat to 11 pm; Sun 11 am–9 pm. Closed Dec 25. Bar. Semi-a la carte: lunch $4.50–$7.50, dinner $7.95–$11.95. Child's meals. Specializes in mesquite-grilled fish, pasta. Parking. Outdoor dining. Antique mirrors, many full-length windows; lobster tank in lobby. Cr cds: A, C, D, DS, MC, V.

D

✔ ★ ★ LA PAREE. 2013 5th Ave N, near civic center, downtown. 205/251-5936. Hrs: 6:30–10 am, 11 am–3 pm. Closed Sat, Sun; major hols. Serv bar. Semi-a la carte: bkfst $2.75–$6.95, lunch $4.25–$6.95. Child's meals. Specializes in fresh gulf seafood, steak, lamb. Family-owned. Cr cds: A, MC, V.

★ ★ ★ MERRITT HOUSE. 2220 Highland Ave, at Five Points. 205/933-9311. Hrs: 11 am–2 pm, 5–10 pm; Sat from 5 pm. Closed Sun; some hols. Continental menu. Bar 11 am–10 pm. Wine cellar. A la carte entrees: lunch $5.50–$8.95, dinner $11.95–$17.95. Complete meals:

dinner $20.95. Specializes in seafood, lamb, beef. Own baking, pasta. Valet parking. Located in restored mansion (1909); 9 distinct dining areas. Cr cds: A, D, DS, MC, V.

D

★ ★ **MICHAEL'S SIRLOIN ROOM.** *431 S 20th St, downtown. 205/322-0419.* Hrs: 11 am–10 pm. Closed Sun; hols. Bar. Semi-a la carte: lunch $3.95–$7.50, dinner $11.95–$21.95. Specializes in steak, seafood, lamb. Photos of famous sports figures. Cr cds: A, C, D, DS, MC, V.

✔ ★ ★ **NIKI'S WEST.** *233 Finley Ave W, north of downtown. 205/252-5751.* Hrs: 6 am–10 pm. Closed Sun; some major hols. Res accepted. Serv bar. Semi-a la carte: bkfst $2.75–$8.25, lunch $4.75–$9, dinner $7.25–$13.50. Cafeteria dining area: avg ck (lunch, dinner) $4.67. Specializes in veal, fish, chicken. Parking. Nautical decor. Family-owned. Cr cds: A, DS, MC, V.

D

✔ ★ ★ **ROSSI'S SOUTH.** *(2737 US 280, Mountain Brook) E on US 280. 205/879-2111.* Hrs: 11 am–10 pm; Fri to 11 pm; Sat 4:30–11 pm. Closed Sun; some major hols. Res accepted. Italian, Amer menu. Bar. Complete meals: lunch $4.95–$8.95, dinner $7.95–$19.95. Child's meals. Specializes in seafood, steak. Valet parking. Multiple dining areas. Cr cds: A, C, D, DS, MC, V.

D

★ ★ ★ **WINSTON'S.** *(See Wynfrey at Riverchase Galleria Hotel) 205/987-1600.* Hrs: 6–10:30 pm. Closed Sun. Continental menu. Bar. Wine list. A la carte entrees: dinner $15–$28. Specializes in seafood, continental cuisine. Own baking, pastries. Valet parking. Cr cds: A, C, D, MC, V.

D **SC**

Unrated Dining Spots

LEO'S CAFETERIA. *401 18th St S, downtown. 205/251-0347.* Hrs: 11 am–9 pm. Closed Sat; most major hols. Avg ck: lunch, dinner $5–$7.50. Specialty: baked snapper. Parking. Lobster tank. Family-owned. Cr cds: MC, V.

MORRISON'S CAFETERIA. *236 Century Plaza, I-20 Oporto exit in Century Plaza Mall, east of downtown. 205/591-1778.* Hrs: 10:45 am–8:30 pm; Sun to 7 pm. Avg ck: lunch $4.30, dinner $4.75. Specializes in roast beef, strawberry shortcake. Cr cds: A, D, MC, V.

D

Clanton (C-3)

Founded: 1873 **Pop:** 7,669 **Elev:** 599 ft **Area code:** 205 **Zip:** 35045

A peach and truck farming area, Clanton also caters to fishermen along the Coosa River and its tributaries. Lay and Mitchell dams, to the north and east respectively, are backed by lakes and furnish power to the region. Clanton is the seat of Chilton County.

What to See and Do

1. **Lay Dam.** 12 mi NE via AL 145, County 55. Hydroelectric generating plant offers 30-minute guided tours (Sat & Sun, also Mon–Fri afternoons). Plant (daily). For reservations phone 755-4520. **Free.**
2. **Confederate Memorial Park.** 10 mi S via US 31 in Mountain Creek. Two Confederate cemeteries are located on 100 acres that once were the grounds of the Confederate Soldiers Home of Alabama. Museum contains mementos of Alabama's role in the Civil War as well as artifacts, records, documents and photographs. Also hiking

trails, picnicking (shelters). (Daily; closed Jan 1, Dec 25) Phone 755-1990. **Free.**

(For further information contact the Chamber of Commerce, PO Box 66; 755-2400.)

(See Montgomery)

Motels

✔ ★ ★ **HOLIDAY INN.** *2000 Holiday Inn Dr, 3 mi SE at jct US 31, AL 22 & I-65. 205/755-0510; FAX 205/755-0510, ext 116.* 100 rms, 2 story. S, D $42–$50; each addl $3; under 19 free. Crib free. Pet accepted. TV. Pool; wading pool. Restaurant 6 am–2 pm, 5–10 pm. Rm serv. Bar 4–11 pm, closed Sun. Ck-out noon. Meeting rms. Valet serv. Free airport transportation. Cr cds: A, C, D, DS, MC, V.

🐾 🏊 ⊘ ⊙ **SC**

★ **KEY WEST INN.** *2045 7th St S, I-65 exit 205. 205/755-8500; res: 800/833-0555; FAX 205/280-0044.* 43 rms, 2 story. S $41; D $46; each addl $5; under 18 free; higher rates fishing tournaments. Crib free. TV; cable. Complimentary coffee in lobby. Restaurant nearby. Ck-out noon. Coin lndry. Totally nonsmoking. Cr cds: A, D, DS, MC.

D 🐾 ⊘ ⊙ **SC**

Cullman (B-3)

Founded: 1873 **Pop:** 13,367 **Elev:** 799 ft **Area code:** 205 **Zip:** 35055

Cullman was founded by Colonel John G. Cullmann, an immigrant whose dream was to build a self-sustaining colony of other German refugees and immigrants. In 1873, 5 German families settled on the 5,400 square miles of land he purchased from the Louisville & Nashville Railroad. He also laid out the town. Cullman's residents still enjoy the 100-foot-wide streets. In 1880 there were 6,300 people, many of them Germans, in the county that had already been named for Cullmann by the legislature. Located on the Cumberland Plateau, the area is rich in timber and coal. Today, Cullman is the center of an agricultural region; poultry-raising and processing are important.

What to See and Do

1. **Ave Maria Grotto.** I-65 exit 308. Brother Joseph Zoettl, a Benedictine monk, spent nearly 50 years building some 150 miniature replicas of famous churches, buildings and shrines, including Bethlehem, Nazareth, Jerusalem, the Basilica of St Peter's and the California missions. He built them using such materials as cement, stone, bits of jewelry and marble. The miniatures cover four acres of a terraced, landscaped garden. Free picnic grounds adj to parking lot. (Daily; closed Dec 25) Sr citizen rate. Phone 734-4110. ¢¢
2. **Clarkson Covered Bridge** (1904). 9 mi W via US 278W. The largest covered bridge in Alabama, the truss-styled Clarkson is 277 feet long and 90 feet high. Also here are a dogtrot cabin and gristmill. Nature trail. Picnic facilities. Phone 739-3530. **Free.**
3. **Cullman County Museum.** 211 2nd Ave, NE. Large, eight-room museum features items related to the origin and history of Cullman. (Daily exc Sat; closed some major hols) Phone 739-1258. ¢
4. **Hurricane Creek Park.** 6 mi N on US 31, near Vinemont. Gorge with observation platform; trail over swinging bridge; unusual rock formations, earthquake fault and waterfalls. Picnic tables. (Daily) Phone 734-2125. ¢¢
5. **Sportsman Lake Park.** N off US 31. Stocked with bream, bass, catfish and other fish; pedal boats. Miniature golf; kiddie rides. Picnicking, concession. Camping. Fee for some activities. (Apr–Sept, daily) Phone 734-3052. **Free.**
6. **William B. Bankhead National Forest.** 25 mi W on US 278. This 180,684-acre forest includes the Sipsey Wilderness Area, which

contains the last remaining stand of old-growth hardwood in the state. Swimming; fishing (bass, bream), hunting (deer, turkey, squirrel); boating. Hiking, horseback riding. Contact District Ranger, PO Box 278, Double Springs 35553; 489-5111. Fee for some activities.

(For further information contact the Convention & Tourism Bureau, Cullman County Chamber of Commerce, 211 Second Ave NE, PO Box 1104; 734-0454.)

(See Birmingham, Decatur)

Motels

✔ ★**DAYS INN.** *1841 4th St SW, jct I-65 & US 278.* 205/739-3800; FAX 205/739-3123. 117 rms, 2 story. S $32–$36; D $38–$44; each addl $4; family, wkly rates. Crib free. Pet accepted; $3. TV; cable. Pool. Playground. Restaurant 6 am–9 pm. Ck-out noon. Meeting rms. Sundries. Picnic tables. Cr cds: A, C, D, DS, MC, V.

★ ★**RAMADA INN.** *(PO Box 1204, 35056) I-65 & AL 69W, ¼ mi E of I-65 Cullman-Good Hope exit.* 205/734-8484; FAX 205/739-4126. 126 rms, 1–2 story. S $40–$56; D $44–$60; each addl $5; under 18 free. Crib free. TV; cable. Indoor pool; whirlpool. Restaurant 6 am–2 pm, 5–10 pm. Rm serv. Ck-out noon. Coin lndry. Meeting rms. Cr cds: A, C, D, DS, MC, V, JCB.

Restaurant

★ ★**ALL STEAK.** *414 2nd Ave SW.* 205/734-4322. Hrs: 6 am–9 pm; Thurs–Sat to 10 pm; Sun 6:30 am–4 pm. Closed major hols. Semi-a la carte: bkfst $2.50–$4.50, lunch $3.98–$5.50, dinner $5–$26. Sun brunch $7.25. Child's meals. Specializes in steak, seafood. No cr cds accepted.

Dauphin Island (F-2)

Pop: 824 **Elev:** 10 ft **Area code:** 205 **Zip:** 36528

Dauphin Island is rich in history. Spaniards visited and mapped it in the 16th century. Pierre Le Moyne, Sieur d'Iberville, used the island as his base for a short time in 1699. Indians left a bit of their past with the "Shell Mound," an ancient monument. Today, the island is part of Mobile County and a playground for Mobile's citizens. It is also a haven for birds; a 60-acre sanctuary is home to many local and migratory species.

The Battle of Mobile Bay began on the island on August 5, 1864. Admiral David G. Farragut assembled a fleet of Union warships near the mouth of the bay and faced cross-fire from Fort Morgan to his east and Fort Gaines, on Dauphin Island, to his west. He proved successful; both forts were captured, and the port of Mobile was blocked.

Dauphin Island is reached from the north on AL 193, via a four-mile-long, high-rise bridge and causeway, which crosses Grants Pass. The island also has a 3,000-foot paved airstrip. A ferry service to Fort Morgan operates year round.

What to See and Do

Fort Gaines. At E end of island. This five-sided fort was begun in 1821 and completed in the 1850s. It was manned by Confederate forces from 1861 until its capture by Union land troops on August 23, 1864. Museum. (Daily; closed Thanksgiving, Dec 25) Phone 861-6992. ¢¢ Nearby is

Fort Gaines Campground. Private path to secluded Gulf beaches; fishing piers; boat launches. Hiking trail to Audubon Bird

Sanctuary. Recreation areas. Camping; tent & trailer sites. For fee information phone 861-2742.

Annual Event

Alabama Deep-Sea Fishing Rodeo. 3rd wkend July.

(For accommodations see Mobile)

Decatur (A-3)

Founded: 1820 **Pop:** 48,761 **Elev:** 590 ft **Area code:** 205

Decatur, center of north Alabama's mountain lakes recreation area, is a thriving manufacturing and market city with historic districts and sprawling public parks.

The town site was selected by President Monroe in 1820. The Surveyor General was instructed to reserve the area near an old Tennessee River crossing. The place was already a settlement called Rhodes Ferry, named for pioneer Dr. Henry Rhodes' ferry business. The new town was named for Commodore Stephen Decatur.

The Civil War placed Decatur in a constant seesaw between invasion and resistance. It was continually attacked and abandoned; in fact, only five buildings were left standing at war's end.

The TVA brought industry to Decatur by creating a nine-foot channel in the Tennessee River, making it a port for vessels from as far away as Minneapolis. Wheeler Lake, formed by the TVA's Wheeler Dam (see FLORENCE) downstream, offers fishing, boating and other recreational activities.

What to See and Do

1. **Old Decatur & Albany historic districts.** Walking tour of Victorian neighborhood begins at restored Old Bank on historic Bank Street; includes 3 antebellum and 194 Victorian structures. Contact Decatur Convention & Visitors Bureau.

2. **Princess Theatre.** 112 2nd Ave, NE. Renovated art deco-style theater. Home of Decatur Chamber Orchestra, children's theatre, dramatic and singing groups. Phone 350-1745.

3. **Cook's Natural Science Museum.** 412 13th St SE. Extensive collection of insects; rocks, minerals, coral, sea shells. Mounted wildlife. (Daily; closed Jan 1, Dec 24–25) Phone 350-9347. **Free.**

4. **Point Mallard Park.** Point Mallard Dr SE. A 749-acre park on the Tennessee River. Includes swimming pool, wave pool, water slide, beach (mid-May–Labor Day). Hiking, bicycle trails; 18-hole golf course, tennis courts. Outdoor ice rink (mid-Nov–mid-Mar). Camping (hookups), recreation center. Fee for activities. Phone 350-3000 or 800/669-WAVE.

5. **Wheeler National Wildlife Refuge.** 2 mi E via AL 67. Alabama's oldest and largest (34,500 acres) wildlife refuge. Wintering ground for waterfowl and home to numerous species of animal and plant life. Fishing, hunting (limited, permit required for hunting); boating. Picnicking. Bird study and photography. Wildlife Visitor Center and Waterfowl Observation Building. (Mar–Oct, Wed–Sun; rest of yr, daily) Phone 350-6639. ¢

6. **Mooresville.** 6 mi E on AL 20 State's oldest incorporated town is preserved as a living record of 19th-century life. Features the house of Andrew Johnson, who was a tailor's apprentice here; community brick church (ca 1840); frame Church of Christ (1854) in which James Garfield is said to have preached during the Civil War; antebellum houses (private). The oldest stage coach tavern in the state (1825). Details at Mooresville Post Office, which has original wooden call boxes (1830), mail hand-stamped. (Daily exc Sun; closed hols) Phone 350-2431. **Free.**

(For further information contact the Convention & Visitors Bureau, 719 6th Ave SE, PO Box 2349, 35602; 350-2028.)

Annual Events

Alabama Jubilee. Point Mallard Park. Highlight of festivities are the hot-air balloon races. Phone 350-2028. Memorial Day wkend.

Spirit of America Festival. Point Mallard Park. Games, contests, beauty pageant, concerts, exhibits, fireworks. Wkend of July 4.

Civil War Reenactment. Point Mallard Park. Re-creates camp life of soldiers; features skirmishes led by General "Fighting Joe" Wheeler. Labor Day wkend.

Racking Horse World Celebration. Southeastern Sports Arena. Well-known event features gaited horses. Last full wk Sept.

Southern Wildlife Festival. Competition and exhibits of wildlife carvings, art work, photography and duck calling. 3rd wkend Nov.

(See Athens, Cullman, Huntsville)

Motels

★★**DAYS INN.** *(Box 2063, 35602) 810 N 6th Ave NE, at jct US 31, 72A.* 205/355-3520; FAX 205/355-7213. 118 rms, 2 story. S, D $44–$48; each addl $5; under 12 free. Crib free. Pet accepted; $10. TV; cable. Pool; wading pool. Restaurant 6 am–10 pm. Rm serv. Bar from 5 pm. Ck-out 11 am. Meeting rms. Lawn games. Cr cds: A, C, D, DS, MC, V.

✔★**QUALITY INN.** *(Box 1050, 35601) 3429 US 31S.* 205/355-0190. 92 rms, 1–2 story. S $34–$38; D $38–$42; each addl $6; under 18 free. Crib free. Pet accepted. TV; cable. Pool. Playground. Complimentary continental bkfst in lobby. Restaurant 11 am–9 pm. Rm serv. Ck-out 11 am. Meeting rms. Cr cds: A, C, D, DS, ER, MC, V, JCB.

Motor Hotels

★★★**AMBERLEY SUITE.** *807 Bank St NE (35601), 4 blks W of jct AL 72, US 31.* 205/355-6800; res: 800/288-7332; FAX 205/350-0965. 110 kit. suites, 3 story. S $49–$64; D $60–$75; each addl $10; under 18 free; wkly, wkend rates. Crib free. TV; cable. Pool. Complimentary coffee in rms. Restaurant 6 am–11 pm, Sat & Sun 7 am–noon. Bar 4–11 pm. Ck-out noon. Coin lndry. Meeting rms. Free airport transportation. Exercise equipt; weight machine, bicycles, whirlpool, sauna. Grills. Cr cds: A, C, D, DS, MC, V.

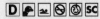

★★★**HOLIDAY INN.** *1101 6th Ave NE (35601), S end of Tennessee River bridge.* 205/355-3150; FAX 205/355-3150, ext 1027. 227 units, 5 story. S $60; D $67; each addl $7; under 19 free; wkend packages. Crib free. Pet accepted. TV; cable. Indoor/outdoor pool; whirlpool. Restaurant 6 am–2 pm, 5–10 pm. Rm serv. Bar 2 pm–1:30 am. Ck-out noon. Free lndry facilities. Meeting rms. Bellhops. Free airport transportation. Some refrigerators. On lake. *LUXURY LEVEL:* **CONCIERGE LEVEL.** 31 units. S $75; D $82. Concierge. Private lounge. Complimentary continental bkfst, refreshments, newspaper. Cr cds: A, C, D, DS, MC, V, JCB.

Unrated Dining Spot

MORRISON'S CAFETERIA. *1801 Beltline Dr, in River Oaks Center.* 205/350-0190. Hrs: 11 am–2:30 pm, 4–8:30 pm; Sat 11 am–8:30 pm; Sun to 7 pm. Avg ck: lunch $4.65, dinner $4.75. Specializes in roast beef, broiled seafood, fried shrimp. Cr cds: MC, V.

Demopolis (C-2)

Founded: 1817 **Pop:** 7,512 **Elev:** 125 ft **Area code:** 205 **Zip:** 36732

Visions of French-made wines and olive oil prompted the first European settlements in this region. The name, meaning "city of the people," is all that remains of the first settlers, a group of French exiles who were, for the most part, habitués of the French court and officers of Napoleon's armies. In July, 1817, they were granted four townships by Congress as the "French Emigrants for the Cultivation of the Vine and Olive." In the end, the colonists failed to cope with the wilderness; and by the mid-1820s, they had scattered.

Americans came afterward to settle on the banks of the Tombigbee River. They established flourishing cotton plantations in this Black Belt area, and many of their fine Greek-revival mansions still can be seen. Agriculture, beef and dairy cattle, as well as a diversified industry support Demopolis today.

What to See and Do

1. **Gaineswood** (1860). 805 S Cedar St. Restored 20-room Greek-revival mansion furnished with many original pieces. (Daily; closed hols) Phone 289-4846. ¢¢

2. **Bluff Hall** (1832). 405 N Commissioners St. Restored antebellum mansion built by the slaves of Allen Glover, a planter and merchant, as a wedding gift for his daughter. The interior has Corinthian columns in drawing room, period furniture, many marble mantels. Also clothing museum and craft shop. (Daily exc Mon; closed major hols) Phone 289-1666. ¢¢

3. **Forkland Park.** 12 mi N on US 43, 1 mi W of Forkland on River Rd. This park is on 10,000-acre Lake Demopolis, which was formed by a 40-foot-high dam on the Tombigbee River. Waterskiing; fishing; boating (ramp). Camping (hookups, dump station; fees). (Mid-Mar–mid-Dec, daily) Phone 289-3540 or -5530.

4. **Foscue Creek Park.** 2 mi W via US 80W, exit Maria St, on Lock & Dam Rd. On Lake Demopolis. Boating (ramps). Trails. Picnic area, pavilion, playground, ballfields. Camping (hookups, dump station; fees). (Daily) Phone 289-3540 or -5535.

5. **Magnolia Grove** (1840). 2 mi S on US 43, then 3 mi E on US 80, then 15 mi NE on AL 69; at 1002 Hobson St in Greensboro. Built for wealthy planter, Col. Isaac Croom, Magnolia Grove was also the home of the builder's nephew, Richmond Pearson Hobson, congressman and admiral who was responsible for sinking the *Merrimac* and for blockading the Spanish fleet in Santiago Harbor in June, 1898. Greek-revival house features an unsupported winding stairway; original furnishings. (Daily exc Mon) Phone 624-8618. ¢¢

(For further information contact the Demopolis Area Chamber of Commerce, 213 N Walnut St, PO Box 667; 289-0270.)

Annual Event

Christmas on the River. Children's parade, evening river boat parade, fireworks. Early Dec.

Motels

✔★**BEST WESTERN-MINT SUNRISE.** *1034 US 80 SE.* 205/289-5772; FAX 205/289-5772, ext 100. 70 rms. S $32.65–$36.50; D $38.85; each addl $2; under 12 free; wkly rates. Crib free. TV; cable. Pool. Complimentary continental bkfst. Ck-out 11 am. Meeting rms. Exercise equipt; weights, bicycles. Refrigerators. Picnic tables. Cr cds: A, C, D, DS, ER, MC, V.

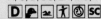

★**WINDWOOD INN.** *628 US 80E. 205/289-1760; res: 800/233-0841 (AL); FAX 205/289-1768.* 94 units, 2 kits. S $28–$31; D $28–$34; each addl $3; kit. units $34–$40; under 12 free. Crib free. TV; cable. Pool. Restaurant adj 5 am–10 pm. Ck-out 11 am. Meeting rm. Cr cds: A, C, D, DS, MC, V.

Restaurants

★**ELLIS V.** *708 US 80E. 205/289-3446.* Hrs: 5 am–10 pm. Closed Dec 25. Bar to 2 am. Semi-a la carte: bkfst $2–$5.25, lunch $3.95–$6.95, dinner $5.95–$14.95. Specializes in prime rib, seafood, country ham. Salad bar. Parking. Cr cds: A, C, D, MC, V.

✔ ★**RIVERVIEW LANDING.** *US 43N. 205/289-1033.* Hrs: 10 am–9 pm; Fri, Sat 11 am–10 pm. Closed Jan 1, Thanksgiving, Dec 25. Bar. Semi-a la carte: lunch, dinner $3.95–$12.95. Child's meals. Specializes in steak, seafood, hush puppies. Parking. Outdoor dining. Overlooks river. Cr cds: A, DS, MC, V.

Dothan (E-4)

Settled: 1858 **Pop:** 53,589 **Elev:** 326 ft **Area code:** 205

This marketing center in the ''wiregrass'' section of Alabama's southeastern corner is the seat of Houston County. Local agricultural products include peanuts, soybeans, corn and cattle. Dothan is also a retail center.

The town had a lusty start. It was a rough pioneer settlement full of lumberjacks and turpentine workers in 1889 when the first railroad reached it. As the railroads developed, Dothan's population grew rapidly. The city owes a large part of its growth to its strategic location—almost equidistant from Atlanta, Birmingham, Jacksonville and Mobile.

What to See and Do

1. **Opera House** (1915). 115 N St Andrews St. Refurbished historical theater; 590 seats. (Daily) Appt recommended. Phone 793-0127. **Free.**
2. **Landmark Park.** US 431N. This 60-acre park features an 1890s living-history farm, natural science and history center, planetarium; nature trails; picnic area. (Daily; closed Jan 1, Thanksgiving, Dec 25) Phone 794-3452. ¢
3. **Westgate Park.** Choctaw St & Westgate Pkwy off Ross Clark Circle. Recreation facility includes Water World, with child's pool, wave pool and giant slide (early May–Labor Day, daily; fee); recreation center with indoor pool, tennis, racquetball, basketball courts and ballfields. (Daily; fee for various activities) Phone 793-0297.
4. **Farley Nuclear Visitors Center.** 16 mi SE via US 52. Features 18 nuclear exhibits, informational videos. Tours. (Mon–Fri) Contact PO Drawer 470, Ashford 36312; 899-5108 or 800/344-8295.

(For further information contact the Dothan Area Convention & Visitors Bureau, 3311 Ross Clark Circle NW, PO Box 8765, 36304; 794-6622.)

Annual Events

Azalea Dogwood Festival. Marked route through residential areas at peak of bloom. Late Mar or early Apr.

National Peanut Festival. Houston County Farm Center. Livestock exhibits, sports events, arts & crafts, midway, beauty pageants, parade. Phone 793-4323. Late Oct–early Nov.

(See Ozark)

Motels

★★**BEST WESTERN-DOTHAN INN.** *2325 Montgomery Hwy (36303). 205/793-4376; FAX 205/793-7720.* 120 rms, 2 story. S $35–$40; D $39–$43; each addl $5; under 12 free. Crib free. TV; cable. Pool. Complimentary coffee in lobby. Restaurant adj open 24 hrs. Ck-out 11 am. Meeting rm. Free airport transportation. Cr cds: A, C, D, DS, MC, V, JCB.

★★**COMFORT INN.** *(Box 1405, 36303) 3591 Ross Clark Circle NW. 205/793-9090; FAX 205/793-4367.* 122 rms, 5 story. S $45–$55; D $50–$69; each addl $5; suites $59–$69; under 18 free. Crib free. Pet accepted. TV; cable. Pool. Continental bkfst. Restaurant open 24 hrs. Ck-out 1 pm. Meeting rm. Exercise equipt; weights, bicycles. Many refrigerators. Cr cds: A, C, D, DS, ER, MC, V, JCB.

✔ ★**DAYS INN.** *2841 Ross Clark Circle SW (36301). 205/793-2550; FAX 205/793-7962.* 120 units, 2 story. S $29–$37; D $34–$43; each addl $5; family rates; some wkend rates. Crib free. Pet accepted. TV; cable. Pool. Coffee in rms. Restaurant adj open 24 hrs. Ck-out noon. Gazebo. Cr cds: A, D, DS, MC, V.

★★**HOLIDAY INN-SOUTH.** *2195 Ross Clark Circle SE (36301). 205/794-8711; FAX 205/671-3781.* 144 rms, 2 story. S $46–$52; D $52–$58; each addl $6; under 18 free; suites $64–$74; wkend rates. TV; cable. Pool. Complimentary full bkfst. Restaurant 6 am–9:30 pm; Sun from 7 am. Rm serv (limited hrs). Bar 2:30 pm–2 am, closed Sun. Ck-out noon. Meeting rms. Cr cds: A, C, D, DS, MC, V, JCB.

✔ ★**MOTEL 6.** *2903 Ross Clark Circle SW (36301). 205/793-6013; FAX 205/793-2377.* 104 rms, 2 story. S, D $34–$36; each addl $5; under 17 free. Crib free. TV; cable. Pool; whirlpool. Complimentary continental bkfst. Coffee in lobby. Ck-out noon. Valet serv. Cr cds: A, C, D, DS, MC, V.

★★**RAMADA INN.** *(Box 1761, 36302) 3001 Ross Clark Circle SW. 205/792-0031; FAX 205/794-3134.* 159 rms, 2 story. S $46–$50; D $52–$56; each addl $6; suites $75–$105; under 18 free; wkly rates; some wkend rates. Crib free. TV; cable. Pool; wading pool. Complimentary bkfst. Restaurant 6 am–11 pm; Sun from 7 am. Rm serv. Bars 2 pm–2 am, closed Sun; entertainment; dancing. Ck-out 1 pm. Meeting rms. Bellhops. Valet serv. Airport transportation. Cr cds: A, C, D, DS, ER, MC, V, JCB.

Restaurant

✔ ★**AUGUST MOON.** *2428 Montgomery Hwy. 205/677-6035.* Hrs: 11 am–2 pm, 5–9 pm. Closed Thanksgiving, Dec 25. Chinese menu. Private club. Semi-a la carte: lunch, dinner $2.75–$8.95. Buffet: lunch, dinner $4.79. Seafood buffet (Thurs–Sat) $6.95. Child's meals. Parking. Cr cds: A, MC, V.

Eufaula (D-5)

Settled: 1823 **Pop:** 13,220 **Elev:** 257 ft **Area code:** 205 **Zip:** 36027

This city stands on a bluff rising 200 feet above Lake Eufaula, a 45,000-acre impoundment of the Chattahoochee River known throughout the area for its excellent bass fishing.

What to See and Do

1. **Shorter Mansion.** 340 N Eufaula Ave. Neoclassical mansion built in 1906; two floors contain antique furnishings, Confederate relics, and memorabilia of six state governors from Barbour County. (Daily; closed major hols) Mini-tour by appt (fee). Phone 687-3793. ¢¢ Mansion is headquarters for the Eufaula Heritage Association and is part of

   Seth Lore and Irwinton Historic District. Second-largest historic district in Alabama, with approximately 582 registered landmarks. Mixture of Greek-revival, Italianate and Victorian houses, churches and commercial structures built between 1834 and 1911. Many are private. Bus tour (fee). Obtain driving tour brochure from the Chamber of Commerce or Eufaula Heritage Association, PO Box 486.

2. **Hart House** (ca 1850). 211 N Eufaula Ave. Single-story, Greek-revival white frame structure with fluted Doric columns on porch serves as headquarters for the Historic Chattahoochee Commission and Visitor Information Center for the Chattahoochee Trace of Alabama and Georgia. (Mon–Fri) Phone 687-9755 or -6631. **Free.**

3. **Lakepoint Resort State Park.** 7 mi N off US 431. A 1,220-acre picturesque park on the shores of the 45,200-acre Lake Eufaula. Swimming; fishing; boating (marina). Hiking; 18-hole golf (fee); tennis. Picnicking, concession, restaurant, resort inn. Camping, cottages. Standard fees. Phone 687-6676 or -8011.

4. **Eufaula National Wildlife Refuge.** 10 mi N on US 431, AL 165. Partially located in Georgia and superimposed on the Walter F. George Reservoir, the refuge was established to provide a feeding and resting area for waterfowl migrating between the Tennessee Valley and the Gulf Coast. Ducks, geese, egrets and herons are among the 281 species of birds found at the refuge; beaver, fox, bobcat and deer are among the 16 species of mammals. Observation tower, nature trail; hunting; photography. (Daily) Contact Refuge Manager, Rte 2, Box 97B; 687-4065. **Free.**

(For further information, including details of walking tours, contact the Chamber of Commerce, 102 N Orange St, PO Box 697; 687-6664 or -6665.)

Annual Events

Eufaula Pilgrimage. Daytime and candlelight tours of antebellum houses and churches, antique show and sales, historic reenactments and Civil War displays. Phone 687-3793. Usually 1st wkend Apr.

Indian Summer Days. Festival including arts & crafts, music, food, children's activities. Phone 687-6664. 1st or 2nd wkend Oct.

Motels

✔ ★**BEST WESTERN INN.** (Mailing address: 1337 S Eufala Ave) On Dothan Hwy (US 431S). 205/687-3900; FAX 205/687-6870. 42 rms, 2 story. S $30–$40; D $34–$46; each addl $4; under 12 free; higher rates: Eufaula Pilgrimage, wkend of July 4. Crib free. TV; cable. Pool. Complimentary continental bkfst, coffee. Restaurant opp 10 am–10 pm. Ck-out 11 am. Some refrigerators. Cr cds: A, D, DS, MC, V.

★★**HOLIDAY INN.** (Box 725) US 82 at Riverside. 205/687-2021; FAX 205/687-2021, ext 4. 96 rms, 2 story. S $40–$49; D $46–$55; each addl $5; suites $52–$56; under 18 free; golf plans. Crib free. TV; cable. Pool. Restaurant 6 am–10 pm. Rm serv. Bar 4 pm–midnight. Ck-out noon. Meeting rms. Bellhops. On lake. Cr cds: A, C, D, DS, MC, V, JCB.

Restaurant

✔ ★★**DOGWOOD INN.** 214 N Eufaula Ave. 205/687-5629. Hrs: 11 am–2 pm, 5–9:30 pm. Closed Sun; major hols. Res accepted. Bar.

Semi-a la carte: lunch $2.50–$5, dinner $6.95–$12.95. Child's meals. Specialties: Charleston shrimp, pecan pie. Parking. Former boardinghouse (1905); Victorian decor, antiques. Cr cds: A, C, D, MC, V.

Evergreen (D-3)

Pop: 3,911 **Elev:** 367 ft **Area code:** 205 **Zip:** 36401

The seat of Conecuh County, this town is appropriately named for its abundance of evergreens. Each year carloads of Christmas trees and other evergreen products for use as decoration are shipped from the town.

What to See and Do

Conecuh National Forest. 25 mi E on US 84, then 11 mi S on on US 29. This 84,400-acre forest, mostly of southern pine, offers swimming (at Blue Pond, fee per vehicle); fishing, hunting; boating. Hiking includes 20 miles of the Conecuh Trail. Campsites at Open Pond only (fee for overnight). Contact District Ranger, US Forest Service, Rte 5, Box 157, Andalusia 36420; 205/222-2555 or Supervisor, 1765 Highland Ave, Montgomery 37170; 205/832-4470.

(For further information contact the Chamber of Commerce, 100 Depot Square; 578-1707.)

Motels

✔ ★**ECONO LODGE.** (Box 564) 1 blk W on AL 83 Business, I-65 exit 96. 205/578-4701. 58 rms, 2 story. S $30–$38; D $36–$45; each addl $4. Crib $4. Pet accepted. TV; cable. Pool. Restaurant adj open 24 hrs. Ck-out 11 am. Cr cds: A, C, D, DS, MC, V.

★★**QUALITY INN.** (Rte 2, Box 393-B) 1 blk E of I-65 exit 96. 205/578-5500. 100 rms, 2 story. S $41; D $46; each addl $6; under 18 free. Crib free. TV; cable. Pool. Restaurant 11 am–2 pm, 5–9 pm. Rm serv. Bar 5–11 pm, Thurs–Sat to 1 am, closed Sun; entertainment, dancing. Ck-out noon. Coin lndry. Meeting rms. Cr cds: A, C, D, DS, ER, MC, V, JCB.

Florence (A-2)

Settled: 1779 **Pop:** 36,426 **Elev:** 541 ft **Area code:** 205 **Zip:** 35630

First settled as a trading post, Florence is still the trading center of a large area. Florence, with Sheffield, Tuscumbia and Muscle Shoals, lies along the Tennessee River's famous shoals area near Wilson Dam. Inexpensive TVA power helped to bring a number of industries to the town.

What to See and Do

1. **Wilson Dam.** 5 mi E on US 72, then 2 mi S on AL 133. This dam is the foundation stone of the Tennessee Valley Authority. For many years, the Muscle Shoals area of the Tennessee River had been discussed as a source of power, and in 1918, the War Department began construction of Wilson Dam as a source of power for making munitions. The dam was completed in 1924, but little use was made of its generating capacity until the TVA took over in 1933. Today, it has the largest generating capacity (630,000 kilowatts) of any TVA dam; its main lock (completed Nov, 1959) is 110 feet by 600 feet and lifts vessels 100 feet, one of the world's highest single lift locks. The treacherous Muscle Shoals are no longer a bottleneck to shipping. The dam, 4,541 feet long and 137 feet high, is one of the many TVA dams that prevents floods, provides 650 miles of

navigable channel and produces electricity for the area's residents, farms and industry. The powerhouse lobby is open to visitors; there is an overlook on the lockmaster's control building. (Daily)   **Free.**

   Wilson Lake extends more than 15 miles upstream to Wheeler Dam (see #2). Swimming; fishing; boating.

2. **Wheeler Dam.** 18 mi E on US 72 to Elgin, then 4 mi S on AL 101. Part of the Muscle Shoals complex, this is a multipurpose TVA dam chiefly built for navigation. It is 72 feet high and 6,342 feet long, impounding a lake 74 miles long. Lobby (daily).   **Free.**

3. **Joe Wheeler State Park.** Named for Confederate General Joseph Wheeler of the Army of Tennessee, the 2,550-acre park is divided into three parts.

   Wheeler Dam. 18 mi E on US 72, then 4 mi S on AL 101. Swimming; fishing (daily); boat liveries and harbor. Tennis. Picnic facilities. Cabins (reservations through Park Manager, phone 685-3306).

   First Creek. 2 mi W of Rogersville via US 72. Beachfront swimming; boating (marina). Nature and hiking trails; 18-hole golf, tennis. Picnicking. Resort lodge overlooking the Tennessee River (see RESORT). Camping (primitive & improved). Phone 247-5466 (office), 247-1184 (campground).

   Elk River. 15 mi W of Athens (see). Fishing; boating (launch). Picnic facilities, playground, concession. Group Lodge. (Daily) Standard fees. Phone 729-8228.

4. **W.C. Handy Home, Museum and Library.** 620 W College St. Restored birthplace of famous composer and "father of the blues" contains hand-written sheet music, personal papers, trumpet and piano on which he composed "St Louis Blues." (Tues–Sat; closed major hols) Phone 760-6434.   ¢

5. **Indian Mound and Museum.** S Court St. Largest ceremonial mound in the Tennessee Valley. Museum has large collection of Indian artifacts. (Tues–Sat; closed major hols) Phone 760-6427.   ¢

6. **Pope's Tavern** (1830). 203 Hermitage Dr. General Andrew Jackson stayed in this stage stop, which served as a hospital for both Union and Confederate soldiers during the Civil War. (Tues–Sat; closed major hols) Phone 760-6439.   ¢

7. **University of North Alabama** (1830). (5,600 students) Wesleyan Ave. Tours. University Art Gallery (Mon–Fri), Planetarium-Observatory (open by appt, phone 760-4284).

8. **Renaissance Tower.** 1 Hightower Place. One of the tallest structures in the state; offers magnificent view of the Tennessee River and Wilson Dam. Educational exhibits. Restaurant. Phone 760-5900.   ¢¢

(For further information contact the Chamber of Commerce of the Shoals, 104 S Pine St; 764-4661.)

Annual Events

   W.C. Handy Music Festival. Week-long celebration of the musical contribution of the "father of the blues." Jazz, blues, gospel concerts, street celebration, running events, bike rides. Phone 766-7642 or -9719. 1st full wk Aug.

   Alabama Renaissance Faire. Renaissance-era arts & crafts, music, food, entertainment. Fair workers in period costumes. Phone 760-9648. 4th wkend Oct.

(See Russellville)

Motels

   ★★**BEST WESTERN EXECUTIVE INN.** *(PO Box Q) 504 S Court St.* 205/766-2331; FAX 205/766-3567. 120 rms, 2 story. S $38; D $42–$48; each addl $5; under 12 free. Crib free. Pet accepted, some restrictions. TV; cable. Pool; whirlpool, poolside serv. Restaurant 6

am–10 pm; Sat, Sun from 7 am. Rm serv. Bar 4 pm–1 am, closed Sun. Ck-out noon. Coin lndry. Meeting rms. Cr cds: A, C, D, DS, MC, V.

   ✔ ★**COMFORT INN.** *400 S Court St.* 205/760-8888; FAX 205/766-1681. 88 rms, 5 story. S $37–$44; D $42–$49; each addl $5; suites $98; under 18 free. Crib free. Pet accepted. TV. Complimentary continental bkfst, coffee. Ck-out noon. Meeting rms. Refrigerator in suites. Cr cds: A, C, D, DS, ER, MC, V, JCB.

Resort

   ★★**JOE WHEELER STATE RESORT LODGE.** *(Drawer K, Rogersville 35652)* 20 mi E on US 72, then 4 mi S. 205/247-5461; res: 800/544-5639; FAX 205/247-5471. 75 rms, 3 story. S $48–$62; D $55–$67; each addl $5; suites $99–$114; under 12 free; golf plans. Crib free. TV; cable. Pool; wading pool. Playground. Dining rm 7 am–9 pm; Fri, Sat to 10 pm. Ck-out 11 am, ck-in 3 pm. Coin lndry. Meeting rms. Sundries. Lighted tennis. 18-hole golf, greens fee, pro, putting green, driving range. Private beach, marina, boat rentals. Hiking trails. Some refrigerators; wet bar in suites. Private patios, balconies. Picnic tables, grills. State-owned; facilities of park avail. Cr cds: A, MC, V.

Restaurant

   ★★**DALE'S.** *US 43 & US 72, ½ mi S.* 205/766-4961. Hrs: 5–10 pm. Closed Sun; major hols. Serv bar. A la carte entrees: dinner $8.95–$23. Specializes in steak, seafood, chicken. Cr cds: A, C, D, MC, V.

Unrated Dining Spot

   MORRISON'S CAFETERIA. *Regency Square Mall, 2 mi NE of US 72 on AL 133.* 205/766-2227. Hrs: 11 am–8:30 pm; Sun to 7 pm. Avg ck: lunch $4.50, dinner $4.90. Specializes in roast beef, fried shrimp, strawberry shortcake. Cr cds: MC, V.

Fort Payne (A-4)

Pop: 11,838 **Elev:** 899 ft **Area code:** 205 **Zip:** 35967

The county seat and market town of DeKalb County, Fort Payne is in an area famed for natural wonders and Native American history. Sequoyah, who invented the Cherokee alphabet, lived in Will's Town, a Cherokee settlement located near Fort Payne.

What to See and Do

1. **DeSoto State Park.** 8 mi NE on County 89. The 5,067-acre park includes Lookout Mountain, Little River Canyon and DeSoto Falls and Lake. The area, rich in Cherokee lore, was a base of military operations prior to the Trail of Tears. The park is noted for its variety of plant life, including spring-blooming rhododendrons, wild azaleas and mountain laurel. Songbirds abound. A scenic drive skirts the canyon, and 20 miles of hiking trail crosses the mountain top. Swimming pool, bathhouse; fishing. Hiking trail; tennis. Picnicking, playground, restaurant, country store, resort inn. Nature center. Camping (all yr), cabins (reservations). Standard fees. Phone 845-5380 (cabins) or -5075 (campground).

2. **Sequoyah Caverns and Kampgrounds.** 16 mi N off US 11, I-59. Thousands of formations, reflecting lakes and rainbow falls with indirect lighting; level walkways. Cave temperature 60° F all year.

Rainbow trout pools, deer, buffalo. Swimming pool. Picnic area. Camping. Guided tours. (Mar–Nov, daily) Phone 635-6423. **¢¢¢**

3. **Landmarks of DeKalb Museum** (1891). 105 Fifth St NE. The museum, Richardsonian Romanesque in style, features Native American artifacts from several different tribes; turn-of-the-century house and farm items; railroad memorabilia; photographs and art work of local historical significance. Special rotating exhibits. (Mon, Wed & Fri, also Sun afternoons; closed hols) Phone 845-5714. **Free.**

4. **Fort Payne Opera House** (1889). 510 Gault Ave N. Alabama's oldest opera house still in use today. Restored and reopened in 1970 as a cultural arts center. Tours of theater include historic murals (by appt). Donation. Phone 845-2741.

5. **Cloudmont Ski Resort.** 5 mi NE via I-59, exit 231 off AL 117 on County Rd 89. 2 pony lifts; patrol, school, rentals; 100% snowmaking; concession area, snack bar. Chalets. Longest run 1,000 ft; vertical drop 150 ft. (Mid-Dec–early-Mar, daily) Summer activities include swimming; fishing. Hiking; 9-hole golf. Phone 634-4344. **¢¢¢¢**

(For further information contact the DeKalb County Tourist Assoc, 2201-J Gault Ave, PO Box 1165; 845-3957.)

Annual Events

June Jam. A week of festivities, including sporting events, street dance, beauty pageant and many others, culminates with an outdoor concert featuring top country entertainers. Phone 845-2741 or -9300 (box office). Mid-June.

DeKalb County VFW Agricultural Fair. VFW Fairgrounds, 18th St NW. Early Oct.

(See Gadsden)

Motels

✔ ★**BEST WESTERN FORT PAYNE.** *1828 Gault Ave N, 1½ mi S of jct I-59, US 11.* 205/845-0481; FAX 205/845-6152. 68 rms, 1–2 story. S $33–$41; D $37–$44. Crib $5. TV; cable. Pool. Restaurant 5 am–9 pm. Rm serv. Ck-out noon. Meeting rms. Free local airport transportation. Downhill ski 10 mi. Cr cds: A, C, D, DS, ER, MC, V.

D 🐕 🏊 🚭 ⊛ **SC**

★★**QUALITY INN.** *(Box 655) 1 mi NW on AL 35 at I-59.* 205/845-4013; FAX 205/845-2344. 79 rms, 2 story. S $37–$42; D $40–$45; each addl $5; under 16 free. Crib free. Pet accepted, some restrictions. TV; cable. Pool. wading pool. Complimentary continental bkfst in lobby. Restaurant 6:30–9:30 am, 5:30–8:30 pm. Rm serv 7 am–9 pm. Ck-out 11 am. Coin lndry. Meeting rms. Cr cds: A, C, D, DS, ER, MC, V, JCB.

D 🐕 🏊 🚭 ⊛ **SC**

Gadsden (B-4)

Founded: 1840 **Pop:** 42,523 **Elev:** 554 ft **Area code:** 205

The town was named for James Gadsden, the man who negotiated the purchase of Arizona and New Mexico in 1853. Today, it is one of the largest industrial centers in the state. Iron, manganese, coal and limestone are found nearby. Steel, rubber, fabricated metal, electrical equipment and electronic devices are among its chief products. It is the seat of Etowah County, a diversified agricultural area.

Union troops sacked Gadsden in 1863 and rode on toward Rome, Georgia. Two heroes were born of this action. Fifteen-year-old Emma Sansom bravely guided General Nathan Bedford Forrest and his men across a ford on Black Creek after the bridge was destroyed. John Wisdom made a night ride of 67 miles to warn the defenders of Rome that the Yankees were coming, a ride the people of Alabama celebrate more than Paul Revere's.

In 1887, electricity came to Gadsden when William P. Lay built an electrical plant. It was the result of years of effort to interest investors in the industrial future of the region. In 1902 it was replaced with a hydroelectric plant on Big Wills Creek. Eventually, Lay's dream of developing the water resources of the Coosa-Alabama river system led to the organization of the Alabama Power Company in 1906.

What to See and Do

1. **Gadsden Museum of Fine Arts.** 2829 W Meighan Blvd. Features works by local, national and international artists. Antique china and crystal collection, historical memorabilia. (Daily exc Sat; closed hols) Phone 546-7365. **Free.**

2. **Center for Cultural Arts.** 501 Broad St. Center features wide variety of cultural and artistic traveling exhibits from the US and Europe; children's museum with "hands on" exhibits features a miniature "walk-through" city. (Daily; closed major hols) Phone 543-2787. **¢**

3. **Noccalula Falls Park.** Noccalula Rd. Black Creek drops 90 feet over a limestone ledge on Lookout Mountain; according to legend, these falls were named for an Indian chief's daughter who leaped to her death after being disappointed in love. A 65-mile trail ending at DeSoto Falls in DeSoto State Park in Fort Payne (see) includes four waterfalls and many Indian sites. Also originating in the park is the Lookout Mountain Parkway, a scenic drive extending 100 miles to Chattanooga, TN. Swimming pool, bathhouse. Nature and hiking trails; miniature golf. Picnic area, playground. Camping, hookups (fee). Pioneer homestead and museum; train. Botanical gardens. (Daily) Phone 549-4663 (office) or 543-7412 (campground). Fee for some activities. Admission **¢**

4. **Weiss Dam and Lake.** 18 mi NE off US 411. An Alabama Power Company project impounds a 30,200-acre lake. Swimming; fishing; boating (daily). Picnicking. Tours of power plant (daily, by appt). Phone 526-8467.

5. **Horton Mill Covered Bridge.** 18 mi W on US 278, then 11 mi S on AL 75. This 220-foot-long structure is the highest covered bridge in the US, 70 feet above the Black Warrior River. Trails. (Daily) **Free.**

(For further information contact the Gadsden-Etowah Tourism Board, PO Box 8267, 35902; 549-0351.)

(See Anniston, Fort Payne, Guntersville)

Motel

✔ ★**ECONO LODGE.** *(507 Cherry St, Attalla 35954)* 4 mi E on I-59, exit 183. 205/538-9925; FAX 205/538-5000. 148 rms, 2 story. S $32.95; D $37.95; each addl $5; under 18 free; higher rates special events. Crib free. Pet accepted; $20 refundable. TV; cable. Pool. Restaurant 5–10 am, 5–10 pm. Bar 5 pm–1 am. Ck-out noon. Meeting rms. Picnic tables, grills. Cr cds: A, C, D, MC, V.

🐕 🏊 🚭 ⊛ **SC**

Unrated Dining Spot

MORRISON'S CAFETERIA. *1001 Rainbow Dr, in Gadsden Mall.* 205/543-9181. Hrs: 11 am–8 pm; Fri & Sat to 8:30 pm; Sun to 7:30 pm. Avg ck: lunch $4.35, dinner $5. Specializes in roast beef, fried shrimp, egg custard pie. Cr cds: A, MC, V.

Greenville (D-3)

Settled: 1819 **Pop:** 7,492 **Elev:** 422 ft **Area code:** 205 **Zip:** 36037

(See Montgomery)

Motel

★ ★HOLIDAY INN. *(Box 126) Jct AL 185, I-65, Greenville exit 130, on Fort Dale Rd. 205/382-2651; FAX 205/382-2651, ext 150.* 96 rms, 2 story. S $42–$47; D $47; each addl $5; under 19 free. Crib free. Pet accepted. TV; cable. Pool. Restaurant 6 am–10 pm. Rm serv. Bar 4–11 pm. Ck-out noon. Meeting rms. Cr cds: A, C, D, DS, MC, V, JCB.

Gulf Shores (F-2)

Pop: 3,261 **Elev:** 6 ft **Area code:** 205 **Zip:** 36542

Located on Pleasure Island, southeast of Mobile, Gulf Shores is separated from the mainland by the Intracoastal Waterway. Between Alabama Point on the east and Mobile Point on the west is a 32-mile stretch of white sand beach. Swimming and fishing in the Gulf are excellent, and charter boats are available. The island also has a number of freshwater lakes. At the eastern end, a bridge across Perdido Bay connects Gulf Shores with Pensacola, Florida.

What to See and Do

1. **Fort Morgan Park.** 21 mi W on AL 180 (Fort Dale Pkwy). This area on the western tip of Mobile Point was explored by the Spanish in 1519. Between that time and 1813, Spain, France, England and, finally, the United States held this strategic point. It was the site of two engagements during the War of 1812. Fishing pier. Picnicking, concessions in restored First Sergeant's Quarters (1900). ¢ Park admission includes

   Fort Morgan. This star-shaped, brick fort was begun in 1819 and replaced a sand and log fort that figured in two battles during the War of 1812. Fort Morgan's most famous moment occurred during the Battle of Mobile Bay (August, 1864). The Confederates' use of mines, then known as torpedoes, was the source of Union Admiral Farragut's legendary command, "Damn the torpedoes, full speed ahead!" Following the battle, the fort withstood a two-week siege before surrendering to Union forces. The fort was in active use during the Spanish-American War and World Wars I and II. (Daily; closed Jan 1, Thanksgiving, Dec 25) Phone 540-7125 or -7127. ¢

   Fort Morgan Museum (1967). Patterned after the 10-sided citadel damaged in 1864, the museum displays military artifacts from the War of 1812 through World War II; local history. (Daily; closed Jan 1, Thanksgiving, Dec 25) **Free.**

2. **Gulf State Park.** 2 mi E on AL 182 from jct AL 59. The 6,000-acre park includes more than 2 miles of white sand beaches on the Gulf and freshwater lakes. Swimming, bathhouse, waterskiing, surfing; fishing in Gulf of Mexico (825-ft pier) and in lakes; marina, boathouse, rentals. Hiking, bicycling; tennis, 18-hole golf (fee). Picnic area, pavilion, grills, restaurant, resort inn (see RESORT). Cabins (for reservations contact Cabin Reservations, 20115 State Hwy 135, phone 948-7275). Camping (14-day max in season). Phone 948-6353 for reservation (Mon–Fri). (Daily) Standard fees. For park information phone 948-7275.

3. **Bon Secour National Wildlife Refuge.** AL 180 W. Consists of 4,500 acres of coastal lands ranging from sand dunes to woodlands; native and migratory birds, small mammals and reptiles including the endangered loggerhead sea turtle. Swimming; fishing (fresh and salt water). Foot trails, hiking. Visitor center (Mon–Fri; closed major hols). Phone 968-8623. **Free.**

4. **Zooland Animal Park.** AL 59 S to 12th Ave. A 15-acre park with native and exotic animals; petting zoo; miniature golf; concession. (Daily; closed Thanksgiving, Dec 25) Phone 968-5731. ¢¢¢

(For additional information contact the Alabama Gulf Coast Area Chamber of Commerce, PO Box 457, 36547; 968-7511.)

Annual Events

Mardi Gras Celebration. Early Mar.

Sea Oats Festival. Early May.

National Shrimp Festival. 2nd wkend Oct.

(See Mobile; also see Pensacola, FL)

Motels

★ ★BEST WESTERN ON THE BEACH. *(Box 481) 337 E Beach Blvd. 205/948-7047; FAX 205/948-7339.* 113 units, 6 story, 50 kits. May–Labor Day: S, D $95–$135; under 12 free; wkly rates; lower rates rest of yr. Crib $5. Pet accepted, some restrictions; $10–$20. TV; cable. 2 pools; whirlpool. Restaurant open 24 hrs. Ck-out 11 am. Meeting rms. Refrigerators. On Gulf beach. Cr cds: A, C, D, DS, MC, V.

✔ ★LIGHTHOUSE. *(Box 233) 455 E Beach Blvd. 205/948-6188.* 160 rms, 1–5 story, 116 kits. May–Labor Day: S, D $65–$130; kit. units $72–$130; wkly rates; lower rates rest of yr. Crib $3. Pet accepted, some restrictions; $40. TV; cable. 2 pools, 1 heated; whirlpool. Restaurant nearby. Ck-out 10 am. Refrigerators. Private patios, balconies. On Gulf beach. Cr cds: A, D, DS, MC, V.

Motor Hotels

★ ★HOLIDAY INN ON THE BEACH. *(Box 417) AL 182, E Beach Blvd. 205/948-6191; FAX 205/948-6191, ext 155.* 118 rms, 4 story. S, D $48–$132; each addl $8; under 19 free; higher rates shrimp festival. Crib free. TV. Pool; wading pool, poolside serv. Restaurant 6 am–2 pm, 4:30–10 pm. Rm serv. Bar from noon (in season); entertainment, dancing. Ck-out noon. Coin lndry. Meeting rms. Sundries. Game rm. Patios, balconies. On private beach. Cr cds: A, C, D, DS, MC, V, JCB.

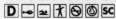

★ ★QUALITY INN BEACHSIDE. *(Box 1013) 931 W Beach Blvd. 205/948-6874.* 158 units, 6 story, 72 kits. May–Labor Day: S, D $99–$129; each addl $6; suites, kits. $129–$195; studio rms $137; under 18 free; wkly rates; packages avail; lower rates rest of yr. Crib $6. TV; cable. 2 pools, 1 indoor; poolside serv. Playground. Restaurant 7 am–9 pm. Rm serv. Bar 5–11 pm. Ck-out 11 am. Coin lndry. Meeting rms. Sundries. Shopping arcade (seasonal). Exercise equipt; weights, bicycles, whirlpool. Some refrigerators. Patios, balconies. On beach. Cr cds: A, C, D, DS, ER, MC, V.

Hotel

★ ★ ★PERDIDO BEACH RESORT (formerly Hilton). *(27200 Perdido Beach Blvd, Orange Beach 36561) 8 mi E of AL 59, on AL 182. 205/981-9811; FAX 205/981-5670.* 345 units, 10 story. May–Labor Day: S, D $119–$154; each addl $10; suites, studio rms $194–$295; family, tennis, honeymoon plans; lower rates rest of yr. Crib free. TV; cable. Indoor/outdoor pool; poolside serv, lifeguard. Restaurant 6 am–11 pm. Bar; entertainment Tues–Sat, dancing. Ck-out noon. Convention facilities. Concierge. Shopping arcade. Some covered parking. Lighted tennis. 18-hole golf privileges, greens fee $42, pro, putting green, miniature golf. Exercise equipt; weights, bicycles, whirlpool, sauna. Game rm. Lawn games. Some refrigerators. Balconies. Fishing pier. On beach. Cr cds: A, C, D, DS, ER, MC, V.

Resort

★ ★GULF STATE PARK RESORT HOTEL. *(Box 437) 1½ mi E of AL 59, on AL 182. 205/948-4853; res: 800/544-GULF; FAX 205/948-*

5998. 144 rms, 2 story, 18 kits. Mid-May–Labor Day: S, D $91; each addl $5; suites $175; under 12 free; lower rates rest of yr. Crib $5. TV. Pool. Dining rm 7 am–9 pm. Bar 4–10 pm (in season), closed Sun. Ck-out 11 am, ck-in 4 pm. Meeting rms. Sundries. Grocery 1½ mi. Package store 2 mi. Lighted tennis. Golf. Lawn games. Refrigerator in suites. Balconies, private patios. On beach. State-owned; facilities of park avail. 825-ft state-operated fishing pier. Fishing guides. Cr cds: A, MC, V.

Restaurants

    ✔ ★**GIFT HORSE.** *(209 W Laurel, Foley) On US 98. 205/943-3663.* Hrs: 11 am–2:30 pm, 5–9 pm; Sun 11 am–8 pm. Closed Dec 25. Buffet: lunch $7.50, dinner $10.50. Sun brunch $10.50. Child's meals. Specialties: apple cheese casserole, fried biscuits, blueberry muffins. Own cakes, candy. Restored building (1912); antique tables. Cr cds: MC, V.

    ★**HAZEL'S.** *(AL 182, Orange Beach) 6 mi E of AL 59, on AL 182. 205/981-4628.* Hrs: 7 am–8:30 pm; Sat to 9:30 pm; May–Oct 6 am–10 pm; Sat, Sun brunch 11 am–4 pm. Closed Dec 25. Serv bar. Semi-a la carte: bkfst $2.99–$6.25, lunch $2.29–$5.25, dinner $5.95–$18.95. Sat, Sun brunch $7.95. Child's meals. Specializes in seafood. Salad bar. Parking. Cr cds: A, DS, MC, V.

    ✔ ★**MIKEE'S.** *1st St N & 2nd Ave E. 205/948-6452.* Hrs: 11 am–10 pm. Bar. Semi-a la carte: lunch $3–$12, dinner $4–$13. Child's meals. Specializes in seafood. Nautical decor. Parking. Cr cds: A, DS, MC, V.

    ★**ORIGINAL SEAFOOD AND OYSTER HOUSE.** *AL 59 at Bayou Village. 205/948-2445.* Hrs: 11 am–10 pm; Fri, Sat to 11 pm. Closed Dec 24–25. Bar. Semi-a la carte: lunch $5–$9.95, dinner $5–$19. Child's meals. Specializes in seafood. Salad bar. Parking. Nautical decor. On Bayou. Cr cds: C, D, DS, MC, V.

    ★★**PERDIDO PASS.** *(27501 Perdido Beach Blvd, Orange Beach 36561) 8 mi E of AL 59, on AL 182, at Alabama Point Bridge. 205/981-6312.* Hrs: 11 am–9 pm. Closed Tues Nov–Jan. Bar. A la carte entrees: lunch $3.99–$7.99, dinner $9.99–$18.99. Child's meals. Specializes in seafood, mesquite grilled steak. Parking. Overlooks Gulf of Mexico. Cr cds: A, DS, MC, V.

    ★**SEA-N-SUDS.** *405 E Beach Blvd. 205/948-7894.* Hrs: 11 am–8 pm; Apr–Aug to 9 pm. Closed Sun off-season; Thanksgiving; also Dec. Bar. Semi-a la carte: lunch, dinner $3.95–$10.95. Specializes in fried seafood. Salad bar. Parking. On pier, overlooking gulf. Cr cds: A, MC, V.

    ✔ ★**ZEKE'S LANDING.** *(26619 Perdido Beach Blvd, Orange Beach) 10 mi E on AL 182. 205/981-4001.* Hrs: 11 am–9 pm; Fri, Sat to 10 pm; Apr–Oct 11 am–10 pm; Fri, Sat to 11 pm; Sun jazz brunch 10:30 am–3 pm. Bar. Semi-a la carte: lunch $5.95, dinner $9.95. Sun brunch $10.95. Child's meals. Specializes in seafood, prime rib. Parking. Overlooking harbor. Cr cds: A, DS, MC, V.

Guntersville (A-3)

Pop: 7,038 **Elev:** 800 ft **Area code:** 205 **Zip:** 35976

A thriving port and power-producing center of the Tennessee Valley Authority, this town was once the site of a Cherokee village. In the 1820s, steamboats plying the river turned Guntersville into a boomtown; still the Cherokees and settlers continued to live alongside each other peacefully. "Boat Day," it was said, was a great occasion for the settlers and Cherokees alike.

    The Cumberland River Trail, the route Andrew Jackson took on his way to the Creek War in 1813, passed through Guntersville, and Cherokees from this area joined and fought bravely with Jackson's troops against the Creeks. But, in 1837, just 24 years later, General Winfield Scott, under the direction of Andrew Jackson, rounded up the area's Cherokees and moved them westward.

    Today, Guntersville receives and distributes river freight. South of town is the plateau of Sand Mountain, one of the great food-producing sections of the state. Part of the growing resort area of north Alabama's TVA lake country, Guntersville's municipal parks have numerous boat docks and launches.

What to See and Do

1. **Guntersville Dam and Lake** (1939). 12 mi W and N via AL 69 and County 240, 50. Fifth of the nine TVA dams on the Tennessee River, it impounds a 67,900-acre lake that is 76 miles long. It is a favorite recreation area for swimming, fishing and boating. Lobby (daily). **Free.**

2. **Lake Guntersville State Park.** 6 mi NE off AL 227 on Guntersville Reservoir. A 5,909-acre park with ridge tops and meadows. Swimming beach, waterskiing; fishing center; boating. Hiking, bicycling; golf (18 holes, fee), tennis. Nature programs. Picnicking, playground, concession, restaurant, chalets, lakeside cottages, resort inn on Taylor Mountain (see RESORT). Camping (hookups). Phone 571-5444.

3. **Buck's Pocket State Park.** 16 mi N & E via AL 227, County 50 to Groveoak. Natural pocket of the Appalachian mountain chain on 2,000 acres. Fishing; boat launch. Hiking trails. Picnic facilities, playground, concession. Primitive and improved camping. Visitor center. Phone 659-2000.

(For further information contact the Chamber of Commerce, 200 Gunter Ave, PO Box 577; 582-3612.)

(See Gadsden, Huntsville)

Motels

    ✔ ★★**BEST WESTERN BOAZ OUTLET CENTER.** *(751 US 431S, Boaz 35957)* Jct US 431 & AL 168. 205/593-8410; FAX 205/593-8410, ext 300. 116 rms, 2 story. S $37–$45; D $42–$49; each addl $5; under 12 free. Crib free. Pet accepted. TV; cable. Pool; wading pool. Restaurant 6 am–2 pm. Ck-out 11 am. Meeting rms. Cr cds: A, C, D, DS, MC, V.

    ★★**HOLIDAY INN.** *(PO Box 937) 2140 Gunter Ave. 205/582-2220; FAX 205/582-2059.* 100 rms, 2–3 story, 20 kits. S $46–$58; D $52–$64; each addl $6; kits. $54–$58; under 19 free. Crib free. TV; cable. Pool. Restaurant 6:30–10 am, 11 am–2 pm, 5–9 pm. Rm serv. Bar; entertainment, dancing exc Sun. Ck-out 11 am. Meeting rms. Refrigerators. Private patios, balconies. View of lake. Cr cds: A, C, D, DS, MC, V, JCB.

    ★**MAC'S LANDING.** *7001 Val-Monte Dr. 205/582-1000; FAX 205/582-1385.* 53 units, 2 story. Apr–Oct: S, D $47–$51; each addl $5; suites, kit. units $78–$93; under 19 free; lower rates rest of yr. Crib $5. Pet accepted. TV; cable. Pool. Complimentary continental bkfst. Restaurant adj 11 am–10 pm. Bar 3:30 pm–1 am, Thurs–Sat noon–2 am. Ck-out 11 am. Coin lndry. Meeting rms. Gift shop. Balconies. Picnic tables, grills. On lake; swimming. Cr cds: A, C, D, DS, MC, V.

Resort

    ★★★**LAKE GUNTERSVILLE LODGE.** *1155 Lodge Dr, 6 mi NE on AL 227. 205/571-5440; res: 800/548-4553; FAX 205/571-5459.* 100 rms in lodge, 2 story, 15 cottages, 20 chalets. Mar–Oct: lodge: S $53–$57; D $55–$59; each addl $5; suites $97; kit. cottages for 4 (2-day min) $97; chalet for 1–6, $97; under 12 free; wkly rates; golf plans; lower rates rest of yr. Maid serv daily in lodge, alternate days in cottages. Crib $5. TV. Pool; wading pool, sauna. Playground. Dining rm 7 am–10 pm; Sun from 11:30 am. Box lunches. Ck-out 11 am. Coin lndry. Meeting rms. Grocery 2 mi. Sports dir. Lighted tennis. 18-hole golf, greens fee $12, pro, putting green. Private beach, waterskiing, launch ramps. Seaplane docking. Rec rm. Hiking, fitness, nature trails. Some fireplaces. Private patios, balconies. Heliport. Native American artifact "gold mine." Cr cds: A, MC, V.

☐D ☐ ☐ ☐ ☐ ☐ ☐ ☐ SC

Restaurant

✔ ★ REID'S. 2½ mi SW on US 431, on Guntersville Lake. 205/582-3162. Hrs: 5:30 am–10 pm; Fri, Sat to 11 pm. Closed Dec 25. Semi-a la carte: bkfst $1.65–$5.25, lunch $2.25–$10.50, dinner $3.25–$10.50. Child's meals. Specializes in fresh river catfish. Parking. Family-owned. Cr cds: A, MC, V.

Hamilton (B-2)

Pop: 5,787 **Elev:** 498 ft **Area code:** 205 **Zip:** 35570

What to See and Do

Natural Bridge of Alabama. 1 mi W of AL 5 on US 278. Two spans of sandstone, longest is 148 feet, created by natural erosion of a tributary stream more than 200 million years ago. Picnicking, camping. (Daily) Phone 486-5330. ¢

(See Russellville)

Motel

★ ★ HOLIDAY INN. (Rte 1, Box 591A) 1 mi S on US 43S, near US 78E, 278W. 205/921-7831; FAX 205/921-7831, ext 601. 80 rms, 2 story. S $48–$53; D $52–$57; each addl $5; under 19 free. Crib free. TV; cable. Pool. Restaurant 6 am–2 pm, 5–10 pm. Rm serv. Ck-out noon. Coin lndry. Meeting rms. Golf privileges. Cr cds: A, C, D, DS, MC, V, JCB.

☐D ☐ ☐ ☐ ☐

Horseshoe Bend National Military Park (C-4)

(13 mi N of Dadeville on AL 49)

Early Spanish explorations, led by De Soto, found the Creeks in Alabama and Georgia living in a settled communal-agricultural society governed by complex rituals and customs. Following the American Revolution, a horde of settlers moved south and west of the Appalachians. Despite territorial guarantees in the Treaty of 1790, the United States repeatedly forced land and road concessions from the Creeks. The Creek Indian Agency was ordered to oversee trade and to reestablish the Indians' prehistoric agricultural economy.

The Lower Creeks of Georgia adjusted to life with the settlers. The Upper Creeks living in Alabama did not and vowed to defend their land and their customs after heeding the preachings of Tecumseh in 1811. When a few Upper Creeks, called Red Sticks, killed settlers near the Tennessee border, the Indian Agency ordered the Lower Creeks to execute the attending warriors. The order produced civil war within the Creek Nation by the spring of 1813. By summer, the settlers became involved in the fray, attacking an Upper Creek munitions convoy at Burnt Corn Creek, fearing the Creeks' intentions. The Upper Creeks retaliated on August 30, 1813, attacking Fort Mims and killing an estimated 250 people. Soon after, the militias of Georgia, Tennessee and the Mississippi Territory were brought in to combat the uprising of the "Red

Sticks." The Georgia troops defeated the Creeks in two battles at Autosee and Calabee Creek, but the Tennessee Militia, under Andrew Jackson, was the most effective force; battles were fought by Jackson's army at Talladega, Emuckfaw and Enitachopco. In March of 1814, they struck and routed the Creeks at the Horseshoe Bend of the Tallapoosa River, the bloodiest battle of the Creek War. The peace treaty that followed soon after this battle cost the Creeks more than 20 million acres of land, opening a vast and rich domain to settlement, and eventually lead to the statehood of Alabama in 1819.

For Jackson, Horseshoe Bend was the beginning; for the Creek Nation, the beginning of the end. In the 1830s, during Jackson's presidency, they were forced to leave Alabama and move to "Indian Territory" (Oklahoma).

A museum at the visitor center depicts the battle. The park contains 2,040 acres of low, forested hills and is situated near the southern end of the Piedmont plateau. Wildflowers bloom from early spring to fall. Dogwoods and other plants and trees as well as a variety of birds and mammals can be seen. A three-mile loop road tour traverses the battle area. There are nature trails and a picnic area, as well as areas for fishing and canoeing. (Daily; closed Dec 25) Contact Rte 1, Box 103, Daviston 36256; 205/234-7111. **Free.**

(For accommodations see Alexander City)

Huntsville (A-3)

Settled: 1805 **Pop:** 159,789 **Elev:** 641 ft **Area code:** 205

In Huntsville, the old and the new in Alabama meet. Now the seat of Madison County, the constitutional convention of Alabama Territory met here in 1819 and set up the state legislature. Many stately houses of that era may be seen. Today, Huntsville is deeply involved in space exploration. The George C. Marshall Space Flight Center of NASA began operations here on July 1, 1960.

Situated in a curving valley, Huntsville was an early textile town processing cotton raised in the surrounding country. Six Alabama governors called it home; so did the Confederate Secretary of War. The University of Alabama–Huntsville is located here.

What to See and Do

1. **US Space and Rocket Center.** 5 mi W on AL 20 just off I-565 at Space Center exit. Hands-on space exhibits, tour of NASA Space Shuttle programs and domed theater comprise this NASA visitor center. (Daily; closed Dec 25) Phone 837-3400 or 800/63-SPACE. Combination ticket ¢¢¢¢

   Space Center. Apollo capsule, space shuttle objects returned from orbit, demonstrations in astronaut gear. Rocket Park displays development of Apollo-Saturn V moon rocket, life-size space shuttle model. Camping. Space Center ¢¢¢

   US Space Camp. Visitors observe trainees fire a rocket engine, guide spacecraft by computer, feel simulated weightlessness on Zero-G machines and go on a simulated shuttle flight. US Space Camp offers one-week programs for children grade 4 and up.

   Spacedome. Space Shuttle and science films photographed by astronauts with Super 70mm Omnimax system, tilt dome screen, 280-seat theater. Actual shuttle footage, multi-speaker stereophonic sound re-create sense of being aboard missions; 45-min films. Spacedome ¢¢¢

   NASA Bus Tours. Escorted 90-min bus trips through Marshall Space Flight Center featuring mission control, Space Shuttle components, large tank where astronauts simulate weightlessness, Space Station development underway. Bus tour ¢¢¢

2. **Von Braun Civic Center.** Downtown, 700 Monroe St. Largest multipurpose complex of its kind in northern Alabama, named for noted space pioneer, Dr Werner von Braun. Center has 9,000-seat arena, 2,171-seat concert hall, 502-seat theater-playhouse; 72,000

square-foot exhibit space, 25,000 square-foot meeting rooms; the city Tourist Info Center (24-hour phone 533-5723); Huntsville Museum of Art (see #6). Phone 533-1953.

3. Big Spring International Park. Spragins St, W of Courthouse Square. The town's water supply, this natural spring produces 24 million gallons daily. The first homesteader was John Hunt, and it was this spring around which the town's nucleus grew.

4. Twickenham Historic District. Downtown, S and E of the Courthouse Sq. A living museum of antebellum architecture, the district contains Alabama's largest concentration of antebellum houses. Several of the houses are occupied by descendants of original builders/owners. Tours can be self-guided; guided tours avail for groups. Contact the Huntsville/Madison County Convention and Visitors Bureau, 551-2230.

5. Huntsville Depot Museum. 320 Church St. Opened in 1860 as "passenger house" and eastern division headquarters for the Memphis & Charleston RR Co, the Huntsville depot was captured by Union troops and used as a prison; Civil War graffiti survives. Street car trips (addl fee); transportation exhibits. (Wed–Sun) Sr citizen rate. Phone 539-1860. ¢¢

6. Huntsville Museum of Art. Von Braun Civic Center, 700 Monroe St SW. Five galleries featuring traditional and contemporary work by regional and national artists; permanent collection and changing exhibits. Tours, lectures, concerts, films. (Daily exc Mon) Phone 535-4350. **Free.**

7. Burritt Museum & Park. 3101 Burritt Dr, just off Monte Sano Blvd. Unusual 11-room house built in shape of a cross. Exhibitions on gems and minerals, archaeology, antiques, historical items. On the grounds of this 167-acre park are 4 authentically furnished cabins, a blacksmith shop, a smokehouse and a church. Nature trails, gardens. Picnicking. Panoramic view of city. Museum (Mar–Nov, Tues–Sun afternoons). Grounds (daily). Phone 536-2882. **Free.**

8. Alabama's Constitution Village. 301 Madison St. Re-created complex of buildings commemorating Alabama's entry into the Union at the 1819 Constitutional Convention; period craft demonstrations and activities; guides in period dress. (Daily exc Sun; closed Dec 24–Feb) Phone 535-6565. ¢¢

9. Monte Sano State Park. 4 mi E, off US 431. A 2,140-acre scenic recreation area on top of 1,800-foot Monte Sano ("Mountain of Health"). Hiking trails. Picnicking (tables, shelters, barbecue pits, fireplaces), playground, concession. Camping, cabins. Amphitheater. Park open all yr. Standard fees. Phone 534-3757 or -6589.

10. Madison County Nature Trail. 12 mi SE on S Shawdee Rd, Green Mountain. Original house on first homestead. Chapel; covered bridge; 16-acre lake, waterfall; wooded hiking trails. (Daily) Braille trail. Phone 883-9501.

(For further information contact the Tourist Information Center, Convention & Visitors Bureau, 700 Monroe St, 35801; 551-2230 or 800/772-2348 or a 24-hr events hot-line at 533-5723.)

Annual Events

Panoply of the Arts Festival. Big Spring Park (see #3). Mid-May.

Northeast Alabama State Fair. Jaycees Fairgrounds. Regional fair involving five area counties. 10 days beginning Thurs prior to Labor Day.

(See Athens, Decatur)

Motels

✔ ★**BUDGETEL INN.** 4890 University Dr NW (35816). 205/830-8999; FAX 205/837-5720. 102 rms, 3 story. S $37.95; D $39.95–$46.95; each addl $7; under 18 free; some wkend rates. Crib free. Pet accepted. TV; cable. Pool. Complimentary continental bkfst, coffee. Restaurant adj open 24 hrs. Ck-out noon. Meeting rm. Cr cds: A, C, D, DS, MC, V.

✔ ★**COMFORT INN.** 3788 University Dr (35816). 205/533-3291; FAX 205/536-7389. 67 rms, 2 story, 8 suites. S $34–$38; D $38–$42; each addl $4; suites $39–$43; under 16 free; wkend rates. Crib $4. TV; cable, in-rm movies avail. Pool. Complimentary continental bkfst. Restaurant opp open 24 hrs. Ck-out 11 am. Meeting rms. Exercise equipt; weights, bicycles. Refrigerators. Cr cds: A, C, D, DS, ER, MC, V, JCB.

★★★**COURTYARD BY MARRIOTT.** 4804 University Dr (35816). 205/837-1400; FAX 205/837-3582. 149 rms, 3 story. S $64; D $74; each addl (after 4th person) $10; suites $74–$84; under 12 free; wkend rates. Crib free. TV; cable. Pool. Restaurant 6–10:30 am. Bar 4–11 pm. Coin lndry. Meeting rms. Valet serv. Exercise equipt; weights, bicycles, whirlpool. Refrigerator in suites. Cr cds: A, C, D, DS, MC, V.

✔ ★**DAYS INN-HUNTSVILLE SPACE CENTER.** 2201 N Memorial Pkwy (35810). 205/536-7441; FAX 205/536-7441, ext 257. 98 rms, 2 story. S $35–$41; D $40–$46; each addl $5; suites $50–$55; under 12 free. Crib free. TV; cable. Pool; wading pool. Complimentary continental bkfst. Restaurant adj open 24 hrs. Ck-out 11 am. Cr cds: A, C, D, DS, MC, V.

★★**ECONO LODGE.** 3772 University Dr NW (35816). 205/534-7061. 82 rms, 2 story. S $24.99–$32; D $32–$39; suites $49; under 18 free. Crib free. Pet accepted, some restrictions; $12.50. TV; cable. Pool. Complimentary coffee in lobby. Restaurant nearby. Ck-out 11 am. Refrigerator in suites. Cr cds: A, C, D, DS, MC, V.

★★**HAMPTON INN.** 4815 University Dr (35816). 205/830-9400; FAX 205/830-9400, ext 104. 128 rms, 3 story. S, D $46–$54; under 18 free. Crib free. Pet accepted, some restrictions. TV; cable. Heated pool; whirlpool. Complimentary continental bkfst. Ck-out noon. Health club privileges. Cr cds: A, C, D, DS, MC, V.

★★**HOLIDAY INN-SPACE CENTER.** 3810 University Dr (35816), W on US 72 at jct AL 53. 205/837-7171; FAX 205/837-7171, ext 301. 179 rms, 2 story. S $56–$66; D $60–$70; under 12 free; some wkend rates. Crib free. Pet accepted, some restrictions; $50 refundable. TV; cable. Pool. Restaurant 6:30 am–2 pm, 5:30–10 pm. Rm serv. Bar 4 pm–midnight. Ck-out 1 pm. Coin lndry. Meeting rms. Bellhops. Valet serv. Sundries. Free airport transportation. Health club privileges. Cr cds: A, C, D, DS, ER, MC, V, JCB.

★★**LA QUINTA.** 3141 University Dr NW (35816). 205/533-0756; FAX 205/539-5414. 130 rms, 2 story. S $43; D $43–$49; each addl $6; under 18 free. Crib free. Pet accepted, some restrictions. TV; cable. Pool. Complimentary continental bkfst. Restaurant adj open 24 hrs. Ck-out noon. Meeting rms. Refrigerators avail. Health club privileges. Cr cds: A, C, D, DS, MC, V.

✔ ★**RED CARPET INN.** 2700 Memorial Pkwy SW (35801). 205/536-6661. 90 rms, 4 story. S $28–$30; D $30–$35; each addl $4; under 14 free. Crib $4. Pet accepted. TV; cable. Pool. Complimentary continental bkfst, coffee. Restaurant adj 11 am–2 pm, 4–9 pm. Ck-out noon. Meeting rms. Beauty shop. Many refrigerators. Balconies. Cr cds: A, C, D, DS, MC, V.

★★**RESIDENCE INN BY MARRIOTT.** 4020 Independence Dr (35816). 205/837-8907; FAX 205/837-5435. 112 kit. suites, 1–2 story. Suites $75–$95; some wkend rates. Crib free. Pet accepted, some restrictions; $50. TV; cable, in-rm movies avail. Pool; whirlpool. Complimentary continental bkfst. Ck-out noon. Valet serv Mon–Fri. Sport court. Health club privileges. Fireplaces. Private patios, balconies. Picnic tables. Cr cds: A, C, D, DS, MC, V.

★**SUPER 8.** *3803 University Dr NW (35805).* 205/539-8881; FAX 205/533-5322. 80 units, 3 story. S $27–$30; D $32–$36; suites $37–$41; under 12 free. Crib free. Pet accepted, some restrictions. TV. Pool. Complimentary coffee. Restaurant adj open 24 hrs. Ck-out 11 am. Cr cds: A, C, D, DS, MC, V, JCB.

Hotels

★ ★**HILTON.** *401 Williams Ave (35801),* at Freedom Plaza. 205/533-1400; FAX 205/533-1400, ext 604. 279 rms, 4 story. S $75–$95; D $85–$105; each addl $10; suites $120–$135. Crib free. Pet accepted. TV; cable. Pool; whirlpool, poolside serv. Restaurant 6:30 am–10 pm. Bars 11 am–midnight; entertainment Mon–Sat. Ck-out noon. Convention facilities. Free airport transportation. Health club privileges. Wet bar in suites. Civic Center, city park opp. 7 minutes from Alabama Space & Rocket Center. *LUXURY LEVEL:* EXECUTIVE FLOOR. 46 rms, 2 suites. S $95; D $105; each addl $10; suites $135. Concierge. Private lounge, honor bar. Wet bars. Complimentary continental bkfst, newspaper, refreshments. Cr cds: A, C, D, DS, ER, MC, V.

★ ★**HOLIDAY INN RESEARCH PARK.** *5903 University Dr (35816),* at Madison Square Mall. 205/830-0600; FAX 205/830-0600, ext 157. 200 rms, 5 story. S, D $70–$86; each addl $8; suites $125–$145; under 19 free; wknd rates. TV; cable. Indoor/outdoor pool. Restaurant 6 am–2 pm, 5–11 pm. Bar 4:30 pm–2 am; entertainment, dancing Tues–Sat. Ck-out noon. Meeting rms. Guest lndry. Airport transportation. Exercise equipt; weights, bicycles, whirlpool, sauna. Cr cds: A, D, DS, MC, V.

★ ★**MARRIOTT.** *5 Tranquility Base (35805),* at Space Center. 205/830-2222; FAX 205/830-2222, ext 6124. 290 rms, 7 story. S, D $69–$120; suites $325; under 18 free; wknd rates. Crib free. Pet accepted, some restrictions. TV; cable. Indoor/outdoor pool; poolside serv. Restaurants 6 am–11 pm. Bar 4 pm–2 am; disc jockey, dancing. Ck-out noon. Convention facilities. Concierge. Airport transportation. Exercise equipt; weights, bicycles, whirlpool, sauna. Game rm. Space & Rocket Museum adj. *LUXURY LEVEL:* CONCIERGE FLOOR. 39 rms. S $113; D $127. Private lounge, honor bar. Complimentary continental bkfst, refreshments, newspaper. In-rm movies. Cr cds: A, C, D, DS, ER, MC, V, JCB.

★ ★**RADISSON SUITE HOTEL.** *6000 S Memorial Pkwy (35802),* at Gate 1 NASA Space Flight Center. 205/882-9400; FAX 205/882-9684. 153 suites, 3 story. May–Oct: S $68–$78; D $73–$83; each addl $5–$10; kit. units $78–$199; under 17 free; wkly rates; lower rates rest of yr. Crib free. Pet accepted, some restrictions; $100 refundable. TV; cable. Complimentary coffee in rms. Restaurant 6 am–2 pm, 5–10 pm. Bar 11 am–midnight. Ck-out noon. Free lndry facilities. Meeting rms. Free airport, RR station, bus depot transportation. Exercise equipt; bicycles, weights, whirlpool. Refrigerators, wet bars. Picnic tables. Cr cds: A, C, D, DS, ER, MC, V, JCB.

★ ★**SHERATON INN-HUNTSVILLE AIRPORT.** *(Box 20068, 35824)* 1000 Glen Hearn Blvd, at Huntsville Intl Airport. 205/772-9661; FAX 205/464-9116. 148 rms, 6 story. S, D $69–$79; each addl $10; suites $89–$109; under 18 free. Crib free. TV; cable. Pool. Restaurant 6 am–10 pm. Rm serv from 7 am. Bar 11 am–midnight. Ck-out noon. Meeting rms. Free parking. Lighted tennis. 18-hole golf, pro. Exercise equipt; weights, bicycles, sauna. Bathrm phone in suites. In air terminal. Offers many facilities of a resort. *LUXURY LEVEL:* EXECUTIVE FLOOR. 31 rms, 4 suites. S, D $99; each addl $10; suites $99–$109. Concierge. Private lounge. Complimentary continental bkfst, refreshments, newspaper. Cr cds: A, C, D, DS, MC, V, JCB.

Restaurants

★ ★**BOOT'S.** *1522 S Memorial Pkwy.* 205/534-9369. Hrs: 11 am–11 pm. Closed Sun; some hols. Res accepted. Bar. Semi-a la carte: lunch $6.25–$18.95, dinner $6.95–$20.50. Child's meals. Specializes in beef, seafood. Salad bar. Parking. Family-owned. Cr cds: A, C, D, MC, V.

✔ ★ ★**FOGCUTTER.** *3805 University Dr NW.* 205/539-2121. Hrs: 11 am–2 pm, 5–10:30 pm. Closed major hols. Res accepted. Bar to midnight. Semi-a la carte: lunch $3.95–$6.95, dinner $9.95–$17.95. Specializes in steak, seafood. Entertainment. Parking. Nautical decor; antiques. Cr cds: A, C, D, MC, V.

✔ ★ ★**OL' HEIDELBERG.** *6125 University Dr NW, Unit E-14.* 205/922-0556. Hrs: 11 am–9 pm; Fri, Sat to 10 pm. Closed some hols. German, Amer menu. Semi-a la carte: lunch $3.75–$6.75, dinner $5.50–$13.50. Specializes in Wienerschnitzel, sauerbraten. Parking. Family-owned. Cr cds: A, MC, V.

★ ★**TWICKENHAM STATION.** *509 Williams Ave SW, opp von Braun Civic Center.* 205/539-3797. Hrs: 11 am–10 pm; Fri, Sat to 11 pm. Closed Sun; Thanksgiving, Dec 25. Res accepted. Bar. Semi-a la carte: lunch $4.95–$7.95, dinner $10.95–$21.95. Child's meals. Specializes in prime rib, fresh seafood. Salad bar. Parking. Converted warehouse, railroad dining car & caboose; railroad memorabilia, photos. Cr cds: C, D, MC, V.

Jasper (B-2)

Settled: 1815 **Pop:** 13,553 **Elev:** 339 ft **Area code:** 205 **Zip:** 35501

(See Birmingham, Cullman)

Motel

★**TRAVEL-RITE INN.** *200 Mallway Dr, opp mall.* 205/221-1161. 60 rms, 2 story. S $23–$25; D $30; each addl $3; under 12 free. Crib $3. Pet accepted. TV; cable. Restaurant adj 6 am–11 pm. Ck-out 11 am. Meeting rm. Cr cds: A, C, D, DS, MC, V.

Motor Hotel

✔ ★ ★**JASPER INN.** *1400 US 78W Bypass.* 205/221-3050; FAX 205/221-3050, ext 508. 153 rms, 2–4 story. S $30–$34; D $40–$44; each addl $6; under 12 free. Crib free. TV. Pool; wading pool. Restaurant 6 am–2 pm, 5–9 pm. Ck-out noon. Meeting rms. Valet serv. Cr cds: A, C, D, DS, MC, V.

Mobile (E-2)

Founded: 1711 **Pop:** 196,278 **Elev:** 7 ft **Area code:** 205

Mobile, Alabama's only port city, blends old Southern grace with new Southern enterprise. The city was begun in 1711 when Jean Baptiste LeMoyne, Sieur de Bienville, moved his colony from Twenty-Seven Mile Bluff to the present site of Mobile.

Shipping, shipbuilding and a variety of manufacturers make Mobile a great industrial center. Today many millions of tons of cargo annually clear this international port. Paper, petroleum products, textiles, food processing and woodworking are among the principal industries.

While remaining very much the vibrant industrial seaport, Mobile has still managed to retain its air of antebellum graciousness and preserve its past in the Church Street, DeTonti Square, Oakleigh Garden and Old Dauphinway historical districts. These areas are famous for azaleas, oak-lined streets and an extraordinary variety of architectural styles.

What to See and Do

1. **Oakleigh.** 350 Oakleigh Place at Savannah St. This 1830s antebellum house stands on the highest point of Simon Favre's old Spanish land grant, surrounded by azaleas and the live oaks for which it was named. Bricks for the first story were made on the site; the main upper portion is of hand-hewn timber. The Historic Mobile Preservation Society has furnished the house in the pre-1850 period; 1850s Cox-Deasy Creole cottage included in tour. Museum collection of local items. (Daily; closed major hols; also day of Mardi Gras & Christmas wk) Phone 432-1281. ¢¢

2. **Bellingrath Gardens and Home.** 20 mi SW via US 90 or I-10 and Bellingrath Hwy, near Theodore. This 800-acre estate comprises natural woodland and some 65 acres of planted gardens on the Isle-aux-Oies (Fowl) River. It is also a bird sanctuary. Many varieties of native and other trees are background for the innumerable flowers and flowering plants that are in bloom all year. Each season has its own special flowers but many bloom for more than one. There are approximately 250,000 azalea plants of 200 varieties, camellias, roses, water lilies, dogwood and hydrangeas. Travels to world-famed gardens abroad inspired the Bellingraths to create their gardens in the 1920s. Visitors receive a pictorial map showing gardens' walks and principal features. Included in the gardens' admission is the world's largest public display of Boehm porcelain. There is a restaurant, a video display at the entrance and a free "pet motel" near the exit. The Bellingrath home, in the center of the gardens, is furnished with antiques, fine china and rare porcelain; it is open to a few people at a time (daily tours). Since the home is located within the gardens, it is not possible to visit the house without visiting the gardens. House & gardens (daily). Phone 973-2365 or -2217. Gardens ¢¢¢;   House & gardens ¢¢¢¢

3. **Bragg-Mitchell Mansion** (1855). 1906 Springhill Ave. Greek-revival, 20-room mansion sits amidst 12 acres of landscaped grounds. Restored interior includes extensive faux-grained woodwork and stenciled moldings; period furnishings. (Daily exc Sat; closed major hols) Phone 471-6364. ¢¢

4. **Richards-DAR House** (ca 1860). 256 N Joachim St. Restored Italianate town house features elaborate ironwork, curved suspended staircase, period furniture. (Daily exc Mon; closed Mardi Gras, Easter, Thanksgiving, late Dec) Phone 434-7320. ¢¢

5. **Cathedral of the Immaculate Conception** (1835). Dauphin and Claiborne Sts. Greek-revival minor basilica with German art glass windows, bronze canopy over altar and hand-carved stations of the cross. (Daily; limited hrs Mon-Fri) Phone 434-1565.

6. **Carlen House Museum** (1842). 54 Carlen St at Willcox St. "Creole cottage" furnished in period style. Guided tours by appt. (Tues-Sat, also Sun afternoons; closed hols) Phone 434-7768. **Free.**

7. **Fine Arts Museum of the South.** Museum Dr on S shore of lake in Langan Park. Permanent collection includes furniture, decorative arts; American and European 19th-century paintings and prints; contemporary arts & crafts; changing exhibits. (Daily exc Mon; closed major hols) Phone 343-2667. **Free.**

8. **Museum of the City of Mobile.** 355 Government St in Bernstein-Bush House (1872), an Italianate town house. Paintings, documents and artifacts of Mobile's French, British, Spanish and Confederate periods; Mobile's maritime history, ship models, antique carriages, arms collection, Mardi Gras and other costumes. World's second largest collection of Edward Marshall Boehm porcelains. Guided tours by appt. (Tues-Sat, also Sun afternoons; closed hols) Phone 434-7569. **Free.**

9. **Eichold-Heustis Medical Museum.** 1504 Springhill Ave. At the University of South Alabama's USA Springhill campus. Named in honor of Dr. James Heustis and Dr. Samuel Eichold, this museum is the largest of its kind in the southeast. It contains displays of medical artifacts and photographs. (Mon-Fri) Phone 434-5055. **Free.**

10. **The Exploreum, Museum of Discovery.** 1906 Spring Hill Ave. Hands-on investigative science and health museum. More than 80 life science, earth science, physical science and "imagination" exhibits and displays. (Daily exc Mon; closed hols) Phone 471-6873. ¢¢

11. **Phoenix Fire Museum.** 203 S Claiborne St. Fire-fighting equipment; memorabilia dating from first Mobile volunteer company (1819); steam fire engines; collection of silver trumpets and helmets. Housed in restored fire station (1859). Guided tours by appt. (Tues-Sat, also Sun afternoons; closed hols) Phone 434-7554. **Free.**

12. **Fort Condé Mobile Visitor Welcome Center.** 150 S Royal St at Church St. Reconstructed 1724-1735 French fort features workable reproductions of 1740s naval cannon, muskets and other arms. Staffed by soldiers dressed in period French uniforms. (Daily; closed Mardi Gras & Dec 25) Phone 434-7304. **Free.**

13. **Condé-Charlotte Museum House** (1822-24). 104 Theatre St, adj to Fort Condé (see #12). Originally a jail, the museum house is now furnished with period antiques and artifacts; period kitchen and Spanish garden. (Tues-Sat; closed hols) Phone 432-4722. ¢¢

14. **University of South Alabama** (1964). (12,000 students). 307 University Blvd. Theater productions presented during school year at USA/Wright Auditorium (phone 460-6305) and at Saenger Theatre (phone 438-5686). Of architectural interest on campus are Seaman's Bethel Theater (1860); the Plantation Creole House (1828), a reconstructed Creole cottage; and Mobile town house (1870), a federal-style building showing Italianate and Greek-revival influences which also houses the USA campus art gallery. Tours of campus. Phone 460-6141 or -6211.

15. **Alabama State Docks.** Port of Mobile. Berths for 35 ocean-going vessels of up to 45-foot draft; 1,000-foot-wide turning basin. (Mon-Fri; closed some hols) Phone 441-7001.

16. **Battleship USS** *Alabama* **Memorial Park.** 1 mi E via Bankhead and Wallace Tunnels on Battleship Pkwy, US 90. Visitors may tour 35,000-ton USS *Alabama,* which serves as a memorial to the state's men and women who served in World War II, the Korean conflict, Vietnam and Desert Storm. Also, submarine USS *Drum,* World War II aircraft, a B-52 bomber and an A-12 Blackbird spy plane. (Daily; closed Dec 25) Parking fee. Phone 433-2703. ¢¢ Also here is

   Sightseeing Cruise. Narrated cruise (1½ hrs); dinner cruise (2½ hrs). (Daily; closed Jan) Phone 433-6101. 1½-hr cruise ¢¢¢

17. **Malbis Greek Orthodox Church** (1965). 13 mi E off I-10 exit 38 or US 90. Impressive Byzantine church, copied from a similar one in Athens, Greece. Pentelic marble is from same quarries that supplied the Parthenon; skilled artists from Greece created the authentic paintings; hand-carved figures and ornaments were brought from Greece. Stained-glass windows, dome with murals, icons and many works of art depicting life of Christ. Guided tours by appt. (Daily exc Dec 25) Phone 626-3050. **Free.**

18. **Greyhound racing. Mobile Greyhound Park.** W via I-10, Theodore-Dawes exit (#13). Parimutuel wagering; restaurant. Minimum age 18. (Nightly exc Sun; matinees Mon, Wed, Sat; closed mid-late Dec) For reservations phone 653-5000.

19. **Gray Line bus tours.** For information and reservations phone 432-2229 or 344-8482.

(For further information contact Mobile Tourism & Travel, PO Box 1827, 36633; 434-7304.)

Annual Events

Senior Bowl Football Game. Ladd Stadium. 3rd Sat Jan.

Mardi Gras. Fifteen parades, balls, other festivities. 10 days ending Shrove Tuesday. Late Feb–early Mar.

Historic Mobile Tours. Houses, buildings open to visitors. Early–mid-Mar.

Blessing of the Shrimp Fleet. Bayou la Batre, 25 mi SW. 4th Sun June.

Greater Gulf State Fair. Commercial, industrial, military and educational exhibits; entertainment. Mid-Oct.

Seasonal Event

Azalea Trail Festival. During the period when the azaleas are usually at full bloom, many events are scheduled to entertain visitors in the city. A 35 mile long driving tour winds through the floral streets in and around Mobile; printed guides available. Azaleas were first introduced to Mobile in the early 18th century, and today they grow throughout the city. The Tourism Department has further details and has maps for self-guided tours of Azalea Trail route and local historic sites. Phone 432-6162. Mar–early Apr.

(See Dauphin Island, Gulf Shores)

Motels

(Rates may be higher during Mardi Gras)

★★**BEST WESTERN BRADBURY INN.** *180 S Beltline Hwy (36608), 2 blks N of jct I-65, Airport Blvd.* 205/343-9345; FAX 205/342-5366. 102 rms, 3 story. S, D $49–$59; each addl $5; suites $65–$75; under 12 free; wknd rates. Crib free. TV; cable. Pool. Complimentary bkfst. Restaurant adj. Ck-out noon. Coin lndry. Meeting rms. Valet serv. Some refrigerators. Cr cds: A, C, D, DS, ER, MC, V.

✔★**DAYS INN.** *5550 I-10 Service Rd (36619).* 205/661-8181; FAX 205/660-0194. 100 rms, 2 story. Apr–Sept: S $39.50; D $45.50; each addl $5; under 18 free; lower rates rest of yr. Crib free. Pet accepted, some restrictions. TV; cable. Pool. Complimentary continental bkfst, coffee. Restaurant adj 6 am–11 pm. Ck-out noon. Coin lndry. Some refrigerators. Cr cds: A, C, D, DS, MC, V.

★★**DRURY INN.** *824 S Beltline Hwy (36609).* 205/344-7700. 110 rms, 4 story. S $51–$63; D $57–$63; each addl $6; under 18 free. Crib free. Pet accepted, some restrictions. TV; cable. Pool. Complimentary continental bkfst. Restaurant adj open 24 hrs. Ck-out noon. Meeting rms. Valet serv. Cr cds: A, C, D, DS, MC, V.

✔★★**HAMPTON INN.** *930 S Beltline Hwy (36609).* 205/344-4942; FAX 205/341-4520. 118 units, 2 story. S $39–$51; D $48–$54; each addl $5; under 18 free. Crib free. Pet accepted, some restrictions. TV; cable. Pool. Complimentary continental bkfst. Ck-out noon. Valet serv. Cr cds: A, C, D, DS, MC, V.

★★**LA QUINTA.** *816 S Beltline Hwy (36609).* 205/343-4051; FAX 205/343-2897. 122 units, 2 story. S $48–$55; D $56–$63; each addl $8; under 18 free. Crib free. Pet accepted. TV; cable. Pool. Complimentary continental bkfst, coffee. Restaurant adj open 24 hrs. Ck-out noon. Meeting rms. Valet serv. Cr cds: A, C, D, DS, MC, V.

★★**RED ROOF INN.** *5450 Coca Cola Rd (36619).* 205/666-1044; FAX 205/666-1044, ext 444. 109 rms, 2 story. S $31–$37; D $33–$41; each addl $6; under 18 free. Crib free. Pet accepted, some restrictions. TV. Complimentary coffee in lobby. Restaurant nearby. Ck-out noon. Cr cds: A, C, D, DS, MC, V.

✔★**SHONEY'S INN.** *5472-A Tillman's Corner Pkwy (36619), at I-10 exit 15B.* 205/660-1520; res: 800/222-2222; FAX 205/666-4240. 120 rms, 3 story, 15 suites. S $44; D $50; each addl $6; suites $65; under 18 free; golf plan. Crib free. Pet accepted; $5 refundable. TV; cable. Pool. Complimentary coffee in lobby. Restaurant adj 6 am–11 pm. Ck-out noon. Some refrigerators. Cr cds: A, C, D, DS, ER, MC, V.

Motor Hotels

★★**HOLIDAY INN.** *6527 AL 90W (36619), AL 90 & I-10 exit 15B.* 205/666-5600; FAX 205/666-2773. 160 units, 5 story. S $51–$78; D $59–$78; each addl $5; suites $75–$95; under 18 free. Crib free. Pet accepted. TV; cable. Pool; whirlpool. Restaurant 6 am–2 pm, 5–10 pm. Rm serv. Bar 11–2 am. Ck-out noon. Coin lndry. Meeting rms. Bellhops. Valet serv. Free airport transportation. *LUXURY LEVEL:* **CLUB FIVE.** 34 rms, D $62–$85. Private lounge. Complimentary continental bkfst. Cr cds: A, C, D, DS, MC, V, JCB.

★★★**RAMADA INN-AIRPORT RESORT.** *600 S Beltline Hwy (36608), jct I-65 & Airport Blvd.* 205/344-8030; FAX 205/344-8055. 236 rms, 4 story. S $59.75–$89.75; D $69.75–$99.75; each addl $10; under 18 free. Crib free. TV; cable. 2 pools, 1 indoor; wading pool. Restaurant 6 am–2 pm, 5–10 pm. Rm serv. Bar 11–2 am; entertainment, dancing. Ck-out noon. Meeting rms. Bellhops. Sundries. Free airport transportation. Lighted tennis. Putting green. Exercise equipt; weights, bicycles, whirlpool. Cr cds: A, C, D, DS, MC, V, JCB.

Hotels

ADAM'S MARK AT RIVERVIEW PLAZA (formerly Stouffer's Riverview Plaza). (New owners, therefore not rated) *64 Water St (36602).* 205/438-4000; FAX 205/438-3719. 375 units, 28 story. S $74–$145; D $74–$157; each addl $12; suites $184; under 18 free; wknd rates. Crib free. Covered parking $3.50. TV; cable. Heated pool; poolside serv. Restaurant 6:30 am–3 pm, 5:30–11 pm. Rm serv 24 hrs. Bar 11–1 am, wkends to 2 am; entertainment. Ck-out 1 pm. Convention facilities. Concierge. Shopping arcade. Airport transportation. Health club privileges. *LUXURY LEVEL:* **THE CLUB LEVEL.** 28 units, 2 floors. S $94–$165; D $94–$177. Private lounge. Complimentary continental bkfst, refreshments, newspaper. Cr cds: A, C, D, DS, ER, MC, V, JCB.

★★**FIESTA PLAZA HOTEL** (formerly Hilton). *3101 Airport Blvd (36606), I-65 Airport Blvd exit.* 205/476-6400; FAX 205/476-9360. 256 rms, 20 story. S $65–$75; D $75–$85; each addl $10; suites $150–$200; family rates. Crib free. Pet accepted, some restrictions. TV; cable. Pool; whirlpool. Restaurant 6:30 am–10 pm. Bar. Ck-out noon. Convention facilities. Some refrigerators. Some balconies. Cr cds: A, C, D, DS, MC, V.

★★★**RADISSON ADMIRAL SEMMES.** *251 Government St (36602).* 205/432-8000; FAX 205/432-8000, ext 7111. 170 rms, 12 story. S, D $85–$125; each addl $10; suites $115–$350; studios $85; under 17 free; wknd rates; varied lower rates. Crib free. Valet parking $3.50. TV; cable. Heated pool; whirlpool, poolside serv. Restaurant 5:45 am–10 pm. Rm serv 24 hrs. Bar; entertainment Wed-Sat. Ck-out 11 am. Meeting rms. Health club privileges. Some refrigerators. Restored landmark hotel in heart of historical district; antiques, artwork. Cr cds: A, C, D, DS, MC, V.

Inn

★★**MALAGA INN.** *359 Church St (36602).* 205/438-4701; *res: 800/235-1586; FAX 205/438-4701, ext 123.* 40 rms, 2–3 story. S $52–$59; D $62–$69; each addl $5; suites $125; studio rms $40. TV. Pool. Complimentary coffee. Dining rm 7 am–10 pm; closed Sun. Rm serv. Bar. Ck-out 11 am, ck-in noon–1 pm. Meeting rms. Bellhops. Private patios, balconies. Twin restored antebellum town houses built 1862; many original antique furnishings. Garden courtyard, fountain. Cr cds: A, C, D, DS, MC, V.

Resort

★★★★**MARRIOTT'S GRAND HOTEL.** *(Point Clear 36564)* 23 mi SE of Mobile on US 98 Scenic. 205/928-9201; FAX 205/928-1149. 306 hotel rms, 2–4 story, 8 multi-unit cottages (2 & 4 bedrm). Mar–Oct: S, D $155–$185; cottage units $200–$225; under 18 free; MAP avail; lower rates rest of yr. Crib free. TV; cable. Pool; poolside serv, lifeguard. Playground. Supervised child's activities (Memorial Day–Labor Day & special wkends). Rm serv. Box lunches, snack bar, picnics avail. Bars 11 am–midnight. Ck-out noon, ck-in 4 pm. Meeting rms. Valet serv. Concierge. Grocery, package store 1 mi. Beauty shop. Airport transportation. Tennis, pro. 36-hole golf, pro. Private beach, luxury yacht, sailboats, paddleboats, jet ski, windsurfing, deep sea fishing. Bicycles. Lawn games. Game rm. Dancing. Exercise equipt; weight machine, bicycles, whirlpool; hydro-therapy. Fishing guides; fish clean & store. Some refrigerators avail. Some private patios, balconies. Picnic tables. 550 landscaped acres on Mobile Bay. Cr cds: A, C, D, DS, ER, MC, V, JCB.

Restaurants

★★★**BAY VIEW.** *(See Marriott's Grand Hotel Resort)* 205/928-9201. Hrs: 6–10 pm. Res accepted. Bar. Semi-a la carte: dinner $10.95–$22.95. Child's meals. Specializes in fresh seafood. Own baking. Parking. Overlooks Mobile Bay. Cr cds: A, C, D, DS, ER, MC, V, JCB.

✔★★**PIER 4.** *Battleship Pkwy.* 205/626-6710. Hrs: 11 am–10 pm; Fri, Sat to 11 pm. Closed Thanksgiving, Dec 25. Continental menu. Semi-a la carte: lunch $4.25–$7.50, dinner $8.95–$16.95. Child's meals. Specialties: shrimp Dijon, snapper Ponchartrain. Own desserts. Parking. View of bay. Cr cds: A, C, D, DS, MC, V.

★★★**THE PILLARS.** *1757 Government St.* 205/478-6341. Hrs: 5–10 pm. Closed Sun; major hols. Res accepted. Continental menu. Serv bar. Wine cellar. Semi-a la carte: dinner $14.50–$17.50. Complete meals: dinner $22.50. Child's meals. Specializes in fresh gulf seafood, veal, Angus beef. Own baking. Valet parking. Restored Southern plantation house. Cr cds: A, C, D, DS, MC, V.

✔★★**ROUSSOS SEAFOOD.** *166 S Royal St, I-10 Water St exit to Fort Condé Historic District Welcome Center.* 205/433-3322. Hrs: 11 am–10 pm; Sun to 9 pm. Closed Dec 25. Res accepted. Bar. Semi-a la carte: lunch, dinner $3.95–$21.95. Child's meals. Specializes in fresh seafood, steak, chicken. Parking. Nautical decor. Extensive seafood menu. Family-owned. Cr cds: A, C, D, DS, MC, V.

★★**RUTH'S CHRIS STEAK HOUSE.** *271 Glenwood St.* 205/476-0516. Hrs: 5–10 pm; also Fri 11 am–2:30 pm. Closed Thanksgiving, Dec 25. Res accepted. Bar. A la carte entrees: lunch, dinner $15–$30. Parking. Cr cds: A, C, D, MC, V.

★★**WEICHMAN'S ALL SEASONS.** *168 S Beltline Hwy, on W Service Rd between Airport Blvd & Dauphin St.* 205/344-3961. Hrs: 11

am–3 pm, 5–10 pm; Sat from 5 pm; Sun 5–9 pm. Res accepted. Bar. Semi-a la carte: lunch $4.95–$12.95, dinner $7.95–$22.95. Child's meals. Specializes in scampi almondine, seafood la Louisiane. Parking. Antique furnishings. Cr cds: A, C, D, DS, MC, V.

Unrated Dining Spot

MORRISON'S CAFETERIA. *3200 Springdale Plaza, W at jct Airport Blvd & I-65.* 205/479-0534. Hrs: 10:45 am–8:30 pm. Avg ck: lunch $4.80, dinner $4.95. Specializes in fried shrimp, char-broiled chicken, fresh pies. Cr cds: MC, V.

Montgomery (C-3)

Settled: 1819 **Pop:** 187,106 **Elev:** 287 ft **Area code:** 205

Between tall, stately columns on the portico of the state capitol, a bronze star marks the spot where Jefferson Davis was inaugurated president of the Confederate States of America on February 18, 1861. At that moment, Montgomery became the Confederacy's first capital. From this city went the telegram "Fire on Fort Sumter" that began the Civil War. Approximately 100 years later, Montgomery became embroiled in another kind of "war," the battle for civil rights.

Today, Montgomery is home to the nation's first Civil Rights Memorial. The memorial chronicles key events and lists the names of approximately 40 people who died in the struggle for racial equality from 1955-1968.

Montgomery is a city of considerable distinction, with many historic houses and buildings. Although Montgomery's most important business is government, it is also a livestock market and a center of manufacturing. As an educational center it offers many cultural activities.

What to See and Do

1. **State Capitol** (1851). Bainbridge between Washington & Monroe Aves. Seat of Alabama's government for more than 100 years. Phone 242-4169. Opposite the capitol are

   First White House of the Confederacy (1835). 644 Washington Ave. This two-story, white frame house was the residence of Jefferson Davis and his family while Montgomery was the Confederate capital. Moved from its original location at Bibb and Lee streets in 1921, it is now a Confederate museum containing period furnishings, personal belongings and paintings of the Davis family and Confederate mementos. Tours. (Daily; closed Jan 1, Easter, Thanksgiving, Christmas hols) Phone 242-1861.   **Free.**

   Alabama Department of Archives and History. 624 Washington Ave. Houses historical museum and genealogical research facilities. Artifact collections include exhibits on the 19th century, the military and early Alabama Indians. Also an interactive children's gallery. (Daily exc Sun; closed hols) Phone 242-4363 or -4443 (recording).   **Free.**

2. **Governor's Mansion.** 1142 S Perry. Tours (Mon–Fri, by appt). Phone 834-3022.   **Free.**

3. **Civil Rights Memorial.** Washington Ave & Hull St at the Southern Poverty Law Center. Designed by Vietnam Veterans Memorial artist Maya Lin.

4. **F. Scott and Zelda Fitzgerald Museum.** 919 Felder Ave. The famous author and his wife lived in this house from 1931–1932. Museum contains personal artifacts detailing the couple's public and private lives. Paintings by Zelda, letters and photographs; 25-minute video presentation. (Wed–Fri, mornings; Sat–Sun, afternoons; closed hols) Phone 264-4222.   **Free.**

5. **Teague House** (1848). 468 S Perry St. Greek-revival mansion used as headquarters for Union General James H. Wilson after April 12,

1865; antiques and period reproductions. (Mon–Fri; closed major hols) Phone 834-6000. **Free.**

6. **Murphy House** (1851). Bibb & Coosa Sts. Fine example of Greek-revival architecture with fluted Corinthian columns and wrought-iron balcony is now headquarters of the Montgomery Water Works. Parlor furnished with period antiques. (Mon–Fri; closed hols) Phone 240-1600. **Free.**

7. **Old Alabama Town.** Includes the Ordemann-Shaw House, an Italianate town house (ca 1850) with period furnishings; service buildings with household items; reconstructed 1840 barn; carriage house; 1820s log cabin depicting pioneer life; shotgun cottage depicting black urban life; urban church (ca 1890); country doctor's office; drugstore museum and cotton gin museum; corner grocery from the late 1890s; one-room schoolhouse; exhibition (Grange) hall. Taped driving tour of historic Montgomery also available. Films, tours, information center. (Daily; closed Jan 1, Easter, Thanksgiving, Dec 25) Phone 240-4500 or -4501. **¢¢¢**

8. **Lower Commerce Street Historic District.** 100 blk of Commerce St. Wholesale and railroad district along the Alabama River. Buildings, primarily Victorian in style, date from the 1880s to turn of the century. Riverfront tunnel to Riverfront Park dates to cotton days.

9. **Montgomery Museum of Fine Arts.** 1 Museum Drive. Collections of 19th- and 20th-century American art; European works on paper; regional and decorative arts. Hands-on children's exhibits. Lectures, concerts. (Daily exc Mon; closed hols) Phone 244-5700. **Free.**

10. **Dexter Avenue King Memorial Baptist Church** (1877). 454 Dexter Ave. The Rev. Dr. Martin Luther King, Jr, was a pastor from 1954 to 1960; from the church he directed the Montgomery bus boycott, which sparked the modern civil rights movement; mural and original painting ''The Beginning of a Dream.'' (Mon–Sat, by appt; closed hols) Phone 263-3970.

11. **St John's Episcopal Church** (1855). 113 Madison Ave and N Perry St. Stained-glass windows, Gothic pipe organ, Jefferson Davis's pew. (Daily) Phone 262-1937.

12. **Montgomery Zoo.** 329 Vandiver Blvd off North Blvd. An 8-acre zoo housing 147 species; 600 mammals, birds, reptiles in geographical groupings. (Daily; closed Jan 1, Dec 25) Phone 240-4900. **¢¢**

13. **Jasmine Hill Gardens & Outdoor Museum.** 8 mi N on US 231, then right on Jasmine Hill Rd, follow signs for 2 mi, near Wetumpka. Extensive 17-acre garden, flowering year round. Designed as setting for statues, fountains and other works of art, including an exact copy of the ruins of the Temple of Hera in Olympia, Greece. Amphitheater offers evening programs in performing arts (phone 263-1440 for schedule). Features a series of pools and avenues of flowering cherries and azaleas and of longleaf pine; 1830s cottage. Gardens (Mar–Sept, daily exc Mon; rest of yr by appt). Phone 567-6463. **¢¢**

14. **Hank Williams' grave.** Hank Williams Memorial Cemetery, adj to Oakwood Cemetery. 1305 Upper Wetumpka Rd. Gravesite memorial to country music legend.

15. **Huntingdon College** (1854). (800 students) 1500 Fairview Ave, 2 mi SE. Founded in Tuskegee to provide higher education for women, the liberal arts school became coeducational after World War II; 58-acre campus of woods and hills; Gothic buildings. Tours (by appt). Phone 265-0511.

16. **Alabama State University** (1874). (5,500 students) S Jackson and I-85. Authorized by the legislature in 1873 as the Lincoln Normal School, this university was moved from Marion to Montgomery in 1887. On campus are an art gallery, Afro-American collection and Tullibody Fine Arts Center. (Daily during academic yr; closed hols) Tours. Phone 293-4291.

17. **Maxwell AFB.** 2 mi S, off I-65. This has been an airfield since 1910, when Wilbur Wright began the world's first flying school on this site. Orville Wright made his first flight in Montgomery on March 26, 1910, four years before the Aviation Section of the Signal Corps was created. Maxwell Field was named Nov 8, 1922, for Lieutenant William C. Maxwell of Atmore, AL, killed while serving with Third Aero Squadron in the Philippines. It is now the site of Air University.

Tours by appt. (Daily; closed hols) Phone 953-1110 or -2014 (tour information). **Free.**

18. **Fort Toulouse/Jackson Park National Historic Landmark.** 12 mi NE, 3 mi W off US 231 near Wetumpka. At the confluence of the Coosa and Tallapoosa rivers, Fort Toulouse was opened by Bienville in 1717 to establish trade in the heart of Creek territory. Abandoned in 1763, Andrew Jackson built a fort on the same site in 1814 after the Battle of Horseshoe Bend. Fort Toulouse has been reconstructed, and Fort Jackson has been partially reconstructed. This is also the site of mounds dating from approximately A.D. 1100. The park features a boat ramp, nature walks, picnicking, improved camping and a museum. A living history program can be seen the third weekend of each month, Apr–Nov. (Daily; closed Jan 1, Thanksgiving, Dec 25) Phone 567-3002. **¢**

19. **Greyhound racing.** VictoryLand Track. 20 mi E via I-85, exit 22, in Shorter. Clubhouse, restaurant. Over 19 yrs only. (Nightly exc Sun; matinees Mon, Wed, Fri & Sat; closed early Jan, Thanksgiving, late Dec) Phone 269-6087. **¢**

20. **Alabama Shakespeare Festival.** The State Theatre. 1 Festival Dr. Professional repertory company performs classic and contemporary comedy and drama. Musical performances as well. Two theaters: 750-seat Festival Stage and 225-seat Octagon. (Nov–Aug, Tues–Sun; wknd matinees) Hotel/play packages available. Inquire about facilities for the disabled and hearing impaired; phone 800/841-4ASF (box office).

Annual Events

Southern Livestock Exposition and World Championship Rodeo. Garrett Coliseum. NE on Federal Dr. Apr.

Jubilee City Fest. Downtown. Memorial Day wkend.

South Alabama Fair. Garrett Coliseum. NE on Federal Dr. Mid-Oct.

Blue-Gray Football Classic. Cramton Bowl. Dec 25.

Additional Visitor Information

The Montgomery Area Chamber of Commerce, 41 Commerce St (between Bibb and Montgomery Sts), PO Box 79, 36101, has information (Mon–Fri). Brochures may be obtained at the Montgomery Visitor Center at 401 Madison Ave; phone 262-0013. Travelers may call Montgomery's Fun Phone, 240-9447, which reports on events and activities in the city.

Motels

✔ ★**BUDGETEL INN.** 5225 Carmichael Rd (36106). 205/277-6000; FAX 205/279-8207. 102 rms, 3 story. S, D $32.95–$43.95; each addl $7; under 18 free. Crib free. TV; cable. Pool. Continental bkfst in rms. Complimentary coffee. Ck-out noon. Meeting rms. Cr cds: A, C, D, DS, MC, V.

★ ★ ★**COURTYARD BY MARRIOTT.** 5555 Carmichael Rd (36117). 205/272-5533; FAX 205/279-0853. 146 units, 3 story. S $69; D $79; each addl $10; suites $84; under 18 free; wkend rates. Crib free. TV; cable. Heated pool; whirlpool. Restaurant 6:30 am–2 pm, 5–10 pm. Bar 4–11 pm. Ck-out noon. Guest lndry. Meeting rms. Valet serv. Refrigerators avail. Some private patios, balconies. Cr cds: A, C, D, DS, MC, V.

✔ ★**DAYS INN.** 2625 Zelda Rd (36107), I-85 exit 3. 205/269-9611; FAX 205/269-9611, ext 286. 120 rms, 2 story. S, D $35–$45; each addl $5; under 12 free. Crib free. Pet accepted. TV; cable. Pool. Complimentary continental bkfst, coffee. Restaurant adj open 24 hrs. Bar 5 pm–2 am. Coin lndry. Ck-out noon. Cr cds: A, C, D, DS, MC, V.

★★**FAIRFIELD INN BY MARRIOTT.** *5601 Carmichael Rd (36117), I-85 exit 6 at East Blvd.* 205/270-0007; FAX 205/270-0007, ext 709. 133 rms, 3 story. S $38.95; D $44.95–$46.95; each addl $7; under 18 free. Crib free. TV; cable. Pool. Complimentary continental bkfst. Restaurant adj 6 am–11 pm. Ck-out noon. Valet serv Mon–Fri. Cr cds: A, C, D, DS, MC, V.

★**HAMPTON INN.** *1401 East Blvd (36117).* 205/277-2400; FAX 205/277-6546. 105 units, 2 story. S $42–$44; D $44–$50; under 18 free. Crib free. Pet accepted. TV; cable. Pool. Complimentary continental bkfst. Restaurant adj. Ck-out noon. Cr cds: A, C, D, DS, MC, V.

★★★**HOLIDAY INN-EAST.** *1185 Eastern Bypass (36117).* 205/272-0370; FAX 205/270-0339. 213 rms, 2 story. S $65–$75; D $75–$85; each addl $10; suites $138–$148; under 16 free; golf plan. Crib free. Pet accepted. TV. Indoor pool. Restaurant 6:30 am–2 pm, 5–10 pm. Rm serv. Bar 4 pm–1 am; dancing. Ck-out noon. Meeting rms. Bellhops. Valet serv. Sundries. Putting green. Exercise equipt; weights, bicycles, whirlpool, sauna. Holidome. Game rm. Rec rm. Cr cds: A, C, D, DS, MC, V, JCB.

✔★★**HOWARD JOHNSON.** *1110 East Blvd (36117), SE at jct I-85, Eastern Bypass exit.* 205/272-8880; FAX 205/272-8880, ext 313. 64 rms, 2 story. S $32–$40; D $42–$57; each addl $5; under 18 free. Crib free. TV; cable. Pool. Complimentary continental bkfst. Ck-out noon. Coin lndry. Meeting rms. Private patios, balconies. Cr cds: A, C, D, DS, ER, MC, V, JCB.

★★**LA QUINTA.** *1280 Eastern Blvd (36117).* 205/271-1620; FAX 205/244-7919. 130 rms, 2 story. S $41; D $47; each addl $6; under 18 free. Crib free. TV; cable. Pool. Complimentary coffee. Restaurant adj 6 am–10 pm; Fri, Sat to 11 pm. Ck-out noon. Meeting rms. Cr cds: A, C, D, DS, MC, V.

★★**RAMADA INN EAST.** *1355 Eastern Bypass (36117).* 205/277-2200; FAX 205/277-2200, ext 295. 154 rms, 2 story. S $54–$57; D $55–$57; each addl $8. Crib free. TV; cable, in-rm movies. Pool. Complimentary continental bkfst. Bar from 4 pm; dancing, entertainment exc Sun. Ck-out noon. Meeting rms. Cr cds: A, C, D, DS, MC, V, JCB.

★★**RIVERFRONT INN.** *200 Coosa St (36104).* 205/834-4300; FAX 205/265-5500. 130 rms, 2 story. S, D $48–$57; each addl $7; suites $125–$175; under 13 free. Crib free. TV; cable. Pool. Restaurant 7 am–2 pm. Bar 5–10 pm. Ck-out noon. Meeting rms. Former Montgomery freight depot (1898). Cr cds: A, C, D, DS, MC, V.

★★**STATEHOUSE INN.** *924 Madison Ave (36104).* 205/265-0741; res: 800/552-7099; FAX 205/834-6126. 162 rms, 6 story. S $44–$60; D $50–$66; each addl $6; suites $75–$125; under 12 free. Crib free. TV; cable. Pool; wading pool. Complimentary coffee in rms. Restaurant 6 am–10 pm. Rm serv. Bar from 2 pm. Ck-out noon. Meeting rms. Sundries. Cr cds: A, C, D, DS, MC, V.

Motor Hotels

✔★★**HOWARD JOHNSON-GOVERNOR'S HOUSE.** *2705 E South Blvd (36116).* 205/288-2800; FAX 205/288-6472. 203 rms, 2 story. S $45–$59; D $45–$64; each addl $5; under 18 free. Crib free. TV; cable. Pool. Restaurant 6:30 am–10 pm. Rm serv. Bar 11 am–midnight. Ck-out noon. Meeting rms. Bellhops. Valet serv. Sundries. Some bathrm phones. Wet bar in some suites. Cr cds: A, C, D, DS, MC, V, JCB.

★★**RADISSON INN.** *5924 Monticello Dr (36117), I-85 exit 6.* 205/272-1013; FAX 205/260-0425. 49 suites, 3 story. Suites $55–$77; wkend rates. Crib free. TV; cable. Pool; whirlpool, sauna. Complimentary full bkfst. Coffee in rms. Restaurant 5–10 pm. Rm serv. Bar from 4 pm. Ck-out noon. Meeting rm. Cr cds: A, C, D, DS, ER, MC, V.

Hotel

★**MADISON.** *120 Madison Ave (36104).* 205/264-2231; FAX 205/263-3179. 190 rms, 6 story. S $60–$75; D $68–$83; suites $105–$200. Crib free. TV. Pool. Restaurant 6 am–10 pm. Bar 11 am–midnight. Ck-out noon. Meeting rms. Free covered parking. Free airport transportation. Cr cds: A, C, D, DS, MC, V.

Restaurants

★★★**CHANTILLY.** *1931 Vaughn Rd (AL 110), 10 mi E.* 205/271-0509. Hrs: 11 am–8 pm. Res required. Southern menu. Bar. Complete meals: lunch $14.50, dinner $17.95–$30. Child's meals. Specializes in chicken, fish, beef. Valet parking. Outdoor dining. Dining in antebellum plantation house (ca 1830). Many original furnishings, much of the original glass still in place. Cr cds: MC, V.

★★**KAT & HARRI'S.** *1061 Woodley Rd.* 205/834-2500. Hrs: 4–11 pm; Fri to midnight; Sun brunch 11 am–3 pm. Closed most major hols. Bar. A la carte entrees: dinner $4.95–$22.50. Sun brunch $8–$10. Specializes in seafood, steak, gourmet pizza. Entertainment wkends. Parking. Outdoor dining. Wood-fired pizza oven. Cr cds: A, MC, V.

★★**MR G'S.** *3080 McGehee Rd.* 205/281-1161. Hrs: 11 am–2 pm, 5–10 pm; Sat from 5 pm; Sun 11 am–3 pm. Bar. Semi-a la carte: lunch $4.75–$7, dinner $9.95–$27.95. Specializes in fresh seafood, steak, prime rib. Cr cds: A, MC, V.

✔★★**SAHARA.** *511 E Edgemont Ave.* 205/262-1215. Hrs: 11 am–10 pm. Closed Sun; most major hols. Bar. Semi-a la carte: lunch $5.25–$8.95, dinner $9.95–$18.95. Specializes in fresh seafood, steak. Cr cds: A, C, D, MC, V.

★★★**VINTAGE YEAR.** *405 Cloverdale Rd.* 205/264-8463. Hrs: 6–10 pm. Closed Sun, Mon; major hols. Bar 4:30 pm–midnight. Wine list. A la carte entrees: dinner $7.95–$18.95. Specializes in seafood, Italian dishes. Art gallery. Cr cds: A, C, D, MC, V.

Unrated Dining Spot

MORRISON'S CAFETERIA. *2929 E South Blvd, in Montgomery Mall.* 205/281-1740. Hrs: 10:45 am–8:30 pm. Avg ck: lunch, dinner $4.70. Specializes in salads, roast beef, egg custard pie. Cr cds: MC, V.

Natural Bridge

(see Hamilton)

Opelika (C-4)

Settled: 1836 **Pop:** 22,122 **Elev:** 822 ft **Area code:** 205 **Zip:** 36801

(See Auburn, Tuskegee; also see Columbus, GA)

Motels

(Rates are generally higher during football season)

✔ ★**BEST WESTERN MARINER INN.** *1002 Columbus Pkwy, jct I-85 & US 280. 205/749-1461.* 95 rms, 2 story. S $29–$34; D $36–$46; each addl $5; under 12 free; wkly rates. Crib $5. TV; cable. Indoor pool; whirlpool. Complimentary coffee in lobby. Restaurant nearby. Bar 3 pm–2 am, Sat to midnight; entertainment, dancing. Cr cds: A, C, D, DS, MC, V.

D ⚐ ≈ ⊘ ◎ SC

★ ★**HOLIDAY INN.** *(Box 391) 1102 Columbus Pkwy, 2 mi SE on US 280 at jct I-85 exit 62. 205/745-6331; FAX 205/749-3933.* 120 rms, 2 story. S $38–$60; D $42–$65; each addl $5; under 18 free; football wkends (2-day min). Crib free. TV; cable. Pool. Restaurant 6 am–2 pm, 5–10 pm. Rm serv. Bar 3 pm–2 am, Sat to midnight; entertainment, dancing exc Sun. Ck-out noon. Meeting rms. Exercise equipt; weights, bicycles. Cr cds: A, C, D, DS, MC, V, JCB.

D ≈ ⊼ ⊘ ◎ SC

✔ ★**RED CARPET INN.** *1107 Columbus Pkwy. 205/749-6154; FAX 205/745-6700.* 115 rms, 2 story. S $21.95–$24.95; D $22.95–$27.95; each addl $5; under 12 free. Crib free. TV; cable. Pool. Restaurant 6 am–1:30 pm. Ck-out 11 am. Cr cds: A, C, D, DS, MC, V.

≈ ⊘ ◎ SC

Ozark (D-4)

Pop: 12,922 **Elev:** 409 ft **Area code:** 205 **Zip:** 36360

What to See and Do

1. **US Army Aviation Museum.** 13 mi SW via AL 249 (Andrews Ave). Located at Fort Rucker, home of the US Army Aviation Center and Aviation School, the museum has early army aircraft, experimental aircraft and a large collection of helicopters ranging from the Army's first R-4 to a prototype of the AH-64 Apache attack helicopter. (Daily; closed some major hols) Phone 255-4443 or -4584. **Free.**

2. **Blue Springs State Park.** 20 mi NE via AL 105, County 33, AL 10. This 103-acre park features a spring-fed pool, swimming pool, bathhouse. Tennis. Picnic facilities, playground, softball field. Primitive and improved campsites. Standard fees. Phone 397-4875.

(For further information contact the Ozark-Dale County Chamber of Commerce, 308 Painter Ave; 774-9321.)

(For accommodations see Dothan, Troy)

Russell Cave National Monument (A-4)

(8 mi W of Bridgeport off US 72 via County 91, then County 98)

This cave shelter, located on the edge of the Tennessee River Valley is part of a much larger cavern system that extends seven miles into the side of a gray limestone hill. Stone Age man made his home here in a giant room 210 feet long, 107 feet wide and averaging 26 feet in height. Excavation of refuse and debris deposited in the cave has been dated to approximately 7000 B.C. Archaeological exploration has revealed a record of almost continuous habitation to A.D. 1650. Archaic, Woodland and Mississippian cultures are represented. The 310-acre site, given to the US by the National Geographic Society, is administered by the National Park Service and is preserved in its natural state.

The visitor center has displays detailing the daily life of the cave's prehistoric occupants including exhibitions of weapons, tools and cooking processes. Audiovisual programs; slide programs within cave shelter. Area and visitor center (daily; closed Dec 25). Contact RR 1, Box 209, Bridgeport 35740; 205/495-2672.   **Free.**

(For accommodations see Scottsboro; also see Chattanooga, TN)

Russellville (A-2)

Pop: 7,812 **Elev:** 764 ft **Area code:** 205 **Zip:** 35653

What to See and Do

Reservoirs. Bear Creek Development Authority has built four dams in the area and, with the assistance of the TVA, has developed recreational facilities at several of the resulting reservoirs. For information and camping fees contact PO Box 670; 332-4392. Four-reservoir user permit per day **¢**

Cedar Creek. 10 mi W via AL 24 & County 41. A 4,300-acre reservoir with 5 recreation areas. Swimming, bathhouses (Slick Rock Ford); boat launches (at dam, Slick Rock Ford, Lost Creek, Hellums Mill, Britton Bridge). Picnicking. Camping, hookups (Slick Rock Ford). Phone 332-9809.

Little Bear Creek. 12 mi W via AL 24. A 1,560-acre reservoir. Boat launch (Williams Hollow, Elliott Branch, McAfee Springs). Picnicking. Camping; tables, grills, electricity (Willams Hollow, Elliott Branch). Phone 332-9804.

Upper Bear Creek. 16 mi S via US 43 near Phil Campbell. A 1,850-acre reservoir. Boat launch (Twin Forks, Quarter Creek, Batestown, Mon Dye). Picnicking. Camping; tables, grills (Twin Forks). Float stream 28 miles below dam.

Bear Creek. 30 mi SW via US 43 & AL 172. A 670-acre reservoir that runs through a deep narrow canyon. Swimming, bathhouse (Piney Point); fishing, pier; boat launch (Piney Point, Horseshoe Bend, Scott's Ford). Picnicking. Camping, electricity (Piney Point, Horseshoe Bend).

(For further information contact the Franklin County Area Chamber of Commerce, PO Box 44; 332-1760.)

(For accommodations see Florence, Sheffield)

Scottsboro (A-4)

Pop: 13,786 **Elev:** 653 ft **Area code:** 205 **Zip:** 35768

(See Huntsville)

Motel

★**DAYS INN.** *(PO Box 518) 1106 John T. Reid Pkwy. 205/574-1212; FAX 205/574-1212, ext 253.* 85 rms, 2 story. S $39–$60; D $42–$60; each addl $5; suite $60; under 18 free; higher rates June Jam. Crib free. Pet accepted. TV; cable. Pool. Complimentary continental bkfst, coffee. Restaurant adj 11 am–9 pm. Ck-out 11 am. Cr cds: A, C, D, DS, MC, V.

Selma (C-3)

Settled: 1815 **Pop:** 23,755 **Elev:** 139 ft **Area code:** 205 **Zip:** 36701

High on a bluff above the Alabama River, Selma is a marketing, agricultural and manufacturing center. William Rufus King, vice president under Franklin Pierce, named the town after a poem by the Gaelic poet Ossian. The classic lines of Greek-revival and elegance of Georgian-colonial architecture blend with early-American cottages, Victorian mansions and modern houses to lend the city an air of the antebellum South. Once an arsenal of the Confederacy–second only to Richmond–Selma was a leading target for Union armies in 1865.

Selma fell on April 2, 1865 when 2,000 troops were captured, ending the city's role as the Confederacy's supply depot. The naval foundry (where the warships *Tennessee, Huntsville, Tuscaloosa* and others were built), a rolling mill, powder works and an arsenal were all destroyed. With defeat came an end to the era of wealthy plantation owners and a leisurely living where horse racing and cockfighting were gentlemanly diversions.

Selma was also the scene of civil rights activity in the mid-1960s with a march on the Edmund Pettus bridge. Spiritual leadership was provided by Dr Martin Luther King, Jr and Andrew Young at the Brown Chapel A.M.E. Church.

County farmers raise cattle, pecan trees, cotton, soybeans, hay, corn and grain. Selma is also the headquarters of a number of industries. The town became an inland port city in 1969 when a nine-foot-deep channel on the Alabama River was completed.

What to See and Do

1. **Sturdivant Hall** (1853). 713 Mabry St. Fine example of Greek-revival architecture designed by Thomas Helm Lee, cousin of Robert E. Lee, features massive Corinthian columns, original wrought iron on balconies and belvedere on roof. Fully restored with period furnishings; kitchen with slave quarters above; smokehouse; wine cellar; carriage house; garden. Guided tour (1 hr). (Daily exc Mon; closed major holidays) Phone 872-5626. ¢¢

2. **Joseph T. Smitherman Historic Building** (1847). 109 Union St. The building has been restored and furnished with artifacts and antiques; art pavilion. (Daily exc Sat; closed hols) Phone 874-2174. **Free.**

3. **Old Town Historic District.** 513 Lauderdale St. District includes over 1,200 structures. Museums, specialty shops, restaurants. Tours (cassette, fee; self-guided). (Daily; Sat, Sun by appt) Contact Chamber of Commerce.

4. **Cahawba.** 9 mi W on AL 22, then 4 mi S on county road. Alabama's first permanent capitol was a flourishing town from 1820 to 1860. By 1822, 184 town lots were sold for $120,000. Nearly swept away by floods in 1825, the capital was moved to Tuscaloosa in 1826; Cahawba was close to being abandoned by 1828 but rose again. By 1830, it had become the most important shipping point on the Alabama River. Despite another flood in 1833 and subsequent rebuilding in 1836, the city reached a peak population of approximately 5,000 by 1850. However, the Civil War and a third flood finally finished the town. Today, only a few of the original buildings remain intact. Ruins include the brick columns of a mansion on the river, old cemeteries and walls enclosing artesian wells. Site currently under development as an historical park; in-progress archeological projects may be viewed by visitors. Welcome center. (Daily) Phone 875-2529. **Free.**

5. **Old Depot Museum** (1891). Water Ave at Martin Luther King, Jr St. Interpretive history museum with artifacts of Selma and Alabama's

"black belt" region. (Mon–Sat, mornings and afternoons; Sun, afternoons only; other times by appt; closed most hols) Phone 875-9918. ¢¢

6. **Black Heritage Tour.** Selma was a leading city in the march towards civil rights. Visit Brown Chapel A.M.E. Church, the Edmund Pettus Bridge, Selma University and the Wilson Building. Tours (Mon–Fri; Sat, Sun by appt). Contact Chamber of Commerce.

7. **Paul M. Grist State Park.** 15 mi N on County 37. This 1,080-acre park has a 100-acre lake. Swimming, bathhouse; fishing; boating (launch rentals). Hiking. Picnic facilities (grills, shelters), playground. Primitive camping. Standard fees. Phone 872-5846.

(For further information on tours and other historic features contact the Chamber of Commerce, 513 Lauderdale St, PO Drawer D; 875-7241.)

Annual Events

Historic Selma Pilgrimage. Guides conduct daylight and candlelight tours of historic houses; antique show. Contact Chamber of Commerce. Mar 26–28.

Cahawba Festival. (See #4) Bluegrass & country music, arts & crafts show; flea market; greased pole climbing contests; games; regional food; walking tours of the old town. 2nd Sat May.

Central Alabama Fair. Early Oct.

Tale Telling Festival. Early Oct.

(See Montgomery)

Motel

✔ ★ ★ **HOLIDAY INN.** *US 80 W, 3 mi W on US 80.* 205/872-0461. 166 rms, 2 story. S $45–$50; D $51–$54; each addl $5; under 19 free. Crib free. TV; cable. Pool; wading pool. Restaurant 6 am–2 pm, 5–10 pm. Rm serv. Bar 5 pm–1 am. Ck-out noon. Meeting rms. Valet serv. Cr cds: A, C, D, DS, MC, V, JCB.

Inn

★ ★ **GRACE HALL BED & BREAKFAST.** *506 Lauderdale St.* 205/875-5744; FAX 205/875-9967. 6 rms, 2 story. S $63–$85; D $73–$95; each addl $15. TV; cable. Complimentary full bkfst, tea/sherry. Ck-out 11 am, ck-in 4 pm. Airport transportation avail. Antiques. Library/sitting rm. Restored antebellum mansion (1857); some original furnishings. Cr cds: A, MC, V.

Restaurants

★ ★ **MAJOR GRUMBLES.** *1 Grumbles Alley.* 205/872-2006. Hrs: 11 am–10 pm. Closed Sun; most major hols. Res accepted Mon–Fri. Bar. Semi-a la carte: lunch $5.95–$10.95, dinner $5.95–$20. Specializes in char-broiled chicken & steak, seafood. Parking. Located on river in former cotton warehouse (1850). Cr cds: A, D, MC, V.

✔ ★ ★ ★ **TALLY-HO.** *507 Mangum Ave.* 205/872-1390. Hrs: 5–10 pm. Closed Sun; major hols. Res accepted. Bar to midnight; Fri–Sun to 1 am. Wine list. Semi-a la carte: dinner $6–$13.50. Child's meals. Own baking. Parking. Entrance & waiting area in old log cabin. Cr cds: A, C, D, MC, V.

Sheffield (A-2)

Settled: 1815 **Pop:** 10,380 **Elev:** 502 ft **Area code:** 205 **Zip:** 35660

One of the Quad-Cities, along with Florence (see), Tuscumbia and Muscle Shoals, Sheffield was named for the industrial city in England. Andrew Jackson is said to be the first white man to foresee the potential of this stretch of the river. Deposits of iron ore spurred the building of five huge iron-making furnaces by 1888, giving Sheffield its start as a part of the major industrial center of the South.

What to See and Do

Ivy Green (1820). 2 mi S on Montgomery Ave, at 300 W North Commons in Tuscumbia. Birthplace and early home of Helen Keller. Anne Sullivan, of Boston's Perkins Institute, was hired to come to Tuscumbia and help Helen Keller, who after an illness was left blind and deaf at the age of 19 months. Miss Sullivan and Helen lived together in a small cottage, which had once been the plantation office. The cottage area includes the pump at which Helen learned her first word, ''water''; the Whistle Path between the house and outdoor kitchen; and many personal items. (Daily; closed major hols) (See ANNUAL EVENT and SEASONAL EVENT) Phone 383-4066. ¢¢

(For information on this area contact the Colbert County Tourism and Convention Bureau, PO Box 440, Tuscumbia, 35674; 383-0783.)

Annual Event

Helen Keller Festival. Ivy Green (see). Late June.

Seasonal Event

The Miracle Worker. Ivy Green (see). Outdoor performance of William Gibson's prize-winning play based on Helen Keller's life. (Fri, Sat) Limited number of tickets available at gate; advance purchase recommended. Price includes tour of Ivy Green preceding play. Phone 383-4066. Mid-June–July.

(See Florence, Russellville)

Motor Hotels

★★★**HOLIDAY INN.** 4900 Hatch Blvd. 205/381-4710; FAX 205/381-4710, ext 403. 203 units, 3 story. S, D $68–$76; each addl $6; suites $158; under 18 free; wkend rates. Crib free. Pet accepted, some restrictions. TV; cable. Pool. Restaurant 6:30 am–2 pm, 5:30–10 pm. Rm serv. Bar 4 pm–2 am; entertainment, dancing exc Sun. Ck-out noon. Coin lndry. Meeting rms. Bellhops. Free local airport transportation. Tennis privileges. Golf privileges. Exercise equipt; weight machine, bicycle, whirlpool. Some refrigerators. Cr cds: A, C, D, DS, MC, V, JCB.

✔★★**RAMADA INN.** 4205 Hatch Blvd. 205/381-3743; FAX 205/381-2838. 150 rms, 2 story. S $39–$53; D $46–$60; each addl $7; suites from $125; under 18 free. Crib free. TV; cable. Pool; whirlpool, poolside serv. Coffee in rms. Restaurant 6 am–10 pm. Rm serv. Bar 5 pm–1 am; entertainment, dancing. Ck-out noon. Meeting rms. Free airport transportation. Golf privileges. Some in-rm hot tubs, refrigerators. Cr cds: A, C, D, DS, MC, V, JCB.

Restaurants

★★**CAFE CONTINENTAL.** 4001 Jackson Hwy. 205/383-2233. Hrs: 11 am–2 pm, 5–10 pm; Mon to 2 pm; Sat from 5 pm. Closed Sun; major hols. Res accepted. Continental menu. Bar. Complete meals: dinner $6.95–$14.95. Child's meals. Specializes in steak, veal, seafood. Parking. Intimate atmosphere with European flair. Cr cds: A, C, D, DS, MC, V.

★★**GEORGE'S STEAK PIT.** 1206 Jackson Hwy. 205/381-1531. Hrs: 4:30–10:30 pm. Closed Sun, Mon; hols. Bar. Semi-a la carte: dinner $11–$24. Specializes in steak, fresh fish. Cr cds: A, C, D, DS, MC, V.

✔★**THE SOUTHLAND.** 1309 Jackson Hwy. 205/383-8236. Hrs: 10 am–9 pm. Closed Mon. Semi-a la carte: lunch $4.50–$6.95, dinner $4.50–$11.95. Specializes in barbecued chicken & pork, catfish, homemade pies. Family-owned. No cr cds accepted.

Unrated Dining Spot

RIGHT TRACK. 1001 Shop Pike Rd. 205/381-8295. Hrs: 11 am–2 pm. Closed Mon, Sat; most major hols. Res accepted. Southern country menu. Semi-a la carte: lunch $2.50–$4.50. Lunch buffet $4.50. Sun brunch $3.50–$5.50. Child's meals. Specializes in baked chicken, roast beef, cinnamon rolls. Restored railroad depot; antiques. Museum adj. Establishment maintained and operated by mentally handicapped citizens of the community. No cr cds accepted.

Sylacauga (C-3)

Pop: 12,520 **Elev:** 600 ft **Area code:** 205 **Zip:** 35150

The city's fortune is literally its foundation—a bed of prized translucent white marble estimated to be 32 miles long, 1.5 miles wide and about 400 feet deep. The bed is, in many places, only 12 feet below ground level. Marble from Sylacauga (said to mean ''meeting place of the Chalaka Indians'') has been used in the United States Supreme Court Building and many other famous buildings in the US and abroad. Sylacauga stone is also crushed and ground for use in products such as paint, putty, plastics, asphalt tile and rubber.

What to See and Do

1. **Isabel Anderson Comer Museum & Arts Center.** 711 N Broadway Ave. Permanent exhibits of local and Native American artifacts; special visiting exhibitions. (Tues–Fri, also Sun afternoons; or by appt) Phone 245-4016. **Free.**

2. **De Soto Caverns Park.** 12 mi NW via AL 21 and County 36; on AL 76, 5 mi E of jct US 280. Scenic 80-acre wooded park, famous for its historic mammoth, onyx caverns. Visited by Hernando De Soto in 1540, the onyx caverns are the historic birthplace of the Creek Nation and the one of the first officially recorded caves in the United States—reported to President Washington in 1796. On display in the caverns is a 2,000-year-old ''Copena'' burial ground, Civil War gunpowder mining center and a moonshine still from prohibition days when the caverns were known as ''the bloody bucket.'' The main cavern, the Great Onyx Cathedral, is larger than a football field and higher than a 12-story building; a sound, laser and water show is presented here. Featured at the park is De Soto's Lost Trail, a 3/4-acre maze (fee). Also, visitors may view a water-powered rock cutting saw in operation, pan for gold and gemstones or visit the Bow and Arrow Arcade. Other facilities include picnic areas; shipboard playground; RV campground and tepee island. Guided tours of the caverns. Fee for activities. Park (daily). For information phone 378-7252.

(For further information and tours contact the Sylacauga Chamber of Commerce, 17 W Ft Williams St, PO Box 185; 249-0308.)

(See Alexander City, Talladega)

Motel

 ★★**TOWNE INN.** *(PO Box 1305) US 280. 205/249-3821.* 76 units, 2 story. S $34–$41; D $37–$42; suites $90; family rates; higher rates Talladega Races. Crib free. TV; cable. Pool. Restaurant adj open 24 hrs. Bar; entertainment, dancing Wed–Sat. Ck-out noon. Meeting rms. Cr cds: A, C, D, MC, V.

Talladega (B-4)

Founded: 1834 **Pop:** 18,175 **Elev:** 555 ft **Area code:** 205 **Zip:** 35160

Andrew Jackson defeated the Creeks in this area on November 9, 1813; it was the first of the battles by which he defeated the Creek Confederacy. Today, Talladega is both a center of diverse manufacturing and a center of preservation with many fine old buildings. It is the home of the Alabama Institute for the Deaf and Blind and Talladega College, founded by two former slaves. Logan Martin Lake, to the northwest, offers excellent water and outdoor recreation activities, and a large section of the Talladega National Forest is to the east. A Ranger District office is located in Talladega as well.

What to See and Do

1. **Talladega Superspeedway.** 10 mi N on AL 77, then 6 mi E on I-20. Said to be one of the world's fastest speedways, with 33 degree banks in the turns. Stock car races include the Winston "500" NASCAR Winston Cup Race and the Talladega "500" NASCAR Winston Cup Stock Car Race. (Early May–late July) Bus tours of track (daily exc during race meets). Phone 362-5002. ¢¢¢¢–¢¢¢¢¢ Also here is
   International Motorsports Hall of Fame. Speedway Blvd. Official hall of fame of the motor sports, with memorabilia and displays of over 100 vehicles. Race car simulator. Gift shop. (Daily) Annual hall of fame induction ceremony (Dec). Phone 362-5002. ¢¢
2. **Historic areas. Silk Stocking District.** District includes much of East Street South, Court Street South and South Street East; many antebellum and turn-of-the-century houses along tree-lined streets. **Talladega Square** (1834), in the heart of town, includes renovated Talladega County Courthouse, the oldest courthouse in continuous use in the state.
3. **Cheaha State Park.** 7 mi NE on AL 21, then 15 mi E on County 96. This park includes Mt Cheaha (2,407 ft), the state's highest point with an observation tower on top, and 2,719 acres of rugged forest country in the surrounding foothills. The area is mentioned in Hernando De Soto's journal of his 1540 expedition. (During the expedition the Spanish introduced hogs and horses to local Indians) Swimming in Lake Cheaha, sand beach, wading area, swimming pool, bathhouse; fishing; boating. Hiking. Picnicking, motel, restaurant. Park (daily). Camping, cabins. Standard fees. Phone 488-5111.
4. **Talladega National Forest.** SE on AL 77. This 364,428-acre forest offers high ridges with spectacular views of valleys heavily wooded with Southern pine and hardwood. Divided into two sections, the park includes the Talladega and the beautiful Oakmulgee, southwest of Birmingham. The Talladega division has lake swimming (fee); fishing. Hiking trails, including the 100-mile Pinhoti National Recreation Trail, National byway extending from AL 78 to Cheaha State Park (#3). Camping (no electric hookup; fee). Contact District Ranger, phone 362-2909; or Forest Supervisor, 1765 Highland Ave, Montgomery 36107, phone 832-4470.

(For further information contact the Chamber of Commerce, 210 East St S, PO Drawer A; 362-9075.)

Seasonal Event

Stock car races (see #1). Early May–late July.

(For accommodations see Anniston, Birmingham, Sylacauga)

Theodore

(see Mobile)

Troy (D-4)

Settled: 1824 **Pop:** 13,051 **Elev:** 543 ft **Area code:** 205 **Zip:** 36081

What to See and Do

1. **Troy State University** (1887). (4,500 students) University Ave, 1½ mi SE. Guided tours of campus. Home of the National Hall of Fame of Distinguished Band Conductors and the Malone Art Gallery. Phone 670-3000 or -3196.
2. **Pike Pioneer Museum.** 2 mi N on US 231. Antique farm and household implements; reconstructed log house, country store and other buildings re-create 19th-century life. (Mon–Sat, also Sun afternoons) Phone 566-3597. ¢

(For further information contact the Pike County Chamber of Commerce, 246 US 231 North; 566-2294.)

(See Montgomery, Ozark)

Motels

 ★**ECONO LODGE.** *(PO Box 1086) 1013 US 231. 205/566-4960.* 69 rms, 2 story. S $32; D $38; each addl $5; under 18 free; higher rates football wkends. Crib free. TV; cable. Pool. Complimentary morning coffee in lobby. Ck-out 11 am. Cr cds: A, C, D, DS, MC, V.

★★**HOLIDAY INN.** *(Box 564) 2 mi NW on US 231 Bypass, ¼ mi N of jct US 29. 205/566-1150; FAX 205/566-7666.* 98 rms, 2 story. S $40–$45; D $45–$50; each addl $5; under 20 free. TV; cable. Pool; wading pool. Restaurant 6 am–10 pm. Rm serv. Bar 4 pm–midnight. Ck-out noon. Meeting rms. Bellhops. Cr cds: A, C, D, DS, MC, V, JCB.

Restaurants

★**MOSSY GROVE SCHOOLHOUSE.** *AL 87S. 205/566-4921.* Hrs: 5–9 pm. Closed Sun, Mon; some major hols. Res accepted. Southern menu. Complete meals: dinner $4.95–$13.95. Child's meals. Specializes in ribeye steak, char-broiled shrimp, seafood. Parking. Restored schoolhouse (1857); original fireplace, blackboard; numerous antiques. Cr cds: MC, V.

★**MR HO'S.** *1400 S Brundidge St. 205/566-4140.* Hrs: 11 am–9 pm; Fri, Sat to 10 pm. Closed Mon. Chinese menu. Beer. Semi-a la carte: lunch $2.95–$3.25, dinner $3.75–$7.50. Buffet: lunch Tues–Sat $4.25, Sun $5.25. Specialties: sweet & sour chicken, pepper steak, moo goo gai pan. Cr cds: MC, V.

Tuscaloosa (C-2)

Founded: 1818 **Pop:** 77,759 **Elev:** 227 ft **Area code:** 205

Located on the Black Warrior River, Tuscaloosa (Choctaw for "Black Warrior") was the capital of Alabama from 1826 to 1846. It was an exciting capital; cotton was a highly profitable crop, and the planters gave extravagant parties. But an increase in cotton production toppled prices, and the capitol was moved to Montgomery. While the Civil War ravaged the university and most of the town, some antebellum houses do remain. After the war, industry and farm trading grew, making Tuscaloosa the busy, pleasant metropolis it is today. It is also the home of the University of Alabama.

What to See and Do

1. **University of Alabama** (1831). (19,800 students) University Blvd (US 11) between Thomas St and 5th Ave E. Tours of the 850-acre campus may be arranged in Rose Administration Building, Rm 151 (daily exc Sun). The information desk is located in Ferguson Student Union. Phone 348-6010. On the campus is an art gallery in Garland Hall with changing exhibits, a museum of natural history and a 60-acre arboretum on Loop Road. Four antebellum buildings remain, the only ones on campus spared from burning by Union troops. Other buildings on campus are

   Gorgas House (1829). 9th Ave and Capstone Dr. A three-story brick structure named for General Josiah Gorgas, former university president. One of the school's original structures, Gorgas now houses a museum with historical exhibits; Spanish-colonial silver display. (Daily; closed all university hols)   **Free.**

   The Old Observatory (1844). The only pre-Civil War classroom building still standing.

   Little Round House (Sentry Box ca 1860). Adj Gorgas Library. Once used by students on guard duty, it was fired on but not destroyed by Union troops.

   Denny Chimes. University Blvd, opp President's Mansion. A 115-foot-high tower erected in honor of former university president Dr. George H. Denny. On the quarter-hours the Westminster Chimes are struck, and selections are played each afternoon on the campanile carillon.

2. **Battle-Friedman House** (ca 1835). 1010 Greensboro Ave. This house was built by Alfred Battle, acquired by the Friedman family in 1875. It contains fine antiques; period gardens occupy ½ block. (Tues–Sun) Phone 758-2238.   ¢¢

3. **Will T. Murphy African American Museum** (ca 1925). 2601 Paul Bryant Dr. House features two rooms with changing exhibits relating to culture and heritage of blacks; antique doll collection; rare books; some period furnishings. (Mon–Fri) Phone 758-2238.   ¢¢

4. **Old Tavern** (1827). University Blvd & 28th Ave, on Historic Capitol Park. Frequented by Governor Gayle (1831–35) and members of the Alabama legislature when Tuscaloosa was capital. (Daily exc Mon; closed Jan 1, Thanksgiving, Dec 25) Phone 758-2238.   ¢¢

5. **National Headquarters of Gulf States Paper Corporation.** 1400 River Rd. Four Oriental buildings house an outstanding collection of sculpture and art, including primitive artifacts from Africa and the South Pacific; Oriental art; large collection of paintings including works by Georgia O'Keeffe, Mary Cassatt and James A.M. Whistler. Guided tours. (Sat & Sun) Phone 553-6200.   **Free.**

6. **Moundville Archaeological Park.** 16 mi S on AL 69 in Moundville, part of the Alabama Museum of Natural History. Group of 20 Indian ceremonial mounds (A.D. 1000–1450); reconstructed village and temple with displays depicting Native American lifestyles and activities. The Archaeological Museum traces prehistory of southeastern Indians and exhibits products of this aboriginal culture. Nature trails along river. Picnic facilities. Tent & trailer sites (fee). (Daily; closed Jan 1, Thanksgiving, Dec 24, 25, 31) Phone 371-2572.   ¢¢

7. **Lake Lurleen State Park.** 12 mi NW off US 82. This 1,625-acre park has a 250-acre lake. Swimming, bathhouses; fishing (piers), bait & tackle shop; boating (ramps, rentals). Hiking. Picnic shelters, playgrounds, concession. Camping. Standard fees. Phone 339-1558.

(For further information contact the Convention & Visitors Bureau, PO Box 032167, 35403; 391-9200 or 800/538-8696.)

(See Bessemer)

Motels

(Rates are generally higher during football season)

✔ ★ ★ **BEST WESTERN-PARK PLAZA.** *3801 McFarland Blvd (35405),* at jct US 82 Bypass, I-20, I-59. 205/556-9690. 120 rms, 2 story. S $39.95–$46.95; D $43.95–$53.95; each addl $5; suites $95–$150. Crib free. TV; cable. Pool; whirlpool. Complimentary continental bkfst. Restaurant adj 11 am–10 pm. Ck-out noon. Cr cds: A, C, D, DS, ER, MC, V, JCB.

D ☂ ⊘ ⊚ SC

★ ★ **HOLIDAY INN.** *(Box 5265, 35405)* 3½ mi S at jct US 82, I-20, I-59. 205/553-1550; FAX 205/553-1550, ext 316. 166 rms, 2 story. S $50–$65; D $65–$70; each addl $5; under 19 free. Crib free. TV; cable. Pool. Playground. Restaurant 6 am–2 pm, 5–10 pm. Rm serv. Bar 5 pm–midnight. Ck-out noon. Coin lndry. Meeting rms. Valet serv. Sundries. Cr cds: A, C, D, DS, MC, V, JCB.

☂ ⊘ ⊚ SC

★ **LA QUINTA.** *4122 McFarland Blvd E (35405).* 205/349-3270; FAX 205/758-0440. 122 rms, 2 story. S $40–$45; D $46–$56; under 18 free. Crib avail. TV; cable. Pool. Complimentary continental bkfst. Restaurant adj open 24 hrs. Ck-out noon. Meeting rms. Cr cds: A, C, D, DS, MC, V, JCB.

D ☂ ☂ ⊘ ⊚ SC

★ ★ **RAMADA INN.** *631 Skyland Blvd E (35405).* 205/759-4431; FAX 205/758-9655. 108 rms, 2 story. S $37–$63; D $47–$72; each addl $8; under 18 free. Crib free. Pet accepted. TV; cable. Pool. Restaurant 6 am–2 pm, 5–10 pm. Rm serv. Bar 4 pm–1 am, Fri & Sat to 2 am; entertainment, dancing exc Sun. Ck-out noon. Meeting rms. Valet serv. Cr cds: A, C, D, DS, MC, V, JCB.

D ☂ ☂ ⊘ ⊚ SC

✔ ★ **SLEEP INN.** *4300 Skyland Blvd E (35405),* I-59/I-20 exit 76. 205/556-5696; FAX 205/556-5696, ext 502. 73 rms, shower only, 2 story, 20 suites. S, D $37–$42; suites $52; each addl $5; under 17 free. Crib free. TV; cable, in-rm movies. Pool. Complimentary continental bkfst. Complimentary coffee in rms. Restaurant adj open 24 hrs. Ck-out noon. Meeting rm. Exercise equipt; weights, bicycles. Cr cds: A, C, D, DS, ER, MC, V, JCB.

D ☂ † ⊘ ⊚ SC

★ **SUPER 8.** *4125 McFarland Blvd E (35405)* I-59, I-20 exit 73. 205/758-8878; FAX 205/758-2602. 62 rms, 3 story. No elvtr. S $31.99; D $36.99; each addl $4; under 12 free. Crib $3.30. TV; cable. Complimentary coffee. Ck-out 11 am. Cr cds: A, C, D, DS, MC, V.

D ⊘ ⊚ SC

Motor Hotel

★ ★ ★ **SHERATON CAPSTONE.** *320 Paul Bryant Dr (35401).* 205/752-3200; FAX 205/759-9314. 152 units, 3 story. S $79–$99; D $89–$99; each addl $10; suites $175–$250; under 17 free. Crib free. TV; cable. Pool; poolside serv. Restaurant 6:30 am–2 pm, 5–10 pm. Rm serv. Bar 4–11 pm. Ck-out noon. Meeting rms. Bellhops. Airport, RR station transportation. Tennis. Refrigerator in suites. Cr cds: A, C, D, DS, MC, V.

Restaurants

✔ ★ ★ **HENSON'S CYPRESS INN.** *501 Rice Mine Rd N. 205/345-6963.* Hrs: 11 am–2 pm, 5:30–9:30 pm; Fri to 10 pm; Sat 5:30–10 pm. Closed some major hols. Bar from 4:30 pm. Semi-a la carte: lunch $5.95–$8.95, dinner $10.95–$15.95. Child's meals. Specializes in fresh fish, steak. Own desserts. Parking. Riverfront view. Cr cds: A, DS, MC, V.

D

★ ★ **THE LANDING.** *2100 McFarland Blvd E. 205/349-1803.* Hrs: 11 am–2:30 pm, 5–9:30 pm; Fri, Sat to 10 pm; Sun to 2 pm. Closed most major hols. Bar 11–2 am. Semi-a la carte: lunch $2.99–$8.95, dinner $6.95–$17.95. Child's meals. Specializes in steak, seafood, prime rib. Salad bar. Own desserts. Parking. Cr cds: A, MC, V.

D

✔ ★ ★ **O'CHARLEY'S.** *3799 McFarland Blvd. 205/556-5143.* Hrs: 10:30–1 am; Fri, Sat to 2 am; Sat, Sun brunch 10 am–3 pm. Closed Dec 25. Bar. Semi-a la carte: lunch $3.99–$6.99, dinner $6.19–$12.99. Sat, Sun brunch $3.99–$12.99. Child's meals. Specializes in seafood, prime rib. Parking. Cr cds: A, C, D, DS, MC, V.

D **SC**

Unrated Dining Spots

MORRISON'S CAFETERIA. *1701 McFarland Ave, in University Mall. 205/556-4960.* Hrs: 11 am–8:30 pm; Sun to 8 pm. Avg ck: lunch $5, dinner $6. Specializes in roast beef, seafood, strawberry shortcake. Cr cds: MC, V.

PICCADILLY CAFETERIA. *2½ mi SE at intersection of US 82, I-20, I-59, in McFarland Mall. 205/752-8327.* Hrs: 11 am–8:30 pm. Closed Dec 25. Avg ck: lunch $4.75, dinner $5.50. No cr cds accepted.

Tuskegee (C-4)

Settled: ca 1763 **Pop:** 12,257 **Elev:** 468 ft **Area code:** 205 **Zip:** 36083

An important part of Tuskegee's history lies in the story of Tuskegee Institute and two well-known men in black history, Booker T. Washington and George Washington Carver. But it was Lewis Adams, a former slave, who was largely responsible for gathering financial support from northern and southern whites to launch Tuskegee Normal and Industrial Institute. It began on July 4, 1881, with 30 students housed in an old frame building; Booker T. Washington was its president. Tuskegee also has a number of antebellum houses and a Ranger District office of the Tuskegee National Forest (see #2).

What to See and Do

1. **Tuskegee Institute National Historic Site** (1881). Booker T. Washington is generally given credit for having founded Tuskegee Institute. In 1965 the college was designated a National Historical Landmark in recognition of the outstanding role it has played in the educational, economic and social advancement of blacks in our nation's history. In 1974, Congress established Tuskegee Institute National Historic Site to include "The Oaks," home of Booker T. Washington, the George Washington Carver Museum and the Historic Campus District. The 5,000-acre campus consists of more than 160 buildings. (Daily; closed Jan 1, Dec 25) Phone 727-6390 for site information, or -3200 for campus tours.

   George Washington Carver Museum. The museum includes Dr Carver's original laboratory, his extensive collection of native plants, minerals, needlework, paintings, drawings, personal belongings and the array of products he developed including the peanut and sweet potato. (Daily; closed Jan 1, Dec 25)   **Free.**

   Booker T. Washington Monument. Larger than life bronze figure of the man who advocated "lifting the veil of ignorance" from the heads of freed slaves.

   Chapel (1969). Paul Rudolph designed this unusual structure with saw-toothed ceilings and deep beams. Adjacent are the graves of George Washington Carver and Booker T. Washington.

2. **Tuskegee National Forest.** E via US 80. An 11,077-acre forest with fishing; hunting; hiking on Bartram National Recreation Trail. Atasi and Taska picnic sites. Primitive camping. Tsinia Wildlife Viewing Area. Contact District Ranger, Rte 1, Box 269; 727-2652 or Supervisor, 1765 Highland Ave, Montgomery 36107; 205/832-4470.

(For further information contact the Office of the Mayor, City Hall, 101 Fonville St; 727-2180.)

(For accommodations see Auburn, Montgomery)

Florida

Population: 12,937,926

Land area: 54,136 square miles

Elevation: 0–345 feet

Highest point: Near Lakewood (Walton County)

Entered Union: March 3, 1845 (27th state)

Capital: Tallahassee

Motto: In God We Trust

Nickname: Sunshine State

State flower: Orange blossom

State bird: Mockingbird

State tree: Sabal palm

State fair: February 4–20, 1994, in Tampa

Time zones: Eastern and Central

Florida is the nation's tropical area, surrounded by balmy waters. The state's first tourist, Ponce de Leon, didn't find the fountain of youth he was searching for in 1513, but modern-day tourists, at the rate of nearly 41 million a year, still are trying. At poolside, on the beach, at a jai alai fronton, in a nightclub or on a park bench, today's visitors look for rejuvenation.

To winter-weary northerners, Florida is a magnetic Eden. The pull of this land of beaches, palms and springs is so mighty that those who cannot come in winter flock here in ever-increasing numbers in summer. More people migrate to Florida to retire than to any other state. Those not yet ready to retire come here seeking a happier balance between work and relaxation. Florida is one of the top 10 states in population, rising dramatically from the early part of the century. Among 12 southeastern states, Florida has moved from last place in 1940 to first place today.

An almost 450-mile-long peninsula, rarely more than 150 miles wide and only a few feet high in many places, Florida has 8,426 miles of tidal coastline including that of the panhandle. The gentle Gulf Stream flows through the Florida straits between Florida and Cuba and north up the Atlantic coast, bestowing a tropical caress on the land. The pines near the Georgia border give way to palms and sea grape, then to bougainvillea and hibiscus, and finally to saw grass and mangrove down in the Everglades. Florida from north to south prides itself on being green and clean.

Florida's east coast has glamour and gloss; the west, a more earthy mood of informality. Between the two is a vast flatland with a spine of shallow ridges—a land that produces approximately $5.8 billion worth of agricultural products a year. Florida leads the nation in citrus fruits and is second only to California in winter vegetables. Cattle ranches and dairy farms prosper in great numbers; forests continue to provide lumber, naval stores and pulp at a seemingly inexhaustible rate; and from the sea, Florida harvests millions of pounds of fish and shellfish each year.

Nevertheless, tourism remains the major industry, providing annual taxable sales of approximately $27.7 billion and 20 percent of the general revenue of the state. Facilities for the tourist trade include 750 hotels, 4,000 motels and more than 45,000 restaurants. Kennedy Space Center, selected in 1961 as the launch facility for the Apollo Moon Mission, is visited by more than three million visitors each year, and Walt Disney World, the gossamer fantasyland of central Florida, has welcomed untold millions since its opening in 1971.

That day in 1513 when Ponce de Leon stepped ashore near St Augustine began Florida's long history. The explorer mapped the coast but failed to find his fountain of youth or to establish a colony. After him, Hernando De Soto traversed the tropical land, beginning his march in 1539 from what is now the Tampa Bay area, to discover the Mississippi River and stake Spain's claim to the Southwest. Spanish settlements became rooted at St Augustine and Pensacola in the 17th century. In the 18th century Florida was taken as a British province. Spanish rule resumed following the British defeat in the American Revolution, but in 1812 a group of Americans took over and declared the peninsula an independent republic. Finally, in 1819 the United States took formal possession of Florida through a treaty of purchase. During the Civil War, Tallahassee was the only Confederate capital east of the Mississippi not captured by Union forces.

Henry Morrison Flagler, a colorful tycoon with a passion for railroads and hotels, was the major figure in the transformation of Florida from a remote and swampy outpost to its present day status. Flagler pushed his Florida East Coast Railroad from Jacksonville to Key West, opening one area after another along the coast to tourist and commercial development. On the west coast, Henry Plant, another millionaire railroader, competed with Flagler on a somewhat more modest scale.

Florida's stock climbed in the 1920s like one of its present-day rockets. A real estate boom unrivaled in history gripped the east coast. Dream cities sprouted everywhere as the voice of the real estate salesperson was heeded. Property values increased from hour to hour and thousands of persons bought uninspected acres, many of them under water. A double disaster—a hurricane and the stock market crash of 1929—burst the bubble. The lure of Florida, however, had by now been implanted in the American soul, and the state's progress since has been at an ever-accelerating pace.

National Park Service Areas

Florida has two national monuments—Castillo de San Marcos (see ST AUGUSTINE) and Fort Matanzas (see)—and two national memorials, De Soto (see BRADENTON) and Fort Caroline (see). Biscayne National Park, Everglades National Park (see), part of the Gulf Islands National Seashore (see PENSACOLA), Canaveral National Seashore (see TITUSVILLE), and Dry Tortugas National Park (see) are also here. In addition, the state has Big Cypress National Preserve (see MIAMI).

National Forests

The following is an alphabetical listing of National Forests and towns they are listed under.

Apalachicola National Forest (see APALACHICOLA): Forest Supervisor in Tallahassee; Ranger offices in Bristol*, Crawfordsville*.

Ocala National Forest (see OCALA and TAVARES): Forest Supervisor in Tallahassee; Ranger offices in Silver Springs, Umatilla*.

Osceola National Forest (see LAKE CITY): Forest Supervisor in Tallahassee; Ranger office in Olustee*.

*Not described in text

State Recreation Areas

The following towns list state recreation areas in their vicinity under What to See and Do; refer to the individual town for directions and park information.

Listed under **Altamonte Springs:** see Wekiwa Springs State Park.

Listed under **Apalachicola:** see St George Island and T.H. Stone Memorial St Joseph Peninsula state parks.

Listed under **Big Pine Key:** see Bahia Honda State Park.

Listed under **Blountstown:** see Torreya State Park.

Listed under **Chiefland:** see Manatee Springs State Park.

Listed under **Dania:** see John U. Lloyd Beach State Recreation Area.

Listed under **De Funiak Springs:** see Ponce de Leon Springs State Recreation Area.

Listed under **DeLand:** see Blue Spring State Park, DeLeon Springs State Recreation Area and Hontoon Island State Park.

Listed under **Destin:** see Grayton Beach State Recreation Area.

Listed under **Dunedin:** see Caladesi Island State Park and Honeymoon Island State Recreation Area.

Listed under **Fernandina Beach:** see Fort Clinch State Park.

Listed under **Fort Lauderdale:** see Hugh Taylor Birch State Recreation Area.

Listed under **Fort Pierce:** see Fort Pierce Inlet State Recreation Area.

Listed under **Gainesville:** see O'Leno, Ichetucknee Springs and Paynes Prairie Preserve state parks.

Listed under **Islamorada:** see Long Key State Recreation Area.

Listed under **Jacksonville:** see Little Talbot Island State Park.

Listed under **Jupiter:** see Jonathan Dickinson State Park.

Listed under **Key Biscayne:** see Bill Baggs Cape Florida State Recreation Area.

Listed under **Key Largo:** see John Pennekamp Coral Reef State Park.

Listed under **Lake Wales:** see Lake Kissimmee State Park.

Listed under **Leesburg:** see Lake Griffin State Recreation Area.

Listed under **Live Oak:** see Suwannee River State Park.

Listed under **Marco Island:** see Collier-Seminole State Park.

Listed under **Marianna:** Florida Caverns State Park, Three Rivers and Falling Waters state recreation areas.

Listed under **Ormond Beach:** see Gamble Rogers Memorial State Recreation Area at Flagler Beach and Tomoka State Park.

Listed under **Panama City Beach:** see St Andrews State Recreation Area.

Listed under **St Augustine:** see Anastasia State Recreation Area.

Listed under **Sarasota:** see Myakka River State Park.

Listed under **Sebring:** see Highlands Hammock State Park.

Listed under **Starke:** see Mike Roess Gold Head Branch State Park.

Listed under **Tallahassee:** see Alfred B. Maclay State Gardens and Edward Ball Wakulla Springs State Park.

Listed under **Venice:** see Oscar Scherer State Recreation Area.

Listed under **Vero Beach:** see Sebastian Inlet State Recreation Area.

Listed under **Zephyrhills:** see Hillsborough River State Park.

Water-related activities, hiking, riding, various other sports, picnicking and visitor centers, as well as camping, are available in many of these areas. Approximately half of the state recreation areas have camping facilities: $8–$19/site/night; $2/day extra for waterfront sites. Stay is limited to two weeks; no pets overnight. Most campsites are available on a first-come, first-serve basis only; however, in 24 parks (26 in summer) reservations are taken by telephone only, no more than 60 days in advance. Electricity fee is $2/night. Camping groups over 4 people (limit 8) will be charged $1 for each additional person. Notification is advised for parties arriving after closing hours. Some parks have vacation cabins, $20–$110/night. Boat ramp use costs $2–$4. Basic state park entrance fee per vehicle is $3.25; additional passenger fee (after 8th person) is $1. Several parks charge additional fees for tours, etc. All parks are open daily, 8 am–sundown. Some parks with camping open wkends preceding holidays and are open until 10 pm; other parks open to 10 pm during busy season. For further information and a free color brochure, *Florida State Parks Guide,* contact the Florida Department of Natural Resources, Marketing Section, MS 535, 3900 Commonwealth Blvd, Tallahassee 32399; 904/488-9872.

Fishing & Hunting

Florida has approximately 600 varieties of fish in its offshore waters and freshwater fish in more than 7,500 lakes. Freshwater fishing is most productive in the spring; sport fishing is good all year. Annual nonresidents saltwater fishing license is $30, residents $12; nonresidents 7-day license is $15; residents 10-day license is $10. Licenses also are required to sell saltwater catch. Annual nonresidents freshwater license is $30, residents $12; nonresidents 7-day license is $15; there is no short-term residents license. Anglers should obtain the proper license, freshwater or saltwater, that covers the species of fish they intend to keep.

Because of the climate and large forest areas, Florida has an abundance of wildlife, including white-tailed deer, small game and game birds. Open seasons are established annually but usually fall between late September and mid-April. Nonresidents (exc AL) annual license is $150; residents annual license is $11; nonresidents (exc GA) 10-day license is $25. An annual residents combination hunting/fishing license is $22. Additional stamps required: bear, no fee; archery or muzzleloaders, $5; turkey, $5; state waterfowl, $3. There is a $25 fee for both residents and nonresidents hunting in state management areas.

Hunting and fishing licenses are not required for persons younger than 16. Residents older than 65 do not need to purchase a hunting or freshwater fishing license, but they must obtain a special permit (free). An additional charge of up to $1.50 may be added to the price of all hunting and fishing licenses and stamps. For further information on saltwater fishing contact the Florida Department of Natural Resources, 3900 Commonwealth Blvd, Tallahassee 32399; 904/488-5757. For information on hunting or freshwater fishing contact the Game and Fresh Water Fish Commission, 620 S Meridian St, Tallahassee 32399-1600; 904/488-4676.

Safety Belt Information

Safety belts are mandatory for all persons in front seat of vehicle. Children under 6 years must be in an approved passenger restraint anywhere in vehicle: ages 4 and 5 may use a regulation safety belt; age 3 and under must use an approved safety seat. For further information phone 904/488-5370.

Interstate Highway System

The following alphabetical listing of Florida towns in *Mobil Travel Guide* shows that these cities are within 10 miles of the indicated interstate highways. A highway map, however, should be checked for the nearest exit.

INTERSTATE 4: Altamonte Springs, Daytona Beach, DeLand, Haines City, Kissimmee, Lakeland, Orlando, St Petersburg Beach, Sanford, Tampa, Winter Haven, Winter Park.

INTERSTATE 10: De Funiak Springs, Jacksonville, Lake City, Live Oak, Marianna, Pensacola, Tallahassee.

INTERSTATE 75: Arcadia, Bonita Springs, Bradenton, Brooksville, Cape Coral, Dade City, Englewood, Fort Myers, Fort Myers Beach, Gainesville, Lake City, Lakeland, Leesburg, Live Oak, Naples, Ocala, Port Charlotte, Punta Gorda, St Petersburg, St Petersburg Beach, Sanibel, Sarasota, Siesta Key, Tampa, Venice, White Springs, Zephyrhills.

INTERSTATE 95: Atlantic Beach, Boca Raton, Boynton Beach, Cocoa, Cocoa Beach, Coral Gables, Dania, Daytona Beach, Deerfield Beach, Delray Beach, Fort Lauderdale, Fort Pierce, Hialeah, Hollywood, Homestead, Jacksonville, Lake Worth, Marineland, Melbourne, Miami, Miami Beach, New Smyrna Beach, Ormond Beach, Palm Beach, Pompano Beach, St Augustine, St Augustine Beach, Stuart, Titusville, Vero Beach, West Palm Beach.

Additional Visitor Information

Details on accommodations and resort facilities throughout the state may be obtained by writing to the Florida Division of Tourism, Visitor Inquiry, 126 Van Buren St, Tallahassee 32399-2000 or the Florida Hotel and Motel Association, Box 1529, Tallahassee 32302-1529; 904/224-2888. For general information contact the Florida Department of Commerce, Bureau of Visitor Services, 904/487-1462. Another source of information is *Florida Living*, monthly, 102 NE 10th Ave, Suite 1, Gainesville 32601; 904/372-8865.

There are several official state welcome stations in Florida; visitors who stop by will find information and brochures most helpful in planning stops at points of interest. Their locations are as follows: at the north central edge of the state, 3 miles north of Campbellton on US 231; in the northeastern part of Florida, 4 miles north of Jennings on I-75, and 3 miles north of Yulee on I-95S; in the northwestern section, 18 miles west of Pensacola on I-10; and in Tallahassee at the Capital Welcome Station. (Daily, 8 am–5 pm)

Altamonte Springs (C-4)

Pop: 34,879 **Elev:** 87 ft **Area code:** 407

What to See and Do

1. **Wekiwa Springs State Park.** 5 mi NW on FL 436, I-4. A 7,000-acre park with springs that flow through limestone caverns beneath Florida's central ridge. Swimming; fishing; canoeing (rentals). Nature trails. Picnicking, concession. Camping (dump station). Standard hrs, fees. Phone 884-2009.

2. **Greyhound racing.** Sanford-Orlando Kennel Club. 6 mi N on US 17/92, at 301 Dog Track Rd in Longwood. (Nov–May, nightly exc Sun; matinees Mon, Wed & Sat) No minors. Phone 831-1600. ¢

(For further information contact the Greater Seminole County Chamber of Commerce, 4590 S US 17/92, Casselberry 32707; 834-4404.)

Seasonal Event

Jai-Alai. Fronton, 1 mi E on US 17/92, in Fern Park. Parimutuels. Wed–Sat evenings, matinees Thurs, Sat & Sun. Phone 339-6221 or 331-9191. June–Apr.

(See Orlando, Sanford, Winter Park)

Motels

★★**CROSBY'S MOTOR INN.** *(1440 W Orange Blossom Trail, Apopka 32712) 12 mi W on Orange Blossom Trail (FL 441).* 407/886-3220; res: 800/821-6685; FAX 407/886-3220, ext 300. 61 rms, 2 story, 14 kit. units. Mid-Oct–mid-Apr: S $46–$99; D $56–$109; each addl $10; suites $125–$175; kit. units $15 addl; under 16 free; higher rates: Daytona 500, golf tournaments, special events; lower rates rest of yr. Crib $6. Pet accepted; $10. TV. Pool. Playground. Complimentary coffee in lobby 7–10 am. Ck-out 11 am. Coin lndry. Meeting rms. Game rm. Some refrigerators. Picnic tables. Cr cds: A, C, D, DS, MC, V.

D 🐾 ⊁ 🚫 🛇 Ⓒ SC

★★**HOLIDAY INN-ALTAMONTE SPRINGS.** *230 W FL 436 (32714), just SW of I-4.* 407/862-4455; FAX 407/682-5982. 202 rms, 4 story. Feb–May, July–Sept: S $95; D $115; each addl $8; suites $250; under 12 free; higher rates special events; lower rates rest of yr. Crib free. TV; cable. Pool; wading pool. Playground. Restaurants 6:30 am–2 pm, 5–10 pm. Rm serv. Bar 4 pm–2 am; entertainment, dancing. Ck-out noon. Coin lndry. Meeting rms. Sundries. Exercise equipt; weight machine, bicycles. Game rm. Cr cds: A, C, D, DS, MC, V, JCB.

D ⊁ 🧍 🚫 🛇 Ⓒ SC

★★**LA QUINTA.** *150 S Westmonte Dr (32714), 3 blks W of I-4 exit 48.* 407/788-1411; FAX 407/788-6472. 115 rms, 2 story, 11 suites. S $61; D $71; each addl $10; suites $24 addl; under 18 free. Crib free. TV; cable. Heated pool. Continental bkfst. Restaurant adj open 24 hrs. Ck-out noon. Meeting rms. Valet serv. Cr cds: A, C, D, DS, ER, MC, V, JCB.

⊁ ⊁ 🚫 🛇 SC

✔★★★**QUALITY INN NORTH.** *(2025 W FL 434, Longwood 32779) On FL 434 at jct I-4, exit 49 (Longwood exit).* 407/862-4000; FAX 407/862-3530. 200 rms, 2 story. Feb–Easter: S $50–$56; D $56–$68; each addl $6; under 18 free; lower rates rest of yr. Crib free. TV; cable. Pool. Restaurant 6:30 am–10 pm; Sun to 2 pm. Rm serv. Bar 11–1 am; entertainment. Ck-out noon. Coin lndry. Meeting rms. Valet serv. Airport, RR station, bus depot transportation. Cr cds: A, C, D, DS, ER, MC, V, JCB.

D ⊁ 🚫 🛇 Ⓒ SC

★★**RESIDENCE INN BY MARRIOTT.** *270 Douglas Ave (32714).* 407/788-7991; FAX 407/869-5468. 128 kit. suites, 1–2 bedrm, 2 story. Suites $109–$159; under 12 free; wkly, monthly rates. Crib free. TV; cable. Heated pool; whirlpools. Complimentary continental bkfst, refreshments. Ck-out noon. Coin lndry. Meeting rm. Valet serv. Tennis, golf privileges. Health club privileges. Fireplaces. Private patios, balconies. Grills. Cr cds: A, C, D, DS, MC, V.

Hotels

★ ★ ★ **EMBASSY SUITES.** *225 E Altamonte Dr (32701). 407/834-2400; FAX 407/834-2117.* 210 suites, 7 story. S, D $129–$144; each addl $15; under 17 free; wkend rates. Crib free. TV; cable. Indoor pool. Complimentary full bkfst. Restaurant 11 am–10 pm. Bar noon–midnight. Ck-out noon. Meeting rms. Gift shop. Airport transportation. Golf privileges. Exercise equipt; weight machine, bicycles, whirlpool, steam rm. Refrigerators. Some private patios, balconies. Cr cds: A, C, D, DS, ER, MC, V.

★ ★ ★ **HILTON-NORTH.** *350 S North Lake Blvd (32701). 407/830-1985; FAX 407/331-2911.* 325 rms, 8 story. S $99–$125; D $109–$135; each addl $10; family rates. Crib free. TV; cable. Heated pool; whirlpool, sauna, poolside serv. Restaurant 6:30 am–10 pm. Bars 11–2 am; entertainment. Ck-out noon. Convention facilities. Gift shop. Airline ticket office. Health club privileges. Opp Altamonte Mall. *LUXURY LEVEL:* **TOWERS.** 84 rms, 4 suites, 2 floors. S $125; D $135; suites $250–$350. Concierge. Private lounge, honor bar. In-rm movies. Library, meeting rm. Complimentary continental bkfst, refreshments, fruit, newspaper.
Cr cds: A, C, D, DS, ER, MC, V, JCB.

★ ★ ★ **SHERATON-ORLANDO NORTH.** *(Box 538300, Orlando 32853) I-4, exit 47 & Maitland Blvd. 407/660-9000; FAX 407/660-2563.* 400 rms, 6 story. Jan–Apr: S $139; D $149; each addl $10; under 17 free; wkend plan; lower rates rest of yr. TV; cable. Heated pool; poolside serv. Restaurant 6:30 am–10:30 pm. Bar. Ck-out noon. Convention facilities. Concierge. Shopping arcade. Beauty shop. Valet parking. Airport, RR station, bus depot transportation. Lighted tennis. Golf privileges. Refrigerators. Balconies. Fountains in lobby. *LUXURY LEVEL:* **TERRACE LEVEL.** 41 rms, 1 suite. S, D $149–$159; suite $425–$625. Private lounge. Complimentary continental bkfst, refreshments, newspaper. Cr cds: A, C, D, DS, ER, MC, V, JCB.

Restaurants

★ ★ ★ **ENZO'S.** *(1130 S US 17/92, Longwood) ¼ mi S of FL 434. 407/834-9872.* Hrs: 11:30 am–2:30 pm, 6–11 pm; Sat from 6 pm. Closed Sun exc Mother's Day, Mon; Jan 1, Dec 25. Res accepted. Central Italian menu. Bar. Semi-a la carte: lunch $6–$15, dinner $13–$29.50. Child's meals. Specialties: bucatini alla Enzo, zuppa di pesce. Own baking. Restored lakeside house. Cr cds: A, C, D, DS, MC, V.

D

★ ★ **FAR PAVILION.** *474 W FL 436. 407/682-4711.* Hrs: 5–10:30 pm; wkends to 11 pm; early-bird dinner 5–6 pm; Sun brunch 11 am–3 pm. Closed Mon. Res accepted. Northern Indian menu. Bar. A la carte entrees: dinner $9.95–$18.95. Sun brunch $11.95. Child's meals. Specialties: tandoori mixed grill, butter chicken. Parking. Clay-oven baking. Indian motif. Cr cds: A, C, D, DS, MC, V.

D

★ ★ **KOBÉ JAPANESE STEAK HOUSE.** *468 W Semoran Blvd, ½ mi W of I-4. 407/862-2888.* Hrs: 5–10:30 pm. Closed Thanksgiving. Res accepted. Japanese menu. Bar. Complete meals: dinner $9.95–$21.95. Child's meals. Specializes in steak & shrimp, filet mignon & lobster tail. Sushi bar. Parking. Meals prepared by Kobé chef on a teppanyaki table. Cr cds: A, D, DS, MC, V.

D

★ ★ ★ **LA SCALA.** *205 Lorraine Dr. 407/862-3257.* Hrs: 11:30 am–2:30 pm, 5–10:30 pm; Fri & Sat to 11 pm. Closed Sun; hols. Res accepted. Italian menu. Bar. Wine cellar. A la carte entrees: lunch $8–$10, dinner $16–$28. Specializes in veal, seafood. Pianist in season. Parking. Elegant decor; crystal chandeliers. Cr cds: A, C, D, MC, V.

D

✔ ★ **MACARONI GRILL.** *884 W FL 436. 407/682-2577.* Hrs: 11 am–10 pm; Fri & Sat to 11 pm. Closed Thanksgiving, Dec 25. Res accepted. Italian menu. Bar. Semi-a la carte: lunch $3.95–$7.95, dinner $6.95–$15.95. Specializes in pizza, pasta. Entertainment. Parking. Italian wine cellar decor. Cr cds: A, C, D, DS, MC, V.

D

★ ★ ★ **MAISON & JARDIN.** *430 S Wymore Rd, ½ mi S of jct FL 436, I-4. 407/862-4410.* Hrs: 6–10 pm; Sun brunch (Oct–mid-June) 11 am–2 pm. Closed Jan 1, Labor Day, Thanksgiving, Dec 25. Res accepted. French, Amer menu. Bar. Extensive wine list. Semi-a la carte: dinner $17.95–$28. Specialties: rack of lamb, fresh fish. Own baking. Strolling guitarist. Mediterranean decor. Antiques. Jacket. Cr cds: A, C, D, MC, V.

★ ★ **RUTH'S CHRIS STEAK HOUSE.** *999 Douglas Ave. 407/682-6444.* Hrs: 5–11 pm; Sun to 10 pm. Closed Thanksgiving, Dec 25. Res accepted. Bar. A la carte entrees: dinner $16–$28. Specializes in steak. Parking. Bi-level dining. Cr cds: A, C, D, ER, MC, V, JCB.

D

★ ★ **STRAUB'S.** *512 E Altamonte Dr. 407/831-2250.* Hrs: 11:30 am–2:30 pm, 4:30–10 pm; Fri to 11 pm; Sat 4:30–11 pm; Sun 4:30–10 pm; early-bird dinner 4:30–6 pm. Closed Thanksgiving, Dec 25. Res accepted. Bar. Semi-a la carte: lunch $5.75–$9, dinner $11–$21. Child's meals. Specialties: red snapper almondine, mesquite-grilled yellowfin tuna, grilled shrimp. Parking. Florida tropical decor. Cr cds: A, C, D, DS, ER, MC, V.

D

Amelia Island (A-4)

Pop: 7,250 (est) **Elev:** 10 ft **Area code:** 904 **Zip:** 32034

Amelia Island is separated from the mainland by the St Mary's River on the north, the Amelia River Intracoastal Waterway on the west and Nassau Sound on the south. Cumberland Island and the Georgia coast can be seen from the north shore.

(For further information about this area contact the Amelia Island-Fernandina Beach-Yulee Chamber of Commerce, 102 Centre St, PO Box 472, Fernandina Beach 32034; 277-0717.)

(See Atlantic Beach, Fernandina Beach, Jacksonville)

Motor Hotel

★ ★ **AMELIA SURF & RACQUET CLUB.** *4800 Amelia Island Pkwy. 904/261-0511; res: 800/323-2001.* 56 kit. villas, 7 story. Mar–Sept: S, D $120–$210; wkly, monthly rates; lower rates rest of yr. Maid serv avail (fee). TV; cable. 2 pools; wading pools. Restaurant nearby. Ck-out 11 am. Lighted tennis, pro. Golf privileges. Balconies. Extensive oceanfront grounds. Cr cds: A, MC, V.

Inns

✔ ★ ★ **FLORIDA HOUSE.** *(PO Box 688) 22 S 3rd St. 904/261-3300; res: 800/258-3301; FAX 904/277-3831.* 11 rms, 2 story. S, D $65–$125; each addl $10; under 6 free. TV; cable. Complimentary full bkfst. Dining rm 11:30 am–8:30 pm. Ck-out 11 am, ck-in 2 pm. Valet serv.

Local airport transportation. Balconies. Old hotel building (1857); wraparound veranda with rocking chairs. Totally nonsmoking. Cr cds: A, D, MC, V.

★**1735 HOUSE.** *584 S Fletcher. 904/261-5878; res: 800/872-8531.* 6 suites, 2 story. No rm phones. S $75–$135; D $85–$150; each addl $10. TV; cable. Complimentary continental bkfst in rms. Coffee in rms. Ck-out 11 am, ck-in 4 pm. Refrigerators. Picnic tables. In 1928 building; named from year island discovered. On ocean, beach. Cr cds: A, DS, MC, V.

Resorts

★★★**AMELIA ISLAND PLANTATION.** *(PO Box 3000, 32035-1307) 3000 First Coast Hwy, on FL A1A, 18 mi SE of I-95 Fernandina Beach-Callahan exit. 904/261-6161; res: 800/874-6878 (exc FL); FAX 904/277-5159.* 24 rms in 2-story inn, 485 kit. apts in 1–6 story villas. Mid-Mar–mid-May: S $188–$223; D $190–$227. Villas, 1-bedrm: S $295; D $300; 2–3 bedrm for 2–6 persons $425–$530. Daily, wkly plans; EP, AP, MAP; hol packages; 3-night min stay hol wkends; serv charge $4/day over 12; varied lower rates rest of yr. Crib $20. TV; cable. 23 indoor/outdoor pools; several wading pools. Supervised child's activities (Mar–early May & Memorial Day–Labor Day). Dining rms 7 am–10:30 pm (public by res on Sun only, brunch at Inn). Rm serv to 10 pm. Ck-out noon, ck-in 4 pm. Convention facilities. Valet serv. Grocery, package store, barber, beauty salon. Sports dir. 26 tennis courts, 3 lighted, pro. 45-hole golf, greens fee $60–$95, putting green, driving range. Beach; lifeguards. Paddleboats. Bicycles; trails; electric cars. Boardwalks through sunken forest (lighted), marshland. Soc dir; entertainment, dancing. Game rm. Rec rms. Exercise rm; instructor, weights, bicycles, whirlpool, steam rm, sauna. Massage. Refrigerators; wet bar in inn rms; dishwasher, washer, dryer in apts; indoor pool in some. Private patios, balconies. Picnic tables. Attractive resort on 1,300 acres. Cr cds: DS, MC, V.

★★★**THE RITZ-CARLTON, AMELIA ISLAND.** *4750 Amelia Island Pkwy, I-95 exit 129E, in the Summer Beach Resort & Country Club. 904/277-1100; FAX 904/277-1145.* 449 units, 8 story, 45 suites. Early Mar–May: S, D $235–$285; each addl $15; suites $520–$675; under 18 free; golf & tennis packages; higher rates Labor Day; lower rates rest of yr. Crib free. Garage parking, valet $7. TV; cable. 2 pools, 1 indoor; poolside serv. Supervised child's activities. Restaurant 6:30 am–11 pm (also see THE GRILL). Afternoon tea 3–5 pm. Rm serv 24 hrs. Bar 11–1 am; entertainment, dancing. Ck-out noon, ck-in 3 pm. Convention facilities. Bellhops. Valet serv. Concierge. Shopping arcade. Beauty shop. Airport transportation. Lighted tennis, pro. 18-hole golf, pro, putting green, driving range. Exercise equipt; weight machines, bicycles, whirlpool, sauna, steam rm. Bathrm phones, refrigerators, minibars, wet bars. Balconies. Located on 1½ mi of white sand beach along the famous First Coast of Florida. Ocean view from all rms. *LUXURY LEVEL: RITZ-CARLTON CLUB.* 61 rms, 3 suites. S, D $315; suites $775–$2,400. Concierge. Private lounge, honor bar. Complimentary food and beverages.
Cr cds: A, C, D, DS, ER, MC, V, JCB.

Restaurant

★★★**THE GRILL.** *(See The Ritz-Carlton, Amelia Island Resort) 904/277-1100.* Hrs: 6–11 pm. Res accepted. Bar to midnight. Wine cellar. A la carte entrees: dinner $15–$35. Specializes in meat & game, fresh Florida seafood. Pianist. Valet parking. Club atmosphere; fireplace. Floor to ceiling windows provide view of ocean. Jacket. Cr cds: A, C, D, DS, ER, MC, V, JCB.

Apalachicola (F-3)

Founded: 1821 **Pop:** 2,602 **Elev:** 16 ft **Area code:** 904 **Zip:** 32320

Once known as West Point, the town took the name of Apalachicola (Indian for "friendly people on the other side") soon after it was incorporated. At one time a leading cotton-shipping port, the town now turns to the sea for its major crop—nearly 90 percent of Florida's oysters are harvested from nearby St George Sound. Local history goes back to 1528, when the Spanish conquistador Narváez stopped to build boats to sail to Mexico. Trinity Church (1839) on Gorrie Square was brought in sections on a schooner from New York; the original bell was melted down to make a Confederate cannon.

What to See and Do

1. **John Gorrie State Museum.** Ave D & 6th St. Memorial to Dr. John Gorrie, who built the first ice-making machine (1845) to cool the rooms of yellow fever victims; replica of first ice machine, scenes of early local history. (Thurs–Mon; closed Jan 1, Thanksgiving, Dec 25) Phone 653-9347. ¢

2. **St George Island.** 7 mi E on US 98/319 to Eastpoint, then S on toll bridge (FL G1A). Swimming beaches; surf fishing. Also here is

   St George Island State Park. More than 1,800 acres with miles of undeveloped beaches, dunes, forest and marshes. Swimming; saltwater fishing. Hiking. Picnicking. Backwoods & improved camping (hookups). Vehicles prohibited in dune areas. Standard hrs, fees. Phone 927-2111.

3. **T.H. Stone Memorial St Joseph Peninsula State Park.** 24 mi W via US 98, then 10 mi W & N on FL 30E. This 2,500-acre park has a 20-mile white sand beach known for its variety of beautiful bird species. Swimming, skin diving; fishing; boating (ramps, marina). Nature trails. Picnicking, concession, playground. Cabins. Tent & trailer sites. Standard hrs, fees. Phone 227-1327.

4. **Apalachicola National Estuarine Research Reserve.** Headquarters located at 261 7th St. This 193,758-acre area, the largest in the US reserve system, preserves the Apalachicola Bay and a large portion of the Apalachicola River, adjoining floodplains, sounds and three barrier islands. Fresh and saltwater marshes, swamp forests, open water and beaches serve as field laboratory; programs, tours. Fishing, boating, hiking. (Daily; building Mon–Fri) Contact Reserve Manager, 261 7th St; 653-8063.

5. **Apalachicola National Forest.** N via US 98/319 or E via FL 65. Many lakes sparkle among oaks, pines, cedars and cypress on this more than 630,000-acre area between Apalachicola and Tallahassee. Three large rivers provide boating and fishing for bass, bream and perch. There are camp and picnic sites and several swimming areas. Fees may be charged at recreation sites. Contact USDA Forest Service, 227 N Bronough St, Suite 4061, Tallahassee 32301; 681-7265.

6. **Fort Gadsden State Historic Site.** E on US 98/319, then 17 mi N on FL 65, just N of Bucks Siding. In 1814 the British built a fort on this 75-acre area as a base for recruitment during the War of 1812. The fort was later destroyed by US forces, but in 1818, Andrew Jackson ordered another built as a supply base. Occupied by Confederate forces from 1862–1863, some earthworks remain visible. Open-sided kiosk has miniature replica of Fort Gadsden, interpretive exhibits. Fishing. Hiking trails. Picnicking. (Fri–Mon & Wed) Phone 670-8988. **Free.**

(For further information contact the Chamber of Commerce, 128 Market St, 32320-1730; 653-9419.)

Annual Event

Florida Seafood Festival. Parade, oyster eating and shucking contests, blessing of the fleet, entertainment. 1st Sat Nov.

(See Panama City)

Arcadia (D-3)

Founded: 1886 **Pop:** 6,488 **Elev:** 57 ft **Area code:** 813 **Zip:** 33821

The seat of De Soto County, Arcadia is a marketplace for cattle and a local government and retail center. It is a predominantly rural community, surrounded by ranches and citrus groves of the Peace River Valley.

(For further information contact the De Soto County Chamber of Commerce, 16 S Volusia Ave, PO Box 149; 494-4033.)

Annual Events

De Soto County Fair. Fairgrounds, S on Brevard Ave, US 17. Feb or Mar.

All-Florida Championship Rodeo. Fenton Arena, S Hillsborough Ave. Professional rodeo circuit; parade, mock shoot-out, barbecue. 2 wkends Mar & July.

(See Port Charlotte)

Motel

✔ ★**BEST WESTERN M & M.** *(PO Box 630) 504 S Brevard Ave (US 17S). 813/494-4884; FAX 813/494-2006.* 37 rms. Feb–Mar: S $43; D $53; each addl $5; under 12 free; lower rates rest of yr. Crib $5. TV; cable. Pool. Complimentary continental bkfst, coffee. Ck-out 10 am. Gift shop. Cr cds: A, C, D, DS, MC, V.

Restaurant

✔ ★**PARADISE.** *903 N Brevard Ave (US 17N). 813/494-2061.* Hrs: 7 am–9 pm; Fri, Sat to 10 pm. Closed Dec 25; also Mon May–Oct. Serv bar. Semi-a la carte: bkfst $2.25–$5, lunch $4.95–$9.95, dinner $5.95–$15.95. Child's meals. Specializes in steak, seafood, chicken. Salad bar. Parking. Cr cds: DS, MC, V.

Atlantic Beach (A-4)

Pop: 11,636 **Elev:** 17 ft **Area code:** 904 **Zip:** 32233

What to See and Do

1. **Mayport Naval Station.** N on Mayport Rd in Mayport. Home port of more than 15 vessels, including an aircraft carrier, cruisers, destroyers and frigates. Guided tours of ships (Sat, Sun). No skirts, high heels; identification required. Phone 270-NAVY. **Free.**
2. **Hanna Park.** Mayport Rd & Wonderwood Dr. This 450-acre recreation area includes 2 plazas overlooking the ocean. Salt- and freshwater fishing. Nature trails. Picnicking. Camping (hookups; fees).

(Daily; closed Jan 1, Thanksgiving, Dec 25) Phone 249-4700 or -2316. Park **¢**

(For further information contact Jacksonville and the Beaches Convention & Visitors Bureau, 3 Independent Dr, Jacksonville 32202; 798-9148.)

(See Amelia Island, Jacksonville, Jacksonville Beach)

Motel

✔ ★**COMFORT INN MAYPORT.** *2401 Mayport Rd. 904/249-0313.* 108 rms, 3 story. No elvtr. S $46.75; D $49.75; each addl $5; under 18 free; higher rates special events. Crib free. TV; cable, in-rm movies avail. Pool. Complimentary continental bkfst. Restaurant adj open 24 hrs. Ck-out noon. Coin lndry. Sundries. Some refrigerators. Cr cds: A, C, D, DS, ER, MC, V, JCB.

Bartow (C-3)

Settled: 1851 **Pop:** 14,716 **Elev:** 125 ft **Area code:** 813 **Zip:** 33830

Bartow, named for a Confederate Army general, is the seat of Polk County. It is noted for the nearby mines, which annually produce more than 70 percent of the country's phosphate, a major ingredient in chemical fertilizers. Citrus and cattle also add to Bartow's economy.

What to See and Do

Polk County Historical and Genealogical Library. 100 E Main St, in Old Courthouse. Extensive collection relating to southeastern US. (Tues–Sat; closed first Tues & Wed of month; also county hols) Phone 534-4380. **¢¢**

(For further information contact the Chamber of Commerce, 510 N Broadway Ave, PO Box 956; 533-7125.)

Annual Event

Bloomin' Arts Festival & Flower Show. Downtown. Juried art show, flower show, entertainment, concessions. Early Apr.

(See Haines City, Lake Wales, Winter Haven)

Motel

✔ ★**DAVIS BROS.** *1035 N Broadway Ave. 813/533-0711; FAX 813/533-0924.* 102 rms, 2 story. Jan–mid-Apr: S $38; D $48; each addl $4; under 16 free; lower rates rest of yr. Crib $4. Pet accepted. TV; cable; wading pool. Restaurant 11 am–2 pm, 4:30–8 pm. Bar 2 pm–1:30 am. Ck-out noon. Meeting rm. Coin lndry. Cr cds: A, C, D, DS, MC, V.

Restaurant

✔ ★**JOHN'S.** *1395 E Main St. 813/533-3471.* Hrs: 6 am–11 pm. Res accepted. Bar 10–2 am. Semi-a la carte: bkfst 99¢–$2.25, lunch $2.25–$5.95, dinner $4.95–$11.95. Child's meals. Specializes in seafood, steak. Salad bar. Entertainment Fri–Sat. Parking. Greek decor. Family-owned. Cr cds: A, C, D, DS, MC, V.

Belle Glade (D-5)

Founded: 1928 **Pop:** 16,177 **Elev:** 20 ft **Area code:** 407 **Zip:** 33430

With Lake Okeechobee's floods tamed by a network of dikes and canals, the incredibly rich Everglades' "black gold" muckland turns out a variety of winter vegetables. Approximately 550,000 acres of sugar cane are processed by 7 mills in the area. The sod and rice industries also are important.

What to See and Do

1. **Lawrence E. Will Museum.** 530 S Main St, in library. Artifacts of Calusa Indians, one of the oldest and least known cultures that ever existed in this country; pioneer and Seminole exhibits; sugar cane display. (Daily exc Sun; closed hols; also Fri after Thanksgiving) Phone 996-3453. **Free.**
2. **Lake Okeechobee.** 3 mi from town. Covering 730 square miles, Okeechobee is the second largest freshwater lake completely within the boundaries of the US. Shallow, only 22 feet at its deepest, with many grassy spots and shoals, the lake is renowned for its bass, crappie, bream and speckled perch; more than one million pounds of fish are caught in the lake annually by commercial and sport fishermen. The Herbert Hoover Dike provides an unobstructed view of the lake. Picnicking; pavilions with cookers.
3. **Belle Glade Marina.** 3 mi W on FL 717, on Lake Okeechobee. Fishing; dock, boat slips, ramps. Picnicking. Camping. Phone 996-6322. Camping/site/night ¢¢¢¢–¢¢¢¢¢

(For further information contact the Chamber of Commerce, 540 S Main St; 996-2745.)

Annual Event

Black Gold Jubilee Celebration. Sports tournaments, parade, arts & crafts, beauty contest, concessions. Usually late Apr.

(For accommodations see Okeechobee, West Palm Beach)

Big Pine Key (F-4)

Pop: 4,206 **Elev:** 8 ft **Area code:** 305 **Zip:** 33043

Largest of all the lower keys, Big Pine consists of 7,700 acres thick with silver palmetto, Caribbean pines and unusual growths of cacti. Rare white herons and the elusive, tiny Key deer, long thought extinct, live on the island and are favorite subjects for photographers. Drivers should be alert to Key deer crossing roadways.

What to See and Do

1. **National Key Deer Refuge.** N of US 1 on Key Deer Blvd (FL 940); refuge headquarters on Watson Blvd, N off Key Deer Blvd. Approximately two-thirds of the present population of Key deer, smallest of all white-tailed deer, inhabit this refuge. The deer can most likely be seen in early morning, late afternoon and evening. A nature walk is located 1.5 miles north of Key Deer and Watson Blvds; nearby is Blue Hole, an old rock quarry that is home to several alligators. (Daily; headquarters Mon–Fri) **Note:** Feeding Key deer and alligators is prohibited by state law; be alert for Key deer crossing roadways. Contact Refuge Manager, PO Box 430510; 872-2239 or 800/872-2239. **Free.**
2. **Bahia Honda State Park.** 5 mi E on US 1. More than 635 acres of beach, dunes, coastal strand hammocks and mangroves cover the skeleton of an ancient coral reef. Swimming, skin and scuba diving, snorkeling trips, rentals; fishing for grouper, mangrove snapper and grunt; boating (ramps, docks, basin). Nature trails. Picnicking,

concession. Camping (dump station). Standard hrs, fees. Phone 872-2353.

(For further information contact the Lower Keys Chamber of Commerce, PO Drawer 430511; 872-2411.)

(For accommodations see Key West, Marathon)

Blountstown (F-3)

Founded: 1823 **Pop:** 2,404 **Elev:** 69 ft **Area code:** 904 **Zip:** 32424

Blountstown is named for John Blount, the Seminole Indian chief who acted as a guide for Andrew Jackson in his campaign against the Creek Indians in 1818. The town sits on a bluff overlooking the Apalachicola River. The Apalachicola National Forest (see APALACHICOLA) is south of here; a ranger district office is located in Bristol.

What to See and Do

Torreya State Park. 4 mi E on FL 20, then NE off FL 12, near Rock Bluff. Park, more than 1,000 acres overlooking the Apalachicola River, is named for a tree native only to a 20-square-mile area at this site. In the park is the antebellum Gregory House of typical plantation architecture (guided tours daily). Confederate gun pits, pylons of old riverboat landing. Nature trails (7 mi). Picnicking. Camping (dump station). Standard hrs, fees. Phone 643-2674.

(For further information contact the Calhoun County Chamber of Commerce, 314 E Central Ave; 674-4519.)

(For accommodations see Marianna, Panama City)

Boca Raton (E-5)

Founded: 1897 **Pop:** 61,492 **Elev:** 16 ft **Area code:** 407

Florida architect Addison Mizner bought several thousand acres of farmland on which to build his dream city, Boca Raton, only to be foiled by the bust that followed the Florida land boom of the 1920s. For three decades, Boca Raton was a small resort town with little more than the architecture of Mizner's Boca Raton Resort and Club to commend it. In recent years, however, the town has been in the forefront of Palm Beach County's explosive growth. Throughout this period, Boca Raton has retained its resort atmosphere while becoming an educational, technical and cultural center.

What to See and Do

1. **Boca Raton Museum of Art.** 801 W Palmetto Park Rd. Exhibits include paintings, photography, sculpture, and glass. Lectures, tours. (Mon–Fri, also Sat & Sun afternoons; closed Jan 1, Thanksgiving, Dec 25) Phone 392-2500. ¢¢
2. **Children's Museum.** 498 Crawford Blvd. Learning experiences in a historical setting; creative exhibits and hands-on activities; nature path. (Tues–Sat afternoons; closed Jan 1, Dec 25) Phone 368-6875. ¢–¢¢
3. **Florida Atlantic University** (1964). (16,000 students) Center of town, 3 mi from ocean. On 850-acre campus are concerts, dance, theater (Nov–mid-Apr); art gallery (Sept–Apr); library. Phone 367-3000.

(For further information contact the Greater Boca Raton Chamber of Commerce, 1800 N Dixie Hwy, 33432-1892; 395-4433.)

Annual Event

KidsFest. At Children's Museum (see #2). Entertainment, zoo & museum booths, theater performances. Apr.

Seasonal Event

Royal Palm Polo. Games played at the Royal Palm Polo Sports Club, considered by many the winter polo capital of the world. Special events. Phone 994-1876. Sun, Jan–Apr.

(See Delray Beach, Fort Lauderdale, Pompano Beach)

Motels

✔ ★ ★ **BEST WESTERN UNIVERSITY INN.** *2700 N Federal Hwy (US 1) (33431).* 407/395-5225; FAX 407/338-9180. 90 rms, 2 story. Mid-Dec–Apr: S, D $69–$89; each addl $8; under 12 free; lower rates rest of yr. Crib free. TV; cable. Heated pool; whirlpool. Complimentary continental bkfst. Restaurant 11:30 am–11 pm. Bar. Ck-out 11 am. Coin lndry. Meeting rm. Valet serv. Sundries. Free airport transportation. Cr cds: A, C, D, DS, ER, MC, V, JCB.

✔ ★ **DAYS INN.** *2899 N Federal Hwy (US 1) (33431).* 407/395-7172. 48 rms, 2 story, 12 kit. units. Feb–Mar: S $79; D $84; each addl $10; kit. units $86; under 12 free; wkly rates; lower rates rest of yr. Crib free. TV. Pool. Complimentary coffee in lobby. Restaurant nearby. Ck-out 11 am. Coin lndry. Cr cds: A, DS, MC, V.

★ **HOLIDAY INN WEST BOCA.** *8144 Glades Rd (33434).* 407/482-7070; FAX 407/482-6076. 97 rms, 4 story. Dec–Apr: S $89–$99; D $95–$105; each addl $6; under 18 free; varied lower rates rest of yr. Crib free. TV; cable. Pool. Restaurant 7 am–1 pm, 5–10 pm. Rm serv. Bar noon–2 am. Ck-out noon. Valet serv. Private patios, balconies. Cr cds: A, C, D, DS, ER, MC, V, JCB.

★ **HOWARD JOHNSON.** *80 E Camino Real (33432).* 407/395-4545; FAX 407/338-5491. 53 rms. Mid-Dec–Apr: S, D $60–$102; under 18 free; lower rates rest of yr. Crib free. TV. Pool. Restaurant 7 am–11 pm. Ck-out noon. Private patios. Picnic tables. Cr cds: A, C, D, DS, MC, V, JCB.

★ ★ **RESIDENCE INN BY MARRIOTT.** *525 NW 77th St (33487).* 407/994-3222; FAX 407/994-3339. 120 kit. suites, 2 story. Early Dec–mid-Apr: suites $175–$205; under 16 free; lower rates rest of yr. Crib free. Pet accepted, some restrictions; $75 non-refundable and $5 per day. TV; cable. Heated pool; whirlpool. Complimentary bkfst buffet. Complimentary coffee in rms. Ck-out noon. Coin lndry. Meeting rms. Valet serv. Tennis privileges, pro. 18-hole golf privileges, pro, putting green, driving range. Health club privileges. Lawn games. Balconies. Picnic tables, grills. Cr cds: A, C, D, DS, MC, V, JCB.

✔ ★ **SHORE EDGE.** *425 N Ocean Blvd (33432).* 407/395-4491. 16 units, 9 kits. Mid-Dec–May: S, D $55–$65; kit. units $55–$95; wkly, monthly rates; varied lower rates rest of yr. TV; cable. Heated pool. Complimentary morning coffee. Ck-out 11 am. Coin lndry. Beach opp. Cr cds: A, MC, V.

Motor Hotels

★ ★ **CROWN STERLING SUITES.** *701 NW 53rd St (33487), in Arvida Park of Commerce.* 407/997-9500; FAX 407/994-3565. 183 suites, 4 story. Mid-Dec–Apr: suites $124–$154; under 12 free; monthly rates; lower rates rest of yr. Crib free. Pet accepted, some restrictions; $25. TV; cable. Heated pool; whirlpool. Complimentary full bkfst. Complimentary coffee in rms. Restaurant 11 am–11 pm. Rm serv. Ck-out 1 pm. Coin lndry. Meeting rms. Bellhops. Valet serv. Sundries. Health club privileges. Refrigerators. Cr cds: A, C, D, DS, ER, MC, V.

★ ★ ★ **HOLIDAY INN I-95 & GLADES.** *1950 Glades Rd (33431).* 407/368-5200; FAX 407/395-4783. 184 rms, 5 story. Jan–Apr: S $109–$139; D $119–$149; each addl $10; suites $129–$199; under 16 free; lower rates rest of yr. Crib free. TV; cable. Heated pool; whirlpool, wading pool, poolside serv. Restaurant 6:30 am–2 pm; dining rm 5:30–10 pm. Rm serv. Bar 11–2 am; dancing. Ck-out noon. Meeting rms. Bellhops. Gift shop. Golf privileges. Refrigerator in suites. Balconies. Cr cds: A, C, D, DS, ER, MC, V, JCB.

★ ★ **SHERATON.** *2000 NW 19th St (33431), I-95 at Glades Rd.* 407/368-5252; FAX 407/750-5437. 192 units, 5 story. Jan–Mar: S, D $110–$144; each addl $10; suites $200; under 17 free; lower rates rest of yr. Crib free. TV; cable. Heated pool; poolside serv. Bkfst buffet. Restaurant 6:30 am–10 pm. Rm serv. Bar 11 am–midnight; entertainment, dancing (seasonal). Ck-out noon. Meeting rms. Bellhops. Valet serv. Sundries. Lighted tennis. Golf privileges. Exercise equipt; weight machine, stair machine. Health club privileges. Some bathrm phones; refrigerators avail. Cr cds: A, C, D, DS, MC, V.

Hotels

★ ★ ★ **BRIDGE.** *999 E Camino Real (33432).* 407/368-9500; res: 800/327-0130; FAX 407/362-0492. 121 units, 11 story. Mid-Dec–Apr: S, D $145–$190; each addl $10; suites $280–$485; under 18 free; lower rates rest of yr. Crib free. TV; cable. Heated pool; poolside serv. Restaurant 7 am–11 pm; dining rm 5–11 pm. Bar 11–1 am; entertainment, dancing. Ck-out noon. Meeting rms. Tennis, golf privileges. Exercise equipt; weights, bicycles, sauna. Some refrigerators. Balconies. Cr cds: A, D, MC, V.

★ ★ ★ **EMBASSY SUITES.** *661 NW 53rd St (33487), at I-95 & Yamato Rd, in Arvida Park of Commerce.* 407/994-8200; FAX 407/994-9518. 261 suites, 7 story. Dec–Apr: S, D $119–$169; lower rates rest of yr. Crib free. TV; in-rm movies. Heated pool. Complimentary full bkfst. Coffee in rms. Restaurant 7 am–10 pm. Bar noon–midnight. Ck-out noon. Convention facilities. Concierge. Gift shop. Free valet parking. Tennis, golf privileges. Exercise equipt; weights, bicycles, whirlpool, sauna. Refrigerators. Balconies. On small lake. Atrium with garden pools, glass-enclosed elvtrs. Cr cds: A, C, D, DS, MC, V.

★ ★ ★ **MARRIOTT-CROCKER CENTER.** *5150 Town Center Circle (33486), at I-95 exit 38.* 407/392-4600; FAX 407/368-9223. 256 rms, 12 story. Jan–Apr: S $129–$179; D $144–$194; each addl $15; suites $250–$400; under 18 free; lower rates rest of yr. Crib free. Pet accepted, some restrictions. TV; cable. Heated pool; poolside serv. Restaurant 6:30 am–11 pm. Bar 10:30–1 am; entertainment. Ck-out noon. Meeting rms. Gift shop. Valet parking. Tennis privileges. 18-hole golf privileges. Exercise equipt; weights, bicycles, whirlpool, sauna. Health club privileges. Refrigerators, minibars. Balconies. *LUXURY LEVEL:* **CONCIERGE LEVEL.** 22 rms. S $169–$199; D $184–$214. Concierge. Private lounge, honor bar. Complimentary continental bkfst, refreshments. Cr cds: A, C, D, DS, ER, MC, V, JCB.

★ ★ **RADISSON SUITE.** *7920 Glades Rd (33434), at Arvida Pkwy Ctr.* 407/483-3600; FAX 407/479-2280. 200 suites, 7 story. Dec–Apr: S, D $135–$350; each addl $10; lower rates rest of yr. Crib free. Pet accepted, some restrictions; $100 non-refundable. TV; cable, in-rm movies. Heated pool. Complimentary full bkfst. Coffee in rms. Restaurants 11:30 am–10:30 pm. Bars. Ck-out noon. Coin lndry. Meeting rms. Gift shop. Exercise equipt; bicycles, treadmill, whirlpool. Health club privileges. Minibars; refrigerators avail. Private patios, balconies. Lake adj. Cr cds: A, C, D, DS, ER, MC, V.

Resort

★ ★ ★ ★ ★ **BOCA RATON RESORT & CLUB.** *501 E Camino Real (33432), 2 blks E of US 1. 407/395-3000; res: 800/327-0101; FAX 407/391-3183.* 963 units in 4 bldgs, 242 rms in 27-story tower, several villa apts with kit., 214 rms in beach club, 327 cloister rms. EP, Mid-Dec-Apr: S, D $210–$410; suites $450–$3,000; MAP avail; lower rates rest of yr. All rms, $9 per rm per day service charge for bellman/maid service; also 18% food & beverage service charge at all dining outlets in lieu of gratuities. Res required. Crib free. TV; cable. 4 pools; poolside serv, lifeguard. Supervised child's activities (summer & hols). Dining rm 7 am–midnight. Box lunches, snack bar. Rm serv 24 hrs. Bar 11–2 am. Ck-out noon. Convention facilities. Barber, beauty shop. Many specialty shops. Airport transportation. Sports dir. 34 tennis courts, 9 lighted, pro. 36-hole golf, 2 putting greens, driving range. Private beach; cabanas. Charter boats. 23 private yacht slips. Bicycles. Lawn games. Soc dir. Entertainment, dancing, movies. Rec rm. Exercise rm; instructor, weights, bicycles, whirlpool, sauna, steam rm. Massage. Many rms with balcony overlook Lake Boca Raton. Luxurious; on 351 landscaped acres. *LUXURY LEVEL:* **PALM COURT CLUB.** 49 units, 5 suites. Mid-Dec–Apr: S, D $310; suites $475. Concierge. Private lounge. Minibars. Wet bars. Complimentary continental bkfst, afternoon tea & refreshments.
Cr cds: A, C, D, DS, ER, MC, V, JCB.

D 🛥 🏊 ⚓ 🏋 🚭 😊 ⌛

Restaurants

★ ★ **ADDISON'S.** *2 E Camino Real. 407/391-9800.* Hrs: 11:30 am–2:30 pm, 4:30–10:30 pm; early-bird dinner Sun–Thurs 4:30–6:30 pm, Fri & Sat 4:30–6 pm; Sun brunch 11:30 am–2:30 pm. Res accepted. Italian menu. Bar. A la carte entrees: lunch $6–$12, dinner $12–$25. Complete meals: dinner $12–$25. Sun brunch $15. Specialties: osso buco, veal Marsala, salmon with mustard dill. Valet parking. Outdoor dining. Eight dining rms; Arbor Room has tree in center, Veranda Area overlooks garden. Cr cds: A, D, DS, MC, V.

D

★ ★ ★ **ARTURO'S RISTORANTE.** *6750 N Federal Hwy (US 1). 407/997-7373.* Hrs: 11:30 am–3 pm, 6–10 pm; Sat, Sun from 6 pm. Closed Thanksgiving, Dec 25. Res required. Northern Italian menu. Bar. Wine cellar. A la carte entrees: lunch $11–$15, dinner $15–$27.95. Complete meal: dinner $30.50. Specialties: veal chop Modenese, zuppa di pesce. Own baking, pasta. Valet parking. Jacket. Cr cds: A, C, D, MC, V.

D

★ ★ ★ **AUBERGE LE GRILLON.** *6900 N Federal Hwy (US 1). 407/997-6888.* Hrs: 6–9:30 pm. Closed Mon in summer. Res accepted. French, continental menu. Wine list. Semi-a la carte: dinner $17–$28. Specialties: Dover sole with lobster and mousseline sauce, roast duckling with apricot and Grand Marnier sauce. Own baking. Parking. Intimate dining; paintings. Cr cds: A, C, D, MC, V.

✔ ★ ★ **BASIL GARDEN.** *5837 N Federal Hwy. 407/994-2554.* Hrs: 5:30–9:30 pm; wkends to 10 pm. Closed Jan 1, Thanksgiving, Dec 25. Res accepted. Italian menu. Wine. A la carte entrees: dinner $10.95–$22.95. Specializes in veal, pasta, fresh seafood. Own pasta, desserts. Parking. Intimate, trattoria-style dining. Cr cds: A, MC, V.

★ ★ **BISTRO L'EUROPE.** *346 Plaza Real, in Mizner Park. 407/368-4488.* Hrs: 11:30 am–11 pm; Sun from 6 pm. Res accepted. Mediterranean menu. Bar. A la carte entrees: lunch $9.25–$11.75, dinner $14.25–$22.50. Semi-a la carte: lunch $9.25–$11.75. Child's meals. Specialties: potato-crusted snapper, osso buco, escargots. Valet parking. Outdoor dining. Sophisticated but informal dining; murals on walls. Cr cds: A, D, MC, V.

D

★ **FIREHOUSE.** *6751 N Federal Hwy (US 1). 407/997-6006.* Hrs: 5–11 pm. Closed Dec 25. Bar. A la carte entrees: dinner $8.95–$26.95. Specializes in prime rib, steak, fresh seafood. Salad bar. Parking. Firehouse decor, memorabilia throughout. Cr cds: A, D, MC, V.

D

★ ★ **GATEHOUSE CAFE.** *741 E Palmetto Park Rd. 407/392-4855.* Hrs: 6–9:30 pm. Closed Sun; Dec 25. Res required. Northern Italian menu. Serv bar. A la carte entrees: dinner $14.50–$25.50. Specializes in veal, pasta, seafood. Parking. Outdoor dining. Historic house (ca 1920); hardwood floors, fireplace. Cr cds: A, MC, V.

D

★ ★ ★ **GAZEBO CAFE.** *4199 N Federal Hwy (US 1). 407/395-6033.* Hrs: 11:30 am–3 pm, 5:30–10 pm; Sat from 5:30 pm; Sun from 5 pm (exc mid-May–Dec). Res accepted. French, continental menu. Serv bar. Wine list. A la carte entrees: lunch $6.95–$16, dinner $16.95–$25.75. Specialties: Dover sole, veal. Parking. Outdoor dining. Jacket (dinner). Cr cds: A, C, D, DS, MC, V.

D

★ ★ ★ **JOE MUER SEAFOOD.** *6450 N Federal Hwy (US 1). 407/997-6688.* Hrs: 4:30–10 pm; Sat–Mon from 3:30 pm. Res accepted. Bar. A la carte entrees: dinner $14.25–$28. Child's meals. Specializes in fresh seafood, beef, pasta. Own pasta, desserts. Piano bar Wed–Sun. Valet parking. Cr cds: A, D, DS, MC, V.

D

★ ★ ★ **LA FINESTRA.** *171 E Palmetto Park Rd. 407/392-1838.* Hrs: 6–10 pm. Closed Sun May–Sept. Res accepted. Northern Italian, French menu. Wine, beer. Semi-a la carte: dinner $12.95–$28.95. Specialties: lobster pescatore, veal chops, yellowtail snapper, Norwegian salmon. Own baking. Guitarist, flutist. Parking. Continental art prints, chandeliers. Chef-owned. Jacket. Cr cds: A, D, MC, V.

D

★ ★ ★ ★ **LA VIEILLE MAISON.** *770 E Palmetto Park Rd. 407/391-6701.* Hrs: May–Oct 6:30–9:30 pm; Nov–Apr 6 and 9:30 pm. 2 sittings: 6/6:30 pm, 9/9:30 pm. Closed Memorial Day, Labor Day. Res accepted; required in season. French menu. Bar. Wine list. A la carte entrees: dinner $17–$35. *Prix fixe*: dinner $49 excluding beverage. "Temptation" menu (May–Nov 1, Sun–Fri) $28.75. Specialties: escargot, shrimp Pernod, medallions of lamb and beef, fresh pompano. Own baking. Treetop balcony dining & outdoor courtyard. Patio & private dining area. Valet parking. Jacket. Cr cds: A, C, D, DS, MC, V.

D

✔ ★ ★ ★ **MARCEL'S.** *1 S Ocean Blvd. 407/362-9911.* Hrs: 11:30 am–2:30 pm, 5–11 pm; wkends to 11 pm. Res accepted. French menu. Semi-a la carte: lunch $4.95–$9.95, dinner $11.95–$25.95. *Prix fixe*: (seasonal) dinner $16.95. Specialties: terrine of pheasant, Dover sole, rack of lamb, fresh seafood. Own baking, desserts. Parking. Bistro atmosphere. Limoges china, paintings. Cr cds: A, DS, MC, V.

D

★ ★ ★ **MAXALUNA.** *21150 Military Trail, in Crocker Center. 407/391-7177.* Hrs: 11:30 am–2:30 pm, 6–10:30 pm; Fri to 11 pm; Sat 6–11 pm; Sun 6–10 pm. Closed Thanksgiving. Italian menu. Res required. Bar. A la carte entrees: lunch $8–$15, dinner $13–$24.95. Specialties: stuffed veal chops, homemade pasta. Valet parking. Outdoor dining. Cr cds: A, C, D, DS, MC, V.

D

★ ★ ★ **MORADA BAR & GRILLE.** *5100 Town Center Circle, suite 100 in Crocker Ctr. 407/395-0805.* Hrs: 11:30 am–2 pm, 6–11 pm. Res accepted; required in season. Bar 4 pm–midnight, wkends & in season to 2 am. A la carte entrees: lunch $4.95–$10.95, dinner $9.95–$24.95. Specialties: Norwegian salmon, sesame charred yellowfin tuna, roasted Sonoma rack of lamb, wildberry gateau. Valet parking. Outdoor dining. Modern contemporary decor; objects d'art. Cr cds: A, D, MC, V.

D

★ ★ **NICK'S ITALIAN FISHERY.** *1 Boca Place, on Glades Rd, 1 blk W of I-95. 407/994-2201.* Hrs: 11:30 am–2:30 pm, 5–11 pm; Sun brunch to 2:30 pm. Res required. Italian, Amer menu. Bar. A la carte entrees: lunch $5.95–$9.95, dinner $14.95–$22.95. Sun brunch $14.95. Specialties: seafood Fra Diavolo, "blue claw crab feast." Raw bar. Entertainment. Valet parking. Glass-enclosed atrium dining; 1,000-gallon fish tank. Jacket. Cr cds: A, D, DS, MC, V.

✔ ★ ★ **PELICAN BISTRO.** 36 SE Third St. 407/391-5922. Hrs: 5–10 pm. Res accepted. French, Northern Italian menu. Bar. Semi-a la carte: dinner $10.95–$21. Specialties: veal chop Normande, chicken Dijonnaise, salmon Alexandrine. Parking. Facade & one dining rm wall of coral rock. Cr cds: A, MC, V.

★ ★ ★ **PETE'S BOCA RATON.** 7940 Glades Rd. 407/487-1600. Hrs: 11:30 am–3 pm, 5–10 pm; wkends 4:30–11 pm; early-bird dinner Mon–Fri 5–6:30 pm. Res accepted. Bar 11–3 am. Wine cellar. Semi-a la carte: lunch $3.95–$8.95, dinner $12.95–$28.95. Specialties: Cajun blackened swordfish, prime rib, seafood Valencia. Entertainment. Valet parking. Outdoor dining. Casual waterfront dining in elegant setting. Cr cds: A, D, MC, V.

★ ★ **TAVERN ON THE GREEN.** 301 Yamato Rd, in the Northern Trust Plaza. 407/241-9214. Hrs: 11:30 am–2:30 pm, 5–9:30 pm; Sat from 5 pm; early-bird dinner 5–6:30 pm. Closed Sun; Jan 1, Memorial Day, July 4. Res required. Continental menu. Bar. A la carte entrees: lunch $5.50–$13.50, dinner $11.50–$21.95. Specialties: pan-roasted duck breast, lamb chop, fresh Florida fish. Own pastries. Entertainment. Parking. Formal dining rm & casual eating area. Sunken atrium garden. Cr cds: A, MC, V.

✔ ★ ★ **UNCLE TAI'S.** 5250 Town Center Circle. 407/368-8806. Hrs: 11:30 am–2:30 pm, 5–10 pm; wkends 5–10:30 pm; early-bird dinner 5–6:30 pm. Res accepted Fri–Sun. Chinese menu. Serv bar. A la carte entrees: lunch $5.95–$8.25, dinner $9.50–$17.75. Specialties: Hunan-style sliced lamb, Uncle Tai's jumbo shrimp. Parking. Outdoor dining. Elegant Oriental decor. Cr cds: A, C, D, MC, V.

✔ ★ ★ **WILDFLOWER.** 551 E Palmetto Park Rd. 407/391-0000. Hrs: 11:30–1:45 am. Bar. A la carte entrees: lunch, dinner $3.95–$14.95. Specializes in salads, steak, pasta, hamburgers. Disc jockey. Parking. Two levels with 5 bars. Overlooks Intracoastal Waterway. Cr cds: A, D, DS, MC, V.

✔ ★ **WILT CHAMBERLAIN'S.** 8903 W Glades Rd. 407/488-8881. Hrs: 11:30 am–11:30 pm; Fri & Sat to 12:30 am. Varied menu. Bar. A la carte entrees: lunch, dinner $4.95–$14.95. Child's meals. Specialties: flatbread pizza, bangko chicken, Wilt's clubhouse sandwich. Magician Sat evenings. Parking. Outdoor dining. Many TVs throughout room; large arcade area. Totally nonsmoking. Cr cds: A, C, D, DS, MC, V.

Bonita Springs (E-3)

Pop: 13,600 **Elev:** 10 ft **Area code:** 813 **Zip:** 33923

Located directly on the Gulf of Mexico, with the Imperial River flowing through the city, Bonita Springs has several popular boat and nature tours.

What to See and Do

1. **Everglades Wonder Gardens.** On US 41 Business. Native reptiles, birds and animals in Everglades setting. Guided tours. (Daily) Sr citizen rate. Phone 992-2591. ¢¢¢

2. **Greyhound racing.** Naples-Fort Myers Greyhound Track, on Old US 41. (Tues–Sat evenings; matinees Wed, Fri–Sun) Phone 992-2411. General admission ¢

(For further information contact the Chamber of Commerce, 8801 W Terry St, PO Box 1240, 33959; 992-2943.)

(See Naples)

Motel

★ ★ **COMFORT INN.** 9800 Bonita Beach Rd. 813/992-5001; FAX 813/992-9283. 69 rms, 3 story. Jan–Apr: S, D $85–$115; each addl $10; under 18 free; lower rates rest of yr. Crib free. TV; cable. Heated pool; whirlpool, poolside serv. Restaurant 7 am–8 pm; off season to 2 pm. Bar from 11 am. Ck-out 11 am. Coin lndry. 18-hole golf privileges, pro, putting green, driving range. Wet bars, refrigerators. Balconies. Cr cds: A, C, D, DS, ER, MC, V, JCB.

Restaurants

✔ ★ **KIM WAH.** 8951 Bonita Beach Rd, in Springs Plaza, #625. 813/992-8881. Hrs: 11:30 am–10 pm; Fri & Sat to 11 pm; Sun to 9 pm. Closed Thanksgiving. Chinese, Amer menu. Bar; Fri, Sat to 2 am. Semi-a la carte: lunch $3.95–$5.95, dinner $5.95–$14.95. Child's meals. Specializes in Cantonese and Szechwan dishes. Entertainment Fri, Sat. Parking. Three dining rms; Oriental motif. Cr cds: A, MC, V.

★ ★ **ROOFTOP.** 25999 Hickory Blvd, in Casa Bonita Plaza. 813/992-0033. Hrs: 11:30 am–2:30 pm, 5–9:30 pm; Fri to 10 pm; Sat 5–10 pm; Sun 5–9:30 pm; Sun brunch 10:30 am–2 pm. Closed Dec 25. Res accepted. Continental menu. Bar. Semi-a la carte: lunch $4.95–$9.95, dinner $7.95–$19.95. Sun brunch $12.95. Child's meals. Specializes in fresh seafood, lamb, prime rib, grouper maison. En-tertainment in season Tues–Sat; summer Fri & Sat. Nautical decor. Scenic view of inlet. Cr cds: A, C, D, MC, V.

★ **TONY ZANGRILLI'S.** 3300 Bonita Beach Rd, #152, at Bonita Springs Shopping Ctr. 813/947-1202. Hrs: 11:30 am–3:30 pm, 5–10 pm. Closed major hols. Italian menu. Wine, beer. Semi-a la carte: lunch $3.50–$6.50, dinner $7.50–$19.95. Child's meals. Specializes in fresh seafood, steaks, chops. Cr cds: DS, MC, V.

Boynton Beach (E-5)

Pop: 46,194 **Elev:** 16 ft **Area code:** 407

Fishing docks and two marinas make Boynton Beach a gateway to Sailfish Alley, five minutes away in the Gulf Stream, and Kingfish Circle, another Gulf Stream spot where king mackerels are found. Boynton Beach Inlet connects the Intracoastal Waterway and Lake Worth with the Atlantic Ocean.

What to See and Do

1. **Fishing, boating.** Pioneer Canal Park at NW 13th Ave and 8th St; drift boat fishing at Sea Mist Marina on E Ocean Ave at Intracoastal Bridge; fishing at Boynton Inlet; launching ramps, fishing pier and picnicking at Boat Club Park, N of town, off US 1 at Oak St.

2. **Arthur R. Marshall Loxahatchee National Wildlife Refuge.** 10 mi W via FL 804 to US 441, then 2 mi S. More than 145,000 acres of freshwater marsh in the Everglades. Fishing; boating (rentals), guided airboat tours (fee). Nature, canoe trails. Concessions. Visitor center. (Daily) Golden Eagle, Golden Age, Golden Access pass-

ports accepted (see INTRODUCTION). Contact Rte 1, Box 278, 33437; 734-8303. Per vehicle ¢¢; Per pedestrian ¢

(For further information contact the Greater Boynton Beach Chamber of Commerce, 639 E Ocean Ave, Suite 108, 33435; 732-9501.)

Annual Events

Boynton's GALA. Civic Center, 128 E Ocean Ave. Selected arts & crafts by area artists. Usually last wkend Mar.

Seafood Fest. Late Sept.

(See Boca Raton, Delray Beach, Palm Beach, Pompano Beach, West Palm Beach)

Motels

★ **ANN MARIE.** *911 S Federal Hwy (US 1) (33435). 407/732-9283.* 14 rms, 3 kits. Mid-Dec–late Apr: S, D $56–$66; each addl $7; lower rates rest of yr. Crib $5. TV; cable. Pool. Restaurant adj open 24 hrs. Ck-out 11 am. Refrigerators. Private patios. Picnic tables, grill. Cr cds: A, DS, MC, V.

✔ ★ **KNIGHTS INN.** *(1255 Hypoluxo Rd, Lantana 33462) N on I-95 exit 45. 407/585-3970; res: 800/843-5644; FAX 407/586-3028.* 131 units, 13 kits. Jan–Apr: S $50–$57; D $52–$59; each addl $3; kits. $62–$75; under 18 free; lower rates rest of yr. Crib free. TV; cable. Pool. Complimentary coffee in lobby. Restaurant adj 6 am–11 pm; wkends to 1 am. Ck-out noon. Cr cds: A, C, D, DS, ER, MC, V.

✔ ★ **SHANE'S.** *2607 S Federal Hwy (US 1) (33435). 407/732-4446; res: 800/782-4446; FAX 407/731-0325.* 21 units, 10 kits. Mid-Dec–mid-Apr: S, D, kit. units $42–$64; each addl $6; under 12 free; varied lower rates rest of yr. TV; cable. Heated pool. Restaurant adj 6 am–3 pm. Ck-out 11 am. Lawn games. Refrigerators. Private patios. Picnic tables, grills. Cr cds: A, D, DS, MC, V.

Motor Hotels

★ ★ ★ **HOLIDAY INN CATALINA.** *1601 N Congress Ave (33426). 407/737-4600; FAX 407/734-6523.* 150 rms, 4 story. Dec–Apr: S $49–$109; D $59–$119; each addl $10; under 18 free; lower rates rest of yr. Crib free. TV; cable. Heated pool; whirlpool. Restaurant 7 am–2 pm, 5–9 pm. Rm serv. Bar 4 pm–2 am, Sat from 8 pm, closed Sun; disc jockey, dancing. Ck-out noon. Meeting rms. Bellhops. Balconies. Cr cds: A, C, D, DS, ER, MC, V, JCB.

★ ★ **RAMADA INN.** *1935 S Federal Hwy (US 1) (33435). 407/736-5805; FAX 407/736-5805, ext 190.* 150 rms, 4 story, 32 suites. Feb–wk after Easter: S, D $84–$99; each addl $10; suites $99–$119; under 18 free; lower rates rest of yr. Crib free. TV; cable. Heated pool; poolside serv. Restaurant 7:30 am–10 pm. Bar from 3 pm. Ck-out noon. Coin lndry. Meeting rms. Lighted tennis. Refrigerator, wet bar in suites. Picnic tables. Cr cds: A, C, D, DS, MC, V, JCB.

Restaurants

★ **BANANA BOAT.** *739 E Ocean Ave. 407/732-9400.* Hrs: 11–2 am; Sun from 9 am. Bar. Semi-a la carte: bkfst $4–$9, lunch $5–$14, dinner $7–$23. Specializes in fresh seafood, conch chowder, shrimp scampi. Reggae band Sun. Parking. Outdoor dining. Nautical artifacts; on Intracoastal Waterway. Cr cds: A, MC, V.

★ ★ ★ **BENVENUTO.** *1730 N Federal Hwy (US 1). 407/364-0600.* Hrs: 4:30–10 pm; Sun brunch 11:30 am–2:30 pm. Italian, Amer menu. Res accepted. Bar. Wine list. Semi-a la carte: dinner $10–$18. Complete meals: dinner $13–$23. Specializes in seafood, veal, beef. Own baking. Valet parking. Outdoor dining. Spanish architecture; lighted garden viewed through large picture windows. Cr cds: MC, V.

★ ★ **CHEF'S TOUCH.** *1002 N Federal Hwy (US 1). 407/732-5632.* Hrs: 5:30–10 pm. Closed Mon; also Sept. Res accepted. Austrian menu. A la carte entrees: dinner $8.75–$25.50. Specialties: Salzburger nocken, veal chops. Valet parking. Cr cds: MC, V.

★ ★ **LUCILLE & OTLEY'S.** *1021 S Federal Hwy (US 1). 407/732-5930.* Hrs: 5–9 pm; Sun from noon. Closed Mon; also mid-May–late Oct. Serv bar. Semi-a la carte: dinner $9.25–$18.25. Child's meals. Specialties: chicken shortcake, lemon meringue pie. Parking. Family-owned. Cr cds: MC, V.

✔ ★ **TWO GEORGES HARBOR HUT.** *728 Casaloma Blvd, on Intracoastal Waterway at E Ocean Ave drawbridge, Boynton Marina. 407/736-2717.* Hrs: 11 am–10 pm. Closed Dec 25. Res accepted. No A/C. Bar. A la carte entrees: lunch $3.95–$8, dinner $5.50–$15. Complete meals: dinner $7.95–$21.95. Specializes in fresh seafood, conch fritters, Key lime pie. Parking. Outdoor dining. Open waterside building with woven thatched roof. Cr cds: DS, MC, V.

Bradenton (D-3)

Settled: 1878 **Pop:** 43,779 **Elev:** 23 ft **Area code:** 813

Located on the Manatee River, Bradenton provides access to river, bay and Gulf fishing, as well as 20 miles of white sand beach. The city took the name of Dr. Joseph Braden, whose nearby fort-like house was a refuge for early settlers during Indian attacks.

What to See and Do

1. **South Florida Museum & Bishop Planetarium.** 201 10th St W. Native American and natural history exhibits; Spanish plaza; historical dioramas; dental and medical exhibits; manatee education & research facility. Planetarium shows. (Daily exc Mon; closed Jan 1, Thanksgiving, Dec 25). Phone 746-4132 or -STAR (planetarium). ¢¢

2. **Manatee Village Historical Park.** 6th Ave E and 15th St E. Park contains five renovated historic buildings: First Court House (1800s); old church (1887); Wiggins Store Museum (1903); one-room schoolhouse (1908); and the Stephens House (1912), built in a style known as Cracker Gothic, and an excellent example of a Florida rural farm house in the period between the 1870s and World War I. (Sept–June, daily exc Sat; rest of yr, Mon–Fri; closed hols & Sun preceding Mon hols) Phone 749-7165. **Free.**

3. **Gamble Plantation State Historic Site.** 1 mi N, then 2 mi E on US 301 in Ellenton. Confederate memorial and the only antebellum house surviving in south Florida. Major Robert Gamble ran a 3,500-acre sugar plantation and refinery here with 190 slaves. In May, 1865, Judah P. Benjamin, Secretary of State of the Confederacy, fled to the plantation to hide from Union troops. Avoiding a surprise raid by Union forces, Benjamin escaped to Bimini and then to Nassau and England. Restored mansion furnished with period pieces. Picnicking. Visitor center with displays (daily; closed Jan 1, Thanksgiving, Dec 25). Mansion (Thurs–Mon, by tour only; closed Jan 1, Thanksgiving, Dec 25). Phone 723-4536. Mansion ¢

4. **De Soto National Memorial.** 2 mi N off FL 64, at end of 75th St NW; on Tampa Bay. At a spot believed to be somewhere near this memorial, Don Hernando De Soto landed on May 30, 1539, with 600 conquistadores to begin the first European expedition into the

interior of what is now the southeastern United States. In a 4,000-mile, 4-year wilderness odyssey, De Soto and his army explored beyond the Mississippi, staking out claims to a vast empire for Spain. Visitor center has weapons and armor of the De Soto era, movie depicting the De Soto expedition; living history area depicts aspects of 16th-century Spanish life (Dec–mid-Apr, daily); self-guided nature trail along beach and through mangrove swamp. (Daily) Phone 792-0458 or -5094. **Free.**

(For further information contact the Manatee County Convention and Visitors Bureau, 1111 3rd Ave W, Suite 180, PO Box 1000, 34206; 746-5989.)

Annual Event

De Soto Celebration. Month-long festival. Phone 747-1998. Late Mar–late Apr.

Seasonal Event

Professional baseball. McKechnie Field, on 9th St at 17th Ave W. Pittsburgh Pirates spring training; exhibition games. Phone 747-3031. Early Mar–early Apr.

(See St Petersburg, Sarasota)

Motels

★★**BEST WESTERN INN-ELLENTON.** *(5218 17th St E, Ellenton 34222)* Off I-75 exit 43. 813/729-8505; FAX 813/729-1110. 73 rms, 2 story, 11 kits. Feb–Apr: S $75–$85; D $80–$90; each addl $5; kits. $100–$110; under 12 free; lower rates rest of yr. Crib free. Pet accepted, some restrictions. TV; cable. Heated pool; whirlpool. Complimentary coffee in lobby. Restaurant nearby. Ck-out noon. Coin lndry. Cr cds: A, C, D, DS, ER, MC, V.

★★**CATALINA BEACH RESORT.** *(1325 Gulf Dr N, Bradenton Beach 34217)* W via FL 64, S on FL 789, on Anna Maria Island. 813/778-6611. 32 units, 2 story, 27 kits. Feb–Apr: S, D $72–$87; each addl $5; 1-bedrm apts $102; 2-bedrm apts $114; wkly rates; lower rates rest of yr. Crib $5. TV. Heated pool. Restaurant 5–10 pm. Ck-out 11 am. Coin lndry. Lawn games. Boat rentals. Picnic tables, grills. Private Gulf beach opp; dock. Cr cds: A, C, D, MC, V.

✔★**HoJo INN.** 6511 14th St W (US 41) (34207), near Sarasota-Bradenton Airport. 813/756-8399; FAX 813/755-1387. 49 units, 2 story, 10 kits. Feb–Apr: S $55; D $70; kits. $60–$70; under 18 free; wkly rates in summer; lower rates rest of yr. Crib free. Pet accepted, some restrictions; $5–$8. TV; cable. Heated pool. Complimentary continental bkfst, coffee. Restaurant adj 9 am–9 pm. Ck-out 11 am. Coin lndry. Free airport transportation. Some refrigerators. Cr cds: A, C, D, DS, MC, V, JCB.

★★**PARK INN CLUB.** 4450 47th St W (34210). 813/795-4633; FAX 813/795-0808. 128 rms, 3 story, 28 suites. Mid-Jan–Easter: S, D $80–$86; each addl $6; suites $98–$105; under 18 free; lower rates rest of yr. Crib free. TV; cable. Heated pool; whirlpool. Complimentary continental bkfst. Restaurant adj 11 am–9 pm. Ck-out noon. Meeting rms. Health club privileges. Bathrm phones. Cr cds: A, C, D, DS, ER, MC, V, JCB.

★**SILVER SURF.** *(1301 Gulf Dr, Bradenton Beach 34217)* 10 mi W on FL 684. 813/778-6626; res: 800/441-7873; FAX 813/778-4308. 49 units, 3 story, 10 kits. Feb–Apr: S, D $66–$91; each addl $8; kits. $79–$91; wkly rates; lower rates rest of yr. Crib $3. TV; cable.

Heated pool. Restaurant adj 7 am–9 pm. Ck-out 11 am. Refrigerators; many wet bars. Picnic tables. Opp Gulf; private beach. Cr cds: MC, V.

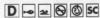

Motor Hotel

★★★**HOLIDAY INN RIVERFRONT.** *100 Riverfront Dr W (34205).* 813/747-3727; FAX 813/746-4289. 153 rms, 5 story, 51 suites. Jan–Apr: S $99–$109; D $109–$119; each addl $10; suites $119–$129; under 18 free; wkend packages off-season; lower rates rest of yr. Crib free. TV. Heated pool; whirlpool, poolside serv. Restaurant 6:30 am–10 pm. Rm serv. Bar 11–2 am; entertainment, dancing. Ck-out noon. Meeting rms. Bellhops. Sundries. Gift shop. Health club privileges. Balconies. Picnic tables. On Manatee River. Cr cds: A, C, D, DS, MC, V, JCB.

Inn

★★**FIVE OAKS.** *(1102 Riverside Dr, Palmetto 34221)* N off US 41. 813/723-1236. 4 rms, 2 story. Some rm phones. Oct–Apr: S, D $65–$100; wkly, monthly rates; lower rates rest of yr. Adults only. TV rm. Complimentary full bkfst, tea & sherry. Ck-out 11 am, ck-in 4 pm. Airport transportation. Bicycles. Umbrella tables, grills. Library. Built 1912 from plans out of Sears Roebuck catalog. Opp river. Cr cds: MC, V.

Restaurants

★★**BEACH BISTRO.** *(6600 Gulf Dr, Holmes Beach)* 813/778-6444. Hrs: 11:30 am–2:30 pm, 5:30–9:30 pm. Closed some major hols. Res accepted. Continental menu. Bar. Semi-a la carte: lunch $5.95–$11.95, dinner $10.95–$26. Specializes in rack of lamb, seafood, bouillabaisse. Parking. Large wine selection. View of gulf. Cr cds: A, D, MC, V.

Ⓓ

★**CAFE ROBAR.** *(204 Pine St, Anna Maria Island)* 813/778-6969. Hrs: 11 am–10 pm; wkends 9:30 am–midnght; Sun brunch to 2 pm. Res accepted. Bar to 2 am. Semi-a la carte: lunch $3.95–$7.95, dinner $9.50–$22.50. Sun brunch $5.25–$7.95. Child's meals. Specializes in steak, veal. Pianist exc Mon. Cr cds: A, DS, MC, V.

Ⓓ

✔★**CHINA PALACE.** 5131 14th St W (US 41). 813/755-3758. Hrs: 11:30 am–9:30 pm; Fri to 10 pm; Sat noon–10 pm. Closed Thanksgiving. Res accepted. Chinese menu. Bar. Semi-a la carte: lunch $3.75–$7, dinner $6.50–$15.50. Buffet: lunch $4.95–$7.25. Specializes in Szechwan, Cantonese dishes. Parking. Authentic Chinese decor. Cr cds: A, C, D, DS, MC, V.

Ⓓ SC

✔★**GULF DRIVE CAFE.** *(900 Gulf Dr N, Bradenton Beach)* 10 mi W on FL 684 (Cortez Rd) to Gulf Dr. 813/778-1919. Hrs: 7 am–9:30 pm. Closed Dec 25. Semi-a la carte: bkfst $1.25–$4.95, lunch $3.70–$5.95, dinner $5.95–$9.25. Child's meals. Specializes in Belgian waffles, fresh fish. Parking. Outdoor dining. Ocean view. No cr cds accepted.

Ⓓ

★★**LEE'S CRAB TRAP II.** *(4815 Memphis Rd, Ellenton)* Off I-75 exit 43. 813/729-7777. Hrs: 11:30 am–9:30 pm; Fri, Sat to 10 pm. Closed Thanksgiving, Dec 25. Bar. Semi-a la carte: lunch $4–$9, dinner $8–$35. Child's meals. Specializes in crab dishes, Florida seafood. Parking. Nautical decor. Cr cds: DS, MC, V.

Ⓓ

✔★**LEVEROCK'S SEAFOOD HOUSE.** 12320 Manatee Ave W. 813/794-8900. Hrs: 11 am–10 pm; early-bird dinner 3–6 pm. Closed Thanksgiving, Dec 25. Bar. Semi-a la carte: lunch $3.95–$7.95, dinner

$7.95–$12.50. Child's meals. Specializes in seafood, steak, chicken. Parking. View of bay. Cr cds: A, D, DS, MC, V.

✔ ★MILLER'S DUTCH KITCH'N. *3401 14th St W (US 41). 813/746-8253.* Hrs: 11 am–8 pm. Closed Sun; some major hols; also 2 wks in summer. Amish menu. Semi-a la carte: lunch $3–$8.50, dinner $5–$9.25. Child's meals. Specialties: Dutch casserole, beef tips & noodles. Own pies. Parking. Totally nonsmoking. No cr cds accepted.

✔ ★ ★REGATTA POINTE GRILLE. *(995 Riverside Dr, Palmetto) 1 mi N on US 41. 813/722-7999.* Hrs: noon–9 pm. Res accepted. Continental menu. Semi-a la carte: lunch $4.95–$8.95, dinner $8.95–$15.95. Child's meals. Specializes in Angus beef. Parking. Outdoor dining. On Manatee River. Cr cds: MC, V.

★ ★SEAFOOD SHACK. *(4110 127th St W, Cortez) 10 mi W on FL 648 (Cortez Rd), east side of bridge. 813/794-1235.* Hrs: 11:30 am–9 pm; Fri, Sat to 10 pm. Closed Thanksgiving, Dec 25. Bar. Semi-a la carte: lunch $3.95–$10.95, dinner $5.95–$19.95. Specializes in seafood. Parking. Paddlewheel boat rides avail. Cr cds: A, MC, V.

Brooksville (C-3)

Pop: 7,440 **Elev:** 230 ft **Area code:** 904

Amid hilly countryside unusual to Florida lies Brooksville, a center for limestone quarrying, cement production, and forest and dairy products.

What to See and Do

1. **Weeki Wachee Spring, the City of Mermaids.** 12 mi W on FL 50 at jct US 19. Underwater amphitheater combines nature and engineering to showcase underwater mermaid shows. The spring, which produces more than 168 million gallons of water daily, has a measured depth of 250 feet, but goes deeper. After a former Navy frogman developed underwater breathing techniques at Weeki Wachee, he recognized the commercial possibilities and, in 1947, had an auditorium built 6 feet below the surface. The first underwater show was so successful that a second, million-dollar auditorium seating 500 was built 16 feet below the surface.

   Today's visitors watch underwater performances through 19 plate-glass windows nearly 3 inches thick. Each performance lasts approximately 30 minutes, with 4 performances daily. Other attractions include Wilderness River Cruise, down the Weeki Wachee River to Pelican Orphanage. Various 30-minute shows include a live performance of Hans Christian Andersen's *The Little Mermaid*; Free-Flying Exotic Birds Show, with macaws and cockatoos performing tricks; and Birds of Prey Show with free-flying eagles, hawks, vultures and owls performing within close view. Also Animal Forest Petting Zoo. (Daily) Phone 596-2062 or 800/678-9335 (FL). ¢¢¢¢

2. **Buccaneer Bay.** 12 mi W on FL 50, at jct US 19, adj to Weeki Wachee Spring (see #1). Natural spring water park features 140-foot sand beach, 3 water flumes, Fantasy Island for children, rope swings, game arcades, 2 volleyball courts; picnicking; concessions. (Apr–Sept, daily) Phone 596-2062 or 800/678-9335 (FL). ¢¢¢

(For further information contact the Greater Hernando Chambers of Commerce, 101 E Fort Dade Ave, 34601; 796-4580.)

Annual Events

Brooksville Raid Festival. Civil War reenactment of the July, 1864 Union attack on Brooksville; more than 700 participants, blue/gray ball, barbecue, museum display. Phone 796-4580. Jan.

Hernando County Fair. Phone 796-4552. 1 wk early Apr.

(For accommodations see Homosassa Springs)

Cape Coral (E-3)

Pop: 74,991 **Elev:** 10 ft **Area code:** 813 **Zip:** 33904

Settled only since 1958 and incorporated since 1970, Cape Coral is rapidly growing and has the second largest area of Florida's cities. Water-related activities on the Caloosahatchee River are popular.

(For information about this area contact the Chamber of Southwest Florida Welcome Center, 2051 Cape Coral Pkwy; 433-3321.)

(See Bonita Springs, Fort Myers, Sanibel & Captiva Islands)

Motels

★ ★CASA LOMA. *3608 Del Prado Blvd. 813/549-6000.* 47 kit. units in 2 bldgs, 2 story. Feb–Mar: S, D $65–$75; each addl $5; wkly rates; lower rates rest of yr. Crib $5. TV; cable. Pool. Restaurant nearby. Ck-out 11 am. Coin lndry. Private patios, balconies. Picnic tables. On canal. Cr cds: A, DS, MC, V.

✔ ★DEL PRADO INN. *1502 Miramar St, at Del Prado Blvd. 813/542-3151; res: 800/231-6818; FAX 813/542-3151, ext 187.* 125 rms, 2 story. Mid-Dec–Apr: S, D $60–$75; each addl $6; under 12 free; lower rates rest of yr. Crib free. Pet accepted, some restrictions. TV; cable. Heated pool; poolside serv. Restaurant 7 am–10 pm. Bar; entertainment. Ck-out 11 am. Coin lndry. Sundries. Lawn games. Refrigerators. Dockage. Cr cds: A, DS, MC, V.

★ ★QUALITY INN. *1538 Cape Coral Pkwy. 813/542-2121; FAX 813/542-6319.* 142 rms, 5 story. Feb–Apr: S, D $75–$80; each addl $10; under 18 free; lower rates rest of yr. Crib free. Pet accepted; $5–$10 per day. TV; cable. Pool; poolside serv. Complimentary continental bkfst. Restaurant nearby. Ck-out 11 am. Coin lndry. Meeting rm. Cr cds: A, C, D, DS, ER, MC, V, JCB.

Resort

★ ★CAPE CORAL GOLF & TENNIS RESORT. *4003 Palm Tree Blvd. 813/542-3191; res: 800/648-1475, ext 276; FAX 813/542-4694.* 100 rms, 2 story. Late Dec–Apr: S, D $90–$110; each addl $10; under 17 free; golf, tennis packages; lower rates rest of yr. Crib free. TV; cable. Heated pool; poolside serv. Restaurant 7 am–9 pm. Rm serv. Bar; entertainment, dancing. Ck-out noon. Meeting rms. 8 tennis courts, 5 lighted, pro. 18-hole golf, greens fee $53 (incl half-cart), pro, putting green, driving range. Lawn games. Cr cds: A, C, D, DS, MC, V.

Restaurants

✔ ★ ★ARIANI. *1529 SE 15th Terrace, in Del Prado Mall. 813/772-8000.* Hrs: 5–10 pm. Closed Sun; Easter, Thanksgiving, Dec 25. Res accepted. Northern Italian menu. Bar. Semi-a la carte: dinner $5.95–$13.95. Child's meals. Specialties: veal & chicken scallopini, eggplant rolatine parmigiana. Intimate dining. Cr cds: A, DS, MC, V.

✔ ★JIMBO'S. *1604 SE 46th St. 813/549-1818.* Hrs: 7 am–9 pm. Closed Jan 1, Thanksgiving, Dec 25. Semi-a la carte: bkfst $1.79–$4.50, lunch $2.50–$3.95, dinner $3.95–$9.50. Specialties:

chicken & steak teriyaki, steak & fried shrimp, barbecued ribs. Parking. No cr cds accepted.

[D]

★★**MR. C'S.** *850 Lafayette St.* 813/542-2001. Hrs: 4:30–10 pm; Sun 4–9 pm; early-bird dinner 4:30–5:45 pm. Closed Mon; Dec 25. Res accepted. Bar. Semi-a la carte: dinner $8.95–$16.95. Child's meals. Specializes in fresh seafood, steak, prime rib. Parking. Cr cds: MC, V.

[D] [SC]

✔ ★★**VELVET TURTLE.** *1404-A Cape Coral Pkwy E.* 813/549-9000. Hrs: 5–9 pm; Fri, Sat to 10 pm. Closed Sun. Res accepted. Continental menu. Bar. A la carte entrees: dinner $7.95–$14.95. Child's meals. Specializes in seafood. Parking. Intimate atmosphere. Cr cds: DS, MC, V.

[D]

Captiva Island
(see Sanibel & Captiva Islands)

Cedar Key (B-2)

Pop: 668 **Elev:** 5 ft **Area code:** 904 **Zip:** 32625

All that remains of the cedars that once lined the shores of this key is the name. Cedar Key, once one of the largest cities in the state, is today a quiet island-city with extensive fishing, crabbing and oystering.

What to See and Do

1. **Cedar Key State Museum.** W of town, on Museum Dr, overlooking Gulf of Mexico. Dioramas and exhibits illustrate history of Cedar Key; shell collection. (Thurs–Mon) Phone 543-5350. ¢
2. **Cedar Key Historical Society Museum.** Corner of 2nd St & FL 24. Early photos, maps, records of Cedar Key; old pencil mill exhibit; self-guided tour. (Daily) Phone 543-5549. ¢

(For further information contact the Cedar Key Area Chamber of Commerce, 2nd St, PO Box 610; 543-5600.)

Annual Event

Seafood Festival. 3rd wkend Oct.

Motel

★★**ISLAND PLACE.** *(Box 687) 1st & C Street.* 904/543-5306 or -5307. 30 kit. condos, 2 story. Kit. condo $75–$130; each addl $5; under 5 free; higher rates: hols, special events. TV; cable. Pool; sauna. Restaurant nearby. Ck-out 11 am. Hot tub. Refrigerators. Balconies. Washer, dryer, dishwasher in all units. Cr cds: DS, MC, V.

Inn

✔ ★★**ISLAND HOTEL.** *(PO Box 460) 2nd & B Streets.* 904/543-5111. 10 rms, 6 with bath, 2 story. No rm phones. S, D $65–$75; each addl $10; under 12 free; wkly rates; wknd package; higher rates special events. TV in sitting rm; cable. Complimentary full bkfst. Restaurant 8–10 am, 6–9:30 pm; hrs vary. Bar 5–11 pm, closed Tues. Ck-out 11 am, ck-in 2 pm. Built 1859; 11-inch tabby exterior walls. Traditional ambience; some feather beds, claw foot tubs. Totally nonsmoking. Cr cds: MC, V.

Restaurant

★★**THE CAPTAIN'S TABLE.** *At west end of Pier.* 904/543-5441. Hrs: 11 am–10 pm. Res accepted. Semi-a la carte: lunch $4.95–$6.95, dinner $8.95–$24.95. Child's meals. Specialties: island lime pie, fresh seafood. Entertainment Fri, Sat. Outdoor dining. Family-owned. Cr cds: MC, V.

Chiefland (B-2)

Founded: 1845 **Pop:** 1,917 **Elev:** 31 ft **Area code:** 904 **Zip:** 32626

Indian and non-Indian farmers once lived harmoniously in the area. The town name honors those Indian neighbors. Peanuts, watermelons, tobacco and corn are processed in and marketed from Chiefland.

What to See and Do

Manatee Springs State Park. 1 mi N on US 19/98, then 6 mi W on FL 320. The major attraction of this 2,075-acre park is a natural spring that produces 117 million gallons of water daily. Swimming, skin and scuba diving, bathhouse, wading pool; fishing; boat dock (canoe rentals). Nature trails, boardwalk. Picnicking, concession. Camping (dump station). Standard hrs, fees. Phone 493-6072.

(For further information contact the Chamber of Commerce, 16 NE 1st Ave, PO Box 1397; 493-1849.)

Annual Event

Watermelon Festival. Watermelon-eating & seed-spitting contests, parade, beauty contest, watermelon auction. 3rd Sat June.

(For accommodations see Cedar Key, Gainesville)

Clearwater (C-3)

Settled: 1842 **Pop:** 98,784 **Elev:** 24 ft **Area code:** 813

Clearwater is a tourist city that has retained its quiet ways under pressure of rapid population growth. The town is the seat of Pinellas County and has numerous light industries.

What to See and Do

1. **Clearwater Marine Science Center.** 249 Windward Passage, off Memorial Causeway. Center, which includes aquarium, research laboratories and educational programs, is the only facility on Florida's west coast equipped for the rescue and treatment of marine mammals and sea turtles. Visitors watch progress and feeding of recuperating sea turtles. (Daily; closed major hols) Phone 441-1790. ¢¢
2. **Florida Gulf Coast Art Center.** 222 Ponce de Leon Blvd in Belleair. Regional and national exhibits; school. (Daily; may be closed between shows) Phone 584-8634. **Free.**
3. **Moccasin Lake Nature Park.** 2750 Park Trail Lane. An environmental and energy education center consisting of 50-acre wilderness preserve; nature trails and boardwalks (1¼ mi); native wildlife and plant exhibits; alternative energy displays. Guided tours (by appt; fee). Special programs (fee). (Daily exc Mon; closed Jan 1, July 4, Thanksgiving, Dec 25) Phone 462-6024. ¢
4. **Heritage Park.** S via US 19, then 5 mi W via FL 688 at 11909 125th St N in Largo. Historical museum and 21-acre village with 22 historic structures. Changing displays; seasonal craft demonstrations. (Tues–Sat, also Sun afternoons; closed some major hols) Donation. Phone 588-8123.

5. Boatyard Village. 16100 Fairchild Dr. Shops and restaurants in 1890s-style fishing village. (Daily) Phone 535-4678.

6. Florida Orchestra concerts. Ruth Eckerd Hall & Tampa Bay Performing Arts Center. Classical and pops performances. (Sept–May) Phone 800/662-7286 or 286-2403 (Tampa).

7. Sightseeing.

   Clearwater Ferry Service. W end of Drew St. Water taxi to Clearwater Beach, Caladesi Island; special tours to Tarpon Springs (Tues–Sat; res required). (Daily exc Mon) Phone 442-7433. Taxi to beach ¢; Tarpon Springs tour (includes lunch) ¢¢¢¢¢

   Gray Line bus tours. Contact PO Box 145, St Petersburg 33731; 822-3577.

(For further information contact the Greater Clearwater Chamber of Commerce, 128 N Osceola Ave, PO Box 2457, 34617, phone 461-0011, or the Pinellas Suncoast Convention & Visitors Bureau, Florida Suncoast Dome, 1 Stadium Dr, Suite A, St Petersburg 37705, phone 800/951-1111.)

Annual Events

Fun 'n Sun Festival. Pageant, parade, city-wide festivities mark end of winter season. 10 days Apr–May.

Jazz Holiday. Coachman Park. One of the Southeast's largest free jazz festivals. 3rd wkend Oct.

Seasonal Event

Professional baseball. Jack Russell Memorial Stadium, 800 Phillies Dr. Philadelphia Phillies spring training, exhibition games, early Mar–early Apr; Class A Clearwater Phillies, Florida State League, Apr–Aug. Phone 441-8638.

(See Clearwater Beach, Dunedin, St Petersburg, Tampa, Tarpon Springs)

Motels

★**BAY QUEEN.** *1925 Edgewater Dr (34615).* 813/441-3295. 18 units, 1–2 story, 16 kits. Mid-Dec–late Apr: S, D $58–$70; each addl $5; kit. units $330–$370/wk; lower rates rest of yr. Crib free. TV. Pool. Restaurant adj 7 am–2 pm. Ck-out 11 am. Lawn games. Refrigerators. Overlooks Clearwater Bay. Cr cds: MC, V.

✔★★**BEST WESTERN CLEARWATER CENTRAL.** *21252 US 19N (34625), 1 blk N of FL 60.* 813/799-1565; FAX 813/797-6801. 270 rms, 2 story. Feb–mid-Apr: S, D $55–$65; each addl $5; under 12 free; lower rates rest of yr. Crib free. TV; cable. 2 heated pools; whirlpool. Restaurant adj. Ck-out noon. Coin lndry. Meeting rm. Tennis. Lawn games. Cr cds: A, C, D, DS, ER, MC, V.

★★★**COURTYARD BY MARRIOTT.** *3131 Executive Dr (34622).* 813/572-8484; FAX 813/572-6991. 149 rms, 3 story. Jan–Apr: S $80–$86; D $90–$96; suites $95–$105; under 12 free; wkend rates; lower rates rest of yr. Crib free. TV; cable. Heated pool. Complimentary coffee in rms. Restaurant 6:30 am–2 pm, 5–10 pm. Bar 4–11 pm. Ck-out noon. Coin lndry. Meeting rms. Valet serv. Exercise equipt; weight machine, bicycles, whirlpool. Health club privileges. Refrigerator in suites. Cr cds: A, C, D, DS, MC, V.

✔★**EDGEWATER DRIVE.** *1919 Edgewater Dr (34615).* 813/446-7858. 22 rms, 1–2 story, 12 kits. Jan–Apr: S, D $38–$65; each addl $5; kit. units $375–$425/wk; some wkend rates; lower rates rest of yr. Crib $5. TV. Pool. Restaurant 7 am–2 pm. Ck-out 11 am (kit. units 10 am). Coin lndry. Refrigerators. Private fishing dock. On Clearwater Bay. Cr cds: A, MC, V.

★★**HAMPTON INN.** *3655 Hospitality Ln (34622), at Ulmerton Rd.* 813/577-9200; FAX 813/572-8931. 118 rms, 2 story, some kits. Jan–Apr: S, D $60–$82; kit. units $70–$93; under 18 free; wkly rates; lower rates rest of yr. Crib free. TV; cable. Pool. Complimentary continental bkfst. Restaurant nearby. Ck-out noon. Coin lndry. Meeting rm. Valet serv. Lighted tennis. Exercise equipt; weights, stair machine, whirlpool, sauna. Cr cds: A, C, D, DS, ER, MC, V.

★★**HOLIDAY INN EXPRESS.** *13625 ICOT Blvd (34620), in Ruben ICOT Ctr.* 813/536-7275; FAX 813/530-3053. 128 rms, 3 story, 28 suites. S $55–$75; D $60–$80; each addl $5; suites $80–$90; under 18 free. Crib free. TV; cable. Heated pool. Complimentary continental bkfst. Restaurant opp 11 am–11 pm. Ck-out noon. Meeting rms. Exercise equipt; weight machine, bicycle, whirlpool. Bathrm phones. Cr cds: A, C, D, DS, ER, MC, V, JCB.

★**HOWARD JOHNSON.** *20788 US 19N (34625), at jct FL 60.* 813/797-5021; FAX 813/797-5021, ext 306. 86 rms, 2 story. Jan–mid-Apr: S, D $43–$95; under 18 free; lower rates rest of yr. Crib free. TV. Pool. Ck-out 11 am. Coin lndry. Meeting rm. Private patios, balconies. Cr cds: A, C, D, DS, ER, MC, V.

★★**LA QUINTA.** *3301 Ulmerton Rd (34622), off I-275 at FL 688 exit.* 813/572-7222; FAX 813/572-0076. 115 units. Jan–May: S $59; D $69; suites $78–$98; under 18 free; lower rates rest of yr. Crib free. Pet accepted, some restrictions. TV; cable. Heated pool. Continental bkfst. Restaurant adj 6 am–10 pm. Ck-out noon. Coin lndry. Meeting rms. Valet serv. Exercise equipt; weights, bicycles, whirlpool, sauna. Cr cds: A, C, D, DS, MC, V.

★★**RESIDENCE INN BY MARRIOTT.** *5050 Ulmerton Rd (34620), at 49th St, 1 mi E of US 19 on FL 688.* 813/573-4444; FAX 813/572-4446. 88 kit. suites, 2 story. Kit. suites $125–$175; wkly, monthly rates. Pet accepted, some restrictions; $200 refundable and $5 per day. TV; cable. Pool; whirlpool. Continental bkfst. Ck-out noon. Coin lndry. Meeting rms. Valet serv. Lawn games. Fireplaces. Private patios, balconies. Grill. Cr cds: A, C, D, DS, MC, V.

✔★**RODEWAY INN.** *20967 US 19N (34625), at Gulf to Bay Blvd (FL 60).* 813/799-1181; FAX 813/797-8504. 114 rms, 2 story. Feb–Easter: S, D $40–$75; each addl $5; under 18 free; wkly rates; lower rates rest of yr. Crib $6. TV; cable. Pool. Complimentary continental bkfst. Restaurant 6:30–11 am, 6:30–8 pm. Bar; comedy club exc Mon. Ck-out 11 am. Coin lndry. Meeting rms. Valet serv. Cr cds: A, D, DS, MC, V.

✔★**TRAVELODGE-DOWNTOWN.** *711 Cleveland St (34615).* 813/446-9183. 48 rms, 3 story. Jan–Apr: S $47–$53; D $56–$73; each addl $8; under 17 free; some wkend rates; lower rates rest of yr. Crib free. TV; in-rm movies avail. Heated pool. Restaurant adj open 24 hrs. Ck-out 11 am. Refrigerators avail. Balconies. Cr cds: A, C, D, DS, ER, MC, V.

Motor Hotels

★★**COMFORT INN.** *3580 Ulmerton Rd (34622), near St Petersburg/Clearwater Intl Airport.* 813/573-1171; FAX 813/573-8736. 120 rms, 3 story. Feb–Apr: S $64; D $74; each addl $10; suites $85–$99; under 16 free; wkly rates; golf plans; higher rates: Super Bowl, Hall of Fame Bowl; lower rates rest of yr. Crib $10. TV; cable. Heated pool. Complimentary continental bkfst, coffee. Restaurant adj 11 am–10 pm. Bar. Ck-out noon. Meeting rms. Bellhops. Valet serv. Sundries. Free airport transportation. Exercise equipt; weights, bicycle, whirlpool. Cr cds: A, C, D, DS, ER, MC, V, JCB.

★ ★ ★**HOLIDAY INN-AIRPORT.** *3535 Ulmerton Rd (34622). 813/577-9100; FAX 813/573-5022.* 174 rms, 5 story. Feb-Apr: S, D $80.50-$105.50; each addl $10; under 18 free; some wkend rates; lower rates rest of yr. Crib free. TV; cable. Heated pool. Restaurant 7 am-2 pm, 5-10 pm. Rm serv. Bar 11-1:30 am; entertainment Tues-Sat, dancing. Ck-out noon. Coin lndry. Meeting rms. Bellhops. Gift shop. Lighted tennis. Exercise equipt; weights, bicycles, whirlpool. Refrigerators avail. *LUXURY LEVEL:* EXECUTIVE LEVEL. 33 rms, 2 suites. S, D $115-$145; suites $230.50. Private lounge, open bar. Complimentary continental bkfst, refreshments, newspaper.
Cr cds: A, C, D, DS, ER, MC, V, JCB.

★ ★**RAMADA INN.** *26508 US 19N (34621), opp Countryside Mall. 813/796-1234; FAX 813/796-0452.* 128 rms, 5 story. Feb-mid-Apr: S, D $49-$89; each addl $10; kit. units, suites $89; under 18 free; wkend rates; lower rates rest of yr. Crib free. TV; cable. Pool; whirlpool. Restaurant 6:30 am-1 pm, 5-10 pm. Rm serv. Bar 5 pm-midnight; entertainment Fri & Sat. Ck-out noon. Coin lndry. Meeting rms. Bellhops. Valet serv. Lighted tennis. In-rm whirlpools. Some private patios, balconies. Cr cds: A, C, D, DS, ER, MC, V, JCB.

Resorts

★ ★ ★ ★**BELLEVIEW MIDO RESORT HOTEL.** *25 Belleview Blvd (34617). 813/442-6171; res: 800/237-8947; FAX 813/443-6361.* 292 rms, 4 story. Jan-Apr: S $112-$165; D $124-$185; each addl $20; suites $240-$445; MAP $45 addl per person; lower rates rest of yr. Crib $5. TV; cable. Heated pools; poolside serv. Dining rm 7 am-10 pm. Bars 11-1 am, Sun 1 pm-midnight; entertainment wknds, dancing exc Sun. Ck-out noon. Convention facilities. Valet serv. Specialty shops. Free parking. Airport transportation avail. 4 clay tennis courts, pro. 18-hole golf, pro, putting greens. Bicycles avail. Lawn games. Rec rm. Exercise rm; instructor, weight machine, stair machine, whirlpool, sauna, steam rm. Massage. Spa & fitness center. Free transportation to Cabana Club and gulf beaches. Historic resort hotel built in 1897. On Intracoastal Waterway with dock, 4 boat slips. Cr cds: A, C, D, DS, MC, V, JCB.

★ ★ ★**SAFETY HARBOR SPA.** *(105 N Bayshore Dr, Safety Harbor 34695) 2 mi N of FL 60. 813/726-1161; res 800/237-0155; FAX 813/726-4268.* 212 hotel units, 3-6 story. AP, mid-Dec-mid-Mar: S $244; D $394; wkend rates; lower rates rest of yr. Crib free. TV; cable. 3 heated pools; 2 whirlpools. Dining rm open 24 hrs. Rm serv 24 hrs. Bar; entertainment, dancing. Coin lndry. Meeting rms. Valet serv. Shopping arcade. Barber, beauty shops. Tennis. 18-hole golf privileges; driving range. Bicycles. Lawn games. Soc dir; movies. 300-seat theater. Exercise rm; instructor, weights, bicycles, whirlpool, steam rm, sauna. Fitness programs; masseur, mineral baths. Constructed over five mineral springs. Cr cds: A, C, D, DS, ER, MC, V, JCB.

Restaurants

★ ★ ★**ALFANO'S.** *1704 Clearwater/Largo Rd, in Marketplace West Shopping Ctr. 813/584-2125.* Hrs: 11:30 am-2 pm, 5-10 pm; Sat 5-11 pm; Sun 5-9:30 pm; early-bird dinner 5-6:15 pm. Closed most major hols; also Sun July & Aug. Res accepted. Italian menu. Bar. Extensive wine list. Complete meals: lunch $4.95-$8.95, dinner $8.95-$18.95. Child's meals. Specialties: Caesar salad, veal sacco, roast duckling amaretto. Pianist Mon, Thurs-Sat. Outdoor dining. Contemporary formal atmosphere. Cr cds: A, D, MC, V.

✔ ★**BELLA BISTRO.** *13505 ICOT Blvd. 813/535-6224.* Hrs: 11:30 am-10 pm; Fri to 11 pm; Sun 5-9 pm; Sat buffet 5-9:30 pm.

Closed most major hols. Northern Italian menu. Bar. Semi-a la carte: lunch $5-$10, dinner $5-$15. Buffet: Sat dinner $9.95. Specialties: pizza e calzone, veal salsa Marsala. Own pasta, pastries. Parking. Outdoor dining. Unique imported wood-burning pizza oven. Cr cds: A, DS, MC, V.

★ ★**EUGEN'S.** *(100 N Indian Rocks Rd, Belleair Bluffs) In Plaza 100 Shopping Center. 813/585-6399.* Hrs: 11:30 am-2:30 pm, 4:30-10 pm; Fri to 10:30 pm; Sat 4:30-10:30 pm; Sun 4-10 pm. Closed July 4. Res accepted. Continental menu. Bar. Complete meals: lunch $4.95-$9.50, dinner $12.75-$35. Child's meals. Specialties: rack of lamb, snapper Oscar, Maine lobster. European decor. Cr cds: A, C, D, MC, V.

★ ★**FORBIDDEN CITY.** *25778 US 19N. 813/797-8989.* Hrs: 11:30 am-10 pm; Fri, Sat to 11 pm; early-bird dinner 3:30-6 pm. Res accepted. Chinese menu. Bar. A la carte entrees: lunch $4.95-$6.35, dinner $7.95-$25. Buffet: lunch $5.95. Specialties: Peking duck, cashew chicken, pan-fried dumpling. Pianist Wed-Sun. Parking. Large imported Chinese wood carving. Cr cds: A, D, MC, V.

★ ★**JESSE'S FLAGSHIP.** *20 Island Way. 813/443-6210.* Hrs: 11:30 am-10 pm. Res accepted. Bar. Semi-a la carte: lunch $5.99-$7.99, dinner $8.99-$25.99. Child's meals. Specializes in seafood, steak, prime rib. Own desserts. Parking. Waterside dining; nautical atmosphere. Cr cds: A, D, DS, MC, V.

★ ★**KEY WEST GRILL.** *2660 Gulf-to-Bay Blvd (FL 60). 813/797-1988.* Hrs: 11:30 am-11 pm; Fri, Sat to midnight; Sun to 10 pm. Closed Thanksgiving, Dec 25. Semi-a la carte: lunch $4.45-$5.95, dinner $5.45-$26.95. Child's meals. Specializes in barbecued ribs, fresh fish, stone crab claws (in season). Parking. Outdoor dining. Key West atmosphere. Cr cds: A, D, DS, MC, V.

★**LA POELE D'OR.** *(7705 Ulmerton Rd, Largo) S via Ulmerton Rd, at Belcher, Plaza de Sunus Shopping Center. 813/531-4975.* Hrs: 11:30 am-2 pm, 5-9 pm. Closed Sun, Mon. Res accepted. French menu. Wine, beer. A la carte entrees: lunch $3.95-$8.95, dinner $6.95-$13.95. Specializes in veal, duck, fish. Cr cds: A, MC, V.

✔ ★**LA TOUR EIFFEL.** *(796 Indian Rocks Rd, Belleair Bluffs) FL Alt 19S to West Bay Dr, then right to Indian Rocks Rd. 813/581-6530.* Hrs: 11 am-2 pm, 5:30-9 pm; Sat from 5:30 pm; Sat, Sun brunch 9 am-2 pm. Closed Mon; Jan 1, July 4, Thanksgiving. Res accepted. French menu. Wine, beer. A la carte entrees: lunch $3.50-$4.95, dinner $8.95-$14.95. Sun brunch $4.95-$7.95. Specialties: quiche crêpes, filet au poivre, coquilles St-Jacques. Parking. Romantic Parisian atmosphere. Cr cds: MC, V.

✔ ★**PANDA.** *1201 Cleveland St, in Cleveland Plaza Shopping Ctr. 813/447-3830.* Hrs: 11:30 am-10 pm; Fri, Sat to 11 pm; Sun 5-10 pm. Closed Thanksgiving, Dec 25. Res accepted. Chinese menu. Bar. A la carte entrees: lunch $3.25-$3.95, dinner $3.50-$10.50. Specialties: lichee duck, Pearls of Seven Seas, chicken with garlic sauce. Carved entrance archway of Chinese cypress. Cr cds: A, D, DS, MC, V.

✔ ★**PEKING PALACE.** *1608 Gulf-to-Bay Blvd (FL 60). 813/461-4414.* Hrs: 11:30 am-9:45 pm; Fri to 10:45 pm; Sat 4:30-10:45 pm; Sun noon-9:45 pm; early-bird dinner 3-6 pm. Closed Thanksgiving. Res accepted. Chinese menu. Bar. A la carte entrees: lunch $3.95-$4.95, dinner $4.95-$12. Specialties: Peking duck, orange chicken, fresh whole fish. Parking. Cr cds: A, D, DS, MC, V.

★ ★ ★ **PEPPER MILL.** 1575 S Fort Harrison Ave. 813/449-2988.
Hrs: 11:30 am–2:30 pm, 5–10 pm; Fri to 11 pm; Sat 5–11 pm; Sun 4–9
pm. Closed Jan 1, Dec 25. Res accepted. New American menu. Bar.
Complete meals: lunch $4.95–$6.50, dinner $10.95–$17.95. Child's
meals. Specialties: Maryland crab cakes, shrimp scampi, Pepper Mill
NY steak. Parking. Garden room dining. High wood-beamed ceiling;
panoramic view. Cr cds: A, MC, V.

D

★ ★ **TIO PEPE.** 2930 Gulf-to-Bay Blvd (FL 60). 813/799-3082.
Hrs: 11 am–2:30 pm, 5–11 pm; Fri to 11:30 pm; Sat 5–11:30 pm; Sun
4–10 pm. Closed Mon; Jan 1, Thanksgiving, Dec 25. Res accepted.
Spanish-Mediterranean menu. Bar. Semi-a la carte: lunch
$4.25–$14.95, dinner $9.25–$31.50. Child's meals. Specialties: paella,
zarzuela de marsicos a la Jesús, pompano relleno. Parking. Extensive
wine selection. Spanish decor. Cr cds: MC, V.

D

✔ ★ **TUCSON'S.** 13563 ICOT Blvd. 813/530-0637. Hrs: 11
am–midnight; Fri, Sat to 1 am. Res accepted. Southwestern menu. Bars.
Semi-a la carte: lunch $3.50–$14.50, dinner $4.95–$14.95. Child's
meals. Specializes in fajitas, steak, sandwiches. Parking. Outdoor dining. Southwestern theme; murals on walls. Cr cds: A, MC, V.

D

Clearwater Beach (C-2)

Elev: 24 ft **Area code:** 813 **Zip:** 34630

This four-mile-long island of white sand beaches is connected to the
mainland by Memorial Causeway. The beach extends the full length of
the island and is between 350 and 1,700 feet wide. There is a fishing
pier, and the marina has slips, docks, boat rentals, sailing and a sport
fishing fleet. Skin diving and shelling are also popular activities.

What to See and Do

Sightseeing Cruises.

Admiral Dinner Boat. Clearwater Beach Marina. Triple-deck,
100-foot, 400-passenger cruiser provides luncheon/sightseeing
and dinner/dance cruises. Two departures (daily exc Mon). Phone
462-2628 or 800/444-4814. ¢¢¢–¢¢¢¢¢

Show Queen. Clearwater Beach Marina. Triple-decked, 150-pas-
senger boat cruises along the Clearwater shoreline. Sightseeing
morning cruise (Tues–Sat) and afternoon cruise (daily exc Mon;
lunch avail); also dinner cruise (Oct–Apr) and sunset cruise
(May–Sept). Phone 461-3113. ¢¢¢–¢¢¢¢

Captain Memo's Pirate Ship Cruise. Clearwater Beach Marina.
Pirate ship sails through the Intracoastal Waterway into the Gulf of
Mexico on two-hour cruises. Free refreshments. Three departures
(daily exc Sun). Phone 446-2587. ¢¢¢¢

(For further information contact the Greater Clearwater Chamber
of Commerce, 128 N Osceola Ave, PO Box 2457, Clearwater 34617,
phone 461-0011, or the Pinellas Suncoast Convention & Visitors Bureau, Florida Suncoast Dome, 1 Stadium Dr, St Petersburg 33705,
phone 800/951-1111.)

(See Clearwater, Dunedin, St Petersburg, Tampa, Tarpon Springs)

Motels

✔ ★ **AEGEAN SANDS.** 421 S Gulfview Blvd. 813/447-3464;
res: 800/942-3432. 80 rms, 4 story, 67 kits. Jan–Apr: S, D $55–$115;
each addl $10; kit. units $75–$130; varied lower rates rest of yr. Crib $5.
Pet accepted, some restrictions; $15 per visit. TV; cable. 2 heated pools.
Ck-out noon. Coin lndry. Sundries. Lawn games. Refrigerators. Many
balconies. Beach opp. Cr cds: A, D, DS, MC, V.

★ ★ ★ **BEST WESTERN SEASTONE RESORT.** 445 Hamden Dr,
at Gulfview Blvd. 813/441-1722; FAX 813/449-1580. 108 rms, 5–6 story.
Mid-Feb–Apr: S, D $99–$119; each addl $8–$12; kit. suites $166–$186;
under 18 free; lower rates rest of yr. Crib free. TV; cable. Heated pool;
hot tub. Supervised child's activities (mid-June–early Sept). Restaurant
7 am–10 pm. Ck-out noon. Coin lndry. Meeting rms. Beauty shop.
Refrigerators. Opp beach, marina. Sun deck. Cr cds: A, C, D, DS, MC, V.

D

★ ★ **CLEARWATER BEACH RESORT.** 678 S Gulfview Blvd.
813/441-3767; res: 800/334-3767; FAX 813/449-2701. 42 kit. units, 3
story. No elvtr. Mid-Feb–Apr: kit. units $100–$150; wkly, monthly rates;
lower rates rest of yr. Crib free. TV; cable. Heated pool; whirlpool.
Complimentary coffee in lobby. Restaurant adj 7 am–11 pm. Ck-out 11
am. Free lndry facilities. Lighted tennis. Lawn games. Covered parking.
In-rm whirlpools. Balconies. Picnic tables, grills. Cr cds: A, C, D, DS, MC,
V.

★ **ECONO LODGE.** 625 S Gulfview Blvd. 813/446-3400;
FAX 813/446-4615. 64 kit. units, 5 story. Mid-Jan–mid-Apr: kit. units
$94–$124; each addl $8; under 18 free; lower rates rest of yr. Crib free.
TV; cable, in-rm movies avail. Heated pool. Complimentary coffee in
lobby. Ck-out noon. Coin lndry. Exercise equipt; weight machine, bicycles, whirlpool. Game rm. Balconies. Picnic tables, grill. On beach. Cr
cds: A, C, D, DS, ER, MC, V.

★ ★ **HoJo INN.** 656 Bayway Blvd. 813/442-6606; FAX 813/
461-0809. 54 rms, 2 story, 38 kit. units. Feb–Apr: S, D $75–$130; each
addl $12; suites $95–$140; kit. units $90–$130; under 18 free; lower
rates rest of yr. Crib free. TV; cable. 2 heated pools. Complimentary
continental bkfst, coffee. Ck-out noon. Coin lndry. 2 blks from beach. Cr
cds: A, C, D, DS, MC, V.

★ **ISLAND QUEEN.** 158 Brightwater Dr. 813/442-8068; FAX
813/442-2412. 14 kit. units, 2 story. Mid-Jan–mid-Apr: S, D $80–$92;
each addl $8; wkly rates; lower rates rest of yr. Crib $4. TV; cable.
Heated pool. Restaurant nearby. Ck-out 10 am. Lawn games. Picnic
tables, grills. Sun deck. On bay; dockage. Cr cds: DS, MC, V.

✔ ★ ★ **NEW YORKER.** 332 Hamden Dr, at Brightwater Dr. 813/
446-2437. 15 rms, 2 story, 13 kits. Feb–Apr: S, D $65–$80; each addl $5;
kit. units $70–$80; lower rates rest of yr. TV. Heated pool. Restaurant
nearby. Ck-out 10 am. Refrigerators. Beach 1 blk. Cr cds: MC, V.

✔ ★ ★ **SEA CAPTAIN RESORT.** 40 Devon Dr. 813/446-7550. 27
rms, 2 story, 23 kits. Mid-Feb–Apr: S, D $65–$70; each addl $5; kit. units
$75–$90; 1-bedrm apts $90–$115; lower rates rest of yr. Crib free. TV.
Heated pool. Restaurant nearby. Ck-out 11 am. Lawn games. Picnic
tables, grills. On bay; dockage, fishing dock. Beach 2 blks. Totally
nonsmoking. Cr cds: A, MC, V.

Motor Hotels

★ ★ **BEST WESTERN SEA WAKE INN.** 691 S Gulfview Blvd.
813/443-7652; FAX 813/461-2836. 110 rms, 6 story, 50 kits. Early
Feb–late Apr: S, D $108–$143; each addl $10; kit. units $118–$143;
under 17 free; lower rates rest of yr. Crib free. TV; cable. Heated pool.
Playground. Free supervised child's activities (mid-June–mid-Aug).
Restaurant 7 am–9:30 pm. Rm serv. Bar 11–1:30 am; entertainment. Ck-
out noon. Meeting rm. Valet serv. Sundries. Gift shop. Some refrigerators. Private balconies. On beach. Cr cds: A, C, D, DS, MC, V, JCB.

D

★ ★ **CLEARWATER BEACH HOTEL.** 500 Mandalay Ave. 813/
441-2425; res: 800/292-2295; FAX 813/449-2083. 160 rms, 2–6 story, 22
suites, 79 kits. Jan–Apr: S, D, kit. units $130–$195; lower rates rest of yr.

Crib free. TV; cable. Heated pool; poolside serv. Restaurant 7:30 am–10:30 pm. Rm serv. Bar 10–2 am; entertainment. Ck-out noon. Meeting rms. Bellhops. Valet serv. Sundries. Gift shop. Free covered parking; valet. Lighted tennis privileges, pro. 36-hole golf privileges. Lawn games. Balconies. On gulf; beach. Cr cds: A, C, D, DS, MC, V.

★★GULF SANDS BEACH RESORT. 655 S Gulfview Blvd. 813/442-7171; res: 800/237-9948 (exc FL); FAX 813/446-7177. 91 rms, 5 story, 45 kits. Early Feb–late Apr: S, D $105–$145; each addl $10; suites $145; kit. units $115–$145; under 17 free; lower rates rest of yr. Crib free. TV; cable. Heated pool. Playground. Free supervised child's activities (mid-June–Sept). Restaurant 7 am–9:30 pm. Bar 11 am–midnight, Sun from 1 pm. Ck-out 11 am. Coin lndry. Valet serv. Lawn games. Private patios, balconies. Grills. Private beach. Cr cds: A, C, D, DS, MC, V.

★★HOLIDAY INN GULFVIEW. 521 S Gulfview Blvd. 813/447-6461; FAX 813/443-5888. 288 rms, 7–9 story, some kits. Mid-Feb–May: S $104.50–$134.50; D $114.50–$144.50; each addl $10; under 18 free; varied lower rates rest of yr. Crib free. TV; cable. Heated pool; wading pool. Restaurant open 24 hrs. Rm serv. Bar 11–1:30 am; entertainment, dancing. Ck-out 11 am. Meeting rms. Bellhops. Valet serv. Sundries. Barber, beauty shop. Game rm. Balconies. On Gulf. Cr cds: A, C, D, DS, ER, MC, V, JCB.

Hotels

★★ADAM'S MARK CARIBBEAN GULF RESORT. 430 S Gulfview Blvd. 813/443-5714; res: 800/444-2326; FAX 813/442-8389. 207 rms, 14 story. Feb–Apr: S, D $139–$169; each addl $10; suites $195–$300; under 18 free; lower rates rest of yr. Crib free. TV; cable. Heated pool; whirlpool, wading pool, poolside serv. Restaurant 7 am–10 pm. Bar noon–1 am; entertainment, dancing. Ck-out 11 am. Coin lndry. Meeting rms. Gift shop. Free garage parking. Private patios, balconies. On Gulf. Cr cds: A, C, D, DS, ER, MC, V, JCB.

★★★HILTON. 715 S Gulfview Blvd. 813/447-9566; FAX 813/447-9566, ext 2168. 207 rms, 2–9 story. Mid-Feb–Apr: S, D $109–$179; each addl $10; suites $310–$425; under 18 free; lower rates rest of yr. Crib free. TV; cable, in-rm movies. Heated pool; wading pool, poolside serv. Playground. Restaurant 7 am–10 pm. Bars open 24 hrs. Ck-out 11 am. Gift shop. Golf privileges. Exercise equipt; weight machine, bicycles. Lawn games. Minibars; some refrigerators. Some balconies. Private beach. Cr cds: A, C, D, DS, ER, MC, V.

★★HOLIDAY INN SURFSIDE. 400 Mandalay Ave, at jct FL 60. 813/461-3222; FAX 813/461-0610. 427 rms, 9 story. Feb–Apr: S $135–$210; D $145–$220; each addl $10; suites $375–$525; under 12 free; lower rates rest of yr. Crib free. TV; cable. Heated pool. Restaurants 6 am–10 pm. Bars 11–2 am; entertainment. Ck-out 11 am. Coin lndry. Convention facilities. Concierge. Shopping arcade. Exercise equipt; weights, bicycles. Balconies. Cabanas. On 10½-acre beach. Cr cds: A, C, D, DS, ER, MC, V, JCB.

★★RADISSON SUITE RESORT ON SAND KEY. 1201 Gulf Blvd, on Sand Key. 813/596-1100; FAX 813/595-4292. 220 suites, 10 story. Jan–Apr: S $165–$225; D $175–$235; under 18 free; wkly rates; lower rates rest of yr. Crib avail. TV; cable. Pool; poolside serv. Playground. Supervised child's activities. Complimentary coffee in rms. Restaurants 6:30 am–11 pm. Bars 11–1 am; entertainment. Ck-out noon. Coin lndry. Meeting rms. Concierge. Shopping arcade. Barber, beauty shop. Free valet parking. Golf privileges. Exercise rm; instructor, weights, bicycles, whirlpool, sauna. Rec rm. On bay; adj Clearwater Sailing Center. Cr cds: A, C, D, DS, ER, MC, V, JCB.

★★★SHERATON-SAND KEY RESORT. 1160 Gulf Blvd, on Sand Key. 813/595-1611; FAX 813/596-8488. 390 rms, 8 story. Feb–Apr: S $118–$158; D $128–$168; each addl $10; suites $235–$425; under 18 free; lower rates rest of yr. Crib $5. TV; cable. Heated pool; wading pool, whirlpool, poolside serv. Supervised child's activities (June–Aug). Restaurants 7–11:30 am, 6–11 pm. Bar 11–2 am; entertainment, dancing exc Sun. Ck-out 11 am. Coin lndry. Convention facilities. Gift shop. Lighted tennis, pro. Golf privileges. Balconies. On Gulf; private beach. Cr cds: A, C, D, DS, ER, MC, V.

Restaurants

✔★★ANCHOR ROOM. 880 Mandalay Ave, in Mandalay Apt building. 813/461-7079. Hrs: 11 am–2 pm, 5–9 pm; early-bird dinner 5–6:30 pm. Closed Mon. Res accepted. French, continental menu. Wine, beer. Semi-a la carte: lunch $5.95–$7.50, dinner $9.50–$16.95. Child's meals. Specialties: bouillabaisse, fresh seafood, steak, veal. Own desserts. View of Gulf. Cr cds: A, MC, V.

★★★BOB HEILMAN'S BEACHCOMBER. 447 Mandalay Ave. 813/442-4144. Hrs: 11:30 am–midnight; Sun noon–10 pm. Res accepted. Bar. Wine cellar. Semi-a la carte: lunch $3.95–$12.95, dinner $8.50–$24.95. Child's meals. Specializes in fresh seafood, aged prime beef, luncheon salads. Own baking. Pianist. Valet parking. Beachcomber murals. Waterfall. Family-owned. Cr cds: A, D, DS, MC, V.

★★THE GALLERY. 1370 Gulf Blvd, ¾ mi S of Sand Key Bridge. 813/596-5657. Hrs: 11:30 am–11:30 pm; Sun 4–10 pm; early-bird dinner 4–6:30 pm. Res accepted. Continental menu. Bar. Semi-a la carte: lunch $4–$7.50, dinner $7.50–$41.95. Child's meals. Specializes in fresh seafood, steak, duckling. Classical pianist. Parking. Old World atmosphere. Overlooks Gulf. Cr cds: A, C, D, MC, V.

✔★JULIE'S SEAFOOD AND SUNSETS. 351 S Gulfview Blvd. 813/441-2548. Hrs: 11 am–10 pm. Res accepted. Wine, beer. Semi-a la carte: lunch, dinner $3.25–$9.95. Child's meals. Specializes in fresh seafood, char-broiled dishes. Parking. Outdoor dining. Scenic sunset view. Cr cds: A, MC, V.

★★RAJAN'S. 435 Mandalay Ave. 813/443-2100. Hrs: 11:30–2 am; Sun from noon. Res accepted. Bar. Semi-a la carte: lunch $3.50–$22.95, dinner $6.95–$22.95. Child's meals. Specializes in fresh seafood, oysters. Nautical decor. Cr cds: A, C, D, DS, MC, V.

Clermont (C-3)

Pop: 6,910 **Elev:** 112 ft **Area code:** 904 **Zip:** 34711

Claiming the highest average elevation of any town in Florida, Clermont has 100 lakes at its doorstep, 17 within the city limits, providing easy access to fishing and waterskiing. The town is named for Clermont, France, the birthplace of its founder.

What to See and Do

Lakeridge Winery & Vineyards. 19239 US 27N, 6 mi N. Tours and tasting of Florida wines; audiovisual presentation; art gallery. (Daily; closed Jan 1, Thanksgiving, Dec 25) Phone 394-8627. **Free.**

(For further information contact the Clermont Area Chamber of Commerce, 691 W Montrose St, PO Box 120417, 34712-0417; 394-4191.)

(See Orlando, Tavares)

Motel

✔ ★**VACATION VILLAGE.** *(Box 120951, 34712) 4 mi S on US 27.* 904/394-4091; *res:* 800/962-9969; *FAX* 904/394-4093. 90 kit. units, villas & lofts. June–Aug & Dec–Apr: villas (up to 6 persons) $64; lofts to 8, $69; wkly rates; lower rates rest of yr. Crib free. TV; cable. Pool; wading pool. Playground. Ck-out 10 am. Coin lndry. Meeting rm. Sundries. Lighted tennis. Lawn games. Private patios, balconies. Picnic tables, grills. On Lake Louise. Cr cds: MC, V.

Restaurant

★**CROWN.** *1340 E FL 50, at US 27.* 904/394-3887. Hrs: 11:30 am–2 pm, 5–9:30 pm; Fri, Sat to 10 pm; Sun brunch Nov–May 11:30 am–3 pm. Closed Memorial Day, Labor Day. Bar to 2 am. Semi-a la carte: lunch $4.95–$8, dinner $10.75–$23.75. Sun brunch $4.95–$9.95. Child's meals. Specializes in prime rib, seafood, back ribs. Parking. Cr cds: A, MC, V.

Cocoa (C-4)

Settled: 1860 **Pop:** 17,722 **Elev:** 25 ft **Area code:** 407

When the name ''Indian River City'' was rejected in 1882 by the US postal authorities because it was too long for a postmark, the boys in the general store chose the town's present name from a box of Baker's cocoa. The city was swept into the space age due to its proximity to both Cape Canaveral and Kennedy Space Center.

What to See and Do

1. **Kennedy Space Center** (see). 2 mi E on FL 520, then N on FL 3.

2. **Brevard Museum of History and Natural Science.** 2201 Michigan Ave. Exhibits include native artifacts, memorabilia of early residents Grace and Albert Taylor, hands-on Discovery Room, mollusk collection, nature center and 22 acres of nature trails through 3 different ecosystems. (Daily exc Mon; closed Jan 1, Dec 25) Phone 632-1830. ¢¢

3. **Historic Cocoa Village.** 434 Delannoy Ave. Guided, walking tour (1 hr) of four-block historic area, including Cocoa Village Playhouse (1924), Porcher House (1916), Gothic church (1886) and eleven other sites; narration by costumed docent, anecdotes, folklore. Also unique shops, restaurants. (Advance res required) Phone 632-1830. ¢¢

(For further information contact the Cocoa Beach Area Chamber of Commerce, 400 Fortenberry Rd, Merritt Island 32952; 459-2200.)

(See Cocoa Beach, Melbourne, Titusville)

Motels

✔ ★ ★**BEST WESTERN-COCOA INN.** *4225 W King St (32926).* 407/632-1065; *FAX* 407/631-3302. 120 rms, 2 story. Jan–Apr: S, D $40–$56; under 12 free; higher rates: special events, hols; lower rates rest of yr. Crib $4. TV; cable. Pool. Restaurant 7 am–1 pm, 5–9 pm. Bar 4 pm–midnight. Ck-out 11:30 am. Coin lndry. Meeting rms. Sundries. Gift shop. Rec rm. Picnic tables, grills. Cr cds: A, C, D, DS, MC, V.

★**DAYS INN.** *5600 FL 524 (32926), at I-95 exit 76.* 407/636-6500; *FAX* 407/631-0513. 115 rms, 2 story. Jan–Mar: S, D $49–$69; each addl $10; under 12 free off-season; wkly rates; higher rates special events; lower rates rest of yr. Crib free. TV; cable. Pool. Complimentary continental bkfst. Ck-out 11 am. Some refrigerators. Cr cds: A, D, DS, MC, V.

★ ★**HOLIDAY INN-MERRITT ISLAND.** *(260 E Merritt Island Causeway, Merritt Island 32952) E on FL 520.* 407/452-7711; *FAX* 407/452-9462. 128 rms, 2 story. Jan–Apr: S $59–$70; D $67–$78; under 18 free; lower rates rest of yr. Crib free. TV; cable. Pool. Restaurant 7 am–2 pm, 5:30–10 pm. Rm serv. Bar 5 pm–2 am; entertainment Tues–Sat, dancing. Ck-out noon. Meeting rms. Tennis. Cr cds: A, C, D, DS, ER, MC, V, JCB.

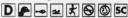

★**RAMADA INN.** *900 Friday Rd (32926).* 407/631-1210; *FAX* 407/636-8661. 150 rms, 2 story. Early Feb–late Apr: S, D $60–$85; each addl $7; package plans; higher rates special events; lower rates rest of yr. Crib free. TV; cable. Heated pool; poolside serv. Restaurant 6 am–10 pm. Rm serv. Bar 4 pm–2 am. Ck-out noon. Coin lndry. Meeting rms. Lawn games. Private lake. Cr cds: A, C, D, DS, ER, MC, V, JCB.

Restaurant

★ ★**BLACK TULIP.** *207 Brevard Ave.* 407/631-1133. Hrs: 11 am–2:30 pm, 5:30–10 pm; Fri, Sat 11 am–2:30 pm, 6–10 pm. Closed Sun; Jan 1, Dec 25. Res accepted. Continental menu. Wine, beer. A la carte entrees: lunch $2.95–$8.95. Semi-a la carte: dinner $9.95–$19.95. Specialties: roasted duckling with apples and cashews, fresh fish baked with bananas and lemon butter. Own pastries, desserts. Former city hall and county jail building. Braille menu. Cr cds: A, D, MC, V.

Cocoa Beach (C-5)

Settled: 1925 **Pop:** 12,123 **Elev:** 12 ft **Area code:** 407 **Zip:** 32931

Inaccessible except by boat until 1923, when a bridge was built to Merritt Island, Cocoa Beach remained a sparsely populated hamlet until about 1940. Located south of the city is Patrick Air Force Base. This facility includes the Logistical and Administrative Center of the Air Force Eastern Test Range. North of the city are Cape Canaveral and the Kennedy Space Center (see).

What to See and Do

1. **Missile and space vehicle watching.** Cocoa Beach offers a good view; missile launches can be seen from almost any point.

2. **Missile exhibit.** Many of the larger missiles tested at Cape Canaveral are on display outside the Technical Laboratory of the Air Force Eastern Space and Missile Center at Patrick Air Force Base (S on FL A1A).

3. **Kennedy Space Center** (see). N on FL A1A, W on FL 520, N on FL 3.

4. **The Cocoa Beach Pier.** 401 Meade Ave, ½ mi N of Causeway (FL 520) off FL A1A. An 800-foot pier, with restaurants, shops, fishing and beach rentals, extends into the ocean. Phone 783-7549.

5. **Port Canaveral.** N on FL A1A, 401. Deep-sea port, connected to the Intracoastal Waterway via Barge Canal and Canaveral Lock, serves downrange missile ships and nuclear submarines, as well as shrimp fleet and major cruise ships. Also available are fishing charters, boat rentals and boat tours.

(For further information contact the Cocoa Beach Area Chamber of Commerce, 400 Fortenberry Rd, Merritt Island, 32952; 459-2200.)

Annual Events

Port Canaveral Seafood Festival. Port Canaveral (see #5). Late Mar.

National Surfing Tourneys. Easter wkend.

Space Coast Art Festival. 3 days following Thanksgiving.

(See Cocoa, Melbourne, Titusville)

Motels

★**DAYS INN OCEANFRONT.** *5600 N Atlantic Ave (FL A1A).* 407/783-7621; FAX 407/799-4576. 120 rms, 2 story. S $69; D $78; each addl $6; kit. units $79–$88; under 12 free. Crib free. TV; cable. Pool. Complimentary coffee in lobby. Restaurant opp open 24 hrs. Ck-out 11 am. Coin lndry. Opp ocean. Cr cds: A, C, D, DS, ER, MC, V, JCB.

✔★**ECONO LODGE.** *5500 N Atlantic Ave (FL A1A).* 407/784-2550; FAX 407/868-7124. 102 rms, 2 story. S $59; D $68; each addl $6; kit. units $69–$78; under 18 free. Crib free. Pet accepted. TV; cable, in-rm movies. Pool. Complimentary coffee in lobby. Restaurant nearby. Ck-out 11 am. Coin lndry. Refrigerators avail. Cr cds: A, C, D, DS, ER, MC, V, JCB.

★**WAKULLA.** *3550 N Atlantic Ave (FL A1A).* 407/783-2230; res: 800/992-5852; FAX 407/783-0980. 116 kit. suites, 2 story. Feb–Apr: kit. suites $79; each addl $5; under 5 free; lower rates rest of yr. Crib free. TV; cable. Heated pool; wading pool. Restaurant nearby. Ck-out 11 am. Coin lndry. Valet serv. Sundries. Lawn games. Balconies. Grills. On beach. Cr cds: A, C, D, DS, MC, V.

Motor Hotels

★★**COMFORT INN AND SUITE RESORT.** *3901 N Atlantic Ave (FL A1A).* 407/783-2221; FAX 407/783-0461. 144 rms, 6 story, 40 kit. units. Jan–Apr: S, D $71–$89; each addl $8; suites $95–$119; kit. units $77–$89; wkly rates; higher rates special events; lower rates rest of yr. Crib $7. TV; cable. Pool; poolside serv. Playground. Restaurant 8 am–3 pm. Bar 11–2 am. Ck-out 11 am. Coin lndry. Meeting rms. Valet serv. Sundries. Rec rm. Lawn games. Some refrigerators. Picnic tables, grill. Beach 1 blk. Cr cds: A, C, D, DS, ER, MC, V, JCB.

★★**OCEAN SUITE.** *5500 Ocean Beach Blvd.* 407/784-4343; res: 800/367-1223; FAX 407/783-6514. 50 suites, 5 story. Feb–Apr, July–Aug: suites $79–$119; each addl $8; under 12 free; package plans off-season; lower rates rest of yr. Crib free. TV; cable. Heated pool. Restaurant 6:30–10:30 am. Ck-out noon. Meeting rms. Valet serv. 18-hole golf privileges, greens fee. Balconies. Ocean view. Cr cds: A, C, D, DS, ER, MC, V.

✔★★**OCEANSIDE INN.** *1 Hendry Ave.* 407/784-3126. 74 rms, 6 story. S, D $59–$109; each addl $10; under 13 free; higher rates special events. Crib $10. TV; cable. Heated pool; poolside serv. Restaurant 6 am–11 pm. Bar 4 pm–midnight. Ck-out 11 am. Balconies. On beach. Cr cds: A, C, D, DS, MC, V.

RADISSON RESORT. (Too new to be rated) *(8701 Astronaut Blvd, Cape Canaveral 32920) N on FL A1A, 1 mi S of Cape Canaveral.* 407/784-0000; FAX 407/783-3070. 200 rms, 2 story. S, D $65–$125; under 18 free. Crib free. TV; cable. Heated pool; wading pool. Playground. Restaurant 6:30 am–11 pm. Rm serv. Bar; entertainment Sat & Sun. Ck-out 11 am. Coin lndry. Convention facilities. Bellhops. Gift shop. Airport transportation. Lighted tennis. Exercise equipt; weights, bicycles, whirlpool. Game rm. Cr cds: A, C, D, DS, ER, MC, V, JCB.

Hotels

★★★**HILTON.** *1550 N Atlantic Ave (FL A1A).* 407/799-0003; FAX 407/799-0344. 300 rms, 7 story. Feb–Apr: S $90–$115; D $100–$125; each addl $15; suites $125–$140; under 18 free; lower rates rest of yr. Crib free. TV; cable. Heated pool; whirlpool, poolside serv. Restaurant 6:30 am–2 pm, 5–10:30 pm. Bar 11–1 am; entertainment Wed–Sat, dancing. Ck-out 11 am. Convention facilities. Concierge. Gift shop. Free valet parking. Sun deck. On ocean. *LUXURY LEVEL:* **EXECUTIVE LEVEL.** 47 rms, 1 suite. S, D $105–$165; suite $450. Concierge. Private lounge. In-rm movies. Complimentary continental bkfst, refreshments, newspaper.
Cr cds: A, C, D, DS, ER, MC, V.

★★**HOWARD JOHNSON PLAZA.** *2080 N Atlantic Ave (FL A1A).* 407/783-9222; FAX 407/799-3234. 210 rms, 6 story. Mid-Feb–mid-May: S, D $75–$145; suites $115–$175; cabanas $65–$125; under 18 free; higher rates special events; lower rates rest of yr. Crib free. TV; cable. 2 pools; wading pool, poolside serv. Restaurants 7 am–midnight; wknds open 24 hrs. Rm serv to 9 pm. Bars. Ck-out 11 am. Coin lndry. Meeting rms. Exercise equipt; weights, bicycles. Game rm. Lawn games. Private patios, balconies. On ocean; beach. *LUXURY LEVEL:* **PLAZA CLUB FLOOR.** 28 rms, 2 suites. S $95–$140; D $110–$150; suites $105–$175. Concierge. Private lounge. Refrigerators. Complimentary continental bkfst, refreshments.
Cr cds: A, C, D, DS, ER, MC, V, JCB.

Restaurants

★★**JACK BAKER'S LOBSTER SHANTY.** *2200 S Orlando Ave.* 407/783-1350. Hrs: 11:30 am–10 pm; early-bird dinner Mon–Sat 3–6 pm. Closed Thanksgiving. Res accepted. Bar. Semi-a la carte: lunch $4.95–$9, dinner $10.95–$24.95. Child's meals. Specializes in seafood. Salad bar. Parking. Outdoor dining. Overlooks Banana River; dock. Cr cds: A, C, D, MC, V.

★★★**MANGO TREE.** *118 N Atlantic Ave (FL A1A).* 407/799-0513. Hrs: 6–9:30 pm. Res accepted. Continental menu. Bar. Wine list. A la carte entrees: dinner $18.95–$36. Child's meals. Specialties: grouper Margarette, veal Française, filet mignon Béarnaise. Own baking. Pianist. Parking. Indoor fish pond. Orchid greenhouse and butterfly collection. Gazebo. One of the first cottages in Cocoa Beach. Braille menu. Cr cds: A, MC, V.

★★**PIER RESTAURANT AND SPINNAKERS.** *401 Meade Ave.* 407/783-7549. Hrs: 11 am–11:30 pm; Sun brunch 10 am–2 pm. Res accepted. Bar 10–1 am. Semi-a la carte: lunch $4.95–$13.95, dinner $6.95–$26.50. Sun brunch $11.95. Child's meals. Specializes in seafood, steak. Multi-level dining area on ocean pier. Nautical decor. Family-owned. Cr cds: A, C, D, DS, MC, V.

Coconut Grove

(see Miami)

Coral Gables (E-5)

Established: 1925 **Pop:** 40,091 **Elev:** 10 ft **Area code:** 305

Coral Gables, one of the 26 seperate municipalities that make up Metropolitan Miami and Dade County, was designed by George Merrick, the son of a Massachusetts minister. Merrick laid out the entire city as the ''American Riviera'' and a ''new Venice,'' but relied on slightly sensational techniques to populate it. To lure prospective buyers from the north, Merrick offered steamship and bus service to Coral Gables, with transportation expense reimbursed for anyone who purchased land. He hired William Jennings Bryan to lecture on the merits of Coral Gables investments and engaged Paul Whiteman and the chorus of Earl Carroll's *Vanities* to entertain buyers. Houses were designed in Mediterranean-Florida style, with sections in French, Italian, Dutch South African and Chinese styles to provide contrast. Today, Coral Gables requires that every new building be approved by its board of architects. The city includes eight planned entrances, two with arched gateways constructed of carved native rock, and fourteen planned plazas.

What to See and Do

1. **Coral Gables Merrick House** (1899). 907 Coral Way. "Coral-rock" plantation house, boyhood home of the city's founder, George Merrick, was built of oolitic limerock and Dade County pine; reflects the Merrick's New England roots while adapting to southern climate; original furnishings, historic pieces; gardens. Guided tours. (Wed & Sun afternoons) Phone 460-5361. ¢–¢¢

2. **Fairchild Tropical Garden.** 10901 Old Cutler Rd. An 83-acre tropical botanical garden featuring rain forest, sunken garden, vine pergola, rare plant house. Hourly tram tour (free). (Daily; closed Dec 25) 667-1651. ¢¢¢

3. **Garden of Our Lord.** Adj to St James Evangelical Lutheran Church, 110 Phoenetia Ave. Consists of shrubs, flowers and trees native to Holy Land and mentioned in Bible; outdoor sanctuary. (Daily) Phone 443-0014. **Free.**

4. **University of Miami** (1925). (14,100 students) Largest independent university in the Southeast; campuses cover 287 acres and contain more than 153 buildings. Gusman Concert Hall and Ring Theater present various programs throughout the year. Phone 284-5500. On the main campus is

   Lowe Art Museum. 1301 Stanford Dr. Permanent collections of fine arts, Asian, pre-Colombian, Native American and African art; Samuel H. Kress Collection of Renaissance and Baroque art; American Art of the 19th & 20th centuries; special exhibitions. (Daily exc Mon; closed Jan 1, July 4, Dec 25) Sr citizen rate. Phone 284-3536. ¢¢

5. **Venetian Pool.** 2701 De Soto Blvd. Much of the coral used to build homes in the city came from a quarry, which afterward was converted into this elaborate swimming pool. It is edged with shady porticos, vine-covered loggias and Spanish towers; palm trees, 2 waterfalls, an island, swim-through caves and a stone and wrought iron bridge complete the landscaping. (Daily exc Mon; closed Jan 1, Thanksgiving & Fri after, Dec 24 & 25) Phone 460-5356. ¢¢

(For further information contact the City of Coral Gables, 405 Biltmore Way, 33134, phone 460-5311; or the Greater Miami Convention & Visitors Bureau, 701 Brickell Ave, Suite 2700, Miami 33131, phone 539-3000.)

Annual Event

Junior Orange Bowl Festival. Events include 5K run, prestigious juniors' golf, gymnastics & tennis tournaments, cheerleading, soccer, queen's pageant and ball, gala evening parade and much more. Phone 662-1210. Nov–Jan.

(See Hialeah, Homestead, Miami, Miami Beach, Miami Intl Airport Area)

Motor Hotel

★ ★ **HOLIDAY INN DOWNTOWN.** *2051 Le Jeune Rd (33134). 305/443-2301; FAX 305/446-6827.* 168 rms, 6 story. S, D $80–$240; each addl $10; suites $140–$240; under 18 free; wkend rates. Crib free. TV; cable. Pool; 2 saunas. Restaurant 6:30 am–11 pm; Sat, Sun from 7

am. Rm serv. Bar; entertainment exc Sun. Ck-out noon. Meeting rms. Bellhops. Valet serv. Cr cds: A, C, D, DS, MC, V, JCB.

Hotels

★ ★ ★ **BILTMORE.** *1200 Anastasia Ave (33134), 1 mi from University of Miami. 305/445-1926; FAX 305/448-9976.* 276 rms, 15 story. Late Dec–mid-Apr: S $129–$169; D $149–$189; each addl $20; suites $289–$329; under 18 free; wkly, wkend rates; golf, tennis plans; lower rates rest of yr. Crib free. Pet accepted, some restrictions. Garage parking $8/night, valet. TV; cable. Pool; lifeguard. Supervised child's activities. Restaurant 6 am–11 pm. Rm serv 24 hrs. Ck-out noon. Meeting rms. Concierge. Barber, beauty shop. Free airport, RR station transportation. Lighted tennis, pro. 18-hole golf, pro, putting green, driving range. Exercise rm; instructor, weight machine, treadmill, whirlpool, sauna, steam rm. Complete spa facilities. Minibars; some refrigerators. Balconies. Landmark hotel with distinctive tower. Biltmore pool is the largest of its kind in the country. Cr cds: A, C, D, DS, ER, MC, V, JCB.

★ ★ ★ **COLONNADE.** *180 Aragon Ave (33134). 305/441-2600; res: 800/533-1337; FAX 305/445-3929.* 157 units, 17 suites; guest rms begin on 10th floor. Jan–mid-Apr: S $229–$249; D $249–$269; each addl $15; suites $309–$699; family rates; wkend rates; lower rates rest of yr. Crib free. Garage parking $7, valet $8.50. TV; cable. Heated pool on 10th-floor terrace; poolside serv. Restaurants 7–1 am (also see ARAGON CAFE). Rm serv 24 hrs. Bars; entertainment. Ck-out noon. Meeting rms. Concierge. Beauty shop. Exercise equipt; weight machines, bicycles, whirlpool, sauna. Minibars; wet bar in suites. Some balconies. European decor; mahogany furnishings throughout. Rotunda off the lobby is part of original Colonnade building (1926). Cr cds: A, C, D, DS, ER, MC, V, JCB.

★ ★ **DAVID WILLIAM.** *700 Biltmore Way (33134). 305/445-7821; res: 800/327-8770; FAX 305/445-5585.* 90 units, 14 story, 80 kits. Dec–Apr: S, D $105–$115; each addl $10; under 12 free; kit. suites $200–$270; lower rates rest of yr. Crib free. TV; cable. Heated rooftop pool; poolside serv. Restaurants 7 am–11 pm. Bar; entertainment. Ck-out noon. Coin lndry. Meeting rm. Valet parking. Refrigerators. Some balconies. Cr cds: A, C, D, MC, V.

★ ★ **HOTEL PLACE ST MICHEL.** *162 Alcazar Ave (33134), at Ponce de Leon Blvd. 305/444-1666; FAX 305/529-0074.* 27 rms, 3 story. S $99; D $115; each addl $10; suites $150. Crib free. TV. Complimentary continental bkfst. Restaurant 7 am–10:30 pm; Sat to 11:30 pm; Sun 11 am–10:30 pm. Piano bar. Ck-out noon. Meeting rms. Restored hotel (1926) with Old World atmosphere; old fashioned brass elvtr; rms decorated with antiques. Cr cds: A, C, D, MC, V.

★ ★ ★ **HYATT REGENCY.** *50 Alhambra Plaza (33134). 305/441-1234; FAX 305/443-7702.* 242 rms, 14 story. Oct–mid-Apr: S $130–$230; D $155–$255; each addl $25; suites $250–$1,200; under 18 free; wkend rates; lower rates rest of yr. Crib free. Valet parking $8.50, garage $7. TV; cable. Heated pool; poolside serv. Restaurant 7 am–11 pm. Rm serv 6–1 am. Bar 11–1 am, Fri, Sat to 2 am; entertainment, dancing Wed, Fri & Sat. Ck-out noon. Meeting rms. Concierge. Gift shop. Exercise equipt; weights, bicycles, whirlpool, sauna. Some balconies. Cr cds: A, C, D, DS, ER, MC, V, JCB.

Restaurants

★ ★ ★ **ARAGON CAFE.** *(See Colonnade Hotel) 305/441-2600.* Hrs: 6–11 pm. Closed Sun, Mon. Res accepted. Bar. Wine list. A la carte entrees: dinner $16–$26. Specialties: Florida seafood, Florida blue crab cakes with jicama salad, macadamia-crusted yellow tail snapper with tropical fruit, grilled Caribbean swordfish. Own baking, desserts.' Valet parking. Casual elegance. Cr cds: A, C, D, DS, ER, MC, V, JCB.

D

★★**THE BISTRO.** 2611 Ponce de Leon Blvd. 305/442-9671. Hrs: 11:30 am–2 pm, 6–10:30 pm; Fri, Sat to 11 pm. Closed Mon. Res accepted; required Fri, Sat. French, continental menu. A la carte entrees: lunch $5–$15.50, dinner $14–$26.50. Specializes in veal, fish, lamb. Cr cds: A, C, D, DS, MC, V.

D

★★★**CAFE BACI.** 2522 Ponce de Leon Blvd. 305/442-0600. Hrs: 11:30 am–2:30 pm, 6–11 pm; Sat from 6 pm. Closed Sun. Italian menu. Wine, beer. A la carte entrees: lunch $5–$12.95, dinner $6.50–$22.50. Child's meals. Specialties: lamb chops prepared in Tuscany oven, breaded lamb chops. Valet parking. Modern decor; brass vaulted ceiling. Cr cds: A, C, D, DS, MC, V.

D

★★**CAFFE ABBRACCI.** 318 Aragon Ave. 305/441-0700. Hrs: 11:30 am–3 pm, 6 pm–midnight. Res required. Italian menu. Bar. A la carte entrees: lunch $5.50–$11, dinner $7.50–$23. Specialties: costoletta tri-color, trio veneziano. Cr cds: A, C, D, MC, V.

D

★★★**CHARADE.** 2900 Ponce de Leon Blvd. 305/448-6077. Hrs: 11:30 am–3 pm, 6–11 pm; Fri, Sat 6 pm–midnight; Sun 6–10:30 pm. Res accepted. Continental menu. Serv bar. Semi-a la carte: lunch $7.50–$13, dinner $18.50–$30. Specialties: lobster Thermidor, Dover sole, center cut veal chops. Own baking. Pianist, violinist. Parking. Former furniture factory (1925); antiques, paintings. Contemporary Mediterranean decor. Cr cds: A, C, D, MC, V.

D

★★**CILANTRO.** 139 Giralda Ave. 305/444-6858. Hrs: 11:30 am–2:30 pm, 5:30–10:30 pm; wkends 6–11:30 pm. Closed Mon. Res accepted. Southwestern menu. Bar. A la carte entrees: lunch $5.95–$8.95, dinner $10.95–$18.95. Specialties: seafood enchilada, wild mushroom quesadilla, duck fajitas. Large dining rm with Southwestern decor. Cr cds: A, C, D, MC, V.

D

✔★★**DIDIER'S.** 325 Alcazar Ave. 305/448-0312. Hrs: 11:30 am–2:30 pm, 6–11 pm; Sat from 6 pm. Closed Sun. Res accepted. French menu. Wine, beer. Semi-a la carte: lunch $7–$9.50, dinner $13.50–$20. Specialties: tuna with mango sauce, escargot, la soupe au pistou. Cr cds: A, D, MC, V.

D

★★**DOMENICO'S.** 2271 Ponce de Leon Blvd. 305/442-2033 or 448-9951. Hrs: 11:30 am–2:30 pm, 6–11 pm; Fri & Sat to midnight. Closed Sun; Dec 25. Res accepted. Italian menu. Bar. Wine list. A la carte entrees: lunch $10–$20, dinner $20–$30. Child's meals. Specialties: spaghettini alla massimo, veal tre colori. Valet parking. Cr cds: A, D, DS, MC, V.

D

★★**GIACOSA.** 394 Giralda, at Le Jeune. 305/445-5858. Hrs: 11 am–2:30 pm, 6 pm–midnight; wkends from 6 pm. Res accepted. Italian menu. Wine. Semi-a la carte: lunch $10–$15, dinner $15–$25. Child's meals. Specialties: risotti, pesce al vapore. Parking. Elegant, informal dining. Cr cds: A, D, MC, V.

D

★★**JOHN MARTIN.** 253 Miracle Mile. 305/445-3777. Hrs: 11:30 am–3 pm, 5:30–10:45 pm; wkends to 11:45 pm; Sun brunch 11:30 am–3 pm. Closed Dec 25. Res accepted. Irish menu. Bar. Complete meals: lunch $6.50–$8.50, dinner $13.50–$18.50. Sun brunch $12.50. Child's meals. Specialties: Gaelic steak, imported Irish oak-smoked salmon. Entertainment. Parking. Authentic Irish pub atmosphere. Cr cds: A, C, D, DS, MC, V.

D

★★★**LE FESTIVAL.** 2120 Salzedo St. 305/442-8545 or 448-5149. Hrs: 11:45 am–2:30 pm, 6–10:30 pm; Fri to 11 pm; Sat 6–11 pm. Closed Sun; major hols; also Sept. Res accepted; required Fri, Sat. French menu. Serv bar. Wine list. A la carte entrees: lunch $7.50–$14, dinner $15.35–$24. Specialties: fresh salmon beurre blanc, grilled veal chop with port wine sauce, chicken à la Normande. Own pastries. Cr cds: A, C, D, MC, V.

D

★★★**LOUISIANA.** 1630 Ponce de Leon Blvd. 305/445-0481. Hrs: 11:30 am–2:30 pm, 6–10 pm; Fri to 11 pm; Sat 6–11 pm; Sun 6–10 pm. Closed Mon. Res accepted. French, continental menu. Beer. Wine list. Semi-a la carte: lunch $5.50–$10.95, dinner $14.50–$22. Specialties: strawberry duck, cassoulet, snapper caprice. Own pastries. Country French decor. Cr cds: A, MC, V.

D

✔★★**MELODY INN.** 83 Andalusia Ave. 305/448-0022. Hrs: 11:30 am–3 pm, 5:30–10:30 pm; Fri to 11 pm; Sat 5:30–11 pm; Sun 5:30–10 pm; summer hrs may vary. Closed Mon; Dec 24, 25. Res accepted. Swiss, continental menu. Beer. Semi-a la carte: lunch $6.50–$9.90, dinner $10.50–$17.95. Specializes in veal, seafood, Swiss dishes. Cr cds: A, C, D, MC, V.

D

★★★**RAMIRO'S.** 2700 Ponce de Leon Blvd. 305/443-7605. Hrs: 11:30 am–3 pm, 6:30–11 pm; Sat 6:30–11:30 pm. Closed Sun; Jan 1, Thanksgiving, Dec 25. Res accepted. Continental menu. Bar. Wine list. A la carte entrees: lunch $8.95–$10.95, dinner $17.95–$25.95. Complete meals: lunch $20–$25, dinner $35–$45. Specialties: spinach flan with black olive sauce, veal mignon with five sauces. Guitarist Wed. Parking. Cr cds: A, D, MC, V.

D

✔★★**SUN INN II.** 112 Giralda Ave. 305/446-8333. Hrs: 11:30 am–10:30 pm; Fri, Sat to 11:30 pm; early-bird dinner Mon–Fri 3–6 pm. Closed Thanksgiving. Res accepted. Chinese menu. Bar. Semi-a la carte: lunch $4.25–$6.95, dinner $7.95–$14.95. Specializes in orange beef, crispy quail, Mongolian firepot, lotus prawn. Chinese artwork, instruments. Cr cds: A, MC, V.

D

★★**THAI ORCHID II.** 317 Miracle Mile. 305/443-6364. Hrs: 11:30 am–3 pm, 5–10:30 pm; Fri, Sat to 11 pm. Closed Thanksgiving, Dec 25. Res accepted. Thai menu. Wine, beer. A la carte entrees: lunch $4.95–$7.95, dinner $7.25–$16.95. Specializes in Thai-style barbecue, sweet & sour snapper, macrobiotic dishes. Outdoor dining. Cr cds: A, MC, V.

D

★★★**YUCA.** 177 Giralda Ave. 305/444-4448. Hrs: noon–11 pm; Sat, Sun from 6 pm. Bar. Wine list. A la carte entrees: lunch $8–$15. Specialties: spicy baby back ribs, pan-seared fillet of yellowtail. Pianist. Parking; valet Fri, Sat. Bi-level dining; modern decor, many art objects. Cr cds: A, D, MC, V.

D

Crystal River (B-3)

Pop: 4,044 **Elev:** 4 ft **Area code:** 904 **Zip:** 34428

Favored by Florida residents as a bountiful fishing ground, the area around Crystal River is also a prime diving area. The town stands where the Crystal River meets King's Bay, and both salt- and freshwater fish are abundant. The river is a designated manatee sanctuary, where the endangered species winters from mid-November through March.

What to See and Do

1. **King's Bay.** Has 110 springs, including Hunter Spring with a flow of 41 million gallons daily. Fishing, duck hunting, scuba diving; also golf, tennis.

2. **Crystal River State Archaeological Site.** 3400 N Museum Point, 2½ mi W off US 19N, State Park Rd exit. Indian burial mounds, trailside displays and interpretive trails; self-guided tours. Visitor center has Indian artifacts. (Daily) Phone 795-3817. Per vehicle ¢

(For further information contact the Chamber of Commerce, 28 NW US 19; 795-3149.)

(See Homosassa Springs)

Motels

✔ ★★**COMFORT INN.** *4486 N Suncoast Blvd (US 19/98). 904/563-1500; FAX 904/563-5426.* 60 rms, 2 story. Mid-Nov–mid-Apr: S $39.95–$65; D $44.95–$65; each addl $5; under 18 free; higher rates some hols; lower rates rest of yr. Crib $7. Pet accepted; $5 per day. TV; cable. Pool. Restaurant 6 am–1 pm. Rm serv. Ck-out 11 am. Coin lndry. Meeting rms. Lighted tennis. Refrigerators avail. Picnic tables. Cr cds: A, D, DS, ER, MC, V.

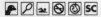

★★**DAYS INN.** *2380 NW US 19. 904/795-2111; FAX 904/795-4126.* 106 rms, 2 story. Jan–Mar: S $49; D $55; each addl $6; under 18 free; lower rates rest of yr. Crib free. Pet accepted; $5 per day. TV; cable. Pool. Restaurant 6 am–10 pm. Rm serv. Bar; entertainment, dancing. Ck-out noon. Coin lndry. Meeting rms. Gift shop. Bus depot transportation. Lawn games. Refrigerators. Boat dock, ramp. Cr cds: A, C, D, DS, MC, V.

✔ ★★**ECONO LODGE CRYSTAL RESORT.** *614 NW US 19, 1 mi N of FL 44. 904/795-3171; FAX 904/795-3179.* 114 rms, 1–2 story. Dec–Easter: S $46–$57; D $50–$61; each addl $4.50; kit. units $53–$61; under 18 free; lower rates rest of yr. Crib free. Pet accepted; $3 per day. TV; cable. Heated pool. Restaurant 6 am–11 pm. Bar from 4 pm. Ck-out noon. Coin lndry. Sundries. Gift shop. Exercise equipt: weight machine, rower, spa. Refrigerators avail. Some balconies. Picnic tables, grill. On Crystal River; dock, launching ramp, boats, guides; skin diving. Cr cds: A, C, D, DS, MC, V.

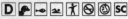

Resort

★★★**PLANTATION INN & GOLF RESORT.** *(Box 1116) West Fort Island Trail, County 44W, ¼ mi off US 19/98. 904/795-4211; res: 800/632-6262; FAX 904/795-1368.* 140 rms, 2 story, 12 villas. Feb–mid-Apr: S, D $88–$107; each addl $15; suites $118; villas to 4, $179; golf condos to 6, $310; under 12 free; wkly rates in villas; golf, tennis packages; lower rates rest of yr. Crib free. Pet accepted, some restrictions; $5 per day. TV; cable. 2 pools, 1 heated; saunas. Complimentary coffee 6–8 am. Dining rm 6 am–2 pm, 5–10 pm. Rm serv. Bar. Ck-out noon, ck-in 2 pm. Coin lndry. Convention facilities. Valet serv. Free local airport, bus depot transportation. Lighted tennis, pro. 27-hole golf, greens fee $32 (cart incl), pro, putting green, lighted driving range. Scuba gear and fishing equipment rentals, fishing guide. Boats avail; dockage. Lawn games. Some refrigerators. Private patios. Picnic tables. On Crystal River. Cr cds: A, C, D, DS, MC, V.

Cypress Gardens

(see Winter Haven)

Dade City (C-3)

Pop: 5,633 **Elev:** 78 ft **Area code:** 904 **Zip:** 33525

A community filled with moss-hung oaks, camphor trees and azalea bushes, Dade City is surrounded by citrus groves, cattle ranches, horse and poultry farms. It is also the seat of Pasco County.

What to See and Do

1. **Pioneer Florida Museum.** ½ mi N via US 301N, at 300 Pioneer Museum Rd. This 25-acre complex contains relics and photographs from pioneer times: clothing, farm implements, wagons; restored 2-story Overstreet House (ca 1864) with period furnishings; one-room school house; 84-year-old church; old train depot, train engine. Also miniature inaugural ball gowns of Florida's first ladies. (Tues–Sun afternoons; closed major hols) (See ANNUAL EVENTS) Phone 567-0262. ¢

2. **Saint Leo Abbey** (1889). 5 mi SW on FL 52, 4 mi E of I-75, on grounds of Saint Leo College. Benedictine Abbey named for Pope Leo I, completed in 1948, is an impressive Lombardic-Romanesque building with 21,000-pound cross, carved from Tennessee rose marble, and reproduction of Lourdes Grotto. (Daily) Donation. Phone 588-2881.

3. **Dade Battlefield State Historic Site.** 22 mi N on US 301, off FL 476W in Bushnell. Site is a memorial to Major Francis L. Dade and the more than 100 men who were ambushed and massacred here by Seminoles in 1835. Museum (daily). Nature trails. Picnicking, playground. Tennis, games. Standard hrs, fees. Phone 793-4781.

(For further information contact the Greater Dade City Chamber of Commerce, 402 E Meridian Ave; 567-3769.)

Annual Events

Pasco County Fair. Fairgrounds, 1 mi W on FL 52. 5 days late Feb.

Pioneer Florida Day. Pioneer Florida Museum (see #1). Commemorates early Florida life with historical exhibits, audiovisual programs; crafts demonstrations, "Cracker" food, traditional music, juried arts & crafts show. Phone 567-0262. Labor Day.

(For accommodations see Zephyrhills, also see Brooksville)

Dania (E-5)

Settled: 1896 **Pop:** 13,024 **Elev:** 11 ft **Area code:** 305 **Zip:** 33004

Little trace remains of the Danish families that originally settled here and little is left of the crops that at one time made Dania the tomato center of the world. Today, Dania attracts tourists with its antique shopping plaza and proximity to the Atlantic Ocean.

What to See and Do

1. **John U. Lloyd Beach State Recreation Area.** ½ mi N, off FL A1A (North Ocean Dr). A 244-acre park with swimming, skin diving; fishing; boating (marina). Nature trails. Picnicking, concession. Standard hrs, fees. Phone 923-2833.

2. **Jai-Alai Fronton.** 301 E Dania Beach Blvd, at jct US 1 & FL A1A. Parimutuel betting; clubhouse dining. (Tues–Sat evenings; matinees Tues, Thurs & Sat; closed 2 wks late Apr) Children over 10 yrs

only; must be with parent. Phone 920-1511, 426-4330 or 945-4345. General admission ¢

(For further information contact the Chamber of Commerce, 102 W Dania Beach Blvd, PO Box 838; 927-3377.)

(See Fort Lauderdale, Hollywood, Pompano Beach)

Hotels

★ ★ ★ **HILTON FORT LAUDERDALE AIRPORT.** *1870 Griffin Rd, at Fort Lauderdale Intl Airport.* 305/920-3300; FAX 305/920-3348. 388 rms, 8 story. Mid-Dec–early Apr: S, D $120–$195; each addl $10; suites $360–$835; family, wkly rates; honeymoon, cruise line, wkend packages; lower rates rest of yr. Crib free. TV; cable. Heated pool. Restaurants 6 am–11 pm. Rm serv to 1 am. Bar 4 pm–1 am; entertainment, dancing exc Sun. Ck-out noon. Convention facilities. Concierge. Gift shop. Free covered parking. Free airport transportation. 2 lighted tennis courts. Exercise rm; instructor, weights, bicycles, whirlpool, saunas. Some refrigerators. Resort-like setting; overlooks waterway. *LUXURY LEVEL:* **CONCIERGE FLOOR.** 27 rms, 2 suites. S $180; D $195. Private lounge. Complimentary continental bkfst, refreshments. Cr cds: A, C, D, DS, ER, MC, V.

★ ★ ★ **SHERATON DESIGN CENTER.** *1825 Griffin Rd, at Fort Lauderdale Intl Airport.* 305/920-3500; FAX 305/920-3571. 251 rms, 12 story. Dec–Apr: S $129–$179; D $139–$199; suites $275–$475; under 12 free; lower rates rest of yr. Crib free. Pet accepted. TV; cable. Pool; poolside serv. Restaurant 7 am–11 pm. Rm serv 24 hrs. Bar 11–3 am; entertainment exc Sun, dancing. Ck-out noon. Convention facilities. Concierge. Gift shop. Deli. Free airport transportation. Lighted tennis. Golf privileges. Exercise equipt; weights, bicycles, whirlpool, sauna, steam rm. Some bathrm phones, refrigerators. 2-story atrium lobby. Cr cds: A, C, D, DS, ER, MC, V.

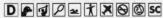

Restaurants

★ ★ ★ **NEVER ON SUNDAY GRAND CAFÉ.** *129 N US 1.* 305/923-1000. Hrs: 5–10 pm; Fri, Sat to 11 pm. Res accepted. French, Italian, continental menu. Wine list. A la carte entrees: dinner $12.95–$23.95. Child's meals. Specialties: Dover sole, sweetbreads, rack of lamb, duckling. Own baking, pasta. Parking. In one of the oldest houses in Dania. Cr cds: A, C, D, DS, MC, V.

★ **SPICED APPLE.** *3281 Griffin Rd.* 305/962-0772. Hrs: 11:30 am–10 pm; Sat 4–10:30 pm; Sun 4–9:30 pm; Sun brunch 11:30 am–4 pm. Res accepted. Bar. A la carte entrees: lunch $3.95–$11.95, dinner $7.95–$24.95. Lunch buffet (Mon–Fri) $6.95. Sun brunch $10.95. Child's meals. Specialties: baby back ribs, jumbo seafood platter, baked stuffed chicken breast. Salad bar. Parking. Six dining rms; rustic decor. Cr cds: A, C, D, MC, V.

Daytona Beach (B-4)

Founded: 1870 **Pop:** 61,921 **Elev:** 10 ft **Area code:** 904

One of the oldest Floridian resorts, Daytona Beach achieved international fame in the early days of the automobile due to its 23-mile, 500-foot-wide beach, which offered a natural speedway. In 1903, Alexander Winton set the world's record of 68 mph on the Daytona beach. Autos are still allowed on certain sections of the beach (daylight hours only), but the speed limit is 10 mph.

The city, with a triple waterfront—the Atlantic Ocean and two sides of the Halifax River—has developed as a year-round vacation spot, especially popular in spring and summer with vacationing students and families. Deep-sea fishing from charter boats at offshore reefs is enjoyed as well as river fishing on the inland waters and from the six bridges spanning the Halifax River. Supplementing tourism are light industry, Bethune-Cookman College, Embry-Riddle Aeronautical University and a branch campus of the University of Central Florida, Orlando.

What to See and Do

1. **Public beach.** Unique in Florida and one of the most unusual in the world, the shoreline of this beach just north and south of the Ponce de Leon Inlet welcomes more than 7 million tourists each year. The water temperature is typically 80°F or warmer during the summer months; ocean lifeguards and beach rangers are on duty year-round. When dampened by the incoming tide, the sand packs to a consistency firm and smooth enough to drive on, and driving is permitted on 30 miles of strand during daylight hours (Feb–early Sept; fee). Swimming, surfing and surf casting. Phone 239-SURF. Beach driving ¢¢

2. **Museum of Arts & Sciences.** 1040 Museum Blvd, in Tuscawilla Park. Exhibits include an extensive Cuban collection of fine and folk art; American fine and decorative arts; African art; graphic art; Pleistocene fossils and a 13-foot-tall giant ground sloth skeleton; planetarium with afternoon star shows; Frischer Sculpture Garden. (Daily exc Mon) Free admission Fri. Phone 255-0285. ¢¢

3. **Sugar Mill Gardens.** 3½ mi S on US 1 to Port Orange, then 1 mi W on Herbert St. Twelve acres of botanical gardens on grounds of ruined sugar mill (1804); flowering trees include magnolia; other flora. Also dinosaur statues. (Daily) Phone 767-1735. **Free.**

4. **Ponce de Leon Inlet & Lighthouse** (1887). S of town, 4931 S Peninsula Dr. The 175-foot lighthouse contains marine museum with much of the original equipment on display; 3 restored keeper's cottages and 3 other buildings. Beaches; fishing. Picnicking, cafes. (Daily) Phone 761-1821. ¢¢

5. **Daytona International Speedway.** 1801 Volusia Ave, on US 92. This 2.5 mile, high-speed, banked track, with a grandstand seating 125,000, is a proving ground for car and accessory manufacturers. Track (daily); tours exc during races & special tests. Most racing events Feb, Mar, July, Oct & Dec. (See ANNUAL EVENT) Phone 253-RACE (tickets) or 254-2700. Tour ¢¢

6. **Daytona Beach Kennel Club.** 2201 W Volusia Ave, W on US 92. Greyhound racing; parimutuel betting. (Mon–Sat evenings; matinees Mon, Wed & Sat) Phone 252-6484. General admission ¢

7. **Sightseeing.** *Dixie Queen* Riverboat. Mainland side of Seabreeze Bridge. Tours (2½ hrs) on the Halifax River aboard 400-passenger, 1890s-style riverboat. Brunch, lunch, dinner cruises; also day cruise to St Augustine. One to three departures (Wed–Sun). Phone 255-1997. ¢¢¢¢–¢¢¢¢¢

8. **Gray Line bus tours.** Contact 3658 S Nova Rd, Port Orange 32119; 761-6506.

(For further information contact ''Destination Daytona,'' 126 E Orange Ave, PO Box 910, 32115; 255-0415 or 800/854-1234.)

Annual Event

Auto races. Daytona International Speedway (see #5). Speed weeks with Rolex 24 & Daytona 500, Feb; Daytona 200 (AMA motorcycle races), early Mar; Pepsi 400 stock car race, early July; several other races. Contact Daytona International Speedway, PO Box 2801, 32120-2801; 253-RACE.

(See DeLand, New Smyrna Beach, Ormond Beach)

Motels

(Rates are usually higher and there is a min 3–5-day stay during hols, race weeks, special events)

★ ★ ★**ACAPULCO INN.** *2505 S Atlantic Ave (32118). 904/761-2210; res: 800/245-3580; FAX 904/761-2216.* 133 rms, 8 story, 91 kit. units. Feb–late Apr: S, D $102; each addl $6–$10; kit. units $109; under 18 free; lower rates rest of yr. Crib free. TV; cable. Heated pool; wading pool, 2 whirlpools. Free supervised child's activities. Restaurant 7 am–8 pm. Bar noon–midnight. Ck-out 11 am. Coin lndry. Bellhops. Valet serv. Gift shop. Tennis & golf privileges. Game rm. Lawn games. Refrigerators. Balconies. Picnic tables. Southwestern-style motel, on beach. Cr cds: A, C, D, DS, ER, MC, V.

[D] [🛎] [⚓] [🏊] [⊘] [◎] [SC]

★ ★**BEACHCOMER INN.** *2000 N Atlantic Ave (32118). 904/252-8513; res: 800/245-3575.* 184 rms, 7 story, 104 kits. Feb–Sept: S, D $83–$107; each addl $6–$10; kit. units $90–$115; under 18 free; lower rates rest of yr. Crib free. TV; cable. Heated pool; wading pool, whirlpool, poolside serv, lifeguard (in season). Free supervised child's activities. Restaurant 7 am–9 pm. Rm serv. Bar. Ck-out 11 am. Coin lndry. Bellhops. Gift shop. Sundries. Golf privileges. Game rm. Lawn games. Refrigerators. Balconies. Picnic tables. On ocean. Cr cds: A, C, D, DS, ER, MC, V.

[D] [🛎] [⚓] [⊘] [◎] [SC]

✔ ★**DAYTONA INN-SEABREEZE.** *730 N Atlantic Ave (32118). 904/255-5491; res: 800/874-1822; FAX 904/255-3680.* 98 rms, 5 story, 51 kits. Feb–mid-Apr, late May–early Sept: S, D $63–$86; each addl $10; kit. units $55–$92; under 17 free; wkly rates; higher rates special events; varied lower rates rest of yr. TV; cable. Pool; wading pool, lifeguard (in season). Free supervised child's activities (June–Aug). Restaurant 7 am–2 pm. Ck-out 11 am. Coin lndry. Golf privileges. Private patios, balconies. Picnic tables. On ocean. Cr cds: A, C, D, DS, ER, MC, V.

[🛎] [⚓] [◎] [SC]

✔ ★ ★**HAMPTON INN-AIRPORT.** *1715 W International Speedway Blvd (US 92) (32114), near Regional Airport. 904/257-4030; FAX 904/257-5721.* 122 rms, 4 story. Jan–Apr: S $62; D $64; under 18 free; lower rates rest of yr. Crib free. TV; cable. Pool; whirlpool. Complimentary continental bkfst, coffee. Restaurant adj 11 am–midnight. Ck-out 11 am. Meeting rms. Valet serv. Free airport transportation. Some refrigerators. Cr cds: A, C, D, DS, ER, MC, V.

[D] [⚓] [✕] [⊘] [◎] [SC]

✔ ★**HoJo INN.** *2015 S Atlantic Ave (32118). 904/255-2446; res: 800/456-2446.* 41 rms, 2 story, 33 kits. Mar–Apr, June–Aug: S, D $60–$80; each addl $5; kit. units $65–$90; under 16 free; wkly, monthly rates; lower rates rest of yr. Crib free. TV; cable. Heated pool. Complimentary coffee in lobby. Restaurant opp 7 am–11 pm. Ck-out 11 am. Coin lndry. Lawn games. Private patios, balconies. Picnic tables, grills. On beach. Cr cds: A, D, DS, MC, V.

[⚓] [⊘] [◎] [SC]

★ ★**HOWARD JOHNSON PIRATE'S COVE.** *3501 S Atlantic Ave (32127), opp Port Orange Causeway. 904/767-8740; FAX 904/788-8609.* 172 rms, 7 story, 99 kits. Feb–mid-Aug: S, D $59–$95; each addl $6; kit. units $65–$99; under 18 free; higher rates special events; lower rates rest of yr. Crib free. TV; cable. Heated pool; wading pool. Restaurant 7 am–2 pm, 5–9 pm. Bars 11–2 am; entertainment, dancing Fri & Sat. Ck-out 11 am. Coin lndry. Gift shop. Game rm. Private patios, balconies. On beach. Cr cds: A, C, D, DS, ER, MC, V.

[⚓] [⊘] [◎] [SC]

★ ★**PERRY'S OCEAN-EDGE.** *2209 S Atlantic Ave (32118). 904/255-0581; res: 800/447-0002; FAX 904/258-7315.* 204 rms, 2–6 story, 140 kits. Feb–Apr, mid-June–Aug: S, D $65–$120; each addl $10; kit. units $10 addl; varied lower rates rest of yr. Crib $10. TV; cable. 3 pools, 1 indoor; whirlpool. Complimentary continental bkfst. Restaurant 7 am–2 pm. Ck-out 11 am. Coin lndry. Bellhops. Valet serv. Gift shop.

Golf privileges, on-site putting green. Game rm. Lawn games. Picnic tables. Oceanfront, beach. Cr cds: A, C, D, DS, MC, V.

[D] [🛎] [⚓] [◎] [SC]

✔ ★**RODEWAY INN-OCEANFRONT.** *1299 S Atlantic Ave (32118). 904/255-4545; FAX 904/248-0443.* 96 rms, 5 story, 62 kit. units. Feb–Easter & June–Aug: S, D $50; suites $65–$85; kit. units $60–$65; under 18 free; wkly rates; higher rates special events; lower rates rest of yr. Crib free. TV; cable. Heated pool; wading pool. Restaurant 7 am–2 pm. Ck-out 11 am. Coin lndry. On beach. Cr cds: A, C, D, DS, MC, V.

[⚓] [⊘] [◎] [SC]

★**SPEEDWAY INN.** *2992 W International Speedway Blvd (US 92) (32124). 904/253-0643; res: 800/553-6499; FAX 904/253-0643, ext 626.* 114 rms, 2 story. Late Jan–Mar: S, D $45–$110; under 12 free; lower rates rest of yr. Crib $5. Pet accepted; $5. TV; cable. Pool. Complimentary coffee in lobby. Restaurant adj open 24 hrs. Bar 3 pm–2 am. Ck-out 11 am. Coin lndry. Cr cds: A, C, D, DS, MC, V.

[🐾] [⚓] [⊘] [◎] [SC]

✔ ★ ★ ★**SUN VIKING LODGE.** *2411 S Atlantic Ave (32118). 904/252-6252; res: 800/874-4469; FAX 904/252-5463.* 91 rms, 2–8 story, 70 kits. Feb–Sept: S, D $46–$75; each addl $6–$10; kit. units $65–$96; under 12 free (limit 2); wkly rates; higher rates special events; lower rates rest of yr. Crib free. TV; cable. 2 heated pools, 1 indoor; wading pool. Free supervised child's activities. Restaurant 7:30 am–2:30 pm. Ck-out 11 am. Coin lndry. Meeting rm. Exercise equipt; weight machine, bicycle, whirlpool, sauna. Lawn games. Game rms. Refrigerators. Balconies. Picnic tables, grills. 60-ft water slide. Rooftop sun deck; on beach. Cr cds: A, C, D, DS, MC, V.

[⚓] [🏃] [⊘] [◎]

Motor Hotels

✔ ★**ALADDIN INN.** *2323 S Atlantic Ave (32118). 904/255-0476; res: 800/874-7517; FAX 904/255-3376.* 120 rms, 6 story, 62 kits. Feb–Aug: S, D $44–$90; suites $73–$150; kit. units $54–$100; under 18 free; wkly rates; higher rates special events; lower rates rest of yr. Crib free. TV; cable. Heated pool; wading pool. Free supervised child's activities (mid-June–mid-Aug). Restaurant 8 am–2 pm. Ck-out 11 am. Coin lndry. Gift shop. Game rm. Lawn games. Refrigerators. Private balconies. On beach. Cr cds: A, C, D, DS, MC, V.

[⚓] [◎] [SC]

★ ★**BEST WESTERN LA PLAYA RESORT.** *2500 N Atlantic Ave (32118). 904/672-0990; FAX 904/677-0982.* 239 rms, 9 story, 35 suites, 165 kits. Feb–Apr: S, D $76–$94; each addl $6–$8; suites $129–$175; kit. units $82–$105; under 18 free; wkly rates; higher rates special events; varied lower rates rest of yr. Crib free. TV; cable. Indoor pool; wading pool. Free supervised child's activities (June–Sept). Restaurant 7 am–1:30 pm. Rooftop bar 5 pm–2 am; entertainment exc Sun. Ck-out 11 am. Meeting rms. Bellhops. Golf privileges. Exercise equipt; bicycles, stair machine, whirlpools, steam rm, sauna. Game rm. Lawn games. Private patios, balconies. Picnic tables. On beach. Cr cds: A, C, D, DS, ER, MC, V, JCB.

[D] [🛎] [⚓] [🏃] [◎] [SC]

★**DAYS INN-OCEANSIDE.** *800 N Atlantic Ave (32118). 904/252-6491; FAX 904/258-1458.* 117 rms, 6–7 story, 55 kits. Feb–Mar: S, D $95–$150; each addl $10; kit. units $10 addl; suites $150; under 12 free; wkly rates; lower rates rest of yr. TV; cable. Heated pool. Restaurant 7–11 am. Ck-out 11 am. Private patios, balconies. On beach. Cr cds: A, C, D, DS, MC, V.

[⚓] [⊘] [◎] [SC]

★ ★**HILTON-DAYTONA BEACH.** *2637 S Atlantic Ave (32118). 904/767-7350; res: 800/525-7350; FAX 904/760-3651.* 212 units, 11 story. Late Feb–Labor Day: S $98–$173; D $103–$173; each addl $15; suites $239–$550; kit. units $173; some wknd rates; varied lower rates rest of yr. Crib free. TV; cable. Heated pool; wading pool, poolside serv (Mar–Sept). Playground. Free supervised child's activities (June–Aug). Restaurant 7 am–5 pm; dining rm 5–10 pm; Fri, Sat to 11 pm. Rm serv.

Bars 10–1:30 am; entertainment. Ck-out 11 am. Meeting rms. Bellhops. Valet serv. Gift shop. Beauty shop. Free underground parking. 2 lighted tennis courts. Golf privileges. Exercise equipt; weights, treadmill, whirlpool. Game rm. Lawn games. Refrigerators. Private patios, balconies. On beach. Cr cds: A, C, D, DS, ER, MC, V, JCB.

[D] [icons] SC

★★HOLIDAY INN-OCEANFRONT. *2560 N Atlantic Ave (32118).* 904/672-1440; FAX 904/677-8811. 143 rms, 4–8 story, 113 studio rms. Feb–Labor Day: S, D $74–$165; each addl $6; studio rms $80–$175; under 18 free; wkly rates; some wknd rates; lower rates rest of yr. Crib free. TV; cable. Heated pool; wading pool, whirlpool. Free supervised child's activities (June–Sept). Restaurant adj 6–11 am. Ck-out 11 am. Coin lndry. Meeting rm. Valet serv. Sundries. Private patios, balconies. On beach. Cr cds: A, C, D, DS, ER, MC, V, JCB.

[D] [icons] SC

★★HOWARD JOHNSON PLAZA HOTEL ON THE BEACH. *600 N Atlantic Ave (32118).* 904/255-4471; FAX 904/253-7543. 323 rms, 14 story, 40 suites, 108 kits. Mid-Jan–Apr: S $74–$114; D $84–$124; each addl $10; suites $119–$225; kit. units $80–$130; under 18 free; golf plans; higher rates special events; lower rates rest of yr. Crib free. TV; cable. Heated pool; poolside serv. Free supervised child's activities (mid-June–mid-Aug). Restaurant 6 am–11 pm. Rm serv. Bar from 11 am; entertainment, dancing. Ck-out noon. Coin lndry. Convention facilities. Bellhops. Valet serv. Gift shop. Golf privileges. Game rm. Lawn games. Some refrigerators. Balconies. On beach. Cr cds: A, C, D, DS, MC, V, JCB.

[D] [icons] SC

★★NAUTILUS INN. *1515 S Atlantic Ave (32118).* 904/254-8600; res: 800/245-0560. 99 rms, 10 story, 72 kits. Jan–Apr: S, D $104–$111; kit. units $111–$127; under 18 free; wkly rates; lower rates rest of yr. Crib free. TV; cable. Heated pool; whirlpool. Free supervised child's activities. Complimentary continental bkfst, afternoon refreshments. Restaurant nearby. Ck-out 11 am. Lawn games. Private patios, balconies. Picnic tables. On ocean, beach. Cr cds: A, C, D, DS, ER, MC, V.

[D] [icons] SC

✔★★PALM PLAZA. *3301 S Atlantic Ave (32118).* 904/767-1711; res: 800/448-2286; FAX 904/756-8394. 98 kit. units, 11 story. June–Sept: S, D $59–$83; under 18 free (limit 2); golf plans; lower rates rest of yr. Crib free. TV; cable. Heated pool; wading pool, whirlpool. Restaurant 7:45 am–3 pm. Ck-out 11 am. Coin lndry. Golf privileges. Game rm. Balconies. On ocean, swimming beach. Cr cds: A, C, D, DS, MC, V.

[icons] SC

✔★★QUALITY INN. *1615 S Atlantic Ave (32118).* 904/255-0921; FAX 904/255-3849. 195 rms, 7 story, 21 suites, 84 kits. S, D $55–$112; each addl $10; suites $77–$132; kit. units $65–$118; under 17 free; monthly rates. Crib free. TV; cable. Heated pool; wading pool. Restaurant 7 am–1 pm. Rm serv. Bar 11–2 am. Ck-out 11 am. Coin lndry. Meeting rm. Bellhops. Valet serv. Gift shop. Putting green. Game rm. Lawn games. Balconies. On ocean, beach. Cr cds: A, C, D, DS, ER, MC, V, JCB.

[icons] SC

★★RAMADA BEACH RESORT. *2700 N Atlantic Ave (32118).* 904/672-3770; FAX 904/673-7262. 383 rms, 12 story, 74 kits. Late Jan–early Apr, June–Aug: S, D $69–$110; each addl $10; kit. units $95–$110; under 18 free; monthly rates; some wknd rates; lower rates rest of yr. Crib free. Pet accepted. TV; cable. 2 pools; wading pool, poolside serv. Free supervised child's activities (mid-May–Aug). Restaurant 6:30 am–2 pm, 5–10 pm. Rm serv. Bar. Ck-out noon. Coin lndry. Convention facilities. Sundries. Rec rm. Balconies. On beach. Cr cds: A, C, D, DS, ER, MC, V, JCB.

[D] [icons] SC

★★SEAGARDEN INN. *3161 S Atlantic Ave (32118).* 904/761-2335; res: 800/245-0575; FAX 904/756-6676. 144 rms, 10 story, 90 kits. Feb–mid-Apr: S, D $97–$104; each addl $6–$10; kit. units $103–$110;

under 12 free; higher rates special events; lower rates rest of yr. Crib free. TV; cable. Heated pool; wading pool, whirlpool, poolside serv. Free supervised child's activities (Mar, Apr & June–Sept). Restaurant 8 am–noon, 4–8 pm. Rm serv. Bar 11 am–midnight. Ck-out 11 am. Coin lndry. Meeting rms. Valet serv. Gift shop. Golf privileges. Private patios, balconies. Picnic tables. On beach. Cr cds: A, C, D, DS, ER, MC, V, JCB.

[D] [icons] SC

★★TREASURE ISLAND INN. *2025 S Atlantic Ave (32118).* 904/255-8371; res: 800/543-5070; FAX 904/255-4984. 228 rms, 11 story, 176 kits. Feb–early Apr: S, D $89–$116; each addl $10; suites $155–$190; studio rms $97–$126; kit. units $8 addl; under 18 free; wkly rates, some wknd rates; lower rates rest of yr. Crib free. TV; cable. 2 pools, 1 heated; wading pool, 2 saunas, poolside serv, lifeguard in season. Free supervised child's activities. Restaurant 7–11:30 am, 5–9:30 pm. Rm serv. Bar 11–2 am; entertainment, dancing. Ck-out 11 am. Coin lndry. Meeting rms. Bellhops. Valet serv. Gift shop. Tennis, golf privileges. Rec rm. Lawn games. Refrigerators. Balconies. Picnic tables. On ocean. Cr cds: A, C, D, DS, ER, MC, V.

[D] [icons] SC

★★WHITEHALL INN. *640 N Atlantic Ave (32118).* 904/258-5435; res: 800/874-7016; FAX 904/253-0735. 204 rms, 11 story, 70 kits. Feb–Apr: S, D $68–$108; each addl $10; kit. units $10 addl; under 18 free; wkly rates; lower rates rest of yr. Crib free. TV; cable. Pool; wading pool, poolside serv, lifeguard in season. Restaurant 7–11 am. Bar noon–2:30 am. Ck-out 11 am. Meeting rms. Bellhops. Game rm. Balconies. On ocean, swimming beach. Cr cds: A, C, D, DS, MC, V.

[D] [icons] SC

Hotel

★★★MARRIOTT. *100 N Atlantic Ave (32118).* 904/254-8200; FAX 904/253-0275. 402 rms, 15 story, 25 suites. S, D $113–$175; each addl $20; suites $265–$450; under 18 free. Crib free. Valet parking $3; garage $8. TV; cable. Indoor/outdoor pool; wading pool, poolside serv. Restaurant 7 am–11 pm. Bar 11–2 am; entertainment, dancing. Ck-out 11 am. Coin lndry. Convention facilities. Concierge. Shopping arcade. Beauty shop. Airport, RR station, bus depot transportation. Tennis & golf privileges. Exercise rm; instructor, weight machine, bicycles, whirlpool, steam rm, sauna. Game rm. Minibars. On beach. *LUXURY LEVEL: EXECUTIVE LEVEL.* 16 rms, 1 suite. S, D $213; suite $750. Private lounge, honor bar. In-rm movies. Bathrm phones. Complimentary coffee 7–9 am, newspaper.
Cr cds: A, C, D, DS, MC, V.

[D] [icons] SC

Inn

✔★★LIVE OAK. *444 & 448 S Beach St (32114).* 904/252-4667; res: 800/881-INNS; FAX 904/255-1871. 16 rms in 2 houses, 4 with bath, 2 story. S, D $70–$99; each addl $10; wkly, wknd rates; golf plan; higher rates: special events, Bike Week. Crib $10. TV; cable, in-rm movies. Complimentary continental bkfst, tea/sherry. Restaurant (see LIVE OAK INN). Rm serv. Ck-out noon, ck-in 2 pm. Concierge. Airport transportation avail. Health club privileges. Two house (1871 & 1881) in historic district. Totally nonsmoking. Cr cds: A, C, MC, V.

[D] [icons]

Resort

★★★HOLIDAY INN CROWN PLAZA-INDIGO LAKES (formerly Hilton). *2620 W International Speedway Blvd (US 92) (32114),* at I-95. 904/258-6333; FAX 904/254-3698. 211 rms, 2 story, 64 suites. Mid-Jan–Apr: S, D $99–$119; each addl $15 (3 or more); suites $129–$175; kit. units $129–$139; family rates; package plans; lower rates rest of yr. Crib free. TV; cable. 2 pools; wading pool, poolside serv (seasonal). Coffee in rms. Restaurants 7 am–10 pm. Rm serv. Bar 9 am–midnight. Ck-out 11 am, ck-in 3 pm. Coin lndry. Meeting rms. Valet serv. Gift shop.

Pro shops. Grocery, package store opp. Free airport transportation. Lighted tennis, pro. 18-hole golf, pro, putting green, driving range. Addl charges for golf, tennis. Bicycle rentals. Lawn games. Exercise equipt; bicycles, treadmill, sauna. Refrigerators. Whirlpool in condo units. Some private patios, balconies. Picnic tables. Cr cds: A, C, D, DS, ER, MC, V, JCB.

Restaurants

★ **AUNT CATFISH'S.** *4009 Halifax Dr, at W end of Port Orange Bridge.* 904/767-4768. Hrs: 11:30 am–10 pm; Sun from 9 am; Sun brunch 9 am–2 pm. Closed Dec 23–25. Res accepted. Bar. Semi-a la carte: lunch $3.99–$7.89, dinner $6.99–$24.95. Sun brunch $8.99. Child's meals. Specializes in seafood, ribs. Salad bar. Pianist (summer). Parking. Southern riverland atmosphere. Antique post office at entrance. Cr cds: A, DS, MC, V.

D **SC**

★ ★ **GENE'S STEAK HOUSE.** *3674 Volusia Ave, 4 mi W of I-95 on US 92.* 904/255-2059. Hrs: 5–10 pm; Sun to 9:30 pm. Closed Mon; most major hols. Res accepted. Bar. Semi-a la carte: dinner $12.95–$28.95. Specializes in char-broiled steak. Parking. Family-owned. Cr cds: A, C, D, MC, V.

✔ ★ ★ **HUNGARIAN VILLAGE.** *424 S Ridgewood.* 904/253-5712. Hrs: 5–9 pm; closing hrs may vary; early-bird dinner 5–6:30 pm. Closed Sun, Mon; also June & Dec. Res accepted. Hungarian, Amer menu. Semi-a la carte: dinner $7.50–$13. Child's meals. Specialties: Wienerschnitzel, Hungarian wooden plate, beef goulash. Parking. Hungarian decor; various musical instruments on display. Cr cds: A, C, D, DS, MC, V.

D

✔ ★ ★ **LIVE OAK INN.** *(See Live Oak Inn)* 904/252-4667. Hrs: 5–9:30 pm. Closed Dec 24. Res accepted. Continental menu. Bar. Complete meals: dinner $13–$17. Child's meals. Specialties: salmon Oscar, chocolate terrine. Parking. Totally nonsmoking. Cr cds: A, C, MC, V.

D

★ ★ **PARK'S SEAFOOD.** *951 N Beach St.* 904/258-7272. Hrs: 5–10 pm; Sat 4:30–11 pm; Sun 4–10 pm; early-bird dinner to 6 pm. Closed Thanksgiving, Dec 25; also 1st 3 wks Dec. Bar. Semi-a la carte: dinner $6.95–$19.95. Child's meals. Specializes in seafood, steak, prime rib. Parking. Rustic setting on waterfront; view of Halifax River. Cr cds: A, D, MC, V.

D

★ ★ **RICCARDO'S.** *610 Glenview Blvd.* 904/253-3035. Hrs: 5–10 pm. Closed Thanksgiving, Dec 24, 25. Res accepted. Northern Italian menu. Wine. Semi-a la carte: dinner $7.25–$22. Child's meals. Specializes in veal, shrimp, pasta. Own ice cream, pastries. Cr cds: A, C, D, MC, V.

D

★ ★ **TOP OF DAYTONA.** *2625 S Atlantic Ave.* 904/767-5791. Hrs: 11 am–10 pm; early-bird dinner 3–6 pm. Sun brunch noon–3 pm. Res accepted. Continental menu. Bar. A la carte entrees: lunch $4.95–$6.95, dinner $8.95–$19.95. Sun brunch $9.95. Child's meals. Specializes in veal, beef, chicken. Salad bar. Pianist. Parking. On 29th floor of high-rise apartment building. Cr cds: A, D, MC, V.

D **SC**

Unrated Dining Spots

MORRISON'S CAFETERIA. *200 N Ridgewood.* 904/258-6396. Hrs: 11 am–8:30 pm. Avg ck: lunch $4.70, dinner $6. Child's meals. Specializes in fried shrimp. Parking. Cr cds: A, DS, MC, V.

D

PICCADILLY CAFETERIA. *1700 International Speedway Blvd, #156, in Volusia Mall.* 904/258-5373. Hrs: 11 am–8:30 pm. Closed Dec 25. Avg ck: lunch $4.50, dinner $4.65. Specialties: Dilly dish, classic American dinner. Cr cds: A, C, D, DS, MC, V.

Deerfield Beach (E-5)

Settled: 1898 **Pop:** 46,325 **Elev:** 12 ft **Area code:** 305

Twenty settlers established the town of Deerfield Beach in 1898. The Hillsboro River, which formed the northern boundary of Deerfield, was later dredged into a canal that linked the town with Lake Okeechobee, 45 miles to the northwest. Although primarily an agricultural area until the late 1940s, during Prohibition the Hillsboro Canal was an unloading site for rumrunners; federal agents occasionally captured a boatload of liquor. Today, tourists come to Deerfield Beach for the excellent fishing and the beautiful beaches.

What to See and Do

Quiet Waters Park. 6601 N Powerline Rd. A 427-acre county park. Swimming, cable water-skiing; fishing; boating (marina, rentals). Nature trails, bicycle rentals. Miniature golf. Picnicking, concessions; playground. Tent camping (rentals). (Daily) Phone 360-1315. Wkends, hols ¢

(For further information contact the Greater Deerfield Beach Chamber of Commerce, 1601 E Hillsboro Blvd, 33441; 427-1050.)

Annual Event

Cracker Day. Celebration in honor of town's early settlers, called ''Crackers,'' who migrated here from Georgia. Parades, rides, games, entertainment, food. Phone 428-4428. Late Mar or early Apr.

(See Boca Raton, Dania, Delray Beach, Fort Lauderdale, Pompano Beach)

Motels

★ ★ **COMFORT SUITES.** *1050 E Newport Center Dr (33442).* 305/570-8887; FAX 305/570-5346. 101 suites, 4 story. Jan–Mar: suites $79–$95; under 18 free; golf plans; lower rates rest of yr. Crib free. Pet accepted, some restrictions. TV; cable. Heated pool; whirlpool. Complimentary continental bkfst. Restaurant adj 6:30 am–3 pm. Bar noon–8 pm. Ck-out noon. Coin lndry. Sundries. Gift shop. Lighted tennis privileges. 18-hole golf privileges, greens fee $30–$60, pro, putting green. Game rm. Refrigerators. Cr cds: A, C, D, DS, ER, MC, V, JCB.

D

★ ★ **RAMADA INN.** *1401 S US 1 (33441).* 305/421-5000; FAX 305/426-2811. 107 rms, 2 story, 7 kits. Mid-Dec–mid-Apr: S $50–$75; D $55–$95; each addl $10; suites $60–$125; kit. units $60–$85; under 16 free; lower rates rest of yr. Crib free. TV; cable. Heated pool; poolside serv. Restaurant 7 am–10 pm. Bar 11 am–midnight. Ck-out noon. Coin lndry. Meeting rms. Sundries. Barber, beauty shop. Refrigerators avail. Cr cds: A, C, D, DS, ER, MC, V, JCB.

★ ★ **WELLESLEY INN.** *100 SW 12th Ave (33442).* 305/428-0661; FAX 305/427-6701. 79 rms, 4 story. Dec–Apr: S $59.99–$69; D $69.99–$79.99; suites $89.99–$99.99; under 12 free; lower rates rest of yr. Crib $5. Pet accepted, some restrictions; $5. TV; cable. Heated pool. Complimentary continental bkfst, coffee. Restaurant nearby. Ck-out 11 am. Coin lndry. Refrigerator in suites. Cr cds: A, C, D, DS, MC, V.

Motor Hotels

✔ ★DAYS INN OCEANSIDE. *50 SE 20th Ave (FL A1A) (33441)*. 305/428-0650. 69 rms, 6 story. Mid-Dec–mid-Apr: S, D $89–$139; each addl $10; under 16 free; lower rates rest of yr. Pet accepted, some restrictions; $10. TV; cable. Pool; wading pool. Restaurant 7–2 am. Rm serv. Bar 4 pm–midnight. Ck-out 11 am. Coin lndry. Meeting rms. Valet serv. Some refrigerators. Beach 1 blk. Cr cds: A, C, D, DS, ER, MC, V.

★ ★HOWARD JOHNSON OCEAN RESORT. *2096 NE 2nd St (33441)*. 305/428-2850; FAX 305/480-9639. 177 rms, 8 story. Early Feb–Mar: S, D $129–$159; under 18 free (max 3); varied lower rates rest of yr. Crib free. TV; cable. Heated pool; poolside serv. Restaurant 6:30 am–10 pm. Bar 11–1 am. Ck-out noon. Meeting rms. Bellhops. Valet serv. Gift shop. Golf privileges. Game rm. Refrigerators avail. Opp ocean, pier. Cr cds: A, C, D, DS, ER, MC, V, JCB.

★ ★RADISSON SUITE HOTEL (formerly Quality Suites). *1050 E Newport Center Dr (33442)*. 305/570-8888; FAX 305/570-5346. 107 suites, 5 story. Jan–Mar: suites $109–$134; under 18 free; golf plans; lower rates rest of yr. Crib free. TV; cable, in-rm movies. Heated pool; whirlpool, poolside serv. Complimentary full bkfst. Restaurant 6:30 am–3 pm. Bar 11 am–8 pm. Ck-out noon. Coin lndry. Meeting rms. Valet serv. Sundries. Gift shop. Lighted tennis privileges. 18-hole golf privileges, greens fee $30–$60, pro, putting green, driving range. Game rm. Refrigerators, wet bars. Balconies. Cr cds: A, C, D, DS, ER, MC, V, JCB.

★ ★SEABONAY BEACH RESORT. *(1159 Hillsboro Mile, Hillsboro Beach 33062)* S on FL A1A. 305/427-2525; res: 800/777-1961; FAX 305/428-8838, ext 105. 78 rms, 6 story, 63 suites. Mid-Dec–Apr: S, D $99; each addl $10; suites $135–$309; under 12 free; wkly rates; lower rates rest of yr. Crib $10. TV; cable. Heated pool. Supervised child's activities. Complimentary coffee in lobby. Restaurant nearby. Ck-out 11 am. Coin lndry. Meeting rms. Bellhops. Sundries. Gift shop. Free garage parking. Refrigerator in suites. Balconies. Picnic tables, grills. At Hillsboro Beach; on ocean. Cr cds: A, DS, MC, V.

Hotels

★ ★DEERFIELD BEACH RESORT. *950 SE 20th Ave (FL A1A) (33441)*. 305/426-0478; res: 800/545-7263; FAX 305/360-0539. 244 kit. suites, 7 story. Dec–Apr: S, D $199–$299; each addl $10; under 12 free; lower rates rest of yr. Crib free. Covered parking $5; valet $7. TV; cable, in-rm movies. Heated pool; whirlpool, poolside serv. Supervised child's activities. Complimentary full bkfst. Restaurant 11 am–11 pm. Bar to 2 am; entertainment. Ck-out noon. Coin lndry. Meeting rms. Concierge. Balconies. Opp ocean. Cr cds: A, C, D, DS, ER, MC, V.

★ ★ ★HILTON. *100 Fairway Dr (33441)*. 305/427-7700; FAX 305/427-2308. 220 rms, 8 story. Jan–Mar: S $119–$139; D $129–$149; each addl $10; family rates; lower rates rest of yr. Crib free. TV; cable. Heated pool; poolside serv. Restaurant 6:30 am–10 pm. Bar from 11 am; entertainment Tues–Sat. Ck-out noon. Meeting rms. Golf privileges. Exercise equipt; weights, bicycles, whirlpool. Refrigerators avail. Mirrored lobby with paintings, Balinese sculpture and artifacts. *LUXURY LEVEL:* TOWER. 44 rms, 2 suites, 2 floors. S $139–$149; D $149–$169; suites $320–$475. Private lounge. Complimentary newspaper. Cr cds: A, C, D, DS, ER, MC, V.

Restaurants

★ ★ ★BROOKS. *500 S Federal Hwy*. 305/427-9302. Hrs: 6 pm–midnight. Closed Dec 25; Mon in May–Oct. Res accepted. Bar.

Semi-a la carte: dinner $17.75–$29.75. Specializes in fresh Florida seafood, mesquite-charcoal broiling. Own baking. Valet parking. Antiques, original oil paintings. Cr cds: A, C, D, MC, V.

★ ★PAL'S CHARLEY'S CRAB. *Cove Yacht Basin, on FL 810, 3 blks E of US 1*. 305/427-4000. Hrs: 11:30 am–3 pm, 4:30–10 pm; Sun brunch 11 am–3 pm. Res accepted. Bar. Semi-a la carte: lunch $6.75–$14.50, dinner $9.95–$24. Sun brunch $16.95. Specializes in fresh seafood. Pianist. Valet parking. Outdoor dining. On Intracoastal Waterway; dockage. Luncheon yacht cruises Mon–Sat. Cr cds: A, C, D, DS, MC, V.

★ ★RIVERVIEW. *1741 Riverview Rd, just off Hillsboro Blvd at the Intracoastal*. 305/428-3463. Hrs: 11:45 am–10 pm; Sun 5:30–8:30 pm. Closed Dec 24. Res accepted. Bar. Semi-a la carte: lunch $3–$12, dinner $9.95–$24. Specializes in fresh seafood, pasta. Parking. Outdoor dining (Sat, Sun). Nautical atmosphere; view of Intracoastal Waterway; dockage. Family-owned. Cr cds: A, C, D, DS, MC, V.

De Funiak Springs (E-2)

Pop: 5,120 **Elev:** 260 ft **Area code:** 904 **Zip:** 32433

In 1881, two members of a surveying party seeking a route for the Louisville and Nashville Railroad passed through this area. They were so impressed by the beauty of the location that they envisioned a prosperous settlement and named the site after Mr. DeFuniak, a prominent official of the Louisville & Nashville Railroad. Lake DeFuniak, located in the center of the city, contains several acres of clear water and is said to be one of two naturally round lakes in the world.

What to See and Do

1. **Walton-DeFuniak Public Library.** 100 Circle Dr. Opened in 1887, this library is believed to be the state's oldest public library operating continuously in its original building; some rare books as old as library itself. Phone 892-3624.

2. **Ponce de Leon Springs State Recreation Area.** E via US 90, then 1 mi S on FL 181A. Within 443-acre park is a natural spring that flows from a horizontal limestone cavity in the center of the pool; the crystal clear water remains at a constant 68°F. Swimming; fishing. Nature trail, ranger-guided walks (on request). Picnicking. Standard hrs, fees. Phone 836-4281 or 638-6130.

(For further information contact the Walton County Chamber of Commerce, Chautauqua Bldg, Circle Dr, PO Box 29; 892-3191.)

Annual Event

Chautauqua Festival Day. Commemorates the Chautauqua, which brought cultural programs to the area for more than 40 years. Many activities during the preceding three months. Last Sat Apr.

Motels

★BEST WESTERN CROSSROADS INN. *(Box 852) At jct I-10, US 331*. 904/892-5111. 100 rms, 2 story. S $35–$45; D $38–$48; each addl $5; under 18 free. Crib avail. TV; cable. Pool. Restaurant 6 am–2 pm, 5–9 pm. Bar 5–11 pm. Ck-out noon. Meeting rm. Cr cds: A, C, D, DS, MC, V.

★COMFORT INN. *1326 S Freeport Rd, off I-10 exit 14*. 904/892-1333; FAX 904/892-0970. 62 rms, 2 story. Mar–Aug: S $42–$52; D $46–$56; each addl $5; under 18 free; lower rates rest of yr. Crib $5. Pet accepted; $25. TV; cable. Pool. Complimentary continental bkfst, coffee. Restaurant nearby. Ck-out 11 am. Cr cds: A, C, D, DS, MC, V, JCB.

DeLand (B-4)

Founded: 1876 **Pop:** 16,491 **Elev:** 77 ft **Area code:** 904

Henry A. DeLand, a New York manufacturer with a dream of establishing an "Athens of Florida," chose this site and planted water oaks 50 feet apart along prospective streets. He encouraged the building of a schoolhouse, a venture subsidized by hat manufacturer John B. Stetson. The school, first known as DeLand Academy, continues to thrive as Stetson University. DeLand is largely sustained by the fern, cut foliage and timber industries, manufacturing companies and government and educational services.

What to See and Do

1. **DeLand Museum of Art.** 600 N Woodland Blvd. Exhibits focusing on the fine arts, concerts, classes, workshops, lectures, films and festivals. Tours. (Daily exc Mon; closed major hols) Phone 734-4371. ¢

2. **Stetson University** (1883). (2,100 students) 516 N Woodland Blvd. Historic campus includes DeLand Hall, Florida's oldest higher educational building in continuous use; William E. Holler Memorial Fountain, part of the Florida exhibit at the 1939 World's Fair; Gillespie Museum of Minerals (academic yr, daily exc Sun); Duncan Art Gallery (academic yr, daily). Tours. Phone 822-8920.

3. **Spring Garden Ranch.** 8 mi N on US 17. At 148 acres, Florida's largest harness training track houses 500 horses; trackside restaurant with observation deck. (Daily) Phone 985-5654.

4. **Houseboat cruises.** On St Johns River. Three companies rent houseboats. For information contact Hontoon Landing Marina, 800/248-2474 (FL) or 800/458-2474 (exc FL); Joy Yacht Club, 800/824-1844; or Holly Bluff Marina, 800/237-5105.

5. **DeLeon Springs State Recreation Area.** 5 mi N via US 17, on Ponce de Leon Blvd, in DeLeon Springs. Operating old sugar mill (early 1800s); 50 acres of gardens. Swimming in "fountain of youth," bathhouse, snorkeling; fishing; paddleboats, canoeing (rentals). Hiking, nature trail. Picnicking, concession. Standard hrs, fees. Phone 985-4212.

6. **Blue Spring State Park.** 5 mi S via US 17/92. A 945-acre park with spring on St Johns River. Manatee return each winter. Historic house. Swimming; fishing; canoeing, boating. Nature trails. Picnicking, playground. Camping, cabins. Standard hrs, fees. Phone 775-3663.

7. **Hontoon Island State Park.** 6 mi SW off FL 44. This 1,650-acre island in St Johns River contains 300-foot-long Timucuan Indian ceremonial mound. Fishing. Nature trails. Picnicking. Tent camping, cabins. Overnight docking. Observation tower. No vehicles; accessible only by ferry boat from parking lot across river (daily; free). Standard hrs, fees. Phone 736-5309.

(For further information contact the DeLand Area Chamber of Commerce, 336 N Woodland Blvd, PO Box 629, 32721-0629; 734-4331 or 800/749-4350.)

Annual Events

Manatee Festival. Volusia County Fairgrounds. Entertainment, endangered animal displays, children's activities, arts & crafts. Phone 775-1112. Late Jan.

DeLand–St Johns River Festival. 4 mi W via FL 44. Raft race competition on St Johns River; also community events. Mid-Sept.

Volusia County Fair & Youth Show. Fairgrounds, 5 mi E via FL 44. Midway, exhibits, stage shows, livestock show and auction. Phone 734-9514. Late Oct–mid-Nov.

(See Altamonte Springs, Daytona Beach, Winter Park)

Motel

 ★ ★**QUALITY INN.** 2801 E New York (32724), off I-4 exit 56. 904/736-3440. 112 rms, 2 story. Mid-Dec–Apr: S $45–$80; D $50–$85; each addl $5; under 16 free; higher rates: Daytona 500, July 4, special events; lower rates rest of yr. Crib free. Pet accepted, some restrictions; $5. TV. Pool; wading pool. Restaurant 6:30 am–10 pm. Rm serv. Bar noon–midnight; entertainment, dancing Tues–Sat. Ck-out 11 am. Coin lndry. Meeting rms. Cr cds: A, C, D, DS, ER, MC, V, JCB.

Hotel

★ ★ ★**HOLIDAY INN.** 350 International Speedway Blvd (32724). 904/738-5200; FAX 904/734-7552. 149 rms, 6 story. S, D $65–$135; each addl $10; suites $89–$145; higher rates special events. Crib free. Pet accepted, some restrictions. TV; cable. Pool; whirlpool. Complimentary coffee in rms. Restaurant 7 am–10 pm. Bar 4 pm–1:30 am; entertainment, dancing exc Sun. Ck-out noon. Meeting rms. Daytona Beach airport transportation. Health club privileges. Some refrigerators. Cr cds: A, C, D, DS, MC, V, JCB.

Restaurant

 ★ ★**PONDO'S.** 1915 Old New York Ave. 904/734-1995. Hrs: 5–10 pm; wkends to 11 pm; early-bird dinner 5–6:30 pm. Res accepted. Continental menu. Bar. Semi-a la carte: dinner $9.95–$15.95. Child's meals. Specializes in veal, duck. Own pasta. Entertainment Fri, Sat. Parking. In historic guest house (1921). Cr cds: A, MC, V.

Delray Beach (E-5)

Settled: 1895 **Pop:** 47,181 **Elev:** 20 ft **Area code:** 407

This placid resort town boasts of beautiful beaches and excellent weather, championship golfing and fishing opportunities along with a historic downtown district. Many noteworthy restaurants and bistros help give Delray Beach a cosmopolitan air.

What to See and Do

Morikami Park. 4000 Morikami Park Rd, off I-95, Linton Blvd exit. Park includes one-mile, self-guided nature trail. Picnicking. (See ANNUAL EVENTS) Phone 495-0233. **Free.** Also here is

The Morikami Museum and Japanese Gardens. Includes gallery, tea ceremony house, theater; bonsai collection and surrounding gardens. (Daily exc Mon) Phone 495-0233 (recording). ¢¢

(For further information contact the Chamber of Commerce, 64 SE 5th Ave, 33483; 278-0424.)

Annual Events

Hatsume Fair. Morikami Park (see). Two-day event featuring Japanese performing arts, food, bonsai exhibits, Asian arts & crafts, exotic plants. Late Feb.

Bon Festival. Morikami Park (see). Japanese summer festival features Japanese folk dancing and music, games, food, special displays. Mid-Aug.

(See Boca Raton, Boynton Beach, Palm Beach)

Motel

★★**BREAKERS ON-THE-OCEAN.** *1875 S Ocean Blvd (33483).* 407/278-4501. 22 kit. suites, 2 story. Feb–Mar: kit. suites $175; each addl $25; lower rates rest of yr. TV; cable. Heated pool. Complimentary continental bkfst. Ck-out 11 am. Free lndry facilities. Putting green. Rec rm. On ocean; private beach, cabanas. No cr cds accepted.

Motor Hotels

★★**HOLIDAY INN HIGHLAND BEACH.** *(2809 S Ocean Blvd, Highland Beach 33487)* 1 mi S on Ocean Blvd. 407/278-6241; FAX 407/278-6241, ext 431. 114 rms, 3–6 story. Mid-Dec–Apr: S, D $99–$169; each addl $6; under 18 free; varied lower rates rest of yr. Crib free. TV; in-rm movies avail. Pool; wading pool. Restaurant 6:30 am–10 pm. Rm serv. Bar 11–1 am. Ck-out noon. Coin lndry. Meeting rms. Beach shop. Golf privileges. Some refrigerators. Private patios, balconies. On beach. Cr cds: A, C, D, DS, ER, MC, V, JCB.

★★**SEAGATE HOTEL & BEACH CLUB.** *400 S Ocean Blvd (33483).* 407/276-2421; res: 800/233-3581; FAX 407/243-4714. 70 suites, 2–3 story. Mid-Jan–mid-Apr: suites $225–$300; studios $155; under 17 free; lower rates rest of yr. Crib free. TV; cable. 2 pools, 1 saltwater. Restaurant 11:30 am–3 pm, 6–9:30 pm; occasional entertainment, dancing. Supervised child's activities. Ck-out noon. Meeting rm. Free valet parking. Opp private beach; bar. Cr cds: A, C, D, MC, V.

Restaurant

★★**ERNY'S.** *1010 E Atlantic Ave.* 407/276-9191. Hrs: 11–1 am. Closed Sun; major hols; also Aug. Bar. Semi-a la carte: lunch $3–$9, dinner $8–$20. Specializes in steak, seafood, lamb chops. Pianist, jazz Tues (in season). Parking. Cr cds: A, C, D, MC, V.

Destin (F-2)

Pop: 8,080 **Elev:** 33 ft **Area code:** 904 **Zip:** 32541

Perched on a narrow strip of land between Choctawhatchee Bay and the Gulf of Mexico, Destin has turned from commercial to sport fishing. Trolling boats ply the waters of the Gulf for king mackerel, cobia, marlin, wahoo and sailfish. Party boats bring in red snapper and grouper. Destin retains the atmosphere of the New England birthplace of its founder, Captain Leonard Destin, who pioneered the snapper fishing industry more than 100 years ago.

What to See and Do

1. **Museum of the Sea & Indian.** 4801 Beach Hwy (Old US 98). Extensive marine and Indian exhibits; two ponds with ducks, alligators, game birds. Gift shop. Audio-guided tour. (Daily) Phone 837-6625. ¢¢

2. **Fishing Museum.** 35 US 98E. Exhibits and displays on history and current sport of fishing, one of Destin's early industries. (Daily exc Mon; closed some hols) Phone 654-1011. ¢

3. **Grayton Beach State Recreation Area.** 20 mi E on US 98, off FL 30A in Santa Rosa Beach. Swimming, skin diving; saltwater fishing. Nature trail. Picnicking. Camping (electric hookups, dump station). Standard hrs, fees. Phone 231-4210.

4. **Eden State Gardens.** 24 mi E on US 98, then N on County 395 to Point Washington, follow signs. Overlooking Choctawhatchee Bay, this was once the site of a large sawmill complex. Eden House, built by William Henry Wesley in 1897, is restored and furnished with antiques. Mansion tours (Thurs–Mon). Gardens, picnic area (daily). Phone 231-4214. Tours ¢

(For further information, including a list of overnight fishing trips, contact the Chamber of Commerce, 1021 US 98 E, PO Box 8, 32540; 837-6241.)

Annual Events

Seafood Festival. Seafood, entertainment; sailing, windsurfing regattas. 1st wkend Oct.

Deep-Sea Fishing Rodeo. $150,000 in prizes. Oct.

(See Fort Walton Beach)

Motels

✔★**COMFORT INN.** *405 US 98E.* 904/837-0007. 131 rms, 2 story. S, D $59–$67; each addl $8; kit. units $69–$77; under 18 free. Crib $5. TV; cable. Pool. Continental bkfst off-season. Restaurant nearby. Bar 4 pm–midnight. Ck-out 11 am. Cr cds: A, D, DS, ER, MC, V, JCB.

✔★**ROBROY LODGE & MARINA.** *(Box 725, 32540)* On US 98. 904/837-6713; res: 800/451-0121. 29 rms, 20 kits. Some rm phones. Mid-May–Labor Day: S, D $43–$128; each addl $5; kit. units $62–$79; 3-day min hols; wkly rates; lower rates rest of yr. Crib free. TV; cable. Pool. Restaurant nearby. Ck-out noon. Meeting rms. Refrigerators. Balconies. Picnic tables, grills. On harbor; marina. No cr cds accepted.

★**SEA OATS.** *(Box 222, 32540)* 5 mi E on US 98. 904/837-6655; res: 800/462-4743. 38 rms, 36 kits. Mid-May–early Sept: S, D $80–$120; kit. units $90–$120; 3-day & 5-day min in season; wkly rates; lower rates rest of yr. Crib $5. TV; cable. Heated pool. Ck-out 10 am. Refrigerators. Balconies. Picnic tables. On beach. All units face Gulf. Cr cds: DS, MC, V.

★**SLEEP INN.** *50,000 Emerald Coast Pkwy, E on US 98.* 904/654-7022. 77 rms, 2 story. May–Labor Day: S $70–$80; D $75–$85; each addl $5; suites $135; family rates; golf plan (off season); lower rates rest of yr. Crib free. TV; cable. Pool. Complimentary continental bkfst, coffee. Restaurant adj 10 am–midnight. Ck-out 11 am. Coin lndry. Refrigerator, wet bar in suites. Ocean 1½ blks; beach. Cr cds: A, C, D, DS, ER, MC, V, JCB.

Motor Hotel

★★**HOLIDAY INN.** *(Box 577) E on US 98.* 904/837-6181; FAX 904/837-1523. 226 rms, 9 story. May–Labor Day: S, D $90–$125; each addl $10; suites $300; under 18 free; golf plan; lower rates rest of yr. Crib free. TV; cable. 2 pools, 1 indoor; wading pool. Restaurant 6:30 am–2 pm, 5–10 pm. Rm serv. Bar 11 am–midnight. Ck-out 11 am. Meeting rms. Bellhops in season. Gift shop. Tennis privileges. Exercise equipt; weight machine, bicycles, whirlpool, sauna. Rec rm. Balconies. On beach. Cr cds: A, C, D, DS, MC, V, JCB.

Hotel

★ ★ ★HILTON SANDESTIN BEACH. *5540 US 98E. 904/267-9500; FAX 904/267-3076.* 400 suites, 15 story. May–Sept: S, D $190–$260; golf, tennis, honeymoon plans; lower rates rest of yr. Crib free. TV; cable. Indoor/outdoor pool; wading pool, poolside serv, lifeguard. Supervised child's activities (May–Sept). Restaurants 7 am–10:30 pm. Bar 10:30–2 am; entertainment, dancing. Ck-out noon. Convention facilities. Concierge. Shopping arcade. Free valet parking. Airport transportation. Tennis, pro. 45-hole golf, greens fee $55, pro, putting green, driving range. Health club privileges. Bathrm phones, refrigerators, minibars. Private patios, balconies. On beach. Cr cds: A, C, D, DS, MC, V.

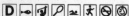

Inn

★ ★HENDERSON PARK INN. *2700 US 98E. 1½ mi E on Old Hwy 98, adj Henderson Beach State Park. 904/654-0400; res: 800/336-4853; FAX 904/837-5390.* 37 rms, 3 story, 19 suites, 18 kit. units. Mar–early Sept: S, D, suites $175–$320; kit. units $158–$178; under 12 free; wkly rates; lower rates rest of yr. Crib $7. TV; cable. Heated pool; whirlpool. Complimentary continental bkfst. Complimentary coffee in rms. Dining rm 7 am–2 pm, 7–9 pm. Ck-out 11 am, ck-in 3 pm. Meeting rm. Bellhops. Balconies. Picnic tables, grills. On beach; swimming. Queen Anne/Victorian-style building. Cr cds: MC, V.

Resorts

★ ★SANDESTIN. *5500 US 98E. 904/267-8000; res: 800/277-0800; FAX 904/267-8222.* 173 rms in hotel, 360 kit. villas (1–4 bedrm). May–Sept: S, D $119; suites $169; tower units $173–$523; villas $170–$380; lower rates rest of yr. Crib free. TV; cable. 10 pools; wading pool, poolside serv. Supervised child's activities (May–Sept). Dining rms 7 am–10 pm (in season). Box lunches. Snack bar. Bar; entertainment, dancing. Ck-out 11 am, ck-in 4 pm. Convention facilities. Grocery. Valet serv. Sports dir. Tennis, pro. 45-hole golf, greens fee, driving range, putting green. Sailing, charter boats. Private beach. Bicycles. Nature trail. Rec rm. Exercise rm; instructor, weights, whirlpool, steam rm, sauna. Refrigerators. Private patios, balconies. On 2,300 acres along Gulf, bay shores. Cr cds: D, DS, MC, V.

★ ★SEASCAPE. *100 Seascape Dr, 7 mi E on Emerald Coast Pkwy. 904/837-9181; res: 800/874-9141; FAX 904/837-4769.* 115 kit. cottages. Mar–early Sept: cottages $105–$220 (3-day min hols); wkly rates; lower rates rest of yr. Crib avail. TV; cable. Pool; wading pool. Supervised children's activities (seasonal). Dining rm from 7 am (seasonal). Box lunches. Snack bar. Picnics. Bar from 2 pm. Ck-out 11 am, ck-in 4 pm. Grocery, package store 2 mi. Convention facilities. Lighted tennis, pro. 18-hole golf, pro, putting green, driving range. Swimming beach. Bicycle rentals. Exercise equipt; weights, rowers. Bathrm phones. Balconies. Picnic tables, grills. On ocean beach. Cr cds: A, D, DS, MC, V.

★ ★ ★TOPS'L BEACH & RACQUET CLUB. *5550 US 98E, 10 mi E on US 98. 904/267-9222; res: 800/476-9222.* 19 rms avail in main bldg, 14 story, 28 villas (2–3 bedrm). EP, late May–Aug: S, D, kit. suites, villas $220–$400. Crib $5. TV; cable. 2 heated pools, 1 indoor; wading pool, poolside serv, whirlpool, steam rm, sauna. Supervised child's activities (May–Aug). Dining rm (public by res in season) 6–10 pm; closed Sun–Tues. Snack bar 11 am–3 pm. Bar. Ck-out 11 am, ck-in 3 pm. Grocery 1½ mi. Lndry facilities. Package store. Meeting rms. Covered parking. Sports dir. 10 lighted clay and 2 hard-surfaced tennis courts, pro. Private swimming beach. Sailboats. Soc dir. Entertainment, dancing, movies. Rec rm. Refrigerators. Many fireplaces. Private patios,

balconies. Picnic tables. Gulf view. 52 acres of dunes, beachfront and wooded terrain. Cr cds: A, MC, V.

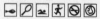

Restaurants

★BEACHSIDE CAFE. *950 Gulfshore Dr. 904/837-1272.* Hrs: 5 pm–closing; early-bird dinner to 6:30 pm. Closed Thanksgiving, Dec 25. Res accepted. French, continental menu. Bar. A la carte entrees: dinner $12.95–$21.95. Specialties: grilled amberjack, chicken Marsala. Entertainment Thurs–Sat. Parking. Country French decor. Cr cds: A, D, DS, MC, V.

★ ★FLAMINGO CAFE. *414 US 98. 904/837-0961.* Hrs: 11 am–2 pm, 5–10 pm; Sun from 5 pm; Sun brunch 10 am–2 pm. Closed Thanksgiving, Dec 25. Res accepted. French, continental menu. Bar. Semi-a la carte: lunch $4.95–$7.95, dinner $15.95–$22.95. Sun brunch $13.95. Child's meals. Specialties: snapper Destin, grouper Flamingo. Own bread, desserts. Pianist Fri & Sat evenings. Parking. Outdoor dining. On waterfront. Cr cds: A, D, DS, MC, V.

D

★ ★LOUISIANA LAGNIAPPE. *775 Gulfshore Dr. 904/837-0881.* Hrs: 6 pm–closing; Fri, Sat from 5:30 pm. Closed Nov–Feb. Cajun menu. Bar. Semi-a la carte: dinner $11.95–$20.95. Child's meals. Specializes in Louisiana seafood, steak, Maine lobster. Own desserts. Parking. Outdoor dining. Overlooks Old Pass Lagoon. Cr cds: A, C, D, DS, MC, V.

D

★ ★MARINA CAFE. *404 US 98E. 904/837-7960.* Hrs: 5–11 pm. Closed Jan 1, Dec 25. Bar. A la carte entrees: dinner $13–$24. Specializes in seafood, prime beef, pasta. Outdoor dining. Cr cds: A, MC, V.

✔ ★SEAFOOD FACTORY. *21 US 98E. 904/837-0999.* Hrs: 11 am–10 pm. Closed Jan 1, Thanksgiving, Dec 25. Wine, beer. Semi-a la carte: lunch, dinner $3.95–$11.95. Specialties: smoked amberjack, fried mullet. Parking. Nautical decor. Cr cds: MC, V.

D

Disney World

(see Walt Disney World)

Dry Tortugas National Park (F-4)

(68 mi W of Key West; reached by boat or seaplane)

Covering approximately 64,000 acres of land and water, this national park includes not only the remains of what was once the largest of the 19th-century American coastal forts, but also the cluster of seven islands known as the Dry Tortugas.

The coral keys, upon which the fort sat, in 1513 were named ''las tortugas'' (the turtles) by Ponce de Leon because so many turtles inhabited these bits of land. The ''dry'' portion of the islands' name warns mariners of a total lack of fresh water. Tropical ocean birds are the chief inhabitants; each year, between May and September, sooty and noddy terns assemble on Bush Key to nest.

Spanish pirates used the Tortugas as a base from which to pillage boats until 1821, when they were driven from the islands. In 1846, the United States, eager to protect its interests in the Gulf of Mexico, began construction of a fort on 10-acre Garden Key. For more than 30 years, laborers worked on the fort, a rampart one-half mile in perimeter with 50-foot-high walls and 3 tiers designed for 450 guns. Called the ''Gibraltar of the Gulf,'' this massive masonry fort was designed for a garrison of 1,500 men. Only partially completed, Fort Jefferson never saw battle. It was occupied by Union troops during the Civil War, but it fired only passing shots at Confederate ships.

Resting on an unstable foundation of sand and coral boulders, Fort Jefferson's walls began to crack and shift, making it unsuitable for military defense. In 1863, it became a military prison, confining some 2,400 men. Among them was Dr. Samuel Mudd, who was imprisoned on the island after innocently setting the broken leg of John Wilkes Booth, Abraham Lincoln's assassin. Following two yellow fever epidemics and a hurricane, the fort was abandoned in 1874. In the 1880s it was reconditioned for use as a naval base, coaling station and wireless station; the USS *Maine* sailed from the fort for Havana, where she was blown up, triggering the Spanish-American War. The fort became Fort Jefferson National Monument in 1935 and was renamed Dry Tortugas National Park in 1992.

The fort and islands are accessible by boat or seaplane trips from Key West (see). There is camping and a picnic area on Garden Key; campers must bring all supplies, including fresh water. Visitor center (daily). Guided tours. Contact the Superintendent, PO Box 279, Homestead 33030; 305/242-7700. For transportation information, contact the Greater Key West Chamber of Commerce, 402 Wall St, Old Mallory Sq, Key West 33040; 305/294-2587.

(For accommodations see Key West)

Dunedin (C-2)

Founded: 1870 **Pop:** 34,012 **Elev:** 11 ft **Area code:** 813 **Zip:** 34698

One of Florida's oldest coastal towns, its name is derived from *Edinburgh,* Scotland. Several buildings in this community are listed on the National Historical Register.

What to See and Do

1. **Caladesi Island State Park.** N via US 19A, W on FL 586 (Dunedin Causeway) to ferry dock on Honeymoon Island (see #2). A 607-acre island accessible only by boat. Swimming; boating (dock). Nature trails. Picnicking. No vehicles. Standard hrs, fees. Ferry service from mainland, weather permitting. Phone 469-5918 or 734-5263 (ferry).

2. **Honeymoon Island State Recreation Area.** 2 mi N via US 19A, W on FL 586 (Dunedin Causeway). One of the few remaining virgin slash pine stands in south Florida may be observed along the island's northern loop trail. These large trees serve as important nesting sites for the threatened osprey. The island, with more than 208 species of plants and a wide variety of shore birds, including several threatened and endangered species, is a prime area for nature study. Swimming; fishing for flounder, snook, redfish, trout, snapper and tarpon. Nature trails. Picnicking. Ferry service to Caladesi Island State Park (see #1). Standard hrs, fees. Phone 469-5942 or 734-5263 (ferry).

(For further information contact the Greater Dunedin Chamber of Commerce, 301 Main St; 736-5066 or 733-3197.)

Annual Event

Highland Games & Scottish Festival. Early Apr.

Seasonal Event

Professional baseball. Dunedin Stadium, 311 Douglas Ave. Toronto Blue Jays spring training; exhibition games. Phone 733-9302. Early Mar–early Apr.

(See Clearwater, St Petersburg, Tampa, Tarpon Springs)

Motels

★ ★ **BEST WESTERN JAMAICA INN.** *150 Marina Plaza, 3 mi W of US 19 on Main St. 813/733-4121; FAX 813/736-4365.* 55 rms, 2 story, 36 kits. Mid-Feb–Apr: S, D $85; kits. $95; under 12 free; lower rates rest of yr. Crib $7. TV; cable. Heated pool. Restaurant 7 am–10 pm. Ck-out 11 am. Overlooks St Joseph's Sound. Cr cds: A, C, D, DS, MC, V.

✔ ★ **INN ON THE BAY.** *1420 Bayshore Blvd (US 19A). 813/734-7689; res: 800/759-5045; FAX 813/734-0972.* 41 kit. units, 4 story. Jan–mid-Apr: S, D $60–$91; wkly rates; lower rates rest of yr. TV; cable. Heated pool. Continental bkfst in lobby. Ck-out 11 am. Balconies. On ocean; fishing dock. Cr cds: A, MC, V.

Restaurants

★ ★ ★ **BON APPETIT.** *148 Marina Plaza. 813/733-2151.* Hrs: 7 am–10 pm; Sun brunch 11:30 am–4 pm. Res accepted. Continental menu. Bar. Wine cellar. Semi-a la carte: bkfst $1.75–$7.25, lunch $4.50–$9.75, dinner $7.77–$17.50. Sun brunch $4.95–$11.95. Child's meals. Specialties: crab cakes, rack of lamb. Pianist. Valet parking. Outdoor terrace dining. Waterfront dining on Intracoastal Waterway. Cr cds: A, C, D, MC, V.

✔ ★ **BOSTON COOKER.** *(3682 Tampa Rd, Oldsmar) FL 584 at Emerald Bay Dr. 813/855-2311.* Hrs: 11:30 am–10 pm; Fri, Sat to 11 pm. Closed Sun; some major hols. Res accepted. New England menu. Bar. Complete meals: lunch $4.95–$7.95, dinner $7.95–$17.95. Child's meals. Specializes in Boston scrod, Ipswich clams, steamed mussels, Maine lobster. Parking. Nautical decor. Cr cds: A, DS, MC, V.

★ ★ **JESSE'S DOCKSIDE.** *345 Causeway Blvd. 813/736-2611.* Hrs: 11:30 am–10 pm; Fri, Sat to 10:30 pm. Res accepted. Bar. Semi-a la carte: lunch $5.99–$8.99, dinner $8.99–$24.95. Child's meals. Specializes in fresh seafood. Parking. Nautical decor; overlooks Intracoastal Waterway. Cr cds: A, DS, MC, V.

★ ★ **SABAL'S.** *315 Main St. 813/734-3463.* Hrs: 6–9 pm; Fri, Sat to 10 pm. Closed Mon; Jan 1, Dec 25. Res required. Nouvelle cuisine. A la carte entrees: dinner $10.95–$21.95. Specialties: filet mignon, octopus, marinated Cornish game hens. Intimate dining. Cr cds: MC, V.

✔ ★ **SEA SEA RIDERS.** *221 Main St. 813/734-1445.* Hrs: 11:30 am–10 pm; Fri, Sat to 11 pm; Sun brunch to 2 pm. Res accepted. Bar. Semi-a la carte: lunch $4.25–$5.95, dinner $5.95–$11.95. Sun brunch $3.95–$5.95. Child's meals. Specializes in fresh Florida seafood. Parking. Outdoor dining on veranda. In 1923 Florida Cracker house. Cr cds: A, MC, V.

✔ ★ **TONG WAH.** *1056 Main St. 813/736-6830.* Hrs: 11:30 am–9:30 pm; Fri, Sat to 10 pm; Sun noon–9:30 pm. Closed Thanksgiving, Dec 25. Res accepted. Chinese, Amer menu. Bar. A la carte entrees: lunch, dinner $4.80–$11. Complete meals: lunch $2.70–$5, dinner $5–$20. Specialties: combination sweet & sour, moo shu pork, combination lo mein. Parking. Tiled wall murals. Cr cds: A, DS, MC, V.

Englewood (D-3)

Pop: 15,025 **Elev:** 13 ft **Area code:** 813

(For information about this area contact the Englewood Area Chamber of Commerce, 601 S Indiana Ave, 34224; 474-5511.)

(See Port Charlotte, Punta Gorda, Venice)

Motels

✔ ★**DAYS INN.** *2540 S McCall Rd (FL 776) (34224). 813/474-5544; FAX 813/475-2124.* 84 rms, 2 story, 48 kit. suites. Feb–mid-Apr: S, D $53–$95; suites $63–$95; each addl $4; under 13 free; advance deposit in winter; lower rates rest of yr. Crib free. Pet accepted, some restrictions; $4. TV; cable. Heated pool. Playground. Restaurant 6 am–8 pm. Ck-out noon. Private patios; some balconies. Cr cds: A, C, D, DS, MC, V.

★**VERANDA INN.** *2073 S McCall Rd (FL 776) (34224). 813/475-6533; res: 800/633-8115.* 38 rms, 3 story. Feb–mid-Apr: S, D $85–$90; each addl $6; under 16 free; wkly rates; lower rates rest of yr. Crib free. Pet accepted; $10. TV. Heated pool. Complimentary coffee in lobby. Restaurant adj 11 am–9 pm. Ck-out 11 am. Coin lndry. On river. Cr cds: A, MC, V.

Resort

★ ★**PALM ISLAND.** *(7092 Placida Rd, Cape Haze 33946) 5 mi S via FL 776 & County Rd 775. 813/697-4800; res: 800/824-5412; FAX 813/697-0696.* 160 kit. villas, 2 story. Mid-Dec–mid-Apr (3-night min): villas $200–$325; wkly rates; package plans; 2-night min off season; lower rates rest of yr. Crib $6. TV; cable. 5 pools, some heated; whirlpools. Playground. Supervised child's activities. Dining rm noon–9:30 pm. Bar to 10:30 pm. Ck-out 11:30 am, ck-in 2:30 pm. Grocery. Free lndry facilities. Package store. Meeting rms. Bellhops. Maid serv wkly. Gift shop. Sports dir. Tennis, pro. Swimming beach. Bicycle rentals. Lawn games. Fishing guides; cleaning. Balconies. Picnic tables, grills. On island in Gulf of Mexico. Cr cds: A, ER, MC, V.

Restaurant

✔ ★**FLYING BRIDGE II.** *2080 S McCall Rd (FL 776). 813/474-2206.* Hrs: 11 am–9 pm. Closed 1–2 wks July. Res accepted major hols. Semi-a la carte: lunch $2.65–$5.50, dinner $5.75–$11.95. Child's meals. Specializes in seafood, barbecued pork ribs, char-grilled grouper. Parking. Outdoor dining. On waterfront. Cr cds: DS, MC, V.

Everglades National Park (F-4)

(S of I-75, W of Miami)

This 2,200-square-mile corner of the United States is the largest subtropical wilderness in North America. The park preserves the spectacular half-land, half-water Everglades that once covered most of the southern third of the Florida peninsula.

From Lake Okeechobee to the northern border of the park, much of the glades have been drained and tamed, leaving an incredibly rich blue-black soil responsible for huge winter vegetable crops. The remaining area, larger than the state of Delaware, has been developed by the South Florida Water Management District into a huge recreation area with hunting, fishing, boating, camping and sightseeing. Easily reached from cities along Florida's east coast are 34 access sites, located along the canals and levees that have been constructed to protect 18 counties from flood and drought. For information write the District at PO Box V, West Palm Beach 33402.

Nowhere else in the world is there an area comparable to this huge, water-sodden saucer, with its prairies of saw grass, stands of dwarf cypress, hammocks of cabbage palm, West Indies mahogany, strangler figs and wild orchids. The mood is serene, but the entire expanse teems with water birds, alligators, snakes, marsh rabbits, deer, raccoons, bobcats, turtles, largemouth bass, garfish and panfish. (Wildlife is visible mainly during the winter months.) This is also part of the traditional domain of the Seminole Indians.

Much of the Everglades is an immense sea of sedges that shoot up 10 feet with barbed blades and needle-sharp edges, appropriately called saw grass. These grassy waters are broken only by clusters of trees and dense vegetation called hammocks. The saw grass glades give way along the coast to huge, shadowy mangrove swamps interlaced by tranquil winding water lanes.

Much of the park is impenetrable except with an experienced guide; however, the National Park Service has set up trails (all improved or marked), exhibits and facilities that make a safe excursion into the Everglades possible for any visitor. Facilities for the disabled include trails developed to accommodate wheelchairs, ramps to visitor centers, rest rooms, designated campsites and wheelchairs.

Note: Fire is a severe danger in the Everglades; ground fires are not permitted. Smoking is also forbidden on nature trails. Pets must be on a leash and are not permitted on the trails or in the backcountry. Hunting is not allowed. Do not feed or disturb the wildlife and stay clear of the alligators—*they are not tame.* Insects, especially mosquitoes, are most plentiful during May–November.

Golden Eagle, Golden Age and Golden Access Passport (see INTRODUCTION) and park passport (fee) accepted. Contact the Park Superintendent, PO Box 279, Homestead 33030; 305/242-7700. Entrance fee per car (7-day permit) ¢¢

What to See and Do

The main road into the park runs southwest from Homestead to Flamingo (50 mi); allow plenty of time. From Homestead it is approximately 12 miles on FL 9336 to the Entrance Station. The visitor center has exhibits, orientation programs and information about the Everglades (daily). From the visitor center it is two miles to

Royal Palm Station turnoff. Here are the Anhinga Trail, one of the best nature and wildlife trails in the park, and Gumbo Limbo Trail, which leads through a tropical hardwood hammock. From Royal Palm turnoff it is two miles to

Long Pine Key Area turnoff. Campgrounds (fee; no reservations; dump station); picnicking facilities. Stays at campsites limited to 14 days Dec–Mar and 30 days Apr–Nov. Campfire talks (mid-Dec–mid-Apr). From here it is approximately three miles to

Pineland Trail. Slender slash pines, saw-palmetto and short-leaf fig trees, marked by signs, line this trail. Approximately six miles beyond is

Pa-hay-okee. An elevated trail leads to a high platform that offers an excellent view of the Shark River Basin, where many small birds and, occasionally, alligators gather; it is an excellent place to take photographs. Seven miles beyond is

Mahogany Hammock. An elevated boardwalk leads into a hardwood hammock with orchids, ferns and strangler figs and a stand of the largest mahogany trees in the US. Five miles further is

Paurotis Pond, with paurotis palms and mangroves. This is the transition zone between fresh and salt water. There is a small lakeside picnic area. Six miles beyond is

West Lake. An elevated boardwalk leads into a mangrove forest. It is approximately eight miles to

Flamingo, with visitor center, museum (daily) and interpretive programs (daily), marina, sightseeing and charter fishing boats, houseboat rentals; it is the starting point for canoe trails. Picnicking, restaurant (Nov–May), lodge, service station. Camping (Nov–May; fee; no trailer hookups; dump station; no reservations). Flamingo is the end of the road; retrace route back to Homestead.

Shark Valley tram tours originate at parking area 30 mi W of Miami on US 41. Two-hour narrated tour along Shark Valley loop road with half-hour stop at observation tower. Abundant wildlife can be seen, especially in winter. No pets. For tram information and reservations phone 305/221-8455. National Park Service entry fee per car (7-day permit) ¢¢

The Western Water Gateway, at Everglades City in the northwest corner of the park, is the starting point for rental-canoe trips along a 99-mile wilderness waterway on the inland route from Everglades City to Flamingo. There is a visitor center. Scenic boat tours leave from the Park Docks, Chokoloskee Causeway on FL 29 (daily). Phone 813/695-2591. Boat tours ¢¢¢¢–¢¢¢¢¢

(For accommodations see Coral Gables, Miami)

Fernandina Beach (A-4)

Settled: 1686 **Pop:** 8,765 **Elev:** 19 ft **Area code:** 904 **Zip:** 32034

The northernmost city on Florida's east coast, Fernandina Beach, which consolidated with Fernandina in 1951, is the only incorporated city on Amelia Island. It received its name in 1811 from King Ferdinand VII of Spain.

During the course of four centuries, eight flags have flown over this area, starting with the French in 1562 and followed by the Spanish. In 1812, the Patriots flag flew, followed in short order by General Sir Gregor MacGregor's personal flag, the Green Cross of Florida, and then, for a brief period, the flag of Mexico. The United States formally took possession of the island in 1821. At the outbreak of the Civil War, the Confederate flag was raised over Fernandina and Fort Clinch, but it was lowered in 1862, when the town was the target of a Union fleet.

Today, Fernandina Beach's harbor provides mooring for a large and prosperous shrimping fleet; two local pulp mills produce linerboard for paper containers and chemical cellulose; a 50-block restored Victorian historical district, including redeveloped Centre Street, is located downtown.

What to See and Do

1. **Fort Clinch State Park.** Entrance on Atlantic Ave off FL A1A. This 1,100-acre park is the most northeasterly point in Florida. The old fort's brick ramparts offer a view of the Georgia shoreline and the Atlantic Ocean. A living history interpretation is provided by park rangers dressed in Union uniforms of the 1864 garrison. Swimming; fishing from 1,500-foot pier, the shore and jetties. Nature trails. Picnicking. Camping (hookups, dump station). Visitor center. Standard hrs, fees. Phone 277-7274.

2. **Amelia Island Museum of History.** 233 S 3rd St. Recited oral history, using artifacts and exhibits, recounts 400 years of settlement under 8 flags; materials from 17th-century Spanish mission archeological site; artifacts from 18th-century shipwrecks; 19th-century "Golden Age" decorative arts and photographs. Docent-guided tours. (Daily exc Sun; closed hols) Phone 261-7378. ¢

3. **Beaches.** 13 mi of sand along Atlantic. Swimming, surfing; surfcasting. Picnicking. Amusement area. Some areas allow limited driving at low tide (Apr–Sept, fee; permit required).

(For further information contact the Amelia Island-Fernandina Beach-Yulee Chamber of Commerce, 102 Centre St, PO Box 472; 277-0717.)

Annual Events

Isle of Eight Flags Shrimp Festival. Blessing of the Shrimp Fleet, art show, folk festival, mock pirates landing. 1st wkend May.

Amateur Invitational Golf Tournament. Fernandina Beach Golf Course, 2800 Bill Melton Rd. June.

(See Amelia Island, Atlantic Beach, Jacksonville)

Motels

★ **BEACHSIDE MOTEL INN.** *3172 S Fletcher Ave.* 904/261-4236. 20 rms, 2 story, 10 kit. units. May–Sept: S $51–$86; D $71–$86; each addl $5; kits. $71–$102; wkly rates; higher rates: major hols, special events; lower rates rest of yr. Crib free. TV; cable. Pool. Complimentary continental bkfst, coffee. Restaurant opp 8 am–10 pm. Ck-out 11 am. On ocean; beach. Cr cds: A, MC, V.

✔ ★ ★ **SHONEY'S INN.** *2707 Sadler Rd.* 904/277-2300; res: 800/222-2222; FAX 904/277-2300, ext 303. 135 rms, 2 story, 8 kits. Apr–Sept: S $61; D $66; kit. units $73; under 18 free; lower rates rest of yr. Crib free. Pet accepted, some restrictions. TV; cable. Pool; whirlpool. Playground. Restaurant 6 am–11 pm; Fri, Sat to midnight. Bar 1 pm–1:30 am; entertainment in season, dancing Tues–Sat. Ck-out 11 am. Coin lndry. Meeting rms. Beauty shop. Lighted tennis. Picnic tables, grills. Ocean 1 blk. Cr cds: A, C, D, DS, ER, MC, V.

Inns

★ ★ **BAILEY HOUSE.** *(Box 805)* 28 S 7th St. 904/261-5390. 4 rms, 2 story. S, D $75–$95; each addl $10; wkly rates; higher rates special events (2-night min). Children over 10 yrs only. TV. Complimentary continental bkfst. Ck-out 10 am, ck-in 4 pm. Bicycles. Queen Anne-style house (1895) with bays, turrets, gables; antiques, hand-made quilts. Totally nonsmoking. Cr cd: A.

★ ★ **ELIZABETH POINTE LODGE.** *98 S Fletcher Ave.* 904/277-4851; FAX 904/277-6500. 20 rms, 3 story. S $95–$115; D $100–$135; each addl $15; under 5 free; higher rates: major hols, special events. Crib $5. TV; cable. Complimentary full bkfst, tea & wine. Dining rm (guests only). Rm serv. Ck-out 11 am, ck-in 3 pm. Bellhops. Valet serv. Concierge. Airport transportation. Grills. 1890s Nantucket shingle-style inn (1992). On ocean; beach. Cr cds: A, MC, V.

✔ ★ ★ **PHOENIX' NEST.** *619 S Fletcher Ave,* off I-95 exit 129. 904/277-2129. 5 suites, 2 story. Rm phones avail. Mar–Nov: S $60–$80; D $65–$85; each addl $10; wkly rates; lower rates rest of yr. TV; in-rm movies. Pool privileges. Complimentary continental bkfst. Complimentary coffee in rms. Ck-out noon, ck-in 4 pm. Free airport transportation. Tennis, golf privileges. Bicycles avail. Balconies. Picnic tables, grills. Beach house (1938); antiques. Extensive video & audio library. On ocean; swimming beach. Cr cds: MC, V.

Restaurant

✔ ★ **BAMBOO HOUSE.** *614 Center St.* 904/261-0508. Hrs: 11:30 am–10 pm; Sat from noon. Closed Sun; Jan 1, Thanksgiving, Dec

25. Res accepted. Chinese, Amer menu. Bar. Semi-a la carte: lunch $5.25-$6.95, dinner $5.25-$16.50. Buffet: lunch $4.95. Child's meals. Specialties: "Happy Family," Bamboo House steak. Parking. Chinese decor, artwork. Cr cds: A, MC, V.

Florida Keys (F-4)

(Extending SW of Miami along US 1)

Like a string of coral beads, the Florida Keys sweep in a graceful arc, southwest from a point south of Miami, 100 miles into the Gulf of Mexico. Forty-two beads in this tropical strand are linked by US 1, Florida's Overseas Highway—a road that goes to sea and ends at Key West. The most spectacular over-water drive in the world, this highway divides the blue waters of the Atlantic from the green of the Gulf of Mexico. Forty-two bridges connect the islands. The entire drive can be made in less than half a day, but few can resist the temptation to stop along the way to admire the seascape and landscape.

Until 1912, the Keys remained largely in tranquil isolation—with interludes of high adventure by boisterous buccaneers, devious freebooters and vengeful Indians. That year, one of the great achievements in railroading was completed when Henry Morrison Flagler extended the Florida East Coast Railroad all the way to Key West, where a train ferry continued to Havana. In 1935, a hurricane made a shambles of Flagler's dream; the US Government took over and opened the Overseas Highway in 1938.

Each major Key is different, and each has its special lure for the visitor. The pristine isolation of many of the islands has given way to mainland lifestyle, but travelers can still find peace and quiet along the route.

Note: In November, 1990, Congress designated the approximately 2,700 square nautical miles of marine environment surrounding the Florida Keys as Florida Keys National Marine Sanctuary, to address increasing public concern about the escalating threats to each of the natural areas that comprise a healthy marine ecosystem. While some areas will continue to be used in the accustomed way, others will be designated for preservation, restoration or scientific research. For information regarding sanctuary regulations and developments contact Education Dept, Florida Keys National Marine Sanctuary, PO Box 1083, Key Largo 33037.

For additional information on the Keys area, see the following towns included in the *Mobil Travel Guide:* Big Pine Key, Islamorada, Key Largo, Key West, Marathon.

(For information about area attractions contact the Key Largo Chamber of Commerce, PO Box 1083, Key Largo 33037, 305/451-1414 or 800/822-1088.)

Fort Caroline National Memorial (A-4)

(13 mi E of Jacksonville on FL 10, then N on Monument Rd, then E on Fort Caroline Rd)

Fort Caroline, a triangular, wood and earthen fortress, once stood at this site. In June, 1564, René de Laudonnière established a short-lived foothold for France in the battle for supremacy in the New World. Unfortunately for France, the group of 300 colonists, mostly Huguenots, spent more time searching for treasure than growing food.

Driven by famine and futility, the colonists were about to abandon the outpost in August, 1565, when reinforcements arrived from France. Almost at the same time, Spanish Captain-General Pedro Menéndez de Avilés was ordered by King Philip II to clear Florida for Spanish colonization. Foiled in his initial efforts to destroy Fort Caroline, Menéndez sailed 30 miles south and established a settlement known today as St Augus-

tine. The French tried to attack, but their fleet was destroyed in a storm. Menéndez took 500 men overland to Fort Caroline, killed about 140 of the French and took approximately 70 women and children prisoner. About 300 shipwrecked Frenchmen also were captured and slain at Matanzas Inlet (see FORT MATANZAS NATIONAL MONUMENT).

In 1568, a French expedition attacked and burned the former Fort Caroline, by then in Spanish hands, killing most of its occupants in vengeance. But Florida was to remain in Spain's control almost continuously for the next 250 years. Nearby St Johns Bluff was the scene of later British and Spanish fortifications. Gun batteries were raised on this site during both the Civil War and the Spanish-American War.

A scale model of the fort has been constructed along 280 feet of riverfront. Descriptions of the fort by its commander and sketches by Jacques Le Moyne, artist and mapmaker, both of whom escaped the early attacks, served as a blueprint. A visitor center overlooks the St Johns River near the former site of the fort. (Daily; closed Dec 25) For further information contact 12713 Ft Caroline Rd, Jacksonville 32225; 904/641-7155.   **Free.**

(For accommodations see Atlantic Beach, Fernandina Beach, Jacksonville)

Fort Lauderdale (E-5)

Pop: 149,377 **Elev:** 10 ft **Area code:** 305

With more than 300 miles of navigable waterways, 23 miles of Atlantic beaches and a myriad of rivers, inlets and man-made canals in the Greater Fort Lauderdale area, the city easily lives up to its nickname "the Venice of America." The abundance of water provides ample room for approximately 40,000 boats, not to mention flotillas of visiting vessels. Water taxis ply waterways to hotels, restaurants and sightseeing attractions. Port Everglades, the deepest and perhaps best-known harbor in the state, is also the world's second largest passenger cruise port. More than one million passengers sail from Fort Lauderdale annually.

Fort Lauderdale was named for Major William Lauderdale, who built a fort in 1838 during the Seminole War. The area remained a sleepy strip of oceanfront until the 1950s and 1960s when college students made it the "spring break capital of the world." More recently, however, Fort Lauderdale has became a recreation area for all ages, as well as a center for commerce and high-tech industry.

What to See and Do

1. **Museum of Art.** 1 E Las Olas Blvd. Permanent and changing exhibits. (Tues–Sat, also Sun afternoons; closed hols) Phone 763-6464 (recording) or 525-5500. Sr citizen rate.   **¢¢**

2. **Museum of Discovery and Science and Blockbuster IMAX Theater.** 401 SW 2nd St; I-95, Broward Blvd E exit, opp Riverwalk's Esplanade Park. Hands-on science museum with seven permanent exhibit areas, including KidScience, Space Base, Choose Health and Florida Ecoscapes. Features Manned Maneuvering Unit space ride, walk-through simulated Florida habitats and Cut-Away House; traveling exhibitions. Blockbuster IMAX Theater features large-format films shown on five-story screen (daily; also Thurs–Sat evenings). (Daily; closed Dec 25) Sr citizen rate. Phone 467-6637.   **¢¢¢**

3. **International Swimming Hall of Fame and Aquatic Complex.** 1 Hall of Fame Dr, 1 blk S of Las Olas Blvd, W of beach. Leading repository for aquatic displays, photos, sculpture, art and memorabilia; computerized exhibits, film & video presentations, library. Also two Olympic-size public swimming pools (daily; fee). Museum (daily). Sr citizen rate. Phone 462-6536 (museum) or 468-1580 (pool).   **¢¢**

4. **Ocean World.** 1701 SE 17th St Causeway, between US 1 & FL A1A. Marine Life Park; performing dolphins, sea lions, sharks and exotic

birds. Sightseeing tour boat (fee); concession. (Daily) Phone 525-6611. ¢¢¢¢

5. **Everglades Holiday Park.** 21940 Griffin Rd, 20 mi SW of town, off I-95 Griffin Rd W exit. Narrated airboat rides, boat rentals, fishing; alligator show; RV campground (fee). (Daily) Phone 434-8111. ¢¢¢¢

6. **Recreation areas.**

Hugh Taylor Birch State Recreation Area. E Sunrise Blvd, at FL A1A. Approximately 180 acres with access to swimming; fishing; canoeing (fee). Nature trails. Picnicking, pavilion. Standard hrs, fees. Phone 564-4521.

Public Beach. Atlantic Blvd. Newly renovated 1½-mi stretch from Sunrise Blvd to Seabreeze Blvd has wide pedestrian promenades, bicycle lanes, palm tree landscaping. Swimming; picnicking; cabanas.

Snyder Park. 3299 SW 4th Ave. Swimming; fishing; boating. Nature trails, bicycling. Picnicking. Botanical areas. Phone 523-0889.

Holiday Park. 1400 E Sunrise Blvd. This 86-acre park has a theater (see SEASONAL EVENTS), playing fields, tennis courts. Picnicking, shelters. Phone 762-5383.

Markham Park. 13 mi W via I-595 (FL 84), just W of Sawgrass Expy in Sunrise. More than 660 acres. Swimming pool; fishing; boating (ramp), canoeing & paddleboating (rentals). Nature trails, bicycle rentals. Tennis. Picnicking, concession. Camping (dump station). Model airplane field. Pistol/rifle, skeet and trap shooting ranges. (Daily) Phone 389-2000. Wkends, hols ¢

7. **Boating, fishing, diving.** Boats of all sizes can be chartered by the hour, day, week or season. Bahia Mar Resort, Pier 66 Resort & Marina, Lauderdale Marina and Marina Bay Club are available for visiting yachtsmen. There are several public fishing piers and boat ramps. Phone 765-4466.

Mercedes I Artificial Reef. 1½ mi offshore of Sunrise Blvd. The *Mercedes I* was sunk in 1985 to provide an artificial reef. This ship lies intact in 97 feet of water and is a popular scuba diving site. Phone 765-4013.

Lowrance Artificial Reef. 1½ mi offshore of Atlantic Blvd near Pompano Beach. (See POMPANO BEACH)

8. **Horseracing.** Gulfstream Park, 12 mi S on US 1 at 901 S Federal Hwy in Hallandale (see HOLLYWOOD).

9. **Sightseeing trips.**

South Florida Trolley Co—"Lolly Trolley." Trolleys make 90-minute narrated route, regularly stopping at points of interest, including Ocean World, Discovery Center Museum, beaches, hotels and restaurants; special excursion tours offered. (Daily) Phone 768-0700. All-day pass ¢¢¢¢

Jungle Queen Cruises. Bahia Mar Yacht Basin, FL A1A. Three-hour cruises (two departures daily); also barbecue-and-shrimp dinner cruise (one departure nightly). Res required. Phone 462-5596. Dinner cruise ¢¢¢¢

(For further information contact the Greater Fort Lauderdale Convention & Visitors Bureau, 200 E Las Olas Blvd, Suite 1500, 33301; 765-4466.)

Annual Event

Winterfest. Month-long festival including a boat parade and downtown New Year's Eve celebration. Phone 767-0686. Dec.

Seasonal Events

Professional baseball. Fort Lauderdale Stadium, 5301 12th Ave NW. New York Yankees spring training; exhibition games. Phone 776-1921. Feb-early Apr.

Parker Playhouse. 707 NE 8th St, in Holiday Park (see #6). Broadway musicals and plays. Phone 764-1441. Nov-May.

(See Boca Raton, Dania, Hollywood, Pompano Beach)

Motels

✔ ★**FORT LAUDERDALE INN.** *5727 N Federal Hwy (US 1) (33308).* 305/491-2500; FAX 305/491-7945. 168 rms, 2 story. Mid-Dec-Mar: S $62-$72; D $68-$78; each addl $10; under 16 free; lower rates rest of yr. Crib $8. TV; cable. Heated pool; wading pool, sauna, poolside serv. Restaurant 7 am-2:30 pm, 5-9:30 pm. Bar 5 pm-2 am; entertainment Wed-Sat. Ck-out 11 am. Coin lndry. Meeting rms. Game rm. Refrigerators avail. Cr cds: A, C, D, DS, ER, MC, V.

★ ★**HAMPTON INN.** *720 E Cypress Creek Rd (33334).* 305/776-7677; FAX 305/776-0805. 122 rms, 4 story. Dec-Apr: S, D $75-$100; under 18 free; lower rates rest of yr. Crib free. TV; cable. Pool; whirlpool. Complimentary continental bkfst. Restaurant nearby. Ck-out 11 am. Meeting rm. Valet serv (Mon-Fri). Cr cds: A, C, D, DS, MC, V.

★★**PELICAN BEACH RESORT.** *2000 N Atlantic Blvd (33305).* 305/568-9431; res: 800/525-6232; FAX 305/565-2622. 77 rms in 7 buildings, 2 story, 19 suites, 37 kit. units. Mid-Dec-Apr: S, D $90-$110; each addl $10; suites $140-$160; kits. $110-$140; under 12 free; wkly rates; higher rates hols; lower rates rest of yr. Crib free. TV; cable. Heated pool. Playground. Complimentary continental bkfst. Restaurant nearby. Ck-out 11 am. Coin lndry. Meeting rms. Bellhops. Valet serv. Concierge. Refrigerators. Balconies. Grills. On ocean; beach. Cr cds: A, C, D, DS, ER, MC, V, JCB.

✔ ★**SEA CHATEAU.** *555 N Birch Rd (33304).* 305/566-8331. 17 rms, 2 story, 5 kit. units. Feb-Apr: S, D $60; each addl $15; kit. units $70; under 16, $5; lower rates rest of yr. Children over 6 yrs only. TV. Pool. Restaurant nearby. Ck-out 11 am. No cr cds accepted.

✔ ★**TRAVELODGE.** *1500 W Commercial Blvd (33309).* 305/776-4222; FAX 305/771-5026. 118 rms, 5 story. Mid-Dec-mid-Apr: S $65, D $75; each addl $8; lower rates rest of yr. Crib free. TV; cable. Pool. Complimentary continental bkfst, coffee. Restaurant nearby. Ck-out noon. Coin lndry. Meeting rms. Valet serv. Sundries. Exercise equipt; weight machine, bicycles. Some refrigerators. Cr cds: A, C, D, DS, ER, MC, V, JCB.

★ ★**VILLAS-BY-THE-SEA.** *(4456 El Mar Drive, Lauderdale-by-the-Sea 33308)* N on FL A1A. 305/772-3550; res: 800/247-8963; FAX 305/772-3835. 150 rms in 6 buildings, 2-4 story, 67 suites, 47 kit. units. Late Dec-mid-Apr: S, D $90-$120; each addl $10; suites $140-$215; kit. units $110-$140; under 12 free; lower rates rest of yr. Crib free. TV; cable. 5 heated pools; whirlpool. Complimentary continental bkfst, coffee. Restaurant adj 7 am-midnight. Ck-out 11 am. Coin lndry. Concierge. Airport transportation. Tennis. Lawn games. Refrigerators. Balconies. Picnic tables, grills. On ocean; swimming beach. Cr cds: A, C, D, DS, MC, V.

★ ★**WELLESLEY INN-PLANTATION.** *(7901 SW 6th St, Plantation 33324)* W via FL 595 to Pine Island Rd, then right on SW 6th St. 305/473-8257; res: 800/444-8888; FAX 305/473-9804. 106 rms, 4 story, 13 suites. Late Dec-mid-Apr: S, D $79.99; suites $99; family rates; lower rates rest of yr. Crib free. Pet accepted, some restrictions; $5. TV; cable. Heated pool. Complimentary continental bkfst, coffee. Restaurant nearby. Bar. Ck-out 11 am. Coin lndry. Meeting rms. Valet serv. Airport transportation. Some refrigerators. Cr cds: A, C, D, DS, ER, MC, V.

Motor Hotels

★ ★ **BEST WESTERN MARINA INN.** *2150 SE 17th St Causeway (33316). 305/525-3484; FAX 305/764-2915.* 157 rms, 4 story. Dec–Apr: S $89–$109; D $99–$119; each addl $10; under 18 free; varied lower rates rest of yr. Crib free. TV; cable. Pool; whirlpool, poolside serv. Complimentary bkfst. Restaurant 7 am–10 pm. Rm serv. Bars 11–2 am; entertainment. Ck-out noon. Coin lndry. Meeting rm. Valet serv. Free local airport, Port Everglades transportation. Putting green. On Intracoastal Waterway; marina; boating. Cr cds: A, C, D, DS, ER, MC, V, JCB.

⊡ ⊷ ⊠ ⊘ ⊙ SC

★ ★ **COMFORT SUITES.** *1800 S Federal Hwy (33316), near Ft Lauderdale-Hollywood Intl Airport. 305/767-8700; FAX 305/524-4112.* 110 suites, 7 story. Jan–Apr: S, D $89–$179; each addl $10; under 18 free; lower rates rest of yr. Crib free. TV. Heated pool. Complimentary continental bkfst. Complimentary coffee in rms. Restaurant nearby. Ck-out noon. Meeting rms. Bellhops. Valet serv. Free airport, RR station, bus depot transportation. Refrigerators. 3 blks from beach. Cr cds: A, D, DS, ER, MC, V.

⊠ ✕ ⊘ ⊙ SC

★ ★ **HILTON SUNRISE.** *3003 N University Dr (33322). 305/748-7000; FAX 305/572-0799.* 297 rms, 6 story, 95 suites. Dec–Apr: S, D $117–$147; each addl $10; suites $137–$350; under 18 free; lower rates rest of yr. Crib free. TV; cable. Heated pool. Restaurant 6:30 am–10 pm. Rm serv. Bar 11–2 am; entertainment exc Sun. Ck-out noon. Meeting rms. Bellhops. Valet serv. Concierge. Lighted tennis privileges. 18-hole golf privileges. Exercise equipt; weights, bicycles, whirlpool, sauna. Some refrigerators. Balconies. Cr cds: A, C, D, DS, ER, MC, V, JCB.

⊡ ⊠♦ ⊘ ⊠ ⊀ ⊘ ⊙ SC

★ ★ **HOWARD JOHNSON BEACH RESORT.** *(4660 Ocean Dr, Lauderdale-by-the-Sea 33308) 6 mi N via FL A1A, just N of Commercial Blvd. 305/776-5660; FAX 305/776-4689.* 181 rms, 5 story, 17 suites, 25 kits. Mid-Dec–Apr: S, D, kit. units $109–$199; each addl $10; suites $109–$189; under 18 free; wkly rates; lower rates rest of yr. Crib free. TV; cable. 2 pools, heated; wading pool, poolside serv. Free supervised child's activities. Restaurant 7 am–10 pm. Rm serv. Bar 4 pm–1 am. Ck-out 11 am. Coin lndry. Meeting rms. Bellhops. Valet serv. Gift shop. Tennis & golf privileges. Exercise equipt; weights, bicycles, steam rm. Many refrigerators. Balconies. On ocean; beach, cabanas. Cr cds: A, C, D, DS, ER, MC, V, JCB.

⊡ ⊠♦ ⊘ ⊠ ⊀ ⊘ ⊙ SC

★ **HOWARD JOHNSON-OCEAN'S EDGE.** *700 N Atlantic Blvd (FL A1A) (33304). 305/563-2451; FAX 305/564-8153.* 144 rms, 9 story. Jan–Apr: S $80–$102; D $85–$112; each addl $10; under 18 free; varied lower rates rest of yr. Crib free. TV; cable. Heated pool; poolside serv. Restaurant 6:30 am–midnight. Rm serv 7 am–10 pm. Bar 11–2 am; entertainment, dancing. Ck-out 11 am. Bellhops. Valet serv. Sundries. Refrigerators. Private patios, balconies. Beach opp. Cr cds: A, C, D, DS, MC, V, JCB.

⊠ ⊘ ⊙ SC

★ ★ **IRELAND'S INN.** *2220 N Atlantic Blvd (FL A1A) (33305). 305/565-6661; res: 800/347-7776; FAX 305/565-8893.* 76 rms, 7 story, 36 kits. Dec–Apr: S, D $69–$195; each addl $15; kit. units $125–$185; suites $140–$195; varied lower rates rest of yr. Crib free. TV; cable. 2 heated pools; poolside serv. Restaurants 7:30 am–3 pm, 5:30–10:30 pm. Bar; entertainment, dancing. Ck-out noon. Gift shop. Refrigerators. Many patios, balconies. On beach. Cr cds: A, C, MC, V.

⊠ ⊙

Hotels

★ ★ **BAHIA MAR RESORT & YACHTING CENTER.** *801 Seabreeze Blvd (33316). 305/764-2233; res: 800/327-8154; FAX 305/523-5424.* 298 rms, 16 story. Mid-Dec–mid-Apr: S, D $115–$165; each addl $10–$20; suites $295–$395; under 17 free; lower rates rest of yr. Crib

free. TV; cable. Heated pool; poolside serv. Restaurant 7 am–10 pm. Bars 11–2 am; entertainment wkends. Ck-out noon. Coin lndry. Convention facilities. Barber, beauty shop. Lighted tennis. Boat rentals. Game rm. Refrigerators avail. Many rms with terrace; some balconies. Complete yachting center on 40 acres at Intracoastal Waterway; dock. Ocean opp; overpass to beach. Cr cds: A, C, D, DS, ER, MC, V.

⊡ ⊷ ⊘ ⊠ ⊘ ⊙ SC

★ ★ **BREAKERS.** *909 Breakers Ave (33304), 1 blk S of Sunrise Blvd, W of FL A1A. 305/566-8800; res: 800/741-7869; FAX 305/566-8802.* 210 units, 18 story. Mid-Dec–mid-Apr: kit. suites $190–$345; studio rms with kitchenette $130; under 18 free; lower rates rest of yr. Crib free. TV; cable. Heated pool; whirlpool, sauna, poolside serv. Restaurant 7 am–10 pm. Bar 11–2 am; entertainment, dancing. Ck-out 11 am. Coin lndry. Concierge. Game rm. Balconies. Opp beach. Cr cds: A, C, D, DS, ER, MC, V.

⊠ ⊙ SC

★ ★ **CROWN STERLING SUITES.** *1100 SE 17th St (33316), adj to Port Everglades. 305/527-2700; FAX 305/760-7202.* 363 suites, 12 story. Jan–mid-Apr: S $139–$159; D $149–$169; each addl $10; under 12 free; lower rates rest of yr. Crib free. TV; cable. Pool; whirlpool, steam rm, sauna, poolside serv. Complimentary full bkfst. Coffee in rms. Restaurant 11 am–11 pm. Bar to 2 am; dancing exc Sun. Ck-out noon. Convention facilities. Free airport, beach, health club transportation. Tennis & golf privileges. Health club privileges. Refrigerators. Private patios, balconies. Waterfall in atrium & lobby. Cr cds: A, C, D, DS, ER, MC, V.

⊡ ⊘ ⊠ ⊘ ⊙ SC

★ ★ **GUEST QUARTERS.** *2670 E Sunrise Blvd (33304). 305/565-3800; FAX 305/561-0387.* 229 kit. suites (1–2 bedrm), 14 story. Mid-Dec–mid-Apr: kit. suites $115–$189; under 18 free; monthly rates; lower rates rest of yr. Crib free. Free covered parking; valet $7. Pet accepted; $10. TV; cable. Heated pool; poolside serv. Complimentary coffee, tea. Restaurant 7 am–11 pm. Rm serv 24 hrs. Bar 11–2 am. Ck-out noon. Coin lndry. Concierge. Gift shop. Free airport transportation. Tennis privileges. Golf privileges. Exercise equipt; weight machine, bicycles, whirlpool, sauna. Minibars; wet bars. Balconies. Overlooks Intracoastal Waterway; dockage. Cr cds: A, C, D, DS, MC, V, JCB.

⊡ ⊷ ⊘ ⊠ ⊀ ⊘ ⊙ SC

★ ★ **LAGO MAR RESORT & CLUB.** *1700 S Ocean Lane (33316). 305/523-6511; res: 800/255-5246; FAX 305/523-6511, ext 609.* 179 rms, 3–5 story, 129 kit. suites. Dec–Apr: S, D $155; each addl $10; kit. suites $245–$285; lower rates rest of yr. Crib $10. TV; cable. 2 heated pools; poolside serv. Playground. Restaurant 7 am–10:30 pm. Bars 11–1 am; entertainment, dancing exc Mon. Ck-out noon. Free lndry facilities. Convention facilities. Shopping arcade. Tennis, pro. 18-hole golf privileges. Miniature golf. Game rm. Lawn games. Some bathrm phones. Private patios, balconies. Private dock. Private beach. Located between Lake Mayan & ocean. Cr cds: A, C, D, MC, V.

⊡ ⊷ ⊘ ⊠ ⊘ SC

★ ★ **MARRIOTT NORTH.** *6650 N Andrews Ave (33309), in Cypress Park West office complex. 305/771-0440; FAX 305/771-7519.* 321 rms, 16 story. Jan–mid-Apr: S $125–$160; D $140–$170; each addl $10; suites $250; under 18 free; wkend rates; honeymoon packages; lower rates rest of yr. Crib free. Valet parking $6; garage free. TV; cable. Heated pool; poolside serv. Restaurant 7 am–11 pm. Bar. Ck-out noon. Convention facilities. Gift shop. Tennis & 18-hole golf privileges, greens fee. Exercise equipt; weights, bicycles, whirlpool, sauna. Minibars; some refrigerators. Balconies. *LUXURY LEVEL:* CONCIERGE LEVEL. 17 rms. S $160; D $175. Concierge. Private lounge, honor bar. Complimentary bkfst, refreshments, newspaper. Cr cds: A, C, D, DS, ER, MC, V.

⊡ ⊘ ⊠ ⊀ ⊘ ⊙ SC

★ ★ **RAMADA BEACH RESORT.** *4060 Galt Ocean Dr (33308). 305/565-6611; FAX 305/564-7730.* 220 rms, 9 story. Mid-Dec–mid-Apr: S $110–$180; D $120–$190; each addl $10; kit. suites $250–$350; under 17 free; lower rates rest of yr. Crib free. TV. Heated pool; poolside serv. Restaurant 7 am–10 pm. Bar 11 am–10 pm; entertainment, dancing. Ck-out noon. Meeting rms. Gift shop. Exercise equipt; bicycle, treadmill. Refrigerators avail. Balconies. On beach. Cr cds: A, C, D, DS, ER, MC, V.

★ ★ **RIVERSIDE.** *620 E Las Olas Blvd (33301).* 305/467-0671; *res:* 800/325-3280; *FAX* 305/462-2148. 107 rms, 6 story. Late Dec–mid-Apr: S $95–$135; D $110–$150; each addl $15; suites $175–$195; under 16 free; varied lower rates rest of yr. Crib free. TV; cable. Pool; poolside serv. Restaurant 11:30–1 am. Bars. Ck-out 11 am. Meeting rms. Free airport transportation. Refrigerators. On New River; dock. Cr cds: A, C, D, MC, V.

★ ★ ★ **SHERATON EXECUPORT.** *2440 W Cypress Creek Rd NW (62nd St) (33309), near Executive Airport.* 305/772-7770; *FAX* 305/772-4780. 139 rms, 4 story. Jan–Apr: S, D $110–$130; each addl $5; under 17 free; lower rates rest of yr. Crib free. TV; cable. Heated pool; poolside serv. Restaurant 6:30 am–10:30 pm. Bar 11–2 am, closed Sun. Ck-out noon. Meeting rms. Free Executive airport, Corporate Center transportation. Health club privileges. Tropical decor. Cr cds: A, C, D, DS, MC, V.

★ ★ ★ **SHERATON SUITES PLANTATION.** *(311 N University Dr, Plantation 33324)* 6½ mi W on Broward Blvd, at Fashion Mall. 305/424-3300; *FAX* 305/452-8887. 264 suites, 9 story. Mid-Dec–mid-Apr: S $118–$165; D $133–$180; each addl $15; under 18 free; wkend rates; lower rates rest of yr. Crib free. Free garage parking. TV; cable, in-rm movies. Heated pool; poolside serv. Complimentary bkfst buffet. Complimentary coffee in rms. Restaurant 6:30 am–10:30 pm; wkends 7 am–10:30 pm. Bar 11 am–midnight. Ck-out noon. Coin lndry. Convention facilities. Shopping arcade. Exercise equipt; weights, bicycles, whirlpool, sauna. Refrigerators, wet bars. Cr cds: A, C, D, DS, ER, V, JCB.

★ ★ ★ **THE WESTIN, CYPRESS CREEK.** *400 Corporate Dr (33334).* 305/772-1331; *FAX* 305/491-9087. 293 rms, 14 story, 33 suites. Dec–Apr: S $160–$185; D $185–$210; each addl $15; suites $235–$455; under 18 free; lower rates rest of yr. Crib free. Pet accepted, some restrictions. TV; cable. Pool; poolside serv. Restaurant 6:30 am–10 pm. Rm serv 24 hrs. Bar 11 am–midnight; entertainment. Ck-out 1 pm. Convention facilities. Concierge. Free valet parking. Free shopping, beach transportation. Tennis & golf privileges. Exercise rm; instructor, weights, bicycles, whirlpool, sauna. Minibars. Some private patios, balconies. Blue-mirrored tile building surrounded by palm trees; 20-ft poolside waterfall, 5-acre lake. Paddleboats. Cr cds: A, C, D, DS, ER, MC, V, JCB.

Resorts

★ ★ ★ **BONAVENTURE.** *250 Racquet Club Rd (33326), 1 mi W of I-595, I-75 & Sawgrass Expy.* 305/389-3300; *FAX* 305/384-0563. 504 rms in 9 bldgs, 4 story, 108 suites. Jan–mid-Apr: S $195–$225; D $225–$275; each addl $15; suites $295–$800; under 17 free; some wkend rates; lower rates rest of yr. Crib free. TV; cable. 5 heated pools; poolside serv. Supervised child's activities. Dining rm 7 am–11 pm. Rm serv 6–2 am. Bar 11–1 am; entertainment, dancing. Ck-out noon, ck-in 4 pm. Convention facilities. Valet serv. Concierge. Gift shop. Barber, beauty shop. 17 clay & 7 hard tennis courts, many lighted, pro. Two 18-hole golf courses, par 70 & par 72, greens fee, pro. Charter excursions avail. Bicycles. Lawn games. Evening programs. Roller skating. Bowling. Exercise rm; instructor, weights, bicycles, whirlpool, steam rm, sauna. Minibars. Cr cds: A, C, D, DS, ER, MC, V.

★ ★ ★ **MARRIOTT'S HARBOR BEACH.** *3030 Holiday Dr (33316).* 305/525-4000; *FAX* 305/766-6152. 624 rms, 15 story. Mid-Dec–Apr: S, D $245–$350; suites $325–$1,700; under 18 free; lower rates rest of yr. Crib free. Garage: self-park $6.95, valet $8.95. TV; cable. Pool; poolside serv. Free supervised child's activities. 6 dining rms 6:30

am–11 pm. Rm serv 24 hrs. Bar 11–2 am. Ck-out 11 am, ck-in 4 pm. Shopping arcade. Convention facilities. Concierge. Barber, beauty shops. Free shopping, golf transportation. Tennis, pro. Golf privileges, pro. Private beach; cabanas. Boats, sailboats. Soc dir. Game rm. Exercise rm; instructor, weights, bicycles, whirlpools, saunas. Some bathrm phones, refrigerators. Private patios, balconies. 16 acres of oceanfront property. Antiques, large chandeliers in lobby. Cr cds: A, C, D, DS, ER, MC, V.

★ ★ ★ **PIER 66 RESORT & MARINA.** *2301 SE 17th St Causeway (33316), southeast of downtown.* 305/525-6666; *res:* 800/327-3796 (exc FL), 800/432-1956 (FL); *FAX* 305/728-3541. 388 rms, 17 story. Mid-Dec–Apr: S, D $180–$270; each addl $15; suites $650–$850; under 17 free; varied lower rates rest of yr. Crib free. Parking $5; valet parking avail. TV; cable. 2 heated pools; wading pool, poolside serv, hot tub. Supervised child's activities. Dining rm 6:30 am–midnight; 7 restaurants and bars. Rm serv 24 hrs. Bars 11–2 am (1 revolving rooftop); entertainment, dancing. Ck-out 11 am. Coin lndry. Convention facilities. Concierge. Gift shop. Full service hair salon. Transportation shuttle to beach by water or vehicle. Tennis, pro. Golf privileges, greens fee $35, pro. Exercise rm; instructor, weights, bicycles, whirlpool, sauna, steam rm. Full service spa. Refrigerators. Many private patios, balconies. Glass-enclosed outside elvtr. 22 acres on Intracoastal Waterway; marina and marina store. Adj to Port Everglades. Cr cds: A, C, D, DS, MC, V, JCB.

Restaurants

★ ★ **ARMADILLO CAFE.** *(4630 SW 64th Ave, Davie) S on I-95 to Griffin Rd, then 5 mi W.* 305/791-4866. Hrs: 5–10 pm; wknds to 11 pm. Closed most major hols; Super Bowl Sun. Res required. Southwestern menu. Bar. A la carte entrees: dinner $4.25–$24. Specialties: smoked barbecued duck, lobster quesadilla, roasted corn & jalapeño fritters. Parking. Outdoor dining. Extensive wine list. Cr cds: A, C, D, DS, MC, V.

★ ★ ★ **BURT & JACKS.** *I-95 to I-595E, follow signs to Port Everglades.* 305/522-5225. Hrs: 5–11 pm; Fri, Sat to midnight. Closed Dec 25. Res accepted. Bar from 4:30 pm. Semi-a la carte: dinner $13.95–$27.95. Specializes in fresh seafood, prime meat. Own baking. Pianist. Valet parking. Spanish mission-style building located at end of pier. Scenic view of port and city skyline. Jacket. Cr cds: A, C, D, MC, V.

★ ★ **BY WORD OF MOUTH.** *3200 NE 12th Ave.* 305/564-3663. Hrs: 11 am–3 pm, 5–10 pm; Sat from 5 pm; Mon, Tues to 3 pm. Closed Sun; major hols; also first wk Aug. Res accepted Wed–Sat. Continental menu. Wine, beer. A la carte entrees: lunch $6.95–$15.95, dinner $14.95–$21.95. Specialties: glazed duckling, tenderloin of beef, sweet & spicy sautéed shrimp. Parking. Cr cds: A, C, D, DS, MC, V.

✔ ★ ★ **CAFÉ DE GENÈVE.** *1519 S Andrews Ave.* 305/522-8928. Hrs: 11:30 am–2:30 pm, 5–10 pm; Sat from 5 pm. Closed Sun. Res accepted. Continental menu. Bar. Semi-a la carte: lunch $5.50–$8.95, dinner $9.95–$19.95. Specializes in veal, fondue, duckling. Parking. Swiss chalet decor. Cr cds: A, C, D, DS, MC, V.

★ ★ **CAFE SEVILLE.** *2768 E Oakland Park Blvd, at Bayview Dr.* 305/565-1148. Hrs: 11:30 am–2 pm, 6–10:30 pm; Sat 6–11 pm; early-bird dinner Mon–Fri 6–7 pm. Closed Sun; some major hols; also 3 wks Aug. Res accepted. Mediterranean menu. Wine, beer. Complete meals: lunch $7.50–$9.95, dinner $11.50–$16.75. Specialties: paella, cazuela de mariscos. Parking. Rustic, Spanish atmosphere. Cr cds: A, C, D, MC, V.

★ ★ **THE CAVES.** *2205 N Federal Hwy (US 1).* 305/561-4622. Hrs: 5:30–11:30 pm. Res accepted. Bar. A la carte entrees: dinner $9.95–$20.95. Child's meals. Specialties: tableau de steak Diane, Caveman filet mignon, lobster tail. Salad bar. Parking. Dining area resembles actual cave interior; tables set in individual alcoves. Wait staff dressed as cave people. Cr cds: A, D, MC, V.

★ ★ ★CHAMELEON. *1095 SE 17th St Causeway. 305/522-6795.* Hrs: 6–10:30 pm; Sat from 5:30 pm. Closed Sun. Res required Fri, Sat. Continental menu. Wine, beer. Semi-a la carte: lunch dinner $14–$24. Child's meals. Specializes in game dishes, loin of lamb, seafood. Own baking, desserts. Parking. Varied antiques; tapestries. Cr cds: A, MC, V.

D

✔ ★ ★CHARLEY'S CRAB. *3000 NE 32nd Ave. 305/561-4800.* Hrs: 11:30 am–3:30 pm, 5–10 pm; wkends to 11 pm; early-bird dinner 5–6 pm; Sun brunch 11 am–3:30 pm. Res accepted. Bar. A la carte entrees: lunch $5.75–$17.50, dinner $9.75–$25.75. Complete meals: dinner $9.95–$14.50. Sun brunch $11.95. Child's meals. Specialties: stone crab, live Maine lobster, shrimp Danielle. Parking. Outdoor dining. On Intracoastal Waterway, boat dockage. Cr cds: A, C, D, DS, MC, V.

D

★ ★ ★CHRYSANTHEMUM. *6000 N Federal Hwy (US 1). 305/493-8888.* Hrs: 11:30 am–2:30 pm, 5–10:30 pm; Fri, Sat 5–11:30 pm; early-bird dinner 5–6 pm. Closed Mon; Thanksgiving. Res accepted. Chinese menu. Bar (Oct–Mar). A la carte entrees: lunch, dinner $8.50–$18.50. Complete meals: lunch $8.50–$12.50. Specialty: sliced chicken with Szechwan pepper. Pianist Oct–Mar. Valet parking. Art deco decor. Cr cds: A, C, D, DS, MC, V.

D

★ ★ ★DANTE'S. *2871 N Federal Hwy (US 1). 305/564-6666.* Hrs: 5:30–11:30 pm. Closed Dec 25. Res accepted. Continental menu. Bar. Semi-a la carte: dinner $12.75–$30. Specializes in prime meats, seafood, pasta, veal. Valet parking. Open-hearth cooking in dining area. Family-owned. Cr cds: A, C, D, MC, V.

★ ★ ★THE DOWN UNDER. *3000 E Oakland Park Blvd. 305/563-4123.* Hrs: 11:30 am–2 pm, 6–11 pm; Sat from 6 pm; Sun 6–10:30 pm. Res required Fri, Sat. Continental menu. Bar. Wine cellar. Semi-a la carte: lunch $7.50–$15, dinner $17–$29. Child's meals. Specializes in fresh local seafood, prime steak, Maine lobster. Own pastries, soups, sauces, ice cream. Pianist. Valet parking. Outdoor dining. At waterfront. Cr cds: A, C, D, DS, MC, V.

D

★ ★ ★FRENCH QUARTER. *215 SE 8th Ave. 305/463-8000.* Hrs: 11:30 am–3 pm, 6–11 pm; Sat from 6 pm. Closed Sun. Res required. French, New Orleans classic menu. Bar. Semi-a la carte: lunch $10–$20, dinner $15.50–$35. Specialty: bouillabaisse Louisiane. Own baking, soups, sauces. Entertainment. Parking. Original residence of city's first mayor (1925). Cr cds: A, C, D, DS, MC, V.

D

★ ★GIBBY'S STEAKS & SEAFOOD. *2900 NE 12th Terrace. 305/565-2929.* Hrs: 5–11 pm. Res accepted. Bar. A la carte entrees: dinner $13.95–$27.95. Specializes in steak, prime rib, rack of lamb. Valet parking. Cr cds: A, C, D, MC, V.

D

✔ ★ ★IL GIARDINO. *609 E Las Olas Blvd. 305/763-3733.* Hrs: 11:30 am–2:30 pm, 6–10:30 pm; Sat from 6 pm. Closed Sun; major hols. Res accepted; required Sat. Northern Italian, Amer menu. Bar to 2 am. Semi-a la carte: lunch $5.25–$8.25, dinner $11.95–$18.95. Child's meals. Specializes in veal, cannelloni, fresh seafood. Parking. Cr cds: A, C, D, MC, V.

D

★ ★LA BONNE AUBERGE. *4300 N Federal Hwy. 305/776-1668.* Hrs: 11:30 am–2:30 pm, 5:30–10:30 pm. Res required. French, continental menu. Serv bar. A la carte entrees: lunch $4.75–$11.15, dinner $13.50–$24.50. Specialties: frogs' legs, Dover sole, rack of lamb. Cr cds: A, D, MC, V.

★ ★ ★LA COQUILLE. *1619 E Sunrise Blvd. 305/467-3030.* Hrs: 5:30–10 pm; Fri also 11:30 am–2 pm. Closed Mon; also Aug. Res accepted. French menu. A la carte entrees: lunch $7–$10, dinner $12.95–$20.50. Specialties: duck breast with peppercorn sauce, salmon with mustard sauce. Own baking. Parking. Cr cds: A, MC, V.

D

★ ★ ★LA FERME. *1601 E Sunrise Blvd. 305/764-0987.* Hrs: 5:30–10 pm. Closed Mon; Dec 25; also Aug. Res accepted. French menu. Serv bar. Wine list. Semi-a la carte: dinner $20–$30. Specializes in calf's liver, rack of lamb. Own pastries. Parking. Cr cds: A, D, MC, V.

D

★ ★ ★LE DOME. *333 Sunset Dr, in Four Season Condominium. 305/463-3303.* Hrs: 6–10 pm. Res accepted. Continental menu. Bar. Semi-a la carte: dinner $17.50–$29. Specializes in châteaubriand, rack of lamb, fresh Norwegian salmon. Pianist. Valet parking. Atop 12-story condominium. Cr cds: A, C, D, DS, MC, V.

★ ★ ★THE LEFT BANK. *214 SE 6th Ave. 305/462-5376.* Hrs: 6 pm–midnight. Res accepted. Florida regional menu. Bar. Semi-a la carte: dinner $14.95–$20.95. Specialties: grilled Atlantic salmon, stone crab salad & white truffle vinaigrette. Parking. Contemporary French decor. Cr cds: A, D, MC, V.

D

★ ★ ★MAI-KAI. *3599 N Federal Hwy (US 1). 305/563-3272.* Hrs: 5 pm–midnight. Res accepted. Oriental, Amer menu. Bar to 2 am. Wine list. A la carte entrees: dinner $12.95–$26.50. Child's meals. Specialties: fresh Peking duck, steamed trout, Maine lobster Tahitienne. Polynesian entertainment (cover in show rm $7.95). Valet parking. Outdoor dining. South Seas setting; exotic gardens. Authentic Polynesian artifacts. Family-owned. Cr cds: A, C, D, DS, MC, V.

D

✔ ★ ★OLD FLORIDA SEAFOOD HOUSE. *1414 NE 26th St. 305/566-1044.* Hrs: 11:30 am–3:30 pm, 4:45–10:15 pm; Sat, Sun from 4:30 pm. Closed Thanksgiving, Dec 25. Bar 11:30 am–midnight. Semi-a la carte: lunch $4.50–$10.95, dinner $9.95–$19.95. Child's meals. Specializes in local fresh fish, shrimp casino, fresh swordfish. Raw bar. Parking. Nautical decor; original pencil sketches; artifacts. Cr cds: A, MC, V.

★ ★ ★THE PLUM ROOM AT YESTERDAY'S. *3001 E Oakland Park Blvd. 305/563-4168.* Hrs: 7–11 pm; Fri 6:30 pm–midnight. Res required. Continental menu. Bar. Wine cellar. A la carte entrees: dinner $23.50–$38.95. Specializes in exotic dishes, including buffalo, elk, pheasant. Classical harpist. Edwardian decor. Secluded dining area upstairs at YESTERDAY'S (see RESTAURANTS). Jacket. Cr cds: A, C, D, DS, MC, V.

★ ★ ★PRIMAVERA. *830 E Oakland Park Blvd. 305/564-6363.* Hrs: 5:30–10:30 pm. Closed Mon; also Sept. Res accepted. Italian menu. Serv bar. Semi-a la carte: dinner $14–$24. Specializes in fresh pasta, osso buco. Own pastries. Cr cds: A, MC, V.

D

★ ★RAINBOW PALACE. *2787 E Oakland Park Blvd. 305/565-5652.* Hrs: 5–10 pm; Thurs & Fri also noon–3 pm; wkends 5–11 pm. Closed July 4, Thanksgiving. Res accepted. Chinese menu. Bar. A la carte entrees: lunch $6.95–$11.95, dinner $16.95–$35. Specialties: orange beef, shrimp gwin jin, seafood Cantonese. Parking. Hand-painted ceiling and wall murals. Cr cds: A, D, DS, MC, V.

D

★ ★SEA WATCH. *6002 N Ocean Blvd. 305/781-2200.* Hrs: 11:30 am–3:30 pm, 5–10 pm; Fri, Sat to 11 pm. Closed Dec 25. Bar. Semi-a la carte: lunch $4.75–$10.50, dinner $13–$30. Specializes in fresh local seafood, prime beef. Valet parking. Outdoor dining. Located on the beach. Nautical decor. Cr cds: A, MC, V.

D

✔ ★ ★SHIRTTAIL CHARLIE'S. *400 SW 3rd Ave. 305/463-3474.* Hrs: 11:30 am–2 pm, 6–10 pm; Sun 11:30 am–9 pm; outdoor dining area 11:30 am–10 pm. Closed Thanksgiving, Dec 25. Res accepted. Bar. Semi-a la carte: lunch $3–$13, dinner $9.95–$18.95. Child's meals. Specialties: swordfish Oscar, scallop primavera, alligator. Entertainment Fri–Sun. Parking. Waterside outdoor dining. On New River; boat cruises avail. Cr cds: A, DS, MC, V.

D

✔ ★ ★STUDIO ONE CAFE. *2447 E Sunrise Blvd, across from Galleria Mall. 305/565-2052.* Hrs: 11:30 am–2:30 pm; 5:30–10 pm; Sat, Sun from 5:30 pm. Closed Mon. Res accepted. French, continental menu. Wine, beer. Complete meals: lunch $2.95–$9, dinner $14.95. Child's meals. Specialties: escargot, grilled salmon, black duck with vanilla sauce, rack of lamb. Parking. Outdoor dining. Cr cds: A, DS, MC, V.

D

★ ★TROPICAL ACRES. *2500 Griffin Rd. 305/761-1744.* Hrs: 4:30–10 pm; Sun 3–9 pm. Closed Dec 24. Res accepted. Bar. A la carte entrees: dinner $7.95–$18.95. Child's meals. Specializes in steak, seafood, chops. Pianist. Family-owned. Cr cds: A, C, D, MC, V.

✔ ★ ★ ★YESTERDAY'S. *3001 E Oakland Park Blvd, on Intracoastal Waterway. 305/561-4400.* Hrs: 5–10:30 pm; Fri, Sat to 11 pm; upstairs 9 pm–2 am. Res accepted. Continental menu. Bars. Wine list. Semi-a la carte: dinner $12.95–$24.95. Complete meals: dinner $12.95–$15.95. Specializes in beef Wellington, fresh seafood. Valet parking. Overlooks Intracoastal Waterway. Cr cds: A, D, DS, MC, V.

D

Fort Matanzas National Monument (B-4)

(On Anastasia Island, 14 mi S of St Augustine on FL A1A)

Fort Matanzas National Monument extends over an area of 298 acres that includes the southern tip of Anastasia Island and Rattlesnake Island, where the fort is actually located. By 1569, the first of several successive wooden watchtowers had been erected on the site to detect approaching vessels; the Spanish realized early that access to the Intracoastal Waterway at Matanzas Inlet provided easy access to St Augustine.

The inlet's importance was clearly demonstrated during a British siege in 1740, when Spanish relief ships ran the blockade and reached the starving defenders in time. Between 1740 and 1742 the Spanish built Fort Matanzas to permanently control the inlet. During 1742–1743, British attempts to destroy the fortification failed. Florida did become British by treaty, in 1763, but reverted to the Spanish in 1784. Fort Matanzas served both the British and the Spanish as an outpost.

After the transfer of Florida to the United States in 1821, the unmanned fort fell into ruin. Later, the fort was stabilized in two phases, one in 1916, the other in 1924, when it was designated a national monument. The fort is considered a fine representative of a vanished style of military architecture.

The fort's name, *Matanzas,* means "slaughters" in Spanish and signifies the 1565 surrender of 245 Frenchmen and their subsequent slaughter by the founder of St Augustine, Pedro Menéndez de Avilés.

A visitor center, with exhibits and information on the fort, is located on Anastasia Island, from which the fort is visible; access, however, is possible only by ferry boat (free). (Daily; closed Dec 25) Contact Superintendent, c/o Castillo de San Marcos National Monument, 1 Castillo Dr, St Augustine 32084; 904/471-0116 or 829-6506. **Free.**

(For accommodations see Marineland, St Augustine)

Fort Myers (E-3)

Founded: 1850 **Pop:** 45,206 **Elev:** 10 ft **Area code:** 813

Fifteen miles upstream from the Gulf of Mexico, on the wide Caloosahatchee River, Fort Myers began as a federal post erected after an Indian raid. Later, settlers came to farm within its protective shadow. Tourism, vegetable and flower growing and commercial and sport fishing are major activities of the area today.

What to See and Do

1. **Edison/Ford Winter Estates.** 2350 McGregor Blvd; from I-75, exit 22 (Colonial Blvd) to McGregor Blvd and turn right. Guided tours. (Daily; closed Thanksgiving, Dec 25) Phone 334-3614 (recording) or -7419. Combination ticket ¢¢¢ includes

    Edison Winter House & Botanical Gardens. In 1885, inventor Thomas Edison, ailing at the age of 38, built this 14-acre riverfront estate, where he wintered for the next half-century. The house and guesthouse, designed by Edison, were brought by ship from Maine. Complex includes museum with inventions, mementos and a chemical laboratory; first modern swimming pool in the state; and extraordinary botanical garden with mature specimens from around the world. Tours every 30 minutes.

    Henry Ford Winter House. "Mangoes," the three-and-one-half-acre winter residence of the world's first billionaire, Henry Ford, is next door to the house of Ford's good friend, Thomas Edison. The house reflects the Midwestern, home-grown values of Henry and his wife, Clara, as well as the effect of extraordinary wealth on their lives. The simply-built bungalow is authentically furnished.

2. **Fort Myers Historical Museum.** 2300 Peck St, in old Atlantic Coastline Railroad Depot. On display are items of local historical significance. (Apr–Oct, daily exc Sat; rest of yr, daily; closed major hols) Phone 332-5955. ¢¢

3. **Everglades Jungle Cruise.** City Yacht Basin, foot of Lee St. Three-hour narrated ride up Caloosahatchee River; birds, rookeries, wild orchids, alligators. Also cruises on Intracoastal Waterway; some with meals, floor shows, music. (Daily) Phone 334-7474. ¢¢¢–¢¢¢¢¢

4. **Nature Center and Planetarium.** On Ortiz Ave, just N of Colonial Blvd near I-75. More than 100 acres of pine flatwoods and bald cypress swamp; Audubon aviary. Planetarium with star shows and laser light and music shows; exhibits; natural history shop; nature trails (2 mi); guided walks. (Daily) Phone 275-3435. ¢¢

(For further information contact the Lee County Visitor & Convention Bureau, 2180 W 1st St, Suite 100, 33901; 335-2631.)

Annual Events

Southwest Florida Fair. Lee County Civic Center, Bayshore Rd & FL 31. 1st wk Feb.

Edison Festival of Light. Tribute to Thomas Edison; includes athletic contests, dances, sailing regattas, entertainment; ends with Parade of Light. Phone 334-2999. 2 wks Feb; parade 3rd Sat.

Seasonal Event

Professional baseball. Minnesota Twins spring training; exhibition games, Lee County Sports Complex, 14100 Six Mile Cypress Pkwy, near Daniels Rd. Phone 768-4270. Early Mar–early Apr.

(See Bonita Springs, Cape Coral, Punta Gorda, Sanibel & Captiva Islands)

Motels

✔ ★BUDGETEL INN. *2717 Colonial Blvd (33907). 813/275-3500.* 122 rms, 4 story. Jan–Apr: S, D $65–$78; lower rates rest of yr. Crib free. Pet accepted. TV; cable. Pool. Complimentary continental bkfst. Complimentary coffee in rms. Ck-out 11 am. Meeting rm. Cr cds: A, C, D, DS, MC, V.

D 🐾 ⌘ 🏊 🚳 ⊘ SC

★★COMFORT SUITES. *13651 Indian Paint Ln (33912), near Southwest Florida Regional Airport. 813/768-0005; FAX 813/768-5458.* 65 suites, 2 story. Jan–mid-Apr: S $85–$105; D $95–$115; each addl $10; under 18 free; lower rates rest of yr. Crib free. Pet accepted. TV; cable, in-rm movies. Heated pool. Complimentary continental bkfst, coffee in rms. Restaurant adj open 24 hrs. Bar 4 pm–midnight. Ck-out 11 am. Coin lndry. Meeting rms. Free airport transportation. Exercise equipt; weight machine, treadmill, whirlpool. Refrigerators, wet bars. Cr cds: A, C, D, DS, ER, MC, V, JCB.

D 🐾 ⌘ 🏃 ✗ 🚳 ⊘ SC

★★★COURTYARD BY MARRIOTT. *4455 Metro Pkwy (33901). 813/275-8600; FAX 813/275-7087.* 149 rms, 3 story. Dec–Apr: S $105; D $115; suites $125; under 12 free; lower rates rest of yr. Crib free. TV; cable. Heated pool. Complimentary coffee in rms. Restaurant 6:30 am–2 pm, 5–10 pm; Sat, Sun from 7 am. Bar 5–11 pm. Ck-out noon. Coin lndry. Meeting rms. Free airport transportation. 18-hole golf privileges, pro, putting green, driving range. Exercise equipt; weights, bicycles, whirlpool. Refrigerator in suites. Balconies. Cr cds: A, C, D, DS, MC, V.

D ▧ ⌘ 🏃 🚳 ⊘ SC

★★DAYS INN-NORTH. *13353 N US 41 (33903). 813/995-0535; FAX 813/656-2769.* 127 rms, 2 story. Mid-Dec–Apr: S $75; D $90; each addl $6; under 18 free; wkly rates off season; lower rates rest of yr. Crib free. Pet accepted; $4 per night. TV; cable. Pool. Complimentary coffee in lobby. Restaurant adj open 24 hrs. Ck-out noon. Coin lndry. Lawn games. Cr cds: A, C, D, DS, MC, V.

D 🐾 ⌘ 🚳 ⊘ SC

★★HAMPTON INN. *13000 N Cleveland Ave (33903). 813/656-4000; FAX 813/656-1612.* 123 rms, 2 story, 4 kits. Dec–Apr: S $67–$75; D $79–$87; kit. units $97–$105; under 18 free; lower rates rest of yr. Crib free. TV; cable. Pool. Complimentary continental bkfst, coffee. Restaurant nearby. Ck-out noon. On river with view. Cr cds: A, C, D, DS, MC, V.

D ⌘ 🚳 ⊘ SC

★★LA QUINTA. *4850 Cleveland Ave (33907). 813/275-3300; FAX 813/275-6661.* 130 rms, 2 story. Jan–Apr: S, D $82–$92; each addl $10; under 18 free; lower rates rest of yr. Crib free. Pet accepted, some restrictions. TV. Heated pool. Complimentary continental bkfst in lobby. Restaurant nearby. Ck-out noon. Meeting rms. Cr cds: A, D, DS, ER, MC, V.

D 🐾 ⌘ 🚳 ⊘ SC

★★RADISSON INN SANIBEL GATEWAY. *20091 Summerlin Rd (33908). 813/466-1200; FAX 813/466-3797.* 153 rms, 3 story. Mid-Feb–Apr: S, D $119–$124; under 16 free; lower rates rest of yr. Crib free. Pet accepted, some restrictions; $25. TV; cable, in-rm movies. Heated pool. Restaurant 6:30 am–10 pm. Rm serv. Bar 11 am–midnight. Ck-out noon. Coin lndry. Meeting rm. Golf privileges, greens fee $45–$60, pro, putting green, driving range. Exercise equipt; bicycles, stair machine, whirlpool. Game rm. Refrigerators. Picnic tables. Cr cds: A, C, D, DS, ER, MC, V, JCB.

D 🐾 ▧ ⌘ 🏃 🚳 ⊘ SC

✔ ★SLEEP INN. *13651 Indian Paint Ln (33912), near Southwest Florida Regional Airport. 813/561-1117; res: 800/358-3170; FAX 813/768-0377.* 50 rms, shower only, 2 story. Jan–mid-Apr: S $50–$70; D $55–$75; each addl $10; under 18 free; lower rates rest of yr. Crib free. Pet accepted. TV; cable. Heated pool. Complimentary continental bkfst, coffee. Restaurant adj open 24 hrs. Bar 4 pm–midnight. Ck-out 11 am. Coin lndry. Meeting rms. Free airport transportation. Exercise equipt; weight machine, treadmill, whirlpool. Cr cds: A, C, D, DS, ER, MC, V, JCB.

D 🐾 ⌘ 🏃 ✗ 🚳 ⊘ SC

✔ ★TA KI-KI. *2631 E 1st St (33916). 813/334-2135.* 23 rms, 5 kits. Mid-Dec–Apr: S, D $52–$58; each addl $5; kit. units $360–$385/wk; varied lower rates rest of yr. Crib free. TV; cable. Heated pool. Complimentary coffee. Restaurant nearby. Ck-out 11 am. Picnic tables, grill. On river; boat dock. Cr cds: A, D, DS, MC, V.

↦ ⌘ ⊘

★★WELLESLEY INNS. *4400 Ford St (33916). 813/278-3949; res: 800/444-8888; FAX 813/278-3670.* 106 rms, 4 story, 13 suites. Jan–mid-Apr: S, D $80–$90; each addl $10; suites $110–$120; lower rates rest of yr. Pet accepted, some restrictions; $10. TV; cable. Heated pool. Complimentary continental bkfst, coffee. Restaurant nearby. Ck-out 11 am. Meeting rm. Valet serv. Refrigerator in suites. Cr cds: A, C, D, DS, MC, V, JCB.

D 🐾 ⌘ 🚳 ⊘ SC

Motor Hotels

★★BEST WESTERN ROBERT E. LEE. *13021 Cleveland Ave (33903). 813/997-5511; FAX 813/656-6962.* 108 rms, 6 story, 24 suites. Late Dec–Apr: S $67–$85; D $85–$125; each addl $5; suites $90–$135; under 18 free; lower rates rest of yr. Crib $5. TV; cable. Heated pool; whirlpool. Restaurant 6:30 am–11 pm. Bar 1 pm–2 am; entertainment. Ck-out 11 am. Coin lndry. Meeting rm. Private patios, balconies. On Caloosahatchee River; fishing pier. Swimming beach adj. Cr cds: A, C, D, DS, ER, MC, V.

D ↦ ⌘ 🚳 ⊘ SC

★★HOLIDAY INN AIRPORT. *13051 Bell Tower Dr (33907), in Bell Tower Center. 813/482-2900; FAX 813/482-2900, ext 7550.* 227 rms, 5 story. Jan–Apr: S $109–$149; D $119–$159; each addl $10; suites $129–$169; under 18 free; lower rates rest of yr. Crib free. TV; cable. Heated pool. Restaurant 6:30 am–2 pm, 5–10 pm. Rm serv. Bar 4 pm–2 am; entertainment, dancing. Ck-out noon. Coin lndry. Meeting rms. Bellhops. Valet serv. Free airport transportation. Exercise equipt; weights, bicycles. Refrigerators; some wet bars. **LUXURY LEVEL: CONCIERGE LEVEL.** 94 rms, 2 floors. S, D $129–$169. Concierge. Private lounge, bar. Complimentary continental bkfst, refreshments. Cr cds: A, C, D, DS, MC, V, JCB.

D ⌘ 🏃 🚳 ⊘ SC

★★RAMADA INN. *12635 Cleveland Ave (33907). 813/936-4300; FAX 813/936-2058.* 222 rms, 2–5 story. Mid-Jan–Apr: S, D $79–$99; each addl $8; suites $129–$149; under 16 free; varied lower rates rest of yr. Crib free. TV; cable. Heated pool; poolside serv. Restaurant 6:30 am–2 pm, 5–10 pm. Rm serv. Bar 2 pm–2 am; entertainment, dancing Tues–Sat. Ck-out noon. Coin lndry. Meeting rms. Sundries. Gift shop. Free airport transportation. Lighted tennis. Spacious grounds. Cr cds: A, C, D, DS, MC, V, JCB.

D 🐾 ⌘ 🚳 ⊘ SC

Hotel

★★SHERATON HARBOR PLACE. *2500 Edwards Dr (33901). 813/337-0300; FAX 813/337-1530.* 417 rms, 25 story, 234 suites. Jan–mid-Apr: S, D $110–$150; each addl $10; suites $150–$450; under 18 free; lower rates rest of yr. Crib free. Pet accepted. TV; cable. 3 pools, 1 indoor, 2 heated; poolside serv. Restaurant 6:30 am–10 pm. Bars 11–2 am. Ck-out noon. Coin lndry. Convention facilities. Gift shop. Free airport transportation. Lighted tennis. Golf privileges. Exercise equipt; weights, bicycles, whirlpool. Game rm. Some wet bars; refrigerator in suites. Opp Caloosahatchee River and harbor; boat dockage avail. Cr cds: A, C, D, DS, ER, MC, V.

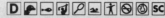

Resort

★ ★ ★ **SANIBEL HARBOUR.** *17260 Harbour Pointe Drive (33908).* 813/466-4000; res: 800/767-7777; FAX 813/466-2150. 325 units, 12 story, 83 condo units. Dec–Apr: S, D $220–$300; suites $350–$850; 2-bedrm condo units $270–$450; under 18 free; monthly rates; tennis plans; lower rates rest of yr. Crib free. TV; cable. 4 pools, 1 indoor; poolside serv. Free supervised child's activities. Dining rm 6:30 am–11 pm. Rm serv. Bar 11–2 am. Ck-out noon, ck-in 3 pm. Convention facilities. Bellhops. Valet serv. Concierge. Gift shop. Barber, beauty shop. Valet parking. Airport and Sanibel Island transportation. Sports dir. 13 lighted tennis courts, pro. 36-hole golf privileges, greens fee $65, putting green, driving range. Private beach; marina, fishing pier. Boat cruises avail; paddleboats. Watersports. Bicycles. Entertainment, dancing. Game rm. Exercise rm; instructor, weights, bicycles, whirlpool, steam rm, sauna. Massage therapy. Refrigerator in condo units; some minibars. Private patios, balconies. Located on 80 landscaped acres; Victorian-style entranceway. Cr cds: A, C, D, DS, ER, MC, V.

Restaurants

★ ★ **CHART HOUSE.** *2024 W 1st St.* 813/332-1881. Hrs: 5–10 pm; Fri, Sat to 11 pm; early-bird dinner 5–6 pm. Res accepted. Bar. Semi-a la carte: dinner $11.95–$22.45. Child's meals. Specializes in hand-cut steak, fresh seafood, prime rib. Salad bar. Built over Caloosahatchee River. Cr cds: A, C, D, DS, MC, V.

D

✔ ★ ★ **MARINER INN.** *3448 Marinatown Lane, off Hancock Bridge Pkwy.* 813/997-8300. Hrs: 11:30 am–9 pm; Fri, Sat to 10 pm. Closed Memorial Day, Dec 24 eve. Res accepted. Bar to midnight. Semi-a la carte: lunch $3.95–$8.50, dinner $6.95–$15.50. Child's meals. Specializes in fresh seafood, prime rib. Outdoor dining. Occasional entertainment. Parking. Waterfront dining; dockage. New England, nautical decor. Cr cds: A, DS, MC, V.

D

★ ★ **PETER'S LA CUISINE.** *2224 Bay St.* 813/332-2228. Hrs: 11:30 am–2 pm, 5:30–9:30 pm; Sat, Sun from 5:30 pm. Closed Dec 25. Res accepted. Continental menu. Bar 4:30 pm–2 am. A la carte entrees: lunch $4.75–$11, dinner $19.50–$26.50. Specializes in veal, lamb, salmon, fresh seafood. Own pastries. Jazz & blues groups upstairs. Parking. In historic riverfront area; modern decor. Cr cds: A, D, MC, V.

D

✔ ★ ★ **THE SHALLOWS SEAFOOD GRILLE.** *1400 Colonial Blvd, in Royal Palms Sq Shopping Mall.* 813/939-4554. Hrs: 11 am–10 pm; Sat from 4 pm; Sun noon–9 pm; early-bird dinner 4–6 pm. Closed Dec 25. Res accepted. Bar. Semi-a la carte: lunch $3.95–$7.50, dinner $6.95–$12.95. Child's meals. Specializes in fresh seafood. Dining in mall courtyard. Cr cds: A, D, DS, MC, V.

D

★ ★ **SMITTY'S.** *2240 W 1st St.* 813/334-4415. Hrs: 11 am–10 pm; Sat from 4 pm; Sun 11:30 am–9 pm. Closed Dec 25. Res accepted. Bar. Semi-a la carte: lunch $3.95–$7.95, dinner $6.95–$24.95. Child's meals. Specializes in steak, fresh seafood, chicken. Parking. Living rm atmosphere, with bookshelves, leather-upholstered chairs. Family-owned. Cr cds: A, MC, V.

D

★ ★ **THE VERANDA.** *2nd St & Broadway, opp county courthouse.* 813/332-2065. Hrs: 11 am–2:30 pm, 5:30–10 pm; Sat from 5:30 pm. Closed Sun exc hols; Dec 25. Res accepted. Continental menu. Bar to 1 am. Wine list. Semi-a la carte: lunch $4.50–$9.50, dinner $13.95–$24.95. Child's meals. Specializes in Southern regional cuisine. Courtyard dining. Own baking. Piano bar. Valet parking (dinner). Turn-of-the-century house; Victorian atmosphere. Cr cds: A, MC, V.

D

Fort Myers Beach (E-3)

Pop: 9,284 **Elev:** 5 ft **Area code:** 813 **Zip:** 33931

Stretching thinly along the seven-mile sliver of Estero Island, this is a town with the Gulf of Mexico on one side and Estero Bay never more than three blocks away on the other. The 18th-century pirates are gone, but tourists love to poke in the sand for treasure; more likely they find sea shells, starfish and sea horses. The beach stretches the entire length of the island and is considered one of the safest in the state.

What to See and Do

1. **Island Tall Ship Excursions.** Adj Snug Harbor Restaurant, San Carlos Blvd, under Mantanzas Bridge. Two-hour sailing in the Gulf of Mexico aboard the 72-foot-long schooner *Island Rover*. Day and sunset cruises. (Three times daily) Sr citizen rate. Phone 765-7447. ¢¢¢¢–¢¢¢¢¢

2. **Fishing.** From 600-foot public pier in Lynn Hall Park (free); Carl Johnson Park on causeway (fee); surf casting from beach; offshore charter boats avail; moonlight "tarpon hunting" (spring–fall).

(For further information contact the Greater Fort Myers Beach Chamber of Commerce, 1661 Estero Blvd, PO Box 6109, Fort Myers 33932; 463-6451.)

Annual Events

Shrimp Festival. Seven-day event culminating with Blessing of Shrimp Fleet. Early Mar.

American Championship Sandsculpting Festival. Nov.

(See Bonita Springs, Cape Coral, Fort Myers, Naples)

Motels

★ **BUCCANEER RESORT INN.** *4864 Estero Blvd.* 813/463-5728; FAX 813/463-5756. 27 rms, 3 story, 25 kits. No elvtr. Late Jan–Apr: S, D $99–$125; each addl $6; under 4 free; 7-day min wk of Dec 25; lower rates rest of yr. Crib $6. TV; cable. Heated pool. Restaurant nearby. Ck-out 10 am. Coin lndry. Lawn games. Sun deck. Picnic tables, grill. On Gulf. Cr cds: DS, MC, V.

✔ ★ **LA FONTAINE INN.** *6950 Estero Blvd.* 813/463-6662. 10 kit. units, 3 story. No elvtr. Feb–Mar & late Dec: S, D $93–$125; wkly rates; lower rates rest of yr. Adults only. TV; cable. Heated pool. Restaurant opp. Ck-out 10 am. Balconies. Grills. On gulf. Cr cds: MC, V.

★ ★ ★ **MARINER'S PINK SHELL BEACH & BAY RESORT.** *275 Estero Blvd.* 813/463-6181; res: 800/237-5786; FAX 813/463-1229. 173 units, 1–5 story, 71 kits., 37 apts, 54 kit. cottages. Late Dec–mid-Apr: S, D $164; each addl $10; kits. $155–$196; apts $185–$251; kit. cottages $202–$316; under 18 free; wkly rates; lower rates rest of yr. Crib $5. TV; cable, in-rm movies. 2 pools, 1 heated; wading pool, poolside serv. Playground. Supervised child's activities. Restaurant 7:30 am–8 pm. Ck-out 11 am. Coin lndry. Sundries. Gift shop. Lighted tennis. Lawn games. Game rm. Many refrigerators. Picnic tables, grills. On 12 acres; fishing pier, dockage, water sports. Cr cds: A, C, D, DS, MC, V.

★ ★ **NEPTUNE INN.** *2310 Estero Blvd.* 813/463-6141. 63 kit. units, 2 story. Mid-Dec–Apr: kit. units $96–$118; each addl $6; under 6 free; monthly rates; lower rates rest of yr. Crib free. TV. 2 pools, 1 heated. Complimentary coffee. Restaurant nearby. Ck-out 11 am. Coin lndry. Lawn games. Some private patios, balconies. Picnic tables, grills. On Gulf. Cr cds: DS, MC, V.

★ ★OUTRIGGER BEACH RESORT. *6200 Estero Blvd. 813/463-3131; res: 800/749-3131; FAX 813/463-6577.* 144 rms, 1–4 story, 68 kits. No elvtr. Mid-Dec–Apr: S, D $90–$125; each addl $8; kit. units $90–$155; lower rates rest of yr. TV; cable. Heated pool. Cafe 7 am–8 pm. Bar noon–8 pm. Ck-out 11 am. Coin lndry. Sundries. Gift shop. Putting green. Lawn games. Refrigerators. On beach. Cr cds: DS, MC, V.

★ ★SANDPIPER GULF RESORT. *5550 Estero Blvd. 813/463-5721.* 63 kit. units, 2–5 story. Mid-Dec–mid-Apr: S, D $98–$115; each addl $7; under 6 free; wkly, monthly rates; higher rates: wkends, major hols; lower rates rest of yr. Crib $1.50. TV; cable. 2 pools, 1 heated; whirlpool. Complimentary coffee in lobby. Restaurant nearby. Ck-out 11 am. Coin lndry. Gift shop. Lawn games. Private patios, balconies. Picnic tables. On beach; swimming. Cr cds: DS, MC, V.

Motor Hotel

★BEST WESTERN BEACH RESORT. *684 Estero Blvd. 813/463-6000; FAX 813/463-3013.* 75 kit. units, 5 story. Feb–Apr, mid-Dec: S, D $175; under 18 free; lower rates rest of yr. Crib free. Pet accepted, some restrictions. TV; cable. Heated pool. Playground. Complimentary coffee in lobby. Restaurant nearby. Ck-out 11 am. Coin lndry. Game rm. Lawn games. Balconies. Picnic tables, grills. On gulf. Cr cds: A, C, D, DS, MC, V.

Hotel

★DAYS INN AT LOVERS KEY. *8701 Estero Blvd, just S of "Big Carlos Pass" Bridge. 813/765-4422; FAX 813/765-4422, ext 160.* 80 kit. suites, 14 story. Late Dec–mid-Apr: suites $95–$179; under 13 free; wkly rates; lower rates rest of yr. Crib free. Pet accepted, some restrictions; $15. TV. Heated pool. Complimentary continental bkfst. Restaurant 7:30 am–3 pm. No rm serv. Ck-out 11 am. Coin lndry. No bellhops. Jet-ski, pontoon boat rentals; boat & seaplane excursions; bicycle rentals. Balconies. Picnic tables, grills. On beach; swimming. Cr cds: A, DS, MC, V.

Restaurants

★ ★BALLENGER'S. *11390 Summerlin Square Dr, at San Carlos Blvd. 813/466-2626.* Hrs: 11 am–10 pm; Sat from 4 pm; Sun 11 am–8 pm; Sun brunch 10:30 am–2 pm. Closed Dec 25. Bar. Semi-a la carte: lunch $4.75–$7, dinner $9–$17.75. Sun brunch $10.95. Specializes in snapper Monte Carlo, fresh local seafood. Salad bar. Parking. Cr cds: A, C, D, DS, MC, V.

★ ★CHARLEY BROWN'S. *6225 Estero Blvd. 813/463-6660.* Hrs: 5–10 pm; Fri, Sat to 10:30 pm; early-bird dinner 5–6 pm. Closed Thanksgiving; also Super Bowl Sun. Bar. Semi-a la carte: dinner $8.95–$20.95. Child's meals. Specializes in New York strip steak, prime rib, fresh seafood. Salad bar. Parking. Cr cds: C, D, DS, MC, V.

🄳

★THE FISH MONGER. *19030 San Carlos Blvd. 813/765-5544.* Hrs: 4–10 pm. Closed major hols; Super Bowl Sun. Res accepted. Bar. Semi-a la carte: dinner $6.95–$16.95. Child's meals. Specializes in pasta, seafood. Parking. Cr cds: MC, V.

🄳

★FISHERMAN'S WHARF. *1821 Estero Blvd. 813/463-4994.* Hrs: 4–11 pm; early-bird dinner 4–6 pm. Res accepted. Continental menu. Bar. Semi-a la carte: dinner $9.95–$30.95. Child's meals.

Specializes in fresh seafood, steak, lamb. Own desserts. Parking. Cr cds: A, MC, V.

★ ★MUCKY DUCK. *2500 Estero Blvd. 813/463-5519.* Hrs: 5–9:30 pm. Closed Thanksgiving, Dec 25. Bar. Semi-a la carte: dinner $9.95–$27.95. Child's meals. Specializes in fresh seafood, steak, duck, grouper Cafe d'Paris. Parking. On Gulf. Cr cds: A, DS, MC, V.

★ ★SKIPPER'S GALLEY. *3040 Estero Blvd. 813/463-6139.* Hrs: 4–10 pm; May–Oct from 4:30 pm; early-bird dinner 4–6 pm. Bar. Semi-a la carte: dinner $8–$19. Child's meals. Specializes in fresh seafood, aged beef. Parking. Dining area resembles a ship's interior. Cr cds: A, DS, MC, V.

★ ★SNUG HARBOR. *645 San Carlos Blvd, under Mantanzas Bridge. 813/463-4343.* Hrs: 11:30 am–3 pm, 4:30–10 pm. Bar to midnight. Semi-a la carte: lunch $4.95–$7.95, dinner $10.95–$15.95. Child's meals. Specializes in fresh seafood, Key lime pie. Parking. On waterfront. Cr cds: DS, MC, V.

Fort Pierce (D-5)

Settled: 1837 **Pop:** 36,830 **Elev:** 24 ft **Area code:** 407

The original Fort Pierce, a US Army garrison established in 1837, during the Seminole War, was located on what is now Indian River Drive. The city formed around the site, with three communities merging into one in 1901. On the west side of the Indian River the city is linked to its ocean beaches by two bridges. It is the marketplace for the cattle ranches, vegetable farms and citrus groves of St Lucie County; tourism and commercial fishing round out the economy.

What to See and Do

1. **St Lucie County Historical Museum.** 414 Seaway Dr, in park at E end of South Beach Bridge. Local and state historical exhibits include 1715 Spanish shipwreck artifacts, military material from Old Fort Pierce, Seminole Indian encampment, items from early industries; restored 1907 house, 1919 American-LaFrance fire engine; changing exhibit gallery. (Daily exc Mon; closed most hols) Phone 468-1795. ¢

2. **Underwater Demolition Team–SEAL Museum.** 5 mi NE via US 1 to 3300 N FL A1A, North Hutchinson Island, in Pepper Park. Diving gear, weapons and apparatus of SEAL ("sea, air and land") commandos—successors to US Navy "frogmen" of World War II. Dioramas trace history of the teams; videos of training process. (Daily exc Mon; closed hols) Phone 489-3597. ¢

3. **Swimming.** Of the more than 20 miles of Atlantic coastline, approx 6 miles are accessible to the public.

   South Beach, on a barrier island more than 15 miles long, includes South Beach Boardwalk, Waveland Beach, Walton Rocks, Frederick Douglass Park. Paved parking, boardwalks, dressing rooms, showers, concession, restrooms; picnicking. **Free.**

   North Beach includes Pepper Beach Park, Jack Island State Preserve and Ft Pierce Inlet State Recreation area (see #5). Fishing docks, tennis, picnicking, rest room. **Free.**

   County beach accesses include Middle Cove Access, Herman's Bay Access, Normandy Beach Access and Dollman Beach, Avalon Beach, John Brooks Park (all three undeveloped). Swimming; surf fishing; boardwalks. Parking. **Free.**

4. **Fishing.** Surfcasting from 20 miles of beach. Free fishing balconies on bridge over Indian River, where world's record sea trout was caught. Deep-sea charter boats. Freshwater fishing in St Lucie

River, lakes and canal. South jetty fishing pier on south side of Ft Pierce Inlet; also oceangoing inlet.

5. Fort Pierce Inlet State Recreation Area. 4 mi E, off FL A1A. More than 300 acres bounded by Atlantic Ocean and Indian River; footbridge to Jack Island. Swimming, skin diving, surfing, dressing rooms, showers; fishing. Nature trails. Picnicking. Standard hrs, fees. Phone 468-3985.

6. The Savannas. 1400 E Midway Rd, off US 1. A 550-acre light marshland. Fishing. Picnicking, playground. Camping (7-day max; fee). Children's petting zoo. Observation tower. Pets on leash only. Park (daily). Phone 464-7855. Entrance fee per car ¢¢

(For further information contact the Fort Pierce/St Lucie County Chamber of Commerce, 2200 Virginia Ave, 34982; 461-2700.)

Seasonal Events

Jai-Alai. 1750 S Kings Highway, 1 mi N of FL Tpke. Parimutuel betting. Mon & Wed–Sat evenings; matinees, Mon, Wed & Sat. Restaurant. Phone 464-7500. Oct–May.

Professional baseball. 10 mi S on US 1, at St Lucie County Sports Complex, Peacock Blvd in Port St Lucie. New York Mets spring training; exhibition games early Mar–early Apr. St Lucie Mets, Florida League, early Apr–Aug. Phone 871-2115.

(See Jensen Beach, Stuart, Vero Beach)

Motels

★★**COMFORT INN.** 3236 S US 1 (34982). 407/461-2323; FAX 407/464-5151. 61 units, 2 story, 14 kits. Jan–Apr: S $60–$68; D $60–$70; each addl $5; kit. units $5 addl; under 18 free; lower rates rest of yr. Crib $5. TV; cable. Pool; whirlpool. Complimentary bkfst. Ck-out 11 am. Cr cds: A, C, D, DS, ER, MC, V.

D ⚮ 🚫 🕑 SC

★★**DAYS INN.** 6651 Darter Ct (34945), W off I-95 exit 65, just S of Okeechobee Rd. 407/466-4066; FAX 407/468-3260. 125 rms, 2 story. Jan–Apr: S, D $65–$70; each addl $5; under 18 free; lower rates rest of yr. TV. Heated pool. Coffee in rms. Restaurant 6 am–11 pm; Fri, Sat to 1 am. Ck-out 11 am. Coin lndry. Meeting rms. Sundries. Some refrigerators. Cr cds: A, C, D, DS, MC, V.

D ⚮ 🚫 🕑 SC

★★**HARBOR LIGHT INN-EDGEWATER MOTEL.** 1160 Seaway Dr (34949), on Hutchinson Island. 407/468-3555; res: 800/433-0004. 35 units, 2 story, 15 kit. suites. Late Dec–Apr: S, D $46.50–$120; each addl $10; suites $77.50–$120; under 12 free (limit 2); wkly rates; lower rates rest of yr. Crib free. TV; cable. Heated pool; whirlpool. Ck-out 11 am. Lawn games. Refrigerators. Balconies. Picnic tables, grills. On inlet; 2 private fishing piers, 2 boat docks. Cr cds: A, C, D, DS, MC, V.

D ⊷ ⚮ 🕑

✔★★**HOLIDAY INN SUNSHINE PARKWAY.** 7151 Okeechobee (34945), W off I-95 exit 65. 407/464-5000; FAX 407/464-5000, ext 287. 161 rms, 2 story. Jan–mid-Apr: S $54–$59; D $60–$65; each addl $6; under 18 free; lower rates rest of yr. Crib free. TV; cable. Pool; wading pool. Restaurant 6 am–2 pm, 5–10 pm. Rm serv. Bar 4–11 pm. Ck-out noon. Coin lndry. Meeting rms. Sundries. Cr cds: A, C, D, DS, ER, MC, V, JCB.

D 🐾 ⚮ 🚫 🕑 SC

✔★★**HOWARD JOHNSON.** 7150 Okeechobee Rd (34945), W off I-95 exit 65. 407/464-4500. 64 rms, 2 story. Feb–mid-Apr: S $55–$59; D $62–$70; each addl $8; under 18 free; varied lower rates rest of yr. Crib free. TV; cable. Pool; wading pool. Restaurant 6 am–8 pm. Ck-out noon. Coin lndry. Sundries. Cr cds: A, C, D, DS, ER, MC, V, JCB.

D ⚮ 🚫 🕑 SC

Restaurants

★**CHUCK'S SEAFOOD.** 822 Seaway Dr. 407/461-9484. Hrs: 4–10 pm; early-bird dinner 4–6 pm. Closed Mon; some major hols. Res accepted. Wine, beer. Semi-a la carte: dinner $8.95–$24.95. Child's meals. Specialties: shrimp scampi, fried shrimp, baked fresh fish. Parking. Outdoor dining overlooking Fort Pierce Inlet. Family-owned. Cr cds: DS, MC, V.

✔★**JOHNNY'S CORNER.** (7180 S US 1, Port St Lucie) 9 mi S on US 1, 1 blk N of Prime Vista Blvd. 407/878-2686. Hrs: 6 am–10 pm; early-bird dinner Mon–Sat 2–5 pm. Closed Dec 25. Italian, Greek, Amer menu. Bar. Semi-a la carte: bkfst $1.95–$4.95, lunch $2.95–$5.25, dinner $4.95–$11.95. Child's meals. Specializes in seafood, steak, chops. Parking. Bakery on premises. Cr cds: MC, V.

D

★★**MANGROVE MATTIE'S.** 1640 Seaway Dr. 407/466-1044. Hrs: 11:30 am–3 pm, 5–10 pm; early-bird dinner 4:30–6 pm. Res accepted. Bar to 11 pm. Semi-a la carte: lunch $4.95–$8.95, dinner $7.95–$19.95. Specializes in fish, shellfish, aged steak. Parking. On Fort Pierce Inlet, view of waterway. Cr cds: A, DS, MC, V.

D

✔★**PEKING.** 1012 S US 1. 407/464-5960. Hrs: 11:30 am–9:30 pm; Fri, Sat to 10 pm. Closed Mon in summer. Res accepted. Chinese menu. Wine, beer. Semi-a la carte: lunch $3.75–$4.95, dinner $5.95–$14.95. Specialties: mixed seafood, Hawaiian duck, imperial shrimp. Parking. Chinese decor. Cr cds: A, MC, V.

D

★★**TOUCAN'S TOP OF THE DOCK.** 201 Fishermans Wharf. 407/465-1334. Hrs: 11:30–2 am; Sun noon–midnight; early-bird dinner 4–6 pm; Sun brunch 10:30 am–2:30 pm. Closed Dec 25. Italian, Amer menu. Bar. Semi-a la carte: lunch $2.95–$7.95, dinner $7.95–$17.95. Lunch buffet (Mon–Fri): $5.95. Sun brunch $12.95. Child's meals. Specializes in seafood, steak. Parking. View of charter fishing activity. Cr cds: DS, MC, V.

D SC

Fort Walton Beach (F-1)

Pop: 21,471 **Elev:** 23 ft **Area code:** 904

Fort Walton Beach covers a six-mile stretch of US 98 along Santa Rosa Sound and the Gulf of Mexico in northwest Florida. Archaeological excavations (begun in 1960) of Indian mounds have added historic significance to the town. Temple Mound (see #1) has yielded artifacts from prehistoric times and between A.D. 1300–1700.

What to See and Do

1. Indian Temple Mound Museum and Park. On US 98, downtown. Covering an acre of land, this mound served as a major religious and civic center for Native Americans of the area. The ancient temple is recreated in a modern shelter on the original site. On the east flank of the mound a museum houses dioramas and exhibits portraying Indian settlement over a span of 12,000 years. Mound (daily; free). Museum (daily exc Sun; closed Jan 1, Thanksgiving, Dec 25). Phone 243-6521. Museum ¢

2. Gulfarium. ½ mi E on US 98, on Okaloosa Island. Exhibition of fish and scuba diving shows; trained dolphins; sea lion shows; harbor seals; shark moat; alligator and saltwater fish displays. Exotic bird exhibits; penguin breeding colonies; otters. (Daily; closed Thanksgiving, Dec 25) Phone 244-5169. ¢¢¢¢

3. Eglin Air Force Base. 13 mi NE via FL 285. Country's largest US Air Force base has 720-square-mile area. Tour (3 hr) includes Climatic Laboratory and Military Working Dog demonstration. Also here is Armament Museum, with various historical aircraft, weapons and

30-minute film (daily). Tours (Jan–Mar & June–Aug; Mon, Wed & Fri) Obtain tour tickets at the Armament Museum. Phone 882-3933. **Free.**

(For further information contact the Greater Fort Walton Beach Chamber of Commerce, 34 Miracle Strip Pkwy SE, PO Drawer 640, 32549; 244-8191.)

Annual Events

Seafood Festival. Fairground bldg, Lewis Turner Blvd. Arts & crafts, demonstrations, entertainment, food. Phone 244-5319. Mid-Apr.

Billy Bowlegs Pirate Festival. Includes mock pirate assault, parades, treasure hunts, coronation pageant. 1st full wkend June.

(See Destin, Pensacola)

Motels

★**ECONO LODGE.** *100 Miracle Strip Pkwy SW (32548). 904/244-0121; FAX 904/244-1094.* 73 rms, 3 story. Mar–early Sept: S, D $59–$74; each addl $5; suite $150–$240; under 16 free; fishing plan; higher rates: wkends & major hols; lower rates rest of yr. Crib free. Pet accepted; $10. TV; cable. Pool. Complimentary coffee in lobby. Restaurant nearby. Ck-out 11 am. Some refrigerators. Ocean 1 blk; beach. Cr cds: A, C, D, DS, MC, V, JCB.

✔★**HOWARD JOHNSON.** *314 Miracle Strip Pkwy SW (32548). 904/243-6162.* 140 rms, 2 story. Late May–Labor Day: S, D $46–$64; each addl $6; under 18 free; higher rates hol wkends; lower rates rest of yr. TV; cable. Pool; wading pool. Restaurant open 24 hrs. Ck-out noon. Coin lndry. Meeting rm. Private patios, balconies. Launching ramp; dockage. Cr cds: A, C, D, DS, MC, V, JCB.

★★**SHERATON INN.** *1325 Miracle Strip Pkwy (32548). 904/243-8116; FAX 904/244-3064.* 153 rms, 2 story. Mar–early Sept: S $80–$115; D $86–$143; each addl $10; under 18 free; 3-night min stay hols; lower rates rest of yr. Crib $5. TV; cable. Pool; poolside serv. Complimentary coffee in rms. Restaurant 6 am–11 pm. Rm serv. Bar 4–11 pm. Ck-out noon. Coin lndry. Meeting rms. Bellhops. Valet serv. Exercise equipt; weight machine, treadmill. Game rm. Many refrigerators, minibars. Some balconies. Picnic tables. On ocean; beach. Cr cds: A, C, D, DS, ER, MC, V, JCB.

✔★**SHONEY'S INN.** *203 Miracle Strip Pkwy (32548). 904/244-8663; res: 800-222-2222.* 102 rms, 3 story, 10 suites, 2 kit. units. Mar–Sept: S, kit. units $49–$60; D $52–$60; each addl $5; suites $60; under 18 free; golf plans; lower rates rest of yr. Crib free. TV; cable. Pool. Complimentary coffee in lobby. Restaurant adj 6 am–midnight. Bar 11–4 am. Ck-out noon. Cr cds: A, C, D, DS, ER, MC, V.

Motor Hotel

★★★**RAMADA BEACH RESORT.** *2 mi SE on US 98 (32548). 904/243-9161; FAX 904/243-2391.* 454 rms, 6 story. Mar–Sept: S, D $95–$140; each addl $10; suites $200–$260; under 18 free; varied lower rates rest of yr. Crib free. TV. 3 pools; wading pool, hot tub. Free supervised child's activities (May–Sept). Restaurants 6 am–10 pm. Rm serv. Bars 11–2 am; entertainment, dancing. Ck-out 11 am. Convention facilities. Bellhops. Sundries. Lighted tennis. Exercise equipt; weights, bicycles, whirlpool, steam rm, sauna. Private patios, balconies. Picnic tables, grills. On beach. Cr cds: A, C, D, DS, MC, V.

Restaurants

✔★**PERRI'S.** *300 Eglin Pkwy NE. 904/862-4421.* Hrs: 11 am–2 pm, 5–10 pm; Fri to 10:45 pm; Sat 5–10:45 pm. Closed Sun, Mon; also mid-Dec–early Jan. Res accepted. Italian, Amer menu. Bar. Semi-a la carte: lunch $4.50–$6.50, dinner $7.50–$16.50. Child's meals. Specialties: saltimbocca, pollo alla Bolognese, veal. Parking. Family-owned. Cr cds: MC, V.

★★**THE SOUND.** *108 W US 98. 904/243-7772.* Hrs: 11 am–10 pm; early-bird dinner 4:30–6 pm. Closed Jan 1, Thanksgiving, Dec 25. Res accepted. Bar. Semi-a la carte: lunch $4–$7, dinner $9–$23. Child's meals. Specializes in fresh seafood, prime rib. Parking. Overlooking Intracoastal Waterway. Cr cds: A, D, MC, V.

Gainesville (B-3)

Settled: 1830 **Pop:** 84,770 **Elev:** 185 ft **Area code:** 904

The seat of Alachua County, Gainesville is a university city with a variety of industries, including the manufacture of archery equipment. Fishing and hunting are excellent in the surrounding area.

What to See and Do

1. **University of Florida** (1853). (34,000 students) University Ave & US 441. A 2,000-acre campus with 16 colleges and 4 schools. Phone 392-3261. Located on campus are

   Florida Museum of Natural History. Museum Rd & Newell Dr. Largest museum of natural history in the southeast United States. Features full-scale North Florida Cave exhibit. Object Gallery has fossilized shark's teeth, live reptiles. (Daily exc Mon; closed Apr 3, Dec 25) (See ANNUAL EVENTS) Phone 392-1721.   **Free.**

   University Art Gallery. Fine Arts Bldg B, off 13th St. Changing, contemporary exhibits. (Tues–Fri, also Sat & Sun afternoons; limited hrs in summer; closed hols & during exhibition changes) Phone 392-0201.   **Free.**

   Lake Alice Wildlife Preserve. Museum Rd, 1 mi W of SW 13th St. Alligators, turtles, birds. Picnicking. (Daily)

2. **Kanapaha Botanical Gardens.** 4625 SW 63rd Blvd. A 62-acre botanical garden featuring butterfly garden, large bamboo garden, vinery; hummingbird garden, herb & palm gardens and others. (Daily exc Thurs) Phone 372-4981.   ¢

3. **Fred Bear Museum.** At jct I-75 & Archer Rd. Collection of archery and bow hunting artifacts, Eskimo and African carvings and artwork, wildlife mounts. (Wed–Sun; closed Dec 25) Phone 376-2411.   ¢¢

4. **Marjorie Kinnan Rawlings State Historic Site.** 11 mi S on US 441 to Micanopy, then 6 mi E via FL 346, then 4 mi via 325 in Cross Creek. Farmhouse and memorabilia of the author of *The Yearling* and *Cross Creek*. Guided tour (limit 10 per hr). (Thurs–Sun; closed Jan 1, Thanksgiving, Dec 25) Phone 466-3672.   ¢

5. **Devil's Millhopper State Geological Site.** 4 mi NW on County 232. Giant sinkhole (500 ft wide, 115 ft deep) was formed when the roof of an underground limestone cavern collapsed. The cool environment allows growth of unique lush vegetation. Access to the bottom is by wooden walkway. Interpretive center; nature walks. Nearby is **San Felasco Hammock State Preserve,** with rare flora and fauna; prehistoric Indian sites; nature trails. Standard hrs, fees. Phone 336-2008.

6. **State parks.**

   O'Leno. 32 mi NW on US 441, 7 mi N of High Springs. The site of an old town, this 5,896-acre park includes a section of the Santa Fe River, which disappears underground through a sinkhole and then emerges nearly three miles to the south. Swimming, fishing. Nature, bridle trails, hiking. Picnicking. Camping (dump station). Standard hrs, fees. Phone 454-1853.

Ichetucknee Springs. 23 mi NW on US 441 to High Springs, then 14 mi NW off US 27, N of Fort White. Crystal-clear springs with limpkins, wood ducks, otters and beavers are found on this 2,241-acre park on the Ichetucknee River. Swimming, scuba and skin diving in Blue Hole (Oct–Mar); canoeing, tubing (daily usage limits on number of people on river). Nature trails; picnicking. Standard hrs, fees. Phone 497-2511.

Paynes Prairie Preserve. 10 mi S off US 441 near Micanopy. Approximately 20,000-acre state preserve is a major wintering ground for sandhill crane. Fishing; boating (ramps; gas motors prohibited), canoeing. Horseback riding, hiking & biking trails. Picnicking. Camping. Visitor center (daily); observation tower. Standard hrs, fees. Phone 466-3397.

7. **Bivens Arm Nature Park.** 3650 S Main St. A 57-acre oak hammock sanctuary and marsh with boardwalk and nature trails. (Daily; closed Jan 1, Thanksgiving, Dec 25) Phone 334-2056. **Free.**

(For further information contact the Alachua County Visitors & Convention Bureau, 10 SW 2nd Ave, Suite 220, 32601; 374-5231.)

Annual Events

Animal Fair. Florida Museum of Natural History (see #1). Celebration includes parrots, snakes, goats, rabbits and others; demonstrations of dog training and snake handling. Late Feb or early Mar.

Gatornationals. NHRA Drag racing at Gainesville Raceway, just N of 53rd Ave & Waldo Rd. Phone 377-0046. Mar.

(See Starke)

Motels

(Rates may be higher during special university events)

★ ★**CABOT LODGE.** 3726 SW 40th Blvd (32608), I-75 exit 75. 904/375-2400; res: 800/843-8735. 208 rms, 3 story. S $49–$52; D $56–$59; each addl $7; under 12 free; higher rates Univ of Florida events. Crib free. TV; cable. Pool. Complimentary continental bkfst, coffee. Restaurant nearby. Ck-out 11 am. Meeting rms. Valet serv. Golf privileges. Health club privileges. Cr cds: A, C, D, DS, MC, V.

✔ ★**FAIRFIELD INN BY MARRIOTT.** 6901 NW 4th Blvd (32607), I-75 exit 76. 904/332-8292; FAX 904/332-8292, ext 709. 135 rms, 3 story. S $36.95–$41.95; D $42.95–$50.95; each addl $3; under 18 free. Crib free. TV; cable. Heated pool. Complimentary coffee in lobby. Restaurant nearby. Ck-out noon. Meeting rms. Valet serv. Cr cds: A, C, D, DS, MC, V.

✔ ★**HOWARD JOHNSON I-75.** 7400 NW 8th Ave (32605). 904/332-3200; FAX 904/332-5500. 64 rms, 2 story. S $39–$58; D $46–$64; each addl $8; under 18 free. Crib free. TV; cable. Pool; wading pool. Playground. Complimentary continental bkfst. Ck-out noon. Meeting rm. Private patios, balconies. Cr cds: A, C, D, DS, MC, V, JCB.

★ ★**LA QUINTA.** 920 NW 69th Terrace (32605). 904/332-6466; FAX 904/332-7074. 134 rms, 4 story. S $46–$60; D $56–$70; each addl $10; under 18 free. Crib free. TV; cable, in-rm movies. Heated pool. Complimentary continental bkfst. Restaurant adj 11 am–10 pm. Ck-out noon. Meeting rms. Valet serv. Golf privileges, pro, putting green, driving range. Health club privileges. Cr cds: A, C, D, DS, MC, V.

★ ★**RESIDENCE INN BY MARRIOTT.** 4001 SW 13th St (32608). 904/371-2101; FAX 904/371-2101, ext 66. 80 suites, 3 story. 1 & 2 bedrm $91–$107. Crib free. Pet accepted, some restrictions; $50 nonrefundable. TV; cable. Pool; whirlpool. Complimentary continental bkfst.

Ck-out noon. Coin lndry. Meeting rms. Valet serv. Picnic tables, grill. Cr cds: A, C, D, DS, MC, V.

Motor Hotel

★ **HOLIDAY INN-UNIVERSITY CENTER.** 1250 W University Ave (FL 26) (32601). 904/376-1661; FAX 904/336-8717. 167 rms, 6 story. S $69–$84; D $74–$89; each addl $10; under 18 free; higher rates special events (2-day min). Crib free. TV; cable. Rooftop pool; poolside serv. Restaurant open 24 hrs. Rm serv. Bar; entertainment, dancing. Ck-out noon. Meeting rms. Beauty shop. Free airport, bus depot transportation. University opp. Cr cds: A, C, D, DS, MC, V, JCB.

Hotel

★ ★**UNIVERSITY CENTRE.** 1535 SW Archer Rd (32608). 904/371-3333; res: 800/824-5637 (exc FL), 800/251-4069 (FL); FAX 904/371-3712. 180 rms, 11 story. S $75; D $85; each addl $8; studio rms $75–$85; suites $155–$350; under 12 free. Crib free. TV; cable. Pool; poolside serv. Restaurant 6–10 pm. Bar 11–2 am. Ck-out noon. Meeting rms. Beauty shop. Free airport, bus depot transportation. Some refrigerators. Balconies. Extensive grounds with decorative pond. Near medical center. Cr cds: A, C, D, MC, V, JCB.

Restaurants

✔ ★ ★**BROWN DERBY.** 5220 SW 13th St. 904/373-0088. Hrs: 11 am–10 pm; Fri to midnight; Sat 11:30 am–midnight; Sun 11:30 am–10 pm; early-bird dinner Mon–Fri 3:30–6 pm. Res accepted. Bar. Semi-a la carte: lunch $3.95–$6.95, dinner $6.95–$14.95. Child's meals. Specializes in prime rib, steak, seafood. Salad bar. Country & Western music Thurs–Sat. Parking. Fireplace. Cr cds: A, DS, MC, V.

★ ★**MR. HAN.** 6944 NW 10th Pl. 904/331-3899 or -6400. Hrs: 11:30 am–10 pm; Fri, Sat to 10:30 pm. Closed Thanksgiving, Dec 24, 25. Res accepted. Chinese, Szechwan menu. Bar. A la carte entrees: lunch $3–$4, dinner $4.50–$19. Specialties: Peking duck, weeping willow chicken. Parking. Elegant Chinese decor; photos of celebrities. Cr cds: A, C, D, MC, V.

★ ★ ★**SOVEREIGN.** 12 SE 2nd Ave. 904/378-6307. Hrs: 5:30–10 pm; Fri, Sat to 11 pm. Closed Sun; major hols. Res accepted. Continental menu. Bar 5–11 pm. Semi-a la carte: dinner $12.95–$23. Own baking. Pianist Thurs–Sat. In restored 1878 carriage house. Cr cds: A, C, D, DS, MC, V.

Unrated Dining Spot

MORRISON'S CAFETERIA. 2620 NW 13th St, in Gainesville Mall. 904/378-7422. Hrs: 11 am–8:30 pm; Sun to 7:30 pm. Avg ck: lunch, dinner $4.75. Child's meals. Specializes in roast beef, fried and broiled seafood. Cr cds: MC, V.

Haines City (C-4)

Pop: 11,683 **Elev:** 161 ft **Area code:** 813 **Zip:** 33844

Haines City lies at the foot of a range of rolling hills known as "The Ridge" and is in the heart of Florida's citrus country. Originally called "Clay Cut," the town eventually took the name of a South Florida Railroad vice-president and was subsequently made a regular stop on the line. Nearby sand pits, electronics, the hydraulics industry and tourism help diversify the economy.

(For information about this area contact the Chamber of Commerce, 908 US 27N, PO Box 986; 422-3751.)

(See Lakeland, Lake Wales, Orlando, Winter Haven)

Motels

★★**BEST WESTERN-TED WILLIAMS.** *(I-4 & US 27, Davenport 33837)* 9 mi N on US 27 at jct I-4 exit 23. 813/424-2511; FAX 813/424-3889. 160 rms, 5 story. Feb-Apr, June-Aug, Dec: S, D $49-$79; each addl $5; under 18 free; lower rates rest of yr. Crib free. TV; cable. Pool. Restaurant nearby. Bar 2 pm-midnight. Ck-out noon. Coin lndry. Cr cds: A, C, D, DS, MC, V.

✔★★**COMFORT INN.** *(PO Box 450850, Kissimmee 34745)* 9 mi N; at jct US 27 & I-4. 813/424-2811; FAX 813/424-1723. 150 rms, 3 story. Mid-Feb-Easter, mid-June-mid-Aug & late Dec: S, D $44; varied lower rates rest of yr. Crib free. TV. Pool. Playground. Complimentary continental bkfst. Restaurant 6 am-midnight. Ck-out noon. Meeting rms. Airport, area attractions transportation. Some refrigerators. Cr cds: A, C, D, DS, ER, MC, V, JCB.

★**HOLIDAY INN.** *(PO Box 1536, Baseball City 33845)* 4825 N US 27, at jct I-4 exit 23. 813/424-2211; FAX 813/424-3312. 251 rms, 2 story. July-Aug & Dec-Mar: S $39-$70.50; D $39-$76.50; each addl $5; under 18 free; lower rates rest of yr. Crib free. Pet accepted, some restrictions; $75 refundable. TV; cable. Pool; wading pool, whirlpool, poolside serv (in season). Playground. Restaurant 6:30 am-2 pm, 5-10 pm. Rm serv. Bar 4 pm-midnight. Ck-out noon. Coin lndry. Meeting rms. Sundries. Gift shop. Lighted tennis. Game rm. Some refrigerators. Cr cds: A, C, D, DS, ER, MC, V, JCB.

Resort

★★★**GRENELEFE.** 3200 FL 546, 6 mi E of jct US 27, FL 544. 813/422-7511; res: 800/237-9549; FAX 813/421-5000. 925 condo units, 1-2 story. Mid-Jan-Apr: Club suites $170; each addl $20; 1-bedrm villa $210; 2-bedrm villa $365; AP, MAP avail; golf, tennis, fishing packages; lower rates rest of yr. Crib free. TV; cable. 5 pools, heated; whirlpool, sauna, poolside serv. Playground. Supervised child's activities. Dining rm (public by res) 7 am-10 pm. Box lunches, snack bar, barbecues, outdoor buffets, picnics. Bar 11-2 am. Ck-out 11 am, ck-in 3 pm. Lndry facilities in all buildings. Grocery. Package store. Gift shop. Convention facilities. Airport transportation. 20 tennis courts, 11 lighted, 2 grass, pros. 54-hole golf, pro, putting green, driving ranges. Pier & marina with 26 slips, boats, sailboats. Boat cruises. Bicycle rentals. 18-hole miniature golf. Lawn games. Activities dir. Entertainment, dancing. Movies. Game rms. Fishing guides. Refrigerators. Private patios, balconies. Picnic tables. 950 acres on Lake Marion. Cr cds: A, C, D, DS, ER, MC, V, JCB.

Hialeah (E-5)

Founded: 1921 **Pop:** 188,004 **Elev:** 6 ft **Area code:** 305

Famous for the racetrack that bears its name, Hialeah is the second largest of the municipalities that make up metropolitan Miami. Many appliance manufacturers, food suppliers and department stores have their distribution headquarters in the community. Glenn Curtiss and James H. Bright, aviation pioneers, were the city's founders.

What to See and Do

1. **Hialeah Park.** E 4th Ave between 21st & 32nd Sts. This lush, "old-world" racetrack is home to a famous pink flamingo colony. Visitors may walk through the grounds and view the tropical gardens, flamingo colony, paddocks and related areas. Horse racing (winter; phone for schedule). Park (Mon-Fri). Phone 885-8000. Grounds ¢

2. **Thompson County Park.** 16665 NW Krome Ave Ext (FL 997), 2 mi S of US 27. Fishing; boating. Biking. Playground. Tent & trailer camping (fee; hookups). Park (Nov-Apr, daily). Some fees. Phone 821-5122.

(For further information contact the Hialeah/Miami Springs/Northwest Dade Area Chamber of Commerce, 59 W 5th St, 33010, phone 887-1515.)

Annual Event

River Cities Festival. Celebrating the Miami River with boat races, demonstrations; Miccosukee Indian activities and exhibits, arts & crafts; all-breed dog & cat show; international foods. 3rd wkend Apr.

(See Coral Gables, Hollywood, Miami, Miami Intl Airport Area)

Motel

★★★**COURTYARD BY MARRIOTT.** 15700 NW 77th Court (33016). 305/556-6665; FAX 305/556-0282. 151 rms, 4 story. Jan-mid-Apr: S $89-$99; D $99-$109; each addl $10; suites $105-$115; under 12 free; lower rates rest of yr. Crib free. TV; cable. Heated pool. Complimentary coffee in rms. Restaurant 6:30 am-noon, 6-11 pm. Bar from 6 pm. Ck-out noon. Coin lndry. Meeting rms. Valet serv. Sundries. Exercise equipt; weight machine, bicycles, whirlpool. Refrigerator in suites. Balconies. Cr cds: A, D, DS, MC, V.

Hotel

★**PARK PLAZA.** *(7707 NW 103rd St, Hialeah Gardens 33016)* Just W of Palmetto Expy (FL 826). 305/825-1000; FAX 305/556-6785. 262 rms, 10 story. S $89; D $99; each addl $10; under 18 free; higher rates special events. Crib free. TV; cable. Pool; poolside serv. Restaurant 7 am-2 pm, 5-11 pm. Bar 4 pm-2 am; entertainment Fri & Sat, dancing. Ck-out noon. Meeting rms. Gift shop. Free airport transportation. Tennis. Exercise equipt; weights, rowers, whirlpool, sauna. Bathrm phones. Balconies. Cr cds: A, C, D, DS, ER, MC, V.

Hollywood (E-5)

Founded: 1921 **Pop:** 121,697 **Elev:** 11 ft **Area code:** 305

Born in the real estate boom of the 1920s, Hollywood still rides the crest of tourism. Joseph W. Young, fresh from adventures in California, developed the city and populated it largely by keeping a fleet of 21 buses on the road to bring in prospective buyers. In addition to the lures of beach and busy boulevard, there are several public golf courses in the area, making it a favorite of the golfing set.

What to See and Do

1. **Gulfstream Park.** US 1 & Hallandale Beach Blvd in Hallandale. Famous racetrack—home of the Florida Derby—has walking ring decorated with leading stable colors; bronze plaques in Garden of Champions honor great Thoroughbreds. (Mid-Jan–Mar, daily exc Mon; Apr, Tues & Thurs–Sun). Phone 454-7000. Grandstand ¢

2. **Recreation areas.**
   Topeekeegee Yugnee Park. 1½ mi NW via I-95, Sheridan St exit, on N Park Rd. Swimming beaches (seasonal), waterslides; marina (rentals). Biking. Picnicking. Tent & trailer camping (fee); store, laundry; dump station. (Daily) Phone 985-1980. Wkends & hols ¢

   C.B. Smith Park. 19 mi W via Hollywood Blvd, N on Flamingo Rd in Pembroke Pines. Swimming beach, waterslides, tube ride; marina (canoe & paddleboat rentals). Racquetball, tennis, miniature golf. Picnicking, concession. Campground (hookups). Outdoor amphitheater. (Daily, weather permitting; some facilities seasonal) Phone 437-2650. Wkends & hols ¢

(For further information contact the Greater Hollywood Chamber of Commerce, 4000 Hollywood Blvd, Suite 265-S, 33021, phone 985-4000; the Information Center, 330 N Federal Hwy, 33020; or the Greater Fort Lauderdale Convention & Visitors Bureau, 200 E Las Olas Blvd, Fort Lauderdale 33301, phone 765-4466.)

Annual Events

Hollywood Festival of the Arts. Young Circle Park. Feb.

Seminole Indian Tribal Fair. Four-day cultural display of Native American heritage; arts & crafts, foods, history; competition powwow with dancers from tribes throughout North America; PRCA rodeo. Phone 584-0400. 2nd wkend Feb.

Florida Derby Festival. Gulfstream Park (see #1). Prior to Derby. Late Feb–early Mar.

Jazz Festival. Young Circle Park. Phone 921-3404. Oct.

Broward County Fair. Gulfstream Park (see #1). Exhibits, rides, entertainment. Late Nov.

Seasonal Events

Greater Hollywood Philharmonic Orchestra. Young Circle Park bandshell. Pop concerts. Phone 921-3404. Dec–Apr.

Dog racing. Hollywood Greyhound Track. US 1 & Pembroke Rd. Phone 454-9400. Dec 26–late Apr.

(See Dania, Fort Lauderdale, Miami, Pompano Beach)

Motel

✔ ★ ★ **DAYS INN AIRPORT SOUTH.** *2601 N 29th Ave (33020). 305/923-7300; FAX 305/921-6706.* 114 rms, 7 story. Mid-Dec–mid-Apr: S $50–$85; D $55–$91; each addl $10; under 12 free; package plans; higher rates: boat shows, Super Bowl; lower rates rest of yr. Crib free. TV; cable. Pool. Complimentary coffee in lobby. Restaurant adj open 24 hrs. Bar 4–10:30 pm. Ck-out noon. Coin lndry. Meeting rms. Exercise equipt; weights, bicycles, whirlpool. Health club privileges. Near airport. Cr cds: A, C, D, DS, MC, V.

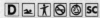

Motor Hotel

★ ★ **HOWARD JOHNSON HOLLYWOOD BEACH RESORT.** *2501 N Ocean Dr (33019). 305/925-1411; FAX 305/921-5565.* 242 rms,

11 story. Late Dec–Apr: S, D $89–$170; each addl $10; under 18 free; varied lower rates rest of yr. Crib free. TV; cable. Heated pool; wading pool, poolside serv. Restaurant 6 am–midnight; Fri, Sat open 24 hrs. Rm serv. Bars 9–4 am. Ck-out noon. Coin lndry. Meeting rms. Bellhops. Valet serv. Sundries. Refrigerators avail. Private patios, balconies. On beach. Cr cds: A, C, D, DS, ER, MC, V, JCB.

Hotels

★ ★ ★ **HILTON-HOLLYWOOD BEACH.** *4000 S Ocean Dr (33019). 305/458-1900; FAX 305/458-7222.* 305 rms, 10 story. Mid-Dec–early Apr: S $119–$189; D $139–$209; each addl $10; suites $235–$450; family rates; lower rates rest of yr. Crib free. TV; cable. Heated pool; whirlpool, poolside serv. 3 restaurants 7 am–11 pm. Bars 11–2 am; entertainment, dancing. Ck-out noon. Convention facilities. Shopping arcade. Barber, beauty shop. Free garage parking; valet. Tennis. Exercise rm; instructor, weights, bicycles, whirlpool, sauna. Rec rm. Lawn games. Private patios, balconies. Beach opp. *LUXURY LEVEL: TOWER FLOOR.* 66 rms, 10 suites, 2 floors. S $189; D $209; suites $385–$450. Concierge. Private lounge. Minibars. Wet bars. Complimentary continental bkfst, newspaper.
Cr cds: A, C, D, DS, ER, MC, V.

★ ★ **HOLLYWOOD BEACH RESORT.** *101 N Ocean Dr (33019). 305/921-0990; res: 800/331-6103; FAX 305/920-9480.* 360 kit. units, 8 story, 35 suites. Mid-Dec–Mar: S, D $95–$155; each addl $10; suites $175–$195; under 18 free; wkly rates; lower rates rest of yr. Crib free. Valet parking $6. TV; cable. Pool; wading pool. Complimentary coffee in rms. Restaurant 11:30 am–midnight. Bar 10–2 am; entertainment, dancing Wed–Sun. Ck-out 11 am. Coin lndry. Meeting rm. Concierge. Shopping arcade. Exercise equipt; weights, bicycles, whirlpool, sauna. Game rm. Large, pink stucco structure with boardwalk-style lobby; enclosed shopping mall; theaters. On ocean. Cr cds: A, D, MC, V.

Restaurants

★ ★ **BAVARIAN VILLAGE.** *1401 N Federal Hwy (US 1). 305/922-7321.* Hrs: 4–11 pm; Sun & hols from noon; early-bird dinner 4–5:30 pm. Closed Dec 24. Res accepted. German, Amer menu. Bar. Semi-a la carte: lunch, dinner $10.95–$22.75. Child's meals. Specializes in Wienerschnitzel, pork shank, prime rib. Accordian player exc Mon. Parking. Old World, Bavarian decor. No cr cds accepted.

★ ★ **DI ANNO'S.** *(308 N Federal Hwy, Hallandale) S on US 1. 305/456-2110.* Hrs: 4:30–11 pm; early-bird dinner to 6 pm. Closed Mon; Dec 25. Res accepted. Italian, Amer menu. Bar to 3 am. Semi-a la carte: dinner $10.95–$24.95. Specialties: veal parmigiana, shrimp Fra Diavolo, chicken scarpariello. Jazz combo exc Sun. Casual atmosphere. Cr cds: A, MC, V.

✔ ★ **LYCHEE GARDEN.** *(680 E Hallandale Beach Blvd, Hallandale) S on US 1 to Hallandale Beach Blvd. 305/457-5900 or 956-9600.* Hrs: 11:30 am–10 pm; early-bird dinner 3–6 pm. Closed Thanksgiving. Chinese, Amer menu. Bar. Complete meals: lunch $4.65–$7.55, dinner $6.55–$8.95. Specialties: jumbo shrimp Cantonese, Lychee gai pan, cashew chicken. Parking. Cr cds: A, C, D, DS, MC, V.

★ ★ **MARTHA'S ON THE INTRACOASTAL.** *6024 N Ocean Dr. 305/923-5444.* Hrs: 11:30–1 am; early-bird dinner 4–5:30 pm; Sun brunch 11 am–3 pm. Res accepted. Continental menu. Bar. A la carte entrees: lunch $6.50–$14.95, dinner $13.95–$35.95. Sun brunch $19.95. Child's meals. Specializes in fresh local seafood, prime beef, snapper Key Largo. Entertainment. Valet parking. Outdoor dining. 2-level dining; tropical decor. Cr cds: A, C, D, DS, MC, V.

★ ★ ★VILLA PERRONE. *(906 E Hallandale Beach Blvd, Hallandale) S on US 1 to Hallandale Beach Blvd, then 1½ mi E. 305/454-8878.* Hrs: 4:30 pm–2 am; early-bird dinner 4:30–6:30 pm. Closed Dec 25. Italian, Amer menu. Bar. Wine list. Complete meals: dinner $10.95–$26. Specialties: costoletta a la Milanese, orecchiette pasta, surf & turf. Pianist. Valet parking. Roman decor; marble statues & entryway. Family-owned. Cr cds: A, D, MC, V.

Homestead (F-5)

Elev: 9 ft **Area code:** 305

This section of southern Florida coastline was the hardest hit by hurricane Andrew in 1992. Most businesses have recovered from hurricane damage, but it is still advisable to phone ahead. Homestead is the gateway to Everglades National Park and to the Florida Keys.

What to See and Do

Everglades National Park (see). 9 mi SW on FL 9336.

(For further information contact the Tropical Everglades Visitor Association, 160 US 1, Florida City 33034; 245-9180 or 800/388-9669.)

(For accommodations see Coral Gables, Key Largo, Miami)

Homosassa Springs (C-3)

Pop: 6,271 **Elev:** 6 ft **Area code:** 904 **Zip:** 32647

What to See and Do

1. **Homosassa Springs State Wildlife Park.** 9225 W Fishbowl Dr. This 45-foot-deep spring, with an hourly flow of millions of gallons at 72°F, is the source of the Homosassa River. Scenic boat tours, underwater observatory for view of fish; bird park; manatee, alligator, crocodile and reptile programs; museum & education center. (Daily) Phone 628-2311. ¢¢¢

2. **Yulee Sugar Mill Ruins State Historic Site.** On FL 490, W of US 19. On six-acre site are remnants of antebellum sugar mill; boiler casing, chimney; engine and connecting gears are scattered. Picnic shelter. Phone 795-3817. **Free.**

(For further information contact the Homosassa Springs Area Chamber of Commerce, 3495 S Suncoast Blvd, PO Box 709, 34447-0709; 628-2666.)

(See Brooksville, Crystal River)

Motel

★ ★RIVERSIDE INN RESORT. *(Box 258, Homosassa 34487) 3 mi W on FL 490, 3 mi W of US 19/98. 904/628-2474; res: 800/442-2040.* 81 rms, 2 story, 8 kits. S, D $59–$69; each addl $7; kit. units $79; under 14 free; wkly rates. Crib $6. Pet accepted; $8. TV; cable. Pool. Restaurant 6 am–9 pm, Mon to 11 am. Bar; entertainment, dancing Fri & Sat. Ck-out noon. Coin lndry. Meeting rms. Tennis. Golf privileges. Lawn games. Marina; charters, boat tours, guides; free dockage for guests. Cr cds: A, C, D, DS, ER, MC, V.

Hotel

 ★ ★ ★CROWN. *(109 N Seminole Ave, Inverness 34450) 18 mi W of I-75 on FL 44. 904/344-5555; FAX 904/726-4040.* 34 rms, 3 story. Nov–Apr: S $40–$60; D $60–$70; each addl $6; lower rates rest of yr. Closed 2 wks Aug. Crib free. TV; cable. Pool. Complimentary continental bkfst. Restaurant (see CHURCHILL'S). Bar 11 am–11 pm. Ck-out 11 am. Meeting rms. Hotel built in late 19th century; Victorian decor; leaded, cut glass windows in lobby; gold-plated bathrm fixtures. Cr cds: A, MC, V.

Restaurant

★ ★ ★CHURCHILL'S. *(See Crown Hotel) 904/344-5555.* Hrs: 5:30–9 pm; Fri, Sat 6–9:30 pm; Sun noon–7 pm. Res required. Continental, traditional English menu. Bar 11 am–11 pm. Wine list. Semi-a la carte: dinner $13.95–$26. Child's meals. Specialties: chicken maison, poached salmon, roast duck l'orange. Own baking. Pianist Fri & Sat. Parking. Victorian decor. Cr cds: A, MC, V.

Indian Rocks Beach

(see St Petersburg Beach Area)

Islamorada (F-5)

Pop: 1,220 **Elev:** 10 ft **Area code:** 305 **Zip:** 33036

Islamorada is made up of 18 miles of coral, limestone and sand on 4 different islands of the Florida Keys. Sport fishing and diving and snorkeling amid coral reefs and shipwrecks are the main tourist attractions. It is the local custom to welcome the spring blossoms of the guaiacum tree, which produces a wood known as lignum vitae that is so dense that it was once used for pulleys and bowling pins. The area got its name, Spanish for purple isles, when early explorers first saw the island as a distant splash of color, which was, perhaps, the purple bloom of the guaiacum tree.

What to See and Do

1. **Theater of the Sea.** On US 1, at mile marker 84.5. Ninety-minute show features dolphins and sea lions; land tour with fish native to Keys area; huge shark and ray collection; bottomless boat ride with performing dolphins. Half-hour seminar and swim with dolphins (res suggested). (Daily) Phone 664-2431. ¢¢¢¢

2. **Long Key State Recreation Area.** S on US 1, at mile marker 67.5 near Layton, on Long Key. This 965-acre park is noted for excellent fishing. Swimming, diving; boating, self-guided canoe trail. Nature trails, guided walks. Picnicking. Camping. Standard hrs, fees. Phone 664-4815.

3. **Indian Key.** State historic site was once seat of Dade County and a salvage area for wrecked ships. With the exception of some stone foundations, all structures on the key were destroyed during an Indian raid in 1840. Boat tour. For schedule phone 664-4815. Tour ¢¢¢

4. **Lignumvitae Key State Botanical Site.** This 332-acre island is covered by a tropical hardwood forest, mostly of West Indian origin, and is named for the lignum vitae, or guaiacum, tree, a gnarled, very hard-wooded species found on this island as well as in the Caribbean and South America. Many unusual plants, some endangered, are protected on this unspoiled key. Boat tour (phone for schedule). Historic house, nature trails. Phone 664-4815. Tour ¢¢¢

5. **Scuba diving, snorkeling.** Many colorful coral reefs, Gardens #1 and #2, and *Herrera*, a wreck of a Spanish galleon, may be reached by dive boat.

6. **Hurricane Monument.** Matecumbe Methodist Church. Memorial to 400 veterans of World War I and others killed in 1935 hurricane while working on Overseas Highway. A few veterans are buried in crypt in center of monument. Ceramic facing on crypt shows map of the Keys.

(For further information contact the Chamber of Commerce, US 1, mile marker 82.5, PO Box 915; 664-4503.)

Annual Events

Sportfishing Festival. Tournaments, seafood festival, arts & crafts, Blessing of the Fleet. Early–mid-Feb.

Rain Barrel Arts Festival. 3rd wkend Mar.

Indian Key Festival. Mid-Apr.

(See Key Largo)

Motels

★ ★ ★**CHESAPEAKE RESORT.** *(Box 909) On Overseas Hwy (US 1), S of Whale Harbor Bridge, at mile marker 83.5.* 305/664-4662; res: 800/338-3395; FAX 305/664-8595. 65 rms, 2 story, 8 suites, 13 kit. villas (1–2 bedrm). Late Dec–Apr: S, D $125–$195; each addl $15; suites $300–$475; kit. villas $140–$375; lower rates rest of yr. TV; cable. 2 heated pools; whirlpool. Playground. Restaurant adj 6:30 am–2 pm, 4:30–10 pm. Ck-out 11 am. Coin lndry. Meeting rm. Tennis. Lawn games. Refrigerators. Screened balconies, patios. Picnic tables, grills. Deep-water lagoon with boat ramp. Gardens. On ocean; harbor adj. Cr cds: A, DS, MC, V.

✔ ★**DROP ANCHOR.** *(Box 222) On Overseas Hwy (US 1), at mile marker 85.* 305/664-4863. 12 rms, 2 story, 8 kits. Mid-Dec–late Apr: S, D $65–$70; each addl $10; kit. units $70–$90; wkly rates in summer; varied lower rates rest of yr. TV; cable. Heated pool. Restaurant nearby. Ck-out 11 am. Refrigerators. Some private patios, balconies. Picnic tables, grill. On beach; boat ramp, dock. Cr cds: A, D, MC, V.

✔ ★**GAMEFISH RESORT.** *(Rte 1, Box 70) On Overseas Hwy (US 1), at mile marker 75.5.* 305/664-5568. 16 rms, 8 kit. units. No rm phones. Dec–Sept: S, D $65; kit. units (3-day min) $75–$95; wkly rates; lower rates rest of yr. Crib $8. TV. Ck-out 11 am. Picnic tables, grills. On Gulf; swimming beach. Cr cds: A, MC, V.

★ ★**HOWARD JOHNSON AT HOLIDAY ISLE.** *84001 Overseas Hwy (US 1), at mile marker 84.5.* 305/664-2711; FAX 305/664-2711, ext 690. 56 rms, 2 story. Mid-Dec–mid-Apr: S, D $115–$145; each addl $15; under 18 free; varied lower rates rest of yr. Crib free. TV. Heated pool. Playground. Restaurant adj 7 am–11 pm. Ck-out 11 am. Coin lndry. Lawn games. Balconies. On beach. Cr cds: A, C, D, DS, MC, V.

★**ISLANDER.** *(Box 766) On Overseas Hwy (US 1), at mile marker 82.1.* 305/664-2031. 114 units in motel, villas, 92 kits. Mid-Dec–mid-Apr: S, D $68–$92; each addl $7; kit. units $71–$89; under 13 free; lower rates rest of yr. Crib free. TV. 2 heated pools (1 saltwater). Ck-out 11 am. Coin lndry. Meeting rm. Lawn games. Private patios. Grills. Spacious grounds on ocean; pier. Cr cds: A, C, D, MC, V.

✔ ★**KON-TIKI RESORT.** *(Rte 1, Box 58) On Overseas Hwy (US 1), at mile marker 81.* 305/664-4702. 18 rms, 12 kits. S, D $50–$60; each addl $10; kit. units $80–$125. TV; cable. Saltwater pool. Coffee in

rms. Restaurant nearby. Ck-out 11 am. Lawn games. Private patios. Picnic tables, grills. On bay; beach, dock. Cr cds: MC, V.

★**PLANTATION YACHT HARBOR.** *87000 Overseas Hwy (US 1), at mile marker 87.* 305/852-2381; res: 800/356-3215 (exc FL), 800/432-3454 (FL). 56 rms, 1–2 story. Dec–Apr & major summer hols: S, D $95; each addl $10; under 13 free; wkly rates; lower rates rest of yr. TV. Pool. Playground. Restaurant (see PLANTATION YACHT HARBOR RESORT). Bar 11–2:30 am; entertainment. Ck-out 11 am. Coin lndry. Meeting rms. Lighted tennis, pro. Picnic tables, grills. On bay, with beach; marina; water sport rentals. Cr cds: A, MC, V.

✔ ★**SHORELINE.** *(Rte 1, Box 57) On Overseas Hwy (US 1), at mile marker 81.* 305/664-4027. 10 units, 4 kits. No rm phones. Mid-Dec–mid-Apr: S, D $60–$90; each addl $7; kits. $70–$80; wkly rates; lower rates rest of yr. TV; cable. Restaurant opp noon–11 pm. Ck-out 11 am. Whirlpool. Grills. On Gulf; boat ramp, dock; sunning beach. Cr cds: MC, V.

Motor Hotels

★**HOLIDAY ISLE.** *84001 Overseas Hwy (US 1), at mile marker 84.5.* 305/664-2321; res: 800/327-7070; FAX 305/664-2703. 71 units, 1–5 story, 22 kits. Mid-Dec–mid-Apr: S, D $110–$175; each addl $15; suites $230–$395; kits. $185; under 18 free; wkly rates; lower rates rest of yr. Crib free. TV. Pool. Restaurant 7 am–11 pm. Bars; entertainment, dancing. Ck-out 11 am. Coin lndry. Meeting rm. Water sport equipment rentals. Private patios, balconies. On ocean; dock, beach. Cr cds: A, C, D, DS, MC, V.

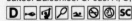

★ ★**PELICAN COVE.** *(Box 633) On Overseas Hwy (US 1), at mile marker 84.5.* 305/664-4435; res: 800/445-4690; FAX 305/664-5134. 63 units, 3 story, 9 suites, 18 kits. Mid-Dec–mid-Apr: S, D $165; each addl $15; suites $285; kit. units $185; under 16 free; wkly rates; lower rates rest of yr (exc hols). TV; cable. Heated pool; whirlpool, poolside serv. Restaurant 11:30 am–4:30 pm. Bar to 7 pm. Ck-out 11 am. Tennis. Lawn games. Balconies. Picnic tables, grills. On ocean, swimming beach; water sports, fishing charters. Cr cds: A, C, D, DS, MC, V.

Resort

★ ★ ★**CHEECA LODGE.** *(Box 527) On Overseas Hwy (US 1), at mile marker 82.* 305/664-4651; res: 800/327-2888; FAX 305/664-2893. 49 rms in lodge, 4 story, 154 villas, 2 story, 64 kits. Mid-Dec–mid-Apr: S, D $200–$475; each addl $25; kit. units $275–$800; under 16 free; AP, MAP avail; golf, tennis, diving plans; lower rates rest of yr. Crib free. TV; cable, in-rm movies. 2 heated pools; wading pool, whirlpools, poolside serv. Playground. Supervised child's activities. Dining rms (public by res) 7 am–10:30 pm. Box lunches. Rm serv. Bar noon–midnight; entertainment. Ck-out noon, ck-in 3 pm. Grocery 1 blk. Coin lndry 3 blks. Package store 2 blks. Meeting rms. Bellhops. Valet serv. Concierge. Gift shop. Lighted tennis, pro. 9-hole golf, greens fee $12, putting green. Beach, boats. Diving shop & gear. On ocean; small boat, sailboat and windsurfing rentals. Soc dir. Fishing guides. Minibars; refrigerator in suites. Balconies. Cr cds: A, C, D, DS, ER, MC, V.

Restaurants

✔ ★ ★**CORAL GRILL.** *On Overseas Hwy (US 1), at mile marker 83.5.* 305/664-4803. Hrs: 4:30–9:30 pm; Sun noon–9 pm. Closed Mon; Dec 25; also Labor Day–mid-Oct. Bar. Semi-a la carte: dinner $7.95–$19.95. Buffet: dinner $14.95. Child's meals. Menu service on 1st floor, buffet on 2nd floor. Specializes in prime rib, steamed shrimp, snow crab clusters, conch chowder. Salad bar. Pianist. Parking. Cr cds: A, D, MC, V.

★ **GREEN TURTLE INN.** *On Overseas Hwy (US 1), at mile marker 81.5.* 305/664-9031. Hrs: noon–10 pm. Closed Mon. Semi-a la carte: lunch $5–$20, dinner $9.95–$28.95. Specializes in seafood, prime rib, steak. Parking. Cr cds: A, C, D, DS, MC, V.

★ ★ **LORELEI.** *On Overseas Hwy (US 1), at mile marker 82.* 305/664-4656. Hrs: 11 am–11 pm. Closed Dec 25. Res accepted. Bar. Semi-a la carte: lunch $3.95–$9.95, dinner $10.95–$24.95. Child's meals. Specializes in steak, seafood. Entertainment. Parking. Outdoor dining. On waterfront. Cr cds: A, C, D, DS, MC, V.

D

★ ★ **MARKER 88.** *On Overseas Hwy (US 1), at mile marker 88.* 305/852-9315. Hrs: 5–10:30 pm. Closed Mon. Res accepted. Bar. Semi-a la carte: dinner $13.95–$28. Child's meals. Specialties: yellowtail Martinique, steak Madagascar, Key lime baked Alaska. Own rolls. Parking. Nautical decor; hatch-covered tables, tropical plants. Overlooks bay. Cr cds: A, C, D, DS, MC, V.

★ ★ **PLANTATION YACHT HARBOR RESORT.** *(See Plantation Yacht Harbor Motel)* 305/852-2381. Hrs: 8 am–3 pm, 5–10 pm. Res accepted. Bar 11–2:30 am. Semi-a la carte: bkfst $2.95–$7.95, lunch $3.95–$10.95, dinner $9.95–$19.95. Child's meals. Specializes in native seafood. Entertainment. Parking. At marina, overlooks bay. Cr cds: A, MC, V.

✔ ★ **WHALE HARBOR INN.** *On Overseas Hwy (US 1), at mile marker 83.5.* 305/664-4959. Hrs: grill 6 am–noon; dining rm 4–9 pm; Fri, Sat to 10 pm; Sun from noon; early-bird dinner Mon–Fri 4–5:30 pm. Bar. Buffet: bkfst $1.95–$5.95, lunch $2.95–$11.95, dinner $15.95–$17.95. Child's meals. Specializes in seafood. Entertainment. Outdoor raw bar. Parking. Nautical decor. Cr cds: A, C, D, DS, MC, V.

Jacksonville (A-4)

Settled: 1822 **Pop:** 635,230 **Elev:** 19 ft **Area code:** 904

Jacksonville, once primarily an industrial, maritime Southern city, now has a sparkling skyline of skyscrapers; yet the city is still graced with tropical scenery, white sandy beaches and a certain Southern flavor and heritage. The Riverwalk near the St Johns River, Jacksonville's financial focal point, and the Jacksonville Landing, a festival marketplace with events and entertainment, are two manifestations of the city's new image as a modern, prosperous city.

Draped around an S curve of the broad St Johns River, Jacksonville is a major tourist and business center in Florida. The river is the hub for cruise boats and sightseeing excursions. Although 12 miles inland from the mouth of the river, Jacksonville berths freighters, ocean liners and a fleet of shrimp boats.

Under the British flag, Jacksonville was known as Cowford, a name that persisted until the purchase of Florida by the United States, when the town was renamed for Andrew Jackson. In the peace following the Seminole Indian War, the city emerged as a prosperous and boisterous harbor town. Jacksonville was occupied by Union troops four times during the Civil War, but emerged during the Reconstruction period as a popular winter resort.

Transportation

Car Rental Agencies: See toll-free numbers under Introduction.

Public Transportation: Buses (Jacksonville Transportation Authority), phone 630-3100.

Airport Information

Jacksonville Intl Airport: Information 741-4902; lost and found 741-2040; weather 741-4311.

Terminals: Concourse A: Delta, TWA; Concourse B: USAir, United; Concourse C: American, Continental

(Airlines and their terminal locations may change. Before leaving for the airport, you should phone the airline to confirm terminal location for your flight.)

What to See and Do

1. **Jacksonville Zoological Park.** 8605 Zoo Rd via Heckscher Dr. More than 700 mammals, birds and reptiles in attractive settings along Trout River. Safari train ride; animal shows; petting zoo; picnic areas. (Daily; closed Jan 1, Thanksgiving, Dec 25) Sr citizen rate. Phone 757-4462 or -4463. ¢¢

2. **Cummer Gallery of Art and Gardens.** 829 Riverside Ave. Contains 14 galleries and the Tudor Room from the original Cummer Mansion. The mansion's formal gardens (2½ acres) were retained as setting for the gallery. Collection ranges from ancient Egypt to the 20th century and features 700 pieces of early Meissen porcelain and important American paintings. Interactive exhibits. (Daily exc Mon; closed major hols, also 1 wk Apr) Phone 356-6857. ¢¢

3. **Museum of Science and History.** 1025 Museum Circle. Interactive exhibits on science and north Florida history, including health; natural and physical sciences; wildlife; Indians; Civil War artifacts from battleship *Maple Leaf.* Free planetarium, science and reptile shows. (Mon–Sat, also Sun afternoons; closed major hols) Sr citizen rate. Phone 396-7062. ¢¢

4. **Jacksonville Art Museum.** 4160 Boulevard Center Dr. Exhibits include pre-Columbian artifacts, contemporary paintings, sculpture and graphics. Classes; lectures; film series. Guided tours. (Daily exc Mon; closed most hols) Phone 398-8336. **Free.**

5. **Jacksonville University** (1934). (2,500 students) N University Blvd, on E bank of St Johns River. This 260-acre riverfront campus houses library of the Jacksonville Historical Society and Charter Marine Science Center. Delius House is restored house of British composer Frederick Delius (1862–1934) (daily, by request). Phone 744-3950. Also here is

   Alexander Brest Museum. Contains large collection of European and Oriental ivory; changing exhibits of painting, pottery, weaving, sculpture; collections of pre-Columbian artifacts, Steuben glass and American, European and Oriental porcelains. (Daily exc Sun; closed most hols). **Free.**

6. **Kingsley Plantation.** N on FL A1A, on Fort George Island at 11676 Palmetto Ave; reached by ferry from Mayport or via FL 105 (Heckscher Dr). Plantation house, kitchen house, barn and tabby slave houses reflect 19th-century life on a Sea Island cotton plantation. Ranger programs. A National Park Service area. Grounds (daily). Phone 251-3537.

7. **Fort Caroline National Memorial** (see). 13 mi E on FL 10, then N on Monument Rd.

8. **Little Talbot Island State Park.** 17 mi NE on FL A1A, near Fort George. More than 2,500 acres of wide Atlantic beaches and extensive salt marshes teem with life, including migrating birds and sea turtles. Sand dunes, forests. Swimming, surfing; fishing. Picnicking, playground. Camping (hookups, dump station). Standard hrs, fees. Phone 251-2320.

9. **Sightseeing tours.**

   Viking Sun **Cruises.** Tours on St Johns River aboard 500-passenger cruise ship. Lunch, dinner and sightseeing cruises. (Fri–Sun; schedule varies rest of wk; closed Dec 25) Phone 398-0797. ¢¢¢–¢¢¢¢¢

   Gray Line bus tours. Contact 420 Wharfside Way, 32207; 398-2242.

10. **Industrial Tour. Anheuser-Busch Brewery.** 111 Busch Dr, N via I-95 toward airport. Tours of brewery conclude in Hospitality Room for beer tasting. Guided and self-guided tours. (Daily exc Sun; closed hols) Phone 751-8118. **Free.**

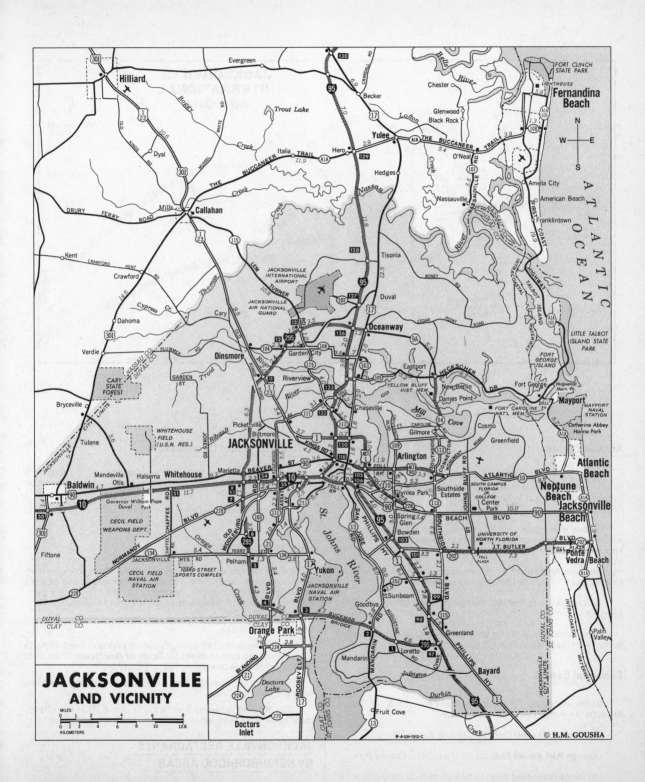

JACKSONVILLE
AND VICINITY

MILES
0 1 2   4   6   8
0 1 2   4   6   8 10   12.8
KILOMETERS

© H.M. GOUSHA

R-4-UH-1312-C

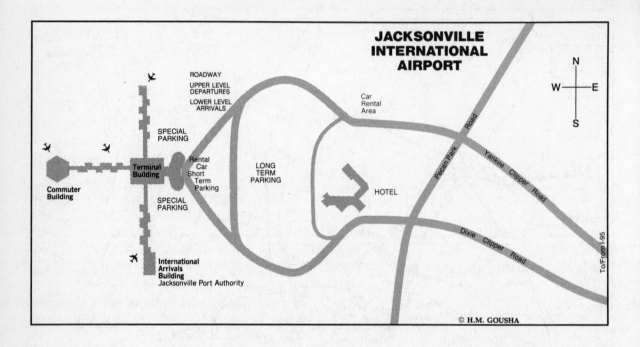

Annual Events

Delius Festival. Event features works by the late 19th-century British-born composer, who had lived in Jacksonville; performances by various musical groups; lectures; exhibits. Phone 744-3950, ext 3371. 1st wk Mar.

Historic Home Tour. Tour representing work of locally prominent architects and builders between 1870–1930. Phone 389-2449. Mid–late Apr.

Riverside Art Festival. Juried art show in variety of media; food, entertainment. Phone 389-4866. Mid- or late Sept.

Jacksonville Jazz Festival. Metropolitan Park, on the river. 2nd wkend Oct.

Gator Bowl Festival. Gator Bowl, Haines & Adams Sts. Climaxed by one of the major college football bowl games. Late Dec.

Seasonal Events

Greyhound racing. Tues & Sun; matinees Wed, Sat & Sun. Phone 646-0001. Year-round seasons rotating among

Jacksonville Kennel Club. 1440 McDuff Ave, N of I-10.

Orange Park Kennel Club. On US 17 at I-295 in Orange Park.

St Johns Greyhound Park. 18 mi S on US 1, at Racetrack Rd in Bayard.

Additional Visitor Information

For brochures, maps and calendar of events contact the Jacksonville and the Beaches Convention and Visitors Bureau, 3 Independent Dr, 32202, phone 798-9148.

(See Atlantic Beach, Fernandina Beach, Jacksonville Beach, St Augustine)

City Neighborhoods

Many of the restaurants, unrated dining establishments and some lodgings listed under Jacksonville include neighborhoods as well as exact street addresses. Geographic descriptions of these areas are given, followed by a table of restaurants arranged by neighborhood.

Baymeadows: Along Baymeadows Rd, east of San Jose Blvd and west of Southside Blvd.

Downtown: South of Beaver St, west of Liberty St, north of the St Johns River and east of Broad St. **South of Downtown:** South of St Johns River. **East of Downtown:** East of Liberty St.

Mandarin: On Mandarin Point south of I-295, east of the St Johns River and Julington Creek.

San Marco/Southbank: Across the St Johns River from Downtown; south of the river, west of US 1A and north of Emerson Rd.

JACKSONVILLE RESTAURANTS BY NEIGHBORHOOD AREAS

(For full description, see alphabetical listings under Restaurants)

BAYMEADOWS

Pagoda. 8617 Baymeadows Rd

Yoshi. 9866 Baymeadows Rd

DOWNTOWN

L & N Seafood. 2 Independent Dr

SOUTH OF DOWNTOWN

Partners. 3585 St Johns Ave

Sterling's Cafe. 3551 St Johns Ave

EAST OF DOWNTOWN

Alhambra Dinner Theatre. 12000 Beach Blvd

Patti's. 7300 Beach Blvd

MANDARIN

Longhorn Steaks. 9965 San Jose Blvd

Sebastian's. 10601 San Jose Blvd

SAN MARCO/SOUTHBANK

Café Carmon. 1986 San Marco Blvd

Cafe on the Square. 1974 San Marco Blvd

Crawdaddy's. 1643 Prudential Dr

Filling Station Cafe. 1004 Hendricks Ave

Note: When a listing is located in a town that does not have its own city heading, it will appear under the city nearest to its location. In these cases, the address and town appear in parenthesis immediately following the name of the establishment.

Motels

(Rates may be higher and there may be a minimum stay on football wkends)

✔ ★**BEST INNS OF AMERICA.** *8220 Dix Ellis Trail (32256), in Baymeadows.* 904/739-3323; FAX 904/739-3323, ext 305. 110 rms, 2 story. S $36–$42; D $44–$50; each addl $6; under 18 free; some wkend rates. Crib free. Pet accepted. TV; cable. Pool. Complimentary continental bkfst. Ck-out 1 pm. Cr cds: A, C, D, DS, MC, V.

D ⏚ 🖙 ☀ ⊘ 🕓 SC

★★**COURTYARD BY MARRIOTT.** *4600 San Pablo Rd (32224), south of downtown.* 904/223-1700; FAX 904/223-1026. 146 rms, 3 story, 12 suites. S, D $85; suites $99; under 12 free; wkend rates. Crib free. TV. Heated pool; whirlpool. Complimentary coffee in rms. Restaurant 6:30 am–10 pm. Bar from 11 am. Ck-out noon. Coin lndry. Meeting rms. Valet serv. Some refrigerators. Cr cds: A, C, D, DS, MC, V.

D 🖙 ⊘ 🕓 SC

✔ ★**ECONOMY INNS OF AMERICA.** *4300 Salisbury Rd (32216), in Baymeadows.* 904/281-0198. 124 rms, 3 story. S $35.90; D $39.90–$44.90; each addl $4. TV; cable. Heated pool. Complimentary continental bkfst. Ck-out 11 am. Meeting rm. Cr cds: A, MC, V.

D ⏚ 🖙 ⊘ 🕓 SC

✔ ★**HAMPTON INN.** *6135 Youngerman Circle (32244), off I-295 exit 4, south of downtown.* 904/777-5313; FAX 904/778-1545. 122 rms, 2 story. S, D $43–$50; under 18 free. Crib free. TV; cable. Heated pool. Complimentary continental bkfst, coffee. Restaurant nearby. Ck-out noon. Meeting rm. Valet serv. Cr cds: A, C, D, DS, MC, V.

D 🖙 ⊘ 🕓 SC

★★★**HOLIDAY INN-BAYMEADOWS.** *9150 Baymeadows Rd (32256), in Baymeadows.* 904/737-1700; FAX 904/737-0207. 250 rms, 2–4 story. S, D $74–$79; each addl $5; under 18 free; higher rates special events. Crib free. TV; cable, in-rm movies. Pool. Restaurant 6:30 am–midnight; Sat, Sun from 7 am. Rm serv. Bar 1 pm–1 am, wkends 11–2 am. Ck-out noon. Coin lndry. Meeting rms. Bellhops. Valet serv. Sundries. Gift shop. Gazebo in pool area. Cr cds: A, C, D, DS, MC, V, JCB.

D 🖙 ⊘ 🕓 SC

★★**HOMEWOOD SUITES.** *8737 Baymeadows Rd (32256), in Baymeadows.* 904/733-9299; FAX 904/448-5889. 116 kit. suites, 2–3 story. Suites $109–$149; wkly, monthly rates; higher rates special events. Crib free. Pet accepted, some restrictions; $75 non-refundable. TV; cable, in-rm movies. Heated pool. Complimentary continental bkfst. Complimentary coffee in rms. Ck-out noon. Coin lndry. Meeting rms. Valet serv. Exercise equipt; weights, stair machine, whirlpool. Balconies. Grills. Apartment-style rms. Cr cds: A, C, D, DS, MC, V.

D 🐾 🖙 🏋 ⊘ 🕓 SC

★★**INN AT BAYMEADOWS.** *8050 Baymeadows Circle W (32256), in Baymeadows.* 904/739-0739; res: 800/831-8183 (exc FL), 800/826-8889 (FL); FAX 904/737-2464. 96 units, 16 suites, 2 story. S $67; D $73–$155; each addl $6; suites $75–$155; under 16 free; wkend, golf, tennis plans. Crib free. TV; cable, in-rm movies. Pool; whirlpool. Complimentary full bkfst wkdays, continental bkfst wkends. Restaurant nearby. Ck-out noon. Meeting rms. Bellhops. Tennis. 18-hole golf, greens fee, pro, putting green, driving range. Private patios, balconies. Cr cds: A, C, D, MC, V.

D ⊶ ⚓ 🏊 🖙 ⊘ 🕓 SC

✔ ★★**LA QUINTA-BAYMEADOWS.** *8255 Dix Ellis Trail (32256), in Baymeadows.* 904/731-9940; FAX 904/731-3854. 106 rms, 2 story. S $46–$58; D $52–$64; each addl $6; under 18 free. Crib free. Pet accepted. TV. Heated pool. Complimentary continental bkfst. Restaurant nearby. Ck-out 1 pm. Meeting rms. Valet serv. Cr cds: A, C, D, DS, ER, MC, V, JCB.

D ⏚ 🖙 ⊘ 🕓 SC

★★**RAMADA INN-MANDARIN CONFERENCE CENTER.** *3130 Hartley Rd (32257), in Mandarin.* 904/268-8080; FAX 904/262-8718. 153 rms, 2 story. S, D $46–$80; each addl $5; family rates. Crib free. Pet accepted, some restrictions. TV; cable. Pool; wading pool. Complimentary full bkfst Mon–Fri; continental bkfst wkends. Restaurant 6:30 am–2 pm, 5–9 pm; Fri, Sat to 10 pm. Rm serv. Bar 3 pm–midnight; pianist, comedy exc Mon. Ck-out noon. Meeting rms. Bellhops. Valet serv. Large stone fireplace in lobby. Cr cds: A, C, D, DS, MC, V.

D 🐾 🖙 ⊘ 🕓 SC

✔ ★**RED ROOF INN.** *6099 Youngerman Circle (32244), south of downtown.* 904/777-1000; FAX 904/777-1005. 109 rms, 2 story. S, D $29.99; each addl $6; under 18 free. Crib free. Pet accepted, some restrictions. TV; cable. Complimentary coffee in lobby. Ck-out noon. Cr cds: A, C, D, DS, MC, V.

D 🐾 ⏚ ⊘ 🕓

★★**RESIDENCE INN BY MARRIOTT.** *8365 Dix Ellis Trail (32256), in Baymeadows.* 904/733-8088; FAX 904/731-8354. 112 kit. suites, 2 story. Kit. suites $130–$160. Crib free. Pet accepted; $50 non-refundable. TV; cable. Heated pool; whirlpools. Complimentary continental bkfst. Restaurant nearby. Refreshments Mon–Thurs. Ck-out noon. Coin lndry. Meeting rms. Health club privileges. Grills. Cr cds: A, C, D, DS, MC, V, JCB.

D 🐾 🖙 ⊘ 🕓

Motor Hotels

✔ ★★★**HOLIDAY INN-AIRPORT.** *(PO Drawer 18409, 32229) 12 mi N on Airport Rd, at I-95, near Intl Airport, north of downtown.* 904/741-4404; FAX 904/741-4907. 498 rms, 2–6 story. S, D, studio rms $60–$65; under 18 free. Crib free. Pet accepted. TV; cable. 3 pools, 1 indoor/outdoor; poolside serv. Restaurant 6 am–10 pm. Rm serv. Bar

11–2 am; dancing. Ck-out noon. Coin lndry. Convention facilities. Bellhops. Sundries. Gift shop. Free airport transportation. Lighted tennis. Exercise equipt; weights, bicycles, sauna. Game rm. *LUXURY LEVEL:* **CONCIERGE FLOOR.** 52 rms. S, D $78. Concierge. Complimentary continental bkfst, refreshments.
Cr cds: A, C, D, DS, MC, V, JCB.

★★**HOLIDAY INN-EAST CONFERENCE CENTER.** *5865 Arlington Expy (32211), east of downtown.* 904/724-3410; FAX 904/727-7606. 270 rms, 2 story, 5 bldgs. S $48–$70; D $53–$75; each addl $5; under 19 free; higher rates special events. Crib free. Pet accepted; $10 non-refundable. TV; cable. Pool. Restaurant 6 am–2 pm, 5–10 pm. Rm serv. Bar; entertainment, dancing. Ck-out noon. Convention facilities. Bellhops. Sundries. Free airport transportation. Tennis. Health club privileges. Private patios, balconies. *LUXURY LEVEL:* **CLUB ROYALE.** 52 rms, 2 floors in separate bldg. S $70; D $76. Complimentary continental bkfst, refreshments, newspaper.
Cr cds: A, C, D, DS, ER, MC, V, JCB.

★★**SKY CENTER INN** (formerly Radisson Inn-Airport). *2101 Dixie Clipper Dr (32229), at Intl Airport, west of downtown.* 904/741-4747; FAX 904/741-0002. 192 rms, 2–6 story. S $55–$65; D $65–$75; suites $75–$110; under 18 free; higher rates sporting events. Crib free. TV; cable. Pool. Restaurant 6 am–2 pm, 5–11 pm. Rm serv. Bar 2 pm–1 am. Ck-out noon. Coin lndry. Meeting rms. Bellhops. Gift shop. Free airport transportation. Golf privileges, greens fee $20, pro, putting green, driving range. Exercise equipt; weight machine, bicycles. Balconies. Cr cds: A, C, D, DS, MC, V.

Hotels

★★**BEST WESTERN BRADBURY SUITES.** *8277 Western Way Circle (32256), in Baymeadows.* 904/737-4477; FAX 904/739-1649. 111 suites, 6 story. S, D $57–$67; each addl $5; under 12 free; wkend rates, special package plans. Crib free. TV; cable. Pool. Complimentary bkfst buffet. Ck-out noon. Coin lndry. Meeting rms. Health club privileges. Refrigerators. Cr cds: A, C, D, DS, MC, V, JCB.

★**DOUBLETREE.** *4700 Salisbury Rd (32256), in Baymeadows.* 904/281-9700; FAX 904/281-1957. 167 rms, 6 story. S, D $99–$119; each addl $10; suites $129–$149; under 12 free. Crib free. TV; cable. Heated pool; whirlpool. Complimentary continental bkfst. Restaurant 7–9 am, 5–10 pm. No rm serv. Bar 5 pm–midnight. Ck-out 1 pm. Meeting rms. Refrigerator in suites. Cr cds: A, C, D, DS, ER, MC, V, JCB.

★★★**EMBASSY SUITES.** *9300 Baymeadows Rd (32256), in Baymeadows.* 904/731-3555; res: 800/432-7272; FAX 904/731-4972. 210 kit. suites, 7 story. S, D $115–$160; each addl $10; under 18 free; wkend packages. Crib free. TV; cable, in-rm movies. Indoor pool; whirlpool, sauna. Complimentary full bkfst. Restaurant 6:30–9:30 am, 11 am–2 pm, 6–10 pm; Sat, Sun 7 am–2 pm, 6–10 pm. Bar 2 pm–midnight. Ck-out noon. Meeting rms. Concierge. Gift shop. Balconies. Glass elevators; atrium lobby. Cr cds: A, C, D, DS, MC, V, JCB.

★★**MARINA HOTEL & CONFERENCE CENTER AT ST JOHNS PLACE.** *1515 Prudential Dr (32207), east of downtown.* 904/396-5100; FAX 904/396-7154. 321 rms, 5 story. S $79–$89; D $89–$99; each addl $10; suites $165–$335; under 18 free; wkend rates. Crib free. TV; cable. Pool. Restaurants 6:30 am–2 pm, 5–10 pm. Rm serv 6:30–1 am. Bar 11:30–1 am. Ck-out noon. Convention facilities. Gift shop. Lighted tennis. 18-hole golf privileges, greens fee. Health club privileges. Game rm. Some refrigerators, bathrm phones. Balconies. On river. Cr cds: A, C, D, MC, V.

★★★**MARRIOTT.** *4670 Salisbury Rd (32256), in Baymeadows.* 904/296-2222; FAX 904/296-7561. 256 units, 9 story, 6 suites. S $118; D $128; suites $175–$275; wkend packages; higher rates special events. Crib free. TV; cable. Indoor & outdoor pools; poolside serv. Restaurant 7 am–10 pm; Fri, Sat to 11 pm. Bar 11–2 am; entertainment, dancing. Ck-out noon. Convention facilities. Gift shop. Golf privileges, pro, putting green, driving range. Exercise equipt; weights, bicycles, whirlpool, sauna. Some refrigerators. Cr cds: A, C, D, DS, ER, MC, V, JCB.

★★★**OMNI.** *245 Water St (32202), downtown.* 904/355-6664; FAX 904/354-2970. 354 rms, 16 story. S $119–$144; D $134–$159; each addl $15; suites from $350; under 18 free; wkend rates. Crib free. Garage $4–$5; valet $7–$8. TV; cable. Heated pool; poolside serv. Restaurant 6:30 am–10:30 pm. Rm serv to 1 am. Bar 11–2 am; entertainment, dancing Fri, Sat. Ck-out noon. Convention facilities. Concierge. Shopping arcade. Airport, bus depot transportation. Lighted tennis privileges, pro. Golf privileges. Exercise equipt; weight machines, bicycles. Minibars. On river. *LUXURY LEVEL:* **OMNI CLUB FLOOR.** 53 rms, 2 suites, 2 floors. S $144; D $159; suites $350–$500. Concierge. Honor bar. In-rm movies. Bathrm phones. Complimentary continental bkfst, newspaper (Mon–Fri).
Cr cds: A, C, D, DS, MC, V, JCB.

Inns

★★**CLUB CONTINENTAL.** *(PO Box 7059, Orange Park 32073, 2143 Astor St, Orange Park 32073) I-295 to US 17, south to Astor St, then left.* 904/264-6070; FAX 904/264-4044. 22 rms, 2 story, 4 kit. suites. S, D $55–$99; kit. suites $135; monthly rates. Crib $5. TV; cable. Pool; wading pool, poolside serv, lifeguard. Complimentary continental bkfst. Dining rm 11:30 am–2 pm, 6:30–9 pm. Ck-out 11 am, ck-in 1 pm. Lighted tennis, pro. Balconies. Mediterranean-style villa (1923) on 30 acres overlooking St Johns River; pools, reflecting ponds. Cr cds: A, MC, V.

★★**HOUSE ON CHERRY STREET.** *1844 Cherry St (32205), west of downtown.* 904/384-1999. 4 rms, 3 story. No rm phones. S $65; D $75; each addl $10. Chidren over 8 yrs only. B/W TV; cable TV in lobby. Complimentary bkfst, coffee & tea/sherry. Ck-out noon, ck-in 3 pm. Health club privileges. Inn (1909) faces St Johns River. Furnished with antiques. Cr cds: MC, V.

Resort

★**INN AT RAVINES.** *(2932 Ravines Rd, Middleburg 32068) On FL 218, 1 mi E of jct FL 21.* 904/282-1111. 40 rms, 2 story. Feb–May, Oct–Nov: S, D $70–$120; under 13 free; golf plans; lower rates rest of yr. TV; cable. Pool; whirlpool. Dining rm (public by res) 7 am–3 pm. Box lunches. Snack bar. Bar 7 am–8 pm. Ck-out noon, ck-in 3 pm. Meeting rms. Lighted tennis. 18-hole golf, pro, driving range. In-rm whirlpools, refrigerators. Private patios, balconies. Cr cds: A, MC, V, JCB.

Restaurants

★**CAFÉ CARMON.** *1986 San Marco Blvd, in San Marco/Southbank.* 904/399-4488. Hrs: 11 am–11 pm; Fri, Sat to midnight; Sun to 3 pm. Closed major hols. Wine, beer. A la carte entrees: lunch $2.15–$7.95, dinner $12.95–$16.95. Specializes in homemade breads, desserts. Outdoor dining. Cr cds: A, C, D, DS, MC, V.

✔★**CAFE ON THE SQUARE.** *1974 San Marco Blvd, in San Marco/Southbank.* 904/399-4848. Hrs: 11 am–closing. Closed some major hols. Res accepted. Bar. Semi-a la carte: lunch $4.95–$7, dinner $11.95–$14.95. Specializes in fresh fish, steak, pasta. Entertainment

Tues–Sat. Outdoor dining. Oldest building in San Marco Square (1926). Cr cds: A, C, D, DS, MC, V.

D

★★**CRAWDADDY'S.** *1643 Prudential Dr, in San Marco/Southbank.* 904/396-3546. Hrs: 11 am–10 pm; Fri, Sat to 11 pm; Sun 3:30–10 pm; early-bird dinner 4:30–6:30 pm; Sun brunch 10:30 am–2:30 pm. Bars to 2 am. Semi-a la carte: lunch $4.95–$10.95, dinner $11.95–$19.95. Buffet: lunch $7.75. Sun brunch $14.95. Child's meals. Specializes in seafood, prime rib. Parking. Outdoor dining. Camp shanty decor. On St John's River. Cr cds: A, C, D, DS, MC, V.

D

★**FILLING STATION CAFE.** *1004 Hendricks Ave, in San Marco/Southbank.* 904/398-3663. Hrs: 11:15 am–2 pm; Fri 11:15 am–2 pm, 6–9 pm; Sat 6–9 pm. Closed Sun; major hols. Res accepted. Wine, beer. Semi-a la carte: lunch $3–$8, dinner $4–$16. Specializes in classic deli & gourmet sandwiches, soup, salad. Parking. Renovated neighborhood filling station. Cr cds: MC, V.

★**L & N SEAFOOD.** *2 Independent Dr, downtown.* 904/358-7737. Hrs: 11 am–10 pm; Fri, Sat to 11:30 pm. Closed Dec 25. Bar to 10 pm; Fri, Sat to 11:30 pm. Semi-a la carte: lunch $4.95–$8.95, dinner $8.95–$18.95. Child's meals. Specializes in mesquite-grilled fish, pasta, salads. Outdoor waterside dining. Cr cds: A, C, D, DS, MC, V.

D

★**LONGHORN STEAKS.** *9965 San Jose Blvd, in Mandarin.* 904/292-2333. Hrs: 11:15 am–10:30 pm; Fri to 11:30 pm; Sat 3–11:30 pm; Sun 3–10 pm. Closed Thanksgiving, Dec 25. Bar. Semi-a la carte: lunch $4.25–$8.25, dinner $9.95–$17.95. Child's meals. Specializes in steak, salmon. Parking. Cr cds: A, C, D, DS, MC, V.

D

✔★**PAGODA.** *8617 Baymeadows Rd, in Baymeadows.* 904/731-0880. Hrs: 11 am–10 pm; Fri to 11 pm; Sat noon–11 pm; Sun noon–10 pm. Closed Thanksgiving, Dec 25. Res accepted. Chinese menu. Bar. Semi-a la carte: lunch $4–$5.95, dinner $4.50–$15. Specialties: lemon chicken, seafood combination. Parking. Cr cds: A, C, D, DS, MC, V.

★**PARTNERS.** *3585 St Johns Ave, south of downtown.* 904/387-3585. Hrs: 11 am–2 pm, 5–10:30 pm; Fri to 11:30 pm; Sat 5–11:30 pm; Sun 5–10:30 pm. Closed some major hols. Continental menu. Bar. Semi-a la carte: lunch $3.50–$9.75, dinner $6.25–$15.75. Child's meals. Specialties: pesto lasagne, shrimp Provençale. Child's meals. Jazz Thurs–Sat. Outdoor dining. Storefront in restored shopping area. Cr cds: DS, MC, V.

✔★★**PATTI'S.** *7300 Beach Blvd, east of downtown.* 904/725-1662. Hrs: 11:30 am–2 pm, 5–10 pm; Fri to 11 pm; Sat 5–11 pm; Sun noon–10 pm; Mon 5–10 pm. Closed Thanksgiving, Dec 25. Res accepted. Italian, Amer menu. Serv bar. Semi-a la carte: lunch $3.50–$6.95, dinner $6.25–$12.95. Child's meals. Specialties: boneless chicken à la parmigiana, lasagne. Parking. Family-owned. Cr cds: A, C, D, DS, MC, V.

✔★**SEBASTIAN'S.** *10601 San Jose Blvd, in Mandarin Landing Shopping Ctr, in Mandarin.* 904/268-4458. Hrs: 5–10 pm; Fri, Sat to 11 pm. Closed Sun & Mon; major hols. Res accepted. Italian menu. Wine, beer. Semi-a la carte: dinner $7.75–$13.95. Child's meals. Specializes in pasta, seafood, veal. Cr cds: A, MC, V.

D **SC**

★★**STERLING'S CAFE.** *3551 St Johns Ave, south of downtown.* 904/387-0700. Hrs: 11 am–2:30 pm, 5:30–10:30 pm; Sun to 2:30 pm. Closed Thanksgiving, Dec 25. Res accepted; required Fri & Sat. Continental menu. Bar. Semi-a la carte: lunch $6–$9, dinner $13.95–$23.95. Sun brunch $10.95. Specialties: black bean cake, the Hemingway. Parking. Outdoor courtyard, patio dining. Cr cds: A, C, D, DS, MC, V.

✔★**YOSHI.** *9866 Baymeadows Rd, in Baymeadows.* 904/642-3978. Hrs: 11:30 am–2 pm, 5:30–10 pm; Fri to 11 pm; Sat 5:30–11

pm. Closed Sun; Jan 1, Easter. Res accepted. Japanese menu. Wine, beer. Semi-a la carte: lunch $5.95–$10.50, dinner $10.50–$15. Child's meals. Specialties: chicken teriyaki, sushi. Parking. Cr cds: A, MC, V.

Unrated Dining Spots

ALHAMBRA DINNER THEATRE. *12000 Beach Blvd, east of downtown.* 904/641-1212. Hrs: Tues–Sun cocktails from 6 pm, buffet 6:30 pm, show 8:15 pm; Sat matinee 11 am, buffet 11:30 am, show 1:15 pm; Sun buffet 12:15 pm, show 2 pm. Closed Mon; Jan 1, Dec 25. Res required. Bar. Buffet & show $24.50–$29.50. Menu changes with each show. Dessert bar. Professional Equity actors & union musicians; Broadway musicals, comedies. Parking. More than 25 yrs of continuous theatrical entertainment. Cr cds: A, DS, MC, V.

SC

THE SISTERS. *(906 Park Ave, Orange Park) 1 mi S of I-295 on US 17.* 904/264-7325. Hrs: 11 am–2:30 pm; tea served to 4 pm. Closed Sun & Mon; hols; also 2 wks Sept. Semi-a la carte: lunch $4.50–$6.95. Tea service $5. Specializes in salads, sandwiches, quiche. Parking. Outdoor dining. Tea room; Victorian country decor, antique tables. Totally nonsmoking. No cr cds accepted.

Jacksonville Beach (A-4)

Settled: 1884 **Pop:** 17,839 **Elev:** 9 ft **Area code:** 904 **Zip:** 32250

This town, 15 miles east of Jacksonville, has a dual personality—as a suburb for many of Jacksonville's commuters and as an ocean resort. With its neighbors, Atlantic Beach (see), Mayport, Neptune Beach and Ponte Vedra Beach, Jacksonville Beach provides a continuous front of sand and amusement areas sometimes referred to as the beaches of Jacksonville. Fishing tournaments, beach events and a variety of other festivities are held year-round.

What to See and Do

1. **Pablo Historical Park.** 425 Beach Blvd. Park includes original house built for section foreman of Florida East Coast Railroad, restored with furnishings from the turn of the century; and the old Mayport Depot, with historic railroad exhibits and memorabilia. Adjacent is a steam locomotive. (Daily; closed some hols) Donation. Phone 246-0093.

2. **Fishing.** Between S 5th & 6th Aves. Lighted fishing pier 1,200-feet long. Jetties on St Johns River. Charter boats.

(For further information contact Jacksonville and the Beaches Convention & Visitors Bureau, 3 Independent Dr, Jacksonville 32202; 798-9148.)

Annual Events

The PLAYERS Championship. PGA event. Tournament Player's Club at Ponte Vedra. Mar.

Beaches Festival Weekend Celebration. Celebration in honor of opening the beaches of Jacksonville; events include sandcastle contests, 5K race, arts & crafts, games, surfing, food and culminating with a spectacular parade. Phone 247-6236. Last wknd Apr.

(See Atlantic Beach, Jacksonville)

Motor Hotel

★★★★**THE LODGE AND BATH CLUB AT PONTE VEDRA BEACH.** *(607 Ponte Vedra Blvd, Ponte Vedra Beach 32082) Approx 8 mi S on FL A1A, E on Corona Rd to Ponte Vedra Blvd.* 904/273-9500; res:

800/243-4304; FAX 904/273-0210. 66 rms, 2 story, 24 suites. Mid-Feb–mid-Nov: S, D $165–$235; each addl $20; suites $235; under 18 free; golf, tennis, honeymoon plans; higher rates: TPC wk, Gator Bowl, FL-GA football game; lower rates rest of yr. Crib free. TV; cable. 3 pools, 2 heated; poolside serv, lifeguard. Supervised child's activities. Restaurant 7 am–10 pm. Rm serv 24 hrs. Bar 11–12:30 am. Ck-out noon. Meeting rms. Concierge. Free valet parking. Tennis, golf privileges. Exercise equipt; weight machines, bicycles, whirlpools, saunas. Bathrm phones, refrigerators; some in-rm whirlpools, minibars, fireplaces. Wet bar in suites. Balconies. Stuccoed, Mediterranean-style structure with red tile roofs; resort atmosphere. On ocean. Cr cds: A, C, D, DS, MC, V.

D ⊷ 🐕 🎿 🏌 ⚓ 🏃 🚭 ⏲ SC

Resorts

★ ★ ★ ★ **MARRIOTT AT SAWGRASS.** *(1000 TPC Blvd, Ponte Vedra Beach 32082) S via FL A1A.* 904/285-7777; res: 800/457-4653; FAX 904/285-0906. 350 rms in hotel, 7 story, 184 villas with kit., 2 story. Mar–June: S, D $189–$210; each addl $21; suites $368–$525; villas $168–$520; under 15 free; tennis & golf plans; higher rates special events; lower rates rest of yr. Crib free. TV; cable. 4 pools, 1 heated; wading pool, poolside serv. Supervised child's activities. Dining rm 6:30 am–10 pm (also see THE AUGUSTINE ROOM). Box lunches, snack bar. Rm serv to 2 am. Bars 11–1 am. Ck-out noon, ck-in 4 pm. Grocery, coin lndry, package store 1 blk. Convention facilities. Valet serv. Gift shop. Airport transportation. Sports dir. Lighted tennis, pro. 99-hole golf, greens fee, pro, shops, putting greens, driving ranges. Private beach, boating. 4 stocked ponds. Bicycles. Soc dir. Exercise rm; instructor, weight machines, bicycles, whirlpool, steam rm, sauna. Many minibars; some fireplaces. Many private patios, balconies. Serpentine-shaped, emerald-glassed hotel offers classic country club elegance; indoor/outdoor waterfalls, natural lagoons, lush tropical foliage and 7-story atrium lobby with extraordinary skylight. Cr cds: A, C, D, DS, MC, V, JCB.

D ⊷ 🏇 🎿 🏌 ⚓ 🏃 🏃 🚭 ⏲ SC

★ ★ ★ **PONTE VEDRA INN & CLUB.** *(200 Ponte Vedra Blvd, Ponte Vedra Beach 32082) 2 mi S via FL A1A, then FL 203.* 904/285-1111; res: 800/234-7842; FAX 904/285-2111. 202 units, 2 story, 64 kits. Mar–May: S, D $175–$195; suites $265–$295; golf plans; MAP, AP avail; lower rates rest of yr. Crib $5. TV; cable. 4 pools, 2 heated; wading pool, poolside serv, lifeguard. Supervised child's activities (June–Sept & hols). Dining rm 7–10 am, 11:30 am–3:30 pm, 6:30–10 pm. Box lunches, snack bar, picnics. Rm serv 24 hrs. Bars 11 am–midnight; entertainment Thurs–Sat. Ck-out noon, ck-in 3 pm. Package store. Convention facilities. Concierge. Gift shops. Valet parking avail. Tennis, pro, shop. Two 18-hole golf courses, greens fee $45–$55, pro, putting green, driving range, shop. Private beach, swimming; boats, rowboats, sailboats, paddleboats. Bicycles. Lawn games. Soc dir; entertainment, dancing. Exercise rm; instructor, weights, bicycles, whirlpool, steam rm, sauna. Health spa facilities; technicians and therapists. Refrigerators, minibars, wet bars; some fireplaces. Private patios, balconies. Picnic tables. Cr cds: A, C, D, DS, MC, V.

D 🏇 🎿 ⚓ 🏃 🏃 🚭 ⏲

Restaurants

★ ★ ★ **THE AUGUSTINE ROOM.** *(See Marriott at Sawgrass Resort)* 904/285-7777. Hrs: 6–10 pm. Closed Sun. Res accepted. French, continental menu. Bar. Wine cellar. Semi-a la carte: dinner $24–$32. Specializes in beef, veal, seafood. Valet parking. Original artwork, fresh floral arrangements. Jacket. Cr cds: A, C, D, DS, MC, V, JCB.

D

✔ ★ ★ **AW SHUCKS.** *(950 Sawgrass Village Dr, Ponte Vedra) In Sawgrass Village, S on FL A1A.* 904/285-3017. Hrs: 11:30 am–11 pm; Fri, Sat to midnight. Closed Thanksgiving, Dec 25. Res accepted. Bar. Semi-a la carte: lunch $3.95–$6.95, dinner $9.95–$15.95. Child's meals. Specializes in gourmet seafood, steak. Parking. Outdoor dining. Tropical decor with outdoor decks overlooking small lake. Cr cds: A, D, MC, V.

★ ★ **KING WU.** *1323 S 3rd St.* 904/246-0567. Hrs: 4–10 pm; Fri, Sat to 11 pm. Chinese menu. Bar. A la carte entrees: dinner $5.50–$16. Specialties: Cantonese pan-fried noodles, diced chicken with cashews, orange flavored beef. Parking. Chinese decor, red & gold inlay. Cr cds: A, MC, V.

Jensen Beach (D-5)

Settled: 1871 **Pop:** 9,884 **Elev:** 50 ft **Area code:** 407 **Zip:** 34957

Jensen Beach, named for Danish sailor John L. Jensen, who first settled the area, was once a major center of pineapple cultivation. Today, the economy is based on tourism and small retail business.

What to See and Do

1. **Hutchinson Island.** Connected to the village by a causeway. The island is the waterfront section of Jensen Beach. Swimming (lifeguards); surf casting, shelling. Picnicking. Also Gilbert's Bar House of Refuge (see STUART), a restored historic site (daily exc Mon; fee), and Elliott Museum (see STUART).

2. **Fishing.** From charter boats, bridges over Indian and St Lucie Rivers; freshwater fishing in savannas; sport fishing in Gulf Stream; surf fishing along beach; fishing pier at Jensen Beach Causeway.

(For further information contact the Chamber of Commerce, 1910 NE Jensen Beach Blvd; 334-3444.)

Annual Events

Sailfish Powerboat Championships. May.

Pineapple Festival. Parade, contests, street fair, exhibits, amusement rides. 2nd wkend Nov.

Seasonal Event

Turtle Watch. Endangered sea turtles, 200–500 pounds, crawl far up onto the beaches of Hutchinson Island (see #1) to lay their eggs. Supervised by the Chamber of Commerce. Reservations required. June–July.

(See Fort Pierce, Stuart)

Motel

✔ ★ ★ **BEST WESTERN.** *(7900 S US 1, Port St Lucie 34952) 2 mi N on US 1.* 407/878-7600. 98 suites, 2 story. Mid-Jan–Mar: suites $55–$89; each addl $5; under 12 free; higher rates special events; lower rates rest of yr. Crib free. TV; cable. Heated pool; whirlpool. Complimentary continental bkfst, coffee. Restaurant adj 11 am–9 pm. Beer, wine. Ck-out 11 am. Coin lndry. Meeting rm. Airport transportation. Cr cds: A, C, D, DS, MC, V.

D ⚓ 🚭 ⏲ SC

Motor Hotels

★ ★ ★ **COURTYARD BY MARRIOTT.** *10978 S Ocean Dr (FL A1A).* 407/229-1000; FAX 407/229-0253. 110 rms, 8 story. Jan–Apr: S $100–$110; D $110–$130; each addl $10; under 17 free; lower rates rest of yr. Crib free. TV; cable. Pool; poolside serv. Coffee in rms. Bkfst avail 7–11 am. Restaurant 11 am–9 pm. Rm serv 5–9 pm. Ck-out noon. Coin lndry. Meeting rooms. Bellhops. Valet serv. Sundries. Tennis, golf privileges. Exercise equipt; weight machine, bicycles. Refrigerators. Some balconies. Exterior glass elvtr to rooftop cafe. On ocean beach. Cr cds: A, D, DS, MC, V.

D ⊷ 🏇 🎿 ⚓ 🏃 🚭 ⏲ SC

★ ★ ★**HOLIDAY INN OCEANSIDE.** *(PO Box 1086, 34958) 3793 NE Ocean Blvd (FL A1A)*, on Hutchinson Island. 407/225-3000; FAX 407/225-1956. 181 rms, 4 story. Mid-Jan–mid-Apr: S, D \$110–\$145; each addl \$10; suites \$245–\$375; under 19 free; varied lower rates rest of yr. Crib free. TV; cable. Heated pool; poolside serv. Restaurant 6 am–10 pm. Rm serv. Bar; entertainment, dancing Tues–Sat. Ck-out 11 am. Coin lndry. Meeting rms. Bellhops. Sundries. Gift shop. Lighted tennis. Game rm. Balconies. On ocean. Cr cds: A, C, D, DS, MC, V, JCB.

★ ★ ★**RADISSON INN.** *(10120 S US 1, Port St Lucie 34952) 2 mi N on US 1, jct Port St Lucie Blvd.* 407/337-2200. 142 rms, 5 story, 72 suites. Jan–mid-Apr: S, D \$89; each addl \$10; suites \$99–\$125; under 18 free; lower rates rest of yr. Crib free. TV; cable. Heated pool; whirlpool. Restaurant 6:30 am–2 pm, 5–10 pm. Rm serv. Bar 11 am–11 pm. Ck-out noon. Coin lndry. Meeting rms. Bellhops. Sundries. Wet bars; some refrigerators. Cr cds: A, C, D, DS, ER, MC, V.

Inn

★ ★**HUTCHINSON INN.** *9750 S Ocean Dr (FL A1A)*, on Hutchinson Island. 407/229-2000. 21 rms, 2 story, 5 suites. Dec–Apr: S, D \$80–\$125; each addl \$20; suites \$165; kit. units \$110; under 3 free; monthly rates; lower rates rest of yr. Crib \$5–\$10. TV; cable. Heated pool. Complimentary full bkfst. Ck-out 11 am, ck-in 2 pm. Bellhops. Concierge. Tennis. Golf privileges, greens fee \$30–\$50, putting green, driving range. Lawn games. Refrigerators. On ocean; miniature waterfall near entrance. Cr cds: MC, V.

Restaurants

★ ★**ADMIRAL'S TABLE.** *4000 NE Indian River Dr.* 407/334-3080. Hrs: 11:30 am–9 pm; Fri, Sat to 10 pm; Sun to 8:30 pm; Sun brunch to 3 pm. Closed Dec 25; also mid-July–Aug. Bar. Semi-a la carte: lunch \$4.10–\$8.50, dinner \$9.50–\$23. Sun brunch \$12.95. Child's meals. Specializes in fresh local fish, Maine lobster, steak. Salad bar. Parking. Nautical decor. View of river. Cr cds: DS, MC, V.

★**CAFE COCONUTS.** *4304 NE Ocean Blvd (FL A1A)*, on Hutchinson Island. 407/225-6006. Hrs: 11:30–2 am; early-bird dinner Mon–Sat 4–6 pm. Closed Dec 25. Bars. Semi-a la carte: lunch \$3.95–\$8.95, dinner \$7.50–\$17.95. Child's meals. Specializes in baby back ribs, steak, seafood. Salad bar. Entertainment. Parking. Outdoor dining. Tropical, nautical atmosphere. Cr cds: MC, V.

★ ★**CONCHY JOE'S SEAFOOD.** *3945 NE Indian River Dr.* 407/334-1130. Hrs: 11:30 am–2:30 pm, 5–10 pm. Closed Thanksgiving, Dec 24; also Super Bowl Sun. Bars. Semi-a la carte: lunch \$3.50–\$10.95, dinner \$9.95–\$25.95. Child's meals. Specializes in local seafood, steak, conch fritters. Entertainment. Raw bar. Parking. Outdoor riverfront dining. Nautical atmosphere; historic pictures of area. Overlooks water; built by Seminole Indians. Cr cds: A, DS, MC, V.

✔ ★ ★**ISLAND REEF.** *10900 S Ocean Dr (FL A1A)*, on Hutchinson Island. 407/229-2600. Hrs: 11:30 am–2:30 pm, 5–9:30 pm; Fri & Sat to 10 pm; Sun brunch to 2:30 pm. Closed Dec 24 eve. Bars. A la carte entrees: lunch \$4.95–\$10.95. Semi-a la carte: dinner \$9.95–\$15.95. Sun brunch \$5.95–\$8.95. Specialties: mango papaya chicken ''cool down,'' mangrove char-grilled Florida dolphin, stuffed jalapeños. Entertainment Fri–Sun. Parking. Outdoor dining. Large open dining rm and deck with view of ocean. Cr cds: A, DS, MC, V.

★ ★**LOBSTER SHANTY.** *999 NE Anchorage Dr.* 407/334-6400. Hrs: 11:30 am–9 pm; Fri, Sat to 10 pm; early-bird dinner Mon–Sat

3–6 pm. Closed Thanksgiving. Bar. Semi-a la carte: lunch \$4.99–\$7.99, dinner \$6.99–\$16.99. Child's meals. Specializes in Maine lobster, local seafood. Salad bar. Parking. Overlooks marina, river. Cr cds: A, D, MC, V.

✔ ★**VILLAGE CORNER.** *2019 Jensen Beach Blvd.* 407/334-8717. Hrs: 6:30 am–8 pm; Sat from 6 am; Sun 6 am–1:30 pm. Bar. A la carte entrees: bkfst \$2–\$4, lunch \$2.35–\$4.25. Complete meals: dinner \$4.39. Specialties: eggs Benedict, veal Parmesan & spaghetti, prime rib. Parking. No cr cds accepted.

✔ ★**WAYSIDE INN.** *2400 Old Dixie Hwy (FL 707).* 407/334-0880. Hrs: 4–8:30 pm; Sun 8 am–8 pm. Closed Mon; Aug; also Tues, Wed June–Sept. Wine, beer. Semi-a la carte: bkfst \$2.49–\$5.75, dinner \$7.95–\$12.95. Child's meals. Specialties: chicken pot pie, Yankee pot roast. Parking. Cr cds: MC, V.

Jupiter (D-5)

Pop: 24,986 **Elev:** 8 ft **Area code:** 407

Jonathan Dickinson, a Quaker, and his party were swept ashore near the present-day site of Jupiter during a storm in 1696. Captured by Indians but set free, the survivors marched 225 miles to St Augustine. Dickinson's tale of his adventures, *God's Protecting Providence*, was widely read in both Europe and America. Jupiter is on the Intracoastal Waterway at the mouth of the scenic Loxahatchee River. A nearly eight-mile stretch of the river, from Riverbend Park in Palm Beach County to the southern boundary of Jonathan Dickinson State Park, forms a component of both the Florida and the National Wild and Scenic Rivers systems.

What to See and Do

1. **Loxahatchee Historical Museum.** On US 1, in Burt Reynolds Park. Exhibits on South Florida culture, Seminole Indians, shipwrecks, railroads; authentic Seminole chickee. (Daily exc Mon; closed hols) Phone 747-6639. ¢¢   The Historical Society also operates

   Jupiter Lighthouse and Museum (1860). On bluff overlooking Jupiter Inlet. This red-brick landmark is one of the oldest lighthouses on the Atlantic coast; now operated by the US Coast Guard. Houses local historical artifacts and memorabilia. (Sun, limited hrs; closed hols) Phone 747-6639.   **Free.**

   Dubois House. NE via FL A1A, Jupiter Beach Rd exit to Dubois Rd. Restored pioneer house (ca 1896) built on Jaega Indian mound faces Jupiter Inlet; many original furnishings and personal memorabilia of first occupants. Tours. (Sun afternoons; closed hols) Phone 747-6639.   **Free.**

2. **Jonathan Dickinson State Park.** 6 mi N on US 1, in Hobe Sound. More than 10,000 acres near where Jonathan Dickinson was shipwrecked between Hobe Sound and the Loxahatchee River; park includes 85-foot-high Hobe Mountain with 25-foot observation tower, pine flatlands and tropical riverfront. Fishing; boating (ramps), canoeing (rentals). Nature trails, bicycling. Picnicking (shelters), playground, concession. Camping (dump station), cottages. Boat trip (2 hrs). Guided tours at Trapper Nelson Interpretive Site on river, accessible only by boat. Standard hrs, fees. Phone 546-2771.

3. **Hobe Sound National Wildlife Refuge.** Approx 5 mi N via US 1, in Hobe Sound. This 970-acre refuge contains 3½ mi of undeveloped ocean beach where sea turtles nest. Nature trails. Hobe Sound Nature Center, visitor center; interpretive signs. (Daily) Golden Eagle, Golden Age and Golden Access passports accepted (see

INTRODUCTION). Contact PO Box 645, Hobe Sound 33475; 546-6141. Per vehicle ¢¢ Pedestrians **Free.**

(For further information contact the Jupiter-Tequesta-Juno Beach Chamber of Commerce, 800 N US 1, 33477; 746-7111.)

(See Lake Worth, Palm Beach, West Palm Beach)

Motels

✔ ★**COMFORT INN.** *810 US 1 (33477).* 407/575-2936. 53 rms, 2 story. Mid-Jan–Apr: S, D $79–$99; each addl $5; under 16 free; lower rates rest of yr. Crib free. TV; cable. Heated pool. Complimentary continental bkfst. Ck-out 11 am. Lndry facilities. On Intracoastal Waterway; observation deck. Cr cds: A, D, MC, V.

D ⩩ ⊘ ⊕ SC

★**COMFORT SUITES.** *(18903 SE Federal Hwy, Tequesta 33469)* 3 mi N on US 1. 407/747-9085. 36 suites, 2 story. Nov–Apr: suites $99–$125; wkly, monthly rates; lower rates rest of yr. Crib free. TV; cable. Pool. Complimentary continental bkfst. Restaurant nearby. Ck-out 11 am. Coin lndry. Some in-rm whirlpools. Balconies. On Intracoastal Waterway. Cr cds: A, C, D, DS, ER, MC, V, JCB.

D ⊷ ⩩ ⊘ ⊕ SC

★★**HOWARD JOHNSON OCEANSIDE.** *(930 US 1, Juno Beach 33408)* S via US 1. 407/626-1531. 108 rms, 2–3 story. Jan–Apr: S, D $79–$159; each addl $10; suites $149–$169; lower rates rest of yr. Crib free. TV; cable. Pool. Restaurant open 24 hrs. Beer, wine. Ck-out noon. Balconies. Patios. Near ocean, beach. Cr cds: A, C, D, DS, MC, V, JCB.

D ⩩ ⊘ ⊕ SC

Motor Hotel

✔ ★★**WELLESLEY INN.** *34 Fisherman's Wharf (33477).* 407/575-7201; res: 800/444-8888; FAX 407/575-1169. 105 rms, 3 story. Mid-Dec–mid-Apr: S $60–$90; D $70–$100; each addl $10; suites $109–$149; under 18 free; wkly rates; diving packages; lower rates rest of yr. Crib $10. TV; cable. Heated pool. Complimentary continental bkfst, coffee. Restaurant adj 6 am–midnight. Ck-out 11 am. Coin lndry. Meeting rm. Valet serv. Golf privileges. Health club privileges. Some refrigerators, wet bars. Cr cds: A, C, D, DS, ER, MC, V, JCB.

D ⊠ ⩩ ⊘ ⊕ SC

Hotel

★★★**JUPITER BEACH RESORT.** *5 N FL A1A (33477),* at Indiantown Rd. 407/746-2511; FAX 407/744-1741. 193 rms, 9 story, 35 kits. Jan–Apr: S $140–$340; D $160–$340; each addl $30; suites $600–$800; kit. suites $340; family rates; varied lower rates rest of yr. Crib free. TV; cable. Heated pool; poolside serv. Restaurant 6:30 am–10 pm. Bar 11–2 am; entertainment, dancing. Ck-out noon. Meeting rms. Concierge. Gift shop. Free valet parking. Free shopping area transportation. Lighted tennis. Golf privileges. Exercise equipt; weight machines, bicycles. Minibars. Balconies. Gazebo overlooks ocean; beach, cabanas. Bicycle rentals. Deep-sea charters, sailing, snorkeling avail; dive shop. Cr cds: A, C, D, DS, ER, MC, V, JCB.

D ⊠ ⏃ ⩩ ⊼ ⊘ ⊕ SC

Restaurants

★★★**BACKSTAGE.** *1061 E Indiantown Rd, in Reynolds Plaza.* 407/747-9533. Hrs: 11:30 am–2:30 pm, 5–10:30 pm; Fri to midnight; Sat 5 pm–midnight. Closed Jan 1, Dec 25. Res accepted. Continental menu. Bar to 2 am; Sat, Sun from 5 pm. Extensive wine list. Semi-a la carte: lunch $3.95–$9.95, dinner $12.95–$25.95. Child's meals. Specialties: red snapper with pecan butter, prime steak, veal chop, New Orleans dishes. Own baking. Jazz 2 nights. Parking. Modern, theatrical atmosphere; autographed photos of celebrities. Cr cds: A, D, MC, V.

D

★★★**CHARLEY'S CRAB.** *1000 N Federal Hwy (US 1).* 407/744-4710. Hrs: 11:30 am–3 pm, 5–10 pm; Fri, Sat to 11 pm; Sun 10 am–2:30 pm, 5–10 pm. Res accepted. Bar to 11 pm. Wine list. Semi-a la carte: lunch $5–$14.50, dinner $9.50–$23. Sun brunch $12.50. Child's meals. Specializes in fresh seafood, homemade pasta, rack of lamb. Own baking. Pianist. Valet parking. Outdoor dining. Overlooks Jupiter Inlet. Cr cds: A, C, D, DS, MC, V.

D

★★**COBBLESTONE CAFE.** *(383 Tequesta Dr, Tequesta)* In Gallery Sq North shopping center. 407/747-4419. Hrs: 11:30 am–2 pm, 6–9:30 pm; May–Oct 6–9 pm. Closed Jan 1, Thanksgiving, Dec 25; also Sun May–Oct & Mon June–Sept. Res accepted. French, Italian menu. Semi-a la carte: lunch $2.75–$10.95, dinner $12.95–$21.95. Complete meals (summer): $40/couple (4 courses). Child's meals. Specializes in fresh Florida fish, rack of lamb. Own sauces, pastas, soups. Country decor. Cr cds: A, MC, V.

D

★★**HARPOON LOUIE'S.** *1065 N FL A1A.* 407/744-1300. Hrs: 8 am–10 pm; Easter–Thanksgiving from 11 am. Closed Dec 25. Bar. Semi-a la carte: bkfst $3.25–$7, lunch $4.25–$11.95, dinner $8.95–$19.95. Complete meals: dinner $15.95. Child's meals. Parking. Outdoor dining. Waterside on Jupiter Inlet with view of lighthouse. Lunch cruises on *Louie's Lady.* Cr cds: A, C, D, DS, MC, V.

D

★★**JUNIPER.** *(205 US 1, Juno Beach)* S on US 1, at Seminole Plaza. 407/624-8997. Hrs: 3–10 pm; Sat, Sun from 5 pm. Closed Mon in summer. Res accepted. Continental menu. Bar to 2 am. Semi-a la carte: dinner $10.95–$18.95. Child's meals. Specialties: chicken Scandinavian, lump Maryland crab, veal & eggplant Palermo. Entertainment Wed–Sun. Parking. Bi-level dining; large, hand-painted mural. Cr cds: A, DS, MC, V.

D

★**JUPITER CRAB CO.** *1511 Old Dixie Hwy,* ½ blk W of US 1. 407/747-8300. Hrs: 11:30 am–10 pm; Fri, Sat to 11 pm. Closed Thanksgiving. Bar. Semi-a la carte: lunch $4.95–$11.95, dinner $9.95–$29.95. Child's meals. Specializes in seafood, crab & grouper baked in a bag. Parking. Nautical decor; marine artifacts. Cr cds: A, DS, MC, V.

D

★**NICK'S TOMATOE PIE.** *1697 W Indiantown Rd.* 407/744-8935. Hrs: 5 pm–closing. Italian menu. Bar. Semi-a la carte: dinner $8.95–$21.95. Child's meals. Specialties: gourmet pizza, shrimp Alfredo, veal saltimbocca. Parking. Italian marketplace decor; intimate seating areas. Cr cds: A, C, D, DS, MC, V.

D

★★**PIERRE'S.** *997 N FL A1A.* 407/746-5959. Hrs: 5–10 pm; early-bird dinner 5–6:30 pm Res accepted. French, Italian, Amer menu. Bar. Wine list. Semi-a la carte: dinner $11.50–$21.95. Child's meals. Specialties: steak au poivre Congolais, saumon en papillote, sea scallops a la Valenciana. Own pastries. Pianist Thurs–Sat (Nov–May). Parking. Elegant, informal atmosphere. Cr cds: A, MC, V.

D

✔ ★**TOO JAY'S-BLUFF'S SQUARE.** *4050 US 1S, in Bluff's Sq Plaza.* 407/627-5555. Hrs: 8 am–9 pm; Sun brunch to 3 pm. Closed Thanksgiving, Dec 25. Wine, beer. Semi-a la carte: bkfst $1.95–$5.95, lunch $4.95–$7.95, dinner $4.95–$9.95. Sun brunch $4.95–$7.95. Child's meals. Specialties: seafood salad, stir-fry chicken, deli sandwiches. Parking. Cr cds: A, D, MC, V.

D

✔ ★**TROPHI'S.** *725 N FL A1A, in Alhambra Shopping Center.* 407/575-2100. Hrs: 5–11 pm; Sun to 10 pm; Dec–Apr also noon–2 pm.

Closed Thanksgiving, Dec 25. Italian menu. Bar. Semi-a la carte: lunch $4.95–$7.45, dinner $6.95–$13.50. Child's meals. Specialties: chicken Francese, veal Marsala, pasta dishes. Own desserts. Autographed pictures of famous athletes. Cr cds: MC, V.

D

Kennedy Space Center (C-5)

(47 mi E of Orlando; 12 mi E of Titusville; 15 mi N of Cape Canaveral. Entrance at visitors center, N or S via US 1 or I-95 exit 78 or 79 to FL 405 NASA Pkwy, then E; N via FL 3; follow signs)

As the launch site for all United States manned space missions since 1968, the Kennedy Space Center on Merritt Island is one of the most historic sites in the world. From here, on July 16, 1969, Apollo 11 astronauts left Earth on man's first voyage to land on the moon. Three Skylab missions, the Apollo/Soyuz Test Project and more than 40 voyages of the space shuttle have all been launched from the Space Center.

The National Aeronautics and Space Administration was established on October 1, 1958. The early focus of NASA's launch operations centered on Cape Canaveral, where manned launches of Project Mercury and Gemini took place. In late 1964, the John F. Kennedy Space Center was relocated to adjacent Merritt Island. The site was selected in 1961 as the launch facility for Apollo, the Moon Mission. Beginning in 1976, these facilities were modified and new ones built to accommodate the launch of the space shuttle. The 140,000-acre John F. Kennedy Space Center is the major launch facility for NASA.

In addition to the historic manned rocket flights, NASA also launches a wide variety of unmanned spacecraft, including weather and communications satellites, orbiting scientific observatories, Earth resources technology satellites and interplanetary probes, such as Galileo and Magellan.

Aside from operational areas, much of Kennedy Space Center is designated a National Wildlife Refuge, portions of which also form part of the Canaveral National Seashore (see TITUSVILLE). Approximately three million visitors annually pass through SPACEPORT USA, the vistor center and starting point for the Center's tours, making the Kennedy Space Center one of the major tourist attractions in the state.

What to See and Do

SPACEPORT USA. Kennedy Space Center's visitor center offers films, exhibits and displays on the past, present and future of space exploration. Available activities include the IMAX Theater, in which the films *The Dream Is Alive* and *Blue Planet* are shown on a 70-foot-wide, 5-story-high screen ($4); "Satellites and You," a 45-minute, simulated journey through a future space station; the Gallery of Space Flight, which displays authentic Mercury, Gemini and Apollo Space capsules and a genuine moon rock; and the outdoor Rocket Garden, where rockets of all types and sizes are displayed. Also at Spaceport USA are the NASA Art Exhibit, the Space Art Gallery and the 42-foot by 50-foot Astronauts Memorial, with the names of the 16 astronauts who have died in the line of duty etched into the surface. Cafeteria, gift shop. Free cameras; free kennel facilities; free parking. Free wheelchairs avail. (Daily; closed Dec 25)   **Free.**   From SPACEPORT USA visitors may take

Bus tours. There are two regularly scheduled, two-hour, guided bus tours, the red and and the blue, aboard double-decker buses from a fleet of 38. Note: Tour routes and availability may be altered because of launch operations. Phone 407/452-2121. The fee for each tour is $7.

Red Tour through Kennedy Space Center includes a simulated launch countdown of the Apollo 11 moon mission. Visitors also view an authentic lunar lander on a lunarscape and are invited to walk around a Saturn V rocket at the Vehicle Assembly Building. Tour also includes a stop near space shuttle launch pads A & B, launch complex 39, where visitors may take photographs.

Blue Tour through Cape Canaveral Air Force Station, the site of early space launches, includes the Air Force Space Museum and mission control for the Mercury and Gemini programs.

(For general and launch information contact SPACEPORT USA, Mail Code TWRS, 32899, phone 407/452-2121.)

(For accommodations see Cocoa, Cocoa Beach, Titusville)

Key Biscayne (E-5)

Pop: 8,854 **Elev:** 10 ft **Area code:** 305 **Zip:** 33149

What to See and Do

1. **Crandon Park.** Beach, cabanas (fee). Golf; marina facilities. Picnic grove, grills, concessions, restaurant. "Pathway to the Sea," specially designed swimming facility for the disabled. (Daily) Parking fee.

2. **Bill Baggs Cape Florida State Recreation Area.** 1200 S Crandon Blvd, off US 1, at S end of island. Approx 900 acres with historic Cape Florida Lighthouse, southern Florida's oldest structure, and replica of the lightkeeper's dwelling. Tours of lighthouse complex; four departures (Thurs–Mon). Swimming; fishing. Bicycle & nature trails. Picnicking, concession. Standard hrs, fees. Phone 361-5811.

(For further information contact the Chamber of Commerce, 95 W McIntire, phone 361-5207; or the Greater Miami Convention & Visitors Bureau, 701 Brickell Ave, Suite 2700, Miami 33131, phone 539-3000.)

Annual Event

Lipton Championship Miami-Dade. Tennis Center. Major two-week tournament attracting top-ranked players. Phone 446-2200. Late Mar.

(For accommodations see Coral Gables, Hollywood, Miami, Miami Beach)

Key Largo (F-5)

Pop: 11,336 **Elev:** 5–14 ft **Area code:** 305 **Zip:** 33037

This island at the north end of the Florida Keys (see) is the longest of the chain. Extending some 30 miles, but seldom more than 2 miles wide, it shares its name with the village. The Overseas Highway (US 1) crosses the first bridge at Jewfish Creek to start its southwestward stretch across the keys to Key West. Scattered on the island are marinas catering to the ever-present fishermen and skin divers.

What to See and Do

1. **Dolphins Plus.** S via Ocean Bay Dr. Research and education center concentrating on the interaction between humans and dolphins; visitors can watch or participate in three- to four-hour programs (res required to participate; experienced swimmers only; equipment provided). Min age 10 yrs; under age 18 must be accompanied by an adult. Programs for the disabled. (2 sessions daily) Phone 451-1993. Program participants ¢¢¢¢ Non-participant observers ¢¢

2. **John Pennekamp Coral Reef State Park.** NE off US 1, mile marker 102.5. The first underwater park in the US, John Pennekamp lies just off the east coast of Key Largo, parallel to its shore. The

55,011-acre park, covering an area more than 21 miles long and more than 3 miles wide, contains fantastic marine and plant life, 650 varieties of tropical fish, brilliantly colored living coral and the wrecks of many ships—a mecca for skin divers and underwater photographers. Swimming; fishing. Nature trails. Picnicking. Camping. Visitor center. Observation tower. Certified scuba instruction, snorkeling, wading; motorboat and canoe rentals (ramp, marina); and glass-bottom boat tours avail through concession (phone 451-1621). Standard hrs, fees. Phone 451-1202. Also in park are

Boat tours over coral reef. Glass-bottom boat cruises (2½ hrs; three departures daily, weather permitting). Scuba and snorkel tours, instruction, rentals; boat rentals. Phone 451-1621. Cruises ¢¢¢¢–¢¢¢¢¢

3. **Jules' Undersea Lodge.** Off US 1, mile marker 103.2, adj to John Pennekamp Coral Reef State Park (see #2). World's only underwater "hotel," five fathoms deep. Designed to accommodate six divers, the Lodge has an entertainment center, fully stocked galley, dining area, bathrooms and 42-inch windows. Available for three-hour or overnight stays. Contact Jules' Habitat Inc, PO Box 3330; 451-2353. ¢¢¢¢¢

(For further information contact the Key Largo Chamber of Commerce, 105950 Overseas Highway; 451-1414 or 800/822-1088.)

Annual Event

Island Jubilee. Harry Harris County Park, mile marker 92.5. Three-day festival with Caribbean flair; arts & crafts, music, entertainment, concessions. 2nd wkend Nov.

(See Islamorada)

Motels

★★**BEST WESTERN THE SUITES AT KEY LARGO.** *201 Ocean Dr, on Overseas Hwy (US 1) at mile marker 100.* 305/451-5081; FAX 305/451-4173. 39 kit. suites, 2 story. Mid-Dec-mid-Apr: kit. suites $125–$150; each addl $10; under 12 free; wkly rates; diving, fishing, honeymoon plans; lower rates rest of yr. Crib free. Pool. Complimentary continental bkfst. Restaurant nearby. Ck-out 11 am. Covered parking. Balconies. Picnic tables, grills. On canal; marina, dockage. Cr cds: A, C, D, DS, MC, V.

★★★**HOLIDAY INN.** *99701 Overseas Hwy (US 1), at mile marker 100.* 305/451-2121; FAX 305/451-5592. 132 rms, 2 story. Dec-Apr: S, D $129–$165; each addl $10; under 18 free; varied lower rates rest of yr. Crib free. TV; cable. 2 heated pools; whirlpool. Restaurant 6:30 am-10:30 pm. Rm serv. Bar 11 am-10 pm. Ck-out 11 am. Coin lndry. Meeting rms. Sundries. Some minibars. On deepwater channel; marina, glass-bottom boat tours. Home port to original *African Queen* used in Humphrey Bogart movie of same name. Cr cds: A, C, D, DS, ER, MC, V, JCB.

★★**HOWARD JOHNSON.** *(Box 1024) On Overseas Hwy (US 1), at mile marker 102.* 305/451-1400. 100 rms, 2 story. Mid-Dec-Apr: S, D $90–$250; each addl $10; under 18 free; lower rates rest of yr. Crib free. TV; cable. Pool. Restaurant 6 am-midnight. Bar 2 pm-2 am. Ck-out noon. Coin lndry. Gift shop. Lawn games. Some refrigerators. On beach; dock. Cr cds: A, C, D, DS, ER, MC, V, JCB.

✔★★★**PORT LARGO RESORT & MARINA.** *99751 Overseas Hwy (US 1), at mile marker 100.* 305/451-3939; FAX 305/451-5592. 56 rms, 3 story, 26 suites. Dec-Apr: S, D $90–$115; suites $180–$250; under 18 free; lower rates rest of yr. Crib avail. TV; cable. Pool. Restaurant adj 6:30 am-10:30 pm. Ck-out 11 am. Coin lndry. Free covered

parking. Minibars. Balconies. On harbor. Cr cds: A, C, D, DS, ER, MC, V, JCB.

Motor Hotels

★★★**MARINA DEL MAR.** *527 Caribbean Dr, at mile marker 100.* 305/451-4107; res: 800/451-3483; FAX 305/451-1891. 76 units, 2–4 story, 28 kit. suites. Dec-Apr: S, D $110–$160; suites $160–$330; wkly rates; lower rates rest of yr. Crib $5. TV; cable. Pool; whirlpool; poolside serv. Complimentary continental bkfst. Restaurant 11 am–11 pm. Bar to 2 am; entertainment, dancing. Ck-out 11 am. Coin lndry. Meeting rm. Tennis. Boat rentals. Refrigerators; many in-rm whirlpools. Private patios, balconies. Located on a deep-water canal, full-service marina with dive shop, fishing fleet. Cr cds: A, C, D, DS, MC, V.

★★★**SHERATON-KEY LARGO RESORT.** *97000 Overseas Hwy (US 1).* 305/852-5553; res: 800/826-1006 (FL); FAX 305/852-8669. 200 rms, 4 story, 10 suites. Mid-Dec-Apr: S, D $175–$250; each addl $15; suites $405; under 17 free; mid-wk plans; lower rates rest of yr. Crib free. TV; cable. 2 heated pools; whirlpool, poolside cafe, bar. Restaurant 6–11 pm. Bar 11–2 am; entertainment exc Sun; dancing nightly. Ck-out 11 am. Convention facilities. Concierge. Gift shop. Beauty shop. Lighted tennis. Minibars. Bathrm phone in suites. Private patios, balconies. West Indies decor. On private beach; pier, dockage. Boat rentals: sailing, windsurfing, scuba diving. 2,000-ft wooded nature trail. Cr cds: A, C, D, DS, ER, MC, V.

Restaurant

✔★★★**ITALIAN FISHERMAN.** *10400 Overseas Hwy (US 1), at mile marker 104.* 305/451-4471. Hrs: 11 am–10 pm; early-bird dinner 4–6 pm. Italian menu. Bar. Semi-a la carte: lunch $3.95–$8.95, dinner $6.95–$15.95. Child's meals. Specialties: linguine marechiaro, char-grilled fish. Parking. Outdoor dining on waterfront. Facing gulf, swimming pool. Cr cds: A, MC, V.

Key West (F-4)

Founded: 1822 **Pop:** 24,832 **Elev:** 5 ft **Area code:** 305 **Zip:** 33040

This southernmost city of the continental US, on the final inhabited island in the string of Florida Keys, is enjoying its busiest days since 1890, when it was the largest city in Florida. Key West is noted for its nineteenth-century gingerbread houses, first introduced to the island by Bahamian settlers. It is also a city of Cuban foods and dialects that have been assimilated into the culture since the time of the big cigar industry, almost a century ago.

Perhaps Ponce de Leon was the first to spot the island, but Florida Indians often made their way here to trade or battle. The original name was "Cayo Hueso," Spanish for Bone Island. English, Bahamians, Cubans, New Englanders and Southerners came to settle here and prospered from salvaging wrecked ships, cigarmaking, sponge gathering, turtling, shrimping and fishing.

Following its early burst of prosperity, the city went bankrupt in the 1930s; an ambitious rehabilitation program was ended by the hurricane that wiped out the Overseas Railroad. However, completion of the Overseas Highway in 1938, along the existing route of the defunct railroad, signaled the start of Key West's present-day affluence. Today, tourism, followed by shrimping and fishing, sustain the economy.

What to See and Do

1. **Ernest Hemingway House Museum** (1851). 907 Whitehead St. Spanish-Colonial-style house of native stone purchased in 1931 by Hemingway, an early "discoverer" of Key West who wrote many of his books here, including *For Whom the Bell Tolls* and *The Snows of Kilimanjaro*. Original furnishings, memorabilia; trees and plants from the Caribbean and other parts of the world, most collected and planted by Hemingway. (Daily) Phone 294-1575. ¢¢¢

2. **Harry S Truman Little White House.** 111 Front St. Vacation home of the 33rd president, who spent eleven working vacations in Key West between 1946–1952. Restored to period with original Truman furnishings. Guided tours; video. (Daily) Phone 294-9911. ¢¢¢

3. **Audubon House and Gardens.** 205 Whitehead St, at Greene St. Gracious antebellum house of sea captain and wrecker John Geiger contains outstanding collection of 18th- and 19th-century furnishings and re-creates the ambiance of the exciting early days of Key West, when Audubon visited the island. Many of the artist's original engravings on display. (Daily) Phone 294-2116. ¢¢

4. **Curry Mansion** (1899). 511 Caroline St. A 26-room Victorian mansion built for the son of Florida's first millionaire; original Audubon prints, period antiques and Tiffany glass; Ernest Hemingway's elephant gun. Self-guided tours. Guest rooms avail (see INNS). (Daily) Phone 294-5349. Tours ¢¢

5. **Key West Lighthouse Museum.** 938 Whitehead St. Exhibits depicting the unique maritime history of the Florida Keys. Tower is open to the public. (Daily; closed Dec 25) Phone 294-0012. ¢¢

6. **East Martello Gallery and Museum.** 3501 S Roosevelt Blvd (FL A1A), at SE end of island. Housed in well-preserved fort constructed in 1861. Changing art exhibits; permanent exhibits depicting history of Florida Keys; antique collections; tropical courtyard garden. Lookout tower. (Daily; closed Dec 25) Phone 296-3913. ¢¢

7. **Wrecker's Museum** (ca 1830). 322 Duval St. The Oldest House in Key West, built with a unique "conch" construction. Once the house of sea captain and wrecker Francis B. Watlington, the museum now houses displays of Key West's wrecking industry, historic documents, ship models, toys, antiques, furnished 1850s doll house. Also old kitchen house and large garden. (Daily) Phone 294-9502. ¢

8. **Key West Aquarium.** Wall & Whitehead Sts. Unique and colorful specimens of sea life from the Gulf of Mexico and the Atlantic Ocean; "touch tank" allows visitors to touch and examine live starfish, horseshoe crabs, sea squirts, sea urchins, conchs and more; watch sharks being hand fed. Guided, narrated tours. (Daily) Sr citizen rate. Phone 296-2051. ¢¢¢

9. **Sunset Celebration—Mallory Pier.** 1 blk from end of Duval St. A roisterous mixture of carnival midway and street-theater entertainment by scores of jugglers, magicians, sword-swallowers and others that draws crowds of spectators each night, especially in season. (Nightly, beginning about 2 hrs before sunset until 2 hrs after). Phone 272-7700 (Key West Cultural Preservation Society). **Free.**

10. **Fishing.** These are some of the best fishing waters in the world. From bridge catwalks, docks, small boats or from many charter boats (fee). Launching ramps at Garrison Bight (fee).

11. **Swimming.** Public areas include Higgs Beach, between White & Reynolds Sts; Smathers Beach, on S Roosevelt Blvd.

12. **Sightseeing and cruises.**

    Personalized Tours of Key West and the Keys. Two- to three-hour personalized auto or walking tours; also step-on guided bus tours. (Daily) Phone 292-8687. ¢¢¢¢

    Conch Tour Train. Board at Mallory Square Depot or Roosevelt Blvd Depot. Fourteen-mile narrated tour (1½ hrs) of the island on a trackless train visiting more than 100 sites. (Daily) No pets. Phone 294-5161. ¢¢¢¢

    Old Town Trolley. Narrated, 1½-hour tours of Key West. Departs every 30 minutes from Mallory Square Depot. (Daily) Phone 296-6688. ¢¢¢¢

    Captain's Corner Charters. At foot of Duval St, behind Ocean Key House Hotel. One-hour narrated history tours on the harbor at sunset. Also snorkeling (equipment provided), scuba diving, fishing charters; sea planes to Dry Tortugas National Park (see). Phone 296-8865. ¢¢¢–¢¢¢¢

    Reef cruises. From N end of Duval St. Two-hour trips in glass-bottom sightseeing boat *Fireball* from Gulf to ocean over coral reef. (Daily, weather permitting) For reservations, phone 296-6293. ¢¢¢¢¢

13. **Industrial tour. Key West Hand Print Fabrics.** 201 Simonton St. View the design and production of hand-screened printed fabrics. (Mon–Fri) Phone 294-9535. **Free.**

14. **Dry Tortugas National Park** (see). 68 mi W, reached by seasonal boat or seaplane; contact chamber of commerce for information.

(For further information contact the Greater Key West Chamber of Commerce, 402 Wall St; 294-2587.)

Annual Events

Old Island Days. House and garden tours; orchid & art shows; conch shell-blowing contest. Usually late Feb.

Hemingway Days. Short story competition, "Papa" Hemingway look-alike contest, arm-wrestling, storytelling Caribbean street festival. 3rd full wk July.

(See Big Pine Key, Marathon)

Motels

✔ ★**BEST WESTERN HIBISCUS.** *1313 Simonton St.* 305/294-3763; FAX 305/293-9243. 61 rms, 2 story, 15 kit. units. Late Dec–Mar: S, D $99–$149; suites $169; kit. units $159; higher rates: hols, Christmas Fantasy Fest; lower rates rest of yr. Crib $7. TV; cable. Heated pool; whirlpool. Complimentary continental bkfst. Restaurant opp 7 am–10 pm. Ck-out 11 am. Refrigerators. Cr cds: A, C, D, DS, ER, MC, V.

D ☞ ◎ SC

★★**BEST WESTERN KEY AMBASSADOR.** *3755 S Roosevelt Blvd (FL A1A), near Intl Airport.* 305/296-3500; FAX 305/296-9961. 100 rms, 2 story. Dec–Mar: S, D $160–$195; each addl $10–$15; higher rates: hol periods, special events; varied lower rates rest of yr. Crib free. TV; cable. Heated pool; poolside serv. Complimentary continental breakfast. Restaurant nearby. Ck-out noon. Coin lndry. Free airport transportation. Lawn games. Refrigerators. Private screened balconies. Picnic tables, grills. Cr cds: A, C, D, DS, MC, V.

☞ ✕ ◎

✔ ★★**BLUE MARLIN.** *1320 Simonton St.* 305/294-2585; res: 800/523-1698 (exc FL), 800/826-5303 (FL). 53 units, 2 story, 10 kits. Late Dec–Apr: S, D $84–$135; each addl $7–$10; kit. units $7–$10 addl (3-night min); under 6 free; higher rates: hols, special events; lower rates rest of yr. Crib $7. TV; cable. Heated pool. Complimentary coffee. Restaurant nearby. Ck-out 11 am. Refrigerators. Cr cds: A, C, D, DS, MC, V.

☞ ◎ SC

★**ECONO LODGE.** *3820 N Roosevelt Blvd (FL A1A).* 305/294-5511; FAX 305/294-5511, ext 7436. 145 rms, 6 story, 17 kits. Mid-Dec–late Apr: S, D $95.50–$250; each addl $10; under 18 free; higher rates: hols, special events; varied lower rates rest of yr. Crib free. TV; cable. Pool. Restaurant open 24 hrs. Bar. Ck-out 11 am. Coin lndry. Cr cds: A, C, D, DS, ER, MC, V, JCB.

☞ ⊘ ◎ SC

★★**HAMPTON INN.** *2801 N Roosevelt Blvd (FL A1A).* 305/294-2917; FAX 305/296-0221. 158 rms, 2 story. Dec–Apr: S $135–$155;

D $145–$165; under 18 free; higher rates: hols, some special events; lower rates rest of yr. Crib free. TV; cable. Pool; whirlpool. Complimentary continental bkfst. Bar 11 am–11 pm. Ck-out noon. Coin lndry. Gift shop. Some covered parking. Two-level sun deck overlooking bay. Cr cds: A, C, D, DS, MC, V.

[D] [≈] [⊘] [◎] [SC]

★ ★ ★HOLIDAY INN BEACHSIDE. 3841 N Roosevelt Blvd (FL A1A), near Intl Airport. 305/294-2571; FAX 305/296-5659. 222 rms, 2–3 story. Late Dec–Apr: S, D $115–$235; each addl $10; higher rates: some hols, special events; lower rates rest of yr. Crib free. TV; cable. Pool; whirlpool, poolside bar. Restaurant 7 am–2 pm, 5–10 pm. Rm serv 7 am–10 pm. Bar 11–1 am. Ck-out noon. Meeting rms. Lighted tennis. Gift shop. Some refrigerators. Private sunning beach; water sport equipt avail. Cr cds: A, C, D, DS, MC, V, JCB.

[D] [🔑] [≈] [✕] [⊘] [◎] [SC]

★ ★HOWARD JOHNSON. 3031 N Roosevelt Blvd (FL A1A). 305/296-6595; FAX 305/296-8351. 64 rms, 2 story. Late Dec–late Apr: S, D $100–$199; each addl $10; under 18 free; higher rates: hols, special events; lower rates rest of yr. Crib free. TV. Pool. Restaurant 6 am–10 pm. Ck-out 11 am. Private patios, balconies. Courtyard. On Gulf. Cr cds: A, C, D, DS, MC, V, JCB.

[≈] [◎] [SC]

★KEY LODGE. 1004 Duval St. 305/296-9915 or -9750; res: 800/458-1296. 24 rms, 7 kit. units. Mid-Dec–Apr: S, D $130–$138; each addl $15; kit. units $135–$148; higher rates: hols, special events; lower rates rest of yr. TV; cable. Heated pool. Restaurant nearby. Ck-out 11 am. Refrigerators. Cr cds: A, DS, MC, V.

[🔑] [≈]

★ ★LA MER. 506 South St. 305/296-5611; res: 800/354-4455; FAX 305/294-8272. 11 units, 2 story, 5 kits. Late Dec–Apr: D, kit. units $170–$240; lower rates rest of yr. Children over 12 yrs only. TV; cable. Pool privileges adj. Complimentary continental bkfst. Restaurant adj. Ck-out 11 am. Private balconies, porches. On ocean. Cr cds: A, MC, V.

[≈] [⊘] [◎]

★ ★PELICAN LANDING. 915 Eisenhower Dr. 305/296-7583; res: 800/527-8108; FAX 305/296-7792. 32 rms, 4 story, 16 kit. suites. Mid-Dec–Apr: S, D $125; each addl $20; kit. suites $225–$475; under 16 free; wkly rates; lower rates rest of yr. Crib free. TV; cable. Pool. Complimentary coffee in lobby. Restaurant nearby. Ck-out 11 am. Balconies. Picnic tables, grills. Marina. Cr cds: A, C, D, DS, MC, V.

[⊷] [≈] [◎] [SC]

★ ★QUALITY INN. 3850 N Roosevelt Blvd (FL A1A). 305/294-6681; FAX 305/294-5618. 148 rms, 2–4 story. Jan–mid-Apr: S, D $99–$199; each addl $10–$15; kit. units, apts $101–$189; under 18 free; higher rates: hols, special events; lower rates rest of yr. TV; cable. Pool. Coffee in rms. Restaurant open 24 hrs. Rm serv 7 am–11 pm. Bar 11:30–2 am. Ck-out 11 am. Coin lndry. Conch tour leaves from depot on property. Cr cds: A, C, D, DS, ER, MC, V, JCB.

[D] [≈] [⊘] [◎] [SC]

✔ ★ ★SANTA MARIA. 1401 Simonton St, at South St. 305/296-5678; res: 800/821-5397. 51 rms, 2 story, 16 kits. Late Dec–late Apr: S, D $95–$155; each addl $20; kit. units $95–$130; under 12 free; higher rates Dec 25; lower rates rest of yr. Crib $10. TV; cable. Heated pool; poolside serv. Restaurant 7 am–2:30 pm. Rm serv. Bar. Ck-out noon. Balconies. Cr cds: A, DS, MC, V.

[≈] [◎]

★SOUTH BEACH OCEANFRONT. 508 South St. 305/296-5611; res: 800/354-4455; FAX 305/294-8272. 47 rms, 2 story. Mid-Dec–mid-Apr: S $99; D, kit. units $155–$200; each addl $15; lower rates rest of yr. Crib free. TV; cable. Pool. Restaurant nearby. Ck-out 11 am. On ocean; pier. Cr cds: A, MC, V.

[⊷] [≈] [⊘] [◎]

★SOUTHERNMOST. 1319 Duval St. 305/296-6577; res: 800/354-4455; FAX 305/294-8272. 127 units, 2–3 story. Late Dec–early Apr: S $99; D $115–$180; each addl $15; lower rates rest of yr. Crib free. TV; cable. 2 pools, 1 heated; whirlpool, poolside serv. Ck-out 11 am. Concierge. Bicycle rentals. Ocean ½ blk. Cr cds: A, MC, V.

[≈] [⊘] [◎]

Motor Hotels

★ ★ ★GALLEON RESORT & MARINA. 617 Front St. 305/296-7711; res: 800/544-3030. 96 kit. units, 4 story. Mid-Dec–Apr: S, D $150–$375; wkly rates; higher rates: hols, special events (3- or 5-day min); lower rates rest of yr. Crib free. TV; cable. Heated pool. Deli 7:30 am–9:30 pm. Bar 11 am–midnight. Ck-out 10 am. Some covered parking. Exercise equipt; weights, bicycles, whirlpool, sauna. Picnic tables, grills. Water sport equipt, moped and bicycle rentals. Observation deck; overlooks gulf, marina; private swimming beach. Docking facilities adj. Fishing charters, guides. Cr cds: A, DS, MC, V.

[⊷] [≈] [🚶] [◎]

★ ★HOLIDAY INN-LA CONCHA. 430 Duval St. 305/296-2991; FAX 305/294-3283. 160 units, 7 story. Mid-Dec–early Apr: S, D $97–$385; each addl $15; suites $197–$500; under 12 free; higher rates special events; lower rates rest of yr. Crib free. TV; cable. Pool; poolside serv. Restaurant 7 am–10 pm. Rm serv. Bar 10–2 am; entertainment. Ck-out 11 am. Meeting rm. Bellhops. Concierge. Gift shop. Limited free parking. Some balconies. 1920s decor. Cr cds: A, C, D, DS, MC, V, JCB.

[D] [≈] [⊘] [◎] [SC]

★ ★ ★PIER HOUSE. #1 Duval St. 305/296-4600; res: 800/327-8340; FAX 305/296-7569. 129 rms, 2–3 story, 13 suites. Mid-Dec–late Apr: S, D $275–$500; each addl $35; suites $500–$1,000; lower rates rest of yr. Crib free. TV; cable. Heated pool; poolside serv. Restaurant 7:30 am–11 pm. Rm serv. Bars; entertainment, dancing. Ck-out noon. Meeting rms. Bellhops. Concierge. Sundries. Gift shop. Beauty shop. Exercise rm; instructor, bicycles, treadmills, sauna. Massage therapy. Minibars. Private patios, balconies. Private beach; fishing, sailboat charters. Bicycle, moped rentals. Unusual architecture, in Old Town Key West. Cr cds: A, C, D, DS, ER, MC, V, JCB.

[D] [⊷] [≈] [🚶] [◎]

Hotels

★ ★ ★HYATT. 601 Front St. 305/296-9900; FAX 305/292-1038. 120 rms, 4 story. Mid-Dec–mid-Apr: S, D $265–$355; each addl $40; suites $635; under 18 free; lower rates rest of yr. Valet parking $6. TV; cable. Heated pool; poolside serv. Restaurant 7 am–10 pm. Rm serv 24 hrs. Bar 11–1 am. Ck-out noon. Meeting rms. Concierge. Gift shop. Exercise equipt; weights, bicycles, whirlpool. Refrigerators. Balconies. Bicycle & moped rentals. Sailboat, fishing boat, wave-runner rentals. On gulf; swimming beach. Cr cds: A, C, D, DS, ER, MC, V, JCB.

[D] [≈] [🚶] [⊘] [◎]

★ ★ ★THE REACH. 1435 Simonton St. 305/296-5000; res: 800/874-4118; FAX 305/296-2830. 149 units, 4–5 story, 79 suites. Mid-Dec–mid-Apr: S, D $220–$325; each addl $40; suites $325–$450; under 12 free; lower rates rest of yr. Crib free. TV; cable. Heated pool; steam rm, sauna. Coffee in rms. Restaurants 7 am–11 pm. Bars; entertainment Tues–Sat. Ck-out 11 am. Meeting rms. Concierge. Gift shop. Free covered parking. Refrigerators; minibar in suites. Private patios, balconies. On ocean beach, with pier; sailboats, windsurfing, snorkeling. Traditional Key West architecture. Cr cds: A, C, D, DS, MC, V.

[D] [≈] [◎] [SC]

Inns

★ ★ARTIST HOUSE. 534 Eaton St. 305/296-3977; res: 800/582-7882. 6 rms, 2 story, 4 suites. Mid-Dec–mid-Apr: S, D $125–$150; suites $150–$250; lower rates rest of yr. Children over 10 yrs only. TV;

cable. Complimentary full bkfst in season; continental bkfst rest of yr. Restaurant nearby. Ck-out 11 am, ck-in 2 pm. Whirlpool. Some fireplaces. Some balconies. Queen Anne/Victorian mansion, former residence of Key West artist Gene Otto (1890); Oriental rugs. Botanical garden in courtyard. Cr cds: A, C, D, DS, MC, V.

★ ★ ★**CURRY MANSION.** *511 Caroline St. 305/294-5349; res: 800/253-3466; FAX 305/294-4093.* 15 rms, 2 story. Mid-Dec–mid-Apr: S, D $150–$190; lower rates rest of yr. TV; cable. Heated pool. Complimentary continental bkfst in courtyard. Restaurant nearby. Pianist. Ck-out 11 am, ck-in 2 pm. Rec rm. Refrigerators, wet bars. Some balconies. Beach access. Victorian-style structure adjoining original mansion (1899); wicker furniture, antiques, sitting rm. Cr cds: A, C, D, DS, MC, V.

★ ★**DUVAL HOUSE.** *815 Duval St. 305/294-1666; res: 800/223-8825.* 30 rms, 2 story, 3 kit. suites. No rm phones. Dec–Apr: S, D $120–$145; each addl $15; lower rates rest of yr. Children over 12 yrs only. TV in some rms, sitting rm. Pool. Complimentary continental bkfst. Restaurant nearby. Ck-out noon, ck-in 3 pm. Private patios, balconies. Historic 1880 Victorian houses; antiques, wicker, individually decorated rms. Cr cds: A, D, DS, MC, V.

★**HERON HOUSE.** *512 Simonton St. 305/294-9227; FAX 305/294-5692.* 19 rms in 3 bldgs, 1–2 story. No rm phones. Mid-Dec–mid-Apr: S, D $125–$185; higher rates: hols, Fantasy Fest; lower rates rest of yr. Children over 16 yrs only. TV; some cable. Pool. Complimentary continental bkfst. Restaurant nearby. Ck-out 11 am, ck-in flexible. Balconies. 3 historical houses (1876); orchid garden. Cr cds: A, C, D, MC, V.

★**ISLAND CITY HOUSE.** *411 William St. 305/294-5702; res: 800/634-8230 (exc FL).* 24 kit. suites, 2–3 story. Mid-Dec–mid-Apr: kit. suites $165–$275; each addl $10; under 12 free; wkly rates; higher rates: some hols, special events; lower rates rest of yr. TV. Pool; whirlpool. Complimentary continental bkfst. Restaurant nearby. Ck-out 11 am, ck-in 2 pm. Street parking. Balconies. Grills. Houses built in 1880s. Cr cds: MC, V.

✔ ★**KEY WEST BED & BREAKFAST.** *415 William St. 305/296-7274.* 8 rms, 4 with bath, 3 story. No rm phones. MAP, mid-Dec–Apr: S $79; D $85–$150; wkly rates in summer; higher rates special events; lower rates rest of yr. Complimentary continental bkfst. Restaurant nearby. Ck-out 11 am, ck-in 2 pm. Concierge. Street parking. Whirlpool, sauna. Balconies. Sun decks. Built by shipbuilders (1890). Cr cds: A, MC, V.

★ ★ ★**THE MARQUESA.** *600 Fleming St. 305/292-1919; res: 800/869-4631; FAX 305/294-2121.* 15 rms, 3 story. No elvtr. Mid-Dec–mid-Apr: S, D $175–$200; suites $235–$250; under 16 free; higher rates some hols; lower rates rest of yr. TV; cable. Heated pool. Dining rm (see CAFÉ MARQUESA). Rm serv. Bar. Ck-out noon, ck-in 3 pm. Bellhops. Valet serv. Concierge. Some minibars. Balconies. 10 blks to beach. Historic Greek-revival house (1884); restored. Antiques. Furnishings are a mixture of traditional and tropical. Cr cds: A, D, MC, V.

Resorts

★ ★ ★**LITTLE PALM ISLAND.** *(Rte 4, Box 1036, Little Torch Key 33042) Accessible only by boat or seaplane. A launch to the island departs from the shore station at Little Torch Key, located 28 mi N on Overseas Hwy (US 1) at mile marker 28.5. Pickup service is also available from the airports in both Key West and Marathon. 305/872-2524; res: 800/343-8567; FAX 305/872-4843.* 28 suites in 14 villas and 1 in greathouse. No rm phones. Mid-Dec–Apr: S, D $465; AP, MAP avail; lower rates rest of yr. Children over 12 yrs only. TV and in-rm movies

avail. Heated pool; poolside serv. Complimentary coffee in rms. Dining rm 7:30–10 am, 11:30 am–2:30 pm, 7–10:30 pm. Picnics. Rm serv. Bar; entertainment Thurs–Sun. Ck-out 11 am, ck-in 3 pm. Coin lndry. Bellhops. Valet serv. Concierge. Gift shop. Airport transportation. Sports dir. Sailing cruises, boat rentals, scuba trips, swimming beach. Lawn games. Social dir. Exercise equipt; weights, bicycles, sauna. Massage avail. Fishing guides; clean & store. Minibars, wet bars. Sun balconies. Picnic tables. Herb garden. Small luxury resort occupies all of historic, 5-acre Little Munson Island; once a retreat and fishing camp that hosted many luminaries. The island is a 15-minute boat ride from Little Torch Key; the launch makes the trip each way once an hour. The 14 thatched-roof villas, each with 2 suites, are selectively situated on this beautifully landscaped tropical island. White sand beach; water sports; nature tours. Dockage avail for 12 deep-draft yachts and 8 shallow-draft boats; complete marine center. Spectacular sunset views from terrace. Cr cds: A, C, D, DS, MC, V.

★ ★ ★**MARRIOTT'S CASA MARINA RESORT.** *1500 Reynolds St, near Intl Airport. 305/296-3535; FAX 305/296-4633.* 312 rms. Mid-Dec–mid-Apr: S, D $199–$345; suites $315–$695; under 18 free; lower rates rest of yr. Crib free. Valet parking $9. TV; cable. Heated pool. Free supervised child's activities. Restaurant (see FLAGLER'S). Rm serv 7–1:30 am (in season). Bar 11–2 am; entertainment. Ck-out 11 am, ck-in 4 pm. Convention facilities. Concierge. Free airport transportation. Lighted tennis, pro. Exercise rm; instructor, weights, bicycles, whirlpool. Sailboats, sailboards. Charter boat, snorkeling & scuba diving trips arranged. Bicycle & moped rentals. Refrigerators. On ocean. Cr cds: A, C, D, DS, MC, V, JCB.

★**SUGAR LOAF LODGE.** *(Box 148, Sugar Loaf Key 33044) 13 mi NE on Overseas Hwy (US 1), at mile marker 17. 305/745-3211; FAX 305/745-3389.* 55 rms, 11 kits. Mid-Dec–mid-Apr: S $85; D $90; each addl $10; kit. units $100; under 12 free; lower rates rest of yr. Crib $5. Pet accepted; $10 per day. TV; cable. Pool. Restaurant 7:30 am–2:30 pm, 5–10 pm. Rm serv. Box lunches. Bar; entertainment, dancing Fri-Sat. Ck-out 11 am, ck-in 1 pm. Grocery. Coin lndry. Tennis. Miniature golf. Lawn games. Balconies. Dolphin show. Marina; charter boats. Cr cds: A, C, D, DS, MC, V.

Restaurants

★ ★**A & B LOBSTER HOUSE.** *700 Front St. 305/294-2536.* Hrs: 11 am–9 pm. Closed Sun; also Sept. Bar. Semi-a la carte: lunch $3.95–$23.95, dinner $10.95–$25. Child's meals. Specialties: broiled seafood platter, Florida lobster, prime rib. Overlooks bay, harbor. Family-owned. Cr cds: MC, V.

★ ★**ANTONIA'S.** *615 Duval St. 305/294-6565.* Hrs: 6–11 pm; May–Sept from 7 pm. Res accepted. Northern Italian menu. Beer, wine. A la carte entrees: dinner $12–$22. Specializes in veal, fish dishes. Own pasta. 1883 building; wood paneling, paintings. Cr cds: A, D, MC, V.

★ ★**BAGATELLE.** *115 Duval St. 305/296-6609.* Hrs: 11:30 am–11 pm. Closed Thanksgiving, Dec 25. Res accepted. Caribbean menu. Bars. Semi-a la carte: lunch $6–$12.95, dinner $13.95–$23.95. Specialties: snapper Rangoon, Bahamian conch steak, Jamaican chicken. Outdoor dining. In sea captain's house (1884) in Old Town Key West. Cr cds: A, D, DS, MC, V.

★ ★**BENIHANA.** *3591 S Roosevelt Blvd (FL A1A). 305/294-6400.* Hrs: 5:30–10 pm; Fri, Sat to 10:30 pm. Res accepted. Japanese, Amer menu. Bar. Complete meals: dinner $12.95–$27.50. Child's meals. Specializes in steak, seafood prepared tableside. Parking. Japanese decor, artifacts. Garden. Ocean view. Cr cds: A, C, D, DS, MC, V.

★ ★**THE BUTTERY.** *1208 Simonton St. 305/294-0717.* Hrs: 6–11 pm; summer 7–10:30 pm. Res accepted. Bar. Semi-a la carte: dinner $15.95–$25.95. Specializes in fresh seafood, steak. Tropical decor. Cr cds: A, C, D, MC, V.

★★**CAFE DES ARTISTES.** *1007 Simonton St. 305/294-7100.* Hrs: 6–11 pm. Res accepted. French menu. Bar. A la carte entrees: dinner $18.75–$24.95. Specializes in seafood. Outdoor dining. Cr cds: A, MC, V.

★★**CAFÉ MARQUESA.** *(See The Marquesa Inn) 305/292-1244.* Hrs: 6 pm–midnight; May–Oct from 7 pm. Closed Tues (Memorial Day–late Oct). Res accepted. Bar. Wine list. A la carte entrees: dinner $18–$26. Specializes in fresh local seafood. Parking. Intimate dining area; trompe l'oiel mural on one wall. Cr cds: A, D, MC, V.

D

★★★**FLAGLER'S.** *(See Marriott's Casa Marina Resort) 305/296-3535 ext 7750.* Hrs: 7 am–2:30 pm, 6–10:30 pm; Sun brunch 10 am–2 pm. Res accepted. Bar. A la carte entrees: bkfst $5.50–$10.95, lunch $10–$12, dinner $19–$30. Sun brunch $24.95. Child's meals. Specializes in seafood. Entertainment (dinner). Valet parking. Outdoor dining. Cr cds: A, C, D, DS, ER, MC, V.

D

✔★**HALF SHELL RAW BAR.** *231 Margaret St, Lands End Village. 305/294-7496.* Hrs: 11 am–11 pm; Sun from noon. Bar. Semi-a la carte: lunch, dinner $5.95–$14.95. Specialties: conch chowder, stone crab claws, oysters, clams. Parking. Outdoor dining. Dock. No cr cds accepted.

✔★**LIGHTHOUSE CAFE.** *917 Duval St. 305/296-7837.* Hrs: 6–11 pm; summer from 7 pm. Closed Easter, Thanksgiving, Dec 25. Res accepted. Italian menu. Semi-a la carte: dinner $10.50–$18.50. Specializes in pasta, seafood. Outdoor dining. Cr cds: C, D, MC, V.

★**LOUIE'S BACKYARD.** *700 Waddell Ave. 305/294-1061.* Hrs: 11:30 am–3 pm, 6–10:30 pm; Apr–Oct 11:30 am–3 pm, 7–11 pm. Closed Dec 25. Res accepted. Bar. A la carte entrees: lunch $8–$15, dinner $23–$30. Specializes in fresh local seafood. Outdoor dining. On oceanfront. Built by early Key West wrecker (1909). Cr cds: A, D, MC, V.

★★**MARTHA'S.** *3591 S Roosevelt Blvd (FL A1A). 305/294-3466.* Hrs: 5:30–10 pm; Fri, Sat to 10:30 pm. Res accepted. Continental menu. Bar. Semi-a la carte: dinner $13–$27. Child's meals. Specializes in steak, fresh local seafood. Pianist. Parking. Outdoor dining. Overlooks ocean. Cr cds: A, C, D, DS, MC, V.

D

★★**PALM GRILL.** *1029 Southard St. 305/296-1744.* Hrs: 6–10 pm; Easter–Thanksgiving from 7 pm. Closed Thurs; also Sept. Res accepted. Continental menu. Wine, beer. A la carte entrees: dinner $15.75–$22. Specialties: cold charred lamb with mint & mango, filet of snapper, roast duck. Outdoor garden dining. Cr cds: DS, MC, V.

Kissimmee (C-4)

Pop: 30,050 **Elev:** 65 ft **Area code:** 407

Although this has been cattle country for more than 75 years (Brahma cattle are raised here), Kissimmee is now known as the gateway to Walt Disney World and several other central Florida attractions.

What to See and Do

1. **Walt Disney World** (see). 10 mi NW on US 192.
2. **Flying Tigers Warbird Air Museum.** 231 N Hoagland Blvd. Restoration projects, exhibits and hands-on displays of World War II aircraft; bombers, early primary and advanced training aircraft; antique planes. (Daily) Sr citizen rate. Phone 933-1942. ¢¢¢
3. **Medieval Life.** On US 192, E of US 17/92. Living museum of the Middle Ages features thatched-roofed buildings set along cobblestone streets; demonstrations by tradesmen and artisans, medieval artifacts, replicas of torture chamber and devices, dungeon. (Daily) Phone 396-1518 or 239-0214 (Orlando). ¢¢¢¢¢

4. **Old Town.** 7 mi W on US 192. Replica turn-of-the-century Florida village with brick-lined streets; specialty shops and restaurants; general store; antique hand-carved wooden carousel and Ferris wheel (fees). (Daily) Phone 396-4888. **Free.**
5. **Water Mania.** On US 192, 1 mi E of I-4. A 38-acre water theme park featuring raft rides, 72-foot free-fall slide, speed slides, flumes and surfing ride; wave pool; kiddie slide area. Also beach; volleyball courts; miniature golf; picnicking; locker room, showers; first-aid station. (Jan–Nov, daily) Phone 396-4994 or -2626. ¢¢¢¢¢
6. **Gatorland.** 4 mi N on US 17/92/441. More than 5,000 alligators, plus other animals. Snakes of Florida, Gator Jumparoo and Gator Wrestlin' shows; walkway through natural cypress swamp; alligator breeding marsh with three-story observation tower. (Daily) Phone 855-5496. ¢¢¢
7. **Alligatorland Safari Zoo.** 4 mi W on US 192. Assortment of exotic animals and alligators in nine-acre natural swamp setting. Trail, petting zoo. (Daily) Phone 396-1012. ¢¢¢
8. **Reptile World Serpentarium.** E on US 192, 4 mi E of St Cloud. Indoor reptile displays; observation of venom laboratories with 1,500 specimens; 3 scheduled venom programs. (Daily exc Mon; closed Thanksgiving, Dec 25; also Sept) Phone 892-6905. ¢¢
9. **Green Meadows Farm.** 5 mi S of US 192 on Ponciana Blvd. Two-hour guided tours encourage hands-on experience with more than 200 farm animals, cows for milking, hay rides, pony rides, free pumpkins in Oct. (Daily; closed Thanksgiving, Dec 25) Phone 846-0770. ¢¢¢

(For further information contact the Kissimmee-St Cloud Convention and Visitors Bureau, 1925 E Irlo Bronson Memorial Hwy, PO Box 422007, 34742-2007; 847-5000 or 800/327-9159.)

Annual Events

Silver Spurs Rodeo. Silver Spurs Arena. Phone 67-RODEO. Feb and July.

Bluegrass Festival. Silver Spurs Arena. Mar.

Boating Jamboree. Late Oct.

Official Florida State Air Fair. Kissimmee Municipal Airport. Aerial acrobatics; jet teams; parachuting; static displays. Phone 933-2173. Late Oct or early Nov.

Seasonal Event

Professional baseball. Osceola County Stadium, 1000 Osceola Blvd. Houston Astros spring training, exhibition games, early Mar–early Apr; Osceola Astros, Florida League, early Apr–late Aug. Phone 933-5400 or -2520.

(See Haines City, Orlando, Winter Haven)

Motels

✔★**BEST WESTERN MAINGATE.** *8600 W Irlo Bronson Memorial Hwy (US 192W) (34747).* 407/396-0100; FAX 407/396-6718. 299 rms, 2 story. Mid-Feb–late Apr, June–Aug, late Dec: S, D $60; each addl $10; under 18 free; lower rates rest of yr. Crib free. TV; cable. Pool; wading pool, poolside serv. Cafe 7–11 am, 5:30–10 pm. Bar 5:30 pm–1 am. Ck-out 11 am. Coin lndry. Sundries. Gift shop. Game rm. Cr cds: A, C, D, DS, MC, V.

★**CHOICE SUITES.** *4694 Irlo Bronson Memorial Hwy (US 192) (34746).* 407/396-1780; res: 800/432-0695; FAX 407/396-6249. 134 suites, 2 story. Feb–Apr, June–Aug & late Dec–Jan 1: S, D $64.95–$79.95; each addl $8; under 16 free (max 2); higher rates Christmas; lower rates rest of yr. Crib $5. TV; cable. Pool. Complimentary continental bkfst, coffee. Restaurant adj 6 am–midnight. Ck-out 11 am.

Coin lndry. Airport transportation. Refrigerators. Cr cds: A, D, DS, ER, MC, V.

[D] [⚌] [🚭] [🕐] [SC]

★★**DAYS SUITES.** *5820 Irlo Bronson Memorial Hwy (US 192E) (34746).* 407/396-7900; FAX 407/396-1789. 604 kit. suites (1–2 bedrm), 2 story. S, D $80–$189; each addl $10; under 18 free. Crib free. TV; cable. 3 pools. Playground. Restaurant 6:30 am–10:30 pm. Ck-out 11 am. Coin lndry. Gift shop. Airport transportation. Game rm. Refrigerators. Private patios, balconies. Picnic tables, grills. Cr cds: A, C, D, DS, ER, MC, V.

[⚌] [🚭] [🕐] [SC]

★**HAMPTON INN.** *3104 Parkway Blvd (34746).* 407/396-8484; FAX 407/396-7344. 164 rms, 4 story. Mid-Feb–mid-Apr, mid-June–Aug, mid-Dec–early Jan: S $65; D $84; under 18 free; higher rates Dec 25–Jan 2; lower rates rest of yr. Crib free. TV; cable. Heated pool. Complimentary continental bkfst, coffee. Restaurant nearby. Ck-out 11 am. Bellhops. Valet serv. Game rm. Cr cds: A, C, D, DS, ER, MC, V, JCB.

[D] [⚌] [🚭] [🕐] [SC]

★★**HOLIDAY VILLAS.** *2928 Vineland Rd (34746).* 407/397-0700; res: 800/344-3959; FAX 407/397-0566. 190 kit. suites, 2 story. Mid-Feb–early Apr & mid-June–late Aug: kit. suites $149–$169; family rates; golf plans; higher rates hols; lower rates rest of yr. Crib free. Maid serv wkly (daily serv $20 addl). TV; cable, in-rm movies. Heated pool. Complimentary continental bkfst. Ck-out 11 am. Meeting rms. Bellhops. Airport transportation. Lighted tennis. Golf privileges, greens fee $40–$50, pro, putting green, driving range. Exercise equipt; bicycles, treadmill, whirlpool, sauna. Picnic tables. Grills. Cr cds: A, DS, MC, V.

[🏌] [🏊] [⚌] [🎿] [🚭] [🕐] [SC]

✔★★**HOWARD JOHNSON.** *2323 E Irlo Bronson Memorial Hwy (US 192) (34744).* 407/846-4900; FAX 407/846-4900, ext 333. 200 rms, 2 story. Mid-Feb–mid-Apr, mid-June–mid-Aug & mid-Dec–Jan 1: S, D $29–$84; each addl $5; under 18 free; lower rates rest of yr. Crib free. Pet accepted, some restrictions; $5. Pool. Restaurant 7:30 am–10 pm. Ck-out noon. Coin lndry. Game rm. Cr cds: A, C, D, DS, ER, MC, V, JCB.

[D] [🐾] [⚌] [🚭] [🕐] [SC]

✔★**KNIGHTS INN ORLANDO MAINGATE EAST.** *2880 Poinciana Blvd (34746).* 407/396-8186; FAX 407/396-8569. 101 rms, 22 kits. Late Dec–early Jan, mid-Feb–Apr & mid-June–mid-Aug: S $43.95; D $55.95; each addl $3; kit. units $3 addl; under 18 free; lower rates rest of yr. Crib free. Pet accepted. TV; cable. Pool. Complimentary coffee. Restaurant adj open 24 hrs. Ck-out noon. Coin lndry. Meeting rm. Attractions transportation. Cr cds: A, C, D, DS, ER, MC, V.

[🐾] [⚌] [🚭] [🕐] [SC]

★**QUALITY INN.** *2039 E Irlo Bronson Memorial Hwy (US 192E) (34744).* 407/846-7814; FAX 407/846-1863. 114 rms, 2 story, 54 kit. suites. Feb-Apr, mid-June–early July & mid-Dec: S, D $67–$97; kit. suites $77–$107; under 16 free; lower rates rest of yr. TV; cable. Pool; whirlpool. Restaurant adj open 24 hrs. Ck-out noon. Meeting rms. Airport transportation. Game rm. Cr cds: A, C, D, DS, ER, MC, V, JCB.

[D] [⚌] [🚭] [🕐] [SC]

★★**RAMADA INN ORLANDO WESTGATE.** *(PO Box 421386, 34742) 9200 Irlo Bronson Memorial Hwy (US 192), at jct US 27.* 813/424-2621; FAX 813/424-4630. 198 rms, 2 story. Feb-Apr, June-Aug, most major hols: S, D $65–$85; each addl $8; under 17 free; lower rates rest of yr. Crib free. TV; cable, in-rm movies. Heated pool. Playground. Restaurant 7–11 am, 6–10 pm. Bar 5 pm–midnight. Ck-out noon. Coin lndry. Valet serv. Sundries. Gift shop. Game rm. Refrigerators. Cr cds: A, C, D, DS, MC, V.

[D] [⚌] [🚭] [🕐] [SC]

★★**RESIDENCE INN BY MARRIOTT ON LAKE CECILE.** *4786 W Irlo Bronson Memorial Hwy (US 192W) (34746).* 407/396-2056; FAX 407/396-2909. 160 kit. suites, 2 story. Mid-Dec–late Apr: S, D $115–$169; lower rates rest of yr. Crib free. TV; cable, in-rm movies. Pool; whirlpool, poolside serv. Playground. Complimentary continental bkfst. Bar noon–7 pm. Ck-out 11 am. Coin lndry. Valet serv. Game rm. Lawn games. Refrigerators; some fireplaces. Balconies. Picnic tables, grills. On Lake Cecile; fishing docks, boats, water sports. Cr cds: A, C, D, DS, ER, MC, V, JCB.

[D] [↤] [⚌] [🚭] [🕐] [SC]

✔★★**SLEEP INN-MAINGATE.** *8536 W Irlo Bronson Memorial Hwy (US 192) (34747).* 407/396-1600; res: 800/225-0086; FAX 407/396-1971. 103 rms, shower only, 3 story. June-Aug, late Dec–early Jan & early Feb–early Apr: S, D $44–$64; each addl $5; under 18 free; lower rates rest of yr. Crib free. TV. Pool. Restaurant adj 6 am–midnight. Ck-out 11 am. Airport transportation. Some refrigerators. Cr cds: A, C, D, DS, ER, MC, V, JCB.

[D] [⚌] [🚭] [🕐] [SC]

★★**TRAVELODGE SUITES.** *5399 W Irlo Bronson Memorial Hwy (US 192) (34746).* 407/396-7666; FAX 407/396-0696. 156 suites, 2 story. Feb-Apr & June-Aug: suites $64–$99; higher rates last wk Dec; lower rates rest of yr. Crib free. TV; in-rm movies. Pool; wading pool, whirlpool. Playground. Complimentary coffee in lobby. Restaurant adj open 24 hrs. Ck-out 11 am. Coin lndry. Meeting rms. Gift shop. Airport transportation. Game rm. Refrigerators. Cr cds: A, C, D, DS, ER, MC, V.

[D] [⚌] [🚭] [🕐] [SC]

★★**WYNFIELD INN MAIN GATE.** *5335 Irlo Bronson Memorial Hwy (US 192) (34746).* 407/396-2121; res: 800/468-8374; FAX 407/396-1142. 216 rms, 3 story. Late Dec–Apr, June-Aug: S, D $62–$79; each addl $5; under 18 free; lower rates rest of yr. Crib free. TV. Heated pool; wading pool, poolside serv. Complimentary coffee, tea in lobby. Ck-out 11 am. Coin lndry. Airport transportation. Game rm. Cr cds: A, C, D, DS, MC, V.

[D] [⚌] [🚭] [🕐] [SC]

Motor Hotels

★★**COMFORT SUITES.** *4018 W Vine St (Irlo Bronson Memorial Hwy/US 192) (34741).* 407/870-2000; FAX 407/870-2010. 225 rms, 3 & 5 story. Feb-Aug, late Dec: S, D $78–$98; under 12 free; lower rates rest of yr. Crib $6. TV; cable. Pool; wading pool, whirlpool, poolside serv. Complimentary continental bkfst. Restaurant adj 8 am–11 pm. Bar. Ck-out 11 am. Coin lndry. Concierge. Sundries. Gift shop. Airport transportation avail. Game rm. Refrigerators. Cr cds: A, C, D, DS, ER, MC, V, JCB.

[D] [⚌] [🚭] [🕐]

★★**HOLIDAY INN MAINGATE.** *7300 Irlo Bronson Memorial Hwy (US 192W) (34747).* 407/396-7300; FAX 407/396-7555. 529 rms, 2 story. Feb-Apr, June-Aug, late Dec: S, D $89–$119; each addl $10; under 19 free; lower rates rest of yr. Crib free. TV; cable. 3 heated pools; 2 wading pools, 3 whirlpools, poolside serv. 2 playgrounds. 3 restaurants 6:30 am–midnight. Rm serv. Bar 6 pm–midnight; entertainment. Ck-out 11 am. Coin lndry. Bellhops. Valet serv. Sundries. Gift shop. Airport transportation; free transportation to Walt Disney World. Lighted tennis. Game rm. Cr cds: A, C, D, DS, ER, MC, V, JCB.

[D] [🏊] [⚌] [🚭] [🕐] [SC]

★★**HOWARD JOHNSON FOUNTAIN PARK PLAZA.** *5150 W Irlo Bronson Memorial Hwy (US 192) (34746).* 407/396-1111; FAX 407/396-1607. 401 rms, 4–10 story. Feb-Aug: S, D $69–$98; suites $125–$200; special package plans; lower rates rest of yr. Crib free. TV; cable, in-rm movies. Heated pool; wading pool, whirlpool, sauna, poolside serv. Playground. Supervised child's activities. Restaurant 7 am–11 pm. Rm serv. Bar 11 am–midnight. Ck-out 11 am. Coin lndry. Meeting rms. Bellhops. Valet serv. Gift shop. Lighted tennis. Putting green. Game rm. Lawn games. Paddle boats. Some refrigerators. Balconies. Picnic tables. Cr cds: A, C, D, DS, ER, MC, V.

[D] [🏊] [⚌] [🚭] [🕐] [SC]

★★**HOWARD JOHNSON MAIN GATE.** *7600 W Irlo Bronson Memorial Hwy (US 192) (34747).* 407/396-2500; FAX 407/396-2096. 206 rms, 3–5 story. Mid-Feb-Apr, mid-June–Aug, late Dec: S, D $70–$90; each addl $10; under 18 free; lower rates rest of yr. Crib free. TV. Pool;

wading pool. Restaurant 7 am–10 pm. Ck-out noon. Coin lndry. Valet serv. Sundries. Gift shop. Airport, attractions transportation. Putting green. Game rm. Lawn games. Some private patios, balconies. Cr cds: A, C, D, DS, ER, MC, V, JCB.

★★**HYATT ORLANDO.** *6375 lrlo Bronson Memorial Hwy (US 192) (34747).* 407/396-1234; FAX 407/396-5090. 924 rms, 2 story. Mid-Dec–Apr: S, D $89–$129; suites $200–$700; under 17 free; lower rates rest of yr. Crib free. TV; cable. 4 heated pools; wading pools, whirlpools, poolside serv. 4 playgrounds. Restaurants 6:30 am–11 pm. Rm serv. Bar; entertainment. Ck-out noon. Coin lndry. Convention facilities. Bellhops. Valet serv. Gift shop. Barber, beauty shop. Valet parking. Airport, Walt Disney World transportation. Golf privileges, greens fee $55. Game rm. Balconies. Helipad. Cr cds: A, C, D, DS, ER, MC, V, JCB.

✔★★**QUALITY INN LAKE CECILE.** *4944 W lrlo Bronson Memorial Hwy (US 192) (34746).* 407/396-4455; FAX 407/396-2856. 222 rms, 5 story. Mid-Feb–late Apr, June–late Aug: S $65; D $75; under 18 free; lower rates rest of yr. Crib free. TV; cable, in-rm movies. Pool. Restaurant 7 am–10 pm. Rm serv. Bar 6 pm–1:30 am. Ck-out 11 am. Coin lndry. Airport, attractions transportation. Game rm. Refrigerators avail. Balconies. On lake; pier, various boats avail. Cr cds: A, C, D, DS, MC, V.

✔★★**QUALITY INN-MAINGATE.** *7675 W lrlo Bronson Memorial Hwy (US 192) (34747).* 407/396-4000; FAX 407/396-0714. 200 rms, 5 story. 84 kit. units. Easter–Aug & mid-late Dec: S, D $64–$74; each addl $7; suites $89; kit. units $89; under 18 free; family rates; lower rates rest of yr. Crib free. TV; cable, in-rm movies. Heated pool; wading pool. Restaurant 7–11 am. Bar 4:30 pm–1 am. Ck-out 11 am. Coin lndry. Meeting rms. Sundries. Gift shop. Airport, bus depot transportation. Tennis privileges. 27-hole golf privileges, greens fee $25–$55, pro, putting green, driving range. Game rm. Cr cds: A, C, D, DS, ER, MC, V, JCB.

★★**QUALITY SUITES.** *5876 W lrlo Bronson Memorial Hwy (US 192W) (34746).* 407/396-8040; FAX 407/396-6766. 225 suites (1–2 bedrm), 5 story. Suites $99–$199; under 19 free. Crib free. TV. Heated pool; wading pool, whirlpool, poolside serv. Playground. Complimentary continental bkfst. Restaurant 6 am–10 pm. Rm serv. Ck-out 11 am. Coin lndry. Bellhops. Valet serv. Sundries. Gift shop. Airport transportation. Game rm. Refrigerators. Cr cds: A, C, D, DS, ER, MC, V.

★★★**RAMADA RESORT-MAINGATE EAST AT THE PARKWAY.** *2900 Parkway Blvd (34747).* 407/396-7000; FAX 407/396-6792. 718 rms, 1–8 story. Mid-Feb–Apr, mid-June–late Aug & late Dec: S $82–$95; D $92–$105; each addl $10; under 18 free; Walt Disney World, honeymoon packages; lower rates rest of yr. Crib free. TV; cable. Heated pool; wading pool, 2 whirlpools, poolside serv. Playground. Restaurant 6:30 am–11 pm. Rm serv. Bar 11–1 am. Ck-out noon. Meeting rms. Bellhops. Valet serv. Gift shop. Airport, attractions transportation. Lighted tennis. Game rm. Lawn games. Located on 20 acres; decorative freshwater ponds. Cr cds: A, C, D, DS, ER, MC, V, JCB.

★★**SHERATON INN-LAKESIDE.** *7769 W lrlo Bronson Memorial Hwy (US 192W) (34747).* 407/396-2222; FAX 407/239-2650. 651 rms, 2 story. Mid-Feb–Apr, mid-June–late Aug & late Dec: S, D $79–$127; each addl $12; under 18 free; lower rates rest of yr. Crib $5. TV; cable. 3 pools, 2 heated; wading pools, poolside serv. Playgrounds. Supervised child's activities. Restaurant 7–11:30 am, 5–10 pm. Rm serv. Bar 5 pm–1 am. Ck-out 11 am. Coin lndry. Meeting rms. Bellhops. Valet serv. Sundries. Gift shop. Airport transportation; free transportation to Walt Disney World. Lighted tennis. Miniature golf. Game rm. Lawn games. Refrigerators. On lake; dock, paddleboats. Cr cds: A, C, D, DS, ER, MC, V, JCB.

★★★**SOL ORLANDO.** *4787 W lrlo Bronson Memorial Hwy (US 192) (34746).* 407/397-0555; FAX 407/397-0553. 150 kit. suites, 2 story. Mid-Feb–Apr, late June–late Aug & mid-late Dec: suites $115–$195; under 18 free; MAP avail; lower rates rest of yr. Crib free. TV; cable. Heated pool. Complimentary coffee in rms. Restaurant 7 am–11:30 pm. Bar 7–11 pm. Ck-out 11 am. Coin lndry. Meeting rms. Valet serv. Concierge. Gift shop. Airport transportation. Lighted tennis. Exercise equipt; bicycles, rowers, whirlpool. Lawn games. Game rm. Balconies. Cr cds: A, D, DS, ER, MC, V.

Hotel

★★★**RADISSON INN MAINGATE.** *7501 W lrlo Bronson Memorial Hwy (US 192W) (34747).* 407/396-1400; FAX 407/396-0660. 580 rms, 7 story. S, D $65–$95; each addl $10; suites $125–$275; under 18 free; package rates. Crib free. TV; cable. Heated pool; whirlpool, poolside serv. Restaurant 7 am–10:30 pm. Bar 11–1 am. Ck-out noon. Coin lndry. Convention facilities. Concierge. Lighted tennis. Game rm. Cr cds: A, C, D, DS, ER, MC, V.

Restaurants

★★**CHARLEY'S STEAK HOUSE.** *2901 Parkway Blvd, at Parkway Pavillion Shops.* 407/396-6055 or 239-1270 (Orlando). Hrs: 5–10:30 pm; Fri, Sat to 11 pm. Closed Dec 25. Res accepted. Bar. Semi-a la carte: dinner $9.95–$26.95. Child's meals. Specializes in flame-broiled steak, seafood. Parking. Nostalgic atmosphere; old-time portraits, Tiffany lamps. Cr cds: A, MC, V.

★**KOBÉ JAPANESE STEAK HOUSE.** *2901 Parkway Blvd.* 407/396-8088. Hrs: 5–10:30 pm. Res accepted. Japanese menu. Bar. Semi-a la carte: dinner $9.95–$21.95. Child's meals. Specializes in fresh seafood, aged beef, sushi. Parking. Tableside preparation. Garden-like entrance with pool. Cr cds: A, DS, MC, V.

Unrated Dining Spots

ARABIAN NIGHTS. *6225 W lrlo Bronson Memorial Hwy (US 192W).* 407/239-9223; res: 800/553-6116. Dinner show hrs vary each season. Res accepted. Bar. Complete meals: $29.95; children 3–11, $17.95. Specializes in beef vegetable soup, prime ribs, baked potato. 25 acts with more than 30 characters; featuring Arabian Dancing Horses, performing Lippizaner horses, "Ben Hur" chariot races. Parking. Arabian-style palace decor. Cr cds: A, C, D, DS, ER, MC, V, JCB.

FORT LIBERTY WILD WEST SHOW. *5260 W lrlo Bronson Memorial Hwy (US 192).* 407/351-5151. Performances: 6:30 & 9 pm. Res accepted. Wine, beer. Complete meals: dinner $28.95; children 3–11, $19.95. Specialties: fried chicken & ribs, vegetarian lasagne. Parking. Two hrs of continuous "wild west" entertainment, featuring can-can dancers, cowboys & Indians; seats more than 600. Cr cds: A, D, DS, MC, V.

MEDIEVAL TIMES. *(Box 422385) 8 mi W of I-4 on lrlo Bronson Memorial Hwy (US 192).* 407/239-0214 (Orlando) or 396-1518 (Kissimmee); res: 800/327-4024 (exc FL), 800/432-0768 (FL). Dinner show hrs vary each season. Res required. Bar. Complete meals: adult $27; children 3–12, $19; under 3 free. Specialties: roasted chicken flambé, spare ribs. Shows of medieval tournament competitions including ring piercing, javelin throwing, sword fighting and jousting. Parking. Reproduction of 11th-century castle; costumed servers. Cr cds: A, MC, V.

Lake Buena Vista

(see Walt Disney World)

Lake City (A-3)

Settled: 1824 **Pop:** 10,005 **Elev:** 196 ft **Area code:** 904 **Zip:** 32055

A hub for major highways, Lake City was one of the important towns of early Florida. Nearby farms grow tobacco, which is auctioned in summer in Lake City. Forest products are another source of income, and the discovery of large deposits of phosphate has spurred mining operations near the Suwannee River.

What to See and Do

Osceola National Forest. N & E via US 90, US 441 or I-10. Almost 184,000 acres dotted with ponds and cypress swamps. Swimming; fishing; boating. Hiking. Picnicking. Camping (fee). Fees may be charged at recreation sites. Contact USDA Forest Service, 227 N Bronough St, Suite 4061, Tallahassee 32301, phone 681-7265; or the ranger district office, E on US 90 in Olustee, phone 752-2537. In forest is

    Olustee Battlefield State Historic Site. 15 mi E on US 90. Site of important battle during War Between the States, resulting in a major Confederate victory. Museum exhibits depict battle scenes; period displays. Battlefield trail; annual battle reenactment (see ANNUAL EVENTS). (Thurs–Mon) Phone 752-3866. **Free.**

(For further information contact the Columbia County Tourist Development Council, 601 Hall of Fame Dr, PO Box 1847, 32056; 758-1312.)

Annual Events

Battle of Olustee Reenactment. Mid-Feb.

North Florida Air Show. Oct.

(See White Springs)

Motels

    ★ ★ **HOLIDAY INN.** *(Drawer 1239) On US 90 at jct I-75. 904/752-3901; FAX 904/752-3901, ext 7100.* 328 rms, 2 story. S $44; D $48; under 18 free. Crib free. Pet accepted. TV; cable. 2 pools; wading pool. Playground. Restaurant 6:30 am–2 pm, 5:30–10 pm. Rm serv. Bar 3 pm–1 am, Sun 4–11 pm. Ck-out noon. Coin lndry. Meeting rms. Bellhops. Sundries. Lighted tennis. Golf privileges. Lawn games. Balconies. 27 acres of grounds. Cr cds: A, C, D, DS, MC, V, JCB.

    ✔ ★ **QUALITY INN.** *On US 90 at I-75. 904/752-7550; FAX 904/752-9405.* 120 rms, 2 story. S $30–$40; D $42–$50; each addl $5; suites $40–$60; under 12 free. Crib $5. TV; cable. Pool; whirlpool. Playground. Continental bkfst. Ck-out 11 am. Cr cds: A, C, D, DS, ER, MC, V, JCB.

Restaurants

    ✔ ★ **FIRELITE.** *On US 90, opp Gleason Mall. 904/758-8534.* Hrs: 11 am–9 pm; Fri, Sat to 10 pm; Sun 4–9 pm. Bar. Semi-a la carte: lunch $3.99–$6.99, dinner $6.95–$14.95. Specializes in steak, prime rib, seafood. Salad bar. Cr cds: A, MC, V.

    ★ **ROBERT'S DOCK.** *On US 90E. 904/752-7504.* Hrs: 11:30 am–9 pm; Fri to 10 pm; Sat 4–10 pm; Sun & Mon 11 am–2:30 pm; Sept–May 11:30 am–2 pm. Closed some major hols; also Mon July–Aug. Wine, beer. Semi-a la carte: lunch, dinner $3.25–$18. Child's meals. Specializes in seafood, chicken. Parking. Rustic decor. Situated in pine grove. Cr cds: MC, V.

    ★ **WAYSIDE.** *On US 90 at jct I-75. 904/752-1581.* Hrs: 6 am–11 pm. Closed Dec 25. Res accepted. Bar. A la carte entrees: bkfst $2.29–$4.95, lunch $2.50–$6.95, dinner $4–$18.95. Child's meals. Specializes in steak, southern-style seafood. Parking. Cr cds: A, C, D, DS, MC, V.

Lakeland (C-3)

Settled: 1884 **Pop:** 70,576 **Elev:** 219 ft **Area code:** 813

Located in central Florida, this city takes its name from the 13 lakes within the city limits. Thousands of acres of citrus groves and several citrus packing and processing plants are in the area. Tourism, agriculture and phosphate mining are integral parts of Lakeland's economy.

What to See and Do

1. **Florida Southern College** (1885). (1,700 students) McDonald St & Johnson Ave. The largest single-site group of structures designed by Frank Lloyd Wright is here, including the Annie Pfeiffer Chapel. Permanent exhibit in Frank Lloyd Wright Visitors Center includes multimedia presentation, photographs and drawings (Tues–Fri, limited hrs Sat & Sun). Guided tours (fee). Maps for self-guided tour may be obtained at Visitor Center or Administration Bldg. Phone 680-4597 or -4110.

2. **Polk Museum of Art.** 800 E Palmetto St. Collection of Pre-Columbian Art, Oriental and decorative art; contemporary and historical photography, sculpture; changing exhibits. Student Gallery. Lectures, films, performances. (Daily exc Mon; closed hols; also Aug) Phone 688-7743. **Free.**

(For further information contact the Chamber of Commerce, 35 Lake Morton Dr, PO Box 3607, 33802-3607; 688-8551.)

Annual Events

Sun & Fun EAA Fly-In. Lakeland Municipal Airport, 4175 Medulla Rd. Week-long convention of aviation enthusiasts; exhibitions, workshops, daily air shows. Phone 644-2431. Begins 2nd wk Apr.

Orange Cup Regatta. Lake Hollingsworth. Hydroplane races. Phone 499-6035. Apr.

Seasonal Event

Professional baseball. Marchant Stadium, 2305 Lakeland Hills Blvd. Detroit Tigers spring training; exhibition games. Phone 682-1401. Early Mar–early Apr.

(See Haines City, Zephyrhills)

Motels

    ★ ★ **BEST WESTERN DIPLOMAT.** *3311 US 98N (33805), off I-4 exit 18 S. 813/688-7972; FAX 813/688-8377.* 120 rms, 2 story. Feb–Apr: S, D $65–$82; each addl $6; under 18 free; lower rates rest of yr. Crib $3. TV. Pool; wading pool. Restaurant 7–11 am. Rm serv. Bar 5 pm–2 am, Sun to midnight; entertainment Fri, Sat. Ck-out 11 am. Meeting rms. Valet serv. Exercise equipt; weights, bicycles. Game rm. Cr cds: A, C, D, DS, ER, MC, V, JCB.

✔ ★ECONO LODGE. *1817 E Memorial Blvd (33801). 813/688-9221; FAX 813/687-4797.* 64 rms, 2 story. Feb–mid-Apr: S, D $49–$60; each addl $4; under 18 free; lower rates rest of yr. Crib free. TV; cable. Pool. Complimentary continental bkfst in lobby. Ck-out 11 am. Opp Lake Parker. Cr cds: A, C, D, DS, MC, V.

★ ★HOLIDAY INN-SOUTH. *3405 S Florida Ave (33803). 813/646-5731; FAX 813/646-5215.* 170 rms, 2 story. Jan–Apr: S, D $59.50–$85; each addl $10; suites $59.50–$154; under 18 free; wkend rates; lower rates rest of yr. Crib free. TV; cable. Pool; whirlpool. Complimentary continental bkfst, refreshments. Coffee in rms. Restaurant 6:30 am–2 pm, 5:30–9 pm. Rm serv. Bar; entertainment, dancing Tues–Sat. Ck-out noon. Meeting rms. Bellhops. Sundries. Health club privileges. Cr cds: A, C, D, DS, MC, V, JCB.

Restaurants

✔ ★RAGAZZI'S. *3605 S Florida Ave, at Merchants Walk. 813/646-7427.* Hrs: 11 am–10 pm; Fri, Sat to 11 pm. Closed Dec 25. Italian menu. Bar. Semi-a la carte: lunch $3.95–$9.95, dinner $4.95–$13.95. Child's meals. Specializes in seafood pasta, lasagne. Entertainment Mon & Tues. Parking. Cr cds: A, C, D, MC, V.

★RED FOX GRILL. *1239 E Memorial Blvd. 813/683-5500.* Hrs: 5–10 pm; early-bird dinner 5–6 pm. Closed Sun; Jan 1, Easter, Dec 25. Res accepted. Bar. Semi-a la carte: dinner $8.95–$16.95. Child's meals. Specializes in prime rib, steak, seafood. Parking. Cr cds: DS, MC, V.

[D]

Lake Placid (D-4)

Pop: 1,158 **Elev:** 136 ft **Area code:** 813 **Zip:** 33852

Located in the central Florida ridge country, halfway between the Atlantic and the Gulf, Lake Placid, with more than 27 freshwater lakes nearby, offers excellent bass fishing and boating.

What to See and Do

1. **Historical Society Museum.** 19 Park Ave W. Four-room museum in historic depot displays exhibits of area history. (Sept–May, Tues–Fri; rest of yr, by appt; closed hols) Phone 465-1771 or -5519. **Free.**
2. **Cypress Knee Museum.** 25 mi S on US 27 near Palmdale. Museum of sculpture-like natural cypress knees; factory; catwalk in cypress swamp. Tours (daily). Phone 675-0128. **¢¢**

(For further information contact the Greater Lake Placid Chamber of Commerce, 10 E Interlake Blvd; 465-4331.)

(For accommodations see Sebring)

Lake Wales (C-4)

Pop: 9,670 **Elev:** 147 ft **Area code:** 813 **Zip:** 33853

Industrial manufacturing, citrus groves and canning make up the commercial life of Lake Wales, but its 23 nearby lakes offer boating, fishing and other recreational sports.

What to See and Do

1. **Bok Tower Gardens.** 3 mi N off US 27A. The 205-foot Bok Singing Tower, established by Edward W. Bok on top of Iron Mountain, is the highest point on the peninsula. Built of Georgia marble and Florida coquina, it houses a carillon of 57 bells (ranging from 17 lbs to 11 tons) that provides music throughout the day (tower closed to public); an audiovisual presentation of the tower's interior can be seen at the visitors center. Surrounding the tower are 128 acres of landscaped gardens; self-guided nature trail, walking paths; seasonal flowers; bird observatory. Picnic area, restaurant. Pet hostel (fee). (Daily) Phone 676-1408. **¢¢**
2. **Depot Museum.** 325 S Scenic Hwy. Built as a passenger station by the Atlantic Coast Line Railroad in 1928, this pink stucco structure now houses memorabilia of early Lake Wales; photographs; turpentine, citrus & ranching exhibits; 1916 train car, 1944 diesel engine, 1926 caboose and old train artifacts. (Daily exc Sun; closed hols) Phone 676-5443. **Free.**
3. **Babson Park Audubon Center.** 7 mi S on US 27A in Babson Park. Nature trails; wildlife museum. (Late Apr–Oct, Mon–Fri mornings; rest of yr, Tues–Sat afternoons & Sat mornings; closed major hols) Phone 638-1355. **Free.**
4. **Lake Kissimmee State Park.** 15 mi E off FL 60, on Camp Mack Rd. More than 5,000 acres bordered by lakes Kissimmee, Tiger and Rosalie. The lakes, flood plain prairies, marshes and pine flatwoods form scenic panoramas where wildlife such as white-tailed deer, bald eagles, sand hill cranes and turkey may be seen. Live oak hammocks and swamps offer additional habitat for other wildlife, including bobcats and Florida scrub jays. Fishing; boating (marina, ramp, docks). Hiking. Picnicking, concession. Primitive & improved camping. Observation platform. Standard hrs, fees. Phone 696-1112. In the park is

    Kissimmee Cow Camp. Re-creation of a Florida frontier cow camp (ca 1875). The history of the region and era is portrayed the way it actually happened by ''cow hunters'' as they round up scrub cows, share campfire coffee and talk to visitors about their life and work. Tours (Sat, Sun & hols).

    (For further information contact the Lake Wales Area Chamber of Commerce, 340 W Central Ave, PO Box 191; 676-3445.)

Seasonal Event

Black Hills Passion Play. Amphitheater, 2 mi S on US 27A. Same cast as Black Hills, South Dakota, production. Tues, Thurs, Sat & Sun evenings; matinees Wed; extra performance on Good Friday. Phone 676-1495. Lenten season, mid-Feb–mid-Apr.

(See Haines City, Winter Haven)

Motel

✔ ★ECONO LODGE. *(Box 1637) 501 S US 27, 1¼ mi S of FL 60. 813/676-7963.* 48 rms, 2 story. Jan–mid-Apr: S $41.50; D $45.50–$48.50; each addl $5; under 19 free; higher rates special events; lower rates rest of yr. Crib free. TV; cable. Restaurant adj open 24 hrs. Ck-out 11 am. Cr cds: A, DS, MC, V.

Inn

★ ★CHALET SUZANNE. *(Box 3800) Chalet Suzanne Dr, 4 mi N on US 17A, at jct US 27. 813/676-6011; res: 800/433-6011; FAX 813/676-1814.* 30 rms, 1–2 story, 5 suites. S $95–$145; D $125–$185; each addl $12; suites $145–$185; kit. units $145; summer, honeymoon packages. Crib $10. TV; cable. Pool; 5 whirlpools, poolside serv. Complimentary refreshments, sherry. Restaurant (see CHALET SUZANNE). Bar. Ck-out 11 am, ck-in 2 pm. Coin lndry. Meeting rms. Bellhops. Gift shop. Tennis, golf privileges. Lawn games. Swiss chalet style with steeples, spires, gables, balconies; garden features tiles signed by celebrities.

Rms individually decorated, many antiques. On 70 acres overlooking lake; airstrip on grounds. Cr cds: A, C, D, DS, MC, V, JCB.

Resort

★ ★ ★ **OUTDOOR RESORTS RIVER RANCH.** *(PO Box 30030, River Ranch 33867) 24700 FL 60E, 25 mi E of town.* 813/692-1321; res: 800/654-8575; FAX 813/692-9134. 178 units, 1 & 2 story, 80 rms, 24 kits., 58 suites, 16 cottages. S, D $72; kits. $82; suites $100; cottages (1–2 bedrm) $115–$180; RV space (complete hookup) $25–$35; under 16 free; wkly, monthly rates. Crib free. TV; cable. 4 pools, poolside serv. Playground. Free supervised child's activities. 2 dining rms 7 am–10 pm. Snack bar. Bar. Ck-out 11 am, ck-in 3 pm. Grocery. Coin lndry. Package store. Meeting rooms. Beauty shop. Sports, soc dir. Lighted tennis. 9-hole golf, greens fee $8.50–$12, putting green, driving range. Boats (rentals). Bicycles (rentals). Lawn games. Archery; trap & skeet stations. Entertainment, dancing, movies. Rec rm. Game rm. Exercise equipt; weights, bicycles; whirlpool, steam rm, sauna. Guided trail rides. Fishing guides, river cruises. Ranch cookouts, fish fries. Petting corral; hay rides; Sat night rodeos. Some fireplaces. Some private patios. Picnic tables. Grills. Library. 1,500 wooded acres on inland waterway; 5,000-ft lighted airstrip. Cr cds: A, DS, MC, V.

Restaurants

★ ★ ★ **CHALET SUZANNE.** *(See Chalet Suzanne Inn)* 813/676-6011. Hrs: 8–11 am, noon–2 pm, 6–9:30 pm. Closed Mon (May–Nov). Res accepted. Amer gourmet menu. Bar. Wine cellars; also wine cave with cheese & wine tasting. Table d'hôte: bkfst $7.25–$15.95, lunch $27.25–$38.95, dinner $52.50–$69.95. Brunch $18.95. Serv charge 18%. Child's meals. Specialties: chicken Suzanne, lobster Newburg, lump crab. Own baking, soups. Entertainment in season. Parking. Country inn; antiques. View of lake. Chef-owned. Cr cds: A, C, D, DS, MC, V, JCB.

★ ★ ★ **VINTON'S.** *229 E Stuart Ave, at The Marketplace.* 813/676-8242. Hrs: 6–10 pm; Oct–May 11:30 am–2 pm, 6–10 pm. Closed Sun; major hols. Res accepted. New Orleans-style menu. Bar 5–10:30 pm. Wine cellar. Semi-a la carte: dinner $15.95–$19.50. Specialties: filet mignon, shrimp jambalaya. Own baking. New Orleans decor. In historic arcade. Cr cds: A, MC, V.

Lake Worth (E-5)

Settled: 1870 **Pop:** 28,564 **Elev:** 19 ft **Area code:** 407

Adjacent to Palm Beach, Lake Worth offers all the advantages of the Gold Coast without straining the budget; a free local transportation system is in use here. On the west shore of saltwater Lake Worth, which is part of the Intracoastal Waterway and separated from the ocean by Palm Beach, the city maintains beach and recreation facilities. Tourism is the principal activity of this town, named for General William J. Worth, a hero of the Seminole and Mexican Wars.

(For information about this area contact the Greater Lake Worth Chamber of Commerce, 1702 Lake Worth Rd, 33460; 582-4401.)

Seasonal Event

Polo. Usually Jan–Apr.

Gulfstream Polo Field. Approx 8 mi W on Lake Worth Rd, ¼ mi W of Sunshine State Pkwy (FL Tpke). Matches Fri & Sun afternoons. Phone 965-2057.

Palm Beach Polo. 12 mi W on Forest Hill Blvd, then left on S Shore Blvd, in Wellington. Matches Sun afternoons. Phone 793-1440.

(See Boca Raton, Delray Beach, Palm Beach, West Palm Beach)

Motel

★ ★ **HOLIDAY INN WEST PALM BEACH TURNPIKE.** *7859 Lake Worth Rd (33467).* 407/968-5000; FAX 407/968-2451. 114 rms, 2 story. Dec–Mar: S, D $68–$78; each addl $6; under 19 free; varied lower rates rest of yr. Crib free. Pet accepted, some restrictions; $5. TV; cable. Heated pool; poolside serv. Restaurant 6:30 am–2 pm, 5–10 pm. Rm serv. Bar 11 am–11 pm, Sun from 2 pm. Ck-out 11 am. Coin lndry. Meeting rms. Tennis. Cr cds: A, C, D, DS, ER, MC, V, JCB.

Restaurants

★ ★ **BOHEMIAN GARDEN.** *(5450 Lake Worth Rd, Green Acres)* 407/968-4111. Hrs: 5–10 pm; Sun 4–9 pm; early-bird dinner 5–6 pm. Closed Mon; also mid-Aug–mid-Sept. Res accepted. Continental menu. Serv bar. Complete meals: dinner $6.50–$16.95. Child's meals. Specializes in prime rib, seafood, duck. Parking. Outdoor dining. Cr cds: A, C, D, DS, MC, V.

✔ ★ ★ **KRISTINE'S.** *1132 N Dixie Hwy.* 407/588-6540. Hrs: 4:30–9 pm; Sun 3:30–8:30 pm; early-bird dinner Tues–Sat 4:30–6 pm, Sun 3:30–5:30 pm. Closed Mon. Res accepted. French, Italian menu. Serv bar. Semi-a la carte: dinner $9–$15. Child's meals. Specialties: broasted chicken, roast duckling, rhubarb. Salad bar. Parking. Cr cds: D, MC, V.

★ ★ **L'ANJOU.** *717 Lake Ave.* 407/582-7666. Hrs: 5–10 pm; early-bird dinner 5–6 pm. Closed Mon from Mother's Day–Aug; also closed Sept. Res required. French menu. Wine, beer. A la carte entrees: dinner $10.50–$17. Specialties: filet Wellington, veal l'orange, pompano Grenoblois, frogs' legs provençale. Parking. French cafe atmosphere. Cr cds: A, MC, V.

Unrated Dining Spot

JOHN G's. *10 S Ocean Blvd.* 407/585-9860. Hrs: 7 am–3 pm. Closed Jan 1, Dec 25; also Sept. Semi-a la carte: bkfst $3–$8.50, lunch $4–$12. Specialties: cinnamon-nut French toast, eggs Benedict, ethnic omelets. Outdoor dining. Casual atmosphere; view of ocean. No cr cds accepted.

Leesburg (C-3)

Founded: 1856 **Pop:** 14,903 **Elev:** 79 ft **Area code:** 904

The largest city in Lake County with 1,400 named lakes, Leesburg is a base for explorations by skiff, motor launch or houseboat. The economy is based on agriculture and light industry. The largest storage plant in the South for frozen citrus concentrates is located here.

What to See and Do

1. **Venetian Gardens.** Off Dixie Ave. An 80-acre park. Miniature islands; swimming pool (fee); boat ramp. Ball fields. Picnicking. Phone 728-9885. **Free.**
2. **Lake Griffin State Recreation Area.** 3 mi N off US 27/441 in Fruitland Park. Approximately 420-acre area noted for its floating islands—marsh plant life floats on dense soil in several feet of water. Fishing; boating, canoeing (rentals). Nature trails. Picnicking.

Camping (hookups, dump station). Standard hrs, fees. Phone 787-7402.

(For further information contact the Leesburg Area Chamber of Commerce, on US 27/441 in Fruitland Park, PO Box 490309, 34749-0309; 787-2131.)

(See Ocala)

Motel

✔ ★**BUDGET HOST INN.** *1225 N 14th St (34748), jct US 27, 441. 904/787-3534; FAX 904/787-0060.* 50 rms, 2 story, 16 kits. Jan–Mar: S, D $46.50; each addl $4; kits. $51.50; family, wkly rates; lower rates rest of yr. TV; cable. Pool. Restaurant opp open 24 hrs. Ck-out 11 am. Coin lndry. Airport transportation. Cr cds: A, DS, MC, V.

Restaurant

✔ ★★**VIC'S EMBERS SUPPER CLUB.** *7940 US 441. 904/728-8989.* Hrs: 4:30–10 pm; Fri, Sat to 11 pm; early-bird dinner 4:30–6 pm; Sun brunch 11:30 am–2:30 pm. Closed some major hols. Bar 3 pm–2 am. Semi-a la carte: dinner $8.95–$14.95. Sun brunch $10.95. Child's meals. Specializes in pasta, seafood, steak. Entertainment Tues–Sat. Valet parking. Cr cds: MC, V.

Live Oak (A-2)

Pop: 6,332 **Elev:** 102 ft **Area code:** 904 **Zip:** 32060

Florida's oldest and largest tobacco market is here, and the town is transformed during July and August by the frenzy of the tobacco auction. Named for a huge live oak that once provided a shaded campground in the area, this is the seat of Suwannee County, which is bordered on three sides by 100 miles of the Suwannee River. This river was picked from an atlas by Stephen Foster and immortalized in his song "Old Folks at Home," which begins "Way down upon the Swanee River..."

What to See and Do

Suwannee River State Park. 14 mi W on US 90. More than 1,800 acres where the Withlacoochee and Suwannee rivers meet. Suwannee River Canoe Trail, which begins in Georgia, ends at the park (although the river may be canoed below the park as well). Panoramic view of rivers and wooded uplands. Earthworks of Confederate fort, escarpments overlook river. Fishing; boating (ramp). Nature trails. Picnicking (grills). Camping (electric hookups). Standard hrs, fees. Phone 362-2746.

(For further information contact Suwannee County Chamber of Commerce, PO Box C; 362-3071.)

(For accommodations see Lake City, also see White Springs)

Longboat Key (& Lido Beach) (D-3)

Pop: 5,937 **Elev:** 9 ft **Area code:** 813 **Zip:** 34228

Situated between Sarasota Bay and the Gulf of Mexico, Longboat Key, nearly 11 miles long, is surrounded by sand beaches. Discovered in 1593 when Hernando De Soto made his historic landing nearby, Longboat Key did not receive recognition until the early 1900s, when circus

magnate John Ringling took an interest in surrounding Sarasota. The area's beaches provide good surf fishing and swimming; several charter-boat companies provide full- and half-day trips.

(For information about this area contact the Chamber of Commerce, 5360 Gulf of Mexico Dr, Suite 107; 383-2466.)

(See Bradenton, Sarasota)

Motels

★**AZURE TIDES RESORT.** *(1330 Ben Franklin Dr, Sarasota 34246)* 1 mi SW of St Armands Circle Dr in Lido Beach. 813/388-2101; res: 800/326-8433; FAX 813/388-3015. 34 kit. suites, 2 story. Late Dec–early May: kit. suites $175–$289; wkly rates; lower rates rest of yr. Crib free. TV; cable, in-rm movies. Heated pool. Restaurant adj. Bar. Ck-out noon. Coin lndry. Balconies. On gulf. Cr cds: A, C, D, DS, ER, MC, V.

★**DIPLOMAT.** *3155 Gulf of Mexico Dr. 813/383-3791; FAX 813/383-0983.* 50 kit. units, 1–2 bedrm, 2 story. Mid-Dec–Apr (2-day min): S, D $115–$187; children over 12, $8, under 12, $4; lower rates rest of yr. Crib free. TV; cable. Heated pool. Restaurant nearby. Ck-out 11 am. Coin lndry. On beach. Cr cds: DS, MC, V.

★★★**HALF MOON BEACH CLUB.** *(2050 Ben Franklin Dr, Sarasota 34236)* ½ mi W of St Armands Circle in Lido Beach. 813/388-3694; res: 800/358-3245; FAX 813/388-1938. 85 rms, 2 story, 12 suites, 30 kits. Late Jan–Apr: S, D $110–$155; each addl $15; suites $225; kit. units $175–$225; under 17 free; lower rates rest of yr. Crib free. TV; cable. Heated pool; poolside serv. Complimentary coffee in rms. Restaurant 7 am–10 pm. Rm serv. Bar 11 am–11 pm; entertainment wkends. Ck-out 11 am. Coin lndry. Meeting rm. Bellhops. Lawn games. Refrigerators. Balconies. Picnic tables. On Gulf; sun deck. Cr cds: A, C, D, DS, ER, MC, V.

★**HOLIDAY BEACH RESORT.** *4765 Gulf of Mexico Dr. 813/383-3704; FAX 813/383-0546.* 22 rms, 20 kits. Late Jan–Apr: S, D $100; each addl $10; suites $110–$150; varied lower rates rest of yr. Crib $1.50. TV; cable. Heated pool. Restaurant nearby. Ck-out 10 am. Coin lndry. Tennis. Lawn games. Refrigerators. Private patios. On Gulf. No cr cds accepted.

★**SEA CLUB I.** *4141 Gulf of Mexico Dr. 813/383-2431; FAX 813/383-2431, ext 71.* 24 kit. units (1–2 bedrm), 1–2 story. Feb–mid-May: S, D $75–$119; 1-wk min (in season); each addl $5; under 6 free; lower rates rest of yr. TV; cable. Heated pool. Restaurant nearby. Ck-out 10 am. Coin lndry. Private patios, balconies. On Gulf beach. Cr cds: MC, V.

★**SEA HORSE BEACH RESORT.** *3453 Gulf of Mexico Dr. 813/383-2417.* 35 kit. apts (1–2 bedrm), 2 story. Feb–Apr: 1-bedrm $130; 2-bedrm $170; studio rms $110; lower rates rest of yr. Crib free. TV; cable. Heated pool. Restaurant opp 8:30 am–6 pm. Ck-out 11 am. Coin lndry. All rms face Gulf. Cr cds: MC, V.

Motor Hotels

★★★**HARBOUR VILLA CLUB AT THE BUCCANEER.** *615 Dream Island Rd. 813/383-9544; res: 800/433-5298; FAX 813/383-8028.* 38 suites, 3 story. Mid-Dec–Apr: suites $250–$265; each addl $15; wkly, monthly rates; lower rates rest of yr. Crib avail. TV; cable. 2 heated pools; whirlpool. Ck-out noon. Lighted tennis. Bathrm phones. Private patios, balconies. On Sarasota Bay Intracoastal Waterway; view of yacht harbor marina. Cr cds: A, MC, V.

★★**HARLEY SANDCASTLE.** *(1540 Benjamin Franklin Dr, Sarasota 34236) 1 mi SW of St Armand Circle Dr in Lido Beach.* 813/388-2181; FAX 813/388-2655. 179 rms, 2–4 story. Feb–May: S, D $135–$205; each addl $15; suites $275; under 18 free; lower rates rest of yr. Crib free. TV; cable. 2 pools, 1 heated; poolside serv. Restaurant 7 am–11 pm. Rm serv. Bar 5 pm–1 am; entertainment Feb–May. Ck-out 11 am. Coin lndry. Meeting rms. Bellhops. Gift shop. Game rm. Lawn games. Refrigerators. Picnic tables. On beach; water sports, boat & bicycle rentals. Cr cds: A, C, D, DS, MC, V.

★★★**HILTON LONGBOAT KEY.** 4711 Gulf of Mexico Dr. 813/383-2451; FAX 813/383-7979. 102 rms, 5 story. Mid-Dec–Apr: S, D $135–$215; each addl $25; 1-bedrm suites $220–$265; 2-bedrm suites $340–$430; family rates; varied lower rates rest of yr. Crib free. TV; cable. Heated pool. Coffee in rms. Restaurant 7 am–10 pm. Rm serv. Bar 11–1 am; entertainment, dancing. Ck-out 11 am. Meeting rms. Bellhops. Valet serv. Sundries. Tennis. Lawn games. Minibars. Refrigerator in suites. Private patios, balconies. Caribbean decor. On 400-ft beach; cabanas, water sports. Cr cds: A, C, D, DS, MC, V.

★★**HOLIDAY INN-LONGBOAT KEY.** 4949 Gulf of Mexico Dr. 813/383-3771; FAX 813/383-7871. 146 rms, 2–3 story. Mid-Jan–Apr: S, D $173–$215; each addl $10; suites $217–$280; kit. units $228–$270; under 19 free; varied lower rates rest of yr. Crib avail. Pet accepted. TV; cable. 2 pools, 1 indoor, 1 heated; saunas, poolside serv. Restaurant 6:30 am–10 pm. Rm serv. 3 bars 11–2 am; entertainment, dancing. Ck-out 11 am. Coin lndry. Meeting rms. Bellhops. Valet serv. Sundries. Gift shop. Lighted tennis, pro. Putting green. Holidome. Lawn games. Private patios, balconies. On Gulf beach. Bicycles, water sports. Cr cds: A, C, D, DS, ER, MC, V, JCB.

★★**HOLIDAY INN-SARASOTA-LIDO BEACH.** *(233 Ben Franklin Dr, Sarasota 34236) 2 blks W of St Armand Circle in Lido Beach.* 813/388-3941; FAX 813/388-4321. 130 rms, 7 story. Feb–Apr: S, D $145–$200; each addl $10; suites $199–$229; under 19 free; lower rates rest of yr. Crib avail. Pet accepted, some restrictions. TV; cable. Heated pool. Restaurant 7 am–10 pm. Rm serv. Bar; entertainment Fri & Sat. Ck-out noon. Coin lndry. Meeting rms. Bellhops. Valet Serv. Gift shop. Balconies. Opp Gulf beach. Cr cds: A, C, D, DS, ER, MC, V, JCB.

Resorts

★★★**COLONY BEACH AND TENNIS RESORT.** 1620 Gulf of Mexico Dr, 2 mi N of Longboat Key Bridge. 813/383-6464; res: 800/426-5669; FAX 813/383-7549. 235 kit. apts (1–2 bedrm), 2–6 story. Late Dec–Apr: kit. apts $295–$465; beach houses $565–$865; clubhouses $435; beach units $485–$535; family rates; varied lower rates rest of yr. Crib $15. TV; cable. Heated pool; poolside serv. Free supervised child's activities. Restaurants 7 am–11 pm. Limited rm serv. Bar 11–2 am; entertainment, dancing. Ck-out 11 am, ck-in 4 pm. Grocery. Coin lndry. Meeting rms. Gift shop. Airport transportation. 21 tennis courts, some lighted, pro, pro shop. Golf privileges. Boat, sailboard, water sport equipt, bicycle rentals. Exercise rm; instructor, weights, bicycles, whirlpool, steam rm, sauna. Private patios, balconies. On gulf beach. Cr cds: A, D, DS, MC, V.

★★★★**THE RESORT AT LONGBOAT KEY CLUB.** *(PO Box 15000)* 301 Gulf of Mexico Dr. 813/383-8821; res: 800/237-8821; FAX 813/383-5396. 233 units, 4–10 story, 213 kits. Mid-Jan–Apr: rms $195–$285; suites $275–$550; 1-bedrm suites $310–$400; 2-bedrm suites $410–$550; varied lower rates rest of yr. TV; cable, in-rm movies. Heated pool; whirlpool, sauna, poolside serv. Supervised child's activities. Complimentary coffee in rms. Dining rm 7 am–midnight. Box lunches. Snack bar. Rm serv from 6:30 am. Bar from 11 am; entertainment, dancing. Ck-out 11 am, ck-in 3 pm. Meeting rms. Valet serv. Concierge. Pro shops. Airport transportation; also transportation on

site and to area attractions. Activities dir. 38 tennis courts, 6 lighted, pro. 45-hole golf, greens fee $86 (incl cart), pro, putting green, driving range. Private beach, boardwalk; water sports. Boat cruises. Bicycles. Lawn games. Health club privileges. Refrigerators, minibars. Extensive library. Private patios. Bird sanctuary. Elaborate landscaping; luxury resort on 1,000 acres; on Gulf. Cr cds: A, C, D, MC, V.

Restaurants

★★★**CAFE L'EUROPE.** 431 St Armands Circle. 813/388-4415. Hrs: 11 am–11 pm; Sun 5–10 pm. Res accepted. Continental menu. Bar to 1 am; pianist & vocalist Tues–Sat from 7 pm. Extensive wine list. Semi-a la carte: lunch $6–$12, dinner $14–$24. Child's meals. Specializes in New Zealand rack of lamb, roast duck, veal, fresh seafood, bouillabaisse. Own pastries. Valet parking. Located in historic bldg; European atmosphere. Cr cds: A, C, D, MC, V.

D

✔★★**CAFE LE RENDEZ-VOUS AT THE FRENCH HEARTH.** 302 John Ringling Blvd, at St Armands Circle Dr in Lido Beach. 813/388-2313. Hrs: 8:30 am–9 pm; Sun brunch 9 am–3 pm. Closed Thanksgiving. French, continental menu. Semi-a la carte: bkfst $1.95–$5.50, lunch $4.50–$7.95, dinner $9.95–$15.95. Own soups. Outdoor dining. European decor. Cr cds: MC, V.

★★**CHART HOUSE.** 201 Gulf of Mexico Dr. 813/383-5593. Hrs: 5–10 pm; early-bird dinner 5–6 pm. Res accepted. Bar. Semi-a la carte: dinner $9.95–$23.95. Child's meals. Specializes in steak, fresh seafood, prime rib. Salad bar. Own desserts. Parking. View of gulf. Cr cds: A, C, D, DS, MC, V.

D

★★**COLUMBIA.** 411 St Armands Circle. 813/388-3987. Hrs: 11 am–11 pm; Sun noon–10 pm; early-bird dinner 4:30–6 pm. Res accepted. Spanish menu. Bar. Semi-a la carte: lunch $7.45–$10.95, dinner $13.95–$20.95. Cover charge Fri & Sat, $2–$3. Child's meals. Specialties: fresh Gulf red snapper alicante, paella Valenciana. Entertainment Tues–Sat. Spanish decor; statuary, paintings, stained-glass windows. Family-owned. Cr cds: A, C, DS, MC, V.

D

★★★**EUPHEMIA HAYE.** 5540 Gulf of Mexico Dr. 813/383-3633. Hrs: 5–10:30 pm; summer: 6–10 pm; Fri, Sat 5–10:30 pm; Sun 5–10 pm. Closed Dec 25; also 3 wks after Labor Day. Res accepted. Eclectic menu. Bar. Wine cellar. A la carte: dinner $15–$33. Child's meals. Specialties: peppered steak, duckling in orange peppercorn sauce, fresh seafood. Own desserts. Parking. Dessert & gourmet coffee room adj. Cr cds: C, D, MC, V.

D

★★**HARRY'S CONTINENTAL KITCHENS.** 525 St Judes Dr. 813/383-0777. Hrs: 11 am–3 pm, 5–10 pm; Sun brunch 10 am–3 pm. Closed Dec 25; also Super Bowl Sun. Res accepted. Continental menu. Wine, beer. A la carte entrees: lunch $5.95–$14.95, dinner $16.95–$28.95. Specializes in seafood, pasta. Jazz pianist Mon–Wed. Parking. Cr cds: MC, V.

D

✔★★★**THE HUNT CLUB.** 5350 Gulf of Mexico Dr. 813/383-0543. Hrs: 9 am–11 pm; early-bird dinner 4:30–6 pm; afternoon tea Wed & Sat 2–4 pm. Closed Dec 25. Res accepted. British, Amer menu. Bar. Wine list. Semi-a la carte: bkfst $1.95–$6.95, lunch $2.95–$6.95, dinner $8.95–$17.95. Child's meals. Specializes in prime rib, veal. Own bread, desserts. Varied entertainment. Parking. Garden atmosphere; trellis and gazebo accents. Cr cds: MC, V.

D

★★**L'AUBERGE DU BON VIVANT.** 7003 Gulf of Mexico Dr. 813/383-2421. Hrs: 5–10 pm. Closed Sun (exc hols); also Sept. Res accepted. French, continental menu. Wine, beer. Semi-a la carte: dinner

$14.75–$28. Child's meals. Specializes in fresh seafood, duck, sweetbreads. Parking. European ambiance. Cr cds: A, D, MC, V.

★ ★ **MOORE'S STONE CRAB.** *800 Broadway.* 813/383-1748. Hrs: 11:30 am–9 pm; Fri & Sat to 9:30 pm. Closed Thanksgiving, Dec 25. Bar. Semi-a la carte: lunch, dinner $4.95–$21.95. Specializes in fresh seafood, stone crab (in season). Child's meals. Parking. Rustic dining on Sarasota Bay; dockage. Family-owned. Cr cds: MC, V.

★ ★ ★ **OSTERIA.** *29 ½ N Blvd of Presidents, St Armands Circle.* 813/388-3671 or -3672. Hrs: 5:30–10 pm; Nov–May from 5 pm. Res accepted. Northern Italian menu. Bar. Wine list. Semi-a la carte: dinner $10–$28. Child's meals. Specializes in fresh seafood, veal, Angus beef, homemade pasta. Own breads. Vocalist. Upstairs dining area; extensive wine display. Cr cds: A, C, D, DS, MC, V.

✔ ★ ★ **SHENKEL'S.** *3454 Gulf of Mexico Dr.* 813/383-2500 or -5700. Hrs: 9 am–2 pm, 5:30–9 pm. Closed Mon. Welsh, Amer menu. Bar. A la carte entrees: bkfst $2.25–$11.95. Semi-a la carte: lunch $3–$10, dinner $7.95–$16.95. Child's meals. Specializes in egg dishes, steak, chicken pot pie. Own desserts. Entertainment. Parking. On waterfront. Family-owned. Cr cds: A, C, D, DS, MC, V.

Madeira Beach
(see St Petersburg Beach Area)

Marathon (F-4)

Settled: 1818 **Pop:** 8,857 **Elev:** 0–7 ft **Area code:** 305 **Zip:** 33050

Transformed from a little fishing village by developers who have spent $15 million in the area, Marathon has become the hub of the Middle Keys. Its name came when an East Coast Railroad engineer groaned "It's getting to be a marathon," after hearing that the construction of the tracks was to continue southward. Today, tourism and commercial and sport fishing are the mainstream of the economy.

What to See and Do

Museum of Natural History of the Florida Keys. 5550 Overseas Hwy (US 1), at mile marker 50. Exhibits on coral reefs, shipwrecks, Indians, wildlife, pirates; nature trail. Also located here is Florida Keys Children's Museum. (Daily; closed some major hols) Phone 743-9100. **¢¢**

(For further information and a list of fishing tournaments contact the Chamber of Commerce, 3330 Overseas Hwy; 743-5417 or 800/842-9580.)

Annual Event

Key Colony Beach Sailfish Tournament. 3 mi NE on US 1 in Key Colony Beach. Mid-Nov.

(See Big Pine Key)

Motels

✔ ★ ★ **CORAL LAGOON.** *12399 Overseas Hwy (US 1), at mile marker 53.* 305/289-0121. 17 kit. units. Dec–Mar & Aug: S, D $100; each addl $7.50; lower rates rest of yr. Crib free. TV; cable. Pool. Complimentary coffee in lobby. Restaurant nearby. Ck-out 11 am. Coin lndry. Tennis. Private patios, hammocks. Grills. Fishing equipt. Boat docks. Cr cds: A, D, MC, V.

★ **DAYS INN RESORT & MARINA.** *13201 Overseas Hwy (US 1), at mile marker 54.* 305/289-0222; FAX 305/743-5460. 134 rms, 2 story. Mid-Dec–mid-Apr: S, D $110–$130; each addl $6; under 12 free; higher rates special events; lower rates rest of yr. Crib free. TV; cable. Pool; wading pool. Restaurant 6:30–11:30 am, 5–10 pm. Bar. Ck-out noon. Coin lndry. Meeting rm. Gift shop. Refrigerators avail. Dive shop; fishing charters. Cr cds: A, D, MC, V.

★ **RAINBOW BEND RESORT.** *(Rte 1, Box 159) On Grassy Key, 5 mi NE on Overseas Hwy (US 1), at mile marker 58.* 305/289-1505; FAX 305/743-0257. 24 units, 1–2 story, 16 kits. Mid-Dec–mid-Apr: S, D, kit. units $120–$205; each addl $17.50; lower rates rest of yr. Deposit required. Crib free. Pet accepted. TV; cable. Pool; whirlpool. Complimentary full bkfst. Restaurant 7:30–9:30 am, noon–2 pm, 5–11 pm. Ck-out noon. Coin lndry. Free local airport transportation. Picnic tables, grills. On Beach; fishing pier; Boston whaler boats, sailboats, canoes. Cr cds: A, MC, V.

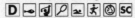

Motor Hotel

★ ★ **SOMBRERO RESORT.** *19 Sombrero Blvd.* 305/743-2250; res: 800/433-8660; FAX 305/743-2998. 124 units, 1–3 story. Mid-Dec–mid-Apr: S, D $115; each addl $10; 2-bedrm suites $240–$280; kit. units $125–$155; under 13 free; lower rates rest of yr. TV; cable. Pool; sauna, poolside serv. Restaurant 11 am–2 pm, 6–10 pm. Bar; entertainment exc Mon. Ck-out 11 am. Coin lndry. Lighted tennis, pro, shop. Some balconies. Picnic tables. Marina; dockage, full hookups. Cr cds: A, D, MC, V.

Resort

★ ★ ★ **HAWK'S CAY.** *(Mile Marker 61, Duck Key 33138) 8 mi N on Overseas Hwy (US 1).* 305/743-7000; res: 800/432-2242; FAX 305/743-5215. 177 rms, 2–5 story, 17 villas. Late Dec–late Apr: S, D $210–$310; each addl $30; suites $325–$600; kit. suites $500; villas (7-day min) $330; under 11 free; lower rates rest of yr. Crib free. TV; cable. Heated pool; whirlpools, poolside serv. Supervised child's activities (summer, hols). Complimentary full bkfst (exc villas). Restaurant 7 am–11 pm. Rm serv. Bar 11–2 am; entertainment, dancing. Ck-out 11 am, ck-in 3 pm. Coin lndry. Meeting rms. Concierge. Gift shop. Free airport transportation. Lighted tennis, pro. 18-hole golf privileges. Private beach, swimming. Marina, boats, glass-bottomed boat, charter boat; wave runners, sailing. Scuba diving, snorkeling. Bicycle rentals. Game rm. Reading rm. Refrigerators. Private patios, balconies. On ocean; dolphin training center. Cr cds: A, C, D, DS, MC, V.

Restaurants

★ ★ **KELSEY'S.** *1996 Overseas Hwy (US 1).* 305/743-9018. Hrs: 6–10 pm. Closed Mon. Res accepted. Bar. Semi-a la carte: dinner $11.95–$29.95. Child's meals. Specializes in rack of lamb, local seafood, beef. Nautical decor. Cr cds: A, MC, V.

✔ ★ **PERRY'S.** *6900 Overseas Hwy (US 1), at mile marker 51.* 305/743-3108. Hrs: 7 am–10 pm. Serv bar. Semi-a la carte: bkfst $1–$3.95, lunch $2.95–$8.50, dinner $6.95–$16.95. Child's meals. Specializes in seafood, steak. Salad bar. Fish tanks. Cr cds: A, C, D, DS, MC, V.

★ ★ **QUAY.** *12650 Overseas Hwy (US 1).* 305/289-1810. Hrs: 11 am–10 pm; Fri, Sat to 11 pm; early-bird dinner 4–6 pm. Res accepted. Bar. Semi-a la carte: lunch $4.50–$9.95, dinner $12.95–$26.95. Child's meals. Specializes in steak, seafood. Entertainment. Parking. Outdoor dining. On Gulf of Mexico. Cr cds: A, C, D, DS, MC, V.

Marco Island (E-4)

Pop: 9,493 **Elev:** 10–52 ft **Area code:** 813 **Zip:** 33937

Marco Island, the largest and northernmost of the Ten Thousand Islands, was once occupied by a cannibalistic tribe of Indians that prevented settlement of the island until the late 1800s. Later, the Doxsee Clam Factory established itself on the island, but it wasn't until the 1960s, when dredges were constructed, that Marco became a flourishing community. Today, the island is noted for fishing and shelling and has been developed as a resort area.

What to See and Do

1. **Marco Island Trolley.** Narrated, 1¾-hour sightseeing tours; more than 100 points of interest; stops at shopping centers, lodgings, restaurants, attractions; also historic Indian Hills area. (9 trips daily; no trips Dec 25) Phone 394-1600. All-day pass ¢¢¢

2. **Collier-Seminole State Park.** 12 mi NE on FL 92. Approx 6,400 acres with historic displays and native plant communities. Fishing; boating (ramp, canoe rentals). Nature trails. Picnicking, concession. Camping (hookups, dump station). Boat tour. Seminole villages nearby. Standard hrs, fees. Phone 394-3397.

3. **Sightseeing. Island Nature Cruises.** Tamiami Trail E to Port of the Islands Hotel. A 14-mile, 2-hour cruise aboard the 49-passenger *Island Princess* or 9-passenger *Princess of the Port* through the Ten Thousand Islands. Two departures (daily). Phone 394-3101. ¢¢¢¢

4. **Everglades National Park** (see). Approx 20 mi SE via US 41. A visitor center is located in Everglades City, S off US 41.

(For further information contact the Marco Island Area Chamber of Commerce, 1102 N Collier Blvd; 394-7549.)

(See Naples)

Motels

★ ★ **BOATHOUSE.** *1180 Edington Place, in Old Marco Village. 813/642-2400; res: 800/528-6345; FAX 813/642-2435.* 19 rms, 2 story. Dec–Apr: S, D $100–$120; each addl $25; wkly rates in season; lower rates rest of yr. Crib avail. Pet accepted, some restrictions; $15. TV; cable. Pool. Restaurant adj 5:30–10 pm. Ck-out 11 am. Coin lndry. Airport transportation. Boat rentals, pedalboats. Balconies. Picnic tables. Built 1883; French doors, antiques. On entrance to Collier Bay; dockage. Cr cds: MC, V.

★ ★ **FLORIDA PAVILION CLUB CONDOMINIUM.** *1170 Edington Pl, in Old Marco Village. 813/394-3345; FAX 813/394-7472.* 20 kit. condos (1–2 bedrm), 2 story. Dec–Apr (3-night min): S, D $135–$215; each addl $25; wkly; monthly rates; lower rates rest of yr. Crib $25. TV; cable. Heated pool. Restaurant adj 7 am–10 pm. Ck-out 11 am. Coin lndry. Private patios, balconies. Picnic tables. Dockage (fee). Cr cds: MC, V.

Motor Hotels

★ ★ ★ **EAGLE'S NEST BEACH RESORT.** *410 S Collier Blvd. 813/394-5167 or 481-3636; res: 800/237-8906; FAX 813/642-1599.* 96 kit. suites, 10 story. Mid-Nov–mid-Apr: suites $260–$285; wkly rates; lower rates rest of yr. TV; cable. Heated pool. Supervised child's activities. Restaurant adj sunrise–sunset. Ck-out 10 am. Gift shop. Lighted tennis. Exercise equipt; weight machine, bicycles, whirlpool, sauna. Game rm. Private patios, balconies. Picnic tables, grills. 3 main buildings

surround courtyard with fountain, pool, lush landscaping. On beach. Cr cds: MC, V.

★ **MARCO BAY RESORT.** *1001 N Barfield Dr, at Bald Eagle Dr. 813/394-8881; res: 800/228-0661; FAX 813/394-8909.* 200 kit. suites (1–2 bedrm), 5 story. Jan–mid-Apr: kit. suites $130–$180; under 17 free; wkly rates; lower rates rest of yr. Crib $7.50. TV; cable. 2 heated pools; 3 whirlpools. Restaurant 7 am–10 pm. Bars 11–1 am. Ck-out 11 am. Coin lndry. Meeting rms. Valet serv. Tennis. Balconies. On bay; dockage, water sports. Cr cds: A, C, D, DS, MC, V.

Hotels

★ ★ ★ **HILTON MARCO ISLAND BEACH RESORT.** *560 S Collier Blvd. 813/394-5000; res: 800/443-4550; FAX 813/394-5251.* 294 rms, 11 story. Mid-Dec–Apr: S, D $200–$295; each addl $20; 1-bedrm suite $395; family rates; special packages; golf, tennis plans; lower rates rest of yr. Crib free. TV; cable, in-rm movies. Heated pool; poolside serv. Supervised child's activities. Coffee in rms. Restaurant 7 am–10 pm (also see SANDCASTLES). Bkfst buffet on patio in season & wkends. Bar noon–2 am; entertainment exc Sun. Ck-out noon. Convention facilities. Concierge. Gift shop. Drugstore. 3 lighted tennis courts, pro. Golf privileges, greens fee $25–$90, pro, putting green, driving range. Exercise rm; instructor, bicycles, weight machines, whirlpool, sauna, steam rm. Massage. Game rm. Bathrm phones & TVs, refrigerators, minibars, wet bars. Private patios, balconies. Oriental antiques, marble floor in lobby. Luxurious hotel with many amenities. On gulf, fishing by arrangement; beach, water sports. Bicycles avail. Cr cds: A, C, D, DS, MC, V.

★ ★ **RADISSON SUITE BEACH RESORT.** *600 S Collier Blvd. 813/394-4100; FAX 813/394-0262.* 269 units, 12 story. Feb–Apr: 1-bedrm $235–$285; 2-bedrm $325–$335; lower rates rest of yr. Crib avail. TV; cable. Heated pool; poolside serv. Supervised child's activities. Restaurants 7 am–midnight. Bar from 11 am; entertainment. Ck-out noon. Coin lndry. Meeting rms. Concierge. Gift shop. Covered parking. Tennis, pro. Golf privileges, greens fee $40–$90 (incl cart), pro, putting green, driving range. Exercise equipt; weights, bicycles, whirlpool. Game rm. Balconies. On Gulf; beach. Cr cds: A, C, D, DS, ER, MC, V, JCB.

Resort

★ ★ ★ **MARRIOTT'S MARCO ISLAND RESORT AND GOLF CLUB.** *400 S Collier Blvd. 813/394-2511; FAX 813/642-2676.* 735 units, 11 story. Mid-Dec–May: S, D $250–$350; 1–2-bedrm suites $580–$890; 1–2-bedrm penthouses $1,000–$1,500; 2-bedrm villas $500–$580; under 18 free; varied lower rates rest of yr. Crib free. TV; cable. 3 pools, 2 heated; poolside serv. Supervised child's activities. Coffee in rms. 5 restaurants 7 am–midnight. Rm serv. Bar 11–2 am; entertainment. Ck-out noon, ck-in 3 pm. Coin lndry. Convention facilities. Valet serv. Concierge. Shopping arcade. Barber, beauty shop. Valet parking. Lighted tennis, pros. 18-hole golf, greens fee $35–$80, pro. Private gulf beach; water sports (rentals). Bicycle rentals. Lawn games. Soc dir; entertainment, dancing. Game rm. Exercise equipt; weights, bicycles, whirlpool. Massage. Refrigerators, minibars. Private patios, balconies. Ice cream parlor. Cr cds: A, C, D, DS, ER, MC, V, JCB.

Restaurants

★ ★ **BAVARIAN INN.** *960 Winterberry Dr. 813/394-7233.* Hrs: 4:30–10 pm; early-bird dinner 4:30–6 pm; light late dinners to 1:30 am. German, Amer menu. Bar 4:30 pm–2 am. Semi-a la carte: dinner

$10–$16.95. Child's meals. Specializes in duck, schnitzel, seafood. German chalet decor. Cr cds: A, C, D, DS, MC, V.

D

★ ★ ★**CAFE DE MARCO.** *244 Royal Palm Dr, off Palm St. 813/394-6262.* Hrs: 5–10 pm. Closed Thanksgiving, Dec 25; Super Bowl Sun; also Sun off-season. Res accepted. Wine list. Semi-a la carte: dinner $10.50–$23.95. Child's meals. Specializes in fresh Florida seafood. Own desserts. Parking. European atmosphere; stained-glass panels. Cr cds: MC, V.

D

✔ ★**HOUTAN'S SEAFOOD & GRILL.** *257 N Collier Blvd. 813/394-8831.* Hrs: 5–9 pm. Closed Sun. Res accepted. Wine, beer. Semi-a la carte: dinner $9.95–$15.95. Specializes in char-broiled dishes, seafood, pasta. Parking. Outdoor dining. Open garden atmosphere. Cr cds: MC, V.

D

★ ★**MARCO POLO.** *30 Marco Lake Dr. 813/394-5777.* Hrs: 5 pm–2 am. Closed Super Bowl Sun. Res accepted. Continental menu. Bar. Semi-a la carte: dinner $9.95–$24.95. Child's meals. Specializes in veal, steak, fresh seafood, pasta. Piano bar. Parking. Cr cds: A, MC, V.

D

✔ ★**NEW SU'S GARDEN.** *537 Bald Eagle Dr. 813/394-4666.* Hrs: 11:30 am–10 pm. Chinese menu. Wine, beer. Semi-a la carte: lunch $4.75–$5.25, dinner $7–$15. Specializes in Cantonese, Szechwan, Hunan and mandarin dishes. Parking. Oriental decor. Cr cds: A, D, MC, V.

D

★ ★**O'SHEAS'.** *1081 Bald Eagle Dr. 813/394-7531.* Hrs: 11:30–12:30 am; Sun brunch 10 am–3 pm. Res accepted. Bar. Semi-a la carte: lunch $3.95–$8.95, dinner $10.95–$21. Sun brunch $16.95. Child's meals. Specializes in fresh seafood, veal, steak. Entertainment. Valet parking. Waterfront view, boat dockage. Cr cds: A, C, D, DS, MC, V.

D

✔ ★ ★**PRAWNBROKER.** *Elkam Circle, rear of Marco Town Center Mall. 813/394-4800.* Hrs: 5–10 pm. Closed July 4, Thanksgiving; also Super Bowl Sun. Res accepted. Bar from 4 pm. Semi-a la carte: dinner $10.95–$15.95. Child's meals. Specializes in fresh seafood. Parking. Fish market on premises. Cr cds: A, MC, V.

D

★ ★ ★**SANDCASTLES.** *(See Hilton Marco Island Beach Resort Hotel) 813/394-5000.* Hrs: 5–10 pm. Res accepted. Continental menu. Bar 5 pm–1 am. Wine list. Semi-a la carte: dinner $21.95–$29.95. Child's meals. Specializes in fresh seafood, steak, veal. Pianist. Valet parking. View of gulf and pool area. Antiques, paintings. Cr cds: A, C, D, DS, MC, V.

D **SC**

★**SNOOK INN.** *1215 Bald Eagle Dr. 813/394-3313.* Hrs: 11 am–10 pm. Closed Thanksgiving, Dec 25. Bar to midnight. Semi-a la carte: lunch $4.95–$7.95, dinner $10.95–$16.95. Child's meals. Specializes in fresh seafood. Salad bar. Entertainment. Outdoor dining. Parking. Nautical decor; aquarium. On Marco River; dockage. Cr cds: A, MC, V.

D

★ ★**VITO'S.** *1079 Bald Eagle Dr. 813/934-7722.* Hrs: 11:30 am–2 pm, 5:30–10 pm; Sun from 5:30 pm. Closed Thanksgiving, Dec 25; also Sept. Res accepted. Italian menu. Bar. Semi-a la carte: lunch $3.75–$6.75, dinner $7.95–$19.95. Specializes in pasta, seafood. Parking. Outdoor dining. Many nautical artifacts; view of bay. Extensive wine selection. Cr cds: A, DS, MC, V.

D

Marianna (E-3)

Founded: 1829 **Pop:** 6,292 **Elev:** 117 ft **Area code:** 904 **Zip:** 32446

The Chipola River bisects Marianna, the seat of Jackson County. East is Merritts Mill Pond and its source, an underwater cave at Blue Springs.

What to See and Do

1. **Florida Caverns State Park.** 3 mi N on FL 166. Approx 1,300 acre includes a limestone cavern and an intriguing network of caves with unusual stalactites and stalagmites. Cavern tours (daily). The Chipola River, which helped form the cavern, flows through the park, going underground for a brief distance. Swimming; fishing; boating (ramp). Nature trails. Picnicking. Camping (hookups, dump station). Visitor center. Standard hrs, fees. Phone 482-9598.
2. **Three Rivers State Recreation Area.** 25 mi E via US 90 to Sneads, then 2 mi N on FL 271. Approx 680 acres on huge, man-made Lake Seminole. Hilly terrain with white-tailed deer, fox squirrel, grey fox and bobwhites. Noted for good fishing. Canoeing, boating (ramp). Nature trails. Picnicking. Camping (hookups, dump station). Standard hrs, fees. Phone 482-9006.
3. **Falling Waters State Recreation Area.** 15 mi W on I-10 to Chipley, then 3 mi S off FL 77A. More than 150 acres with waterfall that flows into a 100-foot sinkhole, which has moss- and fern-covered walls. Swimming. Nature trails. Picnicking. Camping (dump station). Standard hrs, fees. Phone 638-6130.

(For further information contact the Marianna County Chamber of Commerce, 2928 Jefferson St, PO Box 130, 32447; 482-8061.)

(See Blountstown)

Motels

★**COMFORT INN.** *(Box 1507) On FL 71N, at jct I-10 exit 21. 904/526-5600.* 80 rms, 2 story. S $47–$57; D $47–$59; each addl $4; under 18 free. Crib free. Pet accepted. TV; cable. Pool. Complimentary continental bkfst, coffee. Restaurant nearby. Ck-out 11 am. Coin lndry. Cr cds: A, C, D, DS, MC, V, JCB.

D 🐾 🏊 🚫 🕐 **SC**

✔ ★ ★**HOLIDAY INN.** *(Box 979) 2 mi W on US 90, I-10 exit 21. 904/526-3251; FAX 904/482-6223.* 80 rms, 2 story. S $43–$48; D $50–$53; each addl $5; studio rms $46–$52; under 18 free. Crib free. Pet accepted. TV; cable. Pool; wading pool. Restaurant 6 am–2 pm, 5–10 pm. Rm serv. Ck-out noon. Coin lndry. Meeting rms. Bellhops. Cr cds: A, C, D, DS, MC, V, JCB.

D 🐾 🏊 🚫 🕐 **SC**

Restaurant

✔ ★**TONY'S.** *4133 W Lafayette. 904/482-2232.* Hrs: 6 am–9 pm; Fri to 10 pm; Sat 11 am–10 pm. Closed Sun; major hols. Italian, Amer menu. Beer. Semi-a la carte: bkfst from $2.75, lunch from $4.50, dinner $5.95–$13.95. Child's meals. Specializes in steak, seafood. Parking. Cr cds: A, D, MC, V.

Marineland (B-4)

Pop: 21 **Elev:** 11 ft **Area code:** 904

What to See and Do

1. **Marineland of Florida.** Hundreds of fish of all sizes, including dolphins, sharks, moray eels and baracudas in aquatic communities inhabit two of the world's oldest giant oceanariums; they may be photographed through many surrounding portholes. Trained dolphins exhibit their physical and intellectual prowess, as do performing California sea lions; Marine and freshwater exhibits; tropical penguins; 3-D film in Aquarius Theater; Play Port for kids; Shell Museum. Oceanfront promenade; lodging; restaurant; campground opp. (Daily) Phone 471-1111 or 800/874-0492. ¢¢¢¢

2. **Washington Oaks State Gardens.** 2 mi S on FL A1A, just N of Palm Coast. Approximately 400 acres; originally a Spanish land grant to Bautista Don Juan Ferreira in 1815. Citrus groves, rose garden, native plants and shrubs. Nature museum. Swimming; fishing. Nature trails. Picnicking. Standard hrs, fees. Phone 445-3161.

3. **Fort Matanzas National Monument** (see). 4 mi N on FL A1A.

(See Ormond Beach, St Augustine)

Motel

★★**QUALITY INN MARINELAND.** *9507 Ocean Shore Blvd (32086). 904/471-1222; FAX 904/471-3352.* 123 rms, 2–5 story. Feb–Labor Day: S, D $69–$109; each addl $5; suites $84–$109; under 18 free; wkly rates; higher rates: Gator Bowl, races; lower rates rest of yr. Crib $5. TV. 2 pools, 1 heated; wading pool, poolside serv (in season). Playground. Complimentary coffee in rms. Restaurant 7 am–9:30 pm. Bar 11 am–midnight. Ck-out 11 am. Coin lndry. Meeting rms. Sundries. Tennis. Lawn games. Private balconies. Picnic tables. On beach. Cr cds: A, C, D, DS, ER, MC, V, JCB.

Resort

★★★**SHERATON PALM COAST.** *(300 Clubhouse Dr, Palm Coast 32137) S via I-95 exit 91C or FL A1A. 904/445-3000; FAX 904/445-9685.* 154 units, 3 story, 2-bedrm villas in adj Harbor Club. Feb–May, Sept–mid-Nov: S $82–$165; D $92–$175; each addl $20; 2-bedrm suites $250–$350; 2-bedrm villas $270–$400; under 17 free; golf, tennis, family recreation packages; higher rates special events (5-day min); lower rates rest of yr. Pet accepted. TV; cable. 3 pools, 1 heated; wading pool, poolside serv. Playground. Coffee in rms. Restaurant 6:30 am–10:30 pm. Rm serv. Bar 11–1 am; entertainment, dancing Fri, Sat. Ck-out noon, ck-in 3 pm. Grocery, package store 1 mi. Meeting rms. Bellhops. Valet serv. Gift shop. Free area transportation. Sports dir. Lighted tennis, 22-court complex with grass, clay and hard surfaces. 5 golf courses, greens fee $42–$107, putting green, driving range, miniature golf. 80-slip marina. Bicycle rentals. Soc dir. Game rm. Exercise equipt; weights, bicycles, whirlpool, sauna. Minibars. Some private patios, balconies. On Intracoastal Waterway; private beach, club. All rms with view of waterway or marina. Cr cds: A, C, D, DS, ER, MC, V, JCB.

Melbourne (C-5)

Founded: 1878 **Pop:** 59,646 **Elev:** 21 ft **Area code:** 407

On the Indian River, just west of the Atlantic Ocean and neighbor to both Cape Canaveral and Kennedy Space Center (see), Melbourne has tied its present and future to the space age. Many large electronics firms have been established here in the last decade, making the town a leader in technology. There is fishing from the causeways, the rivers, Lake Washington and the Atlantic Ocean. Boating, sailing, waterskiing, boardsailing and jet skiing are also popular.

What to See and Do

1. **Wickham Park.** 1 mi W of US 1 on Parkway Dr. Approximately 480 acres of parkland with 2 lakes, picnic pavilions, camping facilities. Archery range (free). (Daily) Phone 255-4307. **Free.**

2. **Long Point Park.** 2 mi N of Sebastian Inlet, 1 mi W on FL A1A. Approximately 120 acres of park including a freshwater lake. Fishing. Picnicking. Camping facilities (hookups). (Daily) Phone 952-4532. Per car ¢

3. **Florida Institute of Technology** (1958). (6,000 students) Country Club Rd, 1 mi S of New Haven Ave, US 192. On main campus is the Florida Tech Botanical Garden, which features rare and exotic palms (daily; free). Phone 768-8000.

(For further information contact the Melbourne-Palm Bay Area Chamber of Commerce, 1005 E Strawbridge Ave, 32901; 724-5400.)

Seasonal Event

Turtle Crawl. Thousands of baby turtles hatch and make their way to the sea south of Melbourne Beach. June–Sept.

(See Cocoa, Cocoa Beach, Vero Beach)

Motels

★★**COMFORT INN.** *8298 N Wickham Rd (32940). 407/255-0077; FAX 407/259-9633.* 135 rms, 5 story, 18 suites. Feb–Apr: S $50–$85; D $60–$90; each addl $8; suites $65–$95; under 18 free; wkly rates; golf plans; lower rates rest of yr. TV; cable. Pool; poolside serv. Complimentary continental bkfst. Restaurant nearby. Bar 4 pm–1 am. Ck-out noon. Coin lndry. Meeting rms. Bellhops. Airport transportation. Golf privileges, greens fee, pro, putting green, driving range. Health club privileges. Refrigerator in suites. Cr cds: A, C, D, DS, MC, V.

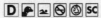

★★★**COURTYARD BY MARRIOTT.** *2101 W New Haven Ave (32904), 4 mi E of I-95 exit 71, near Regional Airport. 407/724-6400; FAX 407/984-4006.* 146 rms, 3 story, 12 suites. S $65; D $75; suites $85–$95; wkly rates. Crib free. TV; cable. Heated pool. Complimentary coffee in rms. Restaurant 6:30–11 am; wkends 7 am–noon. Bar 4–11 pm. Ck-out noon. Coin lndry. Meeting rms. Valet serv. Sundries. Free airport transportation. Exercise equipt; weight machine, bicycles, whirlpool. Some refrigerators. Balconies. Picnic tables. Cr cds: A, D, DS, MC, V.

✔★**DAYS INN.** *4455 W New Haven Ave (32904). 407/724-5840; FAX 407/724-5840, ext 400.* 235 rms, 2 story. Jan–mid-Apr: S, D $39–$55; each addl $5; under 18 free; lower rates rest of yr. Crib free. TV; cable. Pool. Playground. Complimentary continental bkfst. Ck-out noon. Coin lndry. Lighted tennis. Lawn games. Man-made lake. Cr cds: A, D, DS, MC, V.

✔★**ECONO LODGE.** *420 S Harbor City Blvd (US 1) (32901). 407/723-5320; FAX 407/724-0581.* 100 rms, 1–2 story. Jan–Apr: S $44.95; D $49.95; each addl $5; under 18 free; lower rates rest of yr. Crib free. Pet accepted, some restrictions; $50 ($25 refundable). TV; cable. Pool. Bar. Ck-out 11 am. Indian River opp. Cr cds: A, C, D, DS, ER, MC, V, JCB.

Motor Hotel

★★★**HOLIDAY INN MELBOURNE OCEANFRONT.** *(2605 N FL A1A, Indialantic 32903) E on Melbourne Causeway, then N on FL A1A. 407/777-4100; FAX 407/773-6132.* 299 rms, 8 story. S, D $90–$120; each addl $10; suites $159; under 18 free. Crib free. Pet accepted, some restrictions; $100 refundable. TV; cable. Indoor/outdoor pool; whirlpool, poolside serv. Complimentary coffee in rms. Restaurant 6:30 am–2 pm,

5–10 pm. Rm serv. Bar; entertainment Tues–Sat, dancing. Ck-out noon. Bellhops. Valet serv. Gift shop. Tennis. Refrigerator in suites. Balconies. On ocean. Cr cds: A, C, D, DS, ER, MC, V, JCB.

Hotels

★ ★ ★**HILTON AT RIALTO PLACE-MELBOURNE AIRPORT.** *200 Rialto Pl (32901), near Regional Airport.* 407/768-0200; FAX 407/984-2528. 241 rms, 8 story. S $95–$130; D $105–$140; each addl $10; suites $325; under 18 free; package plans. Crib free. TV; cable. Pool; poolside serv. Restaurant 6:30 am–10:30 pm. Bar; entertainment, dancing. Ck-out noon. Convention facilities. Gift shop. Free airport, mall, beach, business transportation. Lighted tennis. Golf privileges. Exercise equipt; weights, bicycles, whirlpool. Some private patios, balconies. **LUXURY LEVEL.** 29 rms, 2 suites. S $125; D $135. Concierge. Private lounge. Wet bars. In-rm whirlpools. Complimentary continental bkfst, refreshments.
Cr cds: A, C, D, DS, ER, MC, V.

★ ★ ★**HILTON OCEANFRONT.** *(3003 N FL A1A, Indialantic 32903)* E via Melbourne Causeway, N on FL A1A. 407/777-5000; FAX 407/777-3713. 118 rms, 11 story. S $80–$120; D $90–$130; each addl $10; suites $130–$150; under 18 free. Crib free. TV; cable. Heated pool; poolside serv. Restaurant 6:30 am–2 pm, 5–10 pm. Bars 11–2 am; outdoor entertainment Sun, dancing Wed–Sun. Ck-out noon. Meeting rms. Airport, RR station, bus depot transportation. Health club privileges. Balconies. On ocean beach. Cr cds: A, C, D, DS, MC, V.

★ ★ ★**QUALITY SUITES OCEANFRONT.** *(1665 N FL A1A, Indialantic 32903)* E via Melbourne Causeway, N on FL A1A. 407/723-4222; FAX 407/768-2438. 208 suites, 9 story. Feb–Apr: suites $89–$130; under 18 free; wkly rates; higher rates hol wkends; lower rates rest of yr. Crib free. TV; cable, in-rm movies. Heated pool; poolside serv. Free buffet bkfst. Cafe 6:30–9:30 am, 11:30 am–2 pm, 5–9 pm. Bar 4 pm–midnight; entertainment Sun in season. Ck-out noon. Coin lndry. Meeting rms. Gift shop. Exercise equipt; weights, bicycles, whirlpool, sauna. Game rm. Minibars. Balconies. On ocean; swimming beach. Cr cds: A, C, D, DS, ER, MC, V, JCB.

★ ★ ★**RADISSON SUITE OCEANFRONT.** *3101 N FL A1A (32903).* 407/773-9260; FAX 407/777-3190. 167 suites, 15 story. Feb–Aug: S, D $109–$159; each addl $10; under 18 free; special package plans; lower rates rest of yr. Crib free. TV; cable. Heated pool; whirlpool, poolside serv. Supervised child's activities (May–Labor Day). Complimentary coffee in rms. Restaurant 7 am–2 pm, 5–10 pm. Bar noon–10 pm. Ck-out noon. Coin lndry. Meeting rms. Gift shop. Balconies. On beach. Cr cds: A, C, D, DS, ER, MC, V.

Restaurants

★ ★**CHART HOUSE.** *2250 Front St.* 407/729-6558. Hrs: 5–10 pm; Fri, Sat to 11 pm; early-bird dinner 5–6 pm. Res accepted. Bar. Semi-a la carte: dinner $13.95–$25.95. Child's meals. Specializes in prime rib, steak, seafood. Salad bar. Parking. On Indian River; view of adj yacht club. Cr cds: A, C, D, DS, MC, V.

✔ ★ ★**NANNIE LEE'S STRAWBERRY MANSION AND MISTER BEAUJEANS.** *1218 E New Haven Ave.* 407/724-8627. Hrs: 8 am–midnight; early-bird dinner 5–6:30 pm. Res accepted. Bar. Semi-a la carte: bkfst $2.75–$5.50, lunch $2.95–$9.95, dinner $9.95–$16.50. Child's meals. Specialties: Mrs. Brown's Cape May crabcakes, duck of the bay, steak Oscar. Own cheesecake. Entertainment in courtyard

Thurs–Sat. Parking. Outdoor dining. Pink mansion (1904); turn-of-the-century decor, fireplace; many antiques. Cr cds: D, MC, V.

✔ ★ ★ ★**NICK'S STEAK HOUSE.** *903 Oak St, on FL A1A.* 407/723-6659. Hrs: 11 am–3 pm, 4–10 pm; Fri to 11 pm; Sat 4–11 pm; early-bird dinner 4–6:30 pm. Res accepted. Bar. Wine list. Semi-a la carte: lunch $4.50, dinner $5.95–$12.95. Child's meals. Specialties: pompano en papillotte, delmonico prime rib. Parking. Original art; antiques. Family-owned. Cr cds: A, C, D, DS, MC, V.

★**O'CHARLEY'S.** *1719 W New Haven Blvd, opp Melbourne Square Mall.* 407/951-2171. Hrs: 11 am–11 pm; Sat, Sun from 9 am; early-bird dinner Mon, Tues, Fri & Sat 3–6 pm; Sun brunch 10:30 am–3 pm. Closed Dec 25. Bar to midnight. A la carte entrees: lunch $3.29–$6.29, dinner $3.99–$15.95. Child's meals (under age 10 eat free). Specializes in prime rib, pasta, seafood. Parking. Cr cds: A, DS, MC, V.

Miami (E-5)

Settled: 1870 **Pop:** 358,548 **Elev:** 5 ft **Area code:** 305

Metropolitan Miami is part bazaar, part Broadway—a place of bikinis and minks, the habitat of boulevardiers and budgeteers; a New World city made up of both North and South America and its peoples; an international place that provides glamour, excitement and sunburn for about 8.5 million visitors each year. It takes more than 600 hotels and motels, 7,000 restaurants, 650 churches and synagogues, 40 foreign consuls and 35 hospitals to cater to the tourists in this sun-drenched conglomeration of 26 separate municipalities.

Put all its fragments together, and Greater Miami's 2,042-square-mile place in the sun seems like a blazing concoction of suntan oil, sand, glitter and gilt. But beyond this, Miami is a place of gleaming skyscrapers, of more than 3,400 manufacturing firms, 170 banks and a half-billion-dollar agricultural industry. With more than $123 million annually in customs collections, and mighty ties in commerce, it is the prime gateway to Latin America.

To most visitors, Miami is an all-encompassing term, including both the city of Miami and its across-the-bay twin, Miami Beach (see). Actually, each is a separate community and, like most sister cities, each is vigorously different in personality. Miami is the older; still a merry lady, but now more settled and sophisticated. Miami Beach is perpetual youth on a fling.

The city of Miami has a touch of Manhattan to it with its business bustle, its rush-hour traffic and its skyscrapers. This is a city of luxury houses, palm-bordered boulevards, art deco architecture and souvenir shops in the midst of a downtown of new ultramodern office towers, hotels, condominiums and shopping malls.

Biscayne Bay serves as the buffer between the two communities. Along this shore, on the Miami side, runs Biscayne Blvd (US 1), lined with hundreds of stately royal palms—a street where anything from a free glass of orange juice to a $2 million yacht can be casually acquired. The Miami River winds through the heart of the city and seven causeways form lifelines to the sandy shores of Miami Beach. Another causeway links the mainland with Key Biscayne to the south.

Although favored by climate and geography, Miami remained a remote tropical village of frame houses until Henry Morrison Flagler brought his East Coast Railway here in 1896, and turned his hand to community development. Miami's growth was persistent but unspectacular until the 1920s when the great Florida land boom brought 25,000 real estate salesmen to town. In 1925, downtown property was selling at $20,000 a front foot, and $100 million was spent in construction. The bubble burst with a mighty hurricane in 1926, but Miami had the natural assets to come back strong. The city's growth continues at an unflinching pace today, solidly based on year-round tourism, interna-

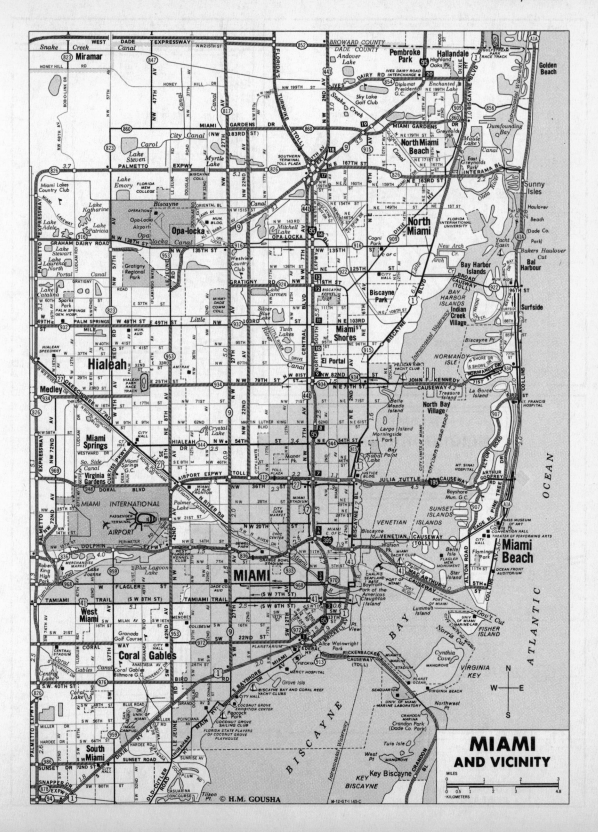

MIAMI
AND VICINITY

© H.M. GOUSHA

MILES

KILOMETERS

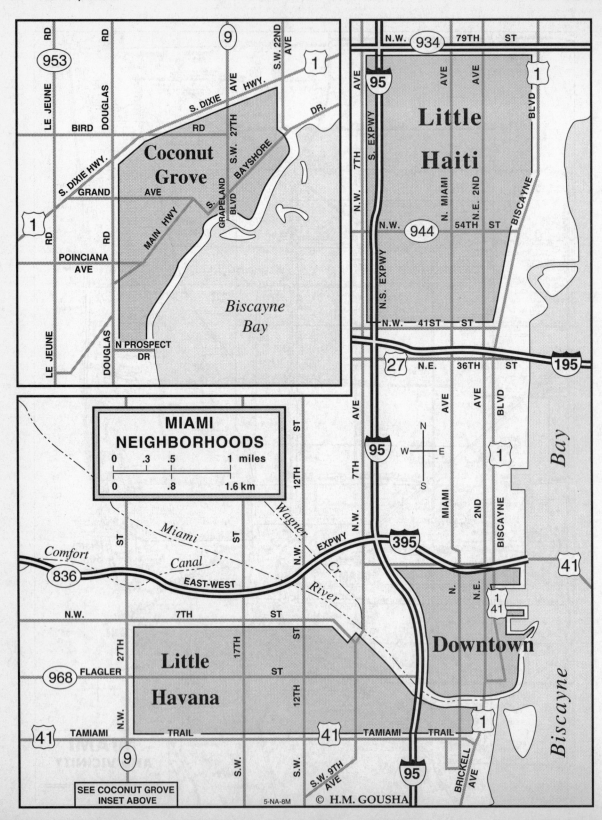

Coconut Grove

Biscayne Bay

Little Haiti

Bay

MIAMI NEIGHBORHOODS

0 .3 .5 1 miles

0 .8 1.6 km

Comfort

Miami Canal

EAST-WEST

River

Downtown

Biscayne

Little Havana

TAMIAMI TRAIL

SEE COCONUT GROVE INSET ABOVE

Biscayne

5-NA-8M © H.M. GOUSHA

tional commerce and trade, industry and agriculture. The Port of Miami is the largest embarkation point for cruise ships in the world.

Transportation

Airport. See MIAMI INTL AIRPORT AREA.

Car Rental Agencies: See toll-free numbers under Introduction.

Public Transportation: Elevated trains and buses (Metro Bus & Rail), phone 638-6700.

Rail Passenger Service: Amtrak 800/872-7245.

What to See and Do

1. **Vizcaya Museum and Gardens.** 3251 S Miami Ave, in Coconut Grove area. Elaborate 70-room Italian Renaissance-style villa with extraordinary collection of European furnishings and art objects from the 1st–19th centuries; 10-acre classical Italian garden with fountains, statuary and grottos. House (1914–1916) of James Deering, International Harvester industrialist. (Daily; closed Dec 25) Phone 579-2708. ¢¢¢

2. **Museum of Science & Space Transit Planetarium.** 3280 S Miami Ave, in Coconut Grove area. More than 150 hands-on displays on light, sound, optics, chemistry, biology, physics, energy, the human body, science-technology and invention; live science demonstrations on electricity, anatomy and endangered species; automated slide presentations, animated dioramas and continuous films; Wildlife Center. Planetarium features multimedia astronomy and laser shows (fee); observatory (Fri–Sun evenings; free). Museum (daily; closed Thanksgiving, Dec 25). Sr citizen rate. Phone 854-4247 (museum) or -2222 (planetarium). Combined museum/planetarium ¢¢¢

3. **Miami Youth Museum.** 5701 Sunset Dr, in Bakery Centre. A hands-on cultural arts museum where children and adults participate in learning experiences that stimulate the imagination and senses. (Daily; closed major hols) Sr citizen rate. Phone 661-ARTS. ¢¢

4. **Historical Museum of Southern Florida.** 101 W Flagler St, in Metro-Dade Cultural Plaza, downtown. Participatory exhibits trace man's experiences in southern Florida from prehistoric to modern times. Includes artifacts from prehistoric and Seminole Indian cultures; maritime history; "boom to bust" era of the Roaring '20s and development as an international city. (Mon–Sat, also Sun afternoons; closed Jan 1, Thanksgiving, Dec 25) Phone 375-1492. ¢¢

5. **American Police Hall of Fame and Museum.** 3801 Biscayne Blvd. Collection of firearms, murder weapons; lie detectors, electric chair; police vehicles; many other exhibits. Memorial to officers killed in the line of duty. (Daily; closed Dec 25) Sr citizen rate. Police officers and family **free.** Phone 573-0070. ¢¢¢

6. **Barnacle State Historic Site.** 5 mi S via I-95, S Miami Ave & S Bayshore Dr to 3485 Main Hwy in Coconut Grove. Historic house and grounds, former residence of Ralph M. Munroe, Coconut Grove pioneer and yacht designer. Oldest remaining residence in Dade County. Designed for the climate, this is an outstanding example of Caribbean architecture. Tours (Thurs–Mon). Phone 448-9445. ¢¢

7. **The Cloisters of the Monastery of St Bernard de Clairvaux.** 16711 W Dixie Hwy, in North Miami Beach. Monastery built in 1141 in Segovia, Spain, and purchased by William Randolph Hearst, who had it disassembled, crated and brought to the US. It wasn't reassembled until 1954, after Hearst's death; it is now owned by the Episcopal Church. Formal garden; guided tours. (Mon–Sat, also Sun afternoons; closed Easter, Thanksgiving, Dec 25) Phone 945-1461. ¢¢

8. **Japanese Garden.** On Watson Island, N side of MacArthur Causeway. Authentic one-acre Japanese garden and pavilion; many sculptural pieces sent from Japan as gifts—pagoda, statues, waterfall, lagoon. (Sat & Sun; also by appt) Phone 575-5240. **Free.**

9. **Metrozoo.** 12400 SW 152nd St (Coral Reef Dr), just W of the FL Tpke exit. Consists of 290 acres with more than 50 cageless exhibits; features rare white Bengal tigers in a moated area, complete with a replica of an ancient Cambodian temple, koalas in a permanent exhibit, and orangutans, elephants, gorillas, chimps, rhinos and bears in areas resembling each animal's native habitat. Wings of Asia, a 1.5-acre free-flight aviary, features 300 tropical birds in a rain forest environment. Also free animal shows (three shows daily); elephant rides, elephant show and an ecology theater; childrens zoo; monorail system; 4 restaurants; and observation deck overlooking African Lobe. (Daily) Phone 251-0400 (recording) or -0401. ¢¢¢

10. **Gold Coast Railroad and Museum.** 12450 SW 152nd St, just W of FL Tpke. Collection of railroad cars and memorabilia; *Ferdinand Magellan*, historic armored private car used by Presidents Roosevelt, Truman, Eisenhower and Reagan; various steam locomotives and passenger cars; 20-minute train ride (Sat & Sun). (Daily) Phone 253-0063. ¢¢

11. **Parrot Jungle and Gardens.** 11000 SW 57th Ave, S off US 1. Parrots, macaws, flamingos in natural tropical jungle; walkways through gardens and cactus ravine; trained macaw and cockatoo shows in geodesic dome amphitheater; baby bird training arena; petting zoo, playground. Cafeteria; gift shop. (Daily) Phone 666-7834. ¢¢¢¢

12. **Miami Seaquarium.** 4400 Rickenbacker Causeway, S on Virginia Key. Tropical marine aquarium on 50 acres of gardens. Home of television's "Flipper"; tanks with viewing windows; tidepool touch tank; killer whale; sea lion & dolphin shows; "Faces of the Rain Forest" exhibit. (Daily; shows run continuously) Sr citizen rate. Phone 361-5705. ¢¢¢¢

13. **Monkey Jungle.** 14805 SW 216th St, W of US 1 & FL Tpke. Unusual setting in which visitors are inside caged walkways and watch nearly 500 monkeys frolic in uncaged freedom; Wild Monkey Swimming Pool, Ape Encounter; three different shows. (Daily) Sr citizen rate. Phone 235-1611. ¢¢¢¢

14. **Bayside Marketplace.** 401 Biscayne Blvd, bounded by Biscayne & Port Blvds, on Biscayne Bay. This 16-acre restaurant, shopping and entertainment complex reflects the South Florida/Caribbean style; more than 150 specialty shops; pushcarts, open-air marketplace, two entertainment pavilions, waterfront promenade, departure point for gondola and boat cruises. (Daily) Phone 577-3344.

15. **Recreation areas.**

    Bayfront Park. 301 N Biscayne Blvd, at Biscayne Bay. Baywalk, laser light tower, amphitheater, fountain. Torch of Friendship symbolizing relationship with Latin American countries; Challenger memorial monument. (Daily) Phone 358-7550. **Free.**

    Lummus Park. 404 NW N River Dr & NW 3rd St. Stone barracks of Fort Dallas, built in 1835 at the mouth of Miami River and once commanded by William Tecumseh Sherman; abandoned in 1838, later moved to this site. Also here is Wagner House, one of the last remaining pioneer structures in Dade County. On Miami River; boat dock. (Daily) Phone 575-5240. **Free.**

    New World Center—Bicentennial Park. Biscayne Blvd, MacArthur Causeway & NE 9th St, on Biscayne Bay. Fishing; picnicking; playground. Trails. Sculpture fountain. The park is used for part of the Grand Prix Miami racecourse (see ANNUAL EVENTS). Park (daily). Phone 575-5240. **Free.**

    Greynolds Park. 17530 W Dixie Hwy, in North Miami. Picnicking, grills, concession. New England-style wooden bridge, observation tower; trails. Fishing; boating, paddleboat rentals; bicycle paths, exercise stations; playground; golf course; bird rookery, bird walks. (Daily) Phone 945-3425. Parking fee (Sat, Sun & hols) ¢

16. **Coconut Grove Playhouse.** 3500 Main Hwy. Regional professional theater produces original comedies, dramas and musicals. (Oct–June, Tues–Sat evenings; matinees Wed, Sat, Sun) Phone 442-4000.

17. **Orange Bowl Stadium.** 1400 NW 4th St. Scene of University of Miami football games (Aug–Jan); Orange Bowl (see ANNUAL

EVENTS). Phone 284-3244 (Univ of Miami) or 643-7100 (Orange Bowl).

18. **Miccosukee Indian Village and Airboat Rides.** 25 mi W on US 41 (Tamiami Trail). Example of an authentic Indian village depicting the traditional lifestyle of the tribe. Guided tours; demonstrations and exhibits of woodcarving, patchwork, beadwork, basket weaving and doll making; alligator wrestling; museum with artifacts & films; airboat rides (fee). Restaurant featuring authentic Miccosukee dishes as well as standard menu; gift shop. (Daily) (See ANNUAL EVENTS) Sr citizen rate. Phone 223-8380 or -8388. Village ¢¢¢

19. **Big Cypress National Preserve.** 47 mi W via US 41. Adjoining the northwest section of Everglades National Park (see), this approximately 570,000-acre area is rich in subtropical plant and animal life. The preserve is a favorite spot of bird watchers and photographers.

20. **Horse racing.**

Calder Race Course. NW 27th Ave at 210th St, in North Miami, just S of FL Tpke. Thoroughbred racing. Includes Florida Stallion Stakes series for more than $1 million in purses. Parking fee. For schedule, fees phone 625-1311.

Gulfstream Park. Approx 15 mi N via US 1 (Biscayne Blvd), at Hallandale Beach Blvd in Hallandale (see HOLLYWOOD).

21. **Jai-Alai.** 3500 NW 37th Ave, at NW 36th St, near airport. Parimutuel betting, courtview restaurant. (Wed–Sat & Mon evenings; matinees Mon, Wed & Sat) Children with adults only. Parking fee. Phone 633-6400. ¢

22. **Boating, fishing.** More than 600 varieties of saltwater and freshwater fish abound in the waters around metropolitan Miami. Persons may fish from bridges, causeways and piers, or boats may be rented; many tournaments throughout the year. Biscayne Bay offers 370 square miles of protected water for boating; anything from a skiff to a yacht can be rented; many marinas and launching ramps are scattered about.

23. **Cruises.** Various types of cruises are available, from lunch or dinner cruises to casino cruises to murder/mystery trips; departure point for many Caribbean cruises; rental boats range from intimate sailboats to 140-foot yachts.

24. **Sightseeing tours.**

Island Queen. Departs from Hyatt Regency Hotel, 400 SE 2nd Ave, or Bayside Marketplace (see #14). Circle cruise (90 min) of Biscayne Bay on the *Island Queen.* Millionaires Row Cruise includes lecture, view of waterfront estates, residential islands, Miami and Miami Beach. (Daily) Phone 379-5119. ¢¢¢

Old Town Trolley Tours. Main depot at Bayside Marketplace (see #14). Replicas of old Miami trolleys make 90-minute, narrated trips, stopping at several locations; trolleys come by every 30 minutes. (Daily) Phone 374-8687. Pass ¢¢¢¢

All Florida Adventure Tours. 8263-B SW 107th Ave. Customized tours of South Florida; history, nature and ecology emphasis. Phone 270-0219. ¢¢¢¢¢

Gray Line bus tours. Contact 1642 NW 21st Terrace, 33142; 325-1000 or 800/826-6754.

Annual Events

Orange Bowl Festival. Orange Bowl Stadium (see #17). Orange Bowl Football Game (Jan 1) and King Orange Jamboree Parade (Dec 31). Two weeks of activities also include tennis tournament, 10K footrace, regatta series and more. Phone 642-1515. Dec–early Jan.

Taste of the Grove. Two-day food and music festival in Coconut Grove. Phone 624-3714. Mid-Jan.

Coconut Grove Arts Festival. 5 mi S via US 1 in Coconut Grove. 300 artists display their works; entertainment; international foods. Phone 447-0401. Mid-Feb.

Doral Ryder Open PGA golf tournament. Held on the famed "Blue Monster" course of the Doral Resort & Country Club. Phone 477-4653. Mid-Feb–early Mar.

Grand Prix of Miami. The streets of downtown Miami are transformed into a European-style raceway. Phone 379-RACE. Last wk Feb or 1st wk Mar.

Carnaval Miami/Calle Ocho Festival. Largest Hispanic-culture festival in the US. Includes Carnaval Night in Orange Bowl, Paseo parade and Calle Ocho Festival in Little Havana. For information phone 324-7349. Early Mar.

Italian Renaissance Festival. Vizcaya (see #1). Re-creation of a Renaissance marketplace with arts, crafts, music, plays, food & drink. Mid-Mar.

Miami/Budweiser Unlimited Hydroplane Regatta. Marine Stadium. At least a dozen of the world's fastest powerboats compete for the Governor's Trophies. Phone 361-6730. June.

Miccosukee Indian Arts Festival. Miccosukee Indian Village (see #18). More than 20 different tribes gather to perform traditional dances and music; arts & crafts; demonstrations; food. Phone 223-8380. Late Dec–early Jan.

Seasonal Events

Professional sports. Dolphins (football), early Sept–Dec, Joe Robbie Stadium, 2269 NW 199th St, phone 620-2578. Heat (basketball), Nov–Apr, Miami Arena, 721 NW 1st Ave, phone 577-4328. Marlins (baseball), Apr–Oct, Joe Robbie Stadium.

Greyhound racing.

Flagler Dog Track. On NW 38th Court, at NW 37th Ave & 7th St, near airport. Races nightly; matinees Tues, Thurs, Sat & hols. Phone 649-3000. June–Dec.

Biscayne Greyhound Track. 320 NW 115th St, just off I-95, in Miami Shores. Parimutuel races nightly; matinees Tues, Thurs & Sat. Phone 754-3484. July–Aug & Nov–Dec.

Opera. Performances at Dade County Auditorium, 2901 W Flagler St. Phone Greater Miami Opera, 854-7890. Jan–Apr.

Additional Visitor Information

The Greater Miami Convention & Visitors Bureau, 701 Brickell Ave, Suite 2700, 33131, phone 539-3000 or 800/283-2707, has brochures and a complete calendar of events available by mail or in person. *South Florida* magazine and *Miami Today*, at newsstands, have up-to-date information on cultural events and articles of interest to visitors.

Miami Area Suburbs

The following suburbs or towns in the Miami area are included in the *Mobil Travel Guide.* For information on any one of them, see the individual alphabetical listing. Coral Gables, Hialeah, Hollywood, Key Biscayne, Miami Beach.

Miami Intl Airport Area

For additional accommodations, see MIAMI INTL AIRPORT AREA, which follows MIAMI.

City Neighborhoods

Many of the restaurants, unrated dining establishments and some lodgings listed under Miami include neighborhoods as well as exact street addresses. A map showing these neighborhoods can be found immediately following the city map. Geographic descriptions of these areas are given, followed by a table of restaurants arranged by neighborhood.

Coconut Grove: South of S Dixie Hwy (US 1), west of SW 22nd Ave, north of Biscayne Bay and east of Douglas Rd.

Downtown: South of NE 12th St, west of Biscayne Bay, north of the Miami River and east of NW 27th St. **North of Downtown:** North of I-395. **South of Downtown:** South of US 41. **West of Downtown:** West of I-95.

Little Haiti: South of NW 79th St, west of Biscayne Blvd (US 1), north of NW 41st St and east of NW 7th St.

Little Havana: South of NW 7th St, west of the Miami River, north of SW 8th St and east of NW 27th St.

MIAMI RESTAURANTS
BY NEIGHBORHOOD AREAS

(For full description, see alphabetical listings under Restaurants)

COCONUT GROVE

Big City Fish. 3015 Grand Ave

Brasserie Le Coze. 2901 Florida Ave

Buccione. 2833 Bird Ave

Cafe Europa. 3159 Commodore Plaza

Cafe Med. 3015 Grand Ave

Cafe Tu Tu Tango. 3015 Grand Ave

Grand Cafe (Grand Bay Hotel). 2669 S Bayshore Dr

Green Street Cafe. 3468 Main Hwy

Janjo's. 3131 Commodore Plaza

Kaleidoscope. 3112 Commodore Plaza

Mayfair Grill (Mayfair House Hotel). 3000 Florida Ave

Monty's Stone Crab. 2550 S Bayshore Dr

Señor Frog's. 3008 Grand Ave

Tuscany Trattoria. 3484 Main Hwy

DOWNTOWN

Las Tappas. 401 Biscayne Blvd

Snappers. 401 Biscayne Blvd

NORTH OF DOWNTOWN

Crabhouse. 1551 79th St Causeway

Il Tulipano. 11052 Biscayne Blvd

Mike Gordon. 1201 NE 79th St

Tony Chan's Water Club. 1717 N Bayshore Dr

SOUTH OF DOWNTOWN

Thai Orchid. 9565 SW 72nd St

Wah Shing. 9503 S Dixie Hwy

WEST OF DOWNTOWN

East Coast Fisheries. 360 W Flagler St

El Cid. 117 NW 42nd Ave

LITTLE HAVANA

Casa Juancho. 2436 SW 8th St

Centro Vasco. 2235 SW 8th St

Note: When a listing is located in a town that does not have its own city heading, it will appear under the city nearest to its location. In these cases, the address and town appear in parenthesis immediately following the name of the establishment.

Motels

(Rates are usually higher during football, Bowl games)

★ ★ ★**COURTYARD BY MARRIOTT.** *3929 NW 79th Ave (33166), west of downtown. 305/477-8118; FAX 305/599-9363.* 145 rms, 4 story. Mid-Jan–mid-Apr: S $109; D $119; each addl $10; suites $140; under 18 free; wkly rates; lower rates rest of yr. Crib free. TV; cable. Heated pool. Complimentary coffee in rms. Restaurant 6:30 am–11 pm. Rm serv. Bar 11 am–11 pm. Ck-out noon. Coin lndry. Meeting rms. Valet serv. Sundries. Free airport transportation. Exercise equipt; weight machine, bicycles, whirlpool. Refrigerator in suites. Balconies. Miami Intl Airport 3 mi SE. Cr cds: A, D, DS, MC, V.

D ⚦ 🛉🍴 ⊘ ⌚ SC

✔ ★ ★**FAIRFIELD INN BY MARRIOTT.** *3959 NW 79th Ave (33166), north of downtown. 305/599-5200; FAX 305/599-5200, ext 709.* 135 rms, 3 story. Jan–mid-Apr: S $68.95; D $74.95; 1st addl $3; under 18 free; lower rates rest of yr. Crib free. TV; cable. Heated pool. Complimentary continental bkfst in lobby. Restaurant nearby. Ck-out noon. Free airport transportation. Cr cds: A, D, DS, MC, V.

D ⚦ ⊘ ⌚ SC

✔ ★ ★**QUALITY INN SOUTH.** *14501 S Dixie Hwy (33176), south of downtown. 305/251-2000; FAX 305/235-2225.* 100 rms, 2 story, 14 kits. Dec–Apr: S $61–$77; D $67–$94; each addl $5; kit. units $92; under 18 free; varied lower rates rest of yr. Crib free. TV; cable. Heated pool. Restaurant 7 am–10 pm; Fri, Sat to 11 pm. Rm serv. Ck-out 11 am. Coin lndry. Cr cds: A, C, D, DS, ER, MC, V, JCB.

⚦ ⊘ ⌚ SC

✔ ★ ★**WELLESLEY INN AT MIAMI LAKES.** *7925 NW 154th St (33016), north of downtown. 305/821-8274; FAX 305/828-2257.* 100 rms, 4 story. Jan–Apr: S $54.99–$69.99; D $59.99–$79.99; each addl $5; suites $89.99; under 18 free; higher rates special events; lower rates rest of yr. Crib free. Pet accepted, some restrictions. TV; cable. Heated pool. Complimentary continental bkfst. Restaurant adj 7–1 am. Ck-out 11 am. Meeting rm. Valet serv. Refrigerator in suites. Cr cds: A, C, D, DS, MC, V.

D 🐾 ⚦ ⊘ ⌚ SC

Motor Hotel

✔ ★ ★**HOLIDAY INN-CALDER/JOE ROBBIE STADIUM.** *21485 NW 27th Ave (33056), University Dr & County Line Rd, north of downtown. 305/621-5801; FAX 305/624-8202.* 214 rms, 9 story. Jan–mid-Mar: S, D $59–$119; each addl $10; under 19 free; varied lower rates rest of yr. Crib free. TV; cable. Pool. Restaurant 6:30 am–2 pm, 5:30–10 pm. Bar 5 pm–midnight; entertainment, dancing. Ck-out noon. Coin lndry. Meeting rms. Bellhops. Valet serv. Gift shop. Private balconies. Panoramic views of Calder Racetrack and Joe Robbie Stadium. Cr cds: A, C, D, DS, MC, V, JCB.

D ⚦ ⊘ ⌚ SC

Hotels

★ ★**DOUBLETREE AT COCONUT GROVE.** *2649 S Bayshore Dr (33133), S on US 1 (S Dixie Hwy) S on SW 27th Ave, then N on S Bayshore Dr, in Coconut Grove. 305/858-2500; FAX 305/858-5776.* 192 rms, 20 story, 19 suites. S $99–$189; D $119–$199; each addl $20; suites $159–$299; under 18 free. Crib free. Valet parking $8. TV; cable. Heated pool; poolside serv. Restaurant 6:30 am–11 pm; Fri, Sat to midnight. Bars from 11 am. Ck-out noon. Meeting rms. Lighted tennis. Health club privileges. Many balconies with ocean view. Fishing, sailing yachts for charter. Opp Coconut Grove Convention Center. Cr cds: A, C, D, DS, ER, MC, V, JCB.

[D] [symbols] SC

★★★★★**GRAND BAY.** 2669 S Bayshore Dr (33133), in Coconut Grove. 305/858-9600; res: 800/327-2788; FAX 305/858-1532. 181 rms, 13 story, 49 suites. S $200–$255; D $200–$270; each addl $15; suites $325–$1,100; under 18 free; wkend rates. Crib free. TV; cable, in-rm movies. Heated pool; poolside serv. Restaurant (see GRAND CAFE). Rm serv 24 hrs. Bar 11:30–2 am; entertainment exc Sun. Ck-out 1 pm. Meeting rms. Concierge. Hair salon. Exercise rm; instructor, weights, bicycles, whirlpool, sauna, steam rm. Massage. Bathrm phones, minibars. Private patios, balconies. European-style villa, crystal chandeliers, objets d'art, commands a breathtaking view of Biscayne Bay. Cr cds: A, C, D, ER, MC, V.

[symbols]

★★★**GRAND PRIX.** 1717 N Bayshore Dr (33132), north of downtown. 305/372-0313; res: 800/872-7749; FAX 305/539-9228. 176 rms, 42 suites, 24 kit. units. Dec-Apr: S, D $125–$375; suites $250–$375; kit. units $175–$375; under 18 free; higher rates Boat Show; lower rates rest of yr. Crib free. TV; cable. Heated pool; poolside serv, lifeguard. Complimentary coffee in rms. Restaurant 7 am–11 pm. Bar; entertainment, dancing Thurs-Sat. Ck-out noon. Coin lndry. Meeting rms. Concierge. Gift shop. Airport, RR station, bus depot transportation. Exercise rm; instructor, weights, treadmill, whirlpool, sauna. Health club privileges. Game rm. Many minibars. Refrigerator, wet bar in suites. Many balconies. On Biscayne Bay. Skywalk connects to Omni International Mall. Cr cds: A, C, D, ER, MC, V, JCB.

[D] [symbols] SC

★★★**HOTEL INTER-CONTINENTAL.** 100 Chopin Plaza (33131), downtown. 305/577-1000; res: 800/327-3005; FAX 305/577-0384. 644 rms, 34 story. S $175–$245; D $195–$270; each addl $20; suites $450–$3,000; under 14 free; wkly, wkend rates. Garage; valet parking $10. TV; cable. Heated pool; poolside serv. Restaurant 7 am–11 pm. Rm serv 24 hrs. Bar 11:30–2 am. Ck-out noon. Convention facilities. Concierge. Minibars. Antiques, original artwork. 5-story domed atrium in lobby. Cr cds: A, C, D, ER, MC, V, JCB.

[D] [symbols]

★★★**MARRIOTT BISCAYNE BAY HOTEL & MARINA.** 1633 N Bayshore Dr (33132), downtown. 305/374-3900; FAX 305/375-0597. 605 rms, 31 story. Mid-Dec-Apr: S $140; D $150; each addl $10; suites $350–$1,050; under 16 free; lower rates rest of yr. Covered parking $7; valet parking $9. TV; cable. Heated pool; poolside serv. Restaurant 7 am–11 pm; Fri, Sat to midnight. Bar 11–1 am. Ck-out noon. Coin lndry. Convention facilities. Shopping arcade. Barber, beauty shop. Exercise rm; instructor, weight machines, treadmill, whirlpool. Game rm. Some bathrm phones. Minibars; refrigerators avail. Balconies. On Biscayne Bay, marina. **LUXURY LEVEL: CONCIERGE FLOOR.** 23 rms. S $160; D $180. Private lounge, honor bar. Complimentary continental bkfst, refreshments.
Cr cds: A, C, D, DS, ER, MC, V, JCB.

[D] [symbols] SC

★★★**MARRIOTT-DADELAND.** 9090 S Dadeland Blvd (33156), south of downtown. 305/670-1035; FAX 305/666-7124. 302 rms, 24 story. S, D $159; suites $275–$450; under 18 free. Crib free. Covered parking $6.50; valet $8. TV; cable. Heated pool; poolside serv. Restaurant 6:30 am–11 pm. Bar 2 pm–midnight; entertainment Thurs-Sat. Ck-out 11 am. Meeting rms. Concierge. Free airport, RR station, shopping transportation. Tennis & golf privileges. Exercise equipt; weights, bicycles, whirlpool, sauna. Game rm. **LUXURY LEVEL.** 50 rms, 2 suites, 3 floors. S, D $175; suites $275–$450. Private lounge, honor bar. Complimentary continental bkfst, refreshments, newspaper.
Cr cds: A, C, D, DS, MC, V.

[D] [symbols] SC

★★★**MAYFAIR HOUSE.** 3000 Florida Ave (33133), in Coconut Grove. 305/441-0000; res: 800/433-4555 (exc FL), 800/341-0809 (FL); FAX 305/447-9173. 182 suites, 5 story. Mid-Dec-Apr: S, D $230–$550;

each addl $35; under 12 free; wkend, honeymoon plans; lower rates rest of yr. Crib free. Valet parking $10. TV; cable, in-rm movies. Rooftop pool. Restaurant 2–11 pm (also see MAYFAIR GRILL). Rm serv 24 hrs. Bars from noon. Ck-out 1 pm. Meeting rms. Concierge. Shopping arcade. Health club privileges. Bathrm phones, refrigerators, honor bars. Private patios, all with hot tub. Elegant setting in World of Mayfair Mall. Cr cds: A, C, D, DS, ER, MC, V, JCB.

[D] [symbols]

★★★**OCCIDENTAL PARC.** 100 SE 4th St (33131), downtown. 305/374-5100; res: 800/521-5100 (exc FL); FAX 305/381-9826. 135 rms, 16 story, 90 suites. Jan-late Mar: suites $110–$180; under 12 free; lower rates rest of yr. Crib free. TV; cable. Pool; poolside serv. Restaurant 7 am–11 pm. Bar. Ck-out noon. Meeting rms. Concierge. Exercise equipt; weights, bicycles. Bathrm phones, minibars. On river. Cr cds: A, D, MC, V.

[D] [symbols]

★★★**OMNI INTERNATIONAL.** 1601 Biscayne Blvd (33132), north of downtown. 305/374-0000; FAX 305/374-0020. 535 rms, 30 story. Jan-late Mar: S $135–$155; D $140–$160; each addl $20; suites $195–$960; studio rms $195; under 17 free; wkend rates; lower rates rest of yr. Crib free. Parking $8.50; self-park $4.50. TV; cable. Heated rooftop pool; poolside serv. Restaurant 6:30 am–11 pm. Rm serv to 2 am. Bar. Ck-out noon. Convention facilities. Concierge. Golf privileges. Health club privileges. Refrigerators. Overlooks bay. 3-level shopping, dining, entertainment complex. **LUXURY LEVEL: OMNI CLUB.** 45 rms, 8 suites. S $165; D $175; suites $195. Minibars. Wet bars. Bathrm phones. Complimentary continental bkfst, newspaper.
Cr cds: A, C, D, ER, MC, V.

[D] [symbols] SC

★★★**SHERATON BISCAYNE BAY BRICKELL POINT.** 495 Brickell Ave (33131), downtown. 305/373-6000; FAX 305/374-2279. 598 rms, 18 story. Jan-Mar: S $129–$169; D $125–$179; each addl $20; suites $250 & $350; under 12 free; lower rates rest of yr. Crib free. TV; cable. Heated pool; poolside serv. Restaurant 6:30 am–11:30 pm. Bar 11–2 am; entertainment, dancing. Ck-out noon. Meeting rms. Concierge. Covered parking. Private patios, balconies. Extensive landscaping; at bayside. Cr cds: A, C, D, DS, ER, MC, V.

[D] [symbols] SC

Inn

✔ ★★★**MIAMI RIVER INN.** 118 SW South River Dr (33130), downtown. 305/325-0045; res: 800/HOTEL-89; FAX 305/325-9227. 40 rms in 4 bldgs, 2–3 story. S, D $60–$125; under 12 free; higher rates some special events. TV; cable. Pool; whirlpool. Complimentary continental bkfst. Restaurant nearby. Ck-out noon, ck-in 2 pm. Meeting rm. Lawn games. Opp river. Restored 1906 houses once owned by Miami's founders. Antiques. Cr cds: A, D, DS, MC, V.

[D] [symbols] SC

Resorts

★★★**DON SHULA'S HOTEL & GOLF CLUB.** (Main St, Miami Lakes 33014) 18 mi NW; N on I-95, W on FL 826 (Palmetto Expy), 1 blk E to Main St. 305/821-1150; res: 800/24-SHULA; FAX 305/821-1150, ext 1150. 301 rms, 3 story, 17 kits. Dec-Mar: S, D $169; each addl $10; suites $190–$270; under 12 free; golf package; varied lower rates rest of yr. Crib $10. TV; cable. 2 pools. Free supervised child's activities. Dining rms 7 am–11 pm. Snack bars 10 am–5 pm; Fri, Sat from 7 am. Bar 11–1 am; entertainment, dancing. Ck-out noon, ck-in 3 pm. Meeting rms. Shopping arcade. Valet parking. Lighted tennis, pro. Two 18-hole golf courses (1 lighted), pro, par 3, 2 putting greens, lighted driving range. Exercise rm; instructor, weights, bicycles, whirlpool, steam rm, sauna. Fishing trips. Wet bars; some refrigerators. Private patios, balconies. **LUXURY LEVEL: PRESS BOX.** 26 rms, 2 suites. S $179; D $189; suites from $229. Private lounge. Complimentary continental bkfst, refreshments, newspapers. Cr cds: A, C, D, DS, MC, V.

D 🍴 🏊 🎾 🏋 🐕 🚫 🕐 SC

★ ★ ★ **DORAL RESORT & COUNTRY CLUB.** *4400 NW 87th Ave (33178), west of downtown. 305/592-2000; res: 800/22-DORAL; FAX 305/594-4682.* 650 rms in 11 buildings. Dec–Apr: S, D $245–$360; each addl $25; suites $360–$1,500; under 17 free (limit 2); some lower rates rest of yr. Crib free. TV; cable. Heated pool; wading pool, poolside serv. Playground. Free supervised child's activities (hols only). Dining rm (public by res) 6:30 am–midnight; off-season to 10:30 pm; also 2 others. Rm serv 24 hrs (in season). Snack bar; box lunches. 3 bars 11–1:30 am. Ck-out 11 am, ck-in 4 pm. Convention facilities. Valet serv. 15 tennis courts (4 lighted), pro. Five 18-hole golf courses; 9-hole par 3 golf, 4 putting greens, lighted driving range, golf school, pro. Bicycle rentals. Lawn games. Soc dir; entertainment, dancing, movies. Rec rm. Game rm. Exercise rm; instructor, weights, bicycles, whirlpool, steam rm. Massage. European spa facilities. Bathrm phones, refrigerators, minibars. Private patios, balconies. Free transportation to Doral Ocean Beach Resort Hotel (see MIAMI BEACH). Luxurious resort hotel on 2,400 elaborately landscaped acres. Cr cds: A, C, D, DS, MC, V, JCB.

D 🔽 🍴 🏊 🎾 🏋 🐕 🚫 🕐

★ ★ ★ ★ **TURNBERRY ISLE RESORT & CLUB.** *(19999 W Country Club Dr, Aventura 33180) Approx 9 mi N via I-95, exit 20 (Ives Dairy Rd), E to US 1 (Biscayne Blvd), to Aventura Blvd. 305/932-6200; res: 800/327-7028; FAX 305/933-3811.* 340 rms in 5 bldgs, 3–7 story. Dec 20–Apr: S, D $275–$380; each addl $30; suites $475–$1,800; under 12 free; golf, tennis and spa plans; lower rates rest of yr. Crib free. TV; cable, in-rm movies. 3 pools; poolside serv. Dining rm for guests 7 am–10 pm. Box lunches, snack bar, picnics. Rm serv 24 hrs. Bars 11–1 am. Ck-out 11 am, ck-in 4 pm. Grocery, package store 1 blk. Coin lndry. Convention facilities. Lighted tennis, pro. 36-hole golf, greens fee $70 ($40 in summer), pro, putting green. Beach, boats, diving, water sports. Entertainment, dancing. Rec rm. Exercise rm; instructor, weights, bicycles, whirlpool, sauna, steam rm. Massage. Refrigerators; many in-rm whirlpools, hot tubs. On 300-acre secluded island with subtropical gardens; marina, private ocean club. Luxurious, gracious, comfortable. Cr cds: A, C, D, DS, ER, MC, V.

D 🔽 🍴 🏊 🎾 🏋 🐕 🚫 🕐

Restaurants

✔ ★ ★ **BIG CITY FISH.** *3015 Grand Ave, in Coconut Grove. 305/445-2489.* Hrs: 11:30 am–midnight; Fri, Sat to 1 am. No A/C. Bar. A la carte entrees: lunch, dinner $5.95–$15.95. Child's meals. Specialties: pan-fried snapper, hurricane shrimp. Raw bar. R & B band Wed–Sat. Parking. Outdoor dining. 2nd floor of Cocowalk complex; fish processing warehouse motif. Outdoor lounge area. Cr cds: A, MC, V.

D

★ ★ **BRASSERIE LE COZE.** *2901 Florida Ave, in Coconut Grove. 305/444-9697.* Hrs: noon–3 pm, 6–11 pm; wkends 6 pm–midnight. Closed Mon. French menu. Bar. Extensive wine list. Complete meals: lunch $14–$22, dinner $29–$40. Specialties: duck confit cassoulet, snapper with basil & olive oil. Salad bar. Valet parking. Outdoor dining. Large beer selection. Casual French brasserie atmosphere. Cr cds: A, D, MC, V.

★ ★ **BUCCIONE.** *2833 Bird Ave, in Coconut Grove. 305/444-4222.* Hrs: noon–2:30 pm, 6–10:30 pm; Mon from 6 pm; wkends 6–11:30 pm. Res accepted. Northern Italian menu. Extensive wine list. A la carte entrees: lunch $11–$25, dinner $25–$50. Specialties: grilled veal chops, lobster ravioli. Valet parking. Cr cds: A, C, D, DS, MC, V.

D

★ ★ **CAFE EUROPA.** *3159 Commodore Plaza, in Coconut Grove. 305/448-5723.* Hrs: 4 pm–midnight; Sat & Sun from noon. Res accepted. French menu. Bar. A la carte entrees: lunch $5.50–$11.95, dinner $8.95–$21.95. Specialties: bouillabaisse, duck à l'orange, rack of lamb. Parking. Outdoor dining. Parisian cafe atmosphere. Cr cds: A, C, D, MC, V.

D

✔ ★ **CAFE MED.** *3015 Grand Ave, in Coconut Grove. 305/443-4392.* Hrs: noon–midnight; wkends to 1 am; Sun brunch to 4 pm. Italian menu. Bar. A la carte entrees: lunch, dinner $4.25–$14.95. Sun brunch $9.95. Child's meals. Specializes in brick oven pizza, fresh pasta dishes, Mediterranean salads. Own desserts. Outdoor dining. Cr cds: A, D, MC, V.

D

✔ ★ ★ **CAFE TU TU TANGO.** *3015 Grand Ave, in Coconut Grove. 305/529-2222.* Hrs: 11:30 am–midnight; Fri, Sat to 2 am. International menu. Bar. A la carte entrees: lunch, dinner $2.50–$7.95. Child's meals. Specialties: Barcelona stir-fry, brick oven pizza. Entertainment. Parking. Outdoor dining. On 2nd floor of Cocowalk complex. Artist loft motif; painters at work. Cr cds: A, MC, V.

D

★ ★ **CASA JUANCHO.** *2436 SW 8th St, in Little Havana. 305/642-2452.* Hrs: noon–midnight; Fri, Sat to 1 am. Res accepted. Spanish menu. Bar. A la carte entrees: lunch $8–$40, dinner $12–$40. Specializes in imported Spanish seafood, fresh seafood, tapas. Strolling musicians. Valet parking. Spanish decor. Cr cds: A, C, D, MC, V.

D

★ ★ **CENTRO VASCO.** *2235 SW 8th St, in Little Havana. 305/643-9606.* Hrs: noon–midnight. Spanish, Amer menu. Res accepted Thurs–Sat. Bar. Semi-a la carte: lunch, dinner $9.95–$27. Specialties: seafood à la Basque, filet madrilène, paella alla Valenciana. Valet parking. Entertainment Wed–Sun. Fireplace. Spanish decor. Family-owned. Cr cds: A, C, D, DS, MC, V.

D

★ ★ ★ **CHEF ALLEN'S.** *(19088 NE 29th Ave, Aventura) Approx 8 mi N on Biscayne Blvd (US 1) to NE 191st St, at jct NE 29th Ave. 305/935-2900.* Hrs: 6–10:30 pm; Sat to 11 pm. Res accepted. Bar. Wine cellar. Semi-a la carte: dinner $19–$27. Child's meals. Specializes in fresh local fish, homemade pasta, dessert soufflés. Own baking. Valet parking. Open-glass kitchen; wood-burning mesquite grill. Cr cds: A, D, MC, V.

D

★ **CRABHOUSE.** *1551 79th St Causeway, north of downtown. 305/868-7085.* Hrs: 11:30 am–11 pm; Fri, Sat to midnight; early-bird dinner 4:30–6:30 pm. Bar. Semi-a la carte: lunch $4.55–$10.95, dinner $9.95–$33.95. Child's meals. Specializes in crab, lobster, fresh fish. Seafood bar. Valet parking. Overlooks bay. Cr cds: A, C, D, DS, MC, V.

D

★ ★ **THE DEPOT.** *(5830 S Dixie Hwy, South Miami) 8 mi S on US 1 (S Dixie Hwy). 305/665-6261.* Hrs: 5 pm–midnight. Res accepted. Serv bar. A la carte entrees: dinner $12.95–$26.95. Specializes in fresh seafood, prime western beef, rack of spring lamb. In historic depot, railroad station decor, memorabilia, miniature trains. Cr cds: A, MC, V.

★ **EAST COAST FISHERIES.** *360 W Flagler St, west of downtown. 305/373-5515.* Hrs: 11:30 am–10 pm. Wine. A la carte entrees: lunch, dinner $9.95–$25. Specialties: roasted garlic mahi mahi, shrimp Chippewa, stone crab claws, lobster. Parking. Authentic retail fish market located at docks on Miami River. Cr cds: A, V.

★ ★ **EL CID.** *117 NW 42nd Ave, west of downtown. 305/642-3144.* Hrs: noon–midnight; wkends to 1 am. Closed Dec 24. Res accepted. Spanish, Amer menu. Bar. A la carte entrees: lunch, dinner $14.95–$23.95. Child's meals. Pianist. Valet parking. Replica of Spanish castle. Strolling minstrels, flamenco dancers. Cr cds: A, C, D, DS, MC, V.

D

★ **GRAND CAFE.** (4-Star 1993; New chef, therefore not rated) *(See Grand Bay Hotel) 305/858-9600.* Hrs: 7 am–11 pm; Fri, Sat to 11:30 pm. Res accepted. International menu. Bar 11:30–2 am; Sun &

Mon to 1 am. A la carte entrees: bkfst $8.50–$17, lunch $8.50–$25, dinner $19–$26. Lunch buffet $11–$16.50. Sun brunch $22. Own baking. Valet parking. Pianist. Windows overlook garden area. Cr cds: A, D, MC, V.

D

✔ ★GREEN STREET CAFE. 3468 Main Hwy, in Coconut Grove. 305/567-0662. Hrs: 6–2 am. No A/C. Italian, Amer menu. A la carte entrees: bkfst $3–$6, lunch $5–$10, dinner $5–$13. Sun brunch $10. Specialties: sun-dried tomato pesto, fettucine, rack of lamb. Parking. Outdoor sidewalk cafe on corner lot. Cr cds: A, MC, V.

D

★ ★ ★IL TULIPANO. 11052 Biscayne Blvd (US 1), north of downtown. 305/893-4811. Hrs: 6–11 pm; Fri, Sat to midnight. Closed Sun; Dec 24; also Sept. Res accepted. Northern Italian menu. Beer. Wine cellar. A la carte entrees: dinner $14–$40. Specialties: pollo scarpariello, rigatini boscaiola "bosco," lobster tail. Own baking. Entertainment Sun–Mon, Wed–Thurs. Cr cds: A, D, MC, V.

D

★ ★JANJO'S. 3131 Commodore Plaza, in Coconut Grove. 305/445-5030. Hrs: 11:30 am–midnight; wkends 10:30–2 am; Sun brunch 11 am–1 pm. Res accepted. Caribbean, Asian menu. Bar. A la carte entrees: lunch $4.95–$16.50, dinner $15.95–$22. Sun brunch $4.25–$7.95. Serv charge 15%. Child's meals. Specializes in veal chops, shrimp pasta, filet mignon. Entertainment. Parking. Outdoor dining. Designed as Caribbean island house. Cr cds: A, C, D, MC, V.

D

★ ★KALEIDOSCOPE. 3112 Commodore Plaza, S on US 1 (S Dixie Hwy) to SW 32nd Ave, SE to Grand Ave, E to Commodore Plaza, in Coconut Grove. 305/446-5010. Hrs: 11:30 am–3 pm, 6–11 pm; Fri, Sat to midnight; Sun 11:30 am–3 pm, 5:30–10:30 pm; Sun brunch to 3 pm. Res accepted Fri, Sat. Wine, beer. Semi-a la carte: lunch $6.95–$10.95, dinner $11.95–$18.95. Sun brunch $16.95. Specialties: red snapper with glazed bananas, pasta. Outdoor dining. On 2nd floor. Cr cds: A, C, D, MC, V.

D

★ ★LAS TAPPAS. 401 Biscayne Blvd, downtown. 305/372-2737. Hrs: 11:30 am–midnight; Fri, Sat to 1 am. Spanish menu. Bar. Semi-a la carte: lunch $6.50–$15, dinner $15–$25. Specialties: seafood paella, serrano ham, seafood. Strolling minstrels. Parking. Outdoor dining. Open kitchen. Cr cds: A, C, D, DS, MC, V.

D

★ ★ ★MARK'S PLACE. (2286 NE 123rd St, N Miami) N on Biscayne Blvd (US 1) to NE 123rd St. 305/893-6888. Hrs: noon–2:30 pm, 6–11 pm; Sat, Sun from 6 pm. Closed Dec 25. Res accepted. Serv bar. Semi-a la carte: lunch $13.95–$17.95, dinner $14.95–$28.50. Specializes in fresh Florida seafood, pasta, gourmet pizza. Cr cds: A, C, D, MC, V.

D

★ ★ ★MAYFAIR GRILL. (See Mayfair House Hotel) 305/441-0000. Hrs: 7 am–11 pm; Sun brunch 11 am–3 pm. Res accepted. Bar 11 am–11 pm. Wine cellar. A la carte entrees: bkfst $6–$8, lunch $7.50–$12.95, dinner $16–$23. Own baking. Valet parking. Victorian setting with South Florida accents; stained-glass ceiling. Cr cds: A, C, D, DS, ER, MC, V, JCB.

D

★ ★MIKE GORDON. 1201 NE 79th St, north of downtown. 305/751-4429. Hrs: noon–10 pm; early-bird dinner 3:30–6 pm. Closed Thanksgiving, Dec 25 from 4 pm. Bar. Semi-a la carte: lunch $5.95–$16.95, dinner $13.75–$18.95. Child's meals. Specializes in fresh seafood. Valet parking; boat docking. Overlooks bay. Family-owned. Cr cds: A, D, MC, V.

D

★ ★MONTY'S STONE CRAB. 2550 S Bayshore Dr, in Coconut Grove. 305/858-1431. Hrs: 11:30 am–4 pm, 5–11 pm; Fri, Sat to midnight. Res accepted. Bar. Complete meals: lunch $6.95–$15, dinner $22–$32. Child's meals. Specializes in Florida seafood, stone crab.

Salad bar. Valet parking. Outdoor dining. Waterfront location overlooking marina. Cr cds: A, D, MC, V.

D

★ ★SEÑOR FROG'S. 3008 Grand Ave, in Coconut Grove. 305/448-0999. Hrs: 5 pm–2 am; wkends from 1 pm. Res accepted. Mexican menu. Bar. A la carte entrees: lunch, dinner $7–$15. Child's meals. Specializes in enchiladas, fajitas, chiles rellenos. Parking. Outdoor dining. Mexican cantina decor. Cr cds: A, D, MC, V.

D

★SNAPPERS. 401 Biscayne Blvd, at Pier #5, downtown. 305/379-0605. Hrs: 7:30 am–midnight. Bar. A la carte entrees: lunch $7.95–$13.95, dinner $11.95–$19.95. Child's meals. Specializes in seafood, pasta. Raw bar. Parking. Outdoor dining at bayside. On pier. Cr cds: A, D, MC, V.

D

✔ ★ ★THAI ORCHID. 9565 SW 72nd St, south of downtown. 305/279-8583. Hrs: 11:30 am–3 pm, 5–10:30 pm. Closed Thanksgiving, Dec 25. Thai menu. Wine, beer. A la carte entrees: lunch $4.25–$7.95, dinner $7.25–$17.95. Specializes in beef, curry, seafood. Parking. Decorated with various types of orchids. Cr cds: A, MC, V.

D

★ ★ ★TONY CHAN'S WATER CLUB. 1717 N Bayshore Dr, in mall area of Grand Prix Hotel, north of downtown. 305/374-8888. Hrs: noon–3 pm, 5–11 pm; Fri to midnight; Sat 5 pm–midnight; Sun 5–11 pm. Closed Thanksgiving, Dec 25. Chinese menu. Bar. A la carte entrees: lunch $6.50–$30, dinner $9–$40. Complete meals: lunch $8–$30, dinner $16–$30. Specialties: Peking duck, honey walnut shrimp, water club sea bass. Valet parking. Outdoor dining. Main dining rm has view of kitchen and of marina. Cr cds: A, D, MC, V.

D

★ ★TUSCANY TRATTORIA. 3484 Main Hwy, in Coconut Grove. 305/445-0022. Hrs: 11:30 am–midnight. Res accepted. Italian menu. Bar. A la carte entrees: lunch $5.95–$12.95, dinner $7.95–$19.95. Complete meals: lunch $10–$15, dinner $20–$30. Child's meals. Specialties: osso buco, snapper Livornese. Parking. Outdoor dining. Cr cds: A, C, D, DS, MC, V.

D

✔ ★UNICORN VILLAGE. (3565 NE 207th St, North Miami Beach) N on Biscayne Blvd (US 1) to NE 207th St. 305/933-8829. Hrs: 11:30 am–9:30 pm; wkends to 10 pm; Sun brunch to 3 pm. Wine, beer. A la carte entrees: lunch $4.95–$8.95, dinner $5.95–$15.95. Sun brunch $4.95–$9.95. Child's meals. Specialties: spinach lasagne, honey mustard chicken, Jamaican-style fish. Salad bar. Valet parking. 100-seat outdoor dining. Large restaurant overlooking Waterways Yacht Harbor. Totally nonsmoking. Cr cds: A, MC, V.

D SC

✔ ★ ★WAH SHING. 9503 S Dixie Hwy (US 1), in Dadeland Plaza, south of downtown. 305/666-9879. Hrs: 11:30 am–11 pm. Closed Thanksgiving. Chinese menu. Wine, beer. A la carte entrees: lunch $4.95–$6.95, dinner $7.95–$12.95. Specializes in Cantonese, mandarin & Szechwan dishes. Oriental decor. Cr cds: A, MC, V.

D

Miami Intl Airport Area *

*5 mi W of Miami (E-5) via FL 112 (toll) or FL 836.

Services and Information

Information: 305/876-7000.

Lost and Found: 305/876-7377.

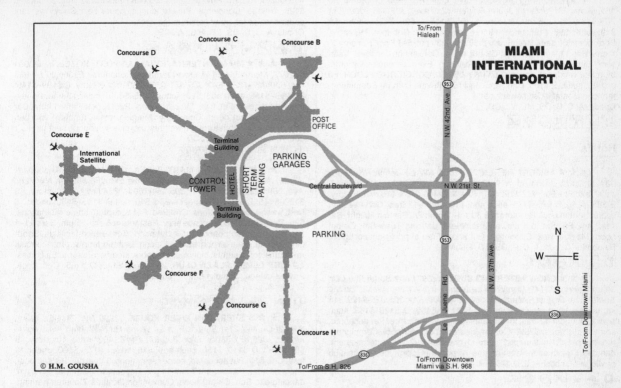

MIAMI INTERNATIONAL AIRPORT

Concourse C

Concourse D

Concourse B

To/From Hialeah

Concourse E

International Satellite

Terminal Building

POST OFFICE

PARKING GARAGES

CONTROL TOWER

HOTEL

SHORT TERM PARKING

Central Boulevard

N.W. 21st. St.

N.W. 42nd Ave

953

Terminal Building

PARKING

953

N.W. 37th Ave

Le Jeune Rd

N
W   E
S

To/From Downtown Miami

Concourse F

Concourse G

Concourse H

836

To/From S.H. 826

To/From Downtown Miami via S.H. 968

836

© H.M. GOUSHA

Weather: 305/661-5065.

Club Lounges: Crown Room (Delta), Concourse H; WorldClub (Northwest), Concourse G.

Terminals

Concourse B: Aero Costa Rica, AeroMexico, Air Aruba, Air France, Air Guadalupe, Air Margarita, Carnival, Copa, Laker, Mexicana, Midwest Express, Virgin Atlantic

Concourse C: ACES, American Trans Air, Continental, Finnair, Guyana, Haiti Trans Air, Air Metro North, Saeta, SAHSA, South African Airways, Taca, Turquoise Air

Concourse D: American, American Eagle

Concourse E: Aero Peru, Air Jamaica, ALM, Alitalia, Avensa, Avianca, Aviateca, British Airways, BWIA, Cayman, Ecuatoriana, El Al, Faucett, LAB, LACSA, Ladeco, LAP, Lufthansa, Russian Intl, Surinam, Trans Brasil

Concourse F: Argentina, Dominicana, Iberia, Lan Chile, LTU, United, VIASA, Zuliana

Concourse G: Air Canada, Northwest, TWA, Varig

Concourse H: Airways International, Bahamasair, Delta, Gulfstream, Paradise Island, USAir

(Airlines and their terminal locations may change. Before leaving for the airport, you should phone the airline to confirm terminal location for your flight.)

(See Coral Gables, Hialeah, Miami)

Motels

✔ ★HAMPTON INN. *(5125 NW 36th St, Miami Springs 33166) N via Le Jeune Rd (NW 42nd Ave) to NW 36th St, opp airport.* 305/887-2153; FAX 305/887-2153, ext 114. 110 units, 6 story. Dec–Apr: S $49.95–$72.95; D $59.95–$72.95; under 18 free; lower rates rest of yr. Crib free. TV; cable. Complimentary continental bkfst. Restaurant nearby. Ck-out noon. Valet serv. Some covered parking. Cr cds: A, C, D, DS, MC, V.

✔ ★ ★WELLESLEY INN. *(8436 NW 36th St, Miami 33166) N via Le Jeune Rd (NW 42nd Ave) to NW 36th St.* 305/592-4799; FAX 305/471-8461. 106 rms, 4 story, 13 suites. Jan–mid-Apr: S $74.99; D $79.99; each addl $10; suites $20 addl; under 18 free; wkly rates; lower rates rest of yr. Crib free. Pet accepted, some restrictions; $10. TV; cable. Heated pool. Complimentary continental bkfst, coffee. Ck-out 11 am. Coin lndry. Meeting rm. Valet serv. Refrigerator in suites. Cr cds: A, C, D, DS, MC, V.

Motor Hotels

★ ★BEST WESTERN MIAMI AIRPORT INN. *(1550 NW Le Jeune Rd, Miami 33126) On Le Jeune Rd (NW 42nd Ave).* 305/871-2345; FAX 305/871-2811. 208 rms, 6 story. S $79–$99; D $84–$104; each addl $5; suites $195; family rates. Crib $5. TV. Pool. Restaurant open 24 hrs. Rm serv. Bar 11–2 am. Ck-out 1 pm. Meeting rms. Bellhops. Sundries. Free airport transportation. Health club privileges. Game rm. Bathrm phones; some refrigerators. Cr cds: A, C, D, DS, ER, MC, V.

★ ★ ★HOLIDAY INN-LEJEUNE CENTRE. *(950 Le Jeune Rd NW, Miami 33126) On Le Jeune Rd (NW 42nd Ave).* 305/446-9000; FAX 305/441-0725. 305 rms, 6 story. S $95–$115; D $95–$125; each addl $10; suites $96–$196; under 19 free; wkend rates. Crib free. TV; cable. Pool; poolside serv. Restaurant 6:30 am–2:30 pm, 5–11 pm. Rm serv to 1 am. Bar 11 am–midnight. Ck-out noon. Convention facilities. Valet serv. Gift shop. Free airport transportation. Exercise equipt; weights, bicycles, whirlpool, sauna. **LUXURY LEVEL: CONCIERGE FLOOR.** 60 units, 1 suite. S $105; D $115; suite $191. Private lounge. Complimentary continental bkfst, newspaper.
Cr cds: A, C, D, DS, MC, V, JCB.

D 🖼 🕴 ✕ 🚫 ◎ SC

Hotels

✔ ★ ★AIRPORT REGENCY. *(1000 NW Le Jeune Rd, Miami 33126) On Le Jeune Rd (NW 42nd Ave).* 305/441-1600; res: 800/367-1039 (exc FL), 800/432-1192 (FL); FAX 305/443-0766. 176 rms, 6 story. S $65–$110; D $75–$125; each addl $10; under 12 free. Crib free. TV; cable. Heated pool. Restaurant 6:30 am–11 pm; Fri, Sat to midnight. Bar 11–2 am; Fri, Sat to 4 am; entertainment, dancing Tues–Sat. Ck-out noon. Meeting rms. Concierge. Gift shop. Free airport transportation. Balconies. Cr cds: A, C, D, DS, ER, MC, V.

D 🖼 ✕ 🚫 ◎ SC

★ ★ ★CROWN STERLING SUITES. *(3974 NW South River Dr, Miami Springs 33142) ½ mi N on Le Jeune Rd (NW 42nd Ave), W on NW South River Dr, just E of airport.* 305/634-5000; FAX 305/635-9499. 318 kit. suites, 10 story. Oct–mid-Apr: S $119–$159; D $129–$169; each addl $10; under 12 free; lower rates rest of yr. Crib free. Pet accepted, some restrictions; $25. TV; cable. Heated pool; whirlpool. Complimentary full bkfst. Restaurant 11 am–11 pm. Bar to 2 am; entertainment, dancing. Ck-out noon. Meeting rms. Airport transportation. Health club privileges. Cr cds: A, C, D, DS, ER, MC, V.

D 🖼 ➰ ✕ 🚫 ◎ SC

★ ★HOLIDAY INN-AIRPORT SOUTH. *(1101 NW 57th Ave, Miami 33126) Jct FL 836 & Red Rd exit (57th Ave).* 305/266-0000; FAX 305/266-9179. 267 rms, 10 story. Jan–Mar: S $80–$125; D $90–$135; each addl $10; suites $175–$215; under 18 free; higher rates Boat Show; lower rates rest of yr. Crib free. TV; cable. Pool; wading pool. Restaurant 6 am–2 pm, 5–10 pm. Bar. Ck-out noon. Coin lndry. Meeting rms. Concierge. Sundries. Free airport transportation. Refrigerators avail. Cr cds: A, C, D, DS, MC, V, JCB.

D 🖼 ➰ ✕ 🕴 ✕ 🚫 ◎ SC

★ ★ ★MIAMI AIRPORT HILTON & TOWERS. *(5101 Blue Lagoon Dr, Miami 33126) S of East-West Expy (Dolphin Expy) via Red Rd (FL 959), E on Blue Lagoon Dr.* 305/262-1000; FAX 305/262-5689. 500 rms, 14 story, 83 suites. Jan–May: S $115–$190; D $135–$210; each addl $20; suites $190–$500; family rates; wkend plans; lower rates rest of yr. Crib free. TV; cable. Pool; whirlpool, poolside serv. Restaurant 6:30 am–11 pm, Sat to midnight. Rm serv 24 hrs. Bar 11–2 am, Fri–Sat to 5 am; entertainment, dancing Tues–Sun. Ck-out noon. Convention facilities. Concierge. Gift shop. Valet parking. Free airport transportation. Lighted tennis. Exercise equipt; weights, bicycles, whirlpool, sauna. Some bathrm phones, refrigerators, minibars. Private patios, balconies. On lake; marina; sailboats, jet skis; waterskiing, windsurfing. Exotic birds in cages, saltwater tanks with exotic fish. **LUXURY LEVEL: THE TOWERS.** 128 units, 16 suites, 3 floors. S $175; D $195; suites $190–$500. Private lounge. Complimentary continental bkfst, refreshments, newspaper.
Cr cds: A, C, D, DS, ER, MC, V, JCB.

D 🖼 ➰ ➰ 🕴 ✕ 🚫 ◎ SC

★ ★MIAMI AIRPORT MARRIOTT HOTEL. *(1201 NW Le Jeune Rd, Miami 33126) On Le Jeune Rd (NW 42nd Ave), SW of FL 836.* 305/649-5000; FAX 305/642-3369. 782 rms, 10 story. S $59–$149; D $59–$169; family, wkend rates. Crib free. Pet accepted, some restrictions. TV; cable. Heated pool. Restaurant 6 am–midnight. Bars 11–2 am; dancing. Meeting rms. Gift shop. Barber, beauty shop. Free airport transportation. Lighted tennis, pro. Exercise equipt; weights, bicycles, 2

whirlpools. Rec rm. Private patios. **LUXURY LEVEL:** 92 rms, 3 floors. S $125; D $135. Concierge. Private lounge, honor bar. Complimentary continental bkfst, newspaper, magazines.
Cr cds: A, C, D, DS, ER, MC, V, JCB.

D 🖼 🕴 ✕ ✕ 🚫 ◎ SC

★ ★ ★MIAMI INTERNATIONAL AIRPORT HOTEL. *(PO Box 592077, Miami 33159) In airport terminal, Concourse E.* 305/871-4100; res: 800/327-1276; FAX 305/871-0800. 260 rms, 8 story. S $109–$149; D $119–$159; each addl $10; suites $195–$600; under 13 free; honeymoon packages. Crib free. TV; cable. Pool. Restaurant 7 am–11 pm. Bar 11–1 am. Ck-out noon. Coin lndry. Meeting rms. Drugstore. Barber, beauty shop. Exercise equipt; weights, bicycles, whirlpool, steam rm. Cr cds: A, C, D, ER, MC, V, JCB.

D 🖼 🕴 🕴 ✕ 🚫 ◎ SC

★ ★ ★RADISSON MART PLAZA. *(711 NW 72nd Ave, Miami 33126) Just S of East-West Expy (Dolphin Expy/FL 836) on NW 72nd Ave.* 305/261-3800; FAX 305/261-7665. 334 rms, 12 story. S $120–$145; D $140–$165; each addl $10; suites $155–$480; under 18 free; wkend package plans. Crib free. Pet accepted, some restrictions; $25. TV; cable. Pool; poolside serv. Restaurant 6 am–11 pm. Bars 11–1 am; entertainment; dancing. Ck-out noon. Convention facilities. Shopping arcade. Free airport transportation. Lighted tennis, pro. Exercise rm; instructor, weights, bicycles, whirlpool, steam rm, sauna. Balconies. **LUXURY LEVEL: PLAZA CLUB.** 30 rms. S $145; D $165. Concierge. Private lounge. Complimentary refreshments.
Cr cds: A, C, D, DS, ER, MC, V.

D 🖼 ➰ ➰ 🕴 ✕ 🚫 ◎ SC

★ ★ ★SHERATON RIVER HOUSE. *(3900 NW 21st St, Miami 33142) On NW 21st St, just E of Le Jeune Rd (NW 42nd Ave), adj to airport.* 305/871-3800; FAX 305/871-0447. 408 rms, 10 story. S $95–$150; D $110–$150; each addl $15; suites $175–$500; under 18 free. Crib $10. Pet accepted, some restrictions. TV; cable. Heated pool; poolside serv. Restaurant 7 am–11 pm. Rm serv to 2 am. Bar 11–2 am; dancing exc Sun. Ck-out noon. Convention facilities. Covered parking. Airport transportation. Lighted tennis. Exercise equipt; weights, bicycles, whirlpool, sauna. Game rm. Bathrm phone in some suites. Golf course adj. On Miami River. Cr cds: A, C, D, DS, ER, MC, V, JCB.

D 🖼 ➰ ➰ ➰ 🕴 🕴 ✕ 🚫 ◎ SC

★ ★ ★SOFITEL. *(5800 Blue Lagoon Dr, Miami 33126) S of East-West Expy (Dolphin Expy, FL 836) via Red Rd (FL 959), W on Blue Lagoon Dr.* 305/264-4888; FAX 305/262-9049. 283 rms, 15 story, 25 suites. S $125–$155; D $135–$175; each addl $15; suites $195–$500; under 17 free; wkend packages. Crib free. Pet accepted, some restrictions. Valet parking $6. TV; cable. Pool. Restaurant 6 am–midnight. Bar 11–2 am; entertainment. Ck-out noon. Meeting rms. Concierge. Gift shop. Free airport transportation. Lighted tennis. Exercise equipt; weights, bicycles, whirlpool, sauna. On lagoon. Cr cds: A, C, D, MC, V.

D 🖼 ➰ ➰ 🕴 ✕ 🚫 ◎ SC

Miami Beach *(E-5)*

Founded: 1915 **Pop:** 92,639 **Elev:** 5 ft **Area code:** 305

Miami Beach is a myriad of hotels, celebrities and sunbathers situated on an island 10 miles long and 1–3 miles wide. The city is an ideal spot from which to sample the sightseeing and recreational opportunities in south Florida and has become an international tourism destination. In the daytime, thousands of people lie in the sun at beaches and pools or enjoy watersports, shopping, museums and sightseeing. In the evening, nightclubs, theater, concerts and world-class dining provide visitors with a variety of entertainment options.

The Miami Beach area was created from what was a wilderness of palmettos: a sandbar infested with snakes and mosquitoes. John S. Collins failed in an attempt to develop avocado groves here and turned to real estate. To join his proposed residential colony with Miami, he built what was then the longest wooden bridge in the US. Collins auctioned off land, then much of it under swamp water, and dredged sand from the bay to transform it into solid ground. This created a yacht basin and several small islands. A pair of elephants, giveaways, super-salesmanship and a talented press agent helped finish the transformation from jungle to resort.

What to See and Do

1. **South Beach.** Extends south from the vicinity of Dade Blvd, concentrated mainly along Ocean Dr. This area was spared from demolition through the efforts of citizens and local designers, who began repainting and restoring art deco buildings from the 1920s, 30s and 40s using bright pastel colors. Subsequent redevelopment of the area has transformed the structures into eclectic boutiques, galleries, hotels, nightclubs and restaurants specializing in alfresco dining overlooking the ocean. Within this area is

    Art Deco District. From 6th to 23rd Sts, Lenox Court to Ocean Dr. A designated national historic district, this is a square-mile concentration of art deco, streamline moderne and Spanish Mediterranean Revival architecture unique in the nation. Former art deco apartment buildings, ballrooms and warehouses have been restored to pastel-and-neon luminosity and sometimes serve as canvases for murals, trompe l'oeil images and elaborate graffiti created by local artists. Special events include classic films, exhibits, music, lectures and fashions. Guided walking tours (Sat mornings). (See ANNUAL EVENTS) Phone 672-2014. Walking tour ¢¢¢

2. **Bass Museum of Art.** 2121 Park Ave. Permanent collection ranging from Old Masters to the moderns. Special exhibitions, lectures, performances, films. Tours by appt. (Daily exc Mon; closed hols & day after Thanksgiving) Phone 673-7533 or -7530. ¢¢¢

3. **Miami Beach Garden Center and Conservatory.** 2000 Convention Center Dr. Approx 200 varieties of tropical plants under 35-foot-high dome; special displays at Easter, Christmas. (Mon–Fri; closed hols) Phone 673-7720. **Free.**

4. **Jackie Gleason Theater of the Performing Arts.** 1700 Washington Ave. Capacity 2,700. Broadway plays, cultural series, contemporary entertainment. For schedule, fees phone 673-7300 (box office).

5. **"Nikko" Gold Coast Cruises.** Haulover Park Marina, 10800 Collins Ave. Sightseeing cruises to Millionaires Row, Miami Seaquarium, Vizcaya, Bayside Marketplace and Fort Lauderdale. Two cruises (daily). Reservations recommended; attraction fee included in some cruises. Phone 945-5461. ¢¢¢

(For further information contact the Chamber of Commerce, 1920 Meridian Ave, 33139, phone 672-1270; or the Greater Miami Convention & Visitors Bureau, 701 Brickell Ave, Suite 2700, Miami 33131, phone 539-3000.)

Annual Events

Art Deco Weekend. Art Deco District (see #1). A celebration of art deco and popular culture in the 1930s. Vintage cars, music, tours and entertainment throughout the district. 2nd wkend Jan.

Festival of the Arts. Collins Ave (FL A1A), between 49th & 53rd Sts. Art, music and drama. Early Feb.

International Boat Show. Miami Beach Convention Center. Phone 531-8410. Early Feb.

South Florida Auto Show. Miami Beach Convention Center. Phone 758-2643. Nov.

(See Coral Gables, Hollywood, Miami)

Motels

✔ ★★**BEACHARBOUR RESORT.** 18925 Collins Ave (33160). 305/931-8900; res: 800/643-0807 (exc FL); FAX 305/937-1047. 240 units, 2–4 story, 83 kits. Mid-Dec–late Apr: S, D $65–$100; each addl $8–$10; kit. units $10 addl; under 12 free; lower rates rest of yr. Crib

free. TV. 2 pools; wading pool. Restaurant 7:30 am–4 pm, 6–10 pm. Bars 11 am–midnight; entertainment exc Mon. Ck-out noon. Bellhops. Sundries. Lawn games. Refrigerators. Private patios, balconies. Cr cds: A, C, D, DS, ER, MC, V.

★★**MONACO.** 17501 Collins Ave (33160), in Sunny Isles. 305/932-2100; FAX 305/931-5519. 113 rms, 2 story, 39 kits. Dec–Apr: S, D $65–$130; each addl $7; kit. units $7 addl; under 15 free; varied lower rates rest of yr. Crib $6. TV; cable. Heated pool; wading pool. Restaurant 7:30 am–3 pm. Rm serv. Bar 11–1 am. Ck-out noon. Coin lndry. Bellhops. Valet serv. Sundries. Exercise equipt; bicycles, rowers, sauna. Rec rm. Lawn games. Refrigerators. Grills. On ocean. Cr cds: A, C, D, DS, ER, MC, V.

★★★**RIU PAN AMERICAN OCEAN RESORT** (formerly Radisson Pan American Ocean Resort). 17875 Collins Ave (33160), in Sunny Isles. 305/932-1100; FAX 305/935-2769. 146 rms, 2–3 story. Mid-Dec–Apr: S, D $149–$189; under 17 free; lower rates rest of yr. Crib free. TV; cable. Heated pool; lifeguard. Supervised child's activities. Restaurant 7 am–10 pm. Rm serv. Bar 11–2 am; entertainment. Ck-out noon. Coin lndry. Meeting rms. Bellhops. Concierge. Beauty shop. Free valet parking. Tennis. Golf privileges. Exercise equipt; bicycles, treadmill. Game rm. Miniature golf. Fishing charters avail. Bathrm phones, refrigerators, minibars. Complimentary newspaper, afternoon tea. Some balconies. On ocean. Cr cds: A, C, D, DS, ER, MC, V.

✔ ★★**SUEZ.** 18215 Collins Ave (33160), in Sunny Isles. 305/932-0661; res: 800/327-5278 (exc FL), 800/432-3661 (FL); FAX 305/937-0058. 196 rms, 2 story, 68 kits. Mid-Dec–Apr: S, D $67–$92; each addl $10; kit. units $15 addl; family rates; lower rates rest of yr. Crib free (kit. units only). TV; cable. 2 pools, heated; wading pool, sauna, poolside serv. Playground. Restaurant 7:30 am–10 pm. Bars. Ck-out noon. Coin lndry. Bellhops. Valet serv. Lighted tennis, pro. Lawn games. Refrigerators. On ocean. Cr cds: A, C, D, ER, MC, V.

Motor Hotels

✔ ★**CHATEAU-BY-THE-SEA.** 19115 Collins Ave (33160), in Sunny Isles. 305/931-8800; res: 800/327-0691; FAX 305/931-6194. 167 units, 2–4 story, 77 kits. Mid-Dec–mid-Apr: S, D $61–$88; each addl $6; under 12 free (limit 2); lower rates rest of yr. Crib free. TV. Heated pool; wading pool. Bar 11–4 am; entertainment, dancing. Ck-out 11 am. Coin lndry. Bellhops. Valet serv. Concierge. Sundries. Beauty shop. Tennis privileges. Lawn games. Refrigerators. Some balconies. On ocean. Cr cds: A, C, ER, MC, V.

★★**ESSEX HOUSE HOTEL.** 1001 Collins Ave (33139). 305/534-2700; FAX 305/532-3827. 60 rms, 3 story. Dec–May: S, D $75–$125; each addl $10; suites $125–$300; under 12 free; wkly rates; higher rates: hol wkends, conventions; lower rates rest of yr. Garage parking; valet $6. TV. Complimentary continental bkfst, coffee. Restaurant opp 4 pm–midnight. Ck-out noon. Bellhops. Valet serv. Concierge. Sundries. Airport transportation. Landmark "streamline moderne" hotel (1938) in Art Deco District. Cr cds: A, MC, V.

★★★**HOLIDAY INN-OCEANSIDE CONVENTION CENTER.** 2201 Collins Ave (33139). 305/534-1511; FAX 305/532-1403. 351 rms, 3–12 story. Mid-Dec–Apr: S $114–$123; D $129–$138; each addl $15; suites $158–$188; under 19 free; higher rates special events; lower rates rest of yr. Crib free. TV; cable. Pool; whirlpool, poolside serv. Restaurant 7 am–10 pm. Rm serv. Bar 5 pm–1 am; entertainment, dancing in season. Ck-out noon. Coin lndry. Convention facilities. Bellhops. Valet serv. Sundries. Barber, beauty shop. Lighted tennis. Game rm. On ocean. Cr cds: A, C, D, DS, MC, V, JCB.

★★**SINGAPORE RESORT.** *(9601 Collins Ave, Bal Harbour 33154) 5 mi N on FL A1A (Collins Ave).* 305/865-9931; res: 800/327-4911; FAX 305/866-2313. 238 units, 7 story, 109 kits. Mid-Dec–Apr: S, D $95–$123; each addl $6; kit. units $8 addl; MAP avail; varied lower rates rest of yr. Crib free. TV; cable. Heated pool; wading pool. Restaurant 8 am–3 pm; dining rm 5–8 pm. Rm serv. Bar; entertainment, dancing exc Mon. Ck-out noon. Coin lndry. Bellhops. Valet serv. Concierge. Tennis privileges. Putting green. Lawn games. On ocean. Cr cds: A, C, D, DS, ER, MC, V, JCB.

🖊️ ⛱️ Ⓦ

✔★★**SURFCOMBER HOTEL.** *1717 Collins Ave (33139).* 305/532-7715; res: 800/336-4264; FAX 305/532-7280. 194 rms, 3 story, 65 kit. units. Mid-Dec–mid-Apr: S, D $70–$110; each addl $10; suites $150–$200; kit. units $5 addl; under 16 free; lower rates rest of yr. Crib $15 (incl set-up). Valet parking $7. TV. Heated pool; poolside serv. Restaurant 7 am–9 pm. Rm serv. Bar noon–midnight; entertainment in season. Ck-out noon. Coin lndry. Meeting rms. Bellhops. Valet serv. Sundries. Gift shop. Exercise equipt; weight machines, treadmill. Some refrigerators. Some balconies. In Art Deco District. Cr cds: A, D, ER, MC, V, JCB.

⛱️ 🧍 Ⓦ

★★**THUNDERBIRD.** *18401 Collins Ave (33160), in Sunny Isles.* 305/931-7700; res: 800/327-2044; FAX 305/932-7521. 177 units, 5 story, 90 kits. Mid-Dec–late Apr: S, D $80–$125; each addl $8; kit. units $10 addl; lower rates rest of yr. Crib free. TV; cable. Heated pool; wading pool, poolside serv. Restaurant 7:30 am–11 pm. Rm serv. Bar noon–2 am; dancing. Ck-out 11 am. Coin lndry. Meeting rms. Bellhops. Valet serv. Concierge. Sundries. Barber, beauty shop. Tennis. Exercise equipt; bicycle, treadmill, whirlpool. Lawn games. Refrigerators. Balconies. On ocean. Cr cds: A, C, D, ER, MC, V.

🖊️ ⛱️ 🧍 Ⓦ

Hotels

★★★**THE ALEXANDER.** *5225 Collins Ave (33140).* 305/865-6500; res: 800/327-6121; FAX 305/864-8525. 178 kit. suites, 17 story. Mid-Dec–mid-Apr: 1-bedrm suites $310–$660; 2-bedrm suites $420–$900; penthouse suites from $1,250; each addl $25; under 17 free; lower rates rest of yr. Crib free. Garage, valet parking $8. TV; cable. 2 heated pools; poolside serv. Restaurants 7 am–11 pm; Fri, Sat to 1 am. Bar 11:30 am–midnight, Fri, Sat to 1 am; entertainment. Ck-out noon. Meeting rms. Concierge. Beauty shop. Golf privileges. Exercise equipt; weights, bicycles, 4 whirlpools, steam rm, sauna. Refrigerators. Private patios, balconies. Elegant decor; many antiques. On ocean; marina, water sport equipt. Cr cds: A, C, D, MC, V, JCB.

Ⓓ 🛥️ ⛱️ 🧍 Ⓦ

✔★**BENTLEY.** *510 Ocean Dr (33139).* 305/538-1700; FAX 305/532-4865. 40 rms, 3 story, 10 kits. S, D $55–$95; wkly rates. Parking $6 in/out. Restaurant noon–midnight. No rm serv. Bar. Ck-out noon. Coin lndry. No bellhops. Shopping arcade. Some refrigerators. Cr cds: A, MC, V.

Ⓦ

★★**BETSY ROSS.** *1440 Ocean Dr (33139).* 305/531-3934; res: 800/755-4601 (exc FL); FAX 305/531-5282. 80 rms, 4 story. Mid-Dec–mid-Apr: S, D $91–$130; each addl $10; suites $131–$185; under 12 free; lower rates rest of yr. Crib free. Valet parking $9; in/out $9. TV; cable. Pool. Restaurant 6 pm–midnight (also see A MANO). No rm serv. Bar. Ck-out noon. Some refrigerators. Colonial-style hotel (1941) in Art Deco District. Beach opp. Cr cds: A, MC, V.

⛱️ Ⓦ

★**BOULEVARD.** *740 Ocean Dr (33139).* 305/532-0376. 39 rms, 3 story, 6 suites. Oct–Apr: S, D $95–$225; each addl $15; suites $225; higher rates special events; lower rates rest of yr. Valet parking $10. TV; cable. Restaurant 7–1 am. Bar. Ck-out 11 am. Valet serv. Beauty shop. Some refrigerators. On beach. Cr cds: A, D, MC, V.

Ⓦ

★★**CARDOZO.** *1300 Ocean Dr (33139).* 305/535-6500; FAX 305/532-3563. 41 rms, 3 story, 6 suites. S, D $110–$135; suites $195–$225; under 12 free. Parking $4–$6. TV; in-rm movies. Restaurant 7–2 am. Rm serv 24 hrs. Bar noon–2 am. Ck-out noon. In Art Deco District. Cr cds: A, C, D, MC, V.

🚫 Ⓦ

★**CAVALIER.** *1320 Ocean Dr (33139).* 305/534-2135; res: 800/338-9076; FAX 305/531-5543. 44 rms, 3 story. Mid-Oct–mid-Apr: D $125; each addl $15; suites $180; under 12 free; lower rates rest of yr. TV. Complimentary continental bkfst, coffee. No rm serv. Ck-out noon. Some refrigerators. In Art Deco District. Cr cds: A, D, DS, MC, V.

🚫 SC

★★★**DORAL OCEAN BEACH RESORT.** *4833 Collins Ave (33140).* 305/532-3600; res: 800/22-DORAL; FAX 305/532-2334. 422 rms, 17 story. Mid-Dec–Apr: S, D $235–$325; each addl $20; suites: 1-bedrm $380–$1,500, 2-bedrm $530–$2,500; under 17 free; lower rates rest of yr. Crib free. Garage $9. TV; cable. Heated pool; wading pool, poolside serv. Free supervised child's activities. Restaurant 6:30–1:30 am (also see ALFREDO L'ORIGINALE DI ROMA). Rm serv 24 hrs (in season). Bar. Ck-out noon. Meeting rms. Shopping arcade. Beauty shop. Use of Doral Resort & Country Club facilities (see MIAMI) and Doral Satornia; free transportation. Lighted tennis. Five 18-hole golf courses, par 3 golf. Exercise rm; instructor, weights, bicycles, whirlpool, steam rm, sauna. Game rm. Rec rms. Lawn games. Bathrm phones, refrigerators, minibars. Some penthouse suites. On ocean; site was once the location of an old plantation. Complete water sports in ocean & Intracoastal Waterway. Cr cds: A, C, D, DS, ER, MC, V.

🚣 🐟 🏌️ 🖊️ ⛱️ 🧍 🏃 Ⓦ 🚫 SC

★★★**FONTAINEBLEAU HILTON RESORT AND SPA.** *4441 Collins Ave (33140).* 305/538-2000; FAX 305/531-9274. 1,206 rms, 17 story. Mid-Nov–May: S $185–$255; D $205–$275; each addl $20; suites $385–$665; family rates; package plans; lower rates rest of yr. Crib free. Pet accepted, some restrictions. Garage $9. TV; cable. Saltwater pool, ½-acre heated lagoon pool; poolside serv. Free supervised child's activities (June–Labor Day). Restaurant 6:30–2 am. Bars; entertainment, dancing. Ck-out 11 am. Convention facilities. Concierge. Shopping arcade. Barber, beauty shop. Golf course transportation. Lighted tennis, pro. Exercise rm; instructor, weights, bicycles, whirlpool, steam rm, sauna. Rec rm. Lawn games. Some refrigerators, minibars. Balconies. Tropical gardens, rocky waterfall into pool. On ocean; dockage, catamarans, windsurfing, paddle boats, para-sailing. Cr cds: A, C, D, DS, ER, MC, V.

Ⓓ 🐟 🖊️ ⛱️ 🧍 🏃 🚫 Ⓦ

★★**HOLIDAY INN NEWPORT PIER RESORT.** *16701 Collins Ave (33160), in Sunny Isles at jct FL A1A, 826.* 305/949-1300; FAX 305/956-2733. 350 rms, 12 story. Mid-Dec–mid-Apr: S, D $135–$175; each addl $10; suites $220–$295; under 18 free; higher rates Feb; lower rates rest of yr. Crib free. Valet parking $4/day. TV; cable. Pool; wading pool, poolside serv. Restaurant 7 am–3 pm; dining rm 4:30–11 pm. Bars. Ck-out noon. Coin lndry. Meeting rms. Beauty shop. Exercise equipt; weights, bicycles, whirlpool. Game rm. Lawn games. Refrigerators. Many balconies. On ocean; fishing pier; water sport rentals. Cr cds: A, C, D, DS, MC, V, JCB.

Ⓓ 🚣 ⛱️ 🧍 🚫 Ⓦ SC

★**LESLIE.** *1244 Ocean Dr (33139).* 305/534-2135; res: 800/338-9076; FAX 305/531-5543. 47 rms, 3 story. Mid-Oct–mid-Apr: S, D $105; each addl $15; suites $225; under 12 free; lower rates rest of yr. TV. Complimentary continental bkfst, coffee. No rm serv. Ck-out noon. Some refrigerators. In Art Deco District. Cr cds: A, C, D, DS, MC, V.

🚫 SC

★★**MARCO POLO RESORT.** *192nd St & Collins Ave (33160), in Sunny Isles.* 305/932-2233; res: 800/327-6363 (exc FL), 800/432-3664 (FL); FAX 305/935-5009. 509 rms, 11 story, 288 kits. Mid-Dec–Apr: S, D $96–$132; each addl $10; kit. units $8 addl; under 12 free (limit 2); lower rates rest of yr. Crib $6. Valet parking $4. TV. Heated pool; wading pool, poolside serv. Restaurant 7 am–11 pm. Bar 11–6 am; entertainment, dancing. Ck-out noon. Coin lndry. Convention facilities. Concierge. Drugstore. Barber, beauty shop. Game rm. Refrigerators. Some balconies. On ocean. Cr cds: A, C, D, MC, V.

★ ★ **MIAMI BEACH OCEAN RESORT.** *3025 Collins Ave (33140). 305/534-0505; res: 800/365-8000; FAX 305/534-0515.* 243 rms, 12 story, 2 suites. Mid-Dec–mid-Apr: S, D $140–$170; each addl $20; suites $450–$500; under 16 free; higher rates Christmas; lower rates rest of yr. Crib free. Valet parking $4–$6. TV; cable. Heated pool; poolside serv. Restaurant 7 am–11 pm. Bar 11–1 am; entertainment. Ck-out noon. Meeting rms. Concierge. Gift shop. Beauty shop. On ocean; swimming beach. Cr cds: A, C, D, MC, V.

★ ★ **QUALITY INN-SHAWNEE BEACH RESORT.** *4343 Collins Ave (33140). 305/532-3311; FAX 305/531-4074.* 479 rms, 4–11 story. Mid-Dec–mid-Apr: S, D $125–$180; each addl $20; suites $295; under 18 free; lower rates rest of yr. Crib free. Valet parking $7. TV. Heated pool; wading pool, whirlpool, poolside serv. Restaurant 6:30 am–11 pm. Bar 11–1 am. Ck-out noon. Coin lndry. Meeting rms. Concierge. Gift shop. Barber, beauty shop. Tennis. Golf privileges. Refrigerators avail. Some balconies. On beach. Cr cds: A, C, D, DS, ER, MC, V, JCB.

★ ★ **SEA VIEW.** *(9909 Collins Ave, Bal Harbour 33154) 5 mi N on FL A1A. 305/866-4441; res: 800/447-1010; FAX 305/866-1898.* 200 rms, 14 story, 13 kits. Mid-Dec–mid-Apr: S, D $179–$245; each addl $18; suites $210–$248; under 12 free; lower rates rest of yr. Crib free. TV; cable. Heated pool; poolside serv. Restaurant 7:30 am–3 pm, 6:30–10:30 pm. Bar; entertainment, dancing in season. Ck-out noon. Meeting rms. Boutique, beauty shop. Garage & valet parking. Solarium. Lawn games. Refrigerators. Many balconies. On ocean. Cr cds: A, C, D, MC, V.

★ ★ **SEACOAST TOWERS.** *5151 Collins Ave (33140). 305/ 865-5152; res: 800/523-3671 (exc FL), 800/624-8769 (FL); FAX 305/868-4090.* 180 kit. suites (1–3 bedrm), 16–17 story. Early Dec–Apr: kit. suites $170–$315; 7-day min special events, hols; lower rates rest of yr. Crib $5. Pet accepted. $100. Garage; valet parking $4. TV; cable, in-rm movies avail. 2 heated pools; poolside serv. Complimentary coffee in rms. Ck-out noon. Coin lndry. Meeting rms. Lighted tennis. Health club privileges. Game rm. Rec rm. Minibars. Balconies. On ocean, private beach; marina. Cr cds: A, D, MC, V.

★ ★ **SEVILLE BEACH.** *2901 Collins Ave (33140). 305/532-2511; res: 800/327-1641; FAX 305/531-6461.* 326 rms, 12 story. Late Dec–mid-Apr: S, D $120–$180; each addl $10; MAP avail; under 12 free; lower rates rest of yr. Crib free. Parking $7. TV; cable. Heated pool. Restaurant open 24 hrs. Bars. Ck-out noon. Meeting rms. Concierge. Drugstore. Barber, beauty shop. Exercise equipt; weights, bicycles, whirlpool. Lawn games. Refrigerators. Some balconies. On ocean. Cr cds: A, C, D, DS, ER, MC, V.

★ ★ ★ **SHERATON BAL HARBOUR.** *(9701 Collins Ave, Bal Harbour 33154) 5 mi N on FL A1A. 305/865-7511; FAX 305/864-2601.* 663 rms, 15 story. Mid-Dec–mid-Apr: S $165–$310; D $175–$315; each addl $25; suites $400–$2,000; under 17 free; lower rates rest of yr. Pet accepted, some restrictions. Valet parking $9. TV; cable. 2 pools, 1 heated. Supervised child's activities. Coffee in rms. Restaurant 6:30 am–11 pm; dining rm 5:30 pm–2 am. Bars noon–2 am. Ck-out noon. Convention facilities. Concierge. Shopping arcade. Tennis. Exercise equipt; weights, bicycles. Game rm. Minibars. Refrigerators avail. Many balconies. 2-story atrium; tropical gardens. On 10 acres at oceanfront; boat rental, aquacycles. Cr cds: A, C, D, DS, ER, MC, V, JCB.

★ ★ **SOL MIAMI BEACH.** *3925 Collins Ave (33140). 305/531-3534; res: 800/531-3534; FAX 305/531-1765.* 271 rms, 12 story, 59 kit. units. Dec–Apr: S, D $100–$140; each addl $15; kit. units $15 addl; under 12 free; wkly rates; higher rates Boat Show; lower rates rest of yr.

Crib avail. Valet parking $6. TV; cable. Pool; poolside serv. Restaurant 7 am–10 pm. Bar; entertainment Fri & Sat. Ck-out noon. Coin lndry. Meeting rms. Concierge. Sundries. Gift shop. Barber, beauty shop. Airport transportation. Tennis. Exercise equipt; bicycles, treadmill. Game rm. Lawn games. Refrigerators. Cr cds: A, D, DS, ER, MC, V.

✔ ★ **TUDOR.** *1111 Collins Ave (33139). 305/534-2934; FAX 305/531-7445.* 66 rms, 3 story. Mid-Dec–mid-Apr: S, D $70–$110; each addl $10; lower rates rest of yr. Garage $3–$5/day. TV; cable. Complimentary coffee in lobby. Restaurant noon–midnight. No rm serv. Ck-out 11 am. Refrigerators. Art Deco design, furnishings. In Art Deco District. Cr cds: A, D, MC, V.

Inn

✔ ★ ★ **BAY HARBOR.** *(9660 E Bay Harbor Dr, Bay Harbor Islands 33154) N via Collins Ave, near Broad Causeway. 305/868-4141; FAX 305/868-4141, ext 602.* 38 rms, 2 story, 12 suites. Dec–Apr: S $80; D $80–$100; each addl $20; suites $105–$115; under 16 free; monthly rates; higher rates holidays (3-night min); lower rates rest of yr. Crib free. Pet accepted, some restrictions; $12. TV; cable. Heated pool. Complimentary continental bkfst. Restaurant 5–11 pm. Ck-out 11 am, ck-in 3 pm. Bellhops. Airport transportation. Some refrigerators. Inn (1948) located on scenic Indian Creek. Cr cds: A, C, D, MC, V.

Restaurants

★ ★ **A FISH CALLED AVALON.** *700 Ocean Dr, in Avalon Hotel. 305/532-1727.* Hrs: 6–11 pm; Sat & Sun to midnight; Sat & Sun brunch noon–4 pm. Res accepted. Bar. A la carte entrees: lunch, dinner $12.95–$21. Sat & Sun brunch $12.95. Specializes in sesame seared tuna, steamed snapper in papillote sauce, steak. Valet parking. Patio dining. Original artwork. Cr cds: A, D, MC, V.

★ ★ ★ **A MANO.** *(See Betsy Ross Hotel) 305/531-6266.* Hrs: 6 pm–midnight; Fri & Sat to 1 am. Closed Mon; Dec 25. Res accepted. Caribbean-influenced Amer menu. Bar. Wine cellar. A la carte entrees: dinner $24–$32. Complete meals: dinner $45–$75. Specialties: soy honey marinated grilled tuna, oven-roasted black bean crusted salmon. Valet parking. Outdoor dining. Partially exposed glass-walled kitchen. In Art Deco District. Cr cds: A, C, D, DS, MC, V.

★ ★ ★ **ALFREDO L'ORIGINALE DI ROMA.** *(See Doral Ocean Beach Resort Hotel) 305/532-3600 ext 3126.* Hrs: 6:30–11:30 pm. Italian menu. Res accepted. Bar. A la carte entrees: dinner $16–$28. Complete meals: dinner $26. Serv charge 17%. Specialties: fettucine Alfredo, seafood, veal. Own baking. Pianist. Valet parking. Italian decor. Ocean view. Cr cds: A, C, D, ER, MC, V.

★ ★ **B.C. CHONG SEAFOOD GARDEN.** *(9601 E Bay Harbor Dr, Bay Harbor Islands) N on Collins Ave, near Broad Causeway. 305/ 866-8888.* Hrs: 11:30 am–10 pm; wknds to 11 pm; early-bird dinner 3–6 pm. Res accepted. Chinese, Amer menu. Bar. A la carte entrees: lunch $4.95–$6.50, dinner $6.95–$32.95. Specialties: Peking duck, lettuce pocket, prawns with black bean sauce. Valet parking. Outdoor dining. Four dining rms. Cr cds: A, D, MC, V.

★ ★ **BRUZZI.** *(3599 NE 207th St, North Miami Beach) N on US 1. 305/937-2400.* Hrs: 11:30 am–3 pm, 5–11 pm; wkends 5 pm–midnight; Sun brunch 11:30 am–3 pm. Res accepted. Italian, Amer menu. Bar. A la carte entrees: lunch $5.95–$9.95, dinner $7.95–$24.95. Sun brunch $5.95–$8.95. Specialties: grilled northern salmon, penne with shrimp & scallops, linguine primavera. Entertainment. Valet parking. Outdoor dining. Modern decor. Cr cds: A, D, MC, V.

★ ★ **CAFE TULIPE.** *9700 Collins Ave, at The Shops of Bal Harbour Shopping Center. 305/861-8556.* Hrs: 11:30 am–10:30 pm.

Italian, French, Amer menu. Bar. A la carte entrees: lunch $5–$16, dinner $10–$21. Specialties: pan-seared snapper, fricassee of seafood, osso buco Milanese. Outoor dining on ground level. Two dining rms, one on second floor. Cr cds: A, D, MC, V.

D

✔ ★ ★ **CAFFÉ MILANO.** *850 Ocean Dr.* 305/532-0707. Hrs: 9 am–5 pm, 7 pm–midnight. Closed Tues. Res accepted. Italian menu. Bar. Complete meals: bkfst $3.50–$5.50. Semi-a la carte: lunch $5–$18, dinner $11–$23. Serv charge 15%. Specialties: risotto al funghi Porcini, cotoletta alla Milanese. Covered patio and sidewalk dining. Art deco furniture on display. Cr cds: D, MC, V.

D

★ ★ **COLONY BISTRO.** *736 Ocean Dr, in Colony Hotel.* 305/673-6776. Hrs: 11:30 am–midnight; wkends to 1 am. Res accepted. Continental menu. Bar. A la carte entrees: lunch $7.50–$15, dinner $7.50–$22. Specialties: steak au poivre, grilled salmon, pasta. Valet parking. Outdoor dining. In Art Deco District. Cr cds: A, MC, V.

D

★ ★ ★ **THE FORGE.** *432 Arthur Godfrey Rd.* 305/538-8533. Hrs: 5 pm–midnight; Fri & Sat to 1 am. Res required. Contemporary American avant-garde cuisine. Bar from 5 pm. Wine cellar. A la carte entrees: dinner $15.95–$25.95. Child's meals. Specializes in steak, pastas, duck, fresh Florida seafood. Own baking. Entertainment, dancing. Valet parking. Elegant decor; 5 unique dining rms; antiques throughout, original artwork, stained glass. Elaborate wine cellar; tours provided; tasting rm. Cr cds: A, C, D, MC, V.

D

✔ ★ **LARIOS ON THE BEACH.** *820 Ocean Dr.* 305/532-9577. Hrs: 11–2 am. Cuban menu. Bar. Semi-a la carte: lunch $6.95–$7.95, dinner $8.95–$16.95. Specializes in roasted chicken, pork loin, black beans & rice. Cuban band Fri & Sat evenings. Valet parking. Outdoor dining. Cr cds: A, D, MC, V.

D

✔ ★ **LAURENZO'S COTILLION.** *2255 NE 164th St.* 305/948-8008. Hrs: 11:30 am–2 pm, 4–10 pm; early-bird dinner 4–6 pm. Closed Sun; Jan 1, Dec 25. Res accepted. Italian, Amer menu. Bar. Semi-a la carte: lunch $4.95–$5.95, dinner $5.95–$15.95. Child's meals. Specializes in seafood, steak, lasagne. Parking. Cr cds: A, MC, V.

D SC

★ ★ **MEZZANOTTE.** *1200 Washington Ave.* 305/673-4343. Hrs: 6 pm–midnight; Fri, Sat to 2 am. Closed Thanksgiving, Dec 25. Northern Italian menu. Bar. Semi-a la carte: dinner $12.95–$25.95. Specializes in pasta, veal. Valet parking. Trendy, neon-lit decor; in Art Deco District. Cr cds: A, C, D, MC, V.

D

✔ ★ **NEWS CAFE.** *800 Ocean Dr.* 305/538-6397. Open 24 hrs. Bar 8–5 am. A la carte entrees: bkfst $2.50–$5, lunch $4.25–$8.75, dinner $4.25–$8.75. Specializes in Middle Eastern cuisine, salads, sandwiches. Valet parking. Outdoor dining. In Art Deco District. Cr cds: A, C, D, MC, V.

D

★ ★ ★ **OSTERIA DEL TEATRO.** *1443 Washington Ave.* 305/538-7850. Hrs: 6 pm–midnight; wkends to 1 am. Closed Tues; major hols. Res accepted. Northern Italian menu. A la carte entrees: dinner $12–$28. Child's meals. Specialties: stuffed zucchini blossom with goat

cheese, stone crab peppardelle, tuna with a Mediterranean sauce. Valet parking. In Art Deco District. Cr cds: A, C, D, MC, V.

D

✔ ★ ★ **PEKING NOODLE.** *(3207 NE 163rd St, North Miami Beach) 6 mi N on FL 1A1, exit 826.* 305/956-9999. Hrs: 4–10 pm; Fri–Sun 11:30 am–10:30 pm. Closed Mon. Res accepted. Chinese menu. A la carte entrees: lunch $2.25–$9.95, dinner $10.95–$14.95. Specialties: Szechwan crispy fish, Peking duck, ly-mein. Parking. Intimate atmosphere. Cr cds: A, MC, V.

✔ ★ **RASCAL HOUSE.** *17190 Collins Ave, in Sunny Isles.* 305/947-4581. Hrs: 7–1:45 am. Closed 2 wks before Yom Kippur. Bar noon–midnight. A la carte entrees: bkfst $2.50–$5.50, lunch $4.25–$6.25, dinner $6.95–$11.95. Specializes in pastrami, stuffed cabbage, corned beef. Jewish, deli-type cafe. Family-owned. No cr cds accepted.

D

Unrated Dining Spot

TIRAMESU. *500 Ocean Dr.* 305/532-4538. Hrs: 6–11 pm; Fri, Sat to midnight; Mon 6:30–11 pm. Res required wkends. Northern Italian menu. Wine, beer. Semi-a la carte: dinner $15–$25. Specializes in pasta. Outdoor dining. Decorated in colors of Italy; in the Art Deco District. Cr cds: A, C, D, MC, V.

D

Naples (E-3)

Settled: 1887 **Pop:** 19,505 **Elev:** 9 ft **Area code:** 813

Named after the Italian city and complete with a "Bay of Naples," this Gulf of Mexico resort community has grown steadily since 1950. In addition to hotel, motel and residential construction, channel dredging has reopened the city to commercial fishing and large pleasure boats. Vacationers enjoy 10 miles of beach and a 1,000-foot fishing pier; shelling also is very good.

What to See and Do

1. **Jungle Larry's Zoological Park at Caribbean Gardens.** 1590 Goodlette Rd, E of Coastland Center. A 52-acre botanical garden with animals, birds and plants from around the world; boat tours; wild animal shows; tropical bird circus; lectures. Picnic area, snack bar, petting zoo, gift shop. (Daily; closed Thanksgiving, Dec 25) Phone 262-4053. ¢¢¢¢

2. **Conservancy Nature Center.** At 14th Ave N, off Goodlette-Frank Rd. Includes natural science museum featuring serpentarium, wildlife, aviary, rehabilitation clinic; trails, free guided boat tours, gift shop. (Hrs vary with season; closed hols) Phone 262-0304. **Free;** Museum ¢¢

3. **Collier County Museum.** 3301 Tamiami Trail E (US 41). Explores 10,000 years of Florida history; 4-acre historical park, archeological lab, 1910 steam locomotive, 1920s swamp buggy, restored house (1926). (Mon–Fri; closed hols) Phone 774-8476. **Free.**

4. **Collier Automotive Museum.** 2500 Horseshoe Dr. Collection of more than 70 classic racing and sports automobiles focuses on their history and significance. Includes one of the largest assemblages of Porsches outside Germany, Gary Cooper's 1935 Dusenberg SSJ and the first Ferrari imported into the US. (Dec–Apr, daily; rest of yr, daily exc Mon) Phone 643-5252. ¢¢¢

5. **Rookery Bay National Estuarine Research Reserve.** Approx 5 mi S, on Shell Island Rd. This 9,400-acre reserve encompasses a variety of habitats, including extensive mangrove forests, sea grasses, salt marshes and upland pine flatwoods; various wildlife and bird species can be observed; slide shows, interpretive displays, nature center with boat & canoe trips (winter) and guided boardwalk

tours (fee). Fishing; hiking. (Daily) Contact Reserve Manager, 10 Shell Island Rd, 33962; 775-8569 (nature center). **Free.**

6. **Corkscrew Swamp Sanctuary.** 20 mi NE on County 846. This National Audubon Society preserve contains one of the largest stands of mature bald cypress trees; two-mile boardwalk loops through the swamp; self-guided tour. Picnic area. Visitor center. (Daily) Phone 657-3771. **¢¢¢**

(For further information contact the Naples Area Chamber of Commerce, 3620 Tamiami Trail N, 33940; 262-6141.)

Annual Events

Collier County Fair. Agriculture and educational displays, entertainment, carnival. Jan.

American Indian Heritage Powwow. Apr.

Tropicool Fest. At City Docks. Includes Taste of Collier, Great Dock Canoe Races. 2 wks beginning early May.

Swamp Buggy Championship Races. Florida Sports Park. Early Mar, late May & last wkend Oct.

(See Bonita Springs, Marco Island)

Motels

★★**BEST WESTERN INN.** *2329 Tamiami Trail (US 41) (33940). 813/261-1148; FAX 813/262-4684.* 80 rms, 2 story. Feb–mid-Apr: S, D $99; suites $109; each addl $6; under 18 free; lower rates rest of yr. Crib $6. TV; cable, in-rm movies. 2 pools, 1 heated. Complimentary continental bkfst. Coffee in rms. Restaurant adj 5–10 pm. Ck-out 11 am. Lawn games. Refrigerators. Private patios, balconies. Cr cds: A, C, D, DS, MC, V.

★**COMFORT INN & EXECUTIVE SUITES.** *3860 Tollgate Blvd (33942). 813/353-9500; FAX 813/353-0035.* 151 units, 4 story, 8 suites, 53 kits. Feb–Apr: S, D $79–$89; each addl $8; suites $139–$189; kit. units $89–$94; under 18 free; wkly rates; lower rates rest of yr. Crib free. TV; cable. Heated pool; whirlpool, poolside serv. Complimentary continental bkfst, coffee. Restaurant adj 6 am–10 pm. Bar 3–9 pm. Ck-out noon. Meeting rms. Gift shop. Golf privileges, greens fee from $30 (cart addl), pro, putting green, driving range. Game rm. Wet bars. Balconies. Cr cds: A, C, D, DS, MC, V, JCB.

✔ ★★**DAYS INN.** *1925 Davis Blvd (33942). 813/774-3117; FAX 813/775-5333.* 158 rms, 3 story, 29 kits. Dec–Apr: S, D $44–$90; each addl $5; kit. suites $65–$115; under 18 free; wkly rates; lower rates rest of yr. Crib free. TV; cable. Heated pool; whirlpool. Playground. Complimentary continental bkfst, coffee. Restaurant adj 6 am–midnight. Ck-out noon. Lawn games. Refrigerators. Private patios. Picnic tables, grills. Marina adj. Beach 1 mi. Cr cds: A, C, D, DS, MC, V.

★★**HAMPTON INN.** *3210 Tamiami Trail (US 41) (33940). 813/ 261-8000; FAX 813/261-7802.* 107 rms, 4 story. Mid-Dec–Apr: S $85–$88; D $89–$94; under 18 free; lower rates rest of yr. Crib free. TV. Heated pool. Complimentary continental bkfst, coffee. Restaurant nearby. Ck-out noon. Meeting rm. Exercise equipt; bicycles, stair machine. Some refrigerators. Cr cds: A, C, D, DS, MC, V.

★★**HOWARD JOHNSON.** *221 9th St S (US 41) (33940). 813/ 262-6181; FAX 813/262-0318.* 100 rms, 2 story. Mid-Dec–mid-Apr: S, D $75–$125; each addl $10; under 18 free; lower rates rest of yr. Crib free. TV; cable. Heated pool; poolside serv. Playground. Restaurant nearby. Ck-out noon. Lawn games. Some refrigerators. Private patios, balconies. Cr cds: A, C, D, DS, ER, MC, V, JCB.

✔ ★**STONEY'S COURTYARD INN.** *2630 N Tamiami Trail (US 41) (33940). 813/261-3870; res: 800/432-3870; FAX 813/261-4932.* 72 rms, 2 story. Jan–Apr: S, D $75–$85; suites $110; lower rates rest of yr. Pet accepted, some restrictions; $5. TV; cable. Heated pool. Complimentary continental bkfst. Restaurant nearby. Ck-out 11 am. Coin lndry. Refrigerators avail. Cr cds: A, C, D, DS, MC, V.

★**THE TIDES.** *1801 Gulf Shore Blvd N (33940). 813/262-6196; res: 800/438-8763; FAX 813/262-3055.* 36 rms, 2 story, 24 kits. Mid-Jan–Apr: S, D $85–$90; kit. units $125–$130; 1-bedrm suites $165–$185; each addl $10; lower rates rest of yr. Crib $6. TV; cable. Heated pool. Complimentary continental bkfst, coffee. Restaurant nearby. Ck-out 11 am. Airport transportation. Refrigerators. Some balconies. On beach. Cr cds: A, MC, V.

★**TROPICS IN OLDE NAPLES.** *312 8th Ave S (33940). 813/ 262-5194; FAX 813/262-4876.* 60 rms, 1–2 story, 45 kits. Jan–Apr: S, D $82; each addl $5; suites $119–$165; kit. units $89–$109; under 16 free; lower rates rest of yr. Crib $5. TV; cable. Complimentary continental bkfst. Restaurant nearby. Ck-out 11 am. Coin lndry. Lawn games. Bicycle rentals. Refrigerators. Picnic tables, grills. Gulf beach 2 blks. Cr cds: A, DS, MC, V.

★★**VANDERBILT BEACH.** *9225 Gulf Shore Dr N (33963). 813/597-3144; res: 800/243-9076; FAX 813/597-2199.* 66 rms in 4 bldgs, 1–4 story, 16 condos, some kit. suites. Mid-Dec–Apr: S, D $80–$99; each addl $10; kit. units $83–$198; under 4 free; lower rates rest of yr. Crib free. TV; cable. Heated pool. Complimentary continental bkfst (motel). Complimentary coffee in motel rms. Restaurant adj 7 am–11 pm. Ck-out 11 am. Coin lndry. Tennis. Lawn games. Refrigerators. Some balconies. Picnic tables, grills. Beachfront property on Gulf. Cr cds: A, MC, V.

★★★**VANDERBILT INN ON THE GULF.** *11000 Gulf Shore Dr N (33963), at Vanderbilt Beach. 813/597-3151; res: 800/643-8654; FAX 813/597-3099.* 147 rms, 2 story, 16 kits. Mid-Feb–Apr: S, D $146–$159; each addl $10; kit. units $254; under 18 free; lower rates rest of yr. Crib free. TV; cable. Heated pool; wading pool, poolside serv. Restaurant 7 am–10 pm. Rm serv. Bar; entertainment wkends. Ck-out 11 am. Coin lndry. Gift shop. Sundries. Some balconies. On Gulf. Wiggins Pass State Park adj. Cr cds: A, C, D, DS, MC, V.

★★**WELLESLEY INN.** *1555 5th Ave S (33942). 813/793-4646; FAX 813/793-5248.* 105 rms, 3 story. Late Dec–Apr: S, D $79–$100; under 18 free; lower rates rest of yr. Crib avail. Pet accepted, some restrictions; $5. TV. Heated pool. Complimentary continental bkfst. Restaurant adj 11 am–10 pm. Ck-out 11 am. Some refrigerators. Cr cds: A, C, D, DS, MC, V.

Motor Hotels

★**COVE INN RESORT & MARINA.** *1191 8th St S (33940), on Naples Bay. 813/262-7161; FAX 813/261-6905.* 102 rms, 3 story. Mid-Dec–Apr: S, D $110; suites $260; kit. units $125; under 18 free; lower rates rest of yr. Crib free. TV; cable. Heated pool; poolside serv. Restaurants 7:30–1 am. Bar 11–1 am. Ck-out 11 am. Coin lndry. Meeting rm. Bellhops. Sundries. Lawn games. Some refrigerators. Picnic tables, grills. Situated on a natural peninsula; balconies overlook waterway. Cr cds: A, D, DS, MC, V.

★★★**INN OF NAPLES AT PARK SHORE.** *4055 Tamiami Trail N (US 41) (33940). 813/649-5500; res: 800/237-8858; FAX 813/649-5500.* 64 rms, 5 story. Mid-Dec–mid-Apr: S, D $100–$140; under 18 free; lower rates rest of yr. Crib $5. TV; cable, in-rm movies. Heated pool; poolside serv. Continental bkfst. Coffee in rms. Restaurant 7:30 am–2:30 pm,

6–10 pm; Sun to 2:30 pm. Rm serv. Bar 11:30 am–11 pm; also Sun noon–6 pm (in season). Ck-out noon. Meeting rms. Bellhops in season. Refrigerators. Private patios, balconies. Spanish-Mediterranean setting. Cr cds: A, D, DS, MC, V.

D **☎** **⊘** **⊙** **SC**

★★**PARK SHORE RESORT.** *600 Neapolitan Way (33940).* 813/263-2222; res: 800/548-2077; FAX 813/263-0946. 156 suites, 2–4 story. Mid-Dec-Apr: 1- & 2-bedrm suites $175–$195; each addl $10; under 18 free; wkly, monthly rates; lower rates rest of yr. Crib free. TV; cable. Heated pool; whirlpool, poolside serv. Restaurant 11:30 am–10 pm. Bar. Ck-out 11 am. Coin lndry. Tennis. Lawn games. Refrigerators. Private patios, balconies. Picnic tables, grills. On 13 landscaped acres; pond, bridge, waterfall. Cr cds: A, MC, V.

⊘ **☎** **⊙** **SC**

★★★**QUALITY INN GOLF & COUNTRY CLUB.** *4100 Golden Gate Pkwy (33999), at FL 951.* 813/455-1010; FAX 813/455-4038. 153 rms, 2–4 story, 24 suites (1–2 bedrm), 32 kit. units. Feb-Apr: S, D $85–$135; each addl $8; suites $150–$210; kit. units $115–$140; under 18 free; monthly rates; golf plans; lower rates rest of yr. Crib free. TV; cable. Heated pool; whirlpool, poolside serv. Restaurant 7 am–9 pm. Bar 10:30 am–11 pm; entertainment. Ck-out noon. Meeting rms. Valet serv. Sundries. Tennis. 18-hole golf, greens fee $39 (incl half-cart), pro, putting green, driving range. Balconies. Cr cds: A, C, D, DS, ER, MC, V, JCB.

D **🖊** **⊘** **☎** **⊘** **⊙** **SC**

Hotel

★★★**EDGEWATER BEACH.** *1901 Gulf Shore Blvd N (33940).* 813/262-6511; res: 800/821-0196 (exc FL); FAX 813/262-1243. 124 kit. suites, 4–7 story. Mid-Dec-Apr: 1-bedrm suites $199–$550; 2-bedrm suites $320–$1,200; under 18 free; golf plans; lower rates rest of yr. Crib free. TV; cable. Heated pool; poolside serv. Restaurant 7 am–11 pm. Bar 4 pm–midnight; entertainment. Ck-out noon. Meeting rms. Gift shop. Valet parking. Tennis privileges. 18-hole golf privileges, greens fee $75 (incl half-cart), putting green, driving range. Private patios, balconies. Overlooks Gulf of Mexico. Grand piano in lobby & dining rm; music in afternoons, evenings. Cr cds: A, C, D, DS, MC, V.

D **🖊** **⊘** **☎** **⊘** **⊙** **⊙** **SC**

Inn

★★★**INN BY THE SEA.** *287 11th Ave S (33940); I-75 exit 16.* 813/649-4124. 5 rms, 2 story. Late Dec-Apr: S, D $117–$170; suite $170; lower rates rest of yr. Children over 16 yrs only. Complimentary continental bkfst, coffee. Restaurant nearby. Ck-out 11 am, ck-in 3 pm. Airport transportation. Located near beach. Built in 1937 of yellow heart pine. Totally non-smoking. Cr cds: MC, V.

⊘ **⊙**

Resorts

★★**NAPLES BEACH HOTEL & GOLF CLUB.** *851 Gulf Shore Blvd N (33940).* 813/261-2222; res: 800/237-7600; FAX 813/261-7380. 315 units in 6 bldgs, 2–8 story, 100 kit. units. Mid-Dec-mid-Apr: S, D $160–$260; each addl $15; suites $210–$375; kit. units $190–$375; under 18 free; AP, MAP avail; golf plans; lower rates rest of yr. Crib $10. TV; cable. Heated pool; poolside serv, lifeguard. Free supervised child's activities. Dining rm 7 am–9:30 pm. Box lunches. Snack bar. Picnics. Rm serv 7 am–midnight. Bar noon–2 am; entertainment, dancing. Ck-out noon, ck-in 4 pm. Grocery. Coin lndry 1 mi. Package store. Convention facilities. Bellhops. Valet serv. Concierge. Gift shop. Airport transportation avail. Sports dir. Tennis, pro. 18-hole golf, greens fee $65 (shared cart), pro, putting green, driving range. Swimming beach. Boats. Bicycle rentals. Lawn games. Soc dir. Rec rm. Game rm. Many refrigerators. Some balconies. Picnic tables. On Gulf. Cr cds: A, D, DS, MC, V.

D **⊷** **🖊** **⊘** **☎** **⊘** **⊙** **⊙** **SC**

★★★**REGISTRY.** *475 Seagate Dr (33940).* 813/597-3232; res: 800/247-9810; FAX 813/597-3147. 424 rms in main building, 18 story, 50 villas. Late Dec-mid-Apr: S, D $290–$455; each addl $35; suites $475–$500; villas $475; under 18 free; tennis, golf plans; honeymoon packages; lower rates rest of yr. Crib free. TV; cable, in-rm movies. 3 heated pools; poolside serv. Supervised child's activities. 4 dining rms 7 am–11 pm (also see LAFITE). Box lunches. Snack bar. Rm serv 24 hrs. Bar 11–2 am. Ck-out noon, ck-in 3 pm. Convention facilities. Valet serv. Concierge. Shopping arcade. Barber, beauty shop. Valet parking. Activities dir. 15 tennis courts, 5 lighted, pro, instruction avail, pro shop. Golf privileges, greens fee (incl cart) $90. Putting green. Swimming beach. Boating; water sports avail. Bicycle rentals. Lawn games. Exercise rm; 3 instructors, weights, bicycles, whirlpool, steam rm, sauna. Entertainment, dancing. Refrigerators, wet bars; mini honor bars. Private patios, balconies. All tower rms with view of gulf. Atrium lobby with 2-story fountain. On 21 lush tropical acres; trolley to beach. Cr cds: A, C, D, DS, ER, MC, V, JCB.

D **🖊** **⊘** **☎** **🎾** **⊘** **⊙** **SC**

★★★★**THE RITZ-CARLTON, NAPLES.** *280 Vanderbilt Beach Rd (33941).* 813/598-3300; res: 800/241-3333; FAX 813/598-6690. 463 units, 14 story, 32 suites. Late Dec-Apr: S, D $295–$450; each addl $15; suites $750–$1,000; under 17 free; monthly, honeymoon plans; MAP avail; lower rates rest of yr. Crib free. TV; cable, in-rm movies. Heated pool; poolside serv. Free supervised child's activities. Dining rms 6:30 am–11 pm (also see THE DINING ROOM and THE GRILL ROOM). Rm serv 24 hrs. Bar 11–1:30 am; entertainment, dancing. Ck-out noon, ck-in 3 pm. Convention facilities. Valet serv. Concierge. Gift shop. Barber, beauty shop. Covered parking, valet. Airport transportation. Lighted tennis, pro. 18-hole golf privileges, greens fee (incl cart) $85, pro, putting green, driving range. On white sand beach; water sports. Complimentary bicycles avail. Lawn games. Activities dir. Rec rm. Exercise rm; instructor, weights, bicycles, whirlpool, sauna, steam rm. Massage therapy. Nutrition & fitness program. Bathrm phones, minibars. Balconies. Classic Mediterranean-style decor with the splendor of a bygone era. On 23 acres, with lush seaside gardens, fountains. *LUXURY LEVEL:* RITZ-CARLTON CLUB. 65 rms, 10 suites, 2 floors. Dec-Apr: S, D $495; suites $759–$2,500. Concierge. Private lounge, honor bar. Complimentary refreshments.
Cr cds: A, C, D, DS, ER, MC, V.

D **⊷** **🖊** **⊘** **☎** **🎾** **⊘** **⊙**

★★**WORLD TENNIS CENTER & RESORT.** *4800 Airport Rd (33942).* 813/263-1900; res: 800/292-6663 (US), 800/621-6665 (CAN); FAX 813/649-7855. 148, 2-bedrm apts, 2 story. Feb-Apr: 1–4 persons $145; wkly, monthly rates; lower rates rest of yr. Crib free. Maid serv avail (fee). TV; cable. Heated pool; whirlpool, sauna. Dining rm 8 am–9 pm. Bar to 10 pm. Ck-out 11 am, ck-in 3 pm. Grocery 1 mi. Meeting rm. 16 tennis courts, 10 lighted, pro. 18-hole golf privileges, greens fee $65–$100, pro, putting green, driving range. Refrigerators, washers & dryers. Private patios, balconies. Mediterranean village atmosphere on 82½ acres. Tennis stadium. Cr cds: A, DS, MC, V.

⊘ **⊷** **🖊** **⊘** **☎** **⊙** **SC**

Restaurants

✔ ★★★**BAYSIDE.** *4270 Gulfshore Blvd N, in Village Shopping Center.* 813/649-5552. Hrs: 11:30 am–11:30 pm; Sun brunch to 2 pm. Res accepted. Continental menu. Bar. Semi-a la carte: lunch $7.75–$13, dinner $14.50–$20. Sun brunch $7.75–$13. Child's meals. Specializes in fresh seafood, lamb, veal, pasta. Pianist. Valet parking. Outdoor dining. View of bay. Cr cds: A, C, D, DS, MC, V.

D

★★★**CHARDONNAY.** *2331 Tamiami Trail N (US 41).* 813/261-1744. Hrs: 5:30–10 pm. Closed Sun June-mid-Dec; also Aug. Res accepted. French, continental menu. Bar from 4 pm. Wine cellar. Semi-a la carte: dinner $16.25–$26.75. Specializes in duck, salmon, escargot. Own baking, desserts. Valet parking. Jacket. Cr cds: A, MC, V.

D

★ ★ ★ **CHEF'S GARDEN.** *1300 3rd St S. 813/262-5500.* Hrs: 11:30 am–2:30 pm, 6–10 pm; Sun from 6 pm; May–Oct 6:30–9:30 pm. Res accepted. Bar; entertainment Tues–Sun. Wine cellar. A la carte entrees: lunch $6.95–$12.50, dinner $16.95–$26.95. Child's meals. Specializes in seafood, pasta, rack of lamb. Own baking, desserts. Valet parking (dinner). Patio. Cr cds: A, C, D, DS, MC, V.

D

★ ★ ★ **THE DINING ROOM.** *(See The Ritz-Carlton, Naples Resort) 813/598-3300.* Hrs: 6–10 pm; Sun brunch (exc May–Oct) 11 am–2:30 pm. Closed Mon–Thurs (May–Oct). Res accepted. Bar 11–1:30 am. Wine list. A la carte entrees: dinner $18–$24. Sun brunch $28. Child's meals. Specializes in fresh Florida seafood, modern American cuisine. Own baking, desserts. Pianist. Valet parking. Old-World grandeur; antiques, crystal chandeliers. Jacket. Cr cds: A, C, D, DS, ER, MC, V.

D

✔ ★ **THE DOCK AT CRAYTON COVE.** *840-B 12th Ave S, at Naples Bay. 813/263-9940.* Hrs: 11:30 am–midnight; Sun from noon. Closed Dec 25. No A/C. Bar. A la carte entrees: lunch $3.95–$7.95, dinner $6.95–$12.95. Child's meals. Specializes in seafood, hamburgers, steak. Rustic, informal atmosphere. Cr cds: A, MC, V.

D

★ ★ ★ **THE GRILL ROOM.** *(See The Ritz-Carlton, Naples Resort) 813/598-3300.* Hrs: 6–10 pm. Res accepted. Bar. Wine cellar. A la carte entrees: dinner $28–$36. Child's meals. Specializes in grilled fresh seafood, hand-cut aged beef. Pianist, vocalist. Valet parking. Old English decor; club atmosphere. Jacket. Cr cds: A, C, D, DS, ER, MC, V.

D

★ **KELLY'S FISH HOUSE.** *1302 5th Ave S. 813/774-0494.* Hrs: 4:30–10 pm. Closed Thanksgiving, Dec 25; also Sept. Bar. Semi-a la carte: dinner $9.95–$18.95. Child's meals. Specializes in fresh seafood, Key lime pie. Parking. Outdoor dining. Nautical decor; decorated with shells. Overlooks Gordon River. Cr cds: A, MC, V.

D

★ ★ ★ **L'AUBERGE.** *602 5th Ave S. 813/261-8148 or -6816.* Hrs: 11 am–2 pm, 5:30–9 pm; June–Sept to 2 pm. Closed Memorial Day, Dec 25; also Sun off season. Res accepted. Southern French menu. Wine list. A la carte entrees: lunch $4.95–$10.95, dinner $16.95–$20.95. Specialties: saumon en papillotte, carré d'agneau (Bearnaise). Ambience of small French village eatery. Cr cds: MC, V.

D

★ ★ ★ **LAFITE.** *(See Registry Resort) 813/597-3232.* Hrs: 6–10:30 pm. Res accepted. Bar. Extensive wine list. A la carte entrees: dinner $22–$35. Child's meals. Specializes in fresh seafood, beef, poultry, lamb, duck. Harpist. Valet parking. Old World elegance; intimate dining alcoves. Tableside food preparation. Jacket. Cr cds: A, C, D, DS, ER, MC, V, JCB.

D

✔ ★ ★ **MARGAUX'S.** *3080 Tamiami Trail N (US 41). 813/434-2773.* Hrs: 11:30 am–2 pm, 5–9 pm; Sat & Sun from 5 pm; early-bird dinner 5–6 pm. Closed Jan 1, July 4, Dec 25. Res accepted. Country French menu. Bar. Semi-a la carte: lunch $4.95–$8.95, dinner $10.95–$17.95. Child's meals. Specialties: bouillabaisse, duck Marseille, veal & lobster. Parking. Intimate atmosphere; French accents. Cr cds: MC, V.

D

★ ★ ★ **MAXWELL'S ON THE BAY.** *4300 Gulf Shore Blvd N, in Village Shopping Center. 813/263-1662.* Hrs: 11 am–10 pm; Sun brunch to 3 pm. Res accepted. Bar. Wine cellar. Semi-a la carte: lunch $5.95–$14.95, dinner $14–$21. Sun brunch $5.95–$14. Child's meals. Specialties: veal & shrimp Maxwell's, lobster, fresh seafood. Valet parking (dinner). Outdoor dining. French country pine furnishings. Overlooks Venetian Bay. Cr cds: A, DS, MC, V.

D

★ ★ **MERRIMAN'S WHARF.** *1200 5th Ave S, at Tin City. 813/261-1811.* Hrs: 11 am–10 pm; Sun from noon. Bar. Semi-a la carte: lunch $5–$10, dinner $12–$18. Specializes in fresh seafood, steak. Parking. Outdoor dining. On wharf; nautical decor. Cr cds: A, C, D, MC, V.

D

✔ ★ **MESON OLÉ.** *2212 Tamiami Trail (US 41). 813/649-6616.* Hrs: 11 am–3 pm, 5–11 pm; Sat noon–11 pm; Sun noon–10 pm. Closed Thanksgiving, Dec 25. Res accepted. Mexican, Spanish menu. Bar. Semi-a la carte: lunch $4.25–$10.75, dinner $9.25–$14.95. Specialties: "las fajitas olé," en pollo al whiskey, la paella Valenciana. Parking. Mexican/Spanish decor. Cr cds: A, C, D, DS, MC, V.

★ ★ **MICHAEL'S CAFE, BAR & GRILL.** *2950 9th St N (US 41), at Hibiscus Ctr. 813/434-2550.* Hrs: 11:30 am–2:30 pm, 5–10 pm; June–Sept from 5 pm; early-bird dinner 5–6:30 pm. Closed Christmas; Super Bowl Sun. Res accepted. Bar. Semi-a la carte: lunch $4.95–$12, dinner $11.95–$21.95. Child's meals. Specializes in beef, poultry, fresh seafood. Parking. Outdoor dining. Art deco decor. Cr cds: A, MC, V.

D **SC**

✔ ★ ★ **NICK'S ON THE WATER.** *1001 10th Ave S. 813/649-7770.* Hrs: 11:30 am–10 pm; Fri & Sat to 11 pm; early-bird dinner 4–5:30 pm; Sun brunch 11:30 am–3 pm. Res accepted. No A/C. Italian menu. Bar. Wine list. Semi-a la carte: lunch $3.25–$6.95, dinner $6.95–$13.95. Specialties: Nick's angel hair, rigatoni a la vodka. Entertainment. Parking. Outdoor dining. Waterfront dining, scenic view. Cr cds: A, DS, MC, V.

D

✔ ★ **THE PALM.** *754 Neapolitan Way. 813/649-6333.* Hrs: 11 am–9 pm; Sun from 8:30 am. Res accepted. Bar. Semi-a la carte: bkfst $2.75–$6, lunch $4–$8, dinner $8–$15. Child's meals. Specializes in roast turkey, lamb shanks, corned beef. Parking. Cr cds: A, C, D, DS, MC, V.

D

★ ★ **PEWTER MUG.** *12300 N Tamiami Trail (US 41). 813/597-3017.* Hrs: 5–10 pm; Fri, Sat to 11 pm. Closed July 4, Thanksgiving, Dec 25; also Super Bowl Sun. Bar. Semi-a la carte: dinner $7.95–$22.95. Child's meals. Specializes in prime rib, steak, fresh fish. Salad bar. Parking. Cr cds: A, C, D, MC, V.

D

✔ ★ ★ **PLUM'S CAFE.** *8920 Tamiami Trail N (US 41). 813/597-8119.* Hrs: 11:30 am–11 pm; Sun from 5 pm. Italian, Amer menu. Bar. Semi-a la carte: lunch, dinner $6.50–$15.50. Child's meals. Specialties: seafood ali-oli, chicken carbonara, Plum's hot club. Own desserts. Valet parking. Cr cds: A, C, D, DS, MC, V.

D

★ ★ **RIVERLIGHTS.** *1355 5th Ave S. 813/775-7772.* Hrs: 11 am–3 pm, 5–10 pm; Sun brunch 10 am–2:30 pm. Closed Mon. Res accepted. French, Italian menu. Bar. Semi-a la carte: lunch $8–$16, dinner $12.95–$33.75. A la carte entrees: dinner $11.95–$25.50. Specialties: Seafood Chef's Delight, The Three Musketeers. Entertainment Tues–Sun. Parking. Outdoor dining. Waterside terraces. Cr cds: A, MC, V.

D

✔ ★ **RIVERWALK FISH & ALE HOUSE.** *1200 5th Ave S, at Old Marine Marketplace at Tin City. 813/263-2734.* Hrs: 11 am–11 pm; Sun from noon. Closed Thanksgiving, Dec 25. Res accepted. No A/C. Bar. Semi-a la carte: lunch, dinner $3.95–$14.95. Child's meals. Specializes in seafood. Valet parking in season. Outdoor dining. In complex of restored waterfront warehouses. Cr cds: A, DS, MC, V.

D

★ **ROSIE'S WATERFRONT CAFE.** *1444 5th Ave S. 813/775-6776.* Hrs: 11–1 am; Sun noon–midnight. Res accepted for paddle wheel boat. No A/C. Bar. Complete meals (paddle wheel boat): bkfst $11.95, lunch $14.95. Semi-a la carte: lunch $5.95–$7.95, dinner $5.95–$13.95. Serv charge (paddle wheel boat) 17%. Child's meals. Specialties: conch fritters, jerk chicken. Steel drum band exc Mon.

Parking. Outdoor dining. Island atmosphere; paddle wheel boat *Rosie* makes regular trips daily. Cr cds: A, D, DS, MC, V.

★★★**ST GEORGE & THE DRAGON.** *936 5th Ave S. 813/262-6546.* Hrs: 11 am–11 pm; Sun 5–9 pm (Jan–Mar). Closed Dec 25. Bar. Wine list. Semi-a la carte: lunch $5.25–$11.75, dinner $8.95–$29.95. Specialties: almond shrimp, conch chowder, prime rib. Own baking. Valet parking. Nautical antiques, decor. Family-owned. Jacket (dinner, dining rm only). Cr cds: A, C, D, MC, V.

★★**TRUFFLES.** *1300 3rd St S, 2nd floor. 813/262-5500.* Hrs: 11 am–11 pm; Sun brunch to 2 pm. Bar. Semi-a la carte: lunch, dinner $4.25–$19.50. Sun brunch $6–$9. Child's meals. Specialties: tuna Caesar salad, crispy fish, pasta. Own desserts. Valet parking. Cafe/bistro atmosphere. Cr cds: A, C, D, DS, MC, V.

★★★**VILLA PESCATORE.** *8920 Tamiami Trail N (US 41). 813/597-8119.* Hrs: 6–10 pm. Res accepted. Northern Italian, Amer menu. Bar. Wine list. Semi-a la carte: dinner $15–$24. Specializes in northern Italian cuisine, seafood. Own breads, desserts. Valet parking. Cr cds: A, C, D, DS, MC, V.

Unrated Dining Spot

NAPLES DINNER THEATER. *1025 Piper Blvd. 813/597-6031 or 337-1101 (Fort Myers).* Evenings: Tues–Sat cocktails 5:30 pm, buffet 6 pm, show 8:15 pm; matinees: Thurs & Sat–Sun cocktails 11 am, buffet 11:15 am, show 1:15 pm. Closed Mon; also early Aug–early Oct. Res required. French, international menu. Serv bar. Oct–Apr, buffet: matinee $30.50, dinner $33.50–$39; prices incl show; lower prices May–July. Big band Sun in season. Parking. Victorian decor. Jacket. Cr cds: A, C, D, DS, MC, V.

New Port Richey (C-3)

Pop: 14,044 **Elev:** 11 ft **Area code:** 813

(For information about this area contact the West Pasco Chamber of Commerce, 5443 Main St, 34652; 842-7651.)

Annual Event

Chasco Fiesta. Celebration of the town's Indian heritage. Street parade, boat parade, entertainment, activities, contests, art show. food. Mid–late Mar.

(See Brooksville, Clearwater, Dunedin)

Motels

★★**COMFORT INN GATEWAY.** *6826 US 19N (34652). 813/842-6800; FAX 813/842-5072.* 66 rms, 2 story, 22 kit. units. Feb–Apr: S $51.50–$59.50; D $56.50–$64.50; each addl $5; kit. units $55–$70; under 18 free; wkly, wkend rates; lower rates rest of yr. Crib free. TV; cable. Heated pool; whirlpool, sauna. Complimentary continental bkfst. Complimentary coffee in lobby. Restaurant adj 7 am–10 pm; Fri, Sat to 11 pm. Ck-out noon. Coin lndry. Meeting rms. Cr cds: A, C, D, DS, ER, MC, V, JCB.

★**DAYS INN AND LODGE.** *(11736 US 19N, Port Richey 34668)* On US 19, ⅛ mi S of FL 52. 813/863-1502; FAX 813/863-1502, ext 185. 156 rms, 2 story, 35 apts. Feb–Apr: S, D $52–$56; each addl $5;

apts $65; under 13 free; monthly rates; lower rates rest of yr. Crib free. Pet accepted; $4 per day. TV; cable. Pool. Ck-out 11 am. Coin lndry. Cr cds: A, C, D, DS, MC, V.

✔★**GULF COAST INN.** *(10826 US 19N, Port Richey 34668)* N on US 19. 813/869-9999. 50 rms, 2 story, 32 kit. units. Jan–Apr: S $44; D $48; kit. units $52; family, wkly rates; lower rates rest of yr. Crib $2. TV; cable, in-rm movies. Heated pool; whirlpool, sauna. Complimentary coffee in lobby. Restaurant nearby. Ck-out 11 am. Coin lndry. Meeting rms. Some in-rm whirlpools. Cr cds: A, DS, MC, V.

★★**HOLIDAY INN BAYSIDE.** *5015 US 19N (34652). 813/849-8551; FAX 813/849-8551, ext 283.* 135 rms, 2 story. Late Feb–Apr: S, D $55–$65; each addl $5; under 19 free; lower rates rest of yr. Crib free. TV; cable. Pool; wading pool, poolside serv. Restaurant 6 am–10 pm. Rm serv. Bar 11–2 am; entertainment Thurs–Sat. Ck-out noon. Lawn games. Dockage behind building. Cr cds: A, C, D, DS, MC, V, JCB.

Restaurants

★★**ELENI'S.** *6818 US 19N. 813/841-0323.* Hrs: 7 am–10 pm; Fri, Sat to 11 pm. Bar. Semi-a la carte: lunch $3.95–$5.95, dinner $4.95–$15.95. Specializes in fresh seafood, steak. Salad bar. Cr cds: MC, V.

✔★**STICKY FINGERS.** *4201 Grand Blvd. 813/845-6266.* Hrs: 11 am–10 pm; Sun noon–9 pm. Closed some major hols. Bar. Semi-a la carte: lunch $3.95–$6.95, dinner $5.95–$13.95. Child's meals. Specializes in seafood, barbecued shrimp & ribs. Parking. Outdoor dining. Cr cds: DS, MC, V.

New Smyrna Beach (B-4)

Founded: 1767 **Pop:** 16,543 **Elev:** 8 ft **Area code:** 904

Dr. Andrew Turnbull, a Scottish doctor, brought a group of settlers from Greece, Italy and the Spanish island of Minorca to work on the sugar and indigo plantations he had developed here. He named the community in honor of Smyrna, Greece, his wife's home, but many of the settlers, dissatisfied with the settlement's administration, went to St Augustine in the late 1770s. Today, New Smyrna, with its moss-hung oaks, palms, tropical shrubbery and citrus trees, is a resort center with agricultural resources, commercial fishing and light manufacturing. Canaveral National Seashore (see TITUSVILLE) is located south of town.

What to See and Do

1. **New Smyrna Sugar Mill Ruins State Historic Site.** 2 mi W of US 1, S off FL 44. Remains of a large sugar mill destroyed by Indians during the Seminole War. Construction of the building began in 1830; it was made of coquina, a native rock made of shells and sand. Today, all that remains is a walking beam from a steam engine and cooking pots. Nature trails. Standard hrs, fees. Phone 428-2126.

2. **New Smyrna Speedway.** W on FL 44 at jct FL 415. Races every Sat night; also special events during Speed Weeks in Feb. For schedule, fees phone 427-4129.

(For further information contact the New Smyrna Beach–Edgewater–Oak Hill Chamber of Commerce, 115 Canal St, 32168; 428-2449.)

Annual Event

"Images" Festival of the Arts. Riverside Park & Old Fort Park. Early Mar.

(See Daytona Beach, DeLand, Ormond Beach)

Motels

★★**COASTAL WATERS INN.** *3509 S Atlantic Ave (32169). 904/428-3800; res: 800/321-7882; FAX 904/432-5002.* 40 rms, 3 story, 32 kits. No elvtr. Late Dec–Labor Day: S, D $65–$80; each addl $7.50; 1 & 2-bedrm kit. units $79–$135; under 12 free; wkly rates; higher rates: race wk, some hols; lower rates rest of yr. Crib $7.50. TV; cable. Heated pool; wading pool. Complimentary coffee in lobby. Restaurant opp 7 am–11 pm. Gift shop. Free Daytona airport transportation. Private patios, balconies. Picnic tables. On beach. Cr cds: A, MC, V.

✔★**NOCTURNE.** *1104 N Dixie Frwy (US 1) (32168). 904/428-6404.* 20 rms, 2 story, 8 kits. Mid-Dec–mid-Apr, mid-June–late Aug: S, D $40; each addl $5; kit. units (3-day min) $5 addl; under 12 free; higher rates special events (5-day min); lower rates rest of yr. TV; cable. Restaurant opp 6 am–11 pm. Ck-out 11 am. Some covered parking. Cr cds: A, MC, V.

✔★**OCEAN AIR.** *1161 N Dixie Frwy (US 1) (32168). 904/428-5748.* 14 rms. Mid-Dec–mid-Apr, June–Sept: S, D $34–$50; each addl $5; wkly rates off-season; higher rates special events; lower rates rest of yr. Crib $5. TV; cable. Pool. Complimentary coffee in lobby. Restaurant nearby. Ck-out 11 am. Lawn games. Refrigerators. Picnic tables. Cr cds: A, C, D, DS, MC, V.

Motor Hotel

★★**ISLANDER BEACH RESORT.** *1601 S Atlantic Ave (32169). 904/427-3452; FAX 904/426-5606.* 114 kit. suites, 7 story. Late Dec–early May, mid-June–Labor Day: suites $60–$120 (3-night min); higher rates special events; lower rates rest of yr. Crib free. TV; cable, in-rm movies. Heated pool; wading pool. Free supervised child's activities. Restaurant 11 am–10 pm. Bar to 2 am. Ck-out 10 am. Coin lndry. Exercise equipt; weight machine, bicycles, whirlpool. Game rm. Lawn games. Many balconies; some private patios. Picnic tables. On beach. Shopping center opp. Cr cds: A, DS, MC, V.

Hotels

★**OCEANIA SUITE.** *421 S Atlantic Ave (32169). 904/423-8400; res: 800/874-1931; FAX 904/423-0254.* 62 kit. suites (2-bedrm), 8 story. Feb–Apr, late May–early Sept: kit. suites $99–$110; under 12 free; higher rates race wk, hols; wkly rates; lower rates rest of yr. Crib $5. TV; cable. Heated pool. Restaurant nearby. Ck-out 11 am. Private patios, balconies. On ocean beach. Cr cds: A, C, D, DS, ER, MC, V.

★★**RIVERVIEW.** *103 Flagler Ave (32169). 904/428-5858; res: 800/945-7416; FAX 904/423-8927.* 18 rms, 3 story, 5 suites. S, D $63–$78; suites $100–$150. TV; cable. Pool; poolside serv. Complimentary continental bkfst. Restaurant adj 11:30 am–9:30 pm; Fri, Sat to 10:30 pm. Bar to 11 pm; occasional entertainment. Ck-out noon. On Indian River; private dock. Rms individually decorated; wicker, paneling. Restored frame building (1885); porches. Elegant turn-of-the-century atmosphere. Cr cds: A, C, D, DS, ER, MC, V.

Restaurants

✔★★**NORWOOD'S SEAFOOD.** *400 2nd Ave. 904/428-4621.* Hrs: 11:30 am–10 pm; early-bird dinner Mon–Fri 4–6 pm. Closed Thanksgiving, Dec 25. Bar. Semi-a la carte: lunch $2.99–$6.99, dinner $5.59–$19.99. Child's meals. Specializes in smoke-house fish, seafood, Black Angus beef. Entertainment summer wkends. Parking. Tropical, nautical decor. Cr cds: A, D, DS, MC, V.

★★**RISTORANTE PIETRO.** *725 3rd Ave. 904/428-0644.* Hrs: 5–10 pm; wkends to 11:30 pm. Res accepted. Northern Italian menu. Bar. Complete meals: dinner $9.95–$25.95. Child's meals. Entertainment. Parking. Multi-level dining area. Cr cds: A, MC, V.

★★**RIVERVIEW CHARLIE'S.** *101 Flagler Ave. 904/428-1865.* Hrs: 11:30 am–10 pm; Fri, Sat to 11 pm; early-bird dinner 4–5:30 pm. Res accepted. Bar. Semi-a la carte: lunch $4.95–$11.95, dinner $7.95–$26.95. Child's meals. Specializes in seafood, pasta, beef. Entertainment Fri, Sat. Parking. On Intracoastal Waterway; nautical decor, view of water. Cr cds: A, C, D, DS, MC, V.

Ocala (B-3)

Settled: 1827 **Pop:** 42,045 **Elev:** 47 ft **Area code:** 904

In the central highlands of the state, Ocala has become a focal point for excursions in the "ridge" country. There are approximately 500 Thoroughbred breeding and training farms here, in addition to many farms with other horse breeds. The Ocala Breeders Sales Pavilion is host to eight horse sales a year. Along with vegetable and citrus growing, limestone mining and manufacturing of mobile homes are major businesses.

What to See and Do

1. **Horse farm.** Ocala Stud Inc. SW 27th Ave, 2 mi W off FL 200. Birthplace of Needles, 1956 Kentucky Derby winner; Carry Back, 1961 Kentucky Derby winner; Roman Brother, 1965 Horse of the Year; and Office Queen, champion three-year-old filly of 1970; also training track; horse swimming pool. (Daily exc Sun, limited hrs; closed hols) Phone 237-2171. **Free.**

2. **Appleton Museum of Art.** 4333 E Silver Springs Blvd. Fifty centuries of fine art and sculpture; galleries dedicated to antiquities, pre-Columbian, African, Oriental and European art; changing exhibits. Guided tours (Tues–Fri). (Tues–Sat, also Sun afternoons; closed some hols) Phone 236-5050. ¢¢

3. **Don Garlits Museum of Drag Racing.** 13700 SW 16th Ave, 8 mi S via I-75, exit 67. Houses racing exhibits, trophies & memorabilia; cars from the beginning of drag racing to the present, starting at the California Dry Lakes in the 1940s and including the finest and most unusual cars in the sport; antique cars. (Daily; closed Dec 25) Phone 245-8661. ¢¢¢

4. **Ocala National Forest.** 10 mi E on FL 40. Largest developed area of this approx 430,000-acre forest is Salt Springs, 26 mi E on FL 19. At a constant temperature of 72°F and a flow of 52 million gallons per day, Salt Springs provides swimming, bathhouse; boating (rentals); hiking; picnicking. camping (some hookups). Juniper Springs and Fern Hammock have a combined daily flow of more than 15 million gallons at a constant 72°F (private canoes allowed, some rentals); swimming, bathhouse; picnicking; camping, trailer facilities; visitor center. Fees may be charged at recreation sites. Contact USDA Forest Service, 227 N Bronough St, Suite 4061, Tallahassee 32301, phone 681-7265; or the ranger district office, 17147 E FL 40 in Silver Springs, phone 625-2520.

5. Jai-Alai. Ocala Jai-Alai Fronton, 15 mi N, E of US 441 on FL 318 in Orange Lake. Parimutuel betting. (May–Sept, Wed, Fri & Sat evenings; matinees Wed, Thurs, Sat & Sun) Phone 591-2345. General admission ¢

(For further information contact the Ocala/Marion County Chamber of Commerce, 110 E Silver Springs Blvd, PO Box 1210, 34478; 629-8051.)

Annual Event

Southeastern Youth Fair. 8 days mid-Feb.

(See Leesburg, Silver Springs)

Motels

★**BUDGET HOST WESTERN.** *4013 NW Blitchton Rd (34475),* I-75 exit 70. 904/732-6940. 21 rms. Jan–Mar: S $27; D $36; each addl $3; under 10 free; lower rates rest of yr. Crib $2. Pet accepted. TV; cable. Restaurant nearby. Ck-out 11 am. Cr cds: A, DS, MC, V.

🄳 ⊘ 🄬 SC

★★**HAMPTON INN.** *3434 SW College Rd (FL 200) (34474),* I-75 exit 68. 904/854-3200; FAX 904/854-5633. 152 rms, 3 story. Jan–Mar: S $65–$75; D $75–$85; each addl $5; suites $85–$135; under 18 free; higher rates: Gator International, FL football games; lower rates rest of yr. Crib free. Pet accepted; $5. TV; cable. Pool. Complimentary continental bkfst, coffee. Restaurant opp open 24 hrs. Ck-out noon. Coin Indry. Meeting rms. Some refrigerators. Cr cds: A, C, D, DS, MC, V.

🄳 🐾 ⊷ ⊘ 🄬 SC

★★**HOLIDAY INN.** *(Box 3308, 34478) 3621 Silver Springs Blvd.* 904/629-0381; FAX 904/629-0381, ext 51. 273 rms, 2 story. Jan–Apr: S $50–$60; D $55–$65; under 18 free; lower rates rest of yr. Crib free. Pet accepted, some restrictions. TV; cable, in-rm movies. Heated pool. Restaurant 6 am–10 pm. Rm serv. Bar 1 pm–2 am; entertainment, dancing. Ck-out noon. Meeting rms. Bellhops. Free RR station, bus depot transportation. Cr cds: A, C, D, DS, MC, V.

🄳 🐾 ⊷ ⊘ 🄬 SC

★★**HOWARD JOHNSON PARK SQUARE INN.** *3712 SW 38th Ave (34474),* I-75 exit 68. 904/237-8000; FAX 904/237-0580. 179 rms, 3 story. Mid-Jan–mid-Apr: S, D $50–$78; suites $95–$150; lower rates rest of yr. Crib free. TV; cable. Complimentary continental bkfst. Restaurant 6 am–10 pm. Bar 4–10 pm. Ck-out noon. Coin Indry. Meeting rms. Sundries. Refrigerator in suites. Balconies. Cr cds: A, C, D, DS, ER, MC, V, JCB.

🄳 🐾 ⊷ ⊘ 🄬 SC

✔★★**RADISSON INN.** *3620 W Silver Springs Blvd (34475).* 904/629-0091; FAX 904/867-8399. 99 units, 2 story. S $39–$65; D $45–$71; under 18 free. Crib free. Pet accepted; $5. TV; cable. Pool; poolside serv. Playground. Restaurant 6:30 am–9 pm. Rm serv. Bar noon–midnight; entertainment Sat. Ck-out noon. Coin Indry. Meeting rms. Private patios, balconies. Cr cds: A, C, D, DS, ER, MC, V, JCB.

🄳 🐾 ⊷ ⊘ 🄬 SC

★★★**RAMADA STEINBRENNER'S YANKEE INN.** *3810 NW Blitchton Rd (34482),* I-75 exit 70. 904/732-3131; FAX 904/732-5692. 134 rms, 2 story. S $40–$50; D $55–$65; each addl $6; suites $85; under 18 free; golf, Silver Springs plans. TV; cable. Heated pool; poolside serv. Playground. Restaurant 6:30 am–10 pm. Rm serv. Bar 11:30–2 am; entertainment, dancing exc Sun. Ck-out noon. Meeting rms. Bellhops. Valet serv. Sundries. Gift shop. Airport, bus depot transportation. 18-hole golf privileges, putting green, driving range. Exercise equipt; weights, bicycles, whirlpool. Lawn games. Bathrm phones; some refrigerators. Balconies. Grills. Display of baseball and New York Yankees memorabilia. Cr cds: A, C, D, DS, ER, MC, V.

🄳 🐿 ⊷ 🕴 ⊘ 🄬 SC

Hotel

★★★**HILTON.** *3600 SW 36th Ave (34474).* 904/854-1400; FAX 904/854-4010. 198 units, 9 story. S, D $49–$119; each addl $10; suites $150–$500; family rates. Crib free. TV; cable. Heated pool; poolside serv. Restaurant 6:30 am–10 pm. Bars 11–1 am; seasonal entertainment. Ck-out noon. Meeting rms. Gift shop. Free local airport, RR station, bus depot transportation. Lighted tennis, pro. Exercise equipt; bicycle, stair machine, whirlpool. Lawn games. Balconies. Park-like setting. Cr cds: A, C, D, DS, MC, V.

🄳 ⊘ ⊷ 🕴 ⊘ 🄬 SC

Inn

★★★**SEVEN SISTERS.** *820 SE Fort King St (34471).* 904/867-1170. 4 rms, 2 with phone, 3 story, 3 suites. S, D $85–$125; each addl $25; suites $115–$125. Children over 12 yrs only. TV in club room; cable. Complimentary full bkfst, coffee. Restaurant nearby. Ck-out 11 am, ck-in 3 pm. Health club privileges. Library, sitting rm. Queen Anne-style, Victorian house (1888); furnished with antiques. Porches. Cr cds: A, DS, MC, V.

🄳 ⊘ 🄬

Restaurants

✔★★**CARMICHAEL'S.** *3105 NE Silver Springs Blvd.* 904/622-3636. Hrs: 7–11 am, 11:30 am–9 pm; Sun to 8 pm; early-bird dinner Mon–Sat 4:30–7:30 pm. Closed Dec 25. Res accepted. Italian, Amer menu. Bar. Semi-a la carte: bkfst $1.99–$5, lunch $4.45–$8.95, dinner $5.95–$16.95. Specialities: baked stuffed flounder imperial, shrimp & crabmeat Alfredo. Parking. Brick fireplace; local historical photographs. Cr cds: A, MC, V.

🄳

★**FIDDLESTIX.** *1016 SE 3rd Ave.* 904/629-8000. Hrs: 11 am–10 pm; Sat 5–11 pm; early-bird dinner 3:30–6 pm. Closed Sun; Memorial Day, Labor Day. Res accepted. Bar. Semi-a la carte: lunch $2.95–$7.95, dinner $6.95–$17.95. Child's meals. Specialties: surf & turf, filet Neptune. Parking. Entry through 2 large, hand-carved redwood doors. Cr cds: A, MC, V.

🄳

★★★**MR. HAN.** *815 SW Pine St.* 904/622-2919. Hrs: 11:30 am–10 pm; Fri to 10:30 pm; Sat & Sun from 5 pm. Closed Thanksgiving, Dec 24 & 25. Res accepted. Chinese menu. Bar. A la carte entrees: lunch $3–$4.75, dinner $5–$25. Specialties: lobster tail with cream sauce, lamb with spring onions, Peking duck. Parking. Chinese decor. Cr cds: C, D, MC, V.

🄳

★★**PETER DINKEL'S.** *725 E Silver Springs Blvd.* 904/732-8003. Hrs: 11:30 am–10 pm; Sat 4–11 pm. Closed Sun. Res accepted. Bar. Semi-a la carte: lunch $3.50–$5.95, dinner $5.95–$17.95. Child's meals. Specializes in prime rib, steak, seafood. Parking. Porch dining. Horse racing memorabilia. Cr cds: A, D, MC, V.

🄳

Unrated Dining Spots

HOLIDAY HOUSE. *4011 E Silver Springs Blvd.* 904/236-3014. Hrs: 11 am–8:30 pm. Closed Dec 24 eve. Avg ck: lunch $5.39, dinner $6.69. Specializes in roast beef, turkey, leg of lamb. Salad bar. Parking. Cr cds: A, MC, V.

🄳

MORRISON'S CAFETERIA. *1602 E Silver Springs Blvd.* 904/622-7447. Hrs: 11 am–8:30 pm; Sun to 8 pm. Avg ck: lunch $4.75, dinner $5. Specializes in fried shrimp, roast beef, custard pie. Parking. Cr cds: MC, V.

Okeechobee (D-4)

Pop: 4,943 **Elev:** 29 ft **Area code:** 813

Located on the northern shore of Lake Okeechobee, this town's primary industry is agriculture centering on livestock and dairies, some of which offer tours. Okeechobee is a fisherman's paradise and is also popular for boating and duck hunting. Not far from the city is the Brighton Indian Reservation.

What to See and Do

Lake Okeechobee. S of city. Covering 730 square miles, with its deepest point at 22 feet, this is the second largest freshwater lake in the US. Shallow, with many grassy spots and shoals, it is renowned for its bass, crappie, bream & speckled perch. More than 1 million pounds of fish are caught here every year. There are many fishing camps, picnic and parking areas along the shores.

(For further information contact the Chamber of Commerce, 55 S Parrott Ave, 34972; 763-6464.)

Annual Events

Speckled Perch Festival. Flagler Park. Fishing contest, parade, art show, rodeo, entertainment. 2nd wkend Mar.

Cattleman's Rodeo. Cattleman's Rodeo Arena, FL 441N. Rodeo, parade, barbecue. Labor Day wkend.

(See Belle Glade)

Motels

 ★ BUDGET INN. *201 S Parrott Ave (34974). 813/763-3185.* 24 units, 5 kits. Nov–Apr: S $35–$65; D $45–$75; each addl $5; kit. units $7 addl; under 12 free; higher rates special events; lower rates rest of yr. Crib $8. Pet accepted; $3. TV; cable. Pool. Complimentary coffee. Restaurant adj. Ck-out 11 am. Cr cds: A, DS, MC, V.

★ OHIO. *507 N Parrott Ave (34972). 813/763-1148.* 24 rms. Nov–Apr: S $45; D $55; each addl $5; lower rates rest of yr. TV; cable. Restaurant nearby. Ck-out 11 am. Cr cds: A, DS, MC, V.

Orlando (C-4)

Settled: 1837 **Pop:** 164,693 **Elev:** 106 ft **Area code:** 407

Orlando was a campground for soldiers during the Seminole Indian War (1835–42), a trading post until 1857, and was then deeded to the county. Since then, it has grown in leaps and bounds, first with the coming of the railroad from Sanford in 1880, then with the establishment of the Kennedy Space Center complex to the southeast.

Orlando is the consistent favorite of a devoted colony of winter visitors. In fact, major roads have enhanced the city's position as a transportation hub, with easy access to Walt Disney World (see) and other entertainment complexes in the area. The city itself has 54 lakes within its limits and retains an open, park-like atmosphere. While still a shipping center for citrus fruits and winter vegetables, Orlando has developed its own crop of aerospace, defense and electronics industries. One of the Navy's three recruit training centers is located here. Orlando is also the home of the University of Central Florida (1963).

Transportation

Car Rental Agencies: See toll-free numbers under Introduction.

Public Transportation: Buses (Orlando Transit Authority), phone 841-8240.

Rail Passenger Service: Amtrak 800/872-7245.

Airport Information

Orlando Intl Airport: Information 825-2001; lost and found 825-2111; weather 851-7510; cash machines, Main Terminal near branch bank office; Crown Room (Delta); USAir Club (US Air).

Terminals: Gates 1–29: American, Continental, TWA; Gates 30–59: All Nippon Airways, Bahamasair, Northwest, United, USAir; Gates 60–99: British Airways, Delta, KLM, TransBrasil, Virgin Atlantic

(Airlines and their terminal locations may change. Before leaving for the airport, you should phone the airline to confirm terminal location for your flight.)

What to See and Do

1. **Walt Disney World** (see). 22 mi SW on I-4 at FL 535.
2. **Kennedy Space Center** (see). 47 mi E via FL 528 to FL 407.
3. **Sea World of Florida.** 7007 Sea World Dr. This 150-acre marine park features a killer whale show with the Shamu family; world's largest collection of dangerous sea creatures in Terrors of the Deep; Penguin Encounter; and Hotel Clyde and Seamore. Mission: Bermuda Triangle is a motion-based deep-dive adventure simulation taking visitors on an exciting submarine voyage to encounter shipwrecks, marine life and an underwater earthquake; 3-acre children's play area; water ski show, sky tower; StarLight Laser Spectacular Show; Polynesian Luau dinner-show (nightly). (Daily; all shows several performances/day) Phone 351-3600. ¢¢¢¢
4. **Leu Botanical Gardens.** 1730 N Forest Ave, at Nebraska. There are 56 acres of stately oaks, flowering shrubs, roses, camellias, orchids and azaleas; desert garden; conservatory. Tours include historic Leu House, restored as a museum to show how people lived in the area from 1910–1930. (Daily; closed Dec 25) Phone 246-2620. ¢¢
5. **Loch Haven Park.** Princeton Blvd & Mills Ave. Here are

    Orlando Science Center. 810 E Rollins St. Hands-on exhibits, shows, demonstrations in science. Planetarium shows (daily; fee; inquire for schedule). (Daily; closed Dec 25) Sr citizen rate. Phone 896-7151. ¢¢¢

    Orange County Historical Museum. 812 E Rollins St. Displays of central Florida pre-history, pioneer life, Victorian era; general store; hot-type newspaper composing room; restored 1926 firehouse. (Mon-Sat, also Sun afternoons; closed hols) Phone 897-6350. ¢

    Orlando Museum of Art. 2416 N Mills Ave. Exhibits of 19th- and 20th-century American art; Pre-Columbian artifacts and African art. (Daily exc Mon; closed some major hols) Phone 896-4231. ¢¢

6. **Municipal recreation areas.**

    Eola Park. Rosalind & Robinson Sts. Around Lake Eola; illuminated fountain, flowers, band shell, concession. (Daily) **Free.**

    Turkey Lake Park. 3401 Hiawassee Rd. Swimming pool; fishing; boating (rentals). Bicycle paths, nature trails. Picnicking, playground, concession. Camping. Petting zoo; ecology center. (Daily) Phone 299-5594. ¢

    Lake Fairview Park. Off Lee Rd. Swimming (fee); boating. Picnicking.

7. **Church Street Station.** 129 W Church St, off I-4 Anderson St/Church St exit. Complex designed with Victorian atmosphere houses sev-

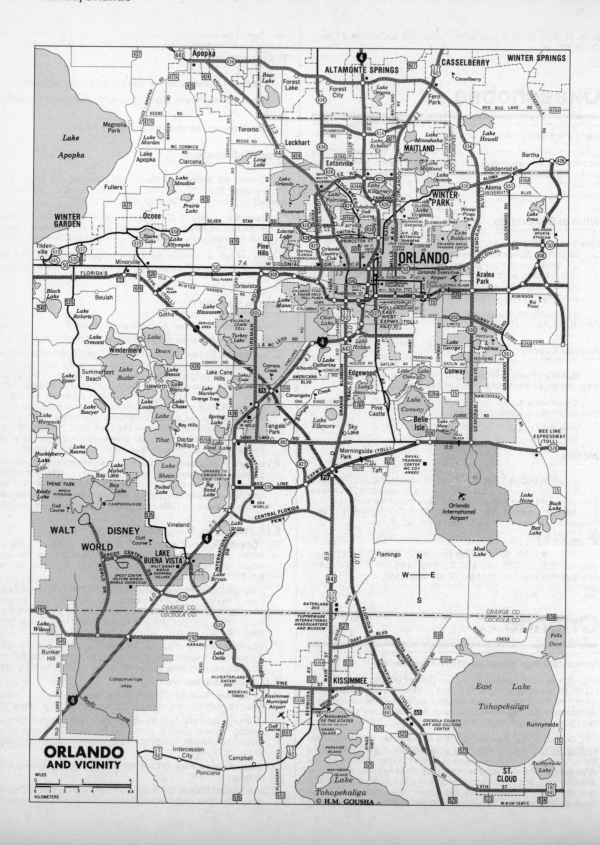

ORLANDO
AND VICINITY

© H.M. GOUSHA

M-9-UH-1241-C

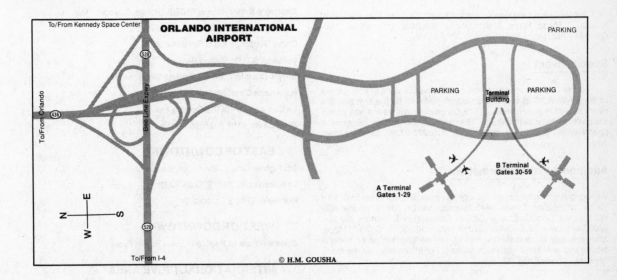

To/From Kennedy Space Center

ORLANDO INTERNATIONAL AIRPORT

PARKING

To/From Orlando

Bee Line Expwy

PARKING

Terminal Building

PARKING

A Terminal Gates 1-29

B Terminal Gates 30-59

N E S W

To/From I-4

© H.M. GOUSHA

eral restaurants and nightclubs, including Rosie O'Grady's Goodtime Emporium, Cheyenne Saloon and Opera House, Apple Annie's Courtyard, Phineas Phogg's Balloon Works, Orchid Garden Ballroom, Crackers Oyster Bar and Wine Cellar, Lili Marlene's Aviators Restaurant & Pub (see RESTAURANTS), Champagne Balloon flights and Commander Ragtime's Midway of Fun, Food and Games; variety of shows and entertainment. Also Church Street Exchange Shopping Emporium. (Daily) Phone 422-2434. Evening cover charge ¢¢¢¢¢

8. **Church Street Market.** Church St between Orange Ave & Garland. Two-story marketplace with 17 shops and 6 restaurants around center courtyard; decor includes streetlamps, benches, fountains, brick walkways. Connected to Church Street Station by second-level footbridge. (Daily) Phone 872-3500.

9. **Universal Studios Florida.** 10 mi SW on I-4, exits 29 & 30B, at jct FL Tpke. A 444-acre lot accommodating more than 40 rides, shows and attractions, 6 working sound stages and realistic street sets from New York City to Hollywood Boulevard. Through technology and special effects, visitors enter the action of such movies as *King Kong, ET, Back to the Future* and *Jaws,* and experience the FUNtastic World of Hanna-Barbera, Hitchcock 3-D Theatre or The Adventures of Rocky & Bullwinkle. Live shows include Wild, Wild Wild West Stunt Show and Beetlejuice Graveyard Revue; shows for the Nickelodeon cable channel are also produced at the facility. Themed concessions, gift shops. (Daily) Phone 363-8000. ¢¢¢¢¢

10. **Wet 'N Wild.** 6200 International Dr, off I-4 at FL 435. This 25-acre water park features waterfalls, rapids, wind and rain tunnels, wave pools and whirlpools. Beach, lifeguards, lockers, showers; raft and towel rentals; kneeboarding; miniature golf; picnicking. (Daily) Phone 351-1800. ¢¢¢¢¢

11. **Mystery Fun House.** 5767 Major Blvd. Walk-through participation in 15-room house featuring crazy-image mirrors, spinning tunnels. Also miniature golf, laser game, arcade; restaurant, gift shops. (Daily) Phone 351-3355. General admission ¢¢¢; Combination ticket ¢¢¢¢

12. **Gray Line bus tours.** Contact PO Box 1671, 32802; 422-0744.

Annual Events

Florida Citrus Sports Holiday. Month of sports activities climaxed by the Florida Citrus Bowl football game (Jan 1). Phone 423-2476. Dec.

Orlando Scottish Highland Games. Fairgrounds. Features pipe band competition, Highland athletic events; other competitions include Highland dancing, piping, drum and country dancing; haggis hurling; special events. Scottish food & merchandise. Phone 672-1682. Last wkend Jan.

Central Florida Fair. Fairgrounds. Horse show, entertainment, midway. Phone 295-3247. Late Feb–early Mar.

The Nestle Invitational. Bay Hill Golf & Country Club, 900 Bay Hill Blvd. PGA tournament. Phone 876-2888. 3rd wk Mar.

Pioneer Days Folk Festival. On the grounds of Pine Castle Folk Arts Center, 6015 Randolph St. Two-day event features sugar cane grinding and syrup making; traditional crafts demonstrations; bluegrass music and clogging; children's activities & games; food. Phone 855-7461. Late Oct.

Seasonal Events

Florida Symphony Orchestra. Classical, pops, chamber, and outdoor concerts. For information phone 894-2011 or 800/393-9376. Sept–May.

Professional basketball. Orlando Magic, Orlando Arena at 600 W Amelia, 1 Magic Place, 32801; phone 896-2442 (box office). Mid-Oct–early Apr.

Special Event

World Cup 94. Orlando will be one of nine US cities to host games of the XV World Cup soccer tournament. This will be the first time the event is held in North America. The Citrus Bowl will be the site of five matches. Tickets avail through Ticketmaster. For further information phone World Cup Public Information, 310/277-9494. Mid-June–mid-July.

Additional Visitor Information

Visitors can obtain further information by contacting the Orlando Official Visitor Information Center, 8445 International Dr, 32819, phone 363-5871 or the Orlando/Orange County Convention & Visitors Bureau, 7208 Sand Lake Rd, Suite 300, 32819, phone 363-5800. *Orlando Magazine*, available at newsstands, has up-to-date information on cultural events and articles of interest to visitors. For information on the many city parks phone 246-2287.

Orlando Area Towns and Suburbs

The following towns and suburbs in the Orlando area are included in the *Mobil Travel Guide*. For information, as well as additional attractions and/or accommodations, see the individual alphabetical listing. Altamonte Springs, Haines City, Kissimmee, Winter Park; also see Walt Disney World.

City Neighborhoods

Many of the restaurants, unrated dining establishments and some lodgings listed under Orlando include neighborhoods as well as exact street addresses. Geographic descriptions of Downtown and the International Drive Area are given, followed by a table of restaurants arranged by neighborhood.

Downtown: South of Colonial Dr (FL 50), west of Magnolia Ave (FL 527), north of Holland East-West Expy and east of Parramore Ave. **North of Downtown:** North of FL 50. **South of Downtown:** South of FL 408. **East of Downtown:** East of Magnolia Ave. **West of Downtown:** West of Parramore Ave.

International Drive Area: Area on and around International Drive between the FL Turnpike on the north and I-4 (exit 27A) on the south.

ORLANDO RESTAURANTS
BY NEIGHBORHOOD AREAS

(For full description, see alphabetical listings under Restaurants)

DOWNTOWN

Crackers. 129 W Church St

Lee's Lakeside. 431 E Central Blvd

Lili Marlene's Aviators Restaurant & Pub. 129 W Church St

Vivaldi. 107 Pine St

NORTH OF DOWNTOWN

Tony Marino's. 729 Lee Rd

SOUTH OF DOWNTOWN

Charley's Steak House. 6107 S Orange Blossom Trail

Chatham's Place. 7575 Dr Phillips Blvd

China Garden. 1303 S Semoran Blvd

Darbar. 7600 Dr Phillips Blvd

Gary's Duck Inn. 3974 S Orange Blossom Trail

Hard Rock Cafe. 5800 Kirkman Rd

Le Coq au Vin. 4800 S Orange Ave

Ming Court. 9188 International Dr

EAST OF DOWNTOWN

4th Fighter Group. 494 Rickenbacker Dr

La Normandie. 2021 E Colonial Dr

Ronnie's. 2702 E Colonial Dr

WEST OF DOWNTOWN

Chris's House of Beef. 801 John Young Pkwy

INTERNATIONAL DRIVE AREA

Caruso's Palace. 8986 International Dr

Charlie's Lobster House. 8445 International Dr

China Coast. 7500 International Dr

King Henry's Feast. 8984 International Dr

Mardi Gras. 8445 International Dr

Passage to India. 5532 International Dr

Siam Orchid. 7575 Republic Dr

Note: When a listing is located in a town that does not have its own city heading, it will appear under the city nearest to its location. In these cases, the address and town appear in parenthesis immediately following the name of the establishment.

Motels

✔ ★★**COMFORT INN-SOUTH.** *8421 S Orange Blossom Trail (32809), at Florida Mall, south of downtown. 407/855-6060; FAX 407/859-5132.* 204 rms, 2 story. Late Dec & Feb-mid-Aug: S, D $49–$99; each addl $6; suites $59–$145; under 18 free; lower rates rest of yr. TV; cable. Heated pool; poolside serv. Playground. Bkfst buffet 7–11 am. Ck-out 11 am. Coin lndry. Meeting rms. Sundries. Gift shop. Free transportation to area attractions. Game rm. Florida Mall adj. Cr cds: A, C, D, DS, ER, MC, V, JCB.

D ⚐ ⊘ ⊛ SC

★★**COMFORT SUITES.** *9350 Turkey Lake Rd (32819), off I-4 exit 29, south of downtown. 407/351-5050; FAX 407/363-7953.* 215 rms, 3 story. Late Dec–early Jan, mid-Feb–mid-Apr, mid-June–Aug: S, D $89–$109; under 12 free; lower rates rest of yr. Crib free. TV; cable. Heated pool; wading pool; whirlpool; poolside serv. Playground. Complimentary continental bkfst. Restaurant 11 am–11 pm. Bar. Ck-out 11 am. Coin lndry. Sundries. Airport transportation. Golf privileges. Game rm. Refrigerators. Cr cds: A, C, D, DS, ER, MC, V, JCB.

D ⚐ ⚐ ⊘ ⊛ SC

★★**COURTYARD BY MARRIOTT.** *7155 Frontage Rd (32812), near Intl Airport, south of downtown. 407/240-7200; FAX 407/240-8962.* 149 rms, 3 story. S, D $92–$102; suites $108–$118; under 18 free;

wkend rates. Crib free. TV; cable. Heated pool; poolside serv. Complimentary coffee in rms. Restaurant 6 am–midnight. Bar from 2 pm. Ck-out noon. Coin lndry. Meeting rms. Free airport transportation. Exercise equipt; weights, bicycles, whirlpool. Some refrigerators. Balconies. Cr cds: A, C, D, DS, MC, V.

★**ECONO LODGE-CENTRAL.** *3300 W Colonial Dr (32808), west of downtown.* 407/293-7221; FAX 407/293-1166. 103 rms, 1–2 story. Feb–Apr, mid-June–mid-Aug: S $46; D $52; each addl $6; under 17 free; lower rates rest of yr. Crib free. TV; cable. Pool. Complimentary coffee in lobby. Restaurant adj open 24 hrs. Bar 11–2 am. Ck-out 11 am. Coin lndry. Meeting rm. Lawn games. Picnic tables. Cr cds: A, C, D, DS, MC, V.

✔★**ECONOMY INNS OF AMERICA.** *8222 Jamaican Ct (32819), south of downtown.* 407/345-1172. 121 rms, 3 story. Mid-Jan–mid-Apr: S, D $39.90–$59.90; lower rates rest of yr. TV; cable. Heated pool. Complimentary continental bkfst. Ck-out 11 am. Cr cds: A, MC, V.

✔★**FAIRFIELD INN BY MARRIOTT.** *8342 Jamaican Ct (32819), south of downtown.* 407/363-1944; FAX 407/363-1944, ext 709. 135 rms, 3 story. Mid-Dec–Aug: S, D $56–$62; each addl $7; under 18 free; lower rates rest of yr. Crib free. TV; cable. Heated pool. Complimentary continental bkfst. Complimentary coffee in lobby. Ck-out noon. Game rm. Cr cds: A, C, D, DS, MC, V.

★★**GATEWAY INN.** *7050 Kirkman Rd (32819), east of I-4, in International Drive Area.* 407/351-2000; res: 800/327-3808 (exc FL), 800/432-1179 (FL), 800/621-3394 (CAN); FAX 407/363-1835. 354 rms, 2 story. Feb–mid-Apr, early June–early Sept, mid-Dec–early Jan: S, D $78–$92; each addl $6; under 18 free; lower rates rest of yr. Crib $6. Pet accepted, some restrictions. TV; cable. 2 pools, heated; wading pool, poolside serv. Playground. Continental bkfst in rms. Restaurant 7 am–10 pm. Bar 11:30–2 am; entertainment, dancing. Ck-out 11 am. Coin lndry. Meeting rm. Bellhops. Valet serv. Sundries. Gift shop. Airport transportation. Free transportation to area attractions. Miniature golf. Game rm. Lawn games. Picnic tables. Cr cds: A, C, D, ER, MC, V.

✔★★**HAMPTON INN.** *7110 S Kirkman (32819), International Drive Area.* 407/345-1112; FAX 407/352-6591. 170 rms, 8 story. Feb–late Apr, early June–early Sept & late Dec–early Jan: S $59–$79; D $69–$84; suites $119; under 17 free; lower rates rest of yr. Crib free. TV; cable. Heated pool; wading pool. Complimentary continental bkfst, coffee. Restaurant adj open 24 hrs. Ck-out 11 am. Coin lndry. Meeting rms. Gift shop. Exercise equipt; weight machine, stair machine. Game rm. Cr cds: A, C, D, DS, MC, V.

★★**HAWTHORN SUITES.** *6435 Westwood Blvd (32821), International Drive Area.* 407/351-6600; FAX 407/351-1977. 150 suites, 5 story. Mid-Feb–Easter & late Dec: suites $135–$185; under 18 free; Walt Disney World plans; lower rates rest of yr. Crib free. TV; cable, in-rm movies. Heated pool; wading pool, poolside serv. Playground. Complimentary bkfst. Complimentary coffee in rms. Restaurant adj 7 am–11 pm. Ck-out 11 am. Coin lndry. Meeting rms. Bellhops. Concierge. Sundries. Airport transportation. Exercise equipt; weights, stair machine, whirlpool. Game rm. Refrigerators, wet bars. Grills. Cr cds: A, C, D, DS, ER, MC, V, JCB.

★★**HERITAGE INN.** *9861 International Dr (32819), in International Drive Area.* 407/352-0008; res: 800/447-1890; FAX 407/352-5449. 150 rms, 2 story. Late Dec–early Jan, Feb–Aug: S, D $79–$109; each addl $10; under 18 free; lower rates rest of yr. Crib free. TV; cable. Heated pool. Restaurant 6:30 am–2 pm, 4–10 pm; dinner theater Tues–Sat from 7 pm. Rm serv. Bar. Ck-out noon. Coin lndry. Meeting

rms. Valet serv. Sundries. Refrigerators. Turn-of-the-century architecture; Victorian decor. Cr cds: A, C, D, DS, ER, MC, V.

✔★★**HOLIDAY INN-CENTRAL PARK.** *7900 S Orange Blossom Trail (32809), south of downtown.* 407/859-7900; FAX 407/859-7442. 266 rms, 2 story. S, D $65–$117; each addl $7; under 18 free. Crib free. TV. Pool; wading pool. Restaurant 6:30 am–2 pm, 5:30–10 pm. Rm serv. Bar 5 pm–midnight. Ck-out 11 am. Coin lndry. Meeting rms. Bellhops. Free airport transportation. Exercise equipt; weight machine, bicycles. Cr cds: A, C, D, DS, MC, V, JCB.

★**INTERNATIONAL GATEWAY INN.** *5859 American Way (32819), in International Drive Area.* 407/345-8880; res: 800/327-0750; FAX 407/363-9366. 192 rms, 4 story. June–early Sept, late Dec: S, D $66–$82; each addl $6; under 18 free; lower rates rest of yr. Crib $6. Pet accepted, some restrictions. TV; cable. Heated pool. Restaurant adj open 24 hrs. Ck-out 11 am. Coin lndry. Game rm. Cr cds: A, C, D, ER, MC, V.

✔★**RAMADA LIMITED.** *8296 S Orange Blossom Trail (32809), 10 mi S on FL 441, near Florida Mall, south of downtown.* 407/240-0570; FAX 407/856-5507. 75 rms, 2 story. Mid-Dec–mid-Apr: S $45–$75; D $49–$75; each addl $6; under 9 free; higher rates: some hols, Daytona 500; lower rates rest of yr. Crib free. TV; cable. Pool. Complimentary coffee in lobby. Restaurant nearby. Ck-out 11 am. Coin lndry. Meeting rm. Bellhops. Airport, RR station, bus depot, Walt Disney World transportation. Golf privileges. Cr cds: A, C, D, DS, ER, MC, V, JCB.

★★**RESIDENCE INN BY MARRIOTT.** *7975 Canada Ave (32819), south of downtown.* 407/345-0117; FAX 407/352-2689. 176 kit. suites (1–2 bedrm). S, D $94–$144; wkly, monthly rates. Crib free. TV; cable. Heated pool; whirlpools. Complimentary continental bkfst. Restaurant nearby. Ck-out 11 am. Coin lndry. Meeting rms. Valet serv. Airport, RR station, bus depot transportation. Many fireplaces. Balconies. Grills. Lighted sports court. Cr cds: A, C, D, DS, MC, V.

✔★**TRAVELODGE.** *409 N Magnolia Ave (32081), downtown.* 407/423-1671; FAX 407/423-1523. 75 rms, shower only, 2 story. Feb–Apr & June–Aug: S $45; D $55; each addl $5; under 18 free; higher rates Citrus Bowl; lower rates rest of yr. TV; cable. Pool. Complimentary coffee in rms. Restaurant nearby. Ck-out noon. Coin lndry. Airport transportation. Cr cds: A, C, D, DS, ER, MC, V, JCB.

✔★★**WYNFIELD INN.** *6263 Westwood Blvd (32821), in International Drive Area.* 407/345-8000; FAX 407/345-1508. 299 rms, 3 story. Feb–late Apr, early June–late Aug: S, D $60–$74; each addl $5; under 18 free; lower rates rest of yr. Crib free. TV; cable. 2 pools, 1 heated; 2 wading pools, poolside serv. Complimentary coffee, fruit. Restaurant adj 6:30 am–midnight. Ck-out 11 am. Coin lndry. Airport, area attraction transportation. Game rm. Cr cds: A, C, D, DS, MC, V.

Motor Hotels

★★**BEST WESTERN PLAZA INTERNATIONAL.** *8738 International Dr (32819), in International Drive Area.* 407/345-8195; FAX 407/352-8196. 673 rms, 4 story, 176 kits. Feb–Apr, mid-June–Aug, mid-Dec–early Jan, hols: S, D $80–$85; each addl $6; suites $100–$105; kit. units $90–$95; under 19 free; lower rates rest of yr. Crib free. TV; cable, in-rm movies. Heated pool; wading pool, whirlpool, poolside serv. Ck-out 11 am. Coin lndry. Bellhops. Sundries. Gift shop. Game rm. Some in-rm whirlpools. Cr cds: A, C, D, DS, MC, V.

✔ ★**COLONY PLAZA.** *(2600 W FL 50, Ocoee 34761) 10 mi W on FL 50.* 407/656-3333; res: 800/821-0136; FAX 407/656-2232. 300 rms, 7 story. Feb–Apr, July–Aug: S $70; D $85; each addl $5; under 18 free; lower rates rest of yr. Crib free. TV. Pool; wading pool, poolside serv. Playground. Restaurant 6:30 am–10 pm. Bar noon–midnight; entertainment, dancing Tues–Sat. Ck-out noon. Coin lndry. Meeting rm. Concierge. Gift shop. Airport, RR station, bus depot transportation. Lighted tennis. Game rm. Lawn games. Private patios, balconies. Cr cds: A, C, D, DS, ER, MC, V.

D ⚷ ≈ 🚭 🕐 SC

★ ★ ★**DELTA ORLANDO RESORT.** *5715 Major Blvd (32819), jct FL 435 & I-4 exit 30B at entrance of Universal Studios, south of downtown.* 407/351-3340; FAX 407/345-2872. 800 units, 4 story. Mid-Feb–Apr, mid-June–Aug, late Dec: S, D $110–$150; suites $175–$475; under 18 free; lower rates rest of yr. Crib free. Pet accepted, some restrictions; $25. TV; cable. 3 pools, heated; wading pools, whirlpools, sauna, poolside serv. Playground. Free supervised child's activities. Restaurants 6:30 am–midnight. Rm serv. Bar 11:30–2 am; entertainment exc Sun. Ck-out 11 am. Coin lndry. Convention facilities. Bellhops. Valet serv. Concierge. Sundries. Gift shop. Lighted tennis. Golf privileges. Miniature golf. Game rm. Lawn games. Private balconies. Cr cds: A, C, D, DS, ER, MC, V, JCB.

D 🏌 ⚷ ≈ 🚭 🕐 SC

★ ★**FLORIDIAN.** *7299 Republic Dr (32819), in International Drive Area.* 407/351-5009; res: 800/445-7299; FAX 407/363-7807. 300 rms, 8 story. Feb–Aug, late Dec: S, D $89–$99; lower rates rest of yr. Crib free. TV; cable, in-rm movies. Heated pool; poolside serv. Restaurant 7–11 am, 5–11 pm. Rm serv. Bar 5 pm–2 am. Ck-out 11 am. Coin lndry. Meeting rms. Bellhops. Valet serv. Concierge. Sundries. Gift shop. Airport transportation. Game rm. Cr cds: A, C, D, DS, MC, V.

D ≈ 🚭 🕐 SC

✔ ★ ★**HAMPTON INN AT UNIVERSAL.** *5621 Windhover Dr (32819), in International Drive Area.* 407/351-6716; FAX 407/363-1711. 120 rms, 5 story. Late May–mid-Aug & late Dec–late Mar: S $69; D $79; under 18 free; golf plan; lower rates rest of yr. Crib free. TV; cable. Heated pool. Complimentary continental bkfst, coffee. Restaurant opp 7 am–midnight. Ck-out noon. Meeting rms. Airport transportation. Game rm. Cr cds: A, C, D, DS, MC, V.

D ≈ 🚭 🕐 SC

✔ ★ ★**HOLIDAY INN.** *626 Lee Rd (32810), north of downtown.* 407/645-5600; FAX 407/740-7912. 201 rms, 5 story. S, D $70–$80; each addl $10; under 18 free; MAP avail. Crib free. TV; cable. Pool. Restaurant 6 am–10 pm. Rm serv. Bar 4 pm–midnight; entertainment Thurs–Sat. Ck-out 11 am. Coin lndry. Meeting rms. Bellhops. Valet serv. Airport, RR station, bus depot transportation. Tennis privileges. Golf privileges, greens fee $18–$30, driving range. Exercise equipt; weight machine, bicycle. Health club privileges. Game rm. Cr cds: A, C, D, DS, MC, V, JCB.

D 🏌 ⚷ ≈ 🏋 🚭 🕐 SC

★ ★ ★**HOLIDAY INN-UNIVERSITY OF CENTRAL FLORIDA.** *12125 High Tech Ave (32817), off University Blvd, north of downtown.* 407/275-9000; FAX 407/381-0019. 250 units, 6 story. S $75–$85; D $85–$95; each addl $10; suites $135; under 18 free. Crib free. TV; cable. Pool. Restaurant 6:30 am–2 pm, 5–10 pm. Rm serv. Bar 11 am–midnight; entertainment, dancing. Ck-out 11 am. Meeting rms. Bellhops. Tennis privileges. Golf privileges. Exercise equipt; weights, bicycles, whirlpool, sauna. Lawn games. Some refrigerators. On lake. **LUXURY LEVEL.** 42 units. S $95; D $110; suites $125–$200. Concierge. Private lounge. Minibars. Complimentary bkfst, refreshments. Cr cds: A, C, D, DS, MC, V, JCB.

D 🏌 ⚷ ≈ 🏋 🏃 🚭 🕐 SC

★**INTERNATIONAL INN.** *6327 International Drive (32819), in International Drive Area.* 407/351-4444; res: 800/999-6327; FAX 407/352-5806. 315 rms, 4–9 story. Mid-Mar–mid-Aug: S, D $55; each addl (after 4th person) $6; suites $65; under 18 free; lower rates rest of yr. Crib free. Pet accepted, some restrictions. TV; cable, in-rm movies.

Heated pool. Restaurant 6:30–10:30 am, 5:30–10 pm. Bar 6 pm–midnight. Ck-out 11 am. Coin lndry. Meeting rms. Bellhops. Sundries. Gift shop. Valet serv. Walt Disney World transportation. Game rm. Refrigerators avail. Cr cds: A, C, D, DS, ER, MC, V, JCB.

🐾 ≈ 🚭 🕐 SC $

★ ★ ★**MARRIOTT.** *8001 International Dr (32819), off I-4 exit 29, in International Drive Area.* 407/351-2420; FAX 407/345-5611. 1,065 units in 16 bldgs, 2 story, 191 kits. S, D $125–$130; suites $210–$450; kit. units $10 addl; under 18 free. Crib free. TV; cable, in-rm movies. 3 pools, heated; 2 wading pools, poolside serv. Playground. Restaurant open 24 hrs. Rm serv. Bar 11–2 am; entertainment, dancing. Ck-out 11 am. Coin lndry. Convention facilities. Bellhops. Sundries. Gift shop. Lighted tennis. Golf privileges. Exercise equipt; weight machine, rowers, whirlpool. Game rm. Balconies. Cr cds: A, C, D, DS, ER, MC, V, JCB.

D 🏌 ⚷ ≈ 🏋 🏃 🚭 🕐 SC

★**QUALITY INN-PLAZA.** *9000 International Dr (32819), in International Drive Area.* 407/345-8585; FAX 407/352-6839. 1,020 rms, 4–10 story. Late Dec–early Jan, mid-Feb–late Apr, mid-June–mid-Aug: S, D $63; lower rates rest of yr. Crib free. Pet accepted, some restrictions. TV; cable. 3 pools, heated; poolside serv in season. Restaurant 6:30–10:30 am, 5:30–9 pm. Bar 5:30 pm–2 am. Ck-out 11 am. Coin lndry. Gift shop. Game rm. Cr cds: A, C, D, DS, ER, MC, V.

D 🐾 ≈ 🚭 🕐 SC

✔ ★ ★**RADISSON INN.** *8444 International Dr (32819), in International Drive Area.* 407/345-0505; FAX 407/352-5894. 300 rms, 5 story. Mid-Dec–Apr: S, D $69–$99; each addl $10; lower rates rest of yr. Crib free. TV; cable. 2 pools, 1 indoor; poolside serv. Playground. Restaurant 6:30 am–10 pm. Bar. Ck-out noon. Meeting rms. Sundries. Gift shop. Airport, RR station, bus transportation. Lighted tennis. Exercise equipt; weights, bicycles. Game rm. Bathrm phones; some refrigerators. Aquatic Center created especially for world-class aquatic training, competition. Shopping center opp. Cr cds: A, C, D, DS, ER, MC, V.

D ⚷ ≈ 🏃 🚭 🕐 SC

✔ ★**RODEWAY INN.** *9956 Hawaiian Court (32819), in International Drive Area.* 407/351-5100; FAX 407/352-7188. 271 rms, 2 story, 49 kit. suites. S $61; D $67; suites $87; under 18 free. Crib free. TV; cable. Pool; whirlpool. Playground. Complimentary coffee in lobby. Restaurant nearby. Bar 5:30 pm–1 am. Ck-out noon. Coin lndry. Meeting rms. Valet serv. Airport, Walt Disney World transportation. Game rm. Refrigerator in suites. Cr cds: A, C, D, DS, ER, MC, V.

D ≈ 🚭 🕐 SC

★ ★ ★**SHERATON WORLD RESORT.** *10100 International Dr (32821), in International Drive Area.* 407/352-1100; res: 800/327-0363 (exc FL), 800/341-4292 (FL); FAX 407/352-3679. 800 units, 2–3 story. Jan–mid-May: S $90–$120; D $105–$135; each addl $15; suites $225–$465; under 18 free; lower rates rest of yr. Crib $5. TV; cable. 3 pools, heated; 2 wading pools, poolside serv. Playground. Supervised child's activities. Restaurants 6:30 am–11 pm. Rm serv. Bar; entertainment. Ck-out 11 am. Coin lndry. Meeting rms. Bellhops. Sundries. Gift shop. Airport transportation. Lighted tennis. Golf privileges. Miniature golf. Exercise equipt; weights, bicycles, whirlpool. Game rm. Cr cds: A, C, D, DS, ER, MC, V, JCB.

D 🏌 ⚷ ≈ 🏃 🚭 🕐 SC

★ ★ ★**SONESTA VILLA RESORT.** *10000 Turkey Lake Rd (32819), I-4 exit 29, south of downtown.* 407/352-8051; res: 800/766-3782; FAX 407/345-5384. 370 villas, 2 story. 1-bedrm $95–$145; 2-bedrm $180–$260. TV; cable. Heated pool; wading pool, poolside serv. Free supervised child's activities. Restaurant 6:30 am–11 pm. Bar 11 am–midnight. Ck-out noon. Meeting rms. Bellhops. Valet serv. Gift shop. Lighted tennis. Exercise equipt; weights, bicycles, 11 whirlpools, sauna. Game rm. Lawn games. Refrigerators. Private patios, balconies. Bicycle rentals. Mediterranean architecture. On lake; paddle boats, jet skis, water-skiing. Cr cds: A, C, D, DS, ER, MC, V.

D ⛵ ⚷ ≈ 🏋 🏃 🚭 🕐 SC

Hotels

★ ★ **CLARION PLAZA.** 9700 International Dr (32819), in International Drive Area. 407/352-9700; FAX 407/351-9111. 810 rms, 14 story. S, D $99–$125; suites $125–$620; under 18 free. Crib free. Valet parking $5. TV; cable. Heated pool; whirlpool. Restaurant 6:30 am–midnight. Bar 11–2 am; entertainment. Ck-out noon. Coin lndry. Convention facilities. Shopping arcade. Airport transportation. Golf privileges, pro, putting green, driving range. Game rm. Refrigerators, minibars; some bathrm phones. Cr cds: A, C, D, DS, ER, MC, V, JCB.

★ ★ ★ **EMBASSY SUITES.** 8978 International Dr (32819), in International Drive Area. 407/352-1400; FAX 407/363-1120. 245 kit. suites, 8 story. Suites $115–$165; each addl $15; under 17 free. Crib free. TV; cable. 2 pools, 1 indoor; whirlpool, steam rm, sauna. Complimentary bkfst. Restaurant 6 am–11 pm. Bar. Ck-out 11 am. Coin lndry. Meeting rms. Gift shop. Airport transportation. Game rm. Refrigerators. Sun deck. Mediterranean-style atrium. Cr cds: A, C, D, DS, MC, V.

★ ★ **EMBASSY SUITES AT PLAZA INTERNATIONAL.** 8250 Jamaican Ct (32819), south of downtown. 407/345-8250; res: 800/327-9797; FAX 407/352-1463. 246 suites, 8 story. Suites $129; under 18 free; package plans. Crib free. TV; cable. Indoor/outdoor pool; poolside serv. Complimentary full bkfst buffet 6–10 am. Bar 5 pm–2 am. Ck-out noon. Gift shop. Tennis & golf privileges. Exercise equipt; weights, rower, whirlpool, sauna. Game rm. Refrigerators. Cr cds: A, C, D, DS, MC, V, JCB.

★ ★ **THE ENCLAVE.** 6165 Carrier Dr (32819), south of downtown. 407/351-1155; res: 800/457-0077; FAX 407/351-2001. 321 kit. suites, 10 story. Mid-Dec–mid-Apr & mid-June–mid-Aug: studio & 2-bedrm suites (to 6 persons) $99–$160; golf, Walt Disney World packages; lower rates rest of yr. Crib $5. TV; cable. 3 pools, 2 heated, 1 indoor; wading pool, poolside serv. Complimentary continental bkfst. Restaurant 11 am–midnight. Bar. Ck-out 11 am. Coin lndry. Meeting rm. Airport, attractions transportation. Lighted tennis. Golf privileges. Exercise equipt; weights, bicycles, whirlpool, sauna, steam rm. Game rm. Private patios, balconies. On lake. Cr cds: A, C, D, MC, V, JCB.

★ ★ **HARLEY.** 151 E Washington St (32801), downtown. 407/841-3220; FAX 407/849-1839. 281 units, 6 story. Mid-Jan–mid-Apr: S, D $75–$85; 2-bedrm suites $105–$200; under 18 free; wkend rates; lower rates rest of yr. Crib free. TV, cable. Heated pool; poolside serv. Restaurant 6:30 am–10:30 pm. Bar 3 pm–midnight; entertainment; dancing Fri-Sat. Ck-out noon. Meeting rms. Garage parking. Airport, Walt Disney World transportation. Golf privileges. Exercise equipt; weights, bicycles. Refrigerators avail. Some balconies. Cr cds: A, C, D, DS, MC, V.

★ ★ **HOLIDAY INN.** 5905 Kirkman Rd (32819), just W of jct FL 435 & I-4 exit 30B, south of downtown. 407/351-3333; FAX 407/351-3333, ext 1000. 256 units, 10 story. Mid-Feb–mid-Apr, mid-June–mid-Aug, last 2 wks Dec: S, D $79–$129; each addl $10; under 18 free; lower rates rest of yr. Crib free. TV; cable. Pool; wading pool. Cafe 6:30–2 am. Rm serv 7 am–10 pm. Bar. Ck-out noon. Coin lndry. Meeting rms. Gift shop. Airport, RR station, bus depot transportation. Game rm. Some refrigerators. Private patios, balconies. Near main entrance to Universal Studios Florida. Cr cds: A, C, D, DS, ER, MC, V, JCB.

✔ ★ ★ **HOWARD JOHNSON UNIVERSAL TOWER.** 5905 International Dr (32819), at jct FL 435 & I-4, in International Drive Area. 407/351-2100; FAX 407/352-2991. 302 units, 21 story. Feb-Aug, late Dec–early Jan: S, D $69–$89; suites $125–$225; under 18 free; lower rates rest of yr. Crib free. TV; cable. Heated pool; wading pool, poolside serv. Restaurant 6:30–11:30 am, 5:30–10 pm. Bar 4:30 pm–2 am; entertainment, dancing. Ck-out noon. Coin lndry. Meeting rms. Concierge. Gift shop. Barber, beauty shop. Airport, RR station, bus depot transpor-

tation. Game rm. Rec rm. Refrigerators avail. Cylindrical building. Cr cds: A, C, D, DS, ER, MC, V, JCB.

★ ★ ★ **HYATT REGENCY ORLANDO INTL AIRPORT.** 9300 Airport Blvd (32827), atop main terminal of Intl Airport, south of downtown. 407/825-1234; FAX 407/856-1672. 446 rms, 10 story, 23 suites. S, D $139–$180; suites $200–$400; under 18 free. Crib avail. Garage parking $8; valet parking $11. TV; cable. Heated pool. Restaurant 6 am–1 pm. Rm serv 24 hrs. Bar. Ck-out noon. Convention facilities. Concierge. Shopping arcade. Golf privileges. Exercise equipt; weights, bicycles, whirlpool. Bathrm phones. Balconies. Dramatic 7-story atrium lobby; airport's main terminal is located 1 level below. **LUXURY LEVEL:** REGENCY CLUB. 48 rms, 2 suites. S, D $164–$205. Concierge. Private lounge, honor bar. Complimentary continental bkfst, refreshments. Cr cds: A, C, D, DS, ER, MC, V, JCB.

★ ★ **MARRIOTT ORLANDO AIRPORT.** 7499 Augusta National Dr (32822), near Intl Airport, south of downtown. 407/851-9000; FAX 407/856-9926. 484 units, 9 story. S, D $59–$169; each addl $12; suites $175–$500; under 18 free; wkend rates. Crib free. TV; cable. Indoor/outdoor pool; wading pool, poolside serv. Restaurant 6 am–11 pm. Bar 11–2 am. Ck-out noon. Convention facilities. Gift shop. Free airport transportation. Lighted tennis. Exercise equipt; weights, bicycles, whirlpool, steam rm, sauna. Game rm. Rec rm. **LUXURY LEVEL:** CONCIERGE LEVEL. 62 rms. S, D $155–$199; suites $175–$500. Private lounge, honor bar. Full wet bar in suites. Bathrm phones. Complimentary coffee. Cr cds: A, C, D, DS, ER, MC, V.

★ ★ ★ **OMNI ORLANDO.** 400 W Livingston St (32801), at Orlando Centroplex Center, downtown. 407/843-6664; FAX 407/648-5414. 290 rms, 15 story. S $79–$160; D $114–$175; each addl $15; suites $220–$415; under 18 free; wkend, special package plans. Crib free. Valet parking $5.50/night. TV; cable. Pool; poolside serv. Restaurant 6:30 am–10 pm. Bar; dancing exc Sun. Ck-out noon. Convention facilities. Gift shop. Airport transportation. Exercise equipt; weights, bicycles, whirlpool. Bathrm phones. Refrigerators avail. Landscaped garden terrace. **LUXURY LEVEL:** OMNI CLUB SERVICE. 39 rms, 8 suites, 2 floors. S $125; D $140; each addl $10; suites $200–$395. Private lounge, honor bar. Complimentary continental bkfst, refreshments. Cr cds: A, C, D, DS, ER, MC, V.

PEABODY ORLANDO. (New general manager, therefore not rated) 9801 International Dr (32819), near Convention & Civic Center, in International Drive Area. 407/352-4000; res: 800/PEABODY; FAX 407/351-0073. 891 units, 27 story, 56 suites. S, D $180–$250; each addl $15; suites $325–$1,200; under 18 free; some lower rates May–Sept. Crib free. Valet parking $7. TV. Heated pool; wading pool, poolside serv. Supervised child's activities. Restaurant open 24 hrs. Bar 11–2 am; entertainment exc Sun. Ck-out noon. Convention facilities. Shopping arcade. Beauty shop. Airport transportation. Lighted tennis, pro shop. 18-hole golf privileges, greens fee. Exercise rm; instructor, weight machines, bicycles, whirlpool, sauna, steam rm. Massage therapy. Game rm. Refrigerators avail. Extensive grounds; fountains at entrance. Guests delight in watching as ducks march to the fountain each morning at 11 am and back to their duck palace at 5 pm. **LUXURY LEVEL:** PEABODY CLUB. 49 rms, 6 suites, 3 story. S, D from $225; suites $325–$1,200. Concierge. Private lounge, honor bar. Full wet bar in suites. Complimentary continental bkfst, refreshments. Cr cds: A, C, D, DS, ER, MC, V, JCB.

★ ★ ★ **PENTA.** 5445 Forbes Place (32812), near Orlando Intl Airport, south of downtown. 407/240-1000; res: 800/762-6222; FAX 407/240-1005. 300 rms, 9 story. S, D $85–$145; each addl $15; suites $290–$435; under 17 free; wkly rates; golf plan. Crib free. TV; cable, in-rm movies. Heated pool; poolside serv. Restaurant 6 am–11 pm. Bar; entertainment exc Sun. Ck-out noon. Convention facilities. Concierge.

Gift shop. Free airport transportation. 36-hole golf privileges. Exercise equipt; weight machines, bicycles, whirlpool, sauna, steam rm. Game rm. Bathrm phones, minibars. *LUXURY LEVEL: EXECUTIVE FLOOR.* 36 suites, 2 floors. Suites $100–$160. Private lounge, honor bar. Complimentary continental bkfst, refreshments.
Cr cds: A, C, D, DS, ER, MC, V, JCB.

D [symbols] **SC**

★ ★ ★ **RADISSON PLAZA.** *60 S Ivanhoe Blvd (32804), I-4 exit 42, north of downtown.* 407/425-4455; FAX 407/843-0262. 337 rms, 15 story. Jan–Apr: S $99; D $140; each addl $15; under 17 free; wkend rates; lower rates rest of yr. TV; cable. Heated pool; poolside serv. Restaurant 6:30–1 am. Bar. Ck-out noon. Meeting rms. Concierge. Gift shop. Lighted tennis. Exercise equipt; weights, bicycles, whirlpool, sauna. Minibars; some refrigerators. *LUXURY LEVEL: PLAZA CLUB.* 46 suites, 2 floors. S $125; D $165; suites $195–$250. Concierge. Private lounge, honor bar. Complimentary continental bkfst, refreshments.
Cr cds: A, C, D, DS, ER, MC, V.

D [symbols] **SC**

★ ★ ★ **STOUFFER ORLANDO RESORT.** *6677 Sea Harbor Dr (32821), in International Drive Area.* 407/351-5555; FAX 407/351-9991. 780 rms, 10 story. Late Dec–mid-May: S, D $189–$229; each addl $20; suites $350–$650; under 18 free; lower rates rest of yr. Crib free. TV; cable, in-rm movies avail. Heated pool; wading pool, poolside serv. Supervised child's activities. Restaurant open 24 hrs. Bar; entertainment. Ck-out noon. Convention facilities. Shopping arcade. Barber, beauty shop. Airport, area attractions transportation avail. Lighted tennis, pro. Golf privileges. Exercise rm; instructor, weights, bicycles, whirlpool, steam rm, sauna. Massage therapy. Game rm. Bathrm phones, minibars. Balconies. Atrium lobby; extensive art collection. *LUXURY LEVEL: CLUB FLOOR.* 94 rms, 8 suites. S, D $209–$249; suites $400–$1,000. Private lounge, honor bar. Full wet bar in suites. Complimentary continental bkfst, refreshments, shoeshine.
Cr cds: A, C, D, DS, ER, MC, V, JCB.

D [symbols] **SC**

★ ★ ★ **TWIN TOWERS.** *5780 Major Blvd (32819), in International Drive Area.* 407/351-1000; res: 800/327-2110; FAX 407/363-0106. 760 rms, 18–19 story. Mid-Feb–mid-Apr: S, D $95–$165; suites $250–$750; under 18 free; lower rates rest of yr. Crib free. TV; cable. Heated pool; wading pool, poolside serv. Playground. Restaurant open 24 hrs. Rm serv 24 hrs. Bar 4:30 pm–2 am; entertainment, dancing Tues–Sat. Ck-out noon. Coin lndry. Convention facilities. Concierge. Shopping arcade. Beauty shop. Airport transportation. Exercise equipt; weight machine, rowers, whirlpool, sauna. Game rm. Refrigerator, wet bar in suites. Located directly in front of Universal Studios entrance. Cr cds: A, C, D, DS, ER, MC, V, JCB.

[symbols] **SC**

Inn

★ ★ ★ **COURTYARD AT LAKE LUCERNE.** *211 N Lucerne Circle E (32801), near Church St Station, downtown.* 407/648-5188; res: 800/444-5289; FAX 407/246-1368. 22 units in 3 bldgs, 2 story. S, D $65–$85; suites $150; kit. unit $85. Crib free. TV; cable. Complimentary continental bkfst. Restaurant nearby. Ck-out 11 am, ck-in 3 pm. Bellhops. Airport, RR station, bus depot transportation. Consists of 3 houses—Victorian, traditional Floridian and art deco—located in historic downtown neighborhood; Victorian Norment-Parry is city's oldest structure (1883). Each guest rm uniquely designed by different artist; large collection of English and American antiques and objets d'art. Gardens. Overlooks lake. Cr cds: A, MC, V.

[symbols] **SC**

Restaurants

★ ★ **CARUSO'S PALACE.** *8986 International Dr, in International Drive Area.* 407/363-7110. Hrs: 5–11 pm. Res accepted. Italian menu. Bar. Wine list. *Prix fixe:* dinner $23.95–$39.95. Child's meals. Specializes in pasta, veal, seafood. Pianist, strolling singers & musi-

cians. Valet parking. Interior replica of European opera house; marble furnishing, frescoes, central garden with sculpture and fountains. Cr cds: A, C, D, DS, MC, V.

D

★ ★ **CHARLEY'S STEAK HOUSE.** *6107 S Orange Blossom Trail, at Oakridge Rd, south of downtown.* 407/851-7130. Hrs: 4:30–10 pm; Fri & Sat to 10:30 pm; Sun 4–9:30 pm. Closed Thanksgiving, Dec 25. Res accepted. Bar. Semi-a la carte: dinner $9.95–$19.95. Child's meals. Specializes in flame-broiled aged steak, fresh seafood. Salad bar. Parking. Antiques. Cr cds: A, MC, V.

D **SC**

★ ★ **CHARLIE'S LOBSTER HOUSE.** *8445 International Dr, at Mercado Shopping Village, in International Drive Area.* 407/352-6929. Hrs: 11 am–10 pm; Fri, Sat to 11 pm. Res accepted. Bar. Semi-a la carte: lunch $4.95–$25.95, dinner $12.95–$36.95. Child's meals. Specializes in seafood, crab cakes. Nautical decor with wood and brass fixtures. Cr cds: A, C, D, DS, ER, MC, V.

D

★ ★ **CHATHAM'S PLACE.** *7575 Dr Phillips Blvd, in Phillips Place, south of downtown.* 407/345-2992. Hrs: 6–9 pm; Fri, Sat to 10 pm. Closed most major hols. Res accepted. Beer. Semi-a la carte: dinner $18.50–$28. Specialties: filet mignon, grouper with pecan butter, rack of lamb. Own specialty desserts. Parking. Intricate wrought-iron grillwork on windows. Totally nonsmoking. Cr cds: A, D, DS, MC, V.

D

✔ ★ **CHINA COAST.** *7500 International Dr, in International Drive Area.* 407/351-9776. Hrs: 11 am–10 pm; Fri, Sat to 11 pm; Sun brunch to 3 pm. Closed Thanksgiving, Dec 25. Chinese menu. Bar. Semi-a la carte: lunch $4.95–$5.95, dinner $4.95–$13.95. Lunch buffet $5.25. Sun brunch $5.25. Child's meals. Parking. Cr cds: A, C, D, DS, MC, V.

D

✔ ★ **CHINA GARDEN.** *1303 S Semoran Blvd, south of downtown.* 407/273-3330. Hrs: 4–10 pm; Fri, Sat to 11 pm; Sun 4–10 pm. Closed Thanksgiving. Res accepted. Chinese menu. Wine, beer. Semi-a la carte: dinner $5.50–$15.95. Complete meals: dinner $10–$16. Specialty: honey garlic ribs. Parking. Modern decor; Chinese artwork. Cr cds: A, MC, V.

D

★ ★ **CHRIS'S HOUSE OF BEEF.** *801 John Young Pkwy, west of downtown.* 407/295-1931. Hrs: 11:30 am–10 pm; Fri & Sat to 11 pm; early-bird dinner Tues–Sat 4–6 pm; Sun champagne brunch 11 am–2:30 pm. Res accepted. Bar. Semi-a la carte: lunch $4.95–$11.95, dinner $7.95–$20.95. Sun champagne brunch $12.95. Child's meals. Specializes in prime rib, steak, seafood. Salad bar. Parking. Atrium garden. Family-owned. Cr cds: A, C, D, DS, ER, MC, V.

D

★ ★ **CRACKERS.** *129 W Church St, at Church Street Station, downtown.* 407/422-2434. Hrs: 11 am–midnight. Bar. Semi-a la carte: lunch $5.50–$9.50, dinner $15–$28. Child's meals. Specialties: seafood gumbo, clam chowder, live Maine lobster. Turn-of-the-century carved and paneled bar. Cr cds: A, D, DS, MC, V.

D

★ ★ **DARBAR.** *7600 Dr Phillips Blvd, in the Marketplace, south of downtown.* 407/345-8128. Hrs: 6–10 pm; Fri & Sat to 10:30 pm; Sun to 9:30 pm. Closed Jan 1, Dec 25. Res accepted. North Indian menu. Bar. Semi-a la carte: dinner $15–$25. Specialties: lobster tandoori, lamb vindaloo. Parking. Indian decor. Cr cds: A, DS, MC, V.

D

★ ★ **4TH FIGHTER GROUP.** *494 Rickenbacker Dr, east of downtown.* 407/898-4251. Hrs: 11 am–10 pm; Fri, Sat to 11 pm; Sun 5–10 pm; early-bird dinner 5–6:30 pm; Sun brunch 10 am–2:30 pm. Res accepted. Bar. Buffet: lunch $6.95. Semi-a la carte: dinner $14.95–$19.95. Sun brunch $14.95. Child's meals. Specializes in prime rib, steak, fresh seafood. Entertainment. Parking. Modeled after WWII English farmhouse; artifacts. Overlooks Orlando Executive Airport. Cr cds: A, C, D, DS, MC, V.

✔ ★★**GARY'S DUCK INN.** *3974 S Orange Blossom Trail, south of downtown.* 407/843-0270. Hrs: 11:30 am–10 pm; Fri to 11 pm; Sat 5–11 pm. Closed Thanksgiving, Dec 25. Res accepted. Bar. Semi-a la carte: lunch $3.95–$8.95, dinner $8.95–$17.95. Child's meals. Specializes in seafood, steak. Parking. Nautical decor. Family-owned. Cr cds: A, MC, V.

★★★**LA NORMANDIE.** *2021 E Colonial Dr (FL 50), east of downtown.* 407/896-9976. Hrs: 11:30 am–2 pm, 5–10 pm; Sat from 5 pm; early-bird dinner 5–7 pm, Sat to 6 pm. Closed Sun; Dec 25. Res accepted. French, continental menu. Bar. Wine list. Semi-a la carte: lunch $7–$11, dinner $10–$19. Specialties: veal fishermen, salmon with lobster sauce, soufflé Grand Marnier. Own baking. Parking. Country French decor. Cr cds: A, C, D, DS, ER, MC, V.

✔ ★★**LE COQ AU VIN.** *4800 S Orange Ave, south of downtown.* 407/851-6980. Hrs: 11:30 am–2 pm, 5:30–10 pm; Sat from 5:30 pm; Sun 5–9 pm. Closed Mon; Jan 1, Easter, Dec 25. Res accepted. French, Amer menu. Wine, beer. Semi-a la carte: lunch $6.50–$12, dinner $12–$16. Child's meals. Parking. Menu changes monthly. Cr cds: A, C, D, MC, V.

★★**LEE'S LAKESIDE.** *431 E Central Blvd, downtown.* 407/841-1565. Hrs: 11 am–11 pm; Sat from 5 pm; early-bird dinner 4–6 pm. Closed Sun; Dec 25. Res accepted. Continental menu. Bar. Semi-a la carte: lunch $7.95–$8.95, dinner $18.95–$22.95. Child's meals. Specializes in fresh seafood, prime rib, veal. Entertainment. Parking. View of skyline across Lake Eola. Cr cds: A, D, DS, MC, V.

★★**LILI MARLENE'S AVIATORS RESTAURANT & PUB.** *129 W Church St, at Church Street Station, downtown.* 407/422-2434. Hrs: 11 am–4 pm, 5:30 pm–midnight; Sun brunch 10:30 am–3 pm. Bar 11–1 am. Semi-a la carte: lunch $4.95–$9.95, dinner $15.95–$23.95. Sun brunch $9.95. Child's meals. Specializes in aged beef, fresh grilled Florida seafood. Entertainment. Valet parking. In historic district; antiques, WWI aviation artifacts. Cr cds: A, C, D, DS, MC, V.

★★★**MING COURT.** *9188 International Dr, south of downtown.* 407/363-0338. Hrs: 11 am–2:30 pm, 4:30 pm–midnight. Res accepted. Chinese menu. Bar. Semi-a la carte: lunch $5–$9, dinner $7–$20. Specialties: Peking duck, dim sum. Own sorbets. Chinese performers. Parking. Chinese-style architecture with undulating "Great Wall" enclosing gardens and waterways. Cr cds: A, C, D, DS, MC, V, JCB.

★★**PASSAGE TO INDIA.** *5532 International Dr, in International Drive Area.* 407/351-3456. Hrs: 11:30 am–10 pm. Res accepted. Indian menu. Wine, beer. Buffet: lunch $5.95. A la carte entrees: dinner $20–$50. Child's meals. Specializes in clay oven preparations, vegetarian dishes. Salad bar (lunch). Parking. Richly carved wooden screens, brass. Cr cds: A, C, D, DS, MC, V.

✔ ★**RONNIE'S.** *2702 E Colonial Dr (FL 50), in Colonial Plaza Shopping Ctr, east of downtown.* 407/894-2943. Hrs: 7 am–11 pm; Fri, Sat to 1 am. Res accepted. Jewish, Amer menu. Semi-a la carte: bkfst $2.45–$7.75, lunch $3.95–$8.95, dinner $4.25–$8.95. Child's meals. Specializes in corned beef, cheesecake. Own baking. Parking. Bakery and deli; large selection of pastries and ice cream specials. Family-owned. No cr cds accepted.

★★★**SIAM ORCHID.** *7575 Republic Dr, in International Drive Area.* 407/351-0821. Hrs: 11 am–2 pm, 5:30–11 pm; Sat, Sun from 5:30 pm. Closed July 4, Dec 25. Res accepted. Thai menu. Bar. Semi-a la carte: dinner $12–$20.95. Specialties: Siam Orchid roast duck, fresh seafood. Parking. Thai decor and artifacts. On lake. Cr cds: A, D, MC, V.

✔ ★**TONY MARINO'S.** *729 Lee Rd, north of downtown.* 407/645-4443. Hrs: 11:30 am–10 pm; Fri to 11 pm; Sat 4–11 pm; Sun 4–10 pm; early-bird dinner 4–6:30 pm. Closed Dec 25. Bar. Semi-a la carte: lunch $4.25–$7.95, dinner $5.95–$13.95. Child's meals. Specializes in steak, seafood, barbecued baby back ribs. Parking. Cr cds: A, D, MC, V.

★★**VIVALDI.** *107 Pine St, downtown.* 407/423-2335. Hrs: 11 am–11 pm; Sat & Sun from 4 pm. Closed Thanksgiving, Dec 25. Res accepted. Italian menu. Bar. A la carte entrees: lunch $6.95–$9.95, dinner $9.90–$22.95. Specialty: Vivaldi's Pride (veal & chicken dish). Parking. Own bread, pasta. Outdoor dining. Intimate gourmet dining. Cr cds: A, D, DS, MC, V.

Unrated Dining Spots

HARD ROCK CAFE. *5800 Kirkman Rd, at Universal Studios Florida, south of downtown.* 407/351-7625. Hrs: 11–2 am. Bar. Semi-a la carte: lunch, dinner $6.95–$15.95. Child's meals. Specializes in hamburgers, "pig sandwich," barbecue dishes. Parking. Outdoor dining. Building shaped like an electric guitar; stained-glass windows depict Elvis Presley, Jerry Lee Lewis and Chuck Berry. Rock & roll and entertainment memorabilia throughout. Cr cds: A, MC, V.

KING HENRY'S FEAST. *8984 International Dr, in International Drive Area.* 407/351-5151; res: 800/347-8181. Dinner show hrs vary each season. Res required. Bar. Complete meals: adult $25.95; children $17.95. Specializes in baked chicken, barbecued ribs. Entertainment includes dueling knights, magicians, jesters. Parking. Medieval palace decor; costumed servers. Cr cds: A, DS, MC, V.

MARDI GRAS. *8445 International Dr, at Mercado Mediterranean Village, in International Drive Area.* 407/351-5151; res: 800/347-8181. Dinner show hrs vary each season. Res accepted. Bar. Complete meals: adult $28.95, children $19.95. Dinner show featuring cabaret-style songs and dances of the world's carnival capitals. Parking. Cr cds: A, C, D, DS, MC, V.

Ormond Beach (B-4)

Founded: 1875 **Pop:** 29,721 **Elev:** 22 ft **Area code:** 904

John D. Rockefeller, Sr, who died here in 1937 at age 97, spent his twilight years giving out dimes to encourage thrift, playing golf with intense seriousness and doggedly trying to live to 100. Partly on the Atlantic Ocean, partly on the Halifax River with the Tomoka River at its back, Ormond Beach still boasts of the healthful climate that contributed to Rockefeller's longevity. One of its main assets is its 23-mile, 500-foot-wide public beach. Auto racing was a popular sport in the early 1900s, when world records were set here. A Stanley Steamer went 127.66 miles per hour in January, 1906. Today, 18 miles of the beach are open to cars.

What to See and Do

1. **Ormond Memorial Art Museum and Gardens.** 78 E Granada Blvd, 3 blks W of FL A1A. Changing exhibits include contemporary art, antiques, and special collections; permanent collection of symbolic religious paintings by Malcolm Fraser; four-acre tropical garden. (Tues–Fri, also Sat & Sun afternoons; closed mid–late Aug & major

hols; also temporarily for exhibit changes) Children only with adults. Phone 677-1857. ¢

2. **The Casements.** 25 Riverside Dr. Former winter home of John D. Rockefeller, Sr now serves as cultural center for city; historical exhibits include Hungarian Historic Room, Boy Scout exhibit; changing art displays. (Daily exc Sun; closed hols) Phone 676-3216. **Free.**

3. **Birthplace of Speed Museum.** 160 E Granada Blvd. Museum interprets the role Ormond Beach has played in the development of automobile racing from 1902, when cars raced up and down its sand beach, to the present; 1922 Model-T, 1929 Model-A, replica of Stanley Steamer. (Daily exc Sun, limited hrs; closed hols) Phone 672-5657. ¢

4. **Tomoka State Park.** 3 mi N on FL A1A, off N Beach St. Approx 900 acres where the Tomoka and Halifax rivers meet. Site of Indian village of Nocoroco. Museum (daily). Fishing; boating (ramp, dock), canoe rentals. Nature trail. Picnicking, playground. Camping (hookups, dump station). Visitor center. Standard hrs, fees. Phone 676-4050.

5. **Gamble Rogers Memorial State Recreation Area at Flagler Beach.** 11 mi N on FL A1A, near Flagler Beach. Approx 145 acres extending across a barrier 3 miles south of town bordered by the Atlantic Ocean and the Intracoastal Waterway. Swimming; fishing; boating (ramp, dock). Nature trails. Picnicking, playground. Camping (hookups, dump station). Standard hrs, fees. Phone 439-2474.

6. **Bulow Plantation Ruins State Historic Site.** 8 mi N off FL A1A, on FL 5, S of Flagler Beach. Bulow Plantation, which flourished in the early 1800s, was destroyed by Seminole Indians in 1836. Now the ruins of its sugar mill remain on this 109-acre park. Canoe rentals; fishing. Nature trails. Picnicking. Interpretive center. Standard hrs, fees. Phone 439-2219.

(For further information contact the Chamber of Commerce, 165 W Granada Blvd, 32175; 677-3454 or -6362.)

Annual Event

Birthplace of Speed Antique Car Show. Parades, antique car competition, beach sprint races. 3 days Thanksgiving wkend.

(See Daytona Beach, DeLand, New Smyrna Beach)

Motels

(Rates may be higher during race week)

★ ★**COMFORT INN ON THE BEACH.** *507 S Atlantic Ave (FL A1A) (32074).* 904/677-8550; res: 800/456-8550; FAX 904/673-6260. 49 units, 4 story, 26 kits. Feb–Apr, June–Labor Day: S, D $60–$90; each addl $5; kit. units $65–$95; under 16 free; higher rates: Easter, July 4, special events; lower rates rest of yr. Crib $5. Pet accepted, some restrictions; $3. TV; cable. Heated pool; wading pool. Ck-out 11 am. Complimentary continental bkfst. Complimentary coffee in lobby. Restaurant adj. Golf privileges. Lawn games. Many private patios, balconies. On ocean, beach. Cr cds: A, C, D, DS, ER, MC, V, JCB.

🅳 🖧 🈂 🏊 🚭 ⓦ SC

★**ECONO LODGE.** *295 S Atlantic Ave (FL A1A) (32176).* 904/672-2651; res: 800/847-8811; FAX 904/672-3180. 58 rms, 4 story, 33 kits. Mid-Feb–Easter: S, D $85; kit. units $87–$95; each addl $7; wkly rates; higher rates: hols, special events (5-day min); lower rates rest of yr. Crib $3. TV; cable. Heated pool; wading pool. Restaurant nearby. Ck-out 11 am. Coin lndry. Golf privileges. Private patios. Picnic tables, grills. On ocean, beach. Cr cds: A, D, DS, MC, V.

🈂 🏊 🚭 ⓦ SC

★ ★**HOWARD JOHNSON NORTH.** *1633 N US 1 (32074), I-95 exit 89.* 904/677-7310; FAX 904/677-7310, ext 310. 64 rms, 2 story. Jan–Apr: S, D $40–$125; each addl $8; under 18 free; higher rates: hols, special events; lower rates rest of yr. Crib free. Pet accepted, some

restrictions. TV; cable. Pool; wading pool. Playground. Ck-out 11 am. Coin lndry. Private patios; some balconies. Cr cds: A, C, D, DS, ER, MC, V, JCB.

🅳 🖧 🈂 🚭 ⓦ SC

★**MAINSAIL.** *281 S Atlantic Ave (FL A1A) (32074).* 904/677-2131; res: 800/843-5142. 50 units, 2–4 story, 33 kits. Mar–Apr: S, D $75–$85; each addl $7; kit. units $90–$95; family, wkly rates; higher rates: hols, special events; lower rates rest of yr. TV; cable. Heated pool; wading pool. Restaurant adj. Ck-out 11 am. Coin lndry. Sundries. 18-hole golf privileges. Exercise equipt; weights, bicycles, sauna. Game rm. Private patios, balconies. Picnic tables, grill. On ocean, beach. Cr cds: A, C, D, DS, MC, V.

🈂 🏊 🚶 ⓦ SC

✔ ★ ★**MAKAI.** *707 S Atlantic Ave (FL A1A) (32176).* 904/677-8060. 110 rms, 4 story, 61 kits. Feb–Apr, June–Labor Day: S, D $45–$85; each addl $5; suites $90–$150; kit. units $49–$85; under 16 free; higher rates: hols, special events; lower rates rest of yr. Crib $4. TV; cable. Heated pool; wading pool, whirlpool. Restaurant nearby. Ck-out 11 am. Coin lndry. Meeting rm. Game rm. Lawn games. Many refrigerators. Private patios, balconies. Picnic tables, grills. On beach. Cr cds: A, C, D, DS, ER, MC, V.

🈂 ⓦ

★ ★**MAVERICK.** *485 S Atlantic Ave (FL A1A) (32074).* 904/672-3550. 138 units, 7 story, no ground floor rms, 138 kits. Early Feb–late Apr, mid-June–early Sept: S, D $90–$115; higher rates: Easter, July 4, special events; varied lower rates rest of yr. Crib free. TV; cable. Heated pool; wading pool, whirlpool, sauna. Free supervised child's activities. Restaurant 7 am–2:30 pm. Ck-out 10 am. Coin lndry. Game rm. Lawn games. Refrigerators. Private patios, balconies. Picnic tables. On ocean, beach. Cr cds: A, D, MC, V.

🈂 ⓦ

✔ ★**QUALITY INN.** *1567 N US 1 (32074), I-95 exit 89.* 904/672-8621. 76 rms, 2 story. Feb–Apr: S, D $39.95–$69.95; under 18 free; higher rates: Daytona races, spring break; lower rates rest of yr. Crib free. TV; cable. Pool. Playground. Complimentary coffee in lobby. Restaurant adj open 24 hrs. Ck-out noon. Coin lndry. Lawn games. Cr cds: A, C, D, DS, ER, MC, V, JCB.

🖧 🈂 🚭 ⓦ SC

★**TRADERS INN.** *1355 Ocean Shore Blvd (32176).* 904/441-1111. 49 kit. units, 5 story. June–Labor Day: kit. units $60–$80; higher rates special events; lower rates rest of yr. Crib $3. TV; cable. Heated pool; wading pool. Restaurant nearby. Ck-out 10 am. Coin lndry. Sundries. Lawn games. Private patios, balconies. Picnic tables, grills. On beach. Cr cds: A, C, D, MC, V.

🅳 🈂 ⓦ

Motor Hotels

★ ★**CASA DEL MAR BEACH RESORT.** *621 S Atlantic Ave (FL A1A) (32176).* 904/672-4550; res: 800/245-1590; FAX 904/672-1418. 151 kit. units, 7 story. May–Sept: kit. units $73–$145; each addl $8; under 16 free; wkly rates; monthly rates Sept–Feb, May–June; higher rates: special events; varied lower rates rest of yr. Crib free. TV; cable. Heated pool; whirlpool, wading pool, poolside serv (seasonal). Restaurant 7 am–1 pm. Rm serv. Bar. Ck-out 11 am. Coin lndry. Meeting rms. Bellhops. Valet serv. Sundries. Game rm. Lawn games. Refrigerators. Balconies. On ocean, beach. Cr cds: A, C, D, DS, ER, MC, V.

🅳 🈂 🚭 ⓦ

★ ★**IVANHOE BEACH RESORT.** *205 S Atlantic Ave (FL A1A) (32176).* 904/672-6711; res: 800/874-9910; FAX 904/676-9494. 146 rms, 7 story, 70 kits. July–mid-Aug: S, D $75–$85; each addl $5; kit. units $80–$85; under 18 free; higher rates: hols, special events (3–7-day min); lower rates rest of yr. Crib $4. TV; cable. Heated pool; wading pool, poolside serv in season. Restaurant 7 am–1 pm. Rm serv. Ck-out

11 am. Coin lndry. Covered parking. Game rm. Lawn games. Refrigerators. Balconies. On beach. Cr cds: A, D, MC, V.

Restaurants

✔ ★ ★ **JULIAN'S.** *88 S Atlantic Ave. 904/677-6767.* Hrs: 4–11 pm. Bar. Semi-a la carte: dinner $8–$16. Child's meals. Specializes in prime beef, seafood. Organist; entertainment exc Mon. Parking. Island decor. Family-owned. Cr cds: A, D, MC, V.

★ ★ **MARIO'S.** *521 S Yonge St. 904/677-2711.* Hrs: 5–10 pm; Sat to midnight. Closed Thanksgiving, Dec 25. Italian, Amer menu. Bar. Semi-a la carte: dinner $8.95–$23. Child's meals. Specialties: veal Marsala, veal à la Française, seafood. Entertainment Fri–Sat. Parking. Italian decor; large oil paintings, brass ceiling lights. Family-owned. Cr cds: A, MC, V.

Unrated Dining Spot

MORRISON'S CAFETERIA. *135 E Granada Blvd. 904/677-0724.* Hrs: 11 am–7:30 pm. Avg ck: lunch $4.89, dinner $5.99. Child's meals. Specializes in fried chicken, roast beef. Salad bar. Parking. Cr cds: MC, V.

Palatka (B-4)

Settled: 1821 **Pop:** 10,201 **Elev:** 22 ft **Area code:** 904 **Zip:** 32177

The name Palatka is derived from the Indian *pilaklikaha,* meaning "crossing over." The town sits at an elbow of the St Johns River, a mighty mile-wide waterway and one of the few north-flowing rivers in the world. After the Civil War, wintering in Florida became fashionable for rich Easterners, who would travel by train to Jacksonville and then take a 50-mile river-steamer trip to Palatka. The city's role as a resort fell into decline with the opening of the railroad in other sections of Florida. Today, more than 30 fishing camps, resorts and lodges along the St Johns River accommodate fishermen angling for bass.

What to See and Do

1. **Bronson-Mulholland House** (1854). 100 Madison St. Three-story antebellum cypress structure built for one of the first circuit judges of the state. (Tues, Thurs & Sun afternoons; closed hols) Phone 329-0140. **Free.**
2. **Ravine State Gardens.** 1 mi SE, off Moseley Ave on Twigg St. Thousands of azaleas of many varieties and other ornamental plants bloom on these 182 landscaped acres. Near entrance is Court of States, with 68-foot obelisk at one end and Civic Center at other; 2-mile drive follows edges of 3 ravines penetrated by 6½ miles of paths. Most spectacular in Feb & Mar. Nature trails. Picnicking. (Daily) Phone 329-3721. **¢** Per car **¢¢**

(For further information contact the Chamber of Commerce, 1100 Reid St, PO Box 550, 32178; 328-1503.)

Annual Events

Azalea Festival. Downtown. Parade, ball, regatta, festival pageant, arts & crafts show. Mar.

Putnam County Fair. Late Mar.

Palatka Horseman's Rodeo. Parade, rodeo. Oct.

(See Gainesville, St Augustine)

Motel

★ **HOLIDAY INN RIVERSIDE.** *201 N 1st St. 904/328-3481; FAX 904/328-3481, ext 315.* 131 rms. S $55–$60; D $60–$65; under 18 free. Crib free. Pet accepted, some restrictions. TV; cable. Pool; poolside serv. Restaurant 6 am–2 pm, 5–10 pm. Rm serv. Bar; entertainment. Coin lndry. Meeting rms. Bellhops. Valet serv. On river; boat dock. Former steamboat landing. Cr cds: A, C, D, DS, MC, V, JCB.

Unrated Dining Spot

HOLIDAY HOUSE. *US 17S, 1 blk S of bridge. 904/325-2125.* Hrs: 11 am–8:30 pm. Avg ck: lunch $4.95–$5.39, dinner $6.95–$7.15. Child's meals. Specializes in lamb, roast beef, ham. Salad bar. Parking. Totally nonsmoking. Cr cds: A, MC, V.

Palm Beach (D-5)

Settled: 1861 **Pop:** 9,814 **Elev:** 15 ft **Area code:** 407 **Zip:** 33480

Although condominiums and office buildings along the main streets have altered the atmosphere of Palm Beach slightly, the image of elegance, beauty and charm remains. Single-family houses and regal estates still dominate the scene, and lush foliage and expert landscaping personify the semi-tropical living. The town prides itself on its world-famous shopping areas: Worth Avenue and the Esplanade, Royal Poinciana Way and South County Road.

Situated on the northern end of a 14-mile-long island, half a mile at its widest point, with Lake Worth to the west and the Atlantic Ocean to the east, Palm Beach probably owes its resort existence to a shipwreck in 1878. The vessel's cargo of coconuts was washed ashore and took root, transforming a barren ribbon of sand into a palm-shadowed haven. Henry Morrison Flagler, the railroad magnate, was the first to recognize the attraction of Palm Beach; he built the famous Royal Poinciana Hotel and directed major civic improvements, including extensive landscaping. The Gulf Stream at Phipps Ocean Park is closer to shore in this area (1–3 miles) than any other point in the US.

What to See and Do

1. **Henry Morrison Flagler Museum (Whitehall).** On Cocoanut Row at Whitehall Way. This 55-room house (1901) was built by Henry Morrison Flagler, developer of the Florida East Coast Railroad. An opulent monument to America's Gilded Age, this marble palace contains porcelains, paintings, silver, glass, dolls, lace, costumes and family memorabilia. Special exhibits illustrate local history and the vast enterprises of the Flagler system. On the grounds is Flagler's private railroad car, refinished and refitted with exact reproductions of the original carpeting, drapery and upholstery materials. (Daily exc Mon; closed Jan 1, Dec 25) (See ANNUAL EVENT) Phone 655-2833. **¢¢¢**
2. **Hibel Museum of Art.** 150 Royal Poinciana Plaza. Located on the shores of Lake Worth, this is the only nonprofit public museum in the world dedicated to the art of a living American woman. Exhibits include paintings, lithographs, drawings, serigraphs, sculpture and porcelain art by Edna Hibel. Also displays of antique Oriental snuff bottles, Italian, English and Oriental furniture, art books and dolls. Gift shop. (Daily exc Mon; closed Dec 25) (See SEASONAL EVENTS) Phone 833-6870. **Free.**
3. **Society of the Four Arts.** Four Arts Plaza, off Royal Palm Way. Complex includes museum, library and gardens (free); also lectures, films, concerts (Jan–Mar, fee). Galleries (mid-Dec–mid-Apr,

daily). Library & gardens (Nov–Apr, daily exc Sun; rest of yr, Mon–Fri; closed most hols). Phone 655-7226.   **Free.**

4. **The Church of Bethesda-by-the-Sea** (1925). S County Rd & Barton Ave. Church of 15th-century Gothic design with embattlement tower, arched main entrance. Adjacent is Cluett Memorial Garden with extensive tropical landscaping. (Daily) Phone 655-4554. **Free.**

5. **Palm Beach Bicycle Trail.** This nearly five-mile, paved trail, beginning south of the Royal Park Bridge at Worth Ave, winds among some of the most beautiful houses in Palm Beach, terminating two blocks north of the Palm Beach Sailfish Club.

(For further information contact the Chamber of Commerce, 45 Cocoanut Row; 655-3282.)

Annual Event

Flagler Anniversary Open House. Henry Morrison Flagler Museum (see #1). Commemorates the opening of Flagler's elaborate mansion as a museum in 1960. Guides in early 1900s costumes, music, antique cars, refreshments, special exhibits and films are featured. 1st Sat Feb.

Seasonal Events

Promenade Concerts. Hibel Museum of Art (see #2). Free Classical & light musical concerts by both beginning and established professional musicians. Limited seating; early arrival suggested. Phone 833-6870. 2nd Sun each month, Nov–May.

Royal Poinciana Playhouse. 70 Royal Poinciana Plaza. Broadway plays and musicals. Phone 659-3310 for tickets. Mid-Dec–Mar.

(See Jupiter, Lake Worth, West Palm Beach)

Motels

 ★**BEACHCOMBER.** 3024 S Ocean Blvd (FL A1A). 407/585-4646. 50 units, 1–2 story, 45 kits. Jan–Apr: S, D $95–$195; each addl $10; varied lower rates rest of yr. Crib free. TV; cable. Saltwater pool. Restaurant nearby. Ck-out noon. Coin lndry. Lawn games. Some patios, balconies. On ocean. Cr cds: A, DS, MC, V.

★**HAWAIIAN OCEAN INN.** 3550 S Ocean Blvd (FL A1A). 407/582-5631; res: 800/457-5631; FAX 407/582-5631, ext 165. 58 units, 2 story, 8 suites. Jan–Apr: S, D $100; each addl $5; suites $129–$185; studio rms $109; under 18 free; wkly rates; lower rates rest of yr. Crib free. TV. Heated pool; poolside serv. Restaurant 7 am–10 pm. Rm serv. Bar 11 am–midnight. Ck-out 11 am. Airport transportation. Refrigerators. On ocean, swimming beach. Cr cds: A, C, D, DS, ER, MC, V.

★★**HEART OF PALM BEACH.** 160 Royal Palm Way. 407/655-5600; res: 800/523-5377; FAX 407/832-1201. 88 rms, 2–3 story. Mid-Dec–Apr: S, D $109–$199; each addl $15; suites $225; under 18 free; varied lower rates rest of yr. Crib free. TV; cable. Heated pool; poolside serv. Restaurant 7–2 am. Rm serv. Bar from 11 am. Ck-out noon. Bellhops. Valet serv. Free underground parking. Refrigerators. Bicycle rentals. Private patios, balconies. Cr cds: A, C, D, MC, V.

Motor Hotel

★★**HOWARD JOHNSON.** 2870 S Ocean Blvd (FL A1A). 407/582-2581; FAX 407/582-7189. 99 rms, 3 story. Mid-Dec–Apr: S, D $102–$120; each addl $10; under 18 free; package plans; varied lower rates rest of yr. Crib free. TV; cable. Pool; poolside serv. Restaurant 6:30

am–11 pm. Rm serv. Bar 3 pm–3 am. Ck-out noon. Coin lndry. Meeting rm. Bellhops. Some balconies. Cr cds: A, C, D, DS, ER, MC, V, JCB.

Hotels

★★★★**BRAZILIAN COURT.** 301 Australian Ave. 407/655-7740; res: 800/552-0335 (US), 800/228-6852 (CAN); FAX 407/655-0801. 134 rms, 2–3 story, 6 suites. Mid-Dec–Apr: S, D $185–$290; each addl $25; suites $525–$850; under 12 free; monthly rates; lower rates rest of yr. Crib free. TV; cable. Heated pool; poolside serv. Restaurants 7 am–10 pm (also see THE DINING ROOM). Rm serv 24 hrs. Bar 11–1 am; entertainment, dancing. Ck-out noon. Meeting rms. Concierge. Tennis & golf privileges. Refrigerators avail. Private patios, balconies. 1920s landmark; renewed in traditional Palm Beach style. Individually decorated rms surround courtyards. Cr cds: A, C, D, DS, MC, V.

★★★**CHESTERFIELD HOTEL.** 363 Cocoanut Row. 407/659-5800; res: 800/243-7871; FAX 407/659-6707. 58 rms, 3 story, 9 suites. Mid-Dec–Apr: S, D $175–$250; suites $325–$700; lower rates rest of yr. Crib free. TV; cable. Heated pool; whirlpool, poolside serv. Restaurant 7 am–10 pm, Fri & Sat to 11 pm (also see BUTLERS). Afternoon tea and scones. Rm serv 24 hrs. Bar 11–1 am; pianist. Ck-out 1 pm. Meeting rms. Concierge. Free valet parking. Airport transportation. Card rm. Library/reading rms. English charm and elegance; service in the European tradition. English-style London taxicab takes guests to and from West Palm Beach and other locations. Ocean 3 blks. Cr cds: A, C, D, DS, ER, MC, V.

★★★**HILTON OCEANSIDE RESORT.** 2842 S Ocean Blvd (FL A1A). 407/586-6542; FAX 407/585-0188. 134 units, 5 story. Mid-Dec–mid-Apr: S, D $210–$260; each addl $25; suites $475–$950; family rates; lower rates rest of yr. Crib free. TV; cable. Heated pool; whirlpool, sauna, poolside serv. Restaurant 7 am–10 pm. Rm serv 24 hrs in season. Bar 11 am–midnight; entertainment. Ck-out noon. Meeting rms. Free covered parking. Tennis. 18-hole golf privileges, greens fee $40. Health club privileges. Refrigerators, honor bars. Private patios, balconies. On ocean beach. Cr cds: A, C, D, DS, ER, MC, V.

★★★★**THE OCEAN GRAND.** 2800 S Ocean Blvd. 407/582-2800; res: 800/432-2335; FAX 407/547-1374. 210 rms, 4 story, 12 suites. Mid-Dec–mid-Apr: S, D $295–$475; suites $750–$1,800; under 17 free; lower rates rest of yr. Crib free. Valet parking $6. TV; cable. Heated pool; poolside serv. Supervised child's activities (Wed–Sun). Restaurant 7 am–10 pm (also see THE RESTAURANT). Rm serv 24 hrs. Bar 4 pm–midnight; pianist. Ck-out noon. Meeting rms. Concierge. Barber, beauty shop. Tennis, pro. 18-hole golf privileges, greens fee $50, pro. Exercise rm; instructor, weight machine, bicycles, whirlpool, sauna, steam rm. Massage. Bathrm phones, minibars; refrigerators avail. Balconies. Combines contemporary design with luxurious detailing of traditional Floridian resorts; views of Atlantic Ocean from all rms. On beach. Cr cds: A, C, D, DS, MC, V, JCB.

★★★★**THE RITZ-CARLTON, PALM BEACH.** (100 S Ocean Blvd, Manalapan 33462) 8 mi S on US A1A. 407/533-6000; res: 800/241-3333; FAX 407/588-4201. 270 rms, 6 story, 56 suites. Mid-Dec–Apr: S, D $310–$500; suites $870–$3,000; under 12 free; golf plans; lower rates rest of yr. Crib free. Garage $10/day. TV; cable. Heated pool; poolside serv. Supervised child's activities. Cafe 6–11 pm (also see THE RESTAURANT). Rm serv 24 hrs. Bar; entertainment. Ck-out noon. Meeting rms. Concierge. Shopping arcade. Barber, beauty shop. Airport transportation. Lighted tennis. 18-hole golf privileges, greens fee $65–$85, pro, putting green, driving range. Exercise rm; instructor, weight machine, bicycles, whirlpool, steam rm. Massage. Bathrm phones, minibars. Balconies. Mediterranean-style beachfront hotel. Distinctive Ritz-Carlton lion atop a crown's crest is carved in stone on an exterior wall; three towers rise above the hotel. *LUXURY LEVEL:* **CLUB LEVEL.** 26 rms, 8 suites. S, D $550; suites $1,250. Concierge. Private lounge, honor bar. Complimentary continental bkfst, refreshments, newspapers. Cr cds: A, C, D, DS, ER, MC, V, JCB.

Inn

★ ★ ★ **PLAZA.** 215 Brazilian Ave. 407/832-8666; res: 800/233-2632; FAX 407/835-8776. 50 rms, 3 story. Mid-Dec-mid-Apr: S, D $125-$155; each addl $15; under 12 free; lower rates rest of yr. Crib free. TV. Heated pool; whirlpool, poolside serv. Complimentary full bkfst. Dining rm 7:30-10 am. Rm serv. Ck-out noon, ck-in 2 pm. Bellhops. Health club privileges. Picnic tables, grills. Art deco building (1939) near ocean. Cr cds: A, MC, V.

Resort

★ ★ ★ ★ **THE BREAKERS.** 1 South County Rd. 407/655-6611; res: 407/659-8440, 800/833-3141; FAX 407/659-8403. 567 rms, 7 story. Mid-Dec-mid-Apr, MAP (serv charge in lieu of tipping): S $245-$395; D $275-$425; each addl $75; suites $370-$775; EP avail; golf, tennis package plans; lower rates rest of yr. Crib avail. TV; cable. Heated pool; wading pool, poolside serv, lifeguard. Playground. Free supervised child's activities. Dining rm (open to public) 7-10:30 am, 6-10 pm; beach club lunch from 11:30 am. Box lunches; snack bar; picnics. Rm serv 24 hrs. Bar 11-2 am. Ck-out noon, ck-in 4 pm. Convention facilities. Valet serv. Concierge. Shopping arcade. Barber, beauty shop. Valet parking. 19 tennis courts, pro. 36-hole golf, greens fee $42, pro, putting green, driving range. Scuba diving instructor. Bicycle rentals. Lawn games. Soc dir; entertainment, dancing, movies. Rec rm. Exercise rm; instructor, weights, bicycles, sauna, steam rm. Masseurs. Language bank. 24 languages spoken. Sign language. Refrigerators, minibars. On ocean, private beach; cabanas, beach club. With Italian Renaissance decor, gourmet food and extensive recreational and relaxation facilities, this historic landmark resort has been frequented by wealthy socialites and celebrities for most of this century. Cr cds: A, C, D, DS, ER, MC, V, JCB.

Restaurants

★ ★ **BICE.** 313½ Worth Ave. 407/835-1600. Hrs: noon-3 pm, 6-10:30 pm; Sat, Sun 6-11 pm. Closed Dec 25; also Sun May-Sept. Res accepted. Italian menu. Bar noon-11 pm. A la carte entrees: lunch $5-$19, dinner $8-$28. Specialties: beef carpaccio, insalata Caprese, tagliolini con gamberoni. Valet parking (dinner). Outdoor courtyard dining. Cr cds: A, D, MC, V.

D

★ ★ ★ **BUTLERS.** (See Chesterfield Hotel) 407/659-5800. Hrs: 7-11 am, noon-2:30 pm, 6-10 pm. Res accepted. Continental menu. Bar 11-1 am. A la carte entrees: bkfst $3.50-$9, lunch $8-$15, dinner $12-$40. Specialties: English-style roast beef & Yorkshire pudding, Chesterfield club sandwich. Pianist exc Sun. Valet parking. Outdoor dining. English country manor decor. Jacket (dinner). Cr cds: A, C, D, DS, ER, MC, V.

D

★ ★ ★ ★ **CAFE L'EUROPE.** 150 Worth Ave, 2nd floor of Esplanade Shopping Area. 407/655-4020. Hrs: 11:30 am-11 pm; Sun 6:30-10 pm. Closed Dec 25. Res accepted. French, continental menu. Bar. Wine list. A la carte entrees: lunch $12-$25, dinner $18-$30. Specialties: fresh Florida snapper sautéed in a potato crust, pinenut-breaded sea scallops, sautéed veal medallions with green asparagus, shiitake mushrooms and fresh thyme sauce, roasted rack of lamb ratatouille. Own baking. Caviar bar. Valet parking. Old World elegance. Jacket (dinner). Cr cds: A, C, D, MC, V.

★ ★ **CHARLEY'S CRAB.** 456 S Ocean Blvd (FL A1A). 407/659-1500. Hrs: 11:30 am-10 pm; Fri, Sat to 11 pm; Sun 10 am-10 pm;

early-bird dinner 5-6 pm; Sun brunch 10:30 am-2:30 pm. Res accepted. Bar. Wine list. Semi-a la carte: lunch $5.95-$16.50, dinner $13.50-$32. Sun brunch $9.95-$19.95. Child's meals. Specializes in fresh seafood, homemade pasta. Own baking. Valet parking. Oceanfront dining. Cr cds: A, C, D, DS, MC, V.

D

★ ★ **CHUCK & HAROLD'S.** 207 Royal Poinciana Way. 407/659-1440. Hrs: 7:30 am-midnight; Fri, Sat to 1 am; Sun from 8 am; early-bird dinner 4:30-6 pm. Res accepted. Continental menu. Bar 11:30-1 am. A la carte entrees: bkfst $2-$9.50, lunch $5.50-$12.50, dinner $13.75-$23. Child's meals. Specializes in homemade pasta, fresh catch of the day. Entertainment. Valet parking (dinner). Outdoor dining. Sidewalk cafe. Convertible roof allows for open-air dining. Cr cds: A, C, D, DS, MC, V.

D

✔ ★ ★ **DEMPSEY'S.** 50 Cocoanut Row. 407/835-0400. Hrs: 11:30 am-3 pm, 5:30-11:30 pm; Sun brunch 9 am-2:30 pm. Closed Dec 25. Bar. Semi-a la carte: lunch $4.50-$11, dinner $7-$22. Sun brunch $3.75-$7.95. Specialties: chicken hash Dempsey, shad roe. Pianist from 9 pm Thurs-Sun. Valet parking. Some antiques; original artwork. Cr cds: A, MC, V.

D

★ ★ ★ **THE DINING ROOM.** (See Brazilian Court Hotel) 407/659-7840. Hrs: 7 am-11 pm; May-Sept to 10 pm; Sun brunch noon-2:30 pm (summer to 2 pm). Res accepted. Bar 11-1 am. Wine list. Semi-a la carte: bkfst $7-$15, lunch $7-$25, dinner $18-$40. Sun brunch $15-$25. Child's meals. Specialties: medallion of Norwegian salmon, rack of lamb, grilled chicken breast. Own baking. Entertainment exc Mon. Valet parking. Outdoor dining. Wrought iron chandeliers; fireplace. Jacket. Cr cds: A, C, D, MC, V.

D

✔ ★ **E.R. BRADLEY'S SALOON.** 111 Bradley Place. 407/833-3520. Hrs: 11-2 am; Sat & Sun from 10 am. Res accepted. Bar. Semi-a la carte: lunch $3.95-$7.50, dinner $10.95-$16.95. Sun brunch $4-$8.50. Child's meals. Specialties: grilled swordfish, sauteed chicken breast. Valet parking. Outdoor dining. Popular local night club; turn-of-the-century atmosphere. Cr cds: A, MC, V.

D

✔ ★ **HAMBURGER HEAVEN.** 314 S County Rd. 407/655-5277. Hrs: 7:30 am-8 pm; May-Oct to 4 pm. Closed Sun; some major hols. Res accepted. Semi-a la carte: bkfst $1.75-$4.75, lunch $3.50-$10, dinner $8.75-$10.95. Specializes in hamburgers, roast turkey dinner, lemon coconut cake. Own soups. No cr cds accepted.

★ ★ **JO'S.** 200 Chilian Ave. 407/659-6776. Hrs: 6:30-9:30 pm. Closed Aug; also Sun Mother's Day-Thanksgiving. Res accepted. French, continental menu. Wine, beer. A la carte entrees: dinner $15-$29. Complete meals: dinner (Mother's Day-Thanksgiving) $19.95. Specialties: crisp roast duckling, osso buco, broiled lump crabcakes. Parking. European bistro atmosphere. Cr cds: MC, V.

★ ★ ★ **RENATO'S.** 87 Via Mizner. 407/655-9752. Hrs: 11:30 am-3 pm, 6-10:30 pm; Sun from 6 pm. Res accepted. French, Italian menu. Bar. A la carte entrees: lunch $11.50-$18, dinner $22-$29. Child's meals. Specialties: scampi alla griglia, penne alla Caprese, snapper alla Livornese. Pianist exc Mon. Valet parking (dinner). Outdoor dining. Elegant country French atmosphere. Cr cds: A, C, D, DS, MC, V.

D

★ ★ ★ **THE RESTAURANT.** (See The Ritz-Carlton, Palm Beach Hotel) 407/533-6000. Hrs: 6 am-11 pm; Sun brunch 11 am-3:30 pm. Res required. Continental menu. Bar. Extensive wine list. A la carte entrees: lunch $8.50-$18, dinner $18-$28. Sun brunch $34. Fri seafood buffet (6-11 pm) $32. Child's meals. Pianist. Valet parking. Elegant decor featuring hand-strung crystal chandeliers; museum-quality works of art. Overlooks Atlantic Ocean. Jacket (dinner). Cr cds: A, C, D, DS, ER, MC, V, JCB.

★ ★ ★ **THE RESTAURANT.** *(See The Ocean Grand Hotel) 407/582-2800.* Hrs: 6–11 pm. Closed Mon & Tues June–Sept. Res required. Southeast regional menu. Bar. Extensive wine list. A la carte entrees: dinner $24–$39. Specialties: West Indies seasoned Maverick Ranch strip steak with wild mushroom yam cake, yellowtale snapper with lemon thyme melon relish, grilled pompano with rock shrimp, cashew & coconut crusted soft-shell crabs. Pianist. Valet parking. Dining area overlooks pool and ocean. Garden on the premises provides fresh fruits & herbs. Trend-setting cuisine is based on history and heritage of the Southeast. Jacket. Cr cds: A, C, D, DS, MC, V, JCB.

✔ ★ ★ **TESTA'S.** *221 Royal Poinciana Way. 407/832-0992.* Hrs: 7 am–midnight; early-bird dinner 4:30–6:30 pm; Sun brunch 11 am–2:30 pm. Closed Thanksgiving. Res accepted. Italian, Amer menu. Bar from 9 am. Semi-a la carte: bkfst $2.75–$6, lunch $4.50–$10, dinner $8.75–$17.95. Sun brunch $11.95. Child's meals. Specializes in steak, seafood, strawberry pie. Valet parking. Outdoor dining. Three individually decorated dining areas. Family-owned. Cr cds: A, C, D, DS, MC, V.

D

Panama City (F-2)

Pop: 34,378 **Elev:** 29 ft **Area code:** 904

On the cooler panhandle of the state, this is a popular destination for vacationers in the summer and for retirees all year. Panama City is known for its stretches of beautiful nearby beach and is considered one of the best fishing centers in the state. To the west, along the Gulf, are 23 miles of white sand for swimming, fishing and relaxing. With a deepwater harbor, the city also ranks as an important coastal port. Boating is possible in the Gulf, the Intracoastal Waterway and several protected bays, and there are a number of public boat ramps and marinas. Carefully nurtured forests are harvested to supply the city's paper and pulp mill.

What to See and Do

1. **Junior Museum of Bay County.** 1731 Jenks Ave. Exhibits include reconstructed log cabin with period furnishings, grist and cane mill; changing art & science exhibits. Nature trail through swamp on elevated walkway. (Tues–Sat; closed hols) Phone 769-6128. **Free.**

2. **Deer Point Dam.** 8 mi NE on FL 77A. Impounds 5,000-acre stocked lake. Fishing for both salt and freshwater fish from same spot; public boat ramp.

3. **Miracle Strip Amusement Park.** 5 mi W on US 98A. Rides; concessions; arcade. (Memorial Day–Labor Day, daily; mid-Mar–mid-May, Fri–Sat) Phone 234-5810 or 800/538-7395. ¢¢¢¢¢ Opposite is

   Shipwreck Island. On W US 98A. Water sports park with a tropical island theme. Unique giant shipwreck. Wave pool, tube ride; Scull Island. (June–Labor Day, daily; Apr, May & early Sept, Sat) Phone 234-0368. ¢¢¢¢¢

(For further information contact the Convention & Visitors Bureau, PO Box 9473, Panama City Beach 32417; 233-6503 or 800/722-3224.)

Annual Events

Spring Festival of the Arts. McKenzie Park. Entertainment, food, art activities for children, crafts displays. 2 days early May.

Open Spearfishing Tournament. Tyndall Air Force Base. Aug.

Bay County Fair. Fairgrounds. Early Oct.

Seasonal Event

Greyhound racing. Ebro Greyhound Track. 15 mi N on FL 79 in Ebro. Parimutuels. Trackside dining. Nightly exc Sun & some Tues; matinee Sat & some Wed. Children only with parent. Phone 234-3943. Early Mar–early Sept.

(See Panama City Beach)

Motels

★ ★ **COMFORT INN.** *1013 E 23rd St (32405). 904/769-6969.* 105 rms, 2 story. May–Sept: S $51–$61; D $55–$66; each addl $6; under 18 free; higher rates: hols, special events; lower rates rest of yr. Crib free. TV; cable. Heated pool. Complimentary continental bkfst, coffee. Ck-out noon. Coin lndry. Meeting rm. Cr cds: A, C, D, DS, ER, MC, V, JCB.

D ⛱ ⊘ ⊙ SC

✔ ★ **ECONO LODGE.** *4411 W US 98 (32401). 904/785-2700.* 51 rms, 2 story, 6 kit. units. Mar–Sept: S $32–$58; D $37–$65; each addl $6; kit. units $37–$65; family, wkly rates; higher rates major hols; lower rates rest of yr. Crib $6. Pet accepted, some restrictions. TV; cable. Pool. Complimentary coffee in lobby. Restaurant adj open 24 hrs. Ck-out 11 am. Cr cds: A, C, D, DS, ER, MC, V, JCB.

🐾 ⛱ ⊘ ⊙ SC

★ ★ **RAMADA INN.** *3001 W 10th St (32401). 904/785-0561; FAX 904/785-3280.* 150 rms, 2–3 story. May–Sept: S $55; D $60; each addl $7; under 18 free; higher rates hols (3-day min); lower rates rest of yr. Pet accepted. TV; cable. Pool. Playground. Restaurant 6 am–10 pm. Rm serv. Bar; entertainment, dancing Tues–Sat. Ck-out noon. Meeting rms. Bellhops. Free airport transportation. Exercise equipt; weight machines, bicycle. Some private patios, balconies. On bay; marina adj. Cr cds: A, C, D, DS, MC, V, JCB.

🐾 ⛱ 🏃 ⊘ ⊙ SC

Motor Hotel

★ ★ **HOLIDAY INN MALL.** *2001 N Cove Blvd (32405). 904/769-0000; FAX 904/763-3828.* 173 rms, 6 story. S, D $64–$73; each addl $7; under 18 free. Crib free. TV; cable. Indoor pool; hot tub. Restaurant 6 am–2 pm, 5:30–10 pm. Rm serv. Bar 3:30 pm–1 am. Ck-out noon. Meeting rms. Bellhops. Free airport transportation. Exercise equipt; weights, bicycles, whirlpool, steam rm, sauna. Bathrm phones. Cr cds: A, C, D, DS, MC, V, JCB.

D ⛱ 🏃 ⊘ ⊙ SC

Restaurants

✔ ★ **BLUE DOLPHIN.** *3101 W 23rd St. 904/763-5025.* Hrs: 6 am–9 pm. Closed Sun; major hols. Res accepted. Semi-a la carte: bkfst $1.29–$3.90, lunch $4.25–$5.05, dinner $5.95–$14.95. Child's meals. Specializes in fresh gulf seafood, steak, chicken. Parking. Antique lamps. Family-owned. Cr cds: DS, MC, V.

✔ ★ **HOUSE OF CHAN.** *4425 US 98W. 904/769-9404.* Hrs: 4–11 pm; Fri to midnight; Sat 4 pm–midnight. Closed Thanksgiving. Res accepted. Chinese, Amer menu. Bar. Semi-a la carte: dinner $4.75–$12.95. Specialties: orange beef, General Tso's chicken. Parking. Mongolian barbecue dining downstairs. Cr cds: A, MC, V.

★ **JP'S.** *4701 US 98W. 904/769-3711.* Hrs: 11 am–11 pm. Closed Sun; major hols. Res accepted. Italian, Amer menu. Bar. Semi-a la carte: lunch $2.95–$6.95, dinner $5.95–$15.95. Child's meals. Specializes in sautéed seafood, hand-cut steak. Classical guitarist Wed, Fri & Sat evenings. Parking. Enclosed patio dining. South Seas atmosphere. Cr cds: A, C, D, DS, MC, V.

Panama City Beach (F-2)

Pop: 4,051 **Area code:** 904 **Zip:** 32407

What to See and Do

1. **Gulf World.** On US 98A, 3 mi E of jct FL 79. Sea lion and dolphin shows; dolphin & stingray petting pools; performing parrot show; shark/sea turtle channel; penguins; scuba demonstration. Also tropical gardens. (Daily) Phone 234-5271. ¢¢¢¢

2. **St Andrews State Recreation Area.** 3 mi E, off US 98 at end of FL 3031. A 1,063-acre point of land between Gulf of Mexico and St Andrews Bay with dunes, white sand beaches. Swimming, skin and scuba diving; fishing in surf and from pier & jetties; boating (ramp, dock). Nature trails, guided tours. Picnicking, concession. Camping (dump station). Interpretive center. Standard hrs, fees. Phone 233-5144.

3. **Fishing. County Pier,** 5 mi W on US 98A. **Panama City Beach City Pier,** 8 mi W on US 98A, a 1600-foot pier (fee). Party and charter boats (inquire locally). Artificial reefs in Gulf. **Dead Lakes State Recreation Area,** 30 mi E on FL 22, then N on FL 71, has excellent fishing for bass, bream and perch; boating; camping. **St Andrews State Recreation Area** (see #2) has a 450-foot pier. Also fishing from several other piers and bridges.

4. **Shell Island Trips.** Capt Anderson's Marina, Thomas Dr at Grand Lagoon. Three-hour sightseeing trip; also dinner cruises (June–Labor Day) & fishing and trolling boats. Shell Island trip (Apr–Oct, two trips daily; Feb & Mar, one trip daily; no trips Nov–Jan). Phone 234-3435. ¢¢¢¢¢

(For further information contact the Convention & Visitors Bureau, PO Box 9473; 233-6503 or 800/722-3224.)

Annual Events

Bay Point Billfish Tournament. July.

Treasure Ship King Mackerel Tournament. Treasure Island Marina. 3rd wkend Sept.

Indian Summer Seafood Festival. Mid-Oct.

Deep Sea Fishing Rodeo. Oct.

(See Panama City)

Motels

★**BEST WESTERN DEL CORONADO.** 11815 W US 98. 904/234-1600. 106 rms, 3 story. May–Labor Day: S $62–$95; D $68–$105; each addl $10; suites $95–$125; under 12 free; lower rates Mar–Apr. Closed rest of yr. Crib free. Pet accepted, some restrictions. TV; cable. Pool. Restaurant adj 7 am–11 pm. Ck-out 11 am. Cr cds: A, C, D, DS, MC, V.

★**BIKINI BEACH.** 11001 Front Beach Rd. 904/234-3392; res: 800/451-5307. 78 rms, 2–5 story. 48 kit. units. Mar–mid-Apr & mid-May–mid-Sept: S $59.50–$79.50; D $69.50–$89.50; suites $89.50–$139.50; kits. $69.50–$109.50; wkly, monthly rates; higher rates: hols, special events; lower rastes rest of yr. Crib free. TV; cable. Pool; poolside serv. Complimentary coffee in lobby. Restaurant adj 10–4 am. Bar 9 am–midnight. Ck-out 11 am. Coin lndry. Meeting rm. Sundries. Game rm. Lawn games. Balconies. Picnic tables, grills. On beach. Cr cds: A, C, D, DS, MC, V.

✔ ★**FIESTA.** 13623 Front Beach Rd. 904/235-1000. 186 rms, 4 story, 131 kits. Mid-May–Labor Day (4-day min hols): S, D $59.95–$73.95; kit. units (up to 4) $84.95–$94.95; higher rates hols; lower rates rest of yr. Crib $10. TV; cable. Pool. Restaurant nearby. Ck-out 10 am. Many private patios, balconies. Picnic tables. On Gulf. Cr cds: A, MC, V.

★ ★**INN AT ST THOMAS SQUARE.** 8730 Thomas Dr. 904/234-0349; res: 800/874-8600. 70 kit. suites, 3 story. Memorial Day–Labor Day: 1-bedrm suites $99–$102; 2-bedrm suites $130; 3-bedrm suites $159; lower rates rest of yr. Crib free. TV; cable. Pool; whirlpool, sauna. Complimentary continental bkfst. Restaurant nearby. Ck-out 11 am. Lighted tennis. Refrigerators. Many private patios, balconies. On lagoon; dockage. Cr cds: A, C, D, DS, MC, V.

✔ ★**SHALIMAR PLAZA.** 17545 Front Beach Rd. 904/234-2133; res: 800/232-2435. 74 units, 3 story, 65 kits. No elvtr. 1-rm kit. units $39–$79; 2-rm kit. units $49–$89; each addl $5. Crib $5. TV; cable. Heated pool. Restaurant adj 6 am–10 pm. Ck-out 10 am. Tennis. Many private patios, balconies. Picnic tables. On Gulf. Cr cds: A, DS, MC, V.

Motor Hotels

★**DAYS INN.** 12818 Front Beach Rd. 904/233-3333; FAX 904/233-9568. 188 rms, 7 story, 82 kit. units. Mar–Sept: S, D $88–$118; each addl (after 4th person) $10; kits. $98–$128; under 12 free; higher rates hols and special events; lower rates rest of yr. Crib free. Pet accepted; some restrictions. TV; cable. Pool; whirlpool, sauna, poolside serv, lifeguard. Restaurant 6 am–10 pm in season. Bar. Ck-out 11 am. Sundries. Gift shop. Lighted tennis privileges. 18-hole golf privileges, putting green, driving range. Lawn games. Balconies. On beach. Cr cds: A, C, D, DS, MC, V.

★ ★**EDGEWATER BEACH.** 11212 W Front Beach Rd. 904/235-4044; FAX 904/233-7599. 530 kit. units, 2-12 story; 163 kit. villas, 1–2 story. Kit. units, villas $95–$350. Crib $5. TV; cable. Pool. Restaurant 7 am–10 pm. Bar. Ck-out 10 am. Lndry facilities. Convention facilities. Sundries. Lighted tennis, pro. 9-hole golf, pro; greens fee $49, putting green. Entertainment. Lawn games. Private patios, balconies. Picnic tables. Private beach. Cr cds: A, C, D, DS, MC, V.

Hotel

★ ★**HOLIDAY INN BEACH.** 11127 Front Beach Rd. 904/234-1111; FAX 904/235-1907. 342 rms, 15 story. Mar–Sept: S, D $98–$168; each addl $10; suites $299–$420; under 19 free; higher rates hols; lower rates rest of yr. Crib free. TV; cable. Pool; poolside serv. Complimentary coffee in rms. Restaurant 7 am–noon, 4–10 pm. Bar 10 am–midnight. Ck-out 11 am. Coin lndry. Meeting rms. Gift shop. Lighted tennis. 18-hole golf privileges, putting green, driving range. Exercise equipt; weights, treadmill, whirlpool, sauna. Game rm. Lawn games. Refrigerators. Wet bar in suites. Some balconies. Picnic tables. On beach. Cr cds: A, C, D, DS, MC, V, JCB.

Resort

★ ★**MARRIOTT'S BAY POINT.** 4200 Marriott Dr (34208). 904/234-3307; FAX 904/233-1308. 355 rms, 14 kits (1- & 2- bedrm). Mar–Oct: S, D $145–$215; each addl $20; suites, kit. units $215–$450; under 18 free; lower rates rest of yr. Crib free. TV; cable. 6 pools, 1 indoor; wading pool, poolside serv, lifeguard in season. Playground. Supervised child's activities (Mar–Oct). Dining rm 6:30 am–10 pm. Rm serv to 11:30 pm. Box lunches. Snack bar. Picnics. Bars 11–1 am. Ck-out 11 am, ck-in 4 pm. Grocery. Coin lndry. Convention facilities. Valet serv. Airport transportation. Lighted tennis, pro. 36-hole golf, pro, greens fee, putting green, driving range. Marina. Waterskiing. Scuba diving. Sailboats, windsurfers. Deep sea fishing. Bicycle rentals. Lawn games. Entertainment, dancing. Game rm. Exercise equipt; weights, bicycles, whirlpool, sauna, steam rm. Refrigerators. Private patios, balconies. Extensive grounds. Cr cds: A, C, D, DS, MC, V.

Restaurants

★ ★ **BOAR'S HEAD.** *17290 Front Beach Rd (US 98A). 904/234-6628.* Hrs: 4:30–10 pm; off-season 5–9 pm. Closed Thanksgiving; Mon off-season. Bar. Semi-a la carte: dinner $11.95–$19.95. Child's meals. Specializes in prime rib, baby back pork ribs, seafood. Own desserts. Parking. Old English tavern decor; fireplaces, stuffed boar's head at entrance. Cr cds: A, C, D, DS, MC, V.

✔ ★ **CAJUN INN.** *477 Beckrich Rd, in the Shoppes at Edgewater. 904/235-9987.* Hrs: 11 am–10 pm. Closed Thanksgiving, Dec 24, 25. Cajun, Creole menu. Wine, beer. Semi-a la carte: lunch $3.95–$5.25, dinner $7.95–$13.95. Child's meals. Specialties: blackened fish, red beans & rice, crawfish etoufée. Parking. Outdoor dining. Hand-crafted wooden booths. Cr cds: MC, V.

★ ★ **CAPT ANDERSON'S.** *5551 N Lagoon Dr, at Thomas Dr on Grand Lagoon. 904/234-2225.* Hrs: 4–10 pm. Closed Nov–Jan; also Sun Sept–May. Bars. Semi-a la carte: dinner $9.95–$28.95. Child's meals. Specialties: charcoal-broiled fish, grilled shrimp, Greek salads. Parking. Nautical decor; overlooks waterfront. Family-owned. Cr cds: A, C, D, DS, MC, V.

D

★ ★ **HAMILTON'S.** *5711 N Lagoon Dr. 904/234-1255.* Hrs: 5–10 pm. Continental menu. Bar. Semi-a la carte: dinner $9.95–$18. Child's meals. Specializes in seafood, pasta, mesquite-grilled dishes. Entertainment Fri & Sat. Parking. Outdoor dining. Victorian decor. Overlooks Grand Lagoon. Cr cds: A, DS, MC, V.

D

★ ★ **HOUSE OF BEEF & SEAFOOD.** *8028 Thomas Dr. 904/234-6913.* Hrs: 4:30–10 pm. Closed Dec 24. Serv bar. Semi-a la carte: dinner $6.95–$18.95. Child's meals. Specializes in beef, seafood. Parking. Circular, 3-level dining rm; formal decor. Cr cds: A, C, D, DS, MC, V.

✔ ★ **SWEET BASIL'S.** *11208 W US 98, in the Shoppes at Edgewater. 904/234-2855.* Hrs: 11 am–11 pm; off-season to 9 pm. Closed Dec 25. Italian menu. Bar. Semi-a la carte: lunch $3.95–$5.95, dinner $6.95–$13.95. Child's meals. Specializes in pasta, pizza. Parking. Family dining. Cr cds: A, DS, MC, V.

★ ★ **TREASURE SHIP.** *3605 S Thomas Dr, on Grand Lagoon. 904/234-8881.* Hrs: 4:30–10 pm; early-bird dinner 4:30–6 pm; Sun brunch 10 am–2 pm. Closed Oct–mid-Feb. Bar to 11 pm. Semi-a la carte: dinner $7.95–$22.95. Sun brunch $8.95. Child's meals. Specializes in steak, seafood. Entertainment in summer. Parking. Gift shop. Dining in replica of 16th-century Spanish galleon with views of gulf, marina. Cr cds: A, C, D, DS, MC, V.

Unrated Dining Spot

ALL AMERICAN DINER. *10590 W US 98. 904/235-2443.* Hrs: Open 24 hrs. Semi-a la carte: bkfst $2–$4.95, lunch $3.50, dinner $4.95–$12.95. Child's meals. Specializes in hamburgers, omelets. Salad bar. Parking. 1950s-style diner. No cr cds accepted.

Pensacola (F-1)

Settled: 1723 **Pop:** 58,165 **Elev:** 11 ft **Area code:** 904

Pensacola is the Old South blended with a bit of modern Florida and a generous dash of Colonial Spain. With its balconies and jutting balustrades, the city clings to the past—a rich brew of 400 years of history under five flags. Pensacola Bay, the largest, natural, landlocked deepwater harbor in Florida, has been the key to the city's history and development. The Spanish established a settlement here in 1559, which lasted only two years. However, in 1698 they reestablished the site and built a fort. After three battles in 1719, the French took over, but Spain returned in 1723. The British flew their flag in 1763, until Spain returned again in 1781. Andrew Jackson led invasions of this Spanish city in 1814 and 1818, and in 1821 returned to accept Florida as a US territory. During the Civil War, it was captured by Union troops and served as a base for the Union blockade of the Confederate Gulf Coast.

After an extensive study, in 1914 the Navy chose Pensacola as a site for its Naval Air Station—because there were more clear days for flying than at any other available place. Since then, the station has been a major factor in the city's personality and its economy. Today, Pensacola also is host to large chemical and nylon plants, pulp and paper mills, wallboard and plywood factories.

Pensacola is the gateway to "the miracle strip," 100 miles of beach-fringed peninsulas and islands stretching to Panama City, and heavily populated by sun worshipers and sports fishermen. Pensacola Beach, on Santa Rosa Island across two bridges from Pensacola, is primarily a resort community. Beaches on both Santa Rosa Sound (Intracoastal Waterway) and the Gulf of Mexico circle the island.

What to See and Do

1. **Naval Air Station Pensacola.** Home of naval aviation and headquarters for the Naval Education and Training Command. Established first as the Navy Yard in 1826, the easy access to the sea made it a prime site for the construction of wooden ships. Confederate troops retreating from the Navy Yard in 1862 reduced most of the facilities to rubble. Rebuilding began but was destroyed by a great hurricane in 1906; construction was brought to a standstill once again two years later by a yellow fever epidemic. Re-opened in 1914 as the first Naval Aeronautic Station, steady growth has produced such additions to the station as the Naval Aviation Depot and many other tenant commands. **Sherman Field** is home of the world-famous precision flying Blue Angels, the Navy's flight demonstration squadron. Phone 452-2311 or -2312. **Free.** Of interest here are

National Museum of Naval Aviation. One of the largest of its kind, this museum features more than 100 historically significant aircraft on display, including the A-1 "Triad," the Navy's first biplane, the NC-4 Flying Boat, the first plane to cross the Atlantic, a vintage 1930s Marine Corp fighter, four A-4 Skyhawks (Blue Angels) suspended in a diamond formation and full-size modern-day jets. Museum traces history of naval aviation from dawn of flight to space exploration; naval aviation and space memorabilia; hands-on childrens exhibits; aviation art & photography. Also here is the Naval Aviation Hall of Honor. Gift shop, book store. (Daily; closed Jan 1, Thanksgiving, Dec 25) Phone 453-2389 or 800/327-5002. **Free.**

USS *Forrestal.* The first "super carrier," manned by a crew of 2,000 men and women, whose current mission is to carrier-qualify student, reserve and fleet naval aviators. Flight training is conducted in Key West, Corpus Christi and Pensacola waters. Tours when in port (Sat, Sun and hols). Phone 432-8802. **Free.**

Fort Barrancas (1839–1844). On the site of 18th-century Spanish fortifications, the historic fort and its attached Water Battery, a 19th-century American fort, have been authentically restored and preserved from old drawings, photos, prints and documents from the National Archives. Now part of Gulf Islands National Seashore (see #6), the area comprises 65 acres in the middle of the Naval Air Station; approx 40 acres of pine and oak forest; visitor center. Tours avail. Phone 455-5167. **Free.**

Old Pensacola Lighthouse (1825). This 176-foot structure is fully automated and remote-controlled from Santa Rosa Island. Owned by the Coast Guard; not open to public.

2. **Historic Pensacola Village.** Seville Square, E Government & S Alcaniz Sts. Historic park contains village buildings (daily exc Sun; closed Jan 1, Thanksgiving, Dec 25). All buildings exc Pensacola Historical Museum are included in admission price. Phone 444-8905. Admission ¢¢¢   Buildings include

 Pensacola Historical Museum (1832). 405 S Adams St, at Zaragoza St. Oldest Protestant church (Old Christ Church) still standing on its original site in Florida; used by Union soldiers as a barracks and hospital. Exhibits cover history of Pensacola from prehistoric times. Extensive photo collection. (Daily exc Sun; closed hols) Phone 433-1559. ¢

 T.T. Wentworth Jr, Florida State Museum. Jefferson and Zaragoza Sts. Exhibits on west Florida history, art, architecture and archaeology; Discovery Gallery for children. Guided tours avail.

 Museum of Industry—Museum of Commerce. 200 E Zaragoza St. Converted warehouses contain exhibits depicting Gulf Coast history.

 Charles LaValle House (1805). 205 E Church St. One of the oldest houses in Pensacola; apron roof and plastered interior are typical of French Creole architecture.

 Dorr House (1871). 311 S Adams St, at Church St. Post-Civil War classical-revival house; restored with antiques of mid-Victorian era.

 Quina House. 204 S Alcaniz St. Pre-Civil War house (1825–1860) with period furnishings.

3. **Pensacola Museum of Art.** 407 S Jefferson St. Housed in the old city jail, the museum has changing art exhibits; library, lectures. (Tues–Sat; closed hols) Phone 432-6247.   **Free.**

4. **The Zoo.** 15 mi E on US 98, at 5701 Gulf Breeze Pkwy in Gulf Breeze. A 50-acre zoo and botanical garden with more than 600 animals including one of the largest lowland gorillas in captivity. Giraffe feeding; petting zoo. Train ride. (Daily; closed Thanksgiving, Dec 25) Sr citizen rate. Phone 932-2229. ¢¢¢

5. **St Michael's Cemetery.** Garden & Alcaniz Sts. In use since 1780s; many graves of Spanish settlers.

6. **Gulf Islands National Seashore.** S on US 98 and FL 399 to Pensacola Beach, then W on Ft Pickens Rd to Ft Pickens Area or E on FL 399 to Santa Rosa Area. The 1,742 acres include old Ft Pickens (1834), one of largest masonry forts in US, where Geronimo was imprisoned; concrete batteries; tours (daily). Swimming, scuba diving; fishing. Picnicking. Camping (fee). Bookstore, museum with historical & maritime exhibits. No pets on beach or in historic fortifications. Santa Rosa area includes beach with pavilion; swimming, picnicking. Golden Eagle, Golden Age & Golden Access Passport (see INTRODUCTION). Phone 934-2600. Per car (Ft Pickens area) ¢¢

 Other areas of the national seashore include Fort Barrancas and other historic fortifications at Naval Air Station (see #1); nearly 1,400 acres of forests with picnicking and nature trails, visitors center; at Naval Live Oaks off US 98, E of Gulf Breeze; beach recreation at Perdido Key, SW on FL 292; and picnic and beach areas at Okaloosa area, E of Fort Walton Beach. Contact Superintendent, Gulf Islands National Seashore, 1801 Gulf Breeze Pkwy, Gulf Breeze 32561; 934-2600.

7. **Scenic drive.** North via Scenic Hwy (US 90) through Gull Point and east around Escambia Bay; provides bluffs and beach views.

8. **Fishing.** Pensacola Beach Pier, Pensacola Beach (fee). Pensacola Bay Pier, Wayside Park (fee). Charter boats for big game fishing in Gulf at Pensacola Beach, Bayou Chico and marinas on Gulf Beach Hwy (FL 292).

9. **Skin diving and scuba diving.** Boats can take divers to the wreck of battleship *Massachusetts,* Russian freighter *San Pablo,* and other spots. Contact the Convention & Visitor Bureau.

10. **Greyhound racing. Pensacola Greyhound Track.** 951 Dog Track Rd, off US 98. (Tues–Sat evenings) Phone 455-8595 or 800/345-3997. General admission ¢

 (For further information and brochures on points of interest contact the Convention & Visitors Bureau, 1401 E Gregory St, 32501; 434-1234 or 800/874-1234 outside FL, 800/343-4321 in FL.)

Annual Events

 Snow Fest '94. Man-made snow is shipped in for snow rides, snowman building contests and other events. Late Jan.

 Mardi Gras. Five days of street dances, parades and musical events. 5 days prior to Ash Wed.

 Fiesta of the Five Flags. Pageant, parades, waterskiing show, races, sports events. June.

 Pensacola Interstate Fair. Mid-Oct.

 Great Gulfcoast Arts Festival. Music, drama; art shows, children's programs. Early Nov.

 Blue Angels Air Show. US Navy's world-renowned precision flight demonstration team performs; also parachuting and static displays of military and civilian aircraft. Nov.

Seasonal Event

 Stock car racing. Five Flags Speedway, Pine Forest Rd. Mid-Mar–early Dec.

 (See Fort Walton Beach; also see Mobile, AL)

Motels

 ✔ ★ ★**BEST WESTERN VILLAGE INN.** *8240 N Davis Hwy (32514).* 904/479-1099. 106 rms, 3 story, 34 kit. suites. S, D $41–$66. TV; cable, in-rm movies avail. Pool. Complimentary continental bkfst. Restaurant nearby. Ck-out noon. Meeting rms. Refrigerators. Balconies. Courtyards with walkways. Near West Florida Medical Center. Cr cds: A, C, D, DS, ER, MC, V.

 ★**COMFORT INN NAS-CORRY.** *3 New Warrington Rd (32506).* 904/455-3233; FAX 904/453-3445. 102 rms, 3 story. S $45.95; D $50.95; each addl $6; under 18 free; wkly rates. Crib free. TV; cable. Pool. Complimentary continental bkfst. Restaurant nearby. Ck-out 11 am. Coin lndry. Meeting rms. Refrigerators. Near Pensacola Naval Air Station. Cr cds: A, C, D, DS, ER, MC, V.

 ★**COMFORT INN-NAVARRE.** *(8680 Navarre Pkwy, Navarre 32566)* E on US 98. 904/939-1761; FAX 904/939-2084. 63 rms, 2 story, 6 suites. June–early Sept: S, D $69–$83; each addl $8; suites $78–$93; under 18 free; golf plans; higher rates major summer hols; lower rates rest of yr. Crib avail. TV; cable. Pool. Complimentary continental bkfst, coffee. Restaurant adj 11 am–9 pm. Ck-out 11 am. Coin lndry. Refrigerator in suites. Picnic tables. Beach ½ mi. Cr cds: A, C, D, DS, ER, MC, V, JCB.

 ★ **HAMPTON INN.** *7330 Plantation Rd (32504),* at University Mall. 904/477-3333. 124 rms, 3 story. S $47–$61; D $51–$58; suites $85; under 18 free. Crib free. TV; cable. Pool privileges. Complimentary continental bkfst. Ck-out noon. Bellhops. Airport transportation. Cr cds: A, C, D, DS, ER, MC, V.

 ★ ★**HOLIDAY INN BAY BEACH.** *(51 Gulf Breeze Pkwy, Gulf Breeze 32561)* S on US 98. 904/932-2214; FAX 904/932-2214, ext 333. 167 rms, 2 story. May–Sept: S $70–$83; D $72–$98; each addl $8; under 18 free; lower rates rest of yr. Crib free. TV; cable. Pool; wading pool.

Restaurant 6 am–2 pm, 5–10 pm. Ck-out 11 am. Coin lndry. Meeting rms. Bellhops. Refrigerators avail. Private patios, balconies. On Pensacola Bay at Pensacola Bay Bridge; opp fishing pier. Cr cds: A, C, D, DS, MC, V.

✔ ★HOLIDAY INN EXPRESS. 6501 Pensacola Blvd (32505). 904/476-7200. 178 rms, 2 story. Mar–Sept: S $43–$45; D $46–$55; suites $125; under 18 free; golf plans; higher rates major hols; lower rates rest of yr. Crib free. Pet accepted, some restrictions. TV; cable. Pool. Complimentary continental bkfst, coffee. Restaurant nearby. Ck-out noon. Coin lndry. Meeting rms. Cr cds: A, C, D, DS, MC, V.

★ ★HOLIDAY INN-UNIVERSITY MALL. 7200 Plantation Rd (32504), at University Mall. 904/474-0100; FAX 904/474-0100, ext 364. 152 rms, 2 story. S $65–$73; D $67–$77; each addl $6; suites $125; studio rms $59; under 19 free. Crib free. TV; cable. Pool. Restaurant 6 am–2 pm, 5–11 pm. Bar from 4:30 pm; entertainment Thurs–Sat, dancing. Ck-out noon. Coin lndry. Meeting rms. Bellhops. Valet serv. Free airport transportation. Cr cds: A, C, D, DS, ER, MC, V, JCB.

★ ★LA QUINTA. 7750 N Davis Hwy (32514). 904/474-0411. 130 rms, 3 story. S $46–$58; D $55–$61; each addl $6; under 18 free. Crib free. TV; cable. Pool. Restaurant open 24 hrs. Ck-out noon. Fireplace in lobby. Near Pensacola Bay. Cr cds: A, C, D, DS, MC, V.

✔ ★QUALITY INN. 6911 Pensacola Blvd (32505). 904/479-3800. 126 rms, 2 story, 26 suites. S $41–$55; D $45–$59; each addl $5; suites $65–$75; under 18 free; golf plans. Crib free. TV; cable. Pool. Restaurant 6:30 am–10 pm. Rm serv. Ck-out noon. Valet serv. Refrigerator, minibar in suites. Cr cds: A, C, D, DS, MC, V.

★RED ROOF INN. 7340 Plantation Rd (32504), at University Mall. 904/476-7960; FAX 904/479-4706. 108 rms, 2 story. S $32.99–$43.99; D $33.99–$43.99; each addl $6; under 18 free. Crib free. TV; cable. Complimentary coffee in lobby. Restaurant nearby. Ck-out noon. Cr cds: A, C, D, DS, MC, V.

★ ★RESIDENCE INN BY MARRIOTT. 7230 Plantation Rd (32504). 904/479-1000; FAX 904/477-3399. 64 kit. suites, 2 story. S, D $75–$102; each addl $8; wkly, wkend rates. Crib free. TV; cable. Pool; whirlpool, sauna. Complimentary continental bkfst. Restaurant adj 11–1 am. Ck-out noon. Meeting rms. Sports court. Fireplaces, refrigerators. Picnic tables, grills. Cr cds: A, C, D, DS, MC, V, JCB.

✔ ★SEVILLE INN. 223 E Garden St (32501). 904/433-8331; FAX 904/432-6849. 128 rms, 2 story. Mid-May–mid-Sept: S, D $44–$69; each addl $5; suites from $79; under 18 free; lower rates rest of yr. Crib free. Pet accepted, some restrictions; $10 non-refundable. TV; cable. 2 pools. Restaurant 7–10 am in season. Bar. Ck-out 11 am. Coin lndry. Meeting rms. Valet serv. Sundries. Cr cds: A, C, D, DS, ER, MC, V.

Motor Hotel

✔ ★DAYS INN. 710 N Palafox St (32501). 904/438-4922. 156 rms, 3 story. S $37–$57; D $47–$52; each addl $5; suites $57–$67; studio rms $38–$45; under 12 free. Crib $5. TV; cable. Pool. Restaurant 6:30 am–1:30 pm; Sat, Sun from 7 am. Rm serv. Bar, closed Sun. Ck-out noon. Coin lndry. Meeting rms. Bellhops. Free airport transportation. Cr cds: A, C, D, DS, MC, V.

Hotels

★ ★HOLIDAY INN-PENSACOLA BEACH. (165 Ft Pickens Rd, Pensacola Beach 32561) S via US 98 & Pensacola Beach Rd, then E on FL 399. 904/932-5361; FAX 904/932-7121. 150 rms, 9 story. Apr–mid-Sept: S, D $90–$110; each addl $10; suites $160; under 18 free; lower rates rest of yr. Crib free. TV; cable. Pool. Supervised child's activities (Easter–Labor Day). Restaurant 6:30 am–10 pm. Rm serv. Bars; dancing. Ck-out 11 am. Coin lndry. Meeting rms. Bellhops. Sundries. Lighted tennis. Game rm. Some refrigerators. Private balconies. On Gulf. Cr cds: A, C, D, DS, MC, V, JCB.

★ ★PENSACOLA GRAND HOTEL (formerly Hilton). 200 E Gregory St (32501). 904/433-3336; FAX 904/432-7572. 212 rms, 15 story. S $80–$99; D $88–$110; each addl $10; suites $140–$408; studio rms $75–$90; family rates; honeymoon, wkend, golf, package plans. Crib free. Pet accepted, some restrictions; $50. TV; cable. Heated pool. Restaurant 7–10 pm. Bars 4 pm–2 am. Ck-out 1 pm. Meeting rms. Shopping arcade. Lobby is restored 1912 Louisville & Nashville Railroad Depot. Cr cds: A, C, D, DS, MC, V.

Inns

★ ★HOMESTEAD INN. 7830 Pine Forest Rd (32526). 904/944-8800; res: 800/937-1735. 6 rms, 2 story. S $59–$69; D $69–$79; each addl $10; family rates. TV. Complimentary full bkfst, coffee/tea. Dining rm 6 am–8 pm. Ck-out noon, ck-in 2 pm. Some fireplaces. Country decor. Cr cds: A, DS, MC, V.

★ ★ ★NEW WORLD. 600 S Palafox (32501). 904/432-4111; FAX 904/435-8939. 16 rms, 2 story. S $65–$75; D $75–$85; each addl $10; suites $90–$100; under 12 free. TV; cable. Continental bkfst. Dining rm 5:30–9:30 pm; closed Sun. Rm serv. Bar from 5 pm. Ck-out noon, ck-in after 2 pm. Meeting rms. Valet serv. Bathrm phones. Cr cds: A, C, D, DS, MC, V.

Restaurants

★THE ANGUS. 1101 Scenic Hwy (US 90E). 904/432-0539 or 432-0475. Hrs: 5–10 pm; Fri, Sat to 11 pm. Closed Sun (exc Sun hols); Thanksgiving, Dec 25. Res accepted. Bar. Semi-a la carte: dinner $7.95–$34.95. Child's meals. Specializes in seafood, prime rib, steak. Parking. Cr cds: A, MC, V.

✔ ★COFFEE CUP. 520 E Cervantes St (US 90E). 904/432-7060. Hrs: 6:30 am–2 pm; Sun 6 am–noon. Closed Dec 25–Jan 1. Semi-a la carte: bkfst $1.50–$3.50, lunch $4.50–$5. Child's meals. Specializes in sandwiches, seafood, bkfst items. Parking. Old-style diner; antique bar stools. No cr cds accepted.

✔ ★DARRYL'S. 7251 Plantation Rd, at University Mall. 904/476-1821. Hrs: 11 am–midnight; Fri, Sat to 1 am; Sun to 11 pm. Closed Dec 25. Res accepted. Bar. Semi-a la carte: lunch, dinner $5.50–$14.95. Child's meals. Specializes in steak, seafood, barbecued ribs. Parking. Turn-of-the-century decor. Cr cds: A, C, D, DS, MC, V.

★ ★ ★JAMIE'S. 424 E Zaragoza St. 904/434-2911. Hrs: 11:30 am–2:30 pm, 6–10 pm; Mon from 6 pm. Closed Sun; most major hols. Res accepted. French menu. Beer. Extensive wine list. Semi-a la carte: lunch $6.50–$8.25, dinner $17.50–$21.75. Specialties: escalope de veau, steak au poivre, fresh seafood. Entertainment exc Thurs. Parking. In restored Victorian house (1870). Cr cds: A, C, D, MC, V.

★McGUIRE'S IRISH PUB & BREWERY. 600 E Gregory St. 904/433-6789. Hrs: 11–2 am; Sun to 1 am. Closed Dec 25. Bar. Semi-a la carte: lunch $4.95–$6.95, dinner $5.95–$17.95. Child's meals. Specializes in steak, hamburgers, Irish stew. Own desserts. Parking. Irish pub atmosphere; Tiffany lamps, brass railings. Beer brewed on premises. Cr cds: A, C, D, DS, MC, V.

✔ ★ ★SKOPELOS SEAFOOD & STEAK. *670 Scenic Hwy (US 90E). 904/432-6565.* Hrs: 5–10:30 pm. Closed Sun & Mon; Dec 25. Res accepted. Bar. Semi-a la carte: dinner $10.50–$14.75. Child's meals. Specializes in seafood, char-broiled steak, homemade Greek baklava. Own pastries. Parking. Outdoor dining. Overlooks Pensacola Bay. Family-owned. Cr cds: A, MC, V.

 D

Unrated Dining Spot

MORRISON'S CAFETERIA. *Town & Country Mall, 3 mi SW on FL 29, N at Fairfield. 904/438-5691.* Hrs: 10:45 am–8 pm; Sun to 7 pm. Avg ck: lunch, dinner $4–$6. Child's meals. Specializes in prime round of beef, shrimp, fried fish almondine. Cr cds: MC, V.

Perry (A-2)

Pop: 7,151 **Elev:** 42 ft **Area code:** 904 **Zip:** 32347

What to See and Do

Forest Capital State Cultural Museum. 204 Forest Park Dr, 1 mi S via US 19, 98. Interprets the story of the forest industry, past, present and future. Exhibits on turpentine production, cutting of virgin forests, cypress swamps and hardwood hammocks; modern forest practices and newly developed techniques are explained; map of the state made of native wood with each of the 67 counties shaped from a different species of Florida tree; visitor center designed in circular shape of a tree; picnic area. (Thurs–Mon) (See ANNUAL EVENT) Phone 584-3227. ¢ Admission includes

Cracker Homestead. Interpretive site depicts typical early Florida homestead constructed of double-notched, squared logs and furnished in the 1860s period. Outbuildings include smokehouse, barn, corn crib, chicken pen, outhouse. Self-guided tours.

(For further information contact the Perry-Taylor County Chamber of Commerce, 428 N Jefferson St, Box 892; 584-5366.)

Annual Event

Florida Forest Festival. Forest Capital State Cultural Museum (see). Activities include parade, chainsaw championship competition, antique car show, arts & crafts, races, free fish fry and pageants. 4th wkend Oct.

Pompano Beach (E-5)

Settled: 1884 **Pop:** 72,411 **Elev:** 10 ft **Area code:** 305

The rapid growth of tourism in this Gold Coast resort has been matched with a comparable increase in year-round residents. Of the town's seven-mile-long ocean beach, more than three remain in the public domain; the rest is fronted with motels. Situated between the Intracoastal Waterway and the Atlantic Ocean, Pompano Beach offers the full range of water sports and fishing activities.

What to See and Do

1. **Butterfly World.** N on FL Tpke, Sample Rd exit, W to Tradewinds Park at 3600 W Sample Rd, in Coconut Creek. Walk among thousands of free-flying butterflies in three, giant, screened aviaries, the largest facility of its kind; botanical vine walk and gardens, breeding laboratory displays, collection of unusual insects. Con-

cessions, gift shop. (Daily; closed Thanksgiving, Dec 25) Sr citizen rates. Phone 977-4400. ¢¢¢

2. **Goodyear Blimp Visitor Center.** 1500 NE 5th Ave. Winter base for the airship *Stars and Stripes.* Visitors are not offered rides, but may view the blimp on the ground. Best time to view blimp in flight is Nov–May. (Wed–Sun) Phone 946-8300. **Free.**

3. **Fishing, boating.** Fishing at 887-foot municipal pier, Pompano Beach Blvd, 2 blks N of Atlantic Blvd; Fish City Marina, 2629 N Riverside Dr; Sands Harbor Marina, 125 N Riverside Dr. Deep-sea fishing and charter boat rentals arranged; public launching ramps located at Alsdorf Park, NE 14th St on W side of Intracoastal Waterway.

4. **Lowrance Artificial Reef.** 1½ mi offshore of Atlantic Blvd. The 435-foot ship *Lowrance* was sunk on March 31, 1984, to form one of the largest artificial reefs on the east coast. This reef, in 190 feet of water, is one of the most popular fishing and diving sites in south Florida.

5. **State Farmers Market.** Hammondville Rd. World's largest wholesale winter vegetable market; visitors may view process, but may not purchase produce. (Daily)

(For further information contact the Greater Pompano Beach Chamber of Commerce, 2200 E Atlantic Blvd, 33062; 941-2940.)

Annual Events

Seafood Festival. Late Apr.

Pompano Beach Fishing Rodeo. Final leg of the south Florida fishing triple crown. Mid-May.

Boat Parade. More than 100 decorated and lighted boats parade up Intracoastal Waterway. Mid–late Dec.

Seasonal Event

Horse racing. Pompano Park Racetrack, off Powerline Rd, W of I-95, Atlantic Blvd exit. Harness racing; 7,500-seat grandstand, dining room. Nightly exc Sun, days vary off-season. Phone 972-2000. Oct–Aug.

(See Boca Raton, Dania, Fort Lauderdale, Hollywood)

Motels

★ ★ ★HOLIDAY INN. *1350 S Ocean Blvd (33062). 305/941-7300; FAX 305/941-7300, ext 7793.* 133 units, 2–3 story, 89 kits. Mid-Dec–mid-Apr: S, D $110–$155; each addl $10; kit. units $120–$180; villa units $150–$180; under 19 free; lower rates rest of yr. Crib free. TV; cable. 2 pools, heated; poolside serv. Restaurant 7 am–10 pm. Rm serv. Bar. Ck-out 11 am. Coin lndry. Meeting rm. Bellhops. Valet serv. Sundries. Tennis. Putting green. Lawn games. Private patios, balconies. On ocean beach; some rms across street. Cr cds: A, C, D, DS, MC, V, JCB.

🐟 🏊 🛥 🚫 🔄 SC

✔ ★THREE SISTERS INN. *2300 NE 10th St (33062). 305/943-3500.* 61 rms, 2 story. Jan–mid-Apr: S, D $45–$70; each addl $5; under 12 free; lower rates rest of yr. Crib free. TV. Complimentary continental bkfst. Restaurant nearby. Ck-out noon. Bathrm phones; Roman tubs. Refrigerators avail. Cr cds: A, MC, V.

🔄

Motor Hotels

★ ★ ★BEST WESTERN BEACHCOMBER HOTEL & VILLAS. *1200 S Ocean Blvd (33062). 305/941-7830; FAX 305/942-7680.* 147 units, 1–8 story, 68 kit. studio rms, 7 kit. apts, 8 kit. villas (1–2 bedrm). Jan–mid-Apr: S, D $87–$172; studio rms $186–$196; apts, villas for 2–4, $172–$241; each addl $15–$25; lower rates rest of yr. TV; cable, in-rm movies. 2 pools, heated; poolside serv. Restaurant 7 am–10 pm. Rm serv. Bar; entertainment, dancing. Ck-out 11 am. Coin lndry. Meeting rm. Bellhops. Valet serv. Gift shop. Putting green. Lawn games. Many private patios, balconies. 300-ft beach, cabanas. Cr cds: A, C, D, DS, ER, MC, V.

✔ ★ ★ **POMPANO BEACH MOTOR LODGE.** *1112 N Ocean Blvd (33062).* 305/943-0630. 55 rms, 6 story, 34 kits. Feb–Mar: S, D $82–$87; each addl $8; kit. units $94–$97; lower rates rest of yr. Crib $5. TV; cable. Heated pool; poolside serv. Restaurant 8 am–2 pm, 5–9 pm. Bar. Ck-out 11 am. Golf privileges (May–Nov). Lawn games. Refrigerators avail. Private patios, balconies. Sun deck. On ocean, beach. Cr cds: A, C, D, MC, V.

★ ★ **QUALITY INN OCEANSIDE RESORT.** *1208 N Ocean Blvd (33062).* 305/782-5300; FAX 305/946-1853. 165 rms, 6–9 story, 32 kits. Dec–Apr: S, D $99; each addl $10; suites $250; kit. units $140; under 16 free; lower rates rest of yr. TV; cable. 2 heated pools; poolside serv. Restaurant 7 am–9 pm. Rm serv. Bar 5 pm–1 am; entertainment, dancing. Ck-out 11 am. Coin lndry. Meeting rms. Bellhops. Tennis privileges. Exercise rm; instructor, weights, treadmill, sauna. Balconies. On ocean, beach. Cr cds: A, C, D, DS, ER, MC, V, JCB.

★ ★ **SANDS HARBOR.** *125 N Riverside Dr (33062).* 305/942-9100; res: 800/227-3353; FAX 305/785-5657. 56 rms, 9 story, 28 kits. Jan–Apr: S, D $70–$130; each addl $10; suites $150–$275; kit. units $80–$130; lower rates rest of yr. Crib $5. TV; cable. Pool; poolside serv. Restaurant 4–9 pm. Bar 11 am–11 pm. Ck-out 11 am. Beauty shop. Boat rentals; scuba diving. Many refrigerators. Balconies. On Intracoastal Waterway. Cr cds: A, C, D, DS, MC, V.

★ ★ **SEA GARDEN BEACH & TENNIS RESORT.** *615 N Ocean Blvd (33062).* 305/943-6200; res: 800/327-8920; FAX 305/783-0047. 144 units, 2–4 story, 90 kit. units. Mid-Dec–mid-Apr: S, D $119; each addl $10; kit. units $159–$199; under 12 free; lower rates rest of yr. Crib free. TV; cable. 2 pools, 1 heated. Restaurant 7 am–10 pm. Bar 11–2 am; entertainment, dancing Wed–Sun. Ck-out noon. Meeting rms. Bellhops. Sundries. Tennis, 4 lighted. Exercise equipt; weights, bicycles. Lawn games. Private patios, balconies. On beach; sailboats. Some rms across street. Cr cds: A, C, D, DS, ER, MC, V.

Hotel

★ ★ **RAMADA.** *1301 S Ocean Blvd (33062).* 305/943-7001; FAX 305/943-7048. 140 suites, 10 story. Dec–Apr: S, D $95–$225; each addl $10; under 18 free; lower rates rest of yr. Crib free. TV. Heated pool; whirlpool, sauna. Restaurant 7 am–10 pm. Ck-out noon. Meeting rms. Refrigerators. Balconies. Across hwy from ocean; dockage. Cr cds: A, C, D, DS, ER, MC, V.

Resort

★ ★ ★ **PALM-AIRE SPA RESORT & COUNTRY CLUB.** *2601 Palm-Aire Dr N (33069).* 305/972-3300; res: 800/2-PALM AIR; FAX 305/968-2744. 191 rms, 2–4 story, 18 kits. Mid-Dec–Apr: S, D $185–$420; each addl $35; spa suites $290–$450; under 12 free (limit 2); lower rates rest of yr. Crib free. TV; cable. Five heated pools; poolside serv. Dining rm 7 am–10 pm; 2 other cafes on premises. Rm serv. Box lunches. Bar; entertainment, dancing. Ck-out noon, ck-in 3 pm. Convention facilities. Valet serv. Concierge. Barber, beauty shop. Valet parking. Airport transportation. Sports dir. Tennis, 31 clay courts, 6 all-weather lighted courts, pro. Five 18-hole golf courses, 2 driving ranges, putting greens. Waterskiing; sailboats. Bicycle rentals nearby. Soc dir. Movies. Racquetball and squash courts. Exercise rm; instructor, weights, bicycles, whirlpools, sauna, steam rm. Massage therapy. Spa with health lectures.

Private patios, balconies. On 1,500 acres. Harness racing opp. Cr cds: A, C, D, MC, V.

Restaurants

★ ★ ★ **CAFE ARUGULA.** *(3150 N Federal Hwy, Lighthouse Point) N on US 1.* 305/785-7732. Hrs: 5:30–10 pm; wkends to 10:30 pm. Closed some major hols. Res accepted. A la carte entrees: dinner $14.95–$29.95. Child's meals. Specialties: pecan-crusted yellowtail snapper, jumbo lump crab cakes, rack of lamb. Parking. Casual elegance with Southwestern flair. Cr cds: A, D, DS, MC, V.

★ ★ **CAFE MAXX.** *2601 E Atlantic Blvd.* 305/782-0606. Hrs: 5:30–10:30 pm; wkdays off-season from 6 pm. Closed July 4; Super Bowl Sunday. Res accepted. Semi-a la carte: dinner $15.95–$28.95. Specialties: caviar pie, grilled veal chop, Norwegian salmon. Own ice creams. Valet parking. Open cooking area; display cases. Cr cds: A, C, D, DS, MC, V.

★ ★ **CAP'S PLACE.** *(2765 NE 28th Ct, Lighthouse Point) N on Federal Hwy (US 1) to NE 24th St, then E and follow signs.* 305/941-0418. Hrs: 5:30–11 pm. Closed Dec 25. Res accepted. Bar. Complete meals: dinner $10.60–$24. Specialties: heart of palm salad, filet mignon, fresh local fish. Historic restaurant established 1928. Accessible by restaurant's launch or private boat only. Cr cds: A, MC, V.

✔ ★ **FRANK'S.** *3428 E Atlantic Blvd.* 305/785-1480. Hrs: 11 am–11 pm. Closed Thanksgiving, Dec 25. Res accepted. Italian menu. Bar. Semi-a la carte: lunch $2–$14, dinner $9.95–$14.95. Specializes in veal, seafood. Own pasta, cheesecake. Entertainment. Parking. Murals depicting scenes of Italy. Cr cds: A, MC, V.

Port Charlotte (D-3)

Pop: 41,535 **Elev:** 5 ft **Area code:** 813

A completely planned community, Port Charlotte has 38 miles of natural shoreline on the Charlotte Harbor, the Peace and Myakka rivers and more than 165 miles of man-made waterways.

(For information about this area contact the Charlotte County Chamber of Commerce, 2702 Tamiami Trail, 33952; 627-2222.)

Seasonal Event

Professional baseball. Charlotte County Stadium, 2300 El Jobean Rd. Texas Rangers spring training; exhibition games. Phone 624-2211. Early Mar–early Apr.

(See Arcadia, Punta Gorda)

Motels

★ ★ **DAYS INN.** *1941 Tamiami Trail (33948).* 813/627-8900; FAX 813/743-8503. 126 rms, 3 story. Jan–Mar: S $52–$80; D $70–$85; each addl $5; under 12 free; lower rates rest of yr. Crib free. TV; cable. Heated pool. Complimentary coffee in lobby. Restaurant adj 6–1 am. Ck-out 11 am. Coin lndry. Meeting rm. Refrigerators. Cr cds: A, C, D, DS, MC, V.

★ **ECONO LODGE.** *4100 Tamiami Trail (33952).* 813/743-2442; FAX 813/743-6376. 60 rms. Late Dec–mid-Apr: S, D $65; each addl $5; under 18 free; lower rates rest of yr. Crib free. TV; cable.

Complimentary coffee in lobby. Restaurant nearby. Ck-out noon. Meeting rm. Cr cds: A, C, D, DS, ER, MC, V, JCB.

Restaurant

✔ ★JOHNNY'S DINER & PUB. *1951 Tamiami Trail.* *813/255-0994.* Hrs: 6–1 am. Res accepted. Bar. Semi-a la carte: bkfst $1.99–$4.99, lunch $1.49–$13.99, dinner $3.99–$13.99. Specializes in fresh seafood, steak, ribs. Parking. Cr cds: A, D, DS, MC, V.

D

Punta Gorda (D-3)

Pop: 10,747 **Elev:** 61 ft **Area code:** 813

At the mouth of the Peace River on Charlotte Harbor, this is an increasingly popular resort city. Fishing, boating and all water sports are particularly good here. Cattle raising, commercial fishing, construction and land development are the important industries.

What to See and Do

1. **Museum of Charlotte County.** 260 W Retta Esplanade. Natural history displays, fossils; mounted exhibits including lions, leopards, bears. Lectures. (Tues–Sat; closed hols) Phone 639-3777. **Free.**

2. **Ponce de Leon Park.** End of W Marion Ave, 3½ mi W on Charlotte Harbor. Commemorates the landing of Spaniards (1513 & 1521) in the area. Boat ramp. Nature trail. Picnicking. Observation mound; shrine. (Daily) Phone 575-5050.   **Free.**

3. **Fishermen's Village.** 1200 W Retta Esplanade. A 40-store specialty shopping mall built on old city fish docks 1,000 feet into Charlotte Harbor. Pool; 98-slip marina, charter fishing boats & services. Tennis. Several restaurants; lodging. (Daily; closed Dec 25) Phone 639-8721.

4. **Babcock Wilderness Adventures.** 3 mi NE on US 17, then 18 mi E on FL 74 to FL 31, then 5 mi S. Offers swamp buggy, nature tours (1½ hr) on 90,000-acre ranch; tours go though cypress swamp and woodland areas, view alligators, bison, panther, hawks and other wildlife, commentary by naturalist. Picnic grounds. (Dec–May, daily; rest of yr, daily exc Mon, limited hrs; no tours Easter, Thanksgiving, Dec 25) Advance reservations required. Phone 338-6367 (recording) or 489-3911.   ¢¢¢¢

(For further information contact the Charlotte County Chamber of Commerce, 2702 Tamiami Trail, Port Charlotte 33952; 627-2222.)

(See Fort Myers, Port Charlotte)

Motels

★ ★BEST WESTERN INN. *26560 N Jones Loop Rd (33950).* *813/637-7200; FAX 813/639-0848.* 74 rms, 2 story, 12 kits. Feb–Apr: S $74–$95; D $80–$100; kit. units $95–$115; under 18 free; wkly rates off season; lower rates rest of yr. Crib free. Pet accepted. TV; cable. Pool; whirlpool. Playground. Complimentary coffee in lobby. Restaurant adj open 24 hrs. Ck-out noon. Coin lndry. Meeting rms. Cr cds: A, C, D, DS, ER, MC, V.

✔ ★SEA COVE. *25000 E Marion Ave (33950).* *813/639-0060.* 30 rms. Feb–Mar: S, D $44–$48; each addl $5; kit. units $300–$335/wk; lower rates rest of yr. Crib free. TV. Complimentary coffee in lobby. Restaurant nearby. Ck-out 11 am. Lawn games. Private patios. Picnic tables, grill. On river; dockage. Cr cds: A, DS, MC, V.

Motor Hotel

★ ★HOLIDAY INN. *300 Retta Esplanade (33950).* *813/639-1165; FAX 813/639-8116.* 183 rms, 2–5 story. Jan–Apr: S, D $82–$104; each addl $5; suites $129–$144; under 19 free; lower rates rest of yr. Crib free. Pet accepted, some restrictions; $12. TV; cable. Heated pool. Restaurant 6:30 am–10 pm. Rm serv. Bar; entertainment, dancing. Ck-out noon. Coin lndry. Meeting rms. Valet serv. Sundries. Gift shop. Private patios, balconies. On river; boat dock. Wilderness tours. Cr cds: A, C, D, DS, MC, V, JCB.

Resort

★ ★MARINA INN BURNT STORE MARINA. *3160 Matecumbe Key Rd (33955), 20 mi S of Punta Gorda via Burnt Store Rd (County 765).* *813/575-4488; res: 800/859-7529; FAX 813/575-7968.* 39 suites, 2–3 story. Jan–Apr: suites $100–$175; each addl $10; under 12 free; wkly, monthly rates; lower rates rest of yr. Crib avail. TV; cable. Heated pool. Restaurant 11 am–11 pm in season. Bar 11:30–1 am; entertainment exc Sun (in season). Ck-out 11 am. Convention facilities. Grocery. Gift shop. Tennis. 27-hole golf, greens fee $15, pro, putting green, driving range. Sailing school; sailing charters. Bicycle rentals. Private patios, balconies. Marina; dockage. Cr cds: A, MC, V.

Restaurant

★OLD POST OFFICE. *121 E Marian Ave.* *813/637-0200.* Hrs: 11 am–9 pm; Fri to 10 pm; Sat 10 am–10 pm; Sun 9 am–2 pm; Sun brunch to 2 pm. Res accepted. Bar. Semi-a la carte: lunch $3.25–$5.35, dinner $6.95–$18.95. Child's meals. Specializes in steak, seafood. Entertainment Fri, Sat. Located in former post office (1926). Cr cds: A, MC, V.

D

Redington Beach

(see St Petersburg Beach Area)

St Augustine (A-4)

Founded: 1565 **Pop:** 11,692 **Elev:** 6 ft **Area code:** 904

Spanish towers and steeples, red-capped roofs and low overhanging balconies are reminders of St Augustine's four centuries of history, which began on September 8, 1565, when Don Pedro Menendez de Aviles dropped anchor and rowed ashore. As a symbol of the cultural ties between the United States and Latin nations, and in an effort to establish an Hispanic counterpart to Williamsburg, Virginia, St Augustine (the oldest permanent settlement in the United States) has been restoring important historic areas to their former Spanish charm.

St Augustine was under a Spanish flag longer than it has been under the Stars and Stripes and has possibly retained more of the languid flavor of a Spanish colony than any other city in the US. Mellowed by time and the sun, the city's Spanish-Renaissance architecture continues to overshadow both 19th-century gingerbread and 20th-century neon and plate glass. Old walled gardens, narrow streets, the plaza and horse-drawn surreys all conspire to maintain St Augustine's Old World mood.

Ponce de Leon and his men are believed to have landed in the vicinity of what is now St Augustine in 1513 to fill their casks with water from a local spring. However, the formal history of Spanish settlement began some 50 years later when Menendez arrived, launching St Augustine on a history often marked by bloody violence. Following orders,

Menendez wiped out the French Huguenot settlement at Fort Caroline (see), using such violent thoroughness that the River of Dolphins became known as the Matanzas—the Spanish word for "slaughters." (See FORT MATANZAS NATIONAL MONUMENT) To protect this strategic outpost, the Spanish built Castillo de San Marcos, a massive gray fortress that still dominates the town today. Through the centuries, St Augustine has been attacked, counterattacked, pillaged, burned, betrayed and defended. The Spanish, British, Confederate and US flags all flew over the city.

St Augustine began its more recent history as a fashionable resort when, in the 1880s, Henry Morrison Flagler, the omnipresent personality in Florida history, built two large hotels here and made the city the headquarters of the Florida East Coast Railroad. St Augustine occupies a peninsula with the Matanzas and North rivers on the east and south and the San Sebastian on the west. Still the headquarters for the Florida East Coast Railroad, the city's industries—other than tourism—include food and seafood processing, farming, boat building, printing, bookbinding and aircraft manufacturing.

What to See and Do

1. **Visitor Information Center.** 10 Castillo Dr. Visitors' guide, maps and descriptive literature available. Continuous film presentation on St Augustine and St Johns County. (Daily; closed Dec 25) Phone 824-1000 or -3335. **Free.**

2. **Castillo de San Marcos National Monument.** Overlooking Matanzas Bay at jct of Castillo Dr & Avenida Menendez (both are FL A1A). Grim but venerable, Castillo de San Marcos is the symbol of Spain's ubiquitous presence in St Augustine and the rest of Florida. This massive, masonry structure, constructed between 1672–95, was built to permanently replace a succession of nine wooden fortifications. It was made of coquina, a natural rock of shells and sand. Hispanic artisans and convicts, Indian laborers, black royal slaves and English prisoners erected walls 25 feet high, 14 feet thick at the base, 9 feet at the top, and 4 feet at the parapet. In 1683, before completion, Castillo served as St Augustine's citadel during a pirate raid.

Castillo de San Marcos was never conquered. It withstood a 50-day siege when St Augustine was captured by the South Carolinians in 1702, and another siege of 38 days in 1740. During the American Revolution, the British imprisoned "rebels" in the Castillo and felt confident the structure could repulse an American or a Spanish attack. The United States used the fort as a battery in the coastal defense system, as a military prison and as a magazine. Wildcat, the Seminole leader, led an escape from Castillo; Confederate and Union troops occupied it during the Civil War; and American deserters were imprisoned here during the Spanish-American War.

As Fort Marion, Castillo de San Marcos was the principal fortification in a regional defense system that reached north to the St Mary's River, south to Matanzas Inlet and west to St Mark's. A unique specimen of a vanished style of military architecture and engineering, it became a national monument in 1924. Area (daily; closed Dec 25). Golden Eagle, Golden Age and Golden Access Passports (see INTRODUCTION), all available at the Fort. Contact Superintendent, Castillo de San Marcos National Monument, 1 Castillo Dr, 32084; 829-6506. **¢**

3. **Mission of Nombre de Dios.** San Marco Ave, 6 blks N of information center. A 208-foot stainless-steel cross marks the site of the founding of St Augustine, September 8, 1565. Here also is the **Shrine of Our Lady of La Leche,** established in 1603 and dedicated to the Motherhood of Mary. (Daily) Phone 824-2809. **Free.**

4. **Oldest House (Gonzalez-Alvarez House).** 14 St Francis St. Located on a site in use since the early 1600s, the house (built 1700s), furnishings and neighborhood reflect periods of Spanish, British and American ownership; other buildings on site include the Manucy Museum of St Augustine History and the Tovar House, which houses the Museum of Florida's Army. (Daily; closed Dec 25) Sr citizen rate. Phone 824-2872. **¢¢**

5. **Spanish Quarter.** Restoration of 18th-century Spanish colonial village by the Historic St Augustine Preservation Board, a state project. The original settlement was founded in 1565. The following buildings are open (daily; closed Dec 25). Tickets may be purchased at ticket booth on St George St. Sr citizen rate. Phone 825-6830. **¢¢** Admission includes

Gallegos House. 21 St George St. Reconstruction of a two-room tabby house occupied in the 1750s by a Spanish soldier and his family. Daily life-style and household activities of the period are depicted; demonstrations of 18th-century outdoor cooking.

Gomez House. 23 St George St. Reconstruction of 18th-century, one-room wooden dwelling occupied by a Spanish infantryman in 1763; small neighborhood shop located in a portion of the room where neighbors came to trade or barter.

Peso de Burgo & Pellicer houses (ca 1780). 55 St George St. Two reconstructed frame houses sharing a common center wall. Houses Spanish Quarter Museum Store.

De Mesa-Sanchez House. 43 St George St. One of 33 original surviving colonial houses recently restored; antique furnishings from the early 1800s, when Florida was still a US Territory.

Gonzales & de Hita houses. 37 St George St. The original Gonzalez House, built of native shellstone, is typical of Spanish colonial houses. The interior contains an area with demonstrations of spinning, weaving and textile arts. The de Hita residence is used for special hands-on learning activities.

Blacksmith Shop. A functioning 18th-century Spanish blacksmith shop, providing hardware for the museum village. This unique Spanish shop is built of tabby, a type of concrete made from oyster shells and lime.

6. **Old Wooden Schoolhouse** (ca 1760). 14 St George St. Served as a private residence and schoolhouse before the Civil War. (Daily; closed Dec 25) Phone 824-0192. **¢**

7. **Pena-Peck House** (ca 1700). 143 St George St. Home of the Spanish Royal Treasurer; later residence of the Peck family (1837–1930). Original 19th-century; guided tours. (Daily; closed some major hols) Phone 829-5064. **¢¢**

8. **Ximenez-Fatio House** (1798). 20 Aviles St. Originally a house and general store built of coquina; used as an inn during 1800s; kitchen in rear is only original remaining in St Augustine. Museum house of the National Society of Colonial Dames of America in the State of Florida. (Feb–Aug, Thurs–Mon) Donation. Phone 829-3575.

9. **Lightner Museum.** 75 King St. In restored 300-room former Alcazar Hotel (1888); fountains and gardens on grounds. Natural science exhibits. Victorian village; collections of art, porcelain, 19th-century musical instruments, needlework, ceramics, Tiffany glass, furniture, dolls. (Daily; closed Dec 25) Phone 824-2874. **¢¢**

10. **Oldest Store Museum.** 4 Artillery Lane. Turn-of-the-century general store museum; more than 100,000 vintage items on display. (Daily; closed Dec 25) Phone 829-9729. **¢¢**

11. **Zorayda Castle** (1883). 83 King St. Inspired by the Alhambra in Spain. Cat rug; court of lions; harem quarters. (Daily; closed Dec 25) Phone 824-3097. **¢¢**

12. **Lighthouse Museum of St Augustine.** 81 Lighthouse Ave, on Anastasia Island. Tours of restored lightkeeper's house; coastal museum with exhibits, video. Gift shop. (Daily; closed Easter, Thanksgiving, Dec 25) Phone 829-0745. **¢¢**

13. **Flagler College** (1968). (1,400 students) King St. The restored main campus building is the former Ponce de Leon Hotel, built in 1887 by railroad magnate Henry Morrison Flagler. Campus tours (May–mid-Aug, daily; free) begin in the rotunda area of the main building. Phone 829-6481.

14. **Potter's Wax Museum.** 17 King St. More than 170 life-size wax figures of famous historical personalities; multi-image presentation; workshop. (Daily; closed Dec 25) Sr citizen rate. Phone 829-9056. **¢¢**

15. **Ripley's Believe It or Not Museum.** 19 San Marco Ave, near City Gate. In historic Castle Warden; three floors of exhibits. (Daily) Sr citizen rate. Phone 824-1606 or -1607. **¢¢¢**

16. **Fountain of Youth.** 155 Magnolia Ave, at William St. A 21-acre tropical setting thought to be the first recorded North American landmark. Indian burial grounds; planetarium and discovery globe (both continuous shows); museum, swan pool, Ponce de Leon statue. (Daily; closed Dec 25) Sr citizen rate. Phone 829-3168. ¢¢

17. **Anastasia State Recreation Area.** 3 mi S on FL A1A. More than 1,000 acres, includes coquina quarries and high white dunes. Swimming; fishing. Nature trails. Picnicking. Camping (hookups, dump station). Standard hrs, fees. Phone 461-2033.

18. **St Augustine Alligator Farm.** 2 mi S of the Bridge of Lions on FL A1A, on Anastasia Island. Farm, established in 1893, offers view of huge alligators and crocodiles; Reptile Show, American Alligator Show, and Snappin' Sam Show; also on the farm are tropical birds, raccoons, monkeys; deer, ducks and goats to feed. (Daily) Phone 824-3337. ¢¢¢

19. **Sightseeing.**

  Scenic Cruise. Departs from Municipal Marina, Avenida Menendez. One-and-one-quarter-hour tour of waterfront and Matanzas Bay aboard *Victory II* and *Victory III*. (Daily; no tours Dec 25) Phone 824-1806. ¢¢¢

  Sightseeing Trains. 170 San Marco Ave; eight boarding stations. Narrated, seven-mile, one-hour trips; stop-off privileges. Departures every 15 minutes (daily; no tours Dec 25). Phone 829-6545. ¢¢¢

  Historical Tours. 167 San Marco Ave. Narrated, one-hour tours aboard green & white, open-air trolleys. (Daily; no tours Dec 24, Dec 25) Phone 829-3800. ¢¢¢

  Colee's Horse-drawn Carriage Tours. Departs from Bayfront near entrance to Fort Castillo de San Marco. St Augustine Transfer Co. Lectured tour of historical area lasts approximately one hour. Night tours avail. (Daily; no tours Dec 25) Phone 829-2818. ¢¢¢

(For further information contact the St Augustine & St Johns County Chamber of Commerce, 1 Riberia St, 32084; 829-5681.)

Annual Events

Blessing of the Fleet. Matanzas Bay. Shrimp fleet as well as privately owned boats are blessed. Palm Sunday.

Spanish Night Watch. St George St. Candlelight procession with colorful Spanish costumes commemorates the presence of the Spanish in St Augustine. Mid-June.

Greek Landing Day Festival. St George St. Music, crafts, food. Late June.

British Night Watch. St George St. Grand illumination ceremony. 1st wkend Dec.

Christmas Tour of Homes. Tour of historic and unusual homes, decorated for the holidays. 1st Sun Dec.

Seasonal Event

Cross and Sword. St Augustine Amphitheater, S on FL A1A. Outdoor drama by Paul Green depicting the founding of St Augustine and its early days; official play of Florida. Nightly exc Sun. Phone 471-1965. Mid-June–late Aug.

(See Jacksonville, Marineland)

Motels

✔ ★**BAYFRONT INN.** 138 Avenida Menendez (32084). 904/824-1681. 39 rms, some kits., 2 story. S $35–$49; D $38–$59; each addl $5; higher rates hols & special events. Crib $5. TV; cable. Pool; whirlpool. Complimentary coffee in lobby. Restaurant nearby. Ck-out 11 am. Balconies. Cr cds: MC, V.

★**COMFORT INN DOWNTOWN.** 1111 Ponce de Leon Blvd (32084). 904/824-5554. 84 rms, 2 story, 5 suites. Feb–Sept: S, D $89; each addl $5; suites $120–$150; under 18 free; higher rates: hols, special events; lower rates rest of yr. Crib $5. Pet accepted; $5 non-refundable. TV; cable. Pool; whirlpool. Complimentary continental bkfst, coffee. Restaurant opp open 24 hrs. Ck-out 11 am. Cr cds: A, C, D, DS, MC, V, JCB.

✔ ★**DAYS INN.** 2800 Ponce de Leon Blvd (32084), in Historical District. 904/829-6581. 124 rms, 2 story. Feb–June–Labor Day: S $38–$75; D $43–$80; each addl $5; under 18, $2; under 12 free; higher rates: hols, special events; lower rates rest of yr. Crib free. Pet accepted, some restrictions; $10 non-refundable. TV. Pool. Playground. Restaurant 6–11:30 am. Ck-out noon. Sundries. Patios. Picnic tables. Cr cds: A, D, DS, MC, V.

★**HOLIDAY INN EXPRESS.** 2310 FL 16 (32095). 904/823-8636; FAX 904/823-8728. 51 rms, 2 story, 2 kit. units. S $45.95–$69.95; D $49.95–$69.95; each addl $6; suites $69.95; kit. units $59.95; under 19 free; higher rates major hols. Crib free. TV; cable. Pool. Complimentary continental bkfst. Complimentary coffee in lobby. Restaurant nearby. Ck-out 11 am. Meeting rm. Valet serv. Cr cds: A, C, D, DS, MC, V, JCB.

★**HOLIDAY INN HISTORIC DOWNTOWN.** 1300 Ponce de Leon Blvd (32084). 904/824-3383; FAX 904/829-0668. 122 rms, 2 story. Feb–Aug: S, D $70–$95; each addl $5; higher rates special events; lower rates rest of yr. Crib free. TV; cable. Pool. Restaurant 6 am–2 pm, 5–10 pm. Rm serv. Bar 4 pm–midnight. Ck-out noon. Meeting rms. Bellhops. Cr cds: A, C, D, DS, MC, V, JCB.

✔ ★**MONTEREY.** 16 Avenida Menendez (32084), opp Fort Castillo de San Marcos. 904/824-4482. 59 rms, 2 story. Feb–Apr, June–Labor Day: S $36–$60; D $38–$70; each addl $7; kit. units $42–$54; family, wkly rates; higher rates: wkends, hols, special events; lower rates rest of yr. Crib $7. TV; cable. Pool. Restaurant 7 am–9 pm. Ck-out 11 am. Bellhops. Sundries. Sun deck. Matanzas Bay opp. Cr cds: A, C, D, DS, ER, MC, V.

★★**QUALITY INN ALHAMBRA.** 2700 Ponce de Leon Blvd (32084). 904/824-2883. 77 rms, 2 story. Feb–Apr, June–Labor Day: S $45–$70; D $50–$75; each addl $5; suites $125–$200; under 18 free; higher rates: Daytona races, Gator Bowl, hols; lower rates rest of yr. Crib free. TV; cable. Pool; whirlpool. Restaurant adj. Ck-out noon. Bellhops. Gift shop. Some in-rm whirlpools. Sightseeing train departure area. Cr cds: A, C, D, DS, ER, MC, V, JCB.

★★**RAMADA INN-HISTORIC AREA.** 116 San Marco Ave (32084). 904/824-4352; FAX 904/824-2745. 100 rms, 5 story. Feb–Labor Day: S, D (up to 4) $49–$110; each addl $5; higher rates: hols, special events; lower rates rest of yr. Crib $7. Pet accepted; $5 non-refundable. TV; cable. Pool; whirlpool. Restaurant 6:30 am–9:30 pm. Rm serv. Bar 2 pm–1 am. Ck-out 11 am. Cr cds: A, C, D, DS, ER, MC, V, JCB.

Inns

★★**CASA DE LA PAZ.** 22 Avenida Menendez (32084). 904/829-2915. 6 rms, 1 with shower only, 3 story, 2 suites. No rm phones. S $50–$85; D $75–$115; each addl $10; suites $85–$115; wkly rates; higher rates: major hols, special events. TV in some rms; cable. Complimentary full bkfst, tea/sherry. Restaurant nearby. Ck-out 11 am, ck-in 2 pm. Concierge. Mediterranean-style house (1915) overlooking Matanzas Bay; antiques. Totally nonsmoking. Cr cds: A, DS, MC, V.

✔ ★CASTLE GARDEN BED & BREAKFAST. *15 Shenandoah St (32084).* *904/829-3839.* 5 rms, 2 with shower only, 2 story. No rm phones. S, D $55–$150; wkend rates; 2-night min hols. TV in sitting rm; cable. Complimentary full bkfst. Complimentary tea/sherry. Restaurant nearby. Ck-out 11 am, ck-in 2 pm. Airport, RR station transportation. Moorish-revival carriage house (ca 1860). Totally nonsmoking. Cr cds: A, DS, MC, V.

  SC

★ ★KENWOOD. *38 Marine St (32084).* *904/824-2116.* 14 rms, 2 story. S $45–$68; D $55–$88; each addl $10. Children over 8 yrs only. TV rm; cable. Pool. Complimentary continental bkfst. Restaurant nearby. Ck-out 11 am, ck-in 2 pm. Restored boarding house (1865–1885); many antiques & reproductions; courtyard. In historic district downtown. Totally nonsmoking. Cr cds: DS, MC, V.

★ST FRANCIS. *279 St George St (32084).* *904/824-6068.* 12 rms, 3 story, 6 kit. suites. S $49–$135; each addl $10; kit. suites $65–$135; monthly, wkly rates. Crib $10. TV; cable. Pool. Complimentary continental bkfst, coffee. Restaurant nearby. Ck-out noon, ck-in 3 pm. Restored inn (1791) near oldest house in country; library, balconies, courtyard. Antiques & modern furnishings. Totally nonsmoking. Cr cds: MC, V.

★VICTORIAN HOUSE. *11 Cadiz St (32084).* *904/824-5214.* 8 rms, 2 story, 5 suites. No rm phones. S, D $60–$65; each addl $10; suites $65–$95. TV in some rms, sitting rm; cable. Complimentary continental bkfst. Restaurant nearby. Ck-out 11 am, ck-in 1 pm. On site of first building in St Augustine; rambling Victorian house; antique textiles. Cr cds: A, MC, V.

★ ★ ★WESTCOTT HOUSE. *146 Avenida Menendez (32084).* *904/824-4301.* 8 rms, 3 story. D $100–$140. TV; cable. Complimentary continental bkfst on silver tray in rms, porch or courtyard. Complimentary bottle of wine. Ck-out 11 am, ck-in 3 pm. Built in 1887; decorated with antiques. Overlooking Matanzas Bay. Cr cds: MC, V.

Resort

★ ★ ★PONCE DE LEON GOLF & CONFERENCE RESORT. *4000 N US 1 (32095).* *904/824-2821;* res: *800/228-2821;* FAX *904/829-6108.* 193 rms, 1–4 story. S $75–$85; D $85–$95; each addl $10; suites $145; under 18 free; MAP, AP avail; golf plans. Crib free. TV; cable. Pool. Complimentary coffee in rms. Dining rm 7 am–2:30 pm, 6–10 pm. Bar 11–1 am; entertainment wkends. Ck-out noon, ck-in 3 pm. Meeting rms. Bellhops. Valet serv. Sundries. Free local airport, bus depot transportation. Tennis. Golf, greens fee $38, pro, putting green, 18-hole putting course. Lawn games. Private patios, balconies. Cr cds: A, C, D, DS, ER, MC, V.

 SC

Restaurants

★ANTONIO'S. *At jct FL 3 & 312.* *904/471-3835.* Hrs: 4–9 pm; early-bird dinner to 6 pm. Closed Thanksgiving, Dec 25. Italian menu. Bar. Semi-a la carte: dinner $6.95–$14.95. Child's meals. Specializes in seafood, veal, homemade pasta. Salad bar. Own desserts. Parking. Cr cds: A, C, D, DS, MC, V.

D

★BARNACLE BILL'S SEAFOOD HOUSE. *14 Castillo Dr.* *904/824-3663.* Hrs: 11 am–9 pm; Sun from 4:30 pm. Closed Thanksgiving, Dec 24, 25. Bar. Semi-a la carte: lunch $3.95–$5.95, dinner $7.95–$14.95. Child's meals. Specializes in seafood, chicken, steak. Parking. Nautical decor. Cr cds: A, C, D, DS, MC, V.

★CHIMES. *12 Avenida Menendez.* *904/829-8141.* Hrs: 7 am–9 pm. Closed Dec 25. Res accepted. Bar. Semi-a la carte: bkfst $3–$6, lunch $4.25–$8, dinner $6.75–$16. Child's meals. Specializes in fresh seafood, lamb, steak. Valet parking. Also 2nd-floor dining with balcony overlooking Matanzas Bay; view of Castillo de San Marcos. Family-owned. Cr cds: A, C, D, DS, MC, V.

✔ ★ ★COLUMBIA. *98 St George St.* *904/824-3341.* Hrs: 11 am–9 pm; Fri, Sat to 10 pm; Sun brunch to 3 pm. Res accepted. Spanish menu. Bar. Semi-a la carte: lunch $2.95–$7.95, dinner $6.95–$14.95. Sun brunch $10.95. Child's meals. Specialties: snapper alicante, paella, black bean soup. Parking. In historic area. Spanish decor; balcony around interior courtyard. Bakery. Family-owned. Cr cds: A, C, D, DS, MC, V.

✔ ★ ★CREEKSIDE DINERY. *160 Nix Boatyard Rd.* *904/829-6113.* Hrs: 11:30 am–2:30 pm, 5–10 pm; Sat & Sun from 5 pm. Closed Dec 24 & 25. Bar. Semi-a la carte: lunch $3.50–$6, dinner $4.99–$13.99. Child's meals. Specializes in seafood, chicken. Parking. Outdoor dining. Waterfront dining in reproduction turn-of-the-century Florida home. Cr cds: MC, V.

★ ★FIDDLERS GREEN. *2750 Anahma Dr, E of Vilano Bridge.* *904/824-8897.* Hrs: 5–10 pm. Closed Thanksgiving, Dec 25; also 2 wks before Dec 25. Res accepted Sun–Fri. Bar 4 pm–1 am. Semi-a la carte: dinner $8.95–$17.95. Specializes in seafood, chicken, steak. Parking. Nautical, Florida decor. View of ocean and St Augustine Inlet. Cr cds: A, D, MC, V.

★ ★LE PAVILLON. *45 San Marco Ave.* *904/824-6202.* Hrs: 11:30 am–2:30 pm, 5–10 pm. Res accepted Fri–Sun. Continental menu. Bar. Semi-a la carte: lunch $4.95–$7.95, dinner $6.95–$16.95. Specialties: rack of lamb, bouillabaisse. Own soups, desserts. Parking. Located in former home built 1890. Cr cds: A, D, MC, V.

✔ ★O'STEEN'S. *205 Anastasia Blvd.* *904/829-6974.* Hrs: 11 am–8:30 pm. Closed Sun, Mon; Jan 1, Thanksgiving, Dec 25. Semi-a la carte: lunch, dinner $4.20–$15.75. Specializes in seafood, fresh vegetables. Fireplace; paintings by local artists. No cr cds accepted.

★ ★OLD CITY HOUSE. *115 Cordova St.* *904/826-0781.* Hrs: 11:30 am–2:30 pm, 6–10 pm; Fri & Sat 6–10 pm; Sun 6–9 pm; Sun brunch 8:30 am–2 pm. Closed Mon; Jan 1, July 4, Dec 25; also 2 wks Jan. Res accepted. Continental menu. Bar. Semi-a la carte: lunch $4.50–$8.95, dinner $10.95–$21.95. Specializes in pasta, seafood, lamb. Parking. Outdoor dining. Fireplace. Cr cds: A, D, MC, V.

★ ★ ★RAINTREE. *102 San Marco Ave.* *904/824-7211.* Hrs: 5–9:30 pm; Fri, Sat to 10 pm; early-bird dinner 5–6 pm. Closed Dec 25. Res accepted. Bar. Wine list. Semi-a la carte: dinner $7.95–$18.95. Serv charge 12%. Child's meals. Specializes in 10-item menu (changes daily). Own baking, dessert crêpes. Parking. In historic house (1879) with glassed atrium overlooking courtyard/garden. Transportation to lodging within city. Cr cds: A, C, D, MC, V.

★RICHARD'S FINE DINING & JAZZ. *77 San Marco Ave.* *904/829-9910.* Hrs: 4 pm–closing. Closed Mon; Dec 25. Res accepted. Continental menu. Bar. A la carte entrees: dinner $8.95–$16.95. Specializes in beef, seafood. Entertainment. Parking. Outdoor dining. Dinner club atmosphere featuring nightly jazz performers. Cr cds: MC, V.

★SAN MARCO GRILLE. *123 San Marco Ave.* *904/824-2788.* Hrs: 11:30 am–2 pm, 5–10 pm; early-bird dinner 5–6 pm. Closed Dec 25. Res accepted. Bar. Semi-a la carte: lunch $3.95–$6.95, dinner $5.95–$18.95. Complete meals: dinner $6.95–$9.95. Child's meals. Specialties: sauerbraten, prime rib. Parking. Contemporary decor. Cr cds: A, MC, V.

St Augustine Beach (A-4)

Pop: 3,657 **Elev:** 10 ft **Area code:** 904 **Zip:** 32084

(See Marineland, St Augustine)

Motels

★**BEACHER'S LODGE.** *(Mailing address: 6970 S FL A1A, St Augustine 32086) At jct FL A1A & FL 206. 904/471-8849; res 800/527-8849.* 142 kit. units, 4 story. Mid-Feb–Sept: kit. units $49–$99; monthly rates Oct–Feb; wkly rates; lower rates rest of yr. Crib $5. TV; cable. Pool. Complimentary coffee in lobby. Ck-out 11 am. Coin lndry. Balconies. On beach. Cr cds: DS, MC, V.

★**BEST WESTERN OCEAN INN.** *3955 FL A1A S. 904/471-8010.* 34 rms, 2 story. Feb–early Sept: S, D $59–$69; each addl $6; under 12 free; higher rates major hols; lower rates rest of yr. Crib $5. Pet accepted, some restrictions; $5 per day. TV; cable. Pool. Complimentary continental bkfst. Restaurant adj 7:30 am–10 pm. Ck-out 11 am. 2 blks to beach. Cr cds: A, C, D, DS, ER, MC, V.

★**COMFORT INN.** *3401 FL A1A S. 904/471-1474.* 70 units, 3 story, 12 kit. units. Feb–Sept: S, D, kit. units $49–$104; each addl $5; under 18 free; wkly rates; higher rates special events; lower rates rest of yr. Crib $5. TV; cable. Heated pool; whirlpool. Complimentary bkfst, coffee. Restaurant nearby. Ck-out 11 am. Coin lndry. Some refrigerators. 3 blks from beach. Cr cds: A, C, D, DS, ER, MC, V, JCB.

★**HOLIDAY INN OCEANFRONT.** *(Box 3127) 3250 FL A1A S. 904/471-2555; FAX 904/461-8450.* 151 rms, 5 story. Apr–mid-Sept: S, D $87–$130; each addl $5; under 19 free; lower rates rest of yr. Crib free. Pet accepted, some restrictions. TV; cable. Pool; poolside serv. Restaurant 7 am–2 pm, 5–10 pm. Rm serv. Bar 5 pm–1 am; dancing. Ck-out noon. Coin lndry. Valet serv. Meeting rms. Balconies. Health club privileges. On beach; ocean views. Cr cds: A, C, D, DS, ER, MC, V, JCB.

★★**LA FIESTA OCEANSIDE INN.** *3050 FL A1A S. 904/471-2220; res: 800/852-6390.* 38 rms, 2 story. Feb–Sept: S, D $60–$95; 3-day min: Easter, July 4, Dec 25, Daytona "500," Gator Bowl; lower rates rest of yr. Crib $5. TV; cable. Pool. Playground. Restaurant 7 am–noon. Ck-out 11 am. Coin lndry. Sundries. Game rm. Lawn games. Picnic tables. Miniature golf. On ocean beach. Cr cds: A, C, D, DS, MC, V.

Restaurants

★★**ARVANNO'S.** *2705 FL A1A S. 904/471-9373.* Hrs: 5–9 pm; wkends to 9:30 pm. Closed Mon; some major hols; also Sun Sept–Feb. Res accepted. Italian menu. Wine, beer. Semi-a la carte: dinner $7.95–$16.95. Child's meals. Specializes in beef, pasta, seafood. Parking. Cr cds: A, MC, V.

★**GYPSY CAB CO.** *828 Anastasia. 904/824-8244.* Hrs: 11 am–3 pm, 5:30–10 pm; Tues to 3 pm; Fri, Sat 5:30–11 pm; Sun 5:30–10 pm; Sun brunch 10:30 am–3 pm. Closed July 4, Thanksgiving, Dec 25. Bar. Semi-a la carte: lunch $4.99–$7.99, dinner $8.99–$15.99. Sun brunch $4.99–$7.99. Child's meals. Specializes in fresh seafood, pasta, unique chicken dishes. Parking. Cr cds: MC, V.

 ★★**SALT WATER COWBOY'S.** *299 Dondanville Rd. 904/471-2332.* Hrs: 5–10 pm. Closed Thanksgiving, Dec 25; also 2nd wk Dec–Dec 25. Serv bar. Semi-a la carte: dinner $4.95–$13.95. Child's meals. Specialties: cucumber fish, baked scallops. Parking. Outdoor dining. Renovated fish camp; on water. Cr cds: MC, V.

St Petersburg (D-3)

Founded: 1876 **Pop:** 238,629 **Elev:** 44 ft **Area code:** 813

The fourth largest city in the state and second only to Miami as a winter resort, St Petersburg is host to more than a million visitors each year. Its chief tourist commodity, of course, is sunshine, drawing golf and boating enthusiasts throughout the year; however, it also has the big-city zest of its aerospace and appliance industries. St Petersburg encompasses a fringe of beaches, parks and yacht basins along Tampa Bay and a string of resort-occupied islands (connected to the mainland by causeways) on the Gulf side, across Boca Ciega Bay. These islands form the St Petersburg Beach Area (see).

Transportation

St Petersburg/Clearwater Intl Airport: Information 535-7600 or 531-1451. **Tampa Intl Airport:** Information 870-8700; lost and found 870-8760; weather 976-1111; cash machines, Landside Building, third level; Crown Room (Delta), Airside C; WorldClub (Northwest), Airside D; USAir Club (US Air), Airside F.

Car Rental Agencies: See toll-free numbers under Introduction.

Public Transportation: Buses, trolley at Clearwater Beach (Pinellas Suncoast Travel Authority), phone 530-9911.

Rail Passenger Service: Amtrak 800/972-7245.

What to See and Do

1. **St Petersburg Historical and Flight One Museum.** 335 2nd Ave NE. Displays concentrate on the history of St Petersburg; changing exhibits gallery. Tours available. (Daily; closed major hols) Phone 894-1052. ¢¢
2. **Salvador Dali Museum.** 1000 3rd St S. Houses the world's largest and most highly acclaimed collection of works by the famous Spanish artist, Salvador Dali. Oils, drawings, watercolors, graphics and sculptures from 1914–1980; tours. (Daily; closed Jan 1, Thanksgiving, Dec 25) Sr citizen rate. Phone 823-3767. ¢¢
3. **Museum of Fine Arts.** 255 Beach Dr NE. Displays include pre-Columbian, European, American, Oriental paintings and sculpture; decorative arts and photography; Georgia O'Keeffe's "Poppy," and a large collection of Steuben glass. Guided tours; films, lectures, concerts. (Daily exc Mon; closed Jan 1, Dec 25) Donation. Phone 896-2667.
4. **Science Center of Pinellas County.** 7701 22nd Ave N. Hands-on educational institution stimulating scientific inquiry for children and adults. Facilities include laboratories, museum, live animal exhibits, computer center, nature trail and gardens. (Mon–Fri; closed hols) Phone 384-0027. **Free.**
5. **Great Explorations.** 1120 4th St S. Hands-on museum arranged in six exploration areas; "Touch Tunnel" lets visitors crawl through 100-foot textured maze in total darkness; flexibility and muscle-strength tests, computerized thinking exhibits. Gift shop. (Daily) Phone 821-8885. ¢¢
6. **Planetarium.** St Petersburg Junior College, off 5th Ave N at 69th St. One-hour planetarium shows (Sept–Apr, Fri evenings; closed univ hols). Observatory open for telescope viewing after shows (weather permitting). Phone 341-4320. **Free.**
7. **Florida's Sunken Gardens.** 1825 4th St N. Botanical garden featuring thousands of tropical and subtropical flowers and plants from around the world; exotic and native birds and animals on exhibit throughout the gardens; bird shows. Inside the complex is a Bibli-

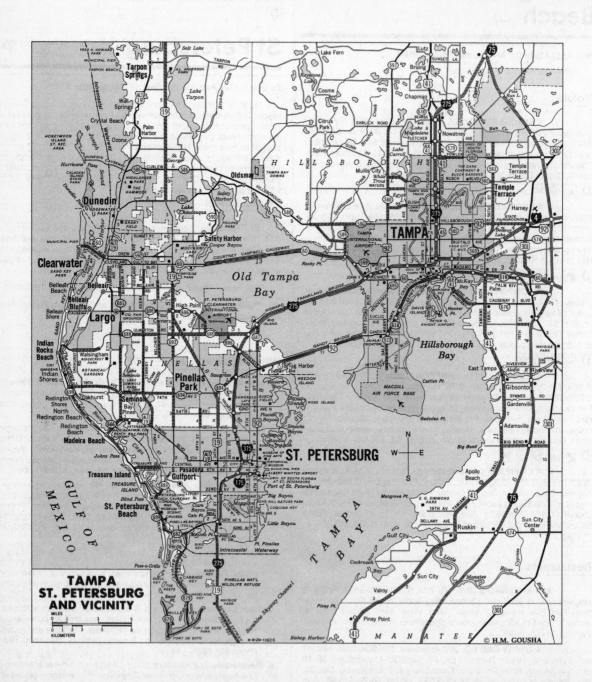

TAMPA
ST. PETERSBURG
AND VICINITY

MILES

KILOMETERS

© H.M. GOUSHA

cal wax museum; also fudge kitchen; gift shop; snack bar; stroller rentals. (Daily) Phone 896-3186. ¢¢¢

8. **The Pier.** 800 2nd Ave NE. A five-story inverted pyramid located at the end of this quarter-mile pier contains observation deck with view of city, restaurants, shops, an aquarium, miniature golf; special events and daily entertainment. Fishing, bait house; boating (rentals), water sports. (Daily) Shuttle trolley. Phone 821-6164.

9. **Boating. Municipal Marina,** 300 2nd Ave SE (dock master). Accommodates 610 boats; 500-foot dock for visiting boats. Electric, water & telephone service; phone 893-7329. **Municipal ramps:** Crisp Park, 35th Ave & Poplar St NE; Grandview Park, 6th St & 39th Ave S; Lake Maggiore (fresh water), west end of 38th Ave S, off 9th St; Maximo Park, 34th St S & W Pinellas Point Dr; Jungle Prada, Elbow Lane & Park St N; Bay Vista, Pinellas Point Dr & 4th St S; Coffee Pot Bayou, 4th St & 31st Ave N; Demens Landing, Bayshore Dr & 2nd Ave S; Sunlit Cove, Sunlit Cove Dr & Bay St NE. Phone 893-7335.

10. **Fort De Soto Park.** On five islands reached by Pinellas Bayway (toll), S to Mullet Key. Historical fort grounds offers swimming, modern bathhouses, waterskiing; fishing piers; boating (ramp). Picnicking, grills; concessions, snack bar. Camping (fee; dump station, hookups; 2-wk max Jan–Apr; reservations required in person). No fires on ground; no pets. Phone 866-2484 or -2662 (camping). **Free.**

11. **Sightseeing.**

   Gray Line bus tours. Contact PO Box 145, 33731; 822-3577.

   Trolley Tour. Serves downtown and beach area.

Annual Events

   Southern Ocean Racing. Mar.

   International Folk Fair. Mar.

   Renaissance Festival. Mar.

   Festival of States. Two-week event with art shows, concerts, sports exhibitions, coronation & ball, youth parade, night parade, Parade of States. Phone 898-3654. Late Mar–mid-Apr.

Seasonal Events

   Greyhound racing. Derby Lane (St Petersburg Kennel Club). 10490 Gandy Blvd. Nightly exc Tues; matinees Sat–Mon & Wed. Phone 576-1361. Jan–July.

   Professional baseball. Al Lang Stadium, 1st St & 2nd Ave S. St Louis Cardinals spring training; exhibition games. Phone 822-3384. Early Mar–early Apr.

   Concerts. The Florida Orchestra. Bayfront Center, Mahaffey Theatre, 400 1st St S. Classical and pops. Phone 447-4210. Sept–May.

   Sailboat regattas. Oct–May.

Additional Visitor Information

The St Petersburg Area Chamber of Commerce (100 2nd Ave N, PO Box 1371, 33731; 821-4715) has free sightseeing literature including maps, brochures, self-guided tour and the comprehensive *Visitors Guide to St Petersburg and its Gulf Beaches.* Visitor information may be obtained at the Suncoast Welcome Center (2001 Ulmerton Rd; 576-1449) and at the Pier (800 2nd Ave NE, 821-6164; see #8). For a recording of current events phone 893-7500.

   (See Bradenton, Clearwater, Dunedin, Tampa)

Motels

   ★**BEACH PARK.** *300 Beach Dr NE (33701). 813/898-6325.* 26 rms, 2 story, 11 kits. Nov–May: S, D $45–$65; each addl $5; kit. units $55; wkly rates; varied lower rates rest of yr. Crib $5. TV. Complimentary

coffee in rms. Restaurant nearby. Ck-out 11 am. Coin lndry. Refrigerators. Balconies. Opp bay, city park. Cr cds: A, DS, MC, V.

   ✔ ★ ★**COMFORT INN CENTRAL.** *1400 34th St N (33713). 813/323-3100; FAX 813/327-5792.* 78 rms, 3 story. Dec–Apr: S $45–$62; D $51–$68; family, wkly rates; lower rates rest of yr. TV. Heated pool; whirlpool. Complimentary full bkfst. Restaurant 6:30–11 am. Ck-out 11 am. Coin lndry. Meeting rms. Cr cds: A, D, DS, MC, V.

🅳 🏊 🛇 SC

   ✔ ★**DAYS INN.** *2595 54th Ave N (33714). 813/522-3191; res: 800/325-2525; FAX 813/527-6120.* 160 rms, 2 story. Feb–mid-Apr: S $42–$50; D $48–$65; each addl $4; under 12 free; lower rates rest of yr. Crib free. TV. Pool; wading pool. Complimentary continental bkfst. Ck-out 11 am. Coin lndry. Meeting rm. Lawn games. Picnic tables. Cr cds: A, C, D, DS, MC, V.

🅳 🏊 🛇 SC

   ★ ★**DAYS INN MARINA BEACH RESORT.** *6800 34th St S (33711). 813/867-1151; FAX 813/864-4494.* 157 rms, 2 story, 20 kits. Feb–mid-Apr: S, D $69–$121; each addl $10; suites, townhouses $121–$259; under 16 free; lower rates rest of yr. TV; cable. 2 pools; whirlpool, poolside serv. Playground. Restaurant 7 am–noon, 5–10 pm. Bar; entertainment Wed–Sat. Ck-out 11 am. Coin lndry. Meeting rms. Valet serv. Sundries. Gift shop. Lighted tennis. Game rm. Lawn games. Many refrigerators; bathrm phone in suites. Private patios, balconies. On bay; water sports, private beach. Marina sailing school, boat charter, deep sea fishing. Attraction tours. Cr cds: A, C, D, DS, MC, V.

🅳 🏊 🏊 🛇 🎣 SC

   ★ ★**ECONO LODGE AND TENNIS RESORT.** *3000 34th St S (33711). 813/867-1111; FAX 813/867-7068.* 120 rms, 3 story. Feb–Apr: S, D $60–$65; each addl $5; suites $80–$85; under 18 free; lower rates rest of yr. Crib free. Pet accepted, some restrictions; $25 refundable. TV; cable. Heated pool. Restaurant 7–2 am. Rm serv. Bar. Ck-out 11 am. Coin lndry. Meeting rms. Beauty shop. Tennis, pro. Some refrigerators. Refrigerator, wet bar in suites. Some balconies. Cr cds: A, C, D, DS, MC, V.

🅳 🏊 🏊 🛇 🛇 SC

   ✔ ★**LA MARK CHARLES.** *(6200 34th St N, Pinellas Park 34665) ½ mi S of FL 694, off I-275. 813/527-7334.* 93 rms, 1–2 story, 35 kits. Feb–Apr: S, D $55; each addl $5; suites $65–$70; kit. units $60; under 12 free; lower rates rest of yr. Crib $3. Pet accepted; $25 refundable and $5 per day. TV. Heated pool; whirlpool. Restaurant 7–10 am. Ck-out 11 am. Meeting rm. Coin lndry. Gift shop. Sundries. Refrigerators avail (3-day min). Cr cds: A, MC, V.

🏊 🏊 🛇 SC

   ✔ ★ ★**LA QUINTA INN.** *4999 34th St N (33714). 813/527-8421; FAX 813/527-8851.* 120 rms, 2 story. Mid-Jan–Apr: S $59; D $69; each addl $10; lower rates rest of yr. Pet accepted, some restrictions. TV; cable. Heated pool. Complimentary continental bkfst. Ck-out noon. Coin lndry. Meeting rm. Exercise equipt; weights, bicycles. Spanish decor. Elaborately landscaped; fountain, palm trees, jasmine & gardenia bushes. Cr cds: A, C, D, DS, MC, V.

🏊 🏊 🏋 🛇 SC

   ★**VALLEY FORGE.** *6825 Central Ave (33710). 813/345-0135; FAX 813/384-1671.* 27 rms, 8 kits. Mid-Jan–mid-Apr: S, D $45–$55; lower rates rest of yr. Crib $5. Pet accepted; $3. TV; cable. Pool. Coffee. Restaurant nearby. Ck-out 11 am. Lawn games. Refrigerators. Private patios. Cr cds: A, D, MC, V.

🏊 🏊 🛇

Hotel

   ★ ★ ★**HILTON.** *333 1st St S (33701). 813/894-5000; FAX 813/894-7655.* 333 units, 15 story, 31 suites. S $89–$114; D $99–$124; each addl $10; suites $129–$454; under 18 free. Crib free. TV; cable. Heated pool; poolside serv. Restaurant 6:30 am–10:30 pm. Bar. Ck-out noon.

Convention facilities. Concierge. Gift shop. Valet parking. Exercise equipt; weights, stair machine, whirlpool. Game rm. Refrigerators avail. Picnic tables. Opp Tampa Bay. *LUXURY LEVEL:* **TOWERS.** 44 units, 3 suites, 2 floors. S from $124; D from $134; suites $139–$449. Private lounge. In-rm movies. Bathrm phones. Kit. area in suites. Complimentary continental bkfst, refreshments. Cr cds: A, C, D, DS, MC, V. JCB.

Resort

STOUFFER VINOY RESORT. (New general manager, therefore not rated) *501 Fifth Ave NE (33701), off I-275 onto I-375, then Beach Dr and left on waterfront, downtown.* 813/894-1000; FAX 813/822-2785. 360 units, 7 story, 29 suites. Mid-Jan–mid-Apr: S, D $239–$399; suites $500–$2,000; under 18 free; wknd packages; golf & tennis plans; lower rates rest of yr. Crib free. Garage, overnight; valet parking $9, self-park $6. TV; cable. 2 heated pools; poolside serv. Supervised child's activities. Complimentary coffee & newspaper in rms. Restaurants 6 am–11 pm (also see TERRACE ROOM). Rm serv 24 hrs. Bar 10–2 am, Sat to midnight; entertainment. Ck-out noon. Lndry facilities. Convention facilities. Concierge. Gift shops. 16 tennis courts, 8 lighted, 4 different surfaces, including grass and clay. 18-hole golf, greens fee $85 (incl cart), pro, putting green, driving range. Exercise rm; instructor, weight machine, bicycles, whirlpool, sauna, steam rm. Masseuse. Complete fitness center. Croquet courts. Minibars. Wet bar in suites. Restored historic landmark (1925) blends the best of the old and the new. Stenciled cypress beams in lobby; leaded-glass windows, hand-painted ceilings and wall murals in the original dining wing; tropical gardens. Situated on a 14-acre site overlooking Tampa Bay; swimming beach; 74-slip private marina. Cr cds: A, C, D, DS, ER, MC, V, JCB.

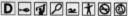

Restaurants

✔ ★ **CHINA DELIGHT.** *1198 Pasadena Ave S.* 813/347-0000. Hrs: 11:30 am–10 pm; Fri to 11 pm; Sat noon–11 pm; Sun 4–10 pm; early-bird dinner Mon–Fri 2:30–5 pm. Closed Thanksgiving. Res accepted. Chinese, Amer menu. Serv bar. Semi-a la carte: lunch $3.95–$4.95, dinner $5.25–$10.95. Child's meals. Specialties: sesame chicken, seafood bird nest. Parking. Decorated with Chinese accents. Cr cds: A, C, D, MC, V.

★ ★ **KEYSTONE CLUB.** *320 4th St N.* 813/822-6600. Hrs: 11 am–2:30 pm, 5–10 pm; Fri to 11 pm; Sat 5–11 pm. Closed Sun; major hols. Res accepted. Bar. Semi-a la carte: lunch $3.95–$6.50, dinner $8.95–$19. Child's meals. Specializes in prime rib, pork chops, fresh fish. Parking. Club-like atmosphere. Cr cds: A, D, MC, V.

★ ★ **LEVEROCK'S.** *4801 37th St S.* 813/864-3883. Hrs: 11:30 am–10 pm; early-bird dinner 3–6 pm. Closed Thanksgiving, Dec 25. Bar. Semi-a la carte: lunch $3.75–$6.95, dinner $5.95–$19.95. Child's meals. Specializes in grouper, Florida fish. Parking. Overlooks bay. Cr cds: A, C, D, MC, V.

✔ ★ **SMOKEY'S TEXAS BAR-B-QUE.** *(8180 49th St N, Pinellas Park) N via 49th St to 82nd Ave.* 813/546-3600. Hrs: 11 am–10 pm. Wine, beer. Semi-a la carte: lunch, dinner $3.50–$12. Specializes in hickory-smoked ribs, prime rib, steak. Parking. Southwestern decor. Cr cds: A, MC, V.

★ ★ **TERRACE ROOM.** *(See Stouffer Vinoy Resort)* 813/894-1000. Hrs: 6 am–3 pm, 5:30–11 pm; early-bird dinner Sun–Thurs 5:30–6:30 pm; Sun brunch 9:30 am–3 pm. Res accepted. Mediterranean menu. Bar 11 am–midnight; wknds to 1 am. Wine cellar. A la carte entrees: bkfst $5–$7.50, lunch $7.25–$15, dinner $12.50–$21.50. Sun brunch $29. Child's meals. Specialties: tortellini with 4 cheeses, bouilla-

baisse, stuffed baked flounder with crabmeat, Caribbean-style snapper. Contemporary jazz band evenings. Valet parking. In historic building; flower and griffin designs on the high ceiling and just above the column were hand-painted as part of an extensive restoration process. The windows are replicas of the original 1920s leaded-glass windows. Jacket (dinner). Cr cds: A, C, D, DS, ER, MC, V, JCB.

St Petersburg Beach Area (D-3)

Elev: 5 ft **Area code:** 813

This strip of islands, connected by bridges and causeways, is separated from the mainland by Boca Ciega Bay. Included here are Indian Rocks Beach, Indian Shores, Madeira Beach, Redington Beach, Redington Shores, St Petersburg Beach and Treasure Island. For a map of the area see ST PETERSBURG.

What to See and Do

1. **Suncoast Seabird Sanctuary.** N on FL 699 (Gulf Blvd) at 18328 Gulf Blvd in Indian Shores. Nonprofit organization specializes in care and recuperation of wild birds; largest wild bird hospital in the US. Visitors may observe rehabilitation and behavior of approx 600 birds of more than 76 different species; excellent photographic opportunities. Guided tours (Wed & Sun afternoons). (Daily) Phone 391-6211. **Free.**

2. *Capt Anderson* **Boat Cruise.** Departs from St Petersburg Beach Causeway. Three-level *Lady Anderson* provides scenic luncheon cruises (days vary), dolphin-watching and bird-feeding cruises (Tues–Fri) and dinner-dance cruises (Tues, Fri & Sat). Cruises (Oct–mid-May; closed Thanksgiving, Dec 25; also 1st wk Jan). Phone 367-7804. ¢¢¢¢¢

(For further information contact the Chamber of Commerce, 6990 Gulf Blvd, St Petersburg Beach 33706, phone 360-6957; or the Pinellas Suncoast Tourist Development Council, 4625 E Bay Dr, Suite 109, Clearwater 34624, phone 800/554-3600.)

Annual Event

Beach Fest. St Petersburg Beach. Off-shore boat racing, other events; entertainment. 1st wkend Sept.

(See Bradenton, St Petersburg, Tampa)

Motels

✔ ★ **ALGIERS.** *(11600 Gulf Blvd, Treasure Island 33706) N on FL 699 (Gulf Blvd), 9 blks N of Treasure Island Causeway.* 813/367-3793. 17 rms, 2 story, 10 kits. Feb–Apr: S, D $75; each addl $5; suites $85–$95; varied lower rates rest of yr. Crib free. TV; cable. Heated pool. Restaurant nearby. Ck-out 10 am. Coin lndry. Lawn games. Refrigerators. On Gulf. Cr cds: MC, V.

★ **ALPAUGH'S GULF BEACH NORTH.** *(1912 Gulf Blvd, Indian Rocks Beach 34635) N on FL 699 (Gulf Blvd).* 813/595-9421. 18 kit. units, 2 story. Dec–Apr: 1-bedrm $72; 2-bedrm $98; each addl $6; under 12, $4; wkly rates; varied lower rates rest of yr. Crib $3. TV; cable. Restaurant nearby. Ck-out 10 am. Coin lndry. Lawn games. Picnic tables, grills. On beach. Cr cds: DS, MC, V.

✔ ★ **CHERI-LYN.** *(11705 Gulf Blvd, Treasure Island 33706) N on FL 699 (Gulf Blvd).* 813/367-3791. 24 rms, 2 story, 18 kits. Feb–Apr:

S, D $55–$69; each addl $7.50; wkly rates; lower rates rest of yr. Crib free. TV; cable. Heated pool. Coffee in rms. Restaurant nearby. Ck-out 10 am. Coin lndry. Lawn games. Refrigerators. Grills. Library. Opp Gulf, beach. Cr cds: A, MC, V.

⊕ ⊚

★★COLONIAL GATEWAY INN. (6300 Gulf Blvd, St Petersburg Beach 33706) S on FL 699 (Gulf Blvd), ¾ mi S of St Petersburg Beach Causeway. 813/367-2711; res: 800/237-8918; FAX 813/367-7068. 200 rms, 1–2 story, 100 kits. Mid-Feb–Apr: S, D $91–$117; each addl $6; kit. units $8 addl; under 12 free; lower rates rest of yr. Crib $6. TV; cable. Heated pool; wading pool. Restaurant 7:30–10:30 am, 11:30 am–2:30 pm, 5–9:30 pm. Beachfront bar; entertainment. Ck-out 11 am. Meeting rms. Sundries. Game rm. On beach. Cr cds: A, C, D, DS, ER, MC, V.

⊕ ⊚

★★DAYS INN ISLAND BEACH RESORT. (6200 Gulf Blvd, St Petersburg Beach 33706) S on FL 699 (Gulf Blvd), approx ¾ mi S of St Petersburg Beach Causeway. 813/367-1902; FAX 813/367-4422. 102 rms, 2 story, 48 kits. Feb–Apr: S, D $129–$149; each addl $20; kit. units $159–$169; under 16 free; lower rates rest of yr. Crib free. TV; cable. 2 heated pools. Complimentary continental bkfst. Restaurant adj. Beachfront bar to 2 am. Ck-out 11 am. Game rm. On 5½ acres of tropical gardens; on Gulf. Cr cds: A, C, D, DS, MC, V.

⊕ ⊘ ⊚ SC

✔★INN ON THE BEACH. (1401 Gulf Way, St Petersburg Beach 33706) At 14th Ave. 813/360-8844. 12 kit. units, 2 story. Jan–Apr: S, D $50–$125; each addl $7; monthly rates; higher rates: Memorial Day, July 4, Dec 25 & 31 (3-day min); lower rates rest of yr. Crib $7. TV; cable. Complimentary continental bkfst Sat & Sun. Restaurant nearby. Ck-out 11 am. Grills. Near beach. Bicycles, beach chairs avail. No cr cds accepted.

⊚ SC

★ISLAND'S END. (1 Pass-a-Grille Way, St Petersburg Beach, 33706) 813/360-5023; FAX 813/367-7890. 6 villas. Mid-Dec–May: S, D $72–$155; each addl $8; wkly rates; lower rates rest of yr. Crib $3. TV; cable. Ck-out 11 am. Free lndry facilities. Some private patios. Cedar cottages with "old-Florida" feeling at point where Pass-a-Grille meets Gulf of Mexico; surrounded on 3 sides by water. Cr cds: MC, V.

D ↦

✔★MALYN. (282 107th Ave, Treasure Island 33706) N on FL 699 (Gulf Blvd), then ¼ mi E on 107th Ave. 813/367-1974; FAX 813/823-0068. 20 kit. units, 2 story. Jan–Apr: S, D $54; each addl $5; studio rms $48–$50; wkly rates; lower rates rest of yr. TV; cable. Heated pool. Restaurant nearby. Ck-out 10 am. Coin lndry. Lawn games. Picnic tables, grills. Overlooks bay; fishing docks, boat dock $5/day. Bayside cabana; beach 4 blks. Cr cds: MC, V.

↦ ⊕ ⊚

★PAGE TERRACE. (10500 Gulf Blvd, Treasure Island 33706) N on FL 699 (Gulf Blvd), 1 blk S of Treasure Island Causeway. 813/367-1997. 35 rms, 3 story, 5 suites, 25 kits. No elvtr. Feb–mid-Apr: S, D $56–$58; each addl $5; suites $90; kit. units $64–$78; under 5 free; wkly rates; lower rates rest of yr. TV; cable. Heated pool; wading pool. Complimentary coffee in lobby. Ck-out 11 am. Coin lndry. Lawn games. Picnic tables, grills. On beach. Cr cds: A, DS, MC, V.

D ⊕ ⊚

★SEA RESORT. (102 Gulf Blvd, Indian Rocks Beach 34635) N on FL 966 (Gulf Blvd). 813/595-0461; FAX 813/595-2092. 29 rms, 2 story, 14 kits. Feb–Apr: S, D $58–$95; each addl $5; kit. units to 4, $80 & $95; varied lower rates rest of yr. TV; cable. Heated pool. Restaurant nearby. Ck-out 10 am. Lndry facilities. Refrigerators. Balconies. On beach. Cr cds: MC, V.

⊕ ⊚

★★SHORELINE ISLAND RESORT. (14200 Gulf Blvd, Madeira Beach 33708) N on FL 699 (Gulf Blvd), ½ mi S of Madeira Beach

Causeway. 813/397-6641; res: 800/635-8373. 70 rms in 5 bldgs, 2–5 story, 65 kits. Feb–Apr: S, D $79–$84; each addl $10; studios $88–$135; 1–2 bedrm kit. units $89–$185; wkly rates; monthly rates off-season; varied lower rates rest of yr. Adults only. TV; cable. Heated pool. Restaurant nearby. Ck-out 11 am. Coin lndry. Lawn games. Private patios, balconies. Picnic tables. Library. 400 ft of beach. On Gulf. Cr cds: DS, ER, MC, V.

⊕ ⊚ SC

★SURFS INN. (14010 Gulf Blvd, Madeira Beach 33708) N on FL 699 (Gulf Blvd), 1 mi N of Johns Pass Bridge. 813/393-4609. 25 rms, 2 story, 17 kits. Feb–Apr: S, D $62; each addl $5; kit. units $67–$72; lower rates rest of yr. Crib free. TV; cable. Heated pool. Ck-out 10:30 am. Lawn games. Refrigerators. Picnic tables, grills. Sun decks. On Gulf; beach. Cr cds: DS, MC, V.

⊕ ⊚

★★THUNDERBIRD. (10700 Gulf Blvd, Treasure Island 33706) N on FL 699 (Gulf Blvd). 813/367-1961; res: 800/367-2473. 64 rms, 2-3 story, 32 kits. No elvtr. Mid-Feb–Apr: S, D $95–$115; each addl $6; kit. units $105–$125; under 13 free; lower rates rest of yr. Crib free. TV; cable. Heated pool; whirlpool, poolside serv. Restaurant 7 am–10 pm. Bar noon–2 am; entertainment, dancing. Ck-out 11 am. Picnic tables. On beach. Cr cds: A, C, D, DS, ER, MC, V.

⊕ ⊚ SC

★★TRAILS END. (11500 Gulf Blvd, Treasure Island 33706) N on FL 699 (Gulf Blvd), 8 blks N of Treasure Island Causeway. 813/360-5541; FAX 813/360-1508. 54 rms, 1–2 story, 32 kits. Feb–Apr: S, D $65–$80; each addl $5; kit. units $73–$90; wkly rates; varied lower rates rest of yr. Crib free. TV; cable. Heated pool. Restaurant adj 8 am–10 pm. Ck-out 11 am. Lawn games. Picnic tables, grill. On beach. Cr cds: A, C, D, DS, MC, V.

⊕ ⊚

Motor Hotels

★★★ALDEN. (5900 Gulf Blvd, St Petersburg Beach 33706) S on FL 699 (Gulf Blvd), ¾ mi S of St Petersburg Beach Causeway. 813/360-7081; res: 800/237-2530 (exc FL), 800/262-3464 (FL); FAX 813/360-5957. 143 rms, 6 story, 139 kits. (1–3 bedrm). Feb–Apr: S, D, kit. units $120–$159; each addl $10; under 12 free; lower rates rest of yr. Crib free. TV; cable. 2 pools, heated; 2 whirlpools. Complimentary coffee in rms. Restaurant nearby. Ck-out 11 am. Coin lndry. Lighted tennis. Game rm. Lawn games. Private patios, balconies. Picnic tables, grills. Sun deck. On Gulf beach. Cr cds: A, C, D, DS, ER, MC, V.

⊘ ⊕ ⊘ ⊚

★★BILMAR BEACH RESORT. (10650 Gulf Blvd, Treasure Island 33706) N on FL 699 (Gulf Blvd) at Treasure Island Causeway. 813/360-5531; res: 800/826-9724; FAX 813/360-2915. 172 rms, 3–8 story, 121 kits. Feb–Apr: S, D, studio rms $110; each addl $5; suites $189; kit. units $120–$125; under 12 free; varied lower rates rest of yr. Crib free. TV; cable. 2 heated pools; whirlpool, poolside serv. Restaurant 7 am–10 pm. Rm serv. Bars 11–2 am; entertainment, dancing. Ck-out 11 am. Meeting rms. Bellhops. Refrigerators. Some private patios. Some balconies. On 550-ft beach. Cr cds: A, C, D, MC, V.

⊕ ⊚

★CORAL REEF BEACH RESORT. (5800 Gulf Blvd, St Petersburg Beach 33706) On FL 699 (Gulf Blvd), approx 1½ mi N of Pinellas Bayway (FL 682). 813/360-0821; res: 800/553-6599; FAX 813/367-2597. 114 units, 4-6 story, 50 apts, 64 condos. Feb–Apr: apts, condos $95–$185; each addl $10; under 12 free; wkly, monthly rates; lower rates rest of yr. Crib $5. TV; cable. Heated pool; whirlpool. Restaurant 4–9 pm. Bar; entertainment. Ck-out 10 am. Coin lndry. Refrigerators. Picnic tables. On beach. Cr cds: A, C, D, MC, V.

⊕ ⊚ SC

★★HILTON RESORT. (5250 Gulf Blvd, St Petersburg Beach 33706) S on FL 699 (Gulf Blvd), approx 1¼ mi S of St Petersburg Beach Causeway. 813/360-1811; FAX 813/360-6919. 151 rms, 11 story.

Jan–Apr: S, D $120–$160; each addl $10; suites $275–$395; family rates; lower rates rest of yr. TV; cable. Heated pool; poolside serv. Restaurant 7 am–10 pm. Rm serv. Revolving rooftop bar 11:30–2 am, Sun from 1 pm, beachfront bar; entertainment exc Mon. Ck-out 11 am. Coin lndry. Meeting rm. Bellhops. Valet serv. Sundries. Tennis privileges. Golf privileges. Some refrigerators. Balconies. On beach. Cr cds: A, C, D, DS, ER, MC, V.

★ ★ **HOLIDAY INN-MADEIRA BEACH.** (15208 Gulf Blvd, Madeira Beach 33708) N on FL 699 (Gulf Blvd), at Madeira Beach Causeway. 813/392-2275; FAX 813/392-2275, ext 7143. 147 rms, 4 story. Feb–Apr: S, D $105.50–$160; each addl $10; family rates; lower rates rest of yr. Crib free. TV; cable. Heated pool; wading pool, poolside serv, poolside bar. Restaurant 6:30 am–10 pm. Rm serv. Bar 11–1 am; Sun from noon. Ck-out 11 am. Coin lndry. Meeting rms. Bellhops. Gift shop. Lighted tennis. Some private patios, balconies. On Gulf; 600-ft beach; sailboat rentals. Cr cds: A, C, D, DS, ER, MC, V, JCB.

★ ★ **HOWARD JOHNSON LODGE.** (11125 Gulf Blvd, Treasure Island 33706) N on FL 699 (Gulf Blvd), 2 blks N of Treasure Island Causeway. 813/360-6971; FAX 813/360-9014. 84 rms, 3 story. Feb–Apr: S, D $90–$98; each addl $10; under 18 free; lower rates rest of yr. Crib free. TV; cable. Heated pool. Restaurant open 24 hrs. Ck-out noon. Coin lndry. Valet serv Mon–Fri. Sundries. Game rm. Lawn games. Refrigerators. Private patios, balconies. Fishing dock. City beach opp. Cr cds: A, C, D, DS, ER, MC, V, JCB.

★ ★ **RAMADA INN.** (12000 Gulf Blvd, Treasure Island 33706) N on FL 699 (Gulf Blvd), ¾ mi N of Treasure Island Causeway. 813/360-7051; FAX 813/367-6641. 121 rms, 4 story, 23 kits. Mid-Feb–Apr: S, D $110–$130; each addl $10; kit. units $120–$130; under 18 free; lower rates rest of yr. Crib free. TV; in-rm movies. Heated pool; whirlpools. Playground. Restaurant 7 am–10 pm. Rm serv. Bar; entertainment, dancing. Ck-out noon. Bellhops. Gift shop. Game rm. Lawn games. On Gulf. Cr cds: A, C, D, DS, ER, MC, V.

★ ★ ★ **SANDPIPER BEACH RESORT.** (6000 Gulf Blvd, St Petersburg Beach 33706) S on FL 699 (Gulf Blvd), approx ¾ mi S of St Petersburg Beach Causeway. 813/360-5551; res: 800/237-0707 (exc FL), 800/282-5553 (FL); FAX 813/360-0417. 153 rms, 7 story, 134 kits. Feb–Apr: S, D $121–$169; each addl $15; 1–3 bedrm kits $149–$225; under 12 free; golf plans; lower rates rest of yr. Crib $5. TV; cable. 2 heated pools, 1 indoor; poolside serv. Free supervised child's activities. Restaurant 7 am–10 pm; dining rm opp 7 am–midnight. Rm serv. Bar; entertainment, dancing exc Sun. Ck-out noon. Coin lndry. Meeting rm. Bellhops. Valet serv. Shopping arcade. Free garage parking. Tennis privileges. Golf privileges. Exercise equipt; weight machine, rowers. Rec rm. Lawn games. Private patios, balconies. Picnic tables, grills. On beach. Cr cds: A, C, D, DS, MC, V.

★ ★ ★ **TRADE WINDS.** (5500 Gulf Blvd, St Petersburg Beach 33706) On FL 699 (Gulf Blvd), 1½ mi N of Pinellas Bayway (FL 682). 813/367-6461; res: 800/237-0707; FAX 813/367-7496. 577 rms, 2–7 story, 150 kits. Feb–Apr: S, D $175–$209; each addl $15; suites $245–$305; under 12 free; lower rates rest of yr. Crib $5. TV; cable. 4 heated pools, 1 indoor; wading pool, poolside serv. Playground. Free supervised child's activities. Restaurant 7 am–10 pm. Rm serv. Bar; entertainment, dancing. Ck-out noon. Coin lndry. Valet serv. Convention facilities. Bellhops. Gift shops. Lighted tennis, pro. Golf privileges. Putting green. Exercise equipt; weight machines, bicycles, sauna. Game rm. Rec rm. Beach games. Bathrm phones, refrigerators. Private patios, balconies. Picnic tables, grills. Lush courtyards with waterfalls, fountains, abundant waterfowl. Cr cds: A, C, D, DS, MC, V.

Hotels

★ ★ ★ ★ **DON CESAR BEACH RESORT.** (3400 Gulf Blvd, St Petersburg Beach 33706) 813/360-1881; res: 800/637-7200; FAX 813/367-6952. 277 rms, 1–10 story. Jan–mid-May: S, D $225–$260; each addl $15; suites $275–$625; penthouse $1,050; under 18 free; lower rates rest of yr. Crib free. TV; cable. Heated pool. Free supervised child's activities. Restaurant 7 am–midnight (also see KING CHARLES). Rm serv 24 hrs. Bars 11–1:30 am. Ck-out noon. Convention facilities. Coin lndry. Concierge. Barber, beauty shop, boutiques. Valet parking. Lighted tennis, pro. Golf privileges. Exercise equipt; weight machine, bicycles, whirlpool, sauna. Massage therapy. Sailboat rentals. Watersport clinics & rentals. Beach cabanas, boardwalk. Lawn games. Some refrigerators, minibars. Some balconies. Ice cream parlor. Art gallery. Historic hotel with Old World elegance. Elaborate landscaping; courtyard, flower gardens. On beach. Cr cds: A, C, D, DS, ER, MC, V.

★ ★ ★ **HILTON NORTH REDINGTON BEACH RESORT.** (17120 Gulf Blvd, North Redington Beach 33708) N on FL 699 (Gulf Blvd), 2 mi S of FL 694 (Park Blvd). 813/391-4000; FAX 813/391-4000, ext 7777. 125 rms, 6 story. Feb–Apr: S, D $120–$195; family rates; wkly rates off-season; lower rates rest of yr. TV; cable, in-rm movies avail. Heated pool; poolside serv. Restaurant 7 am–10 pm. Bars 11:30–2 am; entertainment, dancing May–Aug. Ck-out 11 am. Meeting rms. Gift shop. Minibars. Balconies. On Gulf; beach. Cr cds: A, C, D, DS, ER, MC, V.

★ ★ **HOLIDAY INN TREASURE ISLAND.** (11908 Gulf Blvd, Treasure Island 33706) N on FL 699 (Gulf Blvd), ¾ mi N of Treasure Island Causeway. 813/367-2761; FAX 813/367-9946. 110 rms, 9 story. Jan–May: S, D $108–$149; each addl $10; under 18 free; wkend plans; lower rates rest of yr. Crib free. TV; cable. Heated pool; whirlpool, poolside serv. Restaurant 7 am–2 pm, 5–10 pm. Bar 11–2 am; entertainment, dancing. Ck-out noon. Coin lndry. Gift shop. Private patios. On beach. Cr cds: A, C, D, DS, ER, MC, V, JCB.

Restaurants

✓ ★ **ADAM'S RIB.** (213 Gulf Blvd, Indian Rocks Beach) N on FL 699 (Gulf Blvd). 813/595-4400. Hrs: 4–10 pm; early-bird dinner 4–6 pm. Res accepted. Bar to midnight. Semi-a la carte: dinner $4.95–$11.95. Child's meals. Specializes in ribs, steak, seafood. Parking. Rustic decor. Cr cds: A, C, D, MC, V.

✓ ★ **BALLOON PALACE.** (14995 Gulf Blvd, Madeira Beach) N on FL 699 (Gulf Blvd), 1 mi N of Johns Pass Bridge. 813/393-2706. Hrs: 11 am–midnight; Sun from 1 pm. Closed Thanksgiving, Dec 25. Res accepted Fri, Sat. Bar. Semi-a la carte: lunch 99¢–$4.95, dinner $2.95–$9.95. Child's meals. Specializes in fresh seafood, chicken wings. Own desserts. Entertainment Sun–Tues; sing-along Wed, Fri & Sat. Parking. Hot-air balloon motif. Cr cds: A, MC, V.

★ **BROWN DERBY SANTA MADEIRA.** (601 Blackhawk Rd, Madeira Beach) N on FL 699 (Gulf Blvd), E on Madeira Beach Causeway, N on Blackhawk Rd. 813/397-0020. Hrs: 11 am–11 pm; Fri, Sat to midnight; Sun to 10 pm. Res accepted. Bar. Semi-a la carte: lunch $3.95–$7.95, dinner $6.95–$17.95. Child's meals. Specializes in prime rib, steak, fresh seafood. Salad bar. Parking. Piano bar. Housed in a replica of 3-masted sailing ship; nautical decor. View of bay. Cr cds: A, DS, MC, V.

★ ★ **CAPTAIN KOSMAKOS SEAFOOD & STEAK HOUSE.** (9610 Gulf Blvd, Treasure Island) N on FL 699 (Gulf Blvd), approx 1 blk N of Blind Pass Bridge. 813/367-3743 or 360-6626. Hrs: 3 pm–2 am; early-bird dinner 3–5:30 pm. Res accepted. Continental menu. Bar. Semi-a la carte: dinner $8.95–$22.95. Child's meals. Specializes in steak, prime rib, Maryland crabcakes. Entertainment. Parking. View of bay. Cr cds: A, C, D, MC, V.

★**CAPTAIN'S GALLEY.** *(660 Blackhawk Rd, Madeira Beach)* N on FL 699 (Gulf Blvd), E on Madeira Beach Causeway to Blackhawk Rd, behind shopping center. 813/392-9094. Hrs: 11:30 am–9 pm; Fri, Sat to 10 pm; Sun noon–9 pm; early-bird dinner Mon–Sat 3:30–5:30 pm. Closed Thanksgiving, Dec 25. Bar. Semi-a la carte: lunch $2.95–$6.95, dinner $5.95–$19.95. Child's meals. Specializes in seafood, steak, ribs. Parking. Nautical decor. Overlooks Intracoastal Waterway. Cr cds: DS, MC, V.

✔★**GIGI'S.** *(105 107th Ave, Treasure Island)* N on FL 699 (Gulf Blvd) to Treasure Island Causeway (107th Ave). 813/360-6905. Hrs: 11 am–10:30 pm; early-bird dinner 4–6 pm. Closed Thanksgiving, Dec 25. Italian menu. Wine, beer. Semi-a la carte: lunch $2.49–$4.95, dinner $5.95–$10.95. Child's meals. Specializes in pasta, pizza. Parking. Copper murals. Family-owned. Cr cds: A, D, DS, MC, V.

✔★★**HUNGRY FISHERMAN.** *(19915 Gulf Blvd, Indian Shores)* N on FL 699 (Gulf Blvd), 1 mi S of FL 688. 813/595-4218. Hrs: 11:30 am–10 pm. Closed Thanksgiving, Dec 25. Bar. Semi-a la carte: lunch $3.95–$6.95, dinner $4.95–$14.95. Child's meals. Specializes in Alaskan salmon, ribs. Parking. View of gardens. Family-owned. No cr cds accepted.

★★**HURRICANE.** *(807 Gulf Way, St Petersburg Beach)* 813/360-9558 or -4875. Hrs: 8–2 am. Closed Dec 25. Res accepted Mon–Thurs. Bars. Semi-a la carte: bkfst $1.75–$6.50, lunch, dinner $2.95–$22.95. Specialties: grouper sandwiches, Maryland crabcakes. Jazz Wed–Sun. Beachfront dining; sunset cocktail deck. Cr cds: MC, V.

★★★**KING CHARLES.** *(See Don Cesar Beach Resort Hotel)* 813/360-1881. Hrs: 6–10 pm; Sun 10:30 am–2:30 pm; hrs vary hols. Closed Mon. Res accepted. Continental menu. Extensive wine list. A la carte entrees: dinner $19–$38. Sun brunch $26.95. Specializes in fresh seafood. Own baking. Pianist. Valet parking. Courtyard with fountain. Overlooks Gulf. Jacket. Cr cds: A, C, D, ER, MC, V.

✔★**KINGFISH WHARF.** *(12789 Kingfish Dr, Treasure Island)* N on FL 699 (Gulf Blvd) to 127th Ave, just S of Johns Pass Bridge, E to Kingfish Dr. 813/360-0881. Hrs: 11:30 am–10 pm; Fri & Sat to 11 pm. Closed Thanksgiving, Dec 25. Bar. Semi-a la carte: lunch $3.95–$6.95, dinner $5.45–$9.95. Child's meals. Specializes in shrimp, grouper, steak. Raw bar. Entertainment Fri–Sun. Parking. Nautical decor. On waterfront marina; charter boats avail. Family-owned. Cr cds: D, MC, V.

★★**LE POMPANO.** *(19325 Gulf Blvd, Indian Shores)* N on FL 699 (Gulf Blvd). 813/596-0333. Hrs: 11:30 am–10 pm; early-bird dinner 4–6 pm. Closed Sun. Res accepted. French, continental menu. Bar. Wine cellar. Semi-a la carte: lunch $3.95–$5.95, dinner $9.95–$18.95. Child's meals. Specialties: boneless duckling, shrimp scampi. Parking. Waterfront patio dining. Tableside cooking. Fireplace; antiques. Cr cds: A, C, D, MC, V.

★★**LEVEROCK'S ON THE BAY.** *(565 150th Ave, Madeira Beach)* N on FL 699 (Gulf Blvd) to Madeira Beach Causeway (150th Ave). 813/393-0459. Hrs: 11 am–10 pm; early-bird dinner 3–6 pm. Closed Thanksgiving, Dec 25. Bar. Semi-a la carte: lunch $3.95–$6.95, dinner $5.95–$19.95. Child's meals. Specializes in fresh seafood, steak, ribs. Parking. Overlooks Intracoastal Waterway. Cr cds: A, C, D, DS, MC, V.

★**LITTLE JOE'S OF SAN FRANCISCO.** *(301 N Gulf Blvd, Indian Rocks Beach)* N on FL 699 (Gulf Blvd). 813/596-0062. Hrs: 11:30 am–10 pm; Fri, Sat to 11 pm. Closed Dec 25. Italian menu. Bar. Semi-a la carte: lunch $3.95–$17.95, dinner $5.25–$17.95. Child's meals. Special-

ties: calamari steak, Joe's Special, chicken piccata. Parking. San Francisco theme, decor. Cr cds: MC, V.

★★**THE LOBSTER POT.** *(17814 Gulf Blvd, Redington Shores)* N on FL 699 (Gulf Blvd), 1 mi S of FL 694 (Park Blvd). 813/391-8592. Hrs: 4:30–10 pm; Fri, Sat to 11 pm; early-bird dinner 4:30–6 pm. Closed July 4, Labor Day, Thanksgiving, Dec 25. Res required. Serv bar. Semi-a la carte: dinner $12.75–$28.50. Child's meals. Specializes in fresh seafood, Florida & Maine lobster, apple & banana fritters. Own desserts. Valet parking. Cr cds: A, C, D, DS, MC, V.

✔★★**LUCKY FISHERMAN.** *(5100 Gulf Blvd, St Petersburg Beach)* 813/360-5448. Hrs: 4:30–10 pm; Sun to 9 pm; early-bird dinner 4:30–6:30 pm. Res accepted. Bar. Semi-a la carte: dinner $9.75–$12.95. Child's meals. Specialties: mahi-mahi, red snapper, orange roughy. Parking. Patio dining. Overlooks Gulf of Mexico. Cr cds: D, DS, MC, V.

★★**SCANDIA.** *(19829 Gulf Blvd, Indian Shores)* N on FL 699 (Gulf Blvd). 813/595-5525. Hrs: 11:30 am–9 pm; Sun from noon. Closed Mon. Res accepted. Scandinavian menu. Bar. Semi-a la carte: lunch $4.95–$10.95, dinner $6.95–$19.95. Child's meals. Specializes in roast pork, Danish lobster tails, duck. Parking. Cr cds: A, C, D, DS, MC, V.

✔★**YELLOW FIN.** *(2721 Gulf Blvd, Indian Rocks Beach)* N on FL 699 (Gulf Blvd). 813/593-3346. Hrs: 11:30–1 am; early-bird dinner 4–5:30 pm; Sun brunch 10 am–2 pm. Res accepted. Caribbean, Amer menu. Bar. Semi-a la carte: lunch $4.25–$6.25, dinner $6.95–$14.95. Sun brunch $4.95–$6.45. Child's meals. Specialties: yellowfin tuna, stuffed chicken breast, amberjack. Entertainment nightly. Valet parking. Outdoor dining. 1940s-style roadhouse. Cr cds: A, MC, V.

Sanford (B-4)

Settled: 1837 **Pop:** 32,387 **Elev:** 29 ft **Area code:** 407

Sanford, on the St Johns River and Lake Monroe, was founded near the former site of a federal garrison used for protection against Indians. Fishing for shad, bass, bream and perch in the St Johns River is popular. Light industry and the growing tourism industry are important to the town's economy.

What to See and Do

1. **Central Florida Zoological Park.** On US 17/92 at I-4 exit 52. Hundreds of native and exotic animals; children's zoo, reptile exhibit, pony rides (daily exc Mon; fee) and elephant rides (Sat & Sun; fee); elevated boardwalk, picnic area. Park (daily; closed Thanksgiving, Dec 25). Sr citizen rate. Phone 323-4450. ¢¢

2. **Henry Shelton Sanford Museum.** 520 E 1st St. Exhibits include decorative art objects from New England and Europe (1820–90); photographs and artifacts relating to town's history; re-created library of town's founder. (Tues–Fri; closed hols) Phone 330-5698. **Free.**

3. **Riverboat tours.**

    Rivership *Grand Romance.* Departs from Monroe Harbor Marina. This 135-foot triple-decked sidewheeler cruises the St Johns River for regular 3–4-hour lunch cruise. Also dinner/dance and "showboat" cruises. (Daily) Res required. Phone 321-5091 or 800/225-7999 (exc FL). ¢¢¢¢¢

    St Johns River Cruises. Depart from Osteen Bridge at FL 415. Narrated nature and wildlife cruises along St Johns River; special cruises. (Daily) Res required. Sr citizen rate. Phone 330-1612. ¢¢¢¢

(For further information contact the Greater Sanford Chamber of Commerce, 400 E 1st St, 32771; 322-2212.)

(See Altamonte Springs, DeLand, Orlando, Winter Park)

Motels

✔ ★ ★**BEST WESTERN DELTONA INN.** *(481 Deltona Blvd, Deltona 32725) 10 mi N on I-4, exit 53 Deltona.* 407/574-6693; FAX 407/860-2687. 130 rms, 2 story. Feb–Apr: S, D $39–$59; under 18 free; golf plans; higher rates special events; lower rates rest of yr. TV; cable. Pool. Restaurant 7 am–2 pm, 5:30–10 pm. Bar 11:30–2 am. Ck-out noon. Meeting rms. Golf privileges. Lake. Cr cds: A, C, D, DS, MC, V.

✔ ★**DAYS INN.** *4650 W FL 46 (32771), 1 blk E of I-4.* 407/323-6500. 119 rms, 2 story. Jan–Mar: S $27–$45; D $30–$50; each addl $5; under 18 free; higher rates special events; lower rates rest of yr. TV. Pool. Restaurant 6 am–9 pm. Ck-out noon. Sundries. Cr cds: A, C, D, DS, MC, V.

★**HOLIDAY INN ON LAKE MONROE.** *530 N Palmetto Ave (32771).* 407/323-1910; FAX 407/322-7076. 100 rms, 2 story. Jan–Apr: S $49–$69; D $56–$76; each addl $7; under 18 free; higher rates special events; lower rates rest of yr. Crib free. TV; cable. Pool. Restaurant 6:30 am–10 pm. Rm serv. Bar 11 am–midnight, Fri, Sat to 1 am; entertainment Tues–Sat. Ck-out noon. Coin lndry. Meeting rm. Bellhops. Sundries. Golf privileges. Health club privileges. Holiday Isle Complex on Lake Monroe; marina, dockage; boat rental; water sports, dinner cruise ship. Cr cds: A, C, D, DS, MC, V, JCB.

Restaurant

★**CATTLE RANCH FAMILY STEAKHOUSE.** *2700 S Sanford Ave.* 407/321-5761. Hrs: 5–10 pm; wkends to 11 pm. Closed most major hols. Bar. A la carte entrees: dinner $7.50–$16.99. Child's meals. Specializes in steak, chicken, shrimp. Parking. Western, cowboy atmosphere; antiques. Cr cds: A, C, D, MC, V.

Sanibel & Captiva Islands (E-3)

Pop: 5,468 **Elev:** 5 ft **Area code:** 813 **Zip:** Sanibel, 33957; Captiva, 33924

Sanibel Island, linked to the mainland by a causeway, is considered the third best shelling site in the Western Hemisphere, with deposits on both bay and gulf beaches. North of Sanibel, only a bridge away, is Captiva; legend has it that the pirate Jose Gaspar used the island to harbor his women captives. Together the islands comprise the Sanibel National Wildlife Refuge, haven for more than 200 varieties of birds. The islands are a popular tourist destination, and several marinas line the east pier of Sanibel.

What to See and Do

1. **Island Historical Museum.** 800 Dunlop Rd, Sanibel Island. Former "cracker" style homestead restored and furnished to depict lifestyle of early settlers; antique clothing, tin-type photographs, piano. Re-created Cracker village with grocery store, post office, schoolhouse. (Wed–Sat; closed hols) Phone 472-4648. ¢

2. **Sanibel-Captiva Conservation Foundation.** 3333 Sanibel-Captiva Rd, Sanibel Island. This 250-acre tract contains 4½ miles of nature trails along the properties and the Sanibel River. Guided and self-guided tours to explain the ecosystem of the island; native vegetation and wildlife. Special wetlands exhibits; native plant nursery. (Nov–Apr, daily exc Sun; rest of yr, Mon–Fri; closed most major hols) Phone 472-2329. ¢

3. **J.N. "Ding" Darling National Wildlife Refuge.** Visitor Center 6 mi W of causeway; 5-mile wildlife drive (daily exc Fri); observation tower; walking and canoe trails. Fishing is permitted and crabbing is permitted with use of dipnets only. Feeding of alligators is strictly prohibited. (Daily) Golden Eagle, Golden Age and Golden Access passports accepted (see INTRODUCTION). Phone 472-1100. Per vehicle ¢¢

4. **Bird Sanctuary and Walk.** Tarpon Bay Rd, S side of Sanibel. Tower and trails.

5. **Boat tours.** For shelling and bird-watching. Inquire at Chamber of Commerce.

(For further information contact the Sanibel-Captiva Islands Chamber of Commerce, Causeway Rd, PO Box 166, Sanibel; 472-1080.)

Annual Event

Sanibel Shell Fair. Serious shell collectors display their wares, including specimen shell and live shell exhibits; contests and prizes. 1st full wkend Mar.

(See Fort Myers)

Motels

★**GALLERY.** *541 E Gulf Dr, Sanibel Island.* 813/472-1400. 32 rms, 2 story, 26 kits. Feb–Apr: S, D $148; each addl $10; kit. units $187–$214; apts, cottages $214; wkly rates; lower rates rest of yr. Crib free. TV; cable. Heated pool. Complimentary coffee in lobby. Restaurant nearby. Ck-out 11 am. Coin lndry. Lawn games. Refrigerators. Private patios, balconies. Picnic tables, grills. Library. Bicycles (rentals). On beach. Cr cds: DS, MC, V.

★ ★**ISLAND INN.** *(Box 659) 3111 W Gulf Dr, Sanibel Island.* 813/472-1561; res: 800/851-5088; FAX 813/472-0051. 56 units in motel, lodges, 2–3 story, 28 kits. MAP, mid-Nov–Apr: S, D $88–$160; each addl $30 (child $15); kit. cottages $151–$160; hol wkends (2-day min); varied lower rates rest of yr. Serv charge 10% in season. Crib free. TV; cable. Heated pool. Restaurant 7:30–10:30 am (all yr), 6:30–7:45 pm (mid-Nov–Apr only). Ck-out 11 am. Bellhops. Coin lndry. Tennis. Golf privileges. Lawn games. Refrigerators. Screened porches with most units. Library. On beach. Cr cds: A, DS, MC, V.

★ ★**SANIBEL MOORINGS.** *845 E Gulf Dr, Sanibel Island.* 813/472-4119; res: 800/237-5144; FAX 813/472-8148. 110 kit. units, 2 story. Late-Dec–Apr (3-night min): 1–3 bedrm apts $945–$1,652/wk; each addl $105; 3-day–1-wk min off-season; lower rates rest of yr. Crib $21/wk. Maid serv avail $15/hr. TV; cable. 2 pools, heated; wading pool. Restaurant nearby. Ck-out 11 am. Coin lndry. Tennis. Screened porches. Grills. On beach; dockage. Cr cds: MC, V.

★ ★**SANIBEL SIESTA.** *1246 Fulgur St, Sanibel Island.* 813/472-4117; res: 800/548-2743. 56 condo units (2-bedrm). Mid-Dec–Apr (4-day min): condo units for 4–6, $1,099–$1,435/wk; each addl $70/wk; 7-day min summer hol wkends; lower rates rest of yr. Crib avail. TV; cable. Heated pool. Ck-out 10 am. Coin lndry. Tennis privileges. Lawn games. Private patios, balconies. Grills. On beach. Cr cds: DS, MC, V.

★ ★**SONG OF THE SEA.** *863 E Gulf Dr, Sanibel Island.* 813/472-2220; res: 800/231-1045. 30 kit. units, 2 story. Late Dec–Apr: kit. studios $259; each addl $10; 1-bedrm suites $286; each addl $10; lower rates rest of yr. Crib free. TV; cable, in-rm movies. Heated pool; whirlpool. Complimentary continental bkfst 8–10 am. Ck-out 11 am. Coin lndry. Sundries. Tennis privileges. 18-hole golf privileges, greens fee $20. Lawn games. Library. Screened porches. Picnic tables, grills. Bicycles. On beach. Cr cds: A, C, D, DS, MC, V.

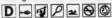

Motor Hotel

★ ★**WEST WIND INN.** *3345 W Gulf Dr, Sanibel Island. 813/472-1541; res 800/824-0476 (exc FL), 800/282-2831 (FL); FAX 813/472-8134.* 104 rms, 2 story, 66 kit. units. Late Dec–Apr: S, D $167–$185; kit. units $188–$206; wkly rates; lower rates rest of yr. Crib free. TV; cable. Heated pool. Restaurant 8 am–2:30 pm; Fri, Sat 5–9 pm. Bar. Ck-out 11 am. Coin lndry. Meeting rm. Tennis. 18-hole golf privileges, putting green. Bicycles, catamarans & windsurfers avail (fee). Lawn games. Refrigerators. Balconies. Grills. On gulf; beach. Cr cds: A, MC, V.

Resorts

★ ★ ★**SOUTH SEAS PLANTATION.** *(PO Box 194) South Seas Plantation Rd, Captiva Island, 13 mi N of Sanibel Causeway at end of Captiva Island. 813/472-5111; res: 800/237-3102 (exc FL), 800/282-3402 (FL); FAX 813/472-7541.* 106 rms in hotel, 2 story, 450 1–3 bedrm kit. villas, beach & tennis, bayside & marina villas. Mid-Feb–late Apr: S, D $260–$275; each addl $25; kit. villas $265–$580; kit. cottages $435–$510; lower rates rest of yr. Crib $10. TV; cable, in-rm movies. 18 pools, heated; poolside serv. Playground. Supervised child's activities. Dining rm 7 am–11 pm. Pizza & ice cream parlors; box lunches. Bar 11–1 am. Ck-out noon, ck-in 4 pm. Grocery, deli. Coin lndry. Package store. Convention facilities. Concierge. Shopping arcade. Barber, beauty shop. 22 tennis courts, 9 lighted, pro. Golf, greens fee $64 for 18 holes (incl cart), pro, putting green. Marina, store; dockage; launching ramp; boats, power motors; waterskiing; wind surfing; para-sailing; jet-skiing; scuba diving, snorkeling; sailing charters; sailing school. Shelling expeditions. Photo safari. Bicycles. Lawn games. Rec dir. Rec rm. Game rm. Entertainment, movies. Exercise equipt; weights, bicycles, whirlpools. Fishing guides, fish clean/shop. Trolley transportation. Refrigerators. Private patios, balconies. Picnic tables, grills. Gracious turn-of-the-century plantation on 330 acres. Elaborate landscaping. 2-mi private beach. Cr cds: C, D, DS, MC, V.

★ ★ ★**SUNDIAL BEACH & TENNIS RESORT.** *1451 Middle Gulf Dr, Sanibel Island. 813/472-4151; res: 800/237-4184; FAX 813/472-1809.* 265 condo units, 4 story. Early Feb–Apr, late Dec: 1-bedrm $247–$358; 2-bedrm $329–$435; each addl $20; under 14 free; tennis, golf, family, honeymoon package plans; lower rates rest of yr. Crib $5. TV; cable. 5 pools, heated; whirlpool, poolside serv. Free supervised child's activities. Restaurant 7–12:30 am. Bar 11:30–1 am; entertainment, dancing. Ck-out 11 am, ck-in 3 pm. Coin lndry. Meeting rms. Valet serv. Gift shop. Lighted tennis, pro, pro shop. 18-hole golf privileges, greens fee $65 (incl cart), putting green, driving range. Boat, watersport equipt rentals. Wind surfing. Bicycle rentals. Lawn games. Rec dir. Game rm. Rec rm. Fishing, shelling guides. Many private patios, balconies. On Gulf. Cr cds: A, C, D, DS, MC, V.

Restaurants

★ ★**BELLINI'S.** *11521 Andy Rosse Ln, Captiva Island. 813/472-6866.* Hrs: 5:30–10:30 pm. Res accepted. Northern Italian menu. Bar. Semi-a la carte: dinner $11–$21.50. Child's meals. Specializes in fresh seafood, pasta, veal, duck. Valet parking. Outdoor dining. Cr cds: A, MC, V.

★ ★ ★**THE GREENHOUSE.** *Captiva Village Square. 813/472-6006.* Hrs: 5:45–10 pm. Res accepted. Continental menu. Extensive wine list, variety of beers. Semi-a la carte: dinner $16.95–$27.95. Child's meals. Specializes in rack of lamb, seafood, duck. Menu changes frequently; seafood daily. Own baking. Parking. Tropical island atmosphere. Cr cds: DS, MC, V.

★**HARBOR HOUSE.** *1244 Periwinkle Way, Sanibel Island. 813/472-1242.* Hrs: 5–10:30 pm; also 11:30 am–2:30 pm in spring. Closed Jan 1, Thanksgiving, Dec 25; also 1 wk in Sept. Bar. Semi-a la carte: lunch (in season) $3.50–$6.95, dinner $7.95–$17.95. Child's meals. Specializes in seasonal seafood, Key lime pie. Parking. Many marine and nautical artifacts. Cr cds: A, MC, V.

★ ★**JACARANDA.** *1223 Periwinkle Way, Sanibel Island. 813/472-1771.* Hrs: 5–10 pm. Closed Dec 25. Res accepted. Continental menu. Bar 4 pm–1 am. Semi-a la carte: dinner $10.95–$19.95. Child's meals. Specializes in seafood, steak, veal, pasta. Entertainment. Parking. Outdoor garden dining. Cr cds: A, C, D, DS, ER, MC, V.

✔ ★**JERRY'S OF SANIBEL.** *1700 Periwinkle Way, Sanibel Island. 813/472-9300.* Hrs: 6 am–11 pm; early-bird dinner Mon–Sat 4–6 pm. Wine, beer. Semi-a la carte: bkfst $2.25–$6.95, lunch, dinner $3.25–$12.95. Specializes in fresh fish, prime rib (Fri, Sat). Salad bar. Parking. Family-owned. Cr cds: MC, V.

★ ★**MAD HATTER.** *6460 Sanibel-Captiva Rd, Sanibel Island. 813/472-0033.* Hrs: 5–9:30 pm. Closed Dec 25; Super Bowl Sun; also early Sept. Res required. Beer, wine. A la carte entrees: dinner $18–$30. Specialties: fresh game, grilled fish, veal chop, lamb. Own desserts. Parking. Overlooks gulf. Totally nonsmoking. Cr cds: A, MC, V.

★ ★**NUTMEG HOUSE.** *2761 W Gulf Dr, Sanibel Island. 813/472-1141.* Hrs: 5:30–9:30 pm. Closed Mon. Res accepted. Wine, beer. Semi-a la carte: dinner $16–$26. Specialties: roast duck with honey, orange and raspberry sauce, stuffed escalope of veal, fresh seafood. Entertainment Tues, Wed, Sun. Parking. Cr cds: A, D, MC, V.

★ ★**TARWINKLES SEAFOOD EMPORIUM.** *2499 Periwinkle Way, at Tarpon Bay Rd, 2½ mi W of Causeway, Sanibel Island. 813/472-1366.* Hrs: 11:30 am–3 pm, 5–10 pm. Res accepted. Bar. Semi-a la carte: lunch $4.95–$7.95, dinner $7.95–$17.95. Child's meals. Specializes in fresh seafood, pasta, steak. Parking. Tropical decor. Cr cds: A, C, D, MC, V.

★ ★**TIMBERS.** *703 Tarpon Bay Rd, Sanibel Island. 813/472-3128.* Hrs: 4:30–10 pm; off-season from 5 pm. Closed Super Bowl Sun, July 4. Bar 4 pm–1 am. Semi-a la carte: dinner $9.95–$21.95. Child's meals. Specializes in fresh seafood, aged steak. Own desserts. Parking. Retail fish market & raw bar. Cr cds: A, MC, V.

★ ★**TRUFFLES AT CASA YBEL.** *2255 W Gulf Dr, Sanibel Island. 813/472-9200.* Hrs: 11 am–9:30 pm. Res accepted. Bar from 11 am. Semi-a la carte: lunch $5–$13, dinner $13–$18. Child's meals. Specializes in fresh seafood, pasta. Guitarist Sun afternoons in season. Parking. Outdoor dining. Victorian-style mansion with 6 dining rms. Cr cds: A, C, D, DS, MC, V.

✔ ★ ★**WIL'S LANDING.** *1200 Periwinkle Way, Sanibel Island. 813/472-4772.* Hrs: 11:30–1 am. Bar. Semi-a la carte: lunch $4.25–$6, dinner $4.95–$16.95. Child's meals. Specializes in fresh seafood, pasta, steak. Raw bar. Entertainment. Parking. Cr cds: A, MC, V.

Sarasota (D-3)

Settled: 1856 **Pop:** 50,961 **Elev:** 27 ft **Area code:** 813

Tourism is the main industry in Sarasota, as it has been since the days before a single house was built and anglers used to pitch tents on the beach. The standard Florida commodities of beach, fishing, golf and sunbathing come in the usual pleasant proportions here, and the city has basis for its claim as ''the cradle of golf'' since the first Florida course was laid out here in 1886 by Col J. Hamilton Gillespie.

Ever since John Ringling selected the city of Sarasota as winter quarters for his circus (1929–59), the two have become synonymous in the minds of many. Ringling did much to develop and beautify the area and surrounding islands. Today, culture, the circus and sportfishing make for a rare blend along Sarasota Bay.

What to See and Do

1. **Ringling Museum of Art.** 3 mi N on US 41. The 66-acre estate of John Ringling is a cultural complex, left to the people of Florida at Ringling's death in 1936. On its beautifully landscaped grounds are a sculpture courtyard and a rose garden. (Daily; closed Easter, Dec 25) Sr citizen rate. Phone 355-5101. Combination ticket for all facilities ¢¢¢   The museum includes

     Ringling Residence (Ca'd'zan) (1924–26). An elaborate Venetian-Gothic mansion patterned after the Doge's Palace in Venice, Italy. Venetian glass windows; hand-wrought iron work; marble floors and 32 rooms; 4,000-pipe organ; tapestries, period furnishings and art objects from around the world.

     Art Gallery. An Italian Renaissance-style villa created by local craftsmen with shiploads of columns, doorways, roof sculptures and marble collected in Italy by John Ringling. One of the most distinguished collections of Baroque art in the Western Hemisphere, assembled by Ringling; also contemporary art; Rubens collection; sculpture garden in courtyard. Admission free on Sat.

     Asolo Theater. Much of the interior decor of the original theater (1798), which occupied the great hall of the castle of Queen Catherine Cornaro in Asolo, near Venice, Italy, was purchased by the state of Florida. It was reassembled here in a specially designed, air-conditioned building. Programs of films, lectures, concerts and more (fees). (See SEASONAL EVENTS)

     Circus Galleries. Extensive collection of circus memorabilia. Multiple galleries include circus wagons, calliopes, costumes, posters and circus-related fine art exhibits.

2. **Bellm's Cars & Music of Yesterday.** 5500 N Tamiami Trail (US 41), opp Ringling Museum of Art. More than 125 restored antique classic cars and 2,000 mechanical antique music boxes and machines are displayed; turn-of-the-century arcade; tours hrly. (Daily) Phone 355-6228. ¢¢¢

3. **Sarasota Visual Art Center.** 707 N Tamiami Trail. Four galleries display works by Florida artists. (Daily; closed most hols) Phone 365-2032. **Free.**

4. **Marie Selby Botanical Gardens.** 811 S Palm Ave, just off US 41. Features orchids, bromeliads and a wide variety of other exotic plants; 11 acres of outside gardens, including Hibiscus, Banyan Grove, Bamboo Grove, Waterfall Garden; Museum of Botany and the Arts; plant, gift and book shops. (Daily; closed Dec 25) Phone 366-5730 or -5731. ¢¢¢

5. **Sarasota Jungle Gardens.** 3701 Bayshore Rd, 1 mi S of airport on US 41, then 2 blks W on Myrtle St. Tropical birds in jungle paradise; more than 5,000 varieties of plants; wild jungle trails; formal gardens; flamingos, swans, peacocks and pelicans roam free; bird and reptile shows; leopards and monkeys; macaws. Kiddie Jungle children's playground. (Daily) Phone 355-5305. ¢¢¢

6. **Mote Marine Laboratory and Marine Aquarium.** 1600 Thompson Pkwy. Aquariums of marine animals collected throughout the central gulf coast region; 30-foot touch tank; display of sharks' jaws; marine research exhibits; 135,000-gallon shark tank. (Daily) Phone 388-2451. ¢¢

7. **Myakka River State Park.** 17 mi E on FL 72. Approx 28,900 acres encompassing one of country's outstanding wildlife areas and breeding grounds. More than 200 species of birds have been identified in the park's diverse habitats. Turkeys, deer, raccoons and many other animals inhabit the park. Birdwalk along lakeshore; bicycles. Tours of park by boat and tram (res advised). No swimming. Fishing in river and lakes, boat rentals. Picnicking at 4 areas, concession. Vacation cottages, tent & trailer sites (hookups, dump station). Standard hrs, fees. Phone 361-6511.

8. **Beaches.** There are 13 public beaches in Sarasota county, including Siesta, Lido and Turtle. Longboat Key (see) reached via John Ringling Blvd (FL 780) to St Armands Key, then N on FL 789; 12 mi of beach on Gulf, fishing in surf, from bridges, docks, fishing pier, picnic area. Siesta Key (see), W on Siesta Bridge, S on FL 789. Lido Beach (see), on Lido Key, W on FL 780, then S on Ben Franklin Dr.

9. **Boating.** Cruising, sailing, outboarding in Sarasota Bay and the Gulf of Mexico. Bayfront municipal marina and Island Park, foot of Main St; marinas at frequent intervals along both city and island shores.

10. *Le Barge* **Cruises.** Leaves from dock at Marina Jack on US 41. Afternoon cruises (2 hrs) aboard the *Le Barge*, includes trips around the bird sanctuary, Mangrove Islands and the Keys; also sunset entertainment cruises; galley serves fresh seafood and sandwiches. (Daily; off season, daily exc Mon) Phone 366-6116. ¢¢¢¢–¢¢¢¢¢

(For further information contact the Convention and Visitors Bureau, 655 N Tamiami Trail, 34236; 957-1877 or 800/522-9799.)

Annual Events

Chrysler Cup. Senior men's Professional Golf Assn, 72-hole championship. Late Feb.

Medieval Fair. Ringling Museum of Art (see #1). Re-creates medieval times; theater, equestrian display; entertainment includes singers and dancers, archers, jesters. Early Mar.

Sarasota Jazz Festival. Van Wezel Performing Arts Hall. 1 wk early Apr.

Sailor Circus. High school campus. Sarasota school students in full circus program. Early Apr.

Sarasota Music Festival. Florida West Coast Symphony Center, on bayfront. Internationally renowned guest artists perform with festival chamber and symphony orchestras at the Van Wezel Performing Arts Hall. Contact 709 N Tamiami Trail, 34236; 953-4252. June.

Sarasota Sailing Squadron Labor Day Regatta. Largest one-design regatta held on the Florida suncoast. Two days of racing. Phone 388-2355. Wkend before Labor Day.

Seasonal Events

Water-ski shows. Bayfront municipal marina. Sun, Jan–Mar.

Sarasota Opera Association. Sarasota Opera House. Contact 61 N Pineapple Ave, 34236-5716; 953-7030 or 366-8450. Early Feb–Mar.

Professional baseball. Ed Smith Sports Complex, 12th St & Tuttle Ave. Chicago White Sox spring training, early Mar–early Apr; phone 366-8451. Florida Winter Instructional League, mid-Sept–Oct. Gulf Coast League, June–Aug.

The Players of Sarasota. Community theater, US 41 & 9th St. Musicals, comedies, dramas. Phone 365-2494. Sept–June.

Asolo Theatre Company. Asolo Center for the Performing Arts, 5555 N Tamiami Trail, adj to Ringling Museum of Art. Professional Equity company presents 7–8 plays. Evening & matinee performances; free tours. For schedule contact 5555 N Tamiami Trail, 34243; 351-8000. Sept–June.

Concert Series. Van Wezel Performing Arts Hall, 777 N Tamiami Trail. Varied programs include concerts, films, lectures, plays, ballet. Contact PO Box 699, 34236; 953-3366. Oct–June.

(See Bradenton, Longboat Key & Lido Beach, Siesta Key, Venice)

Motels

★★**BEST WESTERN MIDTOWN.** *1425 S Tamiami Trail (34239). 813/955-9841; FAX 813/954-8948.* 100 rms, 2–3 story. Feb–Apr: S, D $88–$98; each addl $6; under 18 free; wkly rates May–Jan; lower rates rest of yr. Crib free. TV; cable. Heated pool. Complimentary continental bkfst, coffee. Ck-out 11 am. Airport transportation avail. Exercise equipt; weight machine, bicycle. Cr cds: A, C, D, DS, ER, MC, V.

[D] [≈] [ⅈ] [⊘] [◎] [SC]

✔★**COMFORT INN.** *4800 N Tamiami Trail (34234), near Sarasota-Bradenton Airport. 813/355-7091; FAX 813/359-1639.* 73 rms, 2 story, 16 kit. units. Feb–Mar: S $70–$90; D $75–$95; kits. $105–$110; under 12 free; lower rates rest of yr. Crib free. Pet accepted, some restrictions; $5. TV; cable. Heated pool; whirlpool. Complimentary continental bkfst, coffee. Restaurant nearby. Ck-out 11 am. Coin lndry. Airport transportation avail. Cr cds: A, C, D, DS, ER, MC, V, JCB.

[D] [P] [≈] [✕] [⊘] [◎] [SC]

★★**DAYS INN.** *6600 S Tamiami Trail (34231). 813/924-4900; FAX 813/923-7774.* 132 rms, 4 story. Jan–Apr: S $92; D $99; lower rates rest of yr. Crib free. Pet accepted; $5. TV; cable. Pool; whirlpool. Complimentary coffee in lobby. Restaurant adj open 24 hrs. Bar 5:30–8:30 pm, closed Sun. Ck-out 11 am. Coin lndry. Meeting rm. Valet serv. Cr cds: A, C, D, DS, MC, V.

[D] [P] [≈] [⊘] [◎] [SC]

★★**HAMPTON INN-SARASOTA AIRPORT.** *5000 N Tamiami Trail (34234), near Sarasota-Bradenton Airport. 813/351-7734; FAX 813/351-8820.* 97 rms, 3 story. Jan–mid-Apr: S $83–$87; D $93–$97; under 18 free; golf, dinner theater plans; lower rates rest of yr. Crib free. TV; cable. Heated pool. Complimentary continental bkfst, coffee. Restaurant nearby. Ck-out 11 am. Coin lndry. Meeting rm. Free airport transportation. Exercise equipt; weight machine, bicycle. Cr cds: A, C, D, DS, MC, V.

[D] [≈] [ⅈ] [✕] [⊘] [◎] [SC]

★★**HOLIDAY INN-AIRPORT/MARINA.** *7150 N Tamiami Trail (34243), near Sarasota-Bradenton Airport. 813/355-2781; FAX 813/355-1605.* 177 rms, 2 story. Jan–early Apr: S $68–$78; D $74–$84; each addl $8; suites $100–$108; under 18 free; lower rates rest of yr. Crib free. Pet accepted. TV; cable. Pool; poolside serv. Restaurant 7 am–10 pm. Rm serv. Bar. Ck-out 11 am. Coin lndry. Meeting rms. Bellhops. Valet serv. Free airport transportation. Marina; dockage. Cr cds: A, C, D, DS, MC, V, JCB.

[D] [P] [≈] [✕] [⊘] [◎] [SC]

★★**HOLIDAY INN SARASOTA SOUTH/VENICE.** *(1660 S Tamiami Trail, Osprey 34229) S on US 41. 813/966-2121; FAX 813/966-1124.* 148 rms, 2 story, 18 kits. Mid-Jan–mid Apr: S $82–$108; D $88–$108; kit. units $94–$104; under 18 free; lower rates rest of yr. Crib free. TV; cable. Heated pool; poolside serv. Restaurant 6:30 am–2 pm, 5:30–10 pm. Rm serv. Bar 4 pm–1 am; entertainment Wed, Fri & Sat, dancing exc Sun. Ck-out noon. Coin lndry. Meeting rms. Bellhops. Sundries. Gift shop. Exercise equipt; weights, bicycles, sauna. Cr cds: A, C, D, DS, MC, V, JCB.

[D] [≈] [ⅈ] [⊘] [◎] [SC]

✔★**ISLANDER INN.** *1725 Stickney Point Rd (34231), at Siesta Key Bridge. 813/923-5426; FAX 813/922-0841.* 15 kit. units, 2 story. S, D $78; each addl $8; wkly, monthly rates. TV; cable. Whirlpool, sauna. Restaurant nearby. Ck-out 10:30 am. Coin lndry. Near gulf. Cr cds: DS, MC, V.

[◎] [SC]

Motor Hotel

★★**WELLESLEY INN.** *1803 N Tamiami Trail (34234), near Sarasota-Bradenton Airport. 813/366-5128; res: 800/444-8888; FAX 813/953-4322.* 106 rms, 4 story, 13 suites. Late Dec–early May: S $90; D $95; each addl $15; suites $140; under 18 free; lower rates rest of yr. Crib $5. TV. Heated pool. Complimentary continental bkfst, coffee. Restaurant nearby. Ck-out 11 am. Valet serv. Free airport transportation. Refrigerator, wet bar in suites. Cr cds: A, C, D, DS, ER, MC, V.

[D] [≈] [✕] [⊘] [◎] [SC]

Hotel

★★★**HYATT.** *1000 Blvd of the Arts (34236), on Sarasota Bay. 813/366-9000; FAX 813/952-1987.* 297 rms, 11 story. Late Jan–Apr: S $155–$180; D $180–$205; each addl $25; 1–2-bedrm suites $300–$625; under 18 free; wkend rates in season; lower rates rest of yr. Crib free. TV; cable. Heated pool; poolside serv. Restaurant 6:30 am–midnight. Bar. Ck-out noon. Convention facilities. Concierge. Gift shop. Valet parking. Free airport transportation. Golf privileges, greens fee $37.50 (incl cart). Exercise equipt; weights, treadmill, bicycles. Some bathrm phones. Many balconies. Marina; dockage. View of bay. Cr cds: A, C, D, DS, ER, MC, V, JCB.

[D] [⊞] [≈] [ⅈ] [⊘] [◎] [SC]

Inn

✔★**HARDISTY INN ON THE BAY.** *621 Gulfstream Ave (34236). 813/955-4683.* 4 rms, 2 with bath, 2 story. Jan–May: S, D $75–$85; lower rates rest of yr. Adults preferred. TV; cable. Complimentary continental bkfst (rm serv on request), coffee & tea/sherry. Restaurant nearby. Ck-out 11 am, ck-in 3 pm. Tennis privileges. Picnic table, grill. On bay. Inn (1940) built of cypress. Totally nonsmoking. No cr cds accepted.

[P] [⊘] [◎]

Cottage Colony

★★**TIMBERWOODS VACATION VILLAS.** *7964 Timberwood Circle (34238), I-75 exit 37, 3 mi W to Beneva Rd, then 2 mi S. 813/923-4966; res: 800/824-5444; FAX 813/924-3109.* 112 kit. villas. Jan–mid-Apr (1-wk min): $770/wk; lower rates rest of yr. Crib $20/wk. TV; cable. Heated pool; whirlpool. Restaurant nearby. Ck-out 10 am. Meeting rms. Lighted tennis. Rec rm. Lawn games. Lndry facilities in each villa. Picnic tables, grills. Cr cds: A, DS, ER, MC, V.

[D] [P] [≈] [◎]

Restaurants

★★**ALEXANDER'S.** *5252 S Tamiami Trail. 813/925-1498.* Hrs: 11:30 am–2:30 pm, 5:30–8:30; Fri, Sat to 9 pm. Closed Sun; major hols. Res accepted. Continental. Bar. Semi-a la carte: lunch $6.50–$11.95, dinner $12–$18. Specializes in seafood, beef, duck. Deli, bakery, meat market, gourmet market. In shopping mall along riverfront. Cr cds: MC, V.

★★★**BIJOU CAFE.** *1287 1st St. 813/366-8111.* Hrs: 11:30 am–2 pm, 5:30–10 pm; Sat, Sun from 5:30 pm. Closed some major hols. Res accepted. Continental menu. Beer. Wine list. Semi-a la carte: lunch $4.50–$14, dinner $10–$21. Child's meals. Specializes in seafood, roast duck, Black Angus beef, lamb chops. Own pastries. Parking. Across from Sarasota Opera House. Cr cds: C, D, MC, V.

[D]

★★**BRENTON REEF.** *3808 N Tamiami Trail. 813/355-8553.* Hrs: 11:30 am–10 pm; Fri, Sat to 11 pm; early-bird dinner Mon–Fri 4–6 pm. Res accepted. Bar to 1 am. Semi-a la carte: lunch $3.95–$8.95, dinner $6.95–$24.95. Child's meals. Specializes in hand-carved prime rib, fresh seafood, char-grilled steak. Salad bar. Own desserts. Parking. Outdoor dining. Cape Cod/New England atmosphere. Cr cds: A, DS, MC, V.

D

✔ ★ ★**CAFE OF THE ARTS.** *5230 N Tamiami Trail. 813/351-4304.* Hrs: 8 am–9 pm; Sun brunch 9 am–3 pm. Closed Jan 1, Dec 25. Res accepted. French, Amer menu. Wine, beer. Semi-a la carte: bkfst $3.95–$5.95, lunch $4.50–$6.95, dinner $11.95–$15. Sun brunch $3.95–$7.95. Child's meals. Specializes in regional French cuisine. Parking. Own pastries. Bakery on premises. Cr cds: MC, V.

D

✔ ★**CARAGIULO'S.** *69 S Palm Ave. 813/951-0866.* Hrs: 11 am–10 pm; Fri to 11 pm; Sat noon–11 pm; Sun 5–9 pm. Closed some major hols. Italian menu. Wine, beer. Semi-a la carte: lunch, dinner $5.25–$13.95. Specialties: shrimp Fra Diavolo, gourmet pizza. Outdoor dining. In theater/art district. Cr cds: A, C, D, DS, MC, V.

D

★ ★**CARMICHAEL'S.** *1213 N Palm Ave. 813/951-1771.* Hrs: noon–2:30 pm, 5:30–10:30 pm. Closed Dec 25. Res accepted. Beer. Wine list. Semi-a la carte: lunch $6.95–$8.95, dinner $14.95–$19.95. Child's meals. Specializes in seafood, game, lamb, aged beef. Own baking, ice cream. Outdoor dining. In restored Florida cottage. Cr cds: A, MC, V.

★ ★**CHOPHOUSE GRILLE.** *214 Sarasota Quay (US 41). 813/951-2467.* Hrs: 4:30–10 pm; Fri, Sat to 11 pm; early-bird dinner 4:30–6 pm; Sun brunch 10 am–2 pm. Res accepted. Bar. Extensive wine list. Semi-a la carte: dinner $14.95–$24.95. Sun brunch $14.95. Child's meals. Specializes in oak-grilled aged meats, seafood, veal, pasta. Valet parking. Outdoor dining. English club atmosphere; polished teakwood. Cr cds: A, C, D, MC, V.

D

★ ★**COASTERS.** *1500 Stickney Point Rd, at Boatyard Shopping Village. 813/923-4848.* Hrs: 11:30 am–midnight. Closed Thanksgiving, Dec 25. Bar. Semi-a la carte: lunch $4.95–$8.95, dinner $5.50–$15.95. Child's meals. Specializes in seafood, grilled selections, pasta. Own desserts. Entertainment. Valet parking. Outdoor patio dining. Bistro atmosphere; views of Intracoastal Waterway. Cr cds: A, C, D, DS, MC, V.

D

✔ ★ ★**HILLVIEW GRILL.** *1920 Hillview St. 813/952-0045.* Hrs: 11 am–2:30 pm, 5:30–10 pm; Sat, Sun from 5:30 pm. Closed some major hols; also Sun May–Sept. Res accepted. Bar. Semi-a la carte: lunch $3.50–$7.25, dinner $6.95–$15. Specializes in fresh grilled seafood, chicken, beef, pork. Cr cds: A, MC, V.

D

★ ★**JO-TO JAPANESE STEAK HOUSE.** *7971 N Tamiami Trail. 813/351-4677.* Hrs: 5–10 pm; Fri, Sat to 11 pm. Closed Thanksgiving. Res accepted. Japanese menu. Bar. Semi-a la carte: dinner $9.95–$18.95. Specializes in sushi, authentic Japanese cuisine. Parking. Tableside cooking. Oriental decor. Cr cds: A, MC, V.

D

★ ★**MARINA JACK.** *Marina Plaza, on Island Park Pier. 813/365-4232.* Hrs: 11:45 am–10 pm. Closed Dec 25. Res accepted. Continental menu. Bar to 1 am. Wine list. Semi-a la carte: lunch $4.25–$9.95, dinner $8.25–$21. Child's meals. Specializes in fresh seafood, veal, beef, poultry, pasta. Pianist, soloist Wed–Sun. Valet parking. On bay. Lunch & dinner cruises avail (see MARINA JACK II DINNER BOAT, Unrated Dining). Cr cds: MC, V.

D

★ ★**MICHAEL'S ON EAST.** *1212 East Ave S, in Midtown Plaza. 813/366-0007.* Hrs: 11:30 am–2 pm, 5–10 pm; Fri, Sat 5–11 pm; Sun 5–10 pm. Res accepted. Bar. Wine cellar. A la carte entrees: lunch $4.95–$12.95. Semi-a la carte: dinner $10.95–$23. Child's meals. Specializes in fresh seafood, pasta, veal. Own baking, desserts. Piano

lounge. Valet parking. Contemporary decor; etched-glass windows. Cr cds: A, D, MC, V.

D

★ ★ ★**MIRAMAR AT THE QUAY.** *Tamiami trail (US 41) & 3rd St. 813/954-3332.* Hrs: 11:30 am–10 pm; Fri, Sat to 11 pm; early-bird dinner 4–6 pm. Res accepted. Spanish, Amer menu. Bar. Semi-a la carte: lunch $3.25–$7.95, dinner $8.95–$17.95. Child's meals. Specializes in seafood, chicken, lamb, paella. Entertainment Wed–Sun evenings. Valet parking. Outdoor dining. Contemporary dining with exceptional view of bay. Cr cds: A, C, D, MC, V.

✔ ★ ★ ★**PRIMO.** *8076 N Tamiami Trail. 813/359-3690.* Hrs: 4–10 pm. Closed Easter, Thanksgiving, Dec 25. Res accepted. Italian menu. Bar. Wine list. Semi-a la carte: dinner $4.95–$15.50. Child's meals. Specializes in pasta, veal, fresh seafood. Own baking, desserts. Entertainment. Parking. Cr cds: DS, MC, V.

D

★ ★ ★**ROYAL MARINE ROOM.** *2 N Tamiami Trail, Sarasota Tower, 11th floor. 813/954-7555.* Hrs: 11:30 am–2:30 pm, 5–10 pm; Sat from 5 pm; Sun to 9 pm; Sun brunch 10:30 am–2:30 pm. Res accepted; required Sat. Continental menu. Bar. Wine list. A la carte entrees: lunch $4.95–$12.95, dinner $5.95–$28.95. Buffet: Sun dinner $13.95. Sun brunch $13.95. Specializes in seafood, rack of lamb. Jazz pianist Tues–Fri; 3-piece combo Fri–Sun. Valet parking. Overlooks Sarasota Bay, Gulf of Mexico. Cr cds: DS, MC, V.

D **SC**

✔ ★**SUGAR AND SPICE.** *1850 S Tamiami Trail. 813/953-3340.* Hrs: 11 am–10 pm. Closed Sun; major hols. Semi-a la carte: lunch, dinner $2–$8.75. Child's meals. Specializes in Amish-style dishes. Own desserts. Parking. Country-Amish decor; Amish craftwork. Totally non-smoking. Cr cds: MC, V.

D

Unrated Dining Spot

MARINA JACK II DINNER BOAT. *(See Marina Jack Restaurant) 813/366-9255.* Hrs: noon seating (Jan–May) & 7:30 pm seating (all-yr). Closed Sept; Dec 25. Res required. Continental menu. Bar. Semi-a la carte: lunch $6.95–$9.25 (purchase of 1 lunch entree plus $4 boat fare), dinner from $9.50 (purchase of 1 dinner entree plus $6 boat fare). Specializes in prime rib, seafood. Guitarist during dinner tours. Parking. Dine while cruising aboard 100-ft double-decked sternwheeler, a replica of the steam sternwheel towboat. Excellent view of Sarasota's waterfront & landmarks. Cr cds: MC, V.

D

Sebring (D-4)

Founded: 1912 **Pop:** 8,900 **Elev:** 131 ft **Area code:** 813

With sandy ridge country for citrus, mucklands for vegetables and flowers, and flatlands for cattle, Sebring's (SEE-bring) economy relies upon agriculture, light industry and some tourism. The city has taken over the 2,300 acres that once comprised Hendricks Field Air Force Base and developed them as the Sebring International Raceway, Airport and Industrial Park. The city encircles 3,200-acre Lake Jackson, with 46,000-acre Lake Istokpoga to the southeast.

What to See and Do

Highlands Hammock State Park. 2½ mi W off US 27/98, on FL 634. Approx 4,600 acres of hardwood hammock and cabbage palms with many orchids and air plants. An outstanding nature park with museum, 5 miles of foot trails, 4 miles of scenic drive, 1–1½-hour conducted wildlife tours by tram. Nature trails; bicycle rentals.

Picnic areas (grills, shelters). Camping (hookups, dump station). Standard hrs, fees. Phone 385-0011.

(For further information contact the Chamber of Commerce, 309 S Circle, 33870; 385-8448.)

Annual Event

Sebring 12-Hour Endurance Race. Oldest road race in America. Phone 655-1442. Mid-Mar.

(See Lake Placid)

Motels

(Higher rates Sebring Road Race)

★**ECONO LODGE.** *(2511 US 27 S, Avon Park 33825)* Approx 10 mi N on US 27. 813/453-2000; FAX 813/453-0820. 58 rms, 2 story, 10 kits. Jan–Apr: S $64.95; D $69.95; each addl $5; under 12 free; wkly rates; lower rates rest of yr. Crib free. TV. Pool. Complimentary coffee. Ck-out 11 am. Coin lndry. On Lake Glenada. Cr cds: A, C, D, DS, MC, V.

★ ★ **HOLIDAY INN.** 6525 US 27N (33870). 813/385-4500; FAX 813/382-4793. 148 rms, 2 story. Jan–mid-Apr: S $55–$80; D $60–$85; each addl $5; under 19 free; wkend rates; higher rates special events (4-day min); lower rates rest of yr. Crib free. TV; cable. Pool; wading pool, poolside serv. Restaurant 6:30 am–2 pm, 5–10 pm. Rm serv. Bar 11–1:30 am; entertainment Fri & Sat. Ck-out noon. Coin lndry. Meeting rms. Bellhops. Valet serv. Exercise equipt; weights, bicycles, sauna. Lawn games. Cr cds: A, C, D, DS, MC, V, JCB.

✔ ★**LAKE BRENTWOOD.** *(2060 US 27 N, Avon Park 33825)* Approx 10 mi N on US 27. 813/453-4358. 14 rms, 10 kits. Mid-Dec–Apr: S $36–$48; D $42–$52; each addl $5; kit. units $5 addl; under 12 free; wkly rates; lower rates rest of yr. Crib $5. TV. Coffee in rms. Ck-out 10 am. Coin lndry. 18-hole golf privileges. Lawn games. Picnic tables, grills. On lake; boats avail. Cr cds: A, C, D, DS, MC, V.

Motor Hotel

★ ★ **INN ON THE LAKES.** 3100 Gulfview Rd (33872), at US 27. 813/471-9400; res: 800/531-LAKE; FAX 813/471-9400, ext 195. 161 rms, 3 story, 14 suites. Jan–mid-Apr: S, D $49–$125; suites $125; wkly, monthly rates; golf, fishing plans; higher rates 12 Hours of Sebring; lower rates rest of yr. Crib free. TV; cable. Pool; poolside serv. Restaurant 6:30 am–11 pm. Rm serv. Bar noon–11 pm; entertainment Fri, Sat. Ck-out noon. Coin lndry. Meeting rms. Bellhops. Sundries. Gift shop. Barber, beauty shop. Valet serv. 18-hole golf privileges, greens fee $30, putting green, driving range. Health club privileges. Refrigerator in suites. Overlooks Little Lake Jackson. Cr cds: A, C, D, DS, MC, V.

Siesta Key (D-3)

Pop: 7,772 **Elev:** 10 ft **Area code:** 813 **Zip:** 34242

Back in 1907, Harry L. Higel and Captain Louis Roberts launched an advertising campaign to draw vacationers to "the prettiest spot in the world." Although the claim may be disputed, Siesta Key has been hailed as "the island paradise in the Gulf of Mexico," and Crescent Beach has been rated as one of the top three beaches in the world, along with Waikiki and the French Riviera. Shell hunters and anglers usually have

great success here. With close proximity to Sarasota and its attractions, Siesta Key is a good base from which to take in the sights.

(See Bradenton, Sarasota, Venice)

Motels

★**BEST WESTERN SIESTA BEACH RESORT.** 5311 Ocean Blvd. 813/349-3211; FAX 813/349-7915. 53 units, 2 story, 38 kits. Mid-Jan–Apr: S, D $99–$195; kit. units $135–$145; under 12 free; wkly rates; wkend packages off-season; lower rates rest of yr. TV; cable. Pool; whirlpool. Restaurant nearby. Ck-out 11 am. Picnic tables. Opp Gulf. Cr cds: A, C, D, DS, ER, MC, V, JCB.

★ ★**CRESCENT VIEW BEACH CLUB.** 6512 Midnight Pass Rd. 813/349-2000; res: 800/344-7171. 27 kit. units, 2–4 story. Mid-Dec–early May: kit. units $115–$250; pkg plans; lower rates rest of yr. Crib $12. TV; cable. Heated pool; whirlpool. Complimentary coffee in lobby. Restaurant opp 11 am–11 pm. Ck-out 11 am. Lndry facilities avail. Balconies. Picnic tables, grills. On beach. Cr cds: A, C, D, DS, ER, MC, V.

★ ★**TROPICAL SHORES INN.** 6717 Sarasea Circle, S of Stickney Point Bridge. 813/349-3330; res: 800/235-3493; FAX 813/346-0025. 28 kit. units, 2 motel units, 1–2 story. Late Jan–mid-May: motel units from $125; kits. from $149; each addl $7; suites $175–$245; wkly rates; lower rates rest of yr. Crib free. TV; cable. Heated pool. Playground. Restaurant nearby. Ck-out 10 am. Lawn games. Picnic tables, grills. Cr cds: A, MC, V.

Restaurants

★ ★ ★**THE INN BETWEEN.** 431 Beach Rd, 2 mi N of Stickney Point Bridge. 813/349-7117. Hrs: 5:30–10 pm; early-bird dinner 5–6:30 pm. Closed Sun in summer. Res accepted. Continental, French menu. Bar to 2 am. Semi-a la carte: dinner $9.95–$18.95. Specialties: veal scaloppini, duck with peaches, fresh seafood. Entertainment Tues–Sat. Parking. European ambience; garden room, art collection. Cr cds: MC, V.

D

★ ★ ★**OPHELIA'S ON THE BAY.** 9105 Midnight Pass Rd, 3 mi S of Stickney Point Bridge. 813/349-2212 or -3776. Hrs: 11:30 am–3 pm, 4–10 pm; Sun brunch 11 am–3 pm. Res accepted. Continental menu. Bar. Wine list. Semi-a la carte: lunch $4.95–$9.95, dinner $11.95–$23.95. Sun brunch $9.95. Child's meals. Specialties: fresh seafood, duckling. Valet parking. Outdoor dining. On waterfront; dockage. Cr cds: A, C, D, DS, MC, V.

D

★ ★ ★**SUMMERHOUSE.** 6101 Midnight Pass Rd, ½ mi N of Stickney Point Bridge. 813/349-1100. Hrs: 5–10 pm; Sun to 9 pm. Res accepted. Bar to 12:30 am. Wine cellar. Semi-a la carte: dinner $14–$23. Child's meals. Specializes in fresh seafood, lamb, duck. Own baking, desserts. Band exc Sun. Valet parking. Two-story, glass-walled rm overlooks tropical garden. Art collection. Cr cds: D, DS, MC, V.

D

Silver Springs (B-3)

Pop: 6,421 **Elev:** 98 ft **Area code:** 904

Nearly two million people come to this town each year, principally to see the springs, one of the state's top attractions. This is lake, horse and cattle country, and a Ranger District office of the Ocala National Forest (see OCALA) is located here.

What to See and Do

1. Silver Springs-Source of the Silver River. On FL 40. This 350-acre multi-theme nature park and national landmark includes the main spring from which flows more than one-half billion gallons of water every 24 hours. Estimated to be 100,000 years old, the spring has one large opening through which water, filtered through limestone, surges to the surface from a 65-foot by 12-foot cavern. Four different 30-minute rides let visitors view the area: the famous glass-bottom boats and a jungle cruise pass by 14 springs, various plant and fish species, alligators, waterfowl and exotic wildlife; Lost River Voyage, an environmental boat ride, lets visitors experience Florida as it was 1,000 years ago; and jeep safari trams take people through a 35-acre rainforest where 30 different species of animals live. In addition, the surrounding park includes Doolittle's Petting Zoo, where deer, sheep, goats, llamas and other baby animals can be hand-fed; and animal shows "Creature Feature," "Amazing Pets" and "Reptiles of the World." Strollers, wheelchairs avail. (Daily) Phone 236-2121 or 800/234-7458. ¢¢¢¢

2. Wild Waters. On FL 40. Water park including 450,000-gallon wave pool, 8 flume rides, Water Bonanza play area; miniature golf (fee), arcades (fee); 2 volleyball courts; sun decks, picnic area. (Apr–Sept, daily) Phone 236-2121 or 800/234-7458. ¢¢¢¢

(For further information on the area contact the Ocala/Marion County Chamber of Commerce, 110 E Silver Springs Blvd, PO Box 1210, Ocala 32678; 629-8051.)

(See Ocala)

Motels

 ★**DAYS INN OCALA EAST.** *5001 E Silver Springs Blvd (FL 40) (34488).* 904/236-2891. 56 rms, 2 story. Feb–Apr, mid-June–early Sept: S $30–$40; D $35–$45; each addl $5; under 18 free; higher rates special events; lower rates rest of yr. Crib free. Pet accepted. TV; cable. Pool. Playground. Complimentary coffee in lobby. Restaurant adj 7 am–9 pm. Ck-out 11 am. Coin lndry. Ocala National Forest nearby. Cr cds: A, C, D, DS, MC, V, JCB.

★★**HOLIDAY INN.** *(PO Box 156, 34489)* 5751 Silver Springs Blvd (FL 40). 904/236-2575; FAX 904/236-2575, ext 163. 103 rms, 2 story. Feb–Apr, June–Aug: S, D $49–$60; under 18 free; higher rates hols; lower rates rest of yr. Crib free. TV; cable. Pool; wading pool, poolside serv. Restaurant open 24 hrs. Rm serv. Bar 5–10 pm, closed Sun–Thurs. Ck-out noon. Meeting rms. Bellhops. Valet serv. Fishing guides. Kennels. Cr cds: A, C, D, DS, MC, V, JCB.

★**HOWARD JOHNSON.** *(PO Box 475, 34489)* 5565 E Silver Springs Blvd (FL 40). 904/236-2616; FAX 904/236-1941. 40 rms, 2 story. Feb–Mar & June–Aug: S $40–$45; D $45–$50; each addl $5; under 18 free; higher rates: races, hols, football wkends, special events; lower rates rest of yr. Crib free. TV; cable. Pool. Playground. Restaurant adj 7 am–10 pm. Ck-out noon. Lawn games. Some refrigerators. Patios, balconies. Cr cds: A, C, D, DS, MC, V, JCB.

★**SUN PLAZA.** *(PO Box 216, 34489)* 5461 E Silver Springs Blvd (FL 40). 904/236-2343. 47 rms, 9 kits. Late Dec–Apr, June–Labor Day: S $28; D $30–$40; each addl $4–$5; kit. units $35–$40; lower rates rest of yr. Crib free. Pet accepted; $4. TV. Pool. Playground. Restaurant adj 6 am–11 pm. Ck-out 11 am. Lawn games. Picnic tables, grill. Cr cds: A, C, D, DS, MC, V.

Starke (A-3)

Settled: 1857 **Pop:** 5,226 **Elev:** 160 ft **Area code:** 904 **Zip:** 32091

The pine forests that surround Starke have been the source for turpentine stores since the middle of the 18th century. Extensive mining of ilmenite (ore of iron and titanium) and the winter strawberry crop are also mainstays of the economy.

What to See and Do

1. Camp Blanding Museum. 10 mi E on FL 16. Former training center for nine complete US Army divisions during World War II; museum is refurbished barracks building with photo exhibits and artifacts honoring history of the base and those who trained here. Florida Regimental Memorial is a statue and marble edifice listing Floridians who lost their lives in WWII. Memorial Park is a large area with monuments, displays of weapons and vehicles surrounding a lagoon; fountain and picnic area. (Tues–Fri, also Sat & Sun afternoons; closed Jan 1, Easter, Dec 25) Phone 533-3196. **Free.**

2. Mike Roess Gold Head Branch State Park. 13 mi S on FL 100 to Keystone Heights, then 6 mi NE on FL 21. This park has several lakes and a wildlife refuge on its approx 1,500 acres; ravine with a nature trail and an old mill site. Swimming, bathhouse; fishing; canoes (rentals). Bicycle rentals. Picnicking. Camping (dump station), family vacation cottages. Standard hrs, fees. Phone 473-4701.

(For further information contact the Starke–Bradford County Chamber of Commerce, 202 S Walnut, PO Box 576; 964-5278.)

Annual Event

Bradford County Fair. 5 days Apr.

(See Gainesville)

Motels

★**BEST WESTERN.** *1290 N Temple Ave (US 301).* 904/964-6744. 53 rms, 2 story. S $38–$48; D $45–$55; under 12 free; higher rates special events. Crib free. Pet accepted, some restrictions. TV; cable. Pool. Complimentary continental bkfst, coffee. Restaurant nearby. Ck-out 11 am. Some refrigerators. Cr cds: A, C, D, DS, MC, V.

★**DAYS INN.** *1101 N Temple Ave.* 904/964-7600; FAX 904/964-5201. 100 rms, 2 story. S $47; D $52; each addl $5; under 16 free; higher rates special events. Crib free. Pet accepted; $3. TV; cable. Pool. Restaurant open 24 hrs. Bar from 4 pm. Ck-out 11 am. Coin lndry. Meeting rms. Some refrigerators. Cr cds: A, D, DS, MC, V.

Stuart (D-5)

Pop: 11,936 **Elev:** 13 ft **Area code:** 407

Stuart did not become part of Henry Morrison Flagler's Gold Coast development in the 1890s because the pineapple growers of this area vehemently objected to a railroad going through their lands. Today, the town attracts many fishing enthusiasts and boaters. The St Lucie and Indian rivers meet in Stuart and together they flow through the St Lucie Inlet into the ocean. The bridges and causeways around the town connect Stuart to the attractions and beaches of Hutchinson Island.

What to See and Do

1. **Gilbert's Bar House of Refuge.** 5 mi E on Ocean Blvd to 301 SE MacArthur Blvd on Hutchinson Island, entrance through Indian River Plantation. Originally a US Life Saving Station, now a historic site restored to the late 1800s; aquarium. (Daily exc Mon; closed hols) Phone 225-1875. ¢

2. **Elliott Museum.** 825 NE Ocean Blvd, Hutchinson Island. Gracious Living Wing; antique autos; shell collection; Seminole artifacts; country store; Americana shops; contemporary art gallery. (Daily; closed major hols) Phone 225-1961. ¢¢

(For further information contact the Stuart/Martin County Chamber of Commerce, 1650 S Kanner Hwy, 34994; 287-1011.)

Annual Event

Martin County Fair. Early Mar.

(See Fort Pierce, Jensen Beach, Jupiter)

Motels

★ ★ ★**HOLIDAY INN-DOWNTOWN.** *1209 S Federal Hwy (US 1) (34994).* 407/287-6200; FAX 407/287-6200, ext 100. 119 rms, 2 story. Feb–Mar: S, D $80–$88; each addl $8; under 19 free; varied lower rates rest of yr. Crib free. TV; cable. Pool. Restaurant 6:30 am–2 pm, 5–10 pm. Rm serv. Bar. Ck-out noon. Coin lndry. Meeting rms. Free local airport transportation. Exercise equipt; weight machines, bicycles, sauna. Ocean beach privileges. Cr cds: A, C, D, DS, MC, V, JCB.

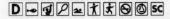

★**HOWARD JOHNSON.** *950 S Federal Hwy (US 1) (34994).* 407/287-3171. 82 rms, 2 story. Jan–Feb: S, D $75–$90; under 18 free; lower rates rest of yr. Crib free. TV; cable. Pool. Restaurant 7 am–11 pm. Rm serv. Bar to 1 am. Ck-out noon. Coin lndry. Meeting rms. Sundries. Cr cds: A, C, D, DS, ER, MC, V, JCB.

Resort

★ ★ ★ ★**INDIAN RIVER PLANTATION BEACH RESORT.** *(555 NE Ocean Blvd, Hutchinson Island 34996)* 407/225-3700; res: 800/444-3389; FAX 407/225-0003. 200 hotel units, 4 story, 107 apts (1–2 bedrm). Feb–Mar: S, D $195; each addl $15; suites $285–$300; 1–2 bedrm kit. units $195–$395; under 18 free; long term rates; varied lower rates rest of yr. Crib free. TV; cable, in-rm movies. 4 pools, heated; poolside serv. Playground. Supervised child's activities. Dining rm 6:30 am–11 pm (also see SCALAWAGS). Rm serv 24 hrs. Box lunches, snack bars. Picnics. Bar. Ck-out 11 am, ck-in 3 pm. Grocery. Coin lndry. Convention facilities. Valet serv. Concierge. Palm Beach Intl Airport transportation. On-site tram service. Lighted tennis, pro. 18-hole golf, pro, putting green. Private beach. Snorkeling equipt. Deep-sea fishing charters; tour boat; boat rentals. Waterskiing. Bicycles. Lawn games. Activities director. Exercise equipt; weight machine, stair machine, whirlpool. Refrigerators, wet bars. Full service marina; store. Cr cds: A, C, D, DS, ER, MC, V.

Restaurants

★ ★ ★**CAFE LA RUCHE.** *(10835 SE Federal Hwy, Hobe Sound)* 10 mi S on US 1. 407/546-2283. Hrs: 4:30–10 pm. Closed Sun; Dec 25; also June–mid-Sept. Res accepted. French, continental menu. Bar. Extensive wine list. Semi-a la carte: dinner $11.95–$24.95. Child's meals. Specialties: rack of lamb, duck framboise, Dover sole, veal rack. Pianist Fri & Sat in season. Parking. 2 dining areas; main rm French

provencial decor; Crystal Rm has oriental rug, antique crystal cabinet, crystal chandelier. Cr cds: A, MC, V.

✔ ★ ★**CHINA STAR.** *1501 S Federal Hwy (US 1).* 407/283-8378. Hrs: 11 am–10 pm; early-bird dinner 3–6:30 pm; Sun brunch to 2 pm. Res accepted. Chinese menu. Wine, beer. Complete meals: lunch $3.50–$4.25, dinner $5.50–$10.95. A la carte entrees: dinner $4.75–$12.95. Sun brunch $5.50. Specialties: Peking duck, lobster Cantonese, orange-flavored beef. Parking. Oriental decor; lacquered screens. Cr cds: A, DS, MC, V.

★ ★**FLAGLER GRILL.** *47 SW Flagler Ave.* 407/221-9517. Hrs: 5:30–9:30 pm. Closed Sun; Dec 25. Res accepted. Wine, beer. A la carte entrees: dinner $11–$17.50. Child's meals. Specialties: pecan-crusted pork tenderloin, corn-crusted yellowfin tuna. Parking. Open kitchen. Totally nonsmoking. Cr cds: A, DS, MC, V.

★ ★ ★**SCALAWAGS.** *(See Indian River Plantation Beach Resort)* 407/225-3700. Hrs: 5–11 pm. Res accepted. Continental menu. Bar to midnight; entertainment. Wine cellar. A la carte entrees: dinner $13.50–$24. Serv charge 15%. Child's meals. Specialties: grilled swordfish, rack of lamb, poached Norwegian salmon. Own baking. Valet parking. Outdoor dining. Display cooking. Overlooks marina and Indian River. Cr cds: A, C, D, DS, ER, MC, V.

Sun City Center *

Pop: 8,326 **Elev:** 50 ft **Area code:** 813
20 mi N of Bradenton (D-3) via I-75.

(For information about this area contact the Chamber of Commerce, 1651 Sun City Center Plaza, 33573; 634-8437.)

(See Bradenton, Tampa, St Petersburg)

Motels

★ ★**COMFORT INN.** *718 Cypress Village Blvd (33573),* I-75 exit 46B. 813/633-3318. 75 rms, 2 story. Jan–Apr: S $65; D $70; each addl $5; kit. units $85; under 12 free; lower rates rest of yr. Crib free. TV; cable. Pool; whirlpool. Complimentary continental bkfst. Restaurant nearby. Ck-out 11 am. Airport transportation. Golf privileges. Cr cds: A, D, DS, MC, V.

★**SUN CITY CENTER HOTEL.** *1335 Rickenbacker Drive (33573).* 813/634-3331; res: 800/237-8200 (exc FL), 800/282-8040 (FL); FAX 813/634-2053. 100 rms, 1–2 story. Dec–early May: S $63; D $68; each addl $3; under 12 free; golf plans; lower rates rest of yr. Crib free. Pet accepted, some restrictions; $10 per day. TV; cable. Pool. Restaurant 7 am–8 pm. Bar; entertainment, dancing. Ck-out 11 am. Meeting rms. Valet serv. 63-hole golf privileges, putting green. Some private patios. Some balconies. Cr cds: A, DS, MC, V.

Restaurant

✔ ★**DANNY BOYS'.** *(3808 FL 674, Ruskin)* W on FL 674, at Cypress Village Shopping Ctr. 813/633-2697. Hrs: 7 am–8:30 pm. Closed Dec 25. Res accepted. Semi-a la carte: bkfst $1.10–$5.25, lunch $2.75–$4.25, dinner $3.95–$10.25. Child's meals. Specializes in chicken, shrimp. Parking. Cr cds: A, MC, V.

Tallahassee (A-1)

Founded: 1824 **Pop:** 124,773 **Elev:** 190 ft **Area code:** 904

The capital of Florida, Tallahassee retains the grace of plantation days and the echoes of its rustic pioneer past. During the Civil War, this majestic city was the only Confederate capital east of the Mississippi not captured by Union forces. The city, as well as Leon County, are now strongly oriented toward state and local government. Lumber and wood production, food production and printing and publishing maintain its economy.

What to See and Do

1. **Historic Old Capitol.** Monroe St and Apalachee Pkwy. Restored to its 1902 grandeur, the building is now a museum, furnished with authentic period pieces and reproductions of original furniture. Historical exhibits; architectural tours (Sat mornings). (Mon–Sat, also Sun afternoons; closed Thanksgiving, Dec 25) Phone 487-1902. **Free.**

2. **State Capitol.** Duval St. At top of Tallahassee's second highest hill, the modern, 22-story capitol building towers above the city; observation level on top floor. Hourly tours (daily). Visitor information center, West Plaza (daily; closed most major hols). Phone 681-9200. **Free.**

3. **Governor's Mansion** (1957). 700 N Adams St. Tours during regular session of legislature (usually Feb–Apr, Mon, Wed & Fri, limited hrs; closed hols). Phone 488-4661. **Free.**

4. **First Presbyterian Church** (1832). Adams St & Park Ave. Florida's oldest public building in continuous use; has galleries where slaves worshiped. (Mon–Fri; closed hols) Phone 222-4504.

5. **Florida State University** (1857). (28,000 students) W Tennessee (US 90) & Copeland Sts. On a 400-acre campus with everything from two supercomputers to its own collegiate circus (see ANNUAL EVENTS). Campus tours (Mon–Fri); maps at Visitor Information Center, 100 S Woodward St; 644-3246. On campus is

   Art Gallery. Fine Arts Bldg, Copeland & W Tennessee Sts. (Sept–May, daily; rest of yr, daily exc Sun; closed university hols) Phone 644-6836. **Free.**

6. **Florida Agricultural and Mechanical University** (1887). (9,300 students) On M.L. King Blvd & Wahnish Way. On campus is the Florida Black Archives, Research Center and Museum (Mon–Fri; closed hols). Phone 599-3000 or -3020 (museum).

7. **Tallahassee Museum of History & Natural Science.** 3945 Museum Dr, on Lake Bradford; W on Orange Ave, then S on Rankin Ave. Fifty-two acres with restored 1880s Big Bend farm and 1854 plantation house; gristmill, schoolhouse, church; hands-on Discovery Center; natural habitat zoo with wild animals native to the area, including the endangered Florida panther; gopher nature trail. Visitors center. (See ANNUAL EVENTS) (Daily; closed some major hols) Sr citizen rate. Phone 575-8684. ¢¢

8. **LeMoyne Art Foundation.** 125 N Gadsden St. Exhibits feature works by Florida and Georgia artists. (Daily exc Mon; closed July 4, Dec 25–early Jan; also Aug) Phone 222-8800. **Free.**

9. **The Columns** (1830). 100 N Duval St. Moved from its original site in 1972, this three-story brick mansion once served as a bank, boarding house, doctor's office and restaurant. Restored and furnished with antiques, it now serves as office of the Chamber of Commerce. (Mon–Fri) Phone 224-8116.

10. **Museum of Florida History.** 500 S Bronough St, at Pensacola St. Contains historical artifacts and information about Florida; changing exhibits. (Daily; closed Thanksgiving, Dec 25) Phone 488-1484. **Free.**

11. **Alfred B. Maclay State Gardens.** 3540 Thomasville Rd, 5½ mi N on US 319. Planted as a private estate garden; outstanding azaleas, camellias, dogwood and others, including some rare plant species, on 308 acres; donated to state in 1953. Museum in house has interpretive display (Jan–Apr). No dogs. The Lake Hall Recreation area has swimming; fishing; boating. Nature trails & gardens. Picnicking. (Daily) Phone 487-4556. ¢¢

12. **Natural Bridge State Historic Site.** 9 mi S on US 363 to Woodville, then 6 mi E on Natural Bridge Rd. This 8-acre monument on the St Marks River marks the spot where a militia of Confederate forces (mostly young boys and old men) stopped Union troops, barring the way to Tallahassee. The battle (Mar 6, 1865) left Tallahassee as the only Confederate capital east of the Mississippi that never fell into Union hands. (See ANNUAL EVENTS) Picnicking. (Daily) Phone 925-6216 or 922-6007. **Free.**

13. **Edward Ball Wakulla Springs State Park.** 14 mi S on FL 61 to FL 267. Located in the heart of this 2,860-acre state park is one of the world's larger and deeper freshwater springs. Glass-bottomed boats allow visitors to see the entrance to the cavern 120 feet below the surface. Wildife observation boat tours encounter alligators, turtles and a variety of birds. Many fossils and artifacts of prehistoric dwellers have been found by skin divers. Facilities include swimming in season; nature trails; picnic area, snack bar, dining rm, lodge and conference center (see MOTELS), gift shop. Glass-bottom boat tour (water visibility permitting) and river boat tour (daily; fees). Standard hrs, fees. Phone 922-3633.

14. **St Marks National Wildlife Refuge.** 15 mi S on FL 363 to St Marks, then 3 mi S on County 59. A 65,000-acre refuge heavily populated with birds, deer, alligators; waterfowl in fall and winter. Freshwater fishing; saltwater boat launching. Nature and primitive walking trails. Picnicking. Visitor center (daily; closed hols). Observation decks. Golden Eagle, Golden Age, Golden Access passports accepted (see INTRODUCTION). (Daily) Phone 925-6121. Per vehicle ¢¢; Per pedestrian ¢

15. **San Marcos de Apalache State Historic Site.** 24 mi S via FL 363, on Canal St in St Marks. Site first visited by Panfilo de Narvaez in 1527 and Hernando de Soto in 1539; ruins of fort (1739); museum on site of old federal marine hospital. Picnicking. Nature trails. (Thurs–Mon) Phone 925-6216 or 922-6007. Museum ¢

16. **Apalachicola National Forest.** S via US 319. (See APALACHICOLA)

(For further information, including a tour map of the capital, contact the Tallahassee Area Visitor Center, New Capitol Bldg, West Plaza, 32302; 681-9200 or 800/628-2866.)

Annual Events

Natural Bridge Battle Reenactment. Natural Bridge State Historic Site (see #12). Reenactment of battle between Confederate and Union forces on this site. Sun nearest Mar 6.

Springtime Tallahassee. Commemorates founding of city. Parades, concerts, art shows, tours of homes and gardens and numerous other activities in various parts of city. Phone 224-5012. 3 wks late Mar–early Apr.

Flying High Circus. Florida State University (see #5). Aproximately 80 students perform in three-ring circus. Evening & matinee performances. Phone 644-4874. 2 wkends Apr.

Spring Farm Days. Tallahassee Museum of History & Natural Science (see #7). Focuses on spring activities on 1880s farm; features sheep shearing. Mid-Apr.

Summer Swamp Stomp. Tallahassee Museum of History & Natural Science (see #7). Continuous musical entertainment from bluegrass to folk and "saltwater" music. Mid-July.

North Florida Fair. Fairgrounds. Exhibits, midway. Phone 878-3247. Late Oct.

December on the Farm. Tallahassee Museum of History & Natural Science (see #7). Focuses on fall activities on 1880s farm; features syrup-making. Early Dec.

Motels

(Rates may be higher university special events)

✔ ★**BEST WESTERN PRIDE INN SUITES.** *2016 Apalachee Pkwy (32301).* 904/656-6312; FAX 904/942-4312. 78 rms, 2 story, 30 suites. S $39–$54; D $46–$59; each addl $5; suites $49–$66; wkly rates. Crib free. Pet accepted, some restrictions; $5. TV; cable. Pool. Complimentary continental bkfst. Restaurant adj 6 am–11 pm. Ck-out 11 am. Coin lndry. Meeting rms. Exercise equipt; weights, bicycles. Cr cds: A, C, D, DS, MC, V.

★★**CABOT LODGE.** *2735 N Monroe St (32303).* 904/386-8880; res: 800/223-1964 (exc FL); FAX 904/386-4254. 160 rms, 2 story. S $53–$59; D $57–$64; each addl $6; under 10 free. Crib free. TV; cable. Pool. Complimentary continental bkfst. Ck-out noon. Health club privileges. Library, fireplace; veranda overlooking pool. Cr cds: A, C, D, DS, MC, V.

★★**COURTYARD BY MARRIOTT.** *1018 Apalachee Pkwy (32301).* 904/222-8822; FAX 904/561-0354. 154 rms, 2 story. S $79; D $89; each addl $5; suites $100–$110; under 12 free; wkend rates. Crib free. TV; cable. Pool. Complimentary coffee in rms. Restaurant 6:30 am–2 pm, 5–10 pm; Fri to 2 pm; Sat & Sun 7 am–2 pm. Bar 4–11 pm. Ck-out noon. Coin lndry. Meeting rms. Valet serv. Exercise equipt; weight machine, bicycles, whirlpool. Refrigerator in suites. Balconies. Cr cds: A, C, D, DS, MC, V.

✔ ★**DAYS INN DOWNTOWN-CAPITOL CENTER.** *722 Apalachee Pkwy (32301).* 904/224-2181. 100 rms, 2 story. S $38–$43; D $48–$53; each addl $5; under 12 free; higher rates special events. Crib free. Pet accepted; $10. TV; cable. Pool. Restaurant open 24 hrs. Ck-out noon. Private patios, balconies. Cr cds: A, C, D, DS, MC, V.

★**ECONO LODGE.** *(PO Box 4131, 32315) 2681 N Monroe St.* 904/385-6155. 82 rms, 2 story. S $28; D $36; each addl $4; under 12 free. Crib free. Pet accepted, some restrictions. TV; cable. Restaurant adj open 24 hrs. Ck-out 11 am. Cr cds: A, C, D, DS, MC, V.

✔ ★**EXECUTIVE SUITE MOTOR INN.** *522 Scotty's Lane (32303).* 904/386-2121. 116 rms, 2 story. S $35–$40; D $40–$45; each addl $5; under 12 free. Crib $5. TV; cable. Pool. Complimentary continental bkfst. Restaurant opp 5–10 pm. Ck-out noon. Meeting rms. Many in-rm whirlpools. Near Tallahassee Mall. Cr cds: A, C, D, DS, ER, MC, V.

★★**LA QUINTA MOTOR INN.** *2905 N Monroe (32303).* 904/385-7172. 154 units, 3 story. S $47–$48; D $53–$55; each addl $6; under 18 free. Crib avail. Pet accepted, some restrictions. TV; cable. Pool. Complimentary continental bkfst, coffee. Restaurant adj 7 am–11 pm. Ck-out noon. Meeting rms. Cr cds: A, C, D, DS, MC, V.

★**RED ROOF INN.** *2930 N Monroe St (32303).* 904/385-7884; FAX 904/385-7884, ext 444. 109 rms, 2 story. S $32.99–$41.99; D $34.99–$41.99; each addl $6; under 18 free. Crib free. Pet accepted, some restrictions. TV. Complimentary coffee in lobby. Ck-out noon. Cr cds: A, C, D, DS, MC, V.

★★**SHONEY'S INN.** *2801 N Monroe (32303).* 904/386-8286; res: 800/222-2222; FAX 904/422-1074. 112 rms, 2 story, 26 suites. S, D $36–$60; each addl $5; suites $74–$120. TV; cable. Heated pool. Complimentary continental bkfst, coffee. Restaurant adj. Ck-out noon. Coin lndry. Meeting rms. Balconies. Cr cds: A, C, D, DS, ER, MC, V.

★★**WAKULLA SPRINGS LODGE & CONFERENCE CENTER.** *(1 Springs Dr, Wakulla Springs 32305) 20 mi S on FL 61 near US 319.* 904/224-5950. 27 rms, 2 story. S $50–$80; D $55–$80; each addl $6; suites $250. Crib $6. TV in lobby. Swimming in springs; 2-level diving board. Restaurant 7:30–10 am, noon–2 pm, 6:30–8:30 pm. Ck-out 11 am. Meeting rms. Sundries. Picnic tables. Boat tours. Atmosphere of an old Southern hotel; located in 2,900-acre state park on Wakulla Springs. Cr cds: MC, V.

Lodge

★★**KILLEARN COUNTRY CLUB & INN.** *100 Tyron Circle (32308),* N off I-10 exit 30, right on Killearny Way, left on Shamrock N to Tyron Circle. 904/893-2186; res: 800/476-4101; FAX 904/668-7637. 39 rms, 2 story. S $59–$65; D $59–$70; each addl $5; under 12 free; higher rates football wkends. Crib avail. TV; cable. Pool; wading pool, poolside serv, lifeguard. Restaurant 7 am–9:30 pm; closed Mon–Wed. Rm serv. Bar. Ck-out noon. Meeting rms. Lighted tennis, pro. 27-hole golf, pro, greens fee, putting green, driving range. Exercise equipt; weight machine, treadmill. Some refrigerators. Some balconies. Cr cds: A, D, DS, MC, V.

Motor Hotel

★**RAMADA INN.** *2900 N Monroe (32303).* 904/386-1027; FAX 904/422-1025. 198 rms, 1–4 story. S $75–$80; D $80–$85; suites $100–$160; under 18 free. Crib free. TV. Pool; poolside serv. Restaurant 6:30 am–10 pm; Fri to 11:30 pm; Sat 7 am–11 pm. Rm serv. Bar 11–2 am; entertainment Fri–Sat. Ck-out noon. Meeting rms. Bellhops. Free airport, area transportation. Health club privileges. Cr cds: A, C, D, DS, MC, V.

Hotel

★★★**RADISSON.** *415 N Monroe (32301).* 904/224-6000; FAX 904/224-6000, ext 4118. 116 units, 7 story. S $87–$109; D $97–$119; each addl $10; suites $130–$195; under 18 free. Crib free. TV; cable. Restaurant 6:30 am–10 pm. Bar to 1 am. Ck-out noon. Meeting rms. Concierge. Free airport, bus depot transportation. Exercise equipt; weights, bicycles, sauna. Some bathrm phones, refrigerators. Cr cds: A, C, D, DS, ER, MC, V.

Inn

★★★**GOVERNORS INN.** *209 S Adams St (32301).* 904/681-6855; res: 800/342-7717 (FL); FAX 904/222-3105. 40 rms, 2–3 story. S $119; D $129–$149; each addl $10; suites $149–$219; wkend rates. Crib free. TV; cable. Free continental bkfst. Ck-out noon, ck-in 3 pm. Meeting rms. Bellhops. Valet parking. Free airport transportation. Wood-burning fireplace in some rms. Individually decorated rooms, antiques, four-poster beds. Complimentary newspaper, shoeshine. Located in Adams Street Commons, this century-old inn has kept original structure. Cr cds: A, C, D, DS, MC, V.

Restaurants

★★**ANDREW'S 2ND ACT.** *228 S Adams St.* 904/222-2759. Hrs: 11:30 am–1:30 pm, 6–10 pm; Fri, Sat to 11 pm; Sun to 9:30 pm. Closed Thanksgiving, Dec 25. Res accepted. Continental menu. Wine cellar. A la carte entrees: lunch $3.50–$8, dinner $15–$27. Child's meals. Specialties: tournedos St Laurent, veal Oscar. Valet parking. Cr cds: A, C, D, MC, V.

★ **ANNELLA'S.** *1400-12 Village Square Blvd, in Village Commons Mall.* 904/668-1961. Hrs: 11:30 am–2:30 pm, 6–9:30 pm; Tues, Wed to 2:30 pm. Closed Sun, Mon; major hols. Res accepted. Continental menu. Serv bar. Semi-a la carte: lunch $4.50–$7, dinner $8–$15. Pianist evenings. Cr cds: A, MC, V.

✔ ★ **BARNACLE BILL'S.** *1830 N Monroe St.* 904/385-8734. Hrs: 11 am–11 pm; Fri, Sat to midnight. Closed Dec 25. Bar. Semi-a la carte: lunch $3.95–$4.95, dinner $3.95–$12.95. Child's meals. Specializes in seafood, grilled & smoked fish, chicken. DJ. Parking. Aquarium. Cr cds: A, MC, V.

[D] [SC]

★ ★ **CHARLEY MAC'S.** *1700-3 Halstead Blvd.* 904/893-0522. Hrs: 11:30 am–10 pm; Sat 5–10 pm; Sun 5–9 pm; Sun brunch 10:30 am–2 pm. Closed some major hols. Res accepted. Varied menu. Bar. Semi-a la carte: lunch $5.50–$8.50, dinner $6.95–$15.95. Sun brunch $10.95. Child's meals. Specializes in fish, beef, pasta. Parking. Contemporary decor. Cr cds: A, MC, V.

✔ ★ **LORENZO LAKE ELLA CAFE.** *1600 N Monroe St.* 904/681-3552. Hrs: 11 am–11 pm; early-bird dinner 5–7 pm. Res accepted. Italian, Amer menu. Bar. Semi-a la carte: lunch $4–$7, dinner $8–$12. Child's meals. Specializes in seafood, veal. Pianist. Parking. Outdoor dining. Cr cds: A, MC, V.

Unrated Dining Spots

CHEZ PIERRE. *115 N Adams St.* 904/222-0936. Hrs: 11 am–2:30 pm, 6–7:30 pm. Closed Sun, Mon; major hols; also 2 wks in late summer. French menu. A la carte entrees: lunch $4–$10, dinner $10–$16. Specializes in homemade soup, French pastries. Parking. Pastry shop 10 am–10 pm; gourmet shop with wines, cheeses, chocolates, croissants. Country French decor. Cr cds: C, D, MC, V.

MILL BAKERY & EATERY. *2136 N Monroe St.* 904/386-2867. Hrs: 6:30 am–midnight. Closed Thanksgiving, Dec 25. Bar. Average ck: bkfst $3, lunch $5, dinner $6.50. Child's meals. Specializes in natural foods, pizza, baked goods. Own baking. Parking. Brew own beer. Cr cds: A, MC, V.

[D]

MORRISON'S CAFETERIA. *2415 N Monroe Ave, in Tallahassee Mall.* 904/385-3471. Hrs: 11 am–8:30 pm; Sun to 8 pm. Avg ck: lunch, dinner $5. Child's meals. Specializes in home-style Southern cooking. Cr cds: A, MC, V.

Tampa (C-3)

Settled: 1824 **Pop:** 280,015 **Elev:** 57 ft **Area code:** 813

This is the business and vacation hub of Florida's west coast. Tampa, Florida's third largest city and its leading industrial metropolis, has a colorful waterfront and a beautiful bay drive. Within it is Ybor City, a Spanish, Cuban, Italian enclave of narrow streets and cigarmakers, and MacDill Air Force Base, headquarters of the 56th TT Wing, US Special Operations Command and the US Central Command.

Sprawled around the mouth of the Hillsborough River at the head of Tampa Bay, the city traces its origins to Fort Brooke, established to oversee Seminole Indians, who recently had moved here from Georgia and northern Florida. An early center for Florida's cattle industry, Tampa enjoyed brisk trade with Cuba and prospered. However, subjected to hit-and-run raids during the Civil War, the city suffered a decline until 1884, when Henry Plant's narrow-gauge South Florida Railroad reached the city. Determined to outdo his East Coast rival Henry Morrison Flagler, Plant built the opulent Tampa Bay Hotel and opened it with a flamboyance undreamed of in this remote outpost. Teddy Roosevelt trained his Rough Riders in the back yard of the hotel. In 1886, Vincente Martinez Ybor moved his cigar factory and its workers here from Key West. Most of the other cigarmakers moved with him, establishing Ybor City.

Today the port of Tampa handles more than 50 million tons of shipping a year. Its cigar factories turn out three million cigars each working day; two huge breweries are in operation in one of 33 industrial parks; two citrus plants and a variety of other factories are here. Some of the world's largest phosphate mines are nearby, and a new technique to extract uranium from mine wastes has revitalized this industry.

Transportation

Tampa International Airport: Information 870-8700; lost and found 870-8760; weather 645-2506; cash machines, Landside Building, third level; Crown Room (Delta), Airside C; WorldClub (Northwest), Airside D; USAir Club (US Air), Airside F.

Car Rental Agencies: See toll-free numbers under Introduction.

Public Transportation: Buses (Rapid Transit Authority), phone 254-4278.

Rail Passenger Service: Amtrak 800/872-7245.

What to See and Do

1. **Ybor City.** 2 mi E of downtown; roughly between I-4, 5th Ave, Nebraska Ave & 22nd St. A link between the past and present, this area retains some of the atmosphere of the original Cuban settlement. Spanish and Italian are spoken as much as English. Many Spanish restaurants, coffeehouses and cigar factories are here. Within the area are

   Ybor Square. A complex of shops and restaurants in a restored 19th-century cigar factory. (Daily) Phone 247-4497.

   Ybor City State Museum. 1818 E 9th Ave. Interprets the beginning (1886) and development of Ybor City and the cigar industry. (Tues–Sat; closed Thanksgiving, Dec 25) Phone 247-6323. ¢

2. **Busch Gardens Tampa.** At Busch Blvd & 40th St, 8 mi N via I-275, then E on Busch Blvd. A 300-acre theme park re-creating some of the sites and sounds of Africa. The area is divided into 8 different regions, including the Timbuktu section that has dolphin theater, rides, craftspeople, German restaurant and entertainment center; the Nairobi section has gorillas and chimpanzees; the Serengeti Plain is home to more than 500 free-roaming animals that can be viewed from a monorail; and the Morocco section has shops, cafes and the 1,200-seat Moroccan Palace Theater with an ice-skating show. Throughout the park are an animal nursery, bird garden and rare white tigers; thrill rides including Questor, a flight simulator ride, Tanganyika Tidal Wave flume ride, Python and Scorpion roller-coaster rides, railway, sky trolley and others. Also self-guided tour of Anheuser-Busch brewery and display of Clydesdale horses. (Daily) Parking fee. Phone 987-5082. Admission includes all rides, shows, attractions. ¢¢¢¢¢

3. **Tampa Museum of Art.** 601 Doyle Carlton Dr, downtown by the river. Traditional and contemporary art; children's exhibitions; Greek and Roman antiquities. Educational programs and films. Tours. (Daily exc Mon; closed major hols) Phone 223-8130. ¢¢

4. **Hillsborough County Historical Commission Museum.** Room 250, County Courthouse, Pierce St between Kennedy Blvd & Twiggs St. County historical exhibits, Indian relics; historical and genealogical library. (Mon–Fri; closed hols) Phone 272-5919. **Free.**

5. **Museum of Science and Industry.** 4801 E Fowler Ave. Large open-air facility features more than 300 hands-on exhibits and participatory programs on a wide range of scientific subjects. Highlights include Gulf Coast Hurricane, Back Woods 40-acre wilderness site and GTE Challenger Learning Center; planetarium. (Daily; closed Jan 1, Thanksgiving, Dec 25) Phone 985-5531. ¢¢¢

6. **Tampa Bay Performing Arts Center.** 1010 N MacInnes Place. Includes 2,400-seat Festival Hall, 900-seat Playhouse Hall and 300-seat Robert and Lorena Jaeb Theater. The Florida Orchestra performs classical and pop concerts here (Sept–May); phone 286-2403); also performances by national artists, touring groups and local artists. Phone 221-1045 (tickets).

7. **Adventure Island.** 4545 Bougainvillea Ave, near Busch Gardens. This 19-acre water theme park features 4 speed slides, inner-tube

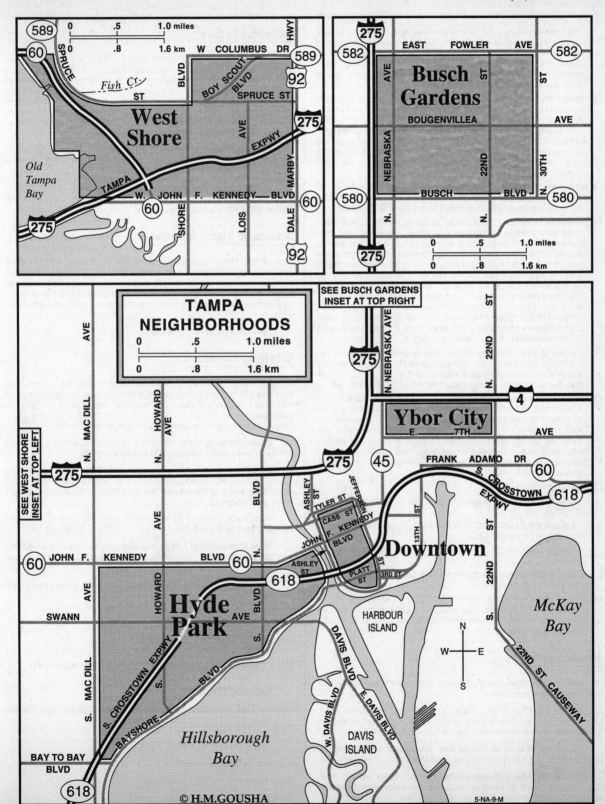

© H.M.GOUSHA

5-NA-9-M

slide, slow-winding tube ride, water-sled ride, 16 water flumes; diving platforms; pool that creates 3–5-foot waves for body- and raft surfing; volleyball complex; large children's water play section; lifeguards. Also includes restaurant, picnicking; dressing room, sunbathing; games; gift shop. (Late Mar–mid-Sept, daily; rest of Sept, Sat & Sun) Phone 987-5660. ¢¢¢¢¢

8. **Lowry Park.** N Boulevard & W Sligh Ave. This 105-acre park contains a section with statues of fable and nursery rhyme characters. Also zoo with Asian, primate & Florida sections, aviary and petting zoo; Safety Village/Children's Museum, which teaches school children bicycle safety; and amusement park with rides. Also boat launch, picnicking, playground. Park (daily). Some fees. Sr citizen rate. Phone 223-8230 (park), 935-8441 (museum) or 932-0245 (zoo). Park **free.**

9. **Waterfront.** From Davis Island, Water St or 13th St. Docks at 139 Twiggs St where stalks of green bananas are unloaded almost daily; shrimp boats unload at docks on the 22nd St Causeway.

10. **University of Tampa** (1931). (1,650 students) 401 W John F. Kennedy Blvd (US 60), at Hillsborough River. Plant Hall, the main building of this 69-acre campus, was the Tampa Bay Hotel, a large, bizarre conglomeration of Victorian, Spanish and Moorish architecture built in 1891 by railroad magnate Henry B. Plant to compete with his east-coast rival Henry Flagler. The structure features several onion-domes, 13 minarets, elaborate filigree work and interlaced gingerbread trim. The 500-room hotel hosted many famous guests, including Teddy Roosevelt and the Rough Riders, Stephen Crane, Richard Harding Davis and others. Historic walking tour leaves from lobby (Sept–May, Tues & Thurs afternoons). Phone 253-6220. **Free.** In the building is

Henry B. Plant Museum. Showcases original Victorian-era furnishings and decorative art objects amassed by Plant for the hotel; exhibits on Plant's railroad & steamship lines; tours. (Tues–Sat, also Sun afternoons; closed major hols) Phone 254-1891. ¢¢

11. **University of South Florida** (1956). (34,000 students) 4202 E Fowler Ave (FL 582), 10 mi N. This 1,700-acre campus has changing art exhibits in Fine Arts Gallery (Mon–Fri; closed hols), Contemporary Art Museum (Mon–Fri, also Sat afternoons; closed hols), Fine Arts Teaching Gallery (Mon–Fri), Anthropology Museum, Social Science Bldg (Mon–Fri; closed school hols). Film, theater, music and athletic events. Sun Dome entertainment center seats 11,183. Phone 974-2235.

12. **Sightseeing tours.**

Gray Line bus tours. Contact PO Box 145, St Petersburg 33731; 273-0845.

Around the Town. 3450 W Busch Blvd, Suite 115, 33618. For information phone 932-7803.

Tampa Tours. 5805 N 50th St, 33610. For information phone 621-6667.

Scenic drive. Bayshore Blvd from Platt St Bridge to Gandy Blvd; 6½ miles along Tampa Bay.

13. **Jai-Alai.** Tampa Fronton. 5 mi SW via I-275, S Dale Mabry Hwy at Gandy Blvd. Parimutuels. (Mon–Wed, Fri & Sat evenings; matinees Mon, Wed & Sat) Children with parent only. Phone 831-1411. General admission ¢

Annual Events

Hall of Fame Bowl. Tampa Stadium. Post-season college football match-up; other events. Jan 1.

Florida State Fair. Florida State Fair and Expo Park. US 301 & I-4. County exhibits, livestock shows, orchid show, industrial exposition, amusement rides, entertainment. Phone 621-7821. Feb 4–20.

Gasparilla Festival of Tampa Bay. Month-long celebration that begins with a "pirate invasion," parade and street party. Early Feb–Mar.

Florida Strawberry Festival/Hillsborough County Fair. In Plant City. Country music, strawberry delicacies and strawberry shortcake eating contest. Phone 752-9194. 10 days early Mar.

Seasonal Events

Professional sports. Tampa Stadium, 4201 N Dale Mabry Hwy: Tampa Bay Buccaneers (football), Sept–Dec, phone 879-BUCS; Tampa Bay Rowdies (soccer), Apr–Aug, phone 877-7800. Expo Mall, Florida State Fairgrounds: Tampa Bay Lightning (hockey), Oct–Apr, phone 229-2658. Plant City Stadium, 2 mi S of I-4 on Park Rd in Plant City: Cincinnati Reds spring training (baseball), early Mar–early Apr, phone 752-REDS. Yankee Complex, Himes Ave & Columbus Dr: Gulf Coast League, Tampa Yankees (baseball), phone 875-7753.

Greyhound racing. Tampa Track. 5 mi N at 8300 Nebraska Ave; US 41 Nebraska Ave exit, I-75 Bird St exit. Nightly exc Tues; matinees Mon, Wed, Sat. Phone 932-4313. July–Dec.

Horse racing. Tampa Bay Downs. 11 mi NW on FL 580 to Oldsmar, then 1 mi N on Race Track Rd. Thoroughbreds. Parimutuels. Daily. Phone 855-4401. Early Dec–early May.

Additional Visitor Information

The Tampa/Hillsborough Convention & Visitors Association, 111 Madison St, Suite 1010, 33602, phone 223-1111, ext 44 or 800/44-TAMPA, has free maps, brochures, listings of current events and information on a free walking tour of Ybor City. *Tampa Bay Magazine*, at newsstands, has up-to-date information on cultural events and articles of interest to visitors.

(See Clearwater, St Petersburg)

City Neighborhoods

Many of the restaurants, unrated dining establishments and some lodgings listed under Tampa include neighborhoods as well as exact street addresses. A map showing these neighborhoods can be found on the preceding page. Geographic descriptions of these areas are given, followed by a table of restaurants arranged by neighborhood.

Busch Gardens: West of Busch Gardens amusement park; south of Fowler Ave, north of Busch Blvd and east of I-275.

Downtown: South of Tyler St, west of Jefferson St, north of Water St and Harbour Island and east of Ashley St. **North of Downtown:** North of US 275. **South of Downtown:** South of FL 618. **West of Downtown:** West of Hillsborough River.

Hyde Park: South of Kennedy Blvd, west and north of Bayshore Blvd and east of MacDill Ave.

West Shore: On Old Tampa Bay south of Courtney Campbell Pkwy and Tampa Intl Airport, west of Dale Mabry Hwy and north of Kennedy Blvd.

Ybor City: South of I-4, west of 22nd St, north of 5th Ave and east of Nebraska Ave.

TAMPA RESTAURANTS
BY NEIGHBORHOOD AREAS

(For full description, see alphabetical listings under Restaurants)

DOWNTOWN

Harbour View (Wyndham Harbour Island Hotel). 725 S Harbour Island Blvd

NORTH OF DOWNTOWN

A.J. Catfish. 8751 N Himes Ave

Rumpelmayers. 4812 E Busch Blvd

Sukothai. 8201 A North Dale Mabry Hwy

SOUTH OF DOWNTOWN

Blueberry Hill. 601 S Harbour Island Blvd

WEST OF DOWNTOWN

Briedy's. 8501 W Hillsborough

Consuelo's. 3814 Neptune

Don Diego's Spanish Steakhouse. 3602 N Armenia Ave

Donatello. 232 N Dale Mabry Hwy

Malios. 301 S Dale Mabry Hwy

HYDE PARK

Bern's Steak House. 1208 S Howard Ave

Cactus Club. 1601 Snow Ave

Chavez at the Royal. 2109 Bayshore Blvd

Colonnade. 3401 Bayshore Blvd

Jimmy Mac's. 113 S Armenia Ave

WEST SHORE

Armani's (Hyatt Regency Westshore Hotel). 6200 Courtney Campbell Causeway

YBOR CITY

Columbia. 2117 E 7th Ave

Spaghetti Warehouse. 1911 N 13th St

Note: When a listing is located in a town that does not have its own city heading, it will appear under the city nearest to its location. In these cases, the address and town appear in parenthesis immediately following the name of the establishment.

Motels

(Rates may be higher during state fair, Gasparilla Festival)

★★**COURTYARD BY MARRIOTT.** *3805 W Cypress St (33607), I-275, exit 23B, near Intl Airport, in West Shore.* 813/874-0555; FAX 813/870-0685. 145 rms, 4 story. Jan–Apr: S $99; D $109; each addl $10; suites $115; under 18 free; lower rates rest of yr. Crib free. Pet accepted; $50 non-refundable. TV; cable. Heated pool. Complimentary coffee in rms. Restaurant 6:30–11 am. Bar 4–11 pm. Ck-out noon. Coin lndry. Meeting rms. Valet serv. Free airport transportation. Exercise equipt; weight machine, bicycles, whirlpool. Refrigerator, minibar in suites. Balconies. Cr cds: A, C, D, DS, MC, V.

D ⊗ ⇨ ⚹ ✕ ⊗ ⊚ SC

✔★**DAYS INN-BUSCH GARDENS NORTH.** *701 E Fletcher Ave (33612), near Busch Gardens.* 813/977-1550; FAX 813/977-6556. 254 rms, 3 story. Jan–Apr: S $37–$55; D $40–$60; each addl $5; family, monthly rates; varied lower rates rest of yr. Crib free. Pet accepted, some restrictions; $5. TV; cable. Pool. Restaurant 6 am–1 pm, 5–9 pm. Ck-out noon. Coin lndry. Meeting rms. Sundries. Cr cds: A, D, DS, ER, MC, V.

⊗ ⇨ ⊗ ⊚ SC

★**DAYS INN-FAIRGROUNDS.** *9942 Adamo Dr (FL 60) (33619), east of downtown.* 813/623-5121; FAX 813/628-4989. 100 rms, 2 story. Jan–Apr: S $49–$58; D $53–$60; each addl $5; under 12 free; lower rates rest of yr. Crib free. TV; cable. Pool. Complimentary continental bkfst. Coffee in rms. Restaurant opp 10:30 am–10 pm. Ck-out noon. Meeting rm. Cr cds: A, C, D, DS, MC, V.

D ⇨ ⊗ ⊚ SC

★**ECONOMY INNS OF AMERICA.** *6606 E Dr Martin Luther King Blvd (33619), I-4 exit 4, east of downtown.* 813/623-6667. 128 rms,

2 story. Jan–mid-Apr: S $33.90; D $39–$51; each addl $6; lower rates rest of yr. Pet accepted. TV; cable. Heated pool. Complimentary coffee in lobby. Restaurant nearby. Ck-out 11 am. Cr cds: A, MC, V.

D ⊗ ⇨ ⊗ SC

✔★★**HAMPTON INN.** *4817 W Laurel St (33607), near Intl Airport, in West Shore.* 813/287-0778; FAX 813/287-0882. 134 rms, 6 story. Jan–Apr: S $58–$64; D $64–$69; under 19 free; higher rates special events; lower rates rest of yr. Pet accepted. TV; cable. Pool. Complimentary continental bkfst, coffee. Ck-out noon. Valet serv. Sundries. Free airport transportation. Cr cds: A, C, D, DS, MC, V.

D ⊗ ⇨ ✕ ⊗ ⊚ SC

★★**HOLIDAY INN BUSCH GARDENS.** *2701 E Fowler Ave (33612), near Busch Gardens.* 813/971-4710; FAX 813/977-0155. 400 rms, 2 story. Jan–Apr: S, D $74–$89; each addl $8; under 18 free; lower rates rest of yr. Crib free. Pet accepted. TV; cable. Pool; poolside serv. Restaurant 6:30 am–10 pm. Rm serv. Bar 11 am–midnight. Ck-out noon. Coin lndry. Meeting rms. Bellhops. Free Busch Gardens transportation. Exercise equipt; weights, bicycles. Tropical garden. Opp shopping mall. Cr cds: A, C, D, DS, MC, V, JCB.

D ⊗ ⇨ ⚹ ⊗ ⊚ SC

✔★★**LA QUINTA INN.** *2904 Melbourne Blvd (33605), I-4 exit 3, east of downtown.* 813/623-3591; FAX 813/620-1375. 129 rms, 3 story. S $43–$58; D $50–$58; each addl $7; suites $75; under 18 free. Crib free. Pet accepted. TV; cable. Heated pool. Complimentary continental bkfst. Ck-out noon. Guest lndry. Meeting rms. Sundries. Cr cds: A, C, D, DS, MC, V.

D ⊗ ⇨ ⊗ ⊚

✔★★**RAMADA INN-STADIUM** (formerly Holiday Inn). *4732 N Dale Mabry Hwy (33614), north of downtown.* 813/877-6061; FAX 813/876-1531. 314 rms, 1–2 story. Late Dec–early Apr: S, D $58–$64; each addl $6; suites $81; kit. units $76; under 18 free; higher rates special stadium events; lower rates rest of yr. Crib free. Pet accepted; $20 non-refundable. TV; cable. Pool. Restaurant 6 am–2 pm, 5–10 pm. Rm serv. Bar 5 pm–midnight; entertainment, dancing Fri & Sat. Ck-out noon. Coin lndry. Meeting rms. Bellhops. Valet serv. Free airport transportation. Picnic table, grill. Cr cds: A, C, D, DS, MC, V, JCB.

D ⊗ ⇨ ⊗ ⊚ SC

★**RED ROOF INN.** *5001 N US 301 (33610), near I-4 exit 6A, east of downtown.* 813/623-5245; FAX 813/623-5240. 109 rms, 2 story. Mid-Jan–mid-Apr: S $34.99–$49.99; D $36–$49.99; under 18 free; lower rates rest of yr. Pet accepted, some restrictions. TV; cable. Complimentary coffee. Restaurant adj open 24 hrs. Ck-out noon. Cr cds: A, C, D, DS, MC, V.

D ⊗ ⊗ ⊚

★★**RESIDENCE INN BY MARRIOTT.** *3075 N Rocky Point Dr (33607), near Intl Airport, west of downtown.* 813/281-5677. 176 kit. units, 1–2 story. Jan–Apr: S, D $105–$150; family rates; lower rates rest of yr. Crib free. Pet accepted; $100 non-refundable and $6 per day. TV. Pool; whirlpool. Complimentary continental bkfst 6:30–9:30 am; Sat & Sun 8–10 am. Ck-out noon. Meeting rms. Bellhops. Valet serv. Airport transportation. Some balconies. On Tampa Bay. Cr cds: A, C, D, DS, MC, V.

D ⊗ ⊸ ⇨ ✕ ⊗ ⊚ SC

★★**SAILPORT RESORT.** *2506 Rocky Point Dr (33607), west of downtown.* 813/281-9599; res: 800/255-9599; FAX 813/281-9510. 237 kit. suites (1–2 bedrm), 4 story. S, D $97–$149; under 12 free; monthly, wkly rates. Crib $5; TV; cable. Heated pool. Complimentary continental bkfst, coffee. Ck-out 11 am. Meeting rms. Coin lndry. Valet serv. Covered parking. Lighted tennis. Private patios, balconies. Some grills. On bay; dock; all waterfront rms. Cr cds: A, D, MC, V.

⊸ 🄿 ⇨ ⊚ SC

✔★**TRAVELODGE AT BUSCH GARDENS.** *9202 N 30th St (33612), near Busch Gardens.* 813/935-7855; FAX 813/935-7958. 146 rms, 3 story. Mid-Jan–Apr: S $45; D $49; each addl $4; suites $70; under 18 free; lower rates rest of yr. Crib free. Pet accepted; $10 refundable.

TV; cable. Pool. Restaurant adj 7 am–11 pm. Ck-out 11 am. Coin lndry avail. Meeting rm. Sundries. Gift shop. Game rm. Cr cds: A, ER, MC, V.

D ⊞ 🏊 ⊗ ◎ SC

Motor Hotels

★ ★ **QUALITY SUITES.** *3001 30th St (33612), near Busch Gardens. 813/971-8930; FAX 813/971-8935.* 150 suites, 3 story. Suites $69–$139; each addl (1–4 persons) $10; under 18 free. Crib free. TV; cable, in-rm movies. Heated pool; whirlpool. Complimentary full bkfst. Complimentary coffee in rms. Restaurant 6–10 am; wkends 7–11 am, 4–7 pm. Ck-out noon. Coin lndry. Meeting rms. Bellhops. Valet serv. Sundries. Gift shop. Balconies. Cr cds: A, C, D, DS, ER, MC, V, JCB.

D 🏊 ⊗ ◎ SC

★ ★ **RAMADA RESORT-BUSCH GARDENS.** *820 E Busch Blvd (33612), near Busch Gardens. 813/933-4011; FAX 813/932-1784.* 255 rms, 2–4 story. Jan–Apr: S $59–$99; D $79–$99; each addl $10; suites $119–$159; under 12 free; wkly, wkend rates; higher rates special events; lower rates rest of yr. Crib free. TV; cable. 2 heated pools, 1 indoor. Restaurant 6:30 am–10 pm. Rm serv. Bar 11–1 am; entertainment, dancing Tues–Sat. Ck-out 11 am. Coin lndry. Convention facilities. Bellhops. Valet serv. Sundries. Gift shop. Free airport, Busch Gardens transportation. Lighted tennis, pro. Exercise equipt; weights, bicycles, sauna. Game rm. Cr cds: A, C, D, DS, ER, MC, V, JCB.

D ⊞ 🏊 🏃 ⊗ ◎ SC

Hotels

★ ★ ★ **EMBASSY SUITES-WEST SHORE.** *555 N Westshore Blvd (33609), near Intl Airport, in West Shore. 813/875-1555; FAX 813/287-3664.* 221 kit. suites, 16 story. Jan–Apr: S, D $109–$149; under 18 free; monthly, wkly, wkend rates; lower rates rest of yr. Pet accepted, some restrictions. TV; cable. Heated pool; poolside serv. Restaurant 6:30 am–2 pm, 5–10 pm; Sat & Sun 7 am–2 pm. Bar noon–midnight. Ck-out noon. Coin lndry. Meeting rms. Gift shop. Free covered parking; valet. Free airport transportation. Exercise equipt; weights, bicycles, whirlpool, sauna. Balconies. Cr cds: A, C, D, DS, ER, MC, V, JCB.

D ⊞ 🏊 🏃 ✕ ⊗ ◎ SC

★ ★ ★ **GUEST QUARTERS ON TAMPA BAY.** *3050 N Rocky Point Dr W (33607), at Courtney Campbell Causeway, near Intl Airport, west of downtown. 813/888-8800; FAX 813/888-8743.* 203 suites, 7 story. Oct–Apr: S $139; D $159; each addl $20; under 13 free; wkend rates; lower rates rest of yr. Crib free. TV; cable. Heated pool. Restaurant 6:30 am–10 pm. Bar 11 am–midnight. Ck-out noon. Coin lndry. Meeting rms. Free airport transportation. Exercise equipt; weights, bicycles, whirlpool, sauna. Refrigerators. Sun deck. Library. On Tampa Bay. Cr cds: A, C, D, DS, MC, V.

D 🏊 🏃 ✕ ◎ SC

★ ★ ★ **HILTON AT METROCENTER.** *2225 Lois Ave (33607), near Intl Airport, in West Shore. 813/877-6688; FAX 813/879-3264.* 238 rms, 12 story. Jan–Apr: S $89–$135; D $99–$145; each addl $10; suites $150–$350; family, wkend rates; lower rates rest of yr. Crib free. TV; cable. Heated pool; poolside serv. Restaurant 6:30 am–11 pm. Bar 11–2 am; pianist evenings. Ck-out noon. Meeting rms. Gift shop. Free airport transportation. Lighted tennis. Exercise equipt; bicycle, stair machine, whirlpool. Cr cds: A, C, D, DS, ER, MC, V, JCB.

D ⊞ 🏊 🏃 ✕ ⊗ ◎ SC

★ ★ **HOLIDAY INN ASHLEY PLAZA CONVENTION CENTER.** *111 W Fortune St (33602), adj to Performing Arts Center, downtown. 813/223-1351; FAX 813/221-2000.* 311 rms, 14 story. Jan–mid-Apr: S $70.50–$95.50; D $80.50–$105.50; each addl $10; suites $151–$186; under 18 free; wkend rates; lower rates rest of yr. Crib free. TV; cable. Heated pool. Restaurant 6:30 am–11 pm. Bar 3 pm–2 am; entertainment Thurs–Sat. Ck-out 11 am. Convention facilities. Gift shop. Free airport

transportation. Exercise equipt; weights, bicycles, whirlpool. Some refrigerators. Cr cds: A, C, D, DS, ER, MC, V, JCB.

D 🏊 🏃 ⊗ ◎ SC

★ ★ ★ **HOLIDAY INN CROWNE PLAZA-SABAL PARK.** *10221 Princess Palm Ave (33610), at I-75 exit 52 S, east of downtown. 813/623-6363; FAX 813/621-7224.* 265 rms, 5 story, 41 suites. Mid-Jan–mid-Apr: S, D $115–$145; suites $145–$500; under 18 free; wkend rates; higher rates special events; lower rates rest of yr. Crib free. Pet accepted, some restrictions. TV; cable. Heated pool; wading pool. Restaurant 6 am–11 pm. Bar 11–2 am. Ck-out noon. Convention facilities. Concierge. Gift shop. Barber, beauty shop. Free airport transportation. Lighted tennis. Exercise equipt; weights, bicycles, whirlpool. Refrigerator in suites. Private patios, balconies. Bldg with distinctive bowed structure located on 9 acres; 3-story atrium lobby with waterfall. *LUXURY LEVEL:* CONCIERGE LEVEL. 67 rms, 12 suites. S, D $135–$170; suites $150–$500. Ck-out 2 pm. Private lounge. Wet bars. Complimentary continental bkfst, refreshments. Cr cds: A, C, D, DS, MC, V, JCB.

D ⊞ 🏊 🏊 🏃 🏃 ⊗ ◎ SC

★ ★ ★ **HYATT REGENCY.** *2 Tampa City Center (33602), off I-275 Ashley exit, bear left onto Tampa St to Jackson St, downtown. 813/225-1234; FAX 813/273-0234.* 518 rms, 17 story. S $150; D $175; each addl $15; 1-bedrm suites $200–$490; 2-bedrm suites $280–$590; under 18 free; wkend rates. Crib free. TV; cable. Heated pool. Restaurant 6:30 am–11 pm. Rm serv 24 hrs. Bar; entertainment. Ck-out noon. Meeting rms. Concierge. Garage, valet parking. Exercise equipt; weights, bicycles, whirlpool, sauna. Massage therapy. *LUXURY LEVEL:* GOLD PASSPORT LEVEL. 105 rms, 7 suites, 4 floors. S $150; D $175; suites $280–$590. Private lounge. Complimentary beverages, newspapers. Cr cds: A, C, D, DS, ER, MC, V, JCB.

D 🏊 🏃 ⊗ ◎ SC

★ ★ ★ **HYATT REGENCY WESTSHORE.** *6200 Courtney Campbell Causeway (33607), on the shores of Tampa Bay, near Intl Airport, in West Shore area. 813/874-1234; FAX 813/281-9168.* 400 rms in main bldg, 14 story, 24 suites, 45 casita villas. Main bldg: S $159; D $184; each addl $25; suites $275–$640; casita villas: S $169; D $194; suites (1–3 bedrm) $275–$515; under 18 free; wkend rates; lower rates May–Sept. Crib free. Covered parking; valet parking $7/night. TV; cable. 2 heated pools; poolside serv. Restaurant 6:30 am–11 pm (also see ARMANI'S). Rm serv 24 hrs. Bar noon–1 am; pianist. Ck-out noon. Convention facilities. Concierge. Gift shop. Free airport transportation. Tennis. Exercise rm; instructor, weights, bicycles, whirlpool, sauna. Massage. Racquetball. Lawn games. Some refrigerators, minibars. On Tampa Bay; boat dock. Elaborate landscaping; courtyard with fountains. Nestled amidst a 35-acre nature preserve. *LUXURY LEVEL:* REGENCY CLUB. 30 units, 5 suites. S $184; D $209; suites $390–$640. Private lounge, honor bar. In-rm movies. Wet bar, whirlpool in some suites. Complimentary full bkfst, refreshments. Cr cds: A, C, D, DS, ER, MC, V, JCB.

D ↺ 🏊 🏃 🏃 ✕ ⊗ ◎ SC

★ ★ ★ **MARRIOTT-TAMPA AIRPORT.** *At Tampa Intl Airport (33607), 1½ mi N of jct FL 60 & I-275, in West Shore. 813/879-5151; FAX 813/873-0945.* 300 rms, 6 story. Jan–Apr: S $129–$160; D $144–$175; each addl $15; suites $250–$600; under 18 free; wkend rates; lower rates rest of yr. Crib free. TV; cable. Pool; poolside serv. Restaurant 6 am–11 pm. Bar 11–1 am. Ck-out 1 pm. Meeting rms. Gift shop. Exercise equipt; weights, bicycles. Refrigerator in suites. Golf nearby. *LUXURY LEVEL:* 55 rms, 4 suites. S $139; D $154; suites $250–$400. Concierge. Private lounge. Wet bar. Complimentary continental bkfst, refreshments, newspaper. Cr cds: A, C, D, DS, ER, MC, V, JCB.

D 🏊 🏃 ✕ ⊗ ◎ SC

★ ★ ★ **MARRIOTT TAMPA WEST SHORE.** *1001 N Westshore Blvd (33607), near Intl Airport, in West Shore. 813/287-2555; FAX 813/289-5464.* 310 rms, 14 story. S $129–$134; D, suites $400; each addl $10; under 18 free; wkend rates. Crib free. TV; cable. Indoor/outdoor pool. Restaurant 6:30 am–11 pm. Bar 11–2 am. Ck-out 1 pm. Conven-

tion facilities. Gift shop. Free airport transportation. Exercise equipt; weights, bicycles, whirlpool, sauna. Game rm. Balconies. Golf, tennis nearby. *LUXURY LEVEL:* **CONCIERGE LEVEL.** 18 rms, 2 suites. S $139; D $154. Concierge. Private lounge. Complimentary continental bkfst, refreshments.
Cr cds: A, C, D, DS, ER, MC, V, JCB.

★ ★ ★ **OMNI AT WESTSHORE.** *700 N Westshore Blvd (33609), near Intl Airport, in West Shore.* 813/289-8200; FAX 813/289-9166. 278 rms, 11 story. Jan–Apr: S $130; D $145; each addl $15; under 18 free; wkend rates; lower rates rest of yr. Crib free. Pet accepted, some restrictions. TV; cable. Heated pool. Complimentary continental bkfst 7:30–9 am. Restaurant 6:30 am–10:30 pm. Bar 11–2 am; entertainment. Ck-out noon. Convention facilities. Airport transportation. Exercise equipt; weights, bicycles, whirlpool, sauna. *LUXURY LEVEL:* **OMNI CLUB.** 26 rms. S $145; D $160; suites $230–$350. Concierge. Private lounge. Bathrm phones.
Cr cds: A, C, D, DS, MC, V.

★ ★ ★ **RADISSON BAY HARBOR INN.** *7700 Courtney Campbell Causeway (33607), west of downtown.* 813/281-8900; FAX 813/281-0189. 257 rms, 6 story. Jan–Apr: S, D $95–$130; each addl $10; suites $150–$450; under 18 free; lower rates rest of yr. Crib free. TV; cable. Heated pool; poolside serv. Restaurant 7 am–11 pm. Bar 11 am–midnight, Sun from 1 pm. Ck-out noon. Meeting rms. Barber, beauty shop. Free airport transportation. Lighted tennis. Golf privileges. Exercise equipt; weight machines, bicycles. Game rm. Private patios, balconies. On Tampa Bay; private beach. Cr cds: A, C, D, DS, MC, V.

★ ★ ★ **SHERATON GRAND HOTEL.** *4860 W Kennedy Blvd (33609), near Intl Airport, in West Shore area.* 813/286-4400; FAX 813/286-4053. 325 rms, 11 story. Jan–Apr: S $120–$180; D $140–$200; each addl $20; suites $240–$550; under 18 free; wkend rates; lower rates rest of yr. Crib free. TV; cable. Heated pool; poolside serv. Coffee in rms. Restaurant 6 am–11 pm. Rm serv 24 hrs. Bar 11–2 am; entertainment. Ck-out noon. Meeting rms. Concierge. Shopping arcade. Free airport transportation. Some bathrm phones, refrigerators. *LUXURY LEVEL:* **GRAND CLUB.** 32 rms, 2 suites. S $175; D $195; suites $240–$375. Concierge. Private lounge. Bathrm phones. Complimentary continental bkfst, refreshments, newspaper.
Cr cds: A, C, D, DS, ER, MC, V.

★ ★ ★ **SHERATON INN & CONFERENCE CENTER.** *7401 E Hillsborough Ave (33610), east of downtown.* 813/626-0999; FAX 813/622-7893. 276 rms, 6 story. Jan–Apr: S $105–$115; D $115–$125; each addl $10; suites $175–$275; under 16 free; wkend rates; lower rates rest of yr. Crib free. Pet accepted; $25 non-refundable. Pool. Restaurant 6:30 am–10:30 pm. Bar 11–2 am. Ck-out noon. Meeting rms. Gift shop. Airport transportation. Exercise equipt; weights, bicycles, whirlpool. Private patios, balconies. Cr cds: A, C, D, DS, MC, V, JCB.

★ ★ ★ ★ **WYNDHAM HARBOUR ISLAND.** *725 S Harbour Island Blvd (33602), downtown.* 813/229-5000; res: 800/822-4200 (US), 800/631-4200 (CAN); FAX 813/229-5322. 300 rms, 12 story. S $139–$199; D $159–$219; each addl $10; suites $295–$850; under 18 free; wkend rates. Crib free. TV; cable. Heated pool; poolside serv. Coffee in rms. Restaurants (also see HARBOUR VIEW). Rm serv to 2 am. Bar; entertainment wkends. Ck-out noon. Convention facilities. Concierge. Shopping arcade. Free airport transportation. Tennis privileges. Health club privileges. Bicycle, boat rentals. Minibars, wet bars; some bathrm phones; refrigerator in suites. Complimentary newspapers Mon–Fri. Formal furnishings. Picturesque bay views, panoramic views of Tampa. Cr cds: A, C, D, DS, MC, V, JCB.

Resort

★ ★ ★ ★ **SADDLEBROOK RESORT.** *(5700 Saddlebrook Way, Wesley Chapel 33543-4499) 25 mi N of Tampa Airport on I-75, exit 58 then 1 mi E on FL 54.* 813/973-1111; res: 800/729-8383; FAX 813/973-4504. 530 units, 2 story, 393 with kits., 131 hotel rms, 157 1-bedrm condos, 242 2-bedrm condos. Mid-Jan–Apr: S, D $175–$325; each addl $20; under 13 free; lower rates rest of yr. TV; cable. 4 pools, 1 heated. Playground. Free supervised child's activities. Dining rm (public by res) (see CYPRESS ROOM). Rm serv 6:30–1 am. Box lunches, snack bar. Bar 11–1 am; entertainment, dancing. Ck-out noon, ck-in 3 pm. Convention facilities. Concierge. Grocery 1 mi. Package store. Gift shop. Barber, beauty shop. Valet parking. Airport transportation. Sports dir. Tennis, 45 courts, 5 lighted, pro. 36-hole golf designed by Arnold Palmer & Dean Refram, pro, putting green, driving range. Home of Arnold Palmer Golf Academy. Nature walks. Bicycle rentals. Game rm. Exercise rm; instructor, weight machines, bicycles, whirlpool, sauna, steam rm. Massage therapy. Minibars. Many refrigerators. Private patios, balconies. Luxury resort secluded on 480 acres of woodlands, lakes, and rolling hills. Accommodations and activities center designed as a walking village. Cr cds: A, C, D, MC, V.

Restaurants

✔ ★ **A.J. CATFISH.** *8751 N Himes Ave, north of downtown.* 813/932-3474. Hrs: 11:30 am–10:30 pm; Sat to 11 pm; Sun 4:30–10 pm. Closed most major hols. Semi-a la carte: lunch $2.95–$8.95, dinner $7.95–$13.95. Child's meals. Specializes in steak, seafood, pasta. Parking. Outdoor dining. Cypress wood interior, 2nd floor balcony. Cr cds: A, MC, V.

★ ★ ★ **ARMANI'S.** *(See Hyatt Regency Westshore Hotel)* 813/281-9165. Hrs: 6–10 pm; Fri & Sat to 11 pm. Closed Sun; most major hols. Res accepted; required Fri & Sat. Northern Italian menu. Bar 5–11 pm; Fri & Sat to midnight. Semi-a la carte: dinner $12–$25. Child's meals. Specialties: veal Armani, lobster ammiraglia. Antipasta bar. Own baking, desserts. Pianist. Valet parking. Outdoor terrace overlooks bay; on rooftop. Jacket. Cr cds: A, C, D, DS, ER, MC, V, JCB.

★ ★ ★ ★ **BERN'S STEAK HOUSE.** *1208 S Howard Ave, 4 blks N of Bayshore Blvd, in Hyde Park.* 813/251-2421. Hrs: 5–11 pm. Closed Dec 25. Res required. Bar. Wine cellars. Semi-a la carte: dinner $15–$45 (serv charge). Specializes in own organically grown vegetables, aged prime beef, variety of roasted and blended coffees. Own baking, ice cream, sherbet, onion soup. Pianist/accordionist. Valet parking. Antiques, paintings, statuary. Chef-owned. Cr cds: C, D, DS, MC, V.

★ **BLUEBERRY HILL.** *601 S Harbour Island Blvd, south of downtown.* 813/221-1157. Hrs: 11–3 am. Bar. A la carte entrees: lunch $3.50–$5, dinner $3.95–$15.95. Child's meals. Specialties: Dagwood club sandwich, 1-lb prime rib, blueberry cobbler. DJ. Parking. Outdoor dining. 50s- and 60s-era decor, memorabilia; 3 halved 1957 Chevys on dance floor. Cr cds: A, MC, V.

★ **BRIEDY'S.** *8501 W Hillsborough, in Buccaneer Square Shopping Center, west of downtown.* 813/886-8148 or 885-3912. Hrs: 11 am–11 pm; Fri, Sat to 12:30 am. Closed Thanksgiving, Dec 25. Res accepted. Italian, Irish, Amer menu. Bar; wkends to 3 am. Semi-a la carte: lunch $3.95–$5, dinner $5.95–$17.95. Child's meals. Specialties: Irish pizza, sirloin strip steak, Italian pastas. Entertainment Wed–Sat. Casual, pub-like atmosphere. Cr cds: A, DS, MC, V.

✔ ★ ★ **CACTUS CLUB.** *1601 Snow Ave, in Old Hyde Park Shopping Center, in Hyde Park.* 813/251-4089. Hrs: 11 am–midnight; Fri, Sat to 1 am; Sun to 11 pm. Closed Thanksgiving, Dec 25. Southwestern menu. Bar. Semi-a la carte: lunch, dinner $5.95–$11.95. Child's meals. Specialties: bluesburger, tacobrito, Mexican pizza. Patio dining. Southwestern decor; ceiling fans. Cr cds: A, C, D, MC, V.

D

★★**CHAVEZ AT THE ROYAL.** *2109 Bayshore Blvd, in rear of Bayshore Royale Condominiums Bldg, in Hyde Park. 813/251-6986.* Hrs: 11 am–3 pm, 5–10 pm; Fri to 11 pm; Sat 5–11 pm. Closed Sun; major hols. Res accepted. Continental menu. Bar. Semi-a la carte: lunch $4.95–$8.50, dinner $8.75–$22.50. Child's meals. Specializes in seafood, steak, lamb. Parking. Cr cds: A, C, D, DS, MC, V.

D

✔★★**COLONNADE.** *3401 Bayshore Blvd, in Hyde Park. 813/839-7558.* Hrs: 11 am–10 pm; Fri, Sat to 11 pm. Closed Thanksgiving, Dec 25. Bar. Semi-a la carte: lunch $4.95–$6.95, dinner $4.95–$11.95. Child's meals. Specializes in fresh seafood, steak, prime rib, desserts. Parking. Nautical decor. Overlooks Tampa Bay. Family-owned. Cr cds: A, C, D, DS, MC, V.

D

★★**COLUMBIA.** *2117 E 7th Ave, in Ybor City. 813/248-4961.* Hrs: 11 am–10 pm; Fri, Sat to 11 pm; Sun noon–9 pm. Res accepted. Spanish menu. Bar. Wine cellars. Semi-a la carte: lunch $4.95–$7.95, dinner $6.95–$16.95. Cover charge $5 (in dining room with show). Child's meals. Specialties: paella a la Valenciana, snapper alicante, filet mignon steak Columbia. Flamenco dancers (dinner) exc Sun. Valet parking. Built 1905; balcony surrounds interior courtyard. Family-owned. Cr cds: A, C, D, DS, MC, V.

D

✔★**CONSUELO'S.** *3814 Neptune, west of downtown. 813/253-5965.* Hrs: 11:30 am–10 pm; Sat 1–11 pm. Closed Sun; Thanksgiving, Dec 25. Res accepted Fri, Sat. Mexican menu. Bar. A la carte entrees: lunch $4.50–$11.50, dinner $7.25–$13.95. Child's meals. Specialties: stuffed jalapeños, enchiladas. Mariachi band Fri, Sat. Strolling guitarists. Cr cds: A, MC, V.

D

★★**CYPRESS ROOM.** *(See Saddlebrook Resort) 813/973-1111, ext 4441.* Hrs: 6:30–10:30 am, 6–10 pm; Fri 6–11 pm; hrs may vary seasonally. Res required. Continental menu. Bar 5 pm–1 am. Semi-a la carte: bkfst $5–$10.50, dinner $19–$24.50. Serv charge 18%. Child's meals. Specializes in steak, veal, seafood buffet. Pastry shop. Entertainment. Valet parking. Creative food presentation. Contemporary decor. View of golf course. Cr cds: A, C, D, MC, V.

D

★★**DON DIEGO'S SPANISH STEAKHOUSE.** *3602 N Armenia Ave, west of downtown. 813/872-7341.* Hrs: 11:30 am–10 pm; Fri to 11 pm; Sat noon–11 pm; Sun noon–9 pm. Res accepted; required Fri, Sat. Spanish, continental menu. Bar. Semi-a la carte: lunch $4.95–$7.95, dinner $6.95–$19.95. Child's meals. Specialties: paella, steak, seafood. Parking. Original Spanish artwork. Cr cds: A, MC, V.

D

★★★**DONATELLO.** *232 N Dale Mabry Hwy, west of downtown. 813/875-6660.* Hrs: noon–3 pm, 6–11 pm; Sat, Sun from 6 pm. Closed Jan 1, Memorial Day, July 4, Dec 25; also Super Bowl Sun. Res accepted. Northern Italian menu. Bar. Wine list. Semi-a la carte: lunch $5.95–$9.95, dinner $15.95–$23.95. Specializes in hand-rolled pasta, veal chops, fresh seafood. Own breads, desserts. Valet parking. Some tableside cooking. Cr cds: A, C, D, DS, MC, V.

D

★★★**HARBOUR VIEW.** *(See Wyndham Harbour Island Hotel) 813/229-5001; or 229-5000.* Hrs: 6:30 am–2 pm, 6–11 pm; Sun brunch 10:30 am–2 pm. Res accepted. Serv bar. A la carte entrees: bkfst $5.25–$9.75, lunch $6.50–$11.50, dinner $16.50–$24.95. Sun brunch $19.95. Pasta bar (Mon–Fri) $9.50. Child's meals. Specializes in contemporary regional cuisine featuring fresh pasta, fresh seafood. Own baking. Valet parking. Waterfront view. Cr cds: A, C, D, DS, ER, MC, V, JCB.

D

★**JESSE'S.** *(5771 Fowler Ave, Temple Terrace) W via Busch Blvd, in Terrace Walk Shopping Center. 813/980-3686.* Hrs: 11 am–midnight; Fri, Sat to 1 am; Sun noon–10 pm. Closed some major hols. Bar. Semi-a la carte: lunch $5.75–$6.75, dinner $5.75–$18.50. Child's meals. Specializes in steak, seafood, prime rib. Extensive beer collection. Two aquariums; fireplace. Cr cds: A, MC, V.

D

★**JIMMY MAC'S.** *113 S Armenia Ave, in Hyde Park. 813/879-0591.* Hrs: 11:30–2 am; Sat from 11 am; Sun 11 am–11 pm; early-bird dinner Mon–Sat 5:30–7:30 pm. Closed most major hols. Bar 11:30–3 am. Semi-a la carte: lunch $4–$7.75, dinner $6.50–$17. Specializes in grilled seasonal seafood, hamburgers. Entertainment Tues–Sat. Parking. Eclectic decor. In 2 restored houses. Cr cds: A, DS, MC, V.

★★**MALIOS.** *301 S Dale Mabry Hwy, west of downtown. 813/879-3233.* Hrs: 11:30 am–2:30 pm, 5–11 pm; Fri, Sat 5–11:30 pm. Closed Sun; most major hols. Res accepted. Bar 11:30–2:30 am. A la carte entrees: lunch $4.95–$6.95, dinner $8.95–$18.95. Specializes in steak, seafood, pasta. Entertainment. Parking. Large central lounge with entertainment. Cr cds: A, D, MC, V.

D

✔★★**RUMPELMAYERS.** *4812 E Busch Blvd, in Ambassador Square Shopping Center, north of downtown. 813/989-9563.* Hrs: 11 am–11 pm. Res accepted. German menu. Complete meals: lunch $3.75–$9.25, dinner $7.50–$16.50. Child's meals. Specialties: Wienerschnitzel, sauerbraten, Black Forest cake. Accordionist evenings. Parking. Extensive German beer selection. Cr cds: A, C, D, DS, MC, V.

✔★**SPAGHETTI WAREHOUSE.** *1911 N 13th St, in Ybor City. 813/248-1720.* Hrs: 11 am–10 pm; Fri to 11 pm; Sat noon–11 pm; Sun noon–10 pm. Closed Thanksgiving, Dec 25. Res accepted. Italian menu. Bar. Semi-a la carte: lunch $2.95–$6.95, dinner $4.10–$8.95. Specialties: lasagne, veal & chicken parmigiana, cannelloni alla Florentina. Parking. Antiques; authentic Dallas trolley. Cr cds: A, C, D, DS, MC, V.

D

★★**SUKOTHAI.** *8201 A North Dale Mabry Hwy, north of downtown. 813/933-7990.* Hrs: 11 am–11 pm; Sat, Sun from 5 pm. Closed Labor Day, Thanksgiving, Dec 25. Res accepted. Thai menu. Wine, beer. Semi-a la carte: lunch $4.95–$6.95, dinner $8.95–$17.95. Specializes in seafood. Original Thai tables, pillows. Parking. Cr cds: A, C, D, MC, V.

D

Tarpon Springs (C-3)

Founded: 1876 **Pop:** 17,906 **Elev:** 10 ft **Area code:** 813

Colorfully Hellenic, Tarpon Springs is famous for its sponge industry, which was most prosperous from the early 1900s to the 1940s and continues today. Greek fishermen go far out to sea in their picturesque boats, from which divers plunge to depths of 150 feet to pluck sponges; in shallow waters they hook sponges with long poles. The city is situated between Lake Tarpon and bayous formed by the Anclote River before it empties into the Gulf of Mexico.

What to See and Do

1. **Dodecanese Blvd.** Along the seawall of this waterfront street are anchored shrimp boats and sponge boats decorated with Greek designs. On the other side are restaurants, curio shops, sponge diving exhibitions, boat rides and stacks of sponges.

2. **Spongeorama Exhibit Center.** Sponge docks, 510 Dodecanese Blvd. Sponge factory, museum on Tarpon Springs, nicknamed "America's sponge-diving birthplace," reproductions of 1900s

sponge docks. Specialty shops. Cinematic theater with film of sponge diving industry. (Daily) Phone 942-3771. Theater ¢

3. **St Nicholas Greek Orthodox Cathedral** (1943). 36 N Pinellas Ave. Neo-Byzantine architecture with interior of sculptured Grecian marble. Beautiful iconography and stained-glass windows. (Daily) Proper attire requested. Phone 937-3540.

4. **Inness Paintings.** Universalist Church, 57 Read St, at Grand Blvd. Eleven symbolic paintings by American landscape painter George Inness, Jr (1854–1926); guided tours. (Oct–May, daily exc Mon, limited hrs; closed hols) Phone 937-4682. ¢

5. **Noell's Ark Chimpanzee Farm.** 4612 Pinellas Ave N, approx 2 mi S on US 19A. Gorillas, chimpanzees, monkeys, orangutans, baboon, alligator, bear, birds; petting zoo. (Daily) ¢¢

(For further information contact the Greater Tarpon Springs Chamber of Commerce, 210 S Pinellas Ave, Suite 120, 34689, phone 937-6109; or the Pinellas Suncoast Tourist Development Council, 1 Stadium Dr, Suite A, St Petersburg 33705, phone 800/554-3600.)

Annual Event

Festival of the Epiphany. St Nicholas Cathedral. Blessing of the waters at noon, followed by Diving for the Cross Ceremony. Colorfully robed dignitaries, costumed children, acolytes, the Byzantine choir and others proceed through the streets from the church to Spring Bayou. There the Archbishop tosses a golden cross into the waters and the young men of the community plunge in to recover it. A benedictory service at the church is followed by banquets and a ball. Jan 6.

(See Clearwater, Dunedin, St Petersburg, Tampa)

Motels

★ ★ **BEST WESTERN TAHITIAN RESORT.** *(2337 US 19N, Holiday 34691)* ½ mi N of jct US 19A. 813/937-4121; FAX 813/937-3806. 140 rms, 2 story, 18 kits. Feb–mid-Apr: S, D $46–$83; each addl $5; kit. units $60–$90; under 12 free; wknd rates; lower rates rest of yr. Crib $3. Pet accepted, some restrictions; $3 per day. TV; cable. Heated pool. Restaurant 6 am–9 pm. Rm serv. Bar 11–2 am; entertainment Fri & Sat evening. Ck-out 11 am. Coin lndry. Cr cds: A, C, D, DS, MC, V.

✔ ★ **KNIGHTS INN.** *(34106 US 19N, Palm Harbor 34684)* S on US 19, 1 blk N of Nebraska Ave. 813/789-2002. 115 rms, 12 kits. Feb–Apr: S $40; D $52; kit. units $54; under 12 free; wkly rates; lower rates rest of yr. Crib avail. Pet accepted, some restrictions; $5 per night. TV; cable. Pool. Restaurant adj 7 am–8 pm. Ck-out noon. Meeting rm. Cr cds: A, C, D, DS, MC, V.

✔ ★ **TARPON SHORES INN.** 40346 US 19N (34689). 813/938-2483; res: 800/633-3802. 51 rms, 2 story, 16 kits. Mar–Apr: S, D $32–$53; kits. $37–$58; under 12 free; lower rates rest of yr. Crib $5. TV; cable. Heated pool; whirlpool, sauna. Complimentary coffee in lobby. Restaurant nearby. Ck-out 11 am. Coin lndry. Meeting rms. Cr cds: A, DS, MC, V.

Inn

★ ★ **SPRING BAYOU BED & BREAKFAST.** *32 W Tarpon Ave (34689).* 813/938-9333. 2 rms, 2 story. Dec–Apr: S $60–$85; D $70–$95; each addl $10; lower rates May–mid-Aug & Nov. Closed rest of yr. Adults only. Complimentary full bkfst, sherry. Restaurant nearby. Ck-out 11 am, ck-in 3–6 pm. Library, sitting area; baby grand piano. Sponge docks nearby. Totally nonsmoking. No cr cds accepted.

Resort

★ ★ ★ **INNISBROOK HILTON RESORT.** *(36750 N US 19, Palm Harbor 34684)* At Klosterman Rd. 813/942-2000; res: 800/456-2000; FAX 813/942-5576. 1,000 condo units in 28 lodges, 2–3 story. Jan–Apr: 1-bedrm, 2-bedrm $187–$360; each addl $10; under 18 free; AP, MAP, family rates; package plans; monthly rates; lower rates rest of yr. Deposit required. Crib free. TV; cable. 6 pools, heated; poolside serv. Supervised child's activities. Coffee in rms. 4 dining rms. Rm serv. 2 snack bars. 4 bars; entertainment. Ck-out noon, ck-in 3 pm. Package store. Free lndry facilities. Convention facilities. Concierge. Gift shop. Beauty shop. Complimentary beach shuttle. 15 tennis courts, 9 lighted, pro shop. 63-hole golf, pro, 4 putting greens, lighted driving range. Instructional tennis and golf. Miniature golf. Bicycle rentals. Lawn games. Rec dir. Game rm. Exercise rm; instructor, weights, bicycles, steam rm, sauna. Honor bars. Private patios, balconies. Popular with golfers; top-rated courses. Extensive wooded setting on 1,000 acres; elaborate landscaping. Wildlife sanctuary with nature walk. Fresh-water stocked lake. Tram service around extensive grounds. Cr cds: A, C, D, DS, MC, V.

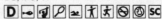

Restaurants

✔ ★ **BRASS KNOCKER.** *(4705 N US 19A, Palm Harbor)* 2 mi S on US 19A, ¼ mi S of Klosterman Rd. 813/943-8251. Hrs: 11 am–9 pm. Closed Mon. Res accepted. Bar. Semi-a la carte: lunch $1.99–$4.99, dinner $4.99–$8.95. Child's meals. Specializes in seafood, steak, chicken. Salad bar. Parking. Cr cds: MC, V.

★ ★ **LOUIS PAPPAS' RIVERSIDE.** *10 W Dodecanese Blvd, at sponge docks.* 813/937-5101. Hrs: 11:30 am–10 pm; Fri, Sat to 11 pm. Res accepted. Greek, Amer menu. Bar. Semi-a la carte: lunch $3.95–$8.95, dinner $4.95–$19.95. Child's meals. Specializes in Greek salad & pastries, prime rib, seafood. Entertainment exc Mon. Valet parking. Panoramic view of sponge boats & pleasure vessels. Family-owned. Cr cds: A, MC, V.

✔ ★ **PAUL'S.** *530 Athens W, at sponge docks.* 813/938-5093. Hrs: 11 am–10 pm; Sun noon–9 pm. Bar. Semi-a la carte: lunch, dinner $3.50–$12.95. Child's meals. Specializes in shrimp. Parking. Nautical decor. Cr cds: MC, V.

Tavares (B-3)

Founded: 1881 **Pop:** 7,383 **Elev:** 77 ft **Area code:** 904 **Zip:** 32778

Nestled between Lake Dora and Lake Eustis, Tavares is linked to seven nearby lakes by a system of rivers and canals and serves as a base for camping, hunting and fishing expeditions.

What to See and Do

1. **Ocala National Forest** (see OCALA). E via FL 44, then N on FL 19. There is a Ranger District office N on FL 19 in Umatilla, phone 669-3153.

2. **Fishing, boating.** Municipal pier, S end of St Clair Abrams Ave; public boat ramps on US 441; Lakes Dora and Eustis, W of town; Tavares Recreation Park on Lake Eustis; Dora Canal Park.

(For further information contact the Chamber of Commerce, 912 Sinclair Ave, PO Box 697; 343-2531.)

(See Clermont, Leesburg)

Motel

✔ ★ ★ **INN ON THE GREEN.** *700 E Burleigh Blvd.* 904/343-6373; res: 800/938-4653; FAX 904/343-7216. 76 rms, 2 story, 14 kit. units. Jan–Apr: S, D $48–$60; each addl $5; kit. units $10 addl; suites $95; under 12 free; wkly rates; higher rates special events; lower rates rest of yr. Crib $6. TV; cable, in-rm movies avail. Pool. Coffee in lobby. Restaurant nearby. Ck-out 11 am. Coin lndry. Sundries. Putting green, practice cages. Lawn games. Picnic tables. On lake. Cr cds: A, C, D, MC, V.

Motor Hotel

★ ★ **LAKESIDE INN OF MT DORA.** *(100 N Alexander St, Mt Dora 32757)* 4 mi S on US 441, then W on Donnelly to Alexander St. 904/383-4101; res: 800/556-5016; FAX 904/735-2642. 86 rms, 2 story. Jan–Apr: S $90–$130; D $105–$145; each addl $10; MAP avail; golf plans; higher rates Bicycle Fest (Oct); lower rates rest of yr. Crib free. TV; cable. Pool. Restaurant 7 am–2:30 pm, 5–10 pm. Rm serv. Ck-out 11 am. Lighted tennis. Golf privileges, pro, putting green. 5 buildings on 5 lakeside acres. Cr cds: A, C, D, DS, MC, V.

Resort

★ ★ ★ **MISSION INN GOLF & TENNIS RESORT.** *(10400 CR 48, Howey-in-the-Hills 34737)* FL 19, 48, 6½ mi N on FL 19 from FL Tpke exit 285. 904/324-3101; res: 800/874-9053 (exc FL); FAX 904/324-3101, ext 7443. 176 rms, 15 villas, 15 kits, 1–4 story. Feb–Apr: S, D $175–$195; suites $230–$335; villas $320–$375; under 12 free; AP, MAP avail; wkly rates; golf, tennis plans; lower rates rest of yr. Crib free. TV; cable. Heated pool; poolside serv. Playground. Dining rm 7 am–2 pm, 6–10 pm (also see EL CONQUISTADOR). Rm serv. Bar 5 pm–midnight; entertainment, dancing. Ck-out noon, ck-in 4 pm. Coin lndry. Convention facilities. Bellhops. Valet serv. Gift shop. Airport, attractions transportation. 6 tennis courts, 4 lighted, pro. 36-hole golf course, greens fee, putting green, driving range, pro, instruction. Pro shop. Private lakes, motor & sail boats; marina. Yacht cruises 3 times wkly. Bicycle rentals. Lawn games. Exercise equipt; weights, bicycles, whirlpool. Rec rm. Some refrigerators; wet bar in suites. Some fireplaces. Private patios, balconies. Picnic tables. Toiletry amenities. Unique furniture, hand-carved. Complimentary newspaper. Extensive grounds, elaborate landscaping, waterfall at entrance. Cr cds: A, C, D, DS, MC, V.

Restaurants

✔ ★ **CAPTAIN APPLEBY'S INN.** *(400 US 441, Mt Dora)* E on US 441, ¼ mi W of FL 44B. 904/383-6662. Hrs: 11:30 am–9:30 pm; Fri, Sat to 10 pm; Sun 10 am–8:30 pm; Sun brunch to 2 pm. Closed Thanksgiving, Dec 25. Bar. A la carte entrees: lunch $3.99–$7.99, dinner $7.99–$13.99. Sun brunch $9.99. Child's meals. Specializes in seafood, steak, prime rib. Salad bar. Parking. Florida cracker country atmosphere. Cr cds: A, DS, MC, V.

★ ★ ★ **EL CONQUISTADOR.** *(See Mission Inn Golf & Tennis Resort)* 904/324-3101. Hrs: 6–9:30 pm. Res required. Continental menu. Bar 5 pm–midnight. Wine list. A la carte entrees: dinner $12–$26. Specializes in fresh seafood, veal. Pianist, vocalists, dancing. Overlooks golf course, small lakes. Family-owned. Jacket in season (Labor Day–Memorial Day). Cr cds: A, C, D, DS, MC, V.

Titusville (C-4)

Founded: 1867 **Pop:** 39,394 **Elev:** 18 ft **Area code:** 407

Located on the Indian River, Titusville has always been known for its saltwater trout, shrimp and crab. Indian River citrus, grown along its banks, is famous the world over. The sleepy atmosphere of the area was forever changed by Kennedy Space Center and the nearby attractions around Orlando.

What to See and Do

1. **Kennedy Space Center** (see). S on US 1, then 12 mi E on FL 405.
2. **US Astronaut Hall of Fame/US Space Camp.** S on NASA Pkwy. **Hall of Fame** features historic artifacts, personal mementos of original Mercury astronauts; rare video footage. Multimedia presentation depicts a shuttle mission aboard full-scale orbiter mock-up. **Space Camp** offers children completing grades 4-7 a 5-day program in which participants tour NASA facilities and experience a simulated astronaut training program (advance reservations required). Hall of Fame (daily; closed Dec 25). Contact 6225 Vectorspace Blvd, 32780; 269-6100. Hall of Fame ¢¢¢
3. **Canaveral National Seashore.** 7 mi E of town via FL 402. Area consists of 24 miles of unspoiled beaches with Apollo Beach at the north (7 mi S of New Smyrna Beach on FL A1A) and Playalinda Beach at the south (12 mi E of Titusville via FL 406 & FL 402); there are no connecting roads between Apollo and Playalinda—the central portion, Klondike Beach, can be reached only by foot, bicycle or on horseback. More than 300 species of birds have been observed within the seashore; Mosquito Lagoon, between the beach and the Intracoastal Waterway, provides a sanctuary for 14 endangered and threatened species. Recreation includes swimming, waterskiing, surfing, beachcombing, crabbing, clamming, shrimping; surf & freshwater fishing; boating (ramps), canoeing. Hiking trails. Picnicking. Primitive camping on beach (Nov–Apr; permit required); backcountry camping in some designated areas. Note: Playalinda Beach and other sections may be periodically closed due to NASA launch-related activities; inquire locally. (Daily) Contact the Superintendent, 308 Julia St, 32796; 267-1110. **Free.** Adjoining the seashore is

Merritt Island National Wildlife Refuge. Located beneath the Atlantic flyway, the refuge is a sanctuary for wintering waterfowl. Bird watching; hunting (in season). Contact Refuge Manager, PO Box 6504, 32782; 861-0667.

(For further information contact the Chamber of Commerce, 2000 S Washington Ave, PO Drawer 2767, 32780; 267-3036.)

Annual Event

Valiant Air Command Air Show. 6600 Tico Rd, 5 mi S via US 1 or I-95 & US 50 at Space Center Executive Airport. World War II airshow; vintage aircraft in aerial display of formation flying, dog-fights, aerobatics and bombing/strafing runs; pyrotechnics, special effects and current military displays. Phone 268-1944 or -1942. Mar.

(See Cocoa, Cocoa Beach)

Motels

★ **HOWARD JOHNSON.** *1829 Riverside Dr (US 1)* (32780). 407/267-7900; FAX 407/267-7080. 104 rms, 2 story. Feb–Apr: S $54–$74; D $59–$79; each addl $10; under 18 free; higher rates: Daytona races, space launches, special events; lower rates rest of yr. Crib free. TV; cable. Pool. Playground. Free coffee in rms. Restaurant open 24 hrs. Bar 3 pm–2 am; dancing. Ck-out noon. Coin lndry. Valet serv.

Sundries. Private patios, balconies. On Indian River; overlooks Kennedy Space Center. Cr cds: A, C, D, DS, ER, MC, V, JCB.

★★QUALITY INN-KENNEDY SPACE CENTER. *3755 Cheney Hwy (32780), I-95 exit 79.* 407/269-4480; FAX 407/383-0646. 142 rms, 2 story. S $45; D $60; each addl $6; kit. units $65; under 17 free; wkly rates; higher rates special events. Crib free. TV; cable. Pool; wading pool. Restaurant 6:30-10:30 am, 5-9 pm. Bar 4 pm-midnight. Ck-out 11 am. Coin lndry. Meeting rms. Lawn games. Refrigerators avail. Cr cds: A, C, D, DS, ER, MC, V, JCB.

★★RAMADA INN. *3500 Cheney Hwy (32780), I-95 exit 79.* 407/269-5510; FAX 407/269-3796. 124 rms, 2 story, 26 kits. S, D $55-$89; each addl $6; suites, kit. units $79-$125; under 18 free; higher rates; Daytona races, space launches. Crib free. TV; cable. Heated pool. Playground. Restaurant open 24 hrs. Rm serv. Bar. Ck-out noon. Coin lndry. Sundries. Meeting rms. Lighted tennis. Exercise equipt; weight machine, bicycles, sauna, whirlpool. Game rm. Space shuttle exhibit in lobby. Cr cds: A, C, D, DS, MC, V.

✔★TRAVELODGE-SPACE CITY USA. *3810 S Washington Ave (US 1) (32780).* 407/267-9111; FAX 407/267-0750. 105 rms, 2 story. Jan-Apr: S, D $40-$50; each addl $7; under 18 free; higher rates: space launches, race wks; lower rates rest of yr. Crib $3. TV; cable. Pool. Restaurant 7 am-10 pm. Rm serv. Ck-out noon. Coin lndry. Valet serv. Refrigerators avail. Indian River opp. View of launch pads. Cr cds: A, C, D, DS, MC, V.

Resort

★★LA CITA COUNTRY CLUB. *777 Country Club Dr (32780).* 407/383-2582; FAX 407/267-4209. 37 condo units (1-2-bedrm), 1-2 story. Nov-Apr: S $80-$120; D $100-$140; each addl $20-$30; under 15 free; package plans; varied lower rates rest of yr. TV; cable. Pool. Ck-out noon, ck-in 3 pm. Grocery, package store 1 blk. Meeting rms. Lighted tennis, pro. 18-hole golf, greens fee $25-$40, pro, putting green, driving range. Water exercise. Entertainment. Exercise rm; instructor, weights, bicycles, whirlpool. Private patios. Shopping center opp. Cr cds: A, D, DS, MC, V.

Restaurants

★DIXIE CROSSROADS. *1475 Garden St.* 407/268-5000. Hrs: 11 am-10 pm. Closed Thanksgiving, Dec 24, 25. Serv bar. Semi-a la carte: lunch $3.95-$7.95, dinner $6.95-$14.95. Child's meals. Specializes in local mullet, shrimp, corn fritters. Parking. Rustic decor; knotty pine walls, display of mounted fish, nautical pictures. Cr cds: A, C, D, DS, MC, V.

✔★★SAND POINT INN. *801 Marina Rd.* 407/269-1012. Hrs: 11 am-10 pm; early-bird dinner Mon-Fri 4-6 pm. Res accepted. Bar. Semi-a la carte: lunch $3.99-$6.99, dinner $6.99-$12.99. Child's meals. Specializes in callico scallops, rock shrimp. Parking. Nautical atmosphere. Overlooks marina and Indian River. Cr cds: A, MC, V.

D

Treasure Island

(see St Petersburg Beach Area)

Venice (D-3)

Pop: 16,922 **Elev:** 18 ft **Area code:** 813

Venice retains the spaciousness planned for it in 1924-25 when it was transformed from an obscure fishing village into a retirement city for the Brotherhood of Locomotive Engineers. The retirement project was discontinued after the 1929 stock market crash, but a small-scale economic boom began in 1960 when the Ringling Bros & Barnum and Bailey Circus moved their winter quarters here from Sarasota. Three public beaches and jetties provide swimming and fishing opportunities while beachcombers can find numerous fossilized shark's teeth on shore.

What to See and Do

1. **Oscar Scherer State Recreation Area.** 6 mi N on US 41 near Osprey. Approximately 1,400 acres of pine and scrubby flatwoods on the banks of a small tidal creek. Swimming; fishing; canoeing (rentals). Nature trails. Picnicking. Camping (no hookups, dump station). Standard hrs, fees. Phone 483-5956.

2. **Warm Mineral Springs and Cyclorama.** 14 mi SE on US 41 to San Servando Ave (I-75 exit 34) in Warm Mineral Springs. Springs produce 9 million gallons of water at 87°F daily. Bathhouse and lockers (fee); Wellness Center. Picnic sites. Cyclorama show in 226-foot enclosed rotunda depicts adventures of Ponce de Leon in 3-dimensional murals. (Daily; closed Dec 25) Phone 426-1692. ¢¢¢

(For further information contact the Venice Area Chamber of Commerce, 257 N Tamiami Trail, 34285; 488-2236.)

Annual Event

Venetian Sun Fiesta. Parade, entertainment, barbecue, contests, fishing tournament. 10 days Oct.

(See Sarasota)

Motels

★★BEST WESTERN SANDBAR BEACH RESORT. *811 The Esplanade North (34285).* 813/488-2251; FAX 813/485-2894. 44 rms, 1-4 story, 30 kits. Feb-Apr: S $110; D $130; kits. $140-$150; under 12 free; lower rates rest of yr. Crib free. TV; cable. Heated pool. Restaurant 7 am-2 pm, 5-8 pm. Ck-out 11 am. Coin lndry. Lawn games. On beach. Cr cds: A, C, D, DS, ER, MC, V.

★★★BEST WESTERN VENICE RESORT INN. *455 N US 41 Bypass (34292).* 813/485-5411; FAX 813/484-6193. 160 rms, 2 story. Feb-Apr: S, D $84-$94; each addl $6; suites $175; under 12 free; wkly rates; lower rates rest of yr. Crib free. Pet accepted, some restrictions; $12. TV; cable. Heated pool; whirlpool. Playground. Bar; entertainment. Ck-out 11 am. Coin lndry. Meeting rms. Lawn games. Dinner theater. Cr cds: A, C, D, DS, ER, MC, V, JCB.

D

Restaurants

★★SHARKY'S. *1600 S Harbor Dr, on Venice Pier.* 813/488-1456. Hrs: 11:30 am-9:30 pm; Fri, Sat to 10:30 pm; Sun brunch 10:30 am-2:30 pm. Res accepted off season. Bar. Semi-a la carte: lunch $3.95-$8.50, dinner $7.95-$15.95. Sun brunch $11.95. Child's meals. Specializes in crab cakes, fresh seafood, steak. Entertainment. Parking. Outdoor dining. Nautical decor. Shark jaw display, souvenirs. Shell valances. On beach, pier. Cr cds: DS, MC, V.

★**SMITTY'S.** *133 S Tamiami Trail (US 41 Business). 813/ 488-2601.* Hrs: 11:30 am–2:30 pm, 4:30–10 pm; Sun noon–9 pm. Closed Dec 25. Res accepted. Bar 11 am–11 pm; Fri, Sat to midnight; Sun noon–9 pm. Semi-a la carte: lunch $3.95–$9.95, dinner $8.95–$29.95. Child's meals. Specializes in fresh seafood, aged prime beef. Parking. Family-owned. Cr cds: A, MC, V.

✔ ★**WEDGWOOD.** *100 W Tampa Ave. 813/488-4017.* Hrs: 11 am–8:30 pm; Sat from 4:30 pm; Sun 11 am–8 pm; early-bird dinner Tues–Fri 3–5:30 pm, Sat 4:30–5:30 pm. Closed Mon; Jan 1, Dec 25; also mid-June–mid-July. Res accepted. Bar to 10 pm. Semi-a la carte: lunch, dinner $2.75–$12.95. Child's meals. Specializes in seafood. Salad bar. Parking. Wedgwood china displayed. Cr cds: MC, V.

D

Vero Beach (D-5)

Pop: 17,350 **Elev:** 20 ft **Area code:** 407

With its broad streets lined with tropical plants and its miles of un-crowded beaches, Vero Beach is a favorite of many perennial Florida visitors. Citrus shipping supplements tourism as a major industry.

What to See and Do

1. **Riverside Park Complex.** Beachland Blvd. Boat launch. One-mile jogging trail, bike path; tennis & racquetball courts (fee). Picnic pavilions (fireplaces). Site of Riverside Theater and Center for the Arts (fees). Phone 567-2144.

2. **Sebastian Inlet State Recreation Area.** 15 mi N on FL A1A, just N of Sebastian. More than 570 acres, bounded by the Indian River and the Atlantic Ocean. Swimming, surfing, skin diving; saltwater fishing; boat ramp. Picnicking, concession. Tent & trailer camping (hookups, dump station). Standard hrs, fees. Phone 984-4852 or 589-9659 (camping). Here is

    McLarty Treasure Museum. Exhibits and artifacts of a Spanish treasure fleet downed in this area in 1715; diorama depicts salvage efforts; slide show on history of site; self-guided audio tour. (Daily) Phone 589-2147. ¢

(For further information contact Vero Beach–Indian River County Tourist Council, 1216 21st St, PO Box 2947, 32961; 567-3491.)

Annual Event

Grant Seafood Festival. N via US 1, in Grant. Feb.

Seasonal Event

Professional baseball. Holman Stadium, Dodgertown, 4000 Walker Ave. Los Angeles Dodgers spring training; exhibition games. Phone 569-4900. Early Mar–early Apr.

(See Fort Pierce, Melbourne)

Motels

★**AQUARIUS NORTH.** *3544 Ocean Dr (32963). 407/231-1133.* 28 kit. units, 10 with shower only, 2 story, 10 suites. Feb–Apr: S, D $85–$115; each addl $5; suites $95–$115; under 12 free; wkly rates off season; lower rates rest of yr. Crib $5. TV; cable. Heated pool. Complimentary coffee in lobby. Restaurant opp 6 am–11 pm. Ck-out 11 am. Coin lndry. On beach; swimming. Cr cds: A, D, DS, MC, V.

✔ ★**AQUARIUS OCEANFRONT RESORT.** *1526 S Ocean Dr (32963). 407/231-5218.* 27 units, 2 story, 25 kits. Feb–Apr: S, D $50;

each addl $5; studios rms $85–$110; 1 & 2-bedrm $95–$110; under 12 free; wkly rates; some wkend rates; lower rates rest of yr. Crib $5. TV; cable. Heated pool. Restaurant opp 5–10 pm. Ck-out 11 am. Coin lndry. Lawn games. Refrigerators. Picnic tables, grills. On ocean, beach. Cr cds: D, DS, MC, V.

★**DAYS INN.** *8800 20th St (32966), I-95 exit 68, FL 60. 407/ 562-9991; FAX 407/562-0716.* 232 rms, 2 story, 4 kits. Feb–Mar: S $60; D $65; each addl $5; wkly rates; lower rates rest of yr. Pet accepted, some restrictions; $5. TV; cable. Pool. Restaurant 6 am–9 pm. Ck-out 11 am. Meeting rms. Cr cds: A, C, D, DS, MC, V.

✔ ★**HoJo INN.** *1985 90th Ave (32966), I-95 exit 68. 407/778-1985; FAX 407/778-1998.* 68 rms, 2 story. Feb–Mar: S $55; D $60; each addl $5; under 18 free; wkly rates; lower rates rest of yr. Pet accepted; $25. TV; cable. Complimentary bkfst. Restaurant opp open 24 hrs. Ck-out noon. Coin lndry. Refrigerators. Cr cds: A, C, D, DS, MC, V.

★ ★**HOLIDAY INN-COUNTRYSIDE.** *8797 20th St (32966), I-95 exit 68 (FL 60). 407/567-8321; FAX 407/569-8558.* 117 rms, 2 story. Mid-Jan–mid-Apr: S $61–$67; D $67–$73; each addl $6; under 18 free; lower rates rest of yr. Crib free. TV; cable. Heated pool; wading pool. Playground. Restaurant 6:30 am–2 pm, 5–10 pm. Rm serv. Bar 4 pm–1 am; dancing. Ck-out noon. Coin lndry. Meeting rms. Valet serv. Free airport transportation. Game rm. Lawn games. Cr cds: A, C, D, DS, MC, V, JCB.

★ ★**ISLANDER.** *3101 Ocean Dr (32963). 407/231-4431; res: 800/952-5886.* 16 units, 2 story. Jan–Apr: S, D from $89; each addl $7; lower rates rest of yr. TV; cable. Pool. Complimentary coffee. Restaurant 7 am–7 pm. Ck-out 11 am. Bicycle rentals. Refrigerators. Some balconies. Beach across street. Cr cds: A, DS, MC, V.

✔ ★ ★**SURF AND SAND.** *1516 S Ocean Dr (32963). 407/231-5700; FAX 407/231-9386.* 15 rms, 2 story, 10 kits. Feb–Apr: S, D $60; each addl $5; kit. units $85–$115; wkly rates; lower rates rest of yr. Crib free. TV; cable. Complimentary coffee. Heated pool. Restaurant opp. Ck-out 11 am. Lawn games. Refrigerators. Grill. On ocean, beach. Cr cds: DS, MC, V.

Motor Hotels

★ ★ ★**DAYS HOTEL-VERO BEACH RESORT.** *3244 Ocean Dr (32963). 407/231-2800; FAX 407/231-3446.* 110 rms, 5 story, 8 kits. Feb–Apr: S, D $79–$135; kit. units $120–$135; under 18 free; package plans; lower rates rest of yr. TV; cable. Pool. Restaurant 6:30 am–10 pm. Bar 11–1 am. Ck-out 11 am. Meeting rms. Private patios, balconies. On ocean, beach. Cr cds: A, D, DS, MC, V.

★ ★**HOLIDAY INN-OCEANSIDE.** *3384 Ocean Dr (32963). 407/231-2300; FAX 407/234-8069.* 104 rms, 3 story, 16 kits. Feb–mid-Apr: S $74–$124; D $81–$131; each addl $7; suites $131; under 19 free; lower rates rest of yr. TV; cable. Heated pool; wading pool, poolside serv. Restaurant 7 am–10 pm. Rm serv. Bar 4 pm–12:30 am; entertainment. Ck-out 11 am. Coin lndry. Meeting rms. Bellhops. Beauty shop. Some refrigerators. Private patios, balconies with ocean view. On beach. Cr cds: A, C, D, DS, ER, MC, V, JCB.

Hotel

★ ★ ★**GUEST QUARTERS SUITE RESORT.** *3500 Ocean Dr (32963). 407/231-5666; FAX 407/234-4866.* 55 suites, 4 story. Mid-Dec–Apr: 1 & 2 bedrm $175–$245; under 19 free; golf, fishing, tennis packages; lower rates rest of yr. Crib free. TV; in-rm movies. Heated pool; wading pool, whirlpool, poolside serv. Restaurant 7 am–10 pm. Ck-out noon. Meeting rms. Garage. Wet bar. Private patios, balconies. On ocean, beach. Cr cds: A, C, D, DS, MC, V.

Restaurants

✔ ★**BEACHSIDE.** *3125 Ocean Dr (FL A1A). 407/234-4477.* Hrs: 6:30 am–8 pm; Sun to 3 pm. Closed Dec 25. Italian, Amer menu. A la carte entrees: bkfst $1.50–$5.95. Semi-a la carte: lunch $2.75–$5.95, dinner $5.50–$13.95. Complete meals: bkfst $2.95–$5.95, lunch $3.95–$8.95. Specializes in fresh grouper, lasagne, Key lime pie. Cr cds: MC, V.

★ ★ ★**BLACK PEARL.** *1409 Ocean Dr (FL A1A). 407/234-4426.* Hrs: 6–10 pm. Closed Jan 1, July 4, Thanksgiving, Dec 25. Res required. Beer. Wine list. Semi-a la carte: dinner $15.50. Specializes in mesquite-grilled local seafood. Own pastries. Parking. Eclectic decor. Cr cds: A, MC, V.

D

★ ★**OCEAN GRILL.** *1050 Sexton Plaza. 407/231-5409.* Hrs: 11:30 am–2:30 pm, 5:45–10 pm; Sat, Sun from 5:45 pm. Closed 2 wks following Labor Day. Bar. Semi-a la carte: lunch $5.95–$13.95, dinner $10.95–$24.95. Child's meals. Specializes in roast duckling, fresh seafood. Parking. Ocean view. European artifacts. Family-owned. Cr cds: A, D, DS, MC, V.

D

★ ★**PATIO.** *1103 Miracle Mile. 407/567-7215.* Hrs: 11–1 am; Sun brunch 10:30 am–2:30 pm. Bar. Semi-a la carte: lunch $3.95–$7.50, dinner $4.95–$22.95. Sun champagne brunch $11.95. Child's meals. Specializes in fresh fish, prime rib. Raw bar. Entertainment. Parking. Outdoor dining. One of oldest eating establishments in Vero Beach; old Spanish decor. Cr cds: A, MC, V.

Wakulla Springs

(see Tallahassee)

Walt Disney World (C-4)

(22 mi SW of Orlando at I-4 and FL 535 in Lake Buena Vista) **Area code:** 407

For the people at Walt Disney World, making dreams come true is a way of life. From its major theme parks to its resort hotels, everything is run with a touch of make-believe in mind. It takes some 35,000 people to keep the Vacation Kingdom going, and every facet of operation is designed to keep visitors happy and content in this gossamer fantasy-land.

The Magic Kingdom, the first of the three major parks, offers more than forty-six attractions as well as shows, shops, exhibits, refreshment areas and special theme areas divided into seven "lands": Adventureland, Frontierland, Liberty Square, Fantasyland, Mickey's Starland, Tomorrowland and Main Street, U.S.A. Since its opening in 1971, Walt Disney World has received untold millions of visitors, making it the most popular tourist attraction in the world.

While the Magic Kingdom may be the best known area of the park, it takes up only a fraction of the 28,000-acre resort complex (almost twice the size of Manhattan Island). Combined with Epcot Center, which opened October 1, 1982, Disney-MGM Studios, which opened May 1, 1989, and the variety of other new attractions, Walt Disney World is a vacation kingdom unique in all the world. Epcot Center, the most dramatic Disney project to date, takes visitors through two distinct "worlds." Future World combines rides and attractions, technical inno-

vations, discovery and scientific achievements, bringing to life a world of new ideas, adventures and entertainment. World Showcase brings together eleven celebrated nations re-created in exact detail through architectural landmarks, shops, authentic food and entertainment.

Disney-MGM Studios explores the world of movies and television, both on-stage and off, and includes a working studio. Palm-lined, art deco-style Hollywood Boulevard offers adventure, entertainment, shopping and dining in true Hollywood style. The park offers a mix of cinema nostalgia, sensational stunt work, television magic and backstage wizardry.

In addition to the Magic Kingdom, Epcot Center and Disney-MGM Studios, Walt Disney World offers many hotels (see); a campground facility with a water recreation park; a 7,500-acre conservation/wilderness area preserving virgin stands of pine, cypress and bay trees; daily parades and fireworks displays; shopping; and several fine restaurants (see). Activities include relaxing on more than 4 miles of beach, fishing, swimming, sailing, motorboating, waterskiing, tennis, steamboat excursions, ranch and trail rides, picnicking and hiking. There are five 18-hole championship golf courses—collectively referred to as the "Magic Linkdom:" the Palm, Magnolia, Lake Buena Vista, Eagle Pines and Osprey Ridge, plus a 9-hole family-play course. All are available for play by the general public.

Walt Disney World's several areas are tied together by a transportation system that includes motorcoaches, 19th-century ferry boats and the famous monorail. Guests at Fort Wilderness Campground and Disney-owned hotels have free use of the transportation system. Special evening shows at Walt Disney World include fireworks, lasers, parades of singers and dancers, moonlight cruises and a variety of after-dark entertainment (see #8).

Walt Disney World is open every day of the year with extended hours in summer and during holiday periods. Guided tours are recommended for first-time visitors. Various ticket combinations are available (inquire about details and limits at time of reservation): a One-park/One-day pass to the Magic Kingdom, Epcot Center or Disney-MGM Studios, $35; a four-day Super Pass with admission to all three of the major theme parks, $125; or a five-day Super-Duper Pass, which also provides 7 consecutive days of admission to Pleasure Island, Typhoon Lagoon, River Country and Discovery Island, $170. Admission to each of the smaller parks also by separate fee. Fees for children ages 3–9 are lower; age 2 and under admitted free. Phone 824-4321.

Transportation

Orlando Intl Airport: Information 825-2001; lost and found 825-2111; weather 851-7510; cash stations, Main Terminal, near bank office; Crown Room (Delta), Main Terminal; USAir Club (US Air), Main Terminal.

Car Rental Agencies: See toll-free numbers under Introduction.

Transportation at Walt Disney World: Monorail, buses, motor launches, basic fare per day $2.50, free with All-Three-Parks Passport and to guests at Disney-owned resorts.

Rail Passenger Service: Amtrak 800/872-7245.

What to See and Do

1. Magic Kingdom. Home of Mickey Mouse and Cinderella, includes

Main St, U.S.A. Depicts 1890–1910 America when, electricity and horseless carriages began replacing gas lamps and horse-drawn vehicles. Steam trains depart from Victorian-style station for tour around the Magic Kingdom.

Fantasyland. Dominated by 18-story Cinderella Castle; highlights include Disney characters, It's A Small World and 20,000 Leagues Under the Sea, featuring Captain Nemo's submarines.

Mickey's Starland. Land of Mickey and friends includes tour of Mickey's house, Mickey's dressing room and a live stage show starring the famous mouse and all his animated pals.

Tomorrowland. Preview of developments for the near and distant future; featuring Grand Prix Raceway; Mission to Mars and Space Mountain.

Adventureland. Jungle cruises to see "live" lions, hippos and headhunters found on rivers around the world. Swiss Family Tree House affords view of the jungle area. Also features Pirates of the Caribbean.

Frontierland. Re-creation of the Old West when pioneers first arrived; wild west stage show at the Diamond Horseshoe Revue; a troupe of bears performs a Western hoedown; Big Thunder Mountain Railroad features a runaway train ride through an Old West mining town. A recent addition is Splash Mountain, a flume ride based on sequences from the Disney film *Song of the South* (1946); guests board eight-passenger hollowed-out logs for a half-mile journey on which they encounter a host of zany characters, including Br'er Rabbit, Br'er Fox and Br'er Bear. The climax of the trip is a thrilling 50-foot, 40-mph drop into the Briar Patch.

Liberty Square. Portrayal of America at the time of its founding; cobblestone streets, colonial shops; Hall of Presidents features 40 life-size, lifelike figures of United States presidents. The Haunted Mansion has an assortment of 999 ghosts, goblins and ghouls waiting to greet visitors.

2. **Epcot Center.** This far-reaching Disney project, the largest of the three theme parks, features these two "worlds."

Future World. Eight themed pavilions present new ideas and technologies in exciting areas such as energy, transportation, communications and imagination; visitors can take a ride through Spaceship Earth, view the 3-D musical film *Captain EO,* take a high-speed simulated flight through the human body, use their imaginations in a state-of-the-art electronic playground, journey through transportation history or participate in various hands-on computer-related exhibits.

World Showcase. These pavilions, surrounding a 40-acre lagoon, showcase some of the world's most fascinating nations— Canada, China, France, Germany, Italy, Japan, Mexico, Morocco, Norway, the United Kingdom and the United States—through treasure-laden shops, enticing restaurants with international specialties, native entertainers, films and attractions.

3. **Disney-MGM Studios.** Just southwest of Epcot Center off the main entrance road, this area houses three film and television soundstages of the Walt Disney Company, giving people a chance to watch a film or television show in the making. Various rides and shows let visitors see the backlots, an animation studio, soundstages of famous films and an explanation of stunt work used in major movies. SuperStar Television and the Monster Sound Show allow guests to work with sound effects, trade quips on a sitcom and prepare for stardom in the "Green Room." Children can play on the *Honey, I Shrunk the Kids* Movie Set Adventure, with 30-foot-tall synthetic grass. New stage shows include Beauty and the Beast and Voyage of the Little Mermaid.

4. **Fort Wilderness Campground.** A 780-acre pine and cypress forest with 785 campsites and 407 "wilderness homes" for rent. The area has swimming pools, beaches; marina, canoeing streams; tennis courts and air-conditioned shower and laundry facilities. All sites have water, power and sewer hookups. Within Fort Wilderness are

River Country. Water slides, flumes, rapids, white-sand beaches and a heated swimming pool round out this Disney version of the "old swimmin' hole."

Discovery Island. An 11-acre island in Bay Lake with exotic birds, animals, flower gardens and nature trails.

5. **Typhoon Lagoon.** A 56-acre water park located between Epcot Center and Disney Village Marketplace. Features world's largest wave pool; 9 waterslides descending from a 95-foot summit; surfing lagoon; saltwater snorkeling in Shark Reef; inner-tube rides. Changing areas, lockers, showers, picnicking and restaurants.

6. **Pleasure Island.** On the shores of Village Lake, linked to Disney Village Marketplace by footbridge. Six-acre entertainment complex featuring six nightclubs with live music and dancing, shows,

comedy, entertainment, shopping and dining. A single cover charge admits guests to all clubs.

7. **Disney Village Marketplace.** Located in Lake Buena Vista. A collection of unique shops, restaurants and nightclubs clustered around a lagoon in a resort community.

8. **Nighttime features.**

SpectroMagic. Magic Kingdom. Musical parade of performers and floats decorated with millions of twinkling lights, covering such Disney themes as *Fantasia* and *The Little Mermaid.* (Nightly, during extended hrs)

IllumiNations. Epcot Center. A dramatic 15-minute laser, pyrotechnic and water show set to symphonic music, presented around World Showcase Lagoon. (Nightly)

Fantasy in the Sky. Magic Kingdom. Fireworks show above Cinderella Castle expends more than 200 shells in under 5 minutes. (Nightly, during extended hrs)

9. **Gray Line bus tours.** Leave from Orlando. Contact PO Box 1671, Orlando 32802; 422-0744.

(For further information contact PO Box 10000, Lake Buena Vista, 32830, 824-4321; for reservations to many of the lodgings phone W-DISNEY.)

Annual Events

Walt Disney World Village Wine Festival. At Disney Village Marketplace (see #7). June.

Fourth of July. Pyrotechnical tour de force over the Seven Seas Lagoon in the Magic Kingdom; also at Disney-MGM Studios and in Epcot Center. July 4.

Walt Disney World Golf Classic. At the "Magic Linkdom." Late Oct.

Halloween. At Disney Village Marketplace (see #7). Villains from Disney films, inclding the Evil Queen from *Snow White and the Seven Dwarfs* and Cruella de Vil from *101 Dalmations,* make appearances after dark. Oct 31.

Festival of the Masters Art Festival. At Disney Village Marketplace (see #7). Early Nov.

(See Altamonte Springs, Clermont, Haines City, Kissimmee, Orlando, Winter Park)

Motor Hotels

✔ ★**COMFORT INN.** *(Box 22776, Lake Buena Vista 32830) 8442 Palm Pkwy, at Vista Ctr.* 407/239-7300; res: 800/999-7300; FAX 407/239-7740. 640 rms, 5 story. Feb–mid-Apr, June–Aug: S, D up to 4, $69; family rates; lower rates rest of yr. Crib free. Pet accepted. TV. 2 pools, 1 heated. Restaurant 6:30–10:30 am, 6–9 pm. Bar 5:30 pm–2 am. Ck-out 11 am. Coin lndry. Valet serv. Sundries. Gift shop. Free Walt Disney World transportation. Game rm. Cr cds: A, C, D, DS, ER, MC, V, JCB.

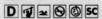

★★★**HOLIDAY INN LAKE SUN SPREE RESORT-LAKE BUENA VISTA.** *(Box 22184, 13351 FL 535, Lake Buena Vista 32830) I-4 exit 27, S on FL 535.* 407/239-4500; FAX 407/239-7713. 507 rms, 6 story. Mid-Feb–mid-Apr, mid-June–mid-Aug, late Dec: S, D $106–$140; under 18 free; lower rates rest of yr. Crib free. TV; cable, in-rm movies. Heated pool; wading pool, whirlpools, poolside serv. Playground. Supervised child's activities. Restaurant 7 am–midnight. Rm serv. Bar from 4:30 pm; entertainment. Ck-out 11 am. Coin lndry. Bellhops. Valet serv. Concierge. Sundries. Shopping arcade. Airport transportation. Free Walt Disney World transportation. 36-hole golf privileges, pro, putting green, driving range. Game rm. Refrigerators. Pink and white stone structure with blue-tiled roofs. Cr cds: A, C, D, DS, ER, MC, V, JCB.

★★**HOWARD JOHNSON PARK SQUARE INN AND SUITES.**
(PO Box 22818, Lake Buena Vista 32830) 8501 Palm Pkwy. I-4 exit 27 to FL 535, N to Vista Center. 407/239-6900; FAX 407/239-1287. 222 rms, 3 story, 86 suites. Feb-mid-Apr, June-Aug, late Dec: S, D $80-$115; each addl $10; suites $90-$140; under 18 free; lower rates rest of yr. Crib free. TV; in-rm movies. 2 pools, heated; wading pool, whirlpool. Playground. Restaurant 7-11 am, 5-10 pm. Bar 4:30 pm-midnight. Ck-out 11 am. Coin lndry. Meeting rms. Bellhops. Sundries. Gift shop. Airport transportation. Free Walt Disney World transportation. Game rm. Lawn games. Refrigerator in suites. Balconies. Landscaped courtyard. Cr cds: A, C, D, DS, ER, MC, V, JCB.

Hotels

★★★**BUENA VISTA PALACE.** *(1900 Buena Vista Dr, Lake Buena Vista 32830) In Walt Disney World Village.* 407/827-2727; res: 800/327-2990; FAX 407/827-6034. 1,028 rms, 27 story, 128 suites. Feb-Apr, late Dec: S, D $145-$240; suites $215-$850; under 18 free; lower rates rest of yr. Crib free. TV; cable. 3 pools, 2 heated; wading pool, poolside serv. Supervised child's activities (June-Labor Day; also wk of Christmas & Easter). Restaurant open 24 hrs (also see ARTHUR'S 27). Bar 11-3 am; entertainment, dancing. Ck-out 11 am. Coin lndry. Convention facilities. Shopping arcade. Barber, beauty shop. Valet parking. Airport transportation. Free Walt Disney World transportation. Lighted tennis. 18-hole golf privileges, pro, pro shop, putting green, driving range. Exercise equipt; weights, bicycles, whirlpool, sauna. Game rm. Some in-rm whirlpools, refrigerators, minibars. Many balconies. *LUXURY LEVEL: CROWN LEVEL.* 78 rms, 2 suites, 2 floors. S, D (to 5 persons) $240; 1-bedrm suites $385-$615. Concierge. Private lounge. Bathrm phones. Some in-rm steam baths. Complimentary continental bkfst, refreshments.
Cr cds: A, C, D, DS, MC, V.

✔★★**DOUBLETREE CLUB.** *(8688 Palm Pkwy, Lake Buena Vista 32836)* I-4 exit 27 to FL 535, N to Vista Center. 407/239-8500; FAX 407/239-8591. 167 rms, 6 story. S, D $85; each addl $10; under 12 free. Crib free. TV; cable. In-rm movies. Heated pool; poolside serv. Restaurant 5-10 pm. Bar to midnight. Ck-out 11 am. Coin lndry. Meeting rms. Concierge. Airport, area attractions transportation. Free Walt Disney World transportation. Exercise equipt; weights, rowing machine, whirlpool. Game rm. Rec rm. Refrigerators avail. Cr cds: A, C, D, DS, ER, MC, V, JCB.

★★★**EMBASSY SUITES RESORT.** *(8100 Lake Ave, Orlando 32836)* Near jct I-4, FL 535. 407/239-1144; FAX 407/239-1718. 280 suites, 6 story. Feb-Apr & mid-Dec-Jan 1: S, D (up to 4 adults) $145-$290; family rates; golf, Disney plans; lower rates rest of yr. Crib free. TV; cable, in-rm movies. 2 heated pools, 1 indoor; wading pool, poolside serv. Supervised child's activities. Complimentary full bkfst. Complimentary coffee in rms. Restaurant 11 am-11 pm. Bar 5 pm-midnight. Ck-out 11:30 am. Coin lndry. Meeting rms. Gift shop. Airport transportation; free scheduled shuttle to all Disney theme parks. Lighted tennis. 18-hole golf privileges, pro, putting green, driving range. Exercise equipt; weight machines, bicycles, whirlpool, sauna. Game rm. Rec rm. Refrigerators, minibars. Cr cds: A, C, D, DS, ER, MC, V, JCB.

★★★**GROSVENOR RESORT.** *(Box 22202, 1850 Hotel Plaza Blvd, Lake Buena Vista 32830) In Walt Disney World Village.* 407/828-4444; res: 800/624-4109; FAX 407/828-8192. 630 rms, 19 story. Feb-late Apr: S, D $99-$160; suites $175-$520; under 18 free; lower rates rest of yr. Crib free. TV; cable, in-rm movies. 2 heated pools; wading pool, whirlpool, poolside serv. Playground. Coffee, tea in rms. Restaurant open 24 hrs. Bar 11-2 am; entertainment in season. Ck-out 11 am. Coin lndry. Convention facilities. Concierge. Shopping arcade. Free Walt Disney World transportation. Lighted tennis. Golf privileges, pro, putting green, driving range. Game rm. Lawn games. Activities dir

(summer). Sherlock Holmes Museum on grounds. Cr cds: A, C, D, DS, ER, MC, V, JCB.

★★★**GUEST QUARTERS SUITE RESORT.** *(2305 Hotel Plaza Blvd, Lake Buena Vista 32830) In Walt Disney World Village.* 407/934-1000; FAX 407/934-1008. 229 suites (1-2 bedrm), 7 story. Late Dec-Apr: S, D $165-$280; each addl $20; lower rates rest of yr. Crib free. TV; cable. Heated pool; wading pool, poolside serv. Playground. Restaurant 6 am-midnight. Bar 2 pm-midnight. Ck-out 11 am. Coin lndry. Meeting rms. Concierge. Gift shop. Airport transportation. Free Walt Disney World transportation. Lighted tennis. 18-hole golf privileges, pro, putting green, driving range. Exercise equipt; weights, bicycles, whirlpool. Game rm. Lawn games. Refrigerators. Some private patios. Cr cds: A, C, D, DS, ER, MC, V.

★★★**HILTON AT WALT DISNEY WORLD VILLAGE.** *(1751 Hotel Plaza Blvd, Lake Buena Vista 32830) In Walt Disney World Village.* 407/827-4000; FAX 407/827-6370. 813 rms, 10 story, 26 suites. Feb-mid-May, late Dec: S, D $155-$230; each addl $20; suites $470-$705; family rates; lower rates rest of yr. Crib free. TV; cable. 2 heated pools; wading pool, poolside serv. Playground. Free supervised child's activities. Restaurant 6:30-1 am. Bar 11-2 am; dancing (seasonal). Ck-out 11 am. Coin lndry. Convention facilities. Barber, beauty shop. Valet parking. Airport transportation. Free Walt Disney World transportation. Lighted tennis, pro. Golf privileges, pro, pro shop, putting green, driving range. Exercise equipt; weight machine, bicycles, whirlpool, sauna. Game rm. Minibars; some bathrm phones, refrigerators. Some private patios, balconies. *LUXURY LEVEL: TOWERS.* 80 rms, 4 suites, 2 floors. S, D $250; suites $585-$820. Private lounge, honor bar. Concierge. Wet bar in suites. Complimentary continental bkfst, refreshments, newspaper.
Cr cds: A, C, D, DS, ER, MC, V, JCB.

★★**HOWARD JOHNSON RESORT.** *(Box 22204, 1805 Hotel Plaza Blvd, Lake Buena Vista 32830) In Walt Disney World Village.* 407/828-8888; FAX 407/827-4623. 323 rms, 14 story. Feb-Apr, mid-June-mid-Aug: S, D $95-$155; each addl $15; suites $395-$595; under 18 free; lower rates rest of yr. Crib free. TV; in-rm movies. 2 pools, heated; wading pool, poolside serv. Playground. Restaurant 6 am-midnight. Rm serv 7 am-10 pm. Bar 4 pm-midnight. Ck-out 11 am. Coin lndry. Convention facilities. Gift shop. Airport transportation. Free Walt Disney World transportation. Tennis & golf privileges. Exercise equipt; weights, bicycles, whirlpool. Game rm. Many private patios, balconies. Cr cds: A, C, D, DS, ER, MC, V, JCB.

★★**ROYAL PLAZA.** *(1905 Hotel Plaza Blvd, Lake Buena Vista 32830) In Walt Disney World Village.* 407/828-2828; res: 800/248-7890; FAX 407/827-6338. 396 rms, 2-17 story. Feb-Apr: S, D $147-$157; suites $404-$550; family rates; lower rates rest of yr. Crib free. TV; cable; in-rm movies. Heated pool; whirlpool, sauna, poolside serv. Playground. Restaurant 6:30 am-midnight. Pizza & beer noon-midnight. Bar 11-2:30 am; entertainment, dancing. Ck-out 11 am. Coin lndry. Convention facilities. Gift shop. Barber, beauty shop. Free valet parking. Airport transportation. Free Walt Disney World transportation. Lighted tennis. 18-hole golf privileges, putting green, driving range. Game rm. Lawn games. Some bathrm phones. Refrigerators avail. Balconies. Cr cds: A, C, D, DS, ER, MC, V.

★★**TRAVELODGE.** *(Box 22205, 2000 Hotel Plaza Blvd, Lake Buena Vista 32830) In Walt Disney World Village.* 407/828-2424; FAX 407/828-8933. 325 rms, 18 story. S, D $109-$169; suites $179-$279. Crib free. TV. Heated pool; wading pool, poolside serv. Playground. Coffee in rms. Restaurant 7 am-midnight. Bar 11:30-2:30 am; entertainment, dancing. Ck-out 11 am. Coin lndry. Meeting rms. Concierge. Gift shop. Airport transportation. Free Walt Disney World transportation. Lighted tennis privileges, pro. 18-hole golf privileges, pro, putting green, driving range. Game rm. Lawn games. Minibars; some refrigerators. Balconies. On lake. Cr cds: A, C, D, DS, ER, MC, V, JCB.

D 🚷 🔎 ⚓ 🚫 Ⓢ SC

Inn

✔ ★ ★ **PERRI HOUSE BED & BREAKFAST.** (PO Box 22005, 10417 FL 535, Orlando 32836) N of I-4 exit 27 on FL 535. 407/876-4830; res: 800/780-4830. 4 rms. S $55; D $65–$75; higher rates special events, major hols. Crib free. Complimentary continental bkfst. Ck-out 11:30 am, ck-in 3 pm. Airport, RR station transportation. Secluded on 20 acres; bird sanctuary. Adj Walt Disney World property. Cr cds: A, DS, MC, V.

⚓ 🚫 Ⓢ SC

Resorts

★ ★ ★ **THE DISNEY INN RESORT.** (1950 W Palm Magnolia Dr, Lake Buena Vista 32830) In Walt Disney World. 407/824-2200; FAX 407/824-3229. 288 rms, 3 story. Mid-Dec–Jan 1, mid-Feb–late Apr, early June–mid-Aug: S, D $205–$225; suites $565–$770; each addl $15; under 18 free; lower rates rest of yr. Crib free. TV; cable. 2 heated pools; wading pool. Playground. Dining rm 7 am–10 pm. Rm serv 6:30 am–midnight. Bar 11 am–11 pm. Ck-out 11 am, ck-in 3 pm. Coin lndry. Meeting rm. Gift shop. Valet parking. Airport transportation. Lighted tennis. 99-hole golf privileges, greens fee, pro shop. Exercise equipt; weight machines, bicycles. Health club privileges. Game rm. Private patios, balconies. Cr cds: A, MC, V.

🐴 🚷 🔎 ⚓ 🧍 🏃 🚫 Ⓢ

★ ★ **DISNEY'S BEACH CLUB RESORT.** (1800 Epcot Resorts Blvd, Lake Buena Vista 32830) In Walt Disney World Village; 5 minute walk to Epcot Center. 407/934-8000; FAX 407/934-3850. 584 rms, 5 story. Mid-Jan–Apr, mid-June–late Aug, major hols: S, D $230–$290; each addl $15; suites $410–$800; under 18 free; Disney packages; lower rates rest of yr. Crib free. TV; cable. 2 pools; poolside serv. Dining rm 7 am–10 pm. Rm serv 24 hrs. Bar 11–1 am; entertainment. Ck-out 11 am, ck-in 3 pm. Coin lndry. Convention facilities. Bellhops. Valet serv. Concierge. Sundries. Gift shop. Barber, beauty shop. Free valet parking. Airport transportation. Free Disney transportation, water transportation to Disney-MGM Studios Theme Park. Lighted tennis, pro. Golf privileges. Mini waterpark; boating, marina. Lawn games. Game rm. Exercise rm; instructor, weight machine, bicycles, sauna, steam rm. Bathrm phones, minibars; wet bar in suites. Balconies. Located on the shores of a 25-acre man-made lake. Architect Robert A.M. Stern has re-created a New England Village with a turn-of-the-century theme. DISNEY'S BEACH CLUB RESORT meets with DISNEY'S YACHT CLUB RESORT (see) in a central courtyard and shares a Fantasy Lagoon. Cr cds: A, MC, V.

🚷 🔎 ⚓ 🧍 🏃 🚫 Ⓢ

✔ ★ ★ **DISNEY'S CARIBBEAN BEACH RESORT.** (PO Box 10000, Lake Buena Vista 32830) 900 Cayman Way, off I-4 exit 36B. 407/934-3400; FAX 407/934-3288. 2,112 rms in several village groups, 2 story. S, D $89–$115; each addl $15; under 18 free. Crib free. TV; cable. 7 heated pools; wading pool, poolside serv, lifeguard. 3 playgrounds. Coffee in rms. Dining rm 5:30 am–midnight; several dining areas. Pizza delivery. Bar noon–1:30 am. Ck-out 11 am, ck-in 3 pm. Coin lndry. Shopping arcade. Tennis privileges. Golf privileges, greens fee. Marina; boat rentals. Game rm. Minibars. Picnic tables. 1½-acre island-like resort with lake. Each village has a pool and beach area, lndry facilities and bus stop. 1¼-mi promenade around lake; island play area for children in middle of lake. Cr cds: A, MC, V.

D 🚷 🔎 ⚓ 🏃 🚫 Ⓢ

★ ★ **DISNEY'S CONTEMPORARY RESORT.** (Box 10000, Walt Disney World 32830) Off US 192, I-4 in Walt Disney World. 407/824-1000; FAX 407/824-3539. 1,053 rms, 14 story tower, 2 3-story bldgs. Mid-Dec–Jan 1, mid-Feb–late Apr, early June–mid-Aug: S, D

$215–$270; each addl $15; 1-bedrm suites $450–$470; under 18 free; lower rates rest of yr. Crib free. TV; cable. 2 heated pools; wading pool, lifeguard. Playground. Restaurant (SEE TOP OF THE WORLD). Rm serv 24 hrs. Snack bar 24 hrs. Bars noon–1 am; entertainment, dancing. Ck-out 11 am, ck-in 3 pm. Convention facilities. Shopping arcade. Barber, beauty shop. Airport transportation. Valet parking. Lighted tennis. 99-hole golf privileges. Exercise rm; instructor, weights, bicycles, sauna. Massage therapy. Lawn games. Refrigerator in suites. Balconies. Monorail runs through 12-story atrium lobby. On lake. **LUXURY LEVEL: SUITE FLOOR.** 33 rms, 11 suites. S, D $350–$365; suites $750–$1,100. Concierge. Private lounge. Bathrm phones. Complimentary bkfst, refreshments.
Cr cds: A, MC, V.

D — 🚷 🔎 ⚓ 🧍 🏃 🚫 Ⓢ

★ ★ ★ **DISNEY'S GRAND FLORIDIAN BEACH RESORT.** (Box 10,000, 4001 Grand Floridian Way, Walt Disney World 32830) In Walt Disney World. 407/824-3000; FAX 407/824-3186. 901 rms: 71 rms in main bldg, 11 suites, 813 rms, 16 suites in 5 lodge bldgs, 4 & 5 story. Mid-Dec–Jan 1, mid-Feb–late Apr, early June–mid-Aug: S, D $250–$430; each addl $15; suites (see LUXURY LEVEL); under 18 free; special package plans; lower rates rest of yr. Crib free. TV; cable. Heated pool; wading pool, poolside serv, lifeguard. Dining rm 7 am–11 pm; five addl dining rms (also see VICTORIA & ALBERT'S); afternoon high tea. Rm serv 24 hrs. Bar 11–1 am. Ck-out 11 am, ck-in 3 pm. Coin lndry. Convention facilities. Valet parking. Barber, beauty shop. Airport transportation; also monorail to Magic Kingdom, Epcot Center & Disney/MGM Studios. Tennis, clay courts, pro. 99-hole golf privileges, greens fee, pro. Private beach; waterskiing, sailing, marina. Boat rentals. Lawn games. Game rm. Exercise rm; instructor, weight machines, bicycles, whirlpool, steam rm. Massage. Fishing guides. Bathrm phones, minibars; wet bar in suites. Balconies. Kennels avail. Complimentary newspaper daily. Striking Victorian-style hotel with broad verandas, cupolas and gingerbread porches, palatial vaulted lobby, open-cage elevator, an aviary, palms and ferns; creates a luxurious, turn-of-the-century atmosphere. On 40 acres, overlooking lagoon. Bldgs #7 and #9 (326 rms) are totally nonsmoking. **LUXURY LEVEL: CONCIERGE.** 71 rms, 11 suites, 5 story (entire main bldg). S, D $420–$440; suites $685–$1,400. Concierge. Private lounge. Deluxe toiletry amenities. Complimentary continental bkfst, refreshments.
Cr cds: A, MC, V.

D — 🐴 🚷 🔎 ⚓ 🧍 🏃 🚫 Ⓢ

★ ★ **DISNEY'S POLYNESIAN RESORT.** (Box 10000, Walt Disney World 32830) Off US 192, I-4 in Walt Disney World. 407/824-2000; FAX 407/824-3174. 853 rms, 2–3 story. Mid-Dec–Jan 1, mid-Feb–late Apr, early June–mid-Aug: S, D $190–$325; each addl $15; suites $350–$750; under 18 free; lower rates rest of yr. Crib free. TV; cable. 2 heated pools; wading pool, poolside serv, lifeguard. Playground. Restaurant open 24 hrs; dining rm 7 am–11 pm (also see PAPEETE BAY VERANDAH). Children's dinner theater. Rm serv 6:30–1 am. Bar 1 pm–1:30 am; entertainment. Ck-out 11 am, ck-in 3 pm. Coin lndry. Sundries. Shopping arcade. Barber, beauty shop. Airport, RR station, bus depot transportation. Lighted tennis, pro. 99-hole golf privileges, greens fee, pro. Health club privileges. Fishing (guides avail). Game rm. Balconies. Kennels. On lake; 2 swimming beaches, boat rentals, waterskiing, marina. **LUXURY LEVEL: KING KAMEHAMEHA SERVICE.** 102 rms, 3 floors. S, D $325. Concierge. Private lounge. Valet parking.
Cr cds: A, MC, V.

D — 🐴 🚷 🔎 ⚓ 🚫 Ⓢ

★ ★ **DISNEY'S PORT ORLEANS.** (PO Box 10,000, Lake Buena Vista 32830) 1662 Old South Rd, off I-4 exit 26B. 407/934-5000; FAX 407/934-5353. 1,008 rms in 7 bldgs, 3 story. S, D $94–$119; each addl $12; under 18 free. Crib free. TV; cable. Pool; wading pool, whirl-pool, sauna. Dining rms 6:30 am–10 pm. Bar 11 am–midnight. Ck-out 11 am, ck-in after 3 pm. Grocery. Coin lndry. Bellhops. Valet serv. Gift shop. Airport transportation. Lighted tennis privileges, pro. Golf privileges, pro, putting green, driving range. Boats. Bicycle rentals. Game rm. Located on a canal, ornate row-house buildings with courtyards and intricate railings are reminiscent of the French Quarter in New Orleans;

cobblestone streets, trips by flat-bottom boats down river to shops and showplaces. Cr cds: A, MC, V.

[icon row]

★★★**DISNEY'S VILLAGE RESORT.** *(PO Box 10150, Lake Buena Vista 32830) 1901 Buena Vista Dr, in Walt Disney World Village. 407/827-1100.* 324 suites, 261 1-3-bedrm villas, 4 townhouses, 1-3 story, 261 kits. No elvtr. Mid-Dec–Jan 1, mid-Feb–late Apr, early June–mid-Aug: suites $190–$270; villas, townhouses $250–$345; homes $725–$800; lower rates rest of yr. Crib free. TV; cable. 6 heated pools; wading pool, poolside serv. 6 playgrounds. Restaurant (see LAKE BUENA VISTA CLUB). Rm serv. Bar 11 am–10 pm. Ck-out 11 am, ck-in 3 pm. Free lndry facilities. Convention facilities. Valet serv. Concierge. Shopping arcade. Lighted tennis. 99-hole golf, greens fee, pro, putting green, driving range. Exercise equipt; weights, bicycles. Electric cart, bicycle and boat rentals. Game rm. Refrigerators; some bathrm phones. Private patios, balconies. Picnic tables, grills. Located on 450 wooded acres. Cr cds: A, MC, V.

[icon row]

★★★**DISNEY'S YACHT CLUB RESORT.** *(1700 Epcot Resort Blvd, Lake Buena Vista 32830) In Walt Disney World Village; 5 minute walk to Epcot Center. 407/934-7000; FAX 407/934-3450.* 635 rms, 5 story, 60 suites. Mid-Jan–Apr, mid-June–late Aug, major hols: S, D $230–$290; each addl $15; suites $410–$800; under 18 free; Disney packages; lower rates rest of yr. Crib free. TV; cable. Pool. Dining rm 7 am–10 pm. Rm serv 24 hrs. Bar 11–1 am; entertainment. Ck-out 11 am, ck-in 3 pm. Coin lndry. Convention facilities. Bellhops. Valet serv. Concierge. Sundries. Gift shop. Barber, beauty shop. Free valet parking. Airport transportation. Free Disney transportation, including water taxi, to Disney-MGM Studios Theme Park. Lighted tennis, pro. Golf privileges. Mini waterpark; boating, marina. Lawn games. Game rm. Exercise rm; instructor, weight machine, bicycles, whirlpool, sauna, steam rm. Massage. Bathrm phones, minibars; wet bar in suites. Located on the shores of a 25-acre man-made lake. Architect Robert A.M. Stern's design echoes New England seaside summer residences of the 1890s. DISNEY'S YACHT CLUB RESORT meets with DISNEY'S BEACH CLUB RESORT (see) in a central courtyard with a "quiet pool" and shares a Fantasy Lagoon with poolside serv. *LUXURY LEVEL: CONCIERGE LEVEL.* 75 rms, 18 suites. S, D $370–$390; suites $410–$800. Concierge. Private lounge, honor bar. Whirlpool in suites. Complimentary continental bkfst, refreshments.
Cr cds: A, MC, V.

[icon row]

★★★**DIXIE LANDINGS.** *(PO Box 10000, 1251 Dixie Dr, Lake Buena Vista 32830) I-4 exit 26B. 407/934-6000; FAX 407/934-5024.* 2,048 units in 15 bldgs, 2-3 story. S, D $94–$119; each addl $12; family rates; golf plans. Crib free. TV; cable. 6 pools, some heated; wading pool, whirlpool, poolside serv, lifeguards. Playground. Restaurant 6:30 am–midnight. Bar; entertainment. Ck-out 11 am, ck-in 3 pm. Grocery, coin lndry, package store. Bellhops. Valet serv. Gift shop. Airport transportation. Lighted tennis, pro. 99-hole golf, greens fee, pro, putting green, driving range. Boat, bicycle rentals. Game rm. Old South plantation-style project located "on the Sassagoula River." Alligator Bayou region is reminiscent of old Cajun country, while Magnolia Bend showcases stately mansions typical of the upriver South. Cr cds: A, MC, V.

[icon row]

★★★★**HYATT REGENCY GRAND CYPRESS.** *(1 Grand Cypress Blvd, Orlando 32836) 2 mi E of I-4 exit 27, Lake Buena Vista exit. 407/239-1234; FAX 407/239-3800.* 750 units, 18 story, 75 suites. Feb–May: S, D $235–$310; suites $450–$1,000; golf plans; lower rates rest of yr. Crib free. Valet parking $7. TV; cable, in-rm movies. Heated pool; poolside serv. Supervised child's activities. Dining rm (see HEMINGWAY'S). 5 restaurants. Rm serv 24 hrs. Bar; entertainment. Ck-out noon, ck-in 4 pm. Convention facilities. Valet serv. Concierge. Shopping arcade. Personal care salon. Walt Disney World transportation. 12 tennis courts, 6 lighted, pro, instruction avail. 45-hole golf, Academy of Golf, pro, putting green, driving range, pitch & putt. Sailing, canoes, paddleboats, windsurfing, scuba diving; rentals avail. Lake with white sand beach. Nature area, Audubon walk; jogging trails. Bicycle rentals.

Lawn games. Game rm. Equestrian center; Western and English trails. Exercise rm; instructor, weights, bicycles, whirlpool, sauna, steam rm. Massage therapy. Minibars. Bathrm phone, refrigerator in some suites. Some private patios. Balconies. Elegant decor. Extensive art collection and artifacts; hotel tours avail. On 1,500 landscaped acres. Trolley and van transport throughout property. *LUXURY LEVEL: REGENCY CLUB.* 68 units, 14 suites. S, D $420; each addl $50; suites $650–$3,000. Concierge. Private lounge. Wet bar in suites. Complimentary continental bkfst, refreshments, newspaper.
Cr cds: A, C, D, DS, ER, MC, V, JCB.

[icon row] SC

★★★**MARRIOTT'S ORLANDO WORLD CENTER.** *(8701 World Center Dr, Orlando 32821) I-4 exit 26A, jct FL 536. 407/239-4200; FAX 407/238-8777.* 1,503 rms, 28 story, 101 suites. S, D $179–$209; suites from $300; under 18 free. Valet parking $3, overnight $8. TV; cable. 3 heated pools, 1 indoor; wading pool, poolside serv. Playground. Free supervised child's activities. Dining rms 6 am–11 pm (also see REGENT COURT). Rm serv 24 hrs. Bar; pianist, dancing. Ck-out 11 am, ck-in 4 pm. Convention facilities. Coin lndry. Concierge. Shopping arcade. Barber, beauty shop. Airport, area attractions transportation. Lighted tennis, pro. 18-hole golf, greens fee $80 (incl half-cart), pro, putting green, driving range. 5-acre activity court with pools, lagoon, waterfalls, sun deck. Lawn games. Game rm. Exercise rm; instructor, weights, bicycles, whirlpool, sauna. Massage therapy. Some refrigerators, minibars. Private patios, balconies. On 200 landscaped acres; view of many lakes. Cr cds: A, C, D, DS, ER, MC, V, JCB.

[icon row] SC

★★**RESIDENCE INN BY MARRIOTT.** *(8800 Meadow Creek Dr, Orlando 32821), 4 mi S, I-4 exit 27. 407/239-7700; FAX 407/239-7605.* 688 kit. villas (1–2 bedrm, 8 villas to unit), 2 story. Mid-Dec–early Jan, mid-Feb–Apr, mid-June–mid Aug: S $125–$175; D $149–$199; wkly, monthly rates; lower rates rest of yr. Crib free. TV; cable, in-rm movies. 3 heated pools; poolside serv. Complimentary coffee in rms. Rm serv. Ck-out 11 am, ck-in 4 pm. Grocery, coin lndry. Meeting rms. Bellhops. Gift shop. Airport, Walt Disney World transportation. Lighted tennis. Balconies. Cr cds: A, C, D, DS, MC, V, JCB.

[icon row] SC

★★★**VISTANA.** *(PO Box 22051, Lake Buena Vista 32830) 8800 Visitana Center Dr; I-4 exit 27, then 1 mi S on FL 535. 407/239-3100; res: 800/877-8787; FAX 407/239-3062.* 820 kit. villas (2-bedrm) 1, 2 & 3 story. Feb–mid-Apr, late Dec: villas $275; family rates; package plans; lower rates rest of yr. Crib $10. TV; in-rm movies. 5 pools, heated; wading pools, poolside serv. Playgrounds. Supervised child's activities. Dining rm 7 am–11 pm. Snack bar. Ck-out 10 am, ck-in 4 pm. Bar. Grocery. Package stores. Sports dir. 13 lighted tennis courts, pro, pro shop. Bicycle rentals. Lawn games. Soc dir. Movies, planned activities. Game rm. Exercise equipt; weights, bicycles, whirlpool, steam rm, sauna. Refrigerators, washers & dryers. Private patios, balconies. Grills. On 110 acres. Cr cds: A, C, D, DS, MC, V.

[icon row]

★★★**WALT DISNEY WORLD DOLPHIN.** *(Box 22653, 1500 Epcot Resorts Blvd, Lake Buena Vista 32830) In Walt Disney World Village, adj to Epcot Center. 407/934-4000; res: 800/227-1500; FAX 407/934-4099.* 1,514 rms, 27 story, 140 suites. Early Feb–late Apr, late Dec: S, D $219–$300; suites $475–$860; under 18 free; Disney packages; lower rates rest of yr. Crib free. TV; cable. 4 pools, 3 heated; wading pool, poolside serv, lifeguard. Playground. Supervised child's activities. Dining rm open 24 hrs. Rm serv 24 hrs. Bars noon–2 am; pianist. Ck-out 11 am, ck-in 3 pm. Coin lndry. Convention facilities. Concierge. Shopping arcade. Barber, beauty shop. Airport transportation. Free Walt Disney World transportation, by both land and water. Lighted tennis, pro. Golf privileges. Exercise rm; instructor, weight machine, bicycles, whirlpool. Game rm. Rec rm. Minibars; many bathrm phones; wet bar in suites. Designed by architect Michael Graves as "entertainment architecture," the hotel features a waterfall cascading down the front of the building into a pool supported by two dolphin statues. *LUXURY LEVEL: DOLPHIN TOWERS.* 172 rms, 35 suites, 8 floors. S, D $325–$350; suites $550–$2,400. Concierge. Private lounge,

honor bar. In-rm whirlpool in suites. Complimentary continental bkfst, refreshments.
Cr cds: A, C, D, DS, ER, MC, V, JCB.

★ ★ ★ **WALT DISNEY WORLD SWAN.** (1200 Epcot Resort Blvd, Lake Buena Vista 32830) In Walt Disney World Village, adj to Epcot Center. 407/934-3000; res: 800/248-SWAN; FAX 407/934-4499. 758 rms, 12 story, 64 suites. S, D $240–$340; each addl $20; suites $450–$1,200; under 18 free; Disney packages. Crib free. Valet parking $7 overnight. TV; cable. 2 pools, 1 rock-sculptured grotto; wading pool, poolside serv, lifeguard (grotto). Playground. Supervised child's activities. Dining rm 6:30 am–11 pm. Rm serv 24 hrs. Bar 3 pm–midnight. Ck-out 11 am, ck-in 3 pm. Convention facilities. Concierge. Gift shop. Beauty shop. Airport transportation. Free transportation, including water taxi, to Epcot Center, Disney-MGM Studios Theme Park and other Kingdom areas. 8 lighted tennis courts, pro. Golf privileges. Exercise equipt; weight machine, bicycles, whirlpool, sauna. Game rm. Minibars; many bathrm phones; some wet bars. Balconies. Situated on 150-acre resort site. Dramatic style of "entertainment architecture," created by Michael Graves; two 28-ton, 47.3-ft high swan statues grace the roofline. *LUXURY LEVEL:* ROYAL BEACH CLUB. 45 rms, 6 suites, 2 floors. S, D $345; suites $895–$1,320. Concierge. Private lounge, honor bar. Complimentary continental bkfst, refreshments.
Cr cds: A, C, D, DS, ER, MC, V, JCB.

Restaurants

★ ★ ★ **ARTHUR'S 27.** (See Buena Vista Palace Hotel) 407/827-3450. Hrs: 6–10:30 pm. Res accepted. International menu. Bar. Wine cellar. Semi-a la carte: dinner $21–$32. Complete meals: dinner $45–$60. Specializes in gourmet dishes, some custom-prepared. Pianist. Valet parking. On 27th floor; view of Walt Disney World. Cr cds: A, C, D, DS, MC, V.

✔ ★ ★ **CHEF MICKEY'S.** In Walt Disney World Village. 407/828-3830 or -3900 (res). Hrs: 9 am–2 pm, 5–10 pm. Res accepted. Family dining with character dinner. Semi-a la carte: bkfst $3.75–$6, lunch $5–$9, dinner $9.75–$18. Child's meals. Specializes in beef, seafood. Parking. Chef Mickey appears at dinner. View of lake. Cr cds: A, MC, V.

D

★ ★ **CRAB HOUSE.** (8496 Palm Pkwy, Lake Buena Vista) I-4 exit 27 to FL 535, N to Vista Center. 407/239-1888. Hrs: 11:30 am–3 pm, 5–11 pm; Sat from 5 pm; Sun 1–11 pm. Bar. Semi-a la carte: lunch $4.95–$10.95, dinner $9.95–$19.95. Child's meals. Specializes in prime rib, fresh seafood, Maryland crab. Salad bar. Parking. Patio dining. Rustic, New England-style decor. Cr cds: A, C, D, DS, MC, V.

D

★ ★ ★ **EMPRESS ROOM.** Aboard the Empress Lilly in Walt Disney World Village. 407/828-3900. Hrs: 6–9:30 pm. Res accepted. Continental menu. Bar to 11 pm. Wine list. A la carte entrees: dinner $30–$40. Serv charge 20%. Specialty: Empress Room Trio. Own baking. Valet parking. Gourmet dining aboard 1890s Mississippi riverboat overlooking lake. Louis XV decor. Jacket. Totally nonsmoking. Cr cds: A, MC, V.

D

★ ★ ★ **FISHERMAN'S DECK.** Aboard the Empress Lilly in Walt Disney World Village. 407/828-3900. Hrs: Disney character bkfst, sittings 8:30 & 10 am (res required); 11:30 am–2 pm, 5:30–10 pm. Res accepted. Continental menu. Bar. Complete meals: bkfst $10.95, children $7.95. A la carte entrees: lunch $6.25–$9.95, dinner $15.75–$23. Child's meals. Valet parking. Aboard 1890s Mississippi riverboat overlooking lake. Totally nonsmoking. Cr cds: A, MC, V.

D

★ ★ ★ **HEMINGWAY'S.** (See Hyatt Regency Grand Cypress Resort) 407/239-1234. Hrs: 11:30 am–2:30 pm, 6–11 pm; Fri, Sat 11:30

am–2:30 pm, 5:30–11 pm; Sun & Mon 6–11 pm. Res accepted. Bar to 1 am. Extensive wine list. A la carte entrees: lunch $7–$14, dinner $14–$30. Child's meals. Specializes in live Maine lobster, Floridita seafood salad, seafood, steak. Valet parking. Outdoor dining. Atmosphere of old Key West with ceiling fans, wicker furnishings, tropical palms. Perched atop a rock precipice, overlooking lagoon-like pool. Cr cds: A, C, D, DS, ER, MC, V, JCB.

D

✔ ★ ★ **KOBÉ JAPANESE STEAK HOUSE.** (8460 Palm Pkwy, Lake Buena Vista) I-4 exit 27 to FL 535, N to Vista Center. 407/239-1119. Hrs: 5–10:30 pm. Res accepted. Japanese menu. Bar. Semi-a la carte: dinner $9.95–$21.95. Child's meals. Specializes in fresh seafood, beef, sushi. Parking. Tableside preparation. Cr cds: A, C, D, DS, MC, V.

D

★ ★ **LAKE BUENA VISTA CLUB.** (See Disney's Village Resort) 407/828-3735. Hrs: 7–11 am, 11:30 am–3 pm, 5:30–10 pm. Res accepted. Bar. A la carte entrees: bkfst $4.25–$7.25, lunch $4.95–$10.25, dinner $8.95–$21.95. Child's meals. Specializes in steak, fresh seafood. Parking. Overlooks golf course at lake. Cr cds: A, MC, V.

D

★ ★ ★ **PAPEETE BAY VERANDAH.** (See Disney's Polynesian Resort) 407/824-1391. Hrs: 7:30–10:30 am, 5:30–10 pm; Sun brunch 10:45 am–2 pm. Res accepted. Polynesian menu. Bar. Character bkfst buffet: $10.95, children 3–11, $5.95. A la carte entrees: dinner $8.95–$16.50. Sun brunch: 12 & over $14.95, 6–11 $8.50, under 3 free. Own baking. Entertainment. Overlooks lagoon. Cr cds: A, MC, V.

D

★ ★ **PEBBLES.** (12551 SR 535, Lake Buena Vista) I-4 to FL 535, right to Crossroads Shopping Center. 407/827-1111. Hrs: 11–1 am. Closed Thanksgiving, Dec 25. Bar. Semi-a la carte: lunch, dinner $5.25–$19.25. Child's meals. Specialties: Mediterranean salad, chicken with avocado and orange sauce, pasta with pesto. Parking. Outdoor dining. Vaulted ceilings. Cr cds: A, D, DS, MC, V.

D

★ ★ ★ **REGENT COURT.** (See Marriott's Orlando World Center Resort) 407/238-4200; ext 8577. Hrs: 6–10 pm. Res accepted. Bar to midnight. Wine list. Semi-a la carte: dinner $19–$30. Child's meals. Specialties: rack of lamb, chocolate fudge torte, fresh Florida seafood. Own baking, desserts. Valet parking. Aquarium. European decor. Cr cds: A, C, D, DS, ER, MC, V, JCB.

D SC

★ ★ ★ **STEERMAN'S QUARTERS.** Aboard the Empress Lilly in Walt Disney World Village. 407/828-3900. Hrs: Disney character bkfst, sittings 8:30 & 10 am (res required); 5:30–10 pm. Res accepted. Continental menu. Bar. Complete meals: bkfst $10.95. A la carte entrees: dinner $18–$27. Child's meals. Valet parking. Aboard 1890s Mississippi riverboat; view of giant paddle wheel. Totally nonsmoking. Cr cds: A, MC, V.

D

★ ★ ★ **TOP OF THE WORLD.** (See Disney's Contemporary Resort) 407/824-3611. Hrs: 6 & 9:15 pm sittings; Sun brunch 9 am–2 pm. Res accepted. Continental menu. Wine list. Dinner & show: $44.50, children ages 3–11, $19.50. Sun brunch (res advised): $23, children $11.95–$18. Own pastries. Broadway musical revue. Valet parking. Rooftop dining; view of the Magic Kingdom. Totally nonsmoking. Cr cds: A, MC, V.

D

★ ★ ★ **VICTORIA & ALBERT'S.** (See Disney's Grand Floridian Beach Resort) 407/824-2383. 2 Sittings: 6 & 9 pm. Res required. Continental menu. Wine cellar. Complete meals: dinner $80. Child's meals. Own baking. Harpist nightly. Valet parking. Gourmet menu changes daily. Victorian decor. Jacket. Totally nonsmoking. Cr cds: A, D, MC, V.

Weeki Wachee Spring

(see Brooksville)

West Palm Beach (D-5)

Settled: 1880 **Pop:** 67,643 **Elev:** 21 ft **Area code:** 407

West Palm Beach has developed as a resort city because of its accessibility to nearby beaches and to the West Palm Beach canal, which leads to the sporting attractions of the Everglades. Golfing also is popular—there are more than 145 courses in the city and vicinity.

What to See and Do

1. **Norton Gallery and School of Art.** 1451 S Olive Ave. Permanent displays include 19th- and 20th-century French paintings; American art from 1900 to present; a distinguished Chinese collection; sculpture patio. (Tues–Sat, also Sun afternoons; closed some major hols) Phone 832-5194 or -5196. ¢¢

2. **Dreher Park Zoo.** 1301 Summit Blvd. Approx 20 acres with more than 100 different species in natural settings. Petting zoo. (Daily) Sr citizen rate. Phone 547-9453. ¢¢

3. **South Florida Science Museum.** 4801 Dreher Trail N, off Summit Blvd, between Forest Hill & Southern Blvds. Participatory & live exhibits; the South Florida Aquarium. Observatory viewing & laser light shows (Fri evenings). Planetarium show (daily, inquire for schedule; fee). Museum (daily; closed Thanksgiving, Dec 25). Sr citizen rate. Phone 832-1988. ¢¢

4. **Lion Country Safari.** On Southern Blvd W, 15 mi W of I-95. A 640-acre wildlife preserve; 5-mile self-guided auto tour; more than 1,000 African, Asian and American wild animals roam free. Animal nursery, dinosaur exhibit, petting zoo. Animal Theater. *Safari Queen* narrated boat ride; paddleboats. Picnic area, restaurant; curio shop. Camping. (Daily) Phone 793-1084. Admission includes all rides and tours. ¢¢¢¢

5. **Star of Palm Beach riverboat cruise.** 3 mi N on US 1 to Blue Heron Blvd in Riviera Beach, on E side of Blue Heron Bridge in Phil Foster Park. Sightseeing cruises on Mississippi paddlewheeler; also lunch and dinner cruises. (Daily; no cruises Dec 25) Res required. Phone 842-0882 or -7827. ¢¢¢

6. **Boating.** Palm Harbor Marina, 400-A N Flagler Dr. There are 166 berths; 8–10-foot-deep and 12-foot-wide channel. Phone 655-4757.

7. **Greyhound racing. Palm Beach Kennel Club.** Belvedere Rd & Congress Ave. Parimutuel races; evenings & matinees. (Daily exc Mon) For schedule, fees phone 683-2222.

8. **Palm Beach Jai Alai.** 1415 W 45th St, ¼ mi E off I-95 exit 54. Parimutuels. (Tues–Sat evenings; matinees Wed, Fri & Sat) For schedule, fees phone 844-2444.

(For further information contact the Palm Beach County Convention & Visitors Bureau, 1555 Palm Beach Lakes Blvd, Suite 204, 33401; 471-3995.)

Annual Events

South Florida Fair & Exposition. Fairgrounds, 9067 Southern Blvd. Livestock shows, entertainment, midway, circus. Phone 793-0333 or 800/527-3247. 17 days, mid-Jan.

SunFest. Flagler Dr. Five-day jazz, art and water festival. Phone 659-5980 or -5992. Late Apr–early May.

Seasonal Events

Polo. (See LAKE WORTH)

Professional baseball. Municipal Sports Stadium, Palm Beach Lakes Blvd & Congress Ave. Atlanta Braves & Montreal Expos spring training. Phone 683-6100 (Braves) or 684-6801 (Expos). Exhibition games early Mar–early Apr.

(See Belle Glade, Boynton Beach, Jupiter, Lake Worth, Palm Beach)

Motels

★★**BEST WESTERN PALM BEACH LAKES.** *1800 Palm Beach Lakes Blvd (33401).* 407/683-8810; FAX 407/478-2580. 197 rms, 2 story. Jan–mid-Apr: S, D $72–$84; each addl $10; suites $85–$125; under 18 free; lower rates rest of yr. Crib free. TV; cable. Pool. Restaurant 6:30 am–10 pm. Bar. Ck-out noon. Meeting rms. Valet serv. Sundries. Airport, RR station, bus depot transportation. 18-hole golf, greens fee $9. Lawn games. Refrigerators. Cr cds: A, C, D, DS, ER, MC, V.

★★**BEST WESTERN SEASPRAY INN.** *(123 Ocean Ave, Palm Beach Shores 33404)* 3 mi N on US 1 to Blue Heron Blvd, then E to Ocean Dr, then right; on Singer Island. 407/844-0233; FAX 407/844-9885. 50 rms, 4 story, 18 kits. Late Dec–late Mar: S $69–$115; D $79–$125; each addl $8–$10; kit. units $99–$139; under 18 free; lower rates rest of yr. Crib $5. TV; cable. Heated pool; poolside serv. Restaurant (rooftop) 8 am–2:30 pm, 6–10 pm. Bar; entertainment, dancing. Ck-out 11 am. Airport, RR station, bus depot transportation. Refrigerators avail. Private patios, balconies. On beach. Cr cds: A, C, D, DS, ER, MC, V.

✔★**COMFORT INN.** *5981 Okeechobee Blvd (33417), FL Tpke exit 99.* 407/697-3388; FAX 407/697-2834. 113 rms, 4 story. Jan–mid-Apr: S $60; D $65; each addl $5; under 18 free; lower rates rest of yr. Crib $5. TV; cable. Pool. Complimentary continental bkfst 6–10 am. Ck-out noon. Meeting rm. Some refrigerators. Cr cds: A, C, D, DS, ER, MC, V, JCB.

✔★**COMFORT INN.** *(11360 US 1, North Palm Beach 33408)* Jct US 1, PGA Blvd. 407/624-7186; FAX 407/622-4258. 88 rms, 4 story. Jan–Apr: S $70; D $75; each addl $5; suites $100; under 18 free; lower rates rest of yr. Crib $5. TV; cable. Complimentary continental bkfst, coffee. Restaurant opp 11 am–11 pm. Ck-out 11 am. Valet serv. Exercise equipt; weights, bicycles. Wet bar in suites. Cr cds: A, C, D, DS, ER, MC, V, JCB.

★★**COURTYARD BY MARRIOTT.** *600 Northpointe Pkwy (33407),* I-95 exit 54. 407/640-9000; FAX 407/471-0122. 149 rms, 3 story. Mid-Jan–mid-Apr: S $64–$119; D $54–$125; each addl $10; suites $95–$145; under 18 free; long-term rates; lower rates rest of yr. Crib free. TV; cable. Heated pool; poolside serv. Complimentary coffee in rms. Restaurant 6:30 am–2 pm, 4–9 pm. Bar. Ck-out noon. Coin lndry. Meeting rms. Sundries. Free airport transportation. Golf privileges. Exercise equipt; weight machine, bicycles, whirlpool. Game rm. Some refrigerators. Balconies. Cr cds: A, D, DS, MC, V.

★★**DAYS INN.** *(2700 Ocean Dr, Riviera Beach 33404)* 3 mi N on US 1 to Blue Heron Blvd, then 1 mi E to Ocean Dr, on Singer Island. 407/848-8661; FAX 407/844-0999. 164 rms, 2 story, 16 kit. units. Feb–Apr: S, D $79–$109; kit. units $109–$199; under 12 free; lower rates rest of yr. Crib free. TV; cable. Heated pool; whirlpool. Restaurant 6 am–10 pm. Bar 10 am–midnight. Ck-out noon. Lawn games. Some refrigerators. On ocean beach; cabanas. Cr cds: A, C, D, DS, MC, V.

✔ ★★DAYS INN AIRPORT NORTH. *2300 45th St (33407), 2 mi NW on I-95, exit 54.* 407/689-0450; FAX 407/686-7439. 234 rms, 2 story. Jan–mid-Apr: S $48–$64; D $55–$89; each addl $10; under 12 free; wkly rates; higher rates: auto races, Sunfest; lower rates rest of yr. Crib free. TV. Heated pool; whirlpool, poolside serv. Restaurant 6 am–9 pm. Bar 4–11 pm. Ck-out 11 am. Coin lndry. Meeting rms. Sundries. Gift shop. Free airport, RR station, bus depot, cruise terminal transportation. Lawn games. Refrigerators avail. Cr cds: A, C, D, DS, MC, V.

⊷ Ⓢ Ⓞ SC

★★DAYS INN TURNPIKE/AIRPORT. *6255 Okeechobee Blvd (33417).* 407/686-6000; FAX 407/687-0415. 154 rms, 2 story. Mid-Dec–Apr: S, D $68–$86; each addl $6; under 12 free; wkly, monthly rates; lower rates rest of yr. Crib free. TV; cable, in-rm movies avail. Heated pool; wading pool. Restaurant 7 am–10 pm. Bar 5 pm–1 am. Ck-out 11 am. Coin lndry. Meeting rms. Exercise equipt; weights, bicycles, whirlpool. Refrigerators avail. Cr cds: A, C, D, DS, MC, V.

Ⓓ ⊷ 大 Ⓢ Ⓞ SC

★★HAMPTON INN. *1505 Belvedere Rd (33406), near Intl Airport.* 407/471-8700; FAX 407/689-7385. 136 rms, 3 story. Dec–Apr: S, D $69–$79; under 18 free; lower rates rest of yr. Crib free. TV; cable. Pool. Complimentary continental bkfst. Ck-out noon. Airport transportation. Cr cds: A, C, D, DS, MC, V.

Ⓓ ⊷ Ⓧ Ⓢ Ⓞ SC

✔ ★HoJo INN. *1901 Okeechobee Blvd (33409), I-95 exit 52B.* 407/683-3222; FAX 407/683-3222, ext 502. 72 rms, 2 story. Dec–mid-Apr: S $55–$85; D $60–$95; each addl $10; under 18 free; lower rates rest of yr. Crib free. TV; cable. Pool; wading pool. Restaurant open 24 hrs. Ck-out noon. Coin lndry. Refrigerators avail. Private patios, balconies. Cr cds: A, C, D, DS, ER, MC, V, JCB.

Ⓓ ⊷ Ⓢ Ⓞ SC

★★PARKVIEW. *4710 S Dixie Hwy (US 1) (33405).* 407/833-4644; res: 800/523-8978. 28 rms, 2 story. Mid-Jan–early-Apr: S $60–$68; D $70–$80; each addl $8; lower rates rest of yr. Crib free. TV; cable. Complimentary continental bkfst. Restaurant adj 7 am–10 pm. Ck-out 11 am. Refrigerators avail. Opp park. Cr cds: A, DS, MC, V.

Ⓢ Ⓞ SC

✔ ★★ROYAL INN. *(675 Royal Palm Beach Blvd, Royal Palm Beach 33411) Approx 10 mi W on US 98/441 (Southern Blvd) to Royal Palm Beach Blvd.* 407/793-3000; res 800/428-5389; FAX 407/795-1502. 75 rms, 1–2 story. Late Dec–Easter: S, D $49.50–$54; kit. units $54–$65; under 12 free; lower rates rest of yr. Crib free. TV; cable. Pool. Restaurant noon–11 pm. Bar 2 pm–1 am. Ck-out noon. Barber shop. Lawn games. Refrigerators. Private patios, balconies. Picnic tables. On lake. Cr cds: A, DS, MC, V.

Ⓓ ⊷ Ⓞ

★★RUTLEDGE INN. *(3730 N Ocean Dr, Riviera Beach 33404) 3 mi N on US 1 to Blue Heron Blvd, 1 mi E to N Ocean Dr, on Singer Island.* 407/848-6621; res: 800/348-7946; FAX 407/840-1787. 60 units, 2 story, 36 kits. Mid-Dec–mid-Apr: S, D $80–$116; each addl $10; suites $140–$200; kit. units $100–$116; under 18 free; varied lower rates rest of yr. Crib free. TV; cable. Heated pool; poolside serv. Restaurant adj. Bars 11 am–7 pm. Ck-out noon. Coin lndry. Private patios, balconies. On beach. Cr cds: A, DS, MC, V.

⊷ Ⓞ

Motor Hotels

★★HOLIDAY INN-PALM BEACH AIRPORT. *1301 Belvedere Rd (33405), off I-95 exit 51, near Intl Airport.* 407/659-3880; FAX 407/655-8886. 200 rms, 11 story. Jan–Apr: S, D $83–$109; each addl $10; suites $150; under 18 free; wkly rates off-season; lower rates rest of yr. Crib free. TV; cable. Pool; poolside serv. Restaurants 6:30 am–2 pm, 5–10 pm. Rm serv. Bar from 4 pm. Ck-out 11 am. Meeting rms. Bellhops.

Valet serv. Free airport, RR station transportation. Exercise equipt; weights, bicycles, sauna. Cr cds: A, C, D, DS, MC, V, JCB.

Ⓓ ⊷ 大 Ⓧ Ⓢ Ⓞ SC

★★★HOLIDAY INN-SINGER ISLAND. *(3700 N Ocean Dr, Riviera Beach 33404) 3 mi N on US 1 to Blue Heron Blvd, 1 mi E to N Ocean Dr, on Singer Island.* 407/848-3888; FAX 407/845-9754. 223 rms, 8 story. Jan–Apr: S, D $115–$195; each addl $10; suites $155–$350; under 19 free; lower rates rest of yr. Crib free. TV; cable. Heated pool; wading pool, poolside serv. Coffee in rms. Restaurant 6:30 am–10 pm. Rm serv. Bar 11–1 am; entertainment, dancing. Ck-out noon. Meeting rms. Bellhops. Valet serv. Tennis & golf privileges. Exercise equipt; weights, bicycles. Minibars; some refrigerators. Balconies. On ocean. Cr cds: A, C, D, DS, MC, V, JCB.

Ⓓ 🏄 🏊 ⊷ 大 Ⓢ Ⓞ SC

★★QUALITY RESORT. *(3800 N Ocean Dr, Riviera Beach 33404) 3 mi N on US 1 to Blue Heron Blvd, 1 mi E to N Ocean Dr, on Singer Island.* 407/848-5502; FAX 407/863-6560. 126 rms, 4 story. Mid-Dec–Apr: S, D $95–$145; each addl $10; suites $210–$240; under 18 free; lower rates rest of yr. TV; cable. Heated pool; wading pool, poolside serv. Restaurant 7 am–10 pm. Rm serv. Bar. Ck-out noon. Meeting rms. Bellhops. Sundries. Lighted tennis. Exercise equipt; weight machine, bicycles, whirlpool, saunas. Lawn games. Refrigerator avail. Private patios, balconies. On beach. Cr cds: A, C, D, DS, ER, MC, V.

Ⓓ 🏊 ⊷ 大 Ⓢ Ⓞ SC

★★RADISSON SUITE INN. *1808 Australian Ave S (33409), near Intl Airport.* 407/689-6888; FAX 407/683-5783. 175 suites, 6 story. Jan–Apr: suites $99–$119; each addl $5; under 18 free; lower rates rest of yr. Crib free. TV; cable. Heated pool. Complimentary continental bkfst in rms. Restaurant 6:30 am–10 pm. Rm serv. Bar from 11:30 am. Ck-out noon. Meeting rms. Bellhops. Valet serv. Sundries. Gift shop. Free airport transportation. Exercise equipt; weights, bicycles, whirlpool, sauna. Refrigerators. Cr cds: A, C, D, DS, ER, MC, V, JCB.

Ⓓ ⊷ 大 Ⓧ Ⓢ Ⓞ SC

★★★SHERATON INN. *1901 Palm Beach Lakes Blvd (33409), near Intl Airport.* 407/689-6100; FAX 407/689-6100, ext 715. 160 rms, 6 story. Jan–mid-Apr: S $79–$99; D $89–$110; each addl $10; suites $200; under 18 free; lower rates rest of yr. Crib free. TV; cable. Heated pool. Complimentary coffee in rms. Restaurant 7 am–11 pm. Rm serv. Bar noon–1 am; entertainment, dancing. Ck-out noon. Meeting rms. Valet serv. Sundries. Gift shop. Free airport transportation. Refrigerators avail. Private patios, balconies. Cr cds: A, C, D, ER, MC, V, JCB.

Ⓓ ⊷ Ⓧ Ⓢ Ⓞ SC   *no good*

★★★SHERATON OCEAN INN. *(3200 N Ocean Dr, Riviera Beach 33404) 3 mi N on US 1 to Blue Heron Blvd, 1 mi E to N Ocean Dr, on Singer Island.* 407/842-6171; FAX 407/848-6842. 202 rms, 9 story. Dec–Apr: S $109–$169; D $128–$158; each addl $10; suites $175; under 17 free; lower rates rest of yr. Crib free. TV; cable. Heated pool; poolside serv. Restaurant 6:30 am–10 pm. Rm serv. Bars; entertainment Tues–Sat, dancing. Ck-out noon. Coin lndry. Bellhops. Valet serv. Sundries. Airport transportation. Golf privileges. Game rm. Refrigerators avail. Private patios, balconies. Beach cabanas. On ocean. Cr cds: A, C, D, DS, ER, MC, V.

Ⓓ 🏄 ⊷ Ⓢ Ⓞ SC

Hotels

★★★EMBASSY SUITES. *(181 Ocean Ave, Palm Beach Shores 33404) 4 mi NE on I-95, exit Blue Heron Blvd E to Ocean Ave.* 407/863-4000; FAX 407/845-3245. 257 suites, 6 story. Mid-Dec–Apr: S, D $199–$400; under 13 free; spa packages; lower rates rest of yr. Crib free. Valet parking $5. TV; cable, in-rm movies. Heated pool; wading pool, poolside serv. Playground. Supervised child's activities. Complimentary full bkfst. Complimentary coffee in rms. Restaurant 11 am–11 pm. Bars to 1 am; entertainment Fri, Sat. Ck-out noon. Coin lndry. Meeting rms. Concierge. Gift shop. Tennis privileges. 18-hole golf privileges, greens fee $95, pro, putting green, driving range. Exercise equipt;

weight machine, treadmill, whirlpool, sauna. Refrigerators, wet bars. Balconies. On ocean; swimming beach. Cr cds: A, D, DS, MC, V.

⊡➖🍴🏌🏊♨🚶🈁🛅🕐

★ ★ ★HILTON-PALM BEACH AIRPORT. *150 Australian Ave (33406), near Intl Airport.* 407/684-9400; FAX 407/689-9421. 247 rms, 10 story. Jan–Apr: S $99–$129; D $109–$139; each addl $10; suites $250–$600; family rates; wkend packages; lower rates rest of yr. TV; cable. Pool; poolside serv. Restaurant 6:30 am–10 pm. Bar 11:30–2 am; dancing. Ck-out noon. Meeting rms. Gift shop. Free valet parking. Free airport transportation. Tennis. 18-hole golf privileges. Health club privileges. Built around Lake Cloud; dock, waterskiing, recreation area. Cr cds: A, C, D, DS, ER, MC, V, JCB.

⊡➖🍴🏌🏊✖🛅🕐SC

★ ★ ★MARRIOTT. *(4000 RCA Blvd, Palm Beach Gardens 33410) N on I-95, PGA exit.* 407/622-8888; FAX 407/622-0052. 279 rms, 11 story, 6 suites. Jan–Apr: S, D $155–$165; each addl $10; suites $295–$395; under 6 free; wkly rates; golf plan; lower rates rest of yr. Crib free. TV; cable. Heated pool; poolside serv. Restaurant 6:30 am–11 pm. Bars 11–3 am; entertainment, dancing. Ck-out noon. Convention facilities. Concierge. Gift shop. Tennis privileges. 18-hole golf privileges. Exercise equipt; weights, bicycles, whirlpool, sauna, steam rm. Health club privileges. Refrigerators avail. Wet bar, bathrm phone in suites. Near beach. Tropical atmosphere. Cr cds: A, C, D, DS, MC, V, JCB.

⊡🍴🏌🏊🚶🛅🕐SC

★ ★ ★OMNI. *1601 Belvedere Rd (33406), near Intl Airport.* 407/689-6400; FAX 407/683-7150. 220 units, 15 story, 108 suites. Dec–Apr: S $119–$129; D $131–$141; each addl $10; suites, kit. units $149–$171; under 18 free; lower rates rest of yr. Crib free. TV; cable. Heated pool; poolside serv. Restaurant 6:30 am–10 pm. Bar; entertainment, dancing. Ck-out noon. Meeting rms. Concierge. Gift shop. Valet, garage parking. Free airport transportation. Lighted tennis. 18-hole golf privileges. Exercise equipt; treadmill, stair machine, whirlpool, sauna. Many refrigerators. Minibar in suites. Balconies. Atrium lobby with 40-ft sculpture. Extensive grounds; elaborate landscaping. Cr cds: A, C, D, DS, ER, MC, V.

⊡🍴🏌🏊🚶🛅🕐SC

★ ★ ★RADISSON SUITE. *(4350 PGA Blvd, Palm Beach Gardens 33410) N on I-95, PGA Blvd exit.* 407/622-1000. 160 units, 10 story. Jan–Apr: suites $149–$225; under 17 free; monthly, wkly rates; golf plan; higher rates PGA tournaments; lower rates rest of yr. Crib free. TV; cable. Heated pool; wading pool; poolside serv. Complimentary coffee in rms. Restaurant 6:30 am–10 pm. Bars 11–1 am; entertainment, dancing. Ck-out noon. Coin lndry. Meeting rms. Gift shop. Beauty shop. Free garage parking; valet. Tennis. 18-hole golf privileges. Exercise equipt; weights, bicycles, whirlpool, sauna. Game rm. Minibars. Picnic tables. Cr cds: A, C, D, DS, ER, MC, V, JCB.

⊡🍴🏌🏊🚶🛅🕐SC

★ ★ ★RAMADA. *630 Clearwater Park Road (33401), near Intl Airport.* 407/833-1234; res: 800/444-7256; FAX 407/833-4689. 350 rms, 10 story. Mid-Dec–mid-Apr: S $95–$145; D $115–$200; each addl $15; suites $175–$535; lower rates rest of yr. Crib free. TV; cable. Heated pool; whirlpool. Restaurant 7 am–10 pm; Fri, Sat to 11 pm. Bar 11 am–midnight; entertainment Tues–Sat. Ck-out noon. Meeting rms. Gift shop. Free airport, beach transportation. Lighted tennis. Exercise equipt; weight machine, bicycle, whirlpool. Some balconies. Cr cds: A, C, D, DS, ER, MC, V.

⊡🏊🚶✖🛅🕐SC

Resorts

PALM BEACH POLO & COUNTRY CLUB. (New owner, therefore not rated) *13198 Forest Hill Blvd (33414), I-95 exit 49W.* 407/798-7000; res: 800/327-4204; FAX 407/798-7052. 105 units, 1–2 story. Mid-Dec–late Apr: studio rms $195; 1-bedrm kit. suite $290; 2–3-bedrm kit. suites $460–$515; wkly, monthly rates; golf packages; lower rates rest of yr. Crib free. TV; cable. 9 pools, 1 heated; wading pool, poolside

serv, lifeguard. Playground. Free supervised child's activities (mid-Dec–late Apr). Dining rm 7–10:30 am, 11:30 am–10 pm. Box lunches. Snack bar. Picnics. Bar. Ck-out noon, ck-in 3 pm. Meeting rms. Valet serv. Gift shop. Sports dir. 24 tennis courts, pro, pro shop. Two 18-hole golf courses, 9-hole course, pro, pro shop, putting green, driving range. Exercise rm; instructor, weights, bicycles, whirlpool, sauna. Massage therapy. Lawn games. 10 polo fields. Horse stabling and equestrian facilities. Skeet shooting. Bicycle rentals. Soc dir, movies. On 2,250 acres; includes 150-acre forest preserve. Cr cds: A, C, D, MC, V.

⊡🐎🍴🏌🏊🚶🏃🕐

★ ★ ★ ★PGA NATIONAL RESORT & SPA. *(400 Ave of the Champions, Palm Beach Gardens 33418) 2 mi W of I-95 on PGA Blvd.* 407/627-2000; res: 800/633-9150; FAX 407/622-0261. 335 units, 4 story. Early Jan–mid-Apr: S $215–$285; D $240–$295; each addl $15; kit. cottages $350; each addl $65; under 17 free; lower rates rest of yr. Crib free. TV; cable. Heated pool; wading pool, poolside serv. Supervised child's activities (June–Sept & hols). Dining rm (see EXPLORERS). Bar 11–2 am. Ck-out noon, ck-in 3 pm. Convention facilities. Valet serv. Concierge. Barber, beauty shop. Pro shops. Valet parking. 19 tennis courts, 12 lighted, pro. 5 golf courses, greens fee $70–$115, pro, 3 putting greens, 2 driving ranges. Boating. Beach volleyball. 5 croquet courts, pro. 6 indoor racquetball/handball courts. Exercise rm; instructor, weight machines, bicycles, whirlpool, sauna, steam rm. Massage. Spa building with gardens; also 6 pools that contain various minerals and salts imported from around the world. Refrigerators, minibars. Balconies. On 2,340 acres; includes 26-acre lake for sailing, swimming; sand beach. Elaborately landscaped grounds. Cr cds: A, C, D, DS, ER, MC, V, JCB.

⊡➖🍴🏌🏊🚶🏃🛅🕐SC

Restaurants

★ALEYDA'S. *1890 S Military Trail.* 407/642-2500. Hrs: 11 am–10 pm; Fri, Sat to 11 pm. Closed Jan 1, Dec 24, 25. Mexican menu. Serv bar. A la carte entrees: lunch, dinner $3.50–$10.75. Lunch buffet $4.99. Child's meals. Specializes in fajitas, burritos, tamales. Parking. Authentic Mexican art & decor. Cr cds: A, C, DS, MC, V.

⊡

★ ★BANGKOK O-CHA. *1687 Forum Pl, E of Palm Beach Mall.* 407/471-3163. Hrs: 11 am–3 pm, 5–10 pm; Sat, Sun from 5 pm. Closed Thanksgiving. Res accepted. Thai, Chinese menu. Wine, beer. A la carte entrees: lunch $4.95–$6.50, dinner $5.95–$15.95. Child's meals. Specialties: mee krob, tom ka kai, chicken Panang curry. Intimate; Thai art and architecture. Cr cds: A, DS, MC, V.

 ★ ★BASIL'S NEIGHBORHOOD CAFE. *771 Village Blvd.* 407/687-3801. Hrs: 11:30 am–10 pm; Sat 5–11 pm; Sun 5–10 pm. Closed Mon July–Nov. Bar. A la carte entrees: lunch $5.95–$11.95, dinner $8.95–$16.95. Child's meals. Specialties: fresh grilled tuna salad, poached salmon, gourmet pizza. Entertainment Sun, Mon evenings. Parking. Hand-painted mural of celebrities & sports figures. Cr cds: MC, V.

⊡

★BEEFEEDER'S STEAK PIT & TAVERN. *3208 Forest Hill Blvd.* 407/964-1900. Hrs: 11:30 am–10 pm; Fri 5–10 pm; Sat 5–9 pm; early-bird dinner Mon–Fri 4–6 pm. Closed Easter, Thanksgiving, Dec 25; also Super Bowl Sun. Bar. Semi-a la carte: lunch $4.50–$8.95, dinner $9.95–$29.95. Child's meals. Specialties: prime rib of beef, steak & lobster. Salad bar. Parking. Five small dining rms. Cr cds: A, C, D, DS, MC, V.

⊡

★ ★ ★CAFE CHARDONNAY. *(4533 PGA Blvd, Palm Beach Gardens) Jct I-95N, PGA Blvd and Military Trail, in Garden Square Shoppes.* 407/627-2662. Hrs: 11:30 am–2:30 pm, 5:30–10 pm; Sat, Sun from 5:30 pm. Closed Jan 1, Thanksgiving, Dec 25. Res accepted. French, Amer menu. Wine, beer. Semi-a la carte: lunch $4.95–$9.95, dinner $12.95–$24.95. Child's meals. Specialties: linguine with lobster and wild mushrooms, grilled stuffed veal chop. Own baking. Parking. Split-level dining areas. Cr cds: A, C, D, MC, V.

D

★ ★ **CAFE DU PARC.** *(612 N Federal Hwy, Lake Park) N on Federal Hwy (US 1).* 407/845-0529. Hrs: 5:30–10 pm. Closed Sept–mid-Oct; also Sun, Mon Apr–Aug & mid-Oct–Nov. Res required. French menu. Beer. Wine list. A la carte entrees: dinner $15.95–$24. Complete meals: dinner $19.95–$22. Specialties: beef Wellington, medallions de veau Normande, sweetbreads. Own pastries, desserts. Parking. French Provincial decor in restored house. Paintings; antique French plate collection. Jacket. Cr cds: A, MC, V.

D

★ ★ **CAFE MONTEREY.** *123 Clematis St.* 407/659-1914. Hrs: 5:30–10 pm; early-bird dinner 5:30–7 pm. Res accepted. Semi-a la carte: dinner $9.95–$20.95. Specializes in seafood, pasta, veal, duck. Collection of African masks. Cr cds: A, MC, V.

✔ ★ ★ **DANICA BISTRO.** *6840 Forest Hill Blvd.* 407/967-1113. Hrs: 5–10 pm. Res required. Continental menu. Bar. Semi-a la carte: dinner $12–$15. Child's meals. Specialties: Wienerschnitzel, bouillabaisse, chicken raspberry. Parking. Three dining areas; European atmosphere. Cr cds: A, MC, V.

★ ★ ★ **EXPLORERS.** *(See PGA National Resort & Spa)* 407/627-2000. Hrs: 6–10 pm. Closed Mon & Tues. Res required. Continental menu. Bar. Wine list. A la carte entrees: dinner $17.95–$28.95. Specializes in venison, fresh seafood. Own pastries, sauces. Piano bar. Valet parking. Dramatic eclectic decor; antiques, artifacts from many places. Cr cds: A, C, D, DS, ER, MC, V, JCB.

D

✔ ★ **GREEK VILLAGE.** *6108 S Dixie Hwy.* 407/582-1666. Hrs: 11 am–2:30 pm, 5–9:30 pm; Sat & Sun from 5 pm. Res accepted. Greek menu. Wine, beer. A la carte entrees: lunch $3.95–$9.95, dinner $7.95–$11.95. Specialties: Greek Village salad, moussaka, stuffed grape leaves. Parking. Intimate atmosphere. Cr cds: A, MC, V.

★ ★ **MORTON'S STEAKHOUSE.** *777 S Flagler Dr, in Phillips Point Bldg.* 407/835-9664. Hrs: 5:30–11 pm; Sun 5–10 pm. Closed major hols. Res accepted. Bar. Wine list. A la carte entrees: dinner $15–$29. Specializes in porterhouse steak, whole baked Maine lobster, shrimp Alexander. Valet parking. Extensive mahogany and brick dining area; original artwork, Oriental rugs. Cr cds: A, C, D, MC, V.

D

✔ ★ **NARCISSUS.** *200 Clematis St.* 407/659-1888. Hrs: 11 am–midnight; wkends to 1 am. Res accepted. Bar. A la carte entrees: lunch $5.95–$14.95, dinner $5.95–$16.95. Child's meals. Specialties: coconut shrimp, Greek salad, hot ham & cheese roll-up. Entertainment. Outdoor dining. Former bank building. Cr cds: A, D, MC, V.

D

★ ★ **PARKER'S LIGHTHOUSE.** *(2401 PGA Blvd, Palm Beach Gardens) In Harbour Shops Ctr, jct PGA Blvd & Prosperity Farms Rd.* 407/627-0000. Hrs: 11:30 am–2:30 pm, 5–10 pm; Fri, Sat to 10:30 pm; Sun 5–9 pm; early-bird dinner 5–6:30 pm; Sun brunch 11 am–2:30 pm. Res accepted. Bar to midnight, Sun to 11 pm. Semi-a la carte: lunch $4.95–$10.95, dinner $8.95–$19.95. Sun brunch $13.95. Child's meals. Specialties: crunchy grouper, seafood linguine, mesquite-grilled seafood. Entertainment Fri & Sat. Parking. Outdoor dining. Floor-to-ceiling windows overlook marina. Cr cds: A, C, D, DS, MC, V.

D

★ ★ **RIVER HOUSE.** *(2373 PGA Blvd, Palm Beach Gardens) I-95N to exit 57, then 2¼ mi E.* 407/694-1188. Hrs: 5–10:30 pm; Sun to 10 pm. Closed July 4, Thanksgiving, Dec 25. Bar. Semi-a la carte: dinner $11.95–$27.95. Child's meals. Specialties: salmon in parchment, grilled swordfish, lamb chops, prime rib. Salad bar. Valet parking. On Intracoastal Waterway; boat dock. Cr cds: A, D, MC, V.

D

★ ★ ★ **ST. HONORÉ.** *(2401 PGA Blvd, Palm Beach Gardens) N via I-95 to PGA Blvd, then 3 mi E.* 407/627-9099. Hrs: noon–2:30 pm, 6–10:30 pm. Closed Mon–Wed in summer. Res required. French, Amer menu. Bar. Wine cellar. A la carte entrees: lunch $10–$25 (min charge $15), dinner $35–$70 (min charge $36). Specialties: lobster sauterne, foie gras. Own baking. Second floor of shopping center; overlooks marina. Jacket. Cr cds: A, C, D, ER, MC, V.

D

★ ★ **THIS IS IT PUB.** *424 24th St.* 407/833-4997. Hrs: 11:30 am–10 pm; Sat from 5:30 pm. Closed Sun; major hols. Res accepted. Bar. Semi-a la carte: lunch $3–$9. Complete meals: dinner $10–$25. Specialties: pub scampi, rack of lamb, seafood chowder. Valet parking. Seascapes, nautical artifacts. Antique bar. Cr cds: A, MC, V.

★ ★ ★ **391ST BOMB GROUP.** *3989 Southern Blvd, on perimeter of Palm Beach Intl Airport.* 407/683-3919. Hrs: 11 am–10:30 pm; Fri to 11 pm; Sat 4:30–11 pm; Sun 4–10 pm; Sun brunch 10 am–2:30 pm. Res accepted. Bar. Wine list. Semi-a la carte: lunch $3.45–$8.95, dinner $14.95–$21.95. Sun brunch $14.95. Child's meals. Specializes in prime rib, steak, lamb & veal chops. DJ Fri & Sat. Parking. Outdoor dining. Replica of English farmhouse surrounded by vintage bombers & WWII relics; patrons use headphones to listen to airport tower communications. Cr cds: A, C, D, DS, MC, V.

D

✔ ★ ★ **WATERWAY CAFE.** *(2300 PGA Blvd, Palm Beach Gardens) I-95N to exit 57A, then 2 mi E.* 407/694-1700. Hrs: 11:30 am–10 pm; wkends to 11 pm; Sun brunch 9 am–3 pm. Closed Dec 25. Res accepted. Bar to 1 am. A la carte entrees: lunch $5.95–$8.95, dinner $9.95–$15.95. Sun brunch $5.95–$8.95. Child's meals. Specialties: lump crab cakes, oysters on half-shell, shrimp fettucine Alfredo. Entertainment Wed–Sun. Valet parking. Outdoor dining. On Intracoastal Waterway. Cr cds: A, MC, V.

D

White Springs (A-3)

Founded: 1826 **Pop:** 704 **Elev:** 138 ft **Area code:** 904 **Zip:** 32096

Considered sacred by the Indians who came here to recuperate after battle, the springs are esteemed by many for their alleged medicinal qualities. White Springs is on the north bank of the Suwannee River and is headquarters for the Suwannee River Water Management District.

What to See and Do

Stephen Foster State Folk Culture Center. W edge of city on US 41. Located on the Suwannee River near the Georgia-Florida state line, this 250-acre center perpetuates the crafts, music and legends of early and contemporary Floridians. A carillon, in a 200-foot tower, gives daily concerts. In the base of tower are two animated dioramas, musical instruments and Foster memorabilia; visitor center has eight animated dioramas and exhibits on Florida folk culture. Tours of the visitor center and tower. Special events throughout the year. (Daily) Phone 397-2733. Per car ¢¢

Annual Event

Florida Folk Festival. Stephen Foster Center (see). Entertaining and educational heritage presentations; traditional singers, tale-tellers, fiddlers, and dancers; craftsmen of native woods and foliage; workshops; puppet shows; ethnic foods. Phone 397-2192. Memorial Day wkend.

(For accommodations see Lake City, also see Live Oak)

Winter Haven (C-4)

Settled: 1883 **Pop:** 24,725 **Elev:** 170 ft **Area code:** 813

Attracting more than one million visitors a year—most of whom come to see Cypress Gardens, many of whom stay on to enjoy the freshwater lakes in this area—Winter Haven is a town bolstered by the twin supports of tourism and citrus growing and processing.

What to See and Do

1. **Cypress Gardens.** 4 mi SW on FL 540, off US 27. Towering cypress trees shelter more than 8,000 varieties of exotic plants and flowers at one of the world's most famous botanical gardens. The 223-acre theme park includes shows, museums, a children's amusement ride and game area; elaborate model railroad; and more than 15 shops in a replica of an antebellum town.

   Highlights include Wings of Wonder, a butterfly conservatory showcasing up to 1,000 free-flying butterflies daily; Cypress Roots, a museum that imparts the history of Florida's first major attraction; and Kodak's Island in the Sky, a 16-story viewing and photo platform provides a panoramic view of the area. Daily shows include Ski! Ski! Ski! Everybody's Skiin' Caribbean, a fast-paced water ski show; Feathered Follies, a colorful revue of performing birds; and Varieté Internationalé, featuring entertainment from around the world. Electric boat rides and pontoon boat cruises provide scenic trips through the park. Lovely Southern belles stroll through the lush gardens, which bloom all year. Strollers; cameras on loan; kennel. Gardens (daily). Phone 324-2111. ¢¢¢¢¢

2. **Water Ski Museum/Hall of Fame.** 799 Overlook Dr. Museum depicts the colorful history of water skiing; the Hall of Fame honors the pioneers of the sport. (Mon–Fri; closed hols) Phone 324-2472. **Free.**

   (For further information contact the Chamber of Commerce, 401 Avenue B NW, PO Box 1420, 33882-1420; 293-2138.)

   (See Haines City, Lakeland, Lake Wales)

Motels

★BUDGET HOST DRIFTWOOD MOTOR LODGE. *970 Cypress Gardens Rd (FL 540) (33880). 813/294-4229; FAX 813/293-2089.* 22 rms, 2 kits. Dec–Apr: S, D $62; each addl $4; kit. units $10 addl; lower rates rest of yr. Crib $6. TV; cable. Heated pool. Restaurant 11:30 am–11 pm. Ck-out 11 am. Gift shop. Lawn games. Some refrigerators. Cr cds: A, DS, MC, V.

★DAYS INN. *200 Cypress Gardens Blvd (33880). 813/299-1151; FAX 813/297-8019.* 105 rms, 2 story. Mar–mid-Apr: S $74; D $78; each addl $4; lower rates rest of yr. Crib free. TV; cable. Pool. Ck-out noon. Coin lndry. Meeting rm. Lighted tennis. Lawn games. Some refrigerators. Cr cds: A, C, D, DS, MC, V.

✔★FLORIDA GARDEN. *2345 8th St NW (33881). 813/294-3537; FAX 813/294-3538.* 29 rms, 4 kits. Mid-Dec–Mar: S $32–$50; D $36–$55; each addl $5; kit. units $5 addl; under 12 free; package plans; lower rates rest of yr. Crib $5. TV; cable. Pool. Complimentary coffee in lobby. Restaurant nearby. Ck-out 11 am. Coin lndry. Lawn games. Refrigerators avail. Picnic tables, grills. Cr cds: DS, MC, V.

★★HOLIDAY INN. *1150 3rd St SW (33880). 813/294-4451; FAX 813/293-9829.* 225 rms, 2 story. Jan–mid-Apr: S, D $59–$90; each addl $8; under 18 free; lower rates rest of yr. Crib free. Pet accepted. TV; cable. Pool; wading pool, poolside serv. Restaurant 6 am–2 pm, 5–10 pm. Rm serv. Bar 11–2 am. Ck-out noon. Coin lndry. Meeting rms. Some refrigerators. Cr cds: A, C, D, DS, MC, V, JCB.

★★HOWARD JOHNSON. *1300 3rd St SW (US 17S) (33880). 813/294-7321; FAX 813/299-1673.* 100 rms, 2 story. Dec–Apr: S, D $74–$88; each addl $7; under 18 free; lower rates rest of yr. Crib free. Pet accepted. TV; cable. Heated pool; wading pool. Restaurant 6:30 am–9 pm. Bar 1 pm–2 am. Ck-out noon. Coin lndry. Valet serv. Miniature golf. Game rm. Lawn games. Some refrigerators. Private patios, balconies. Picnic table. Cr cds: A, C, D, DS, ER, MC, V, JCB.

★LAKE ROY MOTOR LODGE. *1823 Cypress Gardens Blvd (33884). 813/324-6320; FAX 813/324-7894.* 33 rms, 2 story, 20 kits. Mid-Dec–Apr: S, D $75–$80; each addl $6; wkly rates; varied lower rates rest of yr. Crib free. TV. Heated pool. Restaurant nearby. Ck-out 11 am. Coin lndry. Lawn games. Some refrigerators. Private patios. Picnic tables, grill. Adults only section. On Lake Roy; dock. Cr cds: A, C, D, DS, MC, V.

★OLDE ENGLISH. *1901 Cypress Gardens Blvd (33884). 813/324-3954; FAX 813/324-5998.* 23 rms, 4 kit. units, 3 kit. apts. Feb–Mar: S, D $55–$75; each addl $5; kit. units $6 addl; kit. apts $8 addl; wkly rates; lower rates rest of yr. Crib free. TV; cable. Heated pool. Playground. Complimentary English tea, coffee. Restaurant nearby. Ck-out 10 am. Coin lndry. Lawn games. Refrigerators. Picnic tables, grills. Cr cds: DS, MC, V.

★★QUALITY INN TOWN HOUSE. *975 Cypress Gardens Blvd (33880). 813/324-4104.* 32 rms, 6 kits. Feb–Apr, late Dec: S, D $56–$65; each addl $5; lower rates rest of yr. Crib $4. TV; cable. Heated pool. Complimentary continental bkfst. Ck-out 11 am. Coin lndry. Lawn games. Some refrigerators. Cr cds: A, C, D, DS, ER, MC, V, JCB.

★RED CARPET INN. *2000 Cypress Gardens Blvd (33884). 813/324-6334; FAX 813/324-9131.* 36 rms, 1–2 story, 14 kits. Late Dec–late Apr: S $55–$60; D $60–$65; each addl $5; kit. units $5–$10 addl; wkly rates; lower rates rest of yr. Crib $5. TV; cable. Pool. Complimentary coffee. Restaurant opp 7 am–10 pm. Ck-out 11 am. Refrigerators. Opp Lake Ina. Cr cds: A, C, D, DS, MC, V.

Restaurants

★★★CHRISTY'S SUNDOWN. *US 17S, at Ave K & 3rd St SW. 813/293-0069.* Hrs: 11:30 am–11 pm. Closed Sun; major hols. Res accepted. Greek, Amer menu. Bar to 1:30 am. Semi-a la carte: lunch $3.95–$8, dinner $8–$18.95. Child's meals. Specializes in fresh seafood, broiled steak, veal. Own baking, desserts. Entertainment. Parking. Antiques, artwork. Family-owned. Cr cds: A, MC, V.

✔★★HARRISTON'S. *230 Cypress Gardens Blvd. 813/294-1300.* Hrs: 11:30 am–2 pm, 5–10 pm; Mother's Day–Oct 5–10 pm. Closed some major hols; also Sun Mother's Day–Oct. Bar. Semi-a la carte: lunch $3–$7.50, dinner $8.95–$16.95. Child's meals. Specializes in fresh seafood, steak, lamb. Entertainment. Parking. Art deco-style decor; stained-glass pieces. Cr cds: C, D, DS, MC, V.

Winter Park (C-4)

Founded: 1882 **Pop:** 22,242 **Elev:** 94 ft **Area code:** 407

Winter Park is a college town, vacation retreat and artist's haven.

What to See and Do

1. Rollins College (1885). (2,600 students) Park & Holt Aves, on 67 acres bordering Lake Virginia. Coeducational, private, liberal arts. Knowles Memorial Chapel's Spanish/Mediterranean architecture make it the most distinctive building on campus. Walk of Fame is bordered by more than 500 inscribed stones from birthplaces and houses of famous people. Theater and fine arts museum host plays and exhibitions. Phone 646-2000.

2. The Charles Hosmer Morse Museum of American Art. 133 E Welbourne Ave. Turn-of-the-century American arts by Tiffany and other masters include leaded stained-glass windows, blown glass, lamps; pottery; 19th-century American paintings; furniture; also special exhibits. (Daily exc Mon; closed hols) Phone 644-3686. ¢¢

3. Scenic Boat Tour. E end of Morse Blvd at Lake Osceola. A narrated one-hour cruise through canals and three lakes for views of estates, Kraft Azalea Gardens, Rollins College and other sights. Departs hourly. (Daily; no cruises Dec 25) Phone 644-4056. ¢¢¢

(For further information contact the Chamber of Commerce, 150 N New York Ave, PO Box 280, 32790; 644-8281.)

(See Altamonte Springs, Orlando)

Motels

★ ★ ★**BEST WESTERN MT VERNON INN.** *110 S Orlando Ave (32789), I-4 exit 45, then 1 mi E to US 17/92, turn left 1½ blks.* 407/647-1166; *FAX 407/647-8011.* 147 rms, 2 story. S $53.50–$80; D $59.50–$86; each addl $6; under 12 free; wkend rates; higher rates: art festival, Daytona 500. Crib $6. TV; cable. Pool; poolside serv. Restaurant 6:30 am–2 pm. Rm serv. Bar 11–2 am; entertainment. Ck-out 11 am. Meeting rms. Valet serv. Sundries. Health club privileges. Many refrigerators. Some balconies. Opp lake. Cr cds: A, C, D, DS, MC, V, JCB.

✔ ★**DAYS INN.** *901 N Orlando Ave (32789). 407/644-8000; FAX 407/644-0032.* 105 rms, 2 story. Feb–mid-Apr: S $59; D $69; each addl $6; under 12 free; higher rates: Daytona 500, art show; lower rates rest of yr. Crib free. Pet accepted, some restrictions; $35. TV; cable. Pool. Restaurant 6 am–10:30 pm. Bar 5 pm–midnight. Ck-out 11 am. Some refrigerators. Cr cds: A, C, D, DS, ER, MC, V.

★**FAIRFIELD INN BY MARRIOTT.** *951 N Wymore Rd (32789). 407/539-1955.* 135 rms, 3 story. Mid-Dec–late Apr: S $52.95; D $60.95; each addl $3; under 18 free; higher rates Daytona 500; lower rates rest of yr. Crib free. TV; cable. Heated pool. Complimentary continental bkfst. Complimentary coffee in lobby. Restaurant nearby. Ck-out noon. Meeting rms. Airport transportation. Health club privileges. Cr cds: A, C, D, DS, MC, V.

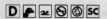

Motor Hotel

★ ★**LANGFORD.** *300 E New England Ave (32789). 407/644-3400; FAX 407/628-1952.* 218 rms, 2-7 story, 10 suites, 82 kits. S $65–$75; D $75–$85; each addl $10; suites $200; kits. addl $10; under 17 free; monthly rates; higher rates art show. Crib free. Pet accepted, some restrictions; $10. TV; cable. Heated pool; whirlpool, sauna, poolside serv. Restaurant 7 am–10 pm. Rm serv. Bar 11–1 am; entertainment, dancing 5 days/wk. Ck-out 11 am. Meeting rms. Bellhops. Valet serv. Sundries. Beauty shop. Game rm. Balconies. Cr cds: A, D, ER, MC, V.

Hotel

★ ★ ★**PARK PLAZA.** *307 Park Ave S (32789). 407/647-1072; res: 800/228-7220; FAX 407/647-4081.* 27 rms, 2 story. S, D $80–$150; higher rates art festival. Children over 5 yrs only. TV; cable. Complimentary continental bkfst in rms or on balcony. Restaurant 11:30 am–3 pm, 6–11 pm. Ck-out noon. Concierge. Free valet parking. Balcony. Restored hotel; antiques, oriental rugs, paintings. Flower, chocolate shops in lobby. Rms individually decorated. Overlooks park. Cr cds: A, C, D, MC, V.

Inns

★**FORTNIGHTLY.** *377 E Fairbanks Ave (32789). 407/645-4440.* 5 rms, 2 story, 2 suites. S, D, suites $75–$95; each addl $10; wkly rates. TV in sitting rm. Complimentary full bkfst, tea/sherry. Restaurant nearby. Ck-out 11 am, ck-in 2 pm. Restored 1920s house; oak floors, clawfoot bathtubs, pedestal sinks, original fixtures. Totally nonsmoking. Cr cds: A, MC, V.

★ ★**THURSTON HOUSE.** *(851 Lake Ave, Maitland 32751) I-4 exit 46 (Lee Rd) E, then N on Wymore, E on Kennedy ¾ mi. 407/539-1911.* 4 rms, 2 story. S, D $70–$80. Children over 12 yrs only. TV in sitting rm; cable, in-rm movies. Complimentary continental bkfst. Ck-out 11 am, ck-in 3 pm. Restored 1885 Queen Anne Victorian house overlooking lake on secluded wooded property. Antiques; screened porches. Totally nonsmoking. Cr cds: A, MC, V.

Restaurants

★**BUBBLE ROOM.** *(1351 S Orlando Ave, Maitland) 1 mi N on US 17/92 (Orlando Ave). 407/628-3331.* Hrs: 11:30 am–2:30 pm, 5:30–10 pm; Fri to 11 pm; Sat 11:30 am–4 pm, 5–11 pm; Sun 11:30 am–4 pm, 5–10 pm. Closed Dec 25. Bar. Semi-a la carte: lunch $5.95–$12.95, dinner $11.95–$26.45. Child's meals. Specializes in fresh filet of grouper, prime rib. Own desserts. Music and memorabilia from 1930s, 40s and 50s. Parking. Festive atmosphere; animated toys, rotating glass chandeliers, traveling electric train. Cr cds: A, C, D, DS, MC, V.

★ ★**CHARLIE'S LOBSTER HOUSE.** *2415 Aloma Ave. 407/677-7352.* Hrs: 11:30 am–9 pm; Sun to 10 pm; some hols to midnight; early-bird dinner 3–6 pm. Res accepted. Bar. Semi-a la carte: lunch $3.95–$7.95, dinner $9.95–$27.95. Child's meals. Specializes in Maine & Florida lobster, Atlantic blue crab, fresh oysters. Parking. Nautical decor. Cr cds: A, C, D, DS, MC, V.

✔ ★ ★**CHINA GARDEN.** *118 S Semoran Blvd. 407/671-2120.* Hrs: 11:30 am–10 pm; Fri, Sat to 11 pm; Sun noon–10 pm. Closed Thanksgiving. Res accepted wkends. Chinese menu. Wine, beer. Semi-a la carte: lunch $4–$5.50, dinner $6.50–$14.95. Specialties: moo shu pork, ginger scallion lobster, braised duck with black mushrooms. Oriental decor. Cr cds: A, MC, V.

★ ★ ★**JORDAN'S GROVE.** *(1300 S Orlando Ave, Maitland) 1 mi N on US 17/92 (Orlando Ave). 407/628-0020.* Hrs: 11:30 am–2:30 pm, 6–10 pm; Sat from 6 pm; Sun brunch to 2:30 pm. Closed Mon; major hols. Res accepted. Beer. Wine cellar. A la carte entrees: lunch $6.95–$12.50, dinner $16.50–$25. Sun brunch $6.95–$12.50. Specializes in fresh seafood, fowl, game. Patio dining. Restored Victorian residence (1912) on 3½ acres. Cr cds: A, C, D, MC, V.

★ ★ ★**LE CORDON BLEU.** *537 W Fairbanks Ave. 407/647-7575.* Hrs: 11:30 am–2:30 pm, 5:30–11 pm. Closed Sun; Jan 1, Dec 25.

Res accepted. French menu. Bar 9–2 am. Semi-a la carte: lunch $5.75–$11.95, dinner $16.95–$24.95. Specialties: filet mignon with Béarnaise sauce, veal scaloppini. Own baking. Entertainment Tues–Sat. Valet parking. Historic establishment; many antiques. Family-owned. Cr cds: A, C, D, DS, MC, V.

★★MAISON DES CRÊPES. 348 N Park Ave. 407/647-4469. Hrs: 11:30 am–3 pm, 5:30–10 pm; Mon to 3 pm; early-bird dinner 5:30–7 pm. Closed Sun; major hols; also 1st 2 wks July. Res accepted. French menu. Semi-a la carte: lunch $6.95–$10.95, dinner $11.95–$25.95. Specialties: filet Royal, crêpes. Country French decor. Cr cds: A, C, D, MC, V.

★★★PARK PLAZA GARDENS. 319 Park Ave S. 407/645-2475. Hrs: 11:30 am–3 pm, 6–10 pm; Fri, Sat to 11 pm, Sun to 9 pm; Sun brunch 11 am–3 pm. Closed Jan 1, Memorial Day, July 4, Dec 25. Res accepted. Continental menu. Bar. Semi-a la carte: lunch $6.95–$12.95, dinner $17.95–$28.95. Sun brunch $17.95. Specializes in seafood, veal, beef. Own baking. Entertainment. Parking. Glass-enclosed garden dining. Tableside cooking. New Orleans decor. Cr cds: A, C, D, DS, MC, V.

✔★TOUCAN WILLIE'S. (829 Eyrie St, Oviedo) N on FL 426. 407/366-6225. Hrs: 4:30–10 pm; Fri, Sat to 11 pm; early-bird dinner 4:30–6 pm. Closed Thanksgiving, Dec 25. Bar to midnight; wkends to 1:30 am. Semi-a la carte: dinner $8.95–$15. Child's meals. Specializes in fresh seafood, barbecued ribs. Guitarist Wed–Sun. Parking. Key West/Caribbean decor. Cr cds: A, C, D, DS, MC, V.

D

Unrated Dining Spot

BRITISH SHOPPE & TEA ROOM. 1917 Aloma Ave, in Winter Park Corners Mall. 407/677-0121. Hrs: Shop 8 am–5 pm; tea rm to 4 pm; Sun 9 am–2 pm. British menu. Wine, beer. A la carte entrees: bkfst, lunch $1.50–$4.50. Specializes in steak & kidney pie, fish & chips, pies & pastry. Large variety of muffins, desserts, meat pies. Own baking. British tearoom decor; travel posters. Shop featuring British candy, cheese, magazines, newspapers, soaps. Cr cds: DS, MC, V.

Zephyrhills (C-3)

Pop: 8,220 **Elev:** 97 ft **Area code:** 813

What to See and Do

Hillsborough River State Park. 6 mi SW on US 301. A 2,994-acre park; one of Florida's oldest. Swinging bridge spans river to nature trail through stands of hammock. The Hillsborough River and rapids are the features of this park. Swimming; fishing; canoeing. Nature trails; biking. Picnic area, concession. Campground (hookups, dump station). Standard hrs, fees. Phone 987-6771.

Ft Foster Historic Site. Reconstruction of fort (ca 1835) built during Second Seminole War; on original site. Living history presentation. Tours (weather permitting) depart from Hillsborough River State Park (Sat, Sun & hols; several departures each day). Phone 987-6771. ¢¢

(For further information contact the Chamber of Commerce, 38415 5th Ave, 33540; 782-1913.)

(See Dade City, Lakeland, Tampa)

Motel

★BEST WESTERN. 5734 Gall Blvd (US 301) (33541), ½ mi N of jct FL 54. 813/782-5527; FAX 813/783-7102. 52 rms, 2 story. Mid-Nov–Apr: S, D $52–$54; each addl $5; under 5, $2; lower rates rest of yr. Crib $5. Pet accepted, some restrictions. TV; cable. Pool. Restaurant adj 7 am–11 pm. Ck-out 11 am. Refrigerators. Picnic tables. Cr cds: A, C, D, DS, MC, V.

Georgia

Population: 6,478,216	
Land area: 58,876 square miles	
Elevation: 0–4,784 feet	
Highest point: Brasstown Bald Mountain (Between Towns, Union counties)	
Entered Union: Fourth of original 13 states (January 1, 1788)	
Capital: Atlanta	
Motto: Wisdom, Justice and Moderation	
State flower: Cherokee rose	
State bird: Brown thrasher	
State tree: Live oak	
State fair: 3rd week October, 1994, in Macon	
Time zone: Eastern	

Georgia, beloved for its antebellum gentility, then devastated by General William Tecumseh Sherman's march to the sea, is now a vibrant, busy state, typifying the economic growth of the New South. Founded with philanthropic and military aims, the only colony where rum and slavery were forbidden, the state nevertheless has the dubious honor of accepting the last shipment of slaves to this country. It boasts Savannah, one of the oldest planned cities in the country, and Atlanta, one of the newest of the South's great cities, rebuilt atop Civil War ashes.

The Georgia Colony was founded by James Oglethorpe on behalf of a private group of English trustees and was named for King George II of England. Georgia's barrier islands not only sheltered the fledgling colony, they provided a bulwark on the Spanish Main for English forts to oppose Spanish Florida and helped end the centuries-old struggle for domination among Spanish, French and English along the South Atlantic Coast.

Today a year-round vacation mecca, the Golden Isles were at times Indian hunting lands, vast sea island plantations, fishing communities isolated after the Civil War and rich men's private preserves. The Colony trustees brought English artisans to found strong colonies at Savannah, Brunswick and Darien, where Scottish Highlanders introduced golf to the New World. The Cherokee Indians made early peace with Oglethorpe and remained within the state to set up the Republic of the Cherokee Nation a century later. Gradually, however, all Indian lands of both Creek and Cherokee were ceded; the Cherokees were banished and their lands, including the capital, distributed by lottery.

From their settlements at Savannah, Brunswick and the coastal islands, Georgia colonists followed the rivers (many of them flowing north) to found inland ports such as Augusta. Colonial boundaries were extended to the Mississippi River by the State of Georgia, but the unfortunate manipulations of land speculators in the legislature deeded all of Mississippi, Alabama, Tennessee, and more, for sale as the Yazoo Tract for one-and-one-half cents an acre. Though repudiated by a subsequent legislature and declared unconstitutional by the Supreme Court, the lands were gone forever, and Georgia no longer extended

from the Mississippi to the sea. It is, however, still the largest state east of the Mississippi.

Georgia's lot in the Civil War was a harsh one from the time Sherman opened his campaign in Georgia on May 4, 1864, until he achieved the Union objective of splitting the South from the Mississippi to the sea. Reconstruction ushered in the reign of carpetbaggers and a long, slow recovery.

Georgia boasts many firsts: the *Savannah,* the first steamship to cross the ocean (1819); America's first nuclear-powered merchant ship, the *Savannah* (1959); the first big American gold strike (1828); the cotton gin, invented by Eli Whitney (1793); and the first use of ether as an anesthetic (1842), by Georgia doctor Crawford W. Long.

Georgia produces peanuts, pecans, cotton, peaches, wood pulp and paper products. Near Atlanta a number of national manufacturing and commercial concerns contribute to a diversified economy. Georgia marble is prized the world over.

Georgia boasts many wonders, from its Blue Ridge vacationlands in the north, where Brasstown Bald Mountain rises 4,784 feet, to the deep "trembling earth" of the ancient and mysterious Okefenokee Swamp bordering Florida. Stone Mountain, a giant hunk of rock that rises from the plain near Atlanta, is the world's largest granite exposure. The coastal Golden Isles, set off by the mysterious Marshes of Glynn, support moss-festooned oaks that grow down to the white sand beaches. Visitors still pan for gold in the country's oldest gold mining town, Dahlonega, and find semiprecious stones in the Blue Ridge.

Historical attractions are everywhere, from the world's largest brick fort near Savannah to the late President Franklin D. Roosevelt's "Little White House" at Warm Springs. There is the infamous Confederate prison at Andersonville and the still lavish splendor of the cottage colony of 60 millionaires of the Jekyll Island Club, now a state-owned resort. The battlefield marking Sherman's campaign before Atlanta and the giant ceremonial mounds of indigenous Indians are equally important national shrines.

Tourism is one of Georgia's primary industries. The state's Visitor Information Centers, which are staffed year-round, offer brochures and computerized information to travelers on major highways.

National Park Service Areas

Georgia has Andersonville National Historic Site (see ANDERSONVILLE), Jimmy Carter National Historic Site (see AMERICUS), Martin Luther King, Jr, National Historic Site (see ATLANTA), Kennesaw Mountain National Battlefield Park (see), Chickamauga and Chattanooga National Military Park (see), Fort Frederica, Fort Pulaski and Ocmulgee national monuments (see all), Cumberland Island National Seashore (see), part of the Appalachian National Scenic Trail (see DAHLONEGA), and the Chattahoochee River National Recreation Area.

National Forests

The following is an alphabetical listing of National Forests and towns they are listed under.

Chattahoochee National Forest (see DAHLONEGA): Forest Supervisor in Gainesville; Ranger offices in Blairsville*, Blue Ridge*, Chatsworth, Clarkesville*, Clayton, Dahlonega, La Fayette*.

Oconee National Forest: Forest Supervisor in Gainesville; Ranger office in Monticello.

*Not described in text

State Recreation Areas

The following towns list state recreation areas in their vicinity under What to See and Do; refer to the individual town for directions and park information.

Listed under **Adel:** see Reed Bingham State Park.

Listed under **Bainbridge:** see Seminole State Park.

Listed under **Blakely:** see Kolomoki Mounds State Park.

Listed under **Carrollton:** see John Tanner State Park.

Listed under **Cartersville:** see Red Top Mountain State Park.

Listed under **Chatsworth:** see Fort Mountain State Park.

Listed under **Cordele:** see Georgia Veterans Memorial State Park.

Listed under **Cumberland Island National Seashore:** see Crooked River State Park.

Listed under **Dahlonega:** see Amicalola Falls and Vogel state parks.

Listed under **Douglas:** see General Coffee State Park.

Listed under **Fort McAllister Historic Park:** see Fort McAllister State Park.

Listed under **Helen:** see Unicoi State Park.

Listed under **Indian Springs:** see Indian Springs State Park.

Listed under **Lumpkin:** see Florence Marina State Park and Providence Canyon State Conservation Park.

Listed under **Okefenokee Swamp:** see Stephen C. Foster State Park.

Listed under **Pine Mountain:** see Franklin D. Roosevelt State Park.

Listed under **Washington:** see Alexander H. Stephens and Elijah Clark state parks.

Listed under **Waycross:** see Laura S. Walker State Park.

Listed under **Winder:** see Fort Yargo State Park.

Water-related activities, hiking, riding, various other sports, picnicking and visitor centers, as well as camping, are available in many of these areas. Most state parks welcome campers, and there are many group camp facilities and comfort stations with hot showers, electric outlets and laundry. All parks listed have trailer dump stations, with the exception of Providence Canyon. Camping is limited to two weeks at any one park. Reservations may be made up to three months in advance (minimum 2-night stay required). Rates in parks are $10/site/night. Walk-in sites, where available, are $6/site/night. Most parks are open year round, 7 am–10 pm.

Georgia park vacationers may enjoy cottages at 24 state parks. These provide complete housekeeping facilities—kitchens with electric ranges and refrigerators, living rooms, one–three bedrooms (linens provided), screened porches, outdoor grills and picnic tables. They are air-conditioned for summer and heated for winter.

Cottages are available at Amicalola Falls, Black Rock Mountain, Cloudland Canyon, Crooked River, Elijah Clark Memorial, Florence Marina, Fort Mountain, Franklin D. Roosevelt, Georgia Veterans Memorial, Hard Labor Creek, Hart, Indian Springs, John Tanner, Little Ocmulgee, Magnolia Springs, Mistletoe, Red Top Mountain, Seminole, Stephen C. Foster, Tugaloo, Unicoi, Vogel and Will-A-Way (in Fort Yargo) parks. Cottages rent for $40–$70 daily with a one-week minimum June–Labor Day if reservations are made more than 30 days in advance. Reservations for cottage rentals must be submitted to the particular park office. Cottage reservations can be made up to 11 months in advance. Reservations are taken (in order of preference) in person, by phone or by mail.

Domestic pets allowed in state parks only if kept on leash not longer than 6 feet and accompanied by owner at all times. No pets allowed in any cottages, site buildings or swimming areas. Fees are subject to change.

Detailed information on state parks may be obtained from the Department of Natural Resources, Public Information Office, 205 Butler St SE, Atlanta 30334; phone 404/656-3530.

Fishing & Hunting

Georgia's range of fresh and saltwater fishing rivals any other state in variety. There are 27 major reservoirs totaling 261,675 acres, and 10 major river systems traverse the state, with thousands of miles of clear, cold-water trout streams and smaller, warm-water streams. Approximately 60,000 small lakes and ponds add to the freshwater total. Some 220 species of freshwater fish are found, 40 of which are considered desirable by game fishermen, including largemouth, shoal and striped bass, as well as crappie and channel catfish. Mountain streams in northern Georgia are a natural source of trout. Fishing in black-water swamp areas in southern Georgia is just as famous for lunker bass and big bream. Coastal waters are good for mackerel, redfish, speckled trout and giant tarpon; no license required.

A state fishing license is required for all freshwater fishing; nonresident: season $24; 5-day permit $7; 1-day permit $3.50; trout stamp (required to fish in trout waters or to keep trout caught): season $13. Fees subject to change. For further information on saltwater fishing contact Dept of Natural Resources, Coastal Resources Division, 1 Conservation Way, Brunswick 31523-8600; 912/264-7218. For further information on freshwater fishing contact Dept of Natural Resources, Game and Fish Division, 2070 US 278SE, Social Circle 30279; 404/918-6418.

There is hunting from the Blue Ridge in northern Georgia to the piney woods of the south. Nonresident: season, $59; 7-day, $25; 1-day, $5.50; big game (deer, wild turkey), $118. Florida resident: 7-day, $144 (incl big game); season, $177 (incl big game). Preserve license, $12; bow hunting permit, $25. Wildlife Management Area stamp, $73. Waterfowl stamp, $5.50 (federal stamp also required). Fees subject to change. For seasons, bag limits, other details write Dept of Natural Resources, Game and Fish Division, 2070 US 278SE, Social Circle 30279; 404/918-6416.

Safety Belt Information

Safety belts are mandatory for all persons in front seat of vehicle and all minors anywhere in vehicle; ages 3 and 4 may use a regulation safety belt; age 2 and under must use an approved safety seat. For further information phone 404/624-7400 or 800/342-9819 (GA).

Interstate Highway System

The following alphabetical listing of Georgia towns in *Mobil Travel Guide* shows that these cities are within 10 miles of the indicated Interstate highways. A highway map, however, should be checked for the nearest exit.

INTERSTATE 16: Dublin, Macon, Savannah.

INTERSTATE 20: Atlanta, Augusta, Carrollton, Madison.

INTERSTATE 75: Adel, Atlanta, Calhoun, Cartersville, Cordele, Dalton, Forsyth, Macon, Marietta, Perry, Tifton, Valdosta.

INTERSTATE 85: Atlanta, Buford, Commerce, La Grange, Norcross.

INTERSTATE 95: Brunswick, Darien, Jekyll Island, St Simons Island, Savannah.

Additional Visitor Information

For visitor information, including brochures and other materials, contact Tourism Dept, PO Box 1776, Atlanta 30301-1776; phone 404/656-3590 or 800/VISIT-GA, ext 1903. Visitor centers are located in Augusta, Columbus, Kingsland, Lavonia, Plains, Ringgold, Savannah, Sylvania, Tallapoosa, Valdosta and West Point. Information available 8:30 am–5:30 pm. Another source of information is *Georgia Journal/Georgia Living*, PO Box 27, Athens 30603; 706/354-0463.

Adel (E-3)

Pop: 5,093 **Elev:** 240 ft **Area code:** 912 **Zip:** 31620

What to See and Do

Reed Bingham State Park. 6 mi W off GA 37. Park includes 400-acre lake. Waterskiing; fishing; boating (ramp). Nature trails. Picnicking; arboretum. Camping. Standard hrs, fees. Contact Superintendent, Rte 2, Box 394B-1; 896-3551.

(For further information contact the Adel-Cook County Chamber of Commerce, 100 S Hutchinson Ave, PO Box 461; 896-2281.)

(For accommodations see Tifton, Valdosta)

Albany (D-2)

Founded: 1836 **Pop:** 78,122 **Elev:** 208 ft **Area code:** 912

Albany lies in a semi-tropical setting of oaks and pines located in the Plantation Trace region of the state. Colonel Nelson Tift, a Connecticut Yankee, led a party up the Flint River from Apalachicola, Florida, and constructed the first log buildings in Albany. Settlers followed when the Native Americans were removed to western lands. Paper-shell pecans grown in surrounding Dougherty County have made this the "pecan capital of the world." Surrounded by numerous plantations, the area is also well-known for quail hunting.

What to See and Do

1. **Thronateeska Heritage Foundation.** 100 Roosevelt Ave. Sponsors Museum of History and Science. Complex of former railroad build-

ings houses exhibits on local and natural history and model trains; also Discovery Room for children. (Daily exc Sun; closed major hols) Phone 432-6955. **Free.** Also here is

Wetherbee Planetarium and Space Museum. In Railway Express Agency Building. Features exhibits of NASA items. Public shows (Sat). ¢

2. **Albany Museum of Art.** 311 Meadowlark Dr. Permanent and changing exhibits of works by national and regional artists. (Daily exc Mon; closed major hols) Phone 439-8400. ¢

3. **Lake Chehaw.** 2 mi NE off GA 91. At the confluence of the Kinchafoonee and Muckalee creeks and the Flint River. Waterskiing; fishing; boating.

4. **Chehaw Park.** 2½ mi NE on GA 91. On 775 acres. Boating. Nature trails. Picnicking. Camping (dump station). Also here is

Chehaw Wild Animal Park. Wildlife preserve (100 acres) where elephant, giraffe, deer, buffalo, llama and other animals roam in natural habitats. Protective trails, elevated walkways. (Daily exc Mon; closed Dec 25) Phone 430-5275. ¢

(For further information contact the Convention & Visitors Bureau, 225 W Broad Ave, 31701; 434-8700.)

Annual Event

Fall on the Flint Festival. Entertainment, parade, exhibits, athletic contests. Last wkend Sept.

(See Americus, Cordele)

Motels

✔ ★**DAYS INN.** 422 W Oglethorpe Blvd (31701). 912/888-2632; FAX 912/435-1875. 189 rms, 2 story. S, D $40–$44. Crib $5. TV; cable. Pool; wading pool. Restaurant 6:30–11 am, 4 pm–midnight. Rm serv. Bar from 4 pm. Ck-out noon. Free airport transportation. Cr cds: A, C, D, DS, MC, V.

D 🐾 🛥 🚫 🎖 ⊘ SC

★ ★**QUALITY INN MERRY ACRES.** (Box 3549, 31708) 1500 Dawson Rd. 912/435-7721; FAX 912/439-9386. 110 rms. S $64–$78; D $69–$83; each addl $5; suites $156–$161. Crib $5. TV; cable. Pool; wading pool. Playground. Restaurant 6:30 am–10 pm. Coffee in rms. Bar 4–10 pm. Ck-out noon. Meeting rms. Valet serv. Sundries. Beauty shop. Exercise equipt; weight machine, stair machine. Some refrigerators, wet bars. Cr cds: A, C, D, DS, ER, MC, V, JCB.

🛥 🕇 ⊘ 🎖 SC

★ ★**RAMADA INN.** 2505 N Slappey Blvd (31701). 912/883-3211; FAX 912/883-3211, ext 113. 158 rms, 2 story. S $54; D $60; each addl $7; suites $90; under 18 free; wkend rates. Crib free. Pet accepted. TV; cable. Pool; wading pool. Restaurant 6:30 am–2 pm, 5–10 pm; Sun 7 am–2 pm. Rm serv 7 am–9 pm. Bar 4 pm–2 am; dancing exc Sun. Ck-out noon. Meeting rms. Bellhops. Valet serv. Sundries. Free airport transportation. Putting green. Cr cds: A, C, D, DS, ER, MC, V, JCB.

D 🐾 🛥 🚫 🎖 ⊘ SC

Motor Hotels

★ ★**BEST WESTERN EXECUTIVE INN.** 911 E Oglethorpe Blvd (US 19/82 Business) (31705). 912/883-1650; FAX 912/883-1650, ext 107. 147 rms, 4 story. S $45–$58; D $51–$64; each addl $5; suites $75–$150; under 17 free. Crib free. TV; cable. Pool. Restaurant 6 am–2 pm, 5–10 pm. Rm serv. Bar 4 pm–midnight. Ck-out noon. Meeting rms. Free airport transportation. Tennis & golf privileges. Health club privileges. Cr cds: A, C, D, DS, MC, V.

D 🚲 🔑 🛥 🚫 🎖 ⊘ SC

✔ ★ ★**HERITAGE HOUSE CONVENTION CENTER.** 732 W Oglethorpe Blvd (US 19/82 Business) (31701). 912/888-1910; FAX 912/888-1910, ext 103. 204 rms, 4 story. S $48; D $52; each addl $6; suites

$65–$105; under 12 free. TV; cable. Pool. Restaurant 6 am–2:30 pm, 6–9:30 pm. Rm serv. Bar 4:30 pm–1:30 am, Sat to midnight; entertainment, dancing exc Sun. Ck-out noon. Meeting rms. Bellhops. Valet serv. Sundries. Free airport transportation. Cr cds: A, C, D, DS, MC, V.

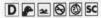

Restaurant

★★CARR'S STEAK HOUSE. *609 N Slappey Blvd. 912/439-8788.* Hrs: 11 am–2 pm, 4 pm–midnight. Closed Sun; major hols. Res accepted. Bar. Semi-a la carte: lunch $4.95–$11.95, dinner $8.95–$17.95. Child's meals. Specializes in steak, seafood. Band. Piano bar Fri, Sat. Parking. Fox-hunting paintings. Cr cds: A, MC, V.

Americus (D-2)

Founded: 1832 **Pop:** 16,512 **Elev:** 355 ft **Area code:** 912 **Zip:** 31709

Americus is at the center of an area once known as the "granary of the Creek nations," so called because Indians favored this area for the cultivation of maize. The town was named, it is said, either for Americus Vespucius or for the settlers themselves, who were referred to as "merry cusses" for their happy-go-lucky ways. The town flourished in the 1890s. Many Victorian/Gothic-revival buildings remain from that period.

Today, peanuts, corn, cotton, small grain and pecans are grown, and bauxite and kaolin are mined in the area. Americus is also a manufacturing center, producing lumber commodities, metal lighting equipment, heating products and textiles. The town's livestock sales are second in volume in the state. Plains, nine miles west via US 280, is the hometown of the 39th president, Jimmy Carter.

What to See and Do

1. **Andersonville National Historic Site.** 11 mi NE on GA 49. (See ANDERSONVILLE)

2. **Georgia Southwestern College** (1906). (2,200 students) Wheatly & Glessner Sts, 2 mi E of jct US 19, 280. On 187-acre campus with a lake is

   Carter Display focusing on former President Jimmy Carter and First Lady Rosalynn Carter; photographs, memorabilia; located in James Earl Carter Library. (Daily exc during school breaks, hols) **Free.**

3. **Americus Historic Driving Tour.** Tour features 38 houses of various architectural styles, including Victorian, Greek revival and classical revival. Contact the Chamber of Commerce.

4. **Jimmy Carter National Historic Site.** 8 mi W on US 280 in Plains. Visitor center is located in railroad depot that served as Jimmy Carter's campaign headquarters for the Georgia presidential primaries in 1976 and 1980; campaign memorabilia; cassette auto driving tour of Plains available (fee). (Daily; closed Dec 25) Phone 824-3413. **Free.**

(For further information contact the Americus-Sumter County Chamber of Commerce, 400 W Lamar St, Box 724; 924-2646.)

(See Albany, Andersonville, Cordele)

Motor Hotel

★★★THE WINDSOR HOTEL. *125 Lamar. 912/924-1555; FAX 912/924-1555, ext 113.* 53 units, 3 story, 8 suites. S, D $65; suites $75–$125; under 14 free. Crib free. TV; cable. Restaurant 6:30 am–10 pm. Rm serv. Bar noon–midnight, closed Sun. Ck-out noon. Meeting rms. Bellhops. Valet serv. Tennis privileges. 18-hole golf privileges, greens fee $12, pro, putting green, driving range. 3-story atrium lobby.

Period-style rms with 12-ft ceilings and ceiling fans. Cr cds: A, C, D, DS, ER, MC, V, JCB.

Restaurant

✔★DRAGON PALACE. *701 Meadowbrook Dr. 912/924-4174.* Hrs: 11 am–2:30 pm, 5–9:30 pm; Fri to 10 pm; Sat 5–10 pm. Closed major hols. Chinese menu. Wine, beer. Semi-a la carte: dinner $4.50–$8.95. Buffet: lunch $4.50. Parking. Cr cds: MC, V.

Andersonville (D-2)

Pop: 277 **Elev:** 390 ft **Area code:** 912 **Zip:** 31711

What to See and Do

1. **Andersonville National Historic Site.** On GA 49. The Confederate Military Prison, Camp Sumter, was built on a 26-acre tract in late 1863 and early 1864 by soldiers and slaves requisitioned from nearby plantations. The lofty pines that grew in the local sandy soil were cut and used to form a stockade. Built to accommodate 10,000 men, the prison at one time held as many as 33,000. Overcrowding, inadequate food, insufficient medicines and a breakdown of the prisoner exchange system resulted in a high death rate. The site is now a memorial to all prisoners of war throughout history. Exhibits, interpretive programs and slide shows depict the role of military prisoners in the history of the nation. Included on grounds are escape tunnels and wells dug by prisoners, Confederate earthworks, three reconstructed sections of stockade wall and state monuments. Park (daily). Visitor center (daily; closed Dec 25). Phone 924-0343. **Free.** Also here are

   Providence Spring. The spring, which bubbled up from the ground after a heavy rain, was said to be in answer to the prisoners' prayers during the summer drought of 1864.

   Andersonville National Cemetery. ½ mi N of prison site. Graves of more than 17,000 Union soldiers and veterans of other wars are in striking contrast to the landscaped grounds. The initial interments were Union soldiers who died in the prison camp. Established as a national cemetery on July 26, 1865.

2. **Civil War Village of Andersonville.** 114 Church St. Restored village from the days of the Civil War. Welcome center, pioneer farm, museum, antique shops. (Daily; closed Dec 25) Phone 924-2558. **Free.**

Annual Event

Andersonville Historic Fair. Center of town. Civil War reenactments, old time craftsmen, antique dealers; RV campsites. Contact Andersonville Historic Fair, PO Box 6; 924-2558. Memorial Day wknd & 1st wknd Oct.

(For accommodations see Americus, Cordele, Perry)

Athens (B-3)

Founded: 1801 **Pop:** 45,734 **Elev:** 775 ft **Area code:** 706

Georgia's "Classic City" is the site of the University of Georgia, chartered in 1785. Diversified industry produces nonwoven fabrics, textiles, clocks, electronic components, precision parts, chemicals and animal feed. Lyman Hall, a signer of the Declaration of Independence, proposed the University and Abraham Baldwin, the acknowledged founding father, wrote the charter. Although allotted 10,000 acres by the legislature in 1784, it was another 17 years before Josiah Meigs, Baldwin's successor and first official president, erected a few log buildings, called it Franklin College and held classes under the tolerant eyes of curious Cherokees.

Athens was incorporated in 1806. Its setting on a hill beside the Oconee River is enhanced by towering oaks and elms, white-blossomed magnolias, old-fashioned boxwood gardens and many well-preserved and still-occupied antebellum houses.

What to See and Do

1. **University of Georgia** (1785). (28,000 students) Consisting of 13 schools and colleges, the main campus extends more than 2 miles south from the Arch (1858), College Ave and Broad St. Nearby are farms managed by the College of Agriculture, a forestry preserve and University Research Park. Historic buildings include Demosthenian Hall (1824); chapel (1832), housing an oil painting (17 by 23½ ft) of the interior of St. Peter's Basilica; Old College (1806), oldest building, designed after Connecticut Hall at Yale; Waddel Hall (1821) and Phi Kappa Hall (1834). Phone 542-3354. Also on campus are

    Georgia Center for Continuing Education. A facility hosting hundreds of conferences yearly, the center has overnight accommodations, conference rooms and an auditorium modeled after the United Nations Assembly Hall. Phone 548-1311.

    Georgia Museum of Art. Contains several permanent collections, including Eva Underhill Holbrook Collection; traveling and special exhibits. (Daily; closed major hols, wk of Dec 25) Phone 542-3255. **Free.**

    State Botanical Garden. 2450 S Milledge Ave. Approximately 300 acres with natural trails, wildlife and special collections. Gardens (daily); conservatory/visitors center (daily); Callaway Bldg (Mon–Fri). Phone 542-1244. **Free.**

    Collegiate Tennis Hall of Fame. Henry Feild Tennis Stadium. Honors great collegiate tennis players of the last 100 years. (Open during home tennis matches and Sat home football games; for other times, phone 542-1622.) **Free.**

2. **Double-barreled cannon** (1863). City Hall lawn, College & Hancock Aves. A unique Civil War weapon cast at Athens' foundry. Believed to be the only double-barreled cannon in the world.

3. **Historic Houses.** For tour information contact Athens Welcome Center in Church-Waddel-Brumby House (see) or contact Athens Convention & Visitors Bureau.

    Taylor-Grady House (1839). 634 Prince Ave. Restored Greek-revival mansion surrounded by 13 columns said to symbolize 13 original states; period furniture. (Mon–Fri; closed major hols) Phone 549-8688. **¢¢**

    Church-Waddel-Brumby House (ca 1820). 280 E Dougherty St. Restored Federal-style house thought to be oldest residence in Athens. Houses **Athens Welcome Center,** which has information on self-guided tours of other historic houses and buildings (days vary). Phone 353-1820.

    University President's House (ca 1855). 570 Prince Ave. Greek-revival mansion surrounded on three sides by massive Corinthian columns. Extensive gardens and picket fences complement classic design. Private residence.

    Founders Memorial Garden and House (1857). 325 S Lumpkin St, on Univ of Georgia campus. Built by University as a residence for professors, house has been restored and furnished with period antiques as museum and headquarters of Garden Club of Georgia. The surrounding gardens are a memorial to founders of Ladies' Garden Club of Athens, the first garden club in the US. House (Mon–Fri; closed hols). Gardens (daily). Phone 542-3631. **¢**

    Other historic houses in Athens include Ross Crane House (Sigma Alpha Epsilon Fraternity) (1842), 247 Pulaski St; Lucy Cobb Institute (1858), 200 N Milledge Ave; Joseph Henry Lumpkin House (1841), 248 Prince Ave; Old Franklin Hotel (1845), 480 E Broad St; Governor Wilson Lumpkin House (1842), South campus, University of Georgia.

4. **Tree That Owns Itself.** Dearing & Finley Sts. White oak, descendant of original tree, stands on plot deeded to it.

5. **Sandy Creek Park.** N on US 441. Swimming (beach); fishing; boating. Hiking; tennis, basketball. Picnicking, playgrounds. Primitive camping. Walkways. (Apr–Sept, daily exc Wed; rest of yr, Thurs–Sun) Phone 613-3631. **¢**

6. **Sandy Creek Nature Center.** ½ mi N of Athens bypass, off US 441. Approximately 200 acres of woods, fields and marshland; includes a live animal exhibit, a 180-year old cabin, nature trails. (Dec–Apr, Mon–Fri; rest of yr, Mon–Fri, also Sat afternoons; closed hols) Phone 613-3615. **Free.**

(For further information contact the Convention & Visitors Bureau, 220 College Ave, 7th floor, PO Box 948, 30603, phone 546-1805; or visit the Athens Welcome Center, 280 E Dougherty St, 30601, phone 353-1820.)

Annual Events

Historic Homes Tour. Held by Athens-Clarke Heritage Foundation. Contact Fire Hall #2, 489 Prince Ave, 30603; 353-1801 or -1820. Last wkend Apr.

Marigold Festival. GA 78 to Cherokee Rd, in Winterville. Arts, crafts, antiques, parades and other events. Phone 742-8600. Wkend after Father's Day.

Crackerland Tennis Tournament. Henry Feild Tennis Stadium, University of Georgia (see #1). Juniors, late July–early Aug. Seniors, mid-Aug.

North Georgia Folk Festival. Sandy Creek Park. Phone 613-3620. Late Sept or early Oct.

(See Commerce, Madison, Winder)

Motel

✔ ★ ★**BEST WESTERN COLONIAL INN.** *170 North Milledge (30601).* 706/546-7311; FAX 706/546-7959. 69 rms, 2 story. S $42; D $48; each addl $4; under 12 free; higher rates: univ football games, graduation. Crib free. Pet accepted; $5. TV; cable. Pool. Complimentary continental bkfst. Restaurant opp 11 am–11 pm. Ck-out noon. Some refrigerators. Cr cds: A, C, D, DS, MC, V.

Motor Hotels

★ ★**COURTYARD BY MARRIOTT.** *166 Finley St (30601).* 706/369-7000; FAX 706/548-4224. 108 rms, 2–3 story. S $65; D $75; each addl $10; kit. units $85; under 18 free; higher rates: univ football games, graduation. Crib free. TV; cable, in-rm movies. Pool. Restaurant adj 11 am–11 pm. Bar. Ck-out 1 pm. Coin lndry. Meeting rms. Free airport transportation. Exercise equipt; weight machine, bicycle, whirlpool. Health club privileges. Some refrigerators. Cr cds: A, C, D, DS, MC, V.

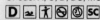

★ ★ ★**HOLIDAY INN.** *(Box 1666, 30603) Broad & Lumpkin Sts. 706/549-4433; FAX 706/549-3031.* 238 rms, 2–6 story. S $60–$79; D $66–$83; each addl $8; suites $87–$135; under 12 free; wknd rates; higher rates football wkends. Crib free. TV; cable. Indoor pool. Coffee in rms. Restaurant 7 am–2 pm, 5:30–10 pm. Rm serv. Bar 4 pm–1 am; closed Sun. Ck-out noon. Coin lndry. Bellhops. Valet serv. Convention facilities. Sundries. Airport transportation. Exercise equipt; weights, bicycles, whirlpool. Some balconies. Adj to Univ of Georgia. *LUXURY LEVEL:* **EXECUTIVE TOWER.** 48 rms, 5 suites, 6 floors. S $83; D $91; suites $114–$122. Concierge. Private lounge. Complimentary continental bkfst, refreshments.
Cr cds: A, C, D, DS, MC, V, JCB.

★ ★**RAMADA INN.** *513 W Broad St (30601), US 29, 78, 129, 441. 706/546-8122; FAX 706/546-8122, ext 586.* 162 rms, 5 story. S, D $51–$65; suites $95; under 18 free; wkend rates; higher rates: graduation, football wkends. Crib free. Pet accepted. TV; cable. Pool. Complimentary continental bkfst Mon–Fri. Restaurant 6 am–10 pm. Rm serv. Bar 4:30 pm–1 am; entertainment, dancing Tues–Sat. Ck-out noon. Bellhops. Valet serv. Meeting rms. Sundries. Free local airport transportation. Cr cds: A, C, D, DS, ER, MC, V, JCB.

Inn

✔ ★ ★**RIVENDELL.** *(3581 S Barnett Shoals Rd, Watkinsville 30677) Approx 8 mi S on US 441, then 5 mi W on Barnett Shoals Rd. 706/769-4522.* 6 rms, 3 with bath, 2 story. Some rm phones. S, D $45–$60; football wkends (2-night min). Children over 10 yrs only. Complimentary full bkfst. Complimentary tea/sherry. Complimentary coffee in library. Ck-out 11 am, ck-in 4–8 pm. Bellhops. Concierge. English country home set upon 5 woodland acres; near Oconee River. Totally nonsmoking. No cr cds accepted.

Restaurant

★ ★**VINCE'S PLACE.** *351 E Broad St, opp univ. 706/546-5629.* Hrs: 6–10:30 pm; Fri, Sat to 11 pm. Closed Sun; major hols. Bar 4 pm–1 am. Semi-a la carte: dinner $12.95–$22. Child's meals. Specializes in steak, prime rib, seafood. Salad bar. Family-owned. Cr cds: A, C, D, MC, V.

Unrated Dining Spots

MORRISON'S CAFETERIA. *3700 Atlanta Hwy (US 29), in Georgia Square Mall. 706/353-0030.* Hrs: 11 am–8:30 pm; Sun to 8 pm. Avg ck: lunch $5, dinner $5.50. Child's meals. Specializes in roast beef, chicken, grilled entrees, fried shrimp. Cr cds: MC, V.

VARSITY. *1000 W Broad St. 706/548-6325.* Hrs: 8 am–midnight. Semi-a la carte: bkfst, lunch, dinner: $1–$1.50. Specializes in hot dogs, hamburgers. Parking. Outdoor dining. School cafeteria atmosphere; pennant flag display. No cr cds accepted.

Atlanta (B-2)

Founded: 1837 **Pop:** 394,017 **Elev:** 1,050 ft **Area code:** 404

When Atlanta was just 27 years old, 90 percent of its houses and buildings were razed by the Union armies after a 117-day siege. Rebuilt by railroads in this century, the city gives an overall impression of 20th-century modernism.

Standing Peachtree, a Creek Indian settlement, occupied Atlanta's site until 1813. Lieutenant George R. Gilmer led 22 recruits to build a fort here because of difficulties among the Creek and Cherokee. This became the first white settlement and grew into an important trading post.

After Georgia's secession from the Union on January 19, 1861, the city became a manufacturing, storage, supply and transportation center for the Confederate forces. This made Atlanta the target and last real barrier on General William Tecumseh Sherman's march to the sea. Although Atlanta had quartered 60,000 Confederate wounded, it was untouched by actual battle until Sherman began the fierce fighting of the Atlanta Campaign on May 7, 1864, with the engagement at Tunnel Hill, just over the Tennessee line. Despairing of capturing the city by battle, Sherman undertook a siege.

Guns were brought in and Atlanta civilians got a foretaste of 20th-century warfare as the population and defenders alike were subjected to continuous bombardment by the Union's heaviest artillery. People took refuge in cellars, trenches and dugouts. Those who could escaped southward by wagon, foot or train until Union forces seized the railroad 20 miles south at Jonesboro on September 1. General Hood evacuated Atlanta that same night, and the mayor surrendered the city the next day, September 2. Although the terms of surrender promised protection of life and property, Sherman ordered the city evacuated. All but 400 of the 3,600 houses and commercial buildings were destroyed in the subsequent burning.

Many citizens had returned to the city by January of 1865. By June, steps had been taken to reorganize business and repair wrecked railroad facilities. In 1866, Atlanta was made federal headquarters for area reconstruction. During the Reconstruction Convention of 1867–68, called by General John Pope in Atlanta, the city offered facilities for the state government if it should be chosen the capital. The convention accepted this proposition, and Atlanta became the capital on April 20, 1868.

Atlanta's recovery and expansion as a rail center was begun by 1872, when two more railroads met here. Today, hundreds of manufacturers produce a wide variety of commodities.

Metropolitan Atlanta's population of 2.8 million is as devoted to cultural activities (such as its famed Alliance Theatre) as it is to its many golf courses and its major sports teams. Peachtree Street today considers itself the South's main street and is more Fifth Avenue than Scarlett O'Hara's beloved lane. Skyscrapers, museums, luxury shops and hotels rub shoulders along this concourse where Coca-Cola was first served; there are few peach blossoms left.

There are 29 colleges and universities in Atlanta. Georgia Institute of Technology, home of "a rambling wreck from Georgia Tech and a hell of an engineer," is one of the nation's top technological institutes. Other schools include Georgia State, Emory and Oglethorpe universities. Atlanta University Center is an affiliation of six institutions of higher learning: Atlanta University, Spelman, Morehouse, Clark, Morris Brown and the Interdenominational Theological Center.

Transportation

Airport: See ATLANTA HARTSFIELD AIRPORT AREA.

Car Rental Agencies: See toll-free numbers under Introduction.

Public Transportation: Buses & subway trains (MARTA), phone 848-4711.

Rail Passenger Service: Amtrak 800/872-7245.

What to See and Do

1. **State Capitol** (1884–89). Capitol Sq. The dome, topped with native gold, is 237 feet high. Inside are historical flags, statues and portraits. Tours (Mon–Fri). Phone 656-2844. **Free.** On the fourth floor is

   Georgia State Museum of Science & Industry. Exhibits of wildlife, snakes, fish, rocks, minerals and fossils. Dioramas of Georgia industry. (Mon–Fri) **Free.**

2. **A.G. Rhodes Memorial Hall** (1903). 1516 Peachtree St NW. Outstanding example of Victorian Romanesque architecture. Open to the public during restoration process (Mon–Fri; closed national hols). Phone 881-9980. ¢¢

3. **Martin Luther King, Jr, National Historic Site.** A two-block area in memory of the famed leader of the civil rights movement and winner of the Nobel Peace Prize. (Daily; closed Jan 1, Thanksgiving, Dec 25) Phone 331-5190. **Free.**

   King Birthplace. 501 Auburn Ave. For tour information phone 331-3920. **Free.**

DOWNTOWN ATLANTA

MILES
0   0.1   0.2   0.3
KILOMETERS
0   0.1   0.2   0.3   0.4   0.48

© H.M. GOUSHA

MARTA Rapid Transit System

Ebenezer Baptist Church. 407 Auburn Ave. Dr. King was co-pastor at Ebenezer from 1960–68. (Daily exc Sun, donation) Next door to the church is the **gravesite** with an eternal flame.

Other features include the Freedom Hall Complex, Chapel of All Faiths, the King Library and Archives and the reflecting pool; films and slides on Dr. King's life and work may be viewed in the screening room (fee). For tour information phone 524-1956. The National Park Service operates an information center (daily exc major hols, phone 331-3920).

4. Robert W. Woodruff Arts Center. 1280 Peachtree St NE. Largest arts complex in the Southeast; headquarters of Atlanta College of Art and

High Museum of Art. European art from the early Renaissance to the present; Samuel H. Kress, J. J. Haverty, Ralph K. Uhry print collection and Richman collection of African art; photographs; decorative arts; traveling exhibitions. (Daily exc Mon; closed some major hols) Also tours, lectures, films; for schedule phone 892-HIGH. Sr citizen rate. For general information phone 898-9540. ¢¢

Symphony Hall. Largest auditorium in Arts Center. Permanent home of Atlanta Symphony Orchestra and Chorus; performances (Sept–May & mid-June–mid-Aug) For schedule, ticket information phone 892-2414.

Alliance Theatre Company. Six mainstage productions, two studio theater productions and two children's theater productions are

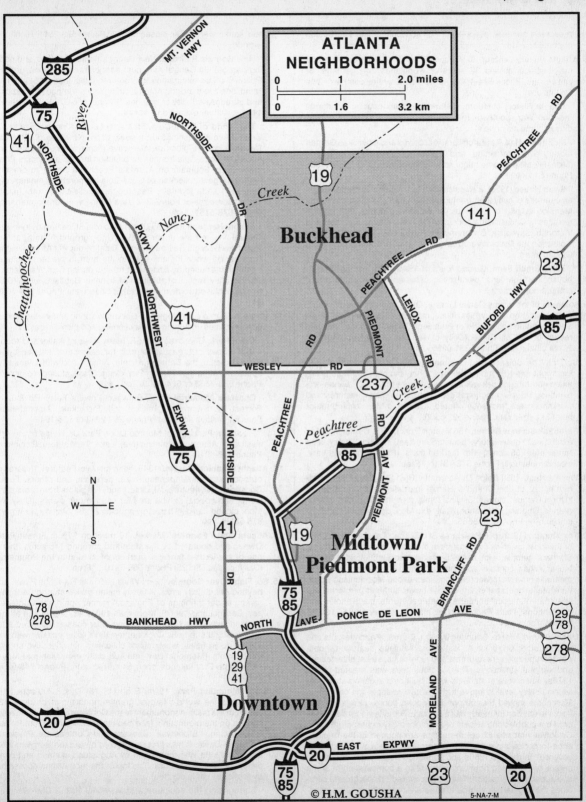

ATLANTA NEIGHBORHOODS

0   1   2.0 miles

0   1.6   3.2 km

Buckhead

Midtown/ Piedmont Park

Downtown

© H.M. GOUSHA

5-NA-7-M

presented annually. (Sept–May) For schedule, ticket information phone 892-2414.

5. **Atlanta History Center.** 130 W Paces Ferry Rd. Center consists of 5 major structures and 32 acres of woodlands and gardens. Sr citizen rate. Phone 814-4000. Admission to entire complex ¢¢¢ On site are

Atlanta History Museum. Historical exhibits relating to Atlanta, the Civil War, Southern folk life and African Americans. (Daily; closed some major hols)

McElreath Hall. Research library, archives and Cherokee Garden Library with gardening and horticulture research collection (Mon–Fri; closed some major hols). Special events. Sr citizen rate. Phone 814-4000.

Swan House (1928), a classically styled mansion is preserved as an example of early 20th-century architecture and decorative arts. Mansion is part of spacious landscaped grounds that include terraces with cascading fountains, formal boxwood garden and Victorian playhouse. On premises is the Philip Trammell Shutze Collection of Decorative Arts. (Daily; closed some major hols) Guided tours.

Tullie Smith Farm. Guided tours of 1840 plantation-style farmhouse, herb gardens, pioneer log cabin and other outbuildings; craft demonstrations.

6. **Museum of the Jimmy Carter Library.** One Copenhill Ave. Museum with exhibits on life in White House, major events during the Carter administration and the life of President Carter. Includes full-scale replica of the Oval Office. (Daily; closed Jan 1, Thanksgiving, Dec 25) Sr citizen rate. Phone 331-0296. ¢¢

7. **SciTrek-The Science and Technology Museum of Atlanta.** 395 Piedmont Ave NE. The worlds of science and high technology are examined through self-guided tour of more than 100 ''hands-on'' exhibits. Traveling exhibits, demonstrations, films, lectures and workshops are frequently offered. (Daily exc Mon; closed major hols) Sr citizen rate. Phone 522-5500. ¢¢¢

8. **Fernbank Science Center.** 156 Heaton Park Dr NE. Center includes exhibit hall, observatory, planetarium (fee), science library; also forest area (65 acres) with marked trails. (Hrs for facilities vary; closed most hols) Phone 378-4311. **Free.**

9. **Wren's Nest.** 1050 Ralph D. Abernathy Blvd SW. Eccentric, Victorian house of Joel Chandler Harris, journalist and transcriber of ''Uncle Remus'' stories. Original family furnishings, books, photographs. Ongoing restoration. (Daily exc Mon; closed major hols) Sr citizen rate. Phone 753-8535. ¢¢

10. **Fox Theatre** (1929). 660 Peachtree St NE. The ''Fabulous Fox,'' one of the most lavish movie theaters in the world, was conceived as a Shriners' temple, with a 4,678-seat auditorium; world's largest Moller organ console and three elaborate ballrooms; restored theater's ornate architecture combines exotic Moorish and Egyptian details. Hosts ballet, Broadway shows, summer film series, full spectrum of musical concerts, theatrical events, trade shows and conventions. Tours (Mon & Thurs; also Sat). Phone 881-2100 for details. Tours ¢¢

11. **Underground Atlanta.** Bounded by Wall, Central, Peachtree Sts and Martin Luther King Jr Dr. A ''festival marketplace'' featuring shops, pushcart peddlers, restaurants and nightclubs, street entertainers and various attractions. The six-block area was created in the 1920s, when several viaducts were built over existing streets at second-story level to move traffic above multiple rail crossings. Merchants moved their shops to second floors, relegating first floors to oblivion for nearly half a century. Today's visitor descends onto the cobblestone streets of a Victorian city in perpetual night. On lower Alabama Street the shops are housed in the original, once-forgotten storefronts. Underground Atlanta was first ''discovered'' in the late 1960s and flourished as a center of nightlife before being closed down in 1981 due to a combination of crime and subway construction. The ''rediscovered'' Underground combines the original below-ground streets with above-ground plazas, promenades, fountains, more shops and restaurants and a 138-foot light tower. (Daily; closed Dec 25) Phone 523-2311. Highlights include

New Georgia Railroad. New Georgia Railroad Depot (and parking garage), 90 Central Ave, near east entrance to Underground. Railroad offers excursions to Stone Mountain (see #16) and narrated loop tours around Atlanta; dining tours. Vintage railroad cars and streamlined diesel engines. Phone 656-0769. Sightseeing ¢¢¢¢; Dinner excursion ¢¢¢¢¢

The World of Coca-Cola. 55 Martin Luther King Jr Dr between Central Ave & Washington St, south of the New Georgia Railroad Depot. A square block of interactive displays and exhibits trace history of Coca-Cola from its introduction in 1886 at Jacob's Pharmacy Soda Fountain on Atlanta's Peachtree Street to present; world's largest collection of Coca-Cola memorabilia; movies; old-fashioned soda fountain. Res suggested. Sr citizen rate. (Daily; closed some major hols & 3–4 days during year for maintenance) Phone 676-5151. ¢¢

Atlanta Heritage Row. 55 Upper Alabama St, between Pryor St & Central Ave, on the upper level of Underground Atlanta, across from New Georgia Railroad Depot. Timeline depicts Atlanta history from period when Indians lived in the area to present; includes bomb shelter used by citizens of Atlanta during Civil War siege, a 1920s trolley, replica of pulpit from Ebenezer Baptist Church. (Daily exc Mon; closed some major hols) Sr citizen rate. Phone 584-7879. ¢¢

12. **Parks** in Atlanta offer dogwood blooms in spring and varied recreational facilities, including golf, swimming and picnic areas.

Grant Park. Cherokee Ave SE. Many miles of walks and roads; visible traces of breastworks built for defense of Atlanta; cyclorama depicting the Battle of Atlanta; Atlanta Zoo with a variety of species. Swimming. Tennis. Picnicking. (Daily; closed major hols) Phone 658-7538 or 624-5600. Zoo ¢¢¢

Chastain Memorial Park. Between Powers Ferry Rd & Lake Forrest Dr. Swimming. Tennis; golf. Picnicking. Amphitheater. Fees for various activities. Phone 252-2927 or 526-1042.

Piedmont Park. Off of Monroe Dr on Park Dr. Home of the Arts Festival of Atlanta. Swimming (fee). Lake. Tennis (fee). Picnicking. Phone 658-6016.

13. **Atlanta Botanical Garden.** 1345 Piedmont Ave. Features 15 acres of outdoor gardens: Japanese, rose, perennial and others. Fuqua Conservatory with tropical, desert and rare plants from around the world; and special exhibit area for carnivorous plants. (Daily exc Mon; closed Jan 1, Thanksgiving, Dec 25) Sr citizen rate. Phone 876-5858. ¢¢

14. **Atlanta State Farmers' Market.** 10 mi S on I-75 in Forest Park. Owned and operated by the state and covering 146 acres, this is one of the largest farmers' markets of its kind in the Southeast. (Daily; closed Dec 25) Phone 366-6910. **Free.**

15. **Six Flags Over Georgia.** 12 mi W via I-20, exit Six Flags Pkwy, just beyond Atlanta city limits. A family theme park featuring Georgia's history under the flags of England, France, Spain, the Confederacy, Georgia and the US. More than 100 rides, shows and attractions, including the Georgia Cyclone roller coaster, modeled after Coney Island's famous Cyclone; the Ninja roller coaster with five upside down turns; water rides; children's activities; live shows. Restaurants. (Memorial Day–late Aug, daily; early Mar–mid-May & early Sept–Oct, wkends only) Sr citizen rate. Phone 948-9290. ¢¢¢¢¢

16. **Stone Mountain Park.** 19 mi E on US 78. This 3,200-acre park surrounds the world's largest granite monolith, which rises 825 feet from the plain. A monument to the Confederacy, the deep relief carving on the mountain's face depicts three figures: Gen. Robert E. Lee, Gen. ''Stonewall'' Jackson and Confederate President Jefferson Davis. It was first undertaken by Gutzon Borglum after the First World War, continued by Augustus Lukeman and completed by Walker Hancock. The top of the mountain is accessible by foot or by cable car (fee).

Surrounding the sculpture are: Memorial Hall, a Civil War museum with commentary in seven languages about the mountain and its carving; an antebellum plantation, featuring 19 buildings restored and furnished with 18th- and 19th-century heirlooms, formal and kitchen gardens, cookhouse, slave quarters, country store and other outbuildings; Antique Auto and Music Museum housing cars dating from 1899 and antique mechanical music collection; riverboat *Scarlett O'Hara*, providing scenic trips around 363-acre lake; scenic railroad with full-size replicas of Civil War trains that make 5-mile trip around base of mountain. Also, a laser show is projected onto the north face of the mountain in 50-minute productions (May–Labor Day, nightly; after Labor Day–October, Fri & Sat) and a 732-bell carillon plays concerts (Wed–Sun).

In addition, the park has 10 miles of nature trails where wild and domestic animals live on 20 wooded acres; beach with bathhouse, fishing, boat rentals; tennis courts, 36-hole golf course, miniature golf; ice-skating; picnicking, snack bars and 3 restaurants, inn; and campground with tent & trailer sites (hookups, dump station). Most attractions are open daily (addl fees; closed Dec 25). For further information contact PO Box 778, Stone Mountain 30086; 498-5600. Per vehicle ¢¢¢

17. **Yellow River Game Ranch.** 4525 US 78 in Lilburn, approx 17 mi E. A 24-acre animal preserve on the Yellow River where more than 600 animals roam free in a natural wooded area. Visitors can pet, feed and photograph the animals. Some of the animals at the park include deer, bears, cougars and buffalo. (Daily; closed Jan 1, Dec 24–25) Phone 972-6643. ¢¢

18. **Kennesaw Mountain National Battlefield Park** (see). 25 mi NW off US 41.

19. **Fort McPherson.** Lee St, US 29, about 3 mi SW via I-75 & Lakewood Freeway to fort. Military reservation since May 4, 1889. Historical tours (Mon–Fri, by appt). Phone 752-2204. **Free.**

20. **Gray Line bus tours.** Contact 3745 Zip Industrial Blvd SE, 30354; 767-0594.

21. **Cable News Network studio tour.** At CNN Center, Techwood Dr & Marietta St. View technicians, writers, editors, producers and on-air journalists in the studio headquarters of a 24-hour all-news cable television network (45-min tour). (Daily; closed major hols) Sr citizen rates. Phone 827-2300. ¢¢

Annual Events

Auto Racing. Atlanta Motor Speedway. S on I-75, exit 77, then approx 15 mi S on US 19/41. NASCAR Winston Cup, Busch Grand National, IMSA and ARCA events. Phone 946-4211. 3 racing wkends, usually Mar, Apr & Nov.

Atlanta Steeplechase. At Seven Branches Farm in Cumming. Phone 237-7436. 1st Sat Apr.

Atlanta Dogwood Festival. Phone 952-9151. Early–mid-Apr.

BellSouth Golf Classic (see MARIETTA). Early May.

Seasonal Events

Georgia Renaissance Festival. Hundreds of costumed characters, authentic crafts, games and food in a re-created 16th-century English village. Phone 964-8575. 8 wkends, late Apr–mid-June.

Theater of the Stars. Fox Theatre (see #10). Six Broadway musicals with professional casts. For ticket information phone 252-8960. Early June–late Aug.

Professional sports. Atlanta–Fulton County Stadium, Capitol Ave. Braves (baseball), phone 522-7630. Georgia Dome, 285 International Blvd, Falcons (football), phone 261-5400. The Omni, 100 Techwood Dr NW, Hawks (basketball), phone 827-3800.

Additional Visitor Information

For information contact the Convention and Visitors Bureau, 233 Peachtree St NE, Suite 2000, 30303; 222-6688. Welcome centers are located at Underground Atlanta, at Peachtree Center Mall, at Lenox Square Mall and at Georgia World Congress Center.

Atlanta Area Suburbs

The following neighborhood and suburbs in the Atlanta area are included in the *Mobil Travel Guide.* For information on them, see the individual alphabetical listing. Buckhead (a neighborhood south of the northern city limits, west of Lenox and Peachtree Rds, north of Wesley Rd and east of Northside Dr), Marietta, Norcross.

Atlanta Hartsfield Airport Area

For additional accommodations, see ATLANTA HARTSFIELD AIRPORT AREA, which follows ATLANTA.

City Neighborhoods

Many of the restaurants, unrated dining establishments and some lodgings listed under Atlanta include neighborhoods as well as exact street addresses. A map showing these neighborhoods can be found immediately following the city map. Geographic descriptions of these areas are given, followed by a table of restaurants arranged by neighborhood.

Downtown: South of North Ave, west of I-75/I-85, north of I-20 and east of Northside Dr. **North of Downtown:** North of North Ave. **East of Downtown:** East of I-75/I-85.

Midtown/Piedmont Park: South of I-85, west of Piedmont Park, north of North Ave and east of I-75/85.

ATLANTA RESTAURANTS
BY NEIGHBORHOOD AREAS

(For full description, see alphabetical listings under Restaurants)

DOWNTOWN

City Grill. 50 Hurt Plaza

Dailey's. 17 International Blvd

Fisherman's Cove. 201 Courtland St

Hsu's Gourmet Chinese Restaurant. 192 Peachtree Center Ave

Lombardi's. 94 Upper Pryor St

Mick's Underground. 75 Upper Alabama St

Morton's of Chicago. 245 Peachtree Center Ave

Nikolai's Roof (Hilton & Towers Hotel). 225 Courtland St NE

Pittypat's Porch. 25 International Blvd

The Restaurant. 181 Peachtree St NE, in The Ritz-Carlton, Atlanta Hotel

NORTH OF DOWNTOWN

Boychick's Deli. 4520-A Chamblee-Dunwoody Rd

Cafe Chanterelle. 4200 Paces Ferry Rd NE

Capri. 5785 Roswell Rd NE

La Paz. 6410 Roswell Rd

The Lark and the Dove. 5788 Roswell Rd

Papa Pirozki's Russian Cafe. 4953 Roswell Rd NE

Patio by the River. 4199 Paces Ferry Rd NW

Piccadilly Cafeteria. 5647 Peachtree Industrial Blvd

Ray's on the River. 6700 Powers Ferry Rd

Winfield's. 1 Galleria Pkwy

EAST OF DOWNTOWN

Partners. 1399 N Highland

MIDTOWN/PIEDMONT PARK

The Abbey. 163 Ponce de Leon Ave NE

Ciboulette. 1529 Piedmont Ave

Country Place. 1197 Peachtree St NE

The Mansion. 179 Ponce de Leon Ave

Mary Mac's Tearoom. 224 Ponce de Leon Ave

Taste of New Orleans. 889 W Peachtree St NE

Varsity. 61 North Ave

Veni Vidi Vici. 41 14th St

Note: When a listing is located in a town that does not have its own city heading, it will appear under the city nearest to its location. In these cases, the address and town appear in parenthesis immediately following the name of the establishment.

Motels

✔ ★ ★ **BEST WESTERN BRADBURY SUITES.** *4500 Circle 75 Pkwy (30339), I-75 exit 110, north of downtown.* 404/956-9919; FAX 404/955-3270. 236 rms in 2 bldgs, 3–5 story. S, D $39.95–$74.95; each addl $5; suites $69.95–$74.95; under 12 free; wkly, wkend rates. Crib $10. TV; cable. Pool; whirlpool. Complimentary full bkfst buffet. Restaurant nearby. Ck-out noon. Coin lndry. Meeting rms. Health club privileges. Some refrigerators. Theme suites. Cr cds: A, C, D, DS, ER, MC, V, JCB.

D ⊠ 🚫 🕐 SC

✔ ★ ★ **COMFORT INN-FOREST PARK.** *3701 Jonesboro Rd SE (30354), south of downtown.* 404/361-1111; FAX 404/366-0294. 73 rms, 2 story. S $40–$60; D $45–$65; each addl $5; suites $65–$75; under 18 free. Crib $5. TV; cable. Pool. Complimentary continental bkfst, coffee. Restaurant nearby. Ck-out 11 am. Coin lndry. Meeting rms. Valet serv. Sundries. Cr cds: A, C, D, DS, ER, MC, V, JCB.

D ⊠ 🚫 🕐 SC

★ ★ ★ **COURTYARD BY MARRIOTT-NORTHLAKE.** *4083 La Vista Rd (30084), adj to Northlake Festival Mall, east of downtown.* 404/938-1200; FAX 404/934-6497. 128 units, 20 suites, 2 story. S $69; D $79; suites $79–$89; under 18 free; wkly, wkend rates. Crib free. TV; cable. Heated pool. Complimentary coffee in rms. Restaurant 6:30–11 am; Sat, Sun from 7 am. Rm serv 5–9:30 pm; Fri, Sat to 10:30 pm. Bar 4–11 pm. Ck-out noon. Coin lndry. Meeting rms. Valet serv. Airport transportation. Exercise equipt; weights, bicycles, whirlpool. Some refrigerators. Private patios, balconies. Picnic tables. Cr cds: A, C, D, DS, MC, V.

D ⊠ 🚶 🚫 🕐 SC

★ ★ **EMORY INN.** *1641 Clifton Rd NE (30329), north of downtown.* 404/712-6700; res: 800/933-6679; FAX 404/712-6701. 107 rms, 2 story. S $86–$96; D $96–$106; each addl $10; under 12 free. Crib free. TV; cable. Pool; poolside serv. Restaurant 7–10 am, 11 am–2 pm, 5–10 pm. Rm serv. Ck-out noon. Meeting rms. Bellhops. Valet serv. Airport, RR station transportation avail. Exercise equipt; weight machine, stair machine, whirlpool. Antiques. Library/sitting rm. Cr cds: A, C, D, DS, ER, MC, V.

D ⊠ 🚶 🚫 🕐 SC

★ ★ **EXECUTIVE VILLAS HOTEL.** *5735 Roswell Rd NE (30342), at I-285 Roswell Rd exit 17, north of downtown.* 404/252-2868; res: 800/241-1013. 130 kit. suites, 1–3 stories. 1-bedrm $99; 2-bedrm $109; 3-bedrm $119; wkend plans; wkly & monthly rates. Crib free. Pet accepted, some restrictions; $150. TV; cable. Pool. Complimentary continental bkfst. Restaurant nearby. Ck-out 11 am. Coin lndry. Meeting

rms. Valet serv. Health club privileges. Private patios, balconies. Picnic tables, grills. Cr cds: A, C, D, MC, V.

D 🐾 ⊠ 🚶 🕐 SC

★ ★ **HAWTHORN SUITES-ATLANTA NORTHWEST.** *1500 Parkwood Circle (30339), I-75 exit 110, north of downtown.* 404/952-9595; FAX 404/984-2335. 200 kit. suites, 2–3 story. Suites $105–$145; each addl $10; under 18 free; wkend, monthly rates. Crib free. Pet accepted, some restrictions; $5. TV; cable. Heated pool. Complimentary continental bkfst. Restaurant nearby. Ck-out noon. Coin lndry. Meeting rms. Valet serv. Airport, bus depot transportation. Lighted tennis. Exercise equipt; weights, bicycles, whirlpool. Refrigerators. Private patios, balconies. Picnic tables, grills. Elaborate landscaping, flowers. Cr cds: A, C, D, DS, MC, V.

D 🐾 🏊 ⊠ 🚶 🚫 🕐 SC

✔ ★ ★ **QUALITY INN-MIDTOWN.** *1470 Spring St NW (30309), in Midtown/Piedmont Park area.* 404/872-5821; FAX 404/874-3602. 179 rms, 4 story. S $50–$75; D $54–$88; each addl $10; suites $145–$195; under 18 free; wkend rates. Crib free. Pet accepted, some restrictions; $25. TV; cable. Pool. Complimentary continental bkfst. Restaurant 7–9 am. Ck-out 11 am. Meeting rms. Bellhops. Valet serv. Airport, RR station, bus depot transportation. Exercise equipt; weights, treadmill. Refrigerator in suites. Balconies. Picnic tables. Cr cds: A, C, D, DS, MC, V.

🏊 ⊠ 🚶 🚫 🕐 SC

★ **RED ROOF INN-DRUID HILLS.** *1960 N Druid Hills Rd (30329), I-85 exit 31, north of downtown.* 404/321-1653; FAX 404/321-1653, ext 444. 115 rms, 3 story. S $30–$42; D $38–$49; each addl $6; under 18 free. Crib free. Pet accepted, some restrictions. TV; cable. Restaurant nearby. Ck-out noon. Cr cds: A, C, D, DS, MC, V.

D 🐾 🚫 🕐

★ ★ **RESIDENCE INN BY MARRIOTT-DUNWOODY.** *1901 Savoy Dr (30341), I-285 at Chamblee-Dunwoody exit, north of downtown.* 404/455-4446; FAX 404/451-5183. 144 kit. suites, 2 story. S, D $79–$99; wkend rates. Crib free. Pet accepted; $35. TV; cable. Heated pool; whirlpool, hot tubs. Complimentary continental bkfst. Ck-out noon. Coin lndry. Meeting rms. Valet serv. Health club privileges. Many fireplaces. Private patios, balconies. Picnic tables, grills. Cr cds: A, C, D, DS, MC, V.

D 🐾 ⊠ 🚫 🕐 SC

★ ★ ★ **STONE MOUNTAIN INN.** *(Box 775, Stone Mountain 30086) 16 mi E on US 78, Stone Mountain Park exit. In Stone Mountain Park.* 404/469-3311; res: 800/277-0007; FAX 404/498-5691. 92 rms, 2 story. $5 park entrance fee (required to reach motel). Late May–early Sept: S $65–$75; D $89–$99; under 12 free; lower rates rest of yr. Crib free. TV; cable. Pool. Restaurant 7 am–9 pm (hrs vary off-season). Ck-out 11 am. Coin lndry. Meeting rms. Bellhops. Gift shop. Lighted tennis. 36-hole golf, pro. Balconies; private patios for poolside rms. Reduced admission to park attractions. Cr cds: A, D, DS, MC, V.

🔜 ⛳ 🏌 ⊠ 🚶 🚫 🕐 SC

★ ★ **SUMMERFIELD SUITES.** *760 Mt Vernon Hwy (30328), north of downtown.* 404/250-0110; res: 800/833-4353; FAX 404/250-9335. 122 kit. suites, 2–3 story. 1-bedrm $119; 2-bedrm $159; family, wkly, wkend rates. Crib free. TV; cable, in-rm movies. Heated pool. Complimentary continental bkfst. Complimentary coffee in rms. Ck-out noon. Coin lndry. Meeting rms. Sundries. Airport, MARTA transportation. Exercise equipt; weights, bicycles, whirlpool. Health club privileges. Balconies. Picnic tables, grills. Cr cds: A, C, D, DS, MC, V, JCB.

D ⊠ 🚶 🚫 🕐 SC

★ **TRAVELODGE-DOWNTOWN.** *311 Courtland St NE (30303), downtown.* 404/659-4545; FAX 404/659-5934. 71 rms, 3 story. S $64–$68; D $76–$80; each addl $8; under 18 free; wkend rates. Crib free. TV; cable, in-rm movies avail. Pool. Coffee in rms. Restaurant adj open 24 hrs. Ck-out noon. Valet serv. Some balconies. Cr cds: A, C, D, DS, ER, MC, V, JCB.

⊠ 🚫 🕐 SC

Motor Hotels

★★COURTYARD BY MARRIOTT-CUMBERLAND. 3000 Cumberland Circle (30339), I-285 Cobb Pkwy exit, north of downtown. 404/952-2555; FAX 404/952-2409. 182 rms, 8 story. S $79; D $89; under 12 free; wkly rates. Crib free. TV; cable, in-rm movies avail. Indoor pool. Complimentary coffee in rms. Restaurant 6:30 am–2 pm, 5–10 pm; wkends 7 am–noon, 5–10 pm. Bar 4–11 pm. Ck-out noon. Meeting rms. Bellhops. Valet serv. Sundries. Exercise rm; instructor, weights, bicycles, whirlpool, sauna. Some refrigerators, wet bars. Balconies. Cr cds: A, C, D, DS, MC, V.

✔★★QUALITY INN-NORTHEAST. 2960 NE Expressway (I-85) (30341), at Shallowford Rd, north of downtown. 404/451-5231; FAX 404/454-8704. 157 rms, 2 story. S, D $34–$49; family, wkly rates. Crib free. Pet accepted, some restrictions. TV; cable. Pool; poolside serv. Continental bkfst 7–10 am. Restaurant open 24 hrs. Rm serv. Ck-out noon. Coin lndry. Meeting rms. Bellhops. Valet serv Mon–Fri. Cr cds: A, C, D, DS, MC, V, JCB.

✔★RAMADA INN-SIX FLAGS. 4225 Fulton Industrial Blvd (30336), I-20W exit 14, west of downtown. 404/691-4100; FAX 404/261-2117. 229 rms, 4–5 story. Apr–mid-Sept: S, D $55–$65; each addl $10; lower rates rest of yr. Crib free. TV; cable. Pool; wading pool. Complimentary full bkfst. Restaurant open 24 hrs. Rm serv. Bar 3 pm–1:30 am; entertainment, dancing Thurs–Sat. Ck-out 11 am. Coin lndry. Meeting rms. Grill. Cr cds: A, C, D, DS, ER, MC, V, JCB.

★★★WYNDHAM GARDEN. 2857 Paces Ferry Rd (30339), I-285 exit 12, north of downtown. 404/432-5555; FAX 404/436-5558. 159 rms, 4 story. S, D $109–$119; suites $119–$129; under 18 free; wkend rates. Crib free. TV; cable. Heated pool; whirlpool, poolside serv. Restaurant 6:30 am–2:30 pm, 5–10 pm. Rm serv from 5 pm. Bar 11:30 am–midnight. Ck-out noon. Meeting rms. Valet serv. Tennis privileges. Health club privileges. Private patios, balconies. Cr cds: A, C, D, DS, ER, MC, V, JCB.

Hotels

★★★ATLANTA PENTA. 590 W Peachtree St NW (30308), at North Ave, in Midtown/Piedmont Park. 404/881-6000; res: 800/633-0000; FAX 404/815-5010. 504 rms, 25 story, 24 suites. S $150–$170; D $165–$185; suites $250–$850; under 12 free; wkend rates. Crib free. Garage parking; valet $9, in/out $7.50. TV; cable. Pool; poolside serv. Restaurant 6:30–1 am. Bar 11–1 am; entertainment. Ck-out noon. Meeting rms. Concierge. Gift shop. Airport, RR station, bus depot transportation. Exercise equipt; weights, bicycles. Health club privileges. Bathrm phones, minibars; some refrigerators, wet bars. Balconies. Luxurious rms; European-style personal service. *LUXURY LEVEL:* EXECUTIVE LEVEL. 48 rms, 2 floors. S $170; D $185; each addl $15; 2-bedrm suite $850. Concierge. Private lounge. Complimentary continental bkfst, refreshments, newspapers.
Cr cds: A, C, D, DS, ER, MC, V, JCB.

★★BILTMORE INN. 30 5th St NE (30308), at W Peachtree St, in Midtown/Piedmont Park. 404/874-0824; res: 800/822-0824; FAX 404/458-5384. 70 kit. suites, 10 story. Kit. suites $95–$225; monthly rates. Crib free. Covered parking $2. TV; cable. Complimentary continental bkfst. Restaurant nearby. Ck-out noon. Airport transportation avail. Health club privileges. Wet bars, in-rm whirlpools. Some balconies. Built 1924; Georgian design with vaulted ceilings, skylights, and limestone detailing. Cr cds: A, D, DS, MC, V.

★★COMFORT INN-DOWNTOWN. 101 International Blvd (30303), downtown. 404/524-5555; FAX 404/221-0702. 260 rms, 11 story. S $59–$119; D $69–$129; each addl $10; under 12 free; wkend rates. Crib free. Garage in/out $6. TV; cable. Pool; whirlpool. Restaurant 6:30–10:30 am, 11:30 am–1:30 pm, 5:30–10 pm. Bar 4 pm–12:30 am. Ck-out noon. Meeting rms. Gift shop. Health club privileges. Adj to Atlanta Market Center and World Congress Center. Cr cds: A, C, D, DS, ER, MC, V, JCB.

★★DAYS INN-DOWNTOWN. 300 Spring St (30308), downtown. 404/523-1144; FAX 404/577-8495. 262 rms, 10 story. S $59–$119; D $69–$129; each addl $10; suites $175; under 18 free. Crib free. Pet accepted; $50. Garage $5/day. TV; Pool. Restaurant 6:30 am–10 pm. Bar 5 pm–midnight. Ck-out noon. Meeting rms. Gift shop. Airport, RR station, bus depot transportation $8–$15. Some refrigerators. Balconies. Cr cds: A, C, D, DS, ER, MC, V.

★★★DOUBLETREE. 7 Concourse Pkwy (30328), north of downtown. 404/395-3900; FAX 404/395-3935. 370 rms, 20 story. S $119–$139; D $129–$149; each addl $10; suites $225–$800; under 17 free; wkend rates. Crib free. TV; cable. Heated pool; whirlpool, sauna, poolside serv. Restaurants 6:30 am–11 pm. Rm serv 24 hrs. Bar 4:30 pm–1 am, Sun to 12:30 am; entertainment. Ck-out noon. Convention facilities. Free covered parking; valet. Tennis privileges. 18-hole golf privileges, greens fee $20, pro. Some refrigerators. *LUXURY LEVEL:* CONCIERGE LEVEL. 40 rms, 2 floors. S $139–$159; D $149–$169. Concierge. Private lounge, honor bar. Complimentary continental bkfst, refreshments, newspaper.
Cr cds: A, C, D, DS, ER, MC, V, JCB.

★★★EMBASSY SUITES-GALLERIA. 2815 Akers Mill Rd (30339), north of downtown. 404/984-9300; FAX 404/955-4183. 261 suites, 9 story. S $99–$134; D $109–$149; each addl $10; under 18 free; wkend rates. Crib free. TV; cable. Indoor pool; whirlpool, sauna. Complimentary full bkfst. Restaurant 11 am–11 pm. Bar to 1 am. Ck-out noon. Meeting rms. Gift shop. Airport transportation avail. Health club privileges. Game rm. Refrigerators. Garden atrium, glass elvtrs. Cr cds: A, C, D, DS, MC, V.

★★★FRENCH QUARTER SUITES. 2780 Whitley Rd (30339), I-285 Cobb Pkwy exit, north of downtown. 404/980-1900; res: 800/843-5858; FAX 404/980-1528. 155 suites, 8 story. Suites $99–$119; under 12 free; wkly, wkend rates. Crib free. TV; cable. Pool. Complimentary full bkfst. Complimentary coffee in rms. Restaurant 5 am–10:30 pm. Rm serv 24 hrs. Bar 11–1 am, Sun to 12:30 am; entertainment, dancing Fri–Sat. Ck-out noon. Meeting rms. Exercise equipt; weights, bicycles, sauna. Health club privileges. Bathrm phones, in-rm whirlpools; some refrigerators. Some private patios, balconies. Cr cds: A, C, D, DS, ER, MC, V, JCB.

★★★GUEST QUARTERS SUITE HOTEL-ATLANTA PERIMETER (formerly Marriott). 6120 Peachtree-Dunwoody Rd (30328), north of downtown. 404/668-0808; FAX 404/668-0008. 224 rms, 6 story. Suites $99–$115; under 18 free; wkend rates. Crib free. TV; cable. Indoor/outdoor pool. Restaurant 6:30–10 am, 11 am–10:30 pm. Bar 11:30–2 am. Ck-out 1 pm. Coin lndry. Meeting rms. Airport transportation. Exercise equipt; weight machine, bicycles, whirlpool, sauna. Refrigerators. Cr cds: A, C, D, DS, ER, MC, V.

★★★HILTON & TOWERS. 255 Courtland St NE (30303), at Harris St, downtown. 404/659-2000; FAX 404/222-2868. 1,224 rms, 29 story. S $165–$195; D $185–$205; each addl $25; suites from $400; family, wkend rates. Crib free. Pet accepted, some restrictions. Valet parking, in/out $9, garage avail. TV; cable. Pool; poolside serv. Restaurant 6–1 am; dining rm (see NIKOLAI'S ROOF), Sun 12:30 pm–midnight; entertainment, dancing. Ck-out 11 am. Convention facilities. Shopping arcade. Airport transportation. Lighted tennis, pro. Exercise rm; instructor, weights, bicycles, whirlpool, sauna. Some bathrm phones. Balconies on 4th floor. Built around 5-story atrium;

glass-enclosed elvtrs. *LUXURY LEVEL:* **THE TOWERS.** 113 rms, 17 suites, 3 floors. S $200; D $225; suites from $450. Concierge. Private lounge, honor bar. Complimentary continental bkfst, refreshments, newspaper.
Cr cds: A, C, D, DS, ER, MC, V, JCB.

[D] [icons] [SC]

★ ★ ★**HOLIDAY INN.** *(1075 Holcomb Bridge Rd, Roswell 30076) N on GA 400 to exit 7B, then NW on Holcomb Bridge Rd.* 404/992-9600; FAX 404/993-6539. 174 rms, 7 story. S $79–$89; D $89–$99; each addl $5; suites $158–$237; under 18 free; wkend rates. Crib free. Pet accepted. TV; cable. Pool. Complimentary coffee in lobby. Restaurant 6:30 am–10:30 pm. Bar 5 pm–2 am. Ck-out noon. Meeting rms. Gift shop. Airport, RR station, bus depot transportation avail. Tennis privileges. Health club privileges. Refrigerators avail. Cr cds: A, C, D, DS, MC, V, JCB.

[D] [icons] [SC]

★ ★ ★**HOLIDAY INN-CROWNE PLAZA.** *4355 Ashford-Dunwoody Rd (30346), 1 blk N I-285 exit 21, north of downtown.* 404/395-7700; FAX 404/392-9503. 495 rms, 14 story, 29 suites. S $125–$162; D $135–$172; each addl $10; suites $125–$950; under 18 free; wkend rates. Crib free. Valet parking $7. TV; cable. Indoor pool. Restaurants 6 am–midnight. Bar; entertainment exc Sun. Ck-out noon. Convention facilities. Concierge. Gift shop. Free covered parking. Airport transportation. Lighted tennis. Exercise equipt; weights, bicycles, whirlpool, sauna. Refrigerator in suites. 3-story greenhouse atrium with waterfalls. On 42 acres, 10 wooded. Adj Perimeter Mall. *LUXURY LEVEL:* **CROWNE PLAZA CLUB.** 25 rms, 3 suites, 1 floor. S $154; D $164; suites $225–$950. Private lounge, honor bar. Minibars. Bathrm phones. Complimentary continental bkfst, refreshments, newspaper.
Cr cds: A, C, D, DS, MC, V, JCB.

[D] [icons] [SC]

★ ★ ★**HYATT REGENCY ATLANTA.** *265 Peachtree St NE (30303), in Peachtree Center, downtown.* 404/577-1234; FAX 404/588-4137. 1,279 rms, 23 story. S $175; D $200; each addl $25; suites $325–$600; under 18 free; wkend plans. Crib free. Garage, in/out $12. TV; cable, in-rm movies avail. Pool; poolside serv. Restaurant 6–1 am. Bar from 11 am. Ck-out noon. Convention facilities. Concierge. Gift shop. Airport transportation. Exercise equipt; weights, bicycles, whirlpool, sauna, steam rm. Minibars. Refrigerator in suites. Many balconies. Built around 23-story atrium lobby; glass-enclosed elvtr. Revolving Polaris dining rm & bar atop roof; panoramic view of city. *LUXURY LEVEL:* **REGENCY CLUB.** 64 rms, 7 suites, 2 floors. S $200; D $225; suites $425–$700. Private lounge. Bathrm phone in suites. Complimentary continental bkfst, refreshments.
Cr cds: A, C, D, DS, ER, MC, V, JCB.

[D] [icons] [SC]

★ ★ ★**HYATT REGENCY SUITES-PERIMETER NORTHWEST.** *2999 Windy Hill Rd NE (30067), I-75N to Windy Hill exit, north of downtown.* 404/956-1234; FAX 404/956-9479. 200 suites, 7 story. S $69–$126; D $69–$151; under 18 free; wkend rates. Crib free. TV (3 per unit); cable. Heated pool. Complimentary coffee in rms. Restaurant 6:30 am–11 pm. Bar 11:30 am–midnight. Ck-out noon. Meeting rms. Tennis privileges. Exercise equipt; weights, bicycles, whirlpool, sauna. Health club privileges. Refrigerators. Atop hill with view of downtown Atlanta. Cr cds: A, C, D, DS, ER, MC, V, JCB.

[D] [icons] [SC]

★**INN AT THE PEACHTREES.** *330 W Peachtree St NW (30308), downtown.* 404/577-6970; res: 800/242-4642; FAX 404/659-3244. 101 rms, 4 story. S $120; D $135; each addl $10; under 12 free. TV; cable, in-rm movies avail. Ck-out 11 am. Meeting rm. Covered parking. Airport transportation. Health club privileges. Near Merchandise Mart & Apparel Mart. Cr cds: A, C, D, DS, MC, V, JCB.

[icons] [SC]

★ ★ ★**THE MARQUE OF ATLANTA.** *111 Perimeter Center West (30346), north of downtown.* 404/396-6800; res: 800/683-6100; FAX 404/399-5514. 276 rms, 12 story, 156 kit. suites. S $105; D $115; each addl $10; kit. suites $119; under 12 free; wkend rates. Crib free. TV;

cable. Pool; poolside serv. Complimentary continental bkfst. Restaurant 6–10 am, noon–2 pm, 6–10 pm. Rm serv 6 am–midnight. Bar. Ck-out noon. Coin lndry. Meeting rms. Concierge. Airport transportation. Exercise equipt; weight machine, bicycles, whirlpool, sauna. Balconies. Situated in park-like setting. Cr cds: A, C, D, DS, MC, V.

[D] [icons] [SC]

★ ★ ★**MARRIOTT MARQUIS.** *265 Peachtree Center Ave (30303), downtown.* 404/521-0000; FAX 404/586-6299. 1,674 rms, 50 story. S, D $200; each addl $20; suites from $350; under 18 free; wkend, honeymoon rates. Crib free. Pet accepted. Garage $12 in/out. TV; cable. Indoor/outdoor pool; lifeguard, poolside serv. 5 restaurants. Rm serv 24 hrs. Bar 11–1 am, Sun from 12:30 pm; entertainment. Ck-out noon. Convention facilities. Shopping arcade. Barber, beauty shop. Exercise rm; instructor, weight machines, bicycles, whirlpool, sauna. Game rm. Rec rm. Some refrigerators. Bathrm phone in suites. *LUXURY LEVEL:* **CONCIERGE LEVEL.** 80 rms, 10 suites, 2 floors. S, D $175; suites $450–$950. Private lounge, honor bar. Complimentary continental bkfst, refreshments.
Cr cds: A, C, D, DS, ER, MC, V, JCB.

[D] [icons] [SC]

OCCIDENTAL GRAND HOTEL. *(Too new to be rated) 75 Fourteenth St (30309), GLG Grand Bldg, in Midtown/Piedmont Park.* 404/881-9898; res: 800/952-0702; FAX 404/873-4692. 246 rms, 19 story, 18 suites. S, D $145–$225; each addl $25; suites $375–$1,500; under 16 free; wkend rates. Crib free. Pet accepted, some restrictions. Garage parking, valet $11. TV; cable. Indoor pool; poolside serv. Restaurant 6 am–11 pm. Rm serv 24 hrs. Bar 11:30–1 am; entertainment. Ck-out noon. Convention facilities. Concierge. Sundries. Barber, beauty shop. Airport, RR station transportation. Exercise rm; instructor, weight machine, bicycles, whirlpool, sauna, steam rm. Masseuse. Spa/health club. Refrigerators, minibars. Complimentary newspaper. Occupies first 20 floors of the GLG Grand Bldg. Three-story grand entry with dramatic grand staircase. Grand ballroom on 3rd floor. A 5th-floor terrace provides scenic view of skyline. Luxury hotel combines Old-World traditions with hospitality of the New South. Cr cds: A, C, D, DS, ER, MC, V, JCB.

[D] [icons] [SC]

★ ★ ★**OMNI HOTEL AT CNN CENTER.** *100 CNN Center (30335), downtown.* 404/659-0000; FAX 404/525-5050. 466 rms, 15 story. S $170; D $190; each addl from $20; suites $250–$1,200; under 18 free; wkend rates. Crib free. Garage $12–$15 in/out. TV; cable. Restaurant 7 am–11 pm. Rm serv 6–2 am. Bars 11–1 am; entertainment Tues–Sat. Ck-out noon. Convention facilities. Concierge. Shopping arcade. Barber, beauty shop. Valet parking. Airport, RR station, bus depot transportation. Tennis, golf privileges. Health club privileges. Minibars. Bathrm phone, wet bar. Balconies. Omni Sports Coliseum, Georgia World Congress Center adj. Underground Atlanta nearby. Cr cds: A, C, D, DS, ER, MC, V, JCB.

[D] [icons] [SC]

★ ★**RADISSON HOTEL.** *165 Courtland St (30303), downtown.* 404/659-6500; FAX 404/524-1259. 754 rms, 12 story. S $119; D $134; each addl $10; suites $150–$650; under 18 free; wkend rates. Crib free. Pet accepted, some restrictions; $25 refundable. Covered parking $5. TV; cable. Indoor/outdoor pool; poolside serv. Restaurant 6:30 am–11 pm. Bar 11–2 am, Sun to 12:30 am; entertainment Fri-Sat, dancing. Ck-out noon. Convention facilities. Concierge. Shopping arcade. Barber, beauty shop. Exercise equipt; weights, whirlpool, sauna. Health club privileges. Game rm. Some bathrm phones. Private patios, balconies. Cr cds: A, C, D, DS, ER, MC, V, JCB.

[D] [icons] [SC]

★ ★**REGENCY SUITES.** *975 W Peachtree St NE (30309), at 10th St, in Midtown/Piedmont Park.* 404/876-5003; res: 800/642-3629. 96 kit. suites, 9 story. Suites $124–$184; under 18 free; wkend, monthly rates. Crib free. Garage, covered parking (fee). TV; cable. Complimentary continental bkfst, coffee. Ck-out 11 am. Coin lndry. Meeting rms. Exercise equipt; weight machines, bicycles. Adj to MARTA station. Cr cds: A, C, D, DS, MC, V.

[D] [icons] [SC]

★ ★ ★SHERATON-CENTURY CENTER. *2000 Century Blvd NE (30345), in Century Center Park, north of downtown.* 404/325-0000; FAX 404/325-4920. 283 rms, 15 story. S $79–$93; D $89–$103; each addl $10; suites from $175; under 18 free; wkend rates. Crib free. TV; cable, in-rm movies avail. Heated pool; poolside serv. Restaurant 6:30 am–2 pm, 5–10 pm. Bar noon–midnight. Ck-out 1 pm. Convention facilities. Gift shop. Barber. Lighted tennis. Exercise equipt; weights, bicycles. Some refrigerators. Cr cds: A, C, D, DS, ER, MC, V, JCB.

D ⊘ 🏊 ⚓ 🏋 🚭 🕐 SC

★ ★ ★SHERATON COLONY SQUARE. *188 14th St NE (30361), in Midtown/Piedmont Park.* 404/892-6000; FAX 404/872-9192. 461 rms, 27 story. S $149–$169; D $169–$189; each addl $20; suites $350–$800; under 18 free; wkend, summer hol plans. Crib free. Valet parking $10 in/out. TV; cable. Pool; poolside serv. Restaurant 6:30–1 am. 2 bars 11–2 am, Sun to midnight. Ck-out noon. Convention facilities. Concierge. Shopping arcade. Airport transportation. Tennis & golf privileges. Exercise equipt; weight machine, bicycles. *LUXURY LEVEL:* COLONY CLUB. 44 rms, 1 suite. S $159–$169; D $179–$189; suite $375. Private lounge. Complimentary continental bkfst, refreshments, newspaper. Cr cds: A, C, D, DS, ER, MC, V, JCB.

D ⊘ 🏊 ⚓ 🏋 🚭 🕐 SC

★ ★ ★SHERATON SUITES-CUMBERLAND. *2844 Cobb Pkwy SE (30339), north of downtown.* 404/955-3900; FAX 404/916-3165. 279 suites, 17 story. Suites $99–$149; each addl $15; under 18 free; wkend rates. Crib free. TV; cable, in-rm movies. 2 pools, 1 indoor; poolside serv. Complimentary full bkfst. Complimentary coffee in rms. Restaurant 6:30 am–10:30 pm. Bar 11 am–midnight. Ck-out noon. Coin lndry. Convention facilities. Gift shop. Free garage parking. Airport, RR station transportation avail. Exercise equipt; weights, bicycles, whirlpool, sauna. Refrigerators. Minibars. Cr cds: A, C, D, DS, ER, MC, V.

D ⚓ 🏋 🚭 🕐 SC

★ ★ ★STOUFFER WAVERLY. *2450 Galleria Pkwy (30339), north of downtown.* 404/953-4500; FAX 404/953-0740. 521 rms, 14 story, 24 suites, 12 conference parlors. S $155–$175; D $175–$195; each addl $20; suites $325–$425; under 18 free; wkend rates. Crib free. TV; cable. 2 pools, 1 indoor. Complimentary coffee. Restaurant open 24 hrs. Rm serv 24 hrs. 3 bars 11:30–1 am. Ck-out noon. Convention facilities. Concierge. Shopping arcade. Airport transportation. Exercise rm; instructor, weight machines, bicycles, whirlpool, sauna, steam rm. Bathrm phones; refrigerator in suites. *LUXURY LEVEL:* THE CLUB LEVEL. 36 rms, 4 suites. S $175–$195; D $195–$215; suites $425–$1,200. Private lounge. Minibars. Complimentary continental bkfst, refreshments, magazines. Cr cds: A, C, D, DS, ER, MC, V, JCB.

D ⚓ 🏋 🚭 🕐 SC

★ ★ ★SUITE HOTEL-UNDERGROUND. *54 Peachtree St (30303), at Underground Atlanta, downtown.* 404/223-5555; res: 800/477-5549; FAX 404/223-0467. 156 suites, 17 story. S $120–$160; D $130–$185; each addl $10; under 16 free; wkend rates. Crib free. Valet $10. TV; cable. Swimming privileges. Restaurant opp 11 am–11 pm. Ck-out noon. Meeting rms. Airport, RR station, bus depot transportation. Health club privileges. Bathrm phones, minibars. Cr cds: A, C, D, DS, ER, MC, V, JCB.

D 🚭 🕐 SC

★ ★ ★THE WESTIN PEACHTREE PLAZA. *(PO Box 56650, 30343) 210 Peachtree St, at International Blvd, downtown.* 404/659-1400; FAX 404/589-7424. 1,068 rms, 73 story. S $155–$220; D $180–$245; each addl $25; suites $325–$1,275; under 18 free; wkend rates. Crib free. Pet accepted, some restrictions. Garage $12.50, valet, in/out $13. TV; cable. Indoor/outdoor pool; poolside serv. Restaurants 6 am–11 pm. Rm serv 24 hrs. Bars (1 revolving rooftop) 11–2 am; entertainment. Ck-out 1 pm. Convention facilities. Concierge. Shopping arcade. Airport, RR station, bus depot transportation. Exercise rm; instructor, weights, bicycles, sauna. Many bathrm phones; some refrigerators. 73-story circular tower built around 8-story atrium. *LUXURY LEVEL:* EXECUTIVE CLUB. 88 rms, 6 suites, 5 floors. S $225; D $250; suites $675. Private lounge, honor bar. Minibar in suites. Bathrm

phones. Complimentary continental bkfst, refreshments, newspaper, shoeshine. Cr cds: A, C, D, DS, ER, MC, V, JCB.

 D 🚲 🏊 ⚓ 🏋 🚭 🕐 🕐

★ ★ ★WYNDHAM MIDTOWN. *125 10th St (30309), at Peachtree St, in Midtown/Piedmont Park.* 404/873-4800; FAX 404/870-1530. 191 rms, 11 story, 5 suites. S $125–$145; D $135–$155; each addl $10; suites $250–$500; under 18 free; wkly, wkend rates. Crib free. Covered parking $7.50, in/out; valet parking $9.50. TV; cable. Indoor pool. In rm coffee avail. Restaurant 6:30 am–11 pm. Bar 4:30 pm–11 pm, Fri, Sat to 1 am. Ck-out noon. Meeting rms. Exercise rm; instructor, weight machines, whirlpool, sauna, steam rm. Many refrigerators. Cr cds: A, C, D, DS, MC, V.

D ⚓ 🏋 🚭 🕐 🕐

Inns

★ ★ANSLEY INN. *253 15th St NE (30309), north of downtown.* 404/872-9000; res: 800/446-5416; FAX 404/892-2318. 15 rms, 3 story. S, D $100–$250; wkly, monthly rates. TV; cable. Complimentary bkfst, coffee. Restaurant nearby. Ck-out 11 am, ck-in 3 pm. Bellhops. Valet serv. Concierge. Airport transportation. Tennis privileges. Health club privileges. In-rm whirlpools. Turn-of-the-century English Tudor house; art gallery. Cr cds: A, C, D, DS, ER, MC, V.

⊘ 🕐

✔ ★ ★SHELLMONT. *821 Piedmont Ave NE (30308), in Midtown/Piedmont Park.* 404/872-9290. 4 rms, 2 story, carriage house. No rm phones. S $65–$70; D $77–$90; each addl $15; carriage house $87–$97. Children under 12 in carriage house only. Crib free. Complimentary full bkfst. Restaurant nearby. Ck-out 11 am, ck-in 3 pm. Some patios, balconies. Restored Victorian house (1891); Tiffany windows, hardwood floors, antiques, artwork. Cr cds: A, MC, V.

🕐 SC

Resort

★ ★ ★EVERGREEN CONFERENCE CENTER. *(1 Lakeview Dr, Stone Mountain 30086) W on US 78, in Stone Mountain State Park.* 404/879-9900; res: 800/722-1000; FAX 404/464-9013. 238 rms, 5 story. $5 park entrance fee (required to reach resort). Apr–Sept: S $120; D $140; each addl $20; suites $200–$300; family, wkend, wkly & hol rates; AP, MAP avail; golf plans; wkends, hols (2–4-night min); higher rates Super Bowl wkend; lower rates rest of yr. Crib free. TV; cable. 2 pools, 1 indoor; wading pool, poolside serv, lifeguard. Restaurant 6 am–11:30 pm. Box lunches. Snacks. Picnics. Rm serv 24 hrs. Bar; entertainment, dancing (in season). Ck-out noon, ck-in 4 pm. Gift shop. Grocery, coin lndry 1 mi. Bellhops. Concierge. Valet serv. Sports dir. Lighted tennis. 36-hole golf, pro, putting green, driving range, greens fee $38. Swimming beach; boats. Horse stables on premises. Hiking. Bicycles (rentals). Social dir. Game rm. Exercise rm; instructor, weight machine, bicycles, whirlpool. Masseuse. Refrigerators. Many balconies. Picnic tables. Situated on lake within Stone Mountain State Park. Cr cds: A, C, D, DS, ER, MC, V.

D 🚣 🐎 🎣 ⚓ 🏊 🏋 🚭 🕐 SC

Restaurants

★ ★ ★THE ABBEY. *163 Ponce de Leon Ave NE, at Piedmont Rd & North Ave, in Midtown/Piedmont Park.* 404/876-8831. Hrs: 6–10 pm. Closed major hols. Res accepted. Continental menu. Bar from 5 pm. Wine cellar. A la carte entrees: dinner $17–$25. Specializes in seafood, chicken, veal. Own baking, desserts. Harpist. Valet parking. Former church; 50-ft arched and vaulted ceiling. Costumed servers. Cr cds: A, C, D, DS, ER, MC, V, JCB.

★ ★CAFE CHANTERELLE. *4200 Paces Ferry Rd NE, north of downtown.* 404/433-9775. Hrs: 11:30 am–2:30 pm, 6–10:30 pm. Closed some major hols. Res accepted. Continental menu. Bar. A la carte entrees: lunch $4.95–$8.95, dinner $7.95–$15.95. Specializes in veal dishes, seafood. Parking. Cr cds: A, MC, V.

★★CAPRI. 5785 Roswell Rd NE, north of downtown. 404/255-7222. Hrs: 11:30 am–2 pm, 6–10:30 pm; Fri, Sat to 11 pm. Closed Sun; major hols. Res accepted. Italian menu. Bar. Semi-a la carte: lunch $5.50–$11.95. A la carte entrees: dinner $8.95–$16.50. Specializes in veal, pasta, northern Italian dishes. Parking. Intimate atmosphere. Cr cds: A, C, D, DS, MC, V.

★★★CIBOULETTE. 1529 Piedmont Ave, in Midtown/Piedmont Park. 404/874-7600. Hrs: 6–10 pm; Fri, Sat to 11 pm. Closed Sun; major hols. French menu. Bar. Semi-a la carte: dinner $14.95–$21.95. Specialties: Amish capon coq au vin "modern-style," nage of fish "Mediterranean-style," duck liver pâté. Parking. Open kitchen. Casual dining in elegant atmosphere. Cr cds: A, D, MC, V.

★★★CITY GRILL. 50 Hurt Plaza, in the Hurt Bldg, downtown. 404/524-2489. Hrs: 11:30 am–2:30 pm, 5:30–10 pm; Sat, Sun from 5:30 pm. Closed most major hols. Res accepted. Contemporary Amer menu. Bar. Wine cellar. A la carte entrees: lunch $4.50–$15, dinner $17–$26. Specializes in crab cakes, chicken. Own pastries. Valet parking (dinner). Rotunda entrance, bronze chandeliers, marble columns, wall murals. Jacket (dinner). Cr cds: A, C, D, DS, MC, V.

★★COUNTRY PLACE. 1197 Peachtree St NE, Colony Square Complex, in Midtown/Piedmont Park. 404/881-0144. Hrs: 11 am–2:30 pm, 5:30–11 pm; Fri to midnight; Sat 5:30 pm–midnight; Sun brunch 11 am–3 pm. Closed Thanksgiving, Dec 25. Bar. Semi-a la carte: lunch $5.95–$10.50, dinner $9.95–$19.95. Sun brunch $5.95–$10.50. Pianist Tues–Sat. Parking. Cr cds: A, C, D, DS, MC, V.

★★DAILEY'S. 17 International Blvd, downtown. 404/681-3303. Hrs: 11 am–3:30 pm, 5:30–11 pm; Fri, Sat to midnight. Closed major hols. Bar. Semi-a la carte: lunch $4.95–$10.50, dinner $11.95–$22. Specialties: New Zealand rack of lamb, swordfish au poivre. Dessert bar. Pianist 7–11 pm. Converted warehouse; vaulted ceiling. Cr cds: A, C, D, DS, MC, V.

★★FISHERMAN'S COVE. 201 Courtland St, downtown. 404/659-3610. Hrs: 11:30 am–2 pm, 5–10 pm; Fri to 10:30 pm; Sat 5–10:30 pm; Sun 5–10 pm. Closed Thanksgiving, Dec 25. Res accepted. Bar from 5 pm. A la carte entrees: lunch $4.95–$12.95, dinner $10.95–$19.95. Child's meals. Specializes in lobster bouillabaisse, Maine lobster, shrimp scampi. Parking. New England fish house decor. Cr cds: A, C, D, MC, V, JCB.

★★★HSU'S GOURMET CHINESE RESTAURANT. 192 Peachtree Center Ave, downtown. 404/659-2788. Hrs: 11 am–11 pm; Sun 5–10 pm. Closed Sun; July 4, Thanksgiving, Dec 25. Res accepted. Chinese menu. Bar from 11 am. Wine list. A la carte entrees: lunch $5.25–$10.95, dinner $10.95–$17.95. Specialties: Peking Duck, asparagus shrimp in black bean sauce, sesame roast chicken, steamed salmon with ginger sauce. Parking (dinner). Chinese decor. Cr cds: A, C, D, MC, V.

✔★LA PAZ. 6410 Roswell Rd, north of downtown. 404/256-3555. Hrs: 5–10 pm; Fri, Sat to 11 pm. Southwestern menu. Bar. A la carte entrees: dinner $3.95–$13. Child's meals. Own desserts. Parking. Outdoor dining. Cr cds: A, C, D, DS, MC, V.

★★★THE LARK AND THE DOVE. 5788 Roswell Rd, north of downtown. 404/256-2922. Hrs: 11:30 am–2:30 pm, 6–10:30 pm; Fri to 11:30 pm; Sat 6–11:30 pm. Closed Sun (exc hols); Jan 1, Memorial Day, Labor Day, Dec 25. Bar. Res accepted. Wine list. A la carte entrees: lunch $4.95–$10.95, dinner $11.95–$25.95. Child's meals. Specializes

in prime rib, seafood, Caesar salad. Entertainment Tues–Sat. Valet parking. Family-owned. Cr cds: A, C, D, MC, V.

★★LOMBARDI'S. 94 Upper Pryor St, downtown. 404/522-6568. Hrs: 11 am–10 pm; Fri to 11 pm; Sat 1–11 pm; Sun 3–10 pm. Closed Jan 1, Easter, Thanksgiving, Dec 25. Res accepted. Northern Italian menu. Bar. A la carte entrees: lunch $7–$16, dinner $9.50–$17.95. Specializes in pasta, veal, seafood. Parking. Cr cds: A, C, D, MC, V.

★★★THE MANSION. 179 Ponce de Leon Ave, in Midtown/Piedmont Park. 404/876-0727. Hrs: 11 am–2 pm, 6–10 pm; Sun brunch 11 am–2:30 pm. Closed some major hols. Res accepted. Continental menu. Bar 11 am–midnight. Wine list. Semi-a la carte: lunch $8.50–$13.95, dinner $16.95–$29.95. Sun brunch $18.95. Specializes in fresh seafood, veal, lamb. Own baking, desserts. Parking. Shingle-style Victorian mansion (1885) with garden, gazebo. Cr cds: A, C, D, DS, ER, MC, V, JCB.

✔★MARY MAC'S TEAROOM. 224 Ponce de Leon Ave, in Midtown/Piedmont Park. 404/876-6604. Hrs: 11 am–4 pm, 5–8 pm; Sat & Sun 11 am–3 pm, 5–8:30 pm. Closed major hols. Complete meals: lunch $5–$6.50, dinner $5–$13. Child's meals. Specializes in baked and fried chicken, fresh vegetables. Own desserts. Parking. Informal neighborhood cafe. Family-owned. No cr cds accepted.

✔★MICK'S UNDERGROUND. 75 Upper Alabama St, downtown. 404/525-2825. Hrs: 11 am–11 pm; Fri, Sat to 1 am; Sun noon–10:30 pm. Closed Thanksgiving, Dec 25. Bar. Semi-a la carte: lunch, dinner $3.50–$14.50. Child's meals. Specializes in hamburgers, chicken, pasta. Own desserts. Cr cds: A, C, D, DS, MC, V.

★★MORTON'S OF CHICAGO. 245 Peachtree Center Ave, in Marquis One Tower office building, downtown. 404/577-4366. Hrs: 5:30–11 pm; Sun 5–10 pm. Closed major hols. Res accepted. Bar. A la carte entrees: dinner $25–$55. Specializes in prime aged steak, veal, lobster. Valet parking. Cr cds: A, C, D, MC, V.

★★★NIKOLAI'S ROOF. (See Hilton & Towers Hotel) 404/659-2000. Sittings: 6:30 & 9:30 pm; open seating wkdays. Closed Jan 1, Dec 25. Res accepted. Classic French menu with Russian flair. Extensive wine list. Prix fixe: five-course dinner $60. Specialties (sample only, menu varies): turbot à la vapeur sur un lit de chanterelles, la coupe royale de gibier aux airells et poivres, piroshkis & borsht. Own baking, desserts. Menu recited. Valet parking. Elegant decor; on 29th floor of hotel. Jacket, tie. Cr cds: A, C, D, DS, ER, MC, V, JCB.

★★PAPA PIROZKI'S RUSSIAN CAFE. 4953 Roswell Rd NE, north of downtown. 404/252-1118. Hrs: 11:30 am–3 pm, 6–11 pm; Sat from 6 pm. Closed Sun; major hols. Res accepted. Russian menu. Bar. Extensive wine list. Semi-a la carte: lunch $4.95–$9.95, dinner $10.95–$22.95. Specialties: rack of lamb, lobster Alexandra. Valet parking. Russian decor and music. Jacket. Cr cds: A, C, D, MC, V.

✔★PARTNERS. 1399 N Highland, east of downtown. 404/876-8104. Hrs: 5:30–11 pm; Fri, Sat to 11:30 pm; Sun 9 am–3 pm; Sat, Sun brunch 9 am–3 pm. Closed Dec 25. Mediterranean menu. Semi-a la carte: dinner $14.95–$17.95. Child's meals. Specializes in seafood. Parking. Midtown bistro. Cr cds: A, C, D, MC, V.

★★★PATIO BY THE RIVER. 4199 Paces Ferry Rd NW, north of downtown. 404/432-2808. Hrs: 11:30 am–2:30 pm, 6–10 pm; Sat from 6 pm; Sun brunch 11:30 am–2:30 pm. Closed most major hols. Res accepted. French menu. Bar. Semi-a la carte: lunch $4–$10, dinner $15.50–$25. Sun brunch $4–$11. Specializes in lamb chops, trout, grilled salmon. Parking. Patio dining. View of Chattahoochee River. Cr cds: A, C, D, DS, MC, V.

✔ ★ ★ **PITTYPAT'S PORCH.** 25 International Blvd, downtown. 404/525-8228. Hrs: from 5 pm. Closed Labor Day, Dec 25; also 1 wk in Dec. Res accepted. Southern menu. Bar. Semi-a la carte: dinner $16.95–$19.95. Child's meals. Specializes in fresh coastal fish, Savannah crab cakes, coastal venison pie. Own desserts. Pianist (dinner). Parking. Collection of rocking chairs in lounge. Cr cds: A, C, D, DS, MC, V.

D

✔ ★ ★ **RAY'S ON THE RIVER.** 6700 Powers Ferry Rd, north of downtown. 404/955-1187. Hrs: 11 am–3 pm, 5:30–10:30 pm; Fri, Sat to midnight; Sun 10 am–3 pm, 5:30–10 pm. Closed Labor Day, Dec 25. Res accepted. Bar 11 am–midnight; Fri, Sat 11–1 am; Sun 12:30–10 pm. Semi-a la carte: lunch $4.95–$9.50, dinner $9.95–$16.95. Sunday brunch $14.95. Child's meals. Specializes in mesquite-grilled seafood, prime rib. Jazz eves Tues–Sat. Valet parking. View of Chattahoochee River. Cr cds: A, C, D, DS, MC, V.

D

★ ★ ★ **THE RESTAURANT.** 181 Peachtree St NE, in The Ritz-Carlton, Atlanta Hotel, downtown. 404/659-0400; ext 6400. Hrs: 11:30 am–2:30 pm, 6–11 pm; Sat, Sun from 6:30 pm. Res accepted. French, continental menu. Wine cellar. A la carte entrees: lunch $10.50–$14, dinner $18–$26. Child's meals. Specialties: sautéed duck foie gras, seared gulf red snapper, baby lamb loin. Own baking, ice cream, pasta. Entertainment Tues–Sat evenings. Valet parking. Private club atmosphere; objets d'art. Jacket. Cr cds: A, C, D, DS, ER, MC, V, JCB.

D

✔ ★ ★ **TASTE OF NEW ORLEANS.** 889 W Peachtree St NE, in Midtown/Piedmont Park. 404/874-5535. Hrs: 11:30 am–2 pm, 6–10 pm; Fri 11:30 am–2 pm, 5:30–11 pm; Sat 5:30–11 pm. Closed Sun; most major hols; also late Dec. Res accepted. Cajun, Creole menu. Bar. Semi-a la carte: lunch $5.99–$7.95, dinner $8.95–$16.95. Specialties: gumbo, seafood etouffee. Parking. Cr cds: A, C, D, MC, V.

★ ★ ★ **VAN GOGH'S.** (70 W Crossville Rd, Roswell) N on GA 400 to exit 7B, then approx 3 mi NW. 404/993-1156. Hrs: 11:30 am–midnight. Closed Sun; Jan 1, Easter, Dec 24–25. Res accepted Mon–Thurs. Continental menu. Bar. Wine list. Semi-a la carte: lunch $4.95–$10.95, dinner $9.95–$22. Child's meals. Specializes in grilled portobello mushrooms, crab cakes. Parking. European ambiance. Cr cds: A, C, D, DS, MC, V.

D

★ ★ **VENI VIDI VICI.** 41 14th St, at W Peachtree, in Midtown/Piedmont Park. 404/875-8424. Hrs: 11 am–11 pm; Fri to midnight; Sat 5 pm–midnight; Sun 5–10 pm. Closed Jan 1, Memorial Day, Thanksgiving, Dec 25. Res accepted. Italian menu. Bar 11:30 am–midnight. A la carte entrees: lunch $6–13, dinner $12–$20. Specializes in seafood, combination platter, risotto. Valet parking. Outdoor dining. Vaulted ceilings. Open kitchen. Cr cds: A, C, D, DS, MC, V.

D

★ ★ **WINFIELD'S.** 1 Galleria Pkwy, north of downtown. 404/955-5300. Hrs: 11:30 am–3 pm, 5:30–10 pm; Fri, Sat to 11 pm; Sun 5–9 pm; Sun brunch 11am–3 pm. Closed Thanksgiving, Dec 25. Bar. Semi-a la carte: lunch $5.50–$9.50, dinner $9.50–$19.95. Sun brunch $5.50–$9.50. Child's meals. Specializes in hickory charcoal-grilled meats & seafoods, homemade desserts. Pianist Tues–Sat evenings. Parking. Cr cds: A, C, D, DS, MC, V.

D

Unrated Dining Spots

BOYCHIK'S DELI. 4520-A Chamblee-Dunwoody Rd, in Georgetown Shopping Center, north of downtown. 404/452-0516. Hrs: 10 am–9 pm; Sat, Sun from 9 am. Closed Dec 25. Semi-a la carte: bkfst $2.25–$4.65, lunch $3.50–$5.25, dinner $5.50–$7.50. Child's meals. Specializes in chopped liver, hot pastrami. New York-style deli. Cr cds: A, MC, V.

PICCADILLY CAFETERIA. 5647 Peachtree Industrial Blvd, north of downtown. 706/451-5364. Hrs: 11 am–8:30 pm. Closed Dec 25. Res accepted. Avg ck: lunch $4.50, dinner $5. Child's meals. Specializes in fried chicken. Parking. Cr cds: A, C, D, DS, MC, V.

D

VARSITY. 61 North Ave, in Midtown/Piedmont Park. 404/881-1706. Hrs: 7–12:30 am; Fri, Sat to 2 am. Specializes in hot dogs, hamburgers, fried peach pie. Avg ck: $4–$4.50. Parking. View of some preparation areas. One of world's largest drive-ins. Graffitiesque decor; tiered seating. Adj Georgia Tech campus. No cr cds accepted.

Atlanta Hartsfield Airport Area *

*8 mi S of Atlanta (B-2) via I-85.

Services and Information

Information: 404/530-6600.

Lost and Found: 404/530-2100.

Weather: 404/762-6151.

Cash Machines: Concourse A.

Club Lounges: Admirals Club (American), Concourse D; Crown Rooms (Delta), Concourses A & B.

Terminals

Concourse A: Delta

Concourse B: Delta

Concourse C: TWA

Concourse D: America West, American, American Eagle, Atlantic Southeast, Continental, Midwest Express, Northwest, United, USAir

International Concourse: Air Jamaica, British Airways, Cayman Airways, Delta, Japan Airlines, KLM, Lufthansa, Swissair

(Airlines and their terminal locations may change. Before leaving for the airport, you should phone the airline to confirm terminal location for your flight.)

(See Atlanta)

Motels

✔ ★ ★ **COMFORT INN.** (1808 Phoenix Blvd, College Park 30349) S on I-85 to I-285, E on I-285, exit 43 (Riverdale Rd S), then W on Phoenix Blvd. 404/991-1099; FAX 404/991-1076. 194 rms, 4 story. S $39–$49; D $44–$74; each addl $5; under 17 free; wkend rates; higher rates Atlanta "500." Crib free. TV; cable. Heated pool; poolside serv. Complimentary coffee in lobby. Restaurant 6–10:30 am, 11:30 am–2 pm, 6–10 pm; Sat, Sun 7–11:30 am, 5:30–10 pm. Rm serv. Bar 5–10 pm. Ck-out 11 am. Coin lndry. Meeting rms. Valet serv. Sundries. Free airport transportation. Balconies. Cr cds: A, C, D, DS, ER, MC, V, JCB.

D 🏊 ✈ 🚫 ◎ **SC**

★ ★ **COURTYARD BY MARRIOTT.** (2050 Sullivan Rd, College Park 30337) S on I-85 to Riverdale Rd, E to Best Rd, S to Sullivan Rd. 404/997-2220; FAX 404/994-9743. 144 rms, 3 story. S $82; D $92; each addl $10; suites $106–$116; under 12 free; wkly, wkend rates. Crib free. TV; cable. Indoor pool. Coffee in rms. Restaurant 6:30 am–1 pm, 6–10 pm. Bar 4–11 pm. Ck-out noon. Coin lndry. Meeting rms. Valet serv. Sundries. Free airport transportation. Exercise equipt; weights, bi-

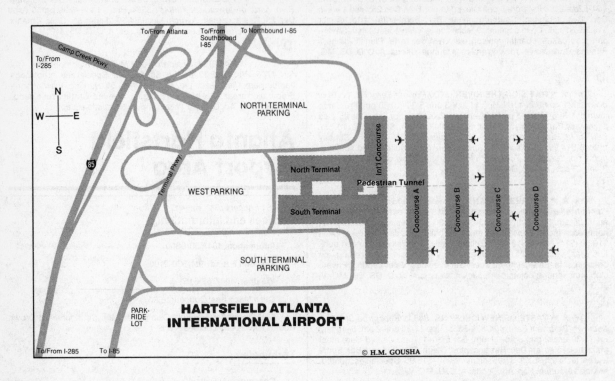

To/From Atlanta
To/From Southbound I-85
To Northbound I-85
To/From I-285
Camp Creek Pkwy.
NORTH TERMINAL PARKING
N W E S
85
Terminal Pkwy.
WEST PARKING
North Terminal
South Terminal
Pedestrian Tunnel
Int'l Concourse
Concourse A
Concourse B
Concourse C
Concourse D
SOUTH TERMINAL PARKING
PARK-RIDE LOT
To/From I-285
To I-85
HARTSFIELD ATLANTA INTERNATIONAL AIRPORT
© H.M. GOUSHA

cycles, whirlpool. Some private patios, balconies. Cr cds: A, C, D, DS, MC, V.

 🏊 👤 ✕ 🚭 ⊙ SC

✔ ★ ★ **HAMPTON INN.** (1888 Sullivan Rd, College Park 30337) S via I-85 exit 18, E on Riverdale Rd to Sullivan Rd. 404/996-2220; FAX 404/996-2488. 130 units, 4 story. S, D $47–$60; under 18 free. Crib free. TV; cable. Pool. Complimentary continental bkfst, coffee. Restaurant adj 6–2 am. Ck-out noon. Meeting rms. Free airport transportation. Public park adj. Cr cds: A, C, D, DS, MC, V.

D 🏊 ✕ 🚭 ⊙ SC

Motor Hotels

★ ★ **DAYS INN.** (4601 Best Rd, College Park 30337) S on I-85, exit Riverdale Rd W, then N on Best Rd. 404/761-6500; FAX 404/763-3267. 160 rms, 6 story. S, D $62–$82; each addl (after 4th person) $10. Crib free. TV; cable. Pool. Playground. Restaurant 6 am–10 pm. Rm serv. Bar 5 pm–midnight. Ck-out noon. Meeting rms. Valet serv. Free airport transportation. Exercise equipt; weights, bicycle. Many refrigerators. Cr cds: A, C, D, DS, MC, V.

D 🏊 👤 ✕ 🚭 ⊙ SC

★ ★ **RAMADA-ATLANTA AIRPORT.** (1419 Virginia Ave, Atlanta 30337) N on I-85, exit Virginia Ave W. 404/768-7800; FAX 404/767-5451. 245 rms, 6 story. S $45–$79, D $55–$80; each addl $6; suites $85–$131; under 18 free. Crib free. TV; cable. Pool; poolside serv. Restaurant 6 am–2 pm, 5–9 pm. Rm serv. Bar 4:30 pm–1 am. Ck-out 1 pm. Coin lndry. Meeting rms. Bellhops. Valet serv. Free airport transpor-

tation. Exercise equipt; weight machines, bicycles, sauna. Cr cds: A, C, D, DS, ER, MC, V, JCB.

D 🏊 👤 ✕ 🚭 ⊙ SC

Hotels

★ ★ ★ **ATLANTA RENAISSANCE HOTEL INTERNATIONAL AIRPORT.** (4736 Best Rd, Atlanta 30337) S on I-85, exit Riverdale Rd W. 404/762-7676; FAX 404/763-4199. 496 units, 10 story. S $105–$165; D $120–$180; each addl $15; suites $175–$600; wkend plans. Crib free. Pet accepted, some restrictions. TV; cable. Indoor/outdoor pool; poolside serv. Restaurant 6:30 am–2:30 pm, 5:30–11 pm. Rm serv Fri, Sat to 1 am. Bar 11–2 am; entertainment exc Sun. Ck-out noon. Convention facilities. Gift shop. Free airport transportation. Exercise equipt; weights, bicycles, whirlpool, sauna. Minibars; some bathrm phones. *LUXURY LEVEL:* **CONCIERGE LEVEL.** 55 units, 4 suites. S $165; D $180; suites $250–$700. Concierge. Private lounge, honor bar. Complimentary continental bkfst, refreshments, newspaper. Cr cds: A, C, D, DS, ER, MC, V, JCB.

D 🐾 🏊 👤 🏃 ✕ 🚭 ⊙ SC

★ ★ ★ **HILTON & TOWERS.** (1031 Virginia Ave, Atlanta 30354) N on I-85, exit 19 Virginia Ave E. 404/767-9000; FAX 404/768-0185. 501 rms, 17 story. S $135–$145; D $150–$160; each addl $15; suites $350–$450; family, wkend rates. Crib free. TV; cable. 2 pools, 1 indoor; poolside serv. Coffee in rms. Restaurant 6 am–midnight. Rm serv 24 hrs. Bar 11:30–1 am; entertainment. Ck-out noon. Convention facilities. Concierge. Gift shop. Barber, beauty shop. Free valet parking. Free airport, RR station, bus depot transportation. Lighted tennis. Exercise rm; instructor, weight machines, bicycles, whirlpool, sauna. Massage. Minibars; some bathrm phones, wet bars. Refrigerators avail. *LUXURY LEVEL:* **TOWERS.** 63 rms, 4 suites, 2 floors. S $165; D $180. Private

lounge, honor bar. Complimentary continental bkfst, refreshments, newspaper.
Cr cds: A, C, D, DS, ER, MC, V, JCB.

★★★MARRIOTT-ATLANTA AIRPORT. *(4711 Best Rd, College Park 30337) S on I-85, exit Riverdale Rd W. 404/766-7900; FAX 404/209-6808.* 639 rms, 16 story. S $140; D $155; suites $200–$600; under 18 free; wkly, wkend, hol rates. Crib free. TV; cable. Indoor/outdoor pool; poolside serv, lifeguard. Restaurant 6:30 am–midnight. Bar 5 pm–2 am, Sun 12:30 pm–midnight; entertainment, dancing. Ck-out noon. Convention facilities. Concierge. Gift shop. Barber, beauty shop. Free airport transportation. Lighted tennis. Exercise equipt; weight machines, bicycles, whirlpool, sauna. Game rm. Refrigerators avail. Some balconies. *LUXURY LEVEL:* CONCIERGE FLOOR. 34 rms. S $150; D $165. Private lounge, honor bar. Complimentary continental bkfst, refreshments.
Cr cds: A, C, D, DS, MC, V, JCB.

STOUFFER CONCOURSE. (Too new to be rated) *(One Hartsfield Pkwy, Atlanta 30354) I-85 exit 20, at Hartsfield Centre. 404/209-9999; FAX 404/209-8934.* 387 rms, 11 story. S $145–$185; D $165–$205; each addl $20; suites $225–$825; family, baseball wkend rates. Crib free. Valet parking $5. TV; cable. 2 pools, 1 indoor; poolside serv. Complimentary coffee in rms. Restaurant 6 am–11 pm. Rm serv 24 hrs. Bar; entertainment, dancing exc Sun. Ck-out 1 pm. Convention facilities. Concierge. Gift shop. Free airport transportation. Exercise rm; instructor, weight machine, bicycles, whirlpool, sauna. Health club privileges. Refrigerators, minibars. Balconies. *LUXURY LEVEL:* CLUB LEVEL. 40 rms, 1 suite. S $165; D $185; suite $825. Concierge. Private lounge, honor bar. Complimentary continental bkfst, refreshments.
Cr cds: A, C, D, DS, ER, MC, V, JCB.

Augusta (B-4)

Founded: 1736 **Pop:** 44,639 **Elev:** 414 ft **Area code:** 706

Augusta was the second town marked off for settlement by General James E. Oglethorpe. Today, it is as famed for golf as for its red Georgia clay bricks. The city has been a military outpost and upriver trading town, the leading 18th-century tobacco center, a river shipping point for cotton, the powder works for the Confederacy, an industrial center for the new south and a winter resort.

During the Revolution, the town changed hands several times, but Fort Augusta, renamed Fort Cornwallis by its British captors, was finally surrendered to "Lighthorse Harry" Lee's Continentals on June 5, 1781.

The Civil War played havoc with many of the wealthy families who had contributed to the Confederate cause. To help revive their depleted bank accounts, some Summerville residents opened their houses to paying guests. Attracted by Augusta's mild winter climate, northern visitors began an annual migration in increasing numbers, and by the turn of the century, Augusta had become a popular winter resort. Many wealthy northerners built winter residences here in the 1920s. Golf courses and country clubs added to the lure. The Masters Tournament attracts the interest of golfers worldwide.

Augusta's many firsts include the state's first medical academy (chartered 1828); the first and oldest newspaper in the South to be published continuously, the *Augusta Chronicle and Herald* (1785); the first steamboat to be launched in southern waters (1790), invented and built by William Longstreet; and the experimental site for one of Eli Whitney's early cotton gins.

Augusta lies at the head of navigation on the Savannah River. Its importance as a cotton market, a producer of cotton textiles, kaolin tiles and brick has been enhanced by diversified manufacturing, processing of cottonseed, farm products and fertilizers. Fort Gordon, an army base southwest of the city, also contributes to the area's economy. With the

Medical College of Georgia, Augusta is a leading medical center in the Southeast.

What to See and Do

1. **Harris House** (ca 1795). 1822 Broad St. House of Ezekiel Harris, tobacco merchant. Period furnishings. Tours (Tues–Fri, afternoons; also Sat mornings) Sr citizen rate. Phone 724-0436. ¢
2. **Meadow Garden.** 1320 Independence Dr. House (1791–1804) of George Walton, signer of the Declaration of Independence. Phone 724-4174. ¢¢
3. **Augusta-Richmond County Museum** (1802). 540 Telfair St. Historic and natural science collections. (Daily exc Mon; closed hols) Sr citizen rate. Phone 722-8454. ¢
4. **Gertrude Herbert Institute of Art.** 506 Telfair St. Old Ware's Folly Mansion (1818) houses changing exhibits; works by local artists. (Tues–Sat; closed major hols) Sr citizen rate. Phone 722-5495. ¢¢
5. **St. Paul's Episcopal Church** (1750). 605 Reynolds St. Granite Celtic cross in churchyard marks site of fort, and the spot where Augusta began, established by Oglethorpe in 1736 in honor of Princess Augusta. Oglethorpe Park, a recreational area on the Savannah river, is located behind the church; picnicking.
6. **Confederate Powder Works Chimney.** 1717 Goodrich St. A memorial honoring war dead, this brick chimney is all that remains of what was once the second largest powder factory in the world.
7. **Augusta College** (1925). (5,600 students) 2500 Walton Way, between Katherine St & Arsenal Ave. Site of Augusta Arsenal (1826–1955), of which portions are preserved. Phone 737-1444.
8. **New Savannah Bluff Lock and Dam.** 12 mi S, near Bush Field Airport. Fishing for shad, bream, yellow perch and jack. Picnicking. (Daily) Sr citizen rate. Phone 821-1706. ¢¢

(For further information contact the Convention & Visitors Bureau, PO Box 1331, 30903-1331; 823-6600.)

Annual Events

Augusta Invitational Rowing Regatta. At Augusta Riverfront Marina. Phone 823-6600. Late Mar or early Apr.

Masters Golf Tournament. Augusta National Golf Course. 1st full wk Apr.

Seasonal Events

Augusta Symphony Orchestra. Phone 826-4705. Fall–spring.

Augusta Opera Association. Phone 826-4710. Fall–spring.

Motels

(Rates are higher Masters Golf Tournament week)

✔ ★★BEST WESTERN BLISSON INN. *(Box 610, 30903) 1103 15th St. 706/724-5560; FAX 706/724-5560, ext 300.* 40 rms, 2 story, 4 suites. S $39.95; D $42.95; each addl $5; suites $49.95; under 12 free. Crib $5. TV; cable. Complimentary continental bkfst, coffee. Restaurant nearby. Ck-out 11 am. Bathrm phones, refrigerators. Cr cds: A, C, D, DS, MC, V.

★★COURTYARD BY MARRIOTT. *1045 Stevens Creek (30907), I-20 at Washington Rd. 706/737-3737; FAX 706/738-7851.* 130 rms, 2 story. S, D $68; each addl $10; suites $84–$94; wkend rates. TV; cable. Pool. Complimentary full bkfst. Restaurant 6:30 am–2 pm, 5–10 pm; Sat 6:30 am–noon; Sun 7 am–2 pm. Bar; closed Sun. Ck-out noon. Coin lndry. Meeting rms. Valet serv. Exercise equipt; weight machines, bicycles, whirlpool. Refrigerators avail. Private patios, balconies. Cr cds: A, C, D, DS, MC, V.

✔ ★★ **VILLAGER LODGE.** *210 Boy Scout Rd (30909).* 706/737-3166; FAX 706/731-9204. 109 rms, 11 kits. S $26.95; D $27.95–$33.95; kits. $32.95–$50.95; wkly rates. Crib free. Pet accepted. TV; cable. Pool. Complimentary coffee. Restaurant nearby. Ck-out noon. Coin lndry. Cr cds: A, C, D, DS, MC, V.

Motor Hotels

★★ **BEST WESTERN BRADBURY SUITES.** *1062 Claussen Rd (30907).* 706/733-4656; FAX 706/736-1133. 111 suites, 6 story. S $49–$69; D $59–$79; each addl $10; under 12 free; wkend rates; golf plan. TV; cable. Pool; whirlpool. Complimentary bkfst, coffee. Restaurant nearby. Ck-out noon. Coin lndry. Meeting rms. Health club privileges. Refrigerators. Picnic table. Suites with different themes avail. Cr cds: A, C, D, DS, MC, V, JCB.

★★★ **RADISSON SUITES INN.** *3038 Washington Rd (30907), at I-20.* 706/868-1800; FAX 706/868-9300. 176 units, 4 story, 152 suites. S $64–$74; D $74–$84; each addl $10; suites $64–$84; under 18 free; monthly rates. Crib free. Pet accepted; $10 per day. TV. Pool. Complimentary bkfst. Complimentary coffee in rms. Restaurant 6 am–10 pm; Sat from 7 am; Sun 7 am–noon. Rm serv. Bar 4–11 pm. Ck-out noon. Coin lndry. Meeting rms. Valet serv. Exercise equipt; weight machine, bicycles. Health club privileges. Some wet bars. Bathrm phone, refrigerator in suites. Cr cds: A, C, D, DS, MC, V, JCB.

★★★ **TELFAIR INN-VICTORIAN VILLAGE.** *326 Greene St (30901).* 706/724-3315; FAX 706/823-6623. 78 rms, 2–3 story, 25 kit. units. S $67–$137; D $77–$157; each addl $10; kit. units $67–$157; under 12 free; golf, honeymoon plans. Crib $10. Pet accepted, some restrictions; $10. TV; cable. Pool. Complimentary coffee in rms. Restaurant 6:30–10 am; also 6–10 pm Thurs-Sat. Rm serv. Bar noon–midnight; entertainment wkends. Ck-out 11 am. Meeting rms. Bellhops. Concierge. Sundries. Free local airport transportation. Lighted tennis. Some bathrm phones, refrigerators, minibars. Grills. Turn-of-the-century buildings in Olde Town area, near River Walk. Cr cds: A, D, DS, MC, V.

Hotels

★★★ **PARTRIDGE INN.** *2110 Walton Way (30904).* 706/737-8888; res: 800/476-6888; FAX 706/731-0826. 105 kit. suites (equipt avail). S $65–$115; D $75–$125; each addl $10; golf, honeymoon plans. Crib $10. TV; cable. Pool. Complimentary bkfst buffet. Coffee in rms. Restaurant 11:30 am–2:30 pm, 5:30–10:30 pm; Sun noon–2:30 pm. Bar 11:30 am–11:30 pm, Fri, Sat to midnight; entertainment wkends. Ck-out noon. Meeting rms. Free garage parking. Balconies. Historic inn (ca 1890) built around original 2-story residence, restored in 1988. Extensive porticos, verandas. Luxurious atmosphere in the tradition of the Old South. Cr cds: A, C, D, DS, MC, V.

★★★ **SHERATON.** *2651 Perimeter Pkwy (30909), I-520 Wheeler Rd exit.* 706/855-8100; FAX 706/860-1720. 179 rms, 6 story, 27 suites. S $79; D $89; each addl $10; suites $129; under 17 free. Crib free. TV; cable. 2 pools, 1 indoor. Complimentary coffee in rms. Restaurant 6:30 am–10:30 pm. Bars. Ck-out noon. Coin lndry. Convention facilities. Concierge. Gift shop. Free airport transportation. Exercise equipt; weight machine, bicycles, whirlpool, sauna, steam rm. Refrigerator, in-rm movies in suites. Cr cds: A, C, D, DS, ER, MC, V, JCB.

Inns

★★★ **OGLETHORPE INN.** *836 Greene St (30901).* 706/724-9774; res: 800/669-9774; FAX 706/724-4200. 19 rms, 3 story, 2 suites. S, D $85; suites $150; wkly, monthly rates. Adults preferred. TV; cable. Complimentary full bkfst, tea/sherry. Restaurant nearby. Ck-out 11 am, ck-in 3 pm. Bellhops. Valet serv. Concierge. Free local airport transportation. Hot tub. Located in 3 refurbished turn-of-the-century houses. Named for town founder General James Oglethorpe. Cr cds: A, C, D, DS, MC, V.

★★★ **PERRIN GUEST HOUSE.** *208 Lafayette Dr (30909).* 706/731-0920; FAX 706/731-9009. 10 rms, 2 story. S, D $65–$150; wkly rates; honeymoon, anniversary plans. TV; cable. Complimentary continental bkfst, evening tea/sherry. Restaurant adj 6–10 pm. Ck-out 11 am, ck-in 1 pm. Bellhops. Valet serv. Concierge. Large country house set among magnolia trees and gardens; gazebo. Totally nonsmoking. Cr cds: A, V.

Restaurants

★★ **GREEN JACKET.** *2567 Washington Rd.* 706/733-2271. Hrs: 11 am–3 pm, 5–10 pm; Fri, Sat to 11 pm; early-bird dinner 5–7 pm. Closed Dec 25. Res accepted. Bar. A la carte entrees: lunch $5.99–$11.99, dinner $7.95–$24.95. Child's meals. Specializes in steak, prime rib, seafood. Salad bar. Parking. Golf motif; Masters Room. Cr cds: A, DS, MC, V.

★★★ **LE MAISON.** *404 Telfair St.* 706/722-4805. Hrs: 6–10 pm. Closed Sun; some major hols. Res accepted. Continental menu. Bar. Wine cellar. Semi-a la carte: dinner $14.50–$25.50. Child's meals. Specializes in rack of lamb, fresh game. Parking. In restored Victorian home (ca 1800). Jacket. Cr cds: A, MC.

✔ ★★★ **TOWN TAVERN.** *15 Seventh St.* 706/724-2461. Hrs: 11:30 am–2:30 pm, 5–10 pm; Sat from 5 pm. Closed Sun; some major hols. Bar. Semi-a la carte: lunch $3.95–$6, dinner $7.95–$16.95. Child's meals. Specializes in live Maine lobster, chicken, steak. Parking. Adj to Riverwalk. Family-owned. Cr cds: A, D, DS, MC, V.

Unrated Dining Spot

S & S CAFETERIA. *1616 Walton Way.* 706/736-2972. Hrs: 11 am–2:15 pm, 4:30–8 pm. Closed Dec 25. Avg ck: lunch $4, dinner $5. Child's meals. Specializes in roast beef, chicken, Southern cooking. Parking. No cr cds accepted.

Bainbridge (E-2)

Founded: 1829 **Pop:** 10,712 **Elev:** 135 ft **Area code:** 912 **Zip:** 31717

On the banks of 37,500-acre Lake Seminole, Bainbridge is Georgia's first inland port. It is a town of giant water oaks and live oaks on the Flint River. Andrew Jackson's troops built an earthworks defense (Ft Hughes) near the present town during the Indian Wars (1817–21). The town was later named in honor of William Bainbridge, commander of the frigate *Constitution*. The forests were so rich in this area that Bainbridge was known as the wealthiest town in the state when fortunes were made in lumbering in the early 20th century.

What to See and Do

1. **Earl May Boat Basin & Park.** W Shotwell St at by-pass. This 600-acre park on Lake Seminole has exhibit of turn-of-the-century

steam engines and locomotives. Beach swimming; boating (ramps). Tennis; playing fields. Camping (hookups). Visitor center (Mon–Sat; closed hols).

2. **Seminole State Park.** 23 mi W on GA 253. Lake Seminole, shallow by Georgia standards, holds a greater number of fish species than any other lake in the state. Swimming beach, waterskiing; fishing; boating. Miniature golf. Picnicking, concession. Camping, cottages. Standard hrs, fees. Contact Superintendent, Rte 2, Donalsonville 31745; 861-3137.

(For further information contact the Bainbridge–Decatur County Chamber of Commerce, PO Box 736; 246-4774.)

Annual Events

Riverside Arts Festival. Arts festival featuring a different state each year. 1st wk May.

Flint River Fair. Carnival, rides, exhibits, livestock show. Late Oct.

(See Thomasville; also see Tallahassee, FL)

Motels

✔ ★ ★ **CHARTER HOUSE INN.** *(Box 308) At jct US 27S, 84 Bypass.* 912/246-8550; res: 800/768-8550; FAX 912/246-0260. 124 rms, 2 story. S $30–$42; D $35–$48; each addl $5; suites $85–$126; under 18 free. Crib free. TV; cable. Pool. Restaurant 6 am–2 pm, 5–10 pm. Bar 4 pm–midnight. Ck-out 1 pm. Valet serv. Meeting rms. Cr cds: A, C, D, DS, MC, V.

★ **HOLIDAY INN EXPRESS.** *751 W Shotwell St.* 912/246-0015; FAX 912/246-9972. 53 rms, 2 story. S $39–$45; D $44–$45; each addl $5; suites $65; under 19 free; wkly rates; higher rates Bass Fishing Tournament. Crib free. TV; cable. Heated pool; whirlpool. Complimentary continental bkfst. Restaurant nearby. Ck-out 11 am. Meeting rms. Refrigerator, wet bar in suites. Cr cds: A, C, D, DS, MC, V, JCB.

Restaurant

✔ ★ **MOBY DICK II.** *US 27 S, 1 mi S of US 84 Bypass.* 912/246-6652. Hrs: 11 am–2 pm, 5–9 pm; Sat from 5 pm; Sun to 2 pm. Closed Mon; July 4, Labor Day, Dec 25. Buffet: lunch $4.25–$5.45. Semi-a la carte: dinner $4.50–$12.95. Child's meals. Specializes in catfish, shrimp. Parking. Cr cds: MC, V.

Blakely (D-1)

Founded: 1826 **Pop:** 5,595 **Elev:** 275 ft **Area code:** 912 **Zip:** 31723

Named for US Navy Captain Johnston Blakely, a hero of the War of 1812, this is an important peanut producing area.

What to See and Do

1. **Courthouse Square.** On square are what may be the world's only monument honoring the peanut and a

   Confederate Flag Pole. The South's last remaining confederate flag pole, erected in 1861.

2. **Coheelee Creek Covered Bridge.** Old River Rd, 9 mi SW via GA 62. Southernmost standing covered bridge in US, built in 1883.

3. **Kolomoki Mounds State Park.** 6 mi N off US 27. Indian mounds, temple mound and some excavation indicate a settlement here between A.D. 800–1200. Swimming pool; fishing; boating (ramps, dock) on Kolomoki Lake. Trails. Picnicking. Camping. Standard

hrs, fees. Contact Superintendent, Rte 1, Box 114; 723-5296. In park is

Indian Museum. Exhibits explain artifacts and civilization of Kolomoki, Weeden Island and Swift Creek cultures. Entry into excavated burial mound. (Daily exc Mon; closed Jan 1, Thanksgiving, Dec 25) ¢

(For further information contact the Chamber of Commerce, 52 Court Square, PO Box 189; 723-3741.)

(See Dothan, AL)

Inn

✔ ★ **LAYSIDE.** *611 River St.* 912/723-8932. 4 rms, 2 baths, 2 story. No rm phones. S $30; D $38; each addl $10. TV in sitting rm; cable. Complimentary full bkfst. Ck-out 11 am. Antiques. Totally nonsmoking. No cr cds accepted.

Restaurant

✔ ★ **OUR PLACE.** *310 S Main St, in Sawyer Shopping Center.* 912/723-8880. Hrs: 6 am–9:30 pm; Sun to 2 pm. Closed Jan 1, July 4, Dec 25. Semi-a la carte: bkfst $1.38–$4.25, lunch, dinner $2.50–$8.29. Buffet (Fri): dinner $5.50. Child's meals. Specializes in fried chicken, hamburgers, steak. Cr cds: MC, V.

Brunswick (E-5)

Settled: 1771 **Pop:** 16,433 **Elev:** 10 ft **Area code:** 912

Brunswick, on the southern third of Georgia's seacoast, separated from the "Golden Isles" by the Marshes of Glynn and the Intracoastal Waterway, was laid out in 1771 by the Colonial Council of the Royal Province of Georgia. Named to honor George III of the House of Brunswick (Hanover), it later became the seat of Glynn County, named in honor of John Glynn, member of the British Parliament and sympathizer with the colonists' struggle for independence.

Gateway to St Simons, Jekyll and Sea Islands (see all), Brunswick is also a manufacturing and seafood processing town. Among its principal products are paints, pulp, paper, lumber machinery, lumber products and processed seafood. Its harbor is a full oceangoing seaport, as well as a home port to coastal fishing and shrimping fleets. Brunswick claims the title of "Shrimp Capital of the World." Natural beauty is enhanced by plantings of palms and flowering shrubs along main avenues, contrasting with moss-covered ancient oaks in spacious parks.

What to See and Do

1. **James Oglethorpe Monument.** Queens Square, E side of Newcastle St. Honors founder of Georgia.

2. **Lover's Oak.** Albany & Prince Sts. Giant oak said to be more than 900 years old; the trunk, at a point 3 feet above ground, measures 13 feet in diameter.

3. **Marshes of Glynn** separate Brunswick from St Simons, Jekyll and Sea islands. Traversed by causeways connecting with US 17, the vast saltwater marshes are bisected by several rivers and the Intracoastal Waterway. Of them Sidney Lanier wrote "Oh, like to the greatness of God is the greatness within the range of the marshes, the liberal marshes of Glynn." Marshes of Glynn Overlook Park has picnic facilities, view of marshes.

4. **Mary Miller Doll Museum.** 1523 Glynn Ave. Collection of 4,000 dolls, dollhouses, miniatures, boats and toys; exhibit subjects include antique dolls, foreign dolls and modern doll artists. (Daily exc Sun; closed Jan 1, Thanksgiving, Dec 25) Phone 267-7569. ¢

5. **Cumberland Island National Seashore** (see). S, off the coast.

6. **Fort Frederica National Monument** (see). 12 mi NE via St Simons/ Sea Island Causeway (toll).

(For further information contact the Brunswick-Golden Isles Visitors Bureau, 4 Glynn Ave, 31520, phone 265-0620; or US 17 Welcome Center, phone 264-5337; or I-95 Welcome Center, phone 264-0202 or 800/933-COAST.)

(See Golden Isles, St Simons Island)

Motels

★ ★**COMFORT INN.** *490 New Jesup Hwy (US 341) (31525), at I-95 Jesup exit 7B.* 912/264-6540. 118 rms, 5 story. S $42–$58; D $49–$67; each addl $6; under 18 free. Crib $2. Pet accepted. TV; cable. Pool. Restaurant adj open 24 hrs. Ck-out noon. Meeting rms. Cr cds: A, C, D, DS, ER, MC, V.

✔ ★**DAYS INN.** *409 New Jesup Hwy (US 341) (31525).* 912/264-4330; FAX 912/264-4330, ext 402. 154 rms, 2 story. S $32–$49; D $37–$54; each addl $5; family rates. Crib free. Pet accepted; $4. TV; cable. Pool. Restaurant 6 am–10 pm; Fri & Sat open 24 hrs. Ck-out noon. Meeting rms. Sundries. Cr cds: A, C, D, DS, MC, V.

★ ★**HOLIDAY INN-US 17.** *3302 Glynn Ave (US 17) (31520).* 912/264-9111; FAX 912/267-6474. 126 rms, 2 story. S $46–$54; D $54–$62; each addl $8; under 16 free. Crib free. Pet accepted. TV; cable. Pool. Restaurant 6:30 am–2 pm, 5:30–9 pm. Rm serv. Bar 4 pm–midnight. Ck-out noon. Coin lndry. Meeting rms. Bellhops. Valet serv Mon–Fri. Cr cds: A, C, D, DS, MC, V, JCB.

✔ ★ ★**HOWARD JOHNSON.** *6 mi N on New Jesup Hwy (US 341) (31520), at I-95.* 912/264-4720; FAX 912/264-5928. 96 rms, 2 story. S $34–$50; D $37–$55; each addl $6; suites $55; under 18 free; higher rates Gator Bowl wk (Dec). Crib free. TV; cable. Pool. Coffee in rms. Restaurant 6 am–10 pm. Ck-out noon. Bellhops 5–11 pm. Sundries. Cr cds: A, C, D, DS, MC, V, JCB.

Hotel

★ ★**GLYNN PLACE MALL SUITES.** *500 Mall Blvd (31525), I-95 exit 8, near Glynco Jet Port Airport.* 912/264-6100; res: 800/432-3229; FAX 912/267-1615. 130 suites, 5 story. S, D $99.95; each addl $10; under 18 free. Crib free. TV; cable. Pool. Complimentary coffee in rms. Restaurant 6:30 am–10 pm. Bar noon–11 pm. Ck-out noon. Meeting rms. Shopping arcade. Free airport, bus depot transportation. Exercise equipt; weight machine, bicycles. Refrigerators, wet bars, in-rm whirlpools. Skylit atrium lobby. Cr cds: A, C, D, DS, ER, MC, V.

Inns

★ ★**BRUNSWICK MANOR.** *825 Egmont St (31520).* 912/265-6889. 4 rms, 2 story. No rm phones. May–Sept: S, D $70–$85; each addl $15; suites $70–$120; 3-night package; lower rates rest of yr. Children over 12 yrs only. Complimentary full bkfst, tea/sherry. Ck-out 11 am, ck-in 3 pm. Some street parking. Antique furnishings, reproductions. Restored Victorian residence (1866) in Old Town section, opp Halifax Square. Cr cds: MC, V.

★**ROSE MANOR GUEST HOUSE.** *1108 Richmond St (31520).* 912/267-6369. 4 rms, 3 with bath, 2 story. Rm phones avail. S $45–$55; D $55–$95; each addl $20; family, wkly rates. Crib free. TV avail; cable. Complimentary full bkfst, afternoon tea/sherry. Dining rm

(by res only). Rm serv avail. Ck-out 11 am, ck-in 3:30 pm. Lawn games. Antiques. Formal garden. Victorian bungalow cottage (ca 1890) on Hanover Square. No cr cds accepted.

Restaurants

✔ ★**CAPTAIN'S TABLE.** *3½ mi N on US 17.* 912/265-2549. Hrs: 5–10 pm; Sun 11:30 am–9 pm. Res accepted. Semi-a la carte: dinner $3.95–$12.95. Complete meals: Sun lunch $4.65–$7.95. Child's meals. Specializes in seafood. Salad bar. Own pies. Parking. Family-owned. Cr cds: A, C, D, MC, V.

✔ ★**MATTEO'S ITALIAN RESTAURANT.** *536 New Jesup Hwy, I-95 & US 341, exit 7B.* 912/267-0248. Hrs: 11 am–10 pm. Closed Sun; most major hols. Italian menu. Wine, beer. Semi-a la carte: lunch, dinner $2.50–$9.50. Specializes in pizza. Parking. Italian cafe atmosphere; wrought-iron booths. Cr cds: MC, V.

★**NEW CHINA.** *3202 Glynn Ave (US 17).* 912/265-6722. Hrs: 11 am–11 pm. Chinese menu. Wine, beer. Semi-a la carte: lunch $2.95–$6, dinner $4.50–$9.50. Child's meals. Specialties: Oriental bird nest, kung bo ding. Parking. Chinese decor. Cr cds: A, C, D, MC, V.

★**OYSTER BOX.** *2129 Glynn Ave (US 17).* 912/265-3698. Hrs: 11:30 am–10 pm. Closed Sun; Thanksgiving, Dec 25. Wine, beer. Semi-a la carte: lunch $4.25–$6, dinner $7.95–$11.95. Child's meals. Specializes in seafood. Parking. Nautical decor. Cr cds: MC, V.

Buckhead *

Area code: 404
A neighborhood of Atlanta (B-2), located S of the northern city limits.

(For general information and attractions see Atlanta.)

Motels

✔ ★ ★**HAMPTON INN-BUCKHEAD.** *3398 Piedmont Rd NE (30305).* 404/233-5656; FAX 404/237-4688. 154 rms, 6 story. S $57–$64; D $64–$71; under 18 free; wkend rates; higher rates major conventions. Crib free. TV; cable. Pool. Complimentary continental bkfst, coffee. Restaurant adj 11 am–11 pm. Ck-out noon. Meeting rms. Valet serv. Health club privileges. Cr cds: A, C, D, DS, MC, V.

★ ★**SUMMERFIELD SUITES.** *505 Pharr Rd NE (30305).* 404/262-7880; res: 800/833-4353; FAX 404/262-3734. 88 suites, 3 story. No elvtr. S, D $124–$164; wkly, wkend rates. Crib $10. Pet accepted, some restrictions; $200 non-refundable. TV; cable, in-rm movies. Heated pool. Complimentary continental bkfst. Complimentary coffee in rms. Restaurant opp 11 am–midnight. Ck-out noon. Coin lndry. Meeting rms. Valet serv. Exercise equipt; weights, bicycles, whirlpool. Refrigerators. Balconies. Picnic tables, grills. Cr cds: A, C, D, DS, MC, V.

Motor Hotel

✔ ★ ★**LENOX INN.** *3387 Lenox Rd NE (30326).* 404/261-5500; res: 800/241-0200; FAX 404/261-6140. 180 rms, 2 story. S $62; D $67; each addl $5; suites $79–$205; under 18 free. Crib free. TV; cable. 2 pools. Complimentary continental bkfst. Restaurant 6:30–9:30 am, Sat & Sun 7–11 am. Bar 5–8 pm. Ck-out noon. Meeting rms. Valet serv. Indoor tennis privileges. Some refrigerators. Cr cds: A, C, D, MC, V.

Hotels

★ ★ ★ **EMBASSY SUITES.** *3285 Peachtree Rd (30305). 404/261-7733; FAX 404/261-6857.* 328 suites, 16 story. Suites $109–$149; under 19 free; wknd rates; higher rates special events. Crib free. TV; cable. 2 pools, 1 indoor. Complimentary full bkfst. Complimentary coffee in rms. Restaurant 11 am–2 pm, 5–10 pm. Bar 11–1 am. Ck-out noon. Coin lndry. Meeting rms. Gift shop. Airport transportation. Exercise equipt; weights, bicycles, whirlpool, sauna. Refrigerators, wet bars. Cr cds: A, C, D, DS, MC, V, JCB.

[D] [≈] [†] [⊘] [◎] [SC]

★ ★ **HOLIDAY INN-BUCKHEAD.** *3340 Peachtree Rd NE (30026). 404/231-1234; FAX 404/231-5236.* 221 rms, 6 story. S, D $78–$98; each addl $10; suites $117–$275; under 18 free; wknd rates. Crib free. Pet accepted. TV; cable. Pool; poolside serv. Restaurant 6:30 am–10:30 pm, Sat & Sun from 7 am. Bar 11:30 am–midnight, Sun from noon. Ck-out noon. Meeting rms. Sundries. Airport, RR station, bus depot transportation. Health club privileges. Some refrigerators. Cr cds: A, C, D, DS, MC, V, JCB.

[🐾] [≈] [⊘] [◎] [SC]

HOTEL NIKKO. (New general manager, therefore not rated) *3300 Peachtree Rd (30305). 404/365-8100; FAX 404/233-5686.* 440 rms, 25 story. S, D $155–$240; each addl $25; suites $385–$1,200; wkend rates. TV; cable, in-rm movies. Pool. Restaurants 6:30 am–11 pm. Rm serv 24 hrs. Bars 11–1 am; entertainment, pianist. Ck-out 1 pm. Convention facilities. Concierge. Gift shop. Garage, valet parking. Airport transportation avail. Tennis & golf privileges. Exercise equipt; bicycles, treadmill, sauna. Bathrm phones, minibars. Tri-level Japanese garden; 35-ft cascading waterfall. *LUXURY LEVEL:* THE NIKKO FLOORS. 43 rms, 5 suites, 3 floors. S, D $240; suites $385–$600. Private lounge. Complimentary continental bkfst, refreshments, newspapers. Cr cds: A, C, D, DS, ER, MC, V, JCB.

[D] [🏊] [🏌] [≈] [†] [⊘] [◎]

★ ★ ★ **J W MARRIOTT.** *3300 Lenox Rd NE (30326), at Peachtree Rd. 404/262-3344; FAX 404/262-8689.* 371 units, 25 story, 43 suites. S, D $115–$199; suites $175–$250; under 18 free. Crib free. Garage $6, valet $8. TV; cable. Indoor pool. Restaurant 6:30 am–11 pm. Rm serv 24 hrs. Bar 11:30–1 am, Fri, Sat to 2 am; entertainment Wed–Sat. Ck-out 1 pm. Convention facilities. Concierge. Shopping arcade. Airport transportation. Tennis privileges. Exercise rm; instructor, weight machine, bicycles, whirlpool, sauna. Health club privileges. Bathrm phones, minibars. *LUXURY LEVEL:* CONCIERGE LEVEL. 28 rms, 6 suites, 3 floors. S $180; D $200; suites $375–$1,100. Private lounge, honor bar. Minibars. Complimentary continental bkfst, refreshments. Cr cds: A, C, D, DS, MC, V, JCB.

[D] [🏌] [≈] [†] [⊘] [◎] [SC]

★ ★ **LANIER PLAZA HOTEL & CONFERENCE CENTER.** *418 Armour Dr NE (30324). 404/873-4661; res: 800/554-8444 (exc GA), 800/282-8222 (GA); FAX 404/872-1292.* 349 units, 5 story. S, D $79–$89; suites $150–$300; under 18 free; wknd rates. Crib free. TV; cable. Pool; poolside serv. Restaurant 6:30 am–2 pm, 5–10:30 pm. Bar 11–1 am. Ck-out noon. Coin lndry. Convention facilities. Concierge. Gift shop. Barber, beauty shop. Airport, RR station, bus depot transportation. Health club privileges. Refrigerators avail. In-rm whirlpool, refrigerator, wet bar, fireplace in suites. Balconies. Cr cds: A, C, D, DS, ER, MC, V, JCB.

[D] [≈] [⊘] [◎] [SC]

★ ★ ★ ★ **THE RITZ-CARLTON, BUCKHEAD.** *3434 Peachtree Rd NE (30326). 404/237-2700; res: 800/241-3333; FAX 404/239-0078.* 553 rms, 22 story. S, D $159–$215; suites $425–$1,100; under 18 free; wknd, honeymoon plans. Crib free. Valet parking $10; self-park in/out $6. TV; cable. Indoor pool; poolside serv, lifeguard. Restaurant 6:30 am–midnight (also see THE CAFE and THE DINING ROOM). Rm serv 24 hrs. Bar 11–2 am; entertainment. Ck-out noon. Convention facilities. Concierge. Shopping arcade. Airport transportation. Tennis privileges, pro. Golf privileges, greens fee $40–$100. Exercise rm; instructor, weight machines, bicycles, whirlpool, sauna, steam rm. Massage. Bathrm phones, minibars. *LUXURY LEVEL:* THE RITZ-CARLTON CLUB. 52

rms, 10 suites, 2 floors. S, D $249. Private lounge. Complimentary continental bkfst, refreshments, afternoon tea. Cr cds: A, C, D, DS, ER, MC, V, JCB.

[D] [🏌] [≈] [†] [⊘] [◎] [SC]

★ ★ ★ **SWISSÔTEL ATLANTA.** *3391 Peachtree Rd NE (30326). 404/365-0065; res: 800/253-1397; FAX 404/365-8787.* 364 rms, 22 story. S $155–$265; D $180–$230; suites $350–$900; under 16 free; wkend rates. Crib free. Garage $6, valet $7, in/out $10. TV; cable. Indoor pool; poolside serv, lifeguard. Restaurant 6:30 am–11 pm. Rm serv 24 hrs. Bar 11 am–midnight, Fri–Sat to 1 am; entertainment. Ck-out 1 pm. Meeting rms. Concierge. Gift shop. Beauty shop. Airport, RR station, bus depot transportation. Tennis privileges. Golf privileges. Exercise rm, instructor, stair machine, weight machine. Bathrm phones, minibars. Art and photo collection. *LUXURY LEVEL:* CLUB FLOOR. 35 rms, 4 suites, 2 floors. S $205–$255; D $230–$280. Private lounge, honor bar. Complimentary continental bkfst, refreshments, newspaper, shoeshine. Cr cds: A, C, D, DS, ER, MC, V, JCB.

[D] [🏌] [≈] [†] [⊘] [◎] [SC]

★ ★ ★ **TERRACE GARDEN INN.** *3405 Lenox Rd NE (30326). 404/261-9250; res: 800/241-8260; FAX 404/848-7391.* 364 rms, 8 story. S $95–$120; D $105–$130; suites $160–$315; under 14 free; wkend rates. Crib free. Covered parking $4. Pet accepted. TV; cable. 2 pools, 1 indoor; wading pool, poolside serv. Restaurant 6 am–2 pm, 6–10 pm. Bars noon–2 am. Ck-out noon. Convention facilities. Concierge. Gift shop. Indoor tennis. Exercise rm; instructor, weight machines, bicycles, whirlpool, sauna. Some refrigerators, wet bars; bathrm phone in suites. Some balconies. *LUXURY LEVEL:* CLUB LEVEL. 69 rms, 2 floors. S $140; D $150. Private lounge. Complimentary continental bkfst, refreshments, newspaper. Cr cds: A, C, D, DS, MC, V.

[D] [🏊] [🏌] [≈] [†] [🏃] [⊘] [◎] [SC]

✔ ★ ★ **TRAVELODGE.** *2061 N Druid Hills Rd NE (30329), at I-85 exit 31. 404/321-4174; FAX 404/636-7264.* 180 rms, 9 story. S $49–$59; D $59–$80; each addl $10; suites to $175; under 18 free; wknd rates. Crib free. TV; cable. Pool. Restaurant 6:30 am–1:30 pm, 6–10 pm. Bar 5 pm–midnight. Ck-out 11 am. Meeting rms. Exercise equipt; weights, bicycles, sauna. Near Lenox Sq. *LUXURY LEVEL:* CLUB LEVEL. 24 rms, 1 suite. S, D $59–$80; suite $175. Private lounge. Complimentary continental bkfst, refreshments, magazines. Cr cds: A, C, D, DS, ER, MC, V, JCB.

[D] [≈] [†] [⊘] [◎] [SC]

Inn

✔ ★ **BEVERLY HILLS.** *65 Sheridan Dr (30305). 404/233-8520; res: 800/331-8520; FAX 404/233-8520, ext 18.* 18 kit. suites, 3 story. S $59–$74; D $68–$120; each addl $5; wkly, monthly rates. Crib avail. Pet accepted, some restrictions. TV. Pool privileges. Complimentary continental bkfst, sherry. Restaurant nearby. Ck-out noon, ck-in 1 pm. Health club privileges. Balconies. European-style hotel restored to 1929 ambiance. Cr cds: A, C, D, DS, ER, MC, V, JCB.

 [🐾] [◎]

Restaurants

★ **ABRUZZI RISTORANTE.** *2355 Peachtree Rd NE, at Peachtree Battle Shopping Center. 404/261-8186.* Hrs: 11:30 am–2:30 pm, 5:30–10:30 pm; Sat 5:30–11 pm. Closed Sun; some major hols. Res required. Italian menu. Bar. Semi-a la carte: lunch from $15, dinner $12.50–$24.45. Specialties: Capellini alla Nico, homemade spinach ravioli, osso buco. Parking. Understated Florentine decor. Jacket. Cr cds: A, D, MC, V.

★ ★ ★ **ANTHONY'S.** *3109 Piedmont Rd NE. 404/262-7379.* Hrs: 6–11 pm. Closed Sun; major hols. Res accepted. Continental menu. Bar. Wine cellar. A la carte entrees: dinner $14.95–$22.95. Specialties: mesquite-grilled fish, châteaubriand. Own baking. Valet parking. Antebellum house (1797); antiques. Cr cds: A, C, D, MC, V, JCB.

Ⓓ

★ ★ **AZALEA.** *3167 Peachtree Rd.* *404/237-9939.* Hrs: 5–11 pm; Fri, Sat to midnight; Sun to 10 pm. Closed July 4, Dec 25. Continental menu. Serv bar. A la carte entrees: dinner $7.95–$16.95. Specialties: catfish, salmon, pizza. Valet parking. West coast atmosphere. Cr cds: A, D, MC, V.

Ⓓ

★ ★ **BASIL'S MEDITERRANEAN CAFE.** *2985 Grandview Ave.* *404/233-9755.* Hrs: 11:30 am–2:30 pm, 6–10 pm; Fri to 11 pm; Sat noon–4 pm, 6–11 pm; Sun 5:30–10 pm. Closed Mon; some major hols. Res accepted. Mediterranean menu. Bar. A la carte entrees: lunch $4.50–$7.25, dinner $10.25–$16.95. Specializes in Middle Eastern cooking. Parking. Outdoor dining. Mediterranean decor. Cr cds: A, D, MC, V.

Ⓓ

★ ★ **BONE'S.** *3130 Piedmont Rd NE, at Peachtree Rd.* *404/237-2663.* Hrs: 11:30 am–2:30 pm, 6–11 pm; Sat & Sun from 6 pm. Closed major hols. Res accepted. Bar. Wine cellar. Semi-a la carte: lunch $8.95–$16.95. A la carte entrees: dinner $18.95–$36. Specializes in aged prime beef, seafood, live Maine lobster. Own desserts. Valet parking. Club atmosphere; wood paneling, fireplace. Cr cds: A, C, D, MC, V.

Ⓓ

✔ ★ ★ **BUCKHEAD DINER.** *3073 Piedmont Rd.* *404/262-3336.* Hrs: 11 am–midnight; Sun to 10 pm. Closed Jan 1, Thanksgiving, Dec 25. Bar. A la carte entrees: lunch $4.25–$12.50, dinner $4.25–$17.50. Specializes in sautéed grouper, veal meat loaf, white chocolate banana cream pie. Valet parking. Update of classic, stainless steel-wrapped diner. Cr cds: A, C, D, DS, MC, V.

Ⓓ

★ ★ ★ **THE CAFE.** *(See The Ritz-Carlton, Buckhead Hotel)* *404/237-2700.* Hrs: 6:30 am–midnight; Sun brunch 11:30 am–2:30 pm. Bar. A la carte entrees: bkfst $7–$15, lunch $10–$22, dinner $15–$30. Sun brunch $32. Child's meals. Specializes in grilled meat, seafood, local dishes. Own pastries. Pianist. Valet parking. Antiques, original art. Cr cds: A, C, D, DS, ER, MC, V, JCB.

Ⓓ

★ ★ **CAFE TU TU TANGO.** *220 Pharr Road.* *404/841-6222.* Hrs: 11:30 am–closing. Eclectic menu. Bar. A la carte entrees: lunch, dinner $3.95–$7.95. Specializes in stir-fry, salad, pizza. Valet parking. Outdoor dining. Artist's studio decor; painters at work. Cr cds: A, MC, V.

Ⓓ

★ ★ ★ **CARBO'S CAFE.** *3717 Roswell Rd.* *404/231-4433.* Hrs: 6–10:30 pm; Fri, Sat to 11:30 pm. Closed major hols. Res accepted. Continental menu. Bar 5 pm–2 am. Wine cellar. Complete meals: dinner $13.95–$29.95. Specializes in seafood, veal, duck. Own baking. Piano bar. Valet parking. Outdoor dining. European decor; antiques, fireplaces, fountain. Cr cds: A, C, D, MC, V.

Ⓓ

★ ★ ★ **CHOPS.** *70 W Paces Ferry Rd.* *404/262-2675.* Hrs: 11:30 am–2:30 pm, 5:30–11 pm; Fri, Sat 5:30–midnight; Sun 5:30–10 pm. Closed some major hols. Res accepted. Bar. A la carte entrees: lunch $6.50–$13.95, dinner $14.50–$29.50. Specializes in steak, fresh seafood. Own pastries. Valet parking. Art deco motif. Cr cds: A, C, D, DS, MC, V.

Ⓓ

★ ★ ★ **COACH AND SIX.** *1776 Peachtree Rd NW.* *404/872-6666.* Hrs: 11 am–2:30 pm, 6–10 pm; Fri to 11 pm; Sat 6–11 pm. Closed Jan 1, Dec 25. Res accepted. Continental menu. Bar. Wine cellar. Semi-a la carte: lunch $6.75–$13.95, dinner $10.95–$24.95. Child's meals. Specializes in steak, Maine lobster, fresh fish, triple-cut lamb chops.

Own baking, desserts. Entertainment Wed–Sat. Valet parking. English club decor; painting collection. Cr cds: A, C, D, DS, MC, V.

Ⓓ

✔ ★ ★ **DANTE'S DOWN THE HATCH.** *3380 Peachtree Rd NE, across from Lenox Square.* *404/266-1600.* Hrs: 4 pm–midnight; Fri, Sat to 1 am; Sun 5–11 pm. Closed Jan 1. Res accepted. Bar. Semi-a la carte: dinner $11–$18.50. Specializes in mixed fondue dinners. Own desserts. Classical guitarist; jazz trio. Parking. Nautical decor. Antique English, Polish ship figureheads. Ship-board dining within multilevel vessel. Family-owned. Cr cds: A, C, D, DS, MC, V.

Ⓓ

★ ★ ★ **THE DINING ROOM.** *(See The Ritz-Carlton, Buckhead Hotel)* *404/237-2700.* Hrs: 6–11 pm. Closed Sun; major hols. Res accepted. Traditional European menu with American regional influences. Bar. Extensive wine cellar. Semi-a la carte: dinner $58–$80. Specializes in light contemporary cuisine. Own baking, pasta, ice cream. Menu changes daily. Valet parking. Elegant decor; Waterford chandeliers, original artwork, antiques. Exquisite paneling. Jacket, tie. Cr cds: A, C, D, DS, ER, MC, V, JCB.

Ⓓ

★ ★ ★ **HEDGEROSE HEIGHTS INN.** *490 E Paces Ferry Rd NE.* *404/233-7673.* Hrs: 6:30–10 pm. Closed Sun, Mon; major hols. Res accepted; required Sat. French, continental menu. Bar. Wine cellar. A la carte entrees: dinner $16–$23. Specializes in seafood, seasonal game dishes, veal. Own pastries. Parking. Restored 1915 house featuring English woodwork. Jacket. Cr cds: A, C, D, MC, V.

Ⓓ

★ ★ ★ **LA GROTTA.** *2637 Peachtree Rd NE.* *404/231-1368.* Hrs: 6–10:30 pm. Closed Sun; major hols; also last wk June–1st wk July. Res required. Northern Italian menu. Bar. Wine list. Semi-a la carte: dinner $15–$23.50. Specialties: vitello tonnato/carpaccio, veal scaloppine. Own pasta, sauces, desserts. Valet parking. Seasonal outdoor dining. Jacket. Totally nonsmoking. Cr cds: A, C, D, DS, MC, V.

Ⓓ

★ ★ ★ **LA TOUR.** *3209 Paces Ferry Place.* *404/233-8833.* Hrs: 6–11 pm. Closed Sun; some major hols. Res accepted. Continental menu. Bar. Wine cellar. Semi-a la carte: dinner $16.95–$26.95. Child's meals. Specializes in seafood, veal. Own pastries, desserts. Pianist. Valet parking. Classic architectural details, faux marbling in formally decorated dining rms. Jacket. Cr cds: A, C, D, DS, ER, MC, V.

Ⓓ

✔ ★ ★ **McKINNON'S LOUISIANE.** *3209 Maple Dr.* *404/237-1313.* Hrs: 6–10 pm; Fri, Sat to 10:30 pm. Closed Sun; major hols. Res accepted. Cajun, Creole menu. Bar. Semi-a la carte: dinner $10.95–$16.95. Specializes in fresh seafood. Parking. Country French decor. Family-owned. Cr cds: A, C, D, DS, MC, V.

Ⓓ

★ ★ ★ **NAKATO.** *1776 Cheshire Bridge Rd NE.* *404/873-6582.* Hrs: 5:30–10 pm; Fri, Sat to 11 pm; Sun 5–10 pm. Closed Jan 1, Dec 25. Res accepted. Japanese menu. Bar. Semi-a la carte: dinner $11–$35. Child's meals. Specializes in sushi, teppan, sashimi. Valet parking. Japanese furniture & decor. Cr cds: A, C, D, MC, V, JCB.

Ⓓ

✔ ★ **OK CAFE.** *1284 W Paces Ferry Rd.* *404/233-2888.* Open 24 hrs; Sat, Sun brunch 11 am–3 pm. Closed some major hols. Wine, beer. Semi-a la carte: bkfst $4–$8, lunch $4–$10, dinner $6–$12. Parking. Diner atmosphere. Cr cds: A, MC, V.

Ⓓ

★ ★ ★ **103 WEST.** *103 W Paces Ferry Rd.* *404/233-5993.* Hrs: 6–11 pm; Fri, Sat from 5:30 pm. Closed Sun; major hols. Res accepted. French, Amer menu. Bar. Wine cellar. A la carte entrees: dinner $14.95–$26.75. Child's meals. Specialties: all lump crab cake, roast breast of duck, broiled noisettes of lamb. Own baking, desserts. Pianist.

Valet parking. Victorian and Renaissance decor; 18th- & 19th-century antiques. Chef-owned. Jacket. Cr cds: A, C, D, DS, MC, V.

D

★ ★ ★ **PANO'S AND PAUL'S.** *1232 W Paces Ferry Rd. 404/261-3662.* Hrs: 6–10:30 pm; Fri & Sat 5:30–11 pm. Closed Sun; major hols. Res accepted. Continental, Amer menu. Bar from 5 pm. Wine cellar. Semi-a la carte: dinner $15–$27. Specialties: fried lobster tail, thick prime veal chop, creative continental/American dishes, white and dark chocolate mousse. Own baking, desserts. Pianist Fri & Sat. Parking. Victorian decor. Chef-owned. Jacket. Cr cds: A, C, D, DS, MC, V.

D

★ ★ **PRICCI.** *500 Pharr Rd. 404/237-2941.* Hrs: 11 am–11 pm; Fri, Sat to midnight; Sun 5–10 pm. Closed Jan 1, Dec 25. Res accepted. Italian menu. Bar. Semi-a la carte: lunch $7–$12, dinner $9–$25. Own breads. Parking. Bakery on premises; view of bread-making process. Cr cds: A, C, D, DS, MC, V.

D

★ ★ **SOUTH OF FRANCE.** *2345 Cheshire Bridge Rd. 404/325-6963 or -6964.* Hrs: 11:30 am–2 pm, 6–10:30 pm; Fri to 11:30 pm; Sat 6–11:30 pm. Closed Sun; major hols. Res accepted. Country French menu. Bar. A la carte entrees: lunch $7.95–$12.95, dinner $12.95–$22.95. Specialties: bouillabaise à la Marseillaise, rack of lamb, duck with orange sauce. Parking. Country French decor. Cr cds: A, C, D, DS, MC, V.

SC

★ ★ **SUNTORY.** *3847 Roswell Rd NE. 404/261-3737.* Hrs: 11:45 am–2 pm, 6–10 pm; Fri, Sat 6–10:30 pm; Sun 5:30–9:30pm. Closed most major hols. Res required. Japanese menu. Bar. Wine list. Semi-a la carte: lunch $6.95–$16.50, dinner $14.50–$22.95. Complete meals: lunch $6.95–$25, dinner $31.25. Sushi bar. Parking. Tableside preparation. Elegant Japanese dining with view of Japanese garden; multiple dining areas featuring traditional Japanese service. Cr cds: A, C, D, DS, MC, V, JCB.

D

Buford (B-2)

Pop: 8,771 **Elev:** 1,187 ft **Area code:** 404 **Zip:** 30518

What to See and Do

1. **Lake Lanier Islands.** N of town, on Lake Lanier. A 1,200-acre, year-round resort owned and operated by the state. Swimming, water-skiing; beach and water park with wave pool, 10 waterslides and other attractions; fishing; boating (ramps, rentals). Horseback riding; 18-hole golf course, tennis. Picnicking; hotel; resort (see); cottages. Tent and trailer camping (hookups). Special events are held May–Oct. Fees for some activities. For further information contact 6950 Holiday Rd, Lake Lanier Islands, 30518; 932-7200.

2. **Winery tours.** Chateau Elan, Ltd. 1½ mi NW on I-85, exit 48, near Braselton. Tours, tastings; restaurant; 18-hole golf course (fee); special events (fee). (Daily; closed Dec 25) Phone 800/233-WINE. **Free.**

(For further information contact the Gwinnett Convention & Visitors Bureau, 6400 Sugarloaf Pkwy, Duluth 30136; 623-4966.)

(See Atlanta, Gainesville)

Motels

✔ ★ **AMERICAN INN.** *4267 GA 20. 404/932-0111.* 40 rms, 2 story. S $31.95; D $35.95; wkly rates. Crib free. TV; cable. Complimen-tary continental bkfst. Restaurant adj 7 am–10 pm. Ck-out 11 am. Cr cds: A, DS, MC, V.

D

★ ★ **BEST WESTERN FALCON INN.** *(I-85 & Suwanee Rd, Suwanee 30174)* S on I-85 exit 44. *404/945-6751; FAX 404/945-6751, ext 303.* 101 rms, 2 story. S $40; D $45; each addl $5; suite $65; under 18 free; wkend rates. Crib free. Pet accepted, some restrictions. TV; cable. Pool. Restaurant 7–10 am, 11 am–1:30 pm, 5–9 pm. Bar. Ck-out 11 am. Meeting rms. Valet serv. Sundries. Gift shop. Airport transportation. Lighted tennis, pro. Exercise equipt; weights, bicycles, whirlpool, sauna. Game rm. Some refrigerators. Owned by Atlanta Falcons football team. Cr cds: A, C, D, DS, MC, V.

D

★ ★ **HOLIDAY INN.** *(2955 GA 317, Suwanee 30174)* Approx 5 mi SW on GA 13, then SE on GA 317. *404/945-4921; FAX 404/945-4921, ext 357.* 120 rms, 2 story. S $45–$63; D $49–$69; each addl $6; under 18 free; wkend rates. Crib free. Pet accepted. TV; cable. Pool; wading pool. Playground. Restaurant 6:30 am–2 pm, 5–10 pm. Rm serv. Bar 11:30 am–midnight, Fri to 2 am, Sat to 3 am. Ck-out noon. Coin lndry. Meeting rms. Valet serv. Sundries. Putting green. Health club privileges. Cr cds: A, C, D, DS, ER, MC, V, JCB.

D

Inn

★ ★ ★ **WHITWORTH.** *(6593 McEver Rd, Flowery Branch 30542)* NE on I-985 exit 2, then N on McEver Rd. *404/967-2386.* 10 rms, 3 story. No rm phones. S, D $55–$65; each addl $10; under 12 free; monthly rates. Crib free. TV in some rms. Complimentary full bkfst, coffee & tea. Ck-out 11 am, ck-in 3 pm. Bellhops. Valet serv. Concierge. Airport transportation avail. Balconies. Picnic tables, grills. Contemporary country inn. Library. Totally nonsmoking. Cr cds: MC, V.

D

Resorts

★ ★ ★ **LAKE LANIER ISLANDS HILTON RESORT.** *(7000 Holiday Rd, Lake Lanier Islands 30518)* I-85 N to I-985 N, exit 1. *404/945-8787; FAX 404/932-5471.* 224 rms, 4 story. Apr–Oct: S, D $109. Crib free. TV; cable, in-rm movies avail. Heated pool; wading pool, poolside serv. Playground. Supervised child's activities (Memorial Day–Labor Day). Dining rm 6:30 am–10 pm. Box lunch, snack bar, picnics. Rm serv. Bar 11–1 am. Ck-out noon, ck-in 3 pm. Grocery 1 mi. Coin lndry, package store 5 mi. Convention facilities. Bellhops. Valet serv. Concierge. Gift shop. Airport transportation avail. Lighted tennis. 18-hole golf, greens fee $47.50 (incl cart), pro, putting green, driving range. Beach, boats, water skiing, swimming. Hiking. Bicycles (rentals). Lawn games. Game rm. Exercise equipt; weights, bicycles, whirlpool, sauna. Some refrigerators. Balconies. Picnic tables, grills. Water park nearby. On lake. Cr cds: A, C, D, DS, ER, MC, V.

D

★ ★ ★ **STOUFFER PINEISLE RESORT.** *(9000 Holiday Rd, Lake Lanier Islands 30518)* 3 mi N on GA 13, then 3 mi W on GA 347. *404/945-8921; FAX 404/945-0351.* 250 rms, 5 story. Apr–Oct, EP: S $145–$225; D $165–$245; each addl $20; 1–2 bedrm suites $385–$900; under 18 free; MAP, golf, tennis, other plans avail; lower rates rest of yr. Crib free. TV; cable, in-rm movies avail. Indoor/outdoor pool; poolside serv & grill (in season). Supervised child's activities (in season). Complimentary coffee, newspaper. Dining rm 6:30–10 pm (also see THE GRILLE ROOM). Rm serv 24 hrs. Box lunches; snack bar. Bar 11–2 am, Sat to midnight, Sun 12:30 pm–midnight. Afternoon tea. Ck-out noon, ck-in 3 pm. Concierge. Laundry avail. Complimentary shoeshine serv. Valet parking. Convention facilities. Gift shop. Airport transportation avail. Tennis, pro. 18-hole golf, greens fee $59–$69 (incl cart), pro, driving range, putting green. Swimming, private beach, waterskiing; water park adj. Boats, motors, sailboats, canoes, pontoon boats, houseboats, docks; instruction avail. Complimentary sunset cruises. Bicycles; horseback riding lessons. Lawn games. Soc dir; entertainment, dancing. Game rm. Exercise rm; instructor, weight machine, bicycles, whirlpool, sauna. Masseuse. Picnic tables. Private patios, balconies. Many decks. Some private enclosed spas. On Lake Lanier. Cr cds: A, C, D, DS, ER, MC, V, JCB.

Restaurants

★★★**CHATEAU ELAN'S LE CLOS & CAFE.** *(7000 Older Winder Hwy, Braselton) Approx 1½ mi NW on I-85N, exit 48, at Chateau Elan Winery.* 404/867-8200. Hrs: Le Clos 6–10 pm; closed Sun–Wed; res accepted. Cafe Elan 10 am–10 pm; Sun brunch 11:30 am–3:30 pm; closed Dec 25; res accepted Thurs–Sat. Classical French menu in Le Clos; southern menu in Cafe Elan. Wine. Le Clos, complete meals: dinner $49. Cafe Elan, semi-a la carte: bkfst $2.95–$5.95, lunch $6.25–$8.95, dinner $6.95–$17.50. Sun brunch $14.95. Two unique dining experiences; Le Clos specializes in genuine classical French cuisine. Cafe Elan specializes in continental and American dishes. Parking. Le Clos offers elegant, formal dining; Cafe Elan offers casual, bistro-style dining. Both provide the festive atmosphere of an authentic French chateau; the restaurant and the cafe are side-by-side in a winery complex; the building also houses a gift shop, museum and offers wine tasting. Cr cds: A, MC, V.

D

★★★**THE GRILLE ROOM.** *(See Stouffer PineIsle Resort)* 404/945-8921. Hrs: 6–10 pm. Closed Sun. Res accepted. Bar 11–2 am; Sat to midnight; Sun 12:30 pm–midnight. A la carte entrees: dinner $12.95–$24. Serv charge 15%. Specializes in grilled steak, seafood. Own baking. Braille menu. Valet parking. View of Lake Lanier. Cr cds: A, C, D, DS, ER, MC, V, JCB.

D

Calhoun (A-1)

Pop: 7,135 **Elev:** 715 ft **Area code:** 706 **Zip:** 30701

Once called Oothcaloga, "place of the beaver dams," the name was changed in 1850 to honor John Caldwell Calhoun, Secretary of State to President John Tyler. Although the town was directly in the path of General Sherman's 1864 march to the sea, Calhoun was not destroyed. Now Calhoun is the seat of Gordon County and center of a dairy, beef cattle and poultry raising area. The town has a major carpet industry and several major manufacturing companies that provide a wide range of products.

What to See and Do

1. **New Echota State Historic Site** (restoration of final Eastern Cherokee capital) (1825–38). ½ mi E of I-75 on GA 225. Includes the Worcester house (1828), the Council House, the print shop, courthouse, the Vann Tavern (1805), an 1830s log store and a museum-orientation center. Citizens of Calhoun bought the 200-acre site in the early 1950s and donated it to the state.

After establishing a government in 1817, the legislature of the Cherokee Indian Nation in 1825 established a capital surrounding the site of their Council House. The written form of the Cherokee language, created by the brilliant Sequoyah, had been developed by 1821, and the print shop was built in 1827. The first issue of the Cherokee newspaper, the *Cherokee Phoenix,* was printed in this shop in 1828 in both Cherokee and English; the paper continued publication until 1834.

Samuel A. Worcester, a most able missionary, arrived from Boston in 1827 and built a house, which is the only original building still standing. The Vann Tavern, built by Cherokees at another location, was moved to the park as part of the restoration. The Cherokee

Nation had a legislative hall, a supreme court house, a mission and several other buildings at New Echota.

At the height of Cherokee prosperity, gold was found in Cherokee territory, then including parts of Georgia, North Carolina, Alabama and Tennessee. In 1835, after a long legal battle, the Cherokees were forced to agree to sell their territory and move to Oklahoma. In the winter of 1838–39 the Cherokees were driven to their new location over the "Trail of Tears," one-fourth of them dying en route. Many hid out in the Great Smoky Mountains; their descendants now form the Eastern Cherokees.

The buildings of the restored New Echota are furnished authentically and are a dramatic reconstruction of a remarkable episode in American Indian history. (Tues–Sat, also Sun afternoons; closed Jan 1, Thanksgiving, Dec 25) Tours. Contact Site Superintendent, 1211 Chatsworth Hwy NE; 629-8151. ¢

2. **Resaca Confederate Cemetery.** 5 mi N on I-75, Resaca exit. Site of the Civil War battle that opened the way to Atlanta for General Sherman. Civil War markers and cemetery. (Daily) **Free.**

(For further information contact the Gordon County Chamber of Commerce, 300 S Wall St; 625-3200.)

(See Dalton, Rome)

Motels

★**DAYS INN.** 742 GA 53 SE, at I-75 exit 129. 706/629-8271; FAX 706/629-8271, ext 163. 120 rms, 2 story. S $30–$42; D $34–$46; each addl $6; under 12 free; lower rates May & Sept. Crib free. Pet accepted. TV; cable. Pool. Playground. Ck-out noon. Coin lndry. Some refrigerators. Cr cds: A, C, D, DS, ER, MC, V.

★★**HOLIDAY INN.** *(Box 252)* On Redbud Rd, I-75 exit 130. 706/629-9191; FAX 706/629-0873. 100 rms, 2 story. S $45; D $50; each addl $5; under 18 free. Crib free. Pet accepted. TV; cable. Pool; poolside serv. Restaurant 6:30 am–2 pm, 5–10 pm. Rm serv. Ck-out noon. Meeting rms. Bellhops. Valet serv. Cr cds: A, C, D, DS, MC, V, JCB.

D

✔★**RED CARPET INN.** 915 GA 53, E off I-75 exit 129. 706/629-9501; FAX 706/629-9502. 100 rms, 2 story. S $21.95–$30.95; D $27.95–$36.95; each addl $3; under 12 free. Crib $2. Pet accepted. TV; cable. Pool; poolside serv. Restaurant 6 am–10 pm. Rm serv. Bar 4 pm–midnight. Ck-out 11 am. Coin lndry. Meeting rms. Picnic tables. Cr cds: A, C, D, DS, MC, V.

Restaurant

✔★**PENG'S PAVILLION.** 1120 South Wall St. 706/629-1453. Hrs: 11 am–9 pm; wkends to 10 pm. Closed Sun; some major hols. Res accepted. Chinese menu. Semi-a la carte: lunch $3.95–$4.50, dinner $5.50–$8.75. Specialty: Mongolian beef. Parking. Chinese decor; murals, lanterns. Cr cds: MC, V.

Carrollton (B-1)

Pop: 16,029 **Elev:** 1,116 ft **Area code:** 404 **Zip:** 30117

Carrollton was named in honor of Charles Carroll, one of the signers of the Declaration of Independence. The town serves as a regional retail, service, manufacturing and health care center for several counties in western Georgia and eastern Alabama. Carrollton is home to Southwire, one of the nation's largest privately owned rod and cable manufacturing companies. The world's largest tape and record manufacturing plant, owned by Sony, is located here as well.

What to See and Do

1. **West Georgia College** (1933). (7,500 students) A unit of the state university system. On campus are John F. Kennedy Memorial Chapel and

   Thomas Bonner House (ca 1840). Maple St. Restored plantation house, campus information center. (Mon–Fri; closed hols, school breaks) Phone 836-6464.

2. **John Tanner State Park.** 6 mi W off GA 16. Two lakes offer the longest beach in the state park system. Swimming; fishing; boating (rentals). Picnicking. Camping, motel. Standard hrs, fees. Contact Superintendent, 354 Tanner's Beach Rd; 830-2222.

   (For further information contact the Carroll County Chamber of Commerce, 200 Northside Dr; 832-2446.)

Motels

✔ ★**COMFORT INN.** *(128 GA 61, Villa Rica 30180) N on GA 61, at jct I-20. 404/459-8000.* 64 rms, 2 story. Memorial Day–mid-Sept: S $40–$50; D $50–$65; each addl $5; under 18 free; higher rates auto races; lower rates rest of yr. Crib $3. TV; cable. Pool. Complimentary continental bkfst, coffee. Restaurant opp 6 am–11 pm. Ck-out 11 am. Some in-rm whirlpools, refrigerators. Cr cds: A, C, D, DS, ER, MC, V, JCB.

★ ★**RAMADA INN.** *1202 S Park St, I-20 exit 5. 404/834-7700; FAX 404/834-1113.* 104 rms, 2 story. S $49–$54; D $54–$59; each addl $5; under 18 free; wkend rates. Crib free. TV; cable. Pool; wading pool. Restaurants 6:30 am–11 pm. Rm serv. Ck-out noon. Coin lndry. Meeting rms. Valet serv. Health club privileges. Cr cds: A, C, D, DS, MC, V, JCB.

Restaurants

★ ★**DANYEL'S.** *911 S Park St. 404/832-9620.* Hrs: 11 am–2 pm, 5–10 pm; Mon to 2 pm; Sat 5–10 pm. Closed Sun; Memorial Day, Thanksgiving, Dec 24–25; also wk of July 4. Res accepted. French, continental menu. Bar. Semi-a la carte: lunch $3.50–$6.75, dinner $7–$19.50. Child's meals. Specializes in steak, veal, seafood. Salad bar. Cr cds: A, DS, MC, V.

★ ★**MAPLE STREET MANSION.** *401 Maple St. 404/834-2657.* Hrs: 11:30 am–2 pm, 4:30–11 pm; Fri to midnight; Sat 4 pm–midnight. Closed Sun; Jan 1, Dec 24–25. Res accepted. Bar. Semi-a la carte: lunch $3.50–$7.95, dinner $5.95–$22. Specializes in prime rib, Chicago pan pizza. Parking. In restored house (1894) built by Georgian industrialist Leroy Mandeville. Cr cds: A, MC, V.

Cartersville (B-1)

Founded: 1832 **Pop:** 12,035 **Elev:** 787 ft **Area code:** 404 **Zip:** 30120

Cartersville is in the center of an area rich in minerals. Its economy is based upon textile manufacturing, plastics, the quarrying of limestone and the mining of ocher, barite and manganese. An Anheuser-Busch brewery also contributes to the economy.

What to See and Do

1. **William Weinman Mineral Museum.** Mineral Museum Dr, jct I-75 & US 411. Displays of cut gemstones, minerals and rocks from Georgia and around the world; simulated limestone cave with waterfall. (Daily exc Mon; closed hols) Sr citizen rate. Phone 386-0576. ¢¢

2. **Etowah Indian Mounds Historic Site & Archaeological Area.** 3 mi S, off GA 113, 61. The most impressive of more than 100 settlements in the Etowah Valley, this village was occupied from A.D. 1000–1500. It was the home of several thousand people of a relatively advanced culture. Six earthen pyramids grouped around two public squares, the largest of which occupies several acres, served as funeral mounds, bases for temples and the residences of the chiefs. Museum displays artifacts from the excavations; crafts, foods, way of life of the Etowah; painted white marble mortuary. (Daily exc Mon; closed Thanksgiving, Dec 25) Phone 387-3747. ¢

3. **Allatoona Lake** (US Army Corps of Engineers). Headquarters is 3 mi N on I-75, exit 125, then E on GA 20, then 4 mi S on GA 294N. Swimming, waterskiing; fishing; boating (ramps). Hiking trails, overlook. Picnicking. Camping (fee). Contact Park Ranger, PO Box 487; 382-4700.

4. **Red Top Mountain State Lodge Park.** 2 mi E of I-75, exit 123. Swimming, waterskiing; boating (ramps, dock, marina). Trails; miniature golf. Picnicking, concession. Restaurant. Lodge. Camping, cottages. Standard hrs, fees. Phone 975-0055.

5. **Kennesaw Mountain National Battlefield Park** (see). Approx 20 mi SE off US 41.

(For further information contact the Cartersville/Bartow County Tourism Council, PO Box 200397; 387-1357 or 800/733-2280.)

(See Atlanta, Marietta, Rome)

Motels

★**BEST WESTERN.** *45 GA 294 SE, at jct I-75 exit 125. 404/382-1515; FAX 404/382-1515, ext 406.* 50 rms, 2 story. S, D $45–$50; each addl $6; under 12 free. Crib $6. TV; cable. Pool. Complimentary coffee in lobby. Restaurant nearby. Ck-out 11 am. Meeting rms. Cr cds: A, C, D, DS, ER, MC, V, JCB.

✔ ★**DAYS INN.** *5618 GA 20 SE, at jct I-75 exit 125. 404/382-1824; FAX 404/325-2525, ext 110.* 52 rms, 2 story. Mar–Aug, Dec: S $28–$40; D $35–$45; each addl $4; suites $58.88; under 12 free; higher rates: baseball, football games; lower rates rest of yr. Crib $4. TV. Pool; wading pool. Complimentary continental bkfst, coffee. Restaurant adj 6 am–11 pm; wkends to 2 am. Ck-out 11 am. Some refrigerators. Cr cds: A, C, D, DS, ER, MC, V.

★ ★**HOLIDAY INN.** *(PO Box 200306) Jct US 411N & I-75 exit 126. 404/386-0830; FAX 404/386-0867.* 150 rms, 2 story. S $52–$68; D $57–$73; each addl $5; under 19 free; wkend rates. Crib free. TV. Pool. Restaurant open 24 hrs. Rm serv. Bar 4 pm–midnight. Ck-out noon. Meeting rms. Valet serv. Sundries. Exercise equipt; weight machine, bicycles, whirlpool. Cr cds: A, C, D, DS, MC, V, JCB.

Restaurants

★**MORRELL'S.** *22 GA 294, at jct I-75 exit 125 & GA 20. 404/382-1222.* Hrs: 5:30 am–10 pm. Closed Dec 25. Semi-a la carte: bkfst $1.50–$4.25, lunch $2.95–$4.95, dinner $2.95–$13.95. Child's meals. Specializes in prime rib, barbecued pork & chicken. Parking. Cr cds: A, DS, MC, V.

✔ ★**WINSTON'S.** *463 E Main St, in Main Street Shopping Center. 404/387-9479.* Hrs: 11 am–10 pm; Fri, Sat to 11 pm; Sun noon–9 pm. Closed Easter, Dec 25. Bar. Semi-a la carte: lunch $3.25–$5.50, dinner $3.25–$12.99. Child's meals. Specializes in fish & chips, salads, hamburgers. Outdoor dining. English pub atmosphere; flags, pictures of British planes on display. Cr cds: A, C, D, DS, MC, V.

Chatsworth (A-1)

Pop: 2,865 **Elev:** 750 ft **Area code:** 706 **Zip:** 30705

Talcum, a mineral that most people know only as a comfort to the skin, was once mined here in large quantities. Murray County has a strong carpet industry, yet almost a third of the land is forest and mountains. Opportunities for fishing, hunting, camping and backpacking abound in the surrounding Cohutta Wilderness and woodlands. A Ranger District office of the Chattahoochee National Forest is located in Chatsworth.

What to See and Do

1. **Fort Mountain State Park.** 7 mi E via GA 52. A mountain park with ruins of a prehistoric stone wall; observation tower. Swimming; fishing; paddleboats (rentals). Self-guided nature trail. Picnicking. Cabins, camping. Standard hrs, fees. Contact Superintendent, Rte 7, Box 7008; 695-2621.

2. **Vann House State Historic Site** (1804). 3 mi W on Alt GA 52 at jct GA 225 in Spring Place. This brick house was the showplace of the Cherokee Nation. James Vann was half Scottish, half Cherokee. His chief contribution to the tribe was his help in establishing the nearby Moravian Mission for the education of the young Cherokees. The three-story house, with foot-thick brick walls, is modified Georgian in style; partly furnished. (Daily exc Mon; closed Jan 1, Thanksgiving, Dec 25) Contact Manager, Rte 7, Box 7655; 695-2598. ¢

3. **Carters Lake.** 15 mi S, off US 411. Swimming; fishing; boating (ramps). Hiking trails, overlooks. Camping (mid-Apr–mid-Sept; fee). For more information visit Resource Manager's office at dam site. Phone 334-2248.

4. **Chattahoochee National Forest.** (See DAHLONEGA)

(For further information contact the Chatsworth-Murray County Chamber of Commerce, Box 327; 695-6060.)

Annual Event

Appalachian Wagon Train. 1 mi E via US 76. Horse and mule shows, trail rides, square dancing, parade. Phone 259-4957. Late June–early July.

(For accommodations see Calhoun, Dalton; also see Chattanooga, TN)

Chickamauga and Chattanooga National Military Park (A-1)

(9 mi S of Chattanooga, TN on US 27)

Established in 1890, this is the oldest and largest national military park in the United States. The two-day battle fought at Chickamauga was one of the Civil War's fiercest, with 36,000 casualties, and was the greatest success of Confederate armies in the West. However, the inability of General Braxton Bragg to follow up the success of September 19 and 20, 1863, and his defeat two months later on Missionary Ridge at Chattanooga, Tennessee, meant the loss of a strategic railway center and opened the gateway to a Union advance into the deep South.

General Bragg had evacuated Chattanooga on September 9 to maintain rail communications southward after Union Commander Rosecrans had abruptly crossed the Tennessee River southwest of the city. However, with the arrival of reinforcements from Lee's army in the East giving him a numerical advantage, Bragg turned back north to surprise Rosecrans' scattered forces. On September 18, the two armies stumbled into each other on the west bank of the Chickamauga Creek.

By the morning of September 19, Union troops attacked and were driven back in heavy fighting. Confederate troops broke the Union line the morning of the 20th, sweeping the entire right wing and part of the center from the field. Union troops on the left, with the aid of the reserve corps, all under the command of General George H. Thomas, took up new positions on Snodgrass Hill, holding under terrific assaults by Confederates until the Union army was able to retreat in good order to Chattanooga. Thomas earned the nickname "Rock of Chickamauga."

US Highway 27 extends more than 3 miles through the 5,400-acre Chickamauga Battlefield, where the battle has been commemorated by markers, monuments, tablets and artillery pieces. Woods and fields are kept as close as possible to the way they were in wartime, and some old buildings lend added atmosphere.

Chickamauga Battlefield is but one of 17 areas forming the National Military Park. Other major areas (all in Tennessee) are Point Park on Lookout Mountain, the Reservations on Missionary Ridge, Signal Point on Signal Mountain and Orchard Knob in Chattanooga—totaling nearly 3,000 acres.

The Chickamauga visitor center, on US 27 at the north entrance to the battlefield, is the logical starting point for auto tours. The center has the Fuller Collection of American Military Shoulder Arms, consisting of 355 weapons, as well as a 26-minute multimedia program (fee) describing the Battle of Chattanooga. Visitor center (daily; closed Dec 25). Park (daily). The National Park Service also offers guided tours, walks, evening programs and musket/cannon firing demonstrations (June–Aug). For further information contact PO Box 2128, Fort Oglethorpe 30742; 706/866-9241. **Free.**

(For accommodations see Dalton; also see Chattanooga, TN)

Clayton (A-3)

Pop: 1,613 **Elev:** 1,925 ft **Area code:** 706 **Zip:** 30525

Located in the mountainous and forested northeast corner of Georgia, Clayton offers visitors a wide variety of activities, including hiking, mountain climbing, camping, boating, fishing, hunting, skiing and whitewater rafting. A Ranger District office of the Chattahoochee National Forest (see DAHLONEGA) is located in Clayton.

What to See and Do

1. **Chattooga Wild and Scenic River.** 8 mi SE via US 76. Originating in the mountains of North Carolina, the Chattooga tumbles southward 57 miles to its terminus, Lake Tugaloo, between Georgia and South Carolina. Designated a Wild and Scenic River by Congress in 1974, the Chattooga is one of the few remaining free-flowing streams in the Southeast. Scenery along the river is spectacular, with gorges, waterfalls and unusual rock formations.

2. **Raft trips. Southeastern Expeditions.** Whitewater raft trips on the Chattooga River in northeast Georgia and Ocoee River in eastern Tennessee ranging in length from half-day to three-day. Contact 2936-H N Druid Hills Rd, Atlanta 30329; 404/329-0433 or 800/868-7238. ¢¢¢¢

(For further information contact the Rabun County Chamber of Commerce, Box 761, phone 782-4812; a Georgia Welcome Center is located on US 441 N, phone 782-5113.)

Annual Event

Homemakers' Harvest Festival. 6 mi N on US 23, 441 in Dillard. Mountain arts & crafts. 3 wkends Oct.

(For accommodations see Hiawassee, also see Toccoa)

Columbus (C-1)

Founded: 1827 **Pop:** 178,681 **Elev:** 250 ft **Area code:** 706

Power from the falls of the Chattahoochee River feeds the industries of this dynamic city. With a nine-foot-deep navigable channel to the Gulf of Mexico, it is at the head of navigation on the Chattahoochee. Originally a settlement of the Creek Indians, the site was chosen as a border stronghold by Governor Forsyth in 1828. The city reached a peak of frenzied manufacturing and commerce between 1861 and 1864, when it supplied the Confederate Army with shoes, caps, swords and pistols.

The Columbus Iron Works (1853) supplied Columbus and the surrounding area with cast iron products, farming equipment, steam engines and industrial and building supplies. It was a major supplier of cannons for the Confederate States during the Civil War. Reconstruction created havoc for a time, but by 1874 Columbus' industries were more numerous and varied than before the war: from 1880 until 1920, a commercial ice-making machine was produced in the town; and by the beginning of World War II, Columbus was a great iron-working center and the second largest producer of cotton in the South.

Much of the original city plan of 1827 is still evident, with streets 99 to 164 feet wide flanked by magnificent trees. Dogwood and wisteria add color in the spring. The atmosphere is exemplified by the brick-lined streets and gaslights in the 28-block historic district and by the Victorian gardens, gazebos and open air amphitheaters on the Chattahoochee Promenade along the banks of the river.

What to See and Do

1. **Fort Benning.** 5 mi S on US 27. Largest infantry post in the US, established during World War I, the fort was named for Confederate General Henry L. Benning of Columbus. Infantry School; demonstrations of Airborne 5000 at Jump Tower (Mon mornings). For information phone 545-2958. **Free.** Here is

   National Infantry Museum. Exhibits of US infantry weapons, uniforms, equipment from the Revolutionary War to the War in the Gulf; experimental and developmental weapons; collection of foreign weapons and equipment. (Daily; closed most major hols) Phone 545-2958. **Free.**

2. **The Columbus Museum.** 1251 Wynnton Rd. Features Chattahoochee Legacy, a regional history gallery with re-created period settings; fine and decorative arts galleries; and Transformations, a youth-oriented participatory gallery. (Daily exc Mon; closed major hols) Phone 649-0713. **Free.**

3. **Columbus Iron Works Convention and Trade Center.** 801 Front Ave, converted from the historic Columbus Iron Works. Exhibit space, banquet facilities, outdoor amphitheater. Phone 327-4522.

4. **Confederate Naval Museum.** 202 4th St. Salvaged remains of Confederate gunboats *Jackson* and *Chattahoochee;* relics, ship models, uniforms, paintings and other exhibits on Confederate naval operations. (Daily exc Mon; closed Thanksgiving, Dec 25) Donation. Phone 327-9798.

5. **Springer Opera House** (1871). 103 10th St at 1st Ave. Restored Victorian theater in which many famous performers have appeared, including Shakespearean actor Edwin Booth; museum. Guided tours. For performance schedule, fee information phone 327-3688 (box office).

(For further information contact the Tourist Dept, Convention and Visitors Bureau, 801 Front Ave, PO Box 2768, 31902, phone 322-1613 or 800/999-1613; or the Georgia Welcome Center, 1751 Williams Rd; 24-hour visitors information hotline, phone 322-3181.)

Annual Event

Riverfest Weekend. At riverfront. 3rd wkend Apr.

(See Pine Mountain; also see Phenix City, AL)

Motels

✔ ★**BUDGETEL INN.** *2919 Warm Springs Rd (31909).* 706/323-4344; FAX 706/596-9622. 102 rms, 3 story, 10 suites. Apr–Oct: S $34.95–$37.95; D $41.95–$44.95; suites $43.95–$50.95; under 18 free; lower rates rest of yr. Crib free. TV; cable. Pool. Complimentary continental bkfst. Complimentary coffee in rms. Restaurant opp 11 am–10 pm. Ck-out noon. Meeting rms. Valet serv. Refrigerator in suites. Cr cds: A, C, D, DS, MC, V.

★★**COURTYARD BY MARRIOTT.** *3501 Courtyard Way (31909), adj to Peachtree Mall.* 706/323-2323; FAX 706/327-6030. 139 rms, 2 story. S $62–$72; D, suites $72–$82; under 12 free; wknd rates. Crib free. TV; cable, in-rm movies. Pool. Restaurant 6:30 am–1 pm. Bar 5–10 pm. Ck-out noon. Coin lndry. Meeting rms. Valet serv. Exercise equipt; weight machine, bicycles, whirlpool. Some refrigerators. Private patios, balconies. Cr cds: A, C, D, DS, MC, V.

✔ ★★**HAMPTON INN-COLUMBUS AIRPORT.** *5585 Whitesville Rd (31904), near Metropolitan Airport.* 706/576-5303. 119 rms, 2 story. S $40–$50; D $46–$56; under 18 free. Crib free. TV; cable, in-rm movies. Pool. Complimentary continental bkfst. Restaurant nearby. Ck-out noon. Meeting rms. Sundries. Free airport transportation. Health club privileges. Cr cds: A, C, D, DS, MC, V.

★**LA QUINTA-MIDTOWN.** *3201 Macon Rd (31906), I-185 exit 4.* 706/568-1740; FAX 706/569-7434. 122 rms, 2 story. S $44–$51; D $49–$56; each addl $7; suites $68–$78; under 18 free; wkly rates. Crib free. Pet accepted. TV; cable. Pool. Complimentary continental bkfst, coffee. Restaurant adj open 24 hrs. Ck-out noon. Coin lndry. Meeting rms. Valet serv. Some refrigerators. Grills. Cr cds: A, C, D, DS, MC, V.

Hotels

★★★**HILTON.** *800 Front Ave (31901).* 706/324-1800; FAX 706/576-4413. 177 rms, 6 story. S $58–$115; D $68–$125; each addl $10; suites $110–$350; family, wknd rates. Crib free. TV; cable. Pool; poolside serv. Restaurant 6:30 am–10 pm. Bar 11:30 am–midnight, Sun from noon; entertainment exc Sun. Ck-out noon. Meeting rms. Gift shop. Airport, bus depot transportation. 18-hole golf privileges, greens fee $35, pro. Exercise equipt; weights, bicycles. Incorporates 100-yr-old grist mill into design. Convention Ctr (former Columbus Iron Works facility) opp. *LUXURY LEVEL:* **CONCIERGE FLOOR.** 17 rms. S $115; D $125. Concierge. Private lounge. Complimentary continental bkfst, refreshments, newspaper. Cr cds: A, C, D, DS, MC, V.

★★**SHERATON AIRPORT.** *5351 Simons Blvd (31904), near Metropolitan Airport.* 706/327-6868; FAX 706/327-0041. 178 rms, 5 story. S $55–$68; D $60–$78; each addl $5; under 16 free; wknd rates. Crib free. Pet accepted. TV; cable. Heated pool; whirlpool, poolside serv. Restaurant 6:30 am–10 pm; Sat, Sun from 7 am. Bar 4 pm–1 am; entertainment. Ck-out noon. Meeting rms. Free airport, bus depot transportation. Health club privileges. Game rm. Some refrigerators. Cr cds: A, C, D, DS, ER, MC, V, JCB.

Restaurants

★ ★ **BLUDAU'S GOETCHIUS HOUSE.** *405 Broadway. 706/324-4863.* Hrs: 5:30–9:45 pm; Fri, Sat to 10:45 pm. Closed Sun. Res accepted. Continental menu. Bar. Semi-a la carte: dinner $13.95–$32.95. Specializes in fresh seafood, veal. Parking. Outdoor dining. In restored antebellum mansion (1839). Cr cds: A, D, DS, MC, V.

✔ ★ **MALONE'S.** *2955 Warm Springs Rd. 706/324-3731.* Hrs: 11–2 am; Sun to midnight. Closed Thanksgiving, Dec 25. Mexican, Amer menu. Bar. Semi-a la carte: lunch $3.95–$6.95, dinner $6.95–$13.95. Child's meals. Specializes in fajitas, mesquite chicken, steak. Parking. Outdoor dining. Cr cds: A, MC, V.

★ **VILLA NOVA.** *2301 Airport Thruway. 706/323-4271.* Hrs: 5–10 pm; wkends to 10:30 pm. Closed some major hols. Italian, Amer menu. Bar 11–2 am. Semi-a la carte: lunch $3.25–$7.95, dinner $5.50–$17.95. Child's meals. Specializes in veal, seafood. Entertainment Wed–Sun. Parking. Cr cds: D, MC, V.

✔ ★ **WD CROWLEY'S.** *3111 Manchester Expy, in Peachtree Mall. 706/324-3463.* Hrs: 11:30 am–10 pm; Fri, Sat to 11 pm; Sun brunch noon–4 pm. Closed Jan 1, Thanksgiving, Dec 24, 25. Bar. Semi-a la carte: lunch $4.95–$7.95, dinner $9.95–$14.95. Sun brunch $4.95. Child's meals. Specializes in prime rib, Australian lobster tail. Cr cds: A, C, D, DS, MC, V.

Unrated Dining Spot

COUNTRY BBQ. *Jct Hamilton & Weems Rds, at Main Street Village. 706/660-1415.* Hrs: 11 am–10 pm; Fri, Sat to 11 pm. Closed some major hols. Res accepted. Semi-a la carte: lunch, dinner $6–$8. Child's meals. Specializes in barbecued chicken, ribs & beef. Outdoor dining. Western decor. Cr cds: MC, V.

Commerce (A-3)

Pop: 4,108 **Elev:** 931 ft **Area code:** 706 **Zip:** 30529

What to See and Do

Crawford W. Long Medical Museum. 10 mi SW via GA 15, on College St in Jefferson. Museum contains diorama of Dr. Long's first use of ether as an anesthetic in surgery, a enormous breakthrough in medicine. Also here are documents, artifacts and history of anesthesia exhibit. Entrance is in Jackson County Historical Society building, which has other exhibits on local history. A third building has an 1840s doctor's office, an apothecary shop and a 19th-century general store exhibit. (Daily exc Mon; closed legal hols) Donation. Phone 367-5307.

(See Athens, Gainesville)

Motels

✔ ★ ★ **HoJo INN.** *(Rte 1, Box 163-D) 3 mi N on US 441 at I-85. 706/335-5581.* 120 rms, 2 story. S $30–$45; D $45–$74; each addl $5; under 18 free. Crib free. Pet accepted. TV; cable. Pool; wading pool. Free full bkfst. Restaurant 6:30 am–9 pm. Ck-out 11 am. Cr cds: A, C, D, DS, ER, MC, V, JCB.

★ ★ **HOLIDAY INN.** *(Box 247) 3 mi N on US 441 at I-85. 706/335-5183; FAX 706/335-6588.* 120 rms, 2–3 story. S, D $46–$65; under 18 free; higher rates special events. Crib free. Pet accepted. TV. Pool;

wading pool. Restaurant 7 am–2 pm, 5:30–10 pm. Rm serv. Bar 5 pm–midnight. Ck-out noon. Coin lndry. Meeting rms. Bellhops. Cr cds: A, C, D, DS, MC, V.

Cordele (D-2)

Founded: 1888 **Pop:** 10,321 **Elev:** 319 ft **Area code:** 912 **Zip:** 31015

Watermelons, sweet potatoes, soybeans, pecans, cotton, peanuts, corn and cantaloupes are produced in Crisp County, of which Cordele is the seat. The local state farmers market sells more watermelons than any other market in the state; Cordele residents thus refer to their city as the "Watermelon Capital of the World." Garment making and the manufacture of enormous baling presses for scrap metals, agricultural implements, air conditioners, foundry products, mobile homes, livestock feed, fiberglass items, steel fittings and several other industries are locally important.

What to See and Do

Georgia Veterans Memorial State Park. 9 mi W via US 280. Swimming pool, waterskiing; fishing; boating; golf. Picnicking, concession. Camping, cabins. Museum; model airplane field with historic aircraft. Standard hrs, fees. Contact Park Manager, 2459-A Hwy 280 West; 276-2371.

(For further information contact the Chamber of Commerce, 302 E 16th Ave, PO Box 158; 273-1668.)

Annual Event

Watermelon Festival. Parade, beach party; watermelon-eating, seed-spitting and largest watermelon contests; fishing rodeo; Miss Heart of Georgia contest. Early–mid-July.

(See Albany, Perry)

Motels

★ **COMFORT INN.** *1601 16th Ave E, I-75 exit 33. 912/273-2371; FAX 912/273-2371, ext 300.* 59 rms, 2 story. Mid-June-Aug: S $46.88–$55.88; D $50.88–$60.88; each addl $5; suites $80–$95; under 18 free; wkend rates; lower rates rest of yr. Crib $5. TV; cable. Pool. Complimentary continental bkfst, coffee. Restaurant opp 6 am–11 pm. Ck-out 11 am. Meeting rm. Some refrigerators. Cr cds: A, C, D, DS, ER, MC, V, JCB.

★ **HOLIDAY INN.** *1711 16th Ave E, at jct US 280, I-75 exit 33. 912/273-4117; FAX 912/273-1344.* 187 rms, 2 story. S $48–$50; D $54–$56; each addl $6; under 18 free; golf plans. Crib free. TV; cable. Pool. Restaurant 6 am–10 pm. Rm serv. Beer, wine, setups. Ck-out noon. Meeting rms. Valet serv. Sundries. Cr cds: A, C, D, DS, MC, V, JCB.

✔ ★ **MASTERS INN.** *566 Farmers Market Rd, I-75 exit 35. 912/276-1008; res: 800/633-3434.* 120 rms, 2 story. S $23.95; D $26.95; under 12 free. TV; cable. Pool. Restaurant 6 am–9 pm. Ck-out noon. Cr cds: A, C, D, DS, MC, V.

Restaurants

★ ★ **DAPHNE LODGE.** *US 280 W. 912/273-2596.* Hrs: 6–10 pm. Closed Sun, Mon; Jan 1, Thanksgiving, Dec 25. Res accepted. Semi-a la carte: dinner $7.95–$18.95. Child's meals. Specializes in catfish, seafood, steak. Parking. Plantation manor house surrounded by pines. Cr cds: MC, V.

D

✔ ★**OLDE INN.** *US 280 W. 912/273-1229.* Hrs: 6–10 pm; Fri, Sat from 5:30 pm. Closed Sun, Mon; July 4, Thanksgiving, Dec 25. Setups. Wine, beer. Semi-a la carte: dinner $7.95–$14.75. Child's meals. Specializes in seafood, steak. Parking. Late 1800s building with original fireplace. Cr cds: A, MC, V.

Cumberland Island National Seashore (E-5)

(Off the coast, NE of St Marys)

Cumberland Island National Seashore, off the coast of Georgia, is an island 16 miles long and 1.5 to 3 miles wide. It is accessible by passenger tour boat, which operates year round. Mainland departures are from St Marys (fee); reservations by phone are necessary.

A visit to the island is a walking experience, and there are no restaurants or shops. The island's western side is fringed with salt marsh, and white sand beaches face the Atlantic Ocean. The interior is forested, primarily by live oak; interspersed are freshwater marshes and sloughs. Activities include viewing the scenery and wildlife, swimming and exploring historical areas led by a ranger. Indians, Spanish and English have all lived on the island; most structures date from the pre-Civil War plantation era, although there are turn-of-the-century buildings built by the Thomas Carnegie family. Camping; reservations by phone necessary. (Mid-Mar–Sept, daily; winter, Thurs–Mon; closed Dec 25) For further information contact the Superintendent, PO Box 806, St Marys 31558; 912/882-4335. Nearby is

Crooked River State Park. 3 mi W of St Marys on GA 40, then 8 mi N on GA 40 Spur. Swimming pool, water sports; fishing in coastal tidewaters; boating. Hiking. Picnicking. Camping, cottages. Contact Superintendent, 3092 GA Spur 40, St Marys 31558; 912/882-5256.

(For accommodations see Brunswick, Jekyll Island, St Simons Island)

Dahlonega (A-2)

Settled: 1833 **Pop:** 3,086 **Elev:** 1,454 ft **Area code:** 706 **Zip:** 30533

Gold fever struck this area in 1828, 20 years before California's Sutter's Mill discovery. Dahlonega, derived from the Cherokee for "yellow metal," yielded so much ore that the federal government established a local mint, which produced $6,115,569 in gold coins from 1838 to 1861. Dahlonega is the seat of Lumpkin County, where tourism, manufacturing, higher education and agri-business are the major sources of employment. A Ranger District office of the Chattahoochee National Forest is located in Dahlonega.

What to See and Do

1. **North Georgia College** (1873). (2,800 students) College Ave. Part of the state university system, North Georgia College's administration building, Price Memorial, was built on the foundation of the old US Branch Mint; unique gold steeple; display of gold coins minted in Dahlonega (Mon–Fri). Liberal arts and military college. Phone 864-1400.
2. **Dahlonega Courthouse Gold Museum State Historic Site.** On the Square, in old Lumpkin County Courthouse (1836). Exhibits on first major gold rush. Film shown every half-hour. (Daily; closed Jan 1, Thanksgiving, Dec 25) Contact Manager, Public Square, Box 2042; 864-2257. ¢

3. **Gold panning.**

   Crisson's Gold Mine. 2½ mi N via US 19 to end of Wimpy Mill Rd, then 1 mi E. Gold and gem panning; indoor panning (winter). Gift shop. (Daily; closed Dec 25) Phone 864-6363 or -7998. ¢

   Gold Miners' Camp. 2½ mi S via GA 60. Gold panning near the Chestatee River in an authentic mining setting. (May–Oct, daily) For further information contact the Chamber of Commerce.

4. **Chattahoochee National Forest.** This vast forest (748,608 acres) includes Georgia's Blue Ridge Mountains toward the north, which have elevations ranging from 1,000 to nearly 5,000 feet. Because the forest ranges from the Piedmont to mountainous areas, the Chattahoochee has a diversity of trees and wildlife. There are 25 developed camping areas, 24 picnicking areas, 10 wilderness areas and 6 swimming beaches. For the Chattahoochee-Oconee National Forest Recreation Area directory, contact the US Forest Service, 508 Oak St NW, Gainesville 30501; 536-0541. Camping and swimming fees at developed recreation sites. In the forest are

   Anna Ruby Falls. Off GA 356, 6 mi N of Helen. Approximately 1,570 acres surrounding a double waterfall, with drops of 50 and 153 feet. This scenic area is enhanced by laurel, wild azaleas, dogwood and rhododendron. Visitor center. Parking fee ¢

   Track Rock Gap. Off US 76, 8 mi SW of Young Harris. Well-preserved rock carvings of ancient Indian origin; figures resemble animal and bird tracks, crosses, circles and human footprints.

   Appalachian National Scenic Trail. Eleven lean-tos are maintained along the 79 miles marking southern portion of the trail. Following the crest of the Blue Ridge divide, the trail continues for 2,000 miles to Mount Katahdin, Maine.

   Cohutta Wilderness (see CHATSWORTH).

5. **Lake Winfield Scott.** 15 mi N on US 19, 129, then 4 mi SW on GA 180. A US Forest Service Recreation Area with an 18-acre lake in the Blue Ridge Mountains. Swimming, bathhouse; fishing. Picnicking. Campsites (fee). (May–Oct) Contact the Ranger District Office, Box 9, Blairsville 30512; 745-6928. Parking ¢

6. **Vogel State Park.** 25 mi N off US 19/129, S of Blairsville. Rugged area in the heart of north Georgia's mountains. At the foot of Blood and Slaughter mountains, 22-acre Lake Trahlyta has swimming, bathhouse; fishing. Picnicking, grills; playground. Camping, 36 furnished cabins. Standard hrs, fees. Contact Superintendent, 7485 Vogel State Park Rd, Blairsville 30512; 745-2628.

7. **Amicalola Falls State Park.** 20 mi W off GA 52. Highest waterfalls in state (729 ft). Trout fishing. Hiking trails. Picnicking, concession. Camping, cabins. For fee information, contact Superintendent, Star Rte, Box 215, Dawsonville 30534; 265-8888.

(For further information contact the Dahlonega-Lumpkin County Chamber of Commerce, 101 S Park St; 864-3711.)

Annual Event

Bluegrass Festival. Mountain music, arts & crafts. Phone 864-7203. Late June.

(See Gainesville)

Motel

★**DAYS INN.** *1065 S Chestatee St. 706/864-2338.* 41 rms, 2 story. Oct–Nov: S $61.50; D $65.50; each addl $5; under 12 free; wkend rates; higher rates: Wildflower, Gold Rush, Bluegrass festivals; lower rates rest of yr. Crib free. TV; cable. Pool. Complimentary continental bkfst, coffee. Restaurant nearby. Ck-out 11 am. Meeting rms. View of mountains. Cr cds: A, D, DS, MC, V.

Resort

★★**FORREST HILLS MOUNTAIN HIDEWAY.** *(Rte 3, Box 510) 12 mi W on GA 52, then right on Wesley Chapel Rd. 706/864-6456; res: 800/654-6313; FAX 706/864-0757.* 20 kit. cottages (1–4 bedrm). MAP: S, D $50–$189; under 18 free; wkly rates: Gold Rush, Memorial Day, July 4. TV; in-rm movies. Pool. Complimentary full bkfst. Complimentary coffee in rms. Dining rm 8:30–10:30 am, 6–8 pm. Ck-out noon, ck-in 3 pm. Grocery 4 mi. Coin lndry. Meeting rms. Maid serv bi-wkly. Gift shop. Tennis. Hiking. Game rm. Porches. Picnic tables. Grills. Surrounded by north Georgia mountain forest. Cr cds: A, DS, MC, V.

Restaurant

✔ ★**SMITH HOUSE.** *202 S Chestatee St. 706/864-3566.* Hrs: 11 am–3 pm, 4–7:30 pm; Fri & Sat 11 am–3 pm, 4:30–8:30 pm; Sun 11 am–7:30 pm; winter hrs vary. Closed Mon. Southern menu. Complete meals: lunch $9.40–$11.47, dinner $11.47–$12.30. Specializes in country cooking, fish, shrimp, chicken. Parking. Family-style dining in Blue Ridge Mountain tradition. Family-owned. Cr cds: A, DS, MC, V.

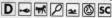

Dalton (A-1)

Founded: 1837 **Pop:** 21,761 **Elev:** 759 ft **Area code:** 706

Once a part of the Cherokee Nation, Dalton was involved in fierce battles and skirmishes in the Civil War as Union forces advanced on Atlanta. Today Dalton, "Carpet Capital of the World," has more than 100 carpet outlets and manufactures a large portion of the world's carpets. Dalton also produces other tufted textiles, chemicals, latex, thread and yarn.

What to See and Do

1. **Crown Garden and Archives.** 715 Chattanooga Ave, 2 mi N via I-75 and US 41, Walnut Ave exit. Headquarters of the Whitfield-Murray Historical Society. Genealogical library; changing exhibits include Civil War items; permanent exhibit on the history of bedspread tufting in the area. (Tues–Sat; closed Jan 1, wk of July 4, Thanksgiving, wk of Dec 25; also closed some Sats) Donation. Phone 278-0217.

2. **Chickamauga and Chattanooga National Military Park** (see). 23 mi N via I-75, GA 2, then 2 mi S via US 27.

(For further information contact the Convention and Visitors Bureau, PO Box 2046, 30722-2046; 272-7676.)

Annual Event

Prater's Mill Country Fair. 10 mi NE on GA 2. Arts & crafts show, food, late 1800s entertainment; canoeing on Coahulla Creek, pony rides, exhibits; 3-story gristmill in operation. Phone 275-6455. Mother's Day wkend & early Oct.

(See Calhoun; also see Chattanooga, TN)

Motels

✔ ★**BEST WESTERN.** *2106 Chattanooga Rd (30720), at I-75 Rocky Face exit. 706/226-5022; FAX 706/226-5022, ext 300.* 97 rms, 2 story. S $34; D $39; each addl $6; under 12 free. Crib $4. Pet accepted. TV; cable. Heated pool. Playground. Restaurant 6 am–9:30 pm. Rm serv. Bar 4 pm–midnight; entertainment, dancing Fri, Sat. Ck-out noon. Coin lndry. Meeting rms. Sundries. Airport, bus depot transportation. Cr cds: A, C, D, DS, MC, V.

★★**HOLIDAY INN.** *515 Holiday Dr (30720), I-75 exit 136. 706/278-0500; FAX 706/226-0279.* 199 rms, 2 story. S $59; D $64; under 17 free; wkend rates. Crib free. TV; cable. Pool; wading pool, poolside serv. Restaurant 6:30 am–1:30 pm, 5:30–10 pm. Rm serv. Bar 4:30 pm–midnight, closed Sun; entertainment, dancing. Ck-out 11 am. Coin lndry. Meeting rms. Valet serv. Exercise equipt; weight machine, bicycles. Cr cds: A, C, D, DS, MC, V, JCB.

✔ ★★**QUALITY INN.** *2107 Chattanooga Rd (30721), at I-75 exit 137. 706/278-1448; FAX 706/278-1448, ext 121.* 104 rms, 2 story. S $33.95–$39.95; D $45.95–$49.95; under 18 free. Crib $2. TV; cable. Pool; wading pool. Complimentary continental bkfst. Restaurant 5:30 am–9:30 pm. Rm serv. Bar 5 pm–midnight; dancing exc Sun. Ck-out 11 am. Meeting rms. Airport transportation. Picnic tables. Cr cds: A, C, D, DS, MC, V.

Darien (D-5)

Founded: 1736 **Pop:** 1,783 **Elev:** 20 ft **Area code:** 912 **Zip:** 31305

James Oglethorpe recruited Scots Highlanders to protect Georgia's frontier on the Altamaha River in 1736. Calling their town Darien, the Scots guarded Savannah from Spanish and Indian attack and carved out large plantations from the south Georgia wilderness. After 1800, Darien thrived as a great timber port until the early 20th century. Today, shrimp boats dock in the river over which Darien Scots once kept watch.

What to See and Do

1. **Fort King George State Historic Site** (1721). 1½ mi E of US 17 on Fort King George Dr. South Carolina scouts built this fort near an abandoned Indian village and Spanish mission to block Spanish and French expansion into Georgia, thereby establishing the foundation for the later English Colony of Georgia. The fort and its blockhouse have been entirely reconstructed to original form. Museum interprets the periods of Indian, Spanish and British occupations, the settlement of Darien and Georgia's timber industry. (Daily exc Mon; closed Thanksgiving, Dec 25) (See ANNUAL EVENT) Contact Superintendent, PO Box 711; 437-4770. ¢

2. **Hofwyl-Broadfield Plantation State Historic Site** (1807). 6 mi S on US 17. The evolution of this working rice plantation (1807–1973) is depicted through tours of the 1851 plantation house, museum and trails. Tours (daily exc Mon; closed Jan 1, Thanksgiving, Dec 25). Contact Manager, Rte 10, Box 83, Brunswick 31525; 264-9263. ¢

3. **Golden Isles** (see). SE off US 17.

Annual Event

Blessing of the Shrimp Fleet. At Darien Bridge. Tours of Fort King George site (see #1). Phone 437-4770. Apr or May.

(For accommodations see Brunswick, Jekyll Island, St Simons Island, Sea Island)

Douglas (D-3)

Founded: 1858 **Pop:** 10,464 **Elev:** 259 ft **Area code:** 912 **Zip:** 31533

The town's central location between I-75 and I-95 has helped Douglas develop into a leading trade and distribution center for the southeast. A number of Fortune 500 companies operate within Coffee County.

What to See and Do

General Coffee State Park. 6 mi E on GA 32. A 1,490-acre park on the Seventeen-Mile River in Coffee County. Swimming pool; fishing. Nature trails. Picnicking, playgrounds. Camping. Standard hrs, fees. Contact Manager, Rte 2, Box 83, Nichols 31554; 384-7082.

(For further information contact the Chamber of Commerce, 404 N Peterson Ave, PO Box 1607; 384-1873.)

Motels

 ★ **DAYS INN.** *907 N Peterson Ave.* *912/384-5190.* 70 rms, 2 story. S, D $32–$38; each addl $5; under 12 free. Crib free. Pet accepted. TV; cable. Pool. Complimentary coffee. Restaurant adj 6 am–midnight. Ck-out noon. Cr cds: A, C, D, DS, MC, V.

★★ **SHONEY'S INN.** *1009 N Peterson Ave.* *912/384-2621; FAX 912/384-2621, ext 304.* 100 rms, 2 story. June–Aug: S $33–$38; D $37–$41; each addl $5; lower rates rest of yr. Crib $2. Pet accepted. TV; cable. Pool. Restaurant 6 am–midnight. Rm serv 9 am–9 pm. Bar 5 pm–2 am; entertainment, dancing Fri, Sat. Ck-out noon. Meeting rms. Grills. Cr cds: A, C, D, DS, MC, V.

Dublin (C-3)

Pop: 16,312 **Elev:** 228 ft **Area code:** 912 **Zip:** 31021

The seat of Laurens County, Dublin sits on land once occupied by Creek Indians. Area industries manufacture a wide range of goods, including textiles, carpeting, missile control systems and computer components. The first aluminum extrusion plant in the US is located here. Agricultural products include soybeans, wheat, grain, peanuts, corn, cotton and tobacco.

What to See and Do

1. **Historic buildings.** Greek-revival and Victorian houses can be found along Bellevue Avenue.
2. **Dublin-Laurens Museum.** Bellevue and Academy at Church. Local history museum featuring Native American artifacts, art, textiles and relics from early settlers. (Tues–Fri; closed Jan 1, Thanksgiving, Dec 25) Phone 272-9242. **Free.**
3. **Fish Trap Cut.** Oconee River, GA 19. Believed to have been built between 1000 B.C. and A.D. 1500, this large rectangular mound, smaller round mound and canal may have been used as an aboriginal fish trap.

(For further information contact the Dublin-Laurens County Chamber of Commerce, PO Box 818; 272-5546.)

Annual Event

St Patrick's Festival. Includes parade, ball, contests, softball and golf tournaments, arts & crafts show, square dancing and entertainment. 2 wks mid-Mar.

Motel

✔ ★★ **HOLIDAY INN.** *(Box 768) 3 mi S on US 319/441 at jct I-16.* *912/272-7862; FAX 912/272-1077.* 184 rms, 2 story. S $39–$48; D $43–$52; each addl $4; suites $73–$77; under 18 free; wkly, wkend rates. Crib free. Pet accepted. TV; cable. Pool. Restaurant 6:30 am–10

pm. Rm serv. Bar 5 pm–1 am; entertainment. Ck-out noon. Meeting rms. Valet serv. Cr cds: A, C, D, DS, MC, V, JCB.

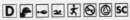

Eatonton (B-3)

Pop: 4,737 **Elev:** 575 ft **Area code:** 706 **Zip:** 31024

In the early 19th century large tracts of land in this area were acquired and put under cultivation; by the mid-1800s the town of Eatonton had become a center of planter culture, that archetypal romantic concept of cotton fields, mansions, wealth and southern grace. Joel Chandler Harris was born in Eatonton in 1848. In creating the character "Uncle Remus" to retell the "Br'er Rabbit" and "Br'er Fox" folk tales heard on the plantation, he successfully immortalized the traditional ways of the Old South.

Eatonton is also the hometown of Alice Walker, author of *The Color Purple,* which may prove to be a classic depiction of the South of a different time. Eatonton, the seat of Putnam County, is known as the largest dairy producer in the state.

What to See and Do

1. **Uncle Remus Museum.** 3 blks S of courthouse on US 441 in Turner Park. Log cabin made from two original slave cabins. Reconstruction of cabin fireplace; shadow boxes with illustrations of 12 tales; mementos of era, first editions; diorama of old plantation; other relics. (June–Aug, daily; rest of yr, daily exc Tues) Phone 485-6856. ¢
2. **Bronson House** (1822). 114 N Madison Ave. Greek-revival mansion purchased in 1985 by Eatonton-Putnam Historical Society to serve as its headquarters. Several rooms have been restored; display of local memorabilia. (By appt only) Phone 485-6442. ¢
3. **Rock Eagle Effigy.** 7 mi N on US 441, located in Rock Eagle 4-H Center. This 8-foot-high mound of milky white quartz is shaped like a great prone bird, wings spread, head turned eastward, 102 feet from head to tail and 120 feet wingtip to wingtip. Archaeologists estimate the monument is more than 5,000 years old and was probably used by aboriginal Indians for religious ceremonies. It may be viewed from an observation tower. Phone 485-2831. **Free.**
4. **Lake Oconee.** E on GA 16 & N on GA 44 (see MADISON). Lawrence Shoals Recreation Area. **Lake Sinclair.** S on US 441 (see MILLEDGEVILLE). Both Georgia Power Co projects created by the impoundment of the Oconee River.
5. **Indian Springs State Park** (see). 35 mi W via GA 16 to Jackson, then 5 mi SE on GA 42.

(For further information contact the Eatonton-Putnam Chamber of Commerce, 105 Sumter St, PO Box 4088; 485-7701.)

Annual Event

Putnam County Dairy Festival. Parade, dairy and farming-related contests, arts & crafts fair, entertainment. 1st Sat June.

(For accommodations see Madison, Milledgeville)

Forsyth (C-2)

Pop: 4,268 **Elev:** 705 ft **Area code:** 912 **Zip:** 31029

What to See and Do

1. **Jarrell Plantation State Historic Site.** 18 mi E of I-75 exit 60 on GA 18E, then N on Jarrell Plantation Rd. Authentic plantation with 20 historic buildings dating from 1847–1940. Plain-style plantation house, sawmill, grist mill, blacksmith shop, farm animals. Seasonal demonstrations. (Daily exc Mon; closed Jan 1, Thanksgiving, Dec 25) Phone 986-5172. ¢

2. **Indian Springs State Park** (see). 17 mi N on GA 42.

(For further information contact the Monroe County Chamber of Commerce, PO Box 811; 994-9239.)

(See Macon)

Motels

✔ ★ ★**BEST WESTERN INN-HILLTOP.** *At jct I-75, exit 63 & GA 42. 912/994-9260; FAX 912/994-9260, ext 101.* 120 rms, 2 story. S $30–$40; D $40–$50; each addl $6; under 12 free. Crib $6. TV; cable, in-rm movies. Pool; wading pool. Restaurant 5:30–9 pm. Ck-out noon. Cr cds: A, C, D, DS, ER, MC, V, JCB.

★★**HAMPTON INN.** *520 Holiday Circle, at I-75 exit 61. 912/994-9697; FAX 912/994-9697, ext 140.* 124 rms, 4 story. S $38–$43; D $41–$48; under 18 free. Crib free. Pet accepted. TV; cable. Pool. Complimentary continental bkfst. Ck-out noon. Meeting rm. Health club privileges. Cr cds: A, C, D, DS, MC, V.

★★**HOLIDAY INN.** *480 Holiday Circle, at I-75 exit 61, Tift College Dr & Juliette Rd. 912/994-5691; FAX 912/994-3254.* 120 rms, 2 story. S, D $39–$56; each addl $5; family rates. Crib free. TV; cable. Pool; wading pool. Restaurant 6 am–10 pm. Rm serv. Bar 4 pm–midnight, closed Sun. Ck-out noon. Coin lndry. Meeting rms. Exercise equipt; weights, bicycles. Game rm. Chapel on premises. Cr cds: A, C, D, DS, ER, MC, V, JCB.

Restaurant

✔ ★**HONG KONG PALACE.** *465 Tift College Dr. 912/994-0973.* Hrs: 11 am–10 pm; Fri to 10:30 pm; Sat 4:30–10:30 pm; Sun noon–9 pm. Closed July 4, Thanksgiving, Dec 25. Chinese menu. Wine, beer. Semi-a la carte: lunch $2.95–$4.25, dinner $4.95–$7.75. Child's meals. Cr cds: DS, MC, V.

Fort Frederica National Monument (D-5)

(12 mi NE of Brunswick via St Simons/Sea Island Causeway-toll)

Fort Frederica was one of the largest and most expensive forts ever built by the British in North America. It was carefully planned by the Trustees in London in 1736 and included the town of Frederica.

Having picked the site of the fort on a bluff commanding the Frederica River, General James Oglethorpe returned to England and helped select families to build and settle it. Forty-four men and 72 women and children landed at St Simons Island on March 16, 1736. In 1738 a regiment of 650 British soldiers arrived. The fort was then strengthened with "tabby" (a kind of cement made of lime, oyster shells,

sand and water) and the whole town was enclosed with earth and timber works from 10 to 13 feet high that included towers and a moat.

Oglethorpe used Fort Frederica as a command post for his invasion of Florida. He built other forts on St Simons and other islands and attacked Spanish outposts to the south. In July, 1742, Spaniards launched an attack on Fort Frederica, but Oglethorpe repulsed this with an ambush at Bloody Marsh, ending Spanish attempts to gain control of Georgia.

Frederica flourished as a military town until after the peace of 1748. With the withdrawal of the regiment the following year, the shopkeepers and tradesman at Frederica had to move elsewhere. The town did not long survive these losses. Archaeological excavations have exposed some of it and stabilization work has been done by the National Park Service. Outdoor exhibits make it easy to visualize the town as it was, and the visitor center has exhibits and a film dealing with its life and history. Self-guided audio tour (fee). (Daily; closed Dec 25) Contact the Superintendent, Rte 9, Box 286-C, St Simons Island 31522; 912/638-3639. Golden Age Passport (see INTRODUCTION). Entrance per vehicle ¢¢

(For accommodations see Brunswick, Jekyll Island, St Simons Island, Sea Island)

Fort McAllister Historic Park (D-5)

(25 mi S of Savannah, via GA 144 from I-95 or US 17; 10 mi E of Richmond Hill off US 17)

This Confederate fort, built for the defense of Savannah, stands on the left bank of the Great Ogeechee River, commanding the river's mouth. Fort McAllister's fall on December 13, 1864, marked the end of Sherman's march to the sea, opening communications between the Union Army and the fleet and rendering further defense of Savannah hopeless.

Prior to this, McAllister had proved that its type of massive earthwork fortifications could stand up against the heaviest naval ordnance. It protected the blockade-running ship *Nashville* from pursuit by Union gunboats in July and November, 1862. It successfully resisted the attacks of *Monitor*-type ironclads of the Union Navy in 1863. The USS *Montauk* shelled the fort with the heaviest shells ever fired by a naval vessel against a shore work up to that time. The fort sustained only one casualty. There were huge holes in its parapets, but the damage was minor. Its gun emplacements were separated by large "traverses," several used to house powder magazines. The fort that seemed to be "carved out of solid earth" was termed "a truly formidable work" by a Union naval officer in 1864. General Sherman called the capture of the fort and overpowering its garrison ". . .the handsomest thing I have seen in this war." Union losses were 24 killed, 110 wounded (mostly by mines outside the fort); the Confederate garrison of 230 men had 70 casualties—16 killed and 54 wounded—in the 15-minute battle.

The earthworks have been restored to approximate conditions of 1863–64. A museum containing mementos of the *Nashville* and the fort was completed in 1963 and opened on the centennial of the great bombardment. (Daily exc Mon; closed Thanksgiving, Dec 25; fee) Fort McAllister has a campground and day-use facilities; boating (ramps, dock). For further information contact the Superintendent, Box 394-A, Richmond Hill 31324; 912/727-2339.

(For accommodations see Savannah)

Fort Pulaski National Monument (D-5)

(15 mi E of Savannah off US 80)

A unit of the Department of the Interior's National Park Service, Fort Pulaski National Monument was established by President Coolidge in 1924. The site, named in honor of Revolutionary war hero Casimir Pulaski, commemorates an international turning point in the history of fortification and artillery. It was here, on April 11, 1862, that newly developed rifled cannons easily overtook a masonry fortification. After centuries of use throughout the world, both masonry forts and smooth-bore cannons were obsolete.

Most visitors begin the tour at the visitor center, which contains a small museum describing the significance of the the fort; the fort's place in the evolution of seacoast fortification and ordnance; and the fort's restoration during the 1930s. The center also has an information desk and a bookstore featuring more than 300 items on the Civil War and other site-related and regional subjects.

Restored to its mid-19th-century appearance, the fort contains several rooms, or casemates, depicting garrison life during its Confederate (1861–62) and Union (1862–1875) occupations. This exhibit includes an officer's quarters and mess, medical dispensary, chapel, quartermaster's office, supply room and enlisted men's quarters. Other displays include several examples of smooth-bore and rifled artillery and carriages. While self-guided tours are available year-round, ranger conducted programs and demonstrations are presented daily in the summer and on weekends the rest of the year.

There are three major trails in the monument. The nature trail is a quarter-mile paved loop through several historic sites. The picnic trail is a half-mile paved trail from the visitor center to the picnic and recreation area, which borders the vast salt marshes and forested hammocks of the Savannah River estuary. The third trail follows the historic dike originally surveyed by Robert E. Lee. A walk on any segment of the trail provides excellent opportunities to see a wide variety of plants and wildlife, as well as scenic views of the fort.

Fishing, boating and other water-related activities are offered at the park. The north channel shoreline and the bridge approaches at the south channel are the best fishing locations. A boat ramp and fishing dock just off US 80 at Lazaretto Creek provide more opportunities for fishing.

All facilities are open daily except Dec 25. Contact Superintendent, PO Box 30757, Savannah 31410; 912/786-5787. Entrance fee per person ¢

(For accommodations see Savannah)

Gainesville (A-2)

Pop: 17,885 **Elev:** 1,249 ft **Area code:** 404

On the shore of 38,000-acre Lake Sidney Lanier, Gainesville is a poultry producing and marketing center with a variety of industries. It is also the headquarters for the Chattahoochee National Forest (see DAHLONEGA). Contact the Forest Supervisor, US Forest Service, 508 Oak St, 30501; 536-0541.

What to See and Do

1. **Brenau University** (1878). (2,000 students) 1 Centennial Circle. Liberal arts residential college for women with coed evening and weekend programs; off-campus, graduate and undergraduate divisions. On campus is Brenau Academy, a four-year preparatory high school for girls. Pearce Auditorium (1897) has fine acoustics, stained glass windows and ceiling frescoes. Trustee Library has displays of American art. Phone 534-6299.
2. **Lake Lanier Islands.** W edge of town (see BUFORD).
3. **Green Street Historical District.** A broad street with Victorian and classical-revival houses dating from the late 19th and early 20th centuries. Here is

Green Street Station. Home of Georgia Mountains Historical and Cultural Trust. Houses historical and arts and crafts exhibits of northeast Georgia as well as the Mark Trail Memorial Exhibit. (Tues–Sat; closed major hols) Phone 536-0889. **Free.**

(For further information contact the Gainesville/Hall County Convention & Visitors Bureau, 830 Green St, 30501; 536-5209.)

Seasonal Event

Auto Racing. Road Atlanta. 8 mi S via GA 53. Sports car and motorcycle racing. Also street-driving and road racing training programs. Phone 967-6143. Mar–Nov.

(See Buford, Dahlonega)

Motel

★ ★ **HOLIDAY INN.** *726 Jesse Jewell Pkwy (30501).* 404/536-4451. 185 rms, 2–3 story. S $54–$60; D $59–$64; each addl $5; under 19 free. Crib free. Pet accepted. TV; cable. Pool. Restaurant 6 am–10 pm. Rm serv. Bar; dancing. Ck-out noon. Coin lndry. Meeting rms. Bellhops. Valet serv. Free RR station, bus depot transportation. Lighted tennis. Cr cds: A, C, D, DS, MC, V, JCB.

Motor Hotel

★ ★ ★ **RAMADA INN-LANIER CENTRE.** *400 E.E. Butler Pkwy (30501).* 404/531-0907; FAX 404/531-0788. 123 rms, 4 story. S $64–$85; D $66–$85; under 18 free; golf plans. Crib free. TV; cable. Pool; whirlpool, poolside serv. Restaurant 6:30 am–9:30 pm. Rm serv. Bar 4:30–10 pm; Fri & Sat to 11 pm. Ck-out noon. Meeting rms. Valet serv. Sundries. Free RR station, bus depot transportation. Lighted tennis privileges. 18-hole golf privileges, greens fee $40, pro, putting green, driving range. Health club privileges. Cr cds: A, C, D, DS, MC, V.

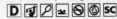

Inn

★ ★ ★ **DUNLAP HOUSE.** *635 Green St (30501).* 404/536-0200. 9 rms, 2 story. S $75–$105; D $85–$115; wkends, hols (2-night min). Closed 1st wk Jan. TV; cable. Complimentary continental bkfst. Complimentary coffee in rms. Restaurant opp 11:30 am–2:30 pm, 5:30–10 pm. Ck-out noon, ck-in 3 pm. Bellhops. Concierge. Library/sitting rm. Built 1910. Totally nonsmoking. Cr cds: A, MC, V.

Restaurants

★ ★ **POOR RICHARD'S.** *1702 Park Hill Dr.* 404/532-0499. Hrs: 11 am–3 pm, 5–10 pm; Fri to 11 pm; Sat 5–11 pm. Closed Sun; most major hols. Res accepted Mon–Thurs. Bar 4:30 pm–midnight. Semi-a la carte: lunch $2.95–$7.95, dinner $5.95–$36.95. Complete meals: dinner $9.95–$17.95. Child's meals. Specializes in prime rib, steaks, seafood. Parking. Cr cds: A, MC, V.

✔ ★ ★ ★ **RUDOLPH'S.** *700 Green St.* 404/534-2226. Hrs: 11:30 am–2:30 pm, 5:30–10 pm; Fri to 11 pm; Sat 5:30–11 pm; early-bird dinner Mon–Thurs 5:30–7 pm. Closed most major hols. Res accepted. Bar. Wine list. Semi-a la carte: lunch $3.95–$7.95, dinner $10.95–$17.95. Child's meals. Specializes in steak Rudolph, fresh seafood. Own baking. Parking. In restored historic residence (1915). Cr cds: A, DS, MC, V.

Golden Isles (D-5)

This chain of lush, subtropical islands stretches from Savannah south to Brunswick. Best known of the group are Sea Island (see), St Simons Island (see) and Jekyll Island (see), all of which may be reached by road. Others are Cumberland, Little St Simons, Ossabaw, St Catherine's and Sapelo, reached only by water.

Indians hunted on these islands for giant turtles, waterfowl, deer and other animals. Spaniards established a chain of missions, which existed for about a century, the largest on St Simons. The French made half-hearted efforts to settle on the islands. James Oglethorpe built Fort Frederica (see) on St Simons in 1736 and later defeated Spanish forces attempting to recapture the island.

Now the islands are resort areas, offering beautiful scenery, swimming, a wide variety of sports facilities and accomodations.

(For accommodations see Brunswick, Jekyll Island, St Simons Island, Sea Island)

Helen (A-2)

Pop: 300 **Elev:** 1,446 ft **Area code:** 706 **Zip:** 30545

The natural setting of the mountains and the Chattahoochee River helped create the atmosphere for this logging town, transformed into a charming alpine village. Helen was reborn in 1969 when the citizens, with the help of a local artist, decided to improve the town's appearance.

The result is the relaxed atmosphere of a small Bavarian town. Quaint cobblestone streets, gift shops with an international flavor, craftsmen, restaurants and festivals—a bit of the Old World in the heart of the mountains of northeast Georgia.

What To See and Do

1. **Museum of the Hills & Fantasy Kingdom.** Main St, in The Castle complex. Authentic reconstruction of rural and village lifestyle in North Georgia at the turn of the century. (Daily; closed Dec 25) Sr citizen rate. Phone 878-3140. ¢¢

2. **Stovall Covered Bridge over Chickamauga Creek.** 7 mi E on GA 255. The smallest covered bridge in Georgia.

3. **Richard B. Russell Scenic Highway.** 5 mi N of Helen. Highway winds around mountainsides, offering spectacular scenic views.

4. **Nacoochee Indian Mound.** 1 mi SE on GA 17. Located in former center of the Cherokee Nation.

5. **Babyland General Hospital.** 19 Underwood St, 9 mi SW via GA 75N, on US 129 in Cleveland. Authentic turn-of-the-century hospital, home of the original "Cabbage Patch Kids"—soft-sculptured "babies" created by artist Xavier Roberts. (Daily; closed Dec 24 & most hols) Phone 865-2171. **Free.**

6. **Anna Ruby Falls.** In Chattahoochee National Forest (see DAHLONEGA).

7. **Unicoi State Park.** 2 mi NE on GA 356. A 1,081-acre park adjacent to Anna Ruby Falls. Swimming beach; fishing; paddleboat (rentals), canoeing (rentals). Nature and hiking trails. Picnicking. Camping, cottages; lodge/conference center (see MOTELS), restaurant, craft shop. Programs on natural resources, folk culture. Standard hrs, fees. Contact Director of Sales, PO Box 849; 878-2201.

(For further information contact the Greater Helen Area Convention & Visitors Bureau, Chattahoochee St, PO Box 730; 878-2181.)

Annual Events

Volksmarch. Bavarian walk in the forest. 3rd wkend Apr.

Mayfest in the Mountains. 1st wkend May.

Hot Air Balloon Race & Festival. 1st wkend June.

Seasonal Events

Fasching Karnival. German Mardi Gras. Jan–Feb.

Oktoberfest. German music & beer festival; one of the longest running Oktoberfests in the country. Sept–Oct.

(See Toccoa)

Motels

★★**COMFORT INN.** *Edelweiss St.* 706/878-8000; *FAX* 404/458-5384. 60 rms, 2 story, 30 suites. Mid-Sept–Oct: S $64–$84; D $69–$89; each addl $5; suites $79–$99; under 18 free; higher rates special events; lower rates rest of yr. Crib $5. TV; cable. Pool. Complimentary continental bkfst, coffee. Restaurant nearby. Ck-out 11 am. Meeting rms. Refrigerator in suites. Cr cds: A, C, D, DS, ER, MC, V, JCB.

★**HEIDI.** *(Box 507) Main St, 4 blks W of town center.* 706/878-2689. 9 rms, 2 story. Sept–Oct (2-day min): S $50–$58; D $80–$85; each addl $5; under 12 free; lower rates rest of yr. TV; cable. Pool. Restaurant nearby. Ck-out 11 am. Cr cds: A, DS, MC, V.

✔★★**UNICOI STATE PARK LODGE.** *Unicoi State Park, 2 mi NE on GA 356.* 706/878-2201; *FAX* 706/878-1897. 100 rms, 2–3 story, 30 kit. cottages. Apr–Nov: S $50; D $56; each addl $6; under 12 free; kit. cottages $40–$70 (2-night min; 1-wk min June–Aug); lower rates rest of yr. Parking $2. TV (exc cottages); in-rm movies avail. Coffee in rms. Restaurant 7 am–8 pm. Ck-out 11 am. Meeting rms. Sundries. Game rm. Access to all facilities of state park. Lighted tennis. Early reservations recommended. Cr cds: A, D, DS, MC, V.

Restaurant

★★**HOFBRAUHAUS.** *1 Main St.* 706/878-2248. Hrs: 11 am–3 pm, 5–10 pm; Fri, Sat to 10:30 pm. Closed Sun; Dec 24, 25. Res accepted. Continental menu. Bar 3 pm–midnight. A la carte entrees: lunch $5–$10, dinner $7.95–$19.50. Child's meals. Specializes in prime rib, veal, seafood. Parking. German decor. Cr cds: A, C, D, DS, MC, V.

Hiawassee (A-2)

Pop: 547 **Elev:** 1,980 ft **Area code:** 706 **Zip:** 30546

A picturesque mountain town in the heart of Georgia's "Little Switzerland," Hiawassee is on Lake Chatuge, surrounded by Chattahoochee National Forest (see DAHLONEGA). Its backdrop is a range of the Blue Ridge Mountains, topped by Brasstown Bald Mt, Georgia's highest peak. Rock hunting, including hunting for the highly prized amethyst crystal, is a favorite activity in surrounding Towns County. Mountaineers of North Georgia gather from 26 surrounding counties to participate in a fair, the rule of which is "everybody can bring something."

What to See and Do

1. **Lake Chatuge.** W edge of town. This approximately 7,000-acre TVA lake provides fishing, boating. Camping.

2. **Brasstown Bald Mountain–Visitor Information Center.** S on GA 17, 75, then W on GA 180, then N on GA 180 spur. At 4,784 feet, this is Georgia's highest peak. Observation deck affords a view of four

states. Visitor Center has interpretive programs presented in mountain-top theater and exhibit hall. Parking/shuttle fee. (June–Oct, daily; late Apr–May, wkends only, weather permitting) Phone 896-2556 or 745-6928 (USDA). **Free.**

Annual Events

Georgia Mountain Fair. Individual accomplishment and ''friendlier living'' is theme of gathering of mountain farm people; arts & crafts, farm produce, flowers, minerals, Indian relics; board splitting, soap and hominy making, quilting; general store, still, farm museum, midway, music hall; entertainment, parade. Camping, beach and tennis courts at Georgia Mountain Fairgrounds and Towns County Recreation Park. Phone 896-4191. 12 days early Aug.

Fall Celebration. At the fairgrounds. Phone 896-4191. Nine days early Oct.

(See Clayton)

Motel

★ ★ ★**FIELDSTONE INN.** *(PO Box 670) 3 mi W on US 76. 706/896-2262.* 66 rms, 2 story. Apr–Nov: S $68–$73; D $75–$80; each addl $7; under 14 free; lower rates rest of yr. Crib $7. TV; cable. Pool. Playground. Complimentary coffee in lobby. Restaurant adj 7 am–3 pm, 5–9 pm; Fri & Sat to 10 pm. Ck-out 11 am. Meeting rm. Street parking. Lighted tennis. Lawn games. Patios, balconies. Picnic tables. On Lake Chatuge. Cr cds: A, MC, V.

Lodge

✔ ★**SALALE.** *(Rte 1, Box 36) 1½ mi S on US 76E. 706/896-3943.* 4 rms, 2 story. July–Oct: S $29–$69; D $34–$74; each addl $5; under 12 free; higher rates: country music season, fall foliage; lower rates rest of yr. Pet accepted, some restrictions. TV; cable. Restaurant nearby. Ck-out 11 am. Refrigerators. On lake; swimming. Cr cds: A, DS, MC, V.

Indian Springs State Park (C-2)

(5 mi SE of Jackson on GA 42)

Called ''the oldest state park in the United States,'' this was originally a gathering place for Creek Indians, who valued sulphur springs for curative powers. General William McIntosh, a Creek, headed the Indian encampment in this area in 1800. In 1821, McIntosh signed a treaty ceding most of the Creek lands between the Flint and Ocmulgee rivers and north to the Chattahoochee. In 1825, he relinquished the rest of the Creek land in Georgia.

The state disposed of all Native American lands except 10 acres called Indian Springs Reserve. Butts County citizens bought an adjoining 513 acres, donating it to the state for a park with a mineral spring, a 105-acre lake and a museum (summer only). Swimming beach; fishing, boating (rentals). Nature trails. Picnicking. Camping, cottages. Standard hrs, fees. Contact Superintendent, Rte 1, Box 439, Flovilla 30216-9715; 404/775-7241.

Jekyll Island (E-5)

Pop: 1500 (est) **Elev:** 5 ft **Area code:** 912

Connected to the mainland by a causeway, Jekyll Island, the smallest of Georgia's coastal islands (see GOLDEN ISLES) with 5,600 acres of highlands and 10,000 acres of marshland, was favored by Indians for hunting and fishing. Spanish missionaries arrived in the late 16th and early 17th centuries and established a mission. In 1734, during an expedition southward, General James Oglethorpe passed by the island and named it for his friend and financial supporter, Sir Joseph Jekyll. Later, William Horton, one of Oglethorpe's officers, established a plantation on the island.

Horton's land grant passed to several owners before the island was sold to Christophe du Bignon, a Frenchman who was escaping the French Revolution. It remained in the du Bignon family as a plantation for almost a century. In 1858, the slave ship *Wanderer* arrived at the island and unloaded the last major cargo of slaves ever to land in the United States. In 1886, John Eugene du Bignon sold the island to a group of wealthy businessmen from the northeast, who formed the Jekyll Island Club.

Club members who wintered at Jekyll in exclusive privacy from early January to early April included J.P. Morgan, William Rockefeller, Edwin Gould, Joseph Pulitzer and R.T. Crane, Jr. Some built fabulous ''cottages,'' many of which are still standing. But by World War II, the club had been abandoned for economic and social reasons, and in 1947 the island was sold to the state. The Jekyll Island Authority was created to conserve beaches and manage the island while maintaining it as a year-round resort.

What to See and Do

1. **Jekyll Island Club Historic District.** Once one of the nation's most exclusive resorts, this restored district is a memorable example of turn-of-the-century wealth. Exhibition buildings and shops are open daily (closed Jan 1, Dec 25). Tours are available (daily, fee; tickets, information at the museum orientation center, the former Jekyll Island Club stables) for Mistletoe Cottage (1900), Indian Mound (or Rockefeller) Cottage (1892), du Bignon Cottage (1884) and the Faith Chapel (1904). Period rooms and changing exhibits can be viewed in several houses.

2. **Horton House.** NW side of Island. Ruins of former house (1742) of William Horton, sent from St Simons as captain by General James Oglethorpe. On Jekyll he established an outpost and plantation. Horton became major of all British forces at Fort Frederica after Oglethorpe's return to England. This house was later occupied by the du Bignon family as part of their plantation.

3. **Summer Waves.** 210 S Riverview Dr. Eleven-acre water park featuring wave pool, two triple-drop slides, serpentine slides, tubing river, children's pool; picnicking, concessions. (Late May–early Sept, daily) Sr citizen rates. Phone 635-2074. ¢¢¢

4. **Public facilities.** Beachfront bathhouses; cable water skiing; pier fishing; charter boats for offshore and inlet fishing and also sightseeing cruises. Bicycle trails, rentals; golf, driving range; miniature golf; 13 clay tennis courts, pro shop. Picnicking on east shore; shopping center. Camping at north end. Some fees.

5. **Cumberland Island National Seashore** (see). S, off the coast.

(For further information contact the Jekyll Island Authority, PO Box 3186, 31527; 635-3636 or 800/841-6586.)

Annual Events

Country by the Sea Music Festival. Top country music stars perform on Jekyll's Beach. Early June.

Beach Music Festival. Famous beach music groups perform all afternoon. Mid-Aug.

(See Brunswick, Golden Isles, St Simons Island, Sea Island)

Motel

★★COMFORT INN ISLAND SUITES. 711 Beachview Dr (31520). 912/635-2211; FAX 912/635-2381. 180 suites, 2 story, 78 kits. Mid-May–mid-Aug: S, D $89–$155; each addl $16; kits. $135; under 16 free; wkly rates; lower rates rest of yr. Crib $4. TV; cable, in-rm movies. Pool; wading pool, whirlpools. Playground. Complimentary full bkfst. Restaurant open 24 hrs. Coin lndry. Meeting rms. Sundries. Local airport transportation. Golf privileges at 3 courses, pro, putting green, driving range. Refrigerators; some in-rm whirlpools. Private patios, balconies. On ocean. Cr cds: A, C, D, DS, ER, MC, V, JCB.

D ⊢ 🖋 🏊 🚭 Ⓜ SC

Motor Hotels

★★CLARION RESORT BUCCANEER. 85 S Beachview Dr (31520). 912/635-2261; FAX 912/635-3230. 206 rms. 2–4 story, 64 kits. Early May–mid-Aug: S, D $99–$149; each addl $10; kit. units $125–$175; under 19 free; wkly rates; lower rates rest of yr. Crib $4. TV; cable. Pool; wading pool, poolside serv (in season). Playground. Supervised child's activities. Restaurant 6:30 am–10 pm. Rm serv. Bar 5 pm–1 am; entertainment exc Sun. Ck-out 11 am. Coin lndry. Meeting rms. Bellhops. Sundries. Tennis. 18-hole golf privileges, pro, putting green. Game rm. Lawn games. Many refrigerators. Private patios, balconies. Beachfront. *LUXURY LEVEL: CONCIERGE LEVEL.* 8 rms. S, D $185. Concierge. Private lounge, honor bar. Complimentary continental bkfst, refreshments. Cr cds: A, C, D, DS, ER, MC, V, JCB.

D ⊢ 🖋 🏊 🚭 Ⓜ SC

✔★★★HOLIDAY INN BEACH RESORT. 200 S Beachview Dr (31527). 912/635-3311; FAX 912/635-2901. 205 units, 2–4 story, 18 kits. S, D $49–$99; each addl $8; suites $109–$259; kit. units $69–$119; under 18 free. Crib free. Pet accepted; $8. TV; cable. Pool; wading pool, poolside serv (in season). Playground. Restaurant 7 am–2 pm, 5:30–10 pm. Rm serv. Bar 5 pm–1 am; entertainment, dancing exc Sun. Ck-out 11 am. Free lndry facilities. Meeting rms. Bellhops. Valet serv. Sundries. Tennis. Sailboats in season. Bicycles. Some in-rm saunas & whirlpools. Private patios, balconies. On beach. Cr cds: A, C, D, DS, ER, MC, V, JCB.

D ⊢ 🏊 🚭 Ⓜ SC

Resorts

★★BEST WESTERN-JEKYLL INN. 975 N Beachview Dr (31527). 912/635-2531; FAX 912/635-2332. 262 rms, 1–2 story, 74 kit. units. May–Aug: S, D $85–$99; each addl $5; suites, kit. units $99–$149; under 12 free; wkly rates; golf, honeymoon plans avail. Crib free. Pet accepted; $20. TV; cable. Pool; wading pool, poolside serv. Playground. Dining rms 7 am–9:30 pm. Snack bar. Bars 4–10 pm, Sat from noon; entertainment, dancing Tues–Sat (in season). Ck-out 11 am, ck-in 4 pm. Coin lndry. Grocery, package store 2 mi. Convention facilities. Valet serv. Lighted tennis privileges, pro. 63-hole golf privileges, pro, putting green, driving range. Swimming beach. Bicycle rentals; trails nearby. Lawn games. Health club privileges. Balconies. Picnic tables. Cr cds: A, C, D, DS, MC, V.

D 🐾 ⊢ 🖋 🏊 🏃 🚭 Ⓜ SC

★★★JEKYLL ISLAND CLUB HOTEL, A RADISSON RESORT. 371 Riverview Dr (31527). 912/635-2600; FAX 912/635-2818. 134 units, 4 story, 15 suites. Early Mar–Labor Day: S, D $99–$125; each addl $20; suites $139–$229; under 18 free; MAP, AP, golf, tennis plans; lower rates rest of yr. Crib free. TV; cable, in-rm movies. Heated pool; poolside serv. Supervised child's activities (Memorial Day–Labor Day). Dining rm 7 am–2 pm, 6–10 pm (also see GRAND DINING ROOM). Bar 4 pm–midnight; pianist. Ck-out noon, ck-in 4 pm. Meeting rms. Concierge. Shopping arcade. Valet parking. Airport transportation avail. 9 tennis courts, 1 indoor & 8 lighted. Three par 72 18-hole golf courses & one 9-hole course, greens fee $24, cart $23, pro, putting green, driving range. Marina; deep sea and sport fishing. Swimming beach. Bicycle rentals;

croquet. Rec dir. Game rm. Extensive grounds; elaborate landscaping. Originally founded as an exclusive retreat for members of high society; historic club house (1887) has been restored to its former splendor, combining turn-of-the-century charm with modern convenience. Cr cds: A, C, D, DS, ER, MC, V, JCB.

D ⊢ 🖋 🏊 🚭 Ⓜ SC

★★VILLAS BY THE SEA. 1175 N Beachview Dr (31527). 912/635-2521; res: 800/841-6262 (exc GA), 800/342-6872 (GA); FAX 912/635-2569. 166 kit. villas, 1–2 story. Late Mar–early Sept: 1-bedrm $99–$119, 2-bedrm $119–$144, 3-bedrm $144–$169; wkly: 1-bedrm $594–$714, 2-bedrm $714–$864; 3-bedrm $864–$1,014; family rates; wkend, tennis, golf, honeymoon plans avail; lower rates rest of yr. Crib free. Pet accepted; $40. TV; cable. Pool; hot tub, wading pool, poolside serv. Playground. Dining rm 7 am–2 pm, 5–10 pm. Bar 5 pm–1 am. Ck-out 11 am, ck-in 4 pm. Grocery 3 mi. Coin lndry. Package store 3 mi. Convention facilities. Gift shop. Lighted tennis privileges, pro. Golf privileges, pro, putting green. Bicycle rentals. Private beach. Some fireplaces. Private patios, balconies. Picnic tables, grills. On 17 acres. Cr cds: A, C, D, DS, MC, V.

D 🐾 ⊢ 🖋 🏊 🚭 Ⓜ SC

Restaurants

★★BLACKBEARD'S. 200 N Beachview Dr. 912/635-3522. Hrs: 11 am–10 pm. Closed Dec 25. Bar. Semi-a la carte: lunch $3.50–$10.95, dinner $9.95–$25.95. Child's meals. Specializes in coastal seafood, steak. Parking. Outdoor dining. Nautical decor. Ocean view. Cr cds: DS, MC, V.

D

★★GRAND DINING ROOM. (See Jekyll Island Club Resort) 912/635-2600. Hrs: 7 am–2 pm, 6–10 pm; Sun brunch 10:45 am–2 pm. Res accepted. Bar. Wine list. Semi-a la carte: bkfst $5.50–$9.95, lunch $6.95–$12.95, dinner $14.95–$29.95. Sun brunch $16.95. Child's meals. Specializes in fresh seafood, steak, baked Alaska. Own baking. Pianist, strolling guitarist. Valet parking. White pillared fireplace, crystal wall lamps. Jacket (dinner). Cr cds: A, C, D, DS, ER, MC, V, JCB.

D

✔★JEKYLL WHARF. 1 Pier Rd. 912/635-3800. Hrs: 11 am–10 pm. Closed Sun; some major hols. Res accepted. Bar. Semi-a la carte: lunch $4.95–$6.95, dinner $9.95–$16.95. Child's meals. Specializes in seafood, smoked prime rib. Parking. Outdoor dining. Dining aboard restored boat house overlooking intracoastal waterway. Cr cds: DS, MC, V.

✔★ZACHRY'S. 44 Beachview Dr. 912/635-3128. Hrs: 8 am–9 pm; Sun to 8 pm; winter to 8 pm. Closed Thanksgiving, Dec 25. Wine, beer. Semi-a la carte: bkfst 95¢–$6.95, lunch, dinner $1.75–$13.95. Child's meals. Specializes in fresh seafood, chicken, steak. Salad bar. Cr cds: MC, V.

D

Kennesaw Mountain National Battlefield Park (B-2)

(Approx 3 mi NW of Marietta off US 41 or I-75 exit 116)

At Kennesaw Mountain in June of 1864, General William Tecumseh Sherman executed the last of a series of flanking maneuvers that were started 100 miles to the north on May 7. The Battle of Kennesaw Mountain stalled but did not halt General Sherman's invasion of Georgia. Kennesaw Mountain National Battlefield Park commemorates the 1864 Atlanta campaign.

In a series of flanking maneuvers and minor battles in May and June, Sherman's 100,000-man Union Army forced the 65,000-man Confederate army, under the command of General Joseph E. Johnston, back from Dalton to the vicinity of Kennesaw Mountain, 20 miles north of Atlanta. On June 19, Johnston took position and dug in, anchoring his right flank on the steep mountain slopes and extending his left flank several miles to the south. He trusted that strong fortifications and rugged terrain would make up for the disparity in numbers.

The Confederates abandoned their positions after a heavy day's fighting and occupied strong points between Kennesaw and Lost mountains. Sherman first tried to march around to an area just south of the Confederate position, but Johnston shifted 11,000 troops to counter the maneuver. In fierce fighting at Kolb's Farm on June 22, Confederate attacks were repulsed, but Sherman was temporarily stymied.

Although the Confederate entrenchments seemed strong, Sherman suspected that they were weakly held. A sharp frontal attack, he decided, might break through and destroy Johnston's entire army. On the morning of June 27, after a heavy artillery bombardment, Sherman struck the Confederate line at two places simultaneously. At Pigeon Hill, 5,500 attackers were quickly driven under cover by sheets of Southern bullets. Two miles to the south, 8,000 Union infantrymen stormed up Cheatham Hill and for a few minutes engaged the Confederates in hand-to-hand combat on top of their earthworks. Casualties were so severe that the location was nicknamed "Dead Angle." By noon both attacks had failed. Sherman had lost 3,000 men, Johnston only 500.

Sherman reverted to his flanking strategy, and on July 2 the Confederates withdrew, eventually to Atlanta. The siege and fall of Atlanta soon followed. Sherman then began his devastating "March to the Sea."

The Visitor Center, on Old US 41 and Stilesboro Rd, north of Kennesaw Mountain, has exhibits, an audiovisual program and information (daily; closed Dec 25). A road leads to the top of Kennesaw Mountain (daily: Mon–Fri, drive or walk; Sat & Sun, bus leaves every ½ hr between the months of Feb and Nov, or walk—no driving). (The Cheatham Hill area, in the south-central section of the park, has the same hours as the Kennesaw Mountain road; closed Dec 25).

Park (daily; closed Dec 25). Self-guided tours. For additional information contact Park Ranger, 900 Kennesaw Mountain Dr, Kennesaw 30144-4854; 404/427-4686. **Free.**

La Grange (C-1)

Pop: 25,597 **Elev:** 772 ft **Area code:** 706 **Zip:** 30240

La Grange is said to be the only town in the Confederacy that organized its own female military company. Legend has it that La Grange was so loyal to the Confederacy that every man marched off to battle. A women's home guard was named for Nancy Hart, Revolutionary heroine. When the defenseless city was about to be invaded by Wilson's Raiders, the Nancy Harts marched out to the fray. The Union colonel, named La Grange, was so affected by this female defense that he marched on without burning the city.

What to See and Do

1. **Bellevue** (1852–53). Ben Hill St. Greek-revival house of US Senator Benjamin Harvey Hill; period furnishings. (Tues–Sat; closed hols) Phone 884-1832. **¢¢**
2. **Chattahoochee Valley Art Museum.** 112 Hines St. Art museum housed in remodeled 1800s jail. Changing exhibits by local, national and international artists. (Daily exc Mon; closed major hols) Phone 882-3267. **Free.**

3. **West Point Lake.** W on GA 109. Approximately 26,000 acres with 525 miles of shoreline. Swimming; fishing, hunting; boating. Camping (fee). Phone 645-2937.

(For further information contact the Troup County Chamber of Commerce, 224 Main St, Box 636, 30241-0636; 884-8671.)

(See Pine Mountain)

Motel

✔ ★**LA GRANGE INN.** *1601 Lafayette Pkwy.* 706/882-9540; FAX 706/882-3929. 101 rms, 2 story. Mar–Sept: S $40–$45; D $45–$50; each addl $5; under 16 free; lower rates rest of yr. Crib free. TV; cable. Pool. Complimentary continental bkfst, coffee. Restaurant nearby. Ckout 11 am. Meeting rms. Health club privileges. Cr cds: A, C, D, DS, ER, MC, V.

Restaurant

★ ★ ★**IN CLOVER.** *205 Broad St.* 706/882-0883. Hrs: 11:30 am–2 pm, 6–10 pm. Closed some major hols. Res accepted Mon–Sat. Bar. Semi-a la carte: lunch $6.50–$12.95, dinner $13.50–$21.95. Child's meals. Specializes in prime beef, seafood. Own baking, desserts. Parking. In restored Victorian house (1892); many engravings, antiques. Cr cds: A, C, D, MC, V.

Lumpkin (D-1)

Pop: 1,250 **Elev:** 593 ft **Area code:** 912 **Zip:** 31815

What to See and Do

1. **Westville.** Living history village featuring buildings circa 1850; decorative arts and work skills of early Georgia. Demonstrations by craftsworkers include quilting, weaving, candlemaking, potterymaking, blacksmithing, and basket weaving; syrup making in season. (Daily exc Mon; closed some major hols; also early Jan) Sr citizen rate. Phone 838-6310. **¢¢¢**
2. **Providence Canyon State Conservation Park.** 7 mi W via GA 39C. Georgia's "Little Grand Canyon" has spectacular erosion gullies up to 150 feet deep. Hiking. Picnicking. Interpretive center (daily). Standard hrs, fees. Contact Superintendent, Rte 1, Box 158; 838-6202.
3. **Lake Walter F. George.** Approx 18 mi W via GA 39C or approx 30 mi SW via GA 27. This 45,000-acre lake, stretching south along the border of Georgia and Alabama, was created by damming the Chattahoochee River. Fishing is good for bass, bream, crappie and catfish, and the lake's 640-mile shoreline provides countless hidden coves and inlets. Phone 768-2516. Various state parks are situated on the lake's border including

   Florence Marina State Park. More than 140 acres at the northern end of Lake Walter F. George. Swimming pool; fishing; boating, johnboat rentals (fee). 18-hole miniature golf (fee); tennis. Camping, cottages. Contact Manager, Rte 1, Box 36, Omaha 31821; 838-4244.

Annual Events

Westville events. Westville (see #1) has many varied events throughout the year. Of special interest are the Spring Festival (early Apr), the May Day celebration (early May), Independence Day (July 4), "Fair of 1850" (late Oct–early Nov) and a variety of Christmas activities (Dec).

(For accommodations see Americus, Columbus; also see Eufaula, AL)

Macon (C-3)

Founded: 1823 **Pop:** 106,612 **Elev:** 325 ft **Area code:** 912

Macon began as a trading post. It served as a fort and rallying point for troops in the War of 1812; later it became a river landing for shipping to the seacoast by oar-propelled flat-bottom boats; then Macon became a major regional cotton market. Having launched *The Pioneer*, a forerunner of all Southern river steamers, Macon was not content to remain just a port. In 1838 a railroad linked Macon with Forsyth; five years later it was connected by rail to Savannah. In 1848, a third line, the Southwestern, connected Macon with the fertile southwest section of the state. The town had become a major railroad center.

Macon's role in the Civil War was to manufacture and distribute quartermaster supplies and ordnance. Harnesses, small weapons, cannon and shot were produced, and the city harbored $1.5 million in Confederate gold. In 1864 refugees poured in from devastated north Georgia. In July and November, Union forces were twice repulsed. The city finally surrendered to Wilson's Raiders in April, 1865.

Sidney Lanier was born and lived here, practicing law before turning to poetry. Macon is also the hometown of rock 'n' roll singer Little Richard.

What to See and Do

1. **City Hall** (1836). 700 Poplar St. Main entrance of classical-revival building is flanked by panels depicting history of Macon area. Building was state capitol Nov 18, 1864–Mar 11, 1865, during the last session of the Georgia General Assembly under the Confederate States of America. Tours. (Mon–Fri; closed hols) Phone 751-7170. **Free.**

2. **Macon Museum of Arts and Sciences & Mark Smith Planetarium.** 4182 Forsyth Rd. Three galleries with permanent and changing art and science exhibits; displays of live amphibians, birds, reptiles and small mammals; nature trails; observatory. Planetarium shows. (Daily) Phone 477-3232. Some fees; **free** Mon, Fri evenings.

3. **Harriet Tubman Museum.** 340 Walnut St. Features African American art, African artifacts and traveling exhibits on the history and culture of African American people. Resource center, workshops and tours (by appt). (Daily exc Sun) Phone 743-8544. **Free.**

4. **Woodruff House** (ca 1836). Greek-revival mansion with massive columns on three sides; owned and operated by Mercer University (see #9). Tours (by appt only). Phone 752-2715. **¢**

5. **Sidney Lanier Cottage** (1840). 935 High St. Gothic-revival house was birthplace of the nationally known poet; period furnishings. Headquarters of Middle Georgia Historical Society. (Daily exc Sun; closed hols) Phone 743-3851. **¢¢**

6. **Old Cannonball House & Macon-Confederate Museum** (1853). 856 Mulberry St. Greek-revival house struck by Union cannonball in 1864. Museum contains Civil War relics and Macon historical items. (Daily; closed Jan 1, Thanksgiving; also Dec 24–31) Sr citizen rate. Phone 745-5982. **¢¢**

7. **Hay House** (1855–59). 934 Georgia Ave. An Italian Renaissance-revival villa with 24 rooms; elaborate ornamental plaster, woodwork, stained glass; ornate period furnishings and objets d'art. (Daily; closed major hols) Phone 742-8155. **¢¢¢**

8. **Macon Historic District.** Downtown. District comprises nearly all of old Macon; 48 buildings and houses have been cited for architectural excellence and listed on National Register of Historic Places; an additional 575 structures have been noted for architectural significance. Walking and driving tours noted on Heritage Tour Markers. For tour maps contact the Convention & Visitors Bureau.

9. **Mercer University** (1833). (6,100 students) 1400 Coleman Ave. Founded as Mercer Institute in Penfield, moved to Macon in 1871.

Liberal arts, business, law, engineering and medicine are offered at Macon campus; also campus in Atlanta. Phone 752-2715.

10. **Wesleyan College** (1836). (500 women) 4760 Forsyth Rd, on US 41. This four-year liberal arts college was chartered to grant degrees to women. Campus tours by appt. Phone 477-1110.

11. **Grand Opera House.** 651 Mulberry St. Originally the Academy of Music (1884), theater was restored in 1970. Tours (exc when stage is in use). (Mon–Fri; closed hols) Phone 749-6580. **¢**

12. **Sightseeing tours.**

    Heart of Georgia Tours. Operated by the Middle Georgia Historical Society, 935 High St (see #5). Guides available for private tours of city or for bus tours. Phone 743-3851.

    Sidney's Old South Historic Tours. 200 Cherry St. Operated by the Macon-Bibb County Convention & Visitors Bureau. Examples of Greek-revival architecture, Victorian cottages, Italianate mansions, antebellum houses; statues, monuments, other landmarks left standing by General Sherman on his march to the sea. (Daily exc Sun; no tours some major hols) Phone 743-3401 or 800/768-3401. **¢¢¢**

13. **Lake Tobesofkee.** 3 mi W via I-475, exit GA 74. A 1,750-acre lake and a 650-acre park. Swimming, waterskiing; fishing; boating (launch). Nature trails; tennis. Picnicking. Camping (hookups). (Daily) Phone 474-8770. Fee for some activities. General admission **¢¢**

14. **Ocmulgee National Monument** (see). 2 mi E on US 80, Alt 129.

(For further information contact the Macon–Bibb County Convention & Visitors Bureau, located in the Terminal Station, 200 Cherry St, PO Box 6354, 31208, phone 743-3401 or 800/768-3401.)

Annual Events

Cherry Blossom Festival. Historic tours, concerts, fireworks, hot air balloons, sporting events, parade. Phone 751-7429. Mid-Mar.

Georgia State Fair. Central City Park. Grandstand shows, midway, exhibit buildings. Phone 746-7184. 3rd wk Oct.

Motels

★ ★ **COMFORT INN NORTH.** 2690 Riverside Dr (31204), I-75 exit 54. 912/746-8855; FAX 912/746-8881. 120 rms, 3 story. June–Dec: S $48; D $51; each addl $7; under 18 free; higher rates Cherry Blossom Festival; lower rates rest of yr. Crib free. TV; cable. Pool. Complimentary continental bkfst 6:30–9 am. Bar 4–10 pm. Ck-out noon. Meeting rms. Some refrigerators. Cr cds: A, C, D, DS, ER, MC, V, JCB.

D ⊠ Ⓧ Ⓞ SC

★ ★ **COURTYARD BY MARRIOTT.** 3990 Sheraton Dr (31210). 912/477-8899; FAX 912/477-4684. 108 rms, 3 story. S $67; D $77; suites $87; wkend rates; higher rates Cherry Blossom Festival. Crib free. TV; cable. Pool. Complimentary coffee in rms. Restaurant 6:30–10 am, 6–9 pm; wkends 7 am–noon, 5–9 pm. Rm serv 6–9 pm. Bar 5–10 pm. Ck-out noon. Meeting rm. Valet serv. Airport transportation avail. Exercise equipt; weights, bicycles, whirlpool. Some refrigerators; minibar in suites. Balconies. Picnic tables. Cr cds: A, C, D, DS, MC, V.

D ⊠ ✦ Ⓧ Ⓞ SC

✔ ★ ★ **HAMPTON INN.** 3680 Riverside Dr (31210), I-75 exit 55A. 912/471-0660; FAX 912/471-2528. 151 rms, 2 story. S $41–$47; D $45–$51; under 18 free. Crib free. Pet accepted. TV; cable. Pool. Complimentary continental bkfst. Ck-out noon. Valet serv. Cr cds: A, C, D, DS, MC, V.

D 🐾 ⊠ Ⓧ Ⓞ SC

✔ ★ **RODEWAY INN.** 4999 Eisenhower Pkwy (31206), I-475 exit 1. 912/781-4343; FAX 912/784-8140. 56 rms, 2 story. S $32–$35; D $35–$39; each addl $4; under 18 free; higher rates Cherry Blossom Festival. Crib $4. Pet accepted. TV; cable; in-rm movies avail. Pool.

Complimentary continental bkfst. Restaurant nearby. Ck-out 11 am. Some refrigerators. Cr cds: A, C, D, DS, MC, V.

Motor Hotel

✔ ★★QUALITY INN-NORTH. *(PO Box 7006, 31298) 2720 Riverside Dr, I-75 exit 54.* 912/743-1482. 87 rms, 6 story. S $30–$35; D $38; each addl $5; under 18 free. Crib free. Pet accepted. TV; cable. Pool. Complimentary continental bkfst. Ck-out 11 am. Meeting rms. Valet serv. Cr cds: A, C, D, DS, ER, MC, V.

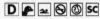

Hotel

★★RADISSON INN-MACON. *108 1st St (31202).* 912/746-1461; FAX 912/746-1461, ext 2560. 306 units, 16 story. S $65; D $75; each addl $10; suites $145–$185; under 18 free. Crib free. TV; cable. Pool. Restaurants 7 am–10 pm. Bar 11–2 am; entertainment. Ck-out noon. Convention facilities. Shopping arcade. Free garage parking. Airport transportation. Tennis, golf privileges. Exercise equipt; weights, bicycles. Some balconies. Cr cds: A, C, D, DS, MC, V.

Inn

★★★1842 INN. *353 College St (31201).* 912/741-1842; res: 800/336-1842; FAX 912/741-1842, ext 41. 21 rms, 2 story. S $65–$95; D $75–$105; each addl $10. Children over 10 yrs only. TV; cable. Complimentary continental bkfst, coffee & tea. Restaurant nearby. Serv bar 8 am–midnight. Ck-out 11 am, ck-in 3 pm. Valet serv. Some in-rm whirlpools. Restored Greek-revival antebellum house (1842). Rms individually decorated & named; fireplaces; antiques. Victorian cottage adj. Cr cds: A, MC, V.

Restaurants

★★★BEALL'S 1860. *315 College St.* 912/745-3663. Hrs: 11 am–2:30 pm, 5–10 pm; Sat from 5 pm. Closed Sun; some major hols. Res accepted. Bar. Semi-a la carte: lunch $3.25–$9.95, dinner $9.95–$21.95. Child's meals. Specializes in prime rib, chicken, seafood. Salad bar. Own baking. Parking. Restored Southern mansion (1860). Cr cds: A, C, D, DS, MC, V.

✔ ★★GREEN JACKET. *325 5th St.* 912/746-4680. Hrs: 11 am–3 pm, 5–10 pm; Fri to 11 pm; Sat 5–11 pm; Sunday buffet 11:30 am–3 pm, 5–10 pm. Closed July 4, Dec 25. Res accepted. Bar 4–7 pm. Semi-a la carte: lunch $3.95–$7.95, dinner $8.50–$17.95. Buffet: Sun $7.95. Child's meals. Specializes in prime rib, seafood, chicken. Salad bar. Parking. Golf motif. Cr cds: A, MC, V.

★★NATALIA'S. *2720 Riverside Dr.* 912/741-1380. Hrs: 6 pm–2 am. Closed Sun; some major hols. Res accepted. Northern Italian menu. Bar. Semi-a la carte: dinner $13.75–$19. Specializes in lamb chops, fish in parchment. Parking. Antiques. Paintings, photographs on display. Cr cds: A, D, MC, V.

★★STEAK AND ALE. *3086 Riverside Dr, I-75 exit 54.* 912/477-1728 or -1729. Hrs: 11 am–2 pm, 5–10 pm; Fri to 11 pm; Sat 4–11 pm; Sun noon–10 pm. Res accepted. Bar. Semi-a la carte: lunch $4.95–$10, dinner $7.95–$17.95. Child's meals. Specializes in prime rib, grilled steak, fish. Salad bar. Parking. Old English decor. Cr cds: A, C, D, DS, MC, V.

Madison (B-3)

Pop: 3,483 **Elev:** 667 ft **Area code:** 706 **Zip:** 30650

General Sherman spared Madison on his Civil War march to the sea. The result is a contemporary city with a wealth of well-preserved antebellum and Victorian residences. Several movies have been filmed in the town to take advantage of the 19th-century atmosphere.

What to See and Do

1. **Madison-Morgan Cultural Center.** 434 S Main St. Romanesque-revival school building (1895) with art galleries, restored schoolroom, museum of local history, original auditorium and ongoing schedule of performances. (Daily exc Mon; closed major hols) Phone 342-4743. ¢
2. **Lake Oconee.** E on I-20. Approximately 19,000-acre lake with 374 miles of shoreline was created by the impoundment of the Oconee River. Beach swimming; fishing; boating, marinas. Picnicking. Camping. For further information phone 485-8704. Some fees at recreation areas. Parking ¢

(For further information contact the Chamber of Commerce, 115 E Jefferson, PO Box 826; 342-4454.)

Annual Event

Spring Tour of Homes. Historic houses, scenic gardens, period furnishings and antiques. Phone 342-4454. Sat in May.

(See Athens, Eatonton)

Motels

★★BEST WESTERN-WHITE COLUMNS INN. *(10130 Alcovy Rd, Covington 30209) 20 mi W on I-20, exit 45A.* 404/786-5800; FAX 404/786-5880. 93 air-cooled rms, 2 story. S $40; D $40–$44; each addl $4; under 12 free. Crib $4. Pet accepted, some restrictions. TV; cable. Complimentary continental bkfst. Restaurant adj open 24 hrs. Ck-out 11 am. Meeting rm. Health club privileges. Cr cds: A, C, D, DS, MC, V.

✔ ★DAYS INN. *2001 Eatonton Hwy, 2 mi S at jct US 129/441, I-20.* 706/342-1839; FAX 706/342-1839, ext 100. 77 rms, 2 story. S $31.95–$35.95; D $38.95–$49.95; each addl $5; under 12 free. Crib free. Pet accepted; $10. TV; cable. Pool; wading pool. Playground. Restaurant (see DAVIS BROS CAFETERIA, Unrated Dining). Ck-out noon. Cr cds: A, C, D, DS, MC, V.

Inns

★★BRADY. *250 N Second St.* 706/342-4400. 7 rms. No rm phones. S $65; D $85; suite $85. TV in sitting rm; cable. Complimentary full bkfst. Restaurant nearby. Ck-out noon, ck-in 6 pm. Restored Victorian cottage in historic downtown. Cr cds: MC, V.

★★BURNETT PLACE. *317 Old Post Rd.* 706/342-4034. 3 rms, 2 story. S $60; D $75; each addl $10. TV. Complimentary full bkfst, tea/sherry. Restaurant nearby. Ck-out 11 am, ck-in 3 pm. Picnic tables, grills. Federal-style house (ca 1830) typical of the Piedmont region. Cr cds: MC, V.

Unrated Dining Spot

DAVIS BROS CAFETERIA. *(See Days Inn Motel)* 706/342-1440. Hrs: 6:30 am–8:30 pm; May–Sept to 9 pm. Avg ck: bkfst $3, lunch $5, dinner $7. Child's meals. Specializes in Southern cooking. Own desserts. Parking. No cr cds accepted.

Marietta (B-2)

Founded: 1834 **Pop:** 44,129 **Elev:** 1,128 ft **Area code:** 404

What to See and Do

1. **Kennesaw Mountain National Battlefield Park** (see). Approx 3 mi NW off US 41 or I-75, follow signs.
2. **White Water.** Marietta Pkwy. Water theme park with 40 rides; body flumes, rapids ride, wave pool, float. (Memorial Day–Labor Day, daily; May, wkends) Phone 424-WAVE. ¢¢¢¢¢ Adj is

   American Adventures. Children's amusement park with over a dozen rides. (Daily; closed some major hols) Fee for various activities. Phone 424-6683. Parking. ¢
3. **Big Shanty Museum.** 6 mi N via US 41 or I-75 to exit 118, at 2829 Cherokee St in Kennesaw. The L & N steam locomotive *General*, permanently housed here, was taken from this spot in 1862 by Union raiders in an attempt to cut Confederate supply lines. The raiders were chased and captured by the train crew. Includes exhibits and video about the raid. (Daily; closed major hols) Phone 427-2117 or 800/742-6897. ¢¢

(For further information contact the Cobb County Convention & Visitors Bureau, Box COBB, 30067-0033; 859-2345. Welcome centers are located at 4 Depot St, phone 429-1115; and at I-75N exit 120, phone 974-7626.)

Annual Event

BellSouth Golf Classic. Atlanta Country Club, Atlanta Country Club Dr. PGA Tour event. Phone 951-8777. Early May.

(See Atlanta, Norcross)

Motels

 ★BEST INNS OF AMERICA. *1255 Franklin Rd (30067). 404/955-0004; res: 800/237-8466; FAX 404/955-0004, ext 345.* 113 rms, 3 story. S $36–$45; D $38–$48; under 18 free. Crib free. TV; cable. Pool. Complimentary coffee in lobby. Restaurant nearby. Ck-out 1 pm. Meeting rms. Cr cds: A, C, D, DS, MC, V.

★★HAMPTON INN. *455 Franklin Rd (30067). 404/425-9977; FAX 404/425-9977, ext 116.* 140 rms, 4 story. S $49–$53; D $57–$60; under 18 free. Crib free. TV; cable. Pool; wading pool. Complimentary continental bkfst, coffee. Restaurant nearby. Ck-out noon. Meeting rm. Valet serv. Cr cds: A, C, D, DS, ER, MC, V, JCB.

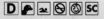

★★LA QUINTA. *2170 Delk Rd (30067). I-75 N Delk Rd exit 111. 404/951-0026; FAX 404/952-5372.* 130 rms, 3 story. S $49; D $55; each addl $6; under 18 free. Crib free. Pet accepted. TV; cable. Pool. Complimentary continental bkfst, coffee. Restaurant adj 6 am–10 pm; wkends to 11 pm. Ck-out noon. Meeting rms. Valet serv. Cr cds: A, C, D, DS, MC, V.

Motor Hotel

★★★SHERATON INN-ATLANTA NORTHWEST. *1775 Parkway Place (30067), I-75 exit 112. 404/428-4400; FAX 404/428-5756.* 219 rms, 10 story. S $85; each addl $10; suites $125–$175; under 17 free; wkend rates. Crib free. TV; cable; B/W in bathrm. Pool. Restaurant 6:30 am–10 pm. Rm serv. Bar 11–2 am, Sun noon–midnight. Ck-out noon. Meeting rms. Bellhops. Valet serv. Some refrigerators. Some balconies. Cr cds: A, C, D, DS, ER, MC, V.

Restaurants

★★★1848 HOUSE. *780 S Cobb Dr. 404/427-4646.* Hrs: 6 pm–closing. Closed Sun; major hols. Res accepted. Bar from 5:30 pm. Wine cellar. A la carte entrees: dinner $12.50–$32.50. Complete meals: dinner $22.50–$42.50. Child's meals. Specializes in seafood, filet mignon, rack of lamb. Own baking. Pianist Mon, Wed, Fri–Sat. Valet parking. Greek-revival plantation house completed in 1848; 13 landscaped acres. Cr cds: A, C, D, DS, MC, V.

✔★★LA STRADA. *2930 Johnson Ferry Rd NE. 404/640-7008.* Hrs: 5–10 pm; Fri, Sat 4:30–11 pm. Closed most major hols. Italian menu. Bar. Semi-a la carte: dinner $7.95–$14.25. Child's meals. Specializes in stuffed shrimp, Fra Diavolo, soft shell crab, tiramisu dessert. Parking. Cr cds: A, C, D, DS, MC, V.

★★SHILLING'S ON THE SQUARE. *19 North Park Square. 404/428-9520.* Hrs: 11 am–midnight; Sun brunch to 3 pm. Closed Jan 1, Dec 25. Res accepted. Bar to 2 am. Semi-a la carte: lunch $4–$10, dinner $11–$20. Sun brunch $3–$6. Specializes in Angus beef, fresh seafood. Pianist. Parking. Tavern decor; century-old wood bar, stained glass panels, tin ceiling. Cr cds: A, C, D, DS, MC, V.

Milledgeville (C-3)

Founded: 1803 **Pop:** 17,727 **Elev:** 335 ft **Area code:** 912 **Zip:** 31061

Milledgeville was laid out to be the state capital and served in that capacity from 1804 through 1868. When the state records were transferred to Milledgeville from Louisville in 1807, wagons were escorted by troops of cavalry from Washington, DC.

Milledgeville's houses typify the development of Southern architecture; the earliest structures had small stoops; houses of the next period had two porches, one above the other; with the third period, the two-story columns become Greek porticos, the second story, a balcony. Later, porches became broad, multi-columned verandas, extending across the front and even around to the sides and back of the house.

What to See and Do

1. **Georgia College** (1889). (5,500 students) 231 W Hancock St. Occupies one of four twenty-acre plots "reserved for public use" when the city was laid out. The Museum and Archives of Georgia Education is located on campus. Phone 453-5350. Also located on campus is

   Old Governor's Mansion. 120 S Clark St. Greek-revival residence of Georgia governors from 1839 to 1868. Guided tours. (Tues–Sat, also Sun afternoons; closed hols, Thanksgiving wkend, wk of Dec 25) Phone 453-4545. ¢¢
2. **Lake Sinclair.** N on US 441, GA 24. This 15,330-acre lake with 417 miles of shoreline was created by the impoundment of the Oconee River. Fishing; boating, marinas. Camping. Phone 706/485-8704.
3. **Historic Guided Trolley Tour.** Includes stops at Governor's Mansion, Stetson-Sanford House. Tour departs from Dept of Tourism

& Trade office, 200 W Hancock. The office also has information on walking tours. Trolley tour (Tues & Fri mornings). ¢¢¢

(For further information contact the Dept of Tourism & Trade, 200 W Hancock St, Box 219, phone 452-4687 or 800/653-1804 Mon–Fri; a Welcome Center, open daily, is located in lobby.)

Annual Events

Old Capital Spring Event. Includes street dance, arts & crafts, cultural and sports events. Apr–May.

Browns Crossing Craftsmen Fair. 9 mi W via GA 22. Features original works, including paintings, weavings, pottery, woodcarvings, graphics. Phone 452-9327. 3rd wkend Oct.

(See Eatonton, Macon)

Motels

★ ★ **HOLIDAY INN.** US 441 N, approx 4 mi N. 912/452-3502; FAX 912/453-3591. 169 rms, 2 story. S $47–$52; D $52–$57; each addl $5; suites $125; under 18 free; wkend rates. Crib free. TV; cable. Pool; wading pool. Restaurant 6 am–2 pm, 5:30–10 pm. Rm serv. Bar. Ck-out noon. Meeting rms. Valet serv. Wet bar, whirlpool in some suites. Cr cds: A, C, D, DS, MC, V, JCB.

D ⊛ ⊗ ⊚ SC

✔ ★ ★ **JAMESON INN.** 2551 N Columbia St. 912/453-8471; res: 800/541-3268. 100 rms, 2 story, 2 kit. units. S $41–$45; D $45–$48; each addl $4; suites $85–$125; under 14 free. Crib $5. TV; cable. Pool; wading pool. Complimentary continental bkfst. Restaurant 11 am–2 pm, 5:30–9 pm. Ck-out 11 am. Meeting rms. Lighted tennis. Exercise equipt; weight machine, bicycles, whirlpool, sauna. Cr cds: A, D, DS, MC, V.

D ⤢ ⊛ ⊼ ⊗ ⊚ SC

Norcross *

Pop: 5,947 **Elev:** 1,057 ft **Area code:** 404
*NE of Atlanta (B-2) via I-85 or US 23 (GA 13).

Norcross, a suburb of Atlanta, is located approximately 20 miles northeast of the city.

(For further information about this area contact the City of Norcross, 65 Lawrenceville St, 30071, phone 448-2122; or the Gwinnett Convention & Visitors Bureau, 6400 Sugarloaf Pkwy, Duluth 30136; phone 623-4966.)

(See Atlanta, Buford, Winder)

Motels

★ ★ **BEST WESTERN BRADBURY INN.** 5985 Oakbrook Pkwy (30093). 404/662-8175; FAX 404/840-1183. 123 rms, 1–3 story. S, D $52; each addl $5; suites $68–$89; under 12 free; wkend rates. Crib free. TV; cable. Heated pool; whirlpool. Complimentary full bkfst. Ck-out noon. Coin lndry. Meeting rms. Valet serv. Health club privileges. Some refrigerators. Cr cds: A, C, D, DS, MC, V, JCB.

D ⊛ ⊗ ⊚ SC

★ ★ **CLUBHOUSE INN.** 5945 Oakbrook Pkwy (30093). 404/368-9400; FAX 404/416-7370. 147 rms, 2–3 story, 25 kit. suites. S, D $57–$67; each addl $10; kit. suites $70–$90; under 10 free; wkly rates. Crib free. TV; cable. Pool; whirlpool. Complimentary full bkfst. Restaurant adj 11–1 am. Ck-out noon. Coin lndry. Meeting rms. Valet serv. Health club privileges. Wet bar in suites. Balconies. Picnic tables, grills. Cr cds: A, C, D, DS, MC, V.

D ⊛ ⊗ ⊚ SC

★ ★ **COURTYARD BY MARRIOTT-JIMMY CARTER BLVD.** 6235 McDonough Dr (30093). 404/242-7172; FAX 404/840-8768. 122 rms, 2 story. S $59; D $69; suites $69–$79; under 12 free; wkend rates. Crib free. TV; cable. Heated pool. Restaurant 6:30 am–2 pm, 5–10 pm. Bar 4–11 pm, Sun from noon. Ck-out noon. Coin lndry. Meeting rms. Valet serv. Sundries. Exercise equipt; weights, bicycles, whirlpool. Bathrm phone in suites. Private patios, balconies. Cr cds: A, C, D, DS, MC, V.

D ⊛ ⊼ ⊗ ⊚ SC

✔ ★ ★ **FAIRFIELD INN.** 6650 Bay Circle Dr (30071). 404/441-1999; FAX 404/441-1999, ext 709. 135 rms, 3 story. S $29.95–$39.95; D $35.95–$45.95; each addl $6; under 18 free. Crib free. TV; cable. Pool. Complimentary continental bkfst, coffee in lobby. Restaurant nearby. Ck-out noon. Meeting rm. Valet serv. Sundries. Airport transportation avail. Cr cds: A, C, D, DS, MC, V.

D ⊛ ⊗ ⊚ SC

★ ★ **HOMEWOOD SUITES-PEACHTREE CORNERS.** 450 Technology Pkwy (30092). 404/448-4663; res: 800/225-5466; FAX 404/242-6979. 92 suites, 3 story. Suites $89–$139; family, wkend rates. Crib free. Pet accepted, some restrictions; $100. TV; cable, in-rm movies. Pool. Complimentary continental bkfst. Complimentary coffee in rms. Restaurant nearby. Ck-out noon. Coin lndry. Meeting rms. Valet serv. Sundries. Exercise equipt; weight machine, bicycles, whirlpool. Refrigerators. Picnic tables, grills. Cr cds: A, C, D, DS, MC, V.

D ⊱ ⊛ ⊼ ⊗ ⊚ SC

★ ★ **LA QUINTA.** 5375 Peachtree Industrial Blvd (30092). 404/449-5144; FAX 404/840-8576. 130 rms, 3 story. S $40–$47; D $46–$53; each addl $6; suites $62; under 18 free; wkend rates. Crib free. TV; cable, in-rm movies. Pool. Complimentary continental bkfst, coffee. Restaurant nearby. Ck-out noon. Meeting rms. Sundries. Airport transportation avail. Some refrigerators. Cr cds: A, C, D, DS, MC, V.

D ⊛ ⊗ ⊚ SC

✔ ★ **RED ROOF INN.** 5171 Indian Trail Industrial Pkwy (30071). 404/448-8944; FAX 404/448-8955. 115 rms, 3 story. S $25–$29; D $25–$34; each addl $7; under 18 free. Crib free. Pet accepted, some restrictions. TV; cable. Complimentary coffee. Restaurant nearby. Ck-out noon. Sundries. Cr cds: A, C, D, DS, MC, V.

D ⊱ ⊗ ⊚

✔ ★ **TRAVELODGE.** 6045 Oakbrook Pkwy (30093). 404/449-7322; FAX 404/368-1868. 112 rms, 2 story. S, D $38–$45; each addl $5; under 18 free; wkly rates; higher rates Super Bowl. Crib free. TV; cable. Complimentary coffee in rms. Restaurant adj 11 am–2 pm, 5–11 pm. Ck-out noon. Sundries. Valet serv. Airport transportation. Refrigerators avail. Cr cds: A, C, D, DS, ER, MC, V, JCB.

D ⊗ ⊚ SC

Motor Hotel

★ ★ ★ **AMBERLEY SUITE HOTEL.** 5885 Oakbrook Pkwy (30093). 404/263-0515; res: 800/365-0659; FAX 404/263-0185. 170 suites, 3 story. Suites $50–$79; under 18 free; wkend, wkly rates. Crib free. TV; cable, in-rm movies. Pool. Complimentary coffee. Restaurant 6:30 am–1:30 pm, 5–9 pm, Sat & Sun 7–11:30 am. Bar 5–11 pm, closed Sat. Ck-out noon. Coin lndry. Meeting rms. Valet serv. Sundries. Exercise equipt; weights, bicycles, whirlpool, sauna. Game rm. Refrigerators. Cr cds: A, C, D, DS, MC, V.

D ⊛ ⊼ ⊗ ⊚ SC

Hotels

★ ★ ★ **HILTON NORTHEAST ATLANTA.** 5993 Peachtree Industrial Blvd (30092). 404/447-4747; FAX 404/448-8853. 272 rms, 10 story. S $89–$109; D $99–$114; each addl $10; suites $185–$295; family, wkend rates. TV; cable. Indoor/outdoor pool; poolside serv. Restaurant 6:30 am–11 pm. Bar 11–2 am. Ck-out noon. Meeting rms. Gift shop. Free valet parking. Airport transportation. Tennis, golf privileges. Exercise equipt; weights, bicycles, whirlpool, sauna. Some refrigerators. Cr cds: A, C, D, DS, ER, MC, V, JCB.

 SC

★★**HOLIDAY INN-PEACHTREE CORNERS.** *6050 Peachtree Industrial Blvd NW (30071).* 404/448-4400; FAX 404/840-8008. 243 rms, 8 story. S $88; D $98; suites $95–$110; under 19 free; wkly, wkend rates. Crib free. TV; cable. Indoor/outdoor pool. Restaurant 6:30 am–2 pm, 5:30–10 pm. Bar 4 pm–2 am; entertainment exc Sun, dancing. Ck-out noon. Meeting rms. Concierge. Exercise equipt; bicycles, rowers, whirlpool. Health club privileges. Minibars. *LUXURY LEVEL:* **CONCIERGE LEVEL.** 32 rms. S $94; D $104. Private lounge. Complimentary continental bkfst, refreshments, newspaper.
Cr cds: A, C, D, DS, MC, V, JCB.

 SC

★★★**MARRIOTT GWINNETT PLACE.** *(1775 Pleasant Hill Rd, Duluth 30136)* Approx 6 mi NE via I-85 exit 40, then NW on Pleasant Hill Rd, adj to Gwinnett Mall. 404/923-1775; FAX 404/923-0017. 300 rms, 17 story. S, D $89–$140; suites $225–$325; under 18 free; wkend rates. Crib free. Pet accepted, some restrictions. TV; cable. Indoor/outdoor pool; poolside serv, lifeguard. Restaurant 6:30 am–10:30 pm. Bar 11–2 am, Sun to midnight; entertainment, dancing. Ck-out 1 pm. Convention facilities. Gift shop. Airport transportation. Lighted tennis. 18-hole golf privileges, greens fee $35–$50. Exercise equipt; weights, bicycles, whirlpool, sauna. Some balconies. On 11 landscaped acres. *LUXURY LEVEL:* **CONCIERGE LEVEL.** 17 rms, 1 suite. S, D $99–$130. Private lounge, honor bar. Complimentary continental bkfst, refreshments, newspaper.
Cr cds: A, C, D, DS, ER, MC, V, JCB.

 SC

Restaurants

★**BROOKWOOD GRILL.** *7050 Jimmy Carter Blvd.* 404/449-0102. Hrs: 11 am–10:30 pm; Fri, Sat to 11 pm; Sun 11 am–10:30 pm; Sun brunch to 3 pm. Closed Thanksgiving, Dec 25. Res accepted. Bar. Semi-a la carte: lunch, dinner $5.95–$14.95. Sun brunch $5.95–$14.95. Child's meals. Specializes in hickory-grilled steaks & chicken, baby back ribs, fresh seafood. Own desserts. Parking. Outdoor dining. Cr cds: A, C, D, DS, MC, V.

D

✔★**ROYAL THAI CUISINE.** *6365 Spalding Dr NW.* 404/449-7796. Hrs: 11:30 am–2:30 pm, 5:30–10 pm; Fri to 10:30 pm; Sat 1:30–10:30 pm; Sun 5:30–9:30 pm. Closed some hols. Thai menu. Wine, beer. Semi-a la carte: lunch $4.25–$4.95, dinner $5.25–$8.95. Specialties: sates, gang ped, spicy catfish. Parking. Outdoor dining. Thai decor. Cr cds: MC, V.

D

Ocmulgee National Monument (C-3)

(2 mi E of Macon on US 80, Alt 129)

Ocmulgee, the most scientifically excavated of the South's major Native American sites, shows evidence of 12,000 years of settlement, including 6 successive occupations from at least 10,000 B.C. to A.D. 1825. The major remains consist of 9 ceremonial mounds, a funeral mound and a restored ceremonial earthlodge of the early Mississippian Period (A.D. 900 to 1100).

Exhibits and dioramas in the museum depict this sequence: Paleo-Indian Period, from more than 12,000 years ago, when Ice Age hunters trailing mammoth and other now-extinct game arrived using stone-tipped spears. During the Archaic Period, after the Ice Age ended, hunter-gathering people hunted small game and supplemented their

diet with mussels, fish, seeds, berries and nuts. They made polished stone tools and camped along the streams. By 2000 B.C., crude pottery was fashioned. During the Woodland Period (beginning 1000 B.C.), some plants were cultivated, villages were larger and mounds were being built. Pottery was stamped with elaborate designs carved into wooden paddles. The Early Mississippian Period began about A.D. 900, when invaders brought cultivated corn, beans, squash and tobacco to the Macon Plateau. They built a large town with burial and temple mounds and circular, earth-covered council chambers. This ceremonial center declined around A.D. 1100. Late Mississippian Period villagers of the Lamar Culture combined elements of the Mississippian and older Woodland ways of life. They may have been direct ancestors of the historic Creek who lived here when Europeans first settled Georgia. The Creeks soon became involved in the struggle between France, Spain and England for possession of the New World.

Exhibits and dioramas in the museum show the Native American from earliest origins to his removal to Oklahoma in the early 1800s. Great Temple Mound, more than 40 feet high, is the largest in the park. An audio program is conducted in the restored earthlodge, which was the Mississippian council chamber. (Daily; closed Jan 1, Dec 25) For information, contact the Superintendent, 1207 Emery Hwy, Macon 31201; 912/752-8257.

Okefenokee Swamp (E-4)

(In SE corner of state, S of Waycross, E of Valdosta)

One of the largest preserved freshwater wetlands in the United States, the Okefenokee Swamp encompasses more than 650 square miles, stretching an average of 20 miles in width and 40 miles in length. The swamp's southern border is beyond the Florida line. Called "land of trembling earth" by Creek Indians, its lakes of dark brown water, lush with moss-draped cypress, are headwaters for the Suwannee and St Marys rivers. The swamp embraces vast marshes, termed "prairies," which comprise 60,000 acres.

What to See and Do

1. **Okefenokee National Wildlife Refuge** occupies more than 90 percent of the swamp region and harbors bears, deer, bobcats, alligators and aquatic birds. Naturalists have discovered many rare plants on the swamp floor, which has been described as "the most beautiful and fantastic landscape in the world."

The cypress stand mile after mile, their dense formations broken by watery "prairies" or covered by deposits of peat on the swamp's floor ranging to 15 feet in thickness. It is possible to cause small trees and shrubs to shake by stamping on the "trembling earth"; these trees take root in the crust of peat beds and never reach the solid bottom. Such forests are interspersed with varied swamp vegetation. The bay, one of the swamp's most distinctive trees, blooms from May to October, producing a white flower in contrast to its rich evergreen foliage. Aquatic flowers, such as yellow spatterdock and white water lily, blend with pickerel-weed and golden-club and swamp iris in the spring. The swamp is also the home of the sandhill crane and round-tailed muskrat. (Hrs vary with season; phone for details) Phone 912/496-3331.

There are three entrances to the refuge. Approximately eight miles southeast of Waycross via US 1/23, GA 177 is the north entrance at

2. **Okefenokee Swamp Park.** This park, located on Cowhouse Island, has a serpentarium and reptile shows. Guided boat tours; canoe rentals. Cypress boardwalk into swamp to 90-foot-high observation tower. Picnicking. Interpretive centers, video. (Daily) Admission includes two-mile boat trip (more extensive boat trips usually possible, depending on water level and guide availability). No

overnight facilities. Camping available at nearby Laura Walker State Park (see WAYCROSS). Sr citizen rate. Phone 912/283-0583. Admission fee ¢¢¢

On the Suwannee Canal, 11 miles southwest of Folkston off GA 23/121 is the east entrance and the

3. **Suwannee Canal Recreation Area.** Recreation Area provides entry to the Chesser, Grand, Mizell and Chase prairies, where small lakes and "gator holes" offer some of the nation's finest bird watching and freshwater fishing. Area also has restored swamp homestead and guided swamp tours. Boating (ramp, boat and motor rentals), canoeing, guided boat tours. Nature trails, boardwalk (¾ mi) with observation tower; bicycle rentals. Picnicking. Visitor center. (Daily; closed Dec 25) Fees for some activities. Phone 912/496-7836. Per vehicle ¢¢

On Jones Island, 18 miles northeast of Fargo via GA 177, is the west entrance at

4. **Stephen C. Foster State Park.** Park offers access to Billy's Lake, Minnie's Lake and Big Water (daily during daylight hours without a guide). Fishing; boating (rentals, basin, dock, ramp), canoeing (rentals), sightseeing boat tours. Nature trails. Picnicking, concession. Camping, cabins. Museum. Standard hrs, fees. Contact 912/637-5274.

5. **Wilderness canoeing.** There are 15 trail combinations that range from two- to five-day trips; wooden platforms for campsites. March to May and October through early November are most popular times. By advance reservation (two months) and special permit from Refuge Manager. Fee per person per night ¢¢

(For further information contact the Refuge Manager, Rte 2, Box 338, Folkston 31537; 912/496-3331.)

(For accommodations see Waycross)

Perry (C-2)

Pop: 9,452 **Elev:** 337 ft **Area code:** 912 **Zip:** 31069

The early-blooming wildflowers and trees of March and April have made Perry a favorite stopover place for spring motorists. The town is full of stately houses and historical churches. Perry is known as the "Crossroads of Georgia" because of its location near the geographic center of the state.

What to See and Do

1. **Massee Lane Gardens.** 14 mi W on GA 127 to Marshallville, then 3 mi N on GA 49. Ten-acre camellia garden reaches height of bloom between November and March; large greenhouse, Japanese garden, rose garden. Colonial-style headquarters contains more than 300 sculptures of Boehm and other porcelains, other items. Headquarters include the Annabelle Lundy Fetterman Educational Museum; exhibition hall (rare books; porcelain); auditorium with presentation on history of gardens; gift shop. Buildings (Nov–Mar, daily; rest of yr, Mon–Fri); grounds (daily). Phone 967-2722 or -2358. ¢

2. **The Andersonville Trail.** A 75-mile loop drive from Perry to Cordele (see). Along drive are American Camellia Society gardens, two state parks, antebellum houses and Andersonville National Historic Site. For information contact the Chamber of Commerce.

3. **Cranshaw's One Horse Farm and Gardens.** Approx 6 mi NE via GA 127, then N on Sandefur Rd. Commercial garden surrounding farmhouse (ca 1850) features thousands of hybrid daylilies; five herb/perennial gardens; Oriental garden; strolling peacocks. Picnicking. Phone 987-3268. **Free.**

(For further information contact the Perry Area Chamber of Commerce, 1105 Washington St, PO Box 592; 987-1234.)

Annual Event

Old Fashioned Christmas at the Crossroads. Downtown open house, community Christmas tree, parade, candlelight service. 1st wk Dec.

(See Andersonville, Cordele, Macon)

Motels

★★**COMFORT INN.** *1602 Sam Nunn Blvd.* 912/987-7710. 102 rms, 2 story, 12 suites. S, D $44–$50; each addl $5; suites $65–$90; under 18 free. Crib $5. TV; cable. Indoor pool. Complimentary continental bkfst, coffee. Restaurant nearby. Bar from 4:30 pm; dancing. Ck-out 11 am. Coin lndry. Meeting rm. Valet serv. Sundries. Exercise equipt; weights, bicycles, whirlpool, sauna. Game rm. Refrigerators; some wet bars. Cr cds: A, C, D, DS, ER, MC, V, JCB.

✔ ★★**DAYS INN.** *800 Valley Dr, US 341 at I-75 exit 43.* 912/987-2142. 80 rms, 2 story. S $37–$42; D $42–$47; each addl $5; under 18 free. Crib free. TV; cable. Pool; wading pool. Complimentary coffee. Restaurant nearby. Ck-out noon. Private patios, balconies. Cr cds: A, C, D, DS, MC, V, JCB.

★★**QUALITY INN.** *(PO Drawer 1012) 1500 Sam Nunn Blvd, US 341 at I-75, exit 43.* 912/987-1345. 75 rms, 1–2 story. No elvtr. S $35–$55; D $40–$55; each addl $5; suites $55; under 18 free. Crib free. TV; cable. Pool; wading pool. Playground. Restaurant adj 11:30 am–2 pm, 5–9:30 pm. Bar; entertainment. Ck-out 11 am. Bellhops. Landscaped gardens. On 15 acres. Cr cds: A, C, D, DS, ER, MC, V, JCB.

✔ ★**TRAVELODGE.** *100 Westview Lane.* 912/987-7355; FAX 912/987-7250. 64 rms, 2 story. May–Aug: S $33; D $37; each addl $4; suites $43; under 17 free; higher rates fair wk. Crib free. TV; cable. Complimentary coffee in rms. Restaurant adj 6 am–10 pm. Ck-out noon. Coin lndry. Refrigerator, wet bar in suites. Cr cds: A, C, D, DS, ER, MC, V, JCB.

Inn

★★**NEW PERRY.** *800 Main St.* 912/987-1000. 39 hotel rms, 3 story, 17 motel rms. S $24–$42; D $35–$44; each addl $2. Crib $2. TV; cable. Pool. Restaurant (see NEW PERRY). Ck-out noon. Meeting rms. Built in 1925; landscaped grounds. Cr cds: A, MC, V.

Restaurants

✔ ★★**NEW PERRY.** *(See New Perry Inn)* 912/987-1000. Hrs: 7–10 am, 11:30 am–2:30 pm, 5:30–9 pm; Sun, hols from 11 am. Res accepted. Semi-a la carte: bkfst $3–$5.50, lunch $4.75–$6, dinner $7.50–$10.50. Specializes in fried chicken, country ham. Parking. Overlooks pool, gardens. Cr cds: A, MC, V.

D

★**RILEY'S.** *1502 Sam Nunn Blvd, US 341 at I-75, exit 43.* 912/987-9494. Hrs: 11:30 am–2 pm, 5–9:30 pm. Closed Dec 25. Bar 5 pm–midnight. Semi-a la carte: dinner $6.95–$13.50. Buffet: lunch $3.99. Child's meals. Specializes in seafood, prime rib. Entertainment Fri, Sat. Parking. Cr cds: A, MC, V.

D

Pine Mountain (Harris Co) (C-1)

Pop: 875 **Elev:** 860 ft **Area code:** 706 **Zip:** 31822

What to See and Do

1. **Callaway Gardens.** On US 27. This distinctive public garden and resort, consisting of 14,000 acres of gardens, woodlands, lakes, recreation areas and wildlife, was conceived by prominent textile industrialist Cason J. Callaway to be "the finest garden on earth since Adam was a boy." Originally, in the 1930s, the family's weekend vacation spot, Callaway and his wife Virginia expanded the area and opened it to the public in 1952. Today, Callaway Gardens is home to more than 50 varieties of butterflies, 230 varieties of birds and more than 50 species of plantlife, including the rare plumleaf azalea, indigenous to the area. The complex offers swimming, boating and other water recreation around 13 lakes, including 175-acre Mountain Creek Lake and the white sand beach of Robin Lake; 23 miles of roads and paths for hiking or jogging; 63 holes of golf (a 9-hole and three 18-hole courses); 17 lighted tennis courts and 2 indoor racquetball courts; skeet and trapshooting ranges, hunting for deer or quail on 1,000-acre preserve; picnicking, country store; cottages, villas and resort (see); dining pavilion; and 5,000-foot paved and lighted runway and terminal. Also on garden grounds are

   John A. Sibley Horticultural Center. Five acres displaying unique collections of exotic and native plants, seasonal flowerbeds and lush green lawns; also sculpture garden and 22-foot waterfall.

   Cecil B. Day Butterfly Center. An 8,000-square-foot, glass-enclosed conservatory housing up to 1,000 free-flying butterflies, as well as ground pheasants; exotic plants and waterfalls.

   Mr. Cason's Vegetable Garden. Vegetable garden (7½ acres) that produces hundreds of varieties of fruits, vegetables and herbs; setting for "Victory Garden South" television show.

   Ida Cason Callaway Memorial Chapel, a woodland chapel patterned after rural wayside chapels of the 16th and 17th centuries; organ concerts year round. **Pioneer Log Cabin** is an authentic 18th-century structure in which life of early Georgia settlers is demonstrated.

   Gardens (daily); Robin Lake Beach (June–Labor Day, daily; May, wkends; seperate fee includes entrance to gardens). Special events include Florida State University Circus at Robin Lake Beach (June–Labor Day); rates may be higher during special events wkends. Bus tours of gardens available. Phone 663-2281 or 800/282-8181. Gardens ¢¢¢

2. **Franklin D. Roosevelt State Park.** 5 mi SE off jct US 27, GA 190. One of the largest parks in the state system has many historic buildings and King's Gap Indian trail. Swimming pool; fishing. Hiking, bridle & nature trails. Picnicking. Camping, cottages. Standard hrs, fees. Contact Superintendent, 2970 Hwy 190E; 663-4858.

3. **Little White House Historic Site.** Approx 15 mi E on GA 18 & GA 194, then ½ mi S on GA 85W in Warm Springs. Cottage in which President Franklin D. Roosevelt died on April 12, 1945, is preserved as it was on the day he died. On display is original furniture, memorabilia and the portrait on which Elizabeth Shoumatoff was working when the president was stricken with a massive cerebral hemorrhage. A film about Roosevelt's life at Warm Springs and in Georgia is shown at the F.D. Roosevelt Museum and Theater. Picnic area, snack bar. (Daily; closed Jan 1, Thanksgiving, Dec 25) Phone 655-3511. ¢¢

(See Columbus, La Grange)

Motels

★★**DAVIS INN.** *(PO Box 830) Jct US 27S & State Park Rd. 706/663-2522; res: 800/346-2668 (SE states only).* 23 rms, 1–2 story, 10 kits., 15 condos (1–2 bedrm). Mar–Dec (2-day min wkends): S, D $80–$90; each addl $10; kits., condos $100–$195; under 6 free; lower rates rest of yr. Crib free. TV; cable. Swimming privileges. Complimentary coffee in rms. Restaurant nearby. Ck-out noon. Meeting rms. Lighted tennis privileges. Golf privileges, pro, putting green, driving range. Health club privileges. Picnic tables, grills. Adj Callaway Gardens. No cr cds accepted.

★**VALLEY INN.** *(14420 US 27, Hamilton 31811) 6 mi S on US 27. 706/628-4454; res: 800/944-9393.* 24 rms, 4 kits. Mar–Dec: S $60; D $65–$75; each addl $12; kit. cottages $95; under 4 free; wkly rates; lower rates rest of yr. Crib $4. TV; cable. Pool. Playground. Coffee in rms. Ck-out noon. Sundries. Tennis privileges. 63-hole golf privileges. Health club privileges. Picnic tables, grills. On 22-acre lake. Cr cds: MC, V.

Resort

★★★★**CALLAWAY GARDENS.** *(PO Box 2000) S on US 27, 1 mi S of GA 18. 706/663-2281; res: 800/282-8181; FAX 706/663-5080.* 349 rms, 1–3 story, 155 cottages (2-bedrm), 55 villas. Inn: S, D $90–$120; each addl $15; suites $275–$350; luxury villas (1–4 bedrm) $190–$475; cottages: 1-bedrm $160; 2-bedrm $260; under 18 free; MAP, golf, tennis plans; monthly rates off season. Crib free. TV; cable. 3 pools; wading pool, lifeguard in summer. Playgrounds (beach only). Supervised child's activities (June–mid-Aug). 6 dining rms 7 am–11 pm (also see GEORGIA ROOM). Rm serv 24 hrs. Box lunches, snack bar. Bar 11:30–1 am, closed Sun. Ck-out noon, ck-in 4 pm. Grocery 1 mi. Coin lndry. Package store. Convention facilities. Bellhops. Valet serv. Concierge. Airport transportation avail. Lighted tennis, pro. Golf (63 holes): three 18-hole, one 9-hole, greens fee $60–$75 (incl cart), pros. Swimming, private beach, waterskiing. Canoes, sailboats. Bicycles avail; 7-mi bicycle trail. Horseback·riding nearby. Skeet & trap shooting. Soc dir; entertainment, dancing, movies. Rec rm. Exercise rm; instructor, weights, bicycles, sauna. Refrigerators avail. Private patios, balconies. Picnic tables, grills. 12,000 acres of woodlands, lakes, gardens. Free admission (for overnight guests) to Callaway Gardens opp, all facilities avail. Cr cds: A, DS, MC, V.

Restaurants

★★★**GEORGIA ROOM.** *(See Callaway Gardens Resort) 706/663-2281.* Hrs: 6–10 pm. Closed Sun. Res accepted. Continental menu. Serv bar. Wine list. Semi-a la carte: dinner $18.50–$22.50. *Prix fixe:* dinner $35–$50. Specializes in lamb, beef, seafood. Own baking. Parking. Cr cds: A, DS, MC, V.

★★★**OAK TREE VICTORIAN RESTAURANT.** *(Box 53, Hamilton 31811) 5 mi S of Callaway Gardens on US 27. 706/628-4218.* Hrs: 6–9:30 pm. Closed Sun; major hols. Res accepted. French, continental menu. Serv bar. Wine cellar. Semi-a la carte: dinner $16.95–$23.95. Specializes in quail, veal, lamb. Parking. Victorian house (1871). Cr cds: A, C, D, DS, MC, V.

Plains

(see Americus)

Rome (A-1)

Founded: 1834 **Pop:** 30,326 **Elev:** 605 ft **Area code:** 706 **Zip:** 30161

According to legend, five men, seven hills, three rivers, a spring and a hat were the equation that led to the founding of Rome, Georgia. The seven hills suggested that "Rome" be one of the names drawn from the hat by the five founders, two of whom had discovered the site at the junction of three rivers. Lying at the head of Coosa Valley, Rome has more than 75 industrial plants that manufacture scores of items from furniture and textiles to electrical transformers and steel wire.

Nobles' Foundry Lathe, one of the few that produced Confederate cannon, is on display on Civic Center Hill and is a reminder of Sherman's occupation. Rome fell despite the frantic ride of Georgia's Paul Revere, a mail carrier named John E. Wisdom, who rode 67 miles by horse from Gadsden, Alabama, in less than 9 hours to warn "the Yankees are coming."

What to See and Do

1. **Berry College** (1902). (1,800 students) On US 27. Campus, forest preserves and 100 buildings comprise more than 26,000 acres, one of the largest campuses in the world. Old overshot waterwheel is one of the largest in the world. Visitor Reception Desk is at Martha Berry Museum (daily exc Mon). Also open to the public are Oak Hill, antebellum plantation house of Martha Berry, with formal gardens and nature trail; and Martha Berry Museum & Art Gallery (daily exc Mon). Phone 291-1883. Fees for Oak Hill and Museum ¢¢

2. **The Old Town Clock** (1871). Surmounting 104-foot high water tower of brick and superstructure of cypress wood, clock face is 9 feet in diameter. Bronze striking bell is 32 inches high, 40 inches in diameter at rim. Tower was built to hold the city's water supply and is located atop one of Rome's seven hills.

3. **Chieftains Museum.** 501 Riverside Pkwy, N off US 27. Eighteenth-century house of prominent Cherokee leader Major Ridge; artifacts with emphasis on Cherokee history. (Tues–Fri, Sun; closed major hols) Phone 291-9494. ¢¢

4. **Capitoline Wolf Statue.** In front of City Hall. Replica of the famous statue of Romulus and Remus in Rome, Italy. Presented by that city as a gift to Rome, Georgia in 1929.

(For further information contact the Greater Rome Convention & Visitors Bureau, 402 Civic Center Hill, PO Box 5823, 30162-5823; 295-5576.)

Annual Event

Heritage Holidays. River rides, parade, tours, wagon train, arts & crafts fair, music. 2nd wkend Oct.

(See Calhoun, Cartersville)

Motor Hotels

✔ ★ ★**DAYS INN.** 840 Turner McCall Blvd, at Broad St (US 27/GA 20). 706/295-0400; FAX 706/295-0400, ext 255. 107 rms, 5 story. S $37–$45; D $40–$48; each addl $4; suites $90–$120; under 17 free. Crib free. TV; in-rm movies avail. Pool. Complimentary full bkfst. Bar 5 pm–midnight, closed Sun. Ck-out noon. Meeting rms. Valet serv (Mon–Fri). Poolside rms open onto pool decks. Cr cds: A, C, D, DS, MC, V.

★ ★**HOLIDAY INN-SKYTOP.** US 411E, 2 mi E of town center. 706/295-1100; FAX 706/291-7128. 200 rms, 2 story. S $52–$58; D $58–$63; each addl $5; under 18 free. Crib free. Pet accepted. TV; cable.

Indoor/outdoor pool; whirlpool, sauna, poolside serv. Restaurant 6:30 am–1:30 pm, 5:30–10 pm. Rm serv. Bar noon–1:30 am, Sat to midnight; entertainment Tues–Sat, dancing. Ck-out noon. Coin lndry. Meeting rms. Bellhops. Valet serv. Sundries. Airport transportation. 18-hole golf privileges, greens fee $8, pro. Holidome. Cr cds: A, C, D, DS, ER, MC, V, JCB.

★**RAMADA INN-RIVERSIDE.** 707 Turner McCall Blvd (US 27/GA 20). 706/291-0101; FAX 706/232-6558. 149 rms, 2 story. S $41–$46; D $44–$49; each addl $5; suite $85; under 18 free. Crib free. TV; cable. Pool. Restaurant 6:30 am–2 pm, 5:30–10 pm. Rm serv. Bar 3 pm–1:30 am, Sat to midnight, closed Sun. Ck-out noon. Free lndry facilities. Meeting rms. Valet serv. Exercise equipt; weight machine, bicycles. Cr cds: A, C, D, DS, MC, V, JCB.

Unrated Dining Spot

MORRISON'S CAFETERIA. 22 Riverbend Dr, in Riverbend Mall. 706/295-4888. Hrs: 11 am–8:30 pm; Sun to 8 pm. Avg ck: lunch $4.45, dinner $4.75. Child's meals. Specializes in Southern cooking, homemade pies. Salad bar. Cr cds: MC, V.

St Simons Island (E-5)

Pop: 12,026 **Elev:** 0–30 ft **Area code:** 912 **Zip:** 31522

One of Georgia's Golden Isles (see), St Simons has been under five flags: Spanish, French, British, United States and Confederate States of America. Fragments of each culture remain.

John and Charles Wesley preached under St Simons' oaks before a church was built at Frederica, and later Aaron Burr spent a month at Hampton's Point after killing Alexander Hamilton in a duel. St Simons' plantations flourished and were noted for the luxurious and sporting life of planters from about 1800 to the Civil War. Cotton and slavery collapsed after Sherman's forces razed the estates. Former slave quarters remained; inhabitants turned to fishing and garden crops for subsistence as St Simons was nearly forgotten until the 20th century.

What to See and Do

1. **Gascoigne Bluff.** Where the bridge crosses the Frederica River, SW side of island. This is a low-wooded, shell-covered bank named for Captain James Gascoigne, commander of HMS Hawk, which convoyed the two ships bringing settlers (1736). Great live oaks cut here were used to build first US Navy vessels, including the Constitution ("Old Ironsides") (1794). St Simons Marina is open to the public.

2. **Museum of Coastal History.** 101 12th St. Housed in restored 1872 lightkeeper's house; exhibits on history of St Simons lighthouse and Golden Isles. (Daily exc Mon; closed most hols) Phone 638-4666. ¢¢ Includes

St Simons Lighthouse. S end of island. The original lighthouse (1810), which was 75 feet high, was destroyed by Confederate troops in 1862 to prevent it from guiding Union invaders onto the island. The present lighthouse, 104 feet high, has been in continuous operation, except during wartime, since 1872. Visitors may climb to the top.

3. **Coastal Alliance for the Arts.** 536 Ocean Blvd, near village. Exhibitions of works by regional artists and craftsmen, national traveling exhibits, lectures. (Daily exc Sun; closed most major hols) Phone 638-8770. **Free.**

4. **Fort Frederica National Monument** (see). N end of island.

5. **Cumberland Island National Seashore** (see). S, off the coast.

(For further information contact the Chamber of Commerce, 530 B Beachview Dr, Neptune Park; 638-9014 or 800/525-8678.)

Annual Events

Homes & Gardens Tour. Tour of houses and gardens on St Simons Island and Sea Island. Varies each yr. Contact the Chamber of Commerce. Late Mar.

Sunshine Festival. Neptune Park. Juried arts & crafts exhibits; food; fireworks on July 4; Navy ships at pier. Early July.

Georgia Sea Island Festival. Casino grounds. Traditional crafts and music. Contact the Chamber of Commerce. 3rd wkend Aug.

Golden Isles Art Festival. Neptune Park. Juried arts and crafts exhibits, demonstrations, entertainment, food. Mid-Oct.

(See Brunswick, Golden Isles, Jekyll Island, Sea Island)

Motels

✔ ★★**COUNTRY HEARTH INN.** *301 Main St. 912/638-7805; res: 800/673-6323; FAX 912/638-7805, ext 128.* 74 units, 2 story, 12 kits. May–Sept: S, D $55–$70; each addl $9; kit. units $65–$80; under 18 free; lower rates rest of yr. Crib free. Pet accepted; $9 per day. TV; cable. Pool; whirlpool, hot tub. Playground. Complimentary continental bkfst. Ck-out 11 am. Cr cds: A, C, D, DS, MC, V.

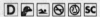

★★**DAYS INN.** *1701 Frederica Rd. 912/634-0660.* 101 rms, 2 story. May–Labor Day: S $75; D $85; each addl $10; under 12 free; lower rates rest of yr. Crib free. TV; cable. Complimentary continental bkfst. Restaurant adj open 24 hrs. Ck-out noon. Meeting rms. Many refrigerators. Cr cds: A, C, D, DS, MC, V.

★★**QUEEN'S COURT.** *437 Kings Way. 912/638-8459.* 23 rms, 2 story. S $45; D $50; each addl $3–$4; suites $55; kit. units $64. Crib free. TV; cable. Pool. Restaurant nearby. Ck-out noon. Some refrigerators. Cr cds: MC, V.

★**SEAGATE INN.** *1014 Ocean Blvd. 912/638-8661.* 48 units, 2–4 story, 16 kits. Early March–Sept: S, D $65–$110; each addl $7; suites $92–$230; kit. units $79–$110; under 10 free; lower rates rest of yr. Crib free. TV; cable. Pool; wading pool. Complimentary continental bkfst. Ck-out noon. Lawn games. Some refrigerators. Balconies. On beach. Cr cds: A, MC, V.

Hotel

★★★**KING & PRINCE BEACH RESORT.** *(Box 798) 201 Arnold Rd, at Downing St. 912/638-3631; res: 800/342-0212; FAX 912/638-3631, ext 399.* 170 units, 4 story. Mid-Mar–early Nov: S, D $69–$139; kit. villas $199–$329; lower rates rest of yr. Crib $10. TV; cable, in-rm movies. 4 pools, 1 indoor; poolside dining (May–Sept), lifeguard (in season). Supervised child's activities (May–Aug). Restaurant 7–10:30 am, 11:30 am–9 pm (also see DELEGAL ROOM). Bar 11 am–midnight, Sun 1–9 pm. Ck-out 11 am. Meeting rms. Airport transportation. 4 tennis courts, pro avail. 18-hole golf, pro. Exercise equipt; weight machine, treadmill, sauna. Hot tub. Sailboats, rafts. Bicycles. Some refrigerators. Some private patios, balconies. Resort-type hotel (1935); on ocean. Cr cds: A, C, D, MC, V.

Resort

★★★**SEA PALMS GOLF & TENNIS RESORT.** *5445 Frederica Rd. 912/638-3351; res: 800/841-6268; FAX 912/634-8029.* 200 units, 1–3 story, 112 kit. villas. Mar–May: S $109; 1-bedrm $139; 2-bedrm $228; 3-bedrm $270; under 14 free; MAP, golf, tennis, honeymoon, other plans; lower rates rest of yr. Crib $5. TV; cable. 2 pools; poolside serv. Playground. Supervised child's activities (June–Labor Day). Dining rm 7 am–10:30 pm. Box lunches, snack bar, outdoor buffets. Bar 11 am–midnight. Ck-out noon, ck-in 3 pm. Convention facilities. Airport transportation. Complimentary transportation on grounds and to beach club. Rec dir (Memorial Day–Labor Day). 12 clay tennis courts, 3 lighted, pro, clinics. 27-hole golf, greens fee $55, golf cart $28, pro, putting greens, driving range. Private beach. Skeet shooting nearby. Exercise equipt; weights, bicycles, whirlpool, sauna. Private patios, balconies, some screened. Cr cds: A, C, D, MC, V.

Restaurants

★★**ALFONZA'S OLDE PLANTATION SUPPER CLUB.** *Harrington Lane. 912/638-9883.* Hrs: 6–10:30 pm. Closed Sun; Thanksgiving, Dec 25. Res accepted. Bar. Semi-a la carte: dinner $10.50–$19.50. Specializes in steak, chicken, seafood. Guitarist. Gospel singers Thurs & Sat. Valet parking. Cr cds: MC, V.

★★**ALLEGRO.** *2465 Demere Rd. 912/638-7097.* Hrs: 6–10 pm; Sun to 9 pm. Closed Mon; some major hols; also first wk Jan. Res accepted. Continental menu. Bar. Wine list. A la carte entrees: dinner $12.95–$19.95. Specialties: Angus beef, seafood, pasta. Parking. Black & white motif. Modern art on display. Cr cds: A, MC, V.

D

★**BENNIE'S RED BARN.** *5514 Frederica Rd. 912/638-2844.* Hrs: 5:45–10:30 pm. Closed Sun; Jan 1, Thanksgiving, Dec 25; also 1 wk Sept. Res accepted wknds. Bar. Semi-a la carte: dinner $9.95–$18.45. Child's meals. Specializes in seafood, steak, chicken. Parking. Family-owned. Cr cds: MC, V.

✔ ★**BLANCHE'S COURTYARD.** *440 Ocean Blvd. 912/638-3030.* Hrs: 5:30–10 pm; winter to 9:30 pm. Closed Thanksgiving, Dec 24–25. Res accepted. Bar. Semi-a la carte: dinner $11.95–$16.50. Specializes in broiled seafood with Cajun spices, steak. Own desserts. Entertainment Sat. Parking. Victorian gaslight decor; antiques; outdoor courtyard. Cr cds: A, C, D, MC, V.

D

✔ ★**BROGEN'S FOOD & SPIRITS.** *200 Pier Alley, in Pier Village. 912/638-1660.* Hrs: 11:30–2 am. Closed Sun; Jan 1, Easter, Dec 25. Bar. A la carte entrees: lunch, dinner $3.45–$5.95. Specialties: hamburgers, chicken Swiss sandwiches. Outdoor dining on porch with view of pier. Cr cds: MC, V.

★★**CHELSEA.** *1226 Ocean Blvd. 912/638-2047.* Hrs: 5:30–10 pm. Res accepted. Continental menu. Bar. Semi-a la carte: dinner $8.95–$21.95. Child's meals. Specializes in seafood, pasta, prime rib, chicken. Parking. Garden rm; ivy. Cr cds: A, MC, V.

D

★★★**DELEGAL ROOM.** *(See King & Prince Beach Resort Hotel) 912/638-3631.* Hrs: 7–10:30 am, 1:30–3 pm, 5:30–10 pm; Sun brunch 11 am–2 pm. Res accepted. Bar. Semi-a la carte: bkfst $4.95–$7.95, lunch $2.95–$8.25, dinner $10.95–$16.95. Sun brunch $14.95. Child's meals. Specializes in local seafood, black Angus steak. Parking. Outdoor dining. Eleven stained-glass windows depict history of island. Overlooks ocean. Cr cds: A, C, D, MC, V.

D

★★**EMMELINE AND HESSIE.** *100 Marina Dr, Golden Isles Marina. 912/638-9084.* Hrs: 11:30 am–10 pm. Bar. Semi-a la carte: lunch $5.50–$10, dinner $10.95–$17.95. Child's meals. Specializes in seafood, steak, desserts. Salad bar. Entertainment Fri & Sat. Valet parking. View of St Simons Bay. Ship decor. Cr cds: DS, MC, V.

🖊 ★ **GOLDEN PALACE.** *260 Red Fern Village. 912/638-9003.* Hrs: 11:30 am–10 pm. Res accepted. Chinese menu. Bar. Semi-a la carte: lunch, dinner $4.95–$15. Lunch buffet $4.95. Specialties: Hong Kong steak, Hawaiian Five ''0''. Parking. Outdoor dining. Chinese decor. Cr cds: C, D, DS, MC, V.

★ **J. MAC'S.** *407 Mallery St. 912/634-0403.* Hrs: 5:30–10 pm. Closed Jan 1, Thanksgiving, Dec 25. Res accepted. Bar. A la carte entrees: dinner $8.95–$21.95. Specializes in seafood & pasta, crab cakes, rack of lamb. Bistro atmosphere. Cr cds: A, MC, V.

★ **KYOTO JAPANESE SEAFOOD & STEAK HOUSE.** *202 Retreat Village Center. 912/638-0885.* Hrs: 5–10 pm; wkends to 11 pm; early-bird dinner 5–6 pm. Closed Thanksgiving, Dec 25; also Super Bowl Sun. Res accepted. Japanese menu. Bar. Semi-a la carte: dinner $9.45–$23.50. Child's meals. Specializes in seafood, steak, chicken. Parking. Tableside preparation. Cr cds: A, C, D, MC, V.

SC

Savannah (D-5)

Founded: 1733 **Pop:** 137,560 **Elev:** 42 ft **Area code:** 912

Savannah has a wealth of history and architecture that few American cities can match. Even fewer have managed to preserve the same air of colonial grace and charm. The city's many rich, green parks are blooming legacies of the brilliance of its founder, General James E. Oglethorpe, who landed at Yamacraw Bluff with 120 settlers on February 12, 1733. His plan for the colony was to make the ''inner city'' spacious, beautiful and all that a city should be. Bull Street, named for Colonel William Bull, one of Oglethorpe's aides, stretches south from the high bluffs overlooking the Savannah River and is punctuated by five handsome squares and Forsyth Park.

Savannah then changed its outer garb of wood palisades to a gray ''Savannah brick'' fort surmounting the bluff. By Revolutionary times, wharves served ocean trade, and sailors caroused in seamen's inns. The town had its liberty pole and a patriots' battalion when news of Lexington came. The Declaration of Independence led to Savannah's designation as capital of the new state. By December, however, the British had retaken the city with 2,000 troops, and the Royal Governor, who had fled earlier, returned. An attempt to recapture Savannah by American troops failed, and more than 1,000 Americans and 700 Frenchmen were killed. General ''Mad Anthony'' Wayne's forces finally drove the British from Savannah in 1782.

In 1795, tobacco culture and Eli Whitney's cotton gin brought prosperity back to Savannah. Meanwhile, the city's growth followed the orderly pattern laid out by Colonel Bull. By the first decade of the new century, classical-revival or Regency-style architecture had superseded Georgian colonial. Savannah, with new forts protecting the estuary and strengthening Fort Wayne on the bluff, fared better during the War of 1812. Afterwards, architect William Jay and master builder Isaiah Davenport added splendid mansions that fronted palm-lined squares. The steamboat *Enterprise* plied upriver from here to Augusta in 1816; and three years later, on May 22, 1819, the SS *Savannah* set sail from Savannah for Liverpool to be the first steamer to cross the Atlantic. Savannah had become the leading market and shipping point for cotton, naval stores and tobacco, and prosperity increased until the Civil War.

Throughout the war, Savannah tried to hold its own. Fort Pulaski (see), which the Confederates took control of even before Secession, was retaken by a Union artillery assault on April 11, 1862, and became a Union military prison. Despite repeated Union naval battering, the Confederates held Fort McAllister (see) until Sherman marched to the sea and captured it on December 13, 1864. Although Confederate troops resisted for three days after Sherman demanded Savannah's surren-

der, Union forces eventually occupied the city, and the Confederates were forced to escape to Hutchison Island.

Reconstruction was painful, but 20 years later cotton was king again. Surrounding pine forests produced lumber and resins; the Cotton and Naval Stores Exchange was launched in 1882 while financiers and brokers strode the streets with confidence. By the 20th century, Savannah turned to manufacturing. With more than 200 industries by World War II, the city's prosperity has been measured by the activity of its port, which included shipbuilding booms during both world wars. Extensive developments by the Georgia Port Authority in the past decade have contributed to the city's commercial, industrial and shipping growth.

Today, more than 1,000 historically and architecturally significant buildings have been restored in Savannah's historic district, making it the largest urban historic landmark district in the country. Another area, the Victorian district, south of the historic district, offers some of the best examples of post-Civil War Victorian architecture in the country. The city that launched the Girl Scouts of America also plays host to modern Girl Scouts, who visit the shrine of founder Juliette Gordon Low (see #13).

What to See and Do

1. **City Hall** (1905). Bull & Bay Sts. A gold dome tops the four-story neoclassic facade of this building, which replaced the original 1799 structure. A tablet outside commemorates sailing of the SS *Savannah;* a model is displayed in the Council Chamber. Another tablet is dedicated to the *John Randolph,* the first iron-sided vessel launched in American waters (1834). (Mon–Fri) **Free.**

2. **US Customs House** (1850). Bull & E Bay Sts. Erected on site of colony's first public building. The granite columns' carved capitals were modeled from tobacco leaves. Tablet on Bull Street marks site where John Wesley preached his first Savannah sermon; tablet on Bay Street marks site of Oglethorpe's headquarters.

3. **Factors Walk.** Between Bull & E Broad Sts. Named by cotton factors of the 19th century, this row of business houses ''on the Bay'' is accessible by a network of iron bridgeways over cobblestone ramps.

4. **Trustees' Garden Site.** E Broad St. Original site of 10-acre experimental garden modeled in 1733 after the Chelsea Gardens in London by colonists who hoped to produce silk, wine and drugs. Peach trees planted in garden were responsible for Georgia's peach industry. Fort Wayne occupied the site in 1762. Not of military importance until the Revolution, the fort was named for General ''Mad Anthony'' Wayne. Strengthened by the British (1779), the Americans rebuilt it during the War of 1812. The massive buttressed brick walls later served as the foundation for a municipal gas company building. The **Pirates' House** (1734), former inn for visiting seamen, has been restored and is a restaurant; Robert Louis Stevenson referred to the inn in *Treasure Island.*

5. **Historic Savannah Waterfront Area.** John P. Rousakis Riverfront Plaza. Restoration of the riverfront bluff to preserve and stabilize the historic waterfront includes a nine-block brick concourse of parks, studios, museums, shops, restaurants and pubs.

6. **Savannah History Museum.** 303 Martin Luther King Jr Blvd, in Battlefield Park, adjacent to the Savannah Visitors Center. This 19th-century railroad shed was renovated to house historical orientation center. Mural in lobby chronicles major events in Savannah's 250-year history. (Daily; closed Jan 1, Thanksgiving, Dec 25) Sr citizen rate. Phone 238-1779. **¢¢** Here are

Main Theater. Orientation film provides an overview of the history of Savannah from 1733 to the present as seen through the eyes of General James E. Oglethorpe.

Exhibit Hall. Artifacts, antiques and memorabilia from Savannah's past; pre-colonial Native American artifacts, Revolutionary and Civil war uniforms and weapons; 1890 Baldwin locomotive; replica of the SS *Savannah,* first steamboat to cross the Atlantic.

Auxiliary Theater. Special audio-visual presentations.

7. **Savannah Science Museum.** 4405 Paulsen St. Exhibits of live reptiles and amphibians; exhibits on the natural, physical, medical and technological sciences. Planetarium shows (Sun afternoons; addl fee). (Tues–Sat, also Sun afternoons; closed hols) Phone 355-6705. ¢¢

8. **Ships of the Sea Museum.** 503 E River St, on Savannah River. Ship models, figureheads; scrimshaw, sea artifacts; ship's carpenter shop. (Daily; closed Jan 1, Thanksgiving, Dec 24–25) Phone 232-1511. ¢¢

9. **Georgia Historical Society.** 501 Whitaker St. Research library and archives for Savannah and Georgia history and genealogy. For hours phone 651-2128. **Free.**

10. **Telfair Mansion and Art Museum.** 121 Barnard St. Site of Royal Governor's residence from 1760 to end of Revolutionary War. Regency Mansion (1818) is one of three surviving buildings in Savannah by William Jay, English architect. Period rooms with family furnishings, silverware, porcelains; Octagon Room. Telfair is the oldest public art museum in the southeast, with a permanent collection of 18th-, 19th- and 20th-century American and European paintings and sculpture; prints, silver, decorative arts. Concerts, lectures; tours. (Daily exc Mon; closed major hols) Sr citizen rate. Phone 232-1177. ¢¢

11. **Owens-Thomas House** (1816–19). 124 Abercorn St. Authentically furnished Regency-style house designed by William Jay. Lafayette was an overnight guest in 1825. Walled garden is designed and planted in 1820s style. (Daily; closed major hols, also Jan) Phone 233-9743. ¢¢

12. **Davenport House** (1815–20). 324 E State St. Built by master builder Isaiah Davenport, this is one of the finest examples of federal architecture in Savannah. Saved from demolition in 1955 by the Historic Savannah Foundation, it is now restored and furnished with period antiques. Gardens. (Daily; closed major hols) Phone 236-8097. ¢¢

13. **Juliette Gordon Low Birthplace** (1818–21). 142 Bull St. Restored Regency town house was birthplace, in 1860, of the founder of Girl Scouts of the USA. Many original Gordon family pieces. Garden restored to Victorian period. (Thurs–Tues; closed some major hols) Phone 233-4501. ¢¢

14. **Andrew Low House** (ca 1848). 329 Abercorn St. Built for Andrew Low, this was later the residence of Juliette Gordon Low, founder of Girl Scouts of America. Period furnishings. (Daily exc Thurs; closed most hols; also mid–late Dec) Phone 233-6854. ¢¢

15. **Green-Meldrim House.** 14 W Macon St. Antebellum house used by General Sherman during occupation of Savannah (1864–65) is now Parish House of St John's Church. Tours. (Tues & Thurs–Sat; closed hols, occasionally for parish activities, also last 2 wks before Easter) Phone 233-3845. Tours ¢

16. **Christ Episcopal Church** (1838). Johnson Sq between E St Julian & E Congress Sts. The mother church of Georgia, the congregation dates from 1733. Among early rectors were John Wesley and George Whitfield. The present church is the third building erected on this site. (Tues & Fri, limited hrs) Phone 232-4131.

17. **Congregation Mickve Israel.** 20 E Gordon St, E side of Monterey Sq. Only Gothic-style synagogue in US contains Torah scroll brought to America by congregation founders, Portuguese and German Jews who came to Savannah in 1733. Synagogue museum has portraits, religious objects, documents, letters from Presidents Washington, Jefferson, Madison. Guided tours (Mon–Fri). Phone 233-1547. **Free.**

18. **Laurel Grove Cemetery (South).** 37th & Ogeechee Rds. Possibly the oldest black cemetery currently in use; both antebellum slave and free black graves. Buried here is Andrew Bryan (1716–1812), pioneer Baptist preacher.

19. **Colonial Park Cemetery** (1753). E Oglethorpe & Abercorn Sts. This was the colony's first and only burial ground for many years; Button Gwinnett, a signer of the Declaration of Independence, is buried in cemetery, as are other distinguished Georgians. Closed since 1853, it has been a city park since 1896.

20. **Wormsloe State Historic Site.** 8 mi SE on Skidaway Rd. Remains of early fortified 18th-century tabby house. (Tabby is a kind of cement made from lime, oyster shells, sand and water.) Visitor center exhibits outline history of site and of Noble Jones family, owners for more than 200 years. Contact Manager, 7601 Skidaway Rd, 31406; 353-3023. ¢

21. **Fort McAllister Historic Park** (see). 25 mi S via GA 144.

22. **Fort Pulaski National Monument** (see). 15 mi E off US 80.

23. **Savannah National Wildlife Refuge.** N via US 17 or US 17A, across the Savannah River in South Carolina.

24. **Sightseeing tours.**

    Helen Salter's Savannah Tours. 1113 Winston Ave. Two-hour guided bus tours of Savannah's historic houses, museums, squares and parks. Phone 355-4296. ¢¢¢¢

    Old Savannah Tours. 516 Lee Blvd. Various guided bus tours of Historic Landmark district and other areas. Tours depart from Visitors Center (see ADDITIONAL VISITOR INFORMATION) and downtown hotels and inns. (Daily; closed St Patrick's Day, Thanksgiving, Dec 25) For details, reservations phone 354-7913. ¢¢¢–¢¢¢¢

    Gray Line bus tours. Contact 215 W Boundary St, 31401; 234-8687.

Annual Events

    Georgia Heritage Festival. Walking tours, open house at historic sites, crafts show, waterfront festival, parade, concerts, Georgia Day. Phone 233-7787. Late Jan–mid-Feb.

    St Patrick's Day Parade. Rivals New York City's in size. Mar.

    Savannah Tour of Homes & Gardens. Sponsored by Christ Episcopal Church with Historic Savannah Foundation. Day and candlelight tours of more than 30 private houses and gardens. Contact 18 Abercorn St, 31401; 234-8054. Late Mar.

    Seafood Festival. Waterfront. Restaurants offer samples; entertainment, arts & crafts. Contact Savannah Waterfront Association, PO Box 572, 31402; 234-0295. Early Apr.

    Night In Old Savannah. At the Savannah Visitors Center. Foods of more than 25 countries; entertainment includes jazz, country and rhythm and blues. Mid-Apr.

    Walking Tour of Old Savannah Gardens. Includes eight private walled gardens in historic Savannah, tea at antebellum Green-Meldrim House (see #15). Phone 238-0248. Apr 8–9.

    Savannah Scottish Games & Highland Gathering. Old Fort Jackson, 2 mi E via President St extension. The clans gather for a weekend of Highland games, piping, drumming, dancing and the traditional "Kirkin' o' th' Tartans." Contact Savannah Scottish Games, Box 13435, 31416; 964-4951 or 897-5781. 2nd Sat May.

    Christmas in Savannah. Month-long celebration includes tours of houses, historical presentations, parades, music, caroling and cultural events. Dec.

Additional Visitor Information

The Savannah Visitors Center, 301 Martin Luther King, Jr Blvd, is open daily, providing information on area attractions (including a free visitors guide with translations in French, German, Spanish and Japanese) and offering a 15-minute audio-visual presentation. All guided bus tours depart from the center on a regular basis.

    Visitor information is also available from the Savannah Area Convention & Visitors Bureau, PO Box 1628, 31402-1628; 944-0456 or 800/444-2427. For additional information on Savannah events phone 233-ARTS.

Motels

(Rates may be higher St Patrick's Day)

★**BEST WESTERN-RIVERFRONT INN.** *412 West Bay St (31401), at Martin Luther King Blvd.* 912/233-1011. 142 rms, 3 story. Mar–Oct: S $52–$62; D $58–$68; each addl $6; under 12 free; higher rates special events; lower rates rest of yr. TV; cable. Pool. Restaurant 6–11 am. Ck-out noon. Meeting rm. Bellhops. Cr cds: A, C, D, DS, ER, MC, V.

⊡ ⊚ SC

✔★**BUDGETEL INN.** *8484 Abercorn St (31406).* 912/927-7660; FAX 912/927-6392. 102 rms, 3 story. June–Oct: S $34.95–$43.95; D $41.95–$50.95; each addl $7; under 18 free; lower rates rest of yr. Crib free. Pet accepted, some restrictions. TV; cable. Pool. Complimentary continental bkfst. Complimentary coffee in rms. Restaurant nearby. Ck-out noon. Coin lndry. Meeting rm. Valet serv. Some refrigerators. Cr cds: A, C, D, DS, MC, V.

🐾 ⊡ ⊚ SC

★**CLUBHOUSE INN.** *6800 Abercorn St (31405).* 912/356-1234; FAX 912/352-2828. 138 rms, 2 story, 16 suites. S $56; D $66; each addl $10; suites $72–$95; under 10 free; wkend rates; higher rates special events. Crib free. TV; cable. Pool; whirlpool. Complimentary full bkfst. Restaurant opp 10 am–10 pm. Ck-out noon. Coin lndry. Meeting rms. Refrigerator, wet bar in suites. Balconies. Grills. Cr cds: A, C, D, DS, MC, V.

⊡ ⊚ SC

★★**COURTYARD BY MARRIOTT.** *6703 Abercorn St (31405).* 912/354-7878; FAX 912/354-1432. 144 rms, 3 story, 12 suites. Feb–Oct: S $68; D $78; suites $80–$90; wkend rates; lower rates rest of yr. Crib free. TV; cable. Pool. Restaurant 6–11:30 am; Sat, Sun to 12:30 pm. Bar 4–11 pm. Ck-out noon. Coin lndry. Meeting rms. Sundries. Exercise equipt; weights, bicycles, whirlpool. Refrigerator in suites. Private patios, balconies. Cr cds: A, D, DS, MC, V.

⊡ ⊚ SC

✔★**DAYS INN ABERCORN.** *11750 Abercorn (31419), at Mercy Blvd.* 912/927-7720; FAX 912/925-8424. 114 rms, 2 story. Mar–Sept: S, D $42–$57; each addl $5; under 12 free; lower rates rest of yr. Crib free. Pet accepted; $10 non-refundable. TV; cable. Complimentary continental bkfst. Restaurant nearby. Ck-out 11 am. Whirlpool. St Joseph's hospital adj. Cr cds: A, C, D, DS, MC, V.

⊡ ⊚ SC

✔★★**HAMPTON INN.** *201 Stephenson Ave (31405).* 912/355-4100; FAX 912/356-5385. 129 rms, 2 story. S $40–$50; D $45–$55; under 18 free; higher rates special events. Crib free. TV; cable. Pool. Complimentary continental bkfst, coffee. Restaurant adj 11 am–10 pm. Ck-out noon. Meeting rms. Cr cds: A, C, D, DS, MC, V.

⊚ SC

★**HAMPTON INN.** *17007 Abercorn (31419).* 912/925-1212; FAX 912/925-1227. 60 rms, 2 story. S $50–$65; D $60–$70; higher rates wkends. Crib free. TV; cable. Pool. Complimentary continental bkfst. Complimentary coffee in lobby. Restaurant adj 7 am–10 pm. Ck-out 11 am. Cr cds: A, C, D, DS, MC, V.

⊡ ⊚ SC

★**HOWARD JOHNSON LODGE.** *224 W Boundary St (31401).* 912/232-4371; FAX 912/232-4371, ext 250. 89 rms, 2 story. Mar–Apr, Oct: S, D $59–$65; each addl $5; suite $85; under 19 free; lower rates rest of yr. Crib free. TV; cable. Pool. Complimentary coffee in lobby. Restaurant adj 6 am–8 pm. Bar 11 am–midnight. Ck-out noon. Valet serv. Cr cds: A, C, D, DS, MC, V, JCB.

⊚ SC

✔★**QUALITY INN AIRPORT.** *(Rte 5, Box 285, 31408) E via I-16, exit Dean Forest Rd, then 4 mi N on Dean Forest Rd, adj to Savannah Intl Airport.* 912/964-1421; FAX 912/966-5646. 171 rms, 2 story. S, D $44–$49; each addl $8; suites $85; under 16 free. Crib free.

TV; cable. Pool. Restaurant 6:30 am–2 pm. Rm serv 7 am–9 pm. Bar 11–2 am; band Wed, Fri. Ck-out noon. Meeting rms. Bellhops. Valet serv. Free airport transportation. Private patios, balconies. Cr cds: A, C, D, DS, ER, MC, V.

⊡ ⊠ ✕ ⊚ SC

Hotels

★**DAYS INN.** *201 W Bay St (31401).* 912/236-4440; FAX 912/232-2725. 253 rms, 7 story, 57 kit. suites. S, D $69–$89; each addl $10; kit. suites $79–$99; higher rates major hols; lower rates rest of yr. Crib free. TV; cable. Pool. Restaurant open 24 hrs. Rm serv 6 am to 10 pm. Ck-out noon. Meeting rms. Free garage parking. Cr cds: A, C, D, DS, MC, V.

⊡ ⊠ ⊚ SC

★★★**HILTON-DE SOTO.** *15 E Liberty St (31401), at Bull St.* 912/232-9000; FAX 912/232-6018. 250 rms, 15 story. S $64–$97; D $85–$112; suites $175–$375; family, wkend rates. Crib free. TV; cable. Pool; poolside serv. Restaurant 6 am–midnight; dining rm 6 am–2 pm, 6–11 pm. Bar 11–2 am; entertainment Tues–Sat. Ck-out 1 pm. Convention facilities. Gift shop. Beauty shop. Free underground parking. Tennis, golf privileges. Health club privileges. Some refrigerators. Balconies; some private patios. Spacious lobby. Carriage tours. Romanesque architecture (1890); social hub of Savannah at turn of the century. Cr cds: A, C, D, DS, ER, MC, V, JCB.

⊡ 🏌 ⚲ ⊠ ⊚ SC

★★★**HYATT REGENCY.** *2 W Bay St (31401), on riverfront.* 912/238-1234; FAX 912/944-3678. 346 rms, 7 story. Mar–July, Sept–Nov: S $125; D $150; each addl $20; suites $185–$500; under 18 free; wkend rates; lower rates rest of yr. Garage $7; valet. TV; cable. Indoor pool. Restaurant 6:30 am–10:30 pm; Fri, Sat to midnight; wkend buffet 9 am–1 pm. Bar 11:30–2 am, Sun noon–midnight; entertainment, dancing Tues–Sat. Ck-out noon. Convention facilities. Concierge. Shopping arcade. Lighted tennis privileges, pro. 18-hole golf privileges, pro, putting green. Exercise equipt; weights, bicycles. Some refrigerators. Heliport. Cr cds: A, C, D, DS, ER, MC, V, JCB.

⊡ 🏌 ⚲ ⊠ ⊡ ⊚ SC

★★★**THE MULBERRY.** *601 E Bay St (31401).* 912/238-1200; FAX 912/236-2184. 122 rms, 26 suites, 3 story. Mid-Mar–June: S $95–$105; D $95–$125; suites $125; under 18 free; honeymoon, other plans avail; higher rates special events; lower rates rest of yr. Crib free. TV; cable. Pool. Complimentary morning coffee, afternoon tea & refreshments. Restaurant nearby. Bar. Ck-out noon. Meeting rms. Rooftop whirlpool. Refrigerator in suites. Early 1800s Victorian structure, in the Historic District. Elegant Old Savannah decor; many objets d'art, antiques, paintings. Cr cds: A, C, D, DS, MC, V, JCB.

⊡ ⊚ SC

★★★**RADISSON PLAZA.** *100 General McIntosh Blvd (31401).* 912/233-7722; FAX 912/233-3765. 384 rms, 8 story, 46 suites. Mar–mid-Nov: S $109–$139; D $119–$159; each addl $15; suites $169–$389; under 18 free; lower rates rest of yr. Crib free. Pet accepted, some restrictions. Garage, in/out $5. TV; cable. Indoor/outdoor pool; poolside serv. Restaurant 6–1 am. Bar 11 am–9 pm; entertainment. Ck-out 11 am. Convention facilities. Concierge. Shopping arcade. Exercise equipt; weight machine, stair machine, whirlpool. Game rm. Balconies. Wet bar in suites. On river. Cr cds: A, C, D, DS, MC, V.

⊡ 🐾 ⚲ 🏌 ⊚ SC

Inns

★★★**BALLASTONE.** *14 E Oglethorpe Ave (31401).* 912/236-1484; res: 800/822-4553; FAX 912/236-4626. 17 rms, 4 story. S, D $95–$200; each addl $15; suites $135–$185. Children over 12 yrs only. Pet accepted, some restrictions. TV; cable, in-rm movies. Complimentary Southern continental bkfst of homemade breads and special brands of tea served in parlor, garden, or rm. Restaurant nearby. Bar. Ck-out 11 am, ck-in 1 pm. Concierge. Gift shop. Each room has a unique decor in this Victorian mansion (1838). Some in-rm whirlpools, fire-places. Period antiques. Courtyard garden with fountain. Cr cds: A, MC, V.

✔★★**BED AND BREAKFAST INN.** *117 W Gordon St (31401). 912/238-0518.* 14 rms, 7 with bath, 4 story. No elvtr. S $33–$69; D $38–$79; each addl $5–$12; garden apts $59–$79. Crib $8. TV; cable. Complimentary full bkfst. Restaurant nearby. Ck-out 11 am, ck-in 2 pm. Some refrigerators. Restored 1853 Federal town house in the Historic District. Cr cds: A, DS, MC, V.

★★★**EAST BAY INN.** *225 E Bay St (31401). 912/238-1225; res: 800/553-6533; FAX 912/232-2709.* 28 rms, 3 story. S $69–$89; D $79–$109; each addl $10. Pet accepted, some restric-tions; $25 non-refundable. TV; cable. Complimentary continental bkfst. Dining rm 11 am–3 pm; Wed–Fri also 6–10 pm; Sat 6–10 pm; closed Sun. Ck-out 11 am, ck-in 3 pm. Bellhop. Built 1853; formerly a cotton ware-house. Furnished with antiques. Opp historic waterfront of Savannah River. Cr cds: A, C, D, DS, MC, V.

★★**ELIZA THOMPSON HOUSE.** *5 W Jones St (31401). 912/236-3620; res: 800/348-9378; FAX 912/238-1920.* 25 units, 3 story. S, D $88–$108; each addl $10; under 12 free; summer rates. Crib $10. TV; cable. Complimentary continental bkfst. Ck-out 11 am, ck-in 2 pm. Meeting rm. Bellhops. Restored 1847 home; period furniture, many antiques. Courtyard with fountain. Cr cds: A, MC, V.

★★**FOLEY HOUSE INN.** *14 W Hull St (31401). 912/232-6622; res: 800/647-3708.* 20 rms, 3–4 story. No elvtr. S, D $85–$175; each addl $10; under 12 free. Crib free. TV; in-rm movies. Complimentary conti-nental bkfst, coffee & refreshments. Ck-out noon, ck-in 3 pm. Bellhops. Fireplaces, some in-rm whirlpools. Some private patios, balconies. Restored 1896 home and carriage house in heart of Historic District. Individually decorated rms; antiques, artwork. Cr cds: A, MC, V.

★★**FORSYTH PARK.** *102 W Hall St (31401), opp Forsyth Park. 912/233-6800.* 10 rms, 2 story. No rm phones. S $60–$145; D $85–$145; each addl $15. Complimentary continental bkfst, wine/sherry. Ck-out 11 am, ck-in 3–9 pm. Balconies. Picnic tables. Restored Victorian mansion (1893); period furnishings, antique marble bathtubs, unique fireplaces. Cr cds: A, DS, MC, V.

★★★★**GASTONIAN.** *220 E Gaston St (31401). 912/232-2869; res: 800/322-6603; FAX 912/232-0710.* 13 units, 4 story. D $98–$250. Children over 12 yrs only. TV; cable. Complimentary full bkfst, fruit, wine, afternoon tea. Ck-out noon, ck-in 3 pm. Concierge. Sun deck with hot tub. Many in-rm whirlpools. Fireplaces. Balconies. Historic home (1868) restored to its original elegance. Each rm individually decorated; antique furnishings throughout; 4-poster and canopied beds. Courtyard with reflecting pond & fountain. Totally nonsmoking. Cr cds: A, MC, V.

★★**JESSE MOUNT HOUSE.** *209 W Jones St (31401), in historic district. 912/236-1774; res: 800/347-1774.* 2 suites (3-bedrm). Some rm phones. S $95; D $125–$225. Crib free. Pet accepted; $25 non-refundable. TV; cable. Complimentary full bkfst, sherry. Restaurant nearby. Ck-out 11 am, ck-in 3 pm. Picnic tables, grills. Georgian brick town house (1854) with Greek-revival detailing; rose garden; rare anti-ques. No cr cds accepted.

★★**LIBERTY INN.** *128 W Liberty St (31401). 912/233-1007; res: 800/637-1007.* 5 kit. suites, 3 story. Mar–Oct: kit. suites $95–$165; each addl $10; lower rates rest of yr. Crib free. TV; cable, in-rm movies. Complimentary continental bkfst, tea. Restaurant nearby. Ck-out 11 am,

ck-in 2 pm. Whirlpool. Picnic tables, grills. Built 1834; many antiques. Cr cds: A, DS, MC, V.

★★★**MAGNOLIA PLACE.** *503 Whitaker St (31401). 912/236-7674; res: 800/238-7674 (exc GA).* 13 rms, 3 story. S, D $89–$195; each addl $15. TV; cable, in-rm movies. Complimentary continental bkfst, refreshments. Ck-out 11 am, ck-in 2:30 pm. Concierge. Some in-rm whirlpools. Fireplaces. Private patios, balconies. Built 1878. Many anti-ques. Cr cds: A, MC, V.

★★★**OLDE HARBOUR.** *508 E Factors Walk (31401). 912/234-4100; res: 800/553-6533; FAX 912/233-5979.* 24 kit. suites, 3 story. S, D $95–$135; each addl $10; under 12 free; wkly, monthly rates; honey-moon plans. Crib $10. Pet accepted, some restrictions; $25 non-refund-able. TV; cable. Complimentary continental bkfst, refreshments. Balco-nies. Antique furnished. Built 1892, originally housed offices and warehouse of an oil company. Cr cds: A, C, D, DS, MC, V.

★★★**PLANTERS.** *29 Abercorn St (31401). 912/232-5678; res: 800/554-1187; FAX 912/232-8893.* 56 rms, 7 story, 6 suites. S $89; D $99–$109; suites $125–$200; wkend plans. Crib $10. TV; cable. Compli-mentary continental bkfst, afternoon tea (4–6 pm). Ck-out noon, ck-in 4 pm. Meeting rms. Valet serv. Bellhops. Concierge. Valet parking. Some balconies. Individually decorated rms; mahogany four-poster beds. Reynolds Square opp. Cr cds: A, C, D, MC, V.

★★★**PRESIDENT'S QUARTERS.** *225 E President St (31401). 912/233-1600; res: 800/233-1776; FAX 912/238-0849.* 9 rms, 4 story, 7 suites. S, D $97–$167; each addl $10; suites $137–$167; under 10 free. Crib free. TV; in-rm movies. Complimentary continental bkfst, sherry. Ck-out 11 am. Tennis, golf, health club privileges. Refrigerators; some in-rm whirlpools. Private patios, balconies. Built 1855; visited by numer-ous US presidents. Cr cds: A, D, DS, MC, V.

★★★**RIVER STREET.** *115 E River St (31401). 912/234-6400; res: 800/253-4229; FAX 912/234-1478.* 44 rms, 5 story. S $79–$135; D $89–$145; each addl $10; under 18 free; higher rates wkend closest to Mar 17. Crib free. Pet accepted, some restrictions. TV; cable. Compli-mentary continental bkfst, wine & cheese. Dining rms 7 am–10 pm, Sat–Sun 8 am–11 pm. Ck-out noon, ck-in 4 pm. Bellhops. Valet serv. Concierge. Health club privileges. Game rm. Balconies. On river. Con-verted cotton warehouse (1817); variety of decors & furnishings; canopy beds, Oriental rugs. Cr cds: A, C, D, ER, MC, V.

★★**17 HUNDRED 90.** *307 E President St (31401). 912/236-7122; res: 800/487-1790.* 14 units, 3 story. S, D $69–$119. Crib free. TV; cable. Complimentary continental bkfst, wine. Dining rm noon–2 pm, 6–10:30 pm; Sat, Sun from 6 pm. Bar noon–1 am. Ck-out 11 am, ck-in 1 pm. Some fireplaces. Antiques. Cr cds: A, MC, V.

Resort

★★**SHERATON SAVANNAH RESORT & COUNTRY CLUB.** *612 Wilmington Island Rd (31410), 10 mi E on US 80. 912/897-1612.* 176 rms, 8 story. Mar–Oct: S $91–$124; D $106–$124; each addl $15; suites $149–$289; under 18 free; golf plan, MAP avail; lower rates rest of yr. Crib free. TV; cable. Pool; wading pool. Playground. Free supervised child's activities (May–Aug). Dining rm 7 am–3 pm, 6–10 pm, Fri & Sat to 11 pm. Box lunches, snack bar. Bar 4 pm–1 am; dancing Tues–Sat. Ck-out noon, ck-in 3 pm. Meeting rms. Package store 2 mi. Gift shop. Recreation dir. Tennis, pro. 18-hole golf, greens fee $28, pro, putting greens, driving range. Private beach. Boats, sailboats, sailing school, waterskiing. Lawn games. Entertainment. Deep-sea fishing, guides avail. On Intracoastal Waterway. Cr cds: A, C, D, DS, MC, V.

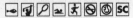

Restaurants

★★**BISTRO SAVANNAH.** *309 W Congress St. 912/233-6266.* Hrs: 6–10:30 pm; Fri, Sat to midnight. Res accepted. Southern coastal cuisine. Bar. A la carte entrees: dinner $8.95–$17.95. Specialties: crispy scored flounder, rack of lamb. Bistro atmosphere. Local art on display. Cr cds: A, MC, V.

★★**CHART HOUSE.** *202 W Bay Street. 912/234-6686.* Hrs: 5–10 pm; Fri, Sat to 11 pm. Res accepted. Bar to midnight. Semi-a la carte: dinner $12.95–$28.95. Child's meals. Specializes in steak, seafood, prime rib. Nautical decor; beamed ceilings, artwork. 3 floors. On historic waterfront. Balcony over Savannah River. Cr cds: A, C, D, DS, MC, V.

✔★★**DAMON'S.** *401 Mall Blvd, Suite 101. 912/354-3331.* Hrs: 11:30 am–10 pm; Fri, Sat to 11 pm. Closed Thanksgiving, Dec 25. Bar. Semi-a la carte: lunch, dinner $3.95–$15.95. Child's meals. Parking. Outdoor dining. Cr cds: A, DS, MC, V.

★★★**ELIZABETH ON 37TH.** *105 E 37th St. 912/236-5547.* Hrs: 6–10 pm. Closed Sun; major hols. Res accepted. Semi-a la carte: dinner $15.75–$24.75. Child's meals. Specializes in local seafood, poultry, lamb. Own baking. Converted turn-of-the-century home; 1800s decor. Cr cds: A, MC, V.

★★★**45 SOUTH.** *20 E Broad St, on grounds of Pirates' House Restaurant. 912/233-1881.* Hrs: 6–9 pm; Fri, Sat to 9:30 pm. Closed Sun; major hols. Res accepted. Bar. Wine list. A la carte entrees: dinner $17.50–$23.50. Specialties: peppered breast of duck, roast rack of lamb, filet of salmon. Own baking. Valet parking. In 1852 building. Jacket. Cr cds: A, MC, V.

★★**GARIBALDI CAFE.** *315 W Congress. 912/232-7118.* Hrs: 6–10:30 pm; Fri, Sat 5:30 pm–midnight. Res accepted. Italian menu. Bar. A la carte entrees: dinner $6.75–$22.95. Specializes in fresh fish, veal. Own desserts. Former 1871 Germania firehouse in historic district. Italian cafe decor. 1842 antique mirror, paintings. Cr cds: A, MC, V.

★★**JOHNNY HARRIS.** *1651 E Victory Dr. 912/354-7810 or -7821.* Hrs: 11:30 am–10:30 pm; Fri, Sat to 12:30 am. Closed Sun; Jan 1, Dec 25. Res accepted Fri, Sat. Bar. Semi-a la carte: lunch $4.95–$7.95, dinner $7.95–$19.95. Child's meals. Specializes in barbecued pork, prime rib, seafood. Entertainment Fri, Sat. Parking. Jacket (Fri, Sat night in main dining rm). Savannah's oldest continuously operating restaurant. Cr cds: A, C, D, DS, MC, V.

✔★**MESA GRILL & CANTINA.** *14045 Abercorn St. 912/927-2077.* Hrs: 11 am–10 pm; Fri & Sat to 11 pm; Sun to 9 pm; Sat & Sun brunch 11 am–2:30 pm. Closed Dec 25. Res accepted Sun–Thurs. Southwestern menu. Bar. Semi-a la carte: lunch $4.95–$6.95, dinner $7.25–$12.95. Sun brunch $2.25–$8.95. Child's meals. Specialties: fajitas, ribs. Parking. Southwestern decor. Cr cds: A, DS, MC, V.

★★**OLDE PINK HOUSE.** *23 Abercorn St. 912/232-4286.* Hrs: 6–10:30 pm. Res accepted. Southern menu. Bar from 4 pm. Semi-a la carte: dinner $13.95–$21.95. Specializes in seafood, beef, veal. Jazz pianist Thurs–Sun. Restored 18th-century mansion. Cr cds: A, MC, V.

✔★★**PALMER'S SEAFOOD HOUSE.** *80 Wilmington Island Rd. 912/897-2611.* Hrs: 11 am–10 pm; Sun to 9 pm; Mon from 5 pm. Closed Thanksgiving, Dec 25. Bar from 5 pm. Semi-a la carte: lunch $3–$6.95, dinner $3–$16.95. Child's meals. Specializes in fresh local seafood.

Salad bar. Parking. Outdoor dining. Overlooks Turner's creek and marsh. Cr cds: A, C, D, DS, MC, V.

★★**RIVER HOUSE.** *125 W River St. 912/234-1900.* Hrs: 11 am–10 pm; Fri, Sat to 11 pm; Sun from noon. Closed Thanksgiving, Dec 25. Res accepted. Bar. Semi-a la carte: lunch $6–$9.95, dinner $8.95–$22.95. Child's meals. Specializes in seafood, poultry, steak. In an old cotton warehouse. Cr cds: A, C, D, MC, V.

★★★**RIVER'S END.** *3122 River Dr. 912/354-2973.* Hrs: 5–10 pm; Fri, Sat to 11 pm. Closed Sun; Thanksgiving, Dec 24, 25. Res accepted. Bar 4–11 pm; Fri, Sat to midnight. Wine list. A la carte entrees: dinner $10.95–$17.95. Child's meals. Specializes in seafood, steak, live Maine lobster. Own baking. Pianist exc Sun. Parking. Overlooks Intracoastal Waterway; dockage. Cr cds: A, C, D, DS, MC, V.

★★**SHRIMP FACTORY.** *313 E River St. 912/236-4229.* Hrs: 11 am–10 pm; Fri, Sat to 11 pm; Sun noon–10 pm. Closed Thanksgiving, Dec 25. Res accepted. Bar. Semi-a la carte: lunch $6.95–$12.95, dinner $13.95–$19.95. Child's meals. Specialties: pine bark stew, fresh fish and shrimp with special sauces, lobster. Located on river. Cr cds: A, C, D, DS, MC, V.

Unrated Dining Spots

MORRISON'S CAFETERIA. *Abercorn Expy, at Oglethorpe Mall. 912/352-3521.* Hrs: 11 am–8:30 pm; Sun to 7 pm. Avg ck: lunch $4.75, dinner $5. Child's meals. Specializes in shrimp, roast beef. Cr cds: A, DS, MC, V.

MRS WILKES' DINING ROOM. *107 W Jones St. 912/232-5997.* Hrs: 8–9 am, 11 am–3 pm. Closed Sat, Sun; major hols. Southern cooking. Complete meals: bkfst $5, lunch $8. Boarding house-style seating and service. Large variety of noted Southern dishes: barbecued pork chops, fried chicken, turnip greens, biscuits, cornbread, banana pudding. Own desserts. 1870 brick house; original wallpaper. Clippings of articles about the boarding house, famous guests. No cr cds accepted.

Sea Island (E-5)

Pop: 750 (est) **Elev:** 11 ft **Area code:** 912 **Zip:** 31561

(See Brunswick, Golden Isles, Jekyll Island, St Simons Island)

Resort

★★★★**THE CLOISTER.** *9 mi E of US 17. 912/638-3611; res: 800/SEA-ISLAND; FAX 912/638-5159.* 263 rms, villas, 1–3 story, 500 kit. cottages. AP, mid-Mar–Nov: S $226–$424; D $276–$474; each addl $60; 6–12 yrs, $26; 3–5 yrs, $18; under 2 free; spa package, golf, tennis, honeymoon, anniversary plans avail. Service charge 15% per rm per day. Garage avail; free parking. TV; cable. 2 pools, 1 heated; wading pool, poolside serv, lifeguard. Free supervised child's activities (spring, summer & Christmas hols). Dining rm 7:30–9:30 am, noon–2 pm, 7–9:30 pm (also see CLOISTER MAIN DINING ROOM). Box lunches, snack bar, outdoor buffets. Rm serv 6:30 am–11 pm. Bar 11 am–midnight, Sat to 2 am, closed Sun. Ck-out 1 pm, ck-in 4 pm. Convention facilities. Valet serv. Package store. Grocery 3 mi. Airport, RR station, bus depot transportation. Sports dir. Tennis, pro, shop. 54-hole golf, greens fee $48, carts required $18 per person, pro, shop, putting greens, driving range. Private beach. Sailboats, charter boats; dock. Nature walks. Bicycles. Lawn games. Trap & skeet shooting & instruction. Soc dir; entertainment, dancing (instruction), movies on Sun. Extra fee for most sports. Rec rm. Exercise rm; instructor, weights, bicycles, whirlpool, sauna, steam rm. Complete spa facilities. Beach club; lockers avail; masseur; steam bath. Luxurious accommodations in exclusive resort on 5-mi private ocean beach on Sea Island. Private patios, balconies. No cr cds accepted.

Restaurant

★★★**CLOISTER MAIN DINING ROOM.** *(See The Cloister Resort)* *912/638-3611.* Hrs: 7–9 pm; Sun noon–2 pm; hrs vary by season. Res accepted. Continental menu. Bar. Wine cellar. Complete meals: dinner $43.50. Child's meals. Specializes in seafood, prime rib, steak. Own baking. Orchestra exc Sun. Valet parking. American colonial decor. Family-owned. Jacket. No cr cds accepted.

D

Statesboro (C-4)

Pop: 15,854 **Elev:** 258 ft **Area code:** 912 **Zip:** 30458

What to See and Do

Georgia Southern University (1906). (14,000 students) ½ mi S on US 301. On campus are art department gallery (Mon–Fri; closed hols); museum (daily exc Sat; closed hols); planetarium (by appt); Herty Nature Trail (daily); and a botanical garden (daily; closed hols). Phone 681-5611.

(For further information and a list of historic tours contact the Convention and Visitors Bureau, PO Box 1516; phone 489-1869.)

Annual Event

Regional Ogeechee Fair. Fairgrounds, GA 67. 2nd wk Oct.

Motels

★**COMFORT INN.** *301 S Main St. 912/489-2626; FAX 912/489-2626, ext 300.* 65 rms, 2 story, 13 kits. S, D $45–$60; each addl $5; kits. $45; under 18 free; higher rates: football wknds, graduation. Crib free. TV; cable. in-rm movies. Pool. Complimentary continental bkfst. Complimentary coffee in rms. Restaurant 4:30 pm–midnight. Serv bar. Ck-out 11 am. Coin lndry. Refrigerators. Cr cds: A, C, D, DS, ER, MC, V.

D ⊷ ⊘ ⊙ SC

★★**HOLIDAY INN.** *230 S Main St (US 25/301). 912/764-6121; FAX 912/764-6121, ext 509.* 129 rms, 2 story. S $44–$46; D $47–$49; each addl $3; under 18 free. Crib free. Pet accepted, some restrictions. TV; cable. Pool; wading pool. Complimentary bkfst buffet Mon–Fri. Restaurant 6:30 am–2 pm, 5–10 pm. Rm serv. Bar 5 pm–midnight. Ck-out noon. Coin lndry. Meeting rms. Valet serv. Cr cds: A, C, D, DS, MC, V, JCB.

D ⊷ ⊷ ⊘ ⊙ SC

✔★★**JAMESON INN.** *1 Jameson Ave. 912/681-7900; res: 800/541-3268.* 40 rms, 2 story. S $42; D $46; each addl $4; suites $65–$85; under 12 free; wkly rates. Crib $4. TV; cable. Complimentary continental bkfst. Restaurant nearby. Ck-out 11 am. Opp Georgia Southern College. Cr cds: A, C, D, DS, MC, V.

D ⊘ ⊙ SC

✔★**MASTER HOSTS-BRYANT'S.** *(Box 249) 461 S Main St (US 25/301). 912/764-5666; FAX 912/489-8193.* 44 rms, 1–2 story. S

$29–$30; D $33–$37; each addl $4; under 12 free. Crib $4. Pet accepted; $4. TV; cable. Pool. Complimentary continental bkfst. Restaurant adj 11 am–10 pm. Ck-out 11 am. Cr cds: A, C, D, DS, MC, V.

Inn

★★★**STATESBORO.** *106 S Main St. 912/489-8628.* 15 rms, 2 story. S $49–$80; D $56–$90; each addl $7. Crib free. TV; cable. Complimentary full bkfst. Dining rm (public by res). Rm serv. Ck-out noon, ck-in 2 pm. Some in-rm whirlpools, fireplaces. Private patios. Built 1904. Many antiques. Cr cds: A, C, D, DS, MC, V.

⊙ SC

Thomasville (E-2)

Pop: 17,457 **Elev:** 285 ft **Area code:** 912 **Zip:** 31792

What to See and Do

1. **Thomasville Cultural Center.** 600 E Washington St. A center for visual and performing arts. Facilities include art galleries with permanent and changing exhibits; fine arts, genealogical library; children's room; and 550-seat auditorium. Concerts, musicals, children's programs, art classes and other programs are offered. Galleries, building tours (daily exc hols; fee). Library (Mon–Fri; closed hols). Phone 226-0588. **Free.**

2. **Thomas County Museum of History.** 725 N Dawson St. Five buildings on property include a log house with period furnishings; an 1877 frame house furnished in middle-class fashion of period; an 1893 Victorian bowling alley; a garage housing historic vehicles; and a 1920s mansion, which houses the main museum. Photographs, period costumes, artifacts. (Afternoons exc Fri; closed Jan 1, Thanksgiving, Dec 24–25, also last wk Sept) Phone 226-7664. ¢¢

3. **Lapham-Patterson House State Historic Site** (1885). 626 N Dawson St. Restored three-story Victorian house features decorative shingle-work, elaborate chinoiserie porches, fanciful gables and cantilevered balconies; built by Chicago merchant as resort cottage. Tours on the hour. (Daily exc Mon; closed Thanksgiving, Dec 25) Phone 225-4004. ¢

4. **Big Oak.** Corner of N Crawford and E Monroe Sts, one blk behind Post Office and Federal Courthouse. Giant live oak is 68 feet tall, has a limb spread of 162 feet and a trunk circumference of 24 feet. The approximately 300-year-old tree was enrolled as a member of the National Live Oak Society in 1936.

5. **Rose Test Garden.** 1840 Smith Ave. Two-acre garden with more than 2,000 rose bushes. (Mid-Apr–mid-Nov, daily) Phone 226-5568. **Free.**

6. **Pebble Hill Plantation.** 5 mi SW via US 319. Historic plantation dates from 1820s; elaborate Greek-revival house furnished with art, antiques, porcelains, crystal, silver and Indian relics belonging to Hanna family of Ohio, who rebuilt house, guest houses, stables and garages after a fire in the 1930s. Gardens; livestock. Wagon rides; tours (daily exc Mon; closed Thanksgiving, Dec 24–25, also Sept). Phone 226-2344. Additional fee for tour of main house (under 6 yrs not admitted). ¢¢¢

7. **Historic tours.** Operated by Chamber of Commerce, 401 S Broad St. Two-hour bus tour of town. (Daily exc Sun; closed hols) Sr citizen rate. For reservations phone 226-9600. ¢¢¢

(For further information contact the Welcome Center, 109 S Broad St, PO Box 1540, 31799; 225-5222.)

Annual Event

Rose Festival. Parade, rose show, arts & crafts. Late Apr.

(See Bainbridge; also see Tallahassee, FL)

Motels

✔ ★ **ECONO LODGE.** *(35 US 84E, Cairo 31728) 13 mi W on US 84. 912/377-4400; FAX 912/377-4400, ext 137.* 34 rms, 2 story. S $35; D $40; each addl $4; suites $40–$45; under 12 free; higher rates: Rose Parade, Rattlesnake Roundup, Mule Day. Crib free. TV; cable. Pool. Complimentary coffee in lobby. Restaurant opp 6 am–11 pm. Ck-out 11 am. Cr cds: A, C, D, DS, MC, V, JCB.

★ ★ **HOLIDAY INN.** *211 US 19S. 912/226-7111; FAX 912/226-7527.* 147 rms, 2 story. S $44.50–$56; D $48.50–$53.50; each addl $5; suite $130; under 19 free; higher rates Rose Festival, Sun Belt Expo (Oct). Crib free. TV; cable. Pool. Restaurant 6:30 am–2 pm, 5:30–10 pm. Rm serv. Bar 5 pm–2 am, Sat to midnight, closed Sun; entertainment, dancing. Ck-out noon. Coin lndry. Meeting rms. Valet serv. Cr cds: A, C, D, DS, MC, V, JCB.

Inn

★ ★ **SUSINA PLANTATION.** *(Rte 3, Box 1010) 12 mi SW via US 319, then 1 mi N via GA 93, then W on GA 156, follow signs. 912/377-9644.* 8 rms, 2 story. No rm phones. MAP: S $125; D $175; family rates. Pool. Ck-out noon, ck-in 2 pm. Airport transportation. Lighted tennis. Picnic tables, grills. 1841 plantation house set amid 115 acres of lawns, oaks and magnolias. No cr cds accepted.

Restaurant

✔ ★ ★ **PLAZA.** *217 S Broad St. 912/226-5153.* Hrs: 6 am–10 pm; Sun 7 am–2:30 pm. Closed some major hols. Greek, Amer menu. Bar. Semi-a la carte: bkfst $1.50–$5.25, lunch $3–$6, dinner $4.95–$16.95. Child's meals. Specializes in seafood, Greek salad, Western steak. Salad bar. Own soups, sauces. Entertainment Fri. Parking. Family-owned. Cr cds: A, MC, V.

Tifton (D-3)

Pop: 14,215 **Elev:** 357 ft **Area code:** 912 **Zip:** 31794

What to See and Do

Georgia Agrirama, 19th-Century Living History Museum. 8th St at I-75, exit 20. Operating exhibits include farms & farmhouses, one-room school, gristmill, newspaper office, blacksmith shop, church, cotton gin, sawmill, turpentine still, country store, drugstore, variety works and more from 1870–1910. Logging train runs spring through fall. Costumed interpreters. (Tues–Sat, also Sun afternoons; closed Jan 1, Thanksgiving, Dec 22–25) Sr citizen rate. Phone 386-3344. ¢¢¢

(For further information, contact the Tifton-Tift County Chamber of Commerce, 100 Central Ave, PO Box 165, 31793; 382-6200.)

(See Adel)

Motels

★ ★ **COMFORT INN.** *1104 King Rd. 912/382-4410; FAX 912/382-4410, ext 102.* 91 rms, 2 story. S $40.88–$45.88; D $45.88–$50.88; each addl $5; suites $69–$79; under 18 free; wknd rates; higher rates Agricultural Expo. Crib free. TV; cable. Indoor/outdoor pool; whirlpool. Complimentary continental bkfst. Restaurant opp open 24 hrs. Ck-out 11 am. Meeting rm. Free local airport transportation. Refrigerator, wet bar in suites. Cr cds: A, D, DS, MC, V.

★ **DAYS INN.** *1008 W 8th St at I-75 exit 20. 912/382-7210; FAX 912/386-8146.* 72 rms, 2 story. S $35; D $40; each addl $5; under 12 free; higher rates special events. TV; cable. Pool. Restaurant 6:30 am–8:30 pm. Ck-out noon. Cr cds: A, D, DS, MC, V.

✔ ★ ★ **RAMADA INN.** *(Box 1450) 2 mi W on US 82 at jct I-75 exit 18. 912/382-8500.* 100 units, 2 story. S, D $34.95–$59; each addl $5; suites $59–$85; under 12 free. Crib free. TV; cable. Pool. Restaurant 6:30 am–2:30 pm, 5–9 pm. Bar 4 pm–midnight, closed Sun; entertainment. Ck-out noon. Meeting rms. Valet serv. Cr cds: A, C, D, DS, MC, V.

Restaurants

✔ ★ **CHARLES SEAFOOD.** *701 W 7th St. 912/382-9696.* Hrs: 6 am–2 pm, 5–10 pm. Closed Sun, Mon; July 4, Dec 25. Semi-a la carte: bkfst $1.19–$4.95, lunch, dinner $1.85–$9.95. Specializes in seafood, BBQ sandwiches. Cr cds: MC, V.

★ **CHINA GARDEN.** *1020 W 2nd St. 912/382-1010.* Hrs: 11 am–2 pm, 5–10 pm. Closed July 4, Thanksgiving, Dec 25. Chinese menu. A la carte entrees: lunch, dinner $4.50–$12.99. Buffet: lunch $4.75, dinner $8.95. Parking. Cr cds: MC, V.

Toccoa (A-3)

Pop: 8,266 **Elev:** 1,017 ft **Area code:** 706 **Zip:** 30577

What to See and Do

1. **Traveler's Rest State Historic Site.** 6 mi NE off US 123. Plantation house (ca 1840) built on land granted in 1785 to Jesse Walton, a Revolutionary soldier and political leader. Two-story structure covers 6,000 square feet. Later owned and enlarged by Devereaux Jarrett, it served as a stagecoach inn and post office. Museum (daily exc Mon; closed Jan 1, Thanksgiving, Dec 25). Phone 886-2256. ¢

2. **Toccoa Falls College** (1907). (911 students) NW edge of town off GA 17A. On November 6, 1977, a 40-year-old earthen dam above the college collapsed, spewing tons of water over the 186-foot Toccoa Falls and inundating the campus—one of the worst such disasters in Georgia history. There is no longer a lake or dam above the falls.

    Toccoa Falls Park is open to the public. (Daily; closed Dec 25) Phone 886-6831. ¢

3. **Hartwell Lake.** 6 mi E on US 123 to lake; continue approx 21 mi E on same road to access Twin Lakes campground, follow signs. This 56,000-acre reservoir with 962-miles of shoreline was created by a dam on the Savannah River. Swimming, waterskiing; fishing; boat-

ing (ramps, marinas). Picnicking. Numerous campsites (Mar–Nov; fee) surround lake. Reservoir (daily). Phone 376-4788.

(For further information contact the Toccoa-Stephens County Chamber of Commerce, 901 E Currahee St, PO Box 577; 886-2132.)

(For accommodations see Commerce, Gainesville, also see Clayton)

Tybee Island (D-5)

Pop: 2,842 **Elev:** 17 ft **Area code:** 912 **Zip:** 31328

A popular year-round Georgia resort has evolved on this V-shaped sandbar fronting the Atlantic for nearly four miles and the Savannah River for over two miles. The beach runs the entire length of the island; its north end is marked by old coastal defenses, a museum and a lighthouse at the tip. Reached by a causeway from Savannah and US 80, the beach has a boardwalk, fishing pier, amusements, hotels, motels and vacation cottages.

What to See and Do

1. **Tybee Museum and Lighthouse.** N end of island. Museum is housed in a coastal artillery battery built 1898. Battery Garland is one of six gun emplacements that made up Fort Screven. Museum traces history of Tybee from colonial times to 1945; exhibits on Martello Tower, Civil War, Fort Screven; doll and gun collections. The lighthouse is one of the oldest active lighthouses in the US; visitors may climb to the top for a scenic view of Tybee and historic Fort Screven. Exhibits and gift shop in 1880s lighthouse keeper's cottage. (Daily exc Tues; closed Jan 1, Thanksgiving, Dec 25) Sr citizen rate. Phone 786-5801. ¢¢

2. **Fort Pulaski National Monument** (see). 3 mi W on US 80.

(For further information contact the Savannah Area Convention & Visitors Bureau, 222 W Oglethorpe Ave, PO Box 1628, Savannah 31402-1628; 944-0456 or 800/444-2427.)

(For accommodations see Savannah)

Restaurant

★**MACELWEE'S SEAFOOD HOUSE.** *101 Lovell Ave (US 80). 912/786-4259.* Hrs: 11 am–11 pm. Closed Easter, Thanksgiving, Dec 25. Bar. Semi-a la carte: lunch $4.50–$18.95, dinner $8.95–$18.95. Child's meals. Specializes in grilled, fried and steamed seafood & steak. Parking. Cr cds: A, D, DS, MC, V.

Valdosta (E-3)

Pop: 39,806 **Elev:** 229 ft **Area code:** 912

When local citizens discovered that surveyors had left the town off the railroad right-of-way, they lost no time in moving the town four miles east of the original community (then called Troupville). Named for Val de Aosta (Vale of Beauty), the governor's estate, Valdosta later became a rail center with seven branch lines of three systems. One of the state's most prosperous small cities, Valdosta's products include timber, tobacco and cattle. Agriculture, tourism, Valdosta State College and Moody Air Force Base, 12 miles to the north, also contribute to the economy. Valdosta is in the center of a large wooded area with many lakes nearby.

What to See and Do

1. **Lowndes County Historical Society Museum.** 305 W Central Ave. Originally a Carnegie library, now contains collection of artifacts

from Civil War to present; genealogical library. (Mon–Fri; closed major hols) Phone 247-4780. ¢

2. **Barber House** (1915). 416 N Ashley St. Restored neo-classical house serves as offices for Valdosta-Lowndes County Chamber of Commerce; elaborate woodwork, original light fixtures and furniture. Self-guided tours. (Mon–Fri) Phone 247-8100. **Free.**

3. **Converse Dalton Ferrell House** (1902). 305 N Patterson St. Neoclassical house with wide two-story porch that wraps around front and two sides. Interior has 20-foot ceilings, 14-foot high pocket doors, golden-oak woodwork, some original light fixtures. (By appt only) Contact the Convention & Visitors Center.

4. **The Crescent (Valdosta Garden Center)** (1898). 904 N Patterson St. Neo-classical house named for the dramatic, two-story, crescent-shaped porch supported by 13 columns. House includes grand staircase, second-floor bathroom with gold-leafed tiles and fireplace, and ballroom on third floor. In garden are chapel and octagonal school house. (Mon–Fri; also by appt) Phone 244-6747. ¢

(For further information contact the Valdosta–Lowndes County Convention & Visitors Center, 1703 Norman Dr, Suite F, PO Box 1964, 31603-1964; 245-0513.)

(See Adel)

Motels

✔ ★★**BEST WESTERN KING OF THE ROAD.** *1403 N St Augustine Rd (31601), 1 blk W of jct GA 94, I-75 exit 5. 912/244-7600; FAX 912/245-1734.* 137 units, 3 story. S $34; D $39; each addl $3; under 12 free. Crib $2. Pet accepted. TV; cable. Pool; wading pool. Playground. Restaurant 6–10 am, 5:30–9 pm. Rm serv. Bar 4 pm–midnight, closed Sun; entertainment. Ck-out 11 am. Meeting rms. Sundries. Airport transportation. Some refrigerators. Cr cds: A, C, D, DS, MC, V.

🐾 🏊 🚭 ⊛ SC

★★**CLUBHOUSE INN.** *1800 ClubHouse Dr (31601), I-75 at GA 94, exit 5. 912/247-7755; res: 800/258-2466; FAX 912/245-1359.* 121 rms, 2 story, 17 suites. S $52–$62; D, suites $62–$72; each addl $10; under 10 free; wkly rates; golf plans. Crib free. TV; cable, in-rm movies. Pool, whirlpool. Complimentary full bkfst buffet. Ck-out noon. Meeting rms. Refrigerator in suites. Private patios, balconies. Cr cds: A, C, D, DS, MC, V.

D 🏊 🚭 ⊛ SC

★★**COMFORT INN.** *(Box 1191, 31603) 2½ mi W at jct US 84, I-75 exit 4. 912/242-1212; FAX 912/242-2639.* 138 rms, 2 story. S $46–$52; D $54–$60; each addl $4; suites $92; under 18 free. TV; cable. Pool. Restaurant 7 am–2 pm. Bar 3 pm–1 am. Ck-out noon. Lndry facilities avail. Airport transportation. Exercise equipt; weight machine, bicycles. Lawn games. Cr cds: A, C, D, DS, ER, MC, V, JCB.

D 🏊 🏋 🚭 ⊛ SC

★★**HAMPTON INN.** *1705 Gornto Rd (31601). 912/244-8800; FAX 912/244-6602.* 101 rms, 2 story. S $40–$45; D $46–$51; each addl $6; under 18 free. Crib free. Pet accepted. TV; cable. Pool. Complimentary continental bkfst. Restaurant adj 6 am–11 pm. Ck-out noon. Meeting rm. Valet serv. Free airport transportation. Health club privileges. Cr cds: A, C, D, DS, MC, V.

🐾 🏊

✔ ★★**QUALITY INN-SOUTH.** *1902 W Hill (31601), I-75 at US exit 4. 912/244-4520; FAX 912/244-4520, ext 55.* 48 rms, 2 story. S $35.95; D $39.95; each addl $4; under 17 free. Crib $4. TV; cable. Pool. Playground. Complimentary continental bkfst. Restaurant 11 am–2 pm, 5–10 pm. Bar 2 pm–2 am, Sat to midnight. Ck-out noon. Sundries. Cr cds: A, C, D, DS, MC, V.

🐾 🏊 🚭 ⊛ SC

★★**RAMADA INN.** *2008 W Hill Ave (31601), 2 mi W at jct US 84, I-75 exit 4. 912/242-1225.* 102 rms, 2 story. S $39; D $45; under 18 free. Crib free. TV; cable. Pool. Restaurant 6 am–10 pm. Rm serv. Bar 5 pm–1 am; entertainment, dancing Wed, Fri–Sat. Ck-out noon. Meeting rms. Valet serv. Game rm. Cr cds: A, C, D, DS, MC, V, JCB.

✔ ★ **SHONEY'S INN.** *1828 W Hill Ave (31601), I-75 exit 4.* 912/244-7711; res: 800/222-2222; FAX 912/244-0361. 96 rms, 2 story. S $36–$42; D $40–$44; each addl $5; suites $65–$75; under 18 free. Crib free. TV; cable. Pool. Complimentary continental bkfst in lobby. Restaurant adj 6 am–midnight. Ck-out noon. Meeting rm. Free airport transportation. Cr cds: A, D, DS, MC, V.

★ **TRAVELODGE.** *1330 N St Augustine Rd (31601), I-75 exit 5.* 912/242-3464; FAX 912/242-3464, ext 189. 88 rms, 2 story. S $36–$41; D $41–$46; each addl $5; suites $43–$48; under 18 free. Crib free. Pet accepted. TV; cable. Pool. Complimentary continental bkfst. Complimentary coffee in rms. Ck-out noon. Valet serv. Some refrigerators. Balconies. Picnic tables, grills. Cr cds: A, C, D, DS, ER, MC, V, JCB.

Restaurants

★ ★ **FIDDLER'S GREEN.** *2575 N Valdosta Rd.* 912/247-0366. Hrs: 6–10 pm. Closed Sun; some major hols. Res accepted. No A/C. Bar from 5 pm. Semi-a la carte: dinner $9.95–$18.95. Child's meals. Specializes in Angus beef, prime rib, steak. Pianist. Parking. Cr cds: A, C, D, DS, MC, V.

✔ ★ **JIMBO'S BAR-B-QUE.** *200 A North Valdosta Hwy (US 41).* 912/247-1000. Hrs: 11 am–10 pm. Closed Thanksgiving, Dec 25. Res accepted. Bar. Semi-a la carte: lunch $3.75–$5.75, dinner $3.75–$8.75. Child's meals. Specializes in seafood, barbeque. Parking. Cr cds: A, MC, V.

★ ★ **JP MULLDOONS.** *1405 Gornto Rd.* 912/247-6677. Hrs: 11 am–10 pm; Fri, Sat to 11 pm. Closed Sun; Thanksgiving, Dec 25. Res accepted. Bar. Semi-a la carte: lunch $1.95–$5.95, dinner $3–$15.95. Specializes in chicken, steak, fresh seafood. Pianist (evenings). Parking. Outdoor dining. Cr cds: A, MC, V.

D

✔ ★ ★ **MOM & DAD'S.** *3840 N Valdosta Rd.* 912/333-0848. Hrs: 5–10 pm. Closed Sun, Mon; most major hols. Italian menu. Bar. Semi-a la carte: dinner $6.95–$13. Child's meals. Specializes in fish, veal, beef. Parking. Cr cds: A, D, DS, MC, V.

D

Warm Springs

(see Pine Mountain)

Washington (B-3)

Settled: 1773 **Pop:** 4,279 **Elev:** 618 ft **Area code:** 706 **Zip:** 30673

The first city incorporated in the name of George Washington, it was the site of the Confederacy's last cabinet meeting (May 5, 1865) and the home of the South's first woman newspaper editor (Sarah Hillhouse of *The Monitor*, who printed editorials about the weather). Natives refer to this town as "Washington-Wilkes" (it is in Wilkes County) to distinguish it from the nation's capital.

Settlers first built a stockade called Heard's Fort. Elijah Clark led them in resistance to British troops, enabling patriots to hold Wilkes County when the rest of Georgia fell in 1779 (Kettle Creek Battleground). The last Confederate cabinet meeting convened in the Heard Building with President Davis and 14 officials on May 5, 1865. On June 4, Union

soldiers seized $100,000 of the $500,000 in gold remaining in the Confederate Treasury, moved to the town from Richmond. Legend persists that the rest of the gold (not recovered when Davis was captured at Irwinville) is buried in or near Washington.

What to See and Do

1. **Courthouse Square.** On square are historic markers noting last cabinet meeting of Confederacy; inscription of first land-grant record; capstone from cotton factory (1811); World War II Memorial; Hill House (ca 1784), first property owned by a woman in northeast Georgia; and a Vietnam Memorial.

2. **Robert Toombs House State Historic Site** (1797). 216 E Robert Toombs Ave. Restored residence of unreconstructed Confederate statesman and soldier. Frame Federal-era house with Greek-revival portico; period furniture, exhibits, video. (Daily exc Mon) Contact Superintendent, PO Box 605; 678-2226. ¢

3. **Washington-Wilkes Historical Museum.** 308 E Robert Toombs Ave. Located in white frame, antebellum house (ca 1836), the museum includes period furnishings, Civil War mementos, Indian items, earthenware. (Tues–Sat, also Sun afternoons; closed Jan 1, Thanksgiving, Dec 25) Phone 678-2105. ¢

4. **Callaway Plantation.** 5 mi W on US 78. Complete working plantation complex includes red brick Greek-revival mansion (1869); gray frame "Federal plainstyle" house (ca 1790) with period furnishings; hewn log kitchen (ca 1785) with utensils, agricultural equipment. RV parking (hookups). (Daily exc Mon; closed major hols) For further information contact the Chamber of Commerce.

5. **Kettle Creek Battleground.** 8 mi SW on Kettle Creek, off GA 44. Marker indicates site of a decisive battle of Revolutionary War.

6. **J. Strom Thurmond Dam and Lake.** 16 mi NE on US 378 to Lincolnton, then S on GA 47, E on GA 150. Swimming; fishing; boating (ramps). Hiking. Picnicking. Camping (yr-round; fee). For information contact Resource Manager's Office (E end of dam), Thurmond Lake, Rte 1, Box 6, Clarks Hill, SC 29821. Phone 722-3770 or 803/333-2476.

7. **State parks.**

Elijah Clark. 23 mi NE on US 378, on western shore of Clark Hill Lake. Park includes log-cabin museum with colonial life demonstrations. Swimming beach, waterskiing; fishing; boating (ramp). Nature trails. Picnicking. Camping, cottages. Standard hrs, fees. Contact Manager, Rte 4, Box 293, Lincolnton 30817; 359-3458.

Alexander H. Stephens. 19 mi SW on GA 47 to Crawfordville, then ½ mi N. In 1,190-acre park is Liberty Hall (ca 1830), restored house of A.H. Stephens, Vice-President of the Confederacy; Confederate Museum (Wed–Sat, also Sun afternoons; closed Thanksgiving, Dec 25; fee). Fishing; boating, rentals. Nature trails. Picnicking. Camping. Standard hrs, fees. Contact Superintendent, PO Box 235, Crawfordville 30631; 456-2602.

(For further information and maps for self-guided walking and driving tours contact the Washington-Wilkes Chamber of Commerce, 104 Liberty St, Box 661; 678-2013.)

(See Athens)

Motel

✔ ★ ★ **JAMESON INN.** *115 Ann Denard Dr.* 706/678-7925; res: 800/541-3268. 41 rms, 2 story. S $40; D $44; each addl $4; suites $95; under 12 free; higher rates Masters Tournament. Crib $4. TV; cable. Complimentary continental bkfst. Restaurant adj open 24 hrs. Ck-out 11 am. Some refrigerators. Cr cds: A, D, DS, MC, V.

Inn

★ ★ **SOUTHERN MANOR.** *412 E Robert Toombs Ave.* 706/678-2614; or 706/285-2247 (evenings). 3 rms, 2 story. S, D $55; under 12 free. Crib free. Complimentary continental bkfst. Complimentary coffee, tea/sherry in library. Ck-out 2 pm, ck-in 4 pm. Refrigerators avail. Restored, turn-of-the-century carriage house; antiques. Cr cds: A, MC, V.

Waycross (E-4)

Settled: 1818 **Pop:** 16,410 **Elev:** 135 ft **Area code:** 912 **Zip:** 31501

The name Waycross reflects the town's strategic location at the intersection of nine railroads and five highways. Situated at the edge of the Okefenokee Swamp, the town's early settlers put up blockhouses to protect themselves from local Indians. The production of naval stores and the marketing of furs were of prime importance before Okefenokee became a national wildlife refuge. Today, the economy of Waycross is based on a diversity of industries, including timber, railroad, mobile homes and tourism.

What to See and Do

1. **Okefenokee Swamp** (see). S via US 1/23.
2. **Laura S. Walker State Park.** 9 mi SE via US 82 & GA 177. Within the park is a 106-acre lake. Swimming pool, waterskiing; fishing; boating. Picnicking, playground. Camping. Standard hrs, fees. Contact Manager, 5653 Laura Walker Rd; 287-4900.
3. **Okefenokee Heritage Center.** 2 mi W on US 82 to N Augusta Ave. Exhibits on Okefenokee area history; art gallery with changing exhibits; social science room with exhibit on Indians of South Georgia exhibit; 1912 train depot and railroad cars; turn-of-the-century print shop; nature trails; Power House building; 1840s pioneer house. (Daily; closed major hols) Phone 285-4260. ¢
4. **Southern Forest World.** 2 mi W between US 1 and US 82 on N Augusta Ave. Exhibits, with audiovisual displays, detail development and history of forestry in the South; logging locomotive, fire tower, 38-foot model of a loblolly pine, giant cypress tree. Nature trails. (Daily exc Mon; closed major hols) Phone 285-4056. ¢

(For further information contact the Tourism & Conference Bureau, Waycross-Ware County Chamber of Commerce, 200 Lee Ave, PO Box 137, 31502; phone 283-3742.)

Annual Events

Okefenokee Spring Fling. Okefenokee Swamp Park (see OKEFE-NOKEE SWAMP). Fish fry, theater, crafts. Mar.

Forest Festival. Parade, exhibits, barbecue. Apr.

Motels

★ ★ ★**HOLIDAY INN.** (Box 1357) 1725 Memorial Dr (US 1/23) at jct US 84. 912/283-4490; FAX 912/283-4490, ext 197. 145 rms, 2 story. S $40–$47; D $47–$51; each addl $5; under 19 free. Crib free. TV; cable. Pool. Playground. Restaurant 6 am–2 pm, 5–10 pm. Rm serv. Bar 3 pm–2 am, Sat 5 pm–midnight, closed Sun; dancing. Ck-out 1 pm. Coin lndry. Meeting rms. Bellhops. Valet serv. Sundries. Airport, bus depot transportation. Putting green. Game rm. Some private patios, balconies. Cr cds: A, C, D, DS, MC, V.

✔ ★**PINE CREST.** 1761 Memorial Dr (US 1/23). 912/283-3580. 30 rms. S $26; D $30; each addl $5; under 18 free. Crib $5. TV; cable. Pool. Continental bkfst. Restaurant adj 6 am–10 pm. Ck-out noon. Cr cds: A, D, MC, V.

Restaurant

✔ ★**CHRISTOPHER'S.** 140 Lee Ave. 912/283-5260. Hrs: 11 am–2 pm, 5–11 pm; Sat from 5 pm. Closed Sun; Dec 24–25. Res accepted. Bar. Semi-a la carte: lunch $3.99–$6.99, dinner $4.99–$15.99. Child's meals. Specializes in pasta, seafood, steak. Entertainment Wed, Fri & Sat. Parking. Casual dining. Cr cds: A, MC, V.

Winder (B-2)

Pop: 7,373 **Elev:** 984 ft **Area code:** 404 **Zip:** 30680

What to See and Do

1. **Fort Yargo State Park.** 1 mi S via GA 81. The park is named for a fort of hand-hewn pine logs built during Indian uprisings in the 1790s. Swimming, beach; fishing; boating and canoeing (rentals). Nature trails. Picnicking. Camping. Contact Manager; 867-3489. At the north end is

   Will-A-Way Recreation Area. Designed to benefit disabled persons. Swimming pool; fishing; boating. Nature trails. Picnicking. Camping area for disabled and special chairs for water access. For hrs, fees phone 867-5313.
2. **Kilgore Mill Covered Bridge** (1874). S on GA 11, 1½ mi beyond Bethlehem. Covered bridge, 117 feet long, 16.5 feet wide, spans Appalachee River between Barrow and Walton counties.

(For further information contact the Barrow County Chamber of Commerce, PO Box 456, phone 867-9444; or visit the Welcome Center, a restored railroad depot, at Porter & Broad Sts.)

(For accommodations see Athens, Atlanta)

Kentucky

Population: 3,685,296

Land area: 40,409 square miles

Elevation: 257–4,145 feet

Highest point: Black Mountain (Harlan County)

Entered Union: June 1, 1792 (15th state)

Capital: Frankfort

Motto: United We Stand, Divided We Fall

Nickname: Bluegrass State

State flower: Goldenrod

State bird: Kentucky cardinal

State tree: Kentucky coffee tree

State fair: August 18-28, 1994, in Louisville

Time zones: Eastern and Central

The spirits of native sons Abraham Lincoln, Daniel Boone and Henry Clay are still present in many aspects of modern-day Kentucky. Known for such traditions as mountain music, mint juleps and the Derby, Kentucky's rich heritage has not faded over time. Although the bluegrass is blue only for a short time in the spring, and although few self-respecting Kentuckians will dilute a good bourbon with sugar and mint leaves, Kentucky has not sought to distance itself from its history. To many, this is still the land where Lincoln was born, where Zachary Taylor spent his youth and where Harriet Beecher Stowe witnessed the auctioning of slaves and found the inspiration to write *Uncle Tom's Cabin.* Such pioneers and visionaries continue to be revered today perhaps more so in Kentucky than anywhere else. The state itself has been assured immortality through the words of Stephen Foster's song, "My Old Kentucky Home."

Kentucky stretches from Virginia to Missouri, a geographic and historic bridge in the westward flow of American settlement. The state can be divided into four sections: the Bluegrass, the south central cave country, the eastern mountains and western lakes. Each differs drastically in geography, culture and economics. A circular area in the north central portion of the state, the Lexington plain, is bluegrass country, home of great horses and gentlemen-farmers. A predominantly rural nature has remained even though a patina of industry has been imposed, thanks to generous tax laws that have added industrial muscle to almost every major community. The great dams of the Tennessee Valley Authority have harnessed floods, generated cheap power, lured chemical plants and created new vacation resources.

More than 450 million pounds of burley and dark tobacco are typically grown in Kentucky each year. The principal crop is followed by corn, soybeans and wheat. Cattle, hogs, sheep and poultry round out the farm family. Not all of Kentucky's corn is served on the cob; much of it winds up as bourbon whiskey, respected and treasured in much of the world. Kentucky is a major mining state as well, with rich deposits of bituminous coal, petroleum, natural gas, fluorspar, natural cement and clay. Tobacco and food products, electronic equipment, transportation equipment, chemicals and machinery are the principal factory products.

The Cumberland Gap, a natural passageway through the mountains that sealed the Kentucky wilderness off from Virginia, was the gateway of the pioneers. Dr. Thomas Walker, the first recorded explorer to make a thorough land expedition into the state, arrived in 1750. Daniel Boone and a company of axmen hacked the Wilderness Road through the Cumberland Gap and far into the wilds. The first permanent settlement was at Harrodsburg in 1774, followed quickly by Boonesborough in 1775. Richard Henderson, founder of the Transylvania company, asked Congress to recognize Transylvania as the fourteenth state; instead Virginia claimed Kentucky as one of its counties, and Transylvania passed into history. Finally, in 1792 Congress admitted Kentucky as a state. The Civil War found Kentucky for the Union but against abolition. It remained officially with the North, but fought on both sides.

National Park Service Areas

With its abundance of mountains, forests, lakes and rivers, Kentucky offers extensive recreation areas. The state has Mammoth Cave National Park, Abraham Lincoln Birthplace National Historic Site (see both) and one interstate park, Breaks (see). It shares the 20,225 acres of Cumberland Gap National Historical Park (see) with Tennessee and Virginia, and it shares the 162,000 acres of the Big South Fork National River and Recreation Area with Tennessee (see DANIEL BOONE NATIONAL FOREST). Land Between the Lakes (see), a 170,000-acre, 40-mile-long peninsula in western Kentucky, was established as a national demonstration in environmental education and resource management.

National Forest

Daniel Boone National Forest (see DANIEL BOONE NATIONAL FOREST): Forest Supervisor in Winchester; Ranger offices in Berea, Big Creek*, London, Morehead, Somerset, Stanton*, Whitley City*.
*Not described in text

State Recreation Areas

The following towns list state recreation areas in their vicinity under What to See and Do; refer to the individual town for directions and park information.

Listed under **Ashland:** see Greenbo Lake State Resort Park.

Listed under **Bardstown:** see Lincoln Homestead and My Old Kentucky Home state parks.

Listed under **Breaks Interstate Park:** see Breaks Interstate Park.

Listed under **Cadiz:** see Lake Barkley State Resort Park.

Listed under **Campbellsville:** see Green River Lake State Park.

Listed under **Carrollton:** see General Butler State Resort Park.

Listed under **Cumberland Falls State Resort Park:** see Cumberland Falls State Resort Park.

Listed under **Gilbertsville:** see Kentucky Dam Village State Resort Park.

Listed under **Glasgow:** see Barren River Lake State Resort Park.

Listed under **Greenville:** see Lake Malone State Park.

Listed under **Harrodsburg:** see Old Fort Harrod State Park.

Listed under **Hazard:** see Buckhorn Lake State Resort Park.

Listed under **Henderson:** see John James Audubon State Park.

Listed under **Jamestown:** see Lake Cumberland State Resort Park.

Listed under **Kenlake State Resort Park:** see Kenlake State Resort Park.

Listed under **London:** see Levi Jackson Wilderness Road State Park.

Listed under **Louisville:** see E.P. "Tom" Sawyer State Park.

Listed under **Madisonville:** see Pennyrile Forest State Resort Park.

Listed under **Maysville:** see Blue Licks Battlefield State Park.

Listed under **Monticello:** see Dale Hollow Lake State Park.

Listed under **Natural Bridge State Resort Park:** see Natural Bridge State Resort Park.

Listed under **Olive Hill:** see Carter Caves State Resort Park and Grayson Lake State Park.

Listed under **Owensboro:** see Ben Hawes State Park.

Listed under **Pineville:** see Pine Mountain State Resort Park.

Listed under **Prestonsburg:** see Jenny Wiley State Resort Park.

Listed under **Rough River Dam State Resort Park:** see Rough River Dam State Resort Park.

Listed under **Somerset:** see General Burnside State Park.

Listed under **Walton:** see Big Bone Lick State Park.

Listed under **Williamstown:** see Kincaid Lake State Park.

Listed under **Winchester:** see Fort Boonesborough State Park.

Water-related activities, hiking, riding and various other sports, picnicking and camping are available in many of these areas. Sixteen areas have lodges and/or cottages (rates vary; phone 800/255-PARK for information); 28 have tent and trailer sites (Apr–Oct: $10.50 for two persons; $1 each addl person over 16 years; sr citizens rate; electricity and water included; primitive camping $8.50; rates subject to change). Thirteen state parks have campgrounds open year-round. Campsites are rented on a first-come, first-served basis; pets on leash only. No entrance fee is charged at state parks. For further information on state parks or camping, contact the Kentucky Department of Parks, 10th Floor, Capital Plaza Tower, Frankfort 40601; 502/564-2172 or 800/255-PARK including the Canadian provinces of Ontario and Quebec.

Fishing & Hunting

Mountain streams, giant lakes and major rivers all invite the angler and are productive throughout the year. Both largemouth bass and crappie can be found throughout the state. Lake Cumberland (see SOMERSET) has walleye; Laurel River Lake (see CORBIN), Lake Cumberland tailwaters and Paintsville Lake have trout; Buckhorn, Cave Run (see MOREHEAD) and Green River lakes have muskie; Lake Barkley, Kentucky Lake (see GILBERTSVILLE) and tailwaters have sauger and Lake Cumberland has striped bass. Statewide nonresident fishing license: $30; trout stamp $5; nonresident 3-day fishing license $12.50; 15-day license $20; no fishing license required for children under age 16. Annual nonresident hunting license: $95; deer permit with two tags, gun or archery $21; 5-day small game license $27.50. For open season dates and other details contact the Department of Fish and Wildlife Resources, #1 Game Farm Rd, Frankfort 40601; phone 502/564-4336.

Tennessee Valley Authority Recreation Sites

Many of Kentucky's major recreation areas have developed around projects of the Tennessee Valley Authority. The flood-control and power projects in the west have created Kentucky Lake (see GILBERTSVILLE, KENLAKE STATE RESORT PARK), with a scenic shoreline of 2,380 miles, big Lake Barkley (see CADIZ) and Land Between the Lakes (see). The TVA (Land Between the Lakes, 100 Van Morgan Dr, Golden Pond, KY 42231; phone 502/924-5602) will furnish material on the authority and its lakes, including recreation maps. Navigation charts are available at nominal cost from Map Sales, TVA, 101 Haney Bldg, Chattanooga, TN 37402-2801.

Safety Belt Information

Children under 40 inches in height must be in an approved safety seat anywhere in vehicle. In addition, Fayette County, Jefferson County, Kenton County and the cities of Louisville, St Matthews, Anchorage, Murray, Bowling Green and Corbin require the use of safety belts by all persons anywhere in vehicle. For further information phone 502/695-6356.

Interstate Highway System

The following alphabetical listing of Kentucky towns in *Mobil Travel Guide* shows that these cities are within 10 miles of the indicated Interstate highways. A highway map should, however, be checked for the nearest exit.

INTERSTATE 24: Cadiz, Gilbertsville, Hopkinsville, Paducah.

INTERSTATE 64: Ashland, Frankfort, Georgetown, Lexington, Louisville, Morehead, Olive Hill, Winchester.

INTERSTATE 65: Bowling Green, Cave City, Elizabethtown, Glasgow, Hodgenville, Horse Cave, Louisville, Mammoth Cave Natl Park, Park City, Shepherdsville.

INTERSTATE 71: Carrollton, Covington, Louisville, Walton.

INTERSTATE 75: Berea, Corbin, Covington, Georgetown, Lexington, London, Mount Vernon, Richmond, Walton, Williamsburg, Williamstown.

Additional Visitor Information

The Department of Travel Development, Dept MR, PO Box 2011, Frankfort 40602, phone 800/225-8747, ext 67, distributes literature and information, including a list of the state's many interesting festivals and fairs. The *Traveller's Guide to Kentucky* is informative, comprehensive and is revised annually.

There are seven welcome centers in Kentucky; visitors who stop by will find information and brochures most helpful in planning stops at points of interest. Their locations are as follows: Florence Welcome Center, I-75 southbound exit 180, Walton; Franklin Welcome Center, I-65 northbound exit 2, Franklin; Hopkinsville Welcome Center, I-24 westbound exit 89, Hopkinsville; Grayson Welcome Center, I-64 westbound exit 181, Grayson; Shepherdsville Welcome Center, I-65 southbound exit 116, Shepherdsville; Whitehaven Welcome Center, I-24 eastbound and US 45, Paducah; and Williamsburg Welcome Center, I-75 northbound exit 11, Williamsburg. (Daily, 8 am–6 pm)

Abraham Lincoln Birthplace National Historic Site (C-6)

(3 mi S of Hodgenville on US 31E/KY 61)

On February 12, 1809, the Sinking Spring Farm, named after a small limestone spring, became the birthplace of Abraham Lincoln, the 16th President of the United States. Less than three years later, in 1811, Thomas Lincoln, the President's father, moved the family to Knob Creek Farm, located about ten miles northeast. Later moves eventually took the Lincoln family to Indiana and Illinois.

The original purchase of the birthplace farm was made in 1905 by the Lincoln Farm Association, using monies raised through popular subscription. The Association then deeded the memorial park over to the US government in 1916. Today 110 acres of the original Lincoln Farm are contained within the 116-acre park. The site includes

Visitor Center. Audiovisual program and exhibits explore Lincoln's background and environment. Thomas Lincoln's Bible is on display.

Memorial Building (1911). More than 100,000 persons contributed funds to construct this granite and marble building. Inside is the log cabin originally believed to be the Lincoln birthplace; research has revealed that this is most likely not the case. The cabin was disassembled, moved, exhibited and stored many times before being reconstructed inside the Memorial Building.

(Daily exc Dec 25) For specific hrs and possible holiday closures contact the Superintendent, 2995 Lincoln Farm Rd, Hodgenville 42748; 502/358-3137. **Free.**

Annual Events

Lincoln's Birthday. Wreath-laying ceremony. Afternoon of Feb 12.

Founders Day. Festivities commemorating the park's founding; includes pioneer craft demonstrations, musical programs, Lincoln-oriented artwork. Wkend nearest July 17.

(For accommodations see Elizabethtown, also see Hodgenville)

Ashland (A-8)

Settled: 1815 **Pop:** 23,622 **Elev:** 548 ft **Area code:** 606

Set in the highlands of northeastern Kentucky, on the Ohio River, Ashland is an industrial city that produces oil, steel and chemicals.

What to See and Do

1. **Kentucky Highlands Museum.** 1624 Winchester. Displays trace history and cultural heritage of the region. Period clothing; Native American artifacts; WW II memorabilia; industrial exhibits. Gift shop. (Daily exc Mon; closed major hols) Phone 329-8888. ¢¢

2. **Central Park.** A 47-acre park with prehistoric Indian mounds. Sport facilities; picnicking. Phone 327-2046.

3. **Covered bridges.**

   Bennett's Mill Bridge. 8 mi W on KY 125 off KY 7. Built in 1855 to service mill customers, bridge spans Tygarts Creek. At 195 feet, this is one of Kentucky's longest single-span covered bridges; original footings and frame intact. Closed to traffic.

   Oldtown Bridge. 14 mi W via US 23, then 9 mi S on KY 1. Built 1880 to Burr's design; 194-foot, dual-span bridge crosses Little Sandy River. Closed to traffic.

4. **Greenbo Lake State Resort Park.** 18 mi W via US 23 to KY 1. A 3,330-acre park, with 225-acre lake, has early buffalo (pig-iron) furnace. Swimming pool (Memorial Day–Labor Day); fishing; boating (marina). Hiking, bicycle rentals; tennis. Picnicking, playground, lodge. Tent & trailer sites (Apr–Oct). Recreation program for children. Phone 473-7324.

(For further information contact the Ashland Area Convention & Visitors Bureau, 207 15th St, PO Box 987, 41101; 329-1007 or 800/377-6249.)

Seasonal Event

Tri-State Fair & Regatta. Various events held in tri-state area of Kentucky, Ohio and West Virginia. Among the highlights are the Regattafest, Central Park Festival, Budweiser Jet Ski Races, the Huntington Miller Classic Power Boat Races and the Industrial Fun O-Limp-ics. Phone 304/525-8141. June–Aug.

(See Olive Hill)

Motels

✔ ★**DAYS INN.** *12700 KY 180. 606/928-3600; FAX 606/928-6515.* 63 rms, 2 story. S $35–$47; D $40–$57; each addl $5; under 18 free. Crib $5. Pet accepted; $5. TV; cable. Pool. Complimentary continental bkfst. Complimentary coffee in rms. Restaurant nearby. Ck-out noon. Meeting rms. Some refrigerators. Picnic tables. Cr cds: A, C, D, DS, MC, V.

★★**KNIGHTS INN.** *7216 US 60 (41102). 606/928-9501; FAX 606/928-4436.* 124 rms. S $33; D $38; kit. units $38–$43; each addl $5; under 18 free. Crib $5. Pet accepted. TV; cable. Pool. Complimentary coffee. Restaurant nearby. Ck-out noon. Meeting rms. Cr cds: A, C, D, DS, ER, MC, V.

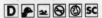

Restaurants

✔ ★**CHIMNEY CORNER.** *1624 Carter Ave, 1 blk S off US 23. 606/324-3300.* Hrs: 10 am–9 pm; Fri & Sat to 10 pm; Sun 8 am–8 pm. Closed most major hols. Res accepted Mon–Sat. Bar. Semi-a la carte: bkfst $2.50–$4.50, lunch $4.25–$6, dinner $6–$15.95. Specializes in char-grilled tuna & salmon, prime rib, fried chicken. Organist Fri & Sat evening. Family-owned. Cr cds: A, C, D, DS, MC, V.

★★**DRAGON PALACE.** *807 Carter Ave. 606/329-8081.* Hrs: 11 am–10 pm; Fri, Sat 11:30 am–11 pm; Sun noon–9 pm. Chinese, Amer menu. Bar. Semi-a la carte: lunch $2.55–$5.25. A la carte entrees: dinner $6.50–$11.95. Specialties: orange chicken, seafood Imperial, sizzling combo. Parking. Cr cds: A, DS, MC, V.

Barbourville (C-7)

Founded: 1800 **Pop:** 3,658 **Elev:** 986 ft **Area code:** 606 **Zip:** 40906

In the valley of the scenic Cumberland River, Barbourville is protected by a $2.5 million flood wall built around the city. Tobacco, coal mining and timber are the area's major industries. The city has also produced two Kentucky governors, a lieutenant governor, three US congressmen, and many other statesmen who served outside Kentucky.

What to See and Do

1. **Dr. Thomas Walker State Historic Site.** 5 mi SW on KY 459. Replica of original log cabin built in 1750 by Dr. Thomas Walker; surrounded by 12 acres of parkland. Miniature golf (fee). Picnic area, shelter, playground. Grounds (daily). Phone 546-4400. **Free.**
2. **Daniel Boone National Forest** (see). 24 mi NW on US 25.

(For further information contact the Knox County Chamber of Commerce, PO Box 128; 546-4300.)

Annual Event

Daniel Boone Festival. Celebrates Boone's search for a route through Kentucky. Square dancing, musket shooting, reenactment of Indian treaty signing, horse show, parade, old time fiddling, long rifle shoot between neighboring states, exhibits, antique displays, arts & crafts, parade, entertainment, homemade candies & cakes. Men grow beards and wear coonskin caps; Cherokee Indians make annual pilgrimage to city. 7 days, 2nd wk Oct.

(For accommodations see Corbin, Pineville)

Bardstown (B-6)

Settled: 1775 **Pop:** 6,801 **Elev:** 647 ft **Area code:** 502 **Zip:** 40004

One of Kentucky's oldest settlements, Bardstown includes many historic sites. It is the seat of Nelson County, home of four bourbon distilleries. Today, the chief agricultural product is tobacco.

What to See and Do

1. **My Old Kentucky Home State Park.** 1 mi E on US 150. The composer Stephen Foster occasionally visited his cousin, Judge John Rowan, at the stately house, Federal Hill (1795). These visits may have inspired him to write "My Old Kentucky Home," a melody that is a lasting favorite. The house and its 290 acres of grounds are now a state park. Attendants wear period costumes; period furnishings. Golf course. Picnic area, playground. Tent & trailer sites (standard fees). Guided tour (fee). Gardens; amphitheater (see SEASONAL EVENT). (Mar–Dec, daily; rest of yr, daily exc Mon; closed Jan 1, Thanksgiving, wk of Dec 25) For information contact Superintendent, PO Box 323; 348-3502. Grounds **Free.**
2. **Lincoln Homestead State Park.** 20 mi SE on US 150 to KY 528. In a compound framed by split rail fences is a replica of the cabin built on this land, which was originally settled in 1782 by Abraham Lincoln, Sr, grandfather of the President. This was the home of Thomas Lincoln until he was 25. Furnished in pioneer style, including several pieces made by Thomas Lincoln. Also, the Berry House, home of Nancy Hanks during her courtship by Thomas Lincoln; pioneer relics, photostatic copies of the Thomas and Nancy Lincoln marriage bonds. A replica of the blacksmith and carpenter shop where Thomas Lincoln worked is also in the compound. Houses (May–Sept, daily; Oct, wkends). The 150-acre park offers 18-hole golf (daily, fee). Picnic facilities, playground. Phone 606/336-7461. Museum **¢**

3. **St Joseph's Cathedral** (1816). 310 W Stephen Foster, at jct US 31E, 62. First Catholic cathedral west of the Allegheny Mountains. Paintings donated by Pope Leo XII. (Daily) Phone 348-3126.
4. **Wickland** (1813–17). E on US 62. Stately Georgian mansion, residence of two Kentucky governors, Charles A. Wickliffe and J.W. Beckham, and former Louisiana governor, R.C. Wickliffe (all of one family). Handsomely furnished with many original antiques. (Daily; closed Easter, Thanksgiving, Dec 25) Phone 348-5428. **¢¢**
5. **Spalding Hall** (ca 1825). Just off N 5th St. Once part of St Joseph College; used as hospital in Civil War. Former dormitory; now houses art and pottery shop. (May–Oct, daily; rest of yr, daily exc Mon) Phone 348-2999. **Free.** Also here are

    Oscar Getz Museum of Whiskey History. 114 N 5th St. Copper stills, manuscripts, documents, bottles and advertising art chronicle the history of whiskey from pre-colonial days to Prohibition era; includes collection of medicinal bottles (1913–33). (May–Oct, daily; rest of yr, Tues–Sat) Phone 348-2999. **Free.**

    Bardstown Historical Museum. Features items covering 200 years of local history. Exhibits include Indian artifacts, Lincoln papers concerning Lincoln-Reed suit, John Fitch papers and replica of first steamboat, Stephen Foster memorabilia, tools and utensils of Trappist Monks, Civil War artifacts, gifts of King Louis Phillipe and King Charles X of France, pioneer items, period costumes (1850s–1890s), natural science display. (May–Oct, daily; rest of yr, daily exc Sun) Phone 348-2999. **Free.**
6. **The Mansion.** 1003 N Third St. House of Ben Johnson, a powerful political figure of Kentucky's past, was site of raising of first Confederate flag in 1861. Tours. Overnight stays avail. (Daily; closed Dec 25) Phone 348-2586. **¢¢**
7. **My Old Kentucky Dinner Train.** Departs from 602 N 3rd St. Scenic dining excursions aboard elegant, restored dining cars from the 1940s. Round trip through countryside encludes four-course meal; five-course meal Fri & Sat evenings. (Apr–Oct, daily; rest of yr, wkends) Phone 348-7500. **¢¢¢¢¢**
8. **Jim Beam American Outpost.** 15 mi NW on KY 245 in Clermont. Educational film showing how Jim Beam bourbon is made. Collection of Jim Beam decanters made from Regal China, many commemorating historic events, famous people and national treasures. Craft shop. (Daily; closed some hols) Phone 543-9877. **Free.**
9. **Bernheim Forest.** 14 mi NW on KY 245 in Shepherdsville (see).

(For further information contact the Bardstown-Nelson County Tourist & Convention Commission, PO Box 867; 348-4877 or 800/638-4877.)

Seasonal Event

The Stephen Foster Story. J. Dan Talbott Amphitheater, in My Old Kentucky Home State Park (see #1). Musical with 50 Foster melodies, tracing composer's triumphs and romance. Nightly exc Mon; Sat also matinee. In the event of rain, indoor theater is used. Phone 348-5971 or 800/626-1563 for prices, reservations. Early June–early Sept.

(See Elizabethtown)

Motels

(Most motels increase their rates for Derby wkend; reservations should be made as far ahead as possible and confirmed)

✔ ★ ★ **BEST WESTERN GENERAL NELSON.** 411 W Stephen Foster Ave (US 62). 502/348-3977; FAX 502/348-7596. 52 rms, 2 story, 4 kits. S $35–$45; D $44–$60; each addl $5; kit. units $44–$55; under 12 free. Crib free. TV; cable. Pool. Restaurant adj 6 am–9 pm. Ck-out noon. Meeting rms. Refrigerators avail. Cr cds: A, C, D, DS, MC, V.

D 🔄 🚫 ⏰ **SC**

★ ★ **HOLIDAY INN.** (Box 520) 2 mi S on US 31E exit 21 at Bluegrass Pkwy. 502/348-9253; FAX 502/348-5478. 103 rms, 2 story.

May–Sept: S, D $58–$70; each addl $5; under 19 free; lower rates rest of yr. Crib free. Pet accepted. TV. Pool; wading pool. Playground. Restaurant 6 am–2 pm, 5–10 pm. Bar 11–1 am; dancing 6 nights/wk. Ck-out noon. Meeting rms. Free local airport transportation. 9-hole par 3 golf; driving range. Miniature golf. Picnic tables. Cr cds: A, C, D, DS, MC, V.

✓ ★OLD BARDSTOWN INN. 510 E Stephen Foster Ave (US 62), off US 150E. 502/348-1700. 35 rms, 2 story. S $30–$45; D $34–$49; each addl $4; under 12 free. Crib $4. TV; cable. Pool. Complimentary coffee in lobby. Restaurant nearby. Ck-out noon. Cr cds: A, MC, V.

★★PARKVIEW. 418 E Stephen Foster Ave (US 62), at jct US 150. 502/348-5983. 40 rms, 1–2 story, 10 kit. units. June–Labor Day: S $44; D $48; each addl $4; suites $60–$80; kit. units $50–$70; lower rates rest of yr. Crib free. Pet accepted. TV; cable. Pool. Complimentary continental bkfst. Restaurant 7 am–10 pm. Bar. Ck-out 11 am. Coin lndry. Picnic tables. My Old Kentucky Home State Park opp. Cr cds: A, MC, V.

Inns

★JAILER'S INN. 111 W Stephen Foster Ave (US 62). 502/348-5551. 5 rms. No rm phones. S, D $55–$80; each addl $5. Closed Jan–Feb. Crib free. TV; cable. Complimentary continental bkfst, coffee and tea/sherry. Restaurant adj 11 am–9 pm. Ck-out 10 am, ck-in 5 pm. Built 1819 as jail, then converted to jailer's residence. Furnished with antiques and oriental rugs. Cr cds: A, DS, MC, V.

★TALBOTT TAVERN/McLEAN HOUSE. 107 W Stephen Foster Ave (US 62). 502/348-3494. 13 rms, 2 story. S, D $50–$69. TV; cable. Complimentary continental bkfst. Restaurant (see OLD TALBOTT TAVERN). Ck-out 11 am, ck-in 2 pm. Talbott Tavern (1779) is oldest western stagecoach stop still in operation. Colonial furnishings; antiques. Cr cds: A, MC, V.

Restaurants

★JONES' KENTUCKY HOME. 4 blks W on US 62. 502/348-3359. Hrs: 6 am–9 pm. Closed Dec 25–Mar 1. Bar. Semi-a la carte: bkfst $3.50–$6, lunch $3.25–$6.95, dinner $6.99–$16.25. Child's meals. Specializes in Kentucky country ham, fried chicken. Parking. Family-owned. Cr cds: A, MC, V.

✓ ★OLD TALBOTT TAVERN. (See Talbott Tavern/McLean House Inn) 502/348-3494. Hrs: 11 am–9 pm. Closed Dec 25. Res accepted. Bar to 1 am. Semi-a la carte: lunch $4.25–$7.50, dinner $9.95–$13.95. Specializes in country ham, rabbit, fried chicken. Entertainment wkends. Historic stagecoach stop (1779). Antique furniture. Cr cds: A, MC, V.

Berea (B-7)

Pop: 9,126 **Elev:** 1,034 ft **Area code:** 606 **Zip:** 40403

Berea College and diverse industry provide the income for this community in the foothills of the Cumberland Mountains. Designated the "Folk Arts and Crafts Capital of Kentucky" by the state legislature, Berea boasts more than 50 antique shops, craft shops and working studios. Indian Fort Mountain nearby is the site of prehistoric fortifications. A Ranger District office of the Daniel Boone National Forest (see) is located here.

What to See and Do

1. **Appalachian Museum.** Jackson St, on campus of Berea College. Collection of rare Appalachian artifacts; restored log smokehouse on grounds; slide-tape programs; changing exhibits. (Daily; closed Thanksgiving, Dec 25) Phone 986-9341, ext 6078. ¢

2. **Churchill Weavers.** Lorraine Ct, exit I-75 to US 25N. Established 1922, Churchill is one of the nation's oldest producers of handwoven goods. Self-guided tours through loomhouse (Mon–Fri; closed Dec 25). Gift shop and outlet shop (daily; closed Dec 25). Phone 986-3127. **Free.**

3. **The Studio Craftspeople of Berea.** An organization of craftspeople working in various media invite visitors to visit their studios. The Tourism Commission has a list of studios open to the public.

(For further information contact the Berea Tourism Commission, 201 N Broadway, PO Box 556; 986-2540 or 800/598-5263.)

Annual Events

Kentucky Guild of Artists & Craftsmen's Fair. Indian Fort Theater. Crafts, art, folk dances, singing. Phone 986-3192. 3rd wkend May and 2nd wkend Oct.

Berea Craft Festival. Indian Fort Theater, at Berea College. Entertainment, regional food, crafts demonstrations. Phone 986-2258. Three days mid-July.

Celebration of Traditional Music Festival. Features traditional music, dancers, concerts. Last wkend Oct.

(See Mount Vernon, Richmond)

Motels

★★DAYS INN. I-75 exit 77, at jct KY 595. 606/986-7373; FAX 606/986-3144. 60 rms, 2 story. S $35–$45; D $39–$45; each addl $5; family rates. Crib free. TV. Pool. Complimentary coffee in lobby. Restaurant adj. Ck-out 11 am. Meeting rm. Miniature golf. Cr cds: A, C, D, DS, MC, V.

✓ ★HOLIDAY. (Box 227) ½ mi E of I-75 exit 76 on KY 21. 606/986-9311. 63 rms. S, D $31.55; each addl $5; suites $44.60. Crib $5. TV; cable. Pool. Restaurant adj 7 am–10 pm. Ck-out 11 am. Cr cds: MC, V.

Hotel

★★★BOONE TAVERN. Main & Prospect Sts, 1 mi E of I-75 exit 76, on KY 21. 606/986-9358 or -9359; FAX 986-7711; res: 800/366-9358. 59 rms. S $47–$69; D $57–$79; each addl $10; under 12 free. Crib $6. Pet accepted, some restrictions. TV. Restaurant 7–9 am, 11:30 am–1:30 pm, 6–7:30 pm. Ck-out noon. Meeting rms. Gift shop. Established 1909. Operated by Berea College; most furniture handmade by students. Cr cds: A, C, D, DS, MC, V.

Restaurants

✓ ★DINNER BELL. I-75 exit 76. 606/986-2777. Hrs: 6 am–10 pm; winter hrs vary. Semi-a la carte: bkfst $1.65–$5.95, lunch $1.99–$4.95, dinner $4.50–$11.95. Child's meals. Specializes in steak, seafood, country ham, pork tenderloin. Parking. Cr cds: MC, V.

★PAPALENO'S. 108 Center St, adj Berea College. 606/986-4497. Hrs: 11 am–11 pm; Fri, Sat to midnight; Sun noon–11 pm. Closed Thanksgiving, Dec 25. Italian menu. Semi-a la carte: lunch, dinner $1.65–$12.50. Child's meals. Specializes in salads, pizza, submarine sandwiches. No cr cds accepted.

Bowling Green (C-5)

Founded: 1780 **Pop:** 40,641 **Elev:** 496 ft **Area code:** 502

In the early days of the community, county court was held in the house of Robert Moore, a founder of the town, and visiting lawyers would idle away their time bowling on the lawn—hence the name. A cultural center for southern Kentucky with a variety of industries, Bowling Green is also sustained by Warren County's dairy cattle, livestock and tobacco farms. For a short time, it was the Confederate capital of Kentucky.

What to See and Do

1. **Western Kentucky University** (1906). College St & 15th St. (15,800 students) High on a hill, Western Kentucky University was built around the site of a Civil War fort. Phone 745-0111. On campus are

    Kentucky Museum. Kentucky Bldg, Kentucky St. Collections include costumes, implements, art works and textiles relating to the cultural history of Kentucky and the region. Exhibits, tours, special programs. Gift shop. (Daily exc Mon; closed univ hols) Phone 745-2592. ¢ In same building is

    Kentucky Library. Contains 30,000 books, manuscripts, maps, broadsides, photographs, sheet music, scrapbooks, materials relating to Kentucky and to genealogical research of Kentucky families. (Daily exc Mon; closed univ hols) Phone 745-2592. **Free.**

    Hardin Planetarium. State St. Varying programs year-round; phone 745-4044 for schedule & fees.

2. **Historic Riverview at Hobson Grove** (1857). 1100 W Main Ave, in Hobson Grove Park. House in Italianate style, furnished with collection of Victorian furniture from 1860–90. (Daily exc Mon; closed hols, late Dec–Jan) Phone 843-5565. ¢¢

3. **Capitol Arts Center.** 416 E Main. Restored art deco building; national and local live presentations, gallery exhibits. (Daily; closed hols) Admission varies with event. Phone 782-2787.

4. **Beech Bend Park.** Beech Bend Rd. Water park includes swimming pool, waterslide, paddleboats, eight rides. Miniature golf. Picnic area. Camping. Separate fee for each activity. (May–Sept, daily) Phone 781-7634. ¢

5. **Industrial tour. General Motors Corvette Plant.** Louisville Road, I-65. Tours of only Corvette assembly plant in the world. No cameras permitted. (Mon–Fri; larger groups by appt) Phone 745-8419. **Free.**

(For further information contact the Bowling Green-Warren County Chamber of Commerce, 812 State St, PO Box 51, 42102; 781-3200.)

Motels

✔ ★ ★ **BEST WESTERN CONTINENTAL INN.** (Box 96, 42102) I-65N exit 28, at US 31W. 502/781-5200. 100 rms, 2 story. S $36–$40; D $40–$45; each addl $3; higher rates car shows. Crib $3. TV; cable. Heated pool; wading pool. Restaurant open 24 hrs. Rm serv. Ck-out noon. Cr cds: A, D, DS, MC, V.

★ ★ **BEST WESTERN MOTOR INN.** (Box 51847, 42102) 1 blk E of I-65 exit 22. 502/782-3800; FAX 502/782-2384. 179 rms, 2–3 story. S, D $50–$62; each addl $3. Crib free. TV; cable. 2 pools, 1 indoor; wading pool, whirlpool, sauna. Playground. Restaurant open 24 hrs. Rm serv. Ck-out noon. Coin lndry. Meeting rms. Sundries. Gift shop. Tennis. Lawn games. Rec rm. Enclosed courtyard. Cr cds: A, C, D, DS, MC, V.

✔ ★ ★ **FAIRFIELD INN BY MARRIOTT.** 1940 Mel Browning St (42104), I-65 exit 22. 502/782-6933; FAX 502/782-6967. 105 rms, 3 story. S $36.95–$41.95; D $42.95–$48.95; each addl $3; under 18 free. Crib free. TV; cable. Heated pool. Complimentary coffee in lobby. Restaurant adj 6 am–11 pm. Ck-out noon. Meeting rms. Refrigerator avail. Cr cds: A, C, D, DS, MC, V.

★ ★ **HAMPTON INN.** 233 Three Springs Rd (42104), I-65 exit 22, W on KY 231. 502/842-4100; 131 rms, 4 story. S $47–$51; D $55–$59; under 18 free; higher rates special events. Crib avail. TV; in-rm movies avail. Pool. Complimentary continental bkfst, coffee. Restaurant nearby. Meeting rms. Ck-out noon. Health club privileges. Cr cds: A, C, D, DS, MC, V.

★ ★ **HOLIDAY INN I-65.** 3240 Scottsville Rd (42104), 2¾ mi SE on US 231, 1 blk W of I-65 exit 22. 502/781-1500; FAX 502/842-0030. 107 rms, 2 story. S $39–$80; D $90; each addl $10; under 12 free. Crib free. TV; cable. Pool; wading pool. Playground. Restaurant 6 am–2 pm, 5–10 pm. Rm serv. Bar 4:30 pm–midnight. Ck-out noon. Sundries. Game rm. Picnic tables. Cr cds: A, C, D, DS, MC, V, JCB.

✔ ★ ★ **NEW'S INN.** 3460 Scottsville Rd (42104), 2½ mi E on US 231; 1 blk W of I-65 exit 22. 502/781-3460. 51 rms. S $32–$40; D $36–$44; each addl $3. Crib free. TV; cable. Pool. Playground. Complimentary coffee. Restaurant adj 6 am–11 pm. Ck-out 11 am. Free airport transportation. Picnic tables, grills. Cr cds: A, D, DS, MC, V.

✔ ★ **TRAVELODGE.** 181 Cumberland Trace (42103), I-65 exit 22. 502/842-6730; FAX 502/842-3692. 122 rms, 2 story. S $30–$36; D $34–$40; each addl $6; under 12 free; higher rates special events. Crib free. TV; cable. Pool. Complimentary continental bkfst. Complimentary coffee in rms. Restaurant 11 am–2 pm, 5–10 pm. Ck-out noon. Cr cds: A, D, DS, MC, V.

Motor Hotels

★ **GREENWOOD EXECUTIVE INN.** (Box 51885, 42102) 2¾ mi SE, just off US 231; 1 blk W of I-65 exit 22. 502/781-6610; res: 800/354-4394; FAX 502/781-7985. 151 rms, 4 story. S $38; D $48; each addl $5; suites $95–$130. Crib $5. TV. Pool; wading pool. Restaurant 6 am–2 pm, 5–10 pm. Rm serv. Bar 11–1 am, Sat to midnight; entertainment, dancing. Ck-out 2 pm. Meeting rms. Airport, bus depot transportation. Cr cds: A, D, DS, MC, V.

★ ★ **HOWARD JOHNSON.** 523 US 31 W Bypass (42101), 1 mi NE. 502/842-9453; FAX 502/842-0228. 143 rms, 2–3 story. No elvtr. S $44–$48; D $50–$74; each addl $8; under 18 free. Crib free. TV; cable. Indoor pool; wading pool. Restaurant 6 am–10 pm. Rm serv. Bar 3 pm–midnight, closed Sun; entertainment Thurs, dancing wkends. Ck-out noon. Meeting rms. Sundries. Game rm. Lawn games. Cr cds: A, C, D, DS, ER, MC, V, JCB.

Restaurants

★ ★ **ANDREW'S.** 2019 Scottsville Rd. 502/781-7680. Hrs: 11 am–9:30 pm; Fri, Sat to 10 pm. Closed Sun. Bar to midnight. Semi-a la carte: lunch $4.95–$7.95, dinner $6.95–$19.95. Child's meals. Specializes in seafood, prime rib. Salad bar. Guitarist Fri. Parking. Red oak paneling with stained & beveled glass. Cr cds: A, D, DS, MC, V.

✔ ★ ★ **MARIAH'S.** 801 State St. 502/842-6878. Hrs: 11 am–1 pm; Fri, Sat to 11 pm; Sun to 9 pm. Closed some major hols. Bar. Semi-a la carte: lunch $4.75–$6.50, dinner $7.75–$13.95. Child's meals. Specialties: filet mignon, marinated chicken, salad dressings. Parking. Outdoor dining. Oldest brick house in Bowling Green (1818); restored to original appearance and furnished with antiques. Cr cds: A, D, DS, MC, V.

★★**RAFFERTY'S.** *1939 Scottsville Rd.* 502/842-0123. Hrs: 11 am–10 pm; Fri, Sat to 11 pm. Closed Thanksgiving, Dec 25. Bar. Semi-a la carte: lunch, dinner $4.75–$16.95. Child's meals. Specializes in barbecued ribs, prime rib. Parking. Outdoor dining. Contemporary decor. Cr cds: A, D, MC, V.

Breaks Interstate Park (C-9)

(7 mi SE of Elkhorn City, KY and 8 mi N of Haysi, VA on KY-VA 80)

Where the Russell Fork of the Big Sandy River plunges through the mountains is called the "Grand Canyon of the South," the major focus of this 4,600-acre park on the Kentucky-Virginia border. From the entrance, a paved road winds through an evergreen forest and then skirts the canyon rim. Overlooks provide a spectacular view of the Towers, a huge pyramid of rocks. Within the park are extraordinary rock formations, caves, springs, a profusion of rhododendron and, of course, the 5-mile-long, 1,600-foot-deep gorge.

The visitor center houses historical and natural exhibits, including a coal exhibit (Apr–Oct, daily). Laurel Lake is stocked with bass and bluegill. Swimming pool; pedal boats. Hiking, bridle trails. Picnicking, playground. Camping (Apr–Oct, fee); cottages (year-round), cafeteria, gift shop. Park (daily); facilities (Apr–Oct, daily). For further information contact Breaks Interstate Park, PO Box 100, Breaks, VA 24607; 703/865-4413 or 800/982-5122. Memorial Day–Labor Day, per car ¢

(For accommodations see Pikeville)

Cadiz (C-4)

Pop: 2,148 **Elev:** 423 ft **Area code:** 502 **Zip:** 42211

With the development of "Land Between The Lakes," a 170,000-acre wooded peninsula between the Tennessee Valley Authority's Kentucky Lake and the Army Corps of Engineers' Lake Barkley on the Cumberland River, Cadiz became a staging area for the major recreation project. The area covers much of Trigg County, of which Cadiz is the seat.

What to See and Do

1. **Barkley Dam, Lock and Lake.** 35 mi NW in Gilbertsville (see). On lakeshore is

   Lake Barkley State Resort Park. 7 mi W on KY 80 to KY 1489. A 3,700-acre park on a 57,920-acre lake. Swimming beach, pool, bathhouse (seasonal); fishing; boating, canoeing (ramps, rentals, marina). Hiking, backpacking, horseback riding (seasonal); 18-hole golf course (yr-round); tennis, trapshooting, shuffleboard, basketball. Picnicking, restaurant, cottages, lodge (see RESORT). Camping (fee). Children's programs. Lighted airstrip. Standard fees. Phone 924-1131 or 800/325-1708.

2. **Recreation areas.**

   Cadiz Public Use Area. On US 68 on W side of town. Fishing; launching ramp. Playground, picnic area. **Free.**

   Hurricane Creek Public Use Area. 12 mi NW via KY 274. Swimming; launching ramp. Playground. Improved campsites (fee). (Apr–mid-Oct, daily) Golden Age Passport accepted (see INTRODUCTION). Phone 522-8821.

3. **Original Log Cabin.** 22 Main St. Four-room log cabin, furnished with 18th- and 19th-century artifacts, was occupied by a single family

for more than a century. (June–Aug, daily exc Sun; rest of yr, Mon–Fri; closed major hols) Phone 522-3892. **Free.**

4. **Kenlake State Resort Park** (see). 16 mi SW on US 68, KY 80.

(For further information contact the Cadiz-Trigg County Tourist Commission, PO Box 735, phone 522-3892; or visit Tourist Information Center, US 68E at I-24 interchange.)

(See Gilbertsville, Land Between The Lakes)

Motel

✔★★**COUNTRY INN BY CARLSON.** *5909 Hopkinsville Rd, I-24 exit 65.* 502/522-7007; res: 800/456-4000; FAX 502/522-3893. 48 rms, 2 story. S $39; D $44; each addl $4; suites $50–$55; under 18 free. Crib free. TV; cable, in-rm movies avail. Pool. Complimentary coffee in lobby, coffee in rms. Restaurant adj. Ck-out noon. Cr cds: A, D, DS, MC, V.

Resort

★★★**LAKE BARKLEY LODGE.** *(Box 790)* 10 mi NW on KY 1489, 3½ mi N of US 68 in Lake Barkley State Resort Park. 502/924-1131; res: 800/325-1708. 124 rms, 2 story, 13 kit. cottages. Apr–Oct: S $49–$55; D $59–$65; each addl $5; suites $140; kit. cottages $120; under 16 free; some lower rates rest of yr. Crib free. TV. Pool; wading pool, lifeguard in summer. Child's program; playground. Dining rm 7–10:30 am, 11:30 am–2:30 pm, 5–9 pm. Ck-out noon (cottages 11 am), ck-in 4 pm. Coin lndry. Meeting rms. Maid serv in lodge. Free transportation to lodge from park airport. Lighted tennis. 18-hole golf, greens fee $15. Beach; waterskiing; boats. Lawn games. Trap shooting. Soc dir; entertainment, movies. Rec rm. Exercise rm; instructor, weight machines, bicycles, whirlpool, sauna, steam rm. Some private patios, balconies. Picnic tables. State-owned; facilities of park available. Cr cds: A, D, DS, MC, V.

Restaurant

✔★**KENTUCKY SMOKEHOUSE.** *I-24 & US 68 (KY 80).* 502/522-8420. Hrs: 6 am–9 pm. Closed Jan 1, Dec 24–25. Res accepted. Semi-a la carte: bkfst 95¢–$5.95, lunch $3.50–$4.95, dinner $5.25–$12.95. Child's meals. Specializes in ham, fish. Salad bar. Parking. Modern country atmosphere. Cr cds: MC, V.

Campbellsville (C-6)

Pop: 9,577 **Elev:** 813 ft **Area code:** 502 **Zip:** 42718

Located geographically in the heart of Kentucky, Campbellsville is near the junction of the Pennyrile, Bluegrass and Knobs regions of the state. Nearby, at Tebbs Bend, the Battle of Green River was fought on July 4, 1863. Also in the vicinity is the town of Greensburg, with its interesting historic district dating to the 18th century.

What to See and Do

Green River Lake State Park. 6 mi S on KY 55. Beach; fishing; boat dock (paddleboat rentals). Picnicking. Camping. (Daily) Standard fees. Phone 465-8255.

(For further information contact the Taylor County Tourist Commission, Court St & Broadway, PO Box 4021; 465-3786.)

(See Jamestown)

Motels

★ ★**BEST WESTERN.** *1400 E Broadway. 502/465-7001; FAX 502/465-7001, ext 302.* 60 rms. S, D $47; each addl $5; suites $50–$73; under 12 free. Crib free. TV; cable. Pool; wading pool, whirlpool. Playground. Coffee in rms. Restaurant nearby. Ck-out 11 am. Meeting rms. Refrigerators. Cr cds: A, C, D, DS, MC, V.

✔ ★**LAKEVIEW.** *1 mi N on KY 289, Lebanon Rd, across from lake. 502/465-8139.* 17 rms. S $31; D $35; each addl $2; under 12 free. Crib free. TV; cable. Complimentary continental bkfst. Coffee in rms. Restaurant nearby. Ck-out 11 am. Some refrigerators. Cr cds: A, DS, MC, V.

Restaurant

✔ ★**CUMBERLAND HOUSE.** *1318 E Broadway. 502/465-7777.* Hrs: 11 am–10 pm; Fri, Sat to 11 pm; Sun buffet to 4 pm. Closed Dec 25. Res accepted Fri–Sun. Semi-a la carte: lunch $1.55–$6.25, dinner $2.25–$10.95. Buffet: dinner (Fri, Sat) $3.95–$8.95. Sun brunch $3.95–$7.95. Child's meals. Specializes in prime rib, seafood. Salad bar. Parking. Cr cds: MC, V.

SC

Carrollton (A-6)

Founded: 1794 **Pop:** 3,715 **Elev:** 469 ft **Area code:** 502 **Zip:** 41008

At the confluence of the Ohio and Kentucky rivers, this tree-shaded residential town is named in honor of Charles Carroll. Originally from Carrollton, Maryland, Carroll was one of the signers of the Declaration of Independence.

What to See and Do

1. **Historic District.** Self-guided auto tour of historic sites and houses. Tour begins at Old Stone Jail, corner of Highland & Court Sts. Tourist center on 2nd floor houses small museum on local history. **Free.**

2. **General Butler State Resort Park.** 2 mi S on KY 227. A 791-acre memorial to William O. Butler, native of Carrollton and hero of Battle of New Orleans. Within the park is a 30-acre lake. Swimming; fishing; boating (rentals). Nature trails; 9-hole golf (fee), tennis. Ski area (fee). Picnic sites, playground, grocery adj; cottages, lodge & dining room (see RESORT). Tent & trailer camping (daily, standard fees). Recreation program. For fees or information phone 732-4384.

(For further information contact the Carroll County Tourism Commission, PO Box 293; 732-7036 or 800/325-4290.)

Annual Event

Kentucky Scottish Weekend. Celebration of Scottish heritage includes pipe bands, bagpipers; Scottish athletic competition, Celtic music; British auto show. Phone 239-2665. 2nd wkend May.

Motels

✔ ★**DAYS INN.** *(Rte 3, Box 108) I-71 exit 44. 502/732-9301; FAX 502/732-6661.* 84 rms. S, D $44; each addl $6; under 19 free; wkend rates; higher rates special events. Crib free. TV; cable. Pool. Restaurant

6:30 am–2 pm, 5:30–10 pm. Ck-out noon. Meeting rms. Downhill ski 2 mi. Cr cds: A, C, D, DS, MC, V.

★ ★**HOLIDAY INN EXPRESS.** *(Rte 3, Box 108) At I-71 exit 44. 502/732-6661.* 62 rms, 2 story. S, D $50; each addl $6; under 19 free; some wkend rates; higher rates special events. Crib free. Pet accepted, some restrictions. TV; cable. Pool. Complimentary continental bkfst. Restaurant adj. Ck-out noon. Meeting rm. Downhill ski 2 mi. Cr cds: A, C, D, DS, MC, V, JCB.

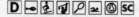

Inn

✔ ★**CARROLLTON INN.** *3rd & Main Sts. 502/732-6905.* 10 rms. S $32.50; D $35.50–$38.50; each addl $5; under 16 free; higher rates special events. Crib free. TV; cable. Restaurant (see CARROLLTON INN). Bar. Ck-out 11 am. Cr cds: A, MC, V.

Resort

★ ★ ★**GENERAL BUTLER LODGE.** *(Box 325) 2 mi N of I-71 exit 44, in General Butler State Resort Park. 502/732-4384; res: 800/325-0078; FAX 502/732-4270.* 57 rms in 2–3 story lodge, 23 kit. cottages. No elvtr in lodge. S $49; D $59; each addl $5; kit. cottages $73–$140; under 17 free. Crib free. TV; cable. Pool; wading pool, lifeguard in summer. Playground. Free supervised child's activities (late May–early Sept). Dining rm 7 am–9 pm. Ck-out noon; cottages 11 am. Meeting rm. Gift shop. Lighted tennis. 9-hole golf, greens fee $10, miniature golf. Swimming in lake; boats, paddleboats. Downhill ski on site. Private patios, balconies. Picnic tables, grills. State-owned; all facilities of state park. Cr cds: A, C, D, DS, MC, V.

Restaurant

✔ ★**CARROLLTON INN.** *(See Carrollton Inn) 502/732-6905.* Hrs: 8 am–10 pm; Fri to 11 pm; Sat 7 am–11 pm; Sun 8 am–9 pm. Closed Dec 25. Res accepted. Bar. Semi-a la carte: bkfst $1.80–$5.95, lunch $2.95–$5.95, dinner $5.95–$14.95. Child's meals. Specializes in prime rib, rib-eye steak. Parking. Cr cds: A, MC, V.

Cave City (C-5)

Pop: 1,953 **Elev:** 636 ft **Area code:** 502 **Zip:** 42127

Situated in an area of many caves, this village primarily serves tourists passing through the region en route to Mammoth Cave and other commercially-operated caves nearby.

What to See and Do

1. **Mammoth Cave Chair Lift and Guntown Mountain.** At jct KY 70, I-65. Lift ascends 1,350 feet to Guntown Mountain. On grounds is authentic reproduction of 1880s frontier town; museums, saloon, entertainment. Train ride (fee). Water slide. Onyx Cave tours (Apr–Nov, daily). (Memorial Day–Labor Day, daily; May–Memorial Day & Labor Day–mid-Oct, Sat, Sun only) Phone 773-3530. Admission includes chair lift. **¢¢¢**

2. **Crystal Onyx Cave.** 2 mi SE on KY 90, off I-65. Helectites, stalagmites, stalactites, onyx columns, rare crystal onyx rimstone formations; Native American burial site dating from 680 B.C. Temperature in cave 54°F. Guided tours every 45 minutes. Improved & primitive camping adj (fee). (Feb–Dec, daily; closed Thanksgiving, Dec 25) Phone 773-2359. Guided tours **¢¢¢**

3. Kentucky Action Park. 1½ mi W on KY 70. Chairlift to top of mountain, slide downhill in individual alpine sleds with braking system. Go-carts, bumper boats, bumper cars (fees); horseback riding (fee). (Memorial Day–Labor Day, daily; Easter–Memorial Day, Labor Day–Oct, wkends) Phone 773-2636. ¢¢

4. Mammoth Cave National Park (see). 10 mi W via I-65, KY 70.

(For further information contact the Cave City Convention Center, PO Box 518; 773-3131 or 800/346-8908.)

(See Glasgow, Horse Cave, Park City)

Motels

★★**DAYS INN.** *(Box 2009) ¾ mi W on KY 70; 2 blks NE of I-65 exit 53. 502/773-2151.* 110 rms, 2 story. Late May–early Sept: S $36–$48; D $48–$56; each addl $5; under 12 free; lower rates rest of yr. Crib free. Pet accepted. TV; in-rm movies. Heated pool; wading pool. Restaurant 5:30 am–8:30 pm. Ck-out noon. Coin lndry. Meeting rms. Game rm. Private patios, balconies. Cr cds: A, C, D, DS, MC, V.

✔★★**HERITAGE INN.** *(Box 2048) ¾ mi W on KY 70; 2 blks NE of I-65 exit 53. 502/773-3121; res: 800/264-1514.* 115 rms, 2 story. Late May–Labor Day: S $25–$40; D $28–$62; each addl $4–$8; under 12 free; golf plans; higher rates hol wkends; lower rates rest of yr. Crib free. TV; cable. Pool; wading pool. Restaurant open 24 hrs. Rm serv 7 am–11 pm. Ck-out noon. Sundries. Miniature golf. Game rm. Cr cds: A, C, D, DS, MC, V.

★★**QUALITY INN.** *Mammoth Cave Blvd, W on KY 70, 90. 502/773-2181.* 101 rms, 2 story. Memorial Day–Labor Day: S $36–$56; D $42–$62; each addl $6; suites $62; under 18 free; lower rates rest of yr. Crib $6. Pet accepted. TV; in-rm movies. Pool. Playground. Restaurant open 24 hrs. Rm serv 6 am–10 pm. Ck-out 11 am. Gift shop. Picnic tables. Cr cds: A, C, D, DS, ER, MC, V.

Restaurant

★**SAHARA STEAK HOUSE.** *413 E Happy Valley St. 502/773-3450.* Hrs: 11 am–9 pm; Sun from 11:30 am. Closed Thanksgiving, Dec 25. Semi-a la carte: lunch $2.95–$6.95, dinner $4.95–$23.95. Child's meals. Salad bar. Parking. Cr cds: A, DS, MC, V.

Corbin (C-7)

Settled: 1883 **Pop:** 7,419 **Elev:** 1,080 ft **Area code:** 606 **Zip:** 40701

What to See and Do

1. Colonel Harland Sanders' Original Restaurant (1940). 2 mi N on US 25. Authentic restoration of the first Kentucky Fried Chicken restaurant. Displays include original kitchen, artifacts, motel room. Original dining area is still in use. (Daily; closed Dec 25)   **Free.**

2. Laurel River Lake. Approx 10 mi W, in Daniel Boone National Forest (see); access from I-75, US 25W, KY 312 & KY 192. A 5,600-acre lake with fishing; boating (launch, rentals). Hiking, recreation areas. Picnicking. Camping (fee). (See ANNUAL EVENT) Contact the US Army Corps of Engineers, Resource Manager, 1433 Laurel Lake Rd, London 40741; 864-6412. For camping information, contact London District Ranger, US Forest Service, PO Box 907, London 40741; 864-4163.   **Free.**

3. Cumberland Falls State Resort Park (see). 19 mi SW via US 18W, KY 90.

(For further information contact the Tourist & Convention Commission, 101 N Lynn Ave; 528-6390 or 800/528-7123.)

Annual Event

Nibroc Festival. Costumes, mountain arts & crafts, parade, horse shows, square dancing, beauty pageant, midway, entertainment, food booths. Boat races on Laurel River Lake (see #2). Early Aug.

(See Barbourville, London, Williamsburg)

Motels

✔★★**BEST WESTERN CORBIN INN.** *2630 Cumberland Falls Rd. I-75 exit 25. 606/528-2100; FAX 606/523-1704.* 63 rms, 2 story. June–Oct: S $32–$39; D $39–$46; each addl $5; under 19 free; wkly rates; higher rates Memorial Day, Labor Day wkends; lower rates rest of yr. Crib free. TV; cable. Pool. Complimentary continental bkfst. Complimentary coffee in rms. Restaurant opp 6 am–10 pm. Ck-out 11 am. Some refrigerators. Cr cds: A, C, D, DS, MC, V.

★**KNIGHTS INN.** *(Rte 11, Box 256) I-75 exit 29. 606/523-1500; FAX 606/523-5818.* 109 rms, 10 kits. S $32–$37.50; D $33–$41.50; each addl $5; kit. units $41–$47; under 18 free; wkly rates. Crib free. TV; cable, in-rm movies avail. Pool. Restaurant nearby. Ck-out noon. Cr cds: A, C, D, DS, MC, V.

Covington (Cincinnati Airport Area) (A-7)

Founded: 1815 **Pop:** 43,264 **Elev:** 531 ft **Area code:** 606

This town is linked to Cincinnati, Ohio, by five broad bridges spanning the Ohio River. Named for a hero of the War of 1812, Covington in its early days had many German settlers who left their mark on the city. East of the city, the Licking River meets the Ohio. The suspension bridge (1867) that crosses from Third and Greenup streets to Cincinnati is the prototype of the Brooklyn Bridge in New York City. The adjacent riverfront area includes Covington Landing, a floating restaurant-entertainment complex.

What to See and Do

1. MainStrasse Village. Approx 5 square blocks in Covington's old German area. Historic district of residences, shops and restaurants in more than 20 restored buildings dating from mid- to late 1800s. (See ANNUAL EVENTS) Phone 491-0458. Also featured is the

Carroll Chimes Bell Tower. Philadelphia St, W end of Village. Completed in 1979, this 100-foot tower has a 43-bell carillon and mechanical figures that portray the legend of the Pied Piper of Hamelin.

2. Devou Park. Western Ave. A 550-acre park with lake overlooking the Ohio River. Golf (fee), tennis. Picnic grounds. Lookout point, outdoor concerts (mid-June–mid-Aug). (Daily) Phone 292-2151. **Free.**   In park is

Behringer-Crawford Museum. 1600 Montague Rd. Exhibits on local archaeology, paleontology, history, fine art and wildlife. (Daily exc Mon) Phone 491-4003. ¢

3. **Cathedral Basilica of the Assumption** (1901). Madison Ave & 12th St. Patterned after the Abbey of St Denis and the Cathedral of Notre Dame, France, the basilica has massive doors, classic stained-glass windows (including one of the largest in the world), murals and mosaics by local and foreign artists. (Daily exc hols) Guided tours (Sun, after 10 am mass; also by appt). Phone 431-2060. Tour ¢

4. **Oldenberg Brewery/Museum.** 4 mi S on I-75, Buttermilk Pike exit in Ft Mitchell. Large brewery/entertainment complex features a 650-seat banquet facility; functioning micro brewery with guided tours; large brewing memorabilia collection; replica 1930s beer truck; beer garden (seasonal); pub; gift shop. (Daily) Phone 341-2804 or 800/323-4917. Museum tour ¢¢

5. **Riverboat cruises.** Sightseeing cruises on the Ohio River; also lunch, dinner and moonlight cruises. Full-day and half-day cruises by appt. Contact BB Riverboats, 1 Madison Ave, 41011, phone 261-8500; or Queen City Riverboats, 303 O'Fallon St, PO Box 131, Dayton 41074, phone 292-8687. ¢¢¢

(For further information, including a list of historic sites in the area, contact the Northern Kentucky Convention and Visitors Bureau, 605 Philadelphia St, 41011; 800/336-3535.)

Annual Events

Jim Beam Stakes Race. Turfway Park Race Track in Florence. One of the largest pursed Thoroughbred races for three-year-olds. Race culminates week-long festival. Phone 371-0200. Last Sat in Mar.

Maifest. MainStrasse Village (see #1). Traditional German spring festival with entertainment, arts & crafts, food, games and rides. Phone 491-0458. 3rd wkend May.

Riverfest. Banks of Ohio River. One of the largest fireworks displays in the country; shot from barges moored on river. Labor Day wkend.

Oktoberfest. MainStrasse Village (see #1). Entertainment, arts & crafts, food. Mid-Sept.

Seasonal Event

Horse racing. Turfway Park Race Course. 3 mi SW at 7500 Turfway in Florence. Thoroughbred racing Wed–Sun. Phone 371-0200 or 800/733-0200. Early Sept–early Oct & late Nov–Mar.

(See Walton)

Motels

✔ ★ ★ **CROSS COUNTRY INN.** *(7810 Commerce Dr, Florence 41042)* I-75 exit 181. 606/283-2030. 112 rms, 2 story. S $29.99–$36.99; D $31.99–$38.99; each addl $7; under 18 free. Crib free. TV; cable. Heated pool. Complimentary coffee in lobby. Restaurant adj 6 am–11 pm. Ck-out noon. Cr cds: A, DS, MC, V.

★ **ENVOY INN.** *(8075 Steilen Dr, Florence 41042)* I-75 exit 180. 606/371-0277. 103 rms, 2 story. S $27.95–$34.95; D $32.95–$42.95; under 18 free. Crib free. TV; cable. Complimentary coffee in lobby. Restaurant nearby. Ck-out noon. Cr cds: A, C, D, DS, MC, V.

✔ ★ ★ **FAIRFIELD INN BY MARRIOTT.** *(50 Cavalier Blvd, Florence 41042)* I-75 exit 182. 606/371-4800. 135 rms, 3 story. S $37.95–$52.95; D $42.95–$55.95; each addl $7; under 18 free; higher rates Jazz Fest. Crib free. TV; cable. Heated pool. Complimentary continental bkfst, coffee in lobby. Restaurant adj 11 am–10 pm. Ck-out noon. Meeting rms. Valet serv. Cr cds: A, C, D, DS, MC, V.

★ ★ **HAMPTON INN.** *(7393 Turfway Rd, Florence 41042)* I-75 exit 182. 606/283-1600; FAX 606/283-1600, ext 156. 118 rms, 4 story. S $57–$62; D $62–$65; under 18 free; higher rates special events, Dec 31. Crib free. TV; cable. Pool. Complimentary continental bkfst. Restaurant adj 7–2 am. Ck-out noon. Meeting rms. Sundries. Free airport transportation. Cr cds: A, C, D, DS, MC, V.

★ ★ **HOLIDAY INN-SOUTH.** *(2100 Dixie Hwy, Ft Mitchell 41011)* 8 mi SW on I-75/71, exit 188B. 606/331-1500; FAX 606/341-2339. 214 rms, 2 story. S, D $75–$95; under 18 free; family, wkend rates; higher rates Jazz Festival. Crib free. Pet accepted, some restrictions. TV; cable. Indoor pool. Playground. Complimentary coffee in rms. Restaurant 6:30 am–2 pm, 5:30–10 pm. Rm serv. Bar 4:30 pm–1 am, closed Sun. Ck-out 11 am. Coin lndry. Meeting rms. Bellhops. Valet serv. Sundries. Free airport transportation. Exercise equipt; weights, rowers, whirlpool, sauna. Holidome. Game rm. Cr cds: A, C, D, DS, ER, MC, V, JCB.

✔ ★ **KNIGHTS INN.** *(8049 Dream St, Florence 41042)* Jct I-75/71 and US 42/127. 606/371-9711. 116 rms, 10 kits. S $33.95–$51; D $34.95–$58; each addl $6; kit. units $43–$55; under 18 free. Crib free. Pet accepted, some restrictions. TV; cable. Pool. Restaurant nearby. Ck-out noon. Meeting rm. Cr cds: A, C, D, DS, ER, MC, V.

★ ★ **SIGNATURE INN.** *(30 Cavalier Ct, Florence 41042)* I-75/71, exit 181 (Turfway Rd). 606/371-0081; FAX 606/371-0081, ext 500. 125 rms, 2 story. S $53–$62; D $54–$65; each addl $7; under 18 free; wkend rates. Crib free. TV; cable. Pool. Complimentary continental bkfst. Restaurant adj 5:30 am–10:30 pm. Ck-out noon. Meeting rms. Valet serv. Free airport transportation. Cr cds: A, C, D, DS, MC, V.

Motor Hotel

★ ★ ★ **DRAWBRIDGE ESTATE.** *(2477 Royal Dr, Ft Mitchell 41017)* At I-75/71 exit 186. 606/341-2800; res: 800/354-9793 (exc KY), 800/352-9866 (KY); FAX 606/341-5644. 505 rms, 2–3 story. S $54–$114; D $67–$129; each addl $10; suites $195–$250; under 18 free; wkend rates. Crib free. TV; cable. 3 pools, 1 indoor; poolside serv, lifeguard. Restaurant open 24 hrs. Rm serv 6:30 am–11 pm. Bars 11:30–2 am, Sun 1 pm–1 am; entertainment, dancing Fri & Sat. Ck-out noon. Convention facilities. Bellhops. Valet serv. Shopping arcade. Free airport transportation. Lighted tennis. Exercise equipt; weights, bicycles, whirlpool, sauna. Lawn games. Tudor decor. Oldenberg brewery adj. **LUXURY LEVEL: DRAWBRIDGE CITADEL.** 29 rms. S $114; D $129. Concierge. Private lounge, honor bar. Complimentary continental bkfst, refreshments.
Cr cds: A, C, D, DS, MC, V, JCB.

Hotels

★ ★ ★ **EMBASSY SUITES AT RIVERCENTER.** 10 E RiverCenter Blvd (41011). 606/261-8400; FAX 606/261-8486. 226 suites, 8 story. Suites $125–$145; under 18 free; wkend rates; higher rates River Fest. Crib free. TV; cable. Indoor pool. Complimentary full bkfst. Complimentary coffee in rms. Restaurant 6:30–1 am. Bar; entertainment. Ck-out noon. Coin lndry. Meeting rms. Gift shop. Free garage. Airport transportation. Exercise equipt; weight machine, bicycles, whirlpool, sauna. Wet bars. Refrigerators. Cr cds: A, C, D, DS, ER, MC, V, JCB.

★ ★ ★ **HILTON COMMONWEALTH.** *(Mailing address: PO Box 75336, Cincinnati, OH 45275)* I-75 exit 182, at Turfway Rd in Florence. 606/371-4400; FAX 606/371-3361. 206 units, 5 story. S $69–$96; D $67–$119; each addl $10; suites $109–$399; family, wkend rates. Crib free. TV; cable. Pool; poolside serv. Restaurant 6:30 am–11 pm. Bar; entertainment, dancing. Ck-out noon. Meeting rms. Concierge. Gift

shop. Free airport transportation. Lighted tennis. Exercise equipt; weight machines, bicycles, sauna. Some refrigerators. Elaborate landscaping. Original artwork. *LUXURY LEVEL:* **EXECUTIVE LEVEL.** 42 rms. S, D $109–$119; suites from $109. Private lounge, honor bar. Complimentary continental bkfst.
Cr cds: A, C, D, DS, ER, MC, V, JCB.

★★HOLIDAY INN-CINCINNATI AIRPORT. *(1717 Airort Exchange Blvd, Erlanger 41018)* I-275 exit Mineola Pike. 606/371-2233; FAX 606/371-5002. 247 rms, 6 story. S, D $86–$149; suites $149–$175; under 18 free; higher rates Jazz Festival. Crib free. TV; cable. Indoor pool. Complimentary coffee in rms. Restaurant 6 am–11 pm. Bar. Ck-out noon. Coin lndry. Convention facilities. Gift shop. Free airport transportation. Exercise equipt; weight machine, bicycles, whirlpool, sauna. Minibar in suites. Cr cds: A, C, D, DS, ER, MC, V, JCB.

★★QUALITY HOTEL-RIVERVIEW. *666 5th St (41011)*, at I-71/75 exit 192. 606/491-1200; FAX 606/491-0326. 235 rms, 18 story. S $68–$78; D $75–$85; each addl $5; suites $140–$180; under 18 free. Crib free. Pet accepted. TV; cable. Indoor/outdoor pool; poolside serv. Restaurants 7–1 am (also see RIVERVIEW ROOM). Rm serv to 11 pm. Bars from 11 am; entertainment exc Sun. Ck-out noon. Meeting rms. Gift shop. Barber. Free airport transportation. Paddle tennis. Exercise equipt; weights, bicycles, whirlpool, steam rm. Cr cds: A, C, D, DS, ER, MC, V, JCB.

Restaurants

★★CROCKETT'S AMERICAN RIVER CAFE. *(1 Riverboat Row, Newport)* Across from the Coliseum on the Ohio River. 606/581-2800. Hrs: 11 am–10 pm; Fri & Sat to 11 pm. Res accepted. Bar to 2 am. Semi-a la carte: lunch, dinner $5–$20. Child's meals. Specialties: steak, scallops, fresh fish. Parking. Outdoor dining. Cr cds: A, C, D, DS, MC, V.

★★MIKE FINK. *Foot of Greenup St, at Covington Landing.* 606/261-4212. Hrs: 11 am–10 pm; Fri & Sat to 11 pm; Sun 10 am–9 pm. Res accepted. Bar. Semi-a la carte: lunch $5–$9, dinner $11–$21. Specializes in fresh seafood. Raw bar. Parking. Old paddlewheel steamer, permanently moored. Scenic view of Cincinnati. Cr cds: A, C, D, DS, MC, V, JCB.

✔★★ORIENTAL WOK. *(317 Buttermilk Pike, Fort Mitchell)* SW via I-75 exit 186, 3 blks E on Buttermilk Pike. 606/331-3000. Hrs: 11 am–10 pm; Fri to 11 pm; Sun 11:30 am–10 pm. Closed Thanksgiving, Dec 25. Res accepted. Chinese, Amer menu. Bar. Semi-a la carte: lunch $4.95–$7.50, dinner $7.50–$15.95. Child's meals. Specializes in Cantonese & Szechwan dishes. Entertainment Fri & Sat. Parking. Outdoor dining. Fountain with goldfish. Cr cds: A, DS, MC, V.

✔★★RIVERVIEW ROOM. *(See Quality Hotel-Riverview)* 606/491-5300. Hrs: 11:30 am–2 pm, 5–10 pm; Fri, Sat to 11 pm; Sun 5–9 pm; Sun brunch 9:30 am–2:30 pm. Closed Dec 25. Res accepted. Bar. Wine list. Semi-a la carte: lunch $3.95–$8.95, dinner $12.95–$18.95. Sun brunch $11.95. Child's meals. Specializes in prime rib, veal. Own baking. Entertainment. Parking. Revolving restaurant overlooking river, Cincinnati skyline. Cr cds: A, C, D, DS, MC, V.

★★★THE WATERFRONT. *14 Pete Rose Pier, on river.* 606/581-1414. Hrs: 5:30–10 pm; Fri to 11 pm; Sat 5–11 pm; Sun 5–9 pm. Res accepted. Bar. Semi-a la carte: dinner $9.95–$23.95. Specializes in seafood, pasta. Raw bar. Valet parking. Outdoor dining. Elegant, 2-story floating restaurant with panoramic view of Cincinnati skyline; Art Deco with tropical accents. Cr cds: A, C, DS, MC, V.

BB RIVERBOATS. *1 Madison Ave, Covington Landing, on riverfront.* 606/261-8500. Hrs: (Office) 9 am–7 pm; Fri, Sat to 11 pm. May–Oct: lunch cruise (exc Sun) 11:30 am–2 pm; dinner cruise (nightly) 7–9 or 9:30 pm. Limited cruises Nov–Apr. Res required. Bar. Complete meals: lunch $14.50–$16.95, dinner $20.95–$28.95. Child's meals. Entertainment. Parking. Dinner cruises on Ohio River, at the Port of Cincinnati. Cr cds: A, C, D, DS, MC, V.

Cumberland Falls State Resort Park (C-7)

(19 mi SW of Corbin via US 25W, KY 90)

In this 1,657-acre park on the Cumberland River is a magnificent waterfall, 65 feet high and 125 feet wide, amid beautiful scenery. Surrounded by Daniel Boone National Forest (see), this awesome waterfall is the second largest east of the Rockies. By night, when the moon is full and the sky clear, a mysterious moonbow appears in the mist. This is the only place in the Western Hemisphere where this phenomenon can be seen. Swimming pool (seasonal); fishing. Nature trails; nature center; riding (seasonal); tennis. Picnicking, playground, lodge (see RESORT), cottages. Tent & trailer campsites (standard fees). Museum, planned recreation. For information phone 606/528-4121 or 800/325-0063.

What to See and Do

1. **Sheltowee Trace Outfitters.** River rafting, canoeing and "funyak" trips in the scenic Cumberland River Gorge below the falls; Big South Fork Gorge, Rockcastle River. Five- to seven-hour trips (Memorial Day–Sept; rafts daily, canoes by appt; Apr–mid-May & Sept–Oct, Sat & Sun). For information contact Sheltowee Trace Outfitters, PO Box 1060, Whitley City 42653; 606/376-5567 or 800/541-7238. ¢¢¢¢¢

2. **Blue Heron Mining Community.** In Big South Fork National River/Recreation Area (KY side); S via US 27 and KY 92 to Stearns, then 9 mi W on KY 742. Re-created 1930s mining town where 300 miners were once employed. Depot has exhibits on history of town with scale models, photographs. Town features giant coal tipple built in 1937 and metal-frame representations of miners' houses, church, school, company store. Snack bar, gift shop. A scenic railway line connects Blue Heron with the town of Stearns (see SOMERSET). Phone 606/376-3787 (KY) or 615/879-3625 (TN). **Free.**

3. **Big South Fork National River/Recreation Area.** Approx 9 mi W on KY 90, then approx 25 mi S on US 27 to Oneida, TN, then 20 mi W on TN 297. (See JAMESTOWN, TN)

(See Corbin, Williamsburg)

Resort

✔★★DUPONT LODGE. *(7351 KY 90, Corbin 40701)* In Cumberland Falls State Resort Park. 606/528-4121; FAX 606/528-0704. 52 rms in 3-story lodge, 26 kit. cottages. Apr–Oct: S $43–$49; D $53–$59; each addl $5; kit. cottages for 1–4, $63–$73; cottages for 6–8, $120–$130; under 17 free; lower lodge rates Nov–Mar. Closed 5 days late Dec. Crib free. TV. Pool; wading pool, lifeguard. Free supervised child's activities (Memorial Day–Labor Day). Dining rm 7–10:30 am, 11:30 am–4 pm, 5–9 pm. Ck-out noon, cottages 11 am; ck-in 4 pm. Meeting rms. Gift shop. Tennis. Lawn games. Rec dir (in season). Rec rm. Hiking trails. Fireplace in most cottages. On river. State-operated. Cr cds: A, C, D, DS, MC, V.

Cumberland Gap National Historical Park (C-7–C-8)

(¼ mi S of Middlesboro on US 25E)

Cumberland Gap, a natural passage through the mountain barrier that effectively sealed off the infant American coastal colonies, was the open door to western development. Through this pass first came Dr. Thomas Walker in 1750, followed by Daniel Boone in 1769. In 1775, Boone and 30 axmen cut a 208-mile swath through the forests from Kingsport, Tennessee, to the Kentucky River, passing through the Cumberland Gap. Settlers poured through the pass and along Boone's "Wilderness Road," and in 1777 Kentucky became Virginia's westernmost county. Although pioneers were harassed by Indians during the Revolution, travel over the Wilderness Road continued to increase and became heavier than ever. After the Revolution, the main stream of western settlement poured through Cumberland Gap and slowed only when more direct northerly routes were opened. During the Civil War, the gap was a strategic point, changing hands several times.

Nearly 22,300 acres of this historic and dramatically beautiful countryside in Kentucky, Tennessee and Virginia have been set aside as a national historical park. Seventy miles of hiking trails provide a variety of walks, long and short. Park (daily; closed Dec 25).

What to See and Do

1. **Visitor Center.** At W end of park (near Middlesboro). Historical exhibits, audiovisual program. (Daily exc Dec 25)
2. **Pinnacle Overlook.** Broad vistas of mountains and forests viewed from a high peak jutting above the Cumberland valley. Vehicles over 20 feet in length and all trailers are prohibited.
3. **Tri-State Peak.** View of meeting point of Kentucky, Virginia and Tennessee.
4. **Civil War fortifications.** Throughout the Gap area.
5. **Camping.** Off US 58. Tables, fireplaces, water and bathhouse. 14-day limit. ¢¢¢
6. **Hensley Settlement.** An isolated mountain community, now a restored historic site, that is accessible by hiking 3.5 miles up the Chadwell Gap trail or by driving up a jeep road.

(For further information contact the Park Superintendent, US 25E, Box 1848, Middlesboro 40965; 606/248-2817.)

(For accommodations see Pineville; also see Harrogate, TN)

Daniel Boone National Forest (B-7 – C-7)

(Stretches roughly north-south from Morehead on US 60 to Whitley City on US 27)

Within these 664,000 acres is some of the most spectacular scenery in Kentucky, from the Cave Run and Laurel River lakes to the Natural Arch scenic area. The forest includes the Red River Gorge Geological Area, known for its natural arches. The gorge has colorful rock formations and cliffs that average 200 to 300 feet high. A scenic loop drive of the gorge begins east of Natural Bridge State Resort Park (see) on KY 77. The nearest camping facilities (fee) are located at Koomer Ridge, near the Slade interchange of the Mountain Parkway.

The Sheltowee Trace National Recreation Trail runs generally north to south, beginning near Morehead (see) and continuing to Pickett State Rustic Park, TN (see JAMESTOWN, TN), a total distance of more than 250 miles. Forest Development Road 918, the main road into the Zilpo Recreation Area, has been designated a National Scenic Byway. The nine-mile road features a pleasant, winding trip through Kentucky hardwood forest, with interpretive signs and pull-overs with views of Cave Run Lake.

Cave Run Lake (see MOREHEAD) has swimming beaches, boat ramps, and camping at Twin Knobs and Zilpo recreation areas. Laurel River Lake (see CORBIN) has boat ramps and camping areas at Holly Bay and Grove (vehicle access). Clay Lick (Cave Run Lake), Grove, White Oak (Laurel River Lake) have boat-in camping. Hunting and fishing permitted in most parts of the forest under Kentucky regulations; backpacking is permitted on forest trails. For further information contact the Forest Supervisor, 100 Vaught Rd, Winchester 40391; 606/745-3100.

(For accommodations see Hazard, London, Morehead, Williamsburg)

Danville (B-6)

Founded: 1775 **Pop:** 12,420 **Elev:** 989 ft **Area code:** 606 **Zip:** 40422

Birthplace of Kentucky government, Danville is near the geographical center of the state. Ten years after the city was founded, it became the first capital of the Kentucky district of Virginia. Later, nine conventions were held leading to admission of the state to the Union. From 1775 to 1792, Danville was the most important center in Kentucky, the major settlement on the Wilderness Road. "Firsts" seem to come naturally to Danville, which claims the state's first college, first log courthouse, first post office, first brick courthouse, first school for the deaf and first law school.

One of the largest tobacco markets in the state, Danville has also attracted several industrial plants.

What to See and Do

1. **Constitution Square State Shrine.** On US 127 in center of town, 105 E Walnut. Authentic reproduction of Kentucky's first courthouse square stands at exact site where first state constitution was framed and adopted in 1792. Original post office; replicas of jail, courthouse, meetinghouse; restored row house, Dr Goldsmith House and Grayson Tavern. Governor's Circle has a bronze plaque of each Kentucky governor. (Daily) Phone 236-5089. ¢
2. **McDowell House and Apothecary Shop.** 125 S 2nd St. Residence and shop of Dr. Ephraim McDowell, noted surgeon of the early 19th century. Restored and refurbished with period pieces. Large apothecary ware collection. Gardens include trees, wildflowers and herbs of the period. (Mar–Oct, daily; rest of yr, daily exc Mon; closed Jan 1, Easter, Thanksgiving, Dec 25) Phone 236-2804. ¢¢
3. **Herrington Lake.** 3 mi N off KY 33. Formed by Dix Dam, one of the world's largest rock-filled dams, Herrington has 333 miles of shoreline. Balanced fish population maintained through conservation program. Swimming; fishing (fee); boat launch (fee; rentals). Camping (hookups), cabins. Phone 236-4286. **Free.**
4. **Pioneer Playhouse Village-of-the-Arts.** 1 mi S on Stanford Ave, US 150. Reproduction of an 18th-century Kentucky village on a 200-acre site; art gallery with changing exhibits, drama school, museum. Camping (fee). (See SEASONAL EVENT) (May–mid-Oct, daily) Phone 236-2747. **Free.**
5. **Perryville Battlefield State Historic Site.** 10 mi W on US 150, 4 mi N on US 68. A 100-acre park, once a field, appears much as it did Oct 8, 1862, when Confederate forces under General Braxton Bragg and Union troops under General Don Carlos Buell clashed. A total of 4,241 Union soldiers and 1,822 Confederate troops were killed, wounded or missing. Still standing are the Crawford House, used by Bragg as headquarters, and Bottom House, center of some of the heaviest fighting. Mock battle is staged each year (wkend

nearest October 8). A 30-acre area at the north end of what was the battle line includes a memorial erected in 1902 to the Confederate dead and one raised in 1931 to the Union dead. Museum with artifacts from battle, 9-by-9-foot, detailed battle map, battle dioramas (fee). Hiking. Picnicking, playground. Self-guided tours. (Apr–Oct, daily; rest of yr by appt) Phone 332-8631. **Free.**

(For further information contact the Danville-Boyle County Tourist Commission, PO Box 1168; 236-7794.)

Seasonal Event

Pioneer Playhouse. Pioneer Playhouse Village-of-the-Arts (see #4). Summer stock; Broadway comedies, musicals. Tues–Sat evenings. Phone 236-2747. Mid-June–late Aug.

(See Harrodsburg)

Motels

★ ★**HOLIDAY INN.** *4th St, at jct US 127S, 127 Bypass, 150 Bypass. 606/236-8600; FAX 606/236-0314.* 113 rms, 2 story. S, D $50; each addl $6; suites $65; under 19 free. Crib free. Pet accepted. TV; cable. Pool. Coffee in rms. Restaurant 6 am–2 pm, 5–10 pm. Rm serv. Ck-out noon. Meeting rms. Refrigerators avail. Cr cds: A, D, DS, MC, V, JCB.

★**SUPER 8.** *3663 US 150, at US 127 Bypass. 606/236-8881; FAX 606/236-8881, ext 301.* 49 units, 2 story. S $37.88; D $43.88–$48.88; each addl $2; suites $50.88; under 12 free. Crib free. TV; cable, in-rm movies avail. Complimentary coffee. Restaurant nearby. Ck-out 11 am. Meeting rms. Some refrigerators. Cr cds: A, C, D, DS, MC, V.

Unrated Dining Spot

TOY BOX DELI. *312 W Main St. 606/236-2876.* Hrs: 9 am–3 pm. Closed Sat, Sun; Dec 25. A la carte entrees: lunch $1–$3.50. Specializes in sandwiches. Own baking. Collection of unusual toys. No cr cds accepted.

Elizabethtown (B-5)

Founded: 1797 **Pop:** 18,167 **Elev:** 731 ft **Area code:** 502 **Zip:** 42701

The Lincoln story has deep roots in this town. Thomas Lincoln, the President's father, owned property and worked in Elizabethtown; it is the town to which Thomas Lincoln brought his bride, Nancy Hanks, immediately after their marriage. Abe's older sister Sarah was born in Elizabethtown. After his first wife's death, Thomas Lincoln returned to marry Sarah Bush Johnston.

What to See and Do

1. **Brown-Pusey Community House** (1825). 128 N Main St, at Poplar St. This former stagecoach inn is an excellent example of Georgian-colonial architecture; General George Custer lived here from 1871–73. Restored as a historical genealogy library and community house; garden. (Daily exc Sun; closed hols) Phone 765-2515. **Free.**

2. **Lincoln Heritage House.** 1 mi N on US 31W in Freeman Lake Park. Double log cabin (1789, 1805) was home of Hardin Thomas. Unusual trim work done by Thomas Lincoln. Pioneer implements, early surveying equipment, period furniture. One-room schoolhouse adjacent. (June–Sept, daily exc Mon) Park facilities include

pavilions, paddle and row boats, canoes. For information contact the Tourism & Convention Bureau. ¢

3. **Abraham Lincoln Birthplace National Historic Site** (see). 13 mi SE via KY 210 (US 31).

4. **Schmidt's Coca-Cola Museum.** 2½ mi W on US 31. Very large private collection of Coca Cola memorabilia includes several thousand items. Complete 1890s marble ice cream parlor; complete tray collection; stained glass chandelier; three-foot, Tiffany-style bottle. Lobby contains magnificent collection of *koi* (carp) in Japanese garden. (Mon–Fri; closed most major hols) Sr citizen rate. Phone 737-4000. ¢¢

(For further information contact the Elizabethtown Tourism & Convention Bureau, 24 Public Square; 765-2175.)

Annual Events

Hardin County Fair. Hardin County Fairgrounds. Mid-July.

Kentucky Heartland Festival. Freeman Lake Park. Antique auto show, arts & crafts, canoe race, running event, hot air balloon, bluegrass music, games, food. Phone 765-4334 or 769-2391. Late Aug.

(See Bardstown, Fort Knox, Hodgenville)

Motels

✔ ★**BEST WESTERN CARDINAL INN.** *642 E Dixie. 502/765-6139.* 67 rms, 2 story. S $24–$40; D $28–$48; each addl $4; under 12 free; higher rates Kentucky Derby. Crib $4. TV; cable, in-rm movies. Pool. Playground. Restaurant 11 am–10 pm. Rm serv. Ck-out 11 am. Coin lndry. Cr cds: A, C, D, DS, MC, V.

★ ★**COMFORT INN.** *1043 Executive Dr, I-65 exit 94. 502/769-3030; FAX 502/769-2516.* 134 rms, 2 story. S $39.50–$59; D $44.50–$64; each addl $5; under 18 free; higher rates Kentucky Derby. Crib free. TV; cable. Indoor pool; poolside serv. Complimentary continental bkfst, coffee. Restaurant adj 6 am–11 pm. Ck-out 11:30 am. Coin lndry. Meeting rms. Indoor putting green. Exercise equipt; weight machine, rowers. Game rm. Many refrigerators. Some wet bars. Picnic tables. Cr cds: A, C, D, DS, ER, MC, V, JCB.

★**DAYS INN.** *(PO Box 903) 2012 N Mulberry, at jct I-65, KY 62 (exit 94). 502/769-5522.* 122 rms, 2 story. S $32–$39; D $37–$44; each addl $5; under 12 free, 12–18, $2; higher rates Derby wkend. Crib free. TV; cable. Pool. Playground. Restaurant open 24 hrs. Ck-out 11 am. Sundries. Gift shop. Game rm. Cr cds: A, D, DS, MC, V.

✔ ★**TOWNE INN.** *2009 N Mulberry, I-65 exit 94, at US 62. 502/765-4166.* 106 rms, 2 story. June–Dec: S, D $26.95–$31.95; higher rates Derby wkend; lower rates rest of yr. Crib free. TV; cable. Pool. Restaurant open 24 hrs. Ck-out noon. Meeting rms. Valet serv. Sundries. Balconies. Cr cds: A, C, D, MC, V.

Restaurants

✔ ★ ★**GREEN BAMBOO.** *902 N Dixie, in Governor's Shopping Center. 502/769-3457.* Hrs: 11 am–2:30 pm, 4:30–9:30 pm. Closed Thanksgiving, Dec 25. Chinese menu. Semi-a la carte: lunch $4.25–$4.50, dinner $8.35–$15. Child's meals. Specialties: Mongolian beef, mandarin chicken. Oriental decor. Cr cds: A, MC, V.

★ ★**STONE HEARTH.** *1001 N Mulberry. 502/765-4898 or 769-3468.* Hrs: 11 am–2 pm, 5–9 pm; Sun 11:30 am–7:30 pm. Closed Jan 1, Dec 25. Semi-a la carte: lunch $3.95–$6.50, dinner

$11.75–$18.95. Child's meals. Specializes in steak, prime rib, seafood. Salad bar. Parking. Old English decor. Cr cds: A, D, MC, V.

Ⓓ

Florence

(see Covington)

Fort Knox (B-5)

Elev: 740 ft **Area code:** 502 **Zip:** 40121

This military post, established in 1918, is home for the US Army Armor Center and School and the Army's home of Armor and Cavalry. Named for Major General Henry Knox, first Secretary of War, the post has been a major installation since 1932, when mechanization of the Army began.

What to See and Do

1. **United States Bullion Depository.** Gold Vault Rd. Two-story granite, steel and concrete building. Opened in 1937, the building houses part of the nation's gold reserves. The depository and the surrounding grounds are not open to the public.

2. **Patton Museum of Cavalry and Armor.** Building 4554, Fayette Ave. The Armor Branch Museum was named in honor of General George S. Patton, Jr. Collection includes US and foreign armored equipment, weapons, art and uniforms; mementos of General Patton's military career, including the sedan in which he was riding when he was fatally injured in 1945. Also on display are a 10-by-12-foot section of the Berlin Wall and foreign armored equipment from Operation Desert Storm. (Daily; closed Jan 1, Dec 24–25, 31) Phone 624-3812.   **Free.**

(For further information contact the Public Affairs Office, US Army Armor Center & Fort Knox, PO Box 995; 624-3351 or -7451.)

Annual Event

Armored Vehicle Presentation. Patton Museum (see #2). Operational armored vehicle demonstration features restored World War II tanks and authentically uniformed troops. July 4.

(For accommodations see Elizabethtown, Louisville, Shepherdsville)

Frankfort (B-6)

Founded: 1786 **Pop:** 25,968 **Elev:** 510 ft **Area code:** 502 **Zip:** 40601

Frankfort is split by the Kentucky River, which meanders through the city. Although rich farmlands funnel burley tobacco and corn through Frankfort, the chief crop is politics, especially when the legislature is in session. Frankfort was chosen as the state capital in 1792 as a compromise to settle the rival claims of Lexington and Louisville. Frankfort was briefly held by the Confederates during the Civil War. Later, the "corn liquor" industry blossomed in this area, utilizing water from flowing limestone springs. Bourbon distilleries carry on this tradition.

What to See and Do

1. **State Capitol** (1910). S end of Capitol Ave, on an elevation overlooking the Kentucky River. Building noted for Ionic columns and the high central dome on an Ionic peristyle, topped with a lantern cupola. In the rotunda are statues of Abraham Lincoln, Jefferson Davis, Henry Clay, Dr. Ephraim McDowell and Alben Barkley, vice-

president under Harry S Truman. Guided tours. (Mon–Sat & Sun afternoons; closed major hols) Phone 564-3000.   **Free.**   On grounds are

Floral Clock. Functioning outdoor timepiece is adorned with thousands of plants and elevated above reflecting pool. Mechanism moves a 530-pound minute hand and a 420-pound hour hand. Visitors toss thousands of dollars in coins into the pool, all of which is turned over to state child-care agencies.

Governor's Mansion (1914). Official residence of the Governor is styled after the Petit Trianon, Marie Antoinette's villa at Versailles. Guided tours (Tues & Thurs mornings). Phone 564-3449.   **Free.**

2. **Old State Capitol Building.** Broadway & Lewis Sts. Kentucky's third capitol building, erected in 1827–29, was used as the capitol from 1829–1909 and was the first Greek-revival statehouse west of the Alleghenies. Completely restored and furnished in period style, the building features an unusual self-balanced double stairway. (Mon–Sat, also Sun afternoons)   **Free.**   In the Old Capitol Annex are

Kentucky History Museum. Exhibits pertaining to the history and development of the state and the culture of its people. (Mon–Sat, also Sun afternoons; closed major hols) Phone 564-3016.   **Free.**

Library. Manuscripts, maps, photographs and special collections cover Kentucky's history; genealogy section. (Daily exc Sun; closed major hols) Phone 564-3016.   **Free.**

3. **Old Governor's Mansion** (1798). 420 High St. Georgian-style residence of 33 governors until 1914, when the new mansion was built (see #1). Restored to the style of the 1800s. Tours (Tues & Thurs afternoons; closed hols). Phone 564-3449 or -3000.   **Free.**

4. **Daniel Boone's Grave.** In Frankfort Cemetery, 215 E Main St. Monument to Boone and his wife. Boone died in Missouri but his remains were brought here in 1845.

5. **Kentucky Vietnam Veterans Memorial.** Adj to State Library & Archives, 300 Coffee Tree Rd. Unique memorial is a 14-foot sun-dial that casts a shadow across veterans' names on the anniversary of their death. Memorial contains more than 1,000 names.

6. **Kentucky Military History Museum.** Old State Arsenal, E Main St. Exhibits trace Kentucky's involvement in military conflicts through two centuries. Weapons, flags, uniforms. (Mon–Fri; closed major hols) Phone 564-3265.   **Free.**

7. **Liberty Hall** (ca 1796). 218 Wilkinson St, at W Main St. Fine example of Georgian architecture, built by the first US senator from Kentucky, John Brown, is completely restored to its original state and furnished with family heirlooms. Period gardens. (Mar–Dec, daily exc Mon; closed some major hols) Phone 227-2560.   ¢¢   On the same block is

Orlando Brown House (1835). 202 Wilkinson St. Early Greek-revival house built for Orlando Brown, son of Senator John Brown; original furnishings and artifacts. (Mar–Dec, daily exc Mon; closed some major hols) Phone 227-2560.   ¢¢   Combination ticket avail for both houses.

8. **Kentucky State University** (1886). (2,550 students) E Main St. Liberal studies institution. Jackson Hall (1887) has art and photo gallery exhibits (Sept–mid-May); King Farouk butterfly collection in Carver Hall. Jackson Hall and Hume Hall (1909) on historic register. Phone 227-6000.

(For further information, including a walking tour map of 32 houses and a map and pamphlet of historic sites, contact the Frankfort Tourist and Convention Commisssion, 100 Capital Ave; 875-8687.)

Annual Event

Capital Expo Festival. Capital Plaza Complex. Traditional music, country music, fiddling; workshops, demonstrations, arts & crafts; balloon race, dancing, games, contests, puppets, museum exhibitions; ethnic & regional foods, entertainment. 1st wkend June.

(See Lexington)

Motels

★★**BEST WESTERN PARKSIDE INN.** *80 Chenault Rd, I-64 exit 58.* 502/695-6111; FAX 502/695-6111, ext 305. 98 rms, 2 story, 12 suites. S $42–$52; D $52–$60; each addl $5; suites $70–$80; under 12 free; higher rates Kentucky Derby. Crib free. TV; cable. Indoor pool; whirlpool. Complimentary continental bkfst, coffee. Restaurant adj 11 am–9 pm. Ck-out noon. Lndry facilities. Meeting rms. Airport transportation. Game rm. Cr cds: A, C, D, DS, ER, MC, V.

✓★**DAYS INN.** *1051 US 127S, I-64 exit 53 B.* 502/875-2200. 122 rms, 2 story. S $35; D $40; each addl $5; 13–17, $1; under 12 free. Crib free. TV; cable. Pool. Continental bkfst. Ck-out 11 am. Sundries. Cr cds: A, C, D, DS, MC, V.

Hotel

★★★**HOLIDAY INN–CAPITAL PLAZA.** *405 Wilkinson Blvd.* 502/227-5100; FAX 502/875-7147. 189 rms, 8 story. S $62; D $72; each addl $10; suites $95–$275; higher rates Kentucky Derby. Crib free. TV; cable. Heated pool. Coffee in rms. Restaurants 7 am–2 pm, 5–10 pm. Bar 11 am–midnight. Ck-out noon. Meeting rms. Shopping arcade. Covered parking. Exercise equipt; weight machine, bicycles, whirlpool, sauna. Game rm. Some refrigerators. Cr cds: A, C, D, DS, MC, V, JCB.

Restaurant

✓★**JIM'S SEAFOOD.** *950 Wilkinson Blvd.* 502/223-7448. Hrs: 11 am–2 pm, 4–10 pm; Sat from 4 pm. Closed Sun; major hols. Res accepted. Wine, beer. Semi-a la carte: lunch $3.95–$6.95, dinner $7.95–$13.95. Child's meals. Specializes in surf & turf. Parking. Outdoor dining. View of river. Family-owned. Cr cds: A, DS, MC, V.

Georgetown (B-7)

Settled: 1776 **Pop:** 11,414 **Elev:** 871 ft **Area code:** 502 **Zip:** 40324

Royal Spring's crystal-clear water flows in the center of this city. This spring attracted pioneer settlers who established an outpost at Georgetown and rebuffed frequent Indian attacks. The town was named for George Washington and was incorporated by the Virginia legislature. Today it remains a quiet college town, with a large portion of the business area designated as a historic district. Georgetown College has a planetarium and many antebellum buildings.

What to See and Do

1. **Scott County Courthouse** (1877). 101 E Main St, at Broadway. Designed in Second Empire style by Thomas Boyd of Pittsburgh. Part of the historic business district. (Mon–Fri; closed hols) Phone 863-7850. **Free.**

2. **Royal Spring Park.** Water St. Location of Royal Spring, largest in Kentucky and source of city water since 1775. Former site of McClelland's Fort (1776), first paper mill in the West, pioneer classical music school and state's first ropewalk. Reputed site of first bourbon distillation in 1789. Cabin of former slave relocated and restored here for use as an information center. Picnicking.

3. **Cardome.** 800 Cincinnati Pike, I-75 exit 125/126. House of Civil War Governor J.F. Robinson and later home of the Academy of the Sisters of the Visitation. Now houses **Scott County Museum** and serves as community center. (Mon–Fri, also by appt; closed Jan 1,

day before Thanksgiving, Thanksgiving, Dec 24, 25 & 31) Phone 863-1575. **Free.**

(For further information, including brochures on historic sites and a walking tour, contact the Georgetown/Scott County Tourist Commission, 160 E Main, PO Box 676; 863-2547.)

(See Frankfort, Lexington, Paris)

Motel

✓★**RAMADA.** *(Box 926) 401 Delaplain Rd, I-75 exit 129.* 502/863-1166. 98 rms, 2 story. S $36–$40; D $38–$45; each addl $5; under 18 free. Crib free. Pet accepted. TV; cable. Pool. Complimentary continental bkfst, coffee in lobby. Restaurant opp open 24 hrs. Ck-out noon. Meeting rm. Cr cds: A, C, D, DS, ER, MC, V, JCB.

Motor Hotel

★**SHONEY'S INN.** *At jct I-75, US 62.* 502/868-9800; res: 800/222-2222; FAX 502/868-9800, ext 141. 104 rms, 3 story, 15 suites. S $39.95; D $44.95; each addl $5; suites $41.95–$59.50; under 18 free. TV; cable. Pool. Complimentary coffee in lobby. Restaurant adj 6 am–11 pm. Ck-out noon. Meeting rms. Cr cds: A, C, D, DS, ER, MC, V.

Gilbertsville (C-3)

Pop: 500 (est) **Elev:** 343 ft **Area code:** 502 **Zip:** 42044

Fishing parties heading for Kentucky Lake stop in Gilbertsville for last-minute provisions. The town also caters to tourists bound for the resorts and state parks in this area. Chemical plants have been built nearby, utilizing Kentucky Dam's hydroelectric power.

What to See and Do

1. **Kentucky Dam Village State Resort Park.** Just S of town off US 62/641 on Kentucky Lake. A 1,352-acre park on a 160,300-acre lake. Fishing. Swimming beach, pool, bathhouse (seasonal), water-skiing; boating (rentals, launching ramps, docks). Hiking; 18-hole and miniature golf (seasonal fee), tennis. Picnicking, playground, shops, grocery. Camping, lodge (see RESORT), cottages. Supervised recreation. Lighted 4,000 ft airstrip. For fees and information phone 362-4271.

2. **Kentucky Dam.** Longest dam in the TVA system, 22 mi upstream from Paducah; 206 ft high, 8,422 ft long, built at cost of $118 million, created lake 184 mi long with 2,380 mi of shoreline. Regulates flow of water from Tennessee River into the Ohio River. Carries US 62/641 across northern end of Kentucky Lake. Viewing balcony (daily); tours of powerhouse (by appt). Phone 362-4221. **Free.**

3. **Barkley Lock and Dam.** 5 mi E. A 1,004-mi shoreline created by damming of the Cumberland River; navigation lock, canal, hydroelectric generating plant, flood control and recreation areas; information & visitor center. Contact the Resource Manager, PO Box 218, Grand Rivers 42045; 362-4236. **Free.**

4. **Kenlake State Resort Park** (see). SE on Purchase Pkwy, US 68.

(For further information contact the Marshall County Chamber of Commerce, Inc, Rte 7, Box 145, Benton 42025; 527-7665.)

(See Cadiz, Land Between The Lakes, Paducah)

Resort

★★**KENTUCKY DAM VILLAGE.** *(Box 69) ¾ mi W of Kentucky Dam on US 62/641; 2 mi E of I-24 exit 27.* 502/362-4271; res: 800/

325-0146; FAX 502/362-8747. 72 lodge rms, 2 story; 68 kit. cottages. Apr–Oct: S \$55; D \$65; each addl \$5.50; kit. cottages for 2–6, \$73–\$150; under 16 free; lower rates rest of yr. Crib free. TV. Pool; wading pool, lifeguard in season. Dining rm 7–10:30 am, 11:30 am–2 pm, 5–9 pm. Ck-out noon (cottages 11 am), ck-in 4 pm. Convention facilities. Airport transportation. Lighted tennis. 18-hole golf, greens fee \$15. Miniature golf. Lawn games. Game rm. Private patios, balconies. Picnic tables. On lake; beach, marina. State-owned; all state park facilities avail. Cr cds: A, C, D, DS, MC, V.

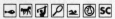

Glasgow (C-5)

Settled: 1799 **Pop:** 12,351 **Elev:** 790 ft **Area code:** 502 **Zip:** 42141

Glasgow was one of the first towns to be settled in the "barrens," then an almost treeless plateau west of the bluegrass section of Kentucky. Today, lumber products are important in Glasgow although tobacco is the leading money crop, followed by dairy products.

What to See and Do

Barren River Dam and Lake. 12 mi SW on US 31E. Impounds waters of Barren River and its tributaries. There is good bass fishing; boating (ramps); water sports. Picnic areas. Camping, lodge, cabins (most have fee). Contact 11088 Finney Rd; 646-2055. Other recreation areas and campsites include Baileys Point, Beaver Creek, Browns Ford (no campsites), the Narrows, Peninsula (no campsites), the Tailwater, Walnut Creek and

  Barren River Lake State Resort Park. Approx 2,100 acres with a 10,000-acre lake. Swimming beach, pool; fishing; boating (rentals). Hiking, horseback riding, bicycle trails; 18-hole golf course, tennis. Picnicking, playground. Tent & trailer sites (Apr–Oct, standard fees), cottages, lodge (see RESORT). Some fees. Phone 646-2151.

(For further information contact the Glasgow-Barren County Chamber of Commerce, 301 W Main St; 651-3161.)

Annual Event

Highland Games and Gathering of Scottish Clans. 14 mi S via US 31E in Barren River Lake State Resort Park (see). Six-day festival. Last wkend in May.

(See Cave City, Horse Cave, Mammoth Cave, Park City)

Motel

✔ ★ ★ **GLASGOW INN.** *½ mi W on US 68; ½ blk W of US 31E Bypass. 502/651-5191.* 80 rms, 2 story. S \$38–\$58; D \$48–\$65; each addl \$8; under 19 free. Crib free. Pet accepted. TV; cable, in-rm movies avail. Heated pool. Complimentary continental bkfst. Restaurant nearby. Ck-out 11 am. Meeting rms. Cr cds: A, C, D, DS, ER, MC, V.

Inn

★ ★ **FOUR SEASONS.** *4107 Scottsville Rd (US 31E). 502/678-1000.* 17 rms, 2 story, 4 suites. S, D \$54.50; each addl \$5; suites \$64.50; wkly rates. Crib \$5. TV; cable. Heated pool. Complimentary continental bkfst, coffee. Restaurant nearby. Ck-out noon, ck-in 2 pm. Some refrigerators. Furnished with antique reproductions. Cr cds: A, C, D, DS, MC, V.

Resort

★ ★ ★ **BARREN RIVER LAKE LODGE.** *(1149 State Park Rd, Lucas 42156) 12 mi SW on US 31E, in state park. 502/646-2151; res: 800/325-0057; FAX 502/646-3645.* 51 rms, 1-3 story, 22 kit. cottages. No elvtr in lodge. S \$49; D \$59; each addl \$5; 2-bedrm kit. cottages (up to 6) \$115–\$135; under 16 free. Closed 5 days wk of Dec 25. Crib free. TV. Pool; wading pool, lifeguard. Free supervised child's activities. Dining rm 7 am–9 pm. Ck-out noon (cottages 11 am), ck-in 4 pm. Meeting rms. Lighted tennis. 18-hole golf, greens fee \$15. Gift shop. Rec rm. Private patios, balconies. Picnic tables. On lake. State-owned; all facilities of state park avail. Cr cds: A, C, D, DS, MC, V.

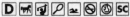

Restaurant

✔ ★ **BOLTON'S LANDING.** *1½ mi S on US 31E. 502/651-8008.* Hrs: 11 am–2 pm, 5–8:30 pm; Sat from 5 pm. Closed Sun; most major hols. Semi-a la carte: lunch \$3.95–\$6.50, dinner \$3.95–\$13.50. Child's meals. Specializes in steak, chicken, catfish. Parking. Original art work. Scottish flair. Cr cds: A, D, MC, V.

Greenville (C-4)

Settled: 1799 **Pop:** 4,689 **Elev:** 538 ft **Area code:** 502 **Zip:** 42345

Located in the heart of the western Kentucky coal, oil and natural gas fields, Greenville is the seat of Muhlenberg County. There is good hunting and fishing in the area.

What to See and Do

Lake Malone State Park. 8 mi S on KY 973, between US 431 and KY 181. A 325-acre park on 788-acre Lake Malone; located in a hardwood tree forest, with tall pines on scenic cliffs. A natural rock bridge, steep sandstone bluffs and a wooded shoreline can be seen from a ride on the lake. Swimming beach; fishing for bass, bluegill, crappie; boating (ramp, rentals, motors). Hiking trail. Picnicking, playground. Tent & trailer camping (Apr–mid-Nov). (Daily) Standard fees. For information contact the Park Superintendent, Dunmor 42339; 657-2111.

(For further information contact the Chamber of Commerce, PO Box 313; 338-5422.)

(For accommodations see Hopkinsville, Madisonville)

Harrodsburg (B-6)

Founded: 1774 **Pop:** 7,335 **Elev:** 886 ft **Area code:** 606 **Zip:** 40330

When James Harrod and a troop of surveyors came here early in 1774 and established a township, they were creating Kentucky's first permanent white settlement. Here, the first corn in Kentucky was grown, the first school was established and the first gristmill in the area was operated. Today the state's oldest city, its sulphur springs and historical sites make it a busy tourist town. Tobacco, cattle, and horse-breeding are important to the economy.

What to See and Do

1. **Old Fort Harrod State Park.** On US 68/127 in town. This 28-acre park includes a reproduction of Old Fort Harrod in an area known as Old Fort Hill, site of the original fort (1774). The stockade shelters Ann McGinty Block House, George Rogers Clark Block House, James

Harrod Block House and the first school, complete with hand-hewn benches. Authentic cooking utensils, tools and furniture are displayed in the cabins. Mansion Museum includes Lincoln Room, Confederate Room, gun collection, Indian artifacts. Lincoln Marriage Temple shelters the log cabin in which Abraham Lincoln's parents were married on June 12, 1806 (moved from its original site in Beech Fork). Pioneer Cemetery. Picnic facilities, playground, gift shop. Living history crafts program in fort (mid-Apr–mid-Oct). Museum (mid-Mar–Nov, daily); fort (daily; closed Jan 1, Thanksgiving, Dec 25). Phone 734-3314. Combination ticket to fort & museum ¢¢

2. **Morgan Row** (1807–45). 220–222 S Chiles St, behind courthouse. Probably the oldest standing row house west of the Alleghenies; once a stagecoach stop and tavern. Houses Harrodsburg Historical Society Museum (Mon–Fri). Phone 734-5985.   ¢¢

3. **Old Mud Meeting House** (1800). 4 mi S off US 68. First Dutch Reformed Church west of the Alleghenies. The original mud-thatch walls have been restored. (By appt only) Phone 734-5985.   Free.

4. **Shaker Village of Pleasant Hill** (1805–1910). 7 mi NE on US 68. Thirty buildings (1805–59) including frame, brick and stone houses. Center Family House has exhibits; Trustees' House (see RESTAURANT) has twin spiral staircases. Craft shops with reproductions of Shaker furniture, Kentucky craft items; craft demonstrations; lodging in 15 restored buildings (see MOTOR HOTEL). Year-round calendar of special events including music, dance and Sept wkend big events. (Daily; closed Dec 24, 25) Sternwheeler offers one-hour excursions on Kentucky River (Late Apr–Oct; fee). Phone 734-5411.   ¢¢¢

5. **Harrodsburg Pottery and Craft Shop.** 1026 Lexington Rd. Demonstrations of candle-dipping, herbal and wreath arrangements; other crafts. Herbal garden; greenhouse. (Mar–Dec, daily; closed Easter, Thanksgiving, Dec 25) Phone 734-9991.   Free.

(For further information contact the Harrodsburg/Mercer County Tourist Commission, PO Box 283; 734-2364.)

Annual Event

Pioneer Days Festival. 3rd wkend Aug.

Seasonal Event

The Legend of Daniel Boone. James Harrod Amphitheater. Outdoor drama traces the story of Boone. Daily exc Sun. For information contact PO Box 365; 734-3346. Mid-June–Aug.

(See Danville)

Motel

✔ ★ ★ **BEST WESTERN.** *1680 Danville Rd, 3 mi S on US 127.* 606/734-9431. 58 rms, 3 story. S $44–$49; D $52–$55; each addl $5; under 12 free. Crib free. TV; cable. Pool. Free continental bkfst, coffee. Restaurant adj 6:30 am–9 pm. Ck-out 11 am. Valet serv. Many refrigerators. Balconies. Golf course adj. Cr cds: A, C, D, DS, MC, V.

Motor Hotel

★ ★ **INN AT PLEASANT HILL.** *3500 Lexington Rd, Shaker Village of Pleasant Hill.* 606/734-5411. 80 rms in 18 bldgs, 1–4 story. S $40–$90; D $52–$150; each addl $8; under 18 free. Closed Dec 24–25. Crib free. TV. Restaurant (see TRUSTEES' HOUSE AT PLEASANT HILL). Ck-out 11 am. Meeting rms. Riverboat cruises. 30 restored buildings (ca 1800) furnished with Shaker reproductions, hand-woven rugs and curtains; some trundle beds. Cr cds: MC, V.

Inn

★ ★ ★ **BEAUMONT.** *638 Beaumont Dr, off US 127.* 606/734-3381; res: 800/352-3992; FAX 606/734-6897. 33 rms. S $50–$75; D $70–$95; each addl $15; under 12, $10. Closed mid-Dec–mid-Mar. TV; cable. Pool; wading pool, lifeguard. Dining rm (public by res) sittings noon & 1:15 pm, 6 & 7:30 pm; Sun, Mon sittings vary. Ck-out noon. Meeting rms. Gift shop. Tennis. Golf privileges. Lawn games. Rms are in 4 buildings; main building furnished with antiques. Cr cds: A, D, DS, MC, V.

Restaurant

✔ ★ ★ **TRUSTEES' HOUSE AT PLEASANT HILL.** *(See Inn at Pleasant Hill Motor Hotel)* 606/734-5411. Sittings: bkfst 7:30, 8:30 & 9:30 am, lunch 11:30 am, 1 & 2:30 pm, dinner 5:30 & 7:15 pm; Sun noon, 1:45, 3:15 & 5:30 pm. Closed Dec 24–25. Res required. Buffet: bkfst $7.50. Semi-a la carte: lunch $6.50–$7.75. Complete meals: dinner $11.25–$17.75. Child's meals. Specializes in traditional Kentucky and Shaker dishes. Parking. Restored Shaker village; Shaker decor. Totally nonsmoking. Cr cds: MC, V.

Hazard (C-8)

Pop: 5,416 **Elev:** 867 ft **Area code:** 606 **Zip:** 41701

In rugged mountain country, Hazard is a coal mining town, a trading center and the seat of Perry County. Both town and county were named for Commodore Oliver Hazard Perry, naval hero of the War of 1812.

What to See and Do

1. **Bobby Davis Memorial Park.** Walnut St. Picnic area, reflecting pool, WWII Memorial, 400 varieties of shrubs and plants. (Daily) In the park is

   Bobby Davis Park Museum. Community museum housing local historical artifacts and photographs relating to life on Kentucky River waterways. (Daily exc Sun; closed most hols) Phone 439-4325.   Free.

2. **Buckhorn Lake State Resort Park.** 25 mi NW via KY 15/28. This 856-acre park encompasses a 1,200-acre lake. Swimming beach, pool, bathhouse (seasonal); fishing; boating (ramp, motors, rentals). Hiking; bicycle rentals, miniature golf, tennis. Picnicking, playground. Lodge (see RESORT), cottages. For fees and information phone 398-7510.

3. **Carr Fork Lake.** 15 mi SE. A 710-acre lake. Beach; fishing; boating (ramps, marina). Picnic shelters. Camping (hookups, dump station; fee). Observation points. Some facilities seasonal. Phone 642-3308.

4. **Daniel Boone National Forest** (see). 10 mi W on KY 15, 80.

(For further information contact the Hazard-Perry County Chamber of Commerce & Tourism Commission, 601 Main St, Suite 3, 439-2659; or the Hazard-Perry County Museum, 439-4325.)

Annual Event

Black Gold Festival. On Main St. Celebrates local coal resources. Food and craft booths, games, entertainment, carnival, parade. Phone 439-1776 or -1212. 3rd full wkend Sept.

Motels

★ ★**HOLIDAY INN.** *200 Dawahare Dr, off Daniel Boone Pkwy. 606/436-4428; FAX 606/436-4428, ext 317.* 81 rms, 2 story. S, D $54–$70; each addl $6; suites $125–$186; under 16 free. Crib avail. TV; cable. 2 pools, 1 indoor; whirlpool. Restaurant 5 am–11 pm. Rm serv. Bar 3 pm–midnight. Ck-out 11 am. Meeting rms. Sundries. Free airport transportation. Cr cds: A, C, D, DS, MC, V.

D ≈ ⊗ ◎ SC

★ **SUPER 8.** *125 Village Lane, off Daniel Boone Pkwy. 606/436-8888; FAX 606/439-0768.* 86 rms, 2 story, 14 suites. S $41.88; D $44.88; each addl $3; suites $48.88–$62.88; under 12 free. Crib free. TV; cable. Complimentary coffee in lobby. Restaurant nearby. Ck-out 11 am. Cr cds: A, C, D, DS, MC, V.

D ⊗ ◎ SC

Resort

✔ ★ ★**BUCKHORN LODGE.** *(HC 36, Box 1000, Buckhorn 41721) 25 mi W on KY 28, in Buckhorn Lake State Resort Park. 606/398-7510; res: 800/325-0058; FAX 606/398-7077.* 36 rms, 2 story. May–Aug: S $43; D $53; each addl $5; cottages $81–$115; under 16 free; lower rates rest of yr. Crib free. TV; cable. Pool; wading pool, lifeguard. Dining rm 7 am–9 pm. Ck-out noon. Meeting rms. Gift shop. Tennis. Miniature golf. Game rm. Rec rm. Lawn games. Balconies. Picnic tables, grills. On lake; beach facilities, boat rental. State-owned; all facilities of state park avail. Cr cds: A, C, D, DS, MC, V.

D ⟋ 𝒫 ≈ ⊗ ◎ SC

Henderson (B-4)

Founded: 1797 **Pop:** 25,945 **Elev:** 409 ft **Area code:** 502 **Zip:** 42420

Henderson was developed by the Transylvania Company and named for its chief executive, Colonel Richard Henderson. This town along the banks of the Ohio River has long attracted residents, most notably naturalist John James Audubon, W.C. Handy, well-known "father of the Blues" and A.B. "Happy" Chandler, former governor and commissioner of baseball.

What to See and Do

John James Audubon State Park. 2 mi N on US 41. Here stand 692 acres of massive hardwood trees, woodland plants, nature preserve, densely forested tracts and two lakes favored by migratory birds and described in Audubon's writings. Swimming beach, bathhouse (seasonal); fishing; paddleboat rentals (seasonal). Nine-hole golf (yr-round; fee). Picnicking, playground. Tent & trailer camping (standard fees), cottages (yr-round). Supervised recreation; guided nature walks. (Daily) Some fees. Phone 826-2247. **Free.**

(For further information contact the Tourist Commission, 2961 US 41N; 826-3128.)

Annual Events

W.C. Handy Blues & Barbecue Festival. Mid June.

Big River Arts & Crafts Festival. Audubon State Park (see). More than 250 exhibitors. Early Oct.

Seasonal Event

Horse Racing.

Ellis Park. 5 mi N on US 41. Thoroughbred racing. Daily exc Mon. Phone 812/425-1456. Late June–Labor Day.

(See Owensboro)

Motels

★ ★**DAYS INN.** *2044 US 41N. 502/826-6600; FAX 502/826-3055.* 115 rms, 2 story. S $40–$55; D $45–$60; each addl $6; suites $70–$100; under 12 free. Crib free. TV; cable. Pool. Coffee in rms. Restaurant 6 am–2 pm, 5–9 pm; Sun to 3 pm. Rm serv. Bars 4 pm–2 am; entertainment, dancing exc Sun. Ck-out 11 am. Coin lndry. Meeting rms. Beauty shop. Some refrigerators. Cr cds: A, C, D, DS, MC, V.

D ≈ ⊗ ◎ SC

✔ ★**SCOTTISH INN.** *2820 US 41N. 502/827-1806; FAX 502/827-1806, ext 113.* 72 rms, 1–2 story. S $26–$29; D $33–$35; each addl $3; under 10 free. Crib free. Pet accepted. TV; cable, in-rm movies avail. Pool; wading pool. Complimentary coffee in lobby. Restaurant nearby. Ck-out 11 am. Cr cds: A, C, D, DS, MC, V.

𝒫 ≈ ⊗ ◎ SC

Hodgenville (B-6)

Founded: 1789 **Pop:** 2,721 **Elev:** 730 ft **Area code:** 502 **Zip:** 42748

Robert Hodgen built a mill and tavern here and entertained many prominent people. Young Abraham Lincoln often came to the mill with corn to be ground from his father's farm seven miles away. Soon after Hodgen's death in 1810, the settlement surrounding his tavern adopted his name and was known thereafter as Hodgenville. In 1909 a bronze statue of Lincoln was erected on the town square.

What to See and Do

1. **Abraham Lincoln Birthplace National Historic Site** (see). 3 mi S on US 31E (KY 61).
2. **Lincoln Museum.** 66 Lincoln Square. Dioramas depicting events in Lincoln's life; memorabilia; special exhibits. (Daily; closed Jan 1, Thanksgiving, Dec 25) Phone 358-3163. ¢¢
3. **Lincoln's Boyhood Home.** 7 mi NE on US 31E, on Knob Creek Farm. Replica of the log cabin where Lincoln lived for five years (1811–1816) during his childhood; contains historic items and antiques. (Apr–Oct, daily) Phone 549-3741. ¢
4. **Lincoln Jamboree.** 2 mi S on US 31E. Family entertainment featuring traditional and modern country music. (Sat evenings; res recommended in summer) Phone 358-3545. ¢¢¢

(For further information contact the LaRue County Chamber of Commerce, 76 Lincoln Square, PO Box 176; 358-3411.)

Annual Events

Founder's Day. Arts, crafts, music. Phone 358-3874. Wkend nearest July 17.

Lincoln Day Celebration. Railsplitting competition; puppet show, arts and crafts exhibits; parade. 2nd wkend Oct.

(For accommodations see Elizabethtown)

Hopkinsville (C-4)

Founded: 1797 **Pop:** 29,809 **Elev:** 548 ft **Area code:** 502 **Zip:** 42240

The tobacco auctioneers' chant has long been the theme song of Hopkinsville. Industry has moved in, and Hopkinsville now manufactures precision springs, magnetic wire, lighting fixtures, bowling balls, hardwood, plastic and cement products, non-woven textiles, wearing apparel and hydraulic motors. Tobacco redrying, flour and cornmeal milling are also done here. Fort Campbell military post has played an important role in the city's growth.

Hopkinsville was the site of the Night Rider War, brought on by farmers' discontent at the low prices they received for their dark tobacco. They raided the town in December, 1907, burning several warehouses. In 1911, the culprits were tried and their group disbanded. Hopkinsville was a stop on the "Trail of Tears." The site of the Cherokee encampment is now a park with a museum and memorial dedicated to those who lost thier lives. Famous sons of the town include Adlai Stevenson, Vice President of the United States 1892–1897; Edgar Cayce, famous clairvoyant, who is buried here; Colonel Wil Starling, Chief of the White House Secret Service 1914–1944; and Ned Breathitt, Governor of Kentucky 1963–1967.

What to See and Do

1. **Fort Campbell.** 16 mi S on US 41A, in both KY and TN. One of the nation's largest military installations (105,000 acres); home of 101st Airborne Div (Air Assault). Wickham Hall houses Don F. Pratt Museum, which displays historic military items (daily; closed Jan 1, Dec 25). Phone 798-2151. **Free.**

2. **Pennyroyal Area Museum.** 217 E 9th St. Exhibits feature area's agriculture and industries, Indian artifacts, miniature circus, old railroad items. Civil War items; 1898 law office furniture; Edgar Cayce exhibit, books. (Daily exc Sun; closed most hols) Phone 887-4270. ¢

3. **Jefferson Davis Monument State Shrine** (see). 11 mi E on US 68 in Fairview.

4. **Pennyrile Forest State Resort Park.** Approx 17 mi NW on KY 109 (see MADISONVILLE).

(For further information contact the Hopkinsville-Christian County Chamber of Commerce, 1209 S Virginia St, PO Box 1382; 885-9096.)

Annual Events

Little River Days. Downtown. Festival consists of road races, canoe races; arts and crafts; entertainment; square dance; children's events. Phone 887-4290 or -4291. Early May.

Western Kentucky State Fair. Midway, rides, concerts, local exhibits and events. Phone 886-7411. 1st wk Aug.

(See Cadiz; also see Clarksville, TN)

Motels

✔ ★ ★ **BEST WESTERN.** 4101 Ft Campbell Blvd. 502/886-9000; FAX 502/886-9000, ext 102. 111 rms, 3 story. S $39–$40; D $43; each addl $4; kit. suites $45–$53; under 12 free. Crib free. TV; cable. Pool. Continental bkfst. Restaurant nearby. Bar 5–10 pm. Ck-out noon. Meeting rms. Cr cds: A, C, D, MC, V.

D ☂ ⚓ 🛇 🕐 SC

★ ★ **HOLIDAY INN.** 2910 Ft Campbell Blvd. 502/886-4413; FAX 502/886-4413, ext 7607. 101 rms, 5 story. S $43–$61; D $49–$67; each addl $6; under 19 free. Crib free. TV; cable. Indoor pool; sauna. Restaurant 6 am–2 pm, 5–10 pm. Rm serv. Bar 4 pm–1 am. Ck-out noon. Meeting rms. Valet serv. Sundries. Cr cds: A, C, D, DS, MC, V, JCB.

D ☂ 🐾 ⚓ 🛇 🕐 SC

Horse Cave (C-5)

Pop: 2,284 **Elev:** 132 ft **Area code:** 502 **Zip:** 42749

Tobacco, livestock and caves are important sources of local income. The town took its name from a nearby cave, which provided water for the area's first settlers ("horse" meant large).

What to See and Do

1. **Kentucky Down Under/Mammoth Onyx Cave.** 2 mi NW on KY 218, just E of I-65, exit 58. Exotic bird garden; wallabies, emus, sheep and other animals in Australian outback setting. Petting zoo; bison and elk overlook. (Apr–Oct, daily) Guided cave tour (45 min) includes Mammoth Onyx Column (45 ft high); colorful stalactites, stalagmites, flowstone and hanging bridges; cave temperature approximately 60°F. Tours (daily; closed Jan 1, Dec 25) Phone 786-2634 or 800/762-2869. ¢¢¢¢

2. **Horse Cave Theatre.** I-65 exit 58, downtown. Southern Kentucky's resident professional theatre. Three of the season's plays run in rotating repertory in summer. Art gallery; gift shop. (July–Dec, nightly exc Mon; matinees Sat, Sun; phone ahead for current schedule) Phone 800/342-2177 for schedule, reservations. ¢¢¢¢

(For accommodations see Cave City, Glasgow)

Jamestown (C-6)

Pop: 1,641 **Elev:** 1,024 ft **Area code:** 502 **Zip:** 42629

What to See and Do

Wolf Creek Dam. 12 mi S via US 127. US Army Corps of Engineers dam; 258 ft high, 5,736 ft long, draining a 5,789-sq-mi area and creating 101-mi-long Lake Cumberland (see SOMERSET). Camping (mid-Mar–Nov; fee). Visitor center. Phone 606/679-6337. On N shore of lake is

Lake Cumberland State Resort Park. 14 mi S on US 127. More than 3,000 acres on a 50,250-acre lake. Swimming pools; fishing; boating (ramps, rentals, dock). Hiking, riding (seasonal), 9-hole/par-3 and miniature golf (seasonal), tennis, shuffleboard. bicycling (rentals). Picnicking, playground, lodge (see RESORTS), rental houseboats, cottages. Tent & trailer camping (Apr–Nov; standard fees). Nature center, supervised recreation. For rates and information phone 343-3111.

(For further information contact the Russell County Tourist Commission, PO Box 64, Russell Springs 42642; 866-4333.)

(See Somerset)

Resorts

★ ★ **JAMESTOWN RESORT & MARINA.** (Box 530) 4 mi S on KY 92E. 502/343-5253; FAX 502/343-5253, ext 687. 40 rms in main bldg, 2 story, 4 kit. units, 17 kit. cottages (1–2 bedrm). Memorial Day–Labor Day, EP: S, D $109.95; each addl $5; kit. units $149.95; kit. cottages $59.95–$99.95; under 17 free; lower rates rest of yr. Crib free. TV; cable, in-rm movies. Pool. Playground. Complimentary coffee in rms. Restaurant adj (seasonal) 7 am–10 pm. Ck-out 10 am, ck-in 2 pm. Grocery. Coin lndry. Meeting rms. Gift shop. Tennis. Boats. Waterskiing. Lake swimming. Hiking. Lawn games. 19-hole miniature golf. Soc dir. Fishing/hunting guides. Refrigerators; some minibars. Balconies. Grills. A 300-acre lakeside development; more than 700 boat slips. Cr cds: A, D, DS, MC, V.

D 🔑 ⚓ 🕐 SC

✔ ★ ★ ★ **LURE LODGE.** (Mailing address: 5465 State Park Rd) 10 mi S, in Lake Cumberland State Park. 502/343-3111; res: 800/325-1709; FAX 502/343-5510. 63 rms in lodge, 13 in annex, 30 kit. cottages (1–2 bedrm). Apr–Oct: S $41–$46; D $51–$64; each addl $5; cottages for 2–4, $79.70–$90.62; under 16 free; lower lodge rates rest of yr. Crib free. TV; cable. 2 pools, 1 indoor; 2 wading pools. Dining rm 7–10:30 am, 11:30

am–2:30 pm, 5–9 pm. Box lunches, snacks. Ck-out noon, cottages 11 am, ck-in 4 pm. Coin lndry. Convention facilities. Gift shop. Sports dir. Tennis. 9-hole golf, greens fee $6, putting green. Miniature golf $1.50. Waterskiing. Marina; boat, houseboat rental. Lawn games. Soc dir. Entertainment. Rec rm. Children's program. Balconies overlook lake. State-owned; all facilities of state park avail. Cr cds: A, C, D, DS, MC, V.

Jefferson Davis Monument State Shrine (C-4)

(10 mi E of Hopkinsville on US 68 in Fairview)

The monument, a cast-concrete obelisk 351 feet tall, ranks as the fourth tallest obelisk in the country and the tallest of such material. It marks the birthplace of Jefferson Davis, the only President of the Confederate States of America. Overlooking a 19-acre park, the monument was built at a cost of $200,000 raised by public subscription and was dedicated in 1924. Visitors may take an elevator to the top (fee).

The son of a Revolutionary War officer, Jefferson Davis was born here in 1808, less than 100 miles from Abraham Lincoln's birthplace. Davis graduated from West Point, became a successful cotton planter in Mississippi, was elected to the US Senate and was Secretary of War in President Franklin Pierce's Cabinet. Elected President of the Confederacy, he served for the duration of the war, was captured in Georgia and imprisoned for two years. (May–Oct, daily) Picnic area; playground. Phone 502/886-1765.

(For accommodations see Hopkinsville)

Kenlake State Resort Park (C-3)

(16 mi NE of Murray on KY 94)

Located 16 miles northeast of Murray (see), Kenlake State Resort Park lies on 1,800 acres with a four-mile shoreline on 160,300-acre Kentucky Lake. Sand beach, pool, bathhouse (seasonal), waterskiing; fishing; boating (ramps, rentals, marina); 9-hole golf (rentals), shuffleboard, tennis (indoor, outdoor, shop). Picnicking, playgrounds, cottages, dining room, lodge (see RESORT). Tent & trailer sites (Apr–Oct, standard fees). For rates and information phone 502/474-2211 or 800/325-0143.

(See Cadiz, Land Between The Lakes)

Motel

✔ ★**EARLY AMERICAN.** *(Rte 1, Aurora 42048) At jct US 68, KY 80 & jct KY 94. 502/474-2241.* 18 rms, 7 kits. Late May–early Sept: S $30.50–$35; D $39.95–$40.25; each addl $4; kit. units $47.95–$58; under 16 free; wkly rates; lower rates Mar–mid-May, mid-Sept–Dec. Closed rest of yr. Crib free. Pet accepted. TV; cable. Pool. Playground. Complimentary coffee in rms. Restaurant opp 6 am–9 pm. Ck-out 10 am. Rec rm. Lawn games. Picnic tables, grills. Cr cds: MC, V.

Resort

★★**KENLAKE.** *(Rte 1, Box 522 Hardin 42048) On KY 94 at jct US 68. 502/474-2211; res: 800/325-0143; FAX 502/474-2018.* 48 rms in lodge, 1–2 story, 34 cottages. Memorial Day–Labor Day: S $49; D $59.50; each addl $5.45; 1–3 bedrm cottages $73–$109; lower rates rest of yr. Closed 1 wk Dec. Crib free. TV. Pool; wading pool, lifeguard May–Sept. Playground. Dining rm 7 am–9 pm. Ck-out noon (lodge rms) & 11 am (cottages), ck-in 4 pm (lodge rms & cottages). Meeting rms. Lighted tennis, some indoor. 9-hole golf, greens fee $10, putting green. Lawn games. Rec rm. Picnic tables, grills. State-owned; all state park facilities avail. Cr cds: A, C, D, MC, V.

Restaurant

★★**BRASS LANTERN.** *(Aurora)* On US 68 at jct KY 80. 502/474-2773. Hrs: 5–9 pm. Closed Mon, Tues exc mid-June–mid-Aug & Thanksgiving–Dec 25; also closed late Dec–late Mar. Res accepted Sun–Fri. Semi-a la carte: dinner $7.95–$21.95. Child's meals. Specializes in prime rib, filet mignon, fresh fish. Salad bar. Parking. Cr cds: A, C, D, DS, MC, V.

Land Between The Lakes (C-3)

A 170,000-acre wooded peninsula, running 40 miles from north to south, located between Kentucky Lake and Lake Barkley in western Kentucky and Tennessee, Land Between The Lakes is one of the largest outdoor recreation areas in the country.

There are three major family campgrounds: Hillman Ferry, Piney and Energy Lake (yr-round; electric hookups; fee). Eleven other lake access areas offer more primitive camping (fee). Reservations for camping at Energy Lake are required. All areas offer swimming; fishing; boating, ramps. Picnic facilities. Family campgrounds have planned recreation programs (summer).

There is a 5,000-acre wooded Environmental Education Area that includes Woodlands Nature Center, which presents films and interpretive displays of native plant and animal life. Within this area are several nature trails and an overlook that offers a panoramic view of Lake Barkley. There is a herd of buffalo living in a 200-acre area near The Homeplace (1850). Nature center (Mar–Nov, daily; fee).

(For further information contact Land Between The Lakes, 100 Van Morgan Dr, Golden Pond 42211; 502/924-5602.)

What to See and Do

1. **Golden Pond Visitor Center.** Main orientation center for Land Between The Lakes visitors. Planetarium presentation (Mar–Dec, Wed–Sun; fee). Seasonal programs. Visitor center (daily).

2. **Woodlands Nature Center.** 14 mi NE of Aurora via US 68, Land Between The Lakes exit. Films and interpretive displays of native animals and plants. (Mar–Nov, daily; rest of yr, Wed–Sun)

3. **The Homeplace–1850.** 17 mi SE of Aurora via US 68, Land Between The Lakes exit. Living history farm. (Mar–Nov, daily) Fee.

(For accommodations see Cadiz, Gilbertsville; also see Paris, TN)

Lexington (B-7)

Founded: 1779 **Pop:** 225,366 **Elev:** 983 ft **Area code:** 606

A midland metropolis rooted in the production of tobacco and Thoroughbreds, Lexington is a gracious city, decorated with rich bluegrass and dotted with aristocratic old houses. The legendary steel-blue tint of the bluegrass is perceptible only in May's early-morning sunshine, but throughout spring, summer and fall it is unrivaled for turf and pasture.

An exploring party, camping here in 1775, got news of the Battle of Lexington and so named the spot. The city was established four years later, rapidly becoming a center for barter and a major producer of hemp (used by New England's clipper ships). Lexington cashed in on its tobacco crop when smoking became popular during the Civil War. Pioneers who settled here brought their best horses with them from Maryland and Virginia; as they grew wealthy, they imported blooded lines from abroad to improve the breed. The first races were held in Lexington in 1780, and the first jockey club was organized in 1797.

Lexington is the world's largest burley tobacco market, with well over 100 million pounds sold each year. Precious bluegrass seed, beef cattle and sheep are also merchandised in Lexington. More than 50 major industries, manufacturing everything from peanut butter and whiskey to air brakes and typewriters, are located here.

What to See and Do

1. **Ashland** (1806). Richmond Rd (E Main St), at Sycamore Rd. Estate on 20 acres of woodland was the home of Henry Clay, statesman, orator, senator and would-be president. Ashland, occupied by the Clay family for four generations, is furnished with family possessions and furniture. The estate was named for the ash trees that surround it. A number of outbuildings still stand. (Daily; closed Thanksgiving, Dec 24, 25, 31; also Jan) Phone 266-8581. **¢¢**

2. **Hunt-Morgan House** (ca 1812–1814). 201 N Mill St, at W 2nd St. In Gratz Park area, a historic district with antebellum residences. Federal-period mansion with a cantilevered elliptical staircase and fanlight doorway. Built for John Wesley Hunt, Kentucky's first millionaire. Later occupied by his grandson, General John Hunt Morgan, known as the "Thunderbolt of the Confederacy." Nobel Prize-winning geneticist Thomas Hunt Morgan was also born in this house. Family furniture, portraits and porcelain. Walled courtyard garden. Gift shop. (Daily exc Mon; closed Thanksgiving, late Dec–Feb) Phone 253-0362. **¢¢**

3. **Mary Todd Lincoln House.** 578 W Main St. Childhood residence of Mary Todd Lincoln is authentically restored; period furnishings, personal items. (Apr–mid-Dec, Tues–Sat; closed major hols) Phone 233-9999. **¢¢**

4. **Headley-Whitney Museum.** 4435 Old Frankfort Pike, 4½ mi NW of New Circle Rd. Unusual buildings house display of bibelots (small decorative objects) executed in precious metals and jewels; Oriental porcelains, paintings, decorative arts, sea shells, special exhibits; library. (Apr–Oct, daily exc Mon; rest of yr, Wed–Sun; closed most hols). Sr citizen rate. Phone 255-6653. **¢¢**

5. **Waveland State Historic Site.** 225 Higbee Mill Rd. Greek-revival mansion (1847) with three original outbuildings. Exhibits depict plantation life of 1840s. Playground. Gift shop. (Mar–Dec, Mon–Sat & Sun afternoons) Phone 272-3611. **¢¢**

6. **Opera House** (1886). 401 W Short St. Restored and reconstructed opera house is a regional performing arts center; performances include Broadway shows and special events. (Sept–June) Contact Lexington Center Corp, Performing Arts, 430 W Vine St, 40507; 233-4567.

7. **University of Kentucky** (1865). (24,000 students) Area of S Limestone St & Euclid Ave. For information on bus and walking tours phone 257-3595. **Free.** On campus are

   Anthropology Museum. Lafferty Hall. Exhibits include cultural history of Kentucky and evolution of man. (Mon–Fri; closed hols) Phone 257-7112. **Free.**

   Art Museum. Singletary Center for the Arts, Euclid Ave & Rose St. Permanent collections; special exhibitions. (Daily exc Mon; closed hols & Dec 26–Jan 2) Phone 257-5716. **Free.**

8. **Transylvania University** (1780). (1,076 students) N Broadway & 3rd St. The oldest institution of higher learning west of the Allegheny Mountains, it has educated two US vice-presidents, 36 state and territorial governors, 34 ambassadors, 50 senators, 112 members

of the US House of Representatives and Confederate President Jefferson Davis. Thomas Jefferson was one of Transylvania's early supporters. Henry Clay taught law courses and was a member of the university's governing board. Administration Building, "Old Morrison" (1833), Greek-revival architecture, was used as hospital during Civil War. Medical museum (Mon–Fri; closed major hols). Tours of campus (by appt). Phone 233-8120. Medical museum **free.**

9. **Lexington Cemetery.** 833 W Main St, on US 421. Buried on these 170 acres are Henry Clay, John C. Breckinridge, General John Hunt Morgan, the Todds (Mrs. Abraham Lincoln's family), coach Adolph Rupp and many other notable persons. Also interred are 500 Confederate and 1,110 Union veterans. Sunken gardens, lily pools, four-acre flower garden, extensive plantings of spring-flowering trees and shrubs. (Daily) Phone 255-5522.

10. **Victorian Square.** Vine St, across Triangle Park from the Convention Center and Rupp Arena. Shopping area located in downtown restoration project. Specialty stores; restaurants; Children's Museum (phone 258-3253); parking in 400-car garage with covered walkway into mall. Phone 252-7575.

11. **Kentucky Horse Park.** 6 mi N via I-75, Kentucky Horse Park exit 120, on Iron Works Pike. More than 1,000 acres of beautiful bluegrass fill the park; features Man O' War grave and memorial, visitors' information center with wide-screen film presentation *Thou Shalt Fly Without Wings*. Also located within park are the International Museum of the Horse, Parade of Breeds (seasonal), Calumet Trophy Collection, Sears Collection of hand-carved miniatures; Hall of Champions stable that houses famous Thoroughbreds and standardbreds; walking farm tour, antique carriage display. Swimming. Tennis. Ball courts. Picnic area, playgrounds. Campground (fee). Special events (see ANNUAL EVENTS); horsedrawn rides (fee). (Mid-Mar–Oct, daily; rest of yr, Wed–Sun; closed Jan 1, Thanksgiving, late Dec) Parking fee (seasonal). Contact Director, 4089 Iron Works Rd, 40511; 800/568-8813. General admission **¢¢¢** Also on grounds is

   American Saddle Horse Museum. 4093 Iron Works Pike. Museum dedicated to the American saddlebred horse, Kentucky's only native breed. Contemporary exhibits on the development and current uses of the American saddlebred. Multimedia presentation. Gift shop. (Apr–Oct, daily; rest of yr, Wed–Sun; closed Jan 1, Thanksgiving, Dec 24–25) Phone 259-2746. **¢¢**

12. **Horse farms.** More than 400 in area, most concentrated in Lexington-Fayette County. Although the majority are Thoroughbred farms, other varieties such as standardbreds, American saddle horses, Arabians, Morgans and quarter horses are bred and raised here as well. Not all are open to the public; they may be seen by taking one of the many tours offered by tour companies in Lexington (see #13).

13. **Sightseeing tours.** There are many tour companies that offer tours of working horse farms in the Lexington area. Many of these companies also offer historic sightseeing tours. For more information contact the Convention & Visitors Bureau.

(For further information, contact the Greater Lexington Convention & Visitors Bureau, 430 W Vine St, Suite 363, 40507; 233-1221 or 800/845-3959.)

Annual Events

Blue Grass Stakes. Keeneland Race Course (see SEASONAL EVENTS). Three-year-olds; one of last major prep races before Kentucky Derby. Mid-Apr.

Rolex-Kentucky Event & Trade Fair. Kentucky Horse Park (see #11). Three-day endurance test for horse and rider in dressage, cross-country and stadium jumping. Fair features boutiques. Phone 233-2362. Late Apr.

High Hope Steeplechase. Kentucky Horse Park (see #11). Mid-May.

Egyptian Event. Kentucky Horse Park (see #11). Activities highlighting rare Egyptian Arabian horses. Show classes, Hall of Champions, Breeder's Sale, saluki dog show, film fest, art exhibit and bazaar. Early June.

Festival of the Bluegrass. Kentucky Horse Park (see #11). Top names in bluegrass music, with more than 20 bands appearing. Includes special shows for children; crafts; workshops with the musicians. The 600-acre park has more than 750 electric hookups for campers. For information, tickets, contact PO Box 644, Georgetown 40324; 846-4995. 2nd full wkend June.

Junior League Horse Show. The Red Mile Track. Contact PO Box 1092, 40589; 252-1893. Six days early July.

Grand Circuit Meet. The Red Mile Track (see SEASONAL EVENTS). Features Kentucky Futurity race, the final leg of trotting's Triple Crown. Daily exc Sun. Phone 255-0752. 2 wks, late Sept–early Oct.

Equifestival of Kentucky. Racing, parade, entertainment. Phone 233-1221. Mid-Oct.

Seasonal Events

Thoroughbred racing. Keeneland Race Course, 6 mi W on US 60. Phone 254-3412. 3 wks Apr & 3 wks Oct.

Harness racing. The Red Mile Track, 1200 Red Mile Rd, 1½ mi S on US 68. Night racing (late Apr–late June & late Sept–early Oct, Wed–Sat). Also site of Grand Circuit racing (see ANNUAL EVENTS). Phone 255-0752.

(See Frankfort, Paris, Richmond, Winchester)

Motels

★★**BEST WESTERN REGENCY.** *2241 Elkhorn (40505), I-75 exit 110.* 606/293-2202; FAX 606/293-2202, ext 300. 112 rms, 2 story. S $42–$47; D $48–$53; each addl $7; suite $64–$75; under 12 free. Crib free. TV; cable. Pool; whirlpool, sauna. Complimentary continental bkfst, coffee. Restaurant nearby. Ck-out 11 am. Coin lndry. Meeting rms. Cr cds: A, C, D, DS, MC, V.

D ▣ ☎ ⊖ ⊘ SC

★★**COMFORT INN.** *2381 Buena Vista (40505), I-75 exit 110.* 606/299-0302; FAX 606/299-0302, ext 500. 124 rms, 3 story. S $47; D $49–$51; each addl $7; suites $82–$89; under 17 free; wkend rates. Crib free. TV; cable. Pool. Complimentary continental bkfst, coffee. Restaurant nearby. Ck-out noon. Meeting rms. Refrigerators avail. Cr cds: A, C, D, DS, ER, MC, V.

D ☎ ⊖ ⊘ SC

★★★**COURTYARD BY MARRIOTT.** *775 Newtown Ct (40511).* 606/253-4646; FAX 606/253-9118. 146 rms, 3 story. S $49–$79; D $49–$89; each addl $10; suites $70–$100; under 18 free. Crib free. TV; cable. Indoor pool. Complimentary coffee in rms. Restaurant 6:30 am–2 pm, 5–10 pm. Rm serv after 5 pm. Bar 4–11 pm. Ck-out noon. Coin lndry. Meeting rms. Valet serv. Sundries. Exercise equipt; weight machine, bicycles, whirlpool. Some refrigerators. Balconies. Cr cds: A, C, D, DS, MC, V.

D ☎ ✝ ⊖ ⊘ SC

★**DAYS INN.** *5575 Athens Boonesboro Rd (40509), off I-75 exit 104.* 606/263-3100. 56 rms, 2 story. S $33–$36; D $36–$42; each addl $5; family rates; higher rates: Kentucky Derby, Keeneland races. Crib free. TV; cable. Complimentary coffee in lobby. Restaurant nearby. Ck-out noon. Sundries. Cr cds: A, C, D, DS, MC, V.

D ⊖ ⊘ SC

✔★**ECONO LODGE.** *925 Newtown Pike (40505), I-64 exit 115.* 606/231-6300. 110 rms, 2 story. S $36–$38; D $40–$47; each addl $5; under 12 free. Crib $4. TV; cable. Pool. Playground. Restaurant 7 am–2 pm; Sat & Sun to noon. Bar 4 pm–1 am. Ck-out noon. Coin lndry.

Meeting rms. Sundries. Refrigerators avail. Cr cds: A, C, D, DS, MC, V, JCB.

☎ ⊘ ⊕ SC

★★**HAMPTON INN.** *2251 Elkhorn Rd (40505), I-75 exit 110.* 606/299-2613; FAX 606/299-9664. 125 rms, 5 story. S $49–$57; D $55–$63; under 18 free. Crib free. TV; cable. Pool. Complimentary continental bkfst, coffee. Restaurant adj open 24 hrs. Ck-out noon. Meeting rm. Cr cds: A, C, D, DS, MC, V.

D ☎ ⊖ ⊘ SC

★★★**HOLIDAY INN–NORTH.** *1950 Newtown Pike (40511), ½ blk S of I-75 exit 115.* 606/233-0512; FAX 606/231-9285. 303 rms, 2 story. S $84; D $89; suites $150; under 18 free. Crib free. Pet accepted, some restrictions. TV; cable. Indoor pool. Coffee in rms. Restaurant 6 am–2 pm, 5–10 pm. Rm serv. Bar 2 pm–1 am; dancing Tues–Sat. Ck-out noon. Coin lndry. Convention facilities. Bellhops. Valet serv. Concierge. Sundries. Gift shop. Free airport transportation. Indoor tennis. Putting green. Exercise equipt; weight machine, bicycle, whirlpool, sauna. Holidome. Game rm. Cr cds: A, C, D, DS, ER, MC, V, JCB.

D ✑ ◿ ☎ ✝ ⊖ ⊘ SC

✔★**KNIGHTS INN.** *1935 Stanton Way (40511), I-75 exit 115.* 606/231-0232; res: 800/843-5644; FAX 606/231-0511. 114 rms, 12 kit. units. S $33–$43; D $40–$44; each addl $6; under 18 free. Crib free. Pet accepted, some restrictions; $6. TV; cable. Pool. Complimentary coffee. Restaurant adj 6 am–10 pm; wkends to midnight. Ck-out noon. Meeting rm. Cr cds: A, C, D, DS, MC, V.

D ✑ ☎ ⊖ ⊘ SC

★★**LA QUINTA INN.** *1919 Stanton Way (40511), I-64/75 exit 115.* 606/231-7551; FAX 606/281-6002. 130 rms, 2 story. S $46; D $54; each addl $8; under 18 free. Crib free. Pet accepted, some restrictions. TV; cable. Pool. Complimentary continental bkfst. Restaurant adj 6 am–10 pm; wkends to 11 pm. Ck-out noon. Meeting rms. Valet serv. Cr cds: A, C, D, DS, MC, V.

D ✑ ☎ ⊖ ⊘ SC

✔★★**QUALITY INN–NORTHWEST.** *1050 Newtown Pike (KY 922) (40511).* 606/233-0561; FAX 606/231-6125. 107 rms, 2 story. S $35.50–$42.50; D $37.50–$50.50; each addl $5; suites $100; under 19 free. Crib $1. TV; cable. Heated pool; poolside serv, lifeguard (in season). Playground. Restaurant 6:30 am–2 pm, 5:30–9:30 pm; Sat & Sun from 7 am. Ck-out noon. Meeting rms. Valet serv. Sundries. Gift shop. Cr cds: A, C, D, DS, ER, MC, V, JCB.

☎ ⊖ ⊘ SC

★**RED ROOF INN.** *483 Haggard Lane (40505), US 27, 68 at jct I-64, I-75 exit 113.* 606/293-2626; FAX 606/299-8353. 109 rms, 2 story. S $28.95–$34; D $38.99–$45; each addl $3; under 18 free. Crib free. TV. Complimentary coffee in lobby. Restaurant nearby. Ck-out noon. Cr cds: A, C, D, DS, MC, V.

D ⊖ ⊘ ⊕ SC

★**SHONEY'S INN.** *2753 Richmond Rd (40509), jct US 25 & KY 4.* 606/269-4999; res: 800/222-2222. 101 rms, 2 story. S $41.95–$43.95; D $46.95–$56.95; each addl $5; under 18 free. Crib free. TV; cable. Pool. Complimentary coffee in lobby. Restaurant adj 6 am–midnight; wkends to 2 am. Ck-out noon. Meeting rms. Valet serv. Sundries. Cr cds: A, C, D, DS, ER, MC, V.

D ☎ ⊖ ⊘ SC

✔★★**SPRINGS INN.** *2020 Harrodsburg Rd (US 68) (40503).* 606/277-5751; res: 800/354-9503; FAX 606/277-3142. 196 rms, 2 story, 13 kits. S $38; D $48; each addl $4; suites $60. Crib free. Pet accepted; $25. TV; cable. Pool; wading pool. Restaurant 7 am–10 pm; Sun to 8:30 pm. Rm serv. Bar 10–1 am; entertainment, dancing Wed–Sat. Ck-out noon. Meeting rms. Valet serv. Gift shop. Some refrigerators. Cr cds: A, C, D, DS, MC, V.

D ✑ ☎ ⊖ ⊘ ⊕ SC

Motor Hotels

✔ ★ ★ **CAMPBELL HOUSE INN, SUITES & GOLF CLUB.** *1375 Harrodsburg Rd (US 68) (40504).* 606/255-4281; res: 800/354-9235 (exc KY), 800/432-9254 (KY); FAX 606/254-4368. 370 rms, 3 story. S $45–$55; D $49–$65; each addl $5; suites $85–$165; under 12 free. Crib $6. TV; cable. Heated pool; poolside serv. Restaurants 6 am–11 pm. Rm serv. Bar 9–1 am; entertainment. Ck-out noon. Coin lndry. Convention facilities. Bellhops. Valet serv. Sundries. Gift shop. Barber, beauty shop. Free airport transportation. Tennis. 18-hole golf, pro. Game rm. Bathrm phones, refrigerators. Sun deck. Cr cds: A, C, D, DS, MC, V.

D 🏌 🅿 ⊛ 😊 ⊚ SC

★ ★ **HARLEY.** *2143 N Broadway (US 27/68) (40505),* at I-75 exit 113. 606/299-1261; res: 800/321-2323; FAX 606/293-0048. 146 rms, 2–3 story. S $76; D $86; each addl $10; under 18 free; wkend rates. Crib free. TV; cable. Indoor/outdoor pools. Restaurant 6:30 am–2 pm, 5–11 pm; Sun 2–10 pm. Rm serv. Bar 4:30 pm–1 am, Sun to 11 pm; entertainment Fri & Sat. Ck-out 1 pm. Meeting rms. Bellhops. Valet serv. Free airport transportation. Lighted tennis. Putting green. Exercise equipt; weights, bicycles, whirlpool, sauna. Rec rm. Balconies. Cr cds: A, C, D, DS, MC, V.

D 🅿 ⊛ 😊 ⊚ SC

Hotels

★ ★ ★ **FRENCH QUARTER SUITES.** *2601 Richmond Rd (40509),* near jct New Circle Rd (KY 4). 606/268-0060; res: 800/262-3774; FAX 606/268-6209. 155 suites, 5 story. S $89–$119; D $99–$129; each addl $10; under 18 free. Crib free. TV; cable. Heated pool. Complimentary full bkfst. Complimentary coffee in rms. Restaurant 11 am–2 pm, 5–10 pm; Fri & Sat to 11 pm. Bar from 11 am; jazz combo Fri, Sat. Ck-out noon. Meeting rms. Shopping arcade. Beauty shop. Free airport transportation. Exercise equipt; weight machine, bicycles, whirlpools. Bathrm phones, refrigerators; some wet bars. Balconies. Cr cds: A, C, D, DS, MC, V, JCB.

D ⊛ 😊 ⊚ SC

★ ★ **HILTON SUITES OF LEXINGTON GREEN.** *3195 Nicholasville Rd (US 27) (40503).* 606/271-4000; FAX 606/273-2975. 174 suites, 6 story. S $85–$125; D $95–$135; each addl $10; family, recreational rates; wkend package plans; higher rates Kentucky Derby. Crib free. TV; cable. Pool; poolside serv. Restaurant 6:30 am–2 pm, 5–10 pm. Bar 11–1 am. Ck-out noon. Meeting rms. Free airport, bus depot transportation. Exercise equipt; weights, bicycles, whirlpool, sauna. Game rm. Refrigerators. *LUXURY LEVEL.* 20 suites. S $105; D $135. Bathrm phones. Complimentary refreshments, newspapers. Cr cds: A, C, D, DS, ER, MC, V, JCB.

D ⊛ 😊 ⊚ SC

★ ★ **HYATT REGENCY.** *400 W Vine St (40507).* 606/253-1234; FAX 606/288-2059. 365 rms, 16 story. S $120; D $145; each addl $25; suites $275–$775; under 18 free; wkend plans. Crib free. TV; cable, in-rm movies avail. Indoor pool. Restaurants 6 am–11 pm. Bar 11–1 am; entertainment, dancing. Ck-out noon. Convention facilities. Concierge. Shopping arcade. Free airport transportation. Tennis privileges. Exercise equipt; bicycles, rowing machine. Sun deck. *LUXURY LEVEL: CLUB LEVEL.* 20 rms. S $145; D $170. Private lounge. Wet bars. Bathrm phones. Complimentary continental bkfst, refreshments. Cr cds: A, C, D, DS, MC, V, JCB.

D 🅿 ⊛ 😊 ⊚ SC

★ ★ ★ **RADISSON PLAZA LEXINGTON.** *Broadway & Vine Sts (40507).* 606/231-9000; FAX 606/281-3737. 367 rms, 22 story. S $115; D $125; each addl $10; suites $175–$365; under 18 free; wkend plans. Crib free. TV; cable. Valet parking $8. TV; cable. Indoor pool; poolside serv. Restaurant 6 am–11 pm. Rm serv to 1 am; wkends to 2 am. Bar 11:30–1 am; entertainment, dancing. Ck-out noon. Convention facilities. Concierge. Gift shop. Free airport transportation. Lighted tennis privileges. Exercise equipt; weights, bicycles, whirlpool, sauna. Rec rm. Some refrigerators. Wet bar in suites. Atrium with fountains. *LUXURY LEVEL: RADIS-*

SON PLAZA CLUB. 46 rms, 3 suites, 2 floors. S $130; D $140; suites $200. Private lounge. Complimentary continental bkfst, refreshments, newspapers, magazines.
Cr cds: A, C, D, DS, ER, MC, V, JCB.

D 🅿 ⊛ 🏌 😊 ⊚ SC

Inn

★ ★ **GRATZ PARK.** *120 W 2nd St (40507).* 606/231-1777; res: 800/227-4362; FAX 606/233-7593. 44 rms, 3 story, 6 suites. S $99; D $104–$114; each addl $10; suites $129–$249; under 12 free. Crib free. TV; cable. Bkfst avail. Ck-out noon, ck-in 3 pm. Meeting rms. Concierge. Free airport transportation. Health club privileges. Elegantly restored building (1887). Cr cds: A, C, D, DS, MC, V.

D ⊛ ⊚ SC

Resort

★ ★ ★ **MARRIOTT'S GRIFFIN GATE RESORT.** *1800 Newtown Pike (KY 922) (40511),* I-64 & I-75 exit 115. 606/231-5100; FAX 606/255-9944. 409 rms, 7 story. S $125; D $137; each addl $10; suite $250–$575; under 18 free; golf plans. Crib free. Pet accepted, some restrictions; $20. TV; cable. 2 pools, 1 indoor; poolside serv, lifeguard. Playground. Dining rm 6:30 am–11 pm (also see MANSION AT GRIFFIN GATE). Rm serv. Bar 11–1 am. Ck-out noon. Coin lndry. Convention facilities. Valet serv. Gift shop. Barber, beauty shop. Package store 1 mi. Free airport transportation. Sports dir. Lighted tennis, pro. 18-hole golf $44–$49, pro, putting green. Seasonal activities include carriage rides, walking tours, pool activities. Dancing. Game rm. Exercise rm; instructor, weights, bicycles, whirlpool, sauna. Refrigerator 1 mi. Private patios, balconies. Picnic tables. Lobby has atrium with waterfalls, mahogany tables, leather chairs. *LUXURY LEVEL.* S $135; D $147; suites $275–$850. Private lounge, honor bar. Most bathrm phones. Complimentary continental bkfst, newspaper.
Cr cds: A, C, D, DS, MC, V, JCB.

D 🐾 🏌 🅿 ⊛ 🏌 😊 ⊚ SC

Restaurants

★ ★ **A LA LUCIE.** *159 N Limestone St,* at Church St. 606/252-5277. Hrs: 6–10 pm. Closed Sun; Thanksgiving, Dec 25. Res accepted. Bar. Semi-a la carte: dinner $9.95–$17.95. Specializes in fresh seafood, ethnic foods. Cr cds: A, C, D, DS, MC, V.

★ ★ **BRAVO PITINO.** *401 W Main St, Victorian Square.* 606/255-2222. Hrs: 5:30–10 pm; Sat 11:30 am–10:30 pm. Closed Sun; some major hols. Res accepted. Northern Italian menu. Bar 11:30–1 am. Semi-a la carte: lunch $4.95–$8.95, dinner $9.95–$19.95. Specialties: tortellini alla panna e pesto, provimi veal, homemade pasta, fresh seafood. Valet parking. Bi-level dining area. Jacket. Cr cds: A, C, D, DS, MC, V.

✔ ★ **CHINA CAFE.** *109 Mt Tabor Rd, off Richmond Rd.* 606/269-8273. Hrs: 11:30 am–10 pm; wkends to 11 pm. Closed Thanksgiving, Dec 25. Chinese menu. Bar. Semi-a la carte: lunch $4.05–$4.95, dinner $4.95–$12.95. Specializes in mandarin, Hunan cuisine. Parking. Entire menu is MSG-free. Cr cds: A, MC, V.

D

★ ★ ★ **COACH HOUSE.** *855 S Broadway (US 68).* 606/252-7777. Hrs: 11 am–2:30 pm, 5–10:30 pm; Sat from 5 pm. Closed Sun; major hols. Res accepted. Continental menu. Bar 11 am–midnight. Wine cellar. Semi-a la carte: lunch $4.50–$7.50, dinner $13–$28. Specialties: Dover sole ''My Way,'' rack of lamb. Own pastries. Pianist Fri & Sat. Parking. Family-owned. Jacket (dinner). Cr cds: A, C, D, DS, MC, V.

D

✔ ★ **DARRYL'S 1891 RESTAURANT & TAVERN.** *3292 Nicholasville Rd (US 27),* 1 blk S of New Circle Rd. 606/272-1891. Hrs: 11 am–11 pm. Closed Dec 25. Res accepted. Bar. Semi-a la carte: lunch, dinner $3.99–$15.99. Child's meals. Specializes in prime rib, pork ribs. Parking. Old English building. Braille menu. Cr cds: A, C, D, DS, MC, V.

★★**DUDLEY'S.** *380 S Mill St, in Dudley Square. 606/252-1010.* Hrs: 11:30 am–2:30 pm, 5:30–10 pm; Fri, Sat to 11 pm. Closed major hols. Res accepted. Continental menu. Bar. Semi-a la carte: lunch $4.50–$7.50, dinner $12–$18. Specializes in seafood, beef, pasta. Parking. Outdoor dining on tree-shaded patio. Restored school (1851); paintings. Cr cds: A, MC, V.

✔★**L & N SEAFOOD.** *3199 Nicholasville Rd (US 27), in Lexington Green Mall. 606/273-7875.* Hrs: 11:30 am–10 pm; Fri, Sat to 11 pm; Sun 11 am–9 pm; early-bird dinner Sun–Fri 3–6 pm; Sun brunch 11 am–2 pm. Closed Dec 25. Res accepted. Bar; Sun from 1 pm. Semi-a la carte: lunch $4.95–$8.95, dinner $8.95–$15.95. Sun brunch $9.95. Child's meals. Specializes in mesquite-grilled seafood. Oyster bar. Outdoor dining overlooking lake. Cr cds: A, C, D, DS, MC, V.

★★**LE CAFE FRANCAIS.** *735 E Main St. 606/266-6646.* Hrs: 11:30 am–2 pm, 6–10 pm; Fri to 11 pm; Sat 6–11 pm; Sun 5–9 pm. Closed Mon; some major hols. Res accepted. French menu. Bar. Semi-a la carte: lunch $5.25–$8.75, dinner $13.95–$22.50. Child's meals. Specialties: duckling with raspberry sauce, lamb, seafood. Jazz pianist Fri, Sat. Parking. Patio dining. Country French atmosphere; fireplace. Cr cds: A, D, MC, V.

★★★**MANSION AT GRIFFIN GATE.** *(See Marriott's Griffin Gate Resort) 606/231-5152.* Hrs: 11:30 am–2 pm, 6–10 pm; Sat & Sun to 10:30 pm. Res accepted. Continental menu. Bar. Semi-a la carte: lunch $6–$9.95, dinner $18.50–$28.95. Specializes in veal, beef, fresh seafood. Parking. On grounds of Marriott's Griffin Gate Resort. Greek-revival mansion built 1873; furnished with antiques; crystal chandeliers. Cr cds: A, C, D, DS, MC, V, JCB.

✔★★**RAFFERTY'S.** *2420 Nicholasville Rd (US 27). 606/278-9427.* Hrs: 11 am–11 pm; Fri, Sat to midnight. Closed Thanksgiving, Dec 25. Bar to midnight; Fri & Sat to 1 am; Sun to 11 pm. Semi-a la carte: lunch, dinner $4.95–$16.95. Child's meals. Specialties: Danish baby back pork ribs, prime rib. Parking. Outdoor dining. Cr cds: A, C, D, MC, V.

✔★**RUBY TUESDAY.** *3199 Nicholasville Rd. 606/273-7985.* Hrs: 11:30 am–midnight; Fri & Sat to 1 am; Sun 11:30 am–9 pm; Sun brunch to 3 pm. Closed Thanksgiving, Dec 25. Res accepted. Bar. Semi-a la carte: lunch, dinner $4.99–$13.99. Child's meals. Specializes in baby-back ribs, chicken. Salad bar. Parking. Patio dining overlooking lake. Sectioned dining areas; Tiffany-style lamps. Cr cds: A, C, D, DS, MC, V.

Unrated Dining Spots

BLUE BOAR CAFETERIA. *2157 Turfland Shopping Ctr, on US 68. 606/277-6180.* Hrs: 11 am–2:30 pm, 4:15–8 pm; Sun 11 am–7 pm. Closed Dec 24–25. Avg ck: lunch $5.50, dinner $6.50. Child's meals. Specializes in country-fried steak, veal parmigiana. Salad bar. Family-owned. No cr cds accepted.

MORRISON'S CAFETERIA. *Lexington Mall, 2 mi W of I-75 exit 110, E on New Circle Rd to Richmond Rd. 606/269-3329.* Hrs: 11 am–8:30 pm; Fri, Sat to 9 pm. Avg ck: lunch $4.50, dinner $6. Child's meals. Cr cds: A, DS, MC, V.

London *(C-7)*

Founded: 1825 **Pop:** 5,757 **Elev:** 1,255 ft **Area code:** 606 **Zip:** 40741

London, seat of Laurel County, has both coal and timber and includes part of Daniel Boone National Forest (see). A Ranger District office of the forest is located in London.

What to See and Do

1. **Levi Jackson Wilderness Road State Park.** 3 mi S on US 25, exit 38 off I-75. A 896-acre park. Descendants of pioneer farmer Levi Jackson deeded some of this land to the state as a historical shrine to those who carved homes out of the wilderness. Boone's Trace and Wilderness Road pioneer trails converge within the park. Recreational facilities include swimming pool (fee); bathhouse. Hiking; archery range; miniature golf (Apr–Oct, fee). Picnicking, playgrounds. Camping (tent & trailer sites). Supervised recreation (Memorial Day–Labor Day). Standard fees. Phone 878-8000. Here are

    Mountain Life Museum. Split-rail fences enclose rustic cabins with household furnishings, pioneer relics, farm tools, Native American artifacts; smokehouse, blacksmith shop, barn with prairie schooner. (Apr–Oct, daily) Phone 878-8000. ¢

    McHargue's Mill. One of the largest collections of millstones in the world. Mill built in 1812, reconstructed on present site in 1939. Tours and demonstrations. (Memorial Day–Labor Day, daily) **Free.**

2. **Canoe trips.** Canoe trips on the Rockcastle River, ranging from three hours to seven days; rentals. Contact Rockcastle Adventures, PO Box 662; 864-9407. ¢¢¢¢–¢¢¢¢¢

3. **Daniel Boone National Forest** (see). 10 mi E on Daniel Boone Pkwy.

    (For further information contact the London-Laurel County Tourist Commission, 140 W Daniel Boone Parkway; 878-6900.)

    (See Corbin)

Motels

★★**BEST WESTERN HARVEST INN.** *207 W KY 80, ¼ mi E of I-75 exit 41. 606/864-2222; FAX 606/878-2825.* 100 rms, 2 story. June–Oct: S $37–$41; D $48–$55; each addl $5; lower rates rest of yr. Crib $3. TV; cable. Indoor pool; whirlpool. Restaurant 6 am–10 pm. Ck-out noon. Meeting rms. Cr cds: A, C, D, MC, V.

✔★★**HOLIDAY INN EXPRESS.** *400 GOP Dr, jct I-75 & KY 80. 606/878-7678; FAX 606/878-7654.* 60 rms, 2 story. S, D $45–$58; each addl $5; under 21 free. Crib avail. TV; cable. Indoor/outdoor pool. Complimentary continental bkfst. Restaurant opp 6 am–11 pm. Ck-out 11 am. Exercise equipt; bicycles, treadmill, whirlpool. Game rm. Cr cds: A, C, D, DS, MC, V.

Louisville *(B-6)*

Founded: 1778 **Pop:** 269,063 **Elev:** 462 ft **Area code:** 502

Louisville is a unique city. It has southern graces and a determined dedication to music and the arts, but to the world, Louisville is "Derby City" for at least one week of every year. Since the first running on May 17, 1875, the Kentucky Derby has generated tremendous excitement. Modeled after England's Epsom Derby, it is the oldest race in continuous existence in the US. The first Saturday in May each year, world attention focuses on Churchill Downs as the classic "run for the roses"

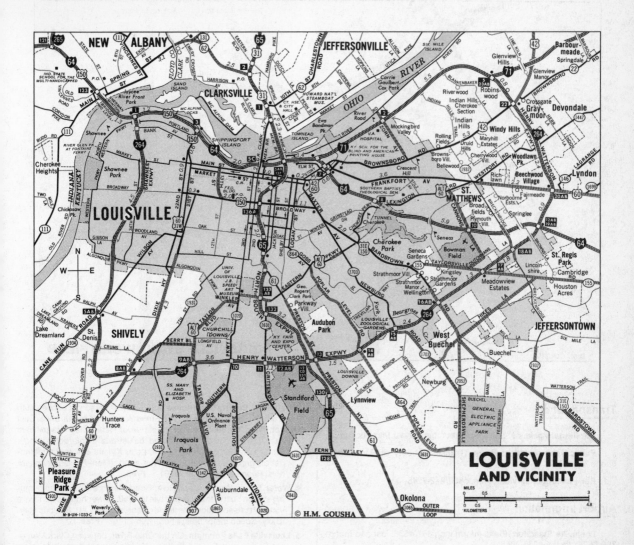

LOUISVILLE AND VICINITY

© H.M. GOUSHA

is played out against its backdrop of Edwardian towers and antique grandstands.

The social highlight of a very social city, Derby festivities are a glamorous melange of carnival, fashion show, spectacle and celebration of the horse. From the opening strains of "My Old Kentucky Home," played before the big race, until the final toast of bourbon is made, Louisville takes on a uniquely festive character. Afterward, the center of Thoroughbred racing quickly returns to normalcy—a city southern in manner, midwestern in pace.

Situated at the falls of the Ohio River, Louisville is a city long nurtured by river traffic. The Spanish, French, English, Scottish, Irish and Germans all had roles in its exploration, settlement and development. George Rogers Clark established the first real settlement, a base

for military operations against the British, on a spit of land above the falls, now entirely erased by the river. Named after Louis XVI of France, the settlement became an important portage point around the falls; later a canal bypassed them. Today, the McAlpine Locks and Dam provide modern navigation around the falls of the Ohio.

Louisville is a top producer of bourbon and a leader in synthetic rubber, paint and varnish, cigarettes, home appliances and aluminum for home use.

This is a community that takes its culture seriously, with a public subscription Fund for the Arts subsidizing the Tony Award-winning Actors Theater. The city also boasts the Kentucky Center for the Arts, home of ballet, opera, art and music groups and other cultural organizations.

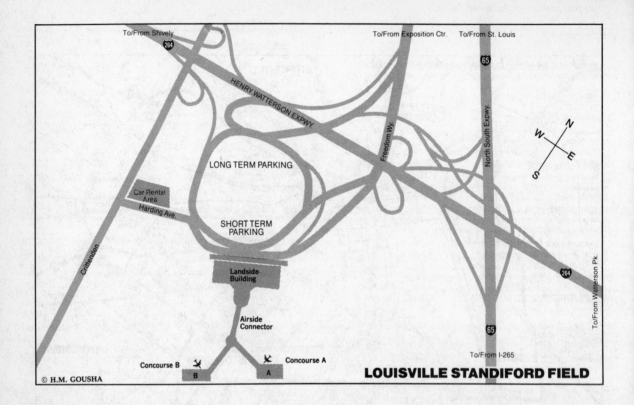

To/From Shively

To/From Exposition Ctr.   To/From St. Louis

HENRY WATTERSON EXPWY.

Freedom Wy.

North South Expwy.

LONG TERM PARKING

Car Rental Area
Harding Ave.

SHORT TERM PARKING

Crittenden

Landside Building

Airside Connector

Concourse B   B   A   Concourse A

© H.M. GOUSHA

To/From Watterson Pk.

To/From I-265

LOUISVILLE STANDIFORD FIELD

Transportation

Car Rental Agencies: See toll-free numbers under Introduction.

Public Transportation: Buses (Transit Authority of River City), phone 585-1234.

Rail Passenger Service: Amtrak 800/872-7245.

Airport Information

Louisville Standiford Field: Information 367-4636; lost and found 368-6524; weather 363-9655.

Terminals: Concourse A: Delta, Northwest, TWA; Concourse B: American, Continental, Midwest Express, Southwest, United, USAir.

(Airlines and their terminal locations may change. Before leaving for the airport, you should phone the airline to confirm terminal location for your flight.)

What to See and Do

1. **Zachary Taylor National Cemetery.** 4701 Brownsboro Rd, 7 mi E on US 42. The 12th President of the US is buried here, near the site where he lived from infancy to adulthood. The Taylor family plot is surrounded by this national cemetery, established 1928. (Daily) Phone 893-3852.

2. **Cave Hill Cemetery.** 701 Baxter Ave, at E end of Broadway. Burial ground of George Rogers Clark. Colonel Harland Sanders, of fried-chicken fame, is also buried here. Rare trees, shrubs and plants; swans, geese, ducks. (Daily) Phone 451-5630.

3. **Jefferson County Courthouse** (1835–60). Jefferson St between 5th & 6th Sts. Designed by Gideon Shryock in Greek-revival style. Cast iron floor in rotunda supports statue of Henry Clay. Magnificent cast iron monumental stair and balustrade in 68-foot rotunda. Statues of Thomas Jefferson and Louis XVI, as well as war memorial on grounds. Guided tours (by appt). (Mon–Fri; closed major hols) Phone 625-5000 or -5761.   **Free.**

4. **Water Tower.** Zorn Ave and River Road. Restored tower and pumping station built in the classic style in 1860. Tower houses Louisville Visual Art Association, Center for Contemporary Art. Exhibits vary. (Daily; closed major hols) Phone 896-2146.   **Free.**

5. **Louisville Falls Fountain.** On the Ohio River, between Clark Memorial Bridge and Conrail Bridge. World's largest floating fountain sprays water 375 feet high. Light shows, with more than 100 colored lights, offered nightly. (May–Nov).

6. **Sightseeing.**

   Riverboat excursion. Riverfront Plaza, wharf, 4th St and River Rd. Two-hour afternoon trips on sternwheeler, *Belle of Louisville.* (Memorial Day–Labor Day, daily exc Mon); sunset cruise (Tues & Thurs); dance cruise (Sat). For rates and schedules phone 547-2355.

   Gray Line bus tours. For information and reservations contact YES Tours Reservations Office, 1601 S Preston St, 40217; 636-5664 or 637-6511.

7. **Industrial tours.**

   American Printing House for the Blind. 1839 Frankfort Ave, 3 mi E. The largest and oldest (1858) publishing house for the blind. In addition to books and music in Braille, it issues talking books, magazines, large type textbooks and educational aids. Tours (Mon–Fri; closed hols). Phone 895-2405.   **Free.**

Philip Morris USA. Broadway & 18th St. Cigarette manufacturers. Displays, audiovisuals; machines produce more than 300,000,000 cigarettes a day. One-hour guided tours, call for schedule. (Mon–Fri; closed most major hols; also wks of July 4, Dec 25) Phone 566-1293. **Free.**

Hillerich & Bradsby's Slugger Park. 4 mi N on I-65, at exit 4, 1525 Charlestown-New Albany Rd in Jeffersonville, IN. Manufacturers of Louisville Slugger baseball bats and Power-bilt golf clubs. Tours (Mon–Fri; closed hols; also last wk Dec & late June–mid-July). No cameras. Children over 8 only; must be accompanied by adult. Phone 585-5226, ext 227. **Free.**

MUSEUMS AND HISTORIC HOUSES

8. **Museum of History and Science.** 727 W Main St. Hands-on scientific exhibits; aerospace hall; IMAX four-story screen film theater (fee); Egyptian mummy's tomb. (Daily; closed Thanksgiving, Dec 24 & 25) Sr citizen rate. Phone 561-6111. ¢¢

9. **The Filson Club.** 1310 S Third St. Historical library (fee); manuscript collection, photographs and prints collection. (Daily exc Sun; closed major hols) Phone 635-5083. Mansion tour **free.**

10. **Farmington** (1810). 3033 Bardstown Rd N, at jct Watterson Expwy (I-264), 6 mi SE on US 31E. Federal-style house built from plans drawn by Thomas Jefferson. Abraham Lincoln visited here in 1841. Furnished with pre-1820 antiques; enclosed stairway, octagonal rooms; museum room; blacksmith shop, stone barn, 19th-century garden. Guided tour (daily; closed some hols) Grounds and gardens (daily; free). Phone 452-9920. ¢¢

11. **Locust Grove** (ca 1790). 6 mi NE on River Rd, then 1 mi SW at 561 Blankenbaker Lane. Home of General George Rogers Clark from 1809–18. Handsome Georgian mansion on 55 acres; original paneling, staircase; authentic furnishings; garden; 8 restored outbuildings. Visitors center features audiovisual program. (Daily; closed hols, Derby Day) Phone 897-9845 or 896-2433. ¢¢

12. **Thomas Edison House.** 731 E Washington. Restored 1850 cottage where Edison lived while working for Western Union after the Civil War. Bedroom furnished in the period; four display rooms with Edison memorabilia and inventions: phonographs, records and cylinders, early bulb collection. (Tues–Thurs & Sat; also by appt) Phone 585-5247. ¢

13. **Colonel Harland Sanders Museum.** 1441 Gardiner Lane. Artifacts and memorabilia relating to Colonel Harland Sanders and Kentucky Fried Chicken. Audiovisual displays, 28-minute film "Portrait of a Legend." (Mon–Thurs, limited hrs Fri; closed hols and 1st Fri in May) Phone 456-8353. **Free.**

14. **Historic districts.** Old Louisville, between Breckinridge and 9th Sts, near Central Park, features renovated Victorian housing; West Main Street Historic District is a concentration of cast iron buildings being renovated on Main Street between 1st and 8th streets; Butchertown is a renovated 19th-century German community between Market St & Story Avenue; Cherokee Triangle is a well-preserved Victorian neighborhood with diverse architectural details; and Portland is an early settlement and commercial port with Irish and French heritage.

EDUCATIONAL CENTERS

15. **University of Louisville** (1798). (23,000 students) 3 mi S at 3rd St & Eastern Pkwy. On Belknap Campus is the Ekstrom Library, with the John Patterson rare book collection, original town charter signed by Thomas Jefferson and the Photo Archives, one of the largest collections of photographs in the country. Also here is an enlarged cast of Rodin's sculpture *The Thinker;* a Foucault pendulum more than 73 feet high, demonstrating the Earth's rotation; and the largest concert organ in the Midwest. Two art galleries feature works by students and locals as well as national and international artists. (daily exc Sat). The grave of Supreme Court Justice Louis D. Brandeis is located under the School of Law portico. Contact information centers at 3rd St entrance or at corner 1st & Brandeis Sts; 588-6565. Also on campus are

J.B. Speed Art Museum. 2035 S 3rd St. Oldest & largest in state. Traditional and modern art, English Renaissance Room, sculpture collection, Kentucky artists; special exhibits. Cafe, shop and bookstore; tours on request. (Daily exc Mon; closed hols) Phone 636-2893. **Free.**

Rauch Memorial Planetarium. Planetarium shows (Sat afternoons) Phone 588-6665. ¢

16. **Bellarmine College** (1950). (2,300 students) Newburg Rd, 5 mi SE. A 115-acre campus. Liberal arts and sciences. The campus houses the Thomas Merton Studies Center, with his manuscripts, drawings, tapes and published works (Tues–Fri, by appt; closed hols); phone 452-8187. Guided campus tours (by appt). Phone 452-8000.

17. **Louisville Presbyterian Theological Seminary** (1853). (250 students) 1044 Alta Vista Rd, ½ mi off US 60 Business, adj to Cherokee Park. On 52-acre campus is Gardencourt, a renovated turn-of-the-century mansion, and the Archaeological Museum, with collection of Palestinian pottery (daily; closed hols). Phone 895-3411. **Free.**

18. **Spalding University** (1814). (1,400 students) 851 S 4th St. Liberal arts college. On campus is Whitestone Mansion (1871), a Renaissance-revival house with period furniture (Mon–Fri; closed hols), art gallery. Phone 585-9911. **Free.**

PARKS AND RECREATIONAL FACILITIES

19. **Churchill Downs.** 700 Central Ave. Founded in 1875, this historic and world-famous Thoroughbred race track is the home of the Kentucky Derby, "the greatest two minutes in sports." (See ANNUAL EVENTS) Spring race meet, late Apr–early July; fall race meet, late Oct–late Nov; Kentucky Derby, 1st Sat May. Phone 636-4400. ¢–¢¢ Adj is

Kentucky Derby Museum. Features exhibits on Thoroughbred racing and the Kentucky Derby. Multi-image show, hands-on exhibits, artifacts, educational programs, tours and special events. Outdoor paddock area with Thoroughbred. Tours of Churchill downs (weather permitting). Gift shop; cafe serving lunch (wkdays). (Daily; closed Thanksgiving, Oaks & Derby Days, Dec 25) Phone 637-1111 or -7097. ¢¢

20. **Kentucky Center for the Arts.** 5 Riverfront Plaza. Three stages present national and international performers showcasing a wide range of music, dance and drama. Distinctive glass-arched lobby features a collection of 20th-century sculpture and provides a panoramic view of Ohio River and Falls Fountain. Restaurant, gift shop, parking garage. For schedule and ticket information phone 584-7777 or 800/775-7777.

21. **Kentucky Fair and Exposition Center.** I-65S at I-264W. More than 400-acre complex includes coliseum, exposition halls, stadium, amusement park. More than 1,500 events take place throughout the year, including Univ of Louisville football, basketball, Louisville Icehawks and St Louis Cardinals minor league affiliate, the Louisville Redbirds. (See ANNUAL EVENTS) Phone 367-5180.

22. **Otter Creek Park.** 30 mi SW via US 31W and KY 1638, near Fort Knox. A 3,000-acre park located on the site of Rock Haven, a town destroyed by 1937 flood. Much of the park that fronts on the Ohio River consists of steep cliffs or very wooded banks. Otter Creek is a small, deeply entrenched stream with steep banks. Artifacts found here indicate that many Indian tribes used the Otter Creek area as hunting and fishing grounds. Swimming pools; fishing; boating (ramp). Miniature golf, tennis, basketball. Picnic facilities. Tent & trailer sites, cabins, lodge and restaurant. Nature center (Mar–Nov; daily exc Mon), wildlife area. Park (daily). For fees, information contact Park Manager, 850 Otter Creek Park Rd, Vine Grove 40175; 583-3577. **Free.**

23. **Louisville Zoo.** 1100 Trevilian Way, 7 mi SE via I-65, I-264 to Poplar Level Road North. Modern zoo exhibits more than 1,600 animals in naturalistic settings. In HerpAquarium are simulated water, desert and rain forest ecosystems. Camel and elephant rides (summer). (Daily; closed Jan 1, Thanksgiving, Dec 25) Sr citizen rate. Phone 459-2181. ¢¢¢

24. E.P. "Tom" Sawyer State Park. 3000 Freys Hill Rd. Approximately 370 acres with swimming pool. Tennis; archery range; BMX track; ballfields; gymnasium, games area. Picnicking. Some fees. Phone 426-8950.

Annual Events

Kentucky Derby Festival. Two-week celebration with Pegasus Parade, Great Steamboat Race (between *Belle of Louisville* and *Delta Queen*), Great Balloon Race, mini-marathon, concerts, sports tournaments, annual running of Kentucky Derby on first Sat of May at Churchill Downs (see #19). For information on tickets for festival events contact Kentucky Derby Festival, 137 W Muhammad Ali Blvd, 40202; phone 584-6383 or 800/928-FEST.

Kentucky State Fair. Kentucky Fair & Exposition Center (see #21). Livestock shows; championship horse show; home & fine arts exhibits; midway, entertainment. Contact VP of Expositions, PO Box 37130, 40233; 367-5180. Aug 18–28.

Corn Island Storytelling Festival. Recaptures bygone days of yarnspinning. Events held at various sites in city. Programs include ghost stories at night in Long Run Park. For information contact Festival Director, 12019 Donohue Ave, 40243; 245-0643. Sept 15–17.

Seasonal Events

Performing arts. Louisville Orchestra (587-8681), Kentucky Opera (584-4500), Broadway Series (584-7469), Louisville Ballet (456-4520); all at Kentucky Center for the Arts; 584-7777 (see #20). Actors Theatre, 316 W Main St, phone 584-1265. Kentucky Shakespeare Festival, free plays in Central Park, daily exc Sun, mid-June–early Aug; phone 634-8237.

Horse racing. Churchill Downs (see #19).

Additional Visitor Information

The Louisville Convention & Visitors Bureau, 400 S First St, 40202, phone 582-3732, provides literature and information. Also available is information about several unique areas of special interest, such as Old Louisville, Butchertown, Phoenix Hill, Cherokee Triangle and the Main Street Preservation District.

The Convention & Visitors Bureau also operates two visitor information centers. The Airport Information Center is located in the central lobby of Standiford Field Airport. The Galleria Information Center is located in the Galleria Shopping Mall, Fourth St & Muhammad Ali Blvd. Phone 800/626-5646 (exc KY) or 800/633-3384 (KY).

For information on parks and courses in the area, phone the Metropolitan Park and Recreation Board, 459-0440.

(See Fort Knox, Shepherdsville)

City Neighborhoods

Many of the restaurants, unrated dining establishments and some lodgings listed under Louisville include neighborhoods as well as exact street addresses. Geographic descriptions of these areas are given, followed by a table of restaurants arranged by neighborhood.

Downtown: South of the Ohio River, west of Shelby St, north of Oak St and east of 9th St. **South of Downtown:** South of Oak St. **East of Downtown:** East of Shelby St.

Old Louisville: South of Breckenridge St, west of I-65, north of Eastern Pkwy and east of 9th St.

LOUISVILLE RESTAURANTS BY NEIGHBORHOOD AREAS

(For full description, see alphabetical listings under Restaurants)

DOWNTOWN

Colonnade Cafeteria. 4th St & Muhammad Ali Blvd

The English Grill (The Brown Hotel). 335 W Broadway

Hasenour's. 1028 Barret Ave

Kunz's. 115 4th Ave

Old Spaghetti Factory. 235 W Market St

Timothy's. 826 E Broadway

Vincenzo's. 150 S 5th St

SOUTH OF DOWNTOWN

Fifth Quarter. 1241 Durrett Lane

Masterson's. 1830 S 3rd St

Uptown Cafe. 1624 Bardstown Rd.

EAST OF DOWNTOWN

Blue Boar Cafeteria. 232 Oxmoor Shopping Center

Cafe Metro. 1700 Bardstown Rd

Darryl's 1815 Restaurant. 3110 Bardstown Rd

Ferd Grisanti's. 10212 Taylorsville Rd

Le Relais. Taylorsville Rd

Mamma Grisanti. 3938 DuPont Circle

New Orleans House East. 9424 Shelbyville Rd

Sichuan Garden. 9850 Linn Station Rd

Note: When a listing is located in a town that does not have its own city heading, it will appear under the city nearest to its location. In these cases, the address and town appear in parenthesis immediately following the name of the establishment.

Motels

(Rates are generally much higher during Kentucky Derby; may be 3-day min)

★★★COURTYARD BY MARRIOTT. *9608 Blairwood Rd (40222), I-64 Hurstbourne Lane exit 15, east of downtown.* 502/429-0006; FAX 502/429-5926. 151 rms, 4 story. S $79; D $89; suites $93–$99; under 18 free; wkend rates. Crib free. TV; cable. Pool. Complimentary coffee in rms. Restaurant 6:30 am–2 pm. Bar 4–11 pm. Ck-out 1 pm. Coin lndry. Meeting rms. Valet serv. Exercise equipt; weights, bicycles, whirlpool. Refrigerators avail. Minibar in suites. Cr cds: A, C, D, DS, MC, V.

🅳 ⛱ 🕴 🚫 ⓞ SC

✔★★FAIRFIELD INN BY MARRIOTT. *9400 Blairwood Rd (40222), I-64 exit 15, east of downtown.* 502/339-1900. 105 rms, 3 story. S $38.95–$47.95; D $45.95–$54.95; each addl $7; under 18 free. Crib free. TV; cable. Pool. Continental bkfst avail. Complimentary coffee in lobby. Restaurant adj 6 am–11 pm. Ck-out noon. Meeting rms. Valet serv. Cr cds: A, C, D, DS, MC, V.

🅳 ⛱ 🚫 ⓞ SC

✔★★HAMPTON INN. *1902 Embassy Square Blvd (40299), I-64 Hurstbourne Lane exit 15, east of downtown.* FAX 502/491-1325. 119 rms, 2 story. S $42–$48; D $49–$55; under 18 free. Crib free. TV; cable. Pool. Continental bkfst. Restaurant nearby. Ck-out noon. Meeting rm. Cr cds: A, C, D, DS, MC, V.

🅳 ⛱ 🚫 ⓞ SC

★RED ROOF INN. *9330 Blairwood Rd (40222), 1 blk N of I-64 exit 15, east of downtown.* 502/426-7621; FAX 502/426-7933. 108 rms, 2 story. S $28.99; D $33.99; 3 or more, $41.99; under 18 free. Crib free. Pet accepted. TV; cable. Complimentary coffee. Restaurant adj 6 am–11 pm. Ck-out noon. Cr cds: A, C, D, DS, MC, V.

[D] [P] [≈] [⊙] [◎]

★ ★ **RESIDENCE INN BY MARRIOTT.** *120 N Hurstbourne Pkwy (40222), east of downtown. 502/425-1821; FAX 502/425-1821, ext 401.* 96 kit. suites, 2 story. 1-bedrm $85–$110; 2-bedrm $105–$130; family rates; some wkend rates. Crib free. Pet accepted; $10 per day. TV; cable. Heated pool; whirlpool, lifeguard. Complimentary continental bkfst. Ck-out noon. Coin lndry. Valet serv. Sport court. Health club privileges. Refrigerators, fireplaces. Grills. Cr cds: A, C, D, DS, MC, V.

[D] [P] [≈] [⊙] [◎] [SC]

✔ ★ ★ **SIGNATURE INN.** *6515 Signature Dr (40213), I-65 exit 128, south of downtown. 502/968-4100; FAX 502/968-4100.* 123 rms, 2 story. S $51–$53; D $58–$60; under 18 free; wkend rates Dec–Feb. Crib free. TV; cable, in-rm movies avail. Pool. Complimentary continental bkfst, coffee. Restaurant adj 6 am–11 pm. Ck-out noon. Meeting rms. Valet serv. Sundries. Free airport transportation. Health club privileges. Cr cds: A, C, D, DS, MC, V.

[D] [≈] [⊙] [◎] [SC]

★ ★ **STUDIO PLUS.** *9801 Bunsen Pkwy (40299), I-64 exit 15, east of downtown. 502/499-6215; FAX 502/495-3551.* 76 kit. suites, 2–3 story. No elvtr. S, D $49–$59; wkly rates. TV. Pool. Restaurant nearby. Ck-out noon. Coin lndry. Exercise equipt; weights, bicycles, sauna. Cr cds: A, C, D, MC, V.

[D] [≈] [☂] [◎] [SC]

★ **SUPER 8.** *4800 Preston Hwy (40213), off I-65 exit 130, south of downtown. 502/968-0088; FAX 968-0088, ext 347.* 100 rms, 3 story. S $37.88; D $47.88; each addl $5; under 12 free. Crib free. TV; cable. Complimentary coffee in lobby. Restaurant opp open 24 hrs. Ck-out 11 am. Airport transportation. Cr cds: A, C, D, DS, MC, V.

[D] [⊙] [◎] [SC]

Motor Hotels

✔ ★ ★ **BRECKINRIDGE INN.** *2800 Breckinridge Lane (40220), I-264 exit 18, south of downtown. 502/456-5050; FAX 502/451-1577.* 123 rms, 2 story. S $52; D $65; each addl $7; suites $65–$95; under 12 free. Crib $7. Pet accepted; $10. TV; cable. 2 pools, 1 indoor; lifeguard. Restaurant 7 am–1:30 pm, 5–10 pm. Rm serv. Bar. Ck-out noon. Meeting rms. Valet serv. Sundries. Gift shop. Barber shop. Free airport transportation. Lighted tennis. Exercise equipt; weights, bicycle, sauna. Cr cds: A, C, D, DS, MC, V.

[P] [P] [≈] [☂] [⊙] [◎] [SC]

★ ★ **EXECUTIVE INN.** *978 Phillips Lane (40213), Watterson Expressway at Fairgrounds, near Standiford Field Airport, south of downtown. 502/367-6161; 800/626-2706 (exc KY), 800/222-8284 (KY); FAX 502/363-1880.* 465 rms, 2–6 story. S $66; D $76; each addl $10; suites $150–$224; under 18 free. Crib free. TV; cable. 2 pools, 1 indoor; wading pool, poolside serv, lifeguard. Restaurants 6:30 am–11:45 pm. Rm serv. Bar 11–1 am, closed Sun. Ck-out 1 pm. Convention facilities. Bellhops. Sundries. Gift shop. Barber, beauty shop. Free airport transportation. Exercise rm; instructor, weights, bicycles, sauna. Lawn games. Some refrigerators. Some private patios, balconies. Tudor-inspired architecture. Cr cds: A, C, D, DS, MC, V.

[D] [≈] [☂] [✕] [⊙] [◎] [SC]

★ ★ **HOLIDAY INN.** *1325 Hurstbourne Lane (40222), at I-64 exit 15, east of downtown. 502/426-2600; FAX 502/423-1605.* 267 rms, 7 story. S, D $76–$99; each addl $10; suites $89–$275; under 16 free. Crib free. TV; cable. Indoor pool; lifeguard. Coffee in rms. Restaurant 6 am–2 pm, 5–10 pm. Rm serv. Bar 4 pm–1 am. Ck-out noon. Meeting rms. Bellhops. Valet serv. Gift shop. Airport transportation. Exercise equipt; weight machines, bicycles, whirlpool, sauna. Game rm. Refrigerator in suites. Cr cds: A, C, D, DS, ER, MC, V, JCB.

[D] [≈] [☂] [⊙] [◎] [SC]

★ ★ **HURSTBOURNE.** *9700 Bluegrass Pkwy (40299), I-64 exit 15, east of downtown. 502/491-4830; res: 800/289-1009; FAX 502/491-2893.* 400 rms, 2–4 story. S $65–$94; D $75–$104; each addl $10; suites $95–$305; under 18 free. Crib free. Pet accepted. TV; cable. 2 indoor pools; poolside serv, lifeguard. Restaurant 6:30 am–10 pm. Rm serv. Bar 11:30–2 am; dancing, entertainment. Ck-out noon. Convention facilities. Bellhops. Valet serv. Gift shop. Barber, beauty shop. Free airport transportation. Exercise equipt; weights, bicycles, whirlpool, sauna. Health club privileges. Game rm. Refrigerator in suites. Cr cds: A, C, D, DS, MC, V.

[D] [P] [≈] [☂] [⊙] [◎] [SC]

★ **QUALITY HOTEL.** *100 E Jefferson St (40202), downtown. 502/582-2481; FAX 502/582-3511.* 104 rms, 6 story. S $52–$63; D $57–$70; each addl $5; suites $120; under 18 free; some wkend rates. Crib free. Pet accepted; $10. TV; cable. Restaurant 6:30 am–2 pm, 5–10 pm. Rm serv 7 am–10 pm. Bar noon–midnight. Ck-out noon. Meeting rms. Bellhops. Valet serv. Free airport transportation. Exercise equipt; weights, bicycles. Refrigerators avail. Sun deck. Cr cds: A, C, D, DS, ER, MC, V, JCB.

[D] [P] [☂] [⊙] [◎] [SC]

✔ ★ **WILSON INN.** *9802 Bunsen Pkwy (40299), I-64 exit 15, east of downtown. 502/499-0000; res: 800/945-7667; FAX 502/499-0000.* 108 rms, 5 story, 32 suites, 50 kit. units. S, D $34.95–$39.95; each addl $5; suites $44.95–$54.95; kit. units $39.95–$45.95; under 18 free. Crib free. Pet accepted, some restrictions. TV; cable. Complimentary continental bkfst 6–10 am, coffee. Restaurant nearby. Ck-out noon. Meeting rms. Valet serv. Sundries. Free airport transportation. Refrigerators. Cr cds: A, C, D, DS, MC, V.

[D] [P] [⊙] [◎] [SC]

Hotels

★ ★ ★ ★ **THE BROWN, A CAMBERLEY HOTEL.** *335 W Broadway (40202), downtown. 502/583-1234; res: 800/866-7666; FAX 502/587-7006.* 294 rms, 16 story. S $125–$145; D $140–$160; each addl $15; suites from $300; family rates; wkend package plans. Crib free. Covered parking $7/night. TV; cable. Restaurants 6:30 am–11 pm (also see THE ENGLISH GRILL). Bar 11–1 am. Ck-out 11 am. Convention facilities. Shopping arcade. Barber, beauty shop. Airport transportation. Exercise equipt; weights, bicycles. Refrigerator in suites. Elegantly restored 1923 hotel; Old English-style furnishings, artwork. *LUXURY LEVEL.* 29 rms, 1 suite. S $150–$180; D $165–$175; suite from $350. Complimentary bkfst, refreshments, newspaper.
Cr cds: A, C, D, DS, ER, MC, V, JCB.

[D] [☂] [⊙] [◎] [SC]

★ ★ ★ **GALT HOUSE.** *140 4th St, at River Rd (40202), downtown. 502/589-5200; res: 800/626-1814; FAX 502/585-4266.* 656 rms, 25 story. S $85–$95; D $95–$120; each addl $12; suites $250; under 16 free; wkend rates. Crib free. TV; cable. Pool; poolside serv, lifeguard. Restaurants 6 am–midnight; dining rm 5:30–10:30 pm. Bar 11:30–1 am; entertainment. Ck-out noon. Convention facilities. Shopping arcade. Garage parking. Refrigerator in suites. Overlooks Ohio River. Cr cds: A, C, D, DS, MC, V.

[D] [≈] [◎] [SC]

★ ★ ★ **GALT HOUSE EAST.** *141 N 4th St (40202), downtown. 502/589-3300; res: 800/843-4258; FAX 502/585-4266.* 600 rms, 18 story. S $110–$125; D $125–$135; each addl $12; 2-bedrm suites $475; under 16 free. Crib free. TV; cable. Pool privileges adj. Restaurant adj 6–1 am. Bar from 11 am. Ck-out noon. Garage parking. Refrigerators, wet bars. Private patios, balconies. Overlooks Ohio River. 18-story atrium. Cr cds: A, C, D, DS, MC, V.

[D] [◎] [SC]

★ ★ **HOLIDAY INN-DOWNTOWN.** *120 W Broadway (40202), downtown. 502/582-2241; FAX 502/584-8591.* 290 rms, 12 story. S $73–$77; D $78–$82; each addl $10; suites $275; under 19 free. Crib free. Pet accepted. TV; cable. Indoor pool; lifeguard. Coffee in rms. Restaurant 6 am–11 pm. Bar 11–2 am. Ck-out noon. Convention facili-

ties. Gift shop. Barber. Free airport transportation. Health club privileges. Some refrigerators, minibars. Some balconies. *LUXURY LEVEL:* **EXECUTIVE LEVEL.** 29 rms. S $88; D $98. In-rm movies. Concierge. Private lounge, honor bar. Complimentary continental bkfst, refreshments, newpapers.
Cr cds: A, C, D, DS, MC, V, JCB.

★ ★ ★ **HYATT REGENCY.** *320 W Jefferson St (40202), downtown.* 502/587-3434; FAX 502/581-0133. 388 rms, 18 story. S, D $75–$165; each addl $20; suites $225–$500; under 18 free. Crib free. TV; cable, in-rm movies avail. Indoor pool; whirlpool. Coffee in suites. Restaurants 6:30 am–midnight. Bars 11–2 am, Sun to midnight. Ck-out noon. Convention facilities. Concierge. Gift shop. Tennis. Health club privileges. Access to shopping center via enclosed walkway. Modern design. *LUXURY LEVEL:* **REGENCY CLUB LEVEL.** 24 rms, 1 suite. S $105–$145; D $105–$165; suite $500. Wet bar in suite. Complimentary continental bkfst, refreshments.
Cr cds: A, C, D, DS, MC, V, JCB.

★ ★ **RADISSON.** *1903 Embassy Square Blvd (40299), E of I-264 at jct I-64, Hurstbourne Lane (exit 15), east of downtown.* 502/499-6220; FAX 502/499-2480. 255 rms, 10 story. S $75–$95; D $85–$105; each addl $10; suites $250–$420; under 18 free. Crib free. Pet accepted, some restrictions; $25. TV; cable. Indoor pool; poolside serv, lifeguard. Restaurant 6:30 am–2 pm, 5–10 pm; Fri, Sat to 11 pm. Bar 2 pm–2 am; entertainment, dancing. Ck-out noon. Convention facilities. Gift shop. Airport transportation. Exercise equipt; weights, bicycles, whirlpool. Health club privileges. Game rm. Balconies. Cr cds: A, C, D, DS, ER, MC, V, JCB.

★ ★ ★ **SEELBACH.** *500 Fourth Ave (40202), downtown.* 502/585-3200; res: 800/333-3399; FAX 502/587-6564. 321 rms, 11 story. S $125–$150; D $144–$160; each addl $10; suites $210–$495; under 18 free; wkend package plans. Crib free. Pet accepted. Parking $7, valet $9.50. TV; cable. Pool privileges. Restaurants 6:30 am–midnight. Bar 4 pm–2 am; entertainment, dancing exc Sun. Ck-out 1 pm. Convention facilities. Concierge. Shopping arcade. Free airport, bus depot transportation. Health club privileges. Restored hotel, originally opened in 1905. Lobby has 8 murals by Arthur Thomas depicting Kentucky pioneers and Indians; rms have 4-poster beds, armoires and marble baths. *LUXURY LEVEL:* **CONCIERGE CLUB.** 39 rms. S $139–$165; D $159–$200. Concierge. Private lounge, honor bar. Complimentary continental bkfst, refreshments, newspaper.
Cr cds: A, C, D, DS, MC, V.

Inn

✔ ★ **OLD LOUISVILLE.** *1359 S 3rd St (40208), in Old Louisville.* 502/635-1574; FAX 502/637-5892. 11 rms, 8 with bath, 3 story. No rm phones. D $55–$85; suites $100–$200; under 12 free. Crib free. TV in sitting rm. Complimentary full bkfst. Restaurant nearby. Ck-out noon, ck-in 3 pm. Individually decorated rms in Victorian house (1901). Ceiling murals. Cr cds: MC, V.

Restaurants

★ ★ **CAFE METRO.** *1700 Bardstown Rd, east of downtown.* 502/458-4830. Hrs: 6–10 pm; Fri, Sat to 11 pm. Closed Sun; hols. Res accepted. Continental menu. Bar. A la carte entrees: dinner $14.75. Specialties: stuffed quail, swordfish, veal. Parking. Collection of pre-WW I German posters. Cr cds: A, MC, V.

✔ ★ ★ **DARRYL'S 1815 RESTAURANT.** *3110 Bardstown Rd, at I-264 exit 16, east of downtown.* 502/458-1815. Hrs: 11 am–11 pm; Fri, Sat to 12:30 am. Bar. Semi-a la carte: lunch $4.99–$9.99, dinner

$4.99–$15.99. Child's meals. Specializes in steak, chicken, ribs. Parking. Cr cds: A, C, D, DS, MC, V.

★ ★ ★ **THE ENGLISH GRILL.** *(See The Brown Hotel)* 502/583-1234. Hrs: 5–11 pm; Sun to 10 pm. Res accepted. Bar. Semi-a la carte: dinner $15.25–$24.95. Specializes in fresh seafood, rack of lamb, pasta, steak. Seasonal menus feature regional foods. English motif; leaded and stained-glass windows, artwork featuring English scenes and Thoroughbred horses. Jacket. Cr cds: A, C, D, DS, ER, MC, V, JCB.

✔ ★ ★ ★ **FERD GRISANTI'S.** *10212 Taylorsville Rd, east of downtown.* 502/267-0050. Hrs: 5–10 pm; Fri, Sat to 11 pm. Closed Sun. Northern Italian menu. Res accepted. Bar. Wine list. Semi-a la carte: dinner $7.25–$16.50. Child's meals. Specializes in veal, pasta. Own baking. Parking. Contemporary Italian decor; artwork. In historic Jeffersontown. Cr cds: A, C, D, MC, V.

✔ ★ ★ **FIFTH QUARTER.** *1241 Durrett Lane, south of downtown.* 502/361-2363. Hrs: 11 am–2:30 pm, 5–10:30 pm; Fri to 11:30 pm; Sat from 4 pm; Sun from 11 am. Closed Dec 25. Bar. Semi-a la carte: lunch $4.59–$7.49, dinner $6.99–$16.99. Specializes in prime rib. Salad bar. Guitarist exc Sun. Parking. Rustic decor. Cr cds: A, DS, MC, V.

★ ★ ★ **HASENOUR'S.** *1028 Barret Ave, downtown.* 502/451-5210. Hrs: 11 am–midnight; Sun 5–11 pm. Closed some major hols. Res accepted. Bar. Semi-a la carte: lunch $4.25–$12.95, dinner $7.95–$24.95, after 10 pm menu $2.75–$8.25. Specializes in sauerbraten, fresh seafood, prime rib. Pianist Wed–Sat. Parking. Family-owned. Varied dining areas. Cr cds: A, C, D, MC, V.

★ ★ ★ **KUNZ'S.** *115 4th Ave, at Market St, downtown.* 502/585-5555. Hrs: 11 am–10:30 pm; Fri & Sat to 11:30 pm; Sun 4–10 pm. Closed Dec 25. Res accepted. Continental menu. Bar. Semi-a la carte: lunch $5.25–$6.95, dinner $10.95–$24.95. Child's meals. Specializes in seafood, steak. Raw bar. Salad bar (lunch). Own breads. Family-owned. Jacket (in formal dining rm). Cr cds: A, C, D, DS, MC, V.

★ ★ **LE RELAIS.** *Taylorsville Rd, near Bownman Field, I-264 exit Taylorsville Rd, east of downtown.* 502/451-9020. Hrs: 11:30 am–2:30 pm, 5:30–10 pm; Fri, Sat 5:30–11 pm; Sun 5:30–9 pm. Closed Mon; Thanksgiving, Dec 25. Res accepted. French menu. Bar. Semi-a la carte: lunch $3.75–$7.50, dinner $10–$19.95. Specializes in fish, tournedos. Parking. Outdoor dining. Jacket (dinner). View of landing strip. Cr cds: A, D, MC, V.

✔ ★ ★ **MAMMA GRISANTI.** *3938 DuPont Circle, east of downtown.* 502/893-0141. Hrs: 11:30 am–2 pm, 5–10 pm; Fri, Sat to 11 pm; Sun to 9 pm. Closed Dec 25. Res accepted. Italian menu. Bar. Semi-a la carte: lunch $3.50–$5.95, dinner $5.49–$12.99. Buffet: lunch $4.75. Child's meals. Specialties: lasagne, fettucini Alfredo, veal scaloppini. Own pasta. Parking. Family-owned. Cr cds: A, MC, V.

★ ★ **MASTERSON'S.** *1830 S 3rd St, south of downtown.* 502/636-2511. Hrs: 8 am–11 pm; Fri, Sat to midnight; Sun brunch 11:30 am–3 pm. Closed July 4, Dec 24 & 25. Res accepted. Greek, Amer menu. Bar from 11 am. Semi-a la carte: bkfst $1.95–$4.95, lunch $3.25–$9.75, dinner $9.25–$19.75. Buffet: bkfst $5.29, lunch $5.25. Sun brunch $7.95. Child's meals. Specialties: souvlakia, chicken stir fry. Parking. Outdoor dining. Near Univ of Louisville. Family-owned. Cr cds: A, C, D, DS, MC, V.

★ ★ **NEW ORLEANS HOUSE EAST.** *9424 Shelbyville Rd, east of downtown.* 502/426-1577. Hrs: 6–9 pm; Fri, Sat 5–10 pm. Closed Sun; Thanksgiving, Dec 25. Res accepted. Seafood menu. Bar. Buffet: dinner $25.95. Child's meals. Specialties: frogs' legs, oysters Rockefeller,

Alaskan crab legs. Salad bar. Parking. 4 dining rms. Cr cds: A, C, D, MC, V.

✔ ★OLD SPAGHETTI FACTORY. *235 W Market St, downtown. 502/581-1070.* Hrs: 11:30 am–2 pm, 5–10 pm; Fri to 11 pm; Sat 5–11 pm; Sun 4–10 pm. Closed Thanksgiving, Dec 24–25. Italian menu. Bar. Semi-a la carte: lunch $2.95–$5.25. Complete meals: dinner $4.25–$8.95. Child's meals. Specializes in spaghetti. Cr cds: DS, MC, V.

✔ ★ ★SICHUAN GARDEN. *9850 Linn Station Rd, in Plainview Shopping Center, east of downtown. 502/426-6767.* Hrs: 11;30 am–2:30 pm, 5–10 pm; Fri to 11 pm; Sat 5–11 pm; Sun brunch 11:30 am–2:30 pm. Closed Thanksgiving, Dec 25. Res accepted. Chinese, Thai menu. Bar. Semi-a la carte: lunch $3.75–$5.95, dinner $5.50–$12.95. Sun brunch $6.95. Specializes in Sichuan orange beef, mandarin seafood-in-a-net, salmon steak. Pianist Wed–Sat evenings. Frosted-glass rm dividers. Cr cds: A, MC, V.

★ ★TIMOTHY'S. *826 E Broadway, downtown. 502/561-0880.* Hrs: 11 am–2 pm, 5:30–11 pm; Fri to midnight; Sat 5:30 pm–midnight. Closed Sun, Mon; Easter, Thanksgiving, Dec 25. Res accepted. Italian, Amer menu. Bar. Semi-a la carte: lunch $5.95–$8.95, dinner $9.95–$20.95. Specializes in pasta, fresh seafood, white chili. Parking. Outdoor dining. Contemporary decor; vintage bar. Cr cds: A, D, DS, MC, V.

★ ★UPTOWN CAFE. *1624 Bardstown Rd, south of downtown. 502/458-4212.* Hrs: 11:30 am–11 pm; Fri & Sat to midnight. Closed Sun; most major hols. Continental menu. Bar. Semi-a la carte: lunch $4–$8, dinner $5.95–$17.50. Specialities: duck ravioli, salmon croquettes, veal pockets. Parking. Converted store front. Cr cds: A, MC, V.

★ ★VINCENZO'S. *150 S 5th St, in the Humana Building, downtown. 502/580-1350.* Hrs: 11:30 am–2:30 pm, 5:30–11 pm; Fri, Sat 5:30 pm–midnight. Closed Sun; major hols. Res accepted. Continental menu. Wine list. A la carte entrees: lunch $4.95–$8.95, dinner $13.95–$22.95. Specialties: crêpes Agostino, veal Gabriele. Own baking. Pianist Fri, Sat. Valet parking. Former Federal Reserve Bank building; original artwork. Jacket. Cr cds: A, C, D, DS, MC, V.

Unrated Dining Spots

BLUE BOAR CAFETERIA. *232 Oxmoor Shopping Center, ½ mi E of I-264 Middletown exit, east of downtown. 502/426-3310.* Hrs: 11 am–8 pm; Fri to 8:30 pm; Sat 11 am–8:30 pm; Sun 11 am–7 pm. Closed Dec 25. Avg ck: lunch $4.40, dinner $5.25. Child's meals. Specializes in roast beef, fried chicken, pecan pie. Family-owned. Cr cds: MC, V.

SC

COLONNADE CAFETERIA. *4th St & Muhammad Ali Blvd, Starks Bldg, lower level, downtown. 502/584-6846.* Hrs: 7–9:30 am; continental bkfst to 10:30 am; 11 am–2 pm. Closed Sat, Sun; major hols. Avg ck: bkfst $3.50, lunch $5–$6. Large variety. No cr cds accepted.

Madisonville (C-4)

Founded: 1807 **Pop:** 16,200 **Elev:** 470 ft **Area code:** 502 **Zip:** 42431

In a region of hills, rivers and creek bottoms, and in the center of a coal-mining area, Madisonville is a growing industrial center and a marketplace for loose-leaf tobacco. Between the Tradewater and the Pond rivers, the town is named for President James Madison.

What to See and Do

1. **Historical Library and Museum.** 107 Union St. More than 4,000 items are on display, including Civil War material, old maps and photos and a 150-gallon whiskey still confiscated in Hopkins County. Adjacent is a restored log cabin, birthplace of Ruby Laffoon, Governor of Kentucky (1931–35); period furnishings (fee). Special events. (Mon–Fri) Phone 821-3986. ¢

2. **Pennyrile Forest State Resort Park.** 10 mi S on US 41, then 14 mi W on Western Kentucky Pkwy, then 7 mi S on KY 109. An 863-acre park surrounding a 55-acre lake. Swimming beach, pool, bathhouse (seasonal); fishing; boating (no motors), rentals. Hiking, riding; 9-hole & miniature golf (seasonal, rentals), tennis, shuffleboard. Picnicking, playground, grocery, cottages & lodge (see RESORT). Tent & trailer sites (Apr–Oct, standard fees), cottages (Mar–Dec). Supervised recreation. For fees and information phone 797-3421 or 800/325-1711.

(For further information contact the Madisonville-Hopkins County Chamber of Commerce, 140 S Main St; 821-3435.)

Annual Event

Hopkins County Fair. Last wk July–first wk Aug.

Motels

✔ ★ ★BEST WESTERN PENNYRILE INN. *(Box 612, Mortons Gap 42440)* 6 mi S on Pennyrile Pkwy, exit 37. *502/258-5201; FAX 502/258-5201, ext 140.* 60 rms, 2 story. S $30.95; D $34.95–$36.95; each addl $2; under 12 free. Crib free. TV; cable. Pool. Restaurant open 24 hrs. Ck-out noon. Meeting rm. Refrigerators avail. Cr cds: A, D, DS, MC, V.

★DAYS INN. *1900 Lantaff Blvd, US 41 Bypass exit 44. 502/821-8620; FAX 502/825-9282.* 141 rms, 2 story. S $39–$59; D $44–$69; each addl $5; suites $65–$100. Crib free. Pet accepted. TV; cable. Indoor pool; sauna. Restaurant 6 am–2 pm, 5–9 pm. Rm serv 7 am–9 pm. Ck-out noon. Meeting rms. Sundries. Local airport transportation. Health club privileges. Cr cds: A, C, D, DS, MC, V.

Resort

★ ★PENNYRILE LODGE. *(20781 Pennyrile Lodge Rd, Dawson Springs 42408)* 9 mi S of Dawson Springs on County Rd 398 in Pennyrile State Forest, 2 mi S of KY 109. *502/797-3421; res: 800/325-1711 (exc KY).* 24 lodge rms, 1–2 story, 13 kit. cottages. Memorial Day–Labor Day: S $45; D $55; each addl $5; kit. cottages $65–$83; under 17 free; lower rates rest of yr. Crib free. TV. Pool; wading pool, lifeguard. Dining rm 7–10:30 am, 11:30 am–2:30 pm, 5–9 pm. Ck-out noon, cottages 11 am, ck-in 4 pm. Meeting rms. Tennis. 9-hole golf, greens fee $10. Miniature golf. Lawn games. Rec rm. Picnic table, grills. Private patios, balconies. State-owned property; all state park facilities avail. Cr cds: A, C, D, DS, MC, V.

Mammoth Cave National Park (C-5)

(On KY 70, 10 mi W of Cave City or 8 mi NW of Park City on KY 255)

This enormous underground complex of intertwining passages, totaling more than 330 miles in length, was carved by mildly acidic water trickling for thousands of years through limestone. Species of colorless, eyeless fish, crayfish and other creatures make their home within. Visible are the remains of a crude system used to mine 400,000 pounds of nitrate to make gunpowder for use in the War of 1812. The cave was the scene of an experiment aimed at the cure of tuberculosis. Mushroom growing was also attempted within the cave.

Above ground the park consists of 52,428 acres with sinkholes, rivers, 70 miles of hiking trails. Picnicking; lodging (see MOTEL). Camping (daily; some fees). An orientation movie is offered at the visitor center (daily exc Dec 25), phone 758-2328. Evening programs are conducted by park interpreters (summer, daily; spring & fall, wkends).

Ranger-led trips of Mammoth Cave vary greatly in distance and length. Trails are solid, fairly smooth and require stooping or bending in places. Most tours involve extensive walking; many are considered strenuous; proper footwear is recommended (no sandals); a sweater or wrap is also advised, even though it may be a hot August day above ground. Tours are conducted by experienced National Park Service interpreters. Contact Superintendent, Mammoth Cave 42259.

What to See and Do

1. **Cave tours** depart from the visitor center (schedules vary with season; no tours Dec 25), phone 502/758-2328. Advance reservations are recommended. Tickets may be purchased in advance through Mistix outlets; phone 800/967-2283. (The following is a partial list of available cave tours.)

   Frozen Niagara. This moderately strenuous tour (2 hrs) explores huges pits and domes and decorative dripstone formations. ¢¢

   Historic. A two-mile guided tour highlighting the cave's rich human history; artifacts of Native Americans, early explorers; ruins of mining operations. ¢¢

   Half-Day. This four-mile tour (4.5 hrs) includes a variety of cave passages, including tubes and canyons. Considered a strenuous tour. Lunch available in Snowball Dining Room, 267 feet underground. ¢¢¢

   Violet City. A three-mile lantern-light tour (3 hrs) of historic features, including tuberclosis hospital huts and some of the cave's largest rooms and passageways. (Summer, daily; spring & fall, Sat & Sun; inquire for schedule) ¢¢

   Travertine. Quarter-mile Travertine (1 hr) is considered an easy tour through Drapery Room, Frozen Niagara and Crystal Lake. Designed for those unable to take many steps. ¢¢

   Disabled Persons. Half-mile tour (1.5 hr) for persons in wheelchairs; assistance necessary. Inquire for schedule and details at visitor center, 502/758-2328. ¢¢

2. *Miss Green River* **Boat Trip.** Round-trip cruise (60 min) through scenic and wildlife areas of the park. (Apr–Oct, daily) Advance tickets may be purchased at visitor center. Phone 502/758-2243. ¢¢

(See Cave City, Horse Cave, Park City)

Motel

★**MAMMOTH CAVE.** *10 mi W of US 31W, I-65 exit 53 on KY 70 to park entrance, or exit 48 on KY 255 to entrance, then 3 mi inside park.* 502/758-2225; FAX 502/758-2301. 42 rms, 2 story. No rm phones. 20-rm motor lodge. Memorial Day-Labor Day: S, D $62–$65; each addl $6; cottages: S, D $40–$48; family rates; lower rates rest of yr. Crib $5. TV. Restaurants 7 am–7:30 pm. Ck-out noon. Coin lndry (summer). Meeting rms (winter). Gift shop. Tennis. Lawn games. Private patios, balconies. Kennel. Cr cds: A, D, MC, V.

Mayfield (C-3)

Settled: 1823 **Pop:** 9,935 **Elev:** 492 ft **Area code:** 502 **Zip:** 42066

Rich clay fields in the area provide clay for all parts of the country. Tobacco is an important crop in this area.

What to See and Do

Wooldridge Monuments. In Maplewood Cemetery, N end of town on US 45. Eccentric horse trader and breeder Henry C. Wooldridge is buried here. Near the stone vault, in which he is interred, are life-size statues of his parents, his brothers, five girls, his favorite dogs, a deer, a fox and a statue of himself mounted on a favorite horse—all facing east. (Daily)

(For further information contact the Mayfield-Graves County Chamber of Commerce, 902 Broadway, PO Box 468; 247-6101.)

(See Murray)

Motel

★**HOLIDAY INN.** *1101 Houseman St, 2 mi W on US 45 Bypass, at jct KY 121.* 502/247-3700; FAX 502/247-3135. 80 rms, 2 story. May–Oct: S $48; D $55; each addl $7; under 19 free; lower rates rest of yr. Crib free. TV; cable. Pool. Restaurant 6 am–2 pm, 5–10 pm. Rm serv. Ck-out noon. Meeting rms. Valet serv. Lawn games. Cr cds: A, C, D, DS, ER, MC, V, JCB.

Maysville (A-7)

Founded: 1787 **Pop:** 7,169 **Elev:** 514 ft **Area code:** 606 **Zip:** 41056

This Ohio River town, first known as Limestone, was established by the Virginia Legislature. By 1792 it had become a leading port of entry for Kentucky settlers. Daniel Boone and his wife maintained a tavern in the town for several years. Maysville is now an important burley tobacco market.

What to See and Do

1. **Blue Licks Battlefield State Park.** 26 mi SW on US 68. Approx 150 acres on the site of one of the bloodiest battles of the frontier and last Kentucky battle of the Revolutionary War (August 19, 1782, one year after Cornwallis' surrender). A monument in the park honors pioneers killed in an ambush. Also here is a museum with exhibits and displays depicting history of the area from the Ice Age through the Revolution. Recreational facilities include swimming pool; fishing. Miniature golf. Picnic shelters, playground. Camping (standard fees). (Apr–Oct, daily) Phone 289-5507. Museum ¢

2. **Old Washington.** 4 mi S on US 68. The original seat of Mason County, Washington was founded in 1786 and soon was the second largest town in Kentucky, with 119 cabins. Restored buildings include Paxton Inn (1810), Albert Sidney Johnston House (1797), Old Church Museum (1848), Mefford Fort, Simon Kenton Trading store and the Cane Brake, thought to be one of the original cabins of 1790. Guided tours (mid-Mar–Dec, daily). (See ANNUAL EVENTS) Contact Old Washington, Inc, PO Box 227, Washington 41096; 759-7411. ¢¢

3. **Mason County Museum.** 215 Sutton St. Restored building (1876) houses art gallery, local historical exhibits, genealogical library. (Apr–Dec, daily exc Sun; rest of yr, Tues–Sat; closed hols) Phone 564-5865. ¢

4. **The Piedmont Art Gallery.** 16 mi NE via KY 8E in Augusta at 115 W Riverside Dr. Located in one of the oldest settlements on the Ohio River, the gallery houses contemporary works by national and regional artists and craftspeople; antiques, paintings, sculpture,

ceramics, American folk art. (Thurs–Sun, afternoons) Phone 756-2216. **Free.**

(For further information and a list of walking tours, contact the Maysville Tourism Commission; 564-6986.)

Annual Events

Sternwheeler Annual Regatta. 16 mi NE in Augusta. Mid-June.

Main Street Festival. Early July.

Simon Kenton Festival. Old Washington (see #2). 3rd wkend Sept.

(For accommodations see Covington, Lexington)

Monticello (C-6)

Pop: 5,357 **Elev:** 923 ft **Area code:** 606 **Zip:** 42633

What to See and Do

Dale Hollow Lake State Park. SE via KY 90, 449. A 3,398-acre park on a 27,700-acre lake. Swimming pool; boat rentals, marina (fee). Playground. Camping (hookups, dump station). Standard fees. Phone 502/433-7431.

(For further information contact the Monticello-Wayne County Chamber of Commerce, PO Box 566.)

Motel

✔ ★**GRIDER HILL DOCK & INDIAN CREEK LODGE.** *(Rte 4, Box 800, Albany 42602) 20 mi W on KY 90, then 5 mi N on KY 734, 1266, on Lake Cumberland.* 606/387-5501. 22 rms, 2 story, 12 kit. cottages, 30 houseboats. Mid-May–mid-Sept: S $43; D $46; each addl $6; kit. cottages for 2–10, $58–$126; houseboats for 6–12, $630–$1,295 (3-day min summer wkends; deposit required); wkly rates; higher rates wkends; lower rates Apr–mid-May, mid-Sept–Oct. Closed rest of yr. TV; cable. Restaurant 6 am–9 pm. Ck-out noon. On lake; swimming, boats, motors, dockage. Cr cds: A, DS, MC, V.

Morehead (B-8)

Pop: 8,357 **Elev:** 748 ft **Area code:** 606 **Zip:** 40351

Seat of Rowan County, Morehead is a university town and a provisioning point for lumbermen and for tourists visiting the northern portions of Daniel Boone National Forest (see). A Ranger District office for the forest is located in Morehead.

What to See and Do

1. **Morehead State University** (1922). (7,800 students) Just off I-64, in center of town. Science Museum (Mon–Fri; free); one-room schoolhouse (by appt); Folk Art Museum, 1st floor of Claypool-Young Art Bldg (Mon–Fri). Phone 783-2766. Also on campus is

   MSU Appalachian Collection. Fifth floor of Julian Carroll Library Tower. Collection includes books, periodicals, geneaological materials, government documents. Special holdings devoted to authors James Still and Jesse Stuart, displays of regional art. (Daily) **Free.**

2. **Cave Run Lake.** In Daniel Boone National Forest (see), 10 mi SW via US 60 then S on KY 801; or S on KY 211. An 8,270-acre lake created by the impoundment of the Licking River. Beach, bath-

house and seasonal interpretive programs at Twin Knobs and Zilpo campgrounds; fishing for bass and muskie; 12 boat ramps, 2 marinas with boat rentals. Hiking. Picnicking. Camping at Twin Knobs and Zilpo campgrounds, boat-in camping at Clay Lick campground. Morehead Visitor Center, on KY 801, has exhibits, information. Scenic roads and views, including Forest Development Road 918, designated a National Scenic Byway. (Mid-Apr–Oct, daily) Some fees. For information contact the Morehead Ranger District, US Forest Service, PO Box 910; phone 784-5624 or 800/283-CAMP (reservations). Per car ¢

3. **Minor Clark State Fish Hatchery.** 10 mi SW on US 60, then 2 mi S on KY 801. Largemouth bass, smallmouth bass, walleye, muskellunge and rockfish are reared here; on display in exhibition pool. (May–Sept, Mon–Fri; closed most hols) Phone 784-6872. **Free.**

(For further information contact the Tourism Commission, 168 E Main St; 784-6221.)

Annual Events

Appalachian Celebration. Week devoted to history & heritage of Appalachia in Kentucky; dances, concerts, arts & crafts, exhibitions. Late June.

Kentucky Hardwood Festival. Appalachian arts & crafts, pageant, parade, contests, antiques, logging contests. 2nd wkend Sept.

(See Olive Hill)

Motels

★**DAYS INN.** *Jct KY 32, I-64 exit 137.* 606/783-1484. 51 rms, 2 story. S $38; D $46; under 12 free; higher rates univ graduation. Crib free. TV; cable. Complimentary coffee. Restaurant adj 7 am–11 pm. Ck-out 11 am. Some refrigerators. Cr cds: A, C, D, DS, MC, V.

✔ ★★**HOLIDAY INN.** *1698 Flemingsburg Rd, jct I-64, KY 32.* 606/784-7591; FAX 606/783-1859. 141 rms, 2 story. S $42–$49; D $45–$53; each addl $6; studio rms $45–$55; under 19 free; higher rates special events. Crib free. TV; cable. Pool. Restaurant 6:30 am–2 pm, 5–9:30 pm. Rm serv. Ck-out noon. Meeting rms. Cr cds: A, C, D, DS, MC, V.

Mount Vernon (C-7)

Pop: 2,654 **Elev:** 1,156 ft **Area code:** 606 **Zip:** 40456

What to See and Do

William Whitley House Historic Site (1785–92). 15 mi NW on US 150. First brick house west of the Alleghenies, building was used as a protective fort from Native Americans and as a haven for travelers on the Wilderness Road. Was called Sportsman's Hill because of the circular racetrack built nearby (first in US), which ran counterclockwise, unlike those in England. Panels symbolizing each of the 13 original states are over the mantel in parlor. Restored and furnished with period pieces. (June–Aug, daily; rest of yr, daily exc Mon) Picnicking, playground. Phone 355-2881. ¢

(See Berea)

Motels

✔ ★★**BEST WESTERN KASTLE INN.** *(Box 637) E of I-75 exit 59.* 606/256-5156. 50 rms, 2 story. S $28–$34; D $34–$40; each addl $5;

under 12 free. Pet accepted, some restrictions. TV; cable. Restaurant 6 am–10 pm. Ck-out 11 am. Sundries. Cr cds: A, C, D, DS, MC, V, JCB.

★ECONO LODGE. *(PO Box 1106) US 25 & I-75 exit 62. 606/ 256-4621.* 35 rms, 2–3 story. S $30–$42, D $34–$54; family rates; higher rates: hol wkends, special events. Crib free. Pet accepted, some restrictions. TV; cable. Pool. Complimentary coffee in lobby. Restaurant nearby. Ck-out 11 am. Some refrigerators. Cr cds: A, C, D, DS, ER, MC, V, JCB.

Murray (D-3)

Pop: 14,439 **Elev:** 515 ft **Area code:** 502 **Zip:** 42071

Located on the banks of the east fork of the Clarks River, Murray has become a staging area for hunters and campers bound for Land Between The Lakes recreation area. In Murray, in 1892, Nathan B. Stubblefield made the first radio broadcast in history. Rainey T. Wells, attorney for the Woodmen of the World, was about one mile away when he heard Stubblefield's voice saying "Hello Rainey! Hello Rainey!" Wells was astounded, and urged Stubblefield to patent his invention. Because of delays and ill-advised deals while perfecting his invention, Stubblefield was not the first to obtain the patent. He finally received one in 1908, but died in poverty in 1928. This is the home of Murray State University (1922), of which Rainey Wells was the second president.

What to See and Do

1. **National Museum, Boy Scouts of America.** N 16th Street on Murray State University campus. Houses the 54 original Norman Rockwell paintings of the scouting movement; several thousand items of scouting memorabilia and artifacts. (Mar–Nov, daily exc Mon) Phone 762-3383. ¢¢

2. **Kenlake State Resort Park** (see). 16 mi NE on KY 94.

3. **Land Between The Lakes** (see). 20 mi NE off KY 94.

(For further information contact the Murray Tourism Commission, PO Box 190; 753-5171.)

Annual Events

Jackson Purchase Arts & Crafts Festival. Kenlake State Resort Park. Early June.

Calloway County Fair. Aug.

(See Mayfield)

Motels

✔ ★HOLIDAY INN. S 12th St (US 641). 502/753-5986. 107 rms, 2 story. S $38–$48; D $43–$51; each addl $5; under 19 free; higher rates homecoming wkend, graduation (2-day min). Crib free. TV; cable. Pool. Restaurant 6 am–10 pm. Rm serv. Ck-out noon. Meeting rms. Valet serv. Cr cds: A, D, DS, MC, V.

★MURRAY PLAZA COURT. *(Box 385) 502 S 12th St (US 641). 502/753-2682.* 40 rms, 1–2 story. S $26.75; D $29.75–$41.75; each addl $3. Crib $5. TV; cable. Restaurant opp 6–2 am. Ck-out noon. Some balconies. Picnic tables. Cr cds: A, MC, V.

Restaurant

✔ ★SEVEN SEAS. *2 mi NW on US 641. 502/753-4141.* Hrs: 4–9 pm. Closed Sun; Jan 1, Thanksgiving, Dec 24–25. Semi-a la carte: dinner $4.99–$10.99. Buffet (Thurs–Sat): dinner $10.99. Child's meals. Specializes in catfish, seafood, steak. Parking. Cr cds: A, C, D, DS, MC, V.

Natural Bridge State Resort Park (B-7)

(On KY 11 near Slade)

Surrounded by 1,899 acres and a 54-acre lake in Daniel Boone National Forest (see), the natural bridge is 78 feet long and 65 feet high. The park has balanced rock, native hemlocks, beautiful Red River Gorge, saltpeter mines. Swimming pool (seasonal); fishing; boating. Nature trails and center; tennis. Picnicking, playground; dining room; cottages, lodge (see RESORT). Tent & trailer sites (Apr–Oct; standard fees), central service buildings. Skylift (mid-Apr–Oct, daily; fee); square dance pavilion; festivals. For prices, information phone 606/663-2214 or 800/325-1710.

(See Winchester)

Resort

✔ ★★HEMLOCK LODGE. *(Slade 40376) 2 mi S of Mountain Pkwy on KY 11, in Natural Bridge State Resort Park. 606/663-2214; res: 800/325-1710; FAX 606/663-5037.* 35 rms, 2 story, 10 kit. cottages. Apr–Nov: S $43–$49; D $53–$59; each addl $5.50; kit. cottages $63–$71; under 16 free; lower rates rest of yr. Closed Christmas hols. Crib free. TV; cable. Pool; wading pool, lifeguard. Playground. Dining rm 7–10:30 am, 11:30 am–4 pm, 5–9 pm. Ck-out noon, cottages 11 am, ck-in 4 pm. Meeting rms. Tennis. Miniature golf. Lawn games. Balconies. Picnic tables, grills. State-owned property; all park facilities avail. Cr cds: A, D, DS, MC, V.

Olive Hill (B-8)

Pop: 1,809 **Elev:** 160 ft **Area code:** 606 **Zip:** 41164

What to See and Do

1. **Carter Caves State Resort Park.** 7 mi NE via US 60, KY 182. This 1,350-acre park lies in a region of cliffs, streams and many caves. Pool (seasonal); boating (rentals); fishing, canoe trips. Nine-hole and miniature golf, tennis, shuffleboard. Picnicking, playground, cottages, lodge (see RESORT); snack shop. Tent & trailer sites (standard fees); central service building. Planned recreation, films, dances, festivals. Several guided cave tours. (Daily; closed late Dec) Some fees. Phone 286-4411.

2. **Grayson Lake State Park.** 15 mi E via US 60, then 8 mi S on KY 7. A 1,500-acre park and 1,512-acre lake. Fishing; boating (boat launch). Hiking. Picnicking, playground. Camping (hookups, dump station). Phone 474-9727.

(See Morehead)

Resort

★★**CAVELAND LODGE.** *(Rte 5, Box 1120) 3 mi N on KY 182, 5 mi NE of I-64 exit 161, in Carter Caves State Resort Park.* 606/286-4411; res: 800/325-0059; FAX 606/286-8165. 28 rms in lodge, 2 story, 15 kit. cottages. Memorial Day–Labor Day: S $49; D $59; each addl $5; kit. cottages $65–$83; under 16 free; lower rates rest of yr. Crib free. TV. 2 pools; 2 wading pools, lifeguard. Playground. Free supervised child's activities (Memorial Day–Labor Day). Dining rm 7–10:30 am, 11:30 am–4 pm, 5–9 pm. Ck-out noon, cottages 11 am, ck-in 4 pm. Meeting rms. Gift shop. Tennis. 9-hole golf, greens fee $10, putting green, miniature golf. Rec rm. Refrigerator in cottages. Private patios, balconies. Picnic tables, grills. State-owned property; all facilities of park avail. Cr cds: A, C, D, DS, MC, V.

Owensboro (B-4)

Settled: 1800 **Pop:** 53,549 **Elev:** 401 ft **Area code:** 502 **Zip:** 42301

Third largest city in Kentucky, Owensboro serves as the major industrial, commercial and agricultural hub of western Kentucky. A progressive arts program has provided Owensboro with a symphony orchestra, fine art museum, dance theatre, science museum and theater workshop. In spring the many historic houses along tree-arched Griffith Avenue are brightened by dogwood and azalea blossoms.

Once known as Yellow Banks from the color of the clay on the Ohio River's high banks, the town saw clashes between Union and Confederate troops during the Civil War. An earlier clash between the values of the North and South occured when Harriet Beecher Stowe found inspiration for her novel *Uncle Tom's Cabin* after a visit to a local plantation.

What to See and Do

1. **Owensboro Area Museum of Science & History.** 2829 S Griffith Ave. Live reptiles, insects; archaeological, geological and ornithological displays; planetarium; historic items. Gift shop. (Daily; closed major hols) Phone 683-0296. **Free.**
2. **Owensboro Museum of Fine Art.** 901 Frederica St. Permanent collection includes 16th–20th-century American, French and English paintings, drawings, sculpture, graphic and decorative arts. Special collection of 19th- and 20th-century regional art; Appalachian folk art. (Daily exc during show change; closed major hols) Phone 685-3181. **Free.**
3. **Windy Hollow Recreation Area.** 10 mi SW off KY 81. Area of 214 acres offers swimming, 240-foot water slide (Memorial Day–Labor Day, fee); fishing. Miniature golf (fee). Grocery. Tent & trailer camping (fee). Park (Apr–Oct, daily). Phone 785-4150.
4. **Ben Hawes State Park.** 4 mi W off US 60. Approximately 300 acres with hiking; 9-hole, 18-hole golf (fee, rentals); tennis. Picnicking, playground. Phone 684-9808 or 685-2011 (golf).

(For further information contact the Owensboro-Daviess County Tourist Commission, 326 St Elizabeth St; 926-1100.)

Annual Events

International Bar-B-Q Festival. Cooks compete with recipes for mutton, chicken, burgoo. Also, tobacco spitting, pie-eating, fiddling contests. Arts & crafts, music, dancing. Early May.

Daviess County Fair. 4 days late July–early Aug.

IBMA Bluegrass FanFest. On riverfront in English Park. Bluegrass musicians perform. Phone 684-9025. Late Sept.

Seasonal Event

Owensboro Symphony Orchestra. RiverPark Center. Includes guest appearances by renowned artists, ballet companies. Phone 684-0661. Oct–Apr.

Motels

✔★**DAYS INN.** 3720 New Hartford Rd, jct US 60 Bypass & US 231. 502/684-9621. 122 rms, 2 story. S $35; D $39; each addl $4; under 12 free. Crib free. TV; cable. Pool. Restaurant 6 am–9 pm. Rm serv 5–9 pm. Ck-out noon. Cr cds: A, C, D, DS, MC, V.

★★**HOLIDAY INN.** 3136 W 2nd St. 502/685-3941; FAX 502/926-2917. 145 rms, 2 story. S $49–$63; D $54–$68; each addl $5; suites $115–$130; under 19 free. Crib free. Pet accepted. TV; cable. Indoor pool. Playground. Restaurant 6 am–2 pm, 5–9 pm. Rm serv. Bar 11–2 am, closed Sun. Ck-out noon. Meeting rms. Exercise equipt; bicycles, treadmill, whirlpool, sauna. Cr cds: A, C, D, DS, MC, V, JCB.

Motor Hotel

★★★**EXECUTIVE INN RIVERMONT.** 1 Executive Blvd. 502/926-8000; res: 800/626-1936. 650 rms, 2–7 story. S $53; D $57; each addl $6; suites $85; under 18 free. Crib free. TV; cable. 2 pools, 1 indoor. Restaurant 6 am–10 pm. Rm serv 7 am–11 pm. Bar 4 pm–2 am, closed Sun; entertainment, dancing. Ck-out noon. Convention facilities. Bellhops. Shopping arcade. Free airport transportation. Lighted indoor tennis. Exercise equipt; weight machines, bicycles, sauna, steam rm. Refrigerators. Patios, balconies. On river. Cr cds: A, C, D, DS, MC, V.

Restaurants

★★**BRIARPATCH.** 2760 Veach Rd. 502/685-3329. Hrs: 11 am–2 pm, 5–9:30 pm; Fri to 10:30 pm; Sat 5–10:30 pm. Closed Thanksgiving, Dec 25. Bar. Semi-a la carte: lunch $3.50–$6.95, dinner $7.95–$18.95. Child's meals. Specializes in steak, seafood. Salad bar. Parking. Cr cds: A, C, D, DS, MC, V.

✔★**MOONLITE BAR B-Q.** 2840 W Parish Ave. 502/684-8143. Hrs: 9 am–9 pm; Sun 10 am–3 pm; Sun brunch 10:30 am–2:30 pm. Closed most major hols. Wine, beer. Semi-a la carte: bkfst $1.50–$4.95, lunch, dinner $3.10–$10.95. Sun brunch $7.95. Child's meals. Specializes in barbecued mutton, ribs and chicken. Parking. Family-owned. Cr cds: A, DS, MC, V.

★**RUBY TUESDAY.** 5000 Frederica St (US 431), in Towne Square Mall. 502/926-8325. Hrs: 11 am–10 pm; Fri, Sat to 11 pm; Sun to 8:30 pm. Res accepted. Semi-a la carte: lunch $4–$6, dinner $13–$18. Sun brunch $5. Child's meals. Specializes in marinated steak, chicken, fresh fish, cajun dishes. Salad bar. Cr cds: A, C, D, DS, MC, V.

Paducah (C-3)

Founded: 1827 **Pop:** 27,256 **Elev:** 339 ft **Area code:** 502

Paducah, historic gateway to western Kentucky, has been shaped and influenced by its location at the convergence of the Ohio and Tennessee rivers. The waters have brought both prosperity and ruin in the form of disastrous floods; the worst occurred in 1937.

Explorer William Clark laid out the town site and named it after his Chickasaw friend, Chief Paduke. Paducah quickly developed as a shipping center and was a strategic point hotly contested during the Civil War. TVA dams have tamed the rivers and created the recreation areas of the Land Between The Lakes (see). Timber, tobacco, soybeans, coal and livestock flow through Paducah as they have for more than a century.

Paducah is perhaps most famous as the birthplace of author and actor Irvin S. Cobb, known for his witty humor and beloved ''Old Judge Priest'' stories.

What to See and Do

1. Memorials.

Irvin S. Cobb Memorial. Oak Grove Cemetery.

Alben W. Barkley Monument. 28th & Jefferson Sts. The senator and vice-president was one of Paducah's most famous citizens.

Chief Paduke Statue. 19th & Jefferson Sts. Memorial to the Chickasaw chief by Lorado Taft.

2. Red Line Scenic Tour. Self-guided driving tour (with map) of city points of interest, including Market House (see #3) and City Hall, designed by Edward Durell Stone. Obtain tour folders at the Tourist Commission, 417 S 4th St, 42002; 443-8783.

3. Market House (1905). S 2nd St & Broadway. Now a cultural center housing

Market House Museum. Early Americana, including complete interior of drugstore more than 100 years old. River lore, Alben Barkley and Irvin S. Cobb memorabilia, Native American artifacts, old tools. (Mar–Dec, daily exc Mon; closed major hols) Phone 443-7759. ¢

Yeiser Arts Center. Monthly changing exhibits; collection ranges from European masters to regional artists. Gift shop. Tours. (Daily exc Mon; closed major hols) Donation. Phone 442-2453.

Market House Theatre. A 250-seat professionally-directed community playhouse. (All yr) Phone 444-6828. ¢¢¢

4. Whitehaven. I-24, exit 7. Antebellum mansion remodeled in classical-revival style in 1903; elaborate plasterwork, stained glass, 1860s furnishings. State uses a portion of the house as a tourist welcome center and rest area. Tours (afternoons). (Daily; closed Jan 1, Thanksgiving, Dec 24, 25) Phone 554-2077. **Free.**

5. Museum of the American Quilter's Society. 215 Jefferson St. More than 200 quilts exhibited. Special exhibits scheduled regularly. Gift shop. (Tues–Sat; closed Jan 1, Thanksgiving, Dec 25) Phone 442-8856. ¢¢

(For further information contact the Paducah-McCracken County Tourist & Convention Commission, 417 S 4th St, PO Box 90, 42002; 443-8783 or 800/359-4775.)

Annual Events

Dogwood Trail Celebration. Blossoming of dogwood and azalea is celebrated with a trail, spotlighted at night, beginning at Paducah City Hall. Mid-Apr.

Kiwanis West Kentucky-McCracken County Fair. Carson Park, 301 Joe Clifton Dr. Society & Western horse shows; harness racing; motorcycle racing; gospel singing. Last full wk June.

Summer Festival. Hot air balloons, symphony & fireworks, free entertainment nightly. Events along river front and throughout city. Last wk July.

Seasonal Event

Bluegrass Downs of Paducah. 2 mi W at 32nd & Park Ave. Parimutuel horse racing featuring Arabian horse racing. Thurs–Sun. Phone 444-7117. Oct.

(See Gilbertsville)

Motels

★**BEST INNS OF AMERICA.** *(Box 9586, 42002) 5001 Hinkleville Rd, I-24 exit 4. 502/442-3334.* 91 rms, 2 story. S $36–$42; D $38–$50; each addl $6; under 18 free. Crib free. Pet accepted. TV; cable. Pool. Restaurant nearby. Ck-out 1 pm. Cr cds: A, C, D, DS, MC, V.

✔ ★**DAYS INN.** *I-24 & US 60W (42001), 3½ mi E on US 60. 502/442-7501.* 122 rms, 2 story. S $36–$40; D $40–$45; each addl $4; under 18, $1. Crib free. TV; cable. Pool. Restaurant 6 am–9 pm. Ck-out noon. Cr cds: A, D, MC, V.

★**DRURY INN.** *4910 Hinckleville Rd (42001). 502/443-3313.* 124 rms, 4 story. S $39–$50; D $52–$58; each addl $5; suites $58–$64; under 18 free. Crib free. TV; cable. Pool. Restaurant open 24 hrs. Ck-out noon. Cr cds: A, C, D, DS, MC, V.

Restaurants

✔ ★**C.C. COHEN.** *Broadway & 2nd St. 502/442-6391.* Hrs: 11 am–9 pm; Fri, Sat to 10 pm. Closed Sun; closed some major hols. Res accepted. Bar. Semi-a la carte: lunch $4.25–$6.50, dinner $9.50–$15. Child's meals. Specializes in prime rib, filet mignon, oversized sandwiches. Entertainment Sat. In Cohen Bldg (ca 1870); early decorative metalwork. Many antiques. Cr cds: A, MC, V.

✔ ★**CHONG'S.** *2708 Jackson St. 502/443-4022.* Hrs: 11 am–9 pm; Fri to 10 pm; Sat 1–10 pm. Closed Sun; Thanksgiving, Dec 25. Chinese, Amer menu. Semi-a la carte: lunch $2.55–$4.70, dinner $3.75–$11.75. Specialties: Hong Kong steak, lobster tail Cantonese. Parking. Chinese hanging lanterns, artifacts throughout. Cr cds: A, D, MC, V.

★**JEREMIAH'S.** *225 Broadway. 502/443-3991.* Hrs: 5–9:30 pm; Fri, Sat to 10:30 pm. Closed Sun; most major hols. Res accepted. Bar 4 pm–midnight. Semi-a la carte: dinner $12.95–$16.95. Specializes in charcoal-grilled steak, frogs' legs. Former bank (1800s); rustic decor. Cr cds: A, C, D, MC, V.

★ ★**NINTH STREET HOUSE.** *323 N 9th St. 502/442-9019.* Hrs: 11 am–2 pm, 5:30–8:30 pm; Fri, Sat to 9 pm. Closed Sun, Mon; most major hols; also 1st 3 wks July. Res accepted. Bar. Semi-a la carte: lunch $3.75–$10.95, dinner $5.95–$19. Specializes in Southern cuisine, chicken salad, 3–5 course dinners. Own baking, ice cream. Pianist Fri, Sat. Recited menu at dinner. Historic house (1886); restored. Antiques. Cr cds: C, D, MC, V.

★ ★**PASTA VINO.** *2711 Jackson St. 502/442-2626.* Hrs: 11 am–10 pm; Sat from 5 pm. Closed Easter, Dec 25. Res accepted. Italian menu. Bar. Semi-a la carte: lunch $3.95–$4.95, dinner $5.95–$17.95. Child's meals. Pasta bar (lunch). Guitarist wkends. Parking. Cr cds: A, MC, V.

★ ★**THE PINES.** *900 N 32nd St. 502/442-9304.* Hrs: 11:30 am–2 pm, 5:30–10 pm; Sat from 5:30 pm. Closed Sun; major hols. Continental menu. Bar to midnight. Semi-a la carte: lunch $4.50–$12, dinner $11–$25. Child's meals. Specializes in steak, seafood. Salad bar. Own ice cream. Parking. Cr cds: A, C, D, DS, MC, V.

✔ ★ ★**STACEY'S.** *1300 Broadway. 502/443-6437.* Hrs: 11 am–11 pm. Closed Sun, Mon; Thanksgiving, Dec 25. Bar. Semi-a la carte: lunch $4.50–$6.75, dinner $11.95–$17.95. Specializes in seafood, prime rib. Entertainment. Parking. Cr cds: A, C, D, DS, MC, V.

★★WHALER'S CATCH. *306 N 13th St. 502/444-7701.* Hrs: 11:30 am–1:30 pm, 5–9 pm; Fri to 10 pm; Sat 5–10 pm. Closed Sun; major hols. Res accepted. Bar. Semi-a la carte: lunch $1.95–$6.95, dinner $5.95–$25.95. Child's meals. Specializes in Southern-style seafood. Parking. Outdoor dining. New Orleans atmosphere. Cr cds: MC, V.

Paris (B-7)

Founded: 1789 **Pop:** 8,730 **Elev:** 845 ft **Area code:** 606 **Zip:** 40361

Both Paris and Bourbon County were named in appreciation of France's aid to the colonies during the Revolution. While the French dynasty is long gone, the whiskey made in this county is a lasting tribute to the royal name. In early days, the limited herds of livestock could not consume all the corn produced, and the surplus grain was used to make corn liquor. Corn liquor made in Paris in 1790 had such respected qualities that soon all Kentucky corn whiskey came to be called bourbon. Fine tobacco and Thoroughbred horse farms are also important to the economy of this town in the Bluegrass region.

What to See and Do

1. **Duncan Tavern Historic Shrine.** 323 High St. Includes Duncan Tavern (1788) and adjoining Anne Duncan House (1800). Daniel Boone and many leading figures of the day were entertained in this tavern. The Anne Duncan House was built flush to the wall of the tavern by the innkeeper's widow, who ran the tavern for many years after his death. Both the tavern, which is made of local limestone, and the old clapboard house of log construction have been restored and furnished with period pieces. (Daily exc Mon; closed hols) Phone 987-1788. Both houses ¢
2. **Old Cane Ridge Meeting House** (1791). 8 mi E on KY 537. Birthplace of the Christian Church (Disciples of Christ). Original log meetinghouse has been restored within an outer building of stone. In the early 1800s, revival meetings outside Old Cane Ridge attracted 20,000 to 30,000 persons at a time. Tours (by appt). Phone 987-5350. **Free.**

(For further information contact the Paris-Bourbon County Chamber of Commerce, 2 Bank Row; 987-3205.)

Annual Events

Central Kentucky Steam and Gas Engine Show. Bourbon County Park. Old operating farm machinery; steam traction engines; old gasoline tractors; threshing grain; flea market; country music. July.

Bourbon County Fair. Carnival; farm and craft exhibits. Late July.

(For accommodations see Georgetown, Lexington)

Park City (C-5)

Pop: 549 **Elev:** 650 ft **Area code:** 502 **Zip:** 42160

What to See and Do

1. **Kentucky Diamond Caverns.** 1 mi NW on KY 255. Guided tours of projecting peaks, rock palaces and some of the world's largest stalactites and stalagmites. Constant 54°F, smooth walks, handrails. For schedule phone 749-2891. ¢¢¢
2. **Mammoth Cave National Park** (see). 2 mi N on KY 70.

(See Bowling Green)

Resort

★★BEST WESTERN PARK MAMMOTH. *(Rte 1) 1½ mi S just off US 31 W; 1½ mi SE of I-65 Park City exit. 502/749-4101.* 92 rms, 2 story. June–Oct: S $44; D $50–$54; each addl $5; under 18 free; golf plan; lower rates rest of yr. Crib free. TV; cable. Indoor pool; wading pool, sauna, poolside serv. Playground. Dining rm 7–10 am, 11:30 am–1 pm, 5–8:30 pm. Ck-out noon. Meeting rms. Gift shop. Lighted tennis. 18-hole golf, greens fee $10. Miniature golf. Lawn games. Rec rm. Miniature train ride. On 2,000 acres. Cr cds: A, C, D, DS, MC, V.

Pikeville (B-8)

Founded: 1824 **Pop:** 6,324 **Elev:** 685 ft **Area code:** 606 **Zip:** 41501

Location of the notorious Hatfield-McCoy feud, Pikeville sits astride the Levisa Fork of the Big Sandy River and is the seat of Pike County, a leading producer of deep-mined coal. The town was named for Zebulon M. Pike, the explorer.

What to See and Do

1. **Breaks Interstate Park** (see). S on US 460.
2. **Fishtrap Lake.** 15 mi SE via US 460 on KY 1789. Created by US Army Corps of Engineers dam on Levisa Fork of Big Sandy River, the lake offers fishing; boating (marina). Picnicking, playground, ballfields. Camping. (Daily) Phone 437-7496. **Free.**
3. **Grapevine Recreation Area.** In Phyllis, S via KY 194. Boating. Picnicking, playground. Camping (May–Sept; fee). Phone 437-7496.

Annual Event

Hillbilly Days Spring Festival. Antique car show, music, arts & crafts. Phone 437-7331. 3rd wkend Apr.

(See Prestonsburg)

Motor Hotel

★★LANDMARK INN. *(Box 2439) 146 S Mayo Trail. 606/432-2545; res: 800/831-1469; FAX 606/432-2545, ext 502.* 104 rms, 4 story. S $49; D $53; each addl $10; under 14 free. Crib free. TV; cable, in-rm movies. Pool. Rooftop restaurant 6 am–10 pm. Rm serv. Bar 1 pm–5 am, Fri & Sat from 2 pm; entertainment. Ck-out noon. Coin lndry. Sundries. Meeting rms. Valet serv. Some balconies. Cr cds: A, C, D, DS, MC, V.

Pineville (C-7)

Settled: 1799 **Pop:** 2,198 **Elev:** 1,015 ft **Area code:** 606 **Zip:** 40977

In 1797 the Kentucky legislature authorized funds for the construction of a tollhouse on the Wilderness Road at a gap called the Narrows. Pineville grew around the tollhouse, which was abandoned in 1830.

What to See and Do

1. **Bell Theatre (1939).** 114 W Kentucky Ave. Restored art deco movie house. For schedule phone 337-7074 or -1319.
2. **Pine Mountain State Resort Park.** 1 mi S on US 25E. Approximately 1,500-acre park, surrounded by 12,000-acre Kentucky Ridge State Forest, has nature center, supervised recreation and the Laurel Cove Amphitheater. Swimming pool (seasonal). Nine-hole and

miniature golf, shuffleboard. Picnicking, playgrounds, cottages, lodge (see RESORT). Camping (Apr–Oct, standard fees), central service building. (See ANNUAL EVENT) Phone 337-3066.

Annual Event

Mountain Laurel Festival. Pine Mountain State Resort Park (see #2). College women from entire state compete for Festival Queen title. Parade, art exhibits, contests, sporting events, concerts. Last wkend May.

(See Barbourville)

Resort

★★**EVANS LODGE.** *1050 Pine Mt State Park Rd, 1 mi S on US 25E. 606/337-3066; res: 800/325-1712; FAX 606/337-7250.* 30 rms, 2 story, 20 1–2 bedrm kit. cottages. Apr–Oct: S $43–$49; D $53–$59; each addl $5.46; kit. cottages $73–$83; under 16 free; lower lodge rates rest of yr. Crib free. TV. Pool; lifeguard. Dining rm 7 am–9 pm; Sun 7–10:30 am, noon–3 pm, 5–9 pm. Ck-out noon, cottages 11 am, ck-in 4 pm. 9-hole golf, greens fee $10, carts $10, miniature golf. Lawn games. Rec rm. Balconies, patios. Picnic tables. State-owned; all park facilities avail. Cr cds: A, C, D, MC, V.

Prestonsburg (B-8)

Settled: 1791 **Pop:** 3,558 **Elev:** 642 ft **Area code:** 606 **Zip:** 41653

Prestonsburg, located between the Big Sandy River and forested hills, is surrounded by coal, oil and natural gas fields. In 1862, Colonel James A. Garfield achieved a decisive Union victory nearby; the first major triumph for the Union cause in the Civil War. This victory elevated Garfield to the rank of general and started him on the road to the presidency.

What to See and Do

Jenny Wiley State Resort Park. 2 mi S on US 23, then 3 mi N on KY 3. Mountainous terrain spanning more than 1,600 acres. Swimming pool (seasonal); fishing in 1,150-acre Dewey Lake; boating (rentals, ramp, dock). Nine-hole golf (seasonal, fee), shuffleboard. Picnicking, playground, cottages, lodge (see RESORT). Tent & trailer sites (Apr–Oct, standard fees). Skylift (Memorial Day–Labor Day, daily; rest of yr, wkends only, weather permitting; fee); amphitheater (see SEASONAL EVENT); recreational programs. Phone 886-2711 or 800/325-0142 (reservations).

(For further information contact the Chamber of Commerce, 130 North Lake Dr; 886-1341.)

Annual Event

Kentucky Apple Festival. In Paintsville, 11 mi N via US 23/460. Parade, amusement rides, antique car show, arts & crafts, flea market, 5K run, postage cancellation, square dancing, music and entertainment. Phone 789-4355. Early Oct.

Seasonal Event

Jenny Wiley Theatre. Jenny Wiley State Resort Park (see). Broadway musicals. For schedule contact General Mgr, PO Box 22; 866-9274. Mid-June–late Aug.

(See Pikeville)

Motel

✔★**HEART O' HIGHLANDS.** *(US 23 Bypass S, Paintsville 41240)* 12 mi N on US 23/460. 606/789-3551. 135 rms, 2–3 story. S $32–$34; D $36–$38; each addl $4; under 12 free; higher rates Apple Festival. Crib free. Pet accepted. TV; cable. Pool. Complimentary coffee in lobby. Restaurant opp 6 am–9:30 pm; Sat from 7 am; Sun 7 am–3 pm. Ck-out noon. Meeting rms. Cr cds: A, C, D, DS, MC, V.

Motor Hotels

★★**CARRIAGE HOUSE.** *(624 2nd St, Paintsville 41240)* Off US 23. 606/789-4242; res: 800/444-3194; FAX 606/789-6788. 150 rms, 3 story. S $43–$46; D $43–$47; each addl $4; suites $95–$107; under 12 free. Crib free. TV; cable. Indoor/outdoor pool; whirlpool, sauna, poolside serv. Restaurant 6 am–2 pm, 5–10 pm; Sun 8 am–4 pm. Rm serv. Private club 5–11 pm; closed Sun. Ck-out noon. Coin lndry. Meeting rms. Indoor putting green. Miniature golf. Balconies. Cr cds: A, C, D, DS, MC, V.

★★**HOLIDAY INN.** *575 US 23S.* 606/886-0001; FAX 606/886-9850. 118 rms, 3 story. S $58–$74; D $64–$80; each addl $6; under 20 free. Crib free. Pet accepted, some restrictions. TV. Heated pool; poolside serv. Restaurant 6 am–10 pm. Rm serv from 7 am. Bar; entertainment Thurs & Fri. Ck-out noon. Coin lndry. Meeting rms. Exercise equipt; weight machine, treadmill, whirlpool. Refrigerators avail. Cr cds: A, C, D, DS, MC, V, JCB.

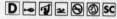

Resort

★★**MAY LODGE.** *(HC 66, Box 200) 2 mi S on US 23, then 1½ mi N on KY 3, in Jenny Wiley State Resort Park.* 606/886-2711; res: 800/325-0142. 49 rms, 2 story, 17 kit. cottages (1–2 bedrm). Apr–Oct: S $49; D $59; each addl $5; suites $60–$90; kit. cottages $67–$83; under 16 free; lower rates rest of yr. Crib free. TV; cable. 2 pools; wading pool. Playground. Dining rm 7 am–9 pm. Ck-out noon, cottages 11 am, ck-in 4 pm. Meeting rms. Social director. 9-hole golf, greens fee $10, miniature golf. Paddleboats. Lawn games. Private patios, balconies. Picnic tables, grills. On lake. State-owned; all park facilities avail. Cr cds: A, C, D, DS, MC, V.

Richmond (B-7)

Founded: 1798 **Pop:** 21,155 **Elev:** 975 ft **Area code:** 606 **Zip:** 40475

Scene of a major Civil War battle—the first Confederate victory in Kentucky—Richmond is an industrial and agricultural center and the home of Eastern Kentucky University (1906).

What to See and Do

1. **Courthouse** (1849). Courthouse Square, Main St between N 1st & N 2nd Sts. Greek-revival courthouse in downtown historic district was used as a hospital by Union and Confederate forces during Civil War. In lobby is

   Squire Boone Rock. One of the Wilderness Road markers.

2. **Hummel Planetarium and Space Theater.** Kit Carson Dr, on Eastern Kentucky University campus. One of the largest and most sophisticated planetariums in the US; state of the art projection and audio systems; large-format film system. Public programs (Thurs–Sun). Phone 622-1547. ¢¢

3. **White Hall State Shrine.** 9 mi N; I-75 exit 95. Restored 44-room house of Cassius M. Clay (1810–1903), emancipationist, diplomat and publisher of *The True American,* an antislavery newspaper. The 1799 Georgian house incorporates an Italianate addition from 1860s. Period furnishings, some original; personal mementos. Picnicking. (Apr–Labor Day, daily; after Labor Day–Oct, Wed–Sun) Phone 623-9178. ¢¢

(For further information contact the Tourism Commission, City Hall, PO Box 250; 623-1000, ext 210.)

Annual Event

Madison County Fair & Horse Show. Last wk July.

(See Berea, Lexington, Winchester)

Motels

 ★ ★ **BEST WESTERN ROAD STAR INN.** *1751 Lexington Rd, near I-75 exit 90.* 606/623-9121; FAX 606/623-3160. 94 rms, 2 story. S $33–$36; D $42–$45; each addl $5; under 12 free. Crib free. TV; cable. Heated pool. Continental bkfst. Restaurant nearby. Ck-out noon. Meeting rm. Cr cds: A, C, D, DS, MC, V.

★ **DAYS INN.** *2109 Belmont Dr, I-75 exit 90B.* 606/624-5769; FAX 606/624-1406. 70 rms, 2 story. S $34; D $36; each addl $5; under 18 free. Pet accepted, some restrictions; $5. TV; cable. Restaurant adj open 24 hrs. Ck-out noon. Meeting rm. Sundries. Cr cds: A, C, D, DS, MC, V.

★ ★ **HOLIDAY INN.** *100 Eastern Bypass (KY 876), I-75 exit 87.* 606/623-9220; FAX 606/624-1458. 141 rms, 2 story. S $47; D $52; each addl $5; under 20 free. Crib free. Pet accepted, some restrictions. TV; cable. Pool. Complimentary coffee in lobby. Restaurant 6:30 am–2 pm, 5–10 pm. Rm serv. Ck-out noon. Meeting rms. Bellhops. Valet serv. Sundries. Picnic tables. Near Eastern Kentucky Univ. Cr cds: A, D, DS, MC, V, JCB.

Rough River Dam State Resort Park (B-5)

(On KY 79 at NE end of Rough River Lake)

This 637-acre park is at the northeast end of 4,860-acre Rough River Lake, on KY 79. Beach with bathhouse, pool (seasonal); fishing; boat dock (ramps, rentals), pedal boats, cruise boat (seasonal). Hiking; fitness trail; 9-hole golf, pro shop, driving range, miniature golf; tennis, shuffleboard. Picnicking, playgrounds, lodge (see RESORT), dining room, cottages. Tent & trailer camping (Apr–Oct, standard fees); central service building. Planned recreation. For fees and information phone 502/257-2311.

Resort

 ★ **ROUGH RIVER LODGE.** *(RR 1, Box 1, Falls of Rough 40119) Just off KY 79 in park.* 502/257-2311; res: 800/325-1713. 40 rms, 2 story. 15 kit. cottages. Memorial Day–Labor Day: S $49; D $59; each addl $5; kit. cottages $83; under 16 free; lower rates rest of yr. Closed Christmas day. Crib free. TV; cable. Pool; wading pool, lifeguard. Playground. Dining rm 7–10:30 am, 11:30 am–4 pm, 5–9 pm; Sun noon–9 pm; winter to 8 pm. Ck-out noon, cottages 11 am, ck-in 4 pm. Coin lndry. Meeting rms. Lighted tennis. 9-hole golf, greens fee $6, driving range. Miniature golf. Sightseeing boat. Airstrip. Private patios, balconies.

Picnic tables, grills (cottages). State-owned property; all facilities of park avail. On lake. Cr cds: A, C, D, DS, MC, V.

Shepherdsville (B-6)

Pop: 4,805 **Elev:** 449 ft **Area code:** 502 **Zip:** 40165

Shepherdsville is the seat of Bullitt County, which was named for Thomas Bullitt, who established Bullitt's Lick in 1773. Salt was produced from this site of prehistoric animal licks. A state information center is located here.

What to See and Do

Bernheim Arboretum and Research Forest. 6 mi S on I-65, exit 112, then 1 mi E on KY 245. This 2,000-acre arboretum offers a nature center with trails, a museum (daily exc Mon), waterfowl lakes and a 12,000-acre research forest. The 200-acre landscape arboretum features 1,800 species of plants. (Mid-Mar–mid-Nov, daily) Phone 543-2451. Mon–Fri (free); Sat, Sun & hols per vehicle ¢¢¢

(See Elizabethtown, Fort Knox, Louisville)

Motels

★ ★ **BEST WESTERN SOUTH.** *(PO Box 96) Lakeview Dr, jct KY 44, I-65 exit 117.* 502/543-7097. 85 rms, 2 story. S $36–$38; D $43–$48; each addl $4; suites $50–$55; under 12 free; higher rates Kentucky Derby. Crib free. TV; cable. Pool; wading pool. Restaurant. Rm serv. Bar 4 pm–midnight; entertainment, dancing Tues–Sat. Ck-out noon. Meeting rm. Cr cds: A, C, D, DS, MC, V.

★ **DAYS INN.** *(PO Box 339) KY 44E, I-65 exit 117.* 502/543-3011. 120 rms, 2 story. S $34; D $40; each addl $6; under 12 free; higher rates Kentucky Derby. Crib free. TV; cable. Pool. Restaurant adj open 24 hrs. Ck-out noon. Cr cds: A, C, D, DS, ER, MC, V.

Somerset (C-7)

Founded: 1801 **Pop:** 10,733 **Elev:** 975 ft **Area code:** 606 **Zip:** 42501

Centrally located, Somerset is only four miles from Lake Cumberland. Many of the state's most popular attractions are within an hour's drive. A Ranger District office of the Daniel Boone National Forest (see) is located in Somerset.

What to See and Do

1. **Big South Fork Scenic Railway.** S on US 27, W on KY 92 in Stearns. Train ride (5.5 mi), through rock tunnel, past abandoned coal camps and along Roaring Paunch Creek to the bottom of a gorge, connects historic Stearns with restored mining town, Blue Heron (see CUMBERLAND FALLS STATE RESORT PARK). (Mid-Apr–Oct) Phone 376-5330 or 800/462-5664. ¢¢¢

2. **Lake Cumberland.** 10 mi S. Man-made lake with 1,255 miles of shoreline has five recreation areas with campsites (mid-Mar–Nov; fee, one free). Swimming; fishing; commercial docks; houseboats, boats, motors for rent. Picnicking. Phone 679-6337.

3. **General Burnside State Park.** 10 mi S on US 27. On Chandler Island in Lake Cumberland. Swimming pool; fishing; boating (ramps). 18-hole golf. Picnicking, playground. Tent & trailer sites (Apr–Oct, standard fees). Square dance pavilion, recreation program (June–Labor Day). Phone 561-4104 or -4192.

4. Beaver Creek Wilderness. 15 mi S on US 27. On 4,791 acres below the cliff lines of the Beaver Creek Drainage within the Daniel Boone National Forest (see). Vertical sandstone cliffs, rockhouses; streams, waterfalls; flowering trees, shrubs and plants; variety of game and wildlife. Trail, compass hiking; backpacking; scenic overlooks. (Daily) Phone 679-2010. **Free.**

(For further information contact the Somerset/Pulaski County Tourist Commission, 522 Ogden St, PO Box 622; 679-6394 or 800/642-6287.)

(See Jamestown, London)

Motels

★★**BEST WESTERN PARKWAY INN.** *101 N US 27.* 606/678-2052; FAX 606/678-8477. 53 rms, 2–3 story. No elvtr. S $36–$42; D $38–$48; each addl $6; under 12 free. Crib free. TV; cable. Indoor pool; whirlpool. Complimentary continental bkfst. Restaurant nearby. Ck-out 11 am. Coin lndry. Cr cds: A, C, D, DS, MC, V.

D ⌂ ⊘ ⊙ SC

★★**HOLIDAY INN.** *606 S US 27, 1 mi S of KY 80.* 606/678-8115; FAX 606/678-8115, ext 323. 157 rms, 2 story. S $46; D $49–$56.50; each addl $7.50; suites $50; under 18 free. Crib free. TV; cable. Pool. Playground. Restaurant 6 am–2 pm, 5–10 pm. Rm serv. Ck-out 11 am. Coin lndry. Meeting rms. Free local airport transportation. Cr cds: A, C, D, DS, MC, V, JCB.

D ⌂ ⊘ ⊙ SC

★**SOMERSET LODGE.** *725 S US 27.* 606/678-4195; FAX 606/679-3299. 100 rms, 1–2 story. S $34; D $38–$42; each addl $4; under 13 free. Crib $5. TV; cable. Pool; wading pool. Playground. Restaurant 6 am–9 pm. Rm serv. Ck-out noon. Meeting rms. Free local airport transportation. Lawn games. Cr cds: A, C, D, DS, MC, V.

D ⌂ ⊘ ⊙

South Union (C-5)

Founded: 1807 **Elev:** 608 ft **Area code:** 502 **Zip:** 42283

The Shakers, officially the United Society of Believers in Christ's Second Appearing, settled this town as a religious community. Craftsmen and farmers of great skill and ingenuity, the Shakers were widely known both for the quality of their products and for their religious observances. When "moved by the spirit" they performed a dance that gave them the name Shakers. Celibacy was part of the religious observance. By 1922 the community had dwindled to only nine members. The property was sold at auction, and the remaining members dispersed. Nearby are many historic buildings, including the Red River Meeting House in Adairville; the Bibb House and the Old Southern Bank in Russellville, robbed by the James Gang in 1868.

What to See and Do

Shaker Museum. On US 68. Located in original 1824 building, museum houses Shaker crafts, furniture, textiles and tools. (Mid-Mar–mid-Nov, daily; rest of yr, by appt) Phone 542-4167. **¢¢**

(For further information contact the Logan County Chamber of Commerce, 116 S Main St, Russellville 42276; 726-2206.)

Annual Events

Shaker Festival. Tour of historic buildings; Shaker foods, music; craft demonstrations. Summer.

Tobacco Festival. 12 mi SW on US 68 in Russellville. Parade; reenactment of the Jesse James bank robbery; house tours in historic

district; tobacco displays; antiques; arts & crafts exhibits; bicycle rides; run (5 mi), fun run (1 mi); entertainment. One wk Oct.

(For accommodations see Bowling Green)

Walton (A-7)

Pop: 2,034 **Elev:** 930 ft **Area code:** 606 **Zip:** 41094

What to See and Do

Big Bone Lick State Park. 7 mi W on KY 338. On 525 acres. Museum and diorama explain prehistoric mammal life preserved in the soft sulphur spring earth around the salt lick (daily; closed Jan); model "dig"; displays of Ice Age formations. Swimming pool (seasonal, campers only). Tennis (free), shuffleboard. Picnicking. Camping (standard fees). Supervised recreation (summer). Phone 384-3522. Museum **¢**

(See Covington)

Motels

★**DAYS INN.** *(Rte 2, Box 85)* Jct I-75, KY 338. 606/485-4151. 137 rms, 2 story. S $34–$38; D $40–$46; each addl $7. Crib free. Pet accepted. TV; cable. Pool. Playground. Restaurant 6–10 am, 6–9 pm. Ck-out 11 am. Sundries. Cr cds: A, C, D, DS, MC, V.

🐾 ⌂ ⊘ ⊙

★**RED CARPET FOUNTAIN INN.** *11165 Frontage Rd, jct I-75, KY 338.* 606/485-4123. 60 rms, 2 story. S $36–$40; D $42–$46; each addl $5; under 12 free; higher rates Jazz Festival. Crib free. Pet accepted, some restrictions. TV; in-rm movies avail. Pool. Playground. Restaurant adj 6–10 am, 6–9 pm. Ck-out 11 am. Cr cds: A, C, D, DS, MC, V.

🐾 ⌂ ⊙ SC

Wickliffe (C-3)

Pop: 851 **Elev:** 330 ft **Area code:** 502 **Zip:** 42087

On high ground, Wickliffe is near the confluence of the Ohio and the Mississippi rivers. The Lewis and Clark Expedition's Fort Jefferson (1789) was at a nearby site, now marked, one mile south on US 51.

What to See and Do

1. Wickliffe Mounds Research Center. On US 51/60/62 in NW area of city. Remnants of a Mississippian culture of 1,000 years ago. Museum exhibits, pottery, ongoing excavations. (Mar–Nov, daily; closed Thanksgiving) Phone 335-3681. **¢¢**

2. Ballard County Wildlife Management Area. 20 mi NE on US 60, exit KY 1105 in LaCenter, headquarters on KY 473 off KY 1105. Waterfowl refuge, 8,000 acres with 11 lakes, borders the Ohio River. Deer, wild turkey, geese and ducks are among the wildlife that may be spotted. Fishing. Hiking. Primitive camping. (Mid-Mar–mid-Oct, daily) Phone 224-2244. **Free.**

(For accommodations see Paducah)

Williamsburg (C-7)

Founded: 1817 **Pop:** 5,493 **Elev:** 951 ft **Area code:** 606 **Zip:** 40769

Shadowed by ridges that rise nearly 2,000 feet, Williamsburg is the seat of Whitley County. Both town and county are named in honor of William Whitley, pioneer.

What to See and Do

1. **Cumberland River,** which runs through Williamsburg and then 18 miles north to Cumberland Falls State Resort Park (see), offers one of the most remote and rustic float trips in the US.

2. **Daniel Boone National Forest** (see). N via US 75, E via Daniel Boone Pkwy.

(For further information contact the Tourist & Convention Commission, PO Box 2; 549-0530.)

(See Corbin, London)

Motels

✔ ★ ★ **BEST WESTERN CONVENIENT MOTOR LODGE.** *(Box 204) 1½ blks W of I-75 exit 11. 606/549-1500; FAX 606/549-1500, ext 500.* 86 rms, 2 story. S $24–$34; D $29–$39; each addl $4; under 12 free. Crib free. TV; cable. Pool. Continental bkfst. Restaurant opp open 24 hrs. Ck-out 11 am. Cr cds: A, C, D, DS, MC, V.

★ ★ **HOLIDAY INN.** *30 KY 92W, I-75 exit 11. 606/549-3450; FAX 606/549-8161.* 100 rms, 2–3 story. No elvtr. S, D $34–$41; under 19 free. Crib free. Pet accepted. TV; cable. Pool. Restaurant 6:30 am–2 pm, 5:30–10 pm. Rm serv. Ck-out noon. Meeting rms. Cr cds: A, C, D, DS, MC, V, JCB.

Williamstown (A-7)

Settled: 1820 **Pop:** 3,023 **Elev:** 974 ft **Area code:** 606 **Zip:** 41097

What to See and Do

1. **Lloyd Wildlife Management Area.** 10 mi N via US 25, E at Gardnersville Rd (KY 491) exit. A 1,200-acre area with archery and shooting ranges (shooting allowed only during sponsored events). Five-acre lake with fishing for catfish, bass and bluegill. Hunting. Forty acres of virgin timberland includes monument to founder Curtis Lloyd; hiking trails. (Daily) Phone 428-3193. **Free.**

2. **Kincaid Lake State Park.** 17 mi NE via KY 22, then 3 mi N off US 27. An 850-acre park with 183-acre lake stocked with bass, bluegill, crappie, channel catfish. Swimming pool (seasonal; fee); fishing; boating (dock, rentals, max 16-ft and 10-HP motor). Hiking; miniature golf. Camping (Apr–Oct). Amphitheater; planned recreation. Phone 654-3531.

(For further information contact the Grant County Chamber of Commerce, 1300 N Main St, PO Box 52; 824-3322.)

(See Covington)

Motels

★ **DAYS INN.** *211 W KY 36, I-75 exit 154. 606/824-5025.* 50 rms, 1–2 story. S $33–$36; D $36–$45; each addl $5; under 12 free. Crib free. Pet accepted, some restrictions. TV. Pool. Restaurant adj. Ck-out 11 am. Cr cds: A, C, D, DS, MC, V.

✔ ★ **HoJo INN.** *1 mi SW on KY 36 at jct I-75, exit 154. 606/824-7177.* 40 rms, 2 story. S $27.95–$33.95; D $34.95–$38.95; each addl $5; under 16 free. Crib free. Pet accepted. TV; cable. Pool. Restaurant adj 6 am–9 pm. Ck-out noon. Picnic table. Cr cds: A, C, D, DS, MC, V, JCB.

Winchester (B-7)

Pop: 15,799 **Elev:** 972 ft **Area code:** 606 **Zip:** 40391

Winchester is the location of several industrial plants. Nearby coal and gas fields and fertile farmland also contribute to the economy. Henry Clay made his first and last Kentucky speeches in the town. The Forest Supervisor's office of the Daniel Boone National Forest (see) is located in Winchester.

What to See and Do

1. **Natural Bridge State Resort Park** (see). 35 mi E via KY 15, 77 in Slade.

2. **Fort Boonesborough State Park.** 9 mi SW via KY 627, located on the Kentucky River. Site of settlement where Daniel Boone defended his fort against Native American sieges. The fort houses craft shops where costumed "pioneers" produce wares; a museum with Boone memorabilia and other historical items; and an audiovisual program (Apr–Labor Day, daily; after Labor Day–Oct, Wed–Sun). Exhibits in cabins and blockhouses recreate life at the fort. Sand beach, bathhouse; fishing; boating (ramp, dock). Miniature golf. Picnicking, playground; snack bar. Tent & trailer sites (standard fees). Rec dir; special events all yr. Phone 527-3131. Museum **¢¢**

3. **Historic Main Street.** Street has a number of restored buildings, most of the Victorian era, and unique shops (daily exc Sun).

4. **Old Stone Church.** 6 mi S off KY 627. Built in the late 1700s, this famous landmark in the Boonesboro section of Clark County is the oldest active church west of the Allegheny Mountains. Daniel Boone and his family worshiped here.

(For further information contact the Winchester-Clark County Tourism Commission, 2 S Maple, Suite A; 744-0556.)

Annual Event

Daniel Boone Pioneer Festival. College & Lykins Parks. Tennis tournaments, juried arts & crafts, street dance, fun runs, concerts, music, food. Phone 744-0556. Labor Day wknd.

(See Lexington)

Mississippi

Population: 2,573,216

Land area: 47,234 square miles

Elevation: 0–806 feet

Highest point: Woodall Mt (Tishomingo County)

Entered Union: December 10, 1817 (20th state)

Capital: Jackson

Motto: By valor and arms

Nickname: Magnolia State

State flower: Magnolia

State bird: Mockingbird

State tree: Magnolia

State fair: 2nd full week October, 1994, in Jackson

Time zone: Central

Bearded Spaniards in rusted armor followed De Soto across Mississippi in search of gold 80 years before the *Mayflower* landed in Massachusetts. De Soto died in the fruitless search. Pierre Le Moyne, Sieur d'Iberville, established Mississippi's first permanent settlement near Biloxi in 1699. There was no gold to be found, but the mighty Mississippi River had created something of infinitely greater value; an immense valley of rich, productive land—land on which cotton could be grown. It was cotton that established the great plantations, but while cotton still ranks first in agricultural production, the state also produces forestry, poultry, soybeans and catfish. However, manufacturing is the number one industry in the state.

Andrew Jackson became a hero in Mississippi after he defeated the Creek Indian nation and was again honored during a triumphal return through the state after winning the Battle of New Orleans in 1815. Mississippians enthusiastically named their capital after "Old Hickory" and they entertained him royally when he returned as an elder statesman in 1840.

For two years northern Mississippi was the scene of some of the fiercest fighting in the Civil War. Following the Union defeat of Confederate forces at the Battle of Shiloh (Tennessee) in April, 1862, General Ulysses S. Grant moved southwest into Mississippi. The following year, Grant besieged Vicksburg for 47 days. When the city finally fell, the fate of the Confederacy, according to some historians, was sealed. Yet battles still seesawed across and up and down the beleaguered state as railroads and telegraph lines were sliced by Northern raiders. Mississippi was left in shambles. It was after General William Tecumseh Sherman burned Jackson that he said, "War is Hell!" For Mississippi the war was indeed hell, and the Reconstruction period was nearly as chaotic.

Today Mississippi's subtropical Gulf Coast provides vast quantities of shrimp and oysters; it is also a tremendously popular resort and vacation area. Fishing is good in many streams, and hunting for waterfowl along the Mississippi River and for deer in other areas is also excellent. The state has beautiful forests, the antebellum traditions and pageantry of Natchez, the beautiful Natchez Trace Parkway and many other attractions.

National Park Service Areas

The Natchez Trace Parkway (see), operated by the National Park Service, will be 445 miles long when completed. About 425 miles are paved and open, most of them in Mississippi. Tupelo National Battlefield, Brices Cross Roads National Battlefield Site (see TUPELO for both) and Vicksburg National Military Park & Cemetery (see VICKSBURG) are on or near the Trace. East and West Ship Islands, with Fort Massachusetts and several offshore islands, are preserved as Gulf Islands National Seashore (see).

National Forests

The following is an alphabetical listing of National Forests and towns they are listed under.

Bienville National Forest (see MENDENHALL): Forest Supervisor in Jackson; Ranger offices in Forest*, Raleigh*.

Delta National Forest (see YAZOO CITY): Forest Supervisor in Jackson; Ranger office in Rolling Fork*.

De Soto National Forest (see HATTIESBURG): Forest Supervisor in Jackson; Ranger offices in Laurel, McHenry*, Wiggins*.

Holly Springs National Forest (see HOLLY SPRINGS): Forest Supervisor in Jackson; Ranger office in Holly Springs.

Homochitto National Forest (see NATCHEZ): Forest Supervisor in Jackson; Ranger offices in Gloster*, Meadville*.

Tombigbee National Forest (see LOUISVILLE and TUPELO): Forest Supervisor in Jackson; Ranger office in Ackerman*.

*Not described in text

State Recreation Areas

The following towns list state recreation areas in their vicinity under What to See and Do; refer to the individual town for directions and park information.

Listed under **Cleveland:** see Great River Road State Park.

Listed under **Columbus:** see Lake Lowndes State Park.

Listed under **Greenville:** see Leroy Percy State Park.

Listed under **Grenada:** see Hugh White State Park.

Listed under **Hattiesburg:** see Paul B. Johnson State Park.

Listed under **Holly Springs:** see Wall Doxey State Park.

Listed under **Kosciusko:** see Holmes County State Park.

Listed under **Louisville:** see Legion State Park.

Listed under **McComb:** see Percy Quin State Park.

Listed under **Meridian:** see Clarkco State Park.

Listed under **Natchez:** see Natchez State Park.

Listed under **Pass Christian:** see Buccaneer State Park.

Listed under **Philadelphia:** see Golden Memorial State Park.

Listed under **Sardis:** see George Payne Cossar and John W. Kyle state parks.

Listed under **Tupelo:** see Tombigbee and Trace state parks.

Water-related activities, hiking, various other sports, picnicking and visitor centers, as well as camping, are available in many of these areas. State parks provide fishing (free); boating, rentals ($4/half-day, $6/day); launching ($5); swimming ($2; children $1); picnicking; tent & trailer facilities ($11–$14/night; 14-day max); primitive tent camping ($6–$8) and cabins ($29–$62/night; 14-day max). Pets on leash only. Scattered throughout the state are 89 roadside parks with picnic facilities. For further information contact Public Information, Dept of Wildlife, Fisheries and Parks, PO Box 451, Jackson 39205-0451; 800/467-2757.

Fishing & Hunting

Anglers find limitless possibilities in Mississippi. There are no closed seasons, and size limits are imposed on game fish in only some areas (except sea-run striped bass and black bass on a few state waters). The Chickasawhay, Pearl, Homochitto and Pascagoula rivers are endless sources for largemouth bass, crappie, bluegill, bream and catfish, as are six large reservoirs and more than 170,000 acres of lakes. There are fishing camps at many lakes and reservoirs and on the Gulf Coast, where boats, bait and tackle are available. Complete charter services for deep-sea fishing and fishing piers are featured along US 90 as well as at Gulf Coast resorts. Nonresident fishing license, 16 yrs & over: annual, $20; 3-day, $6. No license is required for saltwater fishing.

Hunting on some one million acres of the more than 30 state-managed public hunting areas is seasonal: quail, late Nov–late Feb; wild turkey (gobblers only), late Mar–late Apr; squirrel, mid-Oct–mid-Jan; deer, usually Oct–Jan; duck, reservoir areas and major river lowlands, usually Dec–Jan; dove, Sept–Oct and winter. Public waterfowl management areas are located on some reservoirs and river lowlands. Licenses for nonresidents: all game (annual $150, 5-day $75); small game (annual $50, 5-day $30); archery and primitive firearms (must also purchase annual all-game permit) $30; waterfowl, state waterfowl stamp required $2. For detailed information contact the Dept of Wildlife Fisheries and Parks, PO Box 451, Jackson 39205-0451; 601/362-9212.

Safety Belt Information

Safety belts are mandatory for front seat passengers. Children under 2 years must be in an approved safety seat anywhere in vehicle. In addition, safety belts are mandatory for all persons anywhere in vehicle when traveling on the Natchez Trace Parkway. For further information phone 601/987-1336.

Interstate Highway System

The following alphabetical listing of Mississippi towns in *Mobil Travel Guide* shows that these cities are within 10 miles of the indicated Interstate highways. A highway map should, however, be checked for the nearest exit.

INTERSTATE 10: Biloxi, Gulfport, Ocean Springs, Pascagoula, Pass Christian.

INTERSTATE 20: Jackson, Meridian, Vicksburg.

INTERSTATE 55: Grenada, Jackson, McComb, Sardis.

INTERSTATE 59: Hattiesburg, Laurel, Meridian.

Additional Visitor Information

Information booklets are available from the Division of Tourism, Mississippi Dept of Economic and Community Development, PO Box 22825, Jackson 39205; 601/359-3297 or 800/647-2290. A new and up-to-date *Travel Planner to Mississippi* may be obtained free upon request from the Tourism Division and is an excellent aid to travelers.

There are 10 welcome centers in Mississippi; visitors who stop by will receive information, brochures and personal assistance in planning stops at points of interest. Their locations are as follows: at the northern end of the state, on I-55 south of Hernando; along the southern border, on I-55 south of Chatawa, on I-59 north of Nicholson, on I-10 at Waveland and on I-10 at Pascagoula; by the eastern border, on I-20 east of Toomsuba; in the western section, on US 82 & Reed Rd in Greenville, on I-20 near Vicksburg, on US 61 Bypass & Seargent S. Prentiss Dr north of Natchez and on I-78 west of border. Centers are open 8 am–5 pm, daily. For information on road conditions phone the Mississippi Highway Patrol, 601/987-1212.

Biloxi (F-4)

Settled: 1699 **Pop:** 46,319 **Elev:** 25 ft **Area code:** 601

The oldest town in the Mississippi Valley, Biloxi has been a popular resort since the 1840s. It has, since the 1870s, been a leading oyster and shrimp fishing headquarters; shrimp were first canned here in 1883.

The Sieur d'Iberville's first French fort was established at Ocean Springs, just east of Biloxi. In 1721 the third shipment of "Cassette girls" (so called after the boxes or "cassettes" in which they carried their possessions) landed at Ship Island, 12 miles south in the Gulf of Mexico. These 89 girls, carefully selected by a French bishop, were sent to become wives to the settlers.

Magnolia trees, camellias, azaleas, roses and crepe myrtle bloom along Biloxi's streets among the oaks draped with Spanish moss. It is a pretty town on a peninsula, with 25 miles of coastline. There is freshwater, saltwater and deep-sea fishing all year; crabbing, floundering and mullet net casting. Biloxi is the home of Keesler AFB, the electronics and computer training center of the US Air Force.

What to See and Do

1. **"Beauvoir"—Jefferson Davis Shrine.** 2244 Beach Blvd (US 90). Estate where the Confederate president spent the last 12 years of his life. From 1903–1957, "Beauvoir" also served as the Mississippi soldiers' home for Confederate veterans and their widows. Adjoining museums have Davis and Confederate artifacts. The Library Pavilion, where Davis wrote *The Rise and Fall of the Confederate Government* and *A Short History of the Confederate States of America*, contains his desk and books. Landscaped grounds covering 57 acres contain house, museums, 2 pavilions and Confederate cemetery with Tomb of the Unknown Soldier of the Confederate States of America. (Daily; closed Dec 25) Sr citizen rate. Phone 388-1313. ¢¢

2. **Tullis-Toledano Manor** (1856). 360 Beach Blvd. Historic antebellum mansion; oak-shaded grounds. (Mon–Fri) Sr citizen rate. Phone 435-6293. ¢

3. **Old Biloxi Cemetery.** Carter Ave between Father Ryan Ave & Cemetery St. Burial ground of French pioneer families of Biloxi and the Gulf Coast. John Cuevas, hero of Cat Island (War of 1812), is buried here.

4. **Boat trips.** Passenger ferry leaves for trips to Ship Island (see GULF ISLANDS NATIONAL SEASHORE). (Mar–Nov) Schedule varies; for information contact Ship Island Excursions, PO Box 1467, Gulfport 39502; phone 864-1014 (Gulfport, recording), 432-2197 (Biloxi, recording) or 864-3797 (office). Round trip ¢¢¢¢

5. **Deer Island.** Half mile offshore from E Beach Blvd. Called most beautiful of coastal islands, Deer Island is steeped in legends of Indians, explorers, buccaneers and buried pirate treasure.

6. **Harrison County Sand Beach.** This 300-foot-wide white sand beach stretches the entire 26-mile length of the county; a seawall separates the beach from the highway.

7. **Small Craft Harbor.** Jct Main St, US 90. View fishing boats unloading day's catch of Gulf game fish. Deep-sea fishing charter boats. For tour information contact Visitors Center, 435-6248.

8. **Vieux Marché Walking Tour.** Walking tour pamphlets of historic district are available at the Visitors Center, 710 Beach Blvd.

9. **Gulf Islands National Seashore** (see).

(For further information contact the Visitors Center, 710 Beach Blvd, PO Box 346, 39533; 435-6248 or the Office of Cultural Affairs; 432-2563.)

Annual Events

Mardi Gras. Carnival and parade. Shrove Tuesday. Feb 15.

Garden Club Pilgrimage. Guided tour of historic houses, sites and gardens. Mar or Apr.

Shrimp Festival. Gulf of Mexico. Includes *fais do do* (street dance), marine parade and blessing of shrimp fleet. Hundreds of vessels manned by descendants of settlers participate in this ritual of European origin. Wkend May.

Seafood Festival. Point Cadet Plaza, E on US 90. Arts & crafts show, entertainment, seafood booths, contests. Last wkend Sept.

(See Gulfport, Ocean Springs, Pascagoula, Pass Christian)

Motels

(Rates may be higher during Mardi Gras)

★**BREAKERS INN.** 2506 Beach Blvd (US 90) (39531). 601/388-6320; res: 800/624-5031. 28 kit. suites, 1–2 story. May–Sept: S, D $93.50–$137.50; higher rates: Memorial Day wkend, July 4, Labor Day; lower rates rest of yr. Pool; wading pool. Playground. Restaurant nearby. Ck-out 11 am. Lndry facilities in rms. Tennis. Lawn games. Opp ocean. Cr cds: A, C, D, DS, MC, V.

✔ ★★**DAYS INN.** 2046 Beach Blvd (US 90) (39531). 601/385-1155; FAX 601/385-2532 166 rms, 3 story, 83 kit. suites. S $49–$65; D $52–$70; each addl $5; kit. suites $68–$150; under 18 free; golf plans. Crib free. TV; cable. Pool. Complimentary continental bkfst, coffee. Restaurant adj 7 am–11 pm. Ck-out noon. Coin lndry. Meeting rm. Tennis. Balconies. Opp beach and gulf. Cr cds: A, D, DS, MC, V.

★**EDGEWATER INN.** 1936 Beach Blvd (US 90) (39531). 601/388-1100; res: 800/323-9676; FAX 601/385-2406. 30 rms, 2 story. Mar–Sept: S, D $49–$105; each addl $6; suites $139–$225; under 13, $3; wkly rates; package plans; higher rates hols; lower rates rest of yr. Crib $6. TV; cable. Indoor/outdoor pool. Restaurant open 24 hrs. Ck-out noon. Exercise equipt; bicycles, rowing machine, sauna. Lawn games. Refrigerators. Picnic tables, grills. On Gulf; opp beach. Cr cds: A, C, D, DS, ER, MC, V.

★★**QUALITY INN—EMERALD BEACH.** 1865 Beach Blvd (US 90) (39531). 601/388-3212. 62 rms, 2 story. Apr–early Sept: S $57–$65; D $65–$73; each addl $7; lower rates rest of yr. Crib $7. TV; cable. Heated pool; poolside serv. Restaurant 7 am–2 pm, 5–9 pm. Rm serv. Bar 5–10 pm. Ck-out 1 pm. Meeting rms. Bellhops. Sundries. On Gulf; private sand beach. Cr cds: A, C, D, DS, ER, MC, V, JCB.

Hotels

★★**GRANDE BILOXI BEACH RESORT.** 2060 Beach Blvd (US 90) (39531). 601/388-7000; res: 800/325-9384; FAX 601/388-3335. 287 rms, 2-8 story. May–July: S $79–$94; D $89–$104; each addl $10; suites $130–$320; under 18 free; lower rates rest of yr. Crib free. TV; cable. Pool; wading pool, poolside serv, lifeguard. Playground. Restaurant 6:30 am–10 pm. Bar 11 am–midnight, wknd to 2 am. Ck-out noon. Tennis. Balconies. On gulf, opp beach. Cr cds: A, C, D, DS, MC, V.

★★**ROYAL D'IBERVILLE.** 1980 Beach Blvd (US 90) (39531). 601/388-6610; res: 800/388-3955 (exc MS); FAX 601/388-6038. 260 rms, 9 story. S, D $40–$100; each addl $10; suites from $180; under 18 free; varied seasons; golf package. Crib free. TV. 2 pools; wading pool, whirlpool. Complimentary coffee in rms. Restaurant 6:30 am–2 pm, 5:30–9:30 pm; off-season hrs vary. Bar 11–1 am; entertainment, dancing Thurs–Sat. Ck-out 1 pm. Convention facilities. Shopping arcade. Lighted tennis. Game rm. Refrigerator in suites. Balconies. Beach opp. Cr cds: A, C, D, DS, MC, V.

Restaurants

★**CAPTAIN JAKE'S SEA 'N SIRLOIN.** 1983 Beach Blvd (US 90). 601/388-6387 or -6388. Hrs: 10 am–10 pm. Bar. Semi-a la carte: lunch $5–$10, dinner $9–$14.95. Child's meals. Specializes in seafood, steak. Parking. Outdoor dining. Nautical decor. Family-owned. Cr cds: A, DS, MC, V.

✔ ★**FISHERMAN'S WHARF.** 315 Beach Blvd (US 90). 601/436-4513. Hrs: 11 am–10 pm; Sun from noon. Beer. Semi-a la carte: lunch $3.95–$5.95, dinner $6.95–$13.95. Child's meals. Specialties: crabmeat casserole, red snapper. Parking. Overlooks Gulf. Seafood bar on pier in summer. Cr cds: A, C, D, DS, MC, V.

★★★**THE FRENCH CONNECTION.** 1891 Pass Christian Rd. 601/388-6367. Hrs: 11 am–2 pm, 5:30–9:30 pm; Sat from 5:30 pm. Closed Sun; most major hols. French, continental menu. Bar. Semi-a la carte: lunch $5.95–$10.25, dinner $9.95–$23.95. Child's meals. Specialties: tar babies, smoked oysters, shrimp Robert, laughing crab. Own baking. Parking. Outdoor dining. Open-hearth cooking. Antiques. On grounds that were once part of Beauvoir, estate of Jefferson Davis. Cr cds: A, C, D, DS, MC, V.

★HOOK, LINE & SINKER. *2030 Beach Blvd (US 90). 601/388-3757.* Hrs: 11 am–10 pm; Fri & Sat to 11 pm. Closed Mon; also 1 wk in Dec. Bar. Semi-a la carte: lunch $5–$20, dinner $10–$22. Child's meals. Specializes in seafood, broiled stuffed flounder. Parking. Nautical decor; view of gulf. Family-owned. Cr cds: A, C, D, DS, MC, V.

D

★★★MARY MAHONEY'S OLD FRENCH HOUSE. *Rue Magnolia & US 90. 601/374-0163.* Hrs: 11 am–10:30 pm. Closed Sun; Dec 24, 25. Continental menu. Bar. Wine cellar. Semi-a la carte: lunch $6.95–$10.95, dinner $10.95–$20.95. Complete meals: lunch $10.95, dinner $20.95. Child's meals. Specialties: half lobster Georgo, red snapper, oyster soup. Own bread pudding. Parking. Outdoor dining. Colonial house & slave quarters built 1737; antiques, fireplaces. Family-owned. Cr cds: A, C, D, DS, MC, V.

✔★★O'CHARLEY'S. *2590 Beach Blvd (US 90), at Edgewater Mall. 601/388-7883.* Hrs: 11 am–midnight; Fri, Sat to 1 am; Sun 8:30 am–noon. Bar. Semi-a la carte: lunch $5.99–$9.99, dinner $4.99–$16.95. Sun brunch $3.99–$12.99. Child's meals. Specializes in prime rib, seafood. Outdoor dining with view of gulf. Cr cds: A, C, D, DS, MC, V.

D **SC**

Unrated Dining Spot

MORRISON'S CAFETERIA. *Located in Edgewater Mall, 5 mi W on US 90. 601/388-4826.* Hrs: 10:45 am–8:30 pm; Sun to 8 pm. Avg ck: lunch $4.80, dinner $5. Specializes in seafood, roast beef, chicken. Cr cds: MC, V.

D

Brices Cross Roads National Battlefield Site

(see Tupelo)

Clarksdale (B-2)

Founded: 1869 **Pop:** 19,717 **Elev:** 175 ft **Area code:** 601 **Zip:** 38614

Named for John Clark, an Englishman who laid out the town in 1869, Clarksdale shared dual status with Friars Point as Coahoma County seat from 1892 until 1930. Sunflower Landing near Clarksdale is said to be the site where De Soto discovered the Mississippi River.

Clarksdale is located in the heart of the rich delta farmland, one of the state's top-ranking areas in cotton, soybean and grain production. Three lakes in the area make this a water sports center.

What to See and Do

1. **Carnegie Public Library.** 114 Delta Ave. (Daily exc Sun) Phone 624-4461. Located within the library are

   Delta Blues Museum. Videotapes, recordings and memorabilia about blues music. Permanent and changing exhibits; performances. **Free.**

   Archaeology Museum. Native American pottery and other artifacts on exhibit. Collection of books and reports on Lower Mississippi Valley archaeology. **Free.**

2. **North Delta Museum.** Friars Point-Clarksdale Rd, 12 mi NW in Friars Point. Archaeological and historical exhibits of early Delta life,

including Native American artifacts, three original log buildings and Civil War artifacts. (Tues–Sat) Phone 383-2342. **¢**

(For further information contact the Coahoma County Chamber of Commerce, US 49, PO Box 160; 627-7337.)

Annual Event

Delta Jubilee. Statewide arts & crafts festival; Mississippi championship barbecue cooking contest; 5K run, softball, tennis tournaments. First wkend June.

(See Cleveland)

Motel

✔★★COMFORT INN. *½ mi S on US 61. 601/627-9292; FAX 601/627-9292, ext 650.* 93 rms, 2 story. S $45–$48; D $50–$53; each addl $5; under 18 free. Crib free. TV; cable. Indoor/outdoor pool. Complimentary continental bkfst. Restaurant 6 am–11 pm. Rm serv. Ck-out noon. Coin lndry. Meeting rms. Exercise equipt; weights, bicycles, whirlpool. Some refrigerators. Some balconies. Cr cds: A, C, D, DS, ER, MC, V, JCB.

D **≈** **†** **⊗** **⊚** **SC**

Cleveland (B-2)

Pop: 15,384 **Elev:** 142 ft **Area code:** 601 **Zip:** 38732

What to See and Do

1. **Delta State University** (1924). (4,200 students) MS 8. On campus is

   Wright Art Gallery. Exhibits works by southern artists.

2. **Great River Road State Park.** 18 mi W on MS 8 in Rosedale. The 800-acre park is situated on the bluffs of the Mississippi River and has the state's largest campground inside the levee. Fishing in Perry Martin Lake; boating (ramp, rentals). Nature, bicycle trails. Picnicking (shelters), playground, playing field, snack bar, lodge, coin lndry. Improved & primitive camping. Four-level observation tower. Standard fees. Phone 759-6762.

(For further information contact the Chamber of Commerce, Third St, PO Box 490; 843-2712.)

Motel

✔★★CLEVELAND INN. *1 mi S on US 61. 601/846-1411; 800/533-8466; FAX 601/843-1713.* 119 rms, 2 story. S $35–$42; D $40–$47; each addl $5; under 18 free. Crib free. TV; cable. Pool. Restaurant 6 am–2 pm, 5–10 pm. Rm serv. Bar 5–11 pm; closed wkends. Ck-out noon. Cr cds: A, C, D, DS, MC, V.

D **≈** **⊗** **⊚** **SC**

Columbus (B-4)

Settled: 1817 **Pop:** 23,799 **Elev:** 200 ft **Area code:** 601

On the Tennessee-Tombigbee Waterway (also on the Buttahatchie and Luxapalila), Columbus progressed from a trading post to an educational center and repository for traditions and architecture of the Old South.

Mentioned in the state's oldest records, Columbus' site early became a stopover on the Military Road ordered built by Andrew Jackson between New Orleans and Nashville (1817–20). It was first called "Possum Town" because Indians thought that the tavernkeeper who served them looked like a wizened old possum. Columbus welcomed its first steamboat, the *Cotton Plant,* in 1822, a year after Mississippi's first public school, Franklin Academy, was established in the town.

Commerce and education went forward together. The Columbus Female Institute, founded in 1847, later became the first state-supported school in the US to offer education exclusively to women—Mississippi University for Women (1884). Columbus was a favored place for planters to build imposing houses, and in antebellum days it became the cultural center of the rich Black Prairie. During the Civil War a large Confederate arsenal was located in the town, and the state capital was moved here after Jackson fell. Columbus Air Force Base, an ATC training facility, is nine miles north.

What to See and Do

1. **Friendship Cemetery.** 4th St S and 13th Ave. Where first Memorial Day, April 25, 1866, was said to have been observed, as women of Columbus gathered to decorate graves of Union and Confederate soldiers alike.

2. **Blewett-Harrison-Lee Museum.** 316 7th St N. Contains articles of local history as well as Civil War exhibits. (Tues & Thurs afternoons; closed hols) Phone 327-8888.   **Free.**

3. **Historic houses.** Columbus boasts more than 100 antebellum houses. Some are open for tours (daily; fee). For information, free 30-minute auto tour map and narrative of houses contact the Historic Foundation, 329-3533. Tour fee per home ¢¢

4. **Lake Lowndes State Park.** 6 mi SE off MS 69. One of the finest recreation complexes among all the state parks. Approximately 600 acres with a 150-acre lake. Swimming beach, waterskiing; fishing; boating (ramps, rentals). Nature trail, tennis, game fields. Picnicking, playground, concession, indoor recreation complex, coin laundry. Improved & primitive camping, cabins. Standard fees. Phone 328-2110 or -9182.

5. **Waverley Plantation** (1852). 10 mi NW via US 45, MS 50 near West Point. Mansion with twin, circular, self-supporting stairways leading to a 65-foot-high, octagonal observation cupola; original gold-leaf mirrors and Italian marble mantels. (Daily) Phone 494-1399. ¢¢¢

(For further information contact the Columbus Convention & Visitors Bureau, PO Box 789, 39703; 329-1191 or 800/327-2686 exc MS).

Annual Event

Pilgrimage. Costumed guides conduct tours through 13 historic houses. Junior Auxiliary Pageant and Ball. 10 days, early Apr.

(See Starkville)

Motels

✔ ★**COMFORT INN.** *1210 US 45N (39701). 601/329-2422.* 64 rms, 2 story. S $40–$44; D $44–$48; each addl $4; under 12 free. Crib free. TV; cable. Complimentary continental bkfst. Restaurant opp 11 am–9 pm. Ck-out noon. Meeting rms. Cr cds: A, C, D, DS, ER, MC, V, JCB.

★★**HOLIDAY INN.** *506 US 45N (39701),* ¼ *mi S off US 82 Bypass. 601/328-5202; FAX 601/328-5202, ext 141.* 153 rms, 2 story. S, D $43–$56; each addl $5. Crib free. Pet accepted, some restrictions. TV; cable. Pool. Restaurant 6 am–2 pm, 5–10 pm. Rm serv. Bar 4–11 pm. Ck-out noon. Meeting rms. Valet serv. Cr cds: A, C, D, DS, MC, V, JCB.

★★**RAMADA INN.** *1200 US 45N (39701),* at jct US 82 Bypass. *601/327-7077; FAX 601/327-2807.* 121 rms, 4 story. S $47–$51; D $55–$59; each addl $8; suites $85–$175; studio rms $45; under 16 free. Crib free. TV; cable. Pool. Restaurant 6 am–1:30pm, 6–10 pm. Rm serv.

Bar 4 pm–midnight; Sat from 6 pm; entertainment, dancing exc Sun. Ck-out noon. Meeting rms. Bellhops. Cr cds: A, C, D, DS, MC, V.

Restaurants

★★**HARVEY'S.** *200 Main St. 601/327-1639.* Hrs: 11 am–2 pm, 5:30–9:30 pm; Fri, Sat to 10 pm. Closed Sun; some major hols. Res accepted. Bar 4:30–11 pm; Fri, Sat to midnight. Semi-a la carte: lunch $3.95–$13.95, dinner $4.25–$14.95. Serv charge. Child's meals. Specializes in prime rib, seafood, salads. Parking. Restored tannery; antiques. Cr cds: A, DS, MC, V.

D

★**J C GARCIA'S.** *1911 US 45N. 601/329-3616.* Hrs: 11 am–10 pm; Fri, Sat to 11 pm. Closed Dec 25. Mexican, Amer menu. Bar to midnight. Semi-a la carte: lunch $3.50–$17, dinner $4.50–$17. Serv charge. Child's meals. Specializes in traditional Mexican cuisine. Patio entertainment wkends. Parking. Outdoor dining. Cr cds: A, C, DS, MC, V.

D

✔ ★**OLD HICKORY STEAKHOUSE.** *1405 US 45N. 601/328-9793.* Hrs: 11 am–2 pm, 5–10 pm; Mon–Wed to 2 pm. Closed Sun; major hols. Buffet: lunch $5, dinner $10.95. Child's meals. Specializes in prime rib, crab legs. Parking. Casual family dining. Cr cds: MC, V.

D

Corinth (A-4)

Founded: 1855 **Pop:** 11,820 **Elev:** 455 ft **Area code:** 601 **Zip:** 38834

The Memphis and Charleston and the Mobile and Ohio railroads selected this spot as a junction point, calling the town Cross City. Later the name was changed to honor the Greek city.

After being defeated at the Battle of Shiloh (Apr 6–7, 1862), Confederate General P.G.T. Beauregard retreated to Corinth. On Oct 3–4, 1862, Union forces, aiming at Vicksburg, took the town and held it until Jan 25, 1864. The Corinth National Cemetery, established in 1866, has approximately 6,000 markers.

What to See and Do

1. **Curlee House** (1857). 705 Jackson St. Restored antebellum house; served as headquarters for Generals Bragg, Halleck and Hood during Civil War. (Varied hrs; closed Dec 25) Phone 287-9501 or -5269. ¢

2. **Jacinto Courthouse** (1854). 15 mi SE in Jacinto. Fine example of early federal architecture was first courthouse for old Tishomingo County; later used as both school and church. (Daily)   **Free.**

3. **Battery Robinette.** W on Linden St. Union fort constructed on inner defense lines during Battle of Corinth (1862). Monuments mark spots where Confederate heroes died; headstones commemorate color-bearers who fell while trying to plant flag during battle.

(For further information contact the Corinth-Alcorn Area Chamber of Commerce, 810 Tate St, PO Box 1089; 287-5269.)

Motel

✔ ★★**EXECUTIVE INN.** *(Box 2400) US 72, jct US 45 Bypass. 601/286-6071; 800/354-3932; FAX 601/286-9608.* 125 rms, 2–3 story, 6 kits. S $35–$39; D $37–$42; each addl $4; kit. units $45–$49; under 12 free. Crib free. Pet accepted. TV; cable. Pool. Restaurant 6 am–2 pm, 4–9:30 pm. Rm serv. Ck-out noon. Meeting rms. Cr cds: A, C, D, DS, MC, V.

Greenville (C-1)

Settled: 1828 **Pop:** 45,226 **Elev:** 125 ft **Area code:** 601

Greenville, which is not even on the Mississippi, is the state's largest river port. The Mississippi River was, in 1935, finally broken of its habit of stealing whole areas of the town, block by block. Levees forced the channel six miles westward and left a lake for a harbor. Before this, in 1927, the whole town was under water for 70 days. The first Greenville settlement was on the Blantonia Plantation (1828), which was purchased for the site of the third county seat. The first was flooded out; the second burned during shelling by Union gunboats in 1863.

What to See and Do

1. *River Road Queen.* 2 mi W via US 82, near Mississippi River. Replica of 19th-century paddlewheel steamboat. Built for 1984 World's Fair; now serves as town's welcome center. (Daily exc Sun) Phone 332-2378.
2. **Jim Henson Museum.** 8 mi E via US 82, in Leland. Muppet memorabilia from collectors and the family of the late Jim Henson, creator of the Muppets. (Mon–Fri; Sat, Sun & hols by appt) Phone 686-2687. **Free.**
3. **Winterville Mounds State Park.** 3 mi N off MS 1. One of the largest groups of Indian mounds in the Mississippi Valley, the area was a religious site and economic and military center for thousands of Indians of the Mississippian era, who disappeared sometime after De Soto's exploration. Great Temple mound, 55 feet high, is surrounded by 10 smaller mounds used for a variety of purposes. Picnicking (shelters), concession, playground. Museum houses artifacts from mound site and adjoining territory (Wed–Sat & Sun afternoons; closed Dec 25) Phone 334-4684. Museum ¢
4. **Leroy Percy State Park.** 18 mi S on MS 1, then 8 mi E on MS 12. The oldest of Mississippi's state parks is composed of approximately 2,400 acres. One of the four hot artesian wells provides water for an alligator pond (view from boardwalk). Nature trails lead through Delta lowlands. Nearby is live alligator exhibit. Swimming pool (Memorial Day–Labor Day, daily); fishing, hunting; boating (rentals). Picnicking (shelters), playground, game field, snack bar, restaurant, lodge, coin lndry. Improved & primitive camping, cabins. Standard fees. Phone 827-5436.

(For information about recreation in this area contact the Greenville Area Chamber of Commerce, PO Drawer 933, 38701; 378-3141 or the Washington County Convention & Visitors Bureau, PO Box 5217, 38704; 334-2711.)

Annual Event

Delta Blues Festival. 3rd Sat Sept.

Motels

★★**BEST WESTERN REGENCY INN.** *2428 US 82E (38703). 601/334-6900.* 119 rms, 2 story, 13 suites. S, D $45–$51; each addl $6; suites $59–$65; kit. units $46–$52; under 17 free. Crib $5. TV; cable. Heated indoor/outdoor pool; wading pool. Complimentary continental bkfst. Complimentary coffee in rms. Ck-out noon. Coin Indry. Meeting rms. Exercise equipt; weight machines, bicycles, whirlpool. Refrigerators. Cr cds: A, C, D, DS, MC, V.

✔★**DAYS INN.** *(Box 1139, 38701) US 82E, 6 mi W of US 61. 601/335-1999; FAX 601/332-1144.* 153 rms, 2 story. S $29–$35; D $37–$45; each addl $3. TV; cable. Pool. Complimentary continental bkfst. Bar 5 pm–2 am, closed Sun; entertainment, dancing. Ck-out noon. Meeting rms. Game rm. Cr cds: A, C, D, DS, MC, V.

★★**HAMPTON INN.** *2701 US 82E (38701). 601/334-1818; FAX 601/334-1818, ext 295.* 120 units, 2 story. S, D $47–$55; each addl $6; studio rms $50–$56; under 12 free. Crib free. TV; cable. Pool; whirlpool. Complimentary continental bkfst. Ck-out noon. Meeting rm. Cr cds: A, D, DS, MC, V.

★★**RAMADA INN.** *2700 US 82E (38701). 601/332-4411; FAX 601/332-4411, ext 171.* 121 rms, 2 story. S $34–$51; D $47–$55; each addl $5. Crib free. TV; cable. Pool. Playground. Complimentary full bkfst (wkdays). Restaurant 6 am–10 pm. Rm serv. Bar 4 pm–2 am, closed Sun; dancing. Ck-out noon. Meeting rms. Sundries. Some refrigerators. Cr cds: A, C, D, DS, MC, V, JCB.

Greenwood (B-2)

Settled: 1834 **Pop:** 18,906 **Elev:** 140 ft **Area code:** 601 **Zip:** 38930

Lying on both banks of the Yazoo River and surrounded by rich, black delta lands, Greenwood was a river port shipping cotton before the Civil War and a rail center after Reconstruction.

The town grew from a river landing established on 162 acres of land bought for $1.25 an acre by John Williams. Planters who used his landing to ship their cotton included Choctaw Chief Greenwood Leflore. After a quarrel about Williams' storage methods, the chief built his own landing with a warehouse three miles up the river, calling it Point Leflore. However, the original landing flourished and absorbed the trade of its rival. Today Greenwood is one of the nation's largest cotton markets.

What to See and Do

1. **Cottonlandia Museum.** 2 mi W on US 49E, US 82 Bypass W. Exhibits highlight the history of the Mississippi Delta, its people and its land from 10,000 B.C. to the present. Also Mississippi art exhibit; garden; gift shop. (Daily) Phone 453-0925. ¢¢
2. **Florewood River Plantation.** 2 mi W on US 82. Re-creation of 1850s plantation and outbuildings; crops worked and harvested; cotton museum; steam engine displays; crafts demonstrations. Tours (mid-Mar–early Dec, daily exc Mon; limited tours rest of yr). Phone 455-3821. ¢¢

(For further information contact the Convention & Visitors Bureau, PO Box 739; 453-9197.)

(See Grenada)

Motels

★★★**BEST WESTERN REGENCY INN.** *(Box 8288) 635 US 82W. 601/455-5777; FAX 601/455-5777, ext 411.* 100 rms, 2 story. S $45–$48; D $53–$54; each addl $5; under 18 free. Crib free. TV; cable. Indoor/outdoor pool; wading pool. Complimentary continental bkfst. Restaurant 6 am–11 pm. Rm serv. Ck-out noon. Coin Indry. Meeting rms. Valet serv. Tennis. Exercise equipt; weight machines, bicycles, whirlpool. Refrigerators. Some balconies. Cr cds: A, C, D, DS, MC, V.

✔★**COMFORT INN.** *401 US 82W. 601/453-5974.* 60 rms, 2 story. S $35–$37; D $36–$39; each addl $5; under 18 free; wkly rates. Crib $3. TV; cable. Pool. Complimentary continental bkfst, coffee. Restaurant adj 10 am–10 pm. Ck-out noon. Park, picnic grounds opp. Cr cds: A, C, D, DS, MC, V, JCB.

★**DAYS INN.** *621 US 82W. 601/453-0030; FAX 601/453-0030, ext 300.* 50 rms, 2 story. S $30; D $38; each addl $5; under 18 free. Crib free. TV; cable. Pool. Complimentary continental bkfst, coffee.

Restaurant nearby. Ck-out noon. Meeting rms. Bathrm phones; some refrigerators. Cr cds: A, C, D, DS, MC, V.

★ ★**RAMADA INN.** *900 W Park Ave. 601/455-2321; FAX 601/ 455-2321, ext 303.* 147 rms, 2 story. S, studio rms $35–$45; D $43–$48; each addl $5; suites $130–$175; under 12 free. Crib $5. TV. Pool; whirlpool. Restaurant 6 am–10 pm. Rm serv. Bar 4 pm–1 am; entertainment, dancing exc Sun. Ck-out noon. Meeting rms. Sundries. Free airport, bus depot transportation. Cr cds: A, C, D, DS, MC, V, JCB.

Restaurant

★ ★**CRYSTAL GRILL, INC.** *423 Carrollton Ave. 601/453-6530.* Hrs: 10:30 am–10 pm. Closed Mon; most major hols & Dec 24. Res accepted. Bar from 11 am. Semi-a la carte: lunch $4.55–$7.45, dinner $4.75–$18.50. Child's meals. Specializes in seafood, steak. Parking. Family-owned. Cr cds: MC, V.

Grenada (B-3)

Pop: 10,864 **Elev:** 195 ft **Area code:** 601 **Zip:** 38901

The economy of Grenada had from early days been based on cotton. Today, it is diversified; industry and tourism, as well as agriculture, support this town located on the eastern edge of the Mississippi Delta. Founded as two towns by political rivals, the two communities united in 1836. The union was literally symbolized by a wedding in which the bride came from one town and the groom from the other. Confederate General John C. Pemberton headquartered in Grenada while opposing Grant's second Vicksburg campaign.

What to See and Do

1. **Historic Old Grenada.** Motor and walking tour of houses and churches. For brochure contact Chamber of Commerce.

2. **Grenada Lake.** 5 mi NE off MS 8. Covers approximately 35,000 acres, with 200 miles of shoreline. Swimming, water sports; fishing, hunting; boat launch. Fitness trails; archery, tennis, ball fields. Picnicking. Primitive & improved camping (fee at some sites). Visitor center at Grenada Dam on Scenic Loop 333. (Daily) Phone 226-5911. **Free.** On lake is

    Hugh White State Park. 5 mi E on MS 8, then 3½ mi N. A 1,581-acre park with swimming beach, pool, waterskiing; fishing; boating (ramp, rentals). Nature, bicycle trails; tennis nearby. Picnicking (shelters), playground, restaurant (daily exc Mon), lodge. Primitive & improved camping, cabins, camp store. Standard fees. Phone 226-4934.

(For further information contact the Grenada County Chamber of Commerce, 701 Sunset Dr, PO Box 628; 226-2571.)

(See Greenwood)

Motels

★**COMFORT INN.** *1552 Sunset Dr. 601/226-1683; FAX 601/226-9484.* 66 rms, 2 story. May–Sept: S $38–$50; D $40–$55; each addl $5; under 18 free; lower rates rest of yr. Crib $5. TV; cable. Pool; whirlpool. Complimentary continental bkfst, coffee. Restaurant nearby. Ck-out noon. Meeting rms. Refrigerators. Cr cds: A, C, D, DS, MC, V.

✔ ★**DAYS INN.** *1632 Sunset Dr. 601/226-8888.* 53 rms, 2 story. S $34–$38; D $38–$48; each addl $5; under 12 free. Crib free. TV;

cable. Pool; hot tub. Complimentary coffee. Restaurant adj 7 am–10 pm. Ck-out 11 am. Meeting rms. Cr cds: A, C, D, DS, ER, MC, V, JCB.

★ ★**HOLIDAY INN.** *(Box 697) MS 7/8, ⅛ mi E of I-55 exit 206. 601/226-2851; FAX 601/226-5058.* 134 rms, 2 story. S, D $38–$54; each addl $7; suites $165; under 18 free. Crib free. TV; cable. Pool; wading pool. Restaurant 6 am–2 pm, 5–10 pm. Rm serv. Ck-out noon. Coin lndry. Meeting rms. Cr cds: A, C, D, DS, MC, V, JCB.

Restaurant

✔ ★**EVERGREEN.** *Off MS 8W, ½ mi E of I-55, on Frontage Rd. 601/227-1420.* Hrs: 10 am–11 pm; Fri, Sat to midnight. Closed Dec 25. Semi-a la carte: lunch $3.95–$6.25, dinner $6.95–$14.95. Child's meals. Specializes in seafood, char-grilled beef, smoked ribs. Salad bar. Parking. Cr cds: A, DS, MC, V.

Gulf Islands National Seashore (F-4)

Headquarters and campground for the Mississippi district of this beautiful area are in Ocean Springs. Sparkling beaches, coastal marshes and wildlife sanctuaries may be found on the four offshore islands (Petit Bois, Horn, East and West Ship) and the mainland area (Davis Bayou). The mainland areas are open year round and are accessible from US 90.

In 1969, Hurricane Camille split Ship Island in two, leaving East Ship and West Ship Islands. Ship Island was once a base for French exploration and settlement (1699–1753) of the Gulf Coast from Mobile, Alabama, to the mouth of the Mississippi River. What is now East Ship Island once served as the staging area for a 50-ship British armada and an unsuccessful attempt to capture New Orleans in 1815 at the end of the War of 1812.

On West Ship Island is Fort Massachusetts. Construction of this brick coastal defense began in 1859, prior to the outbreak of the Civil War. Two years later the Mississippi militia took control of the fort from the US Army Corps of Engineers after the state seceded from the Union. The Confederates later fortified it, naming it Fort Twiggs in honor of the New Orleans Confederate general. Repeated threats by Northern forces caused the Confederates to withdraw in September, 1861. The fort was then reoccupied by Union soldiers, who called it Fort Massachusetts. For a time, the area east of the fort served as a prisoner-of-war camp, confining some 4,300 Confederate prisoners at one point. Completed in 1866, the fort was never fully armed. Free tours of the fort are offered daily (Mar–Nov). Concession boats run to Fort Massachusetts and West Ship Island from Biloxi (Apr–Nov) and Gulfport (Mar–Oct), depending on weather conditions.

All four offshore islands are accessible year round by boat only and are open to wilderness camping (except on West Ship Island), surf fishing, surf swimming (lifeguard on south shore of West Ship Island only, Memorial Day–Labor Day), boating, picnicking and hiking. No motor vehicles or glass are allowed on the islands. Horn and Petit Bois are designated as wilderness areas, and special restrictions apply.

The mainland campground has water and electric hookups (fee) at 51 sites, a public boat dock and picnic areas. The visitor center offers audiovisual programs, exhibits, boardwalks and nature trails. There are free guided marsh tours through Davis Bayou (Memorial Day–Labor Day, wkends only). Pets are allowed on leash only. **Free.**

(For further information contact Park Office, 3500 Park Rd, Ocean Springs 39564; 601/875-0821.)

(For accommodations see Biloxi, Gulfport, also see Ocean Springs)

Gulfport (F-3)

Founded: 1880 **Pop:** 40,775 **Elev:** 20 ft **Area code:** 601

Although chosen as an ideal site for a port and a railroad terminus in 1887, it was 1902 before the Gulf & Ship Island Railroad's New York owner fulfilled the plan. As a planned city, Gulfport has broad streets laid out in a regular rectangular pattern paralleling the seawall. This was in marked contrast to the narrow-streeted antebellum towns along the rest of the coast. When completed, the railroad, which ran through sparsely settled sections rich in timber, transformed southern Mississippi.

Gulfport turned to the resort business in the 1920s and had a real estate boom in 1925 when the Illinois Central Railroad bought the Gulf & Ship Island line. The boom collapsed a year later after having produced Gulfport's tower apartments and many hotels. After World War II, luxury motels took over. With the Mississippi Sound and a great number of lakes, rivers, bays and bayous within a few minutes drive from downtown, and with excellent facilities for deep-sea fishing, Gulfport is a fisherman's paradise.

Mississippi City, which has been incorporated into Gulfport, was the scene of the bare-knuckles fight for the heavyweight championship of the world on Feb 7, 1882, when John L. Sullivan beat Paddy Ryan under the live oaks now at the corner of US 90 and Texas Street.

What to See and Do

1. **Boat trips.** Passenger ferry leaves from Gulfport Yacht Harbor for trips to Ship Island. (Mar–Nov) Schedule varies; for information contact Ship Island Excursions, PO Box 1467, 39502; 864-1014 (recording), 432-2197 (Biloxi, recording) or 864-3797 (office). Round trip ¢¢¢¢

2. **Small Craft Harbor.** Jct US 49, 90. Launching ramps, charter boats and pleasure craft docking. Adjacent is

   Marine Life Oceanarium. Jones Park. Dolphin and sea lion feedings, giant reef tank, underwater divers, touch pool. Also Aqua Stadium with exotic birds and Captain Crooked's SS *Gravity.* (Daily; closed Dec 25) Phone 863-0651. ¢¢¢

3. **Grass Lawn.** 720 E Beach. Summer house built in 1836 features 10-foot-wide galleries supported by 2-story box columns. (Mon, Wed & Fri; closed major hols) Phone 864-5019. ¢

4. **Port of Gulfport.** Extends seaward from jct US 49, 90, located equidistant between New Orleans and Mobile, AL. One of the largest banana import facilities in the US; the projected depth of the channel is 32 feet; the depth of the harbor is 30 feet at mean low water with a tidal variation of approx 2 feet. The 1,320-foot wide harbor separates the port's 2 parallel piers; 11 berths are available.

5. **John C. Stennis Space Center.** 38 mi W via I-10. Second-largest NASA field installation. Testing site of Saturn V, first and second stages for the Apollo manned lunar program, including those for Apollo 11, which landed first men on moon in 1969. Original test stands were later modified to develop and test space shuttle main engines. The Stennis Space Center hosts NASA and 18 federal and state agencies involved in oceanographic, environmental and national defense programs. Visitor Center with 90-foot Space Tower; films, demonstrations; indoor, outdoor exhibits; guided tours (daily; closed Easter, Thanksgiving, Dec 25). Phone 688-2370. **Free.**

6. **Gulf Islands National Seashore** (see).

   (For further information contact the Chamber of Commerce, 1401 20th Ave, PO Drawer FF, 39502; 863-2933.)

Annual Events

Spring Pilgrimage. Tours of antebellum houses, gardens. Contact Biloxi Community Center for details (432-5836). Late Mar–early Apr.

Mississippi Deep-Sea Fishing Rodeo. Small Craft Harbor. Fishermen from US, Canada and Latin America compete in various types of sportfishing. Phone 388-2271 or 863-2713. Early July.

(See Biloxi, Ocean Springs, Pass Christian)

Motel

★ **GULF VIEW.** *(526 West Beach, Long Beach 39560)* Approx 4 mi W on US 90. 601/863-3713. 50 rms, 2 story, 23 kit. units. May–Sept: S $45–$65; D $60–$68; each addl $3; kit. units $68–$115; lower rates rest of yr. Crib $7. TV; cable. Pool. Playground. Ck-out 1 pm. Cr cds: A, C, D, MC, V.

Motor Hotels

★★ **BEST WESTERN BEACH VIEW INN.** *2922 W Beach Blvd (US 90) (39501).* 601/864-4650; FAX 601/863-6867. 150 rms, 5 story. Mid-May–Labor Day: S $65; D $75; each addl $6; suites $130–$150; under 16 free; higher rates wknds; lower rates rest of yr. Crib free. TV; cable. Pool. Restaurant 6:30 am–2 pm, 5–10 pm. Rm serv. Bar 10–2 am; entertainment, dancing. Ck-out 11 am. Meeting rms. Bellhops. Overlooks harbor. Cr cds: A, C, D, DS, MC, V.

★★ **HOLIDAY INN-BEACHFRONT.** *1600 E Beach Blvd (39501).* 601/864-4310; FAX 601/865-0525. 229 rms, 2–5 story. May–Labor Day: S $65–$76; D $75–$86; 1st addl $10, 2nd addl $5; under 19 free; lower rates rest of yr. Crib free. TV; cable. Pool; wading pool, poolside serv. Restaurant 6 am–10 pm. Rm serv. Bar 2 pm–1 am; entertainment wkends. Ck-out noon. Coin lndry. Meeting rms. Bellhops. Valet serv. Sundries. Free airport transportation. Game rm. Balconies. Opp beach. Cr cds: A, C, D, DS, MC, V, JCB.

Inn

✔ ★ **RED CREEK COLONIAL.** *(7416 Red Creek Rd, Long Beach 39560)* Approx 8 mi W on US 90, N on Menge Ave to Red Creek Rd. 601/452-3080. 3 rms, 2 story. No rm phones. S $39–$59; D $49–$69. Pet accepted, some restrictions. Complimentary continental bkfst. Complimentary coffee in rms. Ck-out noon, ck-in 3 pm. Lawn games. French colonial house (1899) with 6 fireplaces, antique furnishings; 64-ft front porch. Situated on 11 acres of magnolia trees and ancient live oaks. Totally nonsmoking. No cr cds accepted.

Restaurant

✔ ★ **WHITE CAP.** *Gulfport Yacht Harbor.* 601/863-4652. Hrs: 11:30 am–9 pm; Fri, Sat to 9:30 pm; Sun from noon. Closed Tues; Jan 1, Thanksgiving; also last 2 wks Dec. Bar. Semi-a la carte: lunch $4.45–$4.95, dinner $8–$14. Child's meals. Specializes in seafood. Parking. On pier. Nautical decor. Family-owned. Cr cds: MC, V.

Hattiesburg (E-3)

Founded: 1882 **Pop:** 41,882 **Elev:** 161 ft **Area code:** 601

Once known as Twin Forks and Gordonville, the settlement was renamed by an early settler in honor of his wife, Hattie. When railroads were routed through Hattiesburg during the late 19th century, the town began to thrive. Unlike other towns that came and went with the lumber boom of the 1920s, Hattiesburg was able to diversify its economic base with a number of industries. The University of Southern Mississippi (see

#1) makes the town the educational center of the southern sector of the state.

What to See and Do

1. **University of Southern Mississippi** (1910). (12,000 students) 2700 Hardy St. Library houses large collection of original illustrations and manuscripts for children's books by authors and artists from here and abroad. American Rose Society garden on campus, blooms spring–mid-Dec. Also Science & Technology Bldg, Performing Arts Center, Danforth Chapel, Polymer Research Center, art gallery, natatorium and golf course. For tours phone 266-4491.

2. **Paul B. Johnson State Park.** 15 mi S off US 49. More than 805 acres of pine forest. A spring-fed lake provides excellent facilities for water sports. Swimming beach, waterskiing; fishing; boating (ramp, rentals). Nature trail. Picnicking (shelters), playground, playing fields, snack bar, lodge with game rm, coin lndry. Improved & primitive camping, cabins. Visitor center. Standard fees. Phone 582-7721.

3. **De Soto National Forest.** 10 mi SE on US 49. Approximately 500,000 acres. Black Creek Float Trip offers 50 miles of scenic streams. Black Creek Trail has 41 miles of trails, 10 of which go through 5,000 acres of Black Creek Wilderness. Fees may be charged at designated recreation sites. Swimming; fishing. Hiking, bridle trails. Picnicking. Primitive camping. Ranger District offices are located in Laurel, Wiggins and McHenry. Contact Forest Supervisor, 100 W Capitol St, Suite 1141, Jackson 39269; 965-4391 or -5514.

(For further information contact the Chamber of Commerce, PO Box 751, 39403; 545-3300.)

Motels

★ ★ **COMFORT INN.** 6595 US 49 (39401), off I-59 exit 67A. 601/268-2170; FAX 601/261-2504. 119 rms, 2 story. S $46–$52; D $52–$58; each addl $6; under 18 free. Crib free. TV; cable. Pool; poolside serv. Restaurant 6:30 am–2 pm, 5–9 pm. Rm serv. Bar 5 pm–midnight; entertainment, dancing. Ck-out noon. Coin lndry. Meeting rms. Cr cds: A, C, D, DS, MC, V.

✔ ★ ★ **HAMPTON INN.** 4301 Hardy St (39402). 601/264-8080; FAX 601/264-8080, ext 161. 116 units, 2 story. S $43–$47; D $48–$52; under 18 free. Crib free. TV; cable. Pool. Complimentary continental bkfst. Ck-out noon. Meeting rm. Health club privileges. Cr cds: A, C, D, DS, MC, V.

★ ★ **HOLIDAY INN.** 6563 US 49 (39401), off I-59 exit 67A. 601/268-2850; FAX 601/268-2850, ext 309. 128 rms, 2 story. S, D $53–$59; each addl $6; under 18 free. Crib free. TV; cable. Pool; whirlpool. Restaurant 6:30 am–2 pm, 5–10 pm. Rm serv. Bar 4:30 pm–midnight; entertainment, dancing. Ck-out noon. Meeting rms. Lighted tennis. Some refrigerators. Cr cds: A, C, D, DS, MC, V, JCB.

Restaurants

★ ★ **AUSTIN'S.** 304 Broadway. 601/582-3363. Hrs: 11 am–10 pm; Sat from 5 pm; Sun 11 am–2 pm. Closed most major hols & Dec 24. Continental menu. Bar 3 pm–midnight. Semi-a la carte: lunch $5–$10, dinner $10–$16. Child's meals. Specializes in seafood, prime rib. Entertainment, Tues–Sat. Parking. Cr cds: A, C, D, MC, V.

✔ ★ ★ **CHESTERFIELD'S.** 2507 Hardy St. 601/582-2778. Hrs: 11 am–11 pm; Sun to 10 pm. Closed July 4, Thanksgiving, Dec 25. Bar to midnight. Semi-a la carte: lunch, dinner $4.25–$14.95. Child's meals.

Specializes in prime rib, steak, seafood. Parking. Cr cds: A, C, D, DS, MC, V.

✔ ★ ★ **ROCKET CITY DINER.** 4700 Hardy St, at the Arbor in Turtle Creek Shopping Ctr. 601/264-7893. Hrs: 11 am–10 pm; Fri, Sat to 11 pm. Closed July 4, Dec 25. Beer. Semi-a la carte: lunch, dinner $3.50–$10.95. Child's meals. Specializes in hamburgers, country-fried steak. 1950s atmosphere. Cr cds: A, DS, MC, V.

★ ★ **STOCKYARD STEAKS.** 3810 Hardy St. 601/264-0656. Hrs: 11 am–2 pm, 5–10 pm; Sun brunch 11 am–3 pm. Closed Thanksgiving, Dec 25. Res accepted Fri, Sat. French, creole menu. Bar to 2 am. Semi-a la carte: lunch $6–$12, dinner $12–$20. Sun brunch $8–$15. Child's meals. Specializes in steak, pasta, seafood. Jazz combo Sun. Parking. Local original art. Casual, elegant dining. Cr cds: A, MC, V.

Unrated Dining Spots

MACK'S FISH CAMP. 820 River Rd, 3 mi N off US 49. 601/582-5101. Hrs: 4–9 pm; Fri & Sat to 10 pm. Closed Sun; Dec 24, 25. Res accepted. Semi-a la carte: dinner $5.95–$10.95. Buffet: dinner (Tues–Sat) $10.95. Child's meals. Specializes in catfish, shrimp. Salad bar. Parking. Family-style serv. Family-owned. Cr cds: MC, V.

MORRISON'S CAFETERIA. 999 Broadway Dr, in Cloverleaf Mall. 601/545-3241. Hrs: 10:45 am–8:30 pm; Sun to 7:30 pm. Avg ck: lunch $4.65, dinner $4.75. Specializes in fried shrimp, roast beef. Cr cds: MC, V.

Holly Springs (A-3)

Founded: 1835 **Pop:** 7,261 **Elev:** 609 ft **Area code:** 601 **Zip:** 38635

Holly Springs crowns the ridge along which an Indian trail once led from the Mississippi to the tribal home of the Chickasaw Nation. William Randolph, descendant of Virginia's famed John Randolph, is credited with founding the town.

Wealth from cotton went into buying more and more land, driving up real estate prices. Soon lawyers, who were needed to cope with squabbles over land and deeds, outnumbered all other professionals. The town skipped the frontier stage as Georgian and Greek-revival mansions rose instead of log cabins.

Holly Springs suffered 61 raids during the Civil War; the most devastating was by a Southern force led by Confederate General Van Dorn in 1862; the Confederates destroyed General Grant's supply base, delaying the fall of Vicksburg by a year.

What to See and Do

1. **Kate Freeman Clark Art Gallery.** College Ave. Endowed by the artist to permanently house her works, the gallery contains more than 1,000 paintings done while Clark studied under William Merritt Chase in New York in the early 1900s. Clark returned to her native Holly Springs in 1923 and simply stored her work until her death 40 years later. Also here are three canvasses by Chase and one by Rockwell Kent. For schedule inquire at Bank of Holly Springs, phone 252-2511 or First State Bank, phone 252-4211. ¢

2. **Marshall County Historical Museum.** 220 E College Ave at Randolph St. Local historical artifacts; Civil War Room; quilts; dolls; toys; antique clothing; wildlife exhibits. Library. (Daily; closed wk before Christmas) Phone 252-3669. ¢

3. **Rust College** (1866). (1,075 students) Memphis & Rust Aves. Site of campground for General Grant's troops. On campus is Leontyne Price Library, which houses the Roy Wilkins Collection on civil rights. Tours. Phone 252-8000, ext 4074.

4. **Holly Springs National Forest.** NE & SE via US 78, MS 4, 7. Intensive erosion-control measures are carried out within this 152,200-acre area. Fishing, large and small game hunting; boating at Puskus, Chewalla and Tillatoba lakes. Picnicking. Primitive camping. Fees are charged at designated recreation sites. There is a Ranger District station in Holly Springs, 252-2633. Contact Forest Supervisor, 100 W Capitol St, Suite 1141, Jackson 39269; 965-4391.

5. **Wall Doxey State Park.** 7 mi S off MS 7. Park covering 850 acres located on a spring-fed lake. Swimming beach (3-level diving pier); fishing; boating (ramp, rentals). Nature trail. Picnicking (shelters), playground, playing field, snack bar, lodge. Improved & primitive camping, cabins. Standard fees. (See ANNUAL EVENTS) Phone 252-4231. Per car ¢

6. **Green Line Tour.** Driving tour of historic buildings and sites of city outlined in brochure; map shows 90 points of interest with brief history. Obtain guidebook at Chamber of Commerce office, 154 S Memphis, phone 252-2943. ¢¢

(For further information contact the Chamber of Commerce, 154 S Memphis; 252-2943.)

Annual Events

Civil War Living History Expo. In Wall Doxey State Park (see #5). Reenactment of Union and Confederate soldiers in encampment portrays military lifestyle during Civil War. Apr.

Pilgrimage. Historic houses and gardens open to visitors. For schedule and fee information phone 252-2943. Apr.

(See Memphis, TN)

Motel

★**HERITAGE INN.** *(Box 476) MS 7 & US 78 Bypass. 601/252-1120.* 48 rms, 2 story. S $39–$48; D $44–$53; each addl $5; under 12 free. Crib free. TV; cable. Pool. Restaurant 6 am–10 pm. Rm serv. Ckout noon. Meeting rms. Cr cds: A, C, D, DS, MC, V.

Inn

★★**HAMILTON PLACE.** *105 E Mason Ave. 601/252-4368.* 3 rms. S $65; D $75; each addl $15; under 12, $10; wkly rates. TV. Pool. Complimentary full bkfst. Antebellum house (1838); antique furnishings. Carriage house; formal gardens. Cr cds: MC, V.

Jackson (D-2)

Founded: 1821 **Pop:** 196,637 **Elev:** 294 ft **Area code:** 601

The beautiful site of Jackson, along the bluffs above the Pearl River, was selected as a perfect location for commerce by a young French Canadian trader. Although Louis LeFleur succeeded in his aim and set up a trading post after his exploratory voyage up the Pearl from the Gulf of Mexico, the city has throughout its existence been a center of government, rather than business.

It is impossible to separate the town's history from its role as state capital; it was designated such as soon as the state's boundaries had expanded sufficiently, by the ceding of Indian lands, to make Jackson the state's geographical center. The first session of the legislature held in the town convened in January of 1822. By then the city had already been named for Andrew Jackson, idol of Mississippi, and laid out in a checkerboard pattern in accordance with Thomas Jefferson's recommendation to Governor Claiborne 17 years earlier. Evidence still remains of the original plan, which reserved every other square as a park or green.

There were attempts in 1829 to move the capital to Clinton and in the following year to Port Gibson, but these were averted by a legislative act of 1832 that named Jackson as the capital until 1850—by which time it had a permanent stature. Andrew Jackson addressed the legislature in what is now the Old Capitol in 1840, the year after its completion, and a Mississippi Convention assembled to consider Henry Clay's last compromise in 1850. The building was the scene of the Secession Convention in January, 1861.

Jackson was the junction of two great railroads by the time of the Civil War; it played an important role as Confederate capital of Mississippi until it was besieged in 1863, when the capital was removed and the city destroyed. All that was recorded in Jackson of the state's turbulent politics and government went up in smoke when General Sherman's army reduced the city to ashes, bringing it the ironic nickname, "Chimneyville."

The so-called "Black and Tan" convention that met at Jackson in January, 1868, was the first political organization in Mississippi with black representation. It framed a constitution under which Mississippi lived for 22 years, giving blacks the franchise and enabling a few to attain high political office. In the same year, the governor was ejected from his office, and the carpetbaggers reigned until 1876. Jefferson Davis made his last public appearance in Jackson in 1884.

With the coming of the 20th century and half a dozen railroads connecting Jackson with the whole South, the population doubled within five years. Further growth came with the discovery of natural gas fields in 1930. The Ross Barnett Reservoir (see #15), covering 31,000 acres in central Mississippi, created tourist and recreational attractions as well as residential and industrial sites in the greater Jackson area.

What to See and Do

1. **State Capitol** (1903). 400 High St. Impeccably restored in 1979, the lavish, beaux-arts capitol building was patterned after the national capitol in Washington. Houses legislature and governor's office. Tours (Mon–Fri). Phone 359-3114. **Free.**

2. **Governor's Mansion** (1842). 300 E Capitol St, between N Congress & N West Sts. Restored to original plan and Greek-revival style; antiques and period furnishings. Grounds occupy entire block and feature gardens, gazebos; Tours. (Tues–Fri, mornings only; closed during official state functions) Phone 359-3175. **Free.**

3. **Old Capitol.** E end of Capitol St at State St. Houses State Historical Museum. Exhibits tracing state history housed in restored Greek-revival building that was state capitol from 1839 to 1903; collection of Jefferson Davis memorabilia. Monthly exhibits. (Daily; closed major hols) Phone 359-6920. **Free.** Adj are

Confederate Monument (1891). Built with money raised by women of Mississippi and by legislative appropriations.

Archives and History Building. Houses state archives and history collections, research library. Phone 359-6850.

4. **The Oaks House Museum** (1846). 823 N Jefferson St. Greek-revival cottage, built of hand-hewn timber by James H. Boyd, former mayor of Jackson, was occupied by General Sherman during the siege of 1863. Period furniture; garden. (Daily exc Mon; closed Jan 1, Thanksgiving, Dec 25) Phone 353-9339. ¢

5. **Manship House.** 420 E Fortification St. Restored Gothic-revival cottage (ca 1855), was residence of Charles Henry Manship, mayor of Jackson during the Civil War. Period furnishings; fine examples of wood graining and marbling. (Tues–Sat; closed major hols) Phone 961-4724. **Free.**

6. **Museum of Natural Science.** 111 N Jefferson St. Collections, designed for research and education, cover Mississippi's vertebrates, invertebrates, plants and fossils. Exhibits and aquariums depict ecological story of region; educational programs and workshops offered for all ages. Professional library. Division of

Mississippi Department of Wildlife Conservation. (Daily exc Sun; closed Jan 1, July 4, Thanksgiving, Dec 25) Phone 354-7303. **Free.**

7. **Davis Planetarium.** 201 E Pascagoula St. Programs change quarterly; 230-seat auditorium. (Daily; closed major hols) Phone 960-1540 or -1550. ¢¢

8. **Municipal Art Gallery.** 839 N State St. Changing exhibits in a variety of media displayed in antebellum house. (Tues–Sat, also Sun afternoons; closed major hols, Fri of Thanksgiving wk; also Aug) Phone 960-1582. **Free.**

9. **Mississippi Museum of Art.** 201 E Pascagoula. Exhibitions of 19th- and 20th-century works by local, regional, national and international artists. Special exhibitions; sculpture garden; hands-on children's gallery; restaurant, gallery programs, films; instruction, sales gallery. (Daily exc Mon; closed most major hols) Phone 960-1515. ¢¢

10. **Smith Robertson Museum.** 528 Bloom St. History and culture of black Mississippians from Africa to present; large collection of photos, books, documents, art & crafts. (Mon–Fri, Sat mornings, Sun afternoons; closed major hols) Phone 960-1457. ¢

11. **Mynelle Gardens.** 4736 Clinton Blvd, 2 blocks off MS 220. A five-acre display garden with thousands of azaleas, camellias, daylilies, flowering trees and perennials; reflecting pools and statuary; Oriental garden, miniature flower gardens and an all-white garden. Turn-of-the-century Westbrook House is open for viewing. Changing art & photography exhibits. Gift shop. Picnicking. (Daily; closed some major hols) Phone 960-1894. ¢

12. **Jackson Zoological Park.** 2918 W Capitol St. More than 400 mammals, birds and reptiles in naturalized habitats. (Daily; closed Jan 1, Dec 25) Sr citizen rate. Phone 352-2580. ¢¢

13. **Battlefield Park.** Porter St between Langley Ave & Terry Rd. Site of Civil War battle; original cannon and trenches.

14. **Jim Buck Ross/Mississippi Agriculture & Forestry Museum and National Agricultural Aviation Museum.** 1 mi NE on I-55, exit 98 at Lakeland Dr. Complex, covering 39 acres, includes museum exhibit center, forest trail, 1920s living history town and farm. Picnicking. (Daily; closed Jan 1, Dec 25) Phone 354-6113 or 800/844-TOUR. ¢¢

15. **Ross R. Barnett Reservoir.** 7 mi N on I-55, 3 mi E on Natchez Trace Pkwy. Reservoir (43 mi in length) created by damming Pearl River. Swimming, waterskiing; fishing; boating. Picnicking. Camping. Standard fees. (Daily) Phone 354-3448 or 856-6574.

16. **Mississippi Petrified Forest.** 11 mi N on US 49, 1½ mi W via access road. Surface erosion exposed giant (up to 6 ft in diameter) petrified logs that were deposited in Mississippi area as driftwood by a prehistoric river. Self-guided nature trail. Museum at visitor center has dioramas; wood, gem, mineral, fossil displays; ultraviolet (black-light) room. Picnicking. Camping. Gift shop. (Daily; closed Dec 25) Sr citizen rate. Phone 879-8189. ¢¢

(For further information contact the Chamber of Commerce, 201 S President St, 39205, phone 948-7575; or the Convention & Visitors Bureau, PO Box 1450, 39215, phone 960-1891 or 800/354-7695.)

Annual Events

Dixie National Livestock Show. Mississippi Coliseum. Late Jan–mid Feb. Rodeo 2nd wk Feb.

Mississippi State Horse Show. Mississippi Coliseum. Entries from southeastern states participate in walking, trotting and jumping classes. Apr.

Mississippi State Fair. State Fairgrounds, Jefferson St. Agricultural and industrial exhibits and contests; midway, entertainment. 2nd full wk Oct.

(See Mendenhall)

Motels

✔ ★ ★ **BEST WESTERN-NORTHEAST.** *(Box 16275, 39236) 5035 I-55N. 601/982-1011; FAX 601/982-1011, ext 199.* 145 rms, 2 story. S $37–$39; D $41; each addl $4; suites $65–$79; under 17 free. Crib free. TV; cable. Pool. Restaurant 6 am–9 pm; Sat from 7 am; Sun 7 am–noon. Rm serv. Bar 4 pm–1 am. Ck-out noon. Coin lndry. Meeting rms. Valet serv. Sundries. Cr cds: A, C, D, DS, MC, V.

D 🐾 ⛱ 🚫 ⊕ SC

★ **DAYS INN.** *(Box 12864, 39236) 616 Briarwood Dr, just E off I-55N. 601/957-1741; FAX 601/957-1741, ext 195.* 150 rms, 2 story. S $36.95–$38.95, D $42.95–$44.95; each addl $6; under 12 free. Crib free. TV. Pool. Restaurant adj. Ck-out noon. Cr cds: A, C, D, DS, MC, V.

D 🐾 ⛱ 🚫 ⊕ SC

✔ ★ **ECONO LODGE.** *2450 US 80W (39204). 601/353-0340.* 40 rms. S $31.95–$44.95; D $34.95–$54.95; each addl $4; under 12 free. Crib free. TV; cable. Complimentary continental bkfst, coffee. Restaurant nearby. Ck-out 11 am. Cr cds: A, D, DS, MC, V, JCB.

D 🚫 ⊕ SC

★ ★ **LA QUINTA MOTOR INN.** *150 Angle St (39204). 601/373-6110; FAX 601/373-6115.* 101 rms, 2–3 story. S $43; D $45; suites $52–$65; under 18 free. Crib free. TV; cable. Pool. Restaurant adj open 24 hrs. Ck-out noon. Valet serv. Airport transportation. Cr cds: A, C, D, DS, MC, V.

D 🐾 ⛱ 🚫 ⊕ SC

★ ★ **RESIDENCE INN BY MARRIOTT.** *881 E River Pl (39202). 601/355-3599; FAX 601/355-5127.* 120 kit. suites, 2 story. S, D $89–$109; monthly, wkly rates. Crib $10. TV; cable. Pool. Playground. Complimentary continental bkfst. Ck-out noon. Coin lndry. Meeting rms. Health club privileges. Lawn games. Fireplaces. Some private patios, balconies. Picnic tables, grills. Cr cds: A, C, D, DS, MC, V, JCB.

D ⛱ 🏃 🚫 ⊕ SC

★ **SUPER 8.** *2655 I-55 S (39204). 601/372-1006.* 78 rms. S $29–$35; D $33–$38; each addl $5; under 12 free. Crib $5. Heated pool. Restaurant nearby. Ck-out noon. Free airport, RR station, bus depot transportation. Cr cds: A, DS, MC, V.

D ⛱ 🚫 ⊕ SC

✔ ★ **WILSON INN.** *310 Greymont Ave (39202). 601/948-4466; res: 800/333-9457.* 110 rms, 5 story. S $33.95–$48.95; D $38.95–$53.95; each addl $5; under 18 free. Crib free. TV; cable. Complimentary continental bkfst, coffee. Restaurant opp 11 am–9 pm. Ck-out noon. Meeting rms. Bellhops. Some wet bars. Cr cds: A, C, D, DS, MC, V.

D 🚫 ⊕ SC

Motor Hotel

★ ★ **CABOT LODGE MILLSAPS** (formerly Holiday Inn-Medical Center). *2375 N State St (39202). 601/948-8650; res: 800/874-4737; FAX 601/948-8650, ext 198.* 208 rms, 6 story. S $53–$69; D $59–$75; each addl $6; under 12 free; wkend rates. TV. Pool; wading pool. Complimentary continental bkfst. Restaurant 6 am–2 pm, 5–10 pm; Sat–Mon from 7 am. Rm serv. Bar 4 pm–midnight. Ck-out noon. Coin lndry. Meeting rms. Bellhops. Free hospital transportation. Opp University Medical Center. Cr cds: A, C, D, DS, MC, V.

D ⛱ 🚫 ⊕ SC

Hotels

★ ★ ★ **EDISON WALTHALL.** *225 E Capitol St (39201). 601/948-6161; res: 800/932-6161; FAX 601/948-0088.* 208 rms, 8 story. S $50–$70; D $60–$80; each addl $8; suites $90–$175; under 18 free. Crib free. TV; cable. 5th floor pool. Restaurant 6:30 am–10 pm; Sat, Sun from 7 am. Bars 4–10 pm; pianist Mon–Fri. Ck-out noon. Meeting rms. Gift shop. Barber. Free covered parking. Free airport transportation. Exercise equipt; weights, bicycles, whirlpool. Cr cds: A, C, D, DS, MC, V.

★ ★ ★ RAMADA NORTH. (Box 12710, 39211) 1001 County Line Rd. 601/957-2800; FAX 601/957-3191. 300 rms, 14 story. S $84–$110; D $94–$120; each addl $15; suites $200–$500; under 18 free; wkend rates. Crib free. TV; cable. Pool; whirlpool. Restaurants 6 am–10 pm. Bar 11–1 am; entertainment, dancing. Ck-out 1 pm. Convention facilities. Concierge. Barber, beauty shop. Free airport, RR station, bus depot transportation. Tennis privileges. 18-hole golf privileges, driving range. Health club privileges. Bathrm phones, refrigerators. *LUXURY LEVEL:* 32 rms, 4 suites, 2 floors. S $100–$125; D $115–$130; suites $200–$500. Private lounge. Complimentary continental bkfst, cocktail, newspapers.
Cr cds: A, C, D, DS, MC, V.

Inn

★ ★ ★ MILLSAPS BUIE HOUSE. 628 N State St (39202). 601/ 352-0221. 11 units, 3 story. S $80–$150; D $95–$165. Children over 12 yrs only. TV. Complimentary full Southern bkfst, refreshments. Restaurant adj. Ck-out 11 am, ck-in 2 pm. Meeting rm. Bathrm phones; some refrigerators. Private patios, balconies. Picnic tables. Victorian architecture. Restored house built 1888; antique furnishings. Cr cds: A, D, DS, MC, V.

Restaurants

★ ★ ★ DENNERY'S. 330 Greymont Ave. 601/354-2527. Hrs: 11 am–10 pm; Sat from 5 pm; early-bird dinner Mon–Fri 3–6 pm. Closed Sun; major hols. Res accepted. Serv bar. Semi-a la carte: lunch $7–$10, dinner $11.50–$21.50. Child's meals. Specializes in seafood, roast prime rib. Own baking. Parking. Grecian theme. Family-owned. Cr cds: A, C, D, MC, V.

★ IRON HORSE GRILL. 320 W Pearl St. 601/355-8419. Hrs: 11 am–10 pm; Fri, Sat to 11 pm. Closed Sun; major hols. Southwestern menu. Bar. Semi-a la carte: lunch $4.95–$17.95, dinner $5.95–$17.95. Child's meals. Specialties: grilled catfish with red bell pepper sauce, fajitas. Pianist Wed, Fri & Sat. Parking. Once a meat smokehouse. Southwestern decor. Cr cds: A, MC, V.

★ ★ ★ NICK'S. 1501 Lakeland Dr. 601/981-8017. Hrs: 11 am–2 pm, 6–10 pm; Fri, Sat 6–10:30 pm. Closed Sun; Jan 1, Thanksgiving, Dec 25. Continental menu. Bar. Wine list. Semi-a la carte: lunch $5.95–$11.95, dinner $12.95–$22.95. Child's meals. Specializes in seafood, beef, veal. Own pastries. Parking. Cr cds: A, D, MC, V.

✔ ★ POETS. (PO Box 55645) On Lakeland Dr. 601/982-9711. Hrs: 11–1 am. Closed Sun; major hols. Bar. A la carte entrees: lunch, dinner $3.25–$14.95. Specialties: scampi, redfish Kathryn. Entertainment exc Mon. Parking. Outdoor dining. Antique bar, fixtures; stained glass, Tiffany lamps, tin ceiling. Cr cds: A, D, DS, MC, V.

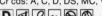

✔ ★ ★ PRIMOS RESTAURANT AT NORTHGATE. 4330 N State St. 601/982-2064. Hrs: 11 am–10 pm; Fri, Sat to 10:30 pm; Sun to 3 pm. Closed July 4, Dec 25. Res accepted. Bar. Semi-a la carte: lunch, dinner $3.50–$15.50. Complete meals: lunch $4–$4.75. Child's meals. Specializes in salads, seafood, steak. Parking. Country French decor. Cr cds: A, MC, V.

★ ★ TICO'S. 1536 E County Line Rd. 601/956-1030. Hrs: 4:30–10:30 pm; Fri, Sat to 11 pm. Closed Sun; major hols. Res accepted

Fri, Sat. Bar. Semi-a la carte: dinner $7.50–$19.50. Specializes in steak, fresh seafood. Own desserts. Parking. Lodge style; fireplace, beamed ceilings. Cr cds: A, D, MC, V.

★ ★ WIDOW WATSON'S. 1000 Metro Center, 1 mi N of I-20, exit Robinson Rd. 601/968-6364. Hrs: 11 am–9 pm; Fri, Sat to 10 pm. Closed Sun; Thanksgiving, Dec 25. Res accepted. Bar to 11 pm; Thurs–Sat to 1 am. Semi-a la carte: lunch $5–$9.95, dinner $8.25–$16.50. Child's meals. Specializes in seafood, steak. Salad bar. Entertainment Fri–Sat. Parking. Antiques. Cr cds: A, MC, V.

Unrated Dining Spot

COCK OF THE WALK. (PO Box 12705, 39236) 15 mi N via I-55, Natchez Trace exit to Ross Barnett Reservoir. 601/856-5500. Hrs: 5:30–9:30 pm; Fri, Sat to 10 pm. Closed Thanksgiving, Dec 24, 25. Bar. A la carte entrees: dinner from $7.95. Child's meals. Specializes in catfish, fried dill pickles, mustard greens. Parking. Rustic decor. Cr cds: A, MC, V.

Kosciusko (C-3)

Pop: 6,986 **Elev:** 488 ft **Area code:** 601 **Zip:** 39090

What to See and Do

1. **Kosciusko Museum-Information Center.** 1½ mi S via S Huntington St, Natchez Trace Pkwy exit. Museum features information on the area, Natchez Trace Pkwy and Polish general Tadeusz Kosciuszko; revolving displays. (Daily; closed Dec 25) Contact Chamber of Commerce. **Free.**

2. **Holmes County State Park.** 25 mi W on MS 12, then S on US 51, between US 51 & I-55. Approximately 450-acre park has 2 lakes. Swimming beach; fishing; boating (rentals). Nature trails; archery range. Picnicking (shelters), playground, skating rink (call for schedule), coin lndry. Camping (water, electric hookups), cabins. Standard fees. Phone 653-3351.

(For further information contact the Kosciusko-Attala Chamber of Commerce, 301 E Jefferson, PO Box 696; 289-2981.)

Annual Event

Central Mississippi Fair and State Dairy Show. Central Mississippi State Fairgrounds. Phone 289-2981. Aug.

(See Louisville)

Laurel (D-3)

Settled: 1882 **Pop:** 18,827 **Elev:** 246 ft **Area code:** 601

Laurel was built by two sawmill men in the piney woods of southeastern Mississippi after Reconstruction. Pushing through northeast Mississippi's pinelands, they picked a spot on the Southern Railroad that they thought was the forest's center. They called it Laurel for the abundant flowering shrubs, but it remained a rough lumber camp for a decade. Laurel bloomed after a midwestern company took over the lumber mill, laying out streets and encouraging workers to buy houses. The ladies of Laurel organized the state's first garden club in the 1890s.

Laurel has been fortunate in the development of a reforestation program and diversified industry. A Ranger District of De Soto National Forest (see HATTIESBURG) lies about eight miles to the southeast.

What to See and Do

Lauren Rogers Museum of Art. 5th Ave & 7th St. Collections of 19th-and 20th-century American and European paintings, 18th-century Japanese woodblock prints, Georgian silver, North American Indian baskets. (Daily exc Mon; closed major hols) Phone 649-6374. **Free.**

(For further information contact the Jones County Chamber of Commerce, PO Box 527, 39441; phone 428-0574.)

(See Hattiesburg)

Motels

★ ★ **DAYS INN.** *(Box 2517, 39440) At jct US 11N, I-59N exit 99.* 601/428-8421; FAX 601/649-0938. 85 rms. S, D $35; each addl $5; under 12 free. Crib free. TV; cable. Pool. Restaurant 6 am–2 pm, 5–9 pm. Rm serv. Ck-out noon. Coin lndry. Meeting rms. Cr cds: A, D, MC, V.

✔ ★ **TOWN HOUSE.** *340 Beacon St.* 601/428-1527; FAX 601/649-2225. 83 rms, 2 story. S $25–$32; D $35–$42; each addl $3. Crib free. TV; cable. Pool. Complimentary continental bkfst in lobby. Ck-out noon. Private patios, balconies. Cr cds: A, C, D, DS, MC, V.

Motor Hotel

★ ★ **RAMADA INN SAWMILL.** *1105 Sawmill Rd (39440).* 601/649-9100. 207 rms, 1–4 story. S $41–$55; D $46–$60; each addl $5; studio rms $58; under 18 free. Crib free. Pet accepted. TV; cable. Pool; poolside serv. Restaurant 6 am–10 pm, Sun to 9 pm. Rm serv. Bar 11–1 am; entertainment, dancing Tues–Sat. Ck-out 1 pm. Meeting rms. Valet serv. Some refrigerators. Cr cds: A, C, D, DS, MC, V.

Restaurant

★ ★ **PARKER HOUSE.** *3115 Audubon Dr.* 601/649-0261. Hrs: 11 am–1:30 pm, 6–9 pm; Fri to 9:30 pm; Sat 6–9:30 pm. Closed Sun, Mon; major hols & Dec 24. Res accepted. Continental menu. Bar 5 pm–midnight. Buffet: lunch $6.25. A la carte entrees: lunch 3.99, dinner $6.95–$19.95. Child's meals. Specializes in seafood, prime rib, stuffed mushrooms. Parking. Cr cds: A, D, DS, MC, V.

Louisville (C-3)

Pop: 7,169 **Elev:** 525 ft **Area code:** 601 **Zip:** 39339

What to See and Do

1. **Tombigbee National Forest.** N on MS 15, which borders west side of forest. This southern section of the forest contains Choctaw Lake. Swimming (fee); fishing; boating. Picnicking. Camping (Mar–mid-Nov; hookups, fee; dump station). Fees are charged at recreation sites. There is a Ranger District station near Ackerman and another section of the forest south of Tupelo (see). Contact Forest Supervisor, 100 W Capitol St, Suite 1141, Jackson 39269, phone 965-4391; or contact the District Ranger, US Forest Service, Rte 1, Box 98A, Ackerman 39735, phone 285-3264. Day use ¢¢

2. **Legion State Park.** On Old MS 25. One of the first parks developed by the Civilian Conservation Corps; original stone lodge still in use.

Swimming beach; two fishing lakes; boating (ramp, rentals). Nature trail. Picnicking (shelters). Tent camping, cabins. (Daily) Standard fees. Phone 773-8323.

3. **Nanih Waiya State Park.** 18 mi SE via MS 397. Legendary birthplace of Choctaw Indians and site of their Sacred Mound; area occupied from approximately the time of Christ until arrival of Europeans. Swinging bridge leads to cave under mound. Picnicking (shelters). Near Pearl River. (Daily; closed Dec 25) Contact Site Manager, Rte 3, Box 251-A; 773-7988. **Free.**

(For further information contact the Louisville-Winston County Chamber of Commerce, 311 W Park, PO Box 551; 773-3921.)

Resort

★ ★ **LAKE TIAK O'KHATA.** *(PO Box 160)* ¼ *mi off MS 15 Bypass S, exit Smyth Rd.* 601/773-7853; FAX 601/773-4555. 74 rms, 2 story; 6 duplex cottages. S $37; D $46; each addl $3.75; kit. cottages $42; wkly rates. Crib $5. TV in hotel rms, lobby; cable. Dining rm 6 am–10 pm; buffet 11 am–2 pm. Snack bar. Ck-out 11 am. Grocery 1 mi. Meeting rms. Convention facilities. Tennis. Private beach; swimming classes (summer), waterslide, lifeguard; boating (ramps, rentals), pedal boats. Nature trails. Picnic tables. 400 acre pine forest; 5 lakes. Cr cds: A, D, DS, MC, V.

McComb (E-2)

Founded: 1872 **Pop:** 11,591 **Elev:** 460 ft **Area code:** 601 **Zip:** 39648

What to See and Do

1. **Percy Quin State Park.** 6 mi S on I-55, exit 13. Park covering 1,700 acres on 700-acre Tangipahoa Lake in oak and pine forests. Lodge area includes arboretum and Liberty White Railroad Museum, housed in a caboose. Pool, bathhouse, waterskiing; fishing; boating (ramp, rentals). Nature; miniature golf. Picnicking (shelters), snack bar, playing field, lodge. Improved & primitive camping, cabins. Standard fees. Phone 684-3938.

2. **Bogue Chitto Water Park.** 12 mi E on US 98. Swimming; tubing, canoeing. Nature trail. Picnicking, playground, pavilion. Primitive/improved camping (fee). Visitor center. (Daily) Phone 684-9568. Per car ¢

(For further information contact the Chamber of Commerce, 202 3rd St, PO Box 83; 684-2291.)

Annual Event

Lighted Azalea Trail. In keeping with the Japanese tradition of lighting cherry blossoms, McComb citizens illuminate their azaleas; arts festival, music programs. Two wks mid-Mar.

Motels

★ ★ **HOLIDAY INN.** *I-55 exit 17 at Delaware Ave.* 601/684-6211; FAX 601/684-6211, ext 179. 143 rms, 2 story. S $42–$48; D $44–$53. Crib free. TV; cable. Pool. Restaurant 6 am–10 pm. Rm serv 7 am–2 pm, 5–9:30 pm. Bar 5 pm–midnight. Ck-out noon. Coin lndry. Free airport, RR station, bus depot transportation. Exercise equipt; weights, bicycles. Cr cds: A, C, D, DS, MC, V, JCB.

✔ ★ **RAMADA INN.** *(Box 1460) I-55 exit 17 at Delaware Ave.* 601/684-5566; FAX 601/684-0641. 151 units, 2 story. S $39–$47; D $44–$52; each addl $6; suites $75–$200; studio rms $47.50–$53; under 18 free. Crib free. TV; cable. Pool. Complimentary full bkfst. Restaurant

6 am–10 pm. Rm serv. Bar 4 pm–midnight; entertainment exc Sun, Mon. Ck-out 1 pm. Meeting rms. Valet serv. Cr cds: A, C, D, DS, MC, V.

D ⚑ ⚓ ⚹ 🚭 ⏰ SC

Unrated Dining Spot

DINNER BELL. *229 5th Ave. 601/684-4883.* Hrs: Tues–Sun 11 am–2 pm; 5:30–8 pm (Fri, Sat, Apr–Sept only). Closed Mon; July 4, Dec 23–third Mon in Jan. Buffet: lunch, dinner $7.50–$8.50. Child's meals. Specializes in fried chicken. Parking. Totally nonsmoking. No cr cds accepted.

Mendenhall (D-3)

Pop: 2,463 **Elev:** 323 ft **Area code:** 601 **Zip:** 39114

What to See and Do

1. **Bienville National Forest.** NW on US 49 to MS 13, then N. This central Mississippi tract of 178,374 acres has numerous forest management demonstration areas of second-growth pine and hardwood. Swimming; boating. Hiking, bridle trails. Picknicking. Camping. Ranger District offices are located in Raleigh and Forest. For information contact Forest Supervisor, 100 W Capitol St, Suite 1141, Jackson 39269; 965-4391. Two major recreation areas are

   Shongelo. 22 mi E & N via MS 540, 35. A five-acre lake. Swimming (fee), bathhouse; fishing. Picnicking. Camping (fee).

   Marathon. 47 mi NE via MS 540, 18, 501, forest service roads. A 58-acre lake. Swimming (fee); fishing; boating. Picnicking. Camping (fee).

2. **D'Lo Water Park.** 3 mi NW via US 49. Park includes 85 acres. Swimming, bathhouse; fishing; canoeing (rentals). Nature trails, lighted playing fields. Picnicking. Camping (hookups; fee). (Daily; closed Jan 1, Thanksgiving, Dec 25) Phone 847-4310. **Free.**

(For accommodations see Jackson)

Meridian (D-4)

Settled: 1831 **Pop:** 41,036 **Elev:** 333 ft **Area code:** 601

Founded at the junction of two railroads, Meridian is now an industrial, agricultural and retailing center in the heart of the South's finest timbergrowing country.

What to See and Do

1. **Merrehope.** 905 Martin Luther King, Jr Memorial Dr. Stately 20-room mansion, begun in 1859, features unusual woodwork, handsome columns, mantels and stairway. (Daily; closed major hols) Special Christmas tours. Phone 483-8439. Nearby is

   Frank W. Williams House. Victorian home (ca 1886) features stained glass, oak paneling, parquet floors and detailed gingerbread. (Days same as Merrehope) Admission to both houses ¢¢

2. **Meridian Museum of Art.** 25th Ave at 7th St. Permanent and changing exhibits of paintings, graphics, photographs, sculpture, crafts by regional artists. (Tues–Sun, afternoons; closed hols) Phone 693-1501. **Free.**

3. **Jimmie Rodgers Museum.** In Highland Park. Fashioned after an old train depot, the museum houses souvenirs and memorabilia of the ''Father of Country Music,'' including a rare Martin 00045 guitar. (Daily; closed Jan 1, Thanksgiving, Dec 25) Phone 485-1808. ¢

4. **Okatibbee Dam and Reservoir.** 7 mi NW off MS 19. A 3,800-acre lake with swimming (seasonal), waterskiing, water slides; fishing;

boating (ramps, marina). Picnicking, lodging. Camping at Twiltley Branch Park (fee; phone 626-8068) and at Okatibbee Water Park (seasonal, fee; phone 737-2370). Phone 626-8431.

5. **Clarkco State Park.** 18 mi S off US 45. Park covering 815 acres situated on 65-acre lake. Swimming beach, waterskiing; fishing; boating (ramp, rentals). Nature trail; lighted tennis. Picnicking (shelters), playground, playing field, lodge, coin lndry. Primitive & improved camping, cabins (each with lake pier). Standard fees. Phone 776-6651.

6. **Bienville National Forest.** 45 mi W off I-20 (see MENDENHALL).

(For further information contact the Meridian/Lauderdale County Partnership, PO Box 790; 483-0083 or 800/748-9970.)

Annual Events

Arts in the Park. Concerts, plays, art shows, children's programs. 1st wkend Apr.

Jimmie Rodgers Memorial Festival. Country and western music. Last full wk May.

Mississippi-Alabama State Fair. Agricultural exhibits, carnival. Oct.

Motels

✔ ★ ★ **BEST WESTERN.** *2219 S Frontage Rd, at jct I-20, I-59.* 601/693-3210. 120 rms, 2 story. S $33–$38; D $38–$44; each addl $5; under 12 free. Crib free. TV; cable. Pool. Restaurant 6–2 am; Sun to 3 pm. Bar 4 pm–1 am, exc Sun; entertainment, dancing. Ck-out noon. Meeting rms. Sundries. Cr cds: A, C, D, DS, MC, V, JCB.

⚓ 🚭 ⏰ SC

★ **BUDGETEL INN.** *1400 Roebuck Dr (39301).* 601/693-2300; FAX 601/485-2534. 102 rms, 3 story. S $32.95–$35.95; D $39.95–$46.95; under 18 free. Crib free. TV; cable. Pool. Restaurant adj open 24 hrs. Ck-out noon. Meeting rms. Cr cds: A, C, D, DS, MC, V.

D ⚓ 🚭 ⏰ SC

★ **COMFORT INN.** *2901 St Paul St (39301).* 601/485-2722. 51 units, 2 story. S $32.98; D $39.98; each addl $5; under 12 free. Crib free. TV; cable. Pool. Ck-out 11 am. Exercise equipt; bicycles, rowing machine, whirlpool, sauna. Game rm. Cr cds: A, D, DS, ER, MC, V.

D ⚓ ⚹ 🚭 ⏰ SC

✔ ★ **DAYS INN.** *530 US 80 East (39301).* 601/483-3812. 122 rms, 2 story. S $31–$35; D $38–$41; each addl $5; studio rms $38–$42; family rates. Crib free. Pet accepted. TV; cable. Pool. Restaurant 6 am–9 pm. Ck-out noon. Cr cds: A, C, D, DS, MC, V.

⚑ ⚓ 🚭 ⏰ SC

★ ★ **HAMPTON INN.** *618 US 11/80, at I-58/20 exit 154B.* 601/483-3000. 118 units, 4 story. S $41–$45; D $41–$47.51; each addl $4; suites $82–$123; under 18 free. Crib free. TV; cable. Pool. Complimentary continental bkfst 6–10 am. Ck-out noon. Meeting rms. Valet serv. Sundries. Free airport, bus depot transportation. Exercise equipt; bicycle, stair machine, whirlpool. Refrigerator in suites. Cr cds: A, C, D, DS, MC, V.

D ⚓ ⚹ 🚭 ⏰ SC

★ ★ **HOLIDAY INN SOUTH.** *(Box 5513, 39302) US 45 at jct I-20, I-59.* 601/693-4521; FAX 601/693-4521, ext 7625. 172 rms, 1–2 story. S, D $46–$51; under 12 free. Crib free. Pet accepted. TV; cable. Pool. Playground. Coffee in rms. Restaurant 6 am–2 pm, 5–10 pm. Rm serv 6:30 am–9:30 pm. Bar 4 pm–midnight, closed Sun. Ck-out noon. Coin lndry. Meeting rms. Valet serv. Cr cds: A, C, D, DS, MC, V, JCB.

⚑ ⚓ 🚭 ⏰ SC

★ ★ **HOWARD JOHNSON.** *(Box 588, 39305) 2 mi E, exit 154 at I-59, I-20.* 601/483-8281. 142 rms, 2 story. S $42–$54; D $44–$58; each addl $4; suites $85–$150; studio rms $45; under 18 free. Crib free. TV. Indoor pool; whirlpool. Restaurant 6 am–10 pm. Bar 11–1 am; entertainment, dancing exc Sun. Ck-out noon. Coin lndry. Meeting rms. Sundries. Private patios, balconies. Cr cds: A, C, D, DS, MC, V, JCB.

Restaurants

★CYPRESS LODGE. *519 Azalea Dr. 601/485-6070.* Hrs: 10 am–2 pm, 5–9 pm; Fri, Sat to 10 pm; Mon 10 am–2 pm. Closed Sun; some major hols. Buffet: lunch $5.75. A la carte entrees: dinner $6.95–$11.95. Child's meals. Specializes in seafood. Salad bar. Parking. Cr cds: A, MC, V.

★★JONATHAN'S. *305 S Frontage Rd. 601/485-6466.* Hrs: 5–10 pm. Closed Sun; Jan 1, July 4. Bar 4 pm–1 am. Semi-a la carte: dinner $7–$18.95. Child's meals. Specializes in prime rib, seafood. Parking. Cr cds: A, C, D, DS, MC, V.

✔★★WEIDMANN'S. *208 22nd Ave. 601/693-1751.* Hrs: 6 am–9:30 pm. Closed Jan 1, July 4, Thanksgiving, Dec 24–25. Continental menu. Bar. Semi-a la carte: bkfst $2.85–$4, lunch $4.25–$10, dinner $8–$15. Child's meals. Specialties: crab Belvedere, trout amandine. Cr cds: A, C, D, MC, V.

Unrated Dining Spot

MORRISON'S CAFETERIA. *22nd Ave, in Village Fair Mall. 601/693-6326.* Hrs: 10:45 am–8:30 pm; Sun to 7 pm. Southern menu. Avg ck: lunch $6, dinner $7.20. Specializes in fried shrimp. Cr cds: MC, V.

Natchez (D-1)

Settled: 1716 **Pop:** 19,460 **Elev:** 215 ft **Area code:** 601 **Zip:** 39120

Natchez lives in the enchantment of the Old South, a plantation atmosphere where everything seems beautiful and romantic. Greek-revival mansions, manicured gardens and lawns, tree-shaded streets and southern hospitality abound in this museum of the antebellum South.

Natchez, named for a Native American tribe, is also a manufacturing town with a history of trapping, trading, hunting and farming. French, Spanish, English, Confederate and US flags have flown over this town, one of the oldest in the Mississippi Valley. Vestiges of the Spanish influence can still be seen along South Wall Street, near Washington Street, a charming neighborhood once restricted to the Spanish dons. The city's modern stores and buildings serve to emphasize how lovingly the citizens of Natchez have preserved their past.

What to See and Do

1. **Canal Street Depot.** Corner of Canal & State St. Houses official Natchez Pilgrimage Tour and Tourist Headquarters. (Daily) Information on historic Natchez and the surrounding area. Offers tours (fee) of 10 antebellum mansions and tickets for spring and fall pilgrimages (see ANNUAL EVENTS).

2. **The House on Ellicott Hill.** Jefferson & Canal Sts. Site where, in 1797, Andrew Ellicott raised the first American flag in the lower Mississippi Valley. Built in 1798, the house overlooks both the Mississippi and the terminus of the Natchez Trace. Restored and authentically furnished. (Daily) Phone 442-2011. ¢¢

3. **Rosalie** (1820–23). 100 Orleans St. Red brick, Georgian mansion with Greek-revival portico served as headquarters for Union Army during occupation of Natchez. Original furnishings date from 1857; gardens on bluff above Mississippi. (Daily; closed Thanksgiving,

Dec 24, 25) Fees vary during scheduled times at the pilgrimages (see ANNUAL EVENTS). Phone 445-4555. ¢¢

4. **Monmouth** (ca 1818). 36 Melrose Ave. Registered as a National Historic Landmark, the monumental, Greek-revival house and auxiliary buildings, once owned by Mexican War hero Gen. John Anthony Quitman, have been completely restored; antique furnishings; extensive gardens. Guest rms (see INNS). Tours (daily; closed Dec 25). Phone 442-5852 or 800/828-4531. ¢¢

5. **Stanton Hall** (1851–57). 401 High St. Highly elaborate antebellum mansion surrounded by giant oaks; original chandeliers, marble mantels, Sheffield hardware, French mirrors. Owned and operated by the Pilgrimage Garden Club. (Daily; days & fees vary during pilgrimages) (See ANNUAL EVENTS) Phone 446-6631 or 800/647-6742. ¢¢

6. **Dunleith** (ca 1856). 84 Homochitto St. National Historic Landmark. Restored antebellum, Greek-revival mansion completely surrounded by colonnaded galleries. Estate includes 40 acres of green pastures and wooded bayous within Natchez. French and English antiques. (Daily; closed Thanksgiving, Dec 25) Guest rms (see INNS). Phone 446-8500 or 800/433-2445 (exc MS). Tours ¢¢

7. **Ravennaside Historical Party House** (ca 1880). 601 S Union St. Designed by original owner for entertainment on lavish scale; restored; most of original furniture retained. (Sept–June, daily) Guest rms (see INNS). Phone 442-8015. Tours ¢¢

8. **Magnolia Hall** (1858). S Pearl at Washington. Last great mansion to be erected in city before outbreak of Civil War, house is an outstanding example of Greek-revival architecture; period antiques; costume museum. (Daily) Phone 442-6672. ¢¢

9. **Longwood.** Lower Woodville Rd. Enormous, Italianate detailed "octagon house" crowned with an onion dome. Under construction at start of Civil War, interiors were never completed above first floor; ca 1840 furnishings. Owned and operated by the Pilgrimage Garden Club. (Daily; days vary during Pilgrimages) (See ANNUAL EVENTS) ¢¢

10. **Historic Jefferson College.** 6 mi E on US 61 in Washington. The Jefferson College campus was the site, in 1817, of the first state Constitutional Convention. Jefferson Davis was among the famous Mississippians who attended the college. No longer in use as a school, the buildings are being restored as a historic site. A museum interprets the early history of the territory, state and campus; nature trails; picnicking. (Daily; closed Jan 1, Thanksgiving, Dec 25) Phone 442-2901. **Free.**

11. **Homochitto National Forest.** NE & SE via US 84, 98, MS 33. This 189,000-acre forest is located near the picturesquely eroded loess country. Visitors view the regular timber management activities. Swimming (Clear Springs Recreation Area); fishing and hunting. Picnicking, camping (Clear Springs Recreation Area). Fees may be charged at recreation sites. Ranger District offices are located in Meadville and Gloster. Contact Forest Supervisor, 100 W Capitol St, Suite 1141, Jackson 39269; 965-4391.

12. **Emerald Mound.** 12 mi NE on Natchez Trace Pkwy (see). This eight-acre Mississippian mound, the second largest in the US, dates roughly from 1250–1600. Unlike earlier peoples, who constructed mounds to cover tombs and burials, the Mississippians (ancestors of the Natchez, Creek and Choctaw) built mounds to support temples and ceremonial buildings. When DeSoto passed through this area in the 1540s the flat-topped temple mounds were still in use. (Daily) Phone 680-4025. **Free.**

13. **Natchez State Park.** 10 mi N off US 61. Park has horse trails believed to be abandoned plantation roads that lead to Brandon Hall, house of the first native Mississippi governor, Gerard Brandon (1826-31). Fishing lake; boating (ramp, rentals). Nature trail. Picnicking. Primitive & improved camping, cabins. Standard fees. Phone 442-2658.

14. **Mount Locust.** 15 mi NE on Natchez Trace Pkwy (see). Earliest inn on the Trace; restored to 1810s appearance. Interpretive program. (Feb–Nov, daily; grounds only, Dec–Jan) Phone 680-4025. **Free.**

15. **Historic Springfield Plantation** (1786–1790). 20 mi NE via US 61, Natchez Trace Pkwy, then 12 mi N on MS 553. Believed to be first

mansion erected in Mississippi; remains nearly intact with little remodeling over the years; original hand-carved woodwork. Built for Thomas Marston Green, Jr, wealthy planter from Virginia; site of Andrew Jackson's wedding. Displays include Civil War equipment, railroad memorabilia, narrow-gauge locomotive. (Daily; closed Dec 25) Phone 786-3802. ¢¢¢

16. **Grand Village of the Natchez Indians.** 400 Jefferson Davis Blvd. Museum, archaeological site, nature trails, picnic area, gift shop. (Daily; closed Jan 1, Thanksgiving, Dec 25) Phone 446-6502. **Free.**

17. *Lady Luck* Riverboat Casino. On riverfront, 21 Silver St. Phone 445-0605 or 800/722-LUCK.

(The Natchez Convention & Visitors Bureau has available walking-tour maps and lists of antebellum houses; 422 Main St, PO Box 1485; 800/647-6724.)

Annual Events

Pilgrimages. Headquarters, Canal Street Depot (see #1). Tours of antebellum houses sponsored by the Natchez Pilgrimage Assn (daily). Also Confederate Pageant at City Auditorium (Mon, Wed, Fri, Sat). Contact PO Box 347 or phone 800/647-6742 for details. Mar–early Apr; Fall Pilgrimage mid-Oct.

Great Mississippi River Balloon Race Weekend. Oct.

Seasonal Event

Natchez Opera Festival. Entire month of May.

Motels

(Rates may be higher during Natchez Pilgrimages)

✔ ★**DAYS INN.** 109 US 61S. 601/445-8291. 121 rms, 2 story. S $33–$60; D $37–$70; each addl $5. Crib free. TV. Pool. Restaurant open 24 hrs. Ck-out 11 am. Sundries. Tennis. Cr cds: A, C, D, DS, MC, V.

★★**HOLIDAY INN.** 271 D'Evereaux Dr (US 61N). 601/442-3686; FAX 601/446-9998. 139 rms, 2 story. S $43–$65; D $49–$75; each addl $5; under 18 free. Crib free. TV; cable. Pool. Restaurant 6 am–10 pm. Rm serv. Bar 4 pm–1 am. Ck-out noon. Meeting rm. Cr cds: A, C, D, DS, MC, V, JCB.

✔ ★**HOWARD JOHNSON.** (Box 1347) US 61, at jct US 65, 84, 98. 601/442-1691; FAX 601/445-5895. 128 units, 1–2 story. S $41–$53; D $41–$68; each addl $5; under 12 free. TV; cable. Pool. Restaurant 5:30 am–9 pm. Rm serv. Bar 4 pm–midnight; entertainment Fri, Sat. Ck-out noon. Meeting rms. Cr cds: A, C, D, DS, MC, V.

★★**RAMADA INN HILLTOP.** (Box 1263) 130 John R. Junkin Dr, at Mississippi River bridge. 601/446-6311; FAX 601/446-6321. 162 rms, 1–3 story. No elvtr. S $48–$68; each addl $5; suites $130; under 18 free. Crib free. TV; cable. Pool; wading pool, poolside serv. Restaurant 6 am–10 pm. Rm serv. Bar; entertainment, dancing Fri, Sat. Ck-out 1 pm. Coin lndry. Meeting rms. Sundries. Airport, bus depot transportation. Some refrigerators. On hilltop overlooking Mississippi River. Cr cds: A, C, D, DS, MC, V, JCB.

Hotels

★★**BEST WESTERN RIVER PARK.** 645 S Canal St. 601/446-6688; FAX 601/442-9823. 145 units, 6 story. S $54–$59; D $64; each addl $5; suites $155; under 18 free. Crib free. Pet accepted. TV; cable. Pool; whirlpool, poolside serv. Restaurant 6:30 am–2 pm, 5:30–8:30 pm.

Bar 4:30 pm–1 am; entertainment Thurs–Sat. Ck-out 1 pm. Meeting rms. Gift shop. Cr cds: A, C, D, DS, MC, V.

★★★**NATCHEZ EOLA.** 110 N Pearl St. 601/445-6000; res: 800/888-9140; FAX 601/446-5310. 125 rms, 7 story. S, D $60–$150; suites $95–$150. Crib $5. Pet accepted. TV; cable. Restaurant 7 am–2 pm, 5:30–9 pm. Bar 11:30 am–midnight; Fri, Sat to 1 am. Ck-out noon. Meeting rms. Valet parking. Balconies; many with view of river. Classic architecture; antique furniture. Cr cds: A, C, D, MC, V.

Inns

★★★**THE BRIARS.** (PO Box 1245) 31 Irving Lane. 601/446-9654; res: 800/634-1818. 13 rms, 2 story. Rm phones avail. S $110; D $120–$135; each addl $40; suite $350. Children over 12 yrs only. TV. Pool. Complimentary full bkfst, coffee. Restaurant adj 11 am, ck-in 1 pm. Balconies. Antebellum mansion (ca 1815–1820) with 80-foot veranda overlooks Mississippi River. Many antiques. Cr cds: A, MC, V.

★★**THE BURN.** 712 N Union. 601/442-1344; res: 800/654-8859. 7 rms, 2 story. No rm phones. S $70; D $85–$125; each addl $20. Closed Dec 25. Children over 6 yrs only. TV. Pool. Complimentary plantation bkfst, wine. Ck-out noon, ck-in 2–6 pm. Early Greek-revival house (1834) with semi-spiral staircase in central hall; used as headquarters and hospital by Union troops during Civil War; antique furnishings. Gardens with many rare camellias. Free tour of house. Cr cds: A, D, DS, MC, V.

★★**DUNLEITH.** 84 Homochitto St. 601/446-8500; res: 800/433-2445. 11 rms, 2 story. S, D $85–$130; each addl $15. Closed Thanksgiving, Dec 25. Children over 14 yrs only. TV. Complimentary full Southern bkfst, refreshments. Ck-out 11 am, ck-in 1 pm. Balconies. Antebellum mansion (ca 1855) on 40 acres; formal gardens, courtyard. Greek-revival architecture; rms individually decorated; antique furnishings; fireplaces. Cr cds: A, DS, MC, V.

★**HOPE FARM.** 147 Homochitto St. 601/445-4848. 4 rms, 2 story. S, D $80–$90; each addl $20. Children over 6 yrs only. Complimentary full bkfst, coffee. Ck-out 11 am, ck-in 1 pm. Built late 18th century as residence of Spanish governor. Antiques. No cr cds accepted.

★**LINDEN.** 1 Linden Place. 601/445-5472. 7 rms, 2 story. No rm phones. S, D $90; each addl $25. Children over 10 yrs only. Complimentary Southern bkfst. Ck-out 11 am, ck-in 1 pm. Antebellum house (ca 1800); antique furnishings; set among mossy oaks, cedars and magnolias. Free tour of house. No cr cds accepted.

★★**MONMOUTH.** (Box 1736) 36 Melrose Ave. 601/442-5852; res: 800/828-4531; FAX 601/446-7762. 19 rms, 2 story. S, D $100–$225; each addl $35. Children over 14 yrs only. TV. Complimentary Southern bkfst. Serv bar. Ck-out 11 am, ck-in 2 pm. Greek-revival mansion (1818) with column-supported galleries on four sides; antique furnishings, Civil War memorabilia; extensive gardens. Free tour of mansion. Cr cds: A, DS, MC, V.

★★**PLEASANT HILL.** 310 S Pearl. 601/442-7674; res: 800/621-7952. 5 rms. S, D $100–$125; each addl $25; wkly rates. Complimentary Southern bkfst. Ck-out 11 am, ck-in 3–6 pm. Greek-revival house (1835); antiques; rms individually decorated. Tour of house. Cr cds: MC, V.

★★RAVENNASIDE. *601 S Union St. 601/442-8015.* 6 rms, 3 story. S, D $75; each addl $25. Closed June–Aug. Crib free. TV in sitting rm. Whirlpool. Complimentary full bkfst. Ck-out 10 am, ck-in 5 pm. Queen Anne/colonial-revival house built circa 1880; many original furnishings. No cr cds accepted.

Restaurants

★BROTHERS CAFE. *209 Franklin. 601/442-1777.* Hrs: 11 am–2 pm, 5:30–9:30 pm; Fri, Sat to 10:30 pm. Closed Sun; most major hols. Res accepted. Bar 4:30–11 pm. A la carte entrees: lunch $5–$11, dinner $7–$20. Child's meals. Specializes in fresh seafood, crawfish, bread pudding. Outdoor dining. Cr cds: A, DS, MC, V.

★★CARRIAGE HOUSE. *401 High St, behind Stanton Hall. 601/445-5151.* Hrs: 11 am–2:30 pm; Mar & Oct Pilgrimages also 5:30–9 pm. Closed Jan 1, Dec 25. Serv bar. Semi-a la carte: lunch $3.65–$12.50, dinner $6.50–$15. Child's meals. Specializes in Southern fried chicken, glazed ham. Carriage house to Stanton Hall (1857). Cr cds: A, MC, V.

✔★COCK OF THE WALK. *200 N Broadway, on the Mississippi River. 601/446-8920.* Hrs: 11:30 am–1:30 pm, 5–9 pm; Fri, Sat to 10 pm; Sun 5–8 pm. Closed most major hols. Limited menu. Serv bar. Complete meals: lunch $5–6, dinner $8–$9.50. Child's meals. Specializes in catfish. Entertainment. Parking. Rustic decor; old train station on river. Cr cds: A, D, DS, MC, V.

★NATCHEZ LANDING. *35 Silver St. 601/442-6639.* Hrs: 5–10 pm; Fri–Sun 11:30 am–2 pm, 5–10 pm; spring & fall pilgrimages 11:30 am–2 pm, 5–10 pm. Closed Thanksgiving, Dec 25. Serv bar. Semi-a la carte: lunch, dinner $3.95–$20. Child's meals. Specializes in barbecued ribs, catfish. Parking. Rustic decor. Cr cds: A, MC, V.

Natchez Trace Parkway (D-1 – A-4)

One of the earliest "interstates," the Natchez Trace stretched from Natchez to Nashville, Tennessee and was the most heavily traveled road in the Old Southwest from approximately 1785 to 1820. Boatmen floated their products downriver to Natchez or New Orleans, sold them and walked or rode home over the Natchez Trace. A "trace" is a trail or road. This one was shown on French maps as far back as 1733. It was still in use, to some extent, as late as the 1830s, although its importance diminished after the War of 1812.

When completed, the Natchez Trace Parkway, operated by the National Park Service, will be a magnificent 445-mile-long road. At this writing about 425 miles are paved and open, most of them in Mississippi; a continuous stretch of 336 miles is open between Jackson and TN 96 west of Franklin, Tennessee. A 79-mile stretch is open west of Jackson to near Natchez.

The parkway crosses and recrosses the original trace, passing many points of historic interest, including Emerald Mound (see NATCHEZ).

The parkway headquarters and visitor center are five miles north of Tupelo, at jct US 45 Business and the parkway. Interpretive facilities include a museum room with exhibits depicting area history and an audiovisual program that tells the story of the trace (daily; closed Dec 25; free). Park Service personnel can furnish information on self-guided trails, wayside exhibits, interpretive programs, camping and picnicking facilities along the parkway. For further information contact Superintendent, Rural Rte 1, NT 143, Tupelo 38801; 601/680-4025.

Ocean Springs (F-4)

Pop: 14,658 **Elev:** 20 ft **Area code:** 601 **Zip:** 39564

This is the site of Old Biloxi, settled by d'Iberville in 1699. The site of the original Fort Maurepas was verified by the discovery here of cannon dredged from the bay and cannonballs unearthed from the land.

Although some soldiers and settlers remained after the French colonial capital was moved to Mobile in 1702, the area languished until the first large influx of summer visitors arrived in the 1850s. It has since become a popular resort.

Headquarters and campground for the Mississippi District of the Gulf Islands National Seashore (see) are in Ocean Springs.

What to See and Do

Shearwater Pottery. 102 Shearwater Dr. Established in 1928. Displays include thrown glazed ware by founder Peter Anderson and his son Jim; original paintings and block prints by Peter's brothers, James McConnell Anderson and Walter Anderson. (Mon–Sat & Sun afternoons; closed major hols) Phone 875-7320. **Free.**

(For further information and copies of a self-guided city tour contact the Chamber of Commerce, 1000 Washington Ave, PO Box 187; 875-4424.)

Annual Events

Garden and Home Pilgrimage. Late Mar or early Apr.

Anniversary of the Landing of d'Iberville. Pageant, other activities commemorating the 1699 event. Last wkend Apr.

(For accomodations see Biloxi, Gulfport, Pascagoula)

Restaurants

✔★AUNT JENNY'S. *1217 N Washington Ave. 601/875-9201.* Hrs: 5–9 pm; Fri, Sat to 9:30 pm; Sun 11:30 am–8 pm. Closed Mon; July 4, Thanksgiving, Dec 24, 25. Res accepted Fri, Sat. Bar. Semi-a la carte: lunch, dinner $7.95–$9.95. Specializes in catfish, chicken, shrimp. Parking. House (1852) overlooks bayou; fireplace. Cr cds: MC, V.

★★GERMAINE'S. *1203 Bienville Blvd (US 90). 601/875-4426.* Hrs: 11:30 am–2 pm, 6–10 pm; Sun to 2 pm. Res accepted. Closed Mon; major hols. Creole, Amer menu. Bar. Semi-a la carte: lunch, dinner $10–$20.50. Child's meals. Specializes in crabmeat, stuffed mushrooms. Parking. Display of antique clocks; changing exhibits of Gulf Coast art. Cr cds: A, D, DS, MC, V.

★JOCELYN'S. *US 90E. 601/875-1925.* Hrs: 5–10 pm. Closed Sun; Jan 1, Thanksgiving, Dec 24, 25. Res accepted. French creole menu. Bar. Semi-a la carte: dinner $10–$18. Child's meals. Specializes in seafood, steak, stuffed mushrooms & eggplant. Parking. Renovated cottage (1890s). Casual dining. No cr cds accepted.

✔★SUMI'S. *503 Porter Ave. 601/875-3791.* Hrs: 5:30–9:30 pm. Closed Sun–Tues; most major hols. Okinawan menu. Bar. Semi-a la carte: dinner $5.95–$8.50. Specialties: Okinawan-style tempura, teriyaki dishes. Parking. Oriental decor. Cr cds: MC, V.

Oxford (B-3)

Settled: 1836 **Pop:** 9,984 **Elev:** 416 ft **Area code:** 601 **Zip:** 38655

Oxford was named for the English university city in an effort to lure the University of Mississippi to the site. Today "Ole Miss," with its forested, hilly 1,194-acre campus, dominates the area, and the town that boasted an opera house before the Civil War still reveres its role as a university town.

Jousting on the greensward and oratory from the courthouse steps were antebellum students' ideas of fun. Planters' sons, who brought their own horses and slaves to the university, reveled in chivalric traditions gleaned from Sir Walter Scott's romances. Future lawyers and statesmen emulated Henry Clay. When the Civil War came, both students and citizens were ready; nine companies of infantry and cavalry were raised, including the University Greys.

William Faulkner, Nobel Prize winning author, lived near the university at ''Rowan Oak'' (see #2). Many landmarks of his fictional Yoknapatawpha County can be found in surrounding Lafayette County.

What to See and Do

1. **University of Mississippi** (1848). (10,000 students) 1 mi W on University Ave. Greek-revival style buildings grouped around the Lyceum Building. Newer buildings follow the classical-revival style. Phone 232-7236 or -7237. On campus are the Center for Study of Southern Culture (232-5993) and

   University Gallery. Fine Arts Center. Faculty, student and traveling art exhibits. (Mon–Fri; closed university hols) Phone 232-7193. **Free.**

   University Museums. Housed in two adjoining buildings, the collections include Greek and Roman antiquities, antique scientific instruments, other historic objects; also Afro-American, Caribbean and Southern folk art. (Daily exc Mon; closed university hols) Phone 232-7073. **Free.**

   University Archives. University Library. Historical and literary works of and by Mississippians; works by William Faulkner in 35 languages, exhibit of his awards, including Nobel Prize, manuscripts and first editions. (Mon–Fri; closed university hols) Phone 232-7408. **Free.**

2. **Rowan Oak.** Old Taylor Rd, 1½ mi SE. Residence of William Faulkner from 1930–62; furnishings and memorabilia are as they were at the time of Faulkner's death. Maintained by the University of Mississippi. (Daily exc Mon; closed university hols) Phone 234-3284. **Free.**

(For further information contact the Oxford Tourism Council, PO Box 965; 234-4651.)

Annual Event

Faulkner Conference. Center for Study of Southern Culture, University of Mississippi (see #1). Various programs celebrate the author's accomplishments. 1st wk Aug.

Motels

✔ ★ ★**BEST WESTERN OXFORD INN.** 1101 Frontage Rd. 601/234-9500. 100 rms, 2 story. S $36–$49, D $41–$55; each addl $5; under 12 free; higher rates college football games. Crib free. TV; cable. Pool. Complimentary coffee in rms. Restaurant 6 am–midnight. Rm serv. Bar 2 pm–midnight; Thurs, Fri to 1 am. Ck-out noon. Meeting rms. Cr cds: A, C, D, DS, ER, MC, V.

★ ★**HOLIDAY INN.** (Box 647) 400 N Lamar, at Jefferson. 601/234-3031; FAX 601/234-2834. 100 rms, 2 story. S $45–$49; D $49–$57; each addl $6; under 19 free. Crib free. TV; cable. Pool. Restaurant 6 am–2 pm, 5–10 pm. Rm serv. Bar 4 pm–midnight. Ck-out 1 pm. Coin lndry. Meeting rms. Valet serv. Free airport transportation. Cr cds: A, C, D, DS, MC, V, JCB.

★**UNIVERSITY INN.** 2201 Jackson Ave W. 601/234-7013. 116 rms, 2 story. S $42; D $48; each addl $6; suites $110; under 12 free;

higher rates football wkends. Crib free. TV; cable. Pool. Complimentary continental bkfst. Ck-out 11 am. Cr cds: A, C, D, DS, MC, V.

Restaurants

★ ★**DOWNTOWN GRILL.** 1115 Jackson Ave. 601/234-2659. Hrs: 11 am–11 pm. Closed Sun; July 4, Labor Day, Dec 25. Res accepted. Bar to midnight; Thurs, Fri to 1 am. Semi-a la carte: lunch $4.95–$7.95, dinner $5.95–$18.95. Specialties: catfish Lafitte, chicken Sicilian, filet Paulette. Entertainment Thurs–Sat. Parking. Elegant dining. On Oxford Square. Cr cds: A, DS, MC, V.

✔ ★ ★**VILLA ELENA.** 2200 W Jackson Ave. 601/236-4413. Hrs: 11 am–2 pm, 5–11 pm; Sat from 5 pm. Closed Sun; most major hols & Dec 24. Res accepted Fri, Sat. Continental menu. Serv bar. Semi-a la carte: lunch $3.45–$7.95, dinner $8.75–$16.50. Serv charge. Specializes in veal, seafood. Parking. Cr cds: A, DS, MC, V.

Pascagoula (F-4)

Pop: 25,899 **Elev:** 15 ft **Area code:** 601 **Zip:** 39567

This resort, shipbuilding center and port offers fresh and salt water fishing, swimming and many other recreational opportunities. The city has a long and fascinating history. Pine ridges and mysterious bayous almost surround it, and its ''singing river'' is famous.

The Pascagoula River gives forth a peculiar singing music, which resembles a swarm of bees in flight. According to legend, the Pascagoula Indians (for whom the city is named) had a young chieftain who wooed and won a princess of the neighboring Biloxi tribe, even though she was betrothed. The Biloxi chief, enraged, attacked the Pascagoula tribe with an overwhelming force. The Pascagoula, realizing they could not win, joined hands and walked, singing, into the river to their death.

What to See and Do

1. **Old Spanish Fort and Museum** (1718). 4602 Fort St, 5 blks N of US 90. Built by the French, later captured by the Spanish, the fort's walls of massive cypress timbers cemented with oyster shells, mud and moss are 18 inches thick. Said to be the oldest structure in the Mississippi Valley. Museum has Native American relics, historic items. (Daily ; closed major hols) Phone 769-1505. ¢

2. **Scranton Museum.** Riverside Park at Pascagoula River. Nautical, marine and wetlands exhibits housed in restored shrimp boat. (Tues–Sat, also Sun afternoons; closed hols) Phone 762-6017 or 938-6612. **Free.**

3. **Singing River.** Pascagoula River, 2 blks W of courthouse. Singing sound is best heard on late summer and autumn nights. The music seems to increase in volume, coming nearer until it seems to be underfoot. Scientists have said it could be made by fish, sand scraping the hard slate bottom, natural gas escaping from sand bed or current sucked past a hidden cave. None of the explanations offered have been proven.

4. **Mississippi Sandhill Crane National Wildlife Refuge.** Off Gautier-Vancleave Rd, ½ mi N of I-10 exit 61, follow signs. Established to protect endangered cranes, the refuge's 3 units total 18,000 acres. Visitor center has slide programs (by request), wildlife exhibit, paintings and maps (Mon–Fri; closed legal hols). Tours (Jan–Feb, by appt). Also here is wildlife trail (¾ mi) with interpretive panels; outdoor exhibit; birdwatching. Contact Manager, 7200 Crane Lane, Gautier 39564; 497-6322. **Free.**

(For further information contact the Jackson County Area Chamber of Commerce, 825 Denny Ave, PO Box 480, 39568-0480; 762-3391.)

Annual Events

Mardi Gras. Month leading to Ash Wednesday.

Garden Club Pilgrimage. Tours of Historic houses and gardens in town. Late Mar–early Apr.

River Jamboree. In Moss Point, N on MS 63. Triathlon, arts & crafts, games. First Sat in May.

Jackson County Fair. Fairgrounds. Late Oct.

(See Biloxi, Ocean Springs; also see Mobile, AL)

Motels

✔ ★**DAYS INN.** *(6700 MS 63, Moss Point 39563)* N on MS 613, at I-10 exit 69. 601/475-0077; FAX 601/475-3783. 51 rms, 2 story. S $39.95–$43.95; D $45.95–$48.95; each addl $5; under 12 free. Crib free. TV. Pool. Complimentary continental bkfst, coffee. Restaurant adj 6 am–10 pm. Ck-out 11 am. Some refrigerators. Cr cds: A, D, DS, MC, V.

D ⩰ 🚫 ⊘ SC

★ ★**LA FONT INN.** *(Box 1028) 2703 Denny Ave. 601/762-7111; res: 800/647-6077 (exc MS), 800/821-3668 (MS); FAX 601/934-4324.* 192 rms, 2 story, 13 kits. S $53–$70; D $58–$70; each addl $5; suites $113–$140; under 14 free. Crib free. TV; cable. Pool; wading pool; poolside serv. Playground. Complimentary coffee in rms. Restaurant 6 am–10 pm. Rm serv. Bar 11 am–midnight. Ck-out 1 pm. Coin lndry. Meeting rms. Bellhops. Valet serv. Sundries. Lighted tennis. 18-hole golf privileges. Exercise equipt; weights, bicycles, whirlpool, steam rm, sauna. Lawn games. Refrigerators. Cr cds: A, C, D, DS, MC, V.

D 🐾 🛎 🏊 ⩰ 🏃 🚫 ⊘ SC

Restaurants

★**CATALINA.** *1925 Denny Ave. 601/762-0501.* Hrs: 11 am–9 pm; Sun, Mon to 8 pm. Closed most major hols. Res accepted Fri, Sat. Semi-a la carte: lunch, dinner $4–$12.95. Child's meals. Specializes in seafood, chicken, hamburgers. Casual family dining. Nautical theme. Cr cds: MC, V.

✔ ★**FILLETS.** *1911 Denny Ave. 601/769-0280.* Hrs: 11 am–9 pm; Fri, Sat to 10 pm. Closed Jan 1, July 4, Thanksgiving, Dec 25. Res accepted Fri, Sat. Semi-a la carte: lunch, dinner $2–$13. Specialties: rock shrimp, seafood platter, po boys. Parking. Casual dining. Cr cds: A, D, DS, MC, V.

D SC

★ ★**TIKI RESTAURANT, LOUNGE & MARINA.** *(PO Drawer 8, Gautier 39553)* 4 mi W off US 90. 601/497-1591. Hrs: 11 am–10 pm; Fri, Sat to midnight. Closed Jan 1, Dec 24–25. Res accepted. Bar to 1 am. Semi-a la carte: lunch $4.50–$5.95, dinner $5.95–$20.95. Child's meals. Specializes in fresh seafood, steak. Entertainment. Parking. On bayou. Family-owned. Cr cds: A, C, D, DS, MC, V.

D SC

Pass Christian (F-3)

Settled: 1704 **Pop:** 5,557 **Elev:** 10 ft **Area code:** 601 **Zip:** 39571

The town was a resort before the Civil War and the site of the South's first yacht club, which was founded in 1849. It is Mrs. Jane Murphy Manders who is generally credited with the "bed sheet surrender" of Pass Christian on April 4, 1862; attempting to save the city from further shelling by the Union fleet after the Confederate forces evacuated, Mrs. Murphy waved a sheet from her doorway. Pass Christian has hosted six vacationing US presidents—Jackson, Taylor, Grant, Theodore Roosevelt, Wilson and Truman. The world's largest oyster reef is offshore.

What to See and Do

1. Buccaneer State Park. 20 mi W on US 90 in Waveland. Located on the Gulf of Mexico, the park features two waterslides. Swimming beach, pool, wading pool; gulf fishing for speckled trout, flounder, redfish, crab, shrimp. Nature, bicycle trails; lighted tennis. Picnicking (shelters), playground, basketball courts, snack bar, lodge with game room, coin lndry. Primitive & improved camping. Standard fees. Phone 467-3822.

2. The Friendship Oak. 6 mi E on US 90, located on the University of Southern Mississippi's Gulf Park campus, beside Hardy Hall in Long Beach. The oak's 16-foot trunk and 5-foot-plus-diameter limbs dwarf Hardy Hall. A plaque dates the tree back to 1487, five years before Columbus' arrival to the new world. Legend proclaims that those who enter the tree's shadow shall remain lifetime friends. Wooden platform provides a peaceful haven. American poet Vachel Lindsay regularly held classes in the shade of the majestic oak.

(For further information contact the Chamber of Commerce, PO Box 307; 452-2252.)

Annual Events

Mardi Gras. Carnival Ball and Parade. Sat, Sun before Shrove Tuesday.

Garden Club Pilgrimage. Information at Chamber of Commerce Bldg, Small Craft Harbor. Visits to several historic houses and gardens in town. Late Mar.

Blessing of the Fleet. Festival; boat decorations competition; band; entertainment. Last Sun May.

Seafood Festival. Entertainment. Mid-July.

(For accommodations see Gulfport)

Restaurant

✔ ★ ★**ANNIE'S.** *120 W Bayview. 601/452-2062.* Hrs: 11:30 am–10 pm; Sun to 9 pm. Closed Mon; also Dec. Res accepted. Continental menu. Bar. Semi-a la carte: lunch, dinner $4–$14.50. Child's meals. Specializes in seafood, steak, veal, chicken. Parking. Mission bells from old Southern plantations displayed on patio. Family-owned. Cr cds: A, MC, V.

Philadelphia (C-3)

Pop: 6,758 **Elev:** 424 ft **Area code:** 601 **Zip:** 39350

This town was settled on Choctaw land. Several thousand Choctaws continue to live in the area. The Choctaw tribe, which once numbered more than 25,000, ceded its lands to the United States by the Treaty of Dancing Rabbit Creek in 1830. The Choctaw Indian Agency, which was founded shortly after the treaty was signed, is located in Philadelphia.

What to See and Do

Golden Memorial State Park. Approx 20 mi SW via MS 21, 5 mi E of Walnut Grove off MS 35. Park covering 120 acres on Golden Lake. Developed as a memorial to one-room schoolhouse that operated on this site after the Civil War. Swimming beach; fishing; boating (rentals). Nature, bicycle trails. Picnicking (shelters), playground. Standard fees. (Wed–Sun) Phone 253-2237.

(For further information contact the Philadelphia-Neshoba County Chamber of Commerce, 410 Poplar Ave, Suite 101, PO Box 51; 656-1742.)

Annual Events

Choctaw Indian Fair. Choctaw Indian Reservation, 8 mi W via MS 16. Entertainment; arts & crafts; cultural programs; princess pageant; music. Mid-July.

Neshoba County Fair. 8½ mi SW via MS 21S. Late July–early Aug.

(For accommodations see Louisville, Meridian)

Port Gibson (D-2)

Settled: 1788 **Pop:** 1,810 **Elev:** 120 ft **Area code:** 601 **Zip:** 39150

Many antebellum houses and buildings remain in Port Gibson, lending support to the story that General Grant spared the town on his march to Vicksburg with the words: "It's too beautiful to burn."

The Samuel Gibson House (ca 1805), oldest existing structure in town, has been restored and now houses the Port Gibson-Claiborne County Chamber of Commerce and Visitor Information Center.

What to See and Do

1. **Grand Gulf Military Park.** 8 mi NW off US 61. This site marks the former town of Grand Gulf, which lost 55 of 75 city blocks to Mississippi floods between 1855 and 1860. The Confederacy chose to fortify the banks when the population was only 160 and the town was dying.

   In the spring of 1862, Admiral David G. Farragut sent his powerful naval squadron upriver; Baton Rouge and Natchez fell, but Vicksburg refused to surrender. Confederate artillery and supporting troops were sent to Grand Gulf, where intermittent fighting between Union warships and Confederate shore batteries continued until a Union column landed at Bayou Pierre, marched on Grand Gulf and burned what remained of the town. War returned to Grand Gulf when Admiral D.D. Porter's ironclads opened fire on forts Cobun and Wade on the morning of April 29, 1863. After more than five hours, two ironclads were disabled and the guns of Fort Wade silenced.

   The park today includes fortifications, an observation tower, a cemetery, sawmill, dog-trot house, memorial chapel, water wheel and grist mill, a carriage house with vehicles used by the Confederates, a four-room cottage reconstructed from early days of Grand Gulf and several other pre-Civil War buildings. A museum in the visitor center displays Civil War, Indian and prehistoric artifacts (daily; closed Jan 1, Thanksgiving, Dec 25; fee). Park (daily). Picnic facilities, 42 camper pads (hookups). Phone 437-5911.

2. **First Presbyterian Church** (1859). Church & Walnut Sts. Gold-leaf hand with a finger pointing skyward tops the steeple; interior features old slave gallery and chandeliers taken from the steamboat *Robert E. Lee.*

3. **Antebellum houses.** Open year round by appointment; special schedule during Spring Pilgrimage. Phone 437-4351. ¢¢

4. **Oak Square** (ca 1850). 1207 Church St, 1 mi off Natchez Trace Pkwy. Restored 30-room mansion with 6 fluted, Corinthian columns, each standing 22 feet tall. Antique furnishings from the 18th and 19th centuries. Extensive grounds, courtyard, gazebo. Guest rms avail (see INNS). Tours (daily). Phone 437-4350 or 800/729-0240. ¢¢

5. **The Ruins of Windsor** Old Rodney Rd. Twenty-three stately columns are all that is left of a four-story mansion built in 1860 at a cost of $175,000 and destroyed by fire in 1890. Its proximity and size made it a natural marker for Mississippi River pilots, including Samuel Clemens.

6. **Energy Central.** 2 mi N on US 61 to Grand Gulf Rd. On grounds of Grand Gulf Nuclear Station. Exhibits and hands-on displays about nuclear energy and electricity. (Mon–Fri) Phone 437-6393 or -6317. **Free.**

7. **Rosswood Mansion** (1857). 9 mi S on US 61 to Lorman, then 2½ mi E on MS 552. Classic Greek-revival mansion designed by David Shroder, architect of Windsor (see #5), features columned galleries, 10 fireplaces, 15-foot ceilings, a winding stairway and slave quarters in the basement. The first owner's diary has survived and offers details of antebellum life on a cotton plantation. The 14 rooms are furnished with antiques. Guest rms avail. (Daily; closed some hols) Phone 800/533-5889. Tours ¢¢¢

(For walking and auto tour information, brochures and maps contact the Port Gibson-Claiborne County Chamber of Commerce, PO Box 491; 437-4351 or -8704.)

Annual Event

Spring Pilgrimage. Tours of historic houses. Phone 437-4351 for dates. Early spring.

(See Vicksburg)

Inns

★★**CANEMOUNT PLANTATION.** *(Rte 2, MS 552W, Lorman 39096)* 10 mi S on US 61, 8 mi W on MS 552. 601/877-3784; res: 800/423-0684 (exc MS). 3 cottages. No rm phones. S, D $145; each addl $65. Children over 12 yrs only. TV. Heated pool. Complimentary full bkfst. Complimentary coffee in rms. Ck-out noon, ck-in 2 pm. Valet serv. On 6,000-acre working plantation. Built 1854; fireplaces. Totally nonsmoking. Cr cds: MC, V.

★★**GIBSON'S LANDING.** *1002 Church St.* 601/437-3432. 5 rms, 3 story. S, D $75–$105; each addl $10. Crib free. TV; cable. Complimentary full bkfst, coffee. Restaurant nearby. Ck-out noon, ck-in 4:30 pm. Built 1830; unusual spiral staircase. Cr cds: MC, V.

★★**OAK SQUARE COUNTRY INN.** *1207 Church St.* 601/437-4350; res: 800/729-0240. 10 rms, 2 story. S $60–$70; D $75–$95. TV. Complimentary Southern bkfst. Wine avail. Ck-out 11 am. Restored antebellum mansion (ca 1850) and guest house; antique furnishings. Courtyard, fountain, gazebo, massive oak trees. Free tour of mansion, grounds. Cr cds: A, MC, V.

Restaurant

✔★**OLD DEPOT.** *1202 Market St.* 601/437-4711. Hrs: 11 am–9 pm; Fri, Sat to 10:30 pm. Closed Sun; major hols. Res accepted Fri, Sat. Bar. Semi-a la carte: lunch, dinner $3.95–$15.75. Child's meals. Specializes in steak, seafood, red beans & rice. Parking. Cr cds: A, MC, V.

Sardis (B-3)

Pop: 2,128 **Elev:** 379 ft **Area code:** 601 **Zip:** 38666

What to See and Do

1. **Heflin House Museum** (1858). 304 S Main. One of the few remaining antebellum structures in Sardis and Panola County; houses exhibits on history of Panola County from Indian times through 1900. (Mon–Fri by appt; closed hols) Donation. Contact Chamber of Commerce.

2. **Sardis Lake and Dam.** 9 mi E off I-55. This lake, with a 260-mile shoreline formed by damming the Little Tallahatchie River, is part of the Yazoo Basin flood control project. Noted for its natural white sand beaches. Swimming, waterskiing; fishing; boating (launching

ramps). Picnicking. Camping (some fees). Interpretive programs. Phone 563-4531. **Free.** Overlooking the lake is

John W. Kyle State Park. On 740 acres overlooking Sardis Lake. Pool (summer, daily exc Mon), waterskiing; fishing; boating (ramps). Nature trails; lighted tennis. Picnicking (shelters), playground, playing field, snack bar, lodge, coin lndry. Improved camping, cabins. Standard fees. Phone 487-1345.

3. **Enid Lake and Dam.** 21 mi S on I-55, then 1 mi E. Shoreline with swimming; boating. Picnicking. Camping (hookups; fee). Amphitheater. Golden Age and Golden Access passports accepted (see INTRODUCTION). Dam is part of the Yazoo Basin Flood Control Plan. Phone 563-4571. On south shore of lake is

George Payne Cossar State Park. 25 mi S on I-55, then 4 mi E on MS 32. Park covering 900 acres situated on a peninsula jutting into Enid Lake. Swimming pool, waterskiing; fishing; boating (ramp). Nature, bicycle trails (rentals); miniature golf. Picnicking (shelters), playground, concession, restaurant (yr round, Wed–Sun), lodge, coin lndry. Improved camping, cabins. Standard fees. Phone 623-7356.

(For further information contact the Chamber of Commerce, 114 W Lee St, PO Box 377; 487-3451.)

Motel

✔ ★ ★ **BEST WESTERN SARDIS INN.** *(Box 279)* 1/8 mi W on MS 315 at I-55, exit 252. *601/487-2424.* 79 rms, 2 story. S $33–$36; D $36–$48; each addl $6; under 12 free. Crib free. TV; cable. Pool; wading pool. Restaurant 6 am–10 pm. Rm serv. Bar 4 pm–midnight. Ck-out 11 am. Some refrigerators. Cr cds: A, C, D, DS, MC, V.

Starkville (C-4)

Founded: 1831 **Pop:** 18,458 **Elev:** 374 ft **Area code:** 601 **Zip:** 39759

Starkville is the seat of Oktibbeha County and the home of Mississippi State University.

What to See and Do

1. **Mississippi State University** (1878). (14,000 students) 1 mi E, on University Dr. Originally Mississippi Agricultural and Mechanical College, it became a state university in 1958. On a 4,200-acre tract, approximately 750 acres make up the campus; the Mississippi Agricultural and Forestry Experiment Station utilizes much of the remaining land for cultivation, pasture and buildings. On campus are the Dunn-Seiler Geology Museum, Cobb Institute of Archaeology, University Art Gallery and the Chapel of Memories. Phone 325-2323.

2. **Oktibbeha County Heritage Museum.** Fellowship & Russell Sts. Artifacts from the county's past housed in former GM&O railroad station. (Tues–Thurs; or by appt; closed hols) Phone 323-0211. **Free.**

3. **Noxubee National Wildlife Refuge.** SE off MS 25; follow signs from stadium at Mississippi State University (see #1). This 46,000-acre refuge, which includes 1,200-acre Bluff Lake, offers space for more than 200 species of birds, including waterfowl, wild turkey, the endangered bald eagle and red-cockaded woodpecker, as well as alligators and deer. Fishing (Mar–Oct), hunting (fall). Hiking. Refuge (daily). Phone 323-5548. **Free.**

(For further information contact the Visitors & Convention Council, 322 University Dr, PO Box 2720; 323-3322.)

(See Columbus)

Motels

★ ★ **HOLIDAY INN.** *(Box 751)* MS 12 & Montgomery St, opp MSU. *601/323-6161; FAX 601/323-8073.* 174 rms, 2 story. S $40, D $44–$50; each addl $6; under 18 free; higher rates football wkends. Crib free. TV; cable. Pool. Restaurant 6 am–2 pm, 5–10 pm. Rm serv. Bar 5 pm–midnight, closed Sun. Ck-out noon. Meeting rms. Cr cds: A, C, D, DS, MC, V, JCB.

✔ ★ **REGAL INN.** *410 Lee St. 601/323-8251.* 62 rms, 2 story. S $32; D $36; each addl $4; under 12 free. Crib $5. TV; cable. Pool. Restaurant 11:30 am–midnight. Bar. Ck-out noon. Meeting rms. Cr cds: A, D, DS, MC, V.

★ **UNIVERSITY INN.** *(Box 905)* MS 12 & Spring St. *601/323-9550; res: 800/475-8648.* 120 units, 2 story. S $34; D $40; each addl $6; suites $125; under 13 free; wkly rates; higher rates football, baseball games. Crib $5. TV; cable. Pool. Complimentary coffee. Ck-out noon. Meeting rms. Some in-rm steam baths, whirlpools. Cr cds: A, C, D, DS, MC, V.

Inn

★ ★ **STATE HOUSE HOTEL.** *(Box 2002)* Main & Jackson Sts. *601/323-2000.* 40 units, 3 story, 20 suites. S $49–$70; D $55–$80; each addl $3–$10; suites $74; under 13 free; higher rates football wkends. Crib $10. TV, cable. Dining rm 6:30 am–2 pm, 6–9:30 pm. Ck-out noon, ck-in 2 pm. Some refrigerators. Balconies. Antique furnishings; courtyard. Cr cds: A, C, D, DS, MC, V.

Restaurant

✔ ★ **HARVEY'S.** *406 MS 12. 601/323-1639.* Hrs: 11 am–2 pm, 5–9:30 pm; Fri, Sat to 10 pm. Closed Sun; most major hols. Res accepted; required Fri, Sat. Bar 5 pm–midnight. Semi-a la carte: lunch $2.95–$9.95, dinner $5.95–$13.95. Child's meals. Specializes in steak, seafood. Parking. Cr cds: A, DS, MC, V.

Tupelo (B-4)

Settled: 1833 **Pop:** 30,685 **Elev:** 290 ft **Area code:** 601 **Zip:** 38801

Tupelo is built on what was formerly Chickasaw Indian land. On May 26, 1736, two forces of French colonists and their Choctaw allies unsuccessfully attacked the Chickasaw in an attempt to rescue prisoners and avenge an attack by Natchez Indians on the French settlement of Natchez. Failure to conquer the Chickasaw prevented the extension of French authority into northern Alabama, Mississippi and western Tennessee.

When the town was ceded by the Treaty of Pontotoc in 1832, settlers moved in and began farming. After the Battle of Shiloh, April 6–7, 1862, Confederate General P.G.T. Beauregard and his defeated troops retreated to Tupelo.

This was the first city to sign for TVA power—on October 11, 1933. Less than four months later service was begun at a tremendous savings. Tupelo is also the birthplace of Elvis Presley (see #2).

What to See and Do

1. **Pvt John Allen National Fish Hatchery** 111 Elizabeth St. This federal hatchery, one of the oldest (1902), operates 15 ponds totaling 17

acres. A warmwater hatchery, it produces striped and largemouth bass, bluegill and redear; it distributes one million fish annually for use in management of reservoirs and coastal waters. (Daily) Phone 842-1341. **Free.**

2. Elvis Presley Park and Museum. 306 Elvis Presley Dr. In park is small white frame house where Presley lived for the first three years of his life. Museum houses collection of Elvis memorabilia. Chapel (free). (Daily; buildings closed Thanksgiving & Dec 25) Phone 841-1245. House **¢**

3. Tupelo Museum. 2 mi W via MS 6 at Ballard Park. Displays include NASA space equipment used in Apollo missions; Elvis Presley room; reproductions of Western Union office, general store, train station, log cabin; Civil War and Chickasaw items. (Daily exc Mon; closed some hols) Phone 841-6438. **¢**

4. Tombigbee State Park. 6 mi SE off MS 6. A 702-acre park with a 102-acre spring-fed lake. Swimming beach (summer, daily). Fishing; boating (ramp, rentals). Nature trail; tennis; archery range. Picnicking (shelters), playground, snack bar, lodge. Primitive & improved camping, cabins. Standard fees. Phone 842-7669.

5. Trace State Park. 10 mi W via MS 6. On 2,500 acres with a 600-acre lake. Swimming beach, waterskiing; fishing for bass, catfish, redear, bluegill and crappie; boating (ramp, rentals). Hiking, horseriding trail; golf. Picnicking; snack bar. Tent & trailer camping (electric hookups, dump station, water), cabins. Standard fees. Phone 489-2958.

6. Natchez Trace Parkway Visitor Center. 5 mi N at jct Pkwy, US 45 (see NATCHEZ TRACE PARKWAY).

7. Tupelo National Battlefield. 1 mi W on MS 6. One-acre tract near area where Confederate line was formed to attack Union position. Marker with texts and maps explains battle. (Daily) **Free.**

8. Brices Cross Roads National Battlefield Site. 17 mi N on US 45 to Baldwyn, then 6 mi W on MS 370. One-acre site overlooks terrain where Confederate soldiers defeated an attacking Union force. Marker with texts and maps identifies landmarks. Adjacent cemetery is burial site of over 100 identified Confederate soldiers. (Daily) Phone 842-1572. **Free.**

9. Tombigbee National Forest. 20 mi S, off Natchez Trace Pkwy. This section of the forest, along with a tract to the south on MS 15 near Louisville (see), totals 66,341 acres. Davis Lake provides swimming (fee); fishing. Picnicking. Camping (electric hookups; fee; dump station). Recreation area (Mar–mid-Nov). Fees are charged at recreation sites. A Ranger District office is located in Ackerman. Contact Forest Supervisor, 100 W Capitol St, Suite 1141, Jackson 39269; 965-4391. Day use **¢¢**

(For further information contact the Convention & Visitors Bureau, 399 E Main St, PO Box 1485; 841-6521 or 800/533-0611.)

Motels

★**COMFORT INN.** 1190 N Gloster. 601/842-5100; FAX 601/844-0554. 83 rms, 2 story. S $35–$39; D $39–$43; each addl $4; under 18 free. Crib $4. TV; cable. Free continental bkfst. Ck-out noon. Meeting rms. Cr cds: A, C, D, DS, MC, V.

✔★**ECONO LODGE.** 1500 McCullough Blvd. 601/844-1904; FAX 601/844-0139. 100 units, 2 story. S $34–$37; D $37–$40; each addl $5; under 16 free; wkly rates; higher rates special events. Crib free. TV; cable. Pool. Complimentary continental bkfst. Ck-out 11 am. Coin lndry. Free airport, RR station, bus depot transportation. Cr cds: A, C, D, DS, MC, V.

★★**RAMADA INN.** (Drawer G) 854 N Gloster St, jct US 45, 78. 601/844-4111; FAX 601/844-4111, ext 2496. 230 rms, 3 story. No elvtr. S $43; D $53; each addl $5; suites $95–$175; studio rms $50–$75; under 18 free. Crib free. TV; cable. Pool; wading pool, poolside serv. Restau-

rant 6 am–10 pm. Rm serv. Bar 4 pm–midnight; entertainment, dancing exc Sun. Ck-out 1 pm. Coin lndry. Convention facilities. Valet serv. Sundries. Barber, beauty shop. Free airport transportation. Cr cds: A, C, D, DS, MC, V.

★★**TRACE INN.** 3400 W Main St. 601/842-5555. 133 rms, 3 story. S, D $39–$44; each addl $5; under 12 free; wkly rates. Crib free. TV; cable. Pool. Ck-out 11 am. Meeting rms. Valet serv. Free airport transportation. Balconies. Cr cds: A, C, D, DS, MC, V.

Motor Hotel

★★**EXECUTIVE INN.** (Box 1603) 1011 N Gloster. 601/841-2222; res: 800/533-3220; FAX 601/844-7836. 115 rms, 5 story. S $39–$63; D $47–$71; each addl $8; suites $150–$200; under 18 free. Crib free. TV; cable. Indoor pool; whirlpool, sauna. Restaurant 5 am–10 pm; Sat, Sun 7 am–2 pm. Rm serv 7 am–2 pm, 5–10 pm. Bar 4 pm–midnight, closed Sun. Ck-out noon. Meeting rms. Bellhops. Cr cds: A, C, D, DS, MC, V, JCB.

Restaurants

★★**FISHERMAN'S BAY.** 1204 N Gloster. 601/844-8440. Hrs: 4:30–9:30 pm. Closed Sun; major hols. Res accepted. Bar. Semi-a la carte: dinner $8.95–$25. Child's meals. Specializes in seafood, steak. Valet parking. Nautical decor. Cr cds: A, C, D, DS, MC, V.

★★**GLOSTER 205.** 205 N Gloster. 601/842-7205. Hrs: 11 am–midnight. Closed Sun; hols. Res accepted. Bar. Semi-a la carte: lunch $3.50–$6.95, dinner $10.95–$19.95. Specializes in prime rib, steak, seafood. Parking. Cr cds: A, C, D, DS, MC, V.

✔★**JEFFERSON PLACE.** 823 Jefferson St. 601/844-8696. Hrs: 11 am–midnight. Closed Sun; Thanksgiving, Dec 25. Bar. Semi-a la carte: lunch $3.95–$9.95, dinner $5.25–$14.95. Specializes in steak, chicken, shrimp. Parking. Cr cds: A, D, MC, V.

★★**PAPA VANELLI'S.** 1302 N Gloster. 601/844-4410. Hrs: 11 am–10 pm. Closed Dec 25. Italian, Greek menu. Bar. A la carte entrees: lunch, dinner $4.95–$14. Child's meals. Specializes in pizza, pasta buffet. Parking. Family-owned. Cr cds: A, C, D, DS, MC, V.

Unrated Dining Spots

JIM'S SHRIMP & OYSTER BAR. 1721 N Gloster. 601/844-4326. Hrs: 5–10 pm. Closed Sun. Bar 4 pm–midnight. Semi-a la carte: dinner $5.95–$16.95. Child's meals. Specializes in seafood, steak, prime rib. Entertainment Fri & Sat. Parking. Outdoor dining. Cr cds: A, DS, MC, V.

MALONE'S FISH & STEAK HOUSE. Just W off MS 6. 601/842-2747. Hrs: 5–10 pm. Closed Sun, Mon; Thanksgiving; also 2 wks late Dec. Semi-a la carte: dinner $3.95–$12.95. Child's meals. Specializes in steak, catfish. Salad bar. Parking. Cr cds: MC, V.

MORRISON'S CAFETERIA. 120 Tupelo Mall, 1 blk S of MS 6. 601/844-5895. Hrs: 11:30 am–8:30 pm; Sun 11 am–8 pm. Avg ck: lunch $6.75, dinner $7.25. Child's meals. Specializes in roast beef, seafood. Cr cds: MC, V.

Vicksburg (D-2)

Settled: 1790 **Pop:** 20,908 **Elev:** 200 ft **Area code:** 601 **Zip:** 39180

In June, 1862, the Union controlled the Mississippi River with the exception of Vicksburg, which was in Confederate hands. The location of the town, partly on high bluffs above the river, made it impossible to move traffic up or down the river without subjecting the boats to withering fire from strong Confederate batteries. This position made it possible to maintain communication lines with Louisiana, which were vital to the Confederacy.

Grant's purpose was to gain complete control of the Mississippi as a waterway and, in doing so, to split the South. In June, Admiral David Farragut sent his fleet of Union gunboats upriver from New Orleans and shelled the town; he was, however, forced to withdraw before taking the city or silencing its guns. General William Tecumseh Sherman, also attempting to take Vicksburg, moved along the west banks of the river, south from Memphis with 30,000 troops. He was repulsed. Meanwhile, Grant's supply lines were being broken and harassed by Confederate cavalry.

Grant was now desperate. He had to take Vicksburg. He ordered Admiral David Porter to move his gunboats south from Memphis and to pass Vicksburg at night. The boats were sighted; two transports were lost. The others got through, and Grant, with an army west of the river, now had transportation across the river. Once in Mississippi, the Union army, living off the land, moved around Vicksburg in a series of brilliant diversionary maneuvers that kept the Confederate cavalry busy accomplishing nothing. Grant now took Jackson and moved toward Vicksburg from the east. He attacked the city with three corps, setting the time of attack and synchronizing watches to make sure all attacked together. But his forces were driven back.

Grant was a more modern and committed general than most of the other Union commanders in the war. He would settle for nothing less than total victory, unconditional surrender of the city of Vicksburg. He realized that to take Vicksburg, the town must be starved; so he surrounded it and laid siege. For 47 days and nights Grant pounded Vicksburg with mortar and cannon fire; and the populace, hiding in caves, nearly starved.

The caves dug by the residents of Vicksburg and the Union army's trenches and tunneling were made easier because the city was built on loess, a wind-blown silt that forms a compacted but soft soil. Grant dug tunnels and planted mines under Confederate positions, but only one charge was set off. On July 4, the Confederates agreed to surrender the city. On that day the South's cause was dealt a mighty blow from which it never recovered.

Modern Vicksburg is nearly surrounded by the Vicksburg National Military Park (see #1), which is as much a part of the town as the streets and fine old houses. Originally an important river port, Vicksburg has a fascinating riverfront on the Yazoo Canal, just off the Mississippi. Plan to spend several days; the town offers much to see and do.

What to See and Do

1. **Vicksburg National Military Park & Cemetery.** This historic park, the site of Union siege lines and a brave Confederate defense, borders the eastern and northern sections of the city. A visitor center is at the park entrance, near US 80 & I-20. Museum; exhibits and audiovisual aids. Self-guided, 16-mile tour. (Daily; closed Dec 25) Phone 636-0583. Per vehicle ¢¢ Within park is

   Cairo Museum. The Union ironclad USS *Cairo*, which sank in 1862, was raised in 1964 and subsequently was restored. An audiovisual program and more than 1,000 artifacts from the sunken gunboat can be viewed inside the museum. (Daily; closed Dec 25) Phone 636-2199. **Free.**

2. **Old Court House Museum** (1858). Court Square, 1008 Cherry St. Built with slave labor, this building offers a view of the Yazoo Canal from its hilltop position. Here Grant raised the US flag on July 4, 1863, signifying the end of fighting after 47 days. Courthouse now houses an extensive display of Americana: Confederate Room contains weapons, documents on the siege of Vicksburg; also Pioneer Room; Furniture Room; Native American displays and objets d'art. (Daily; closed Jan 1, Thanksgiving, Dec 24–25) Phone 636-0741. ¢

3. **Toys and Soldiers Museum.** 1100 Cherry St at Grove. Displays of Sebastian sculptures, Mickey Mouse memorabilia, Civil War artifacts, old model and toy trains, old toys, pewter statuary and other miniatures. More than 32,000 toy soldiers. Gift shop. (Daily; closed Jan 1, Thanksgiving, Dec 24–25) Phone 638-1986. ¢¢

4. **Antebellum houses.**

   Martha Vick House (1830). 1300 Grove St. Built by the daughter of the founder of Vicksburg, Newit Vick. Greek-revival facade; restored original interior furnished with 18th- and 19th-century antiques; outstanding art collection. (Daily; closed some hols) Phone 638-7036. ¢¢

   McRaven Home Civil War Tour Home. 1445 Harrison St. Heaviest-shelled house during Siege of Vicksburg; provides an architectural record of Vicksburg history, from frontier cottage (1797) to Empire (1836) and finally to elegant Greek-revival townhouse (1849); many original furnishings. Original brick walks surround the house; garden of live oaks, boxwood, magnolia and many plants. Guided tours. (Daily; closed Jan) Phone 636-1663. ¢¢

   Cedar Grove (1840). 2200 Oak St. Elegant mansion shelled by Union gunboats in siege; restored, but a cannonball is still lodged in parlor wall; roof garden with view of Mississippi and Yazoo rivers; tea room; many original furnishings. Over four acres of formal gardens; courtyards, fountains, gazebos. (Daily) Guest rms avail (see INNS). Phone 800/862-1300. Guided tours ¢¢

   Anchuca (1830). 1010 First East St. Restored Greek-revival mansion furnished with period antiques and gas-burning chandeliers. Landscaped gardens, brick courtyard. (Daily; closed Dec 25) Guest rms (see INNS). Phone 636-4931 or 800/262-4822 (exc MS). Guided tours ¢¢

   Duff Green (1856). 1114 First East St. Mansion of Paladian architecture shelled by Union forces during siege, then used as hospital for remainder of the war. Restored; antique furnishings. Guided tours. High tea & tour (by reservation). Guest rms avail (see INNS). (Daily) Phone 636-6968. ¢¢

5. **"The Vanishing Glory."** 717 Clay St. Thirty-minute dramatization of Civil War siege of Vicksburg; story based upon diaries and writings of people who lived through the campaign; wide-screen production, quadraphonic sound. (Shown every hour, daily) ¢¢

6. **Biedenharn Candy Company and Museum of Coca-Cola Memorabilia.** 1107 Washington St. Building in which Coca-Cola was first bottled in 1894. Restored candy store; old-fashioned soda fountain; collection of Coca-Cola advertising and memorabilia. (Daily; closed Jan 1, Easter, Thanksgiving, Dec 25) Phone 638-6514. ¢

7. **Waterways Experiment Station.** 2 mi S of I-20 on Halls Ferry Rd. Principal research and testing laboratory of the US Army Corps of Engineers. Research ranges from hydraulics and soils to wetlands, and from concrete and military vehicles to environmental relationships. River, harbor and flood control projects are studied on scale models, some with wave and tide-making machines, others with model towboats. Guided tours (Mon–Fri, mid-morning–early afternoon; closed hols); also self-guided tours. Visitor center (daily). Phone 634-2502. **Free.**

8. **Tourist Information Center.** US 80 E. Furnishes free information, maps and brochures on points of interest and historic houses. Guide service (fee). House (daily; closed Jan 1, Thanksgiving, Dec 25). For information contact PO Box 110; 636-9421 or 800/221-3536.

Annual Events

Spring Pilgrimage. Twelve antebellum houses are open to the public at this time. Three tours daily. Contact tourist information center for details (see #8). Mar 19–Apr 3.

Siege Re-enactment. 500 persons re-enact the siege of Vicksburg. Early July.

(See Port Gibson)

Motels

★ **DAYS INN.** *2 Pemberton Place. 601/634-1622; FAX 601/638-4337.* 85 units, 2 story, 20 suites. June–Aug: S, D $30–$40; each addl $5; suites $35–$45; under 12 free; lower rates rest of yr. Crib free. TV; cable. Pool. Restaurant adj 6 am–midnight. Ck-out 11 am. Cr cds: A, D, DS, MC, V.

✔ ★ ★ **PARK INN INTERNATIONAL.** *4137 I-20 Frontage Rd, exit 4B. 601/638-5811.* 116 rms, 2 story. S $29–$60; D $39–$75; each addl $7; under 16 free. Crib free. TV. Pool. Complimentary buffet bkfst. Restaurant 6–10 am, 5–10 pm. Rm serv 5–9:30 pm. Bar 7:30 pm–1:30 am; entertainment, dancing. Ck-out 12:30 pm. Meeting rms. Bellhops. Some refrigerators. Cr cds: A, C, D, DS, ER, MC, V.

★ ★ **QUALITY INN.** *2390 S Frontage Rd, at I-20. 601/634-8607.* 70 rms, 2 story. S, D $40–$47; each addl $5; under 18 free. Crib $3. TV; cable. Pool; whirlpool, sauna. Continental bkfst. Ck-out 11 am. Refrigerators. Cr cds: A, C, D, DS, MC, V, JCB.

✔ ★ **SUPER 8.** *4127 I-20 Frontage Rd. 601/638-5077.* 62 rms, 2 story. S $35.88; D $41.88; each addl $4; under 12 free; wkly rates. Crib free. TV; cable. Pool. Complimentary continental bkfst, coffe. Restaurant nearby. Ck-out 11 am. Cr cds: A, C, D, DS, MC, V.

Motor Hotel

★ ★ **HOLIDAY INN.** *3330 Clay St. 601/636-4551; FAX 601/636-4552.* 173 rms, 2 story. S $49–$56; D $51–$58; each addl $7; under 18 free. Crib free. TV; cable. Indoor pool; sauna. Playground. Restaurant 6 am–10 pm. Rm serv. Bar noon–4 pm. Ck-out noon. Coin lndry. Meeting rms. Bellhops. Holidome. Game rm. Cr cds: A, C, D, DS, MC, V, JCB.

Inns

★ ★ ★ **ANCHUCA INN.** *1010 First East St. 601/636-4931; res: 800/262-4822.* 12 rms, 2 story. Mar–Dec: S $70–$110; D $75–$175; each addl $20; lower rates rest of yr. Crib free. TV. Pool; hot tub. Complimentary bkfst. Ck-out noon, ck-in 2 pm. Greek-revival house (1830). Gas-lit chandeliers, period antiques and artifacts. Tour of house. Cr cds: A, D, DS, ER, MC, V, JCB.

★ ★ ★ **CEDAR GROVE MANSION.** *2200 Oak St. 601/636-1605; res: 800/862-1300 (exc MS), 800/448-2820 (MS).* 22 rms, 4 story. S $85–$160; D $85–$160; each addl $20. Children over 6 yrs only. Pool. Complimentary Southern bkfst. Ck-out noon, ck-in 2 pm. Gift shop. Tennis courts. Antebellum mansion built 1840. Many original antiques; gas-burning chandeliers. Formal gardens, gazebos, fountains, statues. River view. Cr cds: A, MC, V.

★ ★ **THE CORNERS.** *601 Klein St. 601/636-7421; res: 800/444-7421.* 9 rms, 2 story. Some rm phones. S $75–$95; D $75–$105;

each addl $20; suites $150; extended stay rates. TV; cable. Complimentary full bkfst, coffee. Restaurant nearby. Ck-out 11 am, ck-in noon. Bellhop. Health club privileges. 1 blk from river. Built 1872 as a wedding gift. Antiques; extensive gardens. Totally nonsmoking. Cr cds: A, MC, V.

★ ★ **DUFF GREEN MANSION.** *1114 First East St. 601/638-6662; res: 800/992-0037.* 7 units, 3 story. No rm phones. Mar–Nov: S, D $85–$160; each addl $10; suites $120–$160; under 5 free; wkly plan; lower rates rest of yr. Pet accepted. TV; cable. Pool; whirlpool. Complimentary full bkfst, coffee and tea. Restaurant nearby. Ck-out 11 am, ck-in 3 pm. Paladian mansion (1856), used as both Confederate and Union hospital during Civil war, was shelled during siege; completely restored, many antiques. Cr cds: A, MC, V.

Restaurants

★ ★ ★ **DELTA POINT.** *4144 Washington St. 601/636-5317.* Hrs: 11 am–2 pm, 5–10 pm; Sat 5 pm–11 pm; Sun 11 am–2:30 pm. Closed some major hols. Res accepted. Continental menu. Bar. Wine list. Semi-a la carte: lunch $5–$10.50, dinner $11.25–$27.95. Sun champagne brunch $12.25. Child's meals. Specialties: Black Forest filet, sea scallop sauté. Own baking. Pianist Wed–Sun. Parking. Panoramic view of Mississippi River. Fountain, formal dining. Cr cds: A, C, D, DS, MC, V.

★ ★ **EDDIE MONSOUR'S.** *1903 G Mission 66. 601/638-1571.* Hrs: 11 am–2 pm; 5:30–10 pm; Sat from 5:30 pm. Closed Sun; major hols. Res accepted. Lebanese, Amer menu. Bar. Semi-a la carte: lunch $5–$6, dinner $8.50–$25. Child's meals. Specializes in steak, seafood. Salad bar. Parking. Country-French decor. Cr cds: A, C, D, MC, V.

★ ★ **MAXWELL'S.** *4207 Clay St. 601/636-1344.* Hrs: 11 am–10 pm. Closed Sun; major hols. French, Amer menu. Bar 4:30–11 pm. Semi-a la carte: lunch $5.50–$9.75, dinner $8.95–$17.95 (serv charge 15%). Lunch buffet $6. Child's meals. Specializes in seafood, veal, steak. Salad bar. Pianist. Parking. Cr cds: A, C, D, MC, V.

✔ ★ ★ **NEW ORLEAN'S CAFE.** *1100 Washington St. 601/638-8182.* Hrs: 11 am–10 pm; Sun brunch 10:30 am–2:30 pm. Closed Thanksgiving, Dec 25. New Orleans-style menu. Bar. Semi-a la carte: lunch $2.95–$6.95, dinner $6.95–$14.95. Sun brunch $6.95. Child's meals. Specializes in steak, seafood, po boys. Parking. Casual dining. Cr cds: A, MC, V.

✔ ★ ★ **OLD SOUTHERN TEA ROOM.** *801 Clay St, in Hotel Vicksburg. 601/636-4005.* Hrs: 11 am–2 pm, 5–9 pm; Sun to 2 pm. Closed some major hols. Southern menu. Bar. Semi-a la carte: lunch $4.25–$12.95, dinner $5.95–$12.95. Specialties: southern fried chicken, stuffed baked ham, plantation cooking. Parking. Recipes handed down through families from antebellum days. Cr cds: A, MC, V.

✔ ★ **WALNUT HILLS ROUND TABLES.** *1214 Adams St. 601/638-4910.* Hrs: 11 am–9 pm. Closed Sat; most major hols. Bar. Complete meals: lunch, dinner $5.50–$13.95. Child's meals. Specializes in Southern cooking, fried chicken. Parking. Built 1880. Cr cds: A, D, DS, MC, V.

Woodville (E-1)

Founded: 1811 **Pop:** 1,393 **Elev:** 410 ft **Area code:** 601 **Zip:** 39669

First settled in the 18th century, Woodville grew steadily and became the seat of Wilkinson County. It is the home of *The Woodville Republican*, the oldest newspaper and the oldest business institution in Mississippi. The town still has many beautiful 19th-century houses, and some of the state's first churches. These include the Woodville Baptist (1809), the Woodville Methodist (1824) and St Paul's Episcopal, which has an Erben organ, installed in 1838.

What to See and Do

1. **Rosemont Plantation** (ca 1810). 1 mi E on MS 24 (Main St). The home of Jefferson Davis and his family. His parents, Samuel and Jane Davis, moved to Woodville and built the house when the boy was two years old. The Confederate president grew up here and returned to visit his family throughout his life. Many family furnishings remain, including a spinning wheel that belonged to Jane Davis. Original working atmosphere of the 300-acre plantation. Five generations of the Davis family are buried here. (Mar–mid-Dec, Mon–Fri) ¢¢

2. **Wilkinson County Museum.** Court House Square. Housed in Greek revival-style building; changing exhibits, period room settings. (Mon–Fri, also Sat mornings) Phone 888-3998.   **Free.**

(For further information contact the Woodville Civic Club, PO Box 814; 888-3998.)

(For accommodations see Natchez)

Yazoo City (C-2)

Founded: 1823 **Pop:** 12,427 **Elev:** 120 ft **Area code:** 601 **Zip:** 39194

What to See and Do

1. **Yazoo Historical Museum.** Triangle Cultural Center, 332 N Main St. Exhibits cover history of Yazoo County from prehistoric time to present; Civil War artifacts; fossils. Tours. (Tues–Fri; closed Jan 1, Thanksgiving, Dec 24–26) Phone 746-2273.   **Free.**

2. **Delta National Forest.** W via US 49, 61, MS 16. Numerous small lakes, streams and greentree reservoirs contained on 59,500

acres. Fishing, hunting for squirrel, raccoon, turkey, waterfowl, rabbit, woodcock, deer. Blue Lake picnic area and walking trail; Sweetgum, Overcup Oak and Green Ash natural areas. Primitive camping. A Ranger District office is located in Rolling Fork, phone 873-6256. Contact Forest Supervisor, 100 W Capitol St, Suite 1141, Jackson 39269; 965-4391 or 873-6256.   **Free.**

3. **Casey Jones Railroad Museum.** 1 Main St, in Vaughan, 25 mi E on MS 432, 6 mi S on I-55. Site of famous 1900 Casey Jones train wreck. Now state-owned museum covering story of wreck; local railroad history, folklore and artifacts; 1923 steam locomotive on display. (Daily; closed Jan 1, Thanksgiving, Dec 25) Phone 673-9864. ¢

(For further information contact the Yazoo County Chamber of Commerce, 211 E Broadway, PO Box 172; 746-1273.)

(See Jackson)

Motels

★**DAYSTOP.** *1801 Jerry Clower Blvd.* 601/746-1877. 31 rms. S $30–$34; D $38–$40; each addl $5; under 12 free. Crib free. TV: cable. Pool. Complimentary continental bkfst, coffee. Ck-out 11 am. Cr cds: A, D, DS, MC, V.

★**YAZOO MOTEL.** *(Box 602) At jct US 49, MS 16.* 601/746-2161. 85 rms. S $22–$26.50; D $30.25–$32; each addl $2; under 12 free; wkly rates. Crib free. TV; cable. Pool. Restaurant 5 am–10 pm. Rm serv. Ck-out noon. Cr cds: A, MC, V.

Restaurant

✔ ★**K.O.K.** *101 S Main.* 601/746-7997. Hrs: 9 am–9:30 pm; Sun 11 am–2 pm. Closed most major hols. Thai, Amer menu. Semi-a la carte: lunch $4–$7, dinner $5.95–$10.95. Cr cds: MC, V.

Tennessee

Population:	4,877,185
Land area:	41,154 square miles
Elevation:	182–6,643 feet
Highest point:	Clingmans Dome (Sevier County)
Entered Union:	June 1, 1796 (16th state)
Capital:	Nashville
Nickname:	Volunteer State
State flower:	Iris
State bird:	Mockingbird
State tree:	Tulip poplar
State fair:	Late September, 1994, in Nashville
Time zones:	Eastern and Central

Handsomely rugged and rough-hewn, Tennessee reveals itself most characteristically in a 480-mile stretch from Mountain City at its northeastern boundary, southwest to Memphis and the Mississippi River, with its twisting western shore. In this mountainous land, a place of individualistic, strong-minded people, history and legend blend into folklore based on the feats of Davy Crockett, Daniel Boone, Andrew Jackson and Sam Houston. It is a state of mountain ballads and big-city ballet, of waterpowered mills and atomic energy plants.

The state's economy and its basic patterns of life and leisure were electrified in the 1930s by the Tennessee Valley Authority, that depression-born, often denounced and often praised grand-scale public power, flood control and navigation project. TVA harnessed rampaging rivers, saved cities from the annual plague of floods, created a broad system for navigation and produced inexpensive power and a treasury of recreational facilities. TVA altered the mainstream of the state's economy, achieving a dramatic switch from agriculture to industry. Cheap power, of course, sparked that revolution. Today, Tennessee has manufacturing payrolls in excess of farm income. Chemicals, textiles, foods, apparel, tourism, printing and publishing, metalworking and lumber products are its chief industries.

Farms and forests still produce over 50 different crops, but the emphasis is changing from cotton and tobacco to livestock. With more than 200 species of trees, Tennessee is the nation's hardwood producing center. Mining is also a leading industry in Tennessee, with limestone the major product. The state also ranks high in the production of zinc, pyrite, ball clay, phosphate rock and marble.

In 1541, it is believed, the explorer De Soto planted the flag of Spain on the banks of the Mississippi, near what is now Memphis. Although French traders explored the Tennessee Valley, it was their English counterparts who came over the mountain ranges, settling among the Cherokee and establishing a claim to the area. By the end of the 17th century, the Tennessee region was a territory of North Carolina. With the construction of Fort Loudoun (1756), the first Anglo-American fort garrisoned west of the Alleghenies, settlement began. The first permanent colonies were established near the Watauga River in 1769 and 1771 and are known as the Watauga settlements.

The free-spirited settlers in the outlying regions found themselves far from the seat of their formal government in eastern North Carolina. Dissatisfied and insecure, they formed the independent state of Franklin in 1784. But formal recognition of the independent state was never to come. After four chaotic years, the federal government took over and in 1790 established "The Territory of the United States South of the River Ohio." Tennessee was admitted to the Union six years later. Among the first representatives it sent to Washington was a raw backwoodsman named Andrew Jackson.

During the War of 1812, Tennessee riflemen volunteered in such great numbers that Tennessee was henceforth called the "Volunteer State," and Andrew Jackson emerged from the war a national hero.

Although there was strong abolitionist sentiment in parts of the state, Tennessee finally seceded in 1861 and became a battleground; some of the bloodiest battles of the war, including Shiloh, Stones River, Missionary Ridge, Fort Donelson and the Battle of Franklin, were fought within the state's boundaries. In 1866, shortly after former Tennessee governor Andrew Johnson became president, the state was accepted back into the Union.

National Park Service Areas

Tennessee has Stones River National Battlefield (see MURFREESBORO), Big South Fork National River/Recreation Area (see JAMESTOWN), Fort Donelson National Battlefield and Cemetery, Great Smoky Mountains National Park and Andrew Johnson National Historic Site (see all three), Natchez Trace Parkway (see MISSISSIPPI), and Cumberland Gap National Historical Park (see KENTUCKY), as well as Shiloh National Military Park (see) and Chickamauga and Chattanooga National Military Park (see GEORGIA).

National Forest

Cherokee National Forest (see CHEROKEE NATIONAL FOREST): Forest Supervisor in Cleveland; Ranger offices in Benton*, Elizabethton*, Erwin*, Etowah*, Greeneville, Tellico Plains*.
*Not described in text

State Recreation Areas

The following towns list state recreation areas in their vicinity under What to See and Do; refer to the individual town for directions and park information.

Listed under **Caryville:** see Cove Lake State Park.

Listed under **Celina:** see Standing Stone State Park.

Listed under **Chattanooga:** see Harrison Bay and Booker T. Washington state parks.

Listed under **Cookeville:** see Burgess Falls State Natural Area and Edgar Evins State Park.

Listed under **Covington:** see Fort Pillow State Historic Area.

Listed under **Crossville:** see Cumberland Mountain State Park.

Listed under **Dickson:** see Montgomery Bell State Resort Park.

Listed under **Elizabethton:** see Roan Mountain State Park.

Listed under **Gallatin:** see Bledsoe Creek State Park.

Listed under **Greeneville:** see Davy Crockett Birthplace State Park.

Listed under **Jackson:** see Chickasaw State Rustic Park.

Listed under **Jamestown:** see Pickett State Rustic Park.

Listed under **Jellico:** see Indian Mountain State Park.

Listed under **Kingsport:** see Warriors' Path State Park.

Listed under **Lawrenceburg:** see David Crockett State Park.

Listed under **Lebanon:** see Cedars of Lebanon State Park.

Listed under **Lewisburg:** see Henry Horton State Resort Park.

Listed under **Manchester:** see Old Stone Fort State Archaeological Park.

Listed under **McMinnville:** see Fall Creek Falls State Resort Park and Rock Island State Rustic Park.

Listed under **Memphis:** see Meeman-Shelby Forest and T.O. Fuller state parks.

Listed under **Monteagle:** see South Cumberland State Park.

Listed under **Morristown:** see Panther Creek State Park.

Listed under **Natchez Trace State Resort Park:** see Natchez Trace State Resort Park.

Listed under **Norris:** see Big Ridge State Rustic Park and Norris Dam State Park.

Listed under **Oak Ridge:** see Frozen Head State Park.

Listed under **Paris:** see Nathan Bedford Forrest and Paris Landing state parks.

Listed under **Savannah:** see Pickwick Landing State Resort Park.

Listed under **Tiptonville:** see Reelfoot Lake State Park.

Listed under **Winchester:** see Tims Ford State Rustic Park.

Water-related activities, hiking, riding, various other sports, picnicking and visitor centers, as well as camping, are available in many of these areas. Most state parks have supervised swimming (June–Labor Day; $1.50–$2.25), golf in resort parks (18 holes, $16; 9 holes, $8), boating ($2.25–$2.75/hr), fishing and tent camping (1–2 persons, one must be over 17 yrs: $5.25–$12/day, each addl over 7 yrs, 50¢; 2-wk max). Cabins, rustic to very modern, are available in several parks (wkly,

$190–$400; daily, $35–$80; reservations should be made at park of choice; 1-night deposit required; $5 surcharge added for 1-night-only rental). Reservations for camping at some parks. There is also camping in Cherokee National Forest and Great Smoky Mountains National Park (see both). For further information contact the Public Information Officer, Tennessee Dept of Environment & Conservation, Bureau of State Parks, 401 Church St, Nashville 37243-0446; 615/532-0001 or 800/421-6683.

Fishing & Hunting

There are more than 30 different kinds of fish in the state's mountain streams and lakes, including striped, largemouth, smallmouth and white bass, rainbow trout, walleye, muskie, crappie and catfish. Nonresident licenses: 3-day all species, $20.50; 10-day all species, $30.50; 3-day, no trout $10.50; 10-day, no trout $15.50; annual, no trout $51.00.

Within the constraints of season and limits, everything from squirrel and deer to wild boar can be hunted. Nonresident licenses: 7-day small game and water fowl, $30.50; annual small game and water fowl, $56; 7-day all game, $105.50; annual all game, $156. For detailed information contact the Tennessee Wildlife Resources Agency, Ellington Agricultural Center, PO Box 40747, Nashville 37204; 615/781-6500.

Skiing

Listed under **Gatlinburg:** see Ober Gatlinburg Ski Resort.

Safety Belt Information

Safety belts are mandatory for all persons in front seat of vehicle, and children over 4 years in any seating position. Children under 4 years must be in an approved safety seat anywhere in vehicle. For further information phone 615/251-5313.

Interstate Highway System

The following alphabetical listing of Tennessee towns and parks in *Mobil Travel Guide* shows that these cities are within 10 miles of the indicated Interstate highways. A highway map should be checked, however, for the nearest exit.

INTERSTATE 24: Chattanooga, Clarksville, Manchester, Monteagle, Murfreesboro, Nashville.

INTERSTATE 40: Cherokee Natl Forest, Cookeville, Crossville, Dickson, Hurricane Mills, Jackson, Knoxville, Lebanon, Lenoir City, Memphis, Nashville, Natchez Trace State Resort Park, Newport, Oak Ridge, Sevierville.

INTERSTATE 65: Columbia, Franklin, Lewisburg, Nashville.

INTERSTATE 75: Caryville, Chattanooga, Cleveland, Jellico, Knoxville, Lenoir City, Norris, Sweetwater.

INTERSTATE 81: Kingsport, Morristown.

Additional Visitor Information

The Department of Tourist Development, PO Box 23170, Nashville 37202, publishes a state map and a Tennessee vacation guide booklet highlighting attractions, historic sites and major events and will provide information on vacationing in Tennessee; phone 615/741-2158.

The TVA and the US Army Corps of Engineers have transformed muddy rivers into lovely lakes, making Tennessee home to the "Great Lakes of the South" with more than 29 big lakes in the public province. Also, TVA has developed Land Between The Lakes (see under KENTUCKY), a giant national recreation area spanning the Kentucky-Tennessee border.

There are 12 welcome centers in Tennessee; visitors may find the information and brochures helpful in their state travels. These centers operate year round; they are located on interstate highway entrances to the state.

Andrew Johnson National Historic Site (D-8)

(Monument Ave, College & Depot Sts in Greeneville)

The tailor shop, two houses and the burial place of the 17th president of the United States are preserved. Apprenticed to a tailor during his youth, Andrew Johnson came to Greeneville from his native Raleigh, NC, in 1826. After years of service in local, state and federal governments, Senator Johnson chose to remain loyal to the Union when Tennessee seceded. After serving as military governor of Tennessee, Johnson was elected vice-president in 1864. On April 15, 1865, he became president following the assassination of Abraham Lincoln. Continued opposition to the radical program of Reconstruction led to his impeachment in 1868. Acquitted by the Senate, he continued to serve as president until 1869. In 1875 Andrew Johnson became the only former president to be elected to the US Senate.

What to See and Do

1. **Visitor Center.** Depot & College Sts. The visitor center houses the Johnson tailor shop, preserved with some original furnishings and tools of the craft, as well as a museum with exhibits and memorabilia relating to Johnson's career. (Daily; closed Dec 25) Opp is the Johnson house (1830s–51), occupied during his career as a tailor and as a congressman. **Free.**

2. **Johnson Homestead.** Main St. Occupied by Johnson family from 1851 to 1875, except during Civil War and presidential years, the house is restored and furnished with family heirlooms. (Daily; closed Dec 25) Tickets at Visitor Center. **¢**

3. **Grave and monument.** Monument Ave. An eagle-capped marker sits over the President's grave. Members of his immediate family are also buried in what is now a national cemetery. (Daily)

4. **Park area.** (Daily exc Dec 25) Camping (mid-Mar–Oct) nearby at Kinser Park, phone 615/639-5912, or call US Forest Service, 615/638-4109. For further information about the Historic Site contact Superintendent, PO Box 1088, Greeneville 37744; 615/638-3551.

(For accommodations see Greeneville, Newport)

Caryville (D-7)

Pop: 1,751 **Elev:** 1,095 ft **Area code:** 615 **Zip:** 37714

What to See and Do

Cove Lake State Park. N, off US 25W. Approximately 1,500 acres include 300-acre Cove Lake, where hundreds of Canada geese winter. Pool, wading pool, lifeguard; fishing; boat rentals. Nature trails, programs, bicycles. Picnicking, concession, restaurant, playground, game courts. Camping, tent & trailer sites. Standard fees. Phone 562-8355.

Motels

★ ★**HOLIDAY INN.** *At jct US 25W, TN 63, I-75 exit 134. 615/562-8476; FAX 615/562-8810.* 102 rms, 2 story. S $43–$50; D $50–$64;

each addl $6; family rates. Crib free. Pet accepted. TV; cable, in-rm movies avail. Pool; wading pool. Playground. Restaurant 7 am–2 pm, 6:30–10 pm. Rm serv. Beer. Ck-out noon. Meeting rms. Cr cds: A, C, D, DS, ER, MC, V, JCB.

✔ ★ ★**LAKEVIEW INN.** *(PO Box 250) At US 25W, I-75 exit 134. 615/562-9456; res: 800/431-6887.* 127 rms, 2–3 story. No elvtr. S $20–$34; D $28–$42; each addl $4; under 16 free. Crib $3. TV; cable. Pool. Ck-out 11:30 am. Cr cds: A, C, D, DS, ER, MC, V.

Celina (D-6)

Pop: 1,493 **Elev:** 562 ft **Area code:** 615 **Zip:** 38551

Located in the scenic Upper Cumberland section of Tennessee, Celina is the location of the first law office of Cordell Hull, the revered statesman. Involved in both agriculture (especially cattle raising and truck farming) and industry (notably work clothes and denim sportswear), Celina is also noted for its nearby recreational facilities.

What to See and Do

1. **Dale Hollow Lake** Headquarters is 3 mi E on TN 53. Controlling and harnessing the Obey River is a concrete dam 200 feet high and 1,717 feet long; it creates a 61-mile-long lake with 620 miles of shoreline. Swimming, bathhouse; fishing, hunting; boating (14 commercial docks). Primitive and improved camping (May–Oct; fee; dump station). (Daily) Phone 243-3136. **Free.**

2. **Dale Hollow National Fish Hatchery.** 3 mi E off TN 53. More than 300,000 pounds of rainbow, browns and lake trout are raised annually for stocking streams and reservoirs; aquarium, visitor center. (Daily) Phone 243-2443. **Free.**

3. **Standing Stone State Park.** 10 mi S on TN 52. Approximately 11,000 acres of virgin forest. Swimming pool, bathhouse; fishing; boating (rentals). Hiking; tennis. Picnicking, playground, concessions. Tent & trailer sites, cabins. Standard fees. Phone 823-6347.

4. **Old Mulkey Meeting House State Historic Site (KY)** (1798). 7 mi NW on TN 52, then 10 mi N on TN 51, KY 163 in Tompkinsville, KY. Oldest log meetinghouse in Kentucky, built by Baptist settlers from the Carolinas. Construction is 12-cornered with half-hewn logs. Hannah Boone, sister of Daniel Boone, and 15 soldiers of the Revolutionary War are buried in adjacent graveyard. Picnicking, playground. (Daily) Phone 502/487-8481. **Free.**

(For further information contact the Dale Hollow-Clay County Chamber of Commerce, TN 52, Box 69; 243-3338.)

Resort

★**CEDAR HILL.** *(Rte 1) 3½ mi N on TN 53. 615/243-3201; res: 800/872-8393.* 37 1–4 rm kit. cottages; 10 motel rms, 4 kits. Memorial Day wkend–Labor Day: cottages (no towels; maid serv avail) for 2–6, $45–$110; motel S, D $35–$45; each addl $6; kit. units $38–$50; wkly rates; lower rates rest of yr. Crib $5. Pet accepted. TV. Pool (open to public); lifeguard. Dining rm 6 am–8:30 pm. Box lunches, snack bar. Ck-out 10 am, ck-in 1 pm. Grocery ¼ mi. Sports dir. Boats, motors, guides; waterskiing. Lawn games. Houseboats (drive your own) for 6–8 (3-day min) $95–$300; $395–$2,195 wkly. On Dale Hollow Lake. Cr cds: MC, V.

Chattanooga (E-6)

Settled: 1835 **Pop:** 152,466 **Elev:** 685 ft **Area code:** 615

Walled in on three sides by mountains, Chattanooga is a diversified city—the birthplace of miniature golf, the home of one of the largest civic concert associations in the nation and the site of the first Coca-Cola bottling plant. Industrial leader of the Tennessee Valley, this former outpost of the Cherokee nation has more than 600 major industries, producing more than 1,500 products. River, rails and roads make it a leading distribution center. It has nine trunk-line railroads and the steepest passenger incline railway in the country.

It's a city celebrated in song and heralded in history. The Cherokees called it *Tsatanugi* (rock coming to a point), describing Lookout Mountain, which stands like a sentinel over the city. They called the creek here "Chickamauga" ("river of blood").

Cherokee Chief John Ross founded the city. The tragic "Trail of Tears" started from Chattanooga; Indians from three states were herded by Federal troops and forced to march in bitter winter to distant Oklahoma. The Battle of Chickamauga in the fall of 1863 was one of the turning points of the Civil War. It ended when the Union forces overpowered the entrenched Confederate forces on Missionary Ridge; there were more than 34,500 casualties. Sherman's march to the sea began immediately thereafter.

Chattanooga emerged as an important industrial city at the end of the Civil War, when soldiers from both sides returned to stake their futures in this commercially strategic city. Only 1,500 persons lived in Chattanooga at the war's end, but by 1880 the city had 77 industries.

In 1878, Adolph S. Ochs moved to Chattanooga from Knoxville, purchased the *Chattanooga Times* and made it one of the state's most influential newspapers. Although he later went on to publish the *New York Times*, Ochs retained control of the Chattanooga journal until his death in 1935.

Sparked by the TVA, the city's greatest period of growth began in the 1930s. Today, Chattanooga is a wealthy city, with a polo-playing set, opera-goers and an art league. Much of the city's wealth comes from the world-wide expansion of the soft drink industry.

What to See and Do

1. **Hunter Museum of Art.** 10 Bluff View. Paintings, sculpture, glass, drawings; permanent collection of major American artists; changing exhibits. Gift shop. (Daily exc Mon; closed most hols) Phone 267-0968. ¢

2. **Houston Museum of Decorative Arts.** 201 High St. Glass, porcelain, pottery, music boxes, dolls, collection of pitchers; country-style furniture. (Daily exc Mon; closed hols) Donation. Phone 267-7176.

3. **National Knife Museum.** 7201 Shallowford Rd. Permanent display of knives of every age and description; also changing exhibits. (Daily exc Sun; closed hols) Phone 892-5007. ¢

4. **Tennessee Aquarium.** 1 Broad St, on the banks of the Tennessee River. First major freshwater life center in the country, focusing primarily on the natural habitats and wildlife of the Tennessee River and related ecosystems. Within this 130,000 sq-ft complex are more than 4,000 living specimens. The Aquarium re-creates riverine habitats in 7 major freshwater tanks and 2 terrestial environments and is organized into 5 major galleries: **Appalachian Cove Forest** re-creates the mountain source of the Tennessee River; **Tennessee River Gallery** examines the river at midstream and compares the "original" river with the river as it now exists; **Discovery Falls** is a series of interactive displays and small tanks; **Mississipi Delta** explores the river as it slows to meet the sea; and **Rivers of the World** explores 6 of the world's great river systems. Highlight of the Aquarium is the 60-ft-high central canyon, designed to give visitors a sense of immersion into the river. (Daily; closed Thanksgiving, Dec 25). Phone 265-0695 or 800/262-0695. ¢¢¢

5. **University of Tennessee at Chattanooga** (1886). (7,800 students) 615 McCallie Ave. Fine Arts Center has Arena stage entertainment and special events. Tours of campus by appt. Phone 755-4363.

6. **Tennessee Valley Railroad.** 4119 Cromwell Rd. The South's largest operating historic railroad, with steam locomotives, diesels, passenger coaches of various types. Trains leave hourly for six-mile ride, including tunnel. Audiovisual show, displays; gift shop; dining room. (June–Labor Day, daily; Mar–May & Sept–Nov, wkends only) Phone 894-8028. ¢¢¢

7. **Chattanooga Choo-Choo.** Terminal Station, 1400 Market St. Converted 1909 train station with hotel (see MOTOR HOTELS) and restaurants. Formal gardens, fountains, pools, turn-of-the-century shops, gaslights, trolley ride (fee), model railroad (fee). Phone 266-5000 or 800/872-2529.

8. **Lookout Mountain.** S of town via Ochs Hwy & Scenic Hwy. Mountain towers more than 2,120 feet above the city, offering clear-day views of Tennessee, Georgia, North Carolina, South Carolina and Alabama. During the Civil War, the "Battle above the Clouds" was fought on the slope.

   Lookout Mountain Incline Railway. Lower station at 3917 St Elmo Ave. World's steepest passenger incline railway climbs Lookout Mountain to 2,100-foot altitude; near top, grade is at 72.7˚ angle; passengers ride glass-roofed cars; Smoky Mountains (200 mi away) can be seen from Upper Station observation deck. Round trip approx 60 minutes. (Daily; closed Dec 25) Phone 821-4224. ¢¢¢

   Point Park. Lookout Mt. View of Chattanooga and Moccasin Bend from observatory. Monuments, plaques, museum tell story of battle. Visitor Center. Part of Chickamauga and Chattanooga National Military Park (see under GEORGIA). (Daily; closed Dec 25) Phone 821-7786. **Free.** Opp is

   Cravens House (1866). On Lookout Mt. Oldest surviving structure on mountain, restored with period furnishings. Original house (1856), center of the "Battle Above the Clouds," was largely destroyed; the present structure was erected on the original foundations in 1866. (Apr–Oct, daily) Golden Eagle Passport (see INTRODUCTION). Phone 821-7786. ¢

   Ruby Falls-Lookout Mountain Caverns. Scenic Hwy TN 148, on Lookout Mt. Under the battlefield are twin caves with onyx formations, giant stalactites, stalagmites of various hues; at 1,120 ft below surface Ruby Falls drop 145 ft in a solid sheet of water. View of city from tower above entrance building. Guided tours. (Daily; closed Dec 25) Phone 821-2544. ¢¢¢

   Rock City Gardens. 2½ mi S on TN 58, on Lookout Mt. Fourteen acres of mountaintop trails and vistas. Fairyland Caverns and Mother Goose Village, rock formations, swinging bridge, observation point. Restaurant; shops. (Daily; closed Dec 25) Phone 706/820-2531. ¢¢¢

   Chattanooga Nature Center at Reflection Riding. Garden Rd, 6 mi SW, near jct US 11/64, US 41 & US 72, on Lookout Mt. Park meant for leisurely driving offers winding three-mile drive with vistas: historic sites, trees, wildflowers, shrubs, reflecting pools. Also wetland walkway; nature center; animal diorama, solar energy display; hiking trails; programs. (Daily) Sr citizen rate. Phone 821-1160. ¢¢

   Confederama–Hall of History. 3742 Tennessee Ave, at foot of Lookout Mt. Automated, three-dimensional display re-creates Civil War Battles of Chattanooga using 5,000 miniature soldiers, flashing lights, smoking cannons and crackling rifles. Also here are dioramas of area history prior to Civil War. (Daily; closed Dec 25) Phone 821-2812. ¢¢

9. **Signal Point.** 9 mi N on Ridgeway Ave (US 127). Mountain was used for signaling by Cherokees and later by Confederates. View of "Grand Canyon of the Tennessee" can be seen by looking almost straight down to the Tennessee River from Signal Point Military Park, off St James Blvd.

10. **Raccoon Mountain.**

    Raccoon Mountain Pumped-Storage Plant. 6 mi W. Raccoon Mountain is the largest of the TVA's rock-filled dams, measuring 230 feet high and 8,500 feet long. Water pumped from the Tennessee River flows from the reservoir atop the mountain to the powerhouse below. Cut 1,350 feet inside the mountain, the powerhouse chamber has four of the largest reversible pump-turbines in the world. Visitor center and picnic area atop mountain (daylight hrs);

fishing at base of mountain; overlooks with spectacular views of Tennessee River gorge and Chattanooga. Phone 751-2420. **Free.**

Raccoon Mountain Caverns and Campground. Approx 5 mi W; exit 174 off I-24, 1 mi N on TN 41. Guided tours offer views of beautiful formations, stalagmites and stalactites; also "wild" cave tours through undeveloped sections. Full-facility campground (fee). (Daily) Phone 821-9403 or 821-CAVE. Cave tour ¢¢¢

Raccoon Mountain Alpine Slide. Chairlift to top of mountain and personal-control sled ride (½ mi) to bottom. (Mid-May–Labor Day, daily; Mar–mid-May & early Sept–Nov, wkends only) Phone 825-5666. ¢¢

High Adventure Sports. 4117 Cummings Hwy. Provides simulated hang-gliding flights for all ages on 640-foot-long and 120-foot-high cables; also sky diving & bungee jumping. (Memorial Day–Labor Day, daily; mid-Mar–Memorial Day, Labor Day–Oct, wkends; also by appt) Phone 825-0444. Hang gliding ¢¢¢¢ Sky diving & bungee jumping ¢¢¢¢¢

Grand Prix of Chattanooga. Three-quarter scale Formula cars race against clock on challenging half-mile track; also go-carts. Must have valid driver's license. (Same days as Alpine Slide) Phone 825-5666. Per lap ¢¢

11. Chickamauga Dam and Lake. E edge of city; TN 58, 153. A 129-foot-high, 5,800-foot-long TVA dam impounds lake with 810 miles of shoreline and 35,400 acres of water surface. Swimming, water-skiing; fishing; boating (docks, marina). Powerhouse tours (daily). Phone 751-4200. **Free.**

12. Harrison Bay State Park. 11 mi NE off TN 58. More than 1,200 acres on Chickamauga Lake. Swimming pool; fishing; boating (ramp, rentals, marina). Picnicking, playground, snack bar, restaurant, camp store (all seasonal). Standard fees. Phone 344-6214 or -2272.

13. Booker T. Washington State Park. 13 mi NE on TN 58. More than 350 acres on Chickamauga Lake. Swimming pools; fishing; boating (rentals, launch). Nature trail. Picnicking, playground, lodge. Some facilities seasonal. Standard fees. Phone 894-4955.

14. Chester Frost Park. 2318 Gold Point Circle; 17 mi NE off I-75 exit 4, then TN 153 to Hixson Pike & N to Gold Point Circle, on W shore of Chickamauga Lake. Swimming, sand beach, bathhouse; fishing; boating (ramps). Hiking. Picnicking, concessions. Camping (fee; sr citizen rate; electricity, water). Islands in park are accessible by causeways. Phone 842-0177. **Free.**

15. Nickajack Dam and Lake. 25 mi W on US 41, 64, 72 or I-24. TVA dam impounds lake with 192 miles of shoreline and 10,370 acres of water surface. Fishing; boat launch. Visitor lobby at navigation lock (daily). Phone 837-6380. **Free.**

16. Chickamauga and Chattanooga National Military Park (see under GEORGIA).

(For further information, brochures and maps contact the Chattanooga Area Convention & Visitors Bureau, 1001 Market St, 37402; phone 756-8687.)

Annual Events

Riverbend Festival. Musical & sporting events, children's activities, fireworks display. Phone 265-4112. Late June.

Tennessee Autumn Special. All-day, reserved seat steam-train ride, 130 miles through mountains to Oneida, TN. Air-conditioned and adjustable-window coaches, diner, snack bar and souvenir shop on board. Contact Tennessee Valley Railroad Museum, 4119 Cromwell Rd, 37421; 894-8028. 2 wkends mid-Oct.

Fall Color Cruise & Folk Festival. Riverboat trips, arts & crafts, entertainment. Phone 892-0223. Last 2 wkends Oct.

Seasonal Event

Theatrical, musical productions. Tivoli Theater, 709 Broad St. Variety of events, including plays, concerts, opera; box office, phone 757-5050. Little Theater, 400 River St; box office, phone 267-8534. Memorial Auditorium, 399 McCallie Ave; box office, phone 756-5050. Chattanooga Symphony and Opera Assn, 25 concerts and 2 opera productions yearly, phone 267-8583. Backstage Playhouse, 3264 Brainerd Rd, dinner theater, phone 629-1565.

Motels

✔ ★★★ **BEST WESTERN-SOUTH.** 6710 Ringgold Rd (37412), I-75 at East Ridge. 615/894-6820; FAX 615/490-0824. 131 rms, 3 story. S $37–$39; D $39–$42 each addl $5; suites $95; under 18 free. Crib free. Pet accepted, some restrictions. TV; cable. Pool. Restaurant 6:30–10 am, 5–10 pm. Rm serv. Ck-out noon. Meeting rms. Free airport transportation. Cr cds: A, C, D, DS, MC, V, JCB.

D 🐾 ⊠ 🚫 🕐 SC

★ **CHANTICLEER INN.** (1300 Mockingbird Lane, Lookout Mountain, GA 30750) 8 mi S on GA 157, 3 mi from foot of mountain. 706/820-2015. 16 rms. S $35–$48; D $35–$86; each addl $6. Crib free. TV; cable. Pool. Complimentary continental bkfst. Restaurant nearby. Ck-out 11 am. Meeting rm. Picnic tables, grill. Cr cds: A, MC, V.

D ⊠ 🕐 SC

✔ ★★ **COMFORT INN.** 7717 Lee Hwy (37421). 615/894-5454; FAX 615/894-5454, ext 152. 64 rms, 2 story. S $40–$44; D $42–$52; each addl $4; under 18 free; higher rates hol wkends. Crib free. Pet accepted; $5. TV; cable. Pool. Complimentary continental bkfst, coffee. Restaurant adj open 24 hrs. Ck-out 11 am. Free airport transportation. Cr cds: A, C, D, DS, ER, MC, V, JCB.

D 🐾 ⊠ 🚫 🕐 SC

★★ **DAYS INN AIRPORT.** 7015 Shallowford Rd (37421), at I-75. 615/855-0011; FAX 615/855-0011, ext 72. 132 rms, 2 story. May–Oct: S $38–$45; D $43–$50; each addl $5; suites $55–$100; under 18, $1; lower rates rest of yr. Crib free. TV; cable. Pool. Complimentary coffee. Ck-out 11 am. Some refrigerators. Cr cds: A, C, D, DS, MC, V.

D ⊠ 🚫 🕐 SC

★★ **DAYS INN AND CONVENTION CENTRE.** 1400 Mack Smith Rd (37412), on US 41 at I-75 East Ridge exit. 615/894-0440; FAX 615/899-5819. 237 rms, 2 story. S, D $38–$55; each addl $5; under 18 free. Crib free. Pet accepted, some restrictions. TV; cable. Pool; wading pool. Restaurant 6:30 am–2 pm, 5–9 pm. Ck-out noon. Meeting rms. Valet serv. Free airport transportation. Game rm. Cr cds: A, C, D, DS, MC, V.

D 🐾 ⊠ 🚫 🕐 SC

★★ **DAYS INN RIVERGATE.** 901 Carter St (37402), at M.L. King Blvd. 615/266-7331; FAX 615/265-7504. 135 rms, 2–3 story. S $44–$49; D $49–$56; each addl $7; suites $70; under 18 free. Crib free. TV; cable. Pool. Restaurant 6:30 am–9 pm. Rm serv. Bar 11 am–midnight. Ck-out noon. Health club privileges. Grill. Cr cds: A, C, D, DS, MC, V.

⊠ 🚫 🕐 SC

✔ ★ **ECONO LODGE.** 1417 St Thomas (37412), I-75 exit 1. 615/894-1417. 89 rms, 2 story. S $25.95–$29.95; D $29.95–$36.95; each addl $5; under 12 free. Crib $4. Pet accepted, some restrictions. TV; cable. Pool. Complimentary continental bkfst, coffee. Restaurant adj 6 am–10 pm. Ck-out 11 am. Cr cds: A, C, D, DS, MC, V.

🐾 ⊠ 🚫 🕐 SC

★ **FRIENDSHIP INN.** 7725 Lee Hwy (37421). 615/899-2288. 80 rms, 2 story. June-Aug: S $30–$34; D $36–$40; each addl $4; under 16 free; lower rates rest of yr. Crib $5. Pet accepted, some restrictions; $4. TV; cable. Indoor pool; whirlpool. Complimentary coffee in lobby.

Restaurant adj open 24 hrs. Ck-out 11 am. Cr cds: A, C, D, DS, ER, MC, V.

[D] [🐾] [⊠] [Ⓢ] [Ⓞ] [SC]

★★**HAMPTON INN.** *7013 Shallowford Rd (37421), near Lovell Field Airport.* 615/855-0095; FAX 615/855-0095, ext 501. 126 rms, 2 story. S $50–$55; D $50–$65; under 18 free. Crib free. TV; cable. Pool. Complimentary continental bkfst, coffee. Restaurant adj open 24 hrs. Ck-out 11 am. Meeting rms. Exercise equipt; weights, bicycles. Cr cds: A, C, D, DS, MC, V.

[D] [⊠] [Ⓣ] [⊠] [Ⓢ] [Ⓞ] [SC]

★★★**HOLIDAY INN-LOOKOUT MOUNTAIN.** *3800 Cummings Hwy (37419), 5 mi NW on US 41 at I-24 exit 174.* 615/821-3531; FAX 615/821-8403. 163 rms, 2 story. S $49–$52; D $56–$59; each addl $7; suites from $65; under 19 free. Crib free. TV; cable. Pool. Restaurant 6 am–10 pm. Rm serv. Bar 5 pm–midnight; entertainment, dancing. Ck-out 11 am. Meeting rms. Exercise equipt; weights, bicycles. Game rm. Cr cds: A, C, D, DS, MC, V, JCB.

[D] [⊠] [Ⓣ] [Ⓢ] [Ⓞ] [SC]

✔ ★★**KING'S LODGE.** *2400 West Side Dr (37404), 4 mi NE at jct US 41, I-24 East Ridge, 4th Ave exit.* 615/698-8944; res: 800/251-7702; FAX 615/698-8949. 139 rms, 2 story, 24 suites. S $38; D $45; each addl $5; suites $50–$75; under 12 free. Crib free. Pet accepted, some restrictions. TV; cable. Pool. Restaurant 7 am–11 pm. Rm serv. Bar 1 pm–3 am. Ck-out 11 am. Some balconies. Cr cds: A, C, D, DS, MC, V.

[D] [🐾] [⊠] [Ⓢ] [Ⓞ] [SC]

★**SUPER 8.** *20 Birmingham Hwy (37419), I-24 exit 174.* 615/821-8880. 74 rms, 3 story. Apr–Sept: S $33.88–$38.88; D $41.88–$51.88; each addl $5; under 12 free; lower rates rest of yr. Crib free. Pet accepted, some restrictions. TV; cable. Complimentary coffee in lobby. Restaurant adj open 24 hrs. Ck-out 11 am. Picnic tables. Cr cds: A, C, D, DS, MC, V.

[D] [🐾] [⊠] [Ⓞ] [SC]

Motor Hotel

★★★**HOLIDAY INN CHATTANOOGA CHOO-CHOO.** *1400 Market St (37402), 8 blks S in Terminal Station.* 615/266-5000; FAX 615/265-4635. 360 rms, 48 train-car rms. S $80–$90; D $95–$100; suites $150–$200. Crib free. Pet accepted, some restrictions. TV; cable. 3 pools, 1 indoor. Complimentary coffee in rms. Restaurant 7 am–10 pm. Rm serv 6:30 am–3 pm, 5 pm–midnight. Bars 11:30–2 am. Ck-out 11 am. Meeting rms. Bellhops. Concierge. Shopping arcade. Free airport transportation. Lighted tennis. Golf privileges. Exercise equipt; bicycles, rowing machines, whirlpool. Bathrm phone, wet bar in suites. Some private patios, balconies. Turn-of-the-century atmosphere in restored 1909 train station; gaslights, formal gardens. Many old-style shops. Main lobby under original 85-ft freestanding dome. Bar in authentic Wabash Cannonball club car. 1880 Chattanooga Choo-Choo engine. Cr cds: A, C, D, DS, MC, V, JCB.

[D] [🐾] [🚲] [⊘] [⊠] [Ⓣ] [⊠] [Ⓞ] [SC]

Hotels

★★**COMFORT HOTEL RIVER PLAZA.** *407 Chestnut St (37402), at 4th St; US 27 exit 1 C.* 615/756-5150; FAX 615/265-8708. 205 rms, 12 story. S, D $58–$68; each addl $6; under 18 free; wkend rates. Crib $10. TV; cable, in-rm movies avail. Pool. Restaurant 6:30 am–9:30 pm. Bar 2 pm–midnight; Sun to 10 pm. Ck-out 11 am. Meeting rms. Free airport transportation. Exercise equipt; weights, bicycles. Cr cds: A, C, D, DS, ER, MC, V.

[D] [⊠] [Ⓣ] [Ⓢ] [Ⓞ] [SC]

★★★**MARRIOTT.** *2 Carter Plaza (37402), adj convention center.* 615/756-0002; FAX 615/266-2254. 343 rms, 15 story. S $65–$106; D $65–$121; suites $150–$395; under 12 free. Crib free. Pet accepted, some restrictions. TV; cable. Indoor pool; poolside serv. Restaurant 6:30 am–11 pm. Bar; entertainment, dancing. Ck-out noon.

Convention facilities. Concierge. Shopping arcade. Garage parking. Exercise equipt; weights, bicycles, whirlpool, sauna. Game rm. Bathrm phones, refrigerators. *LUXURY LEVEL:* CONCIERGE LEVEL. 17 rms, 4 suites. S, D $122; suites $175–$350. Private lounge. Complimentary continental bkfst (Mon–Fri), newspapers. Cr cds: A, C, D, DS, ER, MC, V.

[D] [🐾] [🚲] [Ⓣ] [Ⓢ] [Ⓞ] [SC]

★★★**RADISSON READ HOUSE.** *(Box 11165, 37402) M.L. King Blvd & Broad St.* 615/266-4121; FAX 615/267-6447. 243 rms, 10 story. 139 suites. S $66–$92; D $76–$102; each addl $10; suites $82–$112; under 18 free. Crib free. TV; cable. Pool. Restaurants 6 am–11 pm. Bar from 11 am. Ck-out noon. Meeting rms. Shopping arcade. Barber, beauty shop. Free airport transportation. Health club privileges. Wet bars; some bathrm phones, refrigerators. Built to accommodate travelers on the Nashville/Chattanooga Railroad (1847). Cr cds: A, C, D, DS, ER, MC, V, JCB.

[D] [⊠] [Ⓢ] [Ⓞ] [SC]

Restaurants

★★**FIFTH QUARTER.** *5501 Brainerd Rd, 6½ mi E on US 11, 64.* 615/899-0181. Hrs: 11 am–2:30 pm, 5–10 pm; Sat 4–11 pm; Sun 11 am–10 pm; early-bird dinner Sun–Thurs 5–6:30 pm. Closed Dec 24 (dinner), Dec 25. Bar. Semi-a la carte: lunch $4.95–$12.99, dinner $8–$19.99. Child's meals. Specializes in prime rib, fresh seafood. Salad bar. Parking. Cr cds: A, DS, MC, V.

[D] [SC]

✔ ★**MT VERNON.** *3509 Broad St, 1½ mi SW on US 11, 41.* 615/266-6591. Hrs: 11 am–10 pm; Sat from 5 pm. Closed Sun; Jan 1; also wk of Dec 25. Serv bar. Semi-a la carte: lunch $3.75–$6.25, dinner $6.95–$13.95. Child's meals. Specializes in fresh seafood, vegetables, desserts. Parking. Family-owned. Cr cds: A, DS, MC, V.

[D]

★★★**NARROWBRIDGE.** *1420 Jenkins.* 615/855-5000. Hrs: 5:30–10 pm. Closed Sun; some hols. Res accepted. Bar. Semi-a la carte: dinner $11.95–$23.95. Child's meals. Specializes in fresh seafood, steak. Own baking. Parking. Classical Georgian home. Cr cds: A, DS, MC, V.

[D]

★★★**PERRY'S.** *1206 Market St.* 615/267-0007. Hrs: 11:30 am–2:30 pm, 6–10 pm; wkends to 10:30 pm. Closed some major hols. Res accepted. Bar. A la carte entrees: lunch $8–$14, dinner $18–$25. Specializes in fresh seafood. Parking. Built against wall of old freight depot; unique glass atrium structure. Cr cds: A, C, D, DS, MC, V.

[D]

Unrated Dining Spot

VINE STREET MARKET. *414 Vine St.* 615/267-0162. Hrs: 11 am–10 pm. Closed Sun; some hols. Serv bar. A la carte entrees: lunch $4–$8, dinner $10.95–$14.95. Child's meals. Specializes in desserts. Boxed lunches; table service after 4 pm. Chef's choice daily. Menu recited. Parking. Cr cds: A, MC, V.

Cherokee National Forest (D-8 – E-7)

(NE, SE & SW of Johnson City via US 23, 321, TN 91; E of Cleveland on US 64)

Slashed by river gorges and creased by rugged mountains, this 630,000-acre forest lies in two separate strips along the Tennessee-North Carolina boundary, northeast and southwest of Great Smoky

Mountains National Park (see). A region of thick forests, streams and waterfalls, the forest takes its name from the Indian tribe. There are more than 500 miles of hiking trails, including the Appalachian Trail. There are 29 campgrounds, 30 picnic areas, 8 swimming sites and 12 boating sites. Hunting for game, including wild boar, deer and turkey, is permitted under Tennessee game regulations. Fees may be charged at recreation sites. Contact Supervisor, PO Box 2010, Cleveland 37320; 615/476-9700.

(For accommodations see Cleveland, Greeneville, Johnson City, Newport)

Clarksville (D-4)

Founded: 1784 **Pop:** 75,494 **Elev:** 543 ft **Area code:** 615

Clarksville, named for General George Rogers Clark, has achieved a balanced economy with many industries and heavy traffic in tobacco, grain and livestock. Clarksville has long been considered one of the top dark-fired tobacco markets in the world. Natural gas and low-cost TVA power have contributed to the town's industrial development. Clarksville is the home of Austin Peay State University.

What to See and Do

1. **Clarksville-Montgomery County Museum.** 200 S 2nd St. Built in 1898 as a US Post Office and Customs House, the museum houses changing history, science and art exhibits. (Daily exc Mon; closed some major hols) Sr citizen rate. Phone 648-5780. ¢¢

2. **Fort Campbell Military Reservation.** TN 41A, in both TN & KY. Home of the army's famed 101st Airborn Division (Air Assault). The post visitors center is just inside Gate 4; Don F. Pratt Museum is located in Wickham Hall. (Daily; closed Jan 1, Dec 25) Phone 502/798-3215. **Free.**

3. **Port Royal State Historic Area.** 5 mi E via TN 76, near Adams; follow signs. At the confluence of Sulphur Fork Creek and the Red River, Port Royal was one of the state's earliest communities and trading centers. A 300-foot covered bridge spans the river. (Daily) Phone 358-9696.

4. **Dunbar Cave State Natural Area.** 5 mi SE via US 79, Dunbar Cave Rd exit. This 110-acre park with small scenic lake was once a fashionable resort; the cave itself housed big band dances. The old bathhouse has been refurbished to serve as a museum and visitor center. Park (daily); cave (June–Aug, wkends, by res only). Phone 648-5526. **Free.**

5. **Fort Donelson National Battlefield and Cemetery** (see). 30 mi W on US 79.

6. **Land Between The Lakes.** Approx 31 mi E on US 79, Land Between The Lakes exit, then N. (See under KENTUCKY)

7. **Beachhaven Vineyard & Winery.** I-24, exit 4. Tours of vineyard and winery; tasting room; picnic area. (Daily; closed Jan 1, Thanksgiving, Dec 25) Phone 645-8867. **Free.**

(For further information and a walking-tour map of the downtown architectural Historic District contact the Clarksville/Montgomery County Tourist Commission, 180 Holiday Rd, 37041; 648-0001.)

Annual Events

Old-Time Fiddlers Championship. Late Mar.

Historical Tour of Homes. Phone 648-0001. Mid-May.

Walking Horse Show. Fairgrounds. Early July.

(See Hopkinsville, KY)

Motels

✔ ★**DAYS INN.** *1100 Connector Rd (TN 76) (37043), I-24 exit 11.* 615/358-3194. 84 rms, 2 story. S $32–$40; D $40–$45; each addl $5; under 16 free. Crib free. Pet accepted. TV; cable. Pool; whirlpool. Complimentary continental bkfst. Restaurant adj 6 am–9 pm; wkends to 10 pm. Ck-out 11 am. Cr cds: A, C, D, DS, MC, V.

★**ECONO LODGE.** *201 Holiday Rd (37040), I-24 exit 4.* 615/645-6300; FAX 615/645-6300, ext 400. 61 rms, 2 story. S $38–$50; D $50–$60; each addl $5; under 12 free. Crib $5. TV; cable, in-rm movies avail. Pool. Complimentary continental bkfst, coffee. Restaurant nearby. Ck-out 11 am. Some refrigerators, whirlpools. Cr cds: A, C, D, DS, MC, V, JCB.

★★**QUALITY INN.** *803 N 2nd St (37040), 1½ mi NW on US 41A, 79.* 615/645-9084; FAX 615/645-9084, ext 229. 135 rms, 2 story. S $36–$47; D $42–$55; each addl $6; under 18 free. Crib free. Pet accepted, some restrictions. TV; cable. Pool; whirlpool. Complimentary continental bkfst. Bar 3:30 pm–midnight. Ck-out noon. Coin lndry. Meeting rms. Valet serv. Cr cds: A, C, D, DS, MC, V, JCB.

Motor Hotels

✔ ★★**BEST WESTERN COVINGTON INN.** *3075 Guthrie Hwy (37040), US 79 & I-24 exit 4.* 615/645-1400; FAX 615/645-1096. 125 rms, 4 story. S $38–$42; D $44–$47; each addl $5; suites $85; under 18 free. Crib free. Pet accepted. TV; cable. Heated pool; whirlpool. Complimentary coffee in rms. Restaurant 6 am–9 pm. Rm serv. Bar 5:30 pm–midnight. Ck-out noon. Meeting rms. Game rm. Cr cds: A, C, D, DS, MC, V.

★★**HAMPTON INN.** *190 Holiday Rd (37040), I-24 exit 4.* 615/552-2255. 77 air-cooled rms, 2 story. S $43–$48; D $45–$49; each addl $5; under 18 free. Crib free. TV; cable. Pool. Complimentary continental bkfst, coffee in lobby. Restaurant nearby. Ck-out noon. Coin lndry. Meeting rm. Valet serv. Sundries. Exercise equipt; weight machine, bicycles, whirlpool. Some refrigerators. Cr cds: A, C, D, DS, MC, V.

★★**RAMADA INN RIVERVIEW.** *50 College St (37040).* 615/552-3331; FAX 615/647-5005. 154 rms, 7 story. S, D $44–$60; each addl $6; suites $85; under 18 free. Crib free. Pet accepted. TV; cable. Indoor pool; whirlpool, sauna. Restaurant 6 am–2 pm, 5–9 pm; Sat, Sun 7am–2 pm. Bar from 4 pm. Ck-out noon. Meeting rms. Some refrigerators; whirlpool in suites. Cr cds: A, C, D, DS, MC, V, JCB.

Unrated Dining Spot

SADIE'S. *2801 Guthrie Hwy.* 615/645-5997. Hrs: 11 am–3 pm, 4–8:30 pm; Fri, Sat to 9 pm; Sun 11 am–8 pm. Closed Dec 25. Buffet: lunch $4.79, dinner $6.29. Specializes in fried chicken, corn bread. Salad bar. Parking. Cr cds: MC, V.

Cleveland (E-6)

Pop: 30,354 **Elev:** 920 ft **Area code:** 615

Cleveland is the location of the Superintendent's office of the Cherokee National Forest (see).

(See Chattanooga)

Motels

✔ ★ **BUDGETEL INN.** *107 Interstate Dr NW (37312). 615/339-1000.* 102 rms, 3 story, 14 suites. Apr–Sept: S, D, suites $34.95–$62.95; each addl $6; under 18 free; lower rates rest of yr. Crib free. Pet accepted, some restrictions. TV; cable. Pool. Complimentary continental bkfst. Complimentary coffee in rms. Restaurant adj open 24 hrs. Ck-out noon. Coin lndry. Meeting rm. Cr cds: A, C, D, DS, MC, V.

 D 🐾 ⚓ 🚫 ⊙ SC

★ ★ **HOLIDAY INN-NORTH.** *(PO Box 3360, 37320) Jct TN 60 & I-75 exit 25. 615/472-1504; FAX 615/479-5962.* 146 rms, 2 story. S $44–$50; D $49–$55; each addl $7; under 18 free. Crib free. TV; cable. Pool. Restaurant 6 am–2 pm, 5–10 pm. Rm serv 7 am–10 pm. Ck-out noon. Meeting rms. Sundries. Refrigerators. Cr cds: A, C, D, DS, MC, V, JCB.

D ⚓ 🚫 ⊙ SC

★ ★ **QUALITY INN CHALET.** *2595 Georgetown Rd (37311), jct TN 60 & I-75 exit 25. 615/476-8511.* 143 rms, 2–3 story, 23 kits. No elvtr. S, D $40–$47; kit. units $40–$50; under 18 free. Crib free. Pet accepted, some restrictions. TV; cable. 2 pools, 1 indoor; wading pool. Restaurant 11 am–10 pm. Rm serv. Ck-out noon. Coin lndry. Meeting rms. Valet serv. Sundries. Local airport transportation. Some refrigerators. Cr cds: A, C, D, DS, ER, MC, V, JCB.

D 🐾 ⚓ 🚫 ⊙ SC

Restaurant

✔ ★ ★ **ROBLYN'S STEAK HOUSE.** *NW 25th St, 2 blks E of I-75 exit 25. 615/476-8808.* Hrs: 4–10 pm; Sun 11 am–2 pm. Closed major hols. Res accepted. Semi-a la carte: dinner $7–$15. Buffet: (Sun) $5.75. Child's meals. Specializes in steak, seafood. Salad bar. Parking. Family-owned. Cr cds: A, C, D, DS, MC, V.

SC

Columbia (E-4)

Settled: 1807 **Pop:** 28,583 **Elev:** 637 ft **Area code:** 615 **Zip:** 38401

James K. Polk, eleventh president of the United States, spent his boyhood in Columbia and returned to open his first law office. The town is known for its many antebellum houses.

What to See and Do

1. **Ancestral home of James K. Polk** (1816). 301 W 7th St, US 412. Built by Samuel Polk, father of the president, the Federal-style house is furnished with family possessions, including furniture and portraits used at the White House. Gardens link house to adjacent 1818 building owned by the president's sisters. Visitor center. (Daily; closed Jan 1, Thanksgiving, Dec 24–25) Sr citizen rate. Phone 388-2354. ¢¢

2. **The Athenaeum** (1835–37). 808 Athenaeum St. Buildings of Moorish design were after 1852 used as a girls' school; during the Civil War the rectory became headquarters of Union generals Negeley and Schofield. (Memorial Day–Labor Day, Tues–Fri; fall tour Sept) Phone 381-4822. ¢

(For further information contact the Maury County Convention & Visitors Bureau, 308 W 7th St, PO Box 1076, 38402; 388-2155.)

Annual Events

Mule Day. Liar's contest, auction, parade, mule pull, square dance, bluegrass night, pioneer craft festival, knife and coin show. 1st wkend Apr.

National Tennessee Walking Horse Jubilee. Maury County Park. Contact the park, Experiment Station Lane; 388-0303. Late May–early June.

Maury County Fair. Maury County Park Fairgrounds. Phone 388-0303. Late July.

(See Franklin)

Motels

✔ ★ **DAYS INN.** *1504 Nashville Hwy (US 31N). 615/381-3297; FAX 615/381-8692.* 54 rms, 2 story. S $44; D $48; each addl $4; suite $55; under 13 free; wkend rates; higher rates Mule Day. Crib free. TV; cable. Pool. Complimentary continental bkfst, coffee in lobby. Restaurant nearby. Ck-out 11 am. Meeting rm. Cr cds: A, C, D, DS, ER, MC, V.

 D ⚓ 🚫 ⊙ SC

★ **HOLIDAY INN.** *(Box 482) 2½ mi N on US 31. 615/388-2720; FAX 615/388-2360.* 155 rms, 2 story. S $42–$52; D $47–$57; each addl $5. Crib free. Pet accepted. TV; cable. Pool. Restaurant 6 am–2 pm, 5–10 pm. Rm serv. Bar 4 pm–midnight. Ck-out noon. Meeting rms. Cr cds: A, C, D, DS, MC, V, JCB.

D 🐾 ⚓ 🚫 ⊙ SC

Restaurants

★ ★ **ALBERT'S.** *708 N Main St. 615/381-3463.* Hrs: 5–10 pm. Closed Sun, Mon; some hols. Bar. Semi-a la carte: dinner $9.95–$24.95. Specializes in steak, seafood, Jack Daniels charcoal-grilled foods. Parking. Renovated livery stable (1866). Cr cds: A, DS, MC, V.

D

✔ ★ **MARION'S.** *104 W 6th St. 615/388-6868.* Hrs: 11 am–2 pm, 5–9 pm; Fri to 10 pm; Sat & Sun 5–10 pm; Sun brunch 10:30 am–2 pm. Closed some major hols. Res accepted. Bar. Semi-a la carte: lunch $4.95–$9.95, dinner $7.50–$15.50. Sun brunch $3.50–$7.50. Child's meals. Specializes in prime rib, crawfish fettucine, chocolate caramel pecan pie. Parking. Outdoor dining. Colonial decor; in historic building (1846). Cr cds: A, MC, V.

Cookeville (D-6)

Settled: 1854 **Pop:** 21,744 **Elev:** 1,118 ft **Area code:** 615 **Zip:** 38501

Cookeville, a cultural and industrial center for the upper Cumberland area, is the home of Tennessee Technological University.

What to See and Do

1. **Center Hill Dam and Lake.** 25 mi W via I-40, TN 141. This 250-foot-high, 2,160-foot-long concrete and earth-fill dam controls flood waters of the Caney Fork River and provides electric power. The lake has a 415-mile shoreline. Swimming, waterskiing; fishing, hunting; boating. Picnicking at six recreation areas around reservoir. Camping (fee; hookups). Eight commercial docks. Some facilities closed Oct–mid-Apr. Phone 858-3125; 548-4521. Also here is

Edgar Evins State Park. Approximately 6,000-acre park has boat launch facilities. Camping (dump station), cabins. Standard fees. Phone 858-2446 or -2114. Nearby is

Joe L. Evins Appalachian Center for Crafts. W on I-40, 6 mi S on TN 56. On 600 acres overlooking Center Hill Lake. Operated by Tennessee Technological University. Teaching programs in fiber, metal, wood, glass and clay. Exhibition galleries. (Daily; closed major hols) Phone 597-6801. **Free.**

2. **Burgess Falls State Natural Area.** 8 mi S of I-40 exit 286 on TN 135. Scenic riverside trail (¾ mi) leads to an overlook of a 130-foot waterfall, considered one of the most beautiful in the state, located

in a gorge on the Falling Water River. Fishing (Burgess Falls Lake & river below dam). Hiking trails. Picnicking (below dam). For information phone 432-5312.

(For further information contact the Cookeville Area-Putnam County Chamber of Commerce, 302 S Jefferson Ave; 526-2211.)

Motels

✔ ★ ★ BEST WESTERN THUNDERBIRD. *900 S Jefferson Ave, ½ mi N of I-40 Sparta Rd exit 287.* 615/526-7115. 60 rms, 2 story. S $26–$42; D $34–$45; each addl $4; under 12 free. Crib $3. Pet accepted. TV; cable. Pool; wading pool. Complimentary continental bkfst. Restaurant adj 6 am–midnight. Ck-out noon. Meeting rms. Cr cds: A, C, D, DS, ER, MC, V, JCB.

★ COMFORT INN. *1100 S Jefferson Ave, I-40 exit 287.* 615/528-1040. 69 air-cooled rms, 2 story. May–Oct: S $32.95–$36.95; D $34.95–$42.95; each addl $5; suite $49.95; under 10 free; lower rates rest of yr. Crib $5. Pet accepted. TV; cable. Pool. Complimentary continental bkfst, coffee. Ck-out 11 am. Many refrigerators. Cr cds: A, C, D, DS, ER, MC, V, JCB.

★ ★ EXECUTIVE INN. *897 S Jefferson Ave, at jct TN 136 & I-40, exit 287.* 615/526-9521; res: 800/826-2791. 83 rms, 2 story. S $28–$37; D $36–$44; each addl $5. TV; cable. Heated pool; wading pool. Restaurant 11 am–10 pm; Fri, Sat to 11 pm. Rm serv. Beer. Ck-out 11 am. Coin lndry. Meeting rm. Sundries. Cr cds: A, C, D, DS, MC, V.

✔ ★ HOWARD JOHNSON. *2021 E Spring St, on US 70N at I-40 exit 290.* 615/526-3333; FAX 615/528-5039. 64 rms, 2 story. S $30–$38; D $34–$48; each addl $5; under 18 free. Crib free. Pet accepted. TV; cable, in-rm movies avail. Pool; wading pool, whirlpool. Complimentary continental bkfst. Restaurant 11 am–10 pm. Ck-out noon. Coin lndry. Sundries. Free local airport transportation. Refrigerators. Private patios, balconies. Picnic tables. Cr cds: A, C, D, DS, MC, V, JCB.

Motor Hotel

★ ★ HOLIDAY INN. *970 S Jefferson Ave, at jct I-40 & TN 136, exit 287.* 615/526-7125; FAX 615/526-7125, ext 152. 200 rms, 2–3 story. S $56–$59; D $63–$66; suites $75–$200; family rates. Crib avail. Pet accepted. TV; cable. Indoor/outdoor pool; whirlpool; poolside serv. Restaurant 6 am–2 pm, 5–10 pm. Rm serv. Taproom (beer) 4 pm–midnight. Ck-out noon. Meeting rms. Bellhops. Valet serv. Sundries. Holidome. Game rm. Cr cds: A, C, D, DS, MC, V, JCB.

Restaurants

✔ ★ ★ NICK'S. *895 S Jefferson Ave, at jct I-40 & Sparta Hwy.* 615/528-1434. Hrs: 11 am–2:30 pm, 5–10 pm; Sat 5–10:30 pm. Closed Sun. Continental menu. Bar. Semi-a la carte: lunch $4.35–$8.95, dinner $7.75–$13.95. Specializes in char-broiled steak, seafood, ice cream pie. Parking. Cr cds: A, C, D, MC, V.

★ ★ SCARECROW COUNTRY INN. *1720 E Spring St.* 615/526-3431. Hrs: 11 am–2 pm, 5–9:30 pm; Mon to 2 pm; Sat from 5 pm. Closed Sun; major hols. Res accepted. Setups. Semi-a la carte: lunch $4.95–$7.95, dinner $9–$18. Child's meals. Specialties: apple jack pork, hickory ham. Own desserts. Guitarist Tues, Fri & Sat. Parking. Built from logs of original log cabins and schoolhouse. Cr cds: MC, V.

D

Covington (E-2)

Pop: 7,487 **Elev:** 339 ft **Area code:** 901 **Zip:** 38019

What to See and Do

Fort Pillow State Historic Area. 33 mi NW via US 51N & TN 87W. This archaeologically significant area consists of 1,646 acres on the Chickasaw Bluffs, overlooking Mississippi River. It contains substantial remains of a large fort, named for a confederate general, and five miles of earthworks. Fishing. Wooded trails (15 mi). Picnicking. Tent & primitive camping. Visitors center, nature exhibits. (Daily; closed Dec 25) Standard fees. Phone 738-5581.

(For accommodations see Memphis)

Crossville (D-6)

Pop: 6,930 **Elev:** 1,863 ft **Area code:** 615 **Zip:** 38555

More than 36,000 tons of multicolored quartzite are quarried in the Crossville area each year and sold for construction projects throughout the country. This Cumberland Plateau town also markets beef cattle, dairy products, strawberries, beans and potatoes. Hickory handles, charcoal, liquid smoke, rubber mats, office supplies, ceramic tile, exercise equipment, bus and truck mirrors, yarn and apparel are also produced locally.

What to See and Do

1. **Cumberland Mountain State Park.** 4 mi S on US 127. This 1,548-acre park, located along the Cumberland Plateau, is 1,820 feet above sea level. It stands on the largest remaining timberland plateau in America and has a 35-acre lake. Swimming pool, bathhouse, lifeguards; fishing; boating (rentals). Nature trails & programs, tennis. Picnicking, playground, concession, snack bar, dining room. Camping, tent & trailer sites, cabins. Standard fees. Phone 484-6138.

2. **Homesteads Tower Museum & Gallery.** 4 mi S on US 127. The tower was built in 1937–38 to house administrative offices of the Cumberland Homesteads, a New Deal-era project. A winding stairway leads to a lookout platform at the top of the octagonal stone tower. At the base of the tower is a museum with photos, documents and artifacts from the 1930s and 1940s; art gallery is filled with exhibits of local and regional scenes. Museum & gallery (free). (Apr–Nov, daily; closed Easter, Labor Day, Thanksgiving) Donation to climb tower. Phone 456-9663.

3. **Plateau Experiment Station.** Headquarters, 9 mi NW on US 70N. More than 2,000-acre University of TN station used for agricultural research. (Mon–Fri; closed hols) Phone 484-0034. **Free.**

4. **Cumberland County Playhouse.** 1½ mi W on US 70S, overlooking Lake Holiday. Indoor stage presentations by both professional and community actors. Picnic facilities, concession. For schedule and reservations phone 484-5000 or contact PO Box 484, 38557. ¢¢¢¢–¢¢¢¢¢

5. **Cumberland General Store.** 4 mi S via US 127 in Homestead. Old-time country store. (Mid-Mar–Dec, daily; rest of yr, daily exc Sun; closed Jan 1, Thanksgiving, Dec 25) Phone 484-8481. **Free.**

(For further information contact the Greater Cumberland County Chamber of Commerce, 108 S Main St, 38557; 484-8444.)

Annual Event

Cumberland County Fair. Exhibits, horse, cattle and other animal shows, mule pulls, fiddlers' contest. Phone 484-6431. Late Aug–early Sept.

Resort

★ ★ ★**FAIRFIELD GLADE.** *(Box 1500, Fairfield Glade 38557) 10 mi N, 6 mi N of I-40 Peavine Rd exit.* 615/484-7521. 97 rms, 98 villas. June–Oct: S, D $95; villas $105–$150; golf package plan; lower rates rest of yr. Crib free. TV; cable. Indoor/outdoor pool; wading pool. Playground. Supervised child's activities (June–Aug). 3 dining rms 7 am–10 pm. Snack bar. Private club. Ck-out 10 am, ck-in 4 pm. Grocery. Meeting rms. Sports dir. Indoor & lighted tennis, pro. 45-hole golf, greens fee $35–$50, putting green, driving range. Miniature golf. Private beach. Boats, motors, dock. Dancing, entertainment. Lawn games. Rec rm. Exercise equipt; weights, bicycles, sauna. Private patios, balconies. Picnic tables, grills. Cr cds: A, C, D, DS, MC, V.

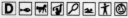

Cumberland Gap National Historical Park

(see Kentucky)

Dickson (D-4)

Founded: 1873 **Pop:** 8,791 **Elev:** 794 ft **Area code:** 615 **Zip:** 37055

What to See and Do

Montgomery Bell State Resort Park. 7 mi E on US 70. A 5,000-acre, wooded park with streams, brooks and three lakes in the Highland Rim. Replica of church on site where Cumberland Presbyterian Church was founded in 1810. Swimming, bathhouse; fishing; boating (rentals). Nature trails, backpacking; golf, tennis. Picnicking, playground, restaurant. Tent & trailer sites, inn, cabins. Standard fees. Phone 797-3101.

(For further information contact the Chamber of Commerce, 119 US 70, PO Box 339; 446-2349.)

Annual Event

Old-Timers' Day. Parades, entertainment and special events. 1st wkend May.

(For accommodations see Hurricane Mills, Nashville)

Dyersburg (D-2)

Pop: 16,317 **Elev:** 295 ft **Area code:** 901 **Zip:** 38024

Motels

✔ ★ ★**COMFORT INN.** *815 Realfoot Dr, I-155 exit 13.* 901/285-6951; FAX 901/285-6956. 82 rms, 2 story. Mar–Sept: S $39.60–$42; D $43–$47; each addl $5; suites $55; under 18 free; lower rates rest of yr. Crib $5. TV; cable, in-rm movies avail. Pool; wading pool. Restaurant adj

11 am–9 pm. Ck-out 11 am. Coin lndry. Meeting rms. Exercise equipt; weights, bicycles. Some refrigerators. Cr cds: A, C, D, DS, ER, MC, V.

★ ★**HOLIDAY INN.** *(Box 490) Jct US 51 Bypass & TN 78, exit 13 on I-155.* 901/285-8601; FAX 901/286-0494. 106 rms, 2 story. S $47; D $54; each addl $8; under 18 free. Crib free. TV; cable. Pool. Restaurant 6 am–2 pm, 5:30–10 pm. Rm serv. Ck-out noon. Meeting rms. Valet serv. Sundries. Cr cds: A, C, D, DS, MC, V, JCB.

Elizabethton (D-9)

Pop: 11,931 **Elev:** 1,530 ft **Area code:** 615 **Zip:** 37643

A monument on the lawn of Carter County Courthouse marks the spot where the Watauga Association was formed in 1772 by settlers in these hills. Isolated from the seaboard colonies, the pioneers were determined to organize for law and self-protection. Their constitution was the first to be adopted by independent Americans. Little is now known about this constitution except that it helped unite the people of eastern Tennessee to fight in the American Revolution.

What to See and Do

1. **Watauga Dam and Lake.** 5 mi SE on US 19E, then 3 mi E on TN 67. Earth and rock-fill TVA dam, 950 feet long and 331 feet high, impounds a 6,430-acre lake. Swimming, waterskiing; boating (docks). Camping, cabins. Visitor overlook (daily). Phone 542-2951. **Free.**

2. **Sycamore Shoals State Historic Area.** 1½ mi W on US 321. First colonial settlement west of the Blue Ridge Mountains has reconstructed fort consisting of five buildings and palisade walls; visitor center with museum and theater (daily). Tours of nearby Carter Mansion available by appointment. Picnic sites. (See ANNUAL EVENTS) Phone 543-5808. **Free.**

3. **Roan Mountain State Park.** 17 mi SE via US 19E, S on TN 143. The 2,104-acre park includes 6,285-foot Roan Mountain, one of the highest peaks in the eastern US. Atop mountain is 600-acre garden of rhododendron, in bloom late June (see ANNUAL EVENTS). Swimming pool; fishing. Nature trail. Cross-country skiing. Picnicking, playground, snack bar. Camping, cabins. Standard fees. Phone 772-3303 or -3314.

(For further information contact the Elizabethton/Carter County Chamber of Commerce, US 19E Bypass, PO Box 190; 543-2122.)

Annual Events

Roan Mt Wild Flower Tours & Bird Walks. Roan Mountain State Park (see #3). May.

Covered Bridge Celebration. Elk Ave Bridge, downtown. Arts & crafts festival, parade, antique show, ice-cream eating contest. Area country music stars and local talent perform. 6 nights early June.

Rhododendron Festival. Roan Mountain State Park (see #3). Mid-late June.

Bluegrass Festival. 2½ mi N on TN 19E at Slagles Pasture. Many nationally known bands perform; camping. Phone 323-3827. June.

Outdoor Drama. Sycamore Shoals State Historic Area (see #2). Depicts muster of Overmountain Men, who marched to King's Mountain, SC, and defeated the British. Phone 543-5808. Mid-July.

Overmountain Victory Trail Celebration. Reenactment in period costume of original 200-mile march. Late Sept.

(For accommodations see Johnson City)

Fort Donelson National Battlefield and Cemetery (D-4)

(1 mi W of Dover on US 79)

"Unconditional and immediate surrender!" demanded General Ulysses S. Grant when Confederate General Simon B. Buckner proposed a truce at Fort Donelson. Thus did Grant contribute to the long list of appropriate and pithy remarks for which American military men have become justly famous.

Nothing helped Grant so much during this four-day battle as weak generalship on the part of Confederate commanders John B. Floyd and Gideon J. Pillow. Although the Confederates repulsed an attack by Federal ironclad gunboats, the responsibility of surrendering the Confederate garrison of 15,000 was thrust upon Buckner on February 16, 1862. Grant's victory at Fort Donelson, coupled with the fall of Fort Henry 10 days earlier, opened the Tennessee and Cumberland rivers into the heart of the Confederacy. In Grant, the people had a new hero. His laconic surrender message stirred the imagination, and he was quickly dubbed "Unconditional Surrender" Grant.

The fort walls, outer defenses and river batteries still remain and are well-marked to give the story of the battle. A visitor center features a 10-minute slide program, museum and touch exhibits (daily; closed Dec 25). A six-mile self-guided auto tour includes a visit to the fort, the cemetery and the Dover Hotel, where General Buckner surrendered. The park is open year round, dawn–dusk. Contact Superintendent, PO Box 434, Dover 37058; 615/232-5706. **Free.**

(For accommodations see Clarksville)

Franklin (D-5)

Founded: 1799 **Pop:** 20,098 **Elev:** 648 ft **Area code:** 615 **Zip:** 37064

Franklin is a favorite of Civil War buffs, who come to retrace the Battle of Franklin, a decisive clash that took place November 30, 1864. General John B. Hood, attempting to prevent two Union armies from uniting, outflanked the troops of General John Schofield. The Union troops, dug in around the Carter House, were discovered by Hood late in the afternoon. For five hours the battle raged. In the morning Hood found that the Schofield troops had escaped across the river to join forces with the Union army at Nashville. The Confederates suffered 6,252 casualties, including the loss of five generals at Carnton Mansion and a sixth general 10 days after the battle. The North suffered 2,326 casualties.

What to See and Do

1. **Historic District.** Downtown area within 1st Ave S to 5th Ave S and N Margin St to S Margin St, centered around the town Square and the Confederate Monument. Earliest buildings of Franklin, dating back to 1815; those along Main St are exceptional in their architectural designs and are part of a historic preservation project.

2. **Carter House** (1830). 1140 Columbia Ave, on US 31. Served as the command post for the Union forces during the Battle of Franklin. Confederate museum has documents, uniforms, flags, guns, maps, Civil War prints. Guided tour of house and grounds, video presentation. (Daily; closed major hols) Phone 791-1861. ¢¢

3. **Carnton Plantation and McGavock Confederate Cemetery.** 1345 Carnton Lane, 1 mi SE off US 431 (Lewisburg Pike). Federal house (1826) modified in the 1840s to reflect Greek-revival style. Built by an early mayor of Nashville, house was a social and politaical center. At the end of the Battle of Franklin, which was fought

nearby, four Confederate generals lay dead on the back porch. The nation's largest private Confederate cemetery is adjacent. (Daily) Phone 794-0903. ¢¢

4. **Heritage Trail.** N and S on US 31. Scenic drive along highway from Brentwood through Franklin to Spring Hill, an area that was, in the mid-1800s, plantation country. Southern culture is reflected in the drive's many antebellum and Victorian houses; Williamson County was one of the richest areas in Tennessee by the time of the Civil War.

(For further information contact the Williamson County Chamber of Commerce, City Hall, PO Box 156; 794-1225.)

Annual Events

Heritage Foundation Town & Country Tour. Contact PO Box 723; 790-0378. 1st wkend May.

Carter House Christmas Candlelight Tour. (See #2). Phone 791-1861. 1st wkend Dec.

(See Columbia, Nashville)

Motels

✔ ★ ★ **BEST WESTERN MAXWELL'S INN.** *1308 Murfreesboro Rd, TN 96 at I-65 exit 65.* 615/790-0570; FAX 615/790-0512. 142 rms, 2 story. S $42; D $48; each addl $5; under 12 free; higher rates Fan Fair. Crib free. Pet accepted; $5. TV. Pool. Complimentary continental bkfst. Restaurant adj 6 am–11 pm. Ck-out noon. Coin lndry. Meeting rms. Cr cds: A, C, D, DS, MC, V.

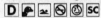

★ ★ ★ **HOLIDAY INN.** *TN 96 at I-65.* 615/794-7591; FAX 615/794-1042. 100 rms, 2 story. S $50–$55; D $55–$65; each addl $7; under 18 free; higher rates Fan Fair Week. Crib free. Pet accepted; some restrictions; $15. TV. Pool; wading pool. Playground. Coffee in some rms. Restaurant 6:30 am–2 pm, 5–10 pm. Rm serv. Bar from 5 pm. Ck-out noon. Meeting rm. Cr cds: A, C, D, DS, MC, V, JCB.

Gallatin (D-5)

Founded: 1802 **Pop:** 18,794 **Elev:** 526 ft **Area code:** 615 **Zip:** 37066

The county seat and market for tobacco and livestock, Gallatin is named for Albert Gallatin, Secretary of the Treasury under John Adams and Thomas Jefferson.

What to See and Do

1. **Cragfont** (1798). 5 mi E on TN 25, in Castalian Springs. This late Georgian-style house was built for General James Winchester, Revolutionary War hero, by masons and carpenters brought from Maryland. It is named for the rocky bluff (with spring below) on which it stands. Galleried ballroom, weaving room, wine cellar; Federal period furnishings. Restored gardens. (Mid-Apr–early Nov, daily exc Mon; rest of yr by appt) Phone 452-7070. ¢¢

2. **Wynnewood** (1828). 7 mi E on TN 25, in Castalian Springs. Log inn, considered the oldest and largest log structure ever built in Tennessee, was originally constructed as a stagecoach stop and mineral springs resort; Andrew Jackson visited here many times. (Apr–Oct, daily; rest of yr, daily exc Sun; closed major hols) Phone 452-5463. ¢¢

3. **Trousdale Place.** 183 W Main St. Two-story brick house built in early 1800s was residence of Governor William Trousdale; period furniture, military history library. (Daily exc Mon; closed Jan 1, Thanksgiving, Dec 25) Phone 452-5648. ¢¢

4. Bledsoe Creek State Park. 6 mi E on TN 25 to Ziegler Fort Rd, then 1½ mi S to Main Park Rd & the park entrance. Waterskiing; fishing; boating (launch). Nature trails. Playground. Camping (hookups, dump station). Standard fees. Phone 452-3706.

(For further information contact the Chamber of Commerce, 118 W Main, PO Box 26; 452-4000.)

Annual Event

Sumner County Pilgrimage. Tour of historic houses. Contact Cragfont, Rte 1, Box 73, Castalian Springs 37031; 452-7070. Last Sat Apr.

(See Nashville)

Motel

★**SHONEY'S INN.** *221 W Main St (TN 25).* 615/452-5433; res: 800/222-2222; FAX 615/452-1665. 86 rms, 2 story. S $36–$45; D $45–$55; each addl $6; under 18 free; higher rates Fanfare. Crib free. TV; cable. Pool. Complimentary coffee in lobby. Restaurant adj 6 am–midnight; Fri, Sat to 2 am. Ck-out noon. Meeting rms. Cr cds: A, C, D, DS, ER, MC, V.

Gatlinburg (D-8)

Pop: 3,417 **Elev:** 1,289 ft **Area code:** 615 **Zip:** 37738

Gatlinburg has shelved its mountain quaintness and has turned its attention to tapping into the stream of tourists that flows through the town on its way into the Great Smoky Mountains National Park, the country's most visited national park. The city has accommodations for 30,000 guests and a $22 million convention center. At the foot of Mount LeConte and at the head of the Pigeon River, Gatlinburg is noted for its many shops that make and sell mountain handicrafts—brooms, candles, candies, pottery and furniture.

What to See and Do

1. Great Smoky Mountains National Park (see).

2. American Historical Wax Museum. 542 Parkway, US 441. American history depicted in tableaux; more than 175 life-size figures. (Mar–Nov, daily) Phone 436-4462. ¢¢

3. Christus Gardens. 510 River Rd. Events from the life of Jesus portrayed in life-size dioramas; music and narration. Floral gardens in season. (Daily; closed Dec 25) Phone 436-5155. ¢¢¢

4. Craft shops. Along Main Street and east along US 321 on Glades Rd.

5. Scenic rides.

Gatlinburg Space Needle. Airport Rd. Glass-enclosed elevator to observation deck for view of the Smokies. (Daily) Sr citizen rate. Phone 436-4629. ¢¢

Sky Lift. 765 Parkway (US 441). Double chairlift ride up Crockett Mountain to 2,300 feet. View of Smokies en route and from observation deck at summit; snack bar; gift shop. (Apr–Oct, daily, weather permitting) Phone 436-4307. ¢¢¢

Sightseeing Chairlift–Ober Gatlinburg Ski Resort (see #6). Ski Mountain Rd, on Mt Harrison. Double chairlift operates to top of Mt Harrison. (Mar–Memorial Day, daily) ¢¢¢

Aerial Tramway–Ober Gatlinburg Ski Resort (see #6). 1001 Parkway. Ten-minute, two-mile tram ride to top of Mt Harrison. (Daily; closed 2 wks Mar) Phone 436-5423. ¢¢¢

6. Ober Gatlinburg Ski Resort. Ski Mountain Rd, on Mt Harrison. Double, 2 quad chairlifts; patrol, school, rentals; snowmaking;

concession area, restaurant, bar. Longest run 5,000 ft; vertical drop 600 ft. (Dec–mid-Mar, daily) Also alpine slide, indoor ice-skating arena (daily; closed 2 wks Mar; fees); aerial tramway and sightseeing chairlift (see #5). Contact Ober Gatlinburg, Inc, 1001 Parkway; 436-5423 or 800/251-9202 (Dec–Mar). ¢¢¢¢¢

(For further information contact the Chamber of Commerce, 520 Parkway, PO Box 527; 430-4148 or 800/568-4748.)

Annual Events

Spring Wild Flower Pilgrimage. Late Apr.

Scottish Festival and Games. Bagpipe marching bands, highland dancing, sheep dog demonstrations. 3rd wkend May.

Dulcimer Harp Festival. In Cosby, 20 mi NE on US 321 to TN 32S. Dulcimer convention; folk music; crafts demonstrations, storytelling, workshops. Participants from throughout the Appalachian region. Admission by advance ticket sales advised. For information contact PO Box 8, Cosby 37722; 487-5543. 2nd wkend June.

Craftsmen's Fairs. Craft demonstrations, folk music. Late July–early Aug; also mid-Oct.

Seasonal Events

Sweet Fanny Adams Theater. 461 Parkway. Professional theater presenting musical comedies, Gay 90s review, old-time sing-along. Nightly exc Sun. Reservations advisable. Phone 436-4039. Late Apr–Nov.

Smoky Mountain Lights. Citywide. Winter celebration including Yule log burnings, more than 2 million lights and other special events. Late Nov–Feb.

(See Pigeon Forge, Sevierville, Townsend)

Motels

★**ALPINE.** *(Box 523) River Rd & Cottage Dr.* 615/436-5651. 37 rms, 2 story, 1 kit. Apr–Dec: S $50–$55; D $55–$60; each addl $5; kit. unit $80–$90. Closed rest of yr. Crib $3. TV; cable. Pool; wading pool. Complimentary coffee. Restaurant nearby. Ck-out 11 am. Refrigerators. Sun deck. Picnic tables, grills. Many rms overlook Little Pigeon River. Cr cds: A, DS, MC, V.

★**ALTO.** *(Box 1277) 404 Airport Rd.* 615/436-5175. 21 rms, 2 story. Late May–Oct: S, D $60–$70; each addl $6; under 16 free; lower rates rest of yr. Crib free. Pet accepted. TV; cable. Pool; wading pool. Playground. Restaurant adj 6 am–11 pm. Ck-out 11 am. Downhill ski 4 mi. Refrigerators. Picnic tables, grills. Cr cds: A, DS, MC, V.

✔ ★★**BEST WESTERN CROSSROADS.** *(PO Box 648) Parkway, at jct US 441 & TN 321.* 615/436-5661. 78 rms, 2–4 story, 10 suites. S $32–$81; D $45–$81; suites, kit. units $85–$125. Crib $3. TV; cable. Pool; wading pool. Restaurant 7 am–11 pm. Ck-out 11 am. Coin lndry. Sundries. Downhill ski 5 mi. Some fireplaces. Covered patio. Cr cds: A, C, D, DS, MC, V.

✔ ★**BON AIR MOUNTAIN INN.** *(Box 36) 950 Parkway.* 615/436-4857; res: 800/848-4857. 37 rms, 2 story, 1 kit. chalet. Apr–Oct: S, D $43–$55; each addl $5–$7; chalet $95; under 12 free; lower rates rest of yr. Crib free. TV; cable. Pool. Restaurant nearby. Ck-out 11 am. Downhill ski 4 mi. Some refrigerators. Balconies. Cr cds: A, DS, MC, V.

★★**BROOKSIDE RESORT.** *463 E Parkway, 3 blks E on US 321.* 615/436-5611; res: 800/251-9597 (exc TN), 800/362-9605 (TN). 227 rms in motel, cottages, 1–2 story, 30 kits. May–Nov: S $55–$110; D $65–$110; each addl $5; suites from $100; kit. units $55–$145; kit.

cottages for 2–4, $60–$150; lower rates rest of yr. Crib free. TV; cable. Pool; wading pool, whirlpool. Playground. Complimentary coffee. Restaurant opp 7 am–10 pm. Ck-out 11 am. Coin lndry. Meeting rm. Downhill ski 6 mi. Lawn games. In-rm steam baths, in-rm whirlpools, refrigerators, fireplaces. Picnic tables, grills. Spacious grounds. By mountain stream. Cr cds: A, C, D, MC, V.

★ ★ COMFORT INN DOWNTOWN. 200 East Parkway (US 321). 615/436-5043; FAX 615/523-8363. 100 rms, 2–4 story. Apr–Oct: S, D up to 4 $59.50–$94.50; each addl $5–$10; suites $89–$129.50; lower rates rest of yr. Crib $5. TV; cable. Pool; wading pool, whirlpool, sauna. Restaurant 7 am–1 pm. Ck-out 11 am. Coin lndry. Meeting rms. Downhill ski 5 mi. Game rm. Some fireplaces. Cr cds: A, C, D, DS, MC, V.

✔ ★ COX'S GATEWAY. 1100 Parkway. 615/436-5656; res: 800/626-0495 (exc TN), 800/331-6831 (TN). 50 rms in motel, cottages, 1–2 story, 5 kits. June–Nov: S $48–$58; D $62–$68; kit. units, kit. cottages for 2–6, $85–$150; higher rates hols; lower rates rest of yr. Crib $5. TV; cable. Pool; wading pool. Complimentary coffee in lobby. Restaurant opp 5:30 am–11 pm. Ck-out 11 am. Some fireplaces. Private patios. Picnic tables, grills. Porches. Cr cds: A, MC, V.

✔ ★ CREEKSIDE. 239 Sycamore Lane. 615/436-5977; res: 800/697-5977. 22 rms, 2 story, 1 kit. Apr–Nov: S $40–$58; D $58–$88; each addl $4; kit. unit $58–$78. Closed rest of yr. Crib $5. TV; cable. Pool; wading pool. Coffee in lobby. Restaurant nearby. Ck-out 11 am. Refrigerators. Picnic tables, grills. Porches overlook creek. Cr cds: A, C, D, DS, MC, V.

★ DOGWOOD. 515 Airport Rd. 615/436-5883. 62 rms, 2–4 story, 8 kits. May–Oct: S, D $51–$67; each addl $5; kit. units $62; lower rates rest of yr. Crib $5. TV; cable. Pool. Restaurant opp 6 am–10 pm. Ck-out 11 am. Downhill ski 5 mi. Refrigerators; some fireplaces. Cr cds: A, C, D, DS, MC, V.

★ ★ EAST SIDE. 315 E Parkway. 615/436-7569. 29 rms, 2–3 story. No elvtr. June–Oct: S $35–$55; D $40–$65; each addl $5; lower rates mid-Mar–May, Nov. Closed rest of yr. Crib $5. TV; cable. Pool; wading pool. Playground. Complimentary coffee in rms. Restaurant nearby. Ck-out 11 am. Refrigerators. Picnic tables, grills. Cr cds: MC, V.

★ ECONO LODGE. (Box 11) 405 Airport Rd. 615/436-5836; FAX 615/523-8363. 33 rms. 1–4 persons $59.50–$89.50; suites $99.50–$129.50. Crib free. TV; cable. Pool. Complimentary coffee in rms. Restaurant adj. Ck-out 11 am. Cr cds: A, D, DS, MC, V.

★ ★ GILLETTE. (Box 231) 235 Airport Rd, opp convention center. 615/436-5601. 80 rms, 3 story, 1 kit. Late May–Oct: S $60; D $65–$75; each addl $10; kit. unit for 2–4, $85; lower rates rest of yr. Crib $10. TV; cable. Pool. Complimentary coffee in rms. Restaurant nearby. Ck-out 11 am. Downhill ski 4 mi. Refrigerators. Balconies. Cr cds: A, C, D, MC, V.

★ ★ JACK HUFF'S MOTOR LODGE. (PO Box 865) 204 Cherokee Orchard Rd. 615/436-5171; res: 800/322-1817. 60 rms, 3 story. June–Oct: S, D $60–$75; each addl $4; lower rates rest of yr. Crib free. TV; cable. Pool; wading pool. Complimentary coffee. Restaurant nearby. Ck-out 11 am. Downhill ski 4 mi. Cr cds: D, DS, MC, V.

★ ★ JOHNSON'S INN. (Box 392) Baskin's Creek Rd. 615/436-4881; res: 800/842-1930. 78 rms, 1–4 story, 4 kits. June–Aug, Oct: D $59–$83.50; each addl $3; under 6 free; higher rates special events; lower rates rest of yr. Crib $5. TV; cable. Pool; wading pool, whirlpool.

Complimentary coffee. Restaurant nearby. Ck-out 11 am. Coin lndry. Refrigerators, fireplaces. Cr cds: DS, MC, V.

★ ★ LE CONTE VIEW. (Box 252) 929 Parkway. 615/436-5032; res: 800/842-5767. 104 rms, 1–5 story. May–Oct: S, D $71–$101; each addl $6; suites $95–$137; under 18 free; fireplace units $14 addl; higher rates some hol wkends; lower rates Jan–Apr, Nov–Dec. Closed Dec 22–25. Crib $4. TV; cable. Indoor/outdoor pool; wading pool. Complimentary coffee in lobby. Restaurant nearby. Ck-out 11 am. Downhill ski 4 mi. Refrigerators. Cr cds: A, C, D, DS, MC, V.

★ ★ LECONTE CREEK INN. 125 LeConte Creek Dr. 615/436-4865; res: 800/473-8319. 69 units, 2 story. Mid-May–early Jan: 1–4 persons $55–$140; each addl $5; suites $125–$140; lower rates rest of yr. Crib free. TV; cable. Pool; wading pool. Complimentary continental bkfst, coffee. Restaurant adj 7 am–10 pm. Ck-out 11 am. Meeting rms. Downhill ski 1 mi. Some in-rm whirlpools, fireplaces. Balconies. Cr cds: A, C, D, DS, MC, V.

★ ★ MIDTOWN LODGE. 805 Parkway. 615/436-5691; res: 800/633-2446. 133 rms, 1–6 story, 13 kits. June–Oct: S, D $65; each addl $10; suites $75–$80; kit. cottages $75–$95; lower rates rest of yr. Crib free. TV; cable. Pool; wading pool. Restaurant opp 7 am–11 pm. Ck-out 11 am. Downhill ski 5 mi. Some refrigerators, fireplaces. Private patios, balconies. Cr cds: A, C, D, MC, V.

★ ★ OAK SQUARE. (Box 1521) 705 Crossroad. 615/436-7582; res: 800/423-5182. 60 kit. suites, 4 story. Suites $69–$115; wkly rates; ski plans; lower rates winter. Crib free. TV; cable. 2 pools, 1 indoor; whirlpool. Restaurant nearby. Ck-out 11 am. Meeting rms. Downhill ski 4 mi. Fireplaces. Balconies. Opp river. Cr cds: A, MC, V.

★ ★ OLDE GATLINBURG PLACE. 306 Baskin's Creek Rd. 615/430-5067; res: 800/874-0233. 91 kit. suites, 7 story. May–Sept, Nov: suites $79–$125; each addl $10; wkly rates; higher rates hols & Oct; lower rates rest of yr. TV; cable. Heated pool. Ck-out 11 am. Coin lndry. Meeting rms. Some in-rm whirlpools. Private patios, balconies. Cr cds: A, DS, MC, V.

★ ★ QUALITY INN CONVENTION CENTER. 938 Parkway. 615/436-5607. 64 rms, 4 story. June–Oct: S, D $47–$95; under 18 free; higher rates hols, special events; lower rates rest of yr. Crib $5. TV; cable. Pool; wading pool. Restaurant adj 7 am–11 pm. Ck-out 11 am. Meeting rm. Downhill ski 4 mi. Refrigerators. Private patios, balconies. Cr cds: A, C, D, DS, MC, V.

★ ★ QUALITY INN SMOKYLAND. 727 Parkway. 615/436-5191. 40 rms, 2 story. Memorial Day wkend–mid-Nov: S, D $73–$99; each addl $10; under 16 free; lower rates rest of yr. Crib $10. TV; cable. Pool; wading pool. Complimentary coffee in rms. Restaurant adj. Ck-out 11 am. Downhill ski 5 mi. Refrigerators; some fireplaces. Cr cds: A, C, D, DS, MC, V.

★ ★ RIVER EDGE MOTOR LODGE. (Box 213) 665 River Rd. 615/436-9292; res: 800/544-2764. 43 rms, 3 story. Memorial Day–Oct: S $55–$75; each addl $5; higher rates hols; lower rates rest of yr. Crib free. TV; cable. Pool; wading pool. Complimentary coffee in rms. Restaurant nearby. Ck-out 11 am. Downhill ski 4 mi. Refrigerators; some fireplaces. Balconies. Cr cds: A, C, D, DS, ER, MC, V.

✔ ★ ROCKY TOP VILLAGE INN. 311 Airport Rd. 615/436-7826; res: 800/553-7738; FAX 615/436-4464. 89 rms, 3 story. No elvtr. Some rm phones. June–Oct: S, D $45–$61; each addl $5; suites $81; kit. cottages $110; lower rates rest of yr. Crib free. TV; cable. Pool; wading pool. Complimentary coffee in lobby. Restaurant adj 7 am–10 pm. Ck-out 11 am. Meeting rms. Many refrigerators. Picnic tables, grills. Cr cds: A, DS, MC, V.

★ ★ROCKY WATERS MOTOR INN. (Box 230) 333 Parkway. 615/436-7861; res: 800/824-1111. 105 rms, 2–3 story. Early May–Oct: S, D $75–$80; each addl $5; lower rates rest of yr. Crib $2. TV; cable. 2 pools; wading pool, whirlpool. Coffee in lobby. Restaurant adj 7 am–11 pm. Ck-out 11 am. Coin lndry. Meeting rm. Downhill ski 6 mi. Refrigerators; some in-rm whirlpools, fireplaces. Private patios. Picnic tables. On river. Cr cds: A, C, D, DS, MC, V.

★ROYAL TOWNHOUSE. 937 Parkway, opp civic auditorium. 615/436-5818; res: 800/433-8792 (exc TN). 81 rms, 3 story. S, D $59.95–$79.95; each addl $5; under 16 free. Crib $5. TV; cable. Pool; wading pool. Complimentary coffee in rms. Restaurant opp 7 am–10 pm. Ck-out 11 am. Meeting rms. Downhill ski 4 mi. Some refrigerators, fireplaces. Balconies. Cr cds: A, DS, MC, V.

✔ ★SKYLAND. (Box 242) 418 Parkway, 1 blk E on US 321. 615/436-5821; res: 800/255-8738. 56 rms, 1–2 story. May–Oct: S, D $49–$69; each addl $5; suites $95–$125; lower rates rest of yr. Crib $3. TV; cable. Pool. Complimentary coffee. Restaurant nearby. Ck-out 11 am. Downhill ski 5 mi. Some refrigerators. Many balconies. Picnic tables. Cr cds: A, C, DS, MC, V.

★ ★TRAVELODGE. 610 Airport Rd. 615/436-7851; FAX 615/430-3580. 126 rms, 4 story, 15 suites. June–Oct: S, D $55–$80; each addl $5; suites $75–$120; under 17 free; higher rates hols; lower rates rest of yr. Crib free. TV; cable. 2 pools, 1 indoor; wading pool, whirlpool, sauna. Coffee in rms. Restaurant 7 am–3 pm. Ck-out 11 am. Coin lndry. Meeting rms. Downhill/x-country ski 4 mi. Game rm. Many refrigerators. Balconies. Picnic tables. On river. Cr cds: A, C, D, DS, MC, V, JCB.

Motor Hotels

★ ★BENT CREEK RESORT. 3919 E Parkway, 11 mi E on US 321. 615/436-2875; res: 800/251-9336; FAX 615/436-3257. 108 rms, 3 story. No elvtr. Apr–Oct: S, D $79–$109; each addl $10; under 18 free; golf plans; lower rates rest of yr. Crib free. TV; cable. Pool; wading pool. Playground. Restaurant 6:30 am–10 pm. Ck-out 11 am. Meeting rms. Lighted tennis. 18-hole golf course, greens fee $28, pro, putting green, driving range. Downhill ski 10½ mi. Lawn games. Some refrigerators. Balconies. Cr cds: A, D, DS, MC, V.

✔ ★ ★DAYS INN GLENSTONE LODGE. 504 Airport Rd. 615/436-9361; FAX 615/436-6951. 216 rms, 5 story. S, D $48–$85; each addl $7; suites $85–$150; under 12 free. Crib free. TV; cable. Indoor pool; wading pool, whirlpool, sauna. Playground. Restaurant 7 am–9 pm. Rm serv. Bar 5–10 pm. Ck-out 11 am. Meeting rms. Bellhops. Valet serv. Downhill/x-country ski 1 mi. Lawn games. Wet bar in suites. Picnic tables, grills. On river. Cr cds: A, C, D, DS, MC, V.

★ ★HOLIDAY INN. (Box 1130) 520 Airport Rd. 615/436-9201; FAX 615/436-9201, ext 234. 402 rms, 2–7 story. May–Oct: S, D $60–$100; each addl $6; suites $150–$250; under 19 free; lower rates rest of yr. Crib free. Pet accepted. TV; cable. 3 pools, 2 indoor; wading pool, whirlpools. Supervised child's activities (summer). Restaurant 7 am–10 pm. Rm serv. Bar 5 pm–1 am. Ck-out 11 am. Free lndry facilities. Convention facilities. Bellhops. Gift shop. Downhill ski 4 mi. Holidome. Rec rm. Cr cds: A, C, D, DS, MC, V, JCB.

★ ★HOWARD JOHNSON. (Box 408) 559 Parkway. 615/436-5621; FAX 615/430-4471. 257 rms, 2–5 story. June–Oct: S, D $56–$92;

each addl $8; suites $68–$136; under 13 free; lower rates rest of yr. Crib free. TV; cable. Heated pool; wading pool. Restaurant adj 7 am–midnight. Ck-out 11 am. Coin lndry. Meeting rms. Downhill ski 4 mi. Fireplace. Balconies. On river. Cr cds: A, C, D, DS, ER, MC, V, JCB.

Hotels

★ ★EDGEWATER. (Box 170) 402 River Rd. 615/436-4151; res: 800/423-9582 (exc TN), 800/423-4532 (TN); FAX 615/436-6947. 200 rms, 8 story. Apr–Oct: S, D $94–$99; each addl $5; suites $175; under 16 free; lower rates rest of yr. Crib $5. TV; cable. Indoor pool; whirlpool. Restaurant 7–11 am, 5–9 pm. Bar; entertainment, dancing. Ck-out 11 am. Meeting rms. Downhill ski 1 mi. Some fireplaces. Balconies. On river. Cr cds: A, C, D, DS, MC, V.

★ ★PARK VISTA. 441 Airport Rd. 615/436-9211; res: 800/421-7275 (exc TN); FAX 615/436-5141. 315 rms, 16 story. S, D $55–$110; suites $150–$230; under 17 free; higher rates special events. Crib free. TV; cable. Indoor pool; wading pool, whirlpool, poolside serv. Restaurant 6:30 am–2 pm, 5–10:30 pm. Rm serv 6:30 am–10:30 pm. Bar noon–1 am; entertainment, dancing. Ck-out noon. Coin lndry. Convention facilities. Gift shop. Valet parking. Downhill ski 5 mi. Exercise equipt; weights, bicycle, sauna. Rec rm. Balconies. Cr cds: A, C, D, DS, MC, V.

Inn

★ ★BUCKHORN. 2140 Tudor Mt Rd; N on US 321, left on Buckhorn Rd, right on Tudor Mt Rd. 615/436-4668. 13 rms, 2 story. S $85–$250; D $95–$250; each addl $20; wkly rates; higher rates Oct. Crib $10. TV in some rms. Complimentary full bkfst. Restaurant (public by res), 7 pm sitting. Ck-out 11 am, ck-in 3 pm. Porch overlooks Mt LeConte. Cr cds: MC, V.

Restaurants

✔ ★BRASS LANTERN. 710 Parkway. 615/436-4168. Hrs: 11 am–10 pm. Bar from noon; Sat to 11 pm. Semi-a la carte: lunch, dinner $3.95–$16.95. Child's meals. Specializes in vegetable soup, prime rib. Parking. Cr cds: A, DS, MC, V.

✔ ★ ★HEIDELBERG. 148 N Parkway. 615/430-3094. Hrs: 11–1 am. Res accepted. German, Swiss, Amer menu. Bar. Semi-a la carte: lunch $4.50–$13.50. A la carte entrees: dinner $8.75–$19.95. Child's meals. Specialties: sauerbraten, schnitzel, steak. German music. Parking. Cr cds: A, C, D, DS, MC, V.

★ ★MAXWELL'S FRESH SEAFOOD & OYSTER BAR. 1103 Parkway. 615/436-3738. Hrs: 5–10 pm; Fri, Sat 4:30–11 pm. Bar. Semi-a la carte: dinner $9.95–$32.95. Child's meals. Specializes in fresh seafood, prime rib. Parking. Cr cds: A, D, MC, V.

★ ★OPEN HEARTH. 1138 Parkway. 615/436-5648. Hrs: 5–10 pm. Closed Dec 24, 25. Bar. Semi-a la carte: dinner $10.95–$22.95. Child's meals. Specializes in prime rib, steak, fresh seafood. Parking. Family-owned. Cr cds: A, C, D, DS, MC, V.

★ ★PEDDLER. 820 River Rd. 615/436-5794. Hrs: 5–10 pm; winter to 9 pm. Closed Dec 25. Bar. Semi-a la carte: dinner $13.95–$24.95. Child's meals. Specializes in New York strip steak, rib eye steak. Salad bar. Own soups, desserts. Parking. Converted log cabin. Overlooks river. Cr cds: A, DS, MC, V.

★ **PIONEER INN.** *373 Parkway.* 615/436-7592. Hrs: 8 am–9 pm. Closed Dec 24, 25. Res accepted. Beer, wine. Semi-a la carte: bkfst, lunch $3–$9.50, dinner $9.95–$18.50. Child's meals. Specializes in prime rib, Southern fried chicken, homemade pies. Early Amer decor; antiques. 4 rms overlook river. Cr cds: A, DS, MC, V.

Great Smoky Mountains National Park (D-7)

(44 mi SE of Knoxville via US 441)

The lofty peaks of the Appalachian Mountains stand tall and regal in this 800-square-mile area. They are products of a slow and powerful uplifting of ancient sediments that took place more than 200 million years ago. Red spruce, basswood, eastern hemlock, yellow birch, white ash, cucumber trees, silverbells, Fraser fir, tulip poplar, red maple and Fraser magnolias tower above hundreds of other species of flowering plants. Perhaps the most spectacular of these are the purple rhododendron, mountain laurel and flame azalea in bloom from early June to mid-July.

The moist, moderate climate has helped make this area a rich wilderness. From early spring to late fall the "coves" (open valleys surrounded by peaks) and forest floors are covered with a succession of flowers unmatched in the United States for colorful variety. Summer brings heavy showers to the mountains, days that are warm, though 15° to 20°F cooler than in the valleys below, and cool nights. Autumn is breathtaking as the deciduous trees change to almost every color in the spectrum. Winter brings snow, which is occasionally heavy, and fog over the mountains; while winter discourages many tourists, it can be a very good time to visit the park. (Some park roads, however, may be temporarily closed.)

A wonderful place to hike, half of the park is in North Carolina, while the other half is in Tennessee. The Appalachian Trail follows the state line for 70 miles along the high ridge of the park. Nearby are the cabins, barns and mills of the mountain people, whose ancestors came years ago from England and Scotland. It is also a place to see the descendants of the Cherokee Indian Nation, whose ancestors hid in the mountains from the soldiers during the winter of 1838–39 to avoid being driven over the "Trail of Tears" to Oklahoma. This is the tribe of Sequoya, a brilliant chief who invented a written alphabet for the Cherokee people.

Stop first at one of the three visitor centers: Oconaluftee (daily; closed Dec 25) in North Carolina, two miles north of Cherokee on Newfound Gap Road, designated US 441 outside of park; Sugarlands (daily; closed Dec 25) in Tennessee, two miles southwest of Gatlinburg; or Cades Cove (Mar–Nov, daily; Dec, wkends), eight miles southwest of Townsend. All three have exhibits and information about the park. There are hundreds of miles of foot trails and bridle paths. Camping is popular; ask at any visitor center for locations, regulations. Developed campgrounds (inquire for fee) are available. Reservations may be made by phoning 800/365-CAMP from mid-May–Oct for Elkmont, Cades Cove and Smokemont; reservations not taken for other sites.

The views from Newfound Gap and the observation platform at Clingmans Dome (closed winter), about seven miles southwest, are spectacular. Cades Cove, about 25 miles west of Sugarlands, is an outdoor museum reflecting the life of the original mountain people. It has log cabins and barns. Park naturalists conduct campfire programs and hikes during the spring and summer. There are also self-guided nature trails. LeConte Lodge, reached only on foot or horseback, is a concession within the park (late Mar–mid-Nov).

Fishing is permitted with a state license. Obtain regulations at visitor centers and campgrounds. The park is a wildlife sanctuary; any disturbance of plant or animal life is forbidden. Dogs and cats are not permitted on trails, but may be brought in if kept on leash or under other physical restrictive controls. Never feed, tease or frighten bears; always give them a wide berth, as they may inflict serious injury. Watch bears from a car with the windows closed. Park (daily). Free.

CCInc Auto Tape Tours, a 90-minute cassette, offers a mile-by-mile self-guided tour of the park. Written in cooperation with the National Park Service, it provides information on history, points of interest and flora and fauna of the park. Available in Gatlinburg at motels and gift shops; in Cherokee, NC, at Raven Craft Shop on Main Street and at Log Cabin Trading Post, across from the cinema. Tapes also may be purchased directly from CCInc, PO Box 227, 2 Elbrook Dr, Allendale, NJ 07401; 201/236-1666. ¢¢¢¢

For further information contact Superintendent, Great Smoky Mountains National Park, 107 Park Headquarters Rd, Gatlinburg 37738; phone 615/436-1200. Lodging is available in the park: LeConte Lodge, phone 615/436-4473.

(For accommodations see Gatlinburg)

Greeneville (D-8)

Settled: 1783 **Pop:** 13,532 **Elev:** 1,531 ft **Area code:** 615 **Zip:** 37743

Greeneville was the capital of the independent sovereign state of Franklin (1785–88), formed by the rugged independent-minded Scotch-Irish settlers who seceded from North Carolina. A Greeneville tailor, Andrew Johnson, was elected to the Board of Aldermen in 1829 and went on to become president of the United States. Davy Crockett was born a few miles outside of town in 1786. Manufacturing, lumber, dairying and tobacco are most important today. A Ranger District office of the Cherokee National Forest is located in Greeneville.

What to See and Do

1. **Andrew Johnson National Historic Site** (see). College & Depot Sts.
2. **Cherokee National Forest** (see). 12 mi S on TN 70.
3. **Davy Crockett Birthplace State Park.** 3 mi E off US 11E. A 66-acre site overlooking Nolichuckey River serves as a memorial to Crockett—humorist, bear hunter, congressman and hero of the Alamo. Small monument marks birthplace; nearby is a replica of the log cabin in which Crockett was born in 1786. Swimming pool (fee). Picnicking. Camping (hook-ups). Museum and visitors center (Mon–Fri, or by appt). Park (daily). Standard fees. Phone 257-2167 or -2168.
4. **Kinser Park.** 6 mi S via TN 70S. A 285-acre park surrounded by woodland, overlooking Nolichuckey River. Swimming pool (bathhouses, waterslide); boating (ramp). Nature trails; tennis courts, golf course; miniature golf, driving range, playing fields, go-cart track. Picnic facilities, playgrounds. Camping (fee; hookups). Fee for some activities. (Mid-Mar–Oct, daily) Sr citizen rate. Phone 639-5912. **Free.**

(For further information contact the Greene County Chamber of Commerce, 207 N Main St; 638-4111.)

(See Newport)

Motels

✔ ★ **CHARRAY INN.** *121 Serral Dr.* 615/638-1331; res: 800/852-4682; FAX 615/639-5289. 36 rms, 2 story. S $31; D $36; each addl $3; under 16 free. Crib free. TV; cable. Restaurant 6–10 am; Sat 7–10:30 am. Ck-out 11 am. Meeting rms. Local airport transportation. Refrigerators. Cr cds: A, C, D, DS, MC, V.

★ ★ **HOLIDAY INN.** *US 11E Bypass.* 615/639-4185. 90 rms, 2 story. S $36–$56; D $46–$56; each addl $5; under 18 free. Crib free. TV;

cable. Pool. Restaurant 7 am–2 pm, 6–10 pm. Rm serv. Bar. Ck-out noon. Meeting rms. Cr cds: A, C, D, DS, MC, V, JCB.

★**PARKWAY.** *US 11E Bypass, 2 mi E. 615/639-2156.* 63 rms, 2 story. S $32–$35; D $35–$40; each addl $3. Crib $3. TV; cable. Complimentary coffee. Restaurant nearby. Ck-out 11 am. Cr cds: A, C, D, DS, MC, V.

Inn

★★**BIG SPRING.** *315 N Main St. 615/638-2917.* 5 rms, 4 with bath, 2 story. Phones avail. S $52–$70; D $60–$78; each addl $10; MAP avail. Adults preferred. TV in parlor. Pool. Complimentary full bkfst. Picnic lunch, dinner by request. Ck-out 11 am, ck-in 4 pm. Airport pick-up serv. Located in historic section of town. Antiques. Cr cds: A, MC, V.

Restaurant

★★**AUGUSTINO'S.** *2679 11E Bypass, 5 mi N on US 11E. 615/639-1231.* Hrs: 11 am–2 pm, 5–10 pm; Sat from 5 pm; Sun brunch to 2 pm. Closed major hols. Italian menu. Private club. A la carte entrees: lunch $3–$8.25, dinner $5.25–$24. Sun brunch $3–$8.25. Child's meals. Specializes in fettucine, prime rib. Pianist Fri, Sat. Parking. Cr cds: A, DS, MC, V.

SC

Harrogate (C-8)

Pop: 2,657 **Elev:** 1,300 ft **Area code:** 615 **Zip:** 37752

What to See and Do

1. **Abraham Lincoln Museum.** S on Cumberland Gap Pkwy, US 25E, on the Lincoln Memorial University campus. Collection, one of the largest of its type in the world, contains more than 25,000 pieces of Lincolniana and items related to Civil War. Research center. (Daily; closed major hols) Sr citizen rate. Phone 869-6235. ¢

2. **Cumberland Gap National Historical Park.** 4 mi N on US 25E. (See under KENTUCKY)

Motor Hotel

★★**HOLIDAY INN.** *(Box 37, Cumberland Gap 37724)* ½ mi E on US 25E. *615/869-3631; FAX 615/869-5953.* 147 rms, 4 story. S $44; D $44–$50; each addl $5; under 12 free. Crib free. Pet accepted, some restrictions. TV; cable. Pool; poolside serv. Playground. Restaurant 6 am–2 pm, 5–10 pm. Rm serv. Bar 5 pm–midnight exc Sun. Ck-out noon. Coin lndry. Meeting rms. Bellhops. Valet serv. Sundries. Free airport transportation. Balconies. Cr cds: A, D, DS, MC, V.

Hurricane Mills (D-4)

Pop: 40 (est) **Elev:** 400 ft **Area code:** 615 **Zip:** 37078

What to See and Do

1. **Loretta Lynn's Ranch.** On TN 13. Tours of country music star's house, museum, Butcher Holler Home and simulated coal mine;

Western and general stores. Swimming; fishing. Hiking; tennis. Camping. Special events including concerts, trail rides, campfires. (Apr–Oct) Fee for most activities. Phone 296-7700.

2. **Nolan House.** 8 mi N via TN 13 in Waverly. Restored, 12-room Victorian house (ca 1870); period furnishings; redoubt trail; dog-trot; family grave yard. Overnight stays avail. Tours (daily exc Sun). Phone 296-2511. ¢

(For further information contact the Humphreys County Chamber of Commerce, 124 E Main St, PO Box 733, Waverly 37185; 296-4865.)

(See Dickson)

Motels

✔★★**BEST WESTERN.** *On TN 13; I-40 exit 143. 615/296-4251; FAX 615/296-9104.* 89 rms, 2 story. June–Aug: S $39–$54; D $46–$61; each addl $4; under 12 free; lower rates rest of yr. Crib $2. Pet accepted, some restrictions. TV; cable. Pool; whirlpool. Playground. Restaurant 6 am–9 pm. Taproom (beer). Ck-out noon. Coin lndry. Meeting rm. Some refrigerators. Cr cds: A, C, D, DS, ER, MC, V.

★**DAYS INN.** *(Rte 1, Box 53A) On TN 13N off I-40 exit 143. 615/296-7647.* 78 rms, 2 story. S $38–$44; D $44–$56; each addl $4. Crib free. Pet accepted. TV; cable. Restaurant nearby. Ck-out 11 am. Cr cds: A, C, D, DS, MC, V.

D 🐾 🚫 🉐 SC

Jackson (E-3)

Founded: 1822 **Pop:** 48,949 **Elev:** 401 ft **Area code:** 901

Railroading is both the tradition and past livelihood of Jackson, home and burial place of John Luther "Casey" Jones, hero of ballad and legend. Because many of General Andrew Jackson's soldiers and many of his wife's relatives settled here, the town was named in his honor. Today, Jackson is an industrial center of western Tennessee.

What to See and Do

1. **Casey Jones Village.** 5 mi NW at US 45 Bypass & I-40. Complex of turn-of-the-century shops and buildings centered around the life of one of America's most famous railroad heroes. Gazebo in center of village on Casey Jones Lane houses the Tourism Association of Southwest Tennessee, offering brochures and visitor information (daily). **Free.** In the village are

   "Casey" Jones Home and Railroad Museum. The original house of the high-rolling engineer who, on April 30, 1900, climbed into the cab of "Old 382" on the Illinois Central Railroad and took his "farewell trip to that promised land"—and a place in American folklore. On display are personal effects of Jones and railroad memorabilia, including railroad passes, timetables, bells and steam whistles; also steam locomotive of the type driven by "Casey" Jones and restored 1890s coach cars. (Daily; closed Easter, Thanksgiving, Dec 25) Phone 668-1222. ¢¢

   Brooks Shaw & Son Old Country Store. Re-creation of a turn-of-the-century general store with more than 15,000 antiques on display; restaurant (see), ice-cream parlor, confectionery shop; museum. (Daily; closed Easter, Thanksgiving, Dec 25) Phone 668-1223. **Free.**

2. **Cypress Grove Nature Park.** Approx 4 mi W on US 70W. Boardwalk more than 1 mile long winds through 165-acre cypress forest; observation tower, nature center, picnic shelter. (Daily) Phone 424-1472. **Free.**

3. **Pinson Mounds State Archaeological Area.** 9 mi S on US 45, then 2½ mi E of Pinson on Ozier Rd. Remains of ancient mounds of the Middle Woodland Mound period and more than 10 ceremonial and

burial mounds of various sizes, including Sauls (72 ft high). Nature trail. Picnicking. Museum (Mar–Nov, daily; rest of yr, Mon–Fri); video programs. Phone 988-5614.   **Free.**

4. **Chickasaw State Rustic Park.** 16 mi SE on US 45, then 8 mi SW on TN 100. Park covering 11,215 acres features two lakes. Swimming; fishing; boating (rentals). Horseback riding. Picnicking, playground, recreation lodge. Tent & trailer sites, cabins. Standard fees. Phone 989-5141.

(For further information contact the Jackson/Madison County Convention & Visitors Bureau, 400 S Highland, 38301; 423-2341.)

Motels

★**BUDGETEL INN.** 2370 N Highland Ave (38305), at I-40 exit 82A. 901/664-1800; FAX 901/664-5456. 102 rms, 3 story. S $29.95–$36.95; D $36.95–$43.95; each addl $7; under 18 free. Crib free. TV; cable. Pool. Coffee in rms. Continental bkfst. Restaurant adj 11 am–10 pm. Ck-out noon. Meeting rms. Cr cds: A, C, D, DS, MC, V.

✓ ★★**DAYS INN.** 1919 US 45 Bypass (38305). 901/668-3444. 120 rms, 3 story. S $25.95–$30; D $34–$38; each addl $4; under 17 free. Crib free. Pet accepted, some restrictions. TV; cable. Pool. Continental bkfst. Ck-out noon. Cr cds: A, C, D, DS, MC, V.

✓ ★**FAIRFIELD INN BY MARRIOTT.** 535 Wiley Parker Rd (38305), I-40 exit 80A. 901/668-1400. 105 rms, 3 story. Mar–Oct: S $27.95–$32.95; D $33.95–$38.95; each addl $6; under 18 free; lower rates rest of yr. Crib free. TV; cable. Heated pool. Complimentary continental bkfst, coffee in lobby. Restaurant adj 10 am–11 pm. Ck-out noon. Meeting rms. Cr cds: A, D, DS, MC, V.

✓ ★★**HAMPTON INN.** 1890 US 45 Bypass (38305). 901/664-4312; FAX 901/664-7844. 123 rms, 2 story. S $37–$46; D $41–$51; under 18 free. Crib free. TV; cable. Pool. Complimentary continental bkfst. Restaurant adj 6 am–midnight. Meeting rm. Health club privileges. Cr cds: A, C, D, DS, MC, V.

★★**QUALITY INN.** 2262 N Highland Ave (38305), at jct US 45, I-40. 901/668-1066. 88 rms, 2 story. May–Aug: S $32; D $40; each addl $5; under 18 free; lower rates rest of yr. Crib $5. TV; cable. Pool. Restaurant adj open 24 hrs. Ck-out noon. Coin lndry. Cr cds: A, C, D, DS, ER, MC, V, JCB.

★★★**RAMADA INN.** 1849 US 45 Bypass (38305), ½ mi S of I-40, exit 80A. 901/668-4222; FAX 901/664-8536. 135 rms, 2 story. S $41–$53; D $47–$59; each addl $6; suites $79; under 18 free. Crib free. TV; cable. Pool; wading pool. Restaurant 6 am–10 pm. Rm serv. Bar 4 pm–1 am; entertainment exc Sun. Ck-out noon. Meeting rms. Whirlpool in some suites. Cr cds: A, C, D, DS, MC, V.

Motor Hotels

★★★**HOLIDAY INN.** 541 Carriage House Dr (38305), I-40 exit 80A. 901/668-6000. 136 air-cooled rms, 5 story, 54 suites. S $47–$57; D $52–$62; each addl $6; suites $57–$67; under 18 free; wkend rates; higher rates special events. Crib free. Pet accepted, some restrictions. TV; cable. Indoor pool. Restaurant 6 am–10 pm. Rm serv. Bar; entertainment Tues–Fri. Ck-out noon. Meeting rms. Bellhops. Sundries. Beauty shop. Valet serv. Health club privileges. Game rm. Refrigerators. Balconies overlooking atrium. Cr cds: A, C, D, DS, MC, V, JCB.

★★★**THE INN AT JACKSON.** US 45 Bypass & I-40 (38305). 901/668-4100; res: 800/362-6717; FAX 901/664-6940. 206 rms, 4 story.

S $39–$44; D $44–$49; suite $69; under 18 free; wkend rates. Crib free. Pet accepted, some restrictions; $5. TV; cable. Pool; wading pool. Restaurant 6 am–2 pm, 5–9 pm. Rm serv. Bar 4:30 pm–midnight. Ck-out noon. Coin lndry. Meeting rms. Valet serv. Sundries. Exercise equipt; weights, bicycles. Some patios, balconies. Cr cds: A, C, D, DS, MC, V, JCB.

★★★**SHERATON OLD ENGLISH INN.** 2267 N Highland Ave (38305), 3 mi N on US 45 at I-40 exit 82. 901/668-1571; FAX 901/664-8070. 103 rms, 2 story, 35 suites. S $57; D $63; each addl $6; suites $66–$82; under 18 free; wkend plans. Crib free. TV; cable. Pool; poolside serv. Complimentary coffee in rms. Restaurant 6 am–10 pm. Bar; entertainment Sat. Ck-out noon. Valet serv. Some refrigerators; bathrm phone in suites. Some fireplaces, patios. English Tudor decor; beamed ceilings, each rm different; antiques, paintings. Cr cds: A, C, D, DS, MC, V.

Restaurant

✓ ★**OLD COUNTRY STORE.** Jct US 45 Bypass, I-40, in Casey Jones Village. 901/668-1223 or -1224. Hrs: 6 am–10 pm. Closed Easter, Thanksgiving, Dec 25. Semi-a la carte: bkfst $1.49–$3.99, lunch, dinner $1.99–$9.99. Buffet: breakfast $3.99, lunch $4.99, dinner $5.99–$8.95. Specializes in Tennessee country ham, catfish, cobblers. Salad bar. Entertainment Fri, Sat. Parking. Turn-of-the-century decor. Family-owned. Cr cds: A, C, D, DS, MC, V.

Unrated Dining Spot

MORRISON'S CAFETERIA. Old Hickory Mall. 901/668-4275. Hrs: 11 am–8:30 pm; Sun to 7 pm. Avg ck: lunch $5, dinner $5.25. Child's meals. Specializes in roast beef, fried chicken, ice cream bars. Cr cds: MC, V.

Jamestown (D-6)

Pop: 1,862 **Elev:** 1,716 ft **Area code:** 615 **Zip:** 38556

Once a hunting ground for Davy Crockett and, later, Sergeant Alvin C. York, Jamestown was also the home of Cordell Hull, FDR's secretary of state.

What to See and Do

1. **Pickett State Rustic Park.** 2 mi N on US 127, then 11 mi NE on TN 154. Park covering 14,000 acres in Cumberland Mountains; unusual rock formations, caves, natural bridges. Sand beach. Swimming; fishing; boating (rentals). Nature trails, backpacking. Picnicking, concession, recreation lodge. Camping, cabins. Standard fees. Phone 879-5821.

2. **Historic Rugby.** 17 mi SE via TN 52. English colony founded in 1880s by author-statesman-social reformer Thomas Hughes. Highest priority was placed on beauty, culture, parks and recreational facilities. When it became difficult to make a living, the colony floundered. However, much has been preserved, and of the 17 original Victorian buildings remaining, 5 are open to the public. Hughes Public Library, unchanged since opening in 1882, contains unique 7,000-volume collection of Victorian era. Visitor center in Rugby Schoolhouse; guided walking tours (daily). (See ANNUAL EVENT) Also picnicking, hiking in surrounding river gorges on trails built by original colonists. Bookshop, traditional craft commissary, lodging in historic houses and cafe. Phone 628-2441.   ¢¢

3. **Big South Fork National River/Recreation Area.** 20 mi NE on TN 154, then TN 297. Approximately 105,000 acres on Cumberland Plateau. Swimming pool; fishing, hunting; whitewater canoeing, rafting, kayaking. Nature trails, hiking, backpacking, bridle trails. Primitive & improved camping (yr-round; fee). Visitor center. Phone 879-3625.

Annual Event

Rugby Pilgrimage. Tours of private historic houses in addition to buildings open regularly (see #2). Contact Historic Rugby, Inc, PO Box 8, Rugby 37733; 628-2441. 1st wkend Oct.

(For accommodations see Cookeville)

Jellico (C-7)

Pop: 2,447 **Elev:** 982 ft **Area code:** 615 **Zip:** 37762

What to See and Do

Indian Mountain State Park. Off I-75, exit 160, between city limits and KY state line. More than 200 acres. Swimming pool; fishing. Hiking trail. Picnicking, shelters; playgrounds. Camping. Standard fees. Phone 784-7958.

(See Caryville)

Motel

✔ ★**DAYS INN.** *(Box 299) ¼ mi S on US 25W at jct I-75 exit 160. 615/784-7281; FAX 615/784-4529.* 125 rms, 2–3 story. No elvtr. S $25–$35; D $28–$41; each addl $4; under 12 free. Crib free. TV; cable. Pool. Playground. Restaurant 6 am–9 pm. Ck-out 11 am. Sundries. Cr cds: A, C, D, DS, MC, V.

Johnson City (D-9)

Settled: 1782 **Pop:** 49,381 **Elev:** 1,692 ft **Area code:** 615

Johnson City is a leading burley tobacco sales center, as well as a market and shipping point for Washington County's cattle, eggs and alfalfa. Chemicals, textiles, building materials, electronics and furniture are also produced in the town.

What to See and Do

1. **Rocky Mount Historic Site & Overmountain Museum.** 4 mi NE on US 11E. Log house (ca 1770), territorial capitol under Governor William Blount from 1790 to 1792, is restored to original simplicity with much 18th-century furniture; log kitchen, slave cabin, barn, blacksmith shop, smokehouse. Costumed interpreters reenact a day in the life of typical pioneer family; tour (1½ hrs) includes Cobb-Massengill house, kitchen and slave cabin, as well as self-guided tour through the adjacent Museum of Overmountain History. (Mar–Dec, daily; rest of yr, Mon–Fri; closed Thanksgiving, Dec 21–Jan 5) Phone 538-7396. ¢¢

2. **Hands On! Regional Museum.** 315 E Main St. More than 20 "hands-on" exhibits designed for children of all ages. Traveling shows. (Daily exc Mon; closed Jan 1, Easter, Thanksgiving, Dec 25) Phone 434-4263. ¢¢

3. **Tipton-Haynes Historic Site.** 1 mi off I-181 exit 31, at S edge of town. Site of the 1788 "Battle of the Lost State of Franklin." Six original buildings and four reconstructions span American history from

pre-colonial days through Civil War. Visitor center with museum display; gift shop. (Apr–Oct, daily; rest of yr, Mon–Fri) Special programs, events. Phone 926-3631. ¢¢

4. **East Tennessee State University** (1911). (12,028 students) Lake and Stout Sts. Campus has 63 buildings on 366 acres; Slocumb Galleries; Memorial Center (sports); James H. Quillen College of Medicine (1974). Tours of campus. Phone 929-4112. Also on campus is

Carroll Reece Museum. Contemporary art and regional history exhibits; gallery tours; concert, film and lecture series. (Daily; closed major hols) Phone 929-4392. **Free.**

5. **Jonesborough.** 6 mi W off US 11 E. Oldest town in Tennessee and the first capitol of the state of Franklin.

Historic District. Four-by-six-block area through the heart of town, reflecting 200 years of history. Private residences, commercial and public buildings of federal, Greek-revival and Victorian styles; brick sidewalks, old-style lampposts, shops. Obtain walking tour brochures at Visitors Center, 117 Boone St; phone 753-5961.

Jonesborough History Museum. 117 Boone St, in Visitors Center. Exhibits highlight history of Jonesborough from pioneer days to early 20th century. (Daily; closed Thanksgiving, Dec 25) Sr citizen rate. Phone 753-9775. ¢

6. **Whitewater rafting. Cherokee Adventures.** 17 mi S on US 19/23, exit 18, then 1 mi N on TN 81. Variety of guided whitewater rafting trips through the Nolichucky Canyon and along the Watauga and Russell Fork rivers. Free camping for rafters. Mountain biking programs. (Mar–Oct) Contact Rte 1, Box 605, Erwin 37650; 743-7733 or 800/445-7238. ¢¢¢¢¢

7. **Cherokee National Forest** (see). E on US 321; S on US 23/19W.

(For further information contact the Convention & Visitors Bureau, 603 E Market St, PO Box 180, 37605; 461-8000.)

Annual Events

Jonesborough Days. 6 mi W, in Jonesborough. Includes parade, art show, crafts, old-time games, traditional music, square dancing and clogging, food. July 4th wkend.

Appalachian Fair. NW, just off I-181 in Gray at fairgrounds. Regional fair featuring livestock, agriculture and youth exhibits, antique display; entertainment. Phone 477-3211. Aug 23–28.

National Storytelling Festival. 6 mi W in Jonesborough. Three-day gathering from across nation features some of the country's best storytellers. Phone 753-2171. Oct 7–9.

Christmas in Jonesborough. 6 mi W. Tours of historic houses, tree decoration, workshops, old-time holiday events. Dec.

(See Elizabethton, Kingsport)

Motels

✔ ★ ★**DAYS INN.** *2312 Brown's Mill Rd (37601). 615/282-2211.* 150 rms, 2 story. S $32; D $36; each addl $4; under 12 free. TV; cable. Pool. Continental bkfst. Restaurant 6–10 am, 5–10 pm. Rm serv. Bar 3 pm–midnight. Ck-out noon. Coin lndry. Meeting rm. Cr cds: A, C, D, MC, V.

✔ ★ ★**FAIRFIELD INN BY MARRIOTT.** *207 E Mountcastle (37601). 615/282-3335; FAX 615/282-3335, ext 702.* 132 rms, 3 story. S $32.95; D $35.95; each addl $6–$9; under 18 free. TV; cable. Pool. Complimentary continental bkfst Mon–Fri 7–9 am, Sat & Sun 8 am. Complimentary coffee in lobby. Restaurant adj 11 am–10 pm. Ck-out noon. Meeting rms. Cr cds: A, C, D, DS, MC, V.

★**SUPER 8.** *108 Wesley St (37601). 615/282-8818.* 63 rms, 3 story. No elvtr. S $31.88–$34.88; D $35.88–$39.88; each addl $4; suites $50; under 12 free; higher rates special events. Crib free. TV;

cable. Complimentary coffee. Restaurant adj open 24 hrs. Ck-out 11 am. Meeting rms. Cr cds: A, C, D, DS, MC, V, JCB.

Motor Hotels

★ ★ ★**GARDEN PLAZA.** *211 Mockingbird Ln (37604). 615/929-2000; res: 800/342-7336; FAX 615/929-2000, ext 168.* 190 rms, 5 story. S $68–$74; D $74–$79; each addl $8; suites $110–$120; under 18 free. Crib free. Pet accepted. TV; cable. Indoor/outdoor pool; poolside serv. Restaurant 6:30 am–2 pm, 5–10 pm. Rm serv. Bar 4 pm–1 am. Ck-out noon. Meeting rms. Bellhops. Valet serv. Free airport transportation. Health club privileges. Wet bar in suites. Cr cds: A, C, D, DS, MC, V.

★ ★**HOLIDAY INN.** *2406 N Roan St (37601). 615/282-2161; FAX 615/282-2161, ext 526.* 197 rms, 2–4 story. S $50–$57; D $54–$61; each addl $4; under 18 free; higher rates special events. Crib free. TV; cable. Pool. Restaurant 7 am–2 pm, 5–10 pm. Rm serv. Bar 5 pm–1 am; entertainment, dancing exc Sun. Ck-out noon. Coin lndry. Free local airport transportation. Cr cds: A, C, D, DS, ER, MC, V, JCB.

Hotel

★ ★ ★**SHERATON PLAZA.** *101 W Springbrook Dr (37604). 615/282-4611; FAX 615/283-4869.* 205 rms, 6 story. S $70–$74; D $80–$84; each addl $10; suites $100–$275; under 18 free. Crib free. TV; cable. Pool; poolside serv. Restaurant 6 am–10 pm. Bar 4:30 pm–1:30 am; entertainment, dancing. Ck-out noon. Meeting rms. Gift shop. Barber, beauty shop. Airport transportation. Exercise equipt; weights, bicycles. Cr cds: A, C, D, DS, ER, MC, V.

Restaurants

✔ ★**FIREHOUSE.** *627 W Walnut. 615/929-7377.* Hrs: 10:30 am–10:30 pm; Sat from 7 am; Sun from 8 am. Closed Easter, Thanksgiving, Dec 24, 25. Serv bar. Semi-a la carte: bkfst $2–$5, lunch $3–$6, dinner $5–$15. Child's meals. Specializes in baby back ribs, barbecue beans. Own desserts. Parking. Converted fire hall (1930). Cr cds: A, MC, V.

★**MAKATO.** *3021 Oakland Ave. 615/282-4441.* Hrs: 11:30 am–2 pm, 5–9 pm; Fri, Sat to 10 pm. Japanese menu. Bar. Complete meals: lunch $3.25–$9.50, dinner $7.25–$25.50. Child's meals. Specializes in seafood, steak. Entertainment Fri, Sat. Parking. Tableside cooking. Cr cds: A, DS, MC, V.

D

★ ★ ★**PARSON'S TABLE.** *(102 Woodrow Ave, Jonesborough)* W on US 11, 321. 615/753-8002. Hrs: 11:30 am–2 pm, 5:30 pm–closing; Sun brunch to 2 pm. Closed Mon; Jan 1, Dec 24, 25. Res accepted. Continental menu. Semi-a la carte: lunch $4.95–$6.75, dinner $10–$20. Sun brunch $9.95. Child's meals. Own baking. Parking. In historic district in 1870s church with loft and parsonage. Victorian decor. Cr cds: A, MC, V.

D

★ ★**PEERLESS STEAK HOUSE.** *2531 N Roan St. 615/282-2351.* Hrs: 4–11 pm. Closed Sun; major hols. Bar. A la carte entrees: dinner $3.50–$21. Child's meals. Specializes in fresh seafood, steak. Parking. Family-owned. Cr cds: A, DS, MC, V.

D

Kingsport (C-8)

Settled: 1761 **Pop:** 36,365 **Elev:** 1,208 ft **Area code:** 615

Located at a natural gateway to the Southwest, this area saw the passage of the Great Indian Warrior & Trader Path and Island Road (1761), the first road built in Tennessee. The trail later became the Great Stage Road and was used for 150 years, marking the beginning of Daniel Boone's Wilderness Road. Kingsport was a little town on the Holston River, but it was converted to a planned industrial city during World War I. The first council-manager form of government in the state was installed in the town. The Tennessee Eastman Company, the largest employer in the state, is located in Kingsport.

What to See and Do

1. **Boat Yard Park.** On banks of the north and south forks of the Holston River. Historical complex includes museum (fee), picnic areas, playgrounds, boating, fishing; footpaths along river (2 mi). Fees for some activities. Phone 246-2010.   **Free.**

   Netherland Inn (1818). Large frame and stone structure on site of King's Boat Yard (1802) was a celebrated stop on the Great Stage Road and was operated for over 150 years as an inn and the town's entertainment center; it was especially popular from 1818 to 1841 and was visited by many prominent individuals, including Andrew Jackson and Andrew Johnson. Now a museum with 18th- and 19th-century furnishings. Complex also includes wellhouse, flatboat, garden, log cabin (1773), children's museum, museum shop. Interpreters. (May–Sept, Sat–Mon; Apr & Oct by appt) Phone 247-3211. ¢¢

2. **Exchange Place.** 4812 Orebank Rd. Restored 19th-century farm once served as a facility for exchanging horses and Virginia currency for Tennessee currency; crafts center; special events (fee). (May–Oct, wkends or by appt) Phone 288-6071.   **Free.**

3. **Fort Patrick Henry Dam and Lake.** 4 mi S on TN 36. Companion to Boone Dam (see #5), this TVA dam, 95 feet high, 737 feet long, impounds a 10-mile-long lake. Swimming; fishing; boating. Overlook. (Daily) Phone 542-2951.   **Free.**   Along lakeshore is

   Warriors' Path State Park. 4 mi S on TN 36; I-81 exit 59. A 950-acre park with swimming pool, water slide, bathhouse; fishing; boating (marina, ramp, rentals). Nature, bridle trails; 18-hole golf, driving range, miniature golf, disc golf. Picnic grove, playground, concessions. Tent, trailer camping. Standard fees. Phone 239-8531.

4. **Bays Mountain Park.** 6 mi SE off TN 93. Plant and animal sanctuary covers 3,000 acres, 25 miles of trails; nature interpretive center, aviary, deer pen; otter, bobcat & wolf habitats; nature programs (summer, daily; rest of yr, wkends); ocean pool; planetarium (shows daily in summer). Exhibition gallery and library. Observation tower. 19th-century farmstead museum. Barge rides on 44-acre lake. Picnic tables. Park (daily). Fee for activities. Phone 229-9447. Parking ¢

5. **Boone Dam and Lake.** 12 mi SE via TN 36, TN 75. TVA dam, 160-feet-high and 1,640-feet-long, impounds a 33-mile-long lake with 130 miles of shoreline. Swimming; fishing; boating (marina). Picnicking. Overlook (daily). Phone 542-2951.   **Free.**

(For further information contact the Convention & Visitors Bureau, 151 E Main St, PO Box 1403, 37662; 392-8820 or 800/743-5282.)

Annual Event

Kingsport Fun Fest. Citywide. More than 100 events including hot-air balloon races, sports events, entertainment. Phone 392-8800. Nine days, late July–early Aug.

(See Johnson City)

Motels

★★**COMFORT INN.** *100 Indian Center Court (37660), at TN 93 & US 11W. 615/378-4418; FAX 615/246-5249.* 122 rms, 2 story. S $48; D $55; each addl $8; suites $65–$77; under 18 free. Crib free. TV; cable. Pool; whirlpool, sauna. Complimentary continental bkfst. Restaurant adj 6:30 am–10 pm. Ck-out noon. Coin lndry. Meeting rms. Bellhops. Valet serv. Some in-rm whirlpools. Cr cds: A, C, D, DS, ER, MC, V, JCB.

✔ ★**ECONO LODGE.** *1704 E Stone Dr (37660). 615/245-0286.* 48 rms, 2 story. S $35; D $39–$42; each addl $4; under 12 free. TV; cable. Complimentary coffee in lobby. Restaurant adj open 24 hrs. Ck-out 11 am. Cr cds: A, C, D, DS, ER, MC, V, JCB.

★★**HOLIDAY INN.** *700 Lynn Garden Dr (37660). 615/247-3133; FAX 615/247-3133, ext 114.* 158 rms, 2–3 story. No elvtr. S $44–$52; D $48–$56; each addl $4; under 18 free. Crib free. TV; cable. Pool. Restaurant 6:30 am–2 pm, 5–10 pm; Sat–Mon from 7 am. Rm serv. Bar 5 pm–midnight; closed Sun. Ck-out noon. Meeting rms. Valet serv. Cr cds: A, C, D, DS, ER, MC, V, JCB.

★★**RAMADA INN.** *2005 La Masa Dr (37660). 615/245-0271; FAX 615/245-7992.* 195 rms, 2 story. S $58–$70; D $64–$75; each addl $6; under 18 free. Crib free. TV; cable. Pool; wading pool. Restaurant 6 am–2 pm, 5–10 pm; Sat, Sun from 7 am. Rm serv 7 am–10 pm. Bar 4 pm–midnight. Ck-out 2 pm. Meeting rms. Sundries. Free airport transportation. Lighted tennis. Health club privileges. Cr cds: A, C, D, DS, MC, V.

Restaurant

★★**SKOBY'S.** *1001 Konnarock Rd. 615/245-2761.* Hrs: 5–10 pm; Fri, Sat 4:30–11 pm. Closed major hols. Res accepted Mon–Sat. Bar. A la carte entrees: dinner $7–$24. Child's meals. Specializes in steak, seafood. Salad bar. Own desserts. Parking. Dining areas with varied themes. Family-owned. Cr cds: A, C, D, DS, MC, V.

Knoxville (D-7)

Settled: 1786 **Pop:** 165,121 **Elev:** 936 ft **Area code:** 615

First capital of Tennessee, Knoxville today is the manufacturing center for the east Tennessee Valley. In its early days, Knoxville was a frontier outpost on the edge of the Cherokee nation, last stop on the way west. Headquarters of the Tennessee Valley Authority, marketplace for tobacco and livestock, Knoxville is also a diversified industrial city, a product of power plant rather than plantation, and also of the atomic age rather than the Old South (Oak Ridge is only 22 miles away). It is a gracious city, with the University of Tennessee as a cultural center and dogwood-lined streets in its residential sections.

Founded by a Revolutionary War veteran from North Carolina, Knoxville, named after Secretary of War Henry Knox, quickly became a provisioning place for westward-bound wagons. It was known for its whiskey and wild times. East Tennessee had many Union sympathizers, and during the Civil War Knoxville was seized by the Confederates and became headquarters for an army of occupation. In 1863, Southern troops withdrew to Chattanooga, and a Union army moved in, only to be besieged by the Confederates. While the battle for Knoxville saw large sections of the city destroyed, the Confederate attack was rebuffed, and Knoxville remained in Union hands for the rest of the war.

The postwar years brought many former Union soldiers, skilled Northern workmen and investment capital to Knoxville. Within two decades its population more than tripled. During and since World War II it has enjoyed a similar period of industrial growth and commercial well-being. In recent years it has been a leader in downtown redevelopment. The University of Tennessee, Knoxville (1794) is located here.

What to See and Do

1. **Sunsphere.** 810 Clinch Ave. Built for the 1982 World's Fair, this 266-ft tower has an observation deck (fee) that provides views of downtown and Smoky Mts. The Convention & Visitors Bureau Information Center is located here. Phone 523-2316.

2. **General James White's Fort.** 205 E Hill Ave. Original pioneer house (1786) built by founder and first settler of Knoxville; restored buildings include smokehouse, blacksmith shop, museum. (Mar–mid-Dec, daily exc Sun; closed major hols) Phone 525-6514. ¢¢

3. **Governor William Blount Mansion** (1792). 200 W Hill Ave. House of William Blount, Governor of the Southwest Territory and signer of the US Constitution, was the center of political and social activity in the territory. Restored to period of late 1700s with period furnishings, Blount memorabilia; 18th-century garden. Tennessee's first state constitution was drafted in the governor's office behind the mansion. (Mar–Oct, daily exc Mon; rest of yr, Tues–Fri; closed Jan 1, Thanksgiving, Christmas wk) Phone 525-2375. ¢¢

    Craighead-Jackson House (1818). Serves as the visitors center for Blount Mansion. Audiovisual presentation, special exhibits. **Free.**

4. **Ramsey House (Swan Pond)** (1797). 6 mi NE on Thorngrove Pike. First stone house in Knox County, built for Colonel Francis A. Ramsey, was social, religious, political center of early Tennessee. Restored gabled house with attached kitchen features ornamental cornices, keystone arches and period furnishings. (Apr–Oct, Tues–Sat & Sun afternoons; rest of yr, by appt) Phone 546-0745. ¢¢

5. **Crescent Bend (Armstrong-Lockett House) and W. Perry Toms Memorial Gardens** (1834). 2728 Kingston Pike. Collections of American and English furniture; English silver (1670–1820); extensive terraced gardens. (Mar–Dec, daily exc Mon) Phone 693-3163. ¢¢

6. **Confederate Memorial Hall.** 3148 Kingston Pike SW. Antebellum mansion with Mediterranean-style gardens served as headquarters of Confederate General James Longstreet during siege of Knoxville. Maintained as a Confederate memorial, the 15-room house is furnished with museum pieces, a collection of Southern and Civil War relics; library of Southern literature. (Tues–Fri) Sr citizens rate. Phone 522-2371. ¢

7. **Marble Springs.** Approx 6 mi S via US 441, TN 33, then W on TN 168. Restored farmhouse of John Sevier, state's first governor (1796–1801, 1803–1809); original cabin and other restored buildings on 36 acres. (Daily) Phone 573-5508 or 577-2834. ¢

8. **Knoxville Museum of Art.** 410 10th St. Four galleries, gardens, great hall, exploratory gallery; collection of graphics. Changing exhibits. Cafe; gift shop. (Daily exc Mon; closed most hols) Sr citizen rate. Phone 525-6101. ¢¢

9. **McClung Historical Collection.** East Tennessee Historical Center, 314 W Clinch Ave. More than 38,000 volumes of history and genealogy covering Tennessee and Southeastern US. (Daily exc Sat; closed most hols) Phone 544-5744. **Free.**

10. **Beck Cultural Exchange Center–Museum of Black History and Culture.** 1927 Dandridge Ave. Research, preservation and display of the achievements of Knoxville's black citizens from the early 1800s. Gallery features changing exhibits of local and regional artists. (Tues–Sat; closed major hols) Phone 524-8461. **Free.**

11. **East Tennessee Discovery Center.** Chilhowee Park. Exhibits on life, energy, transportation, minerals, fossils; includes aquarium and planetarium. (Tues–Fri, also Sat afternoons; closed most hols) Phone 637-1121. ¢¢

12. **Knoxville Zoo.** E via I-40, Rutledge Pike exit. More than 1,000 animals, including big cats, gorillas, reptiles, elephants and marine animals; petting zoo. (Daily; closed Dec 25) Phone 637-5331. ¢¢¢

13. University of Tennessee, Knoxville (1794). (27,018 students) W Cumberland Ave, US 11, 70. On campus are Frank H. McClung Museum (daily exc Sat; phone 974-2144); Clarence Brown Theater on Andy Holt Ave; special collections, 1401 Cumberland Ave (Mon–Fri; phone 974-4480); R. Tait McKenzie Sports Art Collection Gallery, HYPER Building (Mon–Fri; phone 974-0967).

(For further information contact the Knoxville Convention & Visitors Bureau, 810 Clinch Ave, PO Box 15012, 37901; 523-2316.)

Annual Events

Dogwood Arts Festival. More than 150 events and activities throughout the community including arts & crafts exhibits and shows; over 80 public and private gardens on display; musical entertainment; parades; sporting events; more than 60 miles of marked dogwood trails for auto or free bus tours; special children's & sr citizen activities; hot-air balloons. Phone 637-4561. Mid–late Apr.

Tennessee Valley Fair. Chilhowee Park. Entertainment; livestock and agricultural shows; contests, exhibits, fireworks, carnival rides. Phone 637-5840. Early–mid-Sept.

Artfest. Citywide celebration with children's activities; entertainment; changing exhibits, art shows; "Riverfeast," barbecue cooking contest; professional & community theatricals; art auction. Begins with "Saturday Night on the Town," a night of festivities including food, music & dancing. Phone 523-7543. Late Aug–early Oct.

Motels

(Rates may be higher during football wkends)

✔ ★**BUDGETEL INN.** *11341 Campbell Lake Dr (37922), I-40/75 exit 373. 615/671-1010; FAX 615/675-5039.* 100 rms, 3 story. Mar–Oct: S $42.95–$49.95; D $49.95–$59.95; each addl $7; under 18 free; lower rates rest of yr. Crib free. Pet accepted, some restrictions. TV; cable. Pool. Complimentary continental bkfst. Complimentary coffee in rms. Restaurant adj 6 am–10 pm. Ck-out noon. Coin lndry. Meeting rms. Exercise equipt; weight machine, bicycles, sauna. Some refrigerators. Cr cds: A, C, D, DS, MC, V.

★★**CLUBHOUSE INN.** *208 Market Place Ln (37922). 615/531-1900; FAX 615/531-8807.* 120 rms, 2 story, 17 kit. suites. S $66; D $76; each addl $10; kit. suites $80; under 10 free; wkly rates. Crib free. TV; cable. Pool; whirlpool. Complimentary full bkfst 6:30–9 am (wkdays), coffee. Restaurant adj 11:30 am–midnight. Ck-out noon. Coin lndry. Meeting rms. Valet serv. Health club privileges. Refrigerator, wet bar in suites. Balconies. Grills. Cr cds: A, C, D, DS, MC, V.

✔ ★★**COMFORT INN.** *5334 Central Ave Pike (37912). 615/688-1010.* 101 rms, 2 story. S $38–$46; D $44–$56; each addl $5; under 18 free. Crib $5. Pet accepted, some restrictions. TV; cable. Pool. Complimentary continental bkfst. Complimentary coffee in rms. Restaurant nearby. Ck-out noon. Cr cds: A, C, D, DS, ER, MC, V, JCB.

★★**HAMPTON INN.** *119 Cedar Ln (37912), at I-75 & Merchants Rd. 615/689-1011; FAX 615/689-1011, ext 409.* 129 rms, 3 story. May–Sept: S $47.50–$53.50; D $52.50–$60.50; each addl $5; under 18 free; higher rates university football wkends; lower rates rest of yr. Crib free. Pet accepted, some restrictions. TV; cable. Pool. Complimentary continental bkfst, coffee. Restaurant opp 6:30 am–10 pm. Ck-out 11 am. Exercise equipt; bicycles, treadmill. Cr cds: A, C, D, DS, MC, V.

★★**LA QUINTA MOTOR INN.** *258 Peters Rd N (37923). 615/690-9777; FAX 615/531-8304.* 130 rms, 3 story. S $49–$56; D $57–$64; each addl $6; under 18 free. Crib free. Pet accepted, some restrictions.

TV; cable. Heated pool. Restaurant open 24 hrs. Ck-out noon. Meeting rms. Health club privileges. Cr cds: A, C, D, DS, MC, V.

★★**RAMADA INN.** *323 Cedar Bluff Rd (37923). 615/693-7330.* 178 rms, 2 story. S, D $43–$48; each addl $10; suites $49–$59; under 18 free; higher rates special events. Pet accepted, some restrictions. TV; cable. Indoor pool. Restaurant 6 am–2 pm, 5–10 pm. Rm serv. Bar 4:30 pm–2:30 am. Ck-out noon. Meeting rms. Cr cds: A, C, D, DS, MC, V, JCB.

★★**RED ROOF INN.** *5640 Merchants Center Blvd (37912), at I-75 exit 108. 615/689-7100; FAX 615/689-7974.* 85 rms, 2 story. S $34–$52; D $36–$54; each addl $2. Crib free. Pet accepted, some restrictions. TV. Complimentary coffee. Ck-out noon. Cr cds: A, C, D, DS, MC, V.

★★**SUPER 8.** *6200 Paper Mill Rd (37919). 615/584-8511.* 139 rms, 2–3 story. No elvtr. S $42–$52; D $48–$55; each addl $5; under 18 free. Crib free. TV; cable. Pool; wading pool, whirlpool. Complimentary continental bkfst. Ck-out noon. Meeting rm. Cr cds: A, C, D, DS, MC, V.

Motor Hotels

✔ ★**CAMPUS INN.** *1706 W Cumberland (37916), on Univ of TN campus. 615/521-5000; res: 800/448-4144.* 119 rms, 7 story. S $41–$55; D $46–$60; each addl $6; suites $85–$125; under 12 free. Crib free. Pet accepted. TV; cable. Continental bkfst 6–10 am. Bar 5 pm–2 am. Ck-out noon. Meeting rms. Cr cds: A, C, D, DS, MC, V.

★★**DAYS INN.** *5634 Merchants Center Blvd (37912). 615/687-8989; FAX 615/687-3351, ext 11.* 123 rms, 5 story. S $47–$67; D $52–$72; each addl $5. Crib free. TV; cable. Pool. Complimentary continental bkfst. Ck-out noon. Meeting rms. Health club privileges. Cr cds: A, C, D, DS, MC, V.

★★**LUXBURY.** *420 N Peters Rd (37922). 615/539-0058; res: 800/252-7748; FAX 615/539-4887.* 98 rms, 3 story, 23 suites. S, D $55; each addl $6; suites $72–$100; under 18 free; wkend rates; higher rates football season. Crib free. TV. Pool. Complimentary continental bkfst, coffee. Restaurant nearby. Ck-out 11 am. Meeting rms. Valet serv. Health club privileges. Bathrm phone, refrigerator, wet bar in suites. Cr cds: A, C, D, DS, MC, V.

★★**QUALITY INN WEST.** *7621 Kingston Pike (37919). 615/693-8111; FAX 615/690-1031.* 162 rms, 4 story. S $46.50–$55.50; D $58.50–$67.50; each addl $10; suites $100–$180; studio rms $65–$90; under 18 free. Crib free. Pet accepted, some restrictions; $5. TV; cable. Pool. Restaurant 6 am–2 pm, 5–10 pm. Rm serv. Bar 4 pm–2 am; entertainment, dancing. Ck-out noon. Meeting rms. Bellhops. Health club privileges. Cr cds: A, C, D, DS, ER, MC, V, JCB.

★★**SIGNATURE INN-CEDAR BLUFF.** *209 Market Place Ln (37922). 615/531-7444; FAX 615/531-7444, ext 500.* 122 rms, 3 story. S $56; D $59; under 17 free; wkend rates. Crib free. TV; cable. Pool. Complimentary continental bkfst, coffee. Restaurant adj 11 am–10 pm. Ck-out noon. Meeting rms. Valet serv. Health club privileges. Cr cds: A, D, DS, MC, V.

Hotels

★★**HILTON.** *501 Church Ave SW (37902). 615/523-2300; FAX 615/525-6532.* 317 rms, 18 story. S $79–$101; D $89–$111; each addl $12; suites $195–$350; studio rms $115–$155; wkend rates. Crib free. TV; cable. Pool. Restaurant 6:30 am–10 pm. Rm serv. Bar 3 pm–midnight. Ck-out noon. Convention facilities. Gift shop. Valet parking. Free airport transportation. Exercise equipt; weights, bicycles, sauna. Some refrigerators. Cr cds: A, C, D, DS, ER, MC, V, JCB.

⊡ ⛱ ♿ 🚭 ⊚ SC

★ ★ ★HOLIDAY INN WORLD'S FAIR. *525 Henley St (37902). 615/522-2800; FAX 615/523-0738.* 293 rms, 11 story. S, D $72–$102; each addl $10; suites $145–$399; under 18 free; wkend rates; higher rates special events. TV; cable, in-rm movies avail. Indoor pool. Restaurant 6:30 am–1:30 pm, 5:30–10 pm. Bar 4 pm–midnight. Ck-out noon. Coin lndry. Convention facilities. Exercise equipt; weights, bicycles, whirlpool, sauna. Refrigerator in suites. *LUXURY LEVEL:* **THE CONCI-ERGE/EXECUTIVE LEVEL.** 60 rms, 7 suites. S, D $93–$112; suites $144–$399. Concierge. Bathrm phones. Complimentary continental bkfst, refreshments.
Cr cds: A, C, D, DS, MC, V, JCB.

⊡ ⛱ ♿ 🚭 ⊚ SC

★ ★HYATT REGENCY. *500 Hill Ave SE (37915). 615/637-1234; FAX 615/522-5911.* 387 rms, 11 story. S $110; D $125; each addl $15; suites $130–$325; under 18 free; wkend rates. Crib free. Pet accepted, some restrictions; $25. TV; cable. Pool; poolside serv. Playground. Restaurants 6:30 am–midnight. Bars 4 pm–2 am; entertainment, dancing Tues–Sat. Ck-out noon. Convention facilities. Barber, beauty shop. Gift shop. Airport transportation. Exercise equipt; weights, bicycles, sauna. Wet bar in suites. Many balconies. Contemporary decor; 8-story lobby with atrium. Located on hill above the Tennessee River. Cr cds: A, C, D, DS, ER, MC, V, JCB.

⊡ 🏊 ⛱ ✈ ♿ 🚭 ⊚ SC

★ ★ ★RADISSON. *401 Summit Hill Dr (37902). 615/522-2600; FAX 615/522-2600, ext 336.* 198 rms, 12 story. S $75–$85; D $85–$95; each addl $10; suites $150–$250; under 18 free; higher rates special events. Crib free. TV; cable. Indoor pool. Restaurant 6 am–10 pm. Bars 4 pm–midnight. Ck-out noon. Meeting rms. Gift shop. Free airport transportation. Exercise equipt; weights, bicycles, whirlpool. Some refrigerators, wet bars. Cr cds: A, C, D, DS, ER, MC, V, JCB.

⊡ ⛱ ♿ 🚭 ⊚ SC

Inn

★ ★MIDDLETON. *800 W Hill Ave (37902). 615/524-8100.* 13 rms, 3 story. S $65–$150; D $75–$150; each addl $10; under 6 free. Crib free. TV; cable. Complimentary continental bkfst. Ck-out noon, ck-in 3 pm. Concierge. Some refrigerators, in-rm whirlpools. Balcony. Old World atmosphere; antiques, original artwork. Cr cds: A, C, D, DS, MC, V.

🚭 ⊚ SC

Restaurants

✔ ★ARTHUR'S. *4661 Old Broadway. 615/689-4309.* Hrs: 11 am–9:30 pm; Fri & Sat to 10:30 pm. Closed most major hols. Res accepted exc Mother's Day. Bar. Semi-a la carte: lunch, dinner $5–$12.95. Child's meals. Specializes in prime rib, seafood. Salad bar. Parking. Family-owned. Cr cds: A, C, D, MC, V.

✔ ★ ★ASIA. *156 N Seven Oaks Dr, in Windsor Square Shopping Center. 615/693-7408.* Hrs: 11 am–10 pm. Closed Thanksgiving. Res accepted. Chinese menu. Bar. Semi-a la carte: lunch $3.50–$6, dinner $4.95–$14.95. Specializes in beef, chicken, mandarin and Cantonese dishes. High steel-beam ceiling with Chinese kites. Cr cds: A, DS, MC, V.

D

★BUTCHER SHOP. *801 W Jackson Ave. 615/637-0204.* Hrs: 5–10 pm; Fri, Sat to 11 pm; Sun 4–10 pm. Closed major hols. Res accepted. Bar. Semi-a la carte: dinner $13–$23. Child's meals. Special-

izes in steak, seafood, chicken. Parking. Option to select steak and cook it; large, open charcoal grill. In World's Fair Park. Cr cds: A, D, MC, V.

D

✔ ★CALHOUNS. *10020 Kingston Pike. 615/673-3444.* Hrs: 11 am–10 pm; Sat 3–11 pm; Sun to 9:30 pm. Closed Thanksgiving, Dec 25. Res accepted. Bar. Semi-a la carte: lunch $6–$8, dinner $6.95–$16.50. Child's meals. Specializes in baby back ribs, prime rib, hickory-smoked pork. Parking. Rustic decor; antiques, farm implements. Cr cds: A, C, D, DS, MC, V.

D

★ ★CHESAPEAKE'S. *500 N Henley St. 615/673-3433.* Hrs: 11:15 am–2:30 pm, 4:30–10 pm; Fri to 11 pm; Sat 4:30–11 pm. Closed Sun; Jan 1, Thanksgiving, Dec 25. Res accepted. Bar. Semi-a la carte: lunch $5.95–$6.95, dinner $10.95–$24.95. Child's meals. Specializes in fresh seafood, Maine lobster. Parking. Raw oyster bar. Cr cds: A, C, D, DS, MC, V.

D

✔ ★ ★CHINA INN. *6450 Kingston Pike. 615/588-7815.* Hrs: 11 am–3 pm, 5–10 pm; Fri, Sat to 10:30 pm; Sun 11 am–10 pm. Closed Thanksgiving, Dec 24, 25. Chinese menu. Semi-a la carte: lunch $3.50–$8, dinner $5.50–$15. Parking. Cr cds: A, MC, V.

★ ★THE CHOP HOUSE. *9700 Kingston Pike. 615/531-2467.* Hrs: 11 am–10 pm; Fri & Sat to 11 pm. Closed Thanksgiving, Dec 25. Bar. Semi-a la carte: lunch $4.95–$9.95, dinner $5.95–$16.95. Child's meals. Specializes in pork chops, steak. Parking. Outdoor dining. Cr cds: A, MC, V.

D

★ ★COPPER CELLAR. *1807 Cumberland Ave. 615/673-3411.* Hrs: 11 am–10:30 pm; Fri, Sat to 11:30 pm; Sun to 10 pm; Sun brunch to 2 pm. Closed Thanksgiving, Dec 25. Bar. A la carte entrees: lunch $4–$10, dinner $9–$23.95. Child's meals. Specializes in fresh seafood, prime rib. Parking. Cr cds: A, C, D, DS, MC, V.

D

★ ★COPPER CELLAR-CAPPUCCINO'S. *7316 Kingston Pike. 615/673-3422.* Hrs: 11 am–10 pm; Fri to 11 pm; Sat 5–11 pm; Sun 11 am–2 pm, 5–10 pm. Closed some major hols. Res accepted. Italian, Amer menu. Bar. Semi-a la carte: lunch $4.95–$9.95, dinner $8.95–$24.95. Sun brunch $9.95–$11.95. Specializes in prime beef, fresh seafood. Parking. Cr cds: A, C, D, DS, MC, V.

★L & N SEAFOOD GRILL. *401 Henley St. 615/971-4850.* Hrs: 11:30 am–9 pm; Fri to 11 pm, Sat 4–11 pm; Sun 11 am–9 pm. Closed Dec 25. Res accepted. Bar. Semi-a la carte: lunch $4.95–$9.95, dinner $7.95–$18.95. Sun brunch $9.95. Child's meals. Specializes in fresh fish, seafood, steak. Parking. Outdoor dining. In turn-of-the-century building. Cr cds: A, C, D, DS, MC, V.

D

✔ ★LITTON'S. *2803 Essary Rd. 615/688-0429.* Hrs: 11 am–9 pm; Fri, Sat to 10 pm. Closed Sun; most major hols. Semi-a la carte: lunch $4–$6.50, dinner $5–$12.50. Child's meals. Specializes in fresh seafood, steaks, desserts. Parking. Family-owned. No cr cds accepted.

D

✔ ★ ★MANDARIN HOUSE. *8111 Gleason Dr. 615/694-0350.* Hrs: 11 am–2:30 pm, 5–9:30 pm; Sat & Sun to 4 pm. Closed Thanksgiving. Res accepted. Chinese menu. Bar. Semi-a la carte: lunch $3.50–$5, dinner $5–$10. Specializes in buffet. Parking. Cr cds: A, C, D, DS, MC, V.

D

★ ★MICHAEL'S. *7049 Kingston Pike. 615/588-2455.* Hrs: 5 pm–2 am. Res accepted; required football wknds. Greek, Amer menu. Bar 4 pm–3 am. Semi-a la carte: dinner $8.95–$24.95. Child's meals. Specializes in Grecian lamb, beef, seafood. Valet parking. Atrium; brass, oak, beveled glass. Cr cds: A, C, D, DS, MC, V.

D

★★**NAPLES.** *5500 Kingston Pike. 615/584-5033.* Hrs: 11 am–2 pm, 5–10 pm; Fri to 11 pm; Sat 5–11 pm. Closed July 4, Thanksgiving, Dec 24, 25. Res accepted. Italian menu. Bar. Semi-a la carte: lunch $3.95–$8.95. A la carte entrees: dinner $5.95–$15.95. Child's meals. Specializes in pasta, veal, seafood. Parking. Cr cds: A, C, D, DS, MC, V.

 D **SC**

★★★★**THE ORANGERY.** *5412 Kingston Pike. 615/588-2964.* Hrs: 11:30 am–2:30 pm, 6–10 pm; Fri to 11 pm; Sat 6–11 pm. Closed Sun; most major hols. Res accepted. Continental menu. Bar. 2 wine cellars. Semi-a la carte: lunch $4.95–$12, dinner $12.95–$25.95. Specialties: filet "toison d'or," noix panéed saumon, côtelettes d'agneau. Own baking, desserts. Pianist. Valet parking. Formal elegance; Old World charm. European antiques, crystal chandeliers, atrium; wine cellar dining area. Family-owned. Cr cds: A, C, D, MC, V.

D

★★**PERO'S.** *4931 Kingston Pike. 615/584-4215.* Hrs: 11 am–10:30 pm; Fri, Sat to midnight. Closed Mon; major hols. Res accepted Tues–Thurs. Italian, Amer menu. Bar. Semi-a la carte: lunch $3–$5, dinner $4–$24.50. Child's meals. Specializes in lasagne, chicken, steak. Parking. Family-owned. Cr cds: A, C, D, MC, V.

D

★★★**REGAS.** *318 N Gay St, at Magnolia Ave. 615/637-9805.* Hrs: 11 am–2:30 pm, 5–10 pm; Sat 5–10 pm; Sun 11 am–2:30 pm; early-bird dinner Mon–Sat 5–6:30 pm. Closed major hols. Res accepted. Continental menu. Bar. Wine list. Semi-a la carte: lunch $5–$15.25, dinner $8.25–$25. Child's meals. Specializes in clam chowder, prime rib, fresh seafood. Own baking. Pianist. Parking. Dining rms individually decorated; fireplaces, original artwork. Family-owned. Cr cds: A, C, D, DS, MC, V.

D

★★★**TUSCANY.** *5200 Kingston Pike. 615/584-6755.* Hrs: 5–10 pm. Closed Sun; some major hols. Res accepted. Northern Italian, continental menu. Bar. Semi-a la carte: dinner $10.95–$19.95. Specializes in black squid pasta, veal. Strolling troubador. Parking. Intimate dining, trattoria-like atmosphere. Cr cds: A, C, D, MC, V.

D

Unrated Dining Spots

APPLE CAKE TEA ROOM. *Campbell Station Rd, exit 373. 615/966-7848.* Hrs: 11 am–2:30 pm. Closed Sun; major hols. A la carte entrees: lunch $2.25–$6. Child's meals. Specializes in salads, sandwiches, soups, desserts. Parking. Country antique decor. Fireplace, artwork. Cr cds: A, MC, V.

BAGELRY. *5003 Kingston Pike. 615/584-2847.* Hrs: 7:30 am–5 pm; Sat from 8 am; Sun 8:30 am–3 pm. Closed some major hols. Beer. Semi-a la carte: bkfst $1–$5, lunch $2–$5. Specializes in salads, smoked salmon, desserts. Parking. Cr cds: A, MC, V.

 D

MORRISON'S CAFETERIA. *West Town Mall, 10 mi W on US 11, 70, 1 blk SW of I-40, I-75 West Hills exit. 615/693-0383.* Hrs: 11 am–8:30 pm; Sun to 8 pm. Avg ck: lunch $4, dinner $4.40. Child's meals. Specializes in roast beef, fried shrimp, macaroni & cheese. Victorian decor. Cr cds: MC, V.

 D

RAMSEY'S CAFETERIA. *16th & White Ave. 615/522-2520.* Hrs: 10:30 am–8 pm; Sun to 2:30 pm. Closed Jan 1, Labor Day, Dec 24, 25; also wk of July 4. Avg ck: lunch, dinner $3.65. Child's meals. Specializes in roast beef, country steak. Own baking. Parking. No cr cds accepted.

S & S CAFETERIA. *4808 Kingston Pike. 615/584-5191.* Hrs: 11 am–2:15 pm, 4–8 pm; Fri–Sun 11 am–8 pm. Closed Dec 25. Avg ck: lunch, dinner $4.40. Child's meals. Specializes in salads, roast beef, chicken. Parking. No cr cds accepted.

Lawrenceburg (E-4)

Founded: 1815 **Pop:** 10,412 **Elev:** 890 ft **Area code:** 615 **Zip:** 38464

What to See and Do

David Crockett State Park. W on US 64. This 1,000-acre area is located on the banks of Shoal Creek, where Crockett once operated a gristmill. Swimming pool, wading pool, bathhouse; fishing; boating (rentals). Nature, bicycle trails; lighted tennis. Picnicking, playground, concessions; park restaurant doubles as a dinner theater in summer (reservations required). Tent, trailer sites. Visitors center housed in waterpowered gristmill (mid-July–mid-Aug, wkends); amphitheater. Standard fees. Phone 762-9408.

Lebanon (D-5)

Pop: 15,208 **Elev:** 531 ft **Area code:** 615 **Zip:** 37087

Tall red cedars thrive in this area as they did in the Biblical lands of Lebanon. Thus, the founding fathers named the city Lebanon. The dense cedar forest has been used for many industrial purposes including wood, paper and pencils. Since 1842, Lebanon has been the home of Cumberland University.

What to See and Do

1. **Old Hickory Lake.** 6 mi NW. Waterskiing; fishing; boating.
2. **Cedars of Lebanon State Park.** 7 mi S on US 231, TN 10. Approx 831 acres within 9,000-acre state forest. Limestone cavern and sinks were reforested in 1930s, with juniper. Swimming and wading pools. Hiking; game courts. Picnicking, playground, concession, recreation lodge. Tent & trailer sites, cabins. Nature center. Standard fees. Phone 443-2769.

(For further information contact the Lebanon/Wilson County Chamber of Commerce, 149 Public Square; 444-5503.)

(See Murfreesboro, Nashville)

Motels

★**BEST WESTERN EXECUTIVE INN.** *631 S Cumberland St, I-40 exit 238. 615/444-0505; FAX 615/449-8516.* 125 rms, 2 story, 44 suites. June–July: S $37–$47; D $44–$57; each addl $5; suites $47–$75; under 12 free; lower rates rest of yr. Crib free. TV; cable. 2 pools. 1 indoor; whirlpool, sauna. Complimentary continental bkfst, coffee. Restaurant adj 6 am–10:30 pm. Ck-out 11 am. Meeting rms. Picnic tables. Cr cds: A, C, D, DS, MC, V, JCB.

D 🏊 🚫 🏌 **SC**

✔★**DAYS INN.** *914 Murfreesboro Rd. 615/444-5635; FAX 615/449-7969.* 100 rms, 2 story. May–Oct: S $32–$40; D $42–$48; each addl $3; under 18 free; higher rates special events; lower rates rest of yr. Crib free. Pet accepted. TV; cable. Pool. Complimentary continental bkfst, coffee. Restaurant adj open 24 hrs. Ck-out noon. Coin lndry. Valet serv. Airport transportation. Some refrigerators. Cr cds: A, C, D, DS, ER, MC, V, JCB.

🐾 🏊 🚫 🏌 **SC**

★★**HAMPTON INN.** *704 S Cumberland, I-40 exit 238. 615/444-7400; FAX 615/449-7969.* 87 rms, 2 story. S $38–$52; D $44–$58; under 18 free; higher rates Fan Fair. Crib free. Pet accepted. TV; cable. Pool. Complimentary continental bkfst. Restaurant nearby. Ck-out 11 am. Lndry facilities avail. Meeting rms. Exercise equipt; weight machine, bicycle, whirlpool, sauna. Cr cds: A, C, D, DS, MC, V.

✓ ★SHONEY'S INN. *822 S Cumberland St. 615/449-5781; res: 800/222-2222; FAX 615/449-8201.* 111 rms, 3 story. Mid-June–mid-Aug: S, D $39–$57; each addl $5; under 18 free; lower rates rest of yr. Crib free. TV; cable. Indoor pool. Complimentary full bkfst, coffee. Restaurant adj 6 am–midnight. Ck-out noon. Meeting rms. Valet serv. Refrigerators. Cr cds: A, C, D, DS, MC, V.

Lenoir City (D-7)

Founded: 1890 **Pop:** 6,147 **Elev:** 798 ft **Area code:** 615 **Zip:** 37771

What to See and Do

1. **Fort Loudoun Dam and Lake.** On US 11 at S end of city. This TVA dam, 4,190 feet long and 122 feet high, with a lock chamber to permit navigation of the river, transforms a 61-mile stretch of once unruly river into a placid lake extending to Knoxville. Fishing, boating on 14,600-acre lake. Visitor lobby (daily). Phone 986-3737. **Free.**
2. **Tellico Dam and Lake.** Approx 3 mi S off US 321. TVA dam on Little Tennessee River impounds 15,680-acre lake. Upper end of reservoir adjoins the Cherokee National Forest (see). Excellent fishing and boating with the Great Smoky Mountains as backdrop. Summer pool; boat access sites. Picnicking. Camping. Phone 986-3737.

(For further information contact the Loudon County Chamber of Commerce, PO Box 909, Loudon 37774; 458-2067.)

(See Knoxville, Sweetwater)

Motels

★CROSS ROADS INN. *1110 US 321N, at I-75 exit 81. 615/986-2011; res: 800/526-4658; FAX 615/986-7947.* 90 rms, 2 story. S $26–$30; D $31–$40; each addl $3; under 12 free. TV; cable. Pool; wading pool. Restaurant 6 am–8:30 pm. Ck-out 11 am. Meeting rms. Some refrigerators. Cr cds: A, C, D, MC, V.

✓ ★KING'S INN. *1031 US 321N, 2 blks S of I-75 exit 81. 615/986-9091.* 50 rms, 2 story. S $23–$32; D $24–$34; each addl $5; under 12, $3. Crib $4. TV. Pool. Restaurant opp 6 am–10 pm. Ck-out noon. Refrigerators. Cr cds: A, DS, MC, V.

Lewisburg (E-5)

Settled: 1837 **Pop:** 9,879 **Elev:** 734 ft **Area code:** 615 **Zip:** 37091

Named for Meriwether Lewis, of the Lewis and Clark expedition, Lewisburg is largely linked to the dairy industry and is a trading and shipping center for the surrounding farms. Milk-processing plants are supplemented by factories producing air conditioners, furniture and pencils.

What to See and Do

1. **Tennessee Walking Horse Breeders & Exhibitors Association.** 250 N Ellington Pkwy. All registrations, transfers and decisions concerning the walking horse breed are made at this world headquar-

ters. Open to visitors, building contains a gallery of world champions. (Mon–Fri) Phone 359-1574. **Free.**
2. **Dairy Experiment Station.** 3 mi S on US 31A. Operated cooperatively by the US Dept of Agriculture and the University of Tennessee on 615 acres. (Daily) Phone 359-1578. **Free.**
3. **Henry Horton State Resort Park.** 11 mi NE of I-65, on US 31A. Park covering 1,135 acres located on the estate of a former Tennessee governor is bordered by the scenic Duck River, a popular canoeing and fishing river. Facilities include swimming and wading pools. Clubhouse, golf course, lighted tennis; skeet & trap range. Picnicking, restaurant. Tent & trailer sites, cabins, resort inn. Standard fees. Phone 364-2222.

(For further information contact the Marshall County Chamber of Commerce, 227 2nd Ave N; 359-3863.)

(For accommodations see Shelbyville)

Manchester (E-5)

Pop: 7,709 **Elev:** 1,063 ft **Area code:** 615 **Zip:** 37355

What to See and Do

1. **Old Stone Fort State Archaeological Park.** 1½ mi W off I-24. Park covering 600 acres surrounds earthen remains of a more than 2,000 year old walled structure built along the bluffs of the Duck River. Fishing. Picnicking, playground. Camping. Museum. Standard fees. Phone 723-5073.
2. **Normandy Lake.** 8 mi W; 2 mi upstream from Normandy. Completed in 1976, the dam is 2,734 feet high and impounds a 3,160-acre lake. Controlled releases provide a scenic floatway (28 mi) below the dam with public access points along the way. Summer pool; excellent spring and fall fishing. Picnicking. Camping.
3. **Distillery tours.**

    Geo. A. Dickel Distillery. Approx 11 mi SW on TN 55 to Tullahoma, then N on US 41A, follow signs. Distillery built in 1870 and re-created in 1959 produces and matures Tennessee sour mash "whisky." Country store. 30–45-minute guided tours (Mon–Fri; closed major hols, Dec 24; also Friday before some hols) Phone 857-3124. **Free.**

    Jack Daniel Distillery. 25 mi SW on TN 55, in Lynchburg. Nation's oldest registered distillery. One-hour guided tours include rustic grounds, limestone spring cave, old office. (Daily; closed Jan 1, Thanksgiving, Dec 25) Phone 759-4221. **Free.**

(For further information contact the Chamber of Commerce, 110 E Main St; 728-7635.)

Annual Event

Old Timer's Day. City Square. Bluegrass competition; entertainment, games, contests. Early Oct.

(See Monteagle)

Motels

✓ ★★AMBASSADOR INN. *(Rte 6, Box 6022) Interstate Dr, at I-24 exit 110. 615/728-2200; res: 800/237-9228; FAX 615/728-8376.* 105 rms, 1–2 story. S, D $35.90–$39.90; each addl $4; suites $56–$100; under 12 free. Crib $1. Pet accepted, some restrictions. TV; cable. Pool. Complimentary continental bkfst. Restaurant adj 6 am–10 pm. Ck-out 11 am. Exercise equipt; weight machine, bicycles. Refrigerators. Cr cds: A, C, D, DS, MC, V.

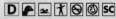

★ ★ **BEST WESTERN OLD FORT INN.** *(Rte 8, Box 8143)* 1 mi S on US 41 at I-24 exit 114. 615/728-9720. 50 rms, 2 story. S $24–$36; D $26–$38; each addl $4; under 12 free; higher rates walking horse show, ball game. Crib $4. Pet accepted, some restrictions. TV; cable. Pool. Complimentary continental bkfst, coffee. Ck-out noon. Cr cds: A, C, D, DS, ER, MC, V.

★ ★ **HOLIDAY INN I-24.** *Hillsboro Hwy, at jct US 41 & I-24 exit 114.* 615/728-9651; FAX 615/728-2208. 141 rms, 2 story. S, D $43–$49; each addl $5; suites $56–$62; under 18 free. Crib free. Pet accepted. TV; cable. Pool. Restaurant 6 am–2 pm, 5–10 pm. Rm serv. Beer, setups 5 pm–midnight. Ck-out noon. Coin lndry. Meeting rms. Some refrigerators. Cr cds: A, C, D, DS, MC, V, JCB.

Restaurant

✔ ★ **OAK FAMILY.** *Interstate Dr, I-24 exit 110.* 615/728-5777. Hrs: 6 am–10 pm; Sun buffet 11 am–3 pm. Closed Dec 25. Res accepted Mon–Sat. Semi-a la carte: bkfst $1.80–$7.99, lunch $3.95–$6.99, dinner $3.89–$12.95. Sun buffet $5.49. Child's meals. Specializes in prime rib, lasagne. Salad bar. Parking. Cr cds: A, D, DS, MC, V.

Maryville (D-7)

Founded: 1795 **Pop:** 19,208 **Elev:** 989 ft **Area code:** 615 **Zip:** 37801

Maryville and its twin city, Alcoa, provide a scenic gateway to the Great Smoky Mountains National Park (see). The seat of Blount County, Maryville was once the home of Sam Houston, the only man in US history to serve as governor of two states; in 1807 he moved to this area from Virginia with his widowed mother and eight brothers.

What to See and Do

1. **Sam Houston Schoolhouse** (1794). 5 mi NE, off US 411 (follow signs), on Old Sam Houston School Rd. Restored log building in which Sam Houston taught in 1812 at tuition rate of $8/term. Museum of Houston memorabilia in nearby visitor center. Picnicking. (Daily; closed Jan 1, Thanksgiving, Dec 25) Phone 983-1550. ¢

2. **Maryville College** (1819). (850 students) E side of town, main entrance on Lamar Alexander Pkwy (US 321). Liberal arts college. Twenty buildings represent architectural trends from 1869–1922. Innovative energy project uses wood chips and sawdust to heat campus. Fine Arts Center has plays, concerts, exhibits. Tours of campus. Phone 981-8000.

(For further information contact the Blount County Chamber of Commerce, 309 S Washington St; 983-2241.)

(See Knoxville, Townsend)

Motel

★ **PRINCESS MOTEL.** *(2614 US 411S)* 2 mi S on US 129, 411. 615/982-2490. 33 rms, 1–2 story. May–Oct: S $40–$50; D $50–$60; each addl $4; kit. units $200–$350/wk; under 12 free; higher rates special events; lower rates rest of yr. Crib $4. TV; cable. Pool. Restaurant adj open 24 hrs. Ck-out 11 am. Cr cds: A, C, D, DS, MC, V.

Inn

★ ★ ★ **INN AT BLACKBERRY FARM.** *(1471 W Millers Cove Rd, Walland 37886)* 10 mi N on TN 321, first right after Foothills Pkwy. 615/984-8166; FAX 615/983-5708. 25 rms, 2 story. No rm phones. AP, Oct–Nov: S $250–$290; D $350–$470; each addl $100; higher rates some hols; lower rates rest of yr (2-day min wkends). Children over 10 yrs only. TV in sitting rms; cable. Heated pool. Complimentary full bkfst, coffee. Dining rm 6 am–9 pm. Rm serv. Ck-out noon, ck-in 3 pm. Valet serv. Concierge. Tennis. Putting green. Game rm. Picnic tables. Antiques. English country house (1930) on 11,000 acres. Cr cds: A, MC, V.

Restaurant

★ ★ **MORNINGSIDE INN.** *1406 Wilkinson Pike.* 615/982-1735. Hrs: 11 am–2 pm, 5–9 pm; Sun–Tues to 2 pm; Sat from 5 pm. Closed Jan 1, Memorial Day, Dec 25. Res accepted. Setups. Semi-a la carte: lunch $1.25–$8.95, dinner $3.95–$17.95. Child's meals. Specializes in aged beef, veal. Pianist, guitarist Fri–Sun. Parking. Cr cds: A, D, DS, MC, V.

McMinnville (D-6)

Pop: 11,194 **Elev:** 976 ft **Area code:** 615 **Zip:** 37110

What to See and Do

1. **Cumberland Caverns Park.** 7 mi SE, just off US 70S. Mined for saltpeter as long ago as the Civil War but not yet fully explored, the Cumberland Caverns offer a variety of underground formations and sights: old saltpeter mines; "Hall of the Mountain King" (600 ft across, 140 ft high); underground dining room; "God of the Mountain," a dramatization of the Creation with spectacular lighting (shown on every tour). Constant 56°F. Picnic area above ground. Tours (1½ hr). (May–Oct, daily) Phone 668-4396. ¢¢¢

2. **Rock Island State Rustic Park.** 14 mi NE via US 70S. Approx 850 acres, located on Center Hill Reservoir. Swimming; fishing; boating (ramp). Picnicking. Camping. Standard fees. Phone 686-2471.

3. **Fall Creek Falls State Resort Park.** 30 mi E via TN 30 to TN 284E. More than 16,000-acre park offers mountain scenery, 256-foot Fall Creek Falls and great fishing. Swimming pool; boating (rentals). Nature trails; backpacking; riding; 18-hole golf, sports facilities. Picnicking, concessions, restaurant, inn. Tent & trailer sites, cabins. Standard fees. Phone 881-3241.

(For further information contact the McMinnville-Warren County Chamber of Commerce, 110 S Court Square, PO Box 574; 473-6611.)

Memphis (E-2)

Settled: 1819 **Pop:** 610,337 **Elev:** 264 ft **Area code:** 901

Memphis, on the Mississippi, is an old town with a new face. It is both "old South" and modern metropolis. The city has towering office buildings, flashy expressways, a $60 million civic center—and ancient Beale Street, where W.C. Handy helped give birth to the blues.

General James Winchester is credited with naming the city for the Egyptian city Memphis, which means "place of good abode." The Nile-like Mississippi, of course, was the inspiration. Winchester, Andrew Jackson and John Overton laid out the town on a land grant from North Carolina, selecting this site because of the high bluffs above the river and the natural harbor at the mouth of the Wolf River. The land deal was somewhat questionable, and General Jackson left under a barrage of criticism. River traffic quickly developed; stores, shops and sawmills

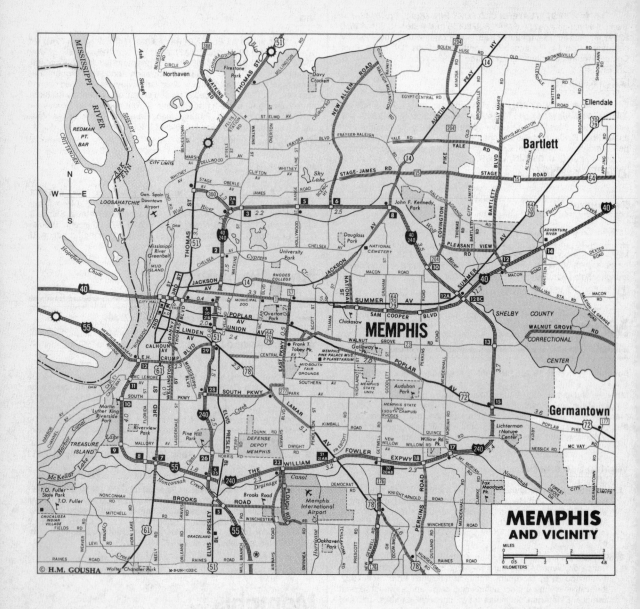

MEMPHIS
AND VICINITY

appeared, and Memphis became one of the busiest and most boisterous ports in America.

For a short time, Memphis was the Confederate capital of the state, also serving as a military supply depot and stronghold for the Southern forces. In 1862, however, Northern troops seized the city after a river battle dominated by an armada of 30 Union ships and held it throughout the war. Plagued by yellow fever epidemics, an impoverished Memphis made a slow postwar recovery. By 1892, however, the city was back on its feet, becoming the busiest inland cotton market and hardwood lumber center in the world.

Memphis dominates the flat, crop-rich, alluvial Mississippi Delta. It serves as hub of 6 railroads, port for millions of tons of river cargo annually and home of over 1,100 manufacturing plants in the Memphis

area. In national competition it has been acclaimed as the Cleanest City, the Safest City and the Quietest City.

As much as one-third of the country's cotton crop is bought or sold in Memphis, known as the cotton center of the world, but the agricultural segment of the city's economy is highly diversified—corn, alfalfa, vegetables, soybeans, rice, livestock and even fish farming. Memphis has the largest medical center in the South and more than a dozen institutions of higher learning, including Memphis State University and Rhodes College. A city with a civic ballet, a symphony orchestra, an opera company, a repertory theater, art galleries and College of Art, Memphis is also a major convention city and distribution center.

Throughout the world, Memphis has become associated with the legendary Elvis Presley. Graceland, Presley's house, and Meditation

Gardens, site of his grave, have become a destination for thousands of visitors annually. Each August, memorial celebrations are held citywide in honor of the ''king of rock and roll.''

Transportation

Memphis Intl Airport: Information 922-8000; lost and found 922-8050; weather 756-4141; Crown Room (Delta); WorldClub (Northwest).

Car Rental Agencies: See toll-free numbers under Introduction.

Public Transportation: Memphis Area Transit Authority, phone 274-6282.

Rail Passenger Service: Amtrak 800/872-7245.

What to See and Do

1. **Pyramid Arena .** Downtown Pinch Historic District, on the Wolf River at Auction St Bridge. This 32-story, 22,000-seat stainless steel and concrete pyramid, overlooking the Mississippi River, is fashioned after the ancient Egyptian Great Pyramid of Cheops and houses a music, sports and entertainment complex. Tours (daily). Phone 526-5177. ¢¢

2. **Mud Island.** Monorail to island at Front St exit off I-40. Fifty-acre island in the Mississippi is a unique park designed to showcase the character of the river. The River Walk is a five-block-long scale model of the Mississippi from Cairo, IL, to the Gulf of Mexico; the River Museum features 18 galleries that chronicle the development of river music, art, lore and history; also here are films, playground, river boat excursions, shops, restaurants, picnicking. For fee information contact the Convention & Visitors Bureau, 543-5333. Also on island is

   Memphis Belle. 280 Mud Island Rd. This B-17 bomber and her crew were the first to complete 25 missions over Nazi targets and return to the US during World War II. Named for the pilot's wartime sweetheart, the *Memphis Belle* was featured in a documentary by director William Wyler; film shown twice daily. Plane displayed under glass dome. ¢

3. **Downtown Mall Trolley.** Electric trolley loop runs up Main St and back in the Pinch Historic District providing transportation to hotels, Beale St and attractions such as Pyramid Arena and the National Civil Rights Museum. (Daily) For fees and schedule phone 274-6282.

4. **Memphis Brooks Museum of Art.** In Overton Park, off Poplar Ave. Paintings, drawings, sculpture, photographs, prints and decorative arts from Renaissance to present. Permanent and changing exhibits. Guided tours, lectures, films, performing arts series. (Daily exc Mon; closed Jan 1, Thanksgiving, Dec 25) Phone 722-3500. ¢¢

5. **Memphis Pink Palace Museum and Planetarium.** 3050 Central Ave. Exhibits focus on natural and cultural history of the mid-South. Many facets of the region, including insects, birds, mammals, geology, pioneer life, medical history, commerce and the Civil War, can be explored; also changing exhibits. (Daily; closed Jan 1, Thanksgiving, Dec 24 & 25) Planetarium has shows weekends and in summer (fee). Phone 320-6320. ¢¢

6. **National Civil Rights Museum.** 450 Mulberry St, at the Lorraine Motel, site of the 1968 assassination of Dr. Martin Luther King, Jr. The nation's first civil rights museum honors the American civil rights movement and the people behind it, from colonial to present times. Exhibits, sound and light displays, audiovisuals and visitor participation programs; auditorium and courtyard. (Daily exc Tues; closed major hols) Phone 521-9699. ¢¢¢

7. **The Children's Museum of Memphis.** 2525 Central Ave. Hands-on museum has created a ''kid-sized city'' including a bank, grocery store and skyscraper, among others. Special workshops. (Daily exc Mon; closed some major hols) Phone 458-2678. ¢¢

8. **National Ornamental Metal Museum.** 374 W California, on the river bluff. Architectural and decorative metalwork. (Daily exc Mon; closed major hols) Phone 774-6380. ¢

9. **Memphis Zoo & Aquarium.** Bounded by N Parkway, E Parkway & Poplar Ave. More than 2,000 animals; aquarium and petting zoo; children's amusement rides (fee). (Daily; closed Thanksgiving, Dec 24, 25) Phone 726-4787. ¢¢

10. **Memphis Botanic Garden.** 750 Cherry Rd in Audubon Park. Goldsmith Civic Garden Center; Japanese and sensory gardens; roses, irises, wildflowers; azalea and dogwood trail; conservatory; cactus, sculpture, conifer and herb gardens; W.C. Paul Arboretum; monthly art exhibits. (Daily; closed Jan 1, Thanksgiving, Dec 25) Phone 685-1566. ¢

11. **Dixon Gallery and Gardens.** 4339 Park Ave. Museum surrounded by 17 acres of formal and woodland gardens with a camellia house and garden statuary; exhibition galleries display American and Impressionist art, British portraits and landscapes, English antique furnishings, 18th-century German porcelain. (Daily exc Mon; closed some major hols) Sr citizen rate. Phone 761-5250. ¢¢

12. **Lichterman Nature Center.** 5992 Quince Rd at Lynnfield. Wildlife sanctuary (65 acres) includes 12-acre lake, greenhouse, hospital for wild animals, interpretive center with ecology room, discovery room and beehive that allows observation of honey production. Hiking trails (3 mi). Picnicking. (Daily exc Mon; closed Jan 1, Thanksgiving, Dec 24, 25) Sr citizen rate. Phone 767-7322. ¢¢

13. **Crystal Shrine Grotto.** 5668 Poplar Ave, in Memorial Park Cemetery. Crystal cave made of natural rock, quartz, crystal and semi-precious stones carved out of a hillside by naturalistic artist Dionicio Rodriguez in the late 1930s. Also scenes by the artist depicting life of Jesus and Biblical characters. (Daily) Phone 767-8930. **Free.**

14. **Victorian Village.** Within 1 mi of downtown area, 600 block of Adams Ave. Eighteen landmark buildings, either preserved or restored, range in style from Gothic revival to neo-classical. The three houses open to the public are

    Magevney House (1836). 198 Adams Ave. Restored house of pioneer schoolmaster Eugene Magevney. Oldest middle-class dwelling in the city, furnished with artifacts of the period. (Tues–Sat; closed Jan 1, Thanksgiving, Dec 24, 25) Donation. Phone 526-4464.

    Woodruff-Fontaine House (1870). 680 Adams Ave. Restored and furnished Second Empire/Victorian mansion with antique textile/costume collection. Gift shop. (Daily; closed July 4, Thanksgiving, Dec 24–25) Sr citizen rate. Phone 526-1469. ¢¢

    Mallory-Neely House (1852). 652 Adams Ave. Preserved Italianate mansion (25 rms) with original furnishings. (Daily exc Mon; closed Jan 1, Thanksgiving, Dec 24, 25) Phone 523-1484. ¢¢

15. **Beale St.** Downtown, off Riverside Dr. Part of a seven-block entertainment district, stretching east from the Mississippi River bluffs, with restaurants, shops, parks and theaters. Statue of W.C. Handy in Handy Park. Also on Beale St is

    W.C. Handy's Home. 325 Beale St. House where W.C. Handy wrote ''Memphis Blues,'' ''St Louis Blues'' and other classic tunes. Collection of Handy memorabilia. (Mon–Fri) Phone 527-2583. ¢

16. **Graceland.** 3764 Elvis Presley Blvd. Elvis Presley house. Mansion tour includes main floor and lower level of house, trophy room, grounds, gravesite. Other attractions include Automobile Museum, Presley's jet airplanes. (Daily; mansion tour, Nov–Feb, daily exc Tues; closed Jan 1, Thanksgiving, Dec 25; res recommended) Contact PO Box 16508, 38186-0508; phone 332-3322 or 800/238-2000. ¢¢–¢¢¢¢

17. **Sun Studio.** 706 Union Ave. Legendary recording studio where Elvis Presley, Jerry Lee Lewis, Roy Orbison, Carl Perkins and Johnny Cash made their first recordings. Tour (30 min). (Daily; closed Jan 1, Thanksgiving, Dec 25) Phone 521-0664 or 800/441-6249. ¢¢

18. **Rhodes College** (1848). (1,400 students) 2000 N Parkway at University St. On campus is the 140-foot-high Richard Halliburton Memorial Tower, with first editions of Halliburton's books; memorabilia. Clough-Hanson Gallery has changing art exhibits (Mon–Fri; closed hols). Tours of campus. Phone 726-3000.

19. **Playhouse on the Square.** 51 S Cooper, in Overton Sq. Professional theater. Phone 725-0776 or ticket office, 726-4656. ¢¢¢¢

20. Circuit Playhouse. 1705 Poplar Ave. Comedies, musicals and dramas. Phone 726-4656.

21. Libertyland. E Parkway at Mid-South Fairgrounds. Educational/historical amusement park; carnival rides, live shows, costumed characters, games; shops; food. (Mid-June–late Aug, Wed–Sun; May–mid-June & late Aug–Labor Day, wkends only) Sr citizen rate. Phone 274-1776. Admission/8-ride ticket ¢¢¢–¢¢¢¢

22. Adventure River Water Park. 6880 Whitten Bend Cove, off I-40E exit 14. Wave-action pool, water slides, free-fall slides, children's pool and play area; arcade, sand volleyball courts, lockers, bathhouse. Picnic area, concessions, gift shop. (Memorial Day–Labor Day, daily; also wkends May) Phone 382-9283. ¢¢¢¢

23. Memphis International Motorsports Park. N on I-240, 5500 Taylor Forge Dr. Multi-use park features four tracks hosting a variety of racing events: drag, circle track, tractor pulls, motorcycle, go-cart and 4-wheeler. (Mar–Nov; daily) For schedule phone 358-7223 or 353-6118. ¢¢¢¢

24. T.O. Fuller State Park. 10 mi S on US 61, then 4 mi W on Mitchell Rd. A 384-acre park where De Soto is believed to have crossed the Mississippi. Swimming pool; bathhouse. Golf. Picnicking, concessions. Campsites (hookups). Standard fees. Phone 543-7581. In the park is

Chucalissa Archaeological Museum. 1987 Indian Village Dr. Archaeological project of Memphis State University at site of Native American village founded about A.D. 900 and abandoned circa 1500. Native houses and temple have been reconstructed; archaeological exhibits. Museum displays artifacts and dioramas; 15-minute slide program. (Daily; closed most hols; no admittance to village area after 4:30 pm) Phone 785-3160. ¢¢

25. Meeman-Shelby Forest State Park. 13 mi N via US 51, near Millington. A 12,500-acre park with 2 lakes bordering the Mississippi River. Swimming pool; fishing; boating. Hiking and bridle trails. Camping, cabins. Nature center. Standard fees. Phone 876-5215.

26. River cruises.

Delta Queen & Mississippi Queen paddle wheelers offer 3- to 12-night cruises on the Mississippi, Ohio, Cumberland and Tennessee rivers. For details contact Delta Queen Steamboat Co, 30 Robin St Wharf, New Orleans, LA 70130-1890; 800/543-1949.

Memphis Queen. Foot of Monroe at Riverside Dr. Sightseeing, dinner cruises aboard Mississippi riverboat. (Sightseeing, Mar–Dec, daily; dinner cruises, May–Sept, Wed–Sun) Phone 527-5694. ¢¢¢–¢¢¢¢

27. Sightseeing tour.

Gray Line bus tours. Contact 2050 Elvis Presley Blvd, 38106; 948-TOUR.

Annual Events

Memphis in May International Festival. Month-long community-wide celebration focuses on cultural and artistic heritage of Memphis while featuring a different nation each year. Major events occur weekends, but activities are held daily. Includes The Beale St Music Festival, World Championship Barbecue Cooking Contest and Sunset Symphony. Phone 525-4611. May.

Beale Street Music Festival. Beale St (see #15). International roster of musicians returns to Memphis for a musical family reunion. Part of the Memphis in May festivities. May.

Carnival Memphis. Features parade, fashion show, salute to industry. Phone 278-0243. 10 days early June.

Elvis Week. More than 30 events take place throughout the city in honor of Presley and his music. Phone 332-3322. Aug 8–16.

Memphis Music Festival. Beale St (see #15). Memphis musicians perform blues, jazz, rhythm and blues, country and rock; at clubs and restaurants throughout the historic district. Phone 526-0110. Sept.

Mid-South Fair and Exposition. Mid-South Fairgrounds, E Parkway S & Southern Ave. Agricultural, commercial, industrial exhibits; midway rides and concerts. Largest rodeo east of the Mississippi. Phone 274-8800. Late Sept–early Oct.

National Blues Music Awards. Celebrates the year's most notable contributors to blues music. Phone 527-2583. Oct.

Seasonal Events

Outdoor concerts. Raoul Wallenberg Overton Park Shell, said to be the true birthplace of rock 'n' roll; Elvis Presley gave one of his first live performances here. Concerts feature local blues, rock and jazz musicians; also theater, movies and dance presentations. For schedule phone 274-6046. Late Mar–early Nov.

Theatre Memphis. 630 Perkins Extended. Internationally acclaimed community theater. Phone 682-8323. Mainstage offers 6-play season Sept–June; Little Theatre features 4-play season July–May.

Additional Visitor Information

For further information contact the Convention & Visitors Bureau, 47 Union Ave, 38103; phone 543-5300. Tourists may also inquire at the visitor information center located at 340 Beale St, phone 543-5333; or the Tennessee Welcome Station, 3910 I-55, phone 345-5956.

City Neighborhoods

Many of the restaurants, unrated dining establishments and some lodgings listed under Memphis include neighborhoods as well as exact street addresses. Geographic descriptions of these areas are given, followed by a table of restaurants arranged by neighborhood.

Beale Street Area: Downtown area along seven blocks of Beale St from Riverside Dr on the west to Danny Thomas Blvd on the east.

Downtown: South of I-40, west of Danny Thomas Blvd (US 51), north of Calhoun Ave and east of the Mississippi River. **East of Downtown:** East of US 51.

Overton Square: South of Poplar Ave, west of Cooper St, north of Union Ave and east of McLean Blvd.

MEMPHIS RESTAURANTS
BY NEIGHBORHOOD AREAS

(For full description, see alphabetical listings under Restaurants)

BEALE STREET AREA

Alfred's. 197 Beale St

Beale Street BBQ. 205 Beale St

Joyce Cobb's Dinner Club. 209 Beale St

DOWNTOWN

Butcher Shop. 101 S Front St

Captain Bilbo's. 263 Wagner Place

Dux (Peabody Hotel). 149 Union Ave

Justines. 919 Coward Place

King Cotton Cafe. 50 N Front St

Pier. 100 Wagner Place

Rendezvous. 52 S 2nd St

EAST OF DOWNTOWN

Benihana of Tokyo. 912 Ridge Lake Blvd

Cooker Bar & Grille. 6120 Poplar Ave

Grisanti's. 1489 Airways Blvd

Hemmings. 25 Belvedere Blvd

OVERTON SQUARE

Bourbon Street Cafe. (French Quarter Suites Hotel). 2144 Madison Ave

Melos Taverna. 2021 Madison Ave

Paulette's. 2110 Madison Ave

The Public Eye. 17 S Cooper

Note: When a listing is located in a town that does not have its own city heading, it will appear under the city nearest to its location. In these cases, the address and town appear in parenthesis immediately following the name of the establishment.

Motels

✔ ★**COMFORT INN.** *2889 Austin Peay Hwy (38128), north of downtown.* 901/386-0033; FAX 901/386-0036. 69 rms, 13 kit. suites. S $49; D $54; each addl $5; kit. suites $65; under 18 free. TV; cable. Indoor pool; whirlpool. Complimentary continental bkfst. Restaurant nearby. Ck-out noon. Meeting rms. Cr cds: A, C, D, DS, ER, MC, V, JCB.

D ⚊ 🚫 ◎ SC

★★**COURTYARD BY MARRIOTT.** *6015 Park Ave (38119), east of downtown.* 901/761-0330; FAX 901/682-8422. 146 units, 3 story. S, D $76; each addl $10; suites $86–$90; under 17 free; wkly rates. Crib free. TV; cable. Heated pool. Complimentary coffee in rms. Restaurant 6:30–11 am, 5–8 pm. Bar 5–11 pm. Ck-out noon. Coin lndry. Meeting rms. Valet serv. Sundries. Exercise equipt; weights, bicycles, whirlpool. Refrigerator, wet bar in suites. Cr cds: A, C, D, DS, MC, V.

D ⚊ 🧍 🚫 ◎ SC

✔ ★★**HAMPTON INN.** *1180 Union Ave (38104), downtown.* 901/276-1175; FAX 901/276-4261. 126 rms, 4 story. S $43–$49; D $48–$55; under 18 free. Crib free. TV; cable. Pool. Complimentary continental bkfst. Restaurant nearby. Ck-out noon. Sundries. Cr cds: A, C, D, DS, MC, V.

D ⚊ 🚫 ◎ SC

★★**LA QUINTA-MEDICAL CENTER.** *42 S Camilla St (38104), east of downtown.* 901/526-1050; FAX 901/525-3219. 130 rms, 2 story. May–Aug: S, D $49–$56; each addl $6; under 18 free; lower rates rest of yr. Crib free. Pet accepted, some restrictions. TV; cable. Pool. Restaurant adj open 24 hrs. Ck-out noon. Meeting rms. Valet serv. Sundries. Free airport transportation. Cr cds: A, C, D, DS, MC, V.

D 🐾 ⚊ 🚫 ◎ SC

★★**QUALITY INN-MEMPHIS AIRPORT.** *2949 Airways Blvd (38131), south of downtown.* 901/345-1250; FAX 901/398-0256. 145 rms, 2 story. Apr–Oct: S $40; D $45; each addl $5; under 18 free; higher rates first two wks Nov; lower rates rest of yr. Crib $5. TV; cable. Pool. Restaurant 6:30 am–10 pm. Bar 4–10 pm, closed Sun. Ck-out noon. Free airport transportation. Cr cds: A, C, D, DS, ER, MC, V, JCB.

D ⚊ 🚫 ◎ SC

✔ ★**RED ROOF INN.** *6055 Shelby Oaks Dr (38134), I-40 exit 12, east of downtown.* 901/388-6111; FAX 901/388-6157. 108 rms, 2 story. S $29.99; D $45.99; each addl $6; under 18 free; higher rates sport events. Crib free. Pet accepted, some restrictions. TV. Complimentary coffee in lobby. Restaurant adj open 24 hrs. Ck-out noon. Cr cds: A, C, D, DS, MC, V.

D 🐾 ⚊ 🚫 ◎

★**RED ROOF INN SOUTH.** *3875 American Way (38118), east of downtown.* 901/363-2335; FAX 901/363-2335, ext 444. 110 rms, 3 story. S $30.99; D $35.99–$43.99; 3–4 persons $45.99; under 18 free. Pet accepted. Crib free. TV. Complimentary coffee. Restaurant adj 6 am–10 pm. Ck-out noon. Cr cds: A, C, D, DS, MC, V.

D 🐾 ⚊ 🚫 ◎

★★**RESIDENCE INN BY MARRIOTT.** *6141 Poplar Pike (38119), south of downtown.* 901/685-9595; FAX 901/685-9595, ext 4001. 105 kit. suites, 4 story. Kit. suites $94–$119; family, monthly rates. Crib free. Pet accepted, some restrictions; $100. TV; cable. Pool; whirlpool. Complimentary continental bkfst. Restaurant nearby. Ck-out noon. Coin lndry. Meeting rms. Valet serv. Health club privileges. Private patios, balconies. Picnic tables. Free grocery shopping serv. Cr cds: A, C, D, DS, MC, V, JCB.

D 🐾 ⚊ 🚫 ◎ SC

Motor Hotels

✔ ★★**COMFORT INN-POPLAR EAST.** *5877 Poplar Ave (38119), east of downtown.* 901/767-6300; FAX 901/767-0098. 126 rms, 5 story. S, D $53–$58; each addl $5; under 18 free. Crib free. Pet accepted, some restrictions. TV; cable. Pool. Complimentary continental bkfst Mon–Fri. Restaurant 7 am–10 pm. Rm serv. Bar noon–11 pm. Ck-out noon. Meeting rms. Bellhops. Valet serv. Sundries. Airport transportation. Exercise equipt; weight machine, bicycles. Cr cds: A, C, D, DS, MC, V.

D 🐾 ⚊ 🧍 🚫 ◎ SC

★★**COUNTRY SUITES BY CARLSON.** *4300 American Way (38118), east of downtown.* 901/366-9333; res: 800/456-4000; FAX 901/366-7835. 120 kit. suites, 3 story. Kit. suites $50–$90; under 16 free. Crib free. TV; cable. Pool; whirlpool. Complimentary continental bkfst. Complimentary coffee in rms. Restaurant adj open 24 hrs. Ck-out noon. Coin lndry. Meeting rms. Valet serv. Sundries. Free airport transportation. Health club privileges. Cr cds: A, C, D, DS, MC, V.

D ⚊ 🚫 ◎ SC

★★**HOLIDAY INN-AIRPORT.** *1441 Brooks Rd (38116), near Intl Airport, south of downtown.* 901/398-9211. 281 rms, 4 story. S $75; D $80; each addl $5; under 18 free; wkend rates. Crib free. TV; cable. Indoor pool. Restaurant 6:30 am–2 pm, 5–10:30 pm. Rm serv. Bar 3 pm–1 am. Ck-out noon. Coin lndry. Meeting rms. Bellhops. Sundries. Gift shop. Free airport transportation. Exercise equipt; weight machine, bicycle, whirlpool, sauna. Cr cds: A, C, D, DS, ER, MC, V, JCB.

D ⚊ 🧍 ✈ ◎ SC

★★**RAMADA CONVENTION CENTER HOTEL.** *160 Union Ave (38103), at 2nd St, downtown.* 901/525-5491; FAX 901/525-5491, ext 2322. 186 rms, 14 story. S $80–$95; D $85–$105; each addl $10; suites $125–$200; under 18 free. Crib free. TV; cable. Pool. Restaurant 6 am–10 pm. Rm serv. Bars 4 pm–midnight, Sat to 2 am. Ck-out noon. Meeting rms. Valet serv. Wet bar in suites. *LUXURY LEVEL:* EXECUTIVE LEVEL. 18 rms. S $95; D $105. Concierge. Complimentary continental bkfst, wine.
Cr cds: A, C, D, DS, ER, MC, V, JCB.

D ⚊ 🚫 ◎ SC

★★★**THE RIDGEWAY INN.** *5679 Poplar Ave (38119), at I-240, east of downtown.* 901/766-4000; res: 800/822-3360; FAX 901/763-1857. 155 rms, 7 story. S, D $85–$105; each addl $15; suites $150–$225; under 12 free. Crib free. Pet accepted, some restrictions. TV. Pool. Restaurant 6:30 am–11 pm; Fri, Sat to 1 am; Sun to 10 pm. Rm serv. Bar from 11 am, Fri, Sat to 1 am, Sun noon–10 pm. Ck-out noon. Meeting rm. Airport transportation. Exercise equipt; weight machine, bicycle. *LUXURY LEVEL:* CONCIERGE LEVEL. 21 rms, 2 suites. S from $105; D from $125; suites $200–$250. Concierge. Private lounge. Complimentary continental bkfst, refreshments.
Cr cds: A, C, D, DS, ER, MC, V.

D 🐾 ⚊ 🧍 🚫 ◎ SC

★★★**SHERATON INN-AIRPORT.** *2411 Winchester Rd (38116), near Intl Airport, south of downtown.* 901/332-2370; FAX 901/398-4085. 211 rms, 3 story. S $72; D $82; each addl $10; suites $116; under 12 free; wkend rates. Crib free. TV; cable. Pool. Complimentary continental bkfst 6–8 am. Restaurant 6 am–11 pm. Rm serv. Bar 4 pm–midnight. Ck-out noon. Meeting rms. Bellhops. Valet serv. Sundries. Free airport transportation. Lighted tennis. Cr cds: A, C, D, DS, ER, MC, V, JCB.

★ ★ **WILSON WORLD.** *2715 Cherry Rd (38118), east of downtown.* 901/366-0000; *res:* 800/872-8366; *FAX* 901/366-6361. 178 rms, 4 story, 90 suites. S $54.95; D $59.95; each addl $5; suites $59.95–$64.95; under 18 free; wkend rates. Crib free. TV; cable. Indoor pool. Restaurant 6 am–2 pm, 5:30–10 pm. Rm serv. Bar from 4 pm; pianist exc Sun. Ck-out noon. Meeting rms. Bellhops. Gift shop. Barber, beauty shop. Free airport transportation. Game rm. Refrigerators, wet bars. Balconies. Cr cds: A, C, D, DS, MC, V.

D 🏊 ⊘ ⊕ SC

Hotels

★ ★ ★ **ADAM'S MARK.** *939 Ridge Lake Blvd (38120), south of downtown.* 901/684-6664; *FAX* 901/762-7411. 379 rms, 27 story. S $115; D $125; each addl $10; suites $175–$425; under 18 free; wkend rates. Crib free. TV; cable. Pool. Restaurant 6:30 am–10 pm; Fri, Sat to 11 pm. Bar noon–1 am; entertainment. Ck-out noon. Convention facilities. Gift shop. Airport transportation. Exercise equipt; weight machines, bicycles. Wet bar in suites. Cr cds: A, C, D, DS, MC, V.

D 🏊 🏋 ⊘ ⊕ SC

★ ★ **BROWNESTONE.** *300 N 2nd (38105), at Market St, downtown.* 901/525-2511; *res:* 800/468-3515; *FAX* 901/525-2511, ext 1220. 243 rms, 11 story. S $75; D $90; each addl $10; suites $125–$275; under 19 free; wkend rates. Crib free. Pet accepted, some restrictions. TV. Pool. Restaurant 6 am–10 pm. Bar 4 pm–midnight. Ck-out noon. Meeting rms. Near Pyramid Arena. *LUXURY LEVEL:* **EXECUTIVE LEVEL.** 24 rms. S $80; D $90. Concierge. Private lounge. Bathrm phones. Complimentary wine.
Cr cds: A, C, D, DS, ER, MC, V.

D 🖉 🏊 ⊘ ⊕ SC

★ ★ **EMBASSY SUITES.** *1022 S Shady Grove Rd (38120), east of downtown.* 901/684-1777; *FAX* 901/685-7702. 220 suites, 5 story. Suites $109–$139; under 12 free; wkend rates. Crib free. Pet accepted, some restrictions; $50. TV; cable. Indoor pool. Complimentary full bkfst. Complimentary coffee in rms. Restaurant 11 am–10 pm. Bar to midnight. Ck-out noon. Coin lndry. Convention facilities. Gift shop. Free airport transportation. Exercise equipt; weight machine, bicycles, whirlpool, sauna. Refrigerators, minibars. Cr cds: A, C, D, DS, MC, V.

D 🖉 🏊 🏋 ⊘ ⊕ SC

★ ★ **FRENCH QUARTER SUITES.** *2144 Madison Ave (38104), in Overton Square.* 901/728-4000; *res:* 800/843-0353 (exc TN); *FAX* 901/278-1262. 105 suites, 4 story. Suites $95–$150; family rates. Crib free. TV; cable. Pool; poolside serv. Complimentary full bkfst. Restaurant (see BOURBON STREET CAFE). Rm serv 24 hrs. Bar 11 am–11 pm, Fri & Sat to midnight; entertainment exc Mon. Ck-out noon. Meeting rms. Free airport transportation. Exercise equipt; weights, bicycles. Some bathrm phones, refrigerators, in-rm whirlpools. Private patios, balconies. Interior atrium; New Orleans decor. Cr cds: A, C, D, DS, ER, MC, V, JCB.

D 🏊 🏋 ⊘ ⊕ SC

★ ★ **HOLIDAY INN CROWNE PLAZA.** *250 N Main St (38103), downtown.* 901/527-7300; *FAX* 901/526-1561. 403 rms, 18 story. S $97–$125; D $107–$135; each addl $10; under 17 free. Crib free. TV; cable. Indoor pool. Restaurant 6 am–10 pm. Bar 11:30–1 am. Ck-out noon. Shopping arcade. Free garage parking. Exercise equipt; weights, bicycles, whirlpool, sauna. Some refrigerators. Balconies. Connected to convention center, near river and Pyramid Arena. *LUXURY LEVEL:* **CONCIERGE LEVEL.** 20 rms, 2 suites. S, D $125–$135; suites $250–$450. Ck-out 1 pm. Private lounge, bar 4–8 pm. Complimentary continental bkfst, refreshments.
Cr cds: A, C, D, DS, ER, MC, V, JCB.

D 🏊 🏋 ⊘ ⊕ SC

★ ★ **HOMEWOOD SUITES.** *5811 Poplar Ave (38119), east of downtown.* 901/763-0500; *res:* 800/225-5466; *FAX* 901/763-0132. 140 kit. suites, 2–3 story. Suites $89–$149; family, wkly, monthly rates. Crib free. Pet accepted, some restrictions; $50. TV; cable, in-rm movies avail. Pool. Complimentary continental bkfst. Complimentary coffee in rms. Restaurant adj 11–2 am. Ck-out noon. Coin lndry. Meeting rms. Gift shop. Free airport transportation. Exercise equipt; weights, bicycles, whirlpool. Cr cds: A, D, DS, MC, V.

D 🐾 🏊 🏋 ⊘ ⊕ SC

★ ★ ★ **MARRIOTT.** *2625 Thousand Oaks Blvd (38118), southeast of downtown.* 901/362-6200; *FAX* 901/360-8836. 320 rms, 12 story. S $125–$127; D $140–$150; suites $165–$275; under 18 free. Crib free. TV; cable. 2 pools, 1 indoor. Restaurant 6 am–2 pm, 5–10 pm; wkends from 7 am. Bars 11–2 am, Fri & Sat to 3 am, closed Sun & Mon; entertainment, dancing. Ck-out noon. Convention facilities. Concierge. Free airport transportation. Exercise equipt; weights, bicycles, whirlpool, sauna. Some bathrm phones, refrigerators. *LUXURY LEVEL:* **EXECUTIVE LEVEL.** 21 rms, 1 suite. S, D $150; suite $275. Concierge. Private lounge, honor bar. Complimentary continental bkfst, refreshments.
Cr cds: A, C, D, DS, ER, MC, V, JCB.

D 🏊 🏋 ⊘ ⊕ SC

★ ★ ★ **MEMPHIS AIRPORT.** *2240 Democrat Rd (38132), near Intl Airport, south of downtown.* 901/332-1130; *FAX* 901/398-5206. 380 rms, 5 story. S $50–$101; D $81–$111; each addl $10; suites $175–$275; under 18 free; wkend rates. Crib free. Pet accepted, some restrictions. TV; cable. 2 pools, 1 indoor; poolside serv. Restaurant 6:30 am–11 pm. Bars 11:30 am–midnight, Fri, Sat to 1 am, Sun 3:30–11 pm; entertainment. Ck-out 1 pm. Convention facilities. Free airport transportation. 2 lighted tennis courts. Exercise equipt; weights, bicycles, sauna. Wet bar in suites. Indoor courtyard. Cr cds: A, C, D, DS, ER, MC, V.

D 🐾 🖉 🏊 🏋 ✕ ⊘ ⊕ SC

★ ★ ★ ★ **PEABODY.** *149 Union Ave (38103) at 2nd St, downtown.* 901/529-4000; *res:* 800/732-2639; *FAX* 901/529-9600. 469 rms, 13 story. S $115–$240; D $140–$275; each addl $25; suites $350–$1,000; under 18 free. Crib free. TV; cable. Heated pool. Restaurant 6:30 am–midnight (also see DUX). Rm serv 24 hrs. Bar 11–2 am; entertainment daily; dancing Thurs–Sat. Ck-out 11 am. Meeting rms. Concierge. Shopping arcade. Barber, beauty shop. Exercise rm; instructor, weights, bicycles, whirlpool, sauna, steam rm. Extensive exercise facilities. A grand hotel, originally opened in 1869, rebuilt in 1925, and restored to former opulence. A symbol of the Peabody is the duck; guests can observe the unique sight of a daily march of these ducks across a red carpet to and from lobby fountain at 11 am & 5 pm. Cr cds: A, C, D, DS, ER, MC, V.

D 🏊 🏋 ⊘ ⊕ SC

★ ★ **RADISSON.** *185 Union Ave (38103), downtown.* 901/528-1800; *FAX* 901/526-3226. 283 rms, 10 story. S, D $99–$109; each addl $10; suites $120–$130; under 18 free. Crib free. Garage/valet $4. TV; cable. Pool. Restaurant 6 am–10 pm. Bar 11 am–midnight. Ck-out noon. Convention facilities. Gift shop. Free airport transportation. Exercise equipt; weight machine, bicycles, whirlpool, sauna. Atrium lobby with trees and fountain, contains reconstructed brick facade of original historic building on site. Near Beale St, Mud Island and Pyramid. Cr cds: A, C, D, DS, ER, MC, V, JCB.

D 🏊 🏋 ⊘ ⊕ SC

Restaurants

✔ ★ **ALFRED'S.** *197 Beale St, in Beale St Area.* 901/525-3711. Hrs: 11–3 am; Sun brunch to 3 pm. Bar. Semi-a la carte: lunch $5.25–$7.95, dinner $6.95–$15.95. Sun brunch $7.95. Specializes in prime rib, blackened catfish. Jazz exc Sun. Parking. Outdoor dining. Cr cds: A, D, DS, MC, V.

D

★ **BEALE STREET BBQ.** *205 Beale Street, in Beale St Area.* 901/525-0880. Hrs: 11–1 am. Beer. Semi-a la carte: lunch $3.50–$17.50, dinner $6–$17.50. Child's meals. Specializes in barbecued ribs, red beans and rice. Parking. Cr cds: A, DS, MC, V.

D

★★**BENIHANA OF TOKYO.** *912 Ridge Lake Blvd, east of downtown.* 901/683-7390. Hrs: 11:30 am–2 pm, 5–10 pm; Fri to 11 pm; Sat 5–11 pm; early-bird dinner 5–7 pm. Res accepted. Japanese menu. Bar 4:30–10 pm. Complete meals: lunch $5.25–$12, dinner $12–$23.50. Child's meals. Parking. Family-owned. Cr cds: A, C, D, DS, MC, V.

D

✔★**BOSCOS PIZZA KITCHEN & BREWERY.** *(7615 W Farmington, Germantown) E on US 72, at Poplar Ave, in Saddle Creek Shopping Plaza.* 901/756-7312. Hrs: 11 am–midnight; Fri & Sat to 1 am. Closed Dec 25. Bar. Semi-a la carte: lunch $3.95–$7.95, dinner $4.95–$14.95. Specializes in wood-fired oven pizza, pasta. Own beer. Parking. Outdoor dining. Mediterranean decor. Cr cds: A, C, D, DS, MC, V.

D

★★**BOURBON STREET CAFE.** *(See French Quarter Suites Hotel)* 901/728-4000. Hrs: 7 am–10 pm; wkends to 11 pm. Cajun menu. Bar. Semi-a la carte: bkfst $3.95–$12.95, lunch $3.95–$12.95, dinner $8.95–$30. Sun brunch $16.95. Specializes in desserts. Patio dining. Jazz. Cr cds: A, C, D, DS, MC, V.

D **SC**

★★**CAPTAIN BILBO'S.** *263 Wagner Place, downtown.* 901/526-1966. Hrs: 5–10:30 pm; Fri, Sat to 11 pm. Closed Jan 1, Thanksgiving, Dec 24, 25. Cajun, Amer menu. Bar 4:30 pm–1 am; Fri, Sat to 2 am. Semi-a la carte: dinner $9.95–$28.95. Child's meals. Specializes in steak, seafood. Entertainment. Valet parking. Former cotton warehouse; nautical decor. Cr cds: A, C, D, MC, V.

D

✔★**COOKER BAR & GRILLE.** *6120 Poplar Ave, east of downtown.* 901/685-2800. Hrs: 11 am–10:30 pm; Fri & Sat to 11:30 pm; Sun to 10 pm. Closed Thanksgiving, Dec 25. Bar. Semi-a la carte: lunch $2.95–$7.95, dinner $6.75–$14.95. Child's meals. Specializes in meat loaf, pot roast, pasta. Parking. Cr cds: A, D, DS, MC, V.

D

★★★**DUX.** *(See Peabody Hotel)* 901/529-4199. Hrs: 6:30–10:30 am, 11:30 am–2:30 pm, 5:30–11 pm; Fri, Sat to midnight; Sun 6:30–11:30 am, 5:30–11 pm; Sun brunch noon–2:30 pm. Res accepted. Bar. Wine list. Semi-a la carte: bkfst $3.75–$8.95, lunch $3.95–$12.95, dinner $7.95–$22.95. Sun brunch $3.75–$11.50. Child's meals. Specializes in mesquite-grilled Black Angus steak and seafood. Own baking. Valet parking. Cr cds: A, C, D, DS, ER, MC, V.

D

★★★**GRISANTI'S.** *1489 Airways Blvd, east of downtown.* 901/458-2648. Hrs: 11 am–2:30 pm, 5–10 pm; Fri, Sat to 10:30 pm. Closed Sun; hols. Res accepted. Northern Italian menu. Bar. Wine cellar. Semi-a la carte: lunch $3.75–$7.50, dinner $8–$23.95. Child's meals. Specialties: cannelloni alla Gusi, fettucine verde al dente, veal cotolétta. Own baking. Parking. Specially prepared gourmet menu on request. Family-owned. Cr cds: A, C, D, DS, MC, V.

D

✔★★**HEMMINGS.** *25 Belvedere Blvd, east of downtown.* 901/276-7774. Hrs: 11:30 am–2:30 pm, 5 pm–midnight; Sat 5 pm–1 am; Sun noon–3 pm. Res accepted. Bar. Semi-a la carte: lunch $5–$9, dinner $8.95–$14.95. Sun brunch $6–$9. Specializes in Southwestern and California-style cooking. Cr cds: A, C, D, DS, MC, V.

D **SC**

★**JOYCE COBB'S DINNER CLUB.** *209 Beale St, in Beale St Area.* 901/525-0484. Hrs: 5 pm–2 am. Bar. Semi-a la carte: dinner $5–$17. Specializes in ribs, grilled chicken, barbecued beef. Parking. Jazz club. Cr cds: A, DS, MC, V.

D

★★★**JUSTINES.** *919 Coward Place, at East St, downtown.* 901/527-3815. Hrs: 5:30–10 pm. Closed Sun, Mon; major hols; also 2 wks Aug. Res accepted. French menu. Wine cellar. A la carte entrees: dinner $35–$40. Specializes in fresh seafood flown in daily. Own baking. Valet parking. In antebellum mansion; gardens. Family-owned. Jacket. Cr cds: A, C, D, DS, MC, V.

★★**KING COTTON CAFE.** *50 N Front St, in Morgan Keegan Tower Bldg, downtown.* 901/576-8150. Hrs: 11:30 am–2:30 pm. Closed Sat & Sun; July 4, Thanksgiving, Dec 25. Bar. Semi-a la carte: lunch $4.50–$12. Child's meals. Specializes in veal, lamb, seafood. Salad bar. Parking. Cr cds: A, D, DS, MC, V.

D

★**MELOS TAVERNA.** *2021 Madison Ave, in Overton Square.* 901/725-1863. Hrs: 4:30–10:30 pm. Closed Sun, Mon; July 4, Thanksgiving, Dec 25. Res accepted; required Fri, Sat. Greek menu. Bar. Semi-a la carte: dinner $8.75–$21. Specializes in lamb, moussaka. Parking. Greek artwork. Cr cds: A, C, D, MC, V.

D

★★★**PAULETTE'S.** *2110 Madison Ave, in Overton Square.* 901/726-5128. Hrs: 11 am–10 pm; Fri & Sat to 11:30 pm; Sat, Sun brunch to 4 pm. Closed major hols. Res accepted. Continental menu. Bar. Semi-a la carte: lunch $5.95–$10, dinner $8–$18.95. Sat, Sun brunch $5–$9. Child's meals. Specialties: filet Paulette, brochettes of prawn. Entertainment Fri–Sun. Parking. Cr cds: A, C, D, DS, MC, V.

D

★★**PIER.** *100 Wagner Place, between Union & Beale Sts, opp Mud Island, downtown.* 901/526-7381. Hrs: 11:30 am–2 pm, 5–10 pm; Sat & Sun 5–10 pm. Bar. Semi-a la carte: lunch $5–$10, dinner $12–$19. Specializes in seafood, prime rib, steak. Located in old, riverfront warehouse. Cr cds: A, D, MC, V.

D

✔★**THE PUBLIC EYE.** *17 S Cooper, in Overton Square.* 901/726-4040. Hrs: 11 am–10 pm; Fri, Sat to midnight; lunch buffet to 2 pm. Closed Jan 1, Dec 25. Bar. Semi-a la carte: lunch $4–$7, dinner $5–$15. Buffet: lunch $5.95. Child's meals. Specializes in barbecued pork, ribs. Parking. Cr cds: A, C, D, DS, MC, V.

Unrated Dining Spots

BUTCHER SHOP. *101 S Front St, downtown.* 901/521-0856. Hrs: 5–10 pm; Fri, Sat to 11 pm. Closed Jan 1, Thanksgiving, Dec 24, 25. Bar. Option to select and cook own steak. Served with salad, potato and bread $14–$19. Child's meals. Salad bar. Grill in dining room; 1907 building. Cr cds: A, D, MC, V.

RENDEZVOUS. *52 S 2nd St, in Gen Washburn Alley, downtown.* 901/523-2746. Hrs: 4:30 pm–midnight; Fri from 11:30 am; Sat from 12:30 pm. Closed Sun, Mon; also 2 wks late July, 2 wks late Dec. Bar (beer). Semi-a la carte: lunch, dinner $3–$10. Specializes in barbecued ribs. In 1890 downtown building; memorabilia, many antiques, collectibles; jukebox. Cr cds: A, C, D, MC, V.

Monteagle (E-6)

Pop: 1,138 **Elev:** 1,927 ft **Area code:** 615 **Zip:** 37356

A popular summer resort for more than a century, Monteagle is also famous for its Chautauqua Assembly, which has been held every summer since 1882.

What to See and Do

1. **University of the South** (1857). (1,100 students) 4 mi SW via US 64, in Sewanee. Campus covering 10,000 acres at an elevation of 2,000 ft features scenic mountain overlooks, hiking trails, waterfalls and caves; Gothic-revival architecture. On campus are duPont Library

Collection of rare books and manuscripts (daily exc Sun); All Saints' Chapel; Leonidas Polk Carillon (concerts Sun). For general information and details on free guided tours phone 598-1286.

2. **South Cumberland State Park.** Extensive park system in southeastern Tennessee comprised of nine separate areas. Visitor Center is located east of Monteagle on US 41. Contact the Park Manager, Rte 1, Box 2196; 924-2980 or -2956. Within the system are

Carter State Natural Area. 5 mi S of Sewanee on TN 56. A 140-acre area that includes the Lost Cove Caves. **Free.**

Sewanee Natural Bridge. 2 mi S of Sewanee on TN 56. A 2-acre area that features a 25-foot sandstone arch overlooking Lost Cove. **Free.**

Foster Falls Small Wild Area. 7 mi S of Tracy City on US 41. Foster Falls has the largest volume of water of any falls in the South Cumberland Recreation Area. Hiking. Picnicking. Camping (mid-Apr–mid-Oct). **Free.**

Grundy Forest State Natural Area. Tracy City. Sycamore Falls, a 12-foot-high waterfall lying in the bottom of the Fiery Gizzard Gorge, and Chimney Rocks, a unique geological formation, are highlights of this 212-acre recreational area. The Fiery Gizzard Hiking Trail winds around moss-laden cliffs and mountain laurel to connect the forest with the Foster Falls Small Wild Area. Picnicking. **Free.**

Grundy Lakes State Park. Tracy City. An 81-acre site features the Lone Rock Coke Ovens. These ovens, operated in the late 1800s with convict labor, were used in making coke for the smelting of iron ore. Swimming. Hiking. Picnicking. **Free.**

Savage Gulf State Natural Area. 27 mi NE, near Palmer on County 399E. Covering 11,500 acres, the area offers 70 miles of wilderness hiking trails, backcountry camping and rock climbing. The Savage Gulf cuts deep into the Cumberland Plateau and shelters virgin timber, rock cliffs, caves and many waterfalls. **Free.**

Great Stone Door. Near Bersheba Springs. A unique rock formation that is a 150-foot-high crevice at the crest of the Cumberland Plateau above Big Creek Gulf. Panoramic view of the area. Hiking. Picnicking. **Free.**

(For further information contact Jim Oliver's Smoke House Motor Lodge and Restaurant, US 64, US 41A, Box 579; 924-2268, 800/489-2091.)

Seasonal Events

Sewanee Summer Music Center Concerts. Guerry Hall, Univ of the South (see #1). 4-day festival concludes season. Phone 598-1225 or -1286. Wkends, late June–early Aug.

Monteagle Chautauqua Assembly. Concerts, lectures, academic courses, art classes. Phone 924-2268. Early July–late Aug.

(See Manchester)

Motels

✓ ★★**COUNTRY INN.** *(Box 188)* I-24 exit 134. 615/924-2221; res: 800/468-6580. 120 rms, 2 story. S $24.95–$28.95; D $32.95–$39.95; each addl $4. Crib free. Pet accepted. TV; cable. Pool. Complimentary full bkfst. Restaurant 5 am–9 pm. Ck-out 11 am. Coin lndry. Cr cds: A, C, D, DS, MC, V.

★★**JIM OLIVER'S SMOKE HOUSE MOTOR LODGE.** *(Box 579)* I-24 exit 134. 615/924-2091; res: 800/489-2091. 100 rms, 2 story. S $24–$41; D $35–$44; each addl $5; suites $75–$125; 1-, 2-bedrm cabins $95–$159; under 12 free. Crib $2. TV; in-rm movies. Pool. Playground. Restaurant 6 am–10 pm. Rm serv. Ck-out 11 am. Meeting rms. Sundries. Shopping arcade. Tennis. Cr cds: A, DS, MC, V.

Inn

★★**ADAMS EDGEWORTH INN.** *Monteagle Assembly Grounds, I-24 exit 134. 615/924-2669; FAX 615/924-3236.* 12 rms, 3 story, 1 suite. S $55–$65; D $65–$95; each addl $25; suite $135. Crib free. TV in library. Complimentary continental bkfst. Complimentary coffee in library. Ck-out 11 am, ck-in 4 pm. Lawn games. Balconies. Antiques, art collection in 1896 building. On grounds of Monteagle Chatauqua Assembly, additional $8 fee July–Aug. Cr cds: MC, V.

Morristown (D-8)

Settled: 1783 **Pop:** 21,385 **Elev:** 1,350 ft **Area code:** 615 **Zip:** 37814

Bounded by Clinch Mountain and the Great Smoky Mountains, Morristown is a major manufacturing center. Davy Crockett lived in the town from 1794 to 1809.

What to See and Do

1. **Rose Center.** 442 W Second North St. Historic building serves as a cultural center and includes a children's "touch" museum, art gallery and historical museum. (Mon–Fri & Sat mornings) Phone 581-4330. **Free.**

2. **Panther Creek State Park.** 4 mi S on US 11E, then 2 mi W on Panther Creek Rd. More than 1,400 acres on Cherokee Lake. Swimming pool; fishing. Hiking trails. Picnic sites, playground. Campground. Visitors center. Standard fees. Phone 587-7046.

3. **Cherokee Dam and Lake.** 14 mi SW on US 11E to Jefferson City, then 5 mi N on TN 92. TVA dam (6,760 ft long, 175 ft high) on Holston River. Fishing; boating. Visitor building & powerhouse tours (daily). Phone 475-7964. **Free.**

(For further information contact the Chamber of Commerce, 825 W 1st North St, PO Box 9, 37815; 586-6382.)

Motels

★★**HOLIDAY INN.** 3230 W Andrew Johnson Hwy. 615/581-8700; FAX 615/581-7128. 118 rms, 2 story. S $46–$60; D $52–$69; each addl $5; suites $146–$168; under 20 free. Crib free. TV; cable. Pool. Restaurant 6 am–2 pm, 5–10 pm; Sat, Sun from 7 am. Rm serv. Ck-out noon. Meeting rms. Sundries. Cr cds: A, C, D, DS, MC, V, JCB.

★★**RAMADA INN.** *(Box 190)* 6 mi S at I-81 & US 25E exit 8. 615/587-2400; FAX 615/581-7344. 113 rms, 2–3 story. No elvtr. S $48–$75; D $53–$75; under 18 free. Crib free. Pet accepted. TV; cable. 2 pools; wading pool. Restaurant 6 am–9 pm. Ck-out noon. Meeting rms. Valet serv. Private patios, balconies. Cr cds: A, C, D, DS, MC, V, JCB.

Murfreesboro (D-5)

Founded: 1811 **Pop:** 44,922 **Elev:** 619 ft **Area code:** 615

Murfreesboro lies in the geographic center of Tennessee. Because of this strategic location, the town was almost named the state capital. The legislature did meet in Murfreesboro from 1819 to 1825, but it never returned after convening in Nashville. The area is rich in Civil War history and is known as the "antique center of the South." Rutherford County is also noted for its production of cattle and prize-winning Tennessee walking horses.

What to See and Do

1. **Oaklands.** 900 N Maney Ave, 2 mi N of I-24. This 19th-century mansion, an architectural blend of four different periods, was a social center before the Civil War and command headquarters for Union Colonel W.W. Duffield, who surrendered Murfreesboro to Confederate General Nathan Bedford Forrest at the house. Rooms restored and furnished with items appropriate to the Civil War period. Grounds landscaped in period style. (Daily exc Mon; closed major hols) Sr citizen rate. Phone 893-0022. ¢¢

2. **Stones River National Battlefield.** 3 mi from I-24 exit 78 on US 41/70S. Park covering approx 400 acres preserves the site of the Battle of Stones River (Dec 31, 1862–Jan 2, 1863), a bitter clash resulting in 10,000 Confederate and 13,000 Union casualties. The Confederates failed in this attempt to halt the Union advance on Chattanooga. The park includes the Hazen Monument (1863), one of the oldest memorials of the Civil War, and the National Cemetery, with 7,000 graves, tablets and markers. Self-guided tours; auto tape tour (1¼ hrs) at visitor center. Living history demonstrations, summer wkends. Visitor center has battlefield museum, films (daily; closed Dec 25). Contact the Superintendent, 3501 Old Nashville Hwy, 37129; 893-9501. **Free.**

(For further information contact the Rutherford County Chamber of Commerce, PO Box 864, 37133; 893-6565.)

Annual Events

Street Festival & Folkfest. International dancers, arts & crafts. May.

International Grand Championship Walking Horse Show. Early Aug.

(See Lebanon, Nashville)

Motels

(Rates may be higher during horse shows)

★ ★ **HAMPTON INN.** 2230 Old Fort Pkwy (37129). 615/896-1172; FAX 615/895-4277. 119 rms, 2 story. S $43–$45; D $48–$50; under 18 free. Crib free. Pet accepted, some restrictions. TV; cable. Pool. Complimentary continental bkfst, coffee. Restaurant adj open 24 hrs. Ck-out noon. Meeting rm. Cr cds: A, C, D, DS, MC, V.

★ ★ **HoJo INN.** 2424 S Church St (37130), at jct US 231 & I-24. 615/896-5522; FAX 615/893-7216. 80 rms, 2 story. S $36–$45; D $39.95–$55; each addl $5; under 12 free. Crib $5. Pet accepted, some restrictions; $5. TV; cable. Pool. Restaurant open 24 hrs. Ck-out noon. Coin lndry. Meeting rm. Game rm. Cr cds: A, C, D, DS, MC, V.

★ ✓ **MURFREESBORO.** 1150 NW Broad St (37129). 615/893-2100. 65 rms. S $25–$32; D $32–$38; each addl $3. Crib $3. Pet accepted, some restrictions. TV; cable. Pool; wading pool. Playground. Restaurant open 24 hrs. Ck-out 11 am. Cr cds: A, C, D, DS, MC, V.

✓ ★ **SHONEY'S INN.** 1954 S Church St (37130). 615/896-6030; res: 800/222-2222; FAX 615/896-6037. 125 rms, 2 story. S $39; D $45; each addl $6; under 18 free; higher rates special events. Crib free. TV; cable. Pool. Complimentary coffee in lobby. Restaurant adj 6 am–11 pm. Ck-out noon. Meeting rms. Valet serv. Health club privileges. Some refrigerators. Cr cds: A, C, D, DS, ER, MC, V.

✓ ★ ★ **WAYSIDE INN.** 2225 S Church St (37130), at jct US 231 & I-24. 615/896-2320. 101 rms, 2 story. S $28.50–$38.50; D $36.50–$69.50; each addl $8; suites $59.50–$74; under 14 free. Crib $4. Pet accepted, some restrictions. TV; cable. Pool. Restaurant 6 am–9 pm. Ck-out 11 am. Meeting rm. Some bathrm phones, refrigerators, wet bars. Cr cds: A, C, D, DS, ER, MC, V, JCB.

Motor Hotels

★ ★ ★ **GARDEN PLAZA.** 1850 Old Fort Pkwy (37129). 615/895-5555; res: 800/342-7336; FAX 615/895-5555, ext 165. 170 rms, 5 story. S $62–$65; D $72–$75; each addl $10; suites $95; under 12 free. Crib free. TV; cable. Indoor pool; whirlpool, poolside serv. Restaurant 6:30 am–2 pm, 5–10 pm. Rm serv. Bar 4 pm–1 am. Ck-out noon. Meeting rms. Bellhops. Valet serv. Health club privileges. Refrigerators; some wet bars. Cr cds: A, C, D, DS, MC, V, JCB.

★ ★ **HOLIDAY INN.** 2227 Old Fort Pkwy (37129), at jct TN 96 & I-24. 615/896-2420; FAX 615/896-8738. 180 rms, 2–4 story. S $50–$65; D $65–$80. Crib free. Pet accepted, some restrictions. TV; cable. Indoor pool; whirlpool, sauna, wading pool. Restaurant 6 am–2 pm, 5–10 pm. Rm serv. Bar 4:30 pm–2 am; dancing exc Sun. Ck-out noon. Coin lndry. Meeting rms. Bellhops. Valet serv. Holidome. Game rm. Cr cds: A, C, D, DS, MC, V, JCB.

Restaurants

★ ★ **CHESNEY'S.** 1695 Memorial Blvd. 615/896-5588. Hrs: 11 am–10 pm; Fri & Sat to midnight; Sun brunch to 3 pm. Closed Thanksgiving, Dec 25. Bar. A la carte entrees: lunch $2.95–$6.45, dinner $6.95–$14.95. Sun brunch $2.95–$6.95. Child's meals. Specializes in steak, prime rib, chicken quesadilla. Parking. Informal dining in relaxed atmosphere. Cr cds: A, MC, V.

✓ ★ **DEMO'S STEAK AND SPAGHETTI HOUSE.** 1115 NW Broad St. 615/895-3701. Hrs: 11 am–10 pm; wkends to 11 pm. Closed Thanksgiving, Dec 24 & 25. Varied menu. Bar. Semi-a la carte: lunch $3.45–$5.95, dinner $4.95–$11.95. Child's meals. Specializes in steak, spaghetti, seafood. Parking. Contemporary decor; three dining areas. Cr cds: C, D, DS, MC, V.

✓ ★ **TRAPPER'S.** 127 SE Broad St. 615/890-3030. Hrs: 11 am–11 pm; Fri & Sat to midnight; early-bird dinner 4–6 pm. Closed Dec 24. Bar. Semi-a la carte: lunch $3.49–$6.95, dinner $4.99–$11.95. Child's meals. Specializes in steak, barbecue ribs, carrot cake. Parking. Cr cds: A, C, D, DS, MC, V.

Nashville (D-5)

Settled: 1779 **Pop:** 488,374 **Elev:** 440 ft **Area code:** 615

Commercial center and capital city, Nashville's heritage is part Andrew Jackson's Hermitage and part Grand Ole Opry. It is often referred to as the "Athens of the South" because of its 16 colleges and universities, religious publishing firms and some 750 churches. To prove this point, it has the Parthenon, the only full-size replica of the Athenian architectural masterpiece.

A city of banks and insurance companies—one of the largest investment banking centers in the South—Nashville also capitalizes on the approximately $1.5 billion payroll of its state and federal employees, the products of its 600 industries and the $5 billion sales of its stores. The world's largest automobile glass plant is in the city. Nashville ranks second in the nation as a music recording center and first in country music recording. Music and related businesses play a multimillion-dollar tune for the city's economy.

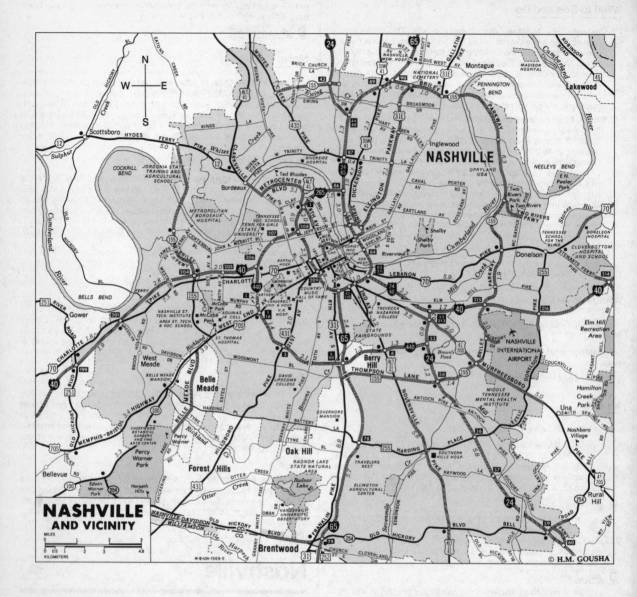

NASHVILLE AND VICINITY

MILES
0 0.5 1 2 3
KILOMETERS
0   4.8

M-S-UH-1569-S

© H.M. GOUSHA

In recent years, millions of dollars in investment capital have been used for new buildings and vast expansion programs. This redevelopment has given the lovely old capital a new and airy setting. Throughout this bustle of commerce and construction, Nashville retains an Old South quality, proud of its gracious homes and its old traditions.

These traditions stem back to the days when, in 1779, a band of pioneers built a log stockade on the west bank of the Cumberland River, naming it Fort Nashborough. The Cumberland Compact established a governing body of 12 judges at this wilderness village. By an act of the North Carolina legislature, the name was changed to Nashville. Nearly 50 years after Tennessee became a state, Nashville was made the permanent capital.

During the Civil War, the city was taken by Union troops in March, 1862. In December, 1864, a Confederate force under General John Bell Hood moved to the hills south of the city in an attempt to recapture it. However, two Union counterattacks virtually wiped out the Confederate army.

Just as the Cumberland Compact of May, 1780, was an innovation in government, so was a new charter, which became effective in 1963, setting up Nashville and Davidson County under a single administration with a legislative body of 40 members.

Transportation

Nashville Intl Airport: Information 275-1675; lost and found 275-1675; weather 244-9393; cash machines, Main Terminal, entry level; Admirals Club (American), South Concourse; Crown Room (Delta), North Concourse.

Car Rental Agencies: See toll-free numbers under Introduction.

Public Transportation: Metro Transit Authority, phone 242-4433.

What to See and Do

1. **State Capitol** (1845–59). 6th & Charlotte Aves. Greek-revival structure with 80-foot tower rising above the city; columns grace the ends and sides. Architect William Strickland died before the building was completed and was buried within its walls. Of special interest are the grand stairway, library, legislative chambers and murals in gubernatorial suite. (Mon–Fri; closed major hols). Phone 741-1621.

2. **Tennessee State Museum.** James K. Polk State Bldg, 5th & Deaderick. Exhibits on life in Tennessee from early man through the early 1900s. (Daily exc Mon; closed major hols) Phone 741-2692. **Free.**

3. **Fort Nashborough.** 170 1st Ave N, at Church St, in N end of Riverfront Park. Patterned after the pioneer fort established several blocks from this site in 1779, replica is smaller and has fewer cabins. Stockaded walls, exhibits of pioneer implements. (Daily; closed major hols) **Free.**

4. **The Parthenon.** In Centennial Park, West End Ave & 25th Ave N. Replica of the Parthenon of Pericles' time was built in plaster for the Tennessee Centennial of 1897 and later reconstructed in concrete aggregate. As in the original, there is not a straight horizontal or vertical line and no two columns are placed the same distance apart. Houses 19th- and 20th-century artworks; changing art exhibits; replicas of Elgin Marbles; 42-foot statue of goddess Athena. (Tues–Sat; closed hols) Sr citizen rate. Phone 862-8431. ¢¢

5. **The Upper Room.** 1908 Grand Ave. Chapel with polychrome wood carving of Leonardo da Vinci's "The Last Supper," said to be largest of its kind in world; also World Christian Fellowship Window. (Mon–Fri; closed major hols) Phone 340-7207. **Free.**

6. **Cumberland Science Museum.** 800 Ridley Blvd, near Greer Stadium. Planetarium, live animal and science programs. (June–Aug, daily; rest of yr, daily exc Mon; closed most hols) Sr citizen rate. Phone 862-5160. ¢¢

7. **Oscar Farris Agricultural Museum.** Ellington Agricultural Center, 6 mi S. Former horse barn on historic estate. Oldest Agricultural Hall of Fame in US. Farm tools, equipment and household items of 19th and early 20th centuries. (Mon–Fri; closed state hols) Phone 360-0197. ¢

8. **Museum of Tobacco Art & History.** 800 Harrison St, at 8th Ave N. Houses exhibits tracing history of tobacco from Native Americans to present. On display are rare antique pipes, tobacco containers, snuff boxes, cigar store figures; art, photographs. (Daily exc Sun; closed major hols) Phone 271-2349. **Free.**

9. **Nashville Toy Museum.** 2613-B McGavock Pike. Features unique displays of antique toys, including German and English bears from early 1900s, china dolls from 1850 and lead soldiers in battle dioramas. Train room contains more than 250 toy and model locomotives and 2 train layouts depicting Tennessee in the 1930s and Britain at the turn of the century. (Daily; closed Thanksgiving, Dec 25) Phone 883-8870. ¢¢

10. **Museum of Beverage Containers and Advertising.** 15 mi N on I-65 to Millersville, 1055 Ridgecrest Dr. More than 30,000 antique soda and beer cans form the largest collection of its kind. Also on display are thousands of period advertising pieces. (Daily; closed Thanksgiving, Dec 25) Phone 859-5236. ¢

11. **Car Collectors Hall of Fame.** 1534 Demonbreun St. Antique car collection featuring cars of country music stars; old-time doctor's office; music parlor with rare musical instruments. (Daily; closed some hols) Phone 255-6804. ¢¢

12. **Belmont Mansion.** 1900 Belmont Blvd, at Acklen Ave, on Belmont University campus. Built in the 1850s in the style of an Italian villa, this mansion, once considered one of the finest private residences in the US, has original marble statues, Venetian glass, gasoliers, mirrors and paintings in the 14 rooms open to public; gardens feature large collection of 19th-century garden ornaments and cast iron gazebos. (Mon–Sat, also Sun afternoons; winter Tues–Sat; closed hols) Phone 269-9537. ¢¢

13. **The Hermitage** (1819; rebuilt after a fire in 1834). 12 mi E off I-40 exit 221A, follow sign. Greek-revival residence of President Andrew Jackson is furnished almost entirely with original family pieces, many of which were associated with Jackson's military career and years in the White House. Also on 660-acre estate are a garden with graves of Jackson and his wife, Rachel; two log cabins; a church; and visitor center and museum with biographical film on Jackson. (Daily; closed Thanksgiving, Dec 25, also 3rd wk Jan) Phone 889-2941. ¢¢¢ Included in fee is

   Tulip Grove (1836). Greek-revival house of Andrew Jackson Donelson, Mrs. Jackson's nephew and President Jackson's private secretary. Interior has examples of 19th-century faux marbling.

14. **Cheekwood/Museum and Gardens.** 8 mi SW on Forrest Park Dr, next to Percy Warner Park. Cultural center on 55 acres includes museum with permanent collection of 19th- and 20th-century American art; Botanic Hall with atrium of tropical flora and changing plant exhibits; public greenhouses featuring orchids, camellias and plants from Central American cloud forests; and five major gardens specializing in dogwood, wildflowers, herbs, daffodils, roses and tulips. (Daily; closed Thanksgiving, Dec 24, Dec 31) Sr citizen rate. Phone 356-8000. ¢¢

15. **Belle Meade** (1853). Harding Rd & Leake Ave, 7 mi SW. Mansion and outbuildings were once part of 5,300-acre working plantation. At turn of the century, Belle Meade was considered the greatest Thoroughbred breeding farm in the country. The 14-room, Greek-revival mansion contains Empire and Victorian furnishings and heirloom showcase with racing trophies and mementos. Also on grounds are Dunham Station log cabin (1793) and the Carriage House (1890s), containing one of the South's largest carriage collections. (Daily; closed Jan 1, Thanksgiving, Dec 25) Phone 356-0501. ¢¢¢

16. **Travellers' Rest Historic House** (1799). I-65 exit 78, S on US 31 (Franklin Rd), follow signs. Restored Federal-style house of Judge John Overton. Maintained as a historical museum with period furniture, records, letters, the building reflects history and development of early Tennessee. Eleven-acre grounds with gardens, kitchen house, smokehouse. Gift shop. Allow at least 45 min for visit. (Tues–Sat, also Sun afternoons; closed Jan 1, Thanksgiving, Dec 25) Phone 832-2962. ¢¢

17. **Sam Davis Home.** 20 mi S off I-24 in Smyrna, at 1399 Sam Davis Rd. Described as "the most beautiful shrine to a private soldier in the US," this stately house and 168-acre working farm have been preserved as a memorial to Sam Davis, Confederate scout caught behind Union lines and tried as a spy. Offered his life if he revealed the name of his informer, Davis chose to die on the gallows. His boyhood home is restored and furnished with many original pieces; grounds include kitchen, smokehouse, slave cabins and family cemetery where Davis is buried. (Daily; closed Jan 1, Thanksgiving, Dec 25) Sr citizen rate. Phone 459-2341. ¢¢

18. **Country Music Hall of Fame & Museum.** 4 Music Square E. Exhibits include Elvis Presley's Cadillac, Johnny Cash tribute, films, costumes, musical instruments, memorabilia of country music notables. Participatory exhibits. (Daily; closed Jan 1, Thanksgiving, Dec 25) Phone 255-5333. ¢¢¢ Also included is a visit to

   RCA Studio B. Studio where music greats recorded. Multimedia exhibit and simulated mix-down session.

19. **Ryman Auditorium & Museum.** 116 5th Ave N. Home of the Grand Ole Opry from 1943–1974. Walking tours include a visit to the stage and the backstage corridors, dressing rooms; view of stage sets

and props, exhibits and gallery of music stars. (Daily; closed Thanksgiving, Dec 25) Phone 254-1445. ¢¢

20. **Country Music Wax Museum and Shopping Mall.** 118 16th Ave S. Sixty wax figures; original stage costumes and memorabilia. Record, western wear, crafts and gift shops; restaurant, entertainment. (Daily; closed Thanksgiving, Dec 25) Phone 256-2490. ¢¢

21. **Music Valley Wax Museum of the Stars.** 2515 McGavock Pike, NE via Briley Pkwy, exit 12. More than 50 lifelike wax figures of famous stars, dressed in authentic costumes. Also features Sidewalk of the Stars with hand and foot imprints of more than 200 country/western stars. (Daily; closed Thanksgiving, Dec 25) Phone 883-3612. ¢¢

22. **Opryland.** 10 mi E on I-40, then 4 mi N on Briley Pkwy, exit 11. A 120-acre entertainment showpark features American music from jazz and blues to pop, Broadway, country, gospel and rock 'n roll in live musical productions. Family thrill rides include the Screamin' Delta Demon, Wabash Cannonball and Chaos, an indoor coaster ride with special effects. Playgrounds; petting zoo; craft shops; restaurants. (Memorial Day–Labor Day, daily; late Mar–Memorial Day, Labor Day–early Nov, wkends) For information phone 889-6611. ¢¢¢¢   Opryland is built around

Grand Ole Opry. Live radio show featuring the best in country music is broadcast from the Grand Ole Opry House, the world's largest broadcast studio, which seats 4,400. The Opry has been broadcast weekends continuously since 1925. (Wkends all yr; extra performances wkends Apr–Oct; also June–Aug, Tues, Thurs; Sat & Sun matinees) Reservations recommended. For information contact Opryland Customer Service, 2802 Opryland Dr, 37214; phone 889-3060. ¢¢¢¢

Grand Ole Opry Tours. Three- to four-hour bus tours include houses of country music stars, Music Row, recording studios, backstage visit to Grand Ole Opry House. Contact 2810 Opryland Dr, 37214; 889-9490. ¢¢¢¢¢

Opryland Museums. Located just outside Opryland Park, in the Plaza area, near the Grand Ole Opry House. **Minnie Pearl Museum** features 50 yrs of memorabilia. **Roy Acuff Museum** includes musical instruments; **Grand Ole Opry Museum** pays tribute to country stars with audio/visual and interactive devices. (Daily) **Free.**

23. **Barbara Mandrell Country.** 1510 Division St. Collection of photos, letters; replicas of the singer's bedroom and makeup room; recording studio; trophy room; video presentations; concession. (Daily; closed Jan 1, Thanksgiving, Dec 25) Phone 242-7800. ¢¢

24. **Jim Reeves Museum.** 1023 Joyce Lane. Housed in one of the city's oldest and most distinguished houses is a collection that chronicles the life and music of "Gentleman" Jim Reeves; contains many personal items. (Daily; closed Jan 1, Thanksgiving, Dec 25) Phone 226-2065. ¢¢

25. **House of Cash.** 20 mi N via I-65, 700 Johnny Cash Pkwy, in Hendersonville. Museum with original Remington bronzes, antique Colt pistols, letter written by Andrew Jackson; Cash's personal memorabilia. (Apr–Oct, daily exc Sun) Phone 824-5110. ¢¢¢

26. **Vanderbilt University** (1873). (9,700 students) West End Ave & 21st Ave S. The 330-acre campus features 19th- and 20th-century architectural styles. The Fine Arts Building has a permanent collection supplemented by traveling exhibits. Blair School of Music offers regular concerts. For campus tours (all yr) phone 322-7771.

27. **Fisk University** (1866). (900 students) 17th Ave N. A National Historic District with Jubilee Hall, a historic landmark. Carl Van Vechten Art Gallery houses Stieglitz Collection of modern art and African art. Phone 329-8710. Gallery ¢¢

28. **Boat trips.**

Belle Carol Riverboats: *Music City Queen* or *Captain Ann.* Boarding at Riverfront Park Dock, just off Broadway near Fort Nashborough. Daytime sightseeing cruises on the Cumberland River. Late-night party cruises. Dinner-entertainment cruises by reservation. For information, reservations phone 244-3430. Daytime sightseeing cruise ¢¢¢

General Jackson. A 300-foot paddle wheel showboat on Cumberland River highlights a musical stage show in its Victorian Theater. Two-hour day cruises offer entertainment and optional food service; three-hour night cruises offer entertainment and dinner. (All yr; addl cruises in summer) For schedule and departure times, contact Customer Service, 2802 Opryland Dr, 37214; 889-6611. ¢¢¢¢¢

29. **J. Percy Priest Lake.** 11 mi E off I-40. Waterskiing; fishing; boating (ramps, commercial boat docks). Picnicking. Tent & trailer sites (fee). Visitor center near dam (Mon–Fri). Some areas closed Nov–Mar. Phone 889-1975.

30. **Old Hickory Lake.** 15 mi NE via US 31E, near Hendersonville. Several recreation areas around reservoir have swimming; fishing; boating (commercial docks). Hiking, archery. Picnicking. Tent & trailer sites (fee). (All yr; some areas closed mid-Sept–mid-Apr) Phone 822-4846 or 847-2395.

31. **Cheatham Lake, Lock and Dam.** 30 mi NW on TN 12, near Ashland City. Some recreation areas have swimming; fishing; boating (commercial docks). Camping (fee; electricity addl); also free primitive camping area. Some areas closed Nov–Mar. Fees for some areas. Phone 792-5697 or 254-3734.

32. **Radnor Lake State Natural Area.** 7 mi S on US 31, then 1½ mi W on Otter Creek Rd. A 1,058-acre environmental preserve with an 85-acre lake. Provides scenic, biological and geological areas for hiking and nature study. (Daily) Phone 373-3467. **Free.**

33. **Gray Line bus tours.** Contact 3250 Dickerson Rd, Suite 300, 37207; 227-2270 or 800/251-1864.

Annual Events

Running of the Iroquois Memorial Steeplechase. Old Hickory Blvd at entrance to Percy Warner Park. Natural amphitheater seats 100,000. Phone 322-7450. 2nd Sat May.

Music festivals. Nashville is host to many festivals, including Summer Lights (late May–early June), the International Country Music Fan Fair with its Grand Master Old-Time Fiddling Championship (1st full wk June) and the National Quartet Convention (late Sept).

Tennessee State Fair. Fairgrounds, Wedgewood Ave & Rains. Contact Box 40208-Melrose Station, 37204; 862-8980. Late Sept.

Longhorn Rodeo. Municipal Auditorium. Professional cowboys compete for world championship points. Phone 876-1016. Nov.

Nashville's Country Holidays. Citywide. More than 60 events examine the holiday celebrations of country, antebellum and international cultures. Phone 259-4700. Nov–Jan 1.

Additional Visitor Information

The Nashville Area Chamber of Commerce, 161 4th Ave N, 37219, has maps, brochures, lists of tour companies and calendar of events; phone 259-4700. Advance reservations are strongly advised for the summer season (mid-May–mid-Sept) and all weekends. The Nashville Tourist Information center, I-65 & James Robertson Pkwy, exit 85 has area information; phone 259-4747.

(See Franklin, Lebanon, Murfreesboro)

City Neighborhoods

Many of the restaurants, unrated dining establishments and some lodgings listed under Nashville include neighborhoods as well as exact street addresses. Geographic descriptions of these areas are given, followed by a table of restaurants arranged by neighborhood.

Downtown: South of Harrison St, west of I-24/65, north of McGavock St and east of 10th Ave N. **South of Downtown:** South of McGavock St. **East of Downtown:** East of I-24/I-65. **West of Downtown:** West of I-40.

Music Row: Area includes 16th Ave S from West End Ave to Demonbreun St; Music Square E from South St to Demonbreun St; Music Square W from South St to Division St; and Division and Demonbreun Sts from 18th Ave S to I-40.

Opryland Area: South of McGavock Pike, west of Briley Pkwy (TN 155) and north and east of the Cumberland River.

NASHVILLE RESTAURANTS
BY NEIGHBORHOOD AREAS

(For full description, see alphabetical listings under Restaurants)

DOWNTOWN

Arthur's (Union Station Hotel). 1001 Broadway

Captain's Table. 313½ Church St

Gerst Haus. 228 Woodland St

Jamaica. 1901 Broadway

Mario's. 2005 Broadway

The Merchants. 401 Broadway

Old Spaghetti Factory. 160 2nd Ave N

Prime Cut Steakhouse. 170 2nd Ave N

Stock-Yard. 901 2nd Ave N

Towne House Tea Room & Restaurant. 165 8th Ave N

SOUTH OF DOWNTOWN

Belle Meade Brasserie. 101 Page Rd

Trapper's. 902 Murfreesboro Rd

EAST OF DOWNTOWN

New Orleans Manor. 1400 Murfreesboro Rd

101st Airborne. 1362 A Murfreesboro Rd

WEST OF DOWNTOWN

Applebee's. 2400 Elliston Place

Belle Meade Buffet Cafeteria. 4534 Harding Rd

F Scott's. 2220 Bandywood Dr

Golden Dragon. 81 White Bridge Rd

J Alexander's. 73 White Bridge Rd

Jimmy Kelly's. 217 Louise Ave

Sperry's. 5109 Harding Rd

Valentino's. 1907 West End Ave

MUSIC ROW

Toucan. 26 Music Square East

OPRYLAND AREA

Cock of the Walk. 2624 Music Valley Dr

Note: When a listing is located in a town that does not have its own city heading, it will appear under the city nearest to its location. In these cases, the address and town appear in parenthesis immediately following the name of the establishment.

Motels

(Rates may be higher during Fan Fair Week)

★**BUDGETEL INN.** *5612 Lenox Ave (37209), I-40 exit 204, west of downtown.* 615/353-0700; FAX 615/352-0361. 110 rms, 3 story. S $42.95–$55.95; D $49.95–$62.95; each addl $7; under 18 free; wkly rates; higher rates special events. Crib free. TV; cable. Pool. Complimentary continental bkfst. Complimentary coffee in rms. Restaurant adj 5–1 am. Ck-out noon. Meeting rms. Sundries. Cr cds: A, C, D, DS, MC, V.

✔★**BUDGETEL INN GOODLETTSVILLE.** *(120 Cartwright Court, Goodlettsville 37072) 14 mi N on I-65, at exit 97.* 615/851-1891; FAX 615/851-4513. 102 rms, 3 story. Apr–Oct: S $39.95–$45.95; D $40.95–$46.95; each addl $6; under 18 free; lower rates rest of yr. Crib free. Pet accepted, some restrictions. TV; cable. Complimentary continental bkfst, coffee. Restaurant nearby. Ck-out noon. Meeting rm. Valet serv. Sundries. Cr cds: A, C, D, DS, MC, V.

★★**CLUBHOUSE INN.** *2435 Atrium Way (37214), east of downtown.* 615/883-0500; FAX 615/889-4827. 135 rms, 3 story, 17 suites. Apr–Oct: S $66, D $76; each addl $10; suites $79; under 10 free; wknd rates; lower rates rest of yr. TV; cable. Heated pool; whirlpool. Complimentary full bkfst, coffee. Ck-out noon. Coin lndry. Meeting rms. Valet serv. Free airport transportation. Refrigerator, wet bar in suites. Balconies. Cr cds: A, C, D, DS, MC, V.

★★★**COURTYARD BY MARRIOTT-AIRPORT.** *2508 Elm Hill Pike (37214), near International Airport, east of downtown.* 615/883-9500; FAX 615/883-0172. 145 rms, 4 story. S, D $72–$82; suites $88–$98; wknd rates. Crib free. TV; cable. Pool. Complimentary coffee in rms. Restaurant 6:30 am–2 pm, 5–10 pm. Bar 4–11 pm. Ck-out noon. Coin lndry. Meeting rms. Valet serv. Sundries. Free airport transportation. Exercise equipt; weight machines, bicycles, whirlpool. Refrigerator avail. Some balconies. Cr cds: A, C, D, DS, MC, V.

✔★**DAYS INN RIVERGATE.** *(809 Wren Rd, Goodlettsville 37072) 12 mi N on I-65, Rivergate exit 96.* 615/859-1771. 45 units, 3 story, 25 suites. No elvtr. May–Aug: S, D $35–$55; suites $39.95–$75; each addl $5; under 12 free; wkly rates; lower rates rest of yr. Pet accepted, some restrictions. TV; cable. Complimentary continental bkfst, coffee. Restaurant nearby. Ck-out 11 am. Cr cds: A, C, D, DS, MC, V.

★★**ECONO LODGE OPRYLAND.** *2460 Music Valley Dr (37214), in Opryland Area.* 615/889-0090. 86 rms, 3 story. May–Sept: S, D $59.95; each addl $5; under 18 free; lower rates rest of yr. Crib free. Pet accepted, some restrictions. TV; cable. Pool. Complimentary coffee in lobby. Restaurant nearby. Ck-out noon. Gift shop. Cr cds: A, C, D, DS, MC, V.

★**FIDDLERS INN-NORTH.** *2410 Music Valley Dr (37214), in Opryland Area.* 615/885-1440. 202 rms, 2–3 story. Apr–Oct: S $34–$45; D $45–$65; each addl $5; varied lower rates rest of yr. Crib $5. TV. Pool. Restaurant adj 6:30 am–10 pm. Ck-out 11 am. Coin lndry. Sundries. Trailer park. Cr cds: A, DS, MC, V.

★★**HAMPTON INN-BRENTWOOD.** *(5630 Franklin Pike Circle, Brentwood 37027) S on I-65, exit 74B.* 615/373-2212; FAX 615/373-2212, ext 162. 114 air-cooled rms, 5 story. S $49–$59; D $57–$67; under 18 free; wkly rates. Crib free. TV; cable. Complimentary continental bkfst, coffee in lobby. Restaurant adj 6 am–midnight. Ck-out noon. Meeting rms. Cr cds: A, C, D, DS, ER, MC, V.

✔ ★★**HoJo INN.** 323 Harding Place (37211), I-24E exit 56, south of downtown. 615/834-0570; FAX 615/831-2831. 112 rms, 14 suites, 10 kits. May–Sept: S $39; D $45; each addl $3; suites $42–$49; kit. units $49–$55; under 18 free; lower rates rest of yr. Crib free. Pet accepted, some restrictions; $10. TV; cable. Pool. Complimentary continental bkfst, coffee. Restaurant nearby. Ck-out noon. Meeting rm. Free airport transportation. Cr cds: A, C, D, DS, MC, V.

D ⚑ ≈ ⊘ ⊙ SC

★★**LA QUINTA.** 2001 Metrocenter Blvd (37228), north of downtown. 615/259-2130; FAX 615/242-2650. 121 rms, 2 story. S $47–$59; D $53–$65; each addl $6; under 18 free. Crib free. TV; cable. Pool. Complimentary continental bkfst, coffee in lobby. Restaurant adj open 24 hrs. Ck-out noon. Valet serv. Cr cds: A, D, DS, MC, V.

D ≈ ⊘ ⊙ SC

✔ ★★**PEAR TREE INN-NORTH.** 2306 Brick Church Pike (37207), I-65 exit 87B, north of downtown. 615/226-9560. 95 rms, 4 story. S $42.95–$48.95; D $48.95–$56.95; each addl $6; under 18 free. Crib free. Pet accepted. TV; cable. Pool. Complimentary continental bkfst. Restaurant adj open 24 hrs. Ck-out noon. Cr cds: A, C, D, DS, MC, V.

D ⚑ ≈ ⊘ ⊙ SC

★★**RAMADA INN SUITES.** 2425 Atrium Way (37214), near International Airport, east of downtown. 615/883-5201; FAX 615/883-5594. 120 suites, 3 story. S, D $56–$106; each addl $6; under 16 free. Crib free. Pet accepted, some restrictions; $6. TV; cable. Pool; whirlpool. Coffee in rms. Complimentary continental bkfst 6:30–8:30 am. Ck-out noon. Coin lndry. Meeting rms. Valet serv. Airport transportation. Refrigerators. Cr cds: A, C, D, DS, MC, V, JCB.

D ⚑ ≈ ✕ ⊘ ⊙ SC

✔ ★**RED ROOF INN-SOUTH.** 4271 Sidco Dr (37204), at jct I-65 & Harding Pl, south of downtown. 615/832-0093; FAX 615/832-0097. 85 rms, 3 story. Mar–Sept: S $30–$36; D $38–$48; each addl $8; under 18 free; lower rates rest of yr. Crib free. Pet accepted. TV; cable. Complimentary coffee in lobby. Restaurant nearby. Ck-out 11 am. Cr cds: A, C, D, DS, MC, V.

D ⚑ ⊘ ⊙

★★**RESIDENCE INN BY MARRIOTT.** 2300 Elm Hill Pike (37214), near International Airport, eastof downtown. 615/889-9600; FAX 615/871-4970. 168 kit. suites, 2 story. Suites: 1-bedrm studio $86–$106; 2-bedrm penthouse $116–$126; under 12 free. TV; cable. Pool; whirlpool. Complimentary continental bkfst. Ck-out noon. Coin lndry. Meeting rms. Airport transportation. Refrigerators; many fireplaces. Balconies. Cr cds: A, C, D, DS, MC, V.

D ≈ ✕ ⊘ ⊙ SC

★**SHONEY'S INN NORTH.** (100 Northcreek Blvd, Goodlettsville 37072) 13 mi N on I-65, exit 97. 615/851-1067; res: 800/222-2222; FAX 615/851-6069. 111 rms, 3 story. S $41–$45; D $45–$59; each addl $6; under 17 free. Crib free. TV; cable. Pool. Complimentary coffee in lobby. Restaurant adj 6 am–midnight; Fri & Sat to 2 am. Ck-out noon. Meeting rms. Cr cds: A, C, D, DS, ER, MC, V.

D ≈ ⊘ ⊙ SC

★**SUPER 8.** 412 Robertson Ave (37209), I-40 exit 204, west of downtown. 615/356-0888; FAX 615/356-0888, ext 118. 73 rms, 3 story. June–July: S $41.80–$48.80; D $48.88–$54.88; each addl $5; suites $58.88–$68.88; under 12 free; wkly rates; lower rates rest of yr. Crib free. Pet accepted. TV; cable. Complimentary continental bkfst, coffee. Restaurant adj open 24 hrs. Ck-out 11 am. Meeting rm. Cr cds: A, C, D, DS, MC, V.

D ⚑ ⊘ ⊙ SC

✔ ★**TRAVELERS REST INN.** (107 Franklin Rd, Brentwood 37027) 1 blk W of I-65 exits 74 B, Brentwood, Old Hickory Blvd. 615/373-3033; res: 800/852-0618. 35 rms, 1–2 story. 2 kits. S $33–$40; D $45–$52; each addl $4; under 18 free. Crib $2. TV; cable. Pool; wading

pool. Complimentary coffee in rms. Restaurant nearby. Ck-out noon. Coin lndry. Some refrigerators. Picnic table. Cr cds: A, C, D, DS, MC, V.

≈ ⊘ ⊙ SC

Motor Hotels

★★**AMERISUITES.** 220 Rudy's Circle (37214), in Opryland Area. 615/872-0422; FAX 615/872-9283. 125 suites, 5 story. June–mid-Sept: S, D $76–$95; each addl $6; under 18 free; higher rates special events; lower rates rest of yr. Crib free. TV; cable, in-rm movies. Pool. Complimentary continental bkfst. Complimentary coffee in rms. Restaurant nearby. Ck-out 11 am. Coin lndry. Meeting rms. Bellhops. Valet serv. Free airport, Opryland Hotel transportation. Refrigerators. Cr cds: A, C, D, DS, ER, MC, V.

D ≈ ⊘ ⊙ SC

★**HAMPTON INN-NORTH.** 2407 Brick Church Pike (37207), I-65 exit 87B, north of downtown. 615/226-3300; FAX 615/226-0170. 125 rms, 5 story. S, D $47–$63; under 18 free; higher rates special events. Crib free. Pet accepted, some restrictions. TV; cable. Pool. Continental bkfst. Restaurant adj 6 am–10 pm. Ck-out noon. Meeting rms. Valet serv. Exercise equipt; weights, bicycles. Game rm. Cr cds: A, C, D, DS, MC, V.

D ⚑ ≈ 🏃 ⊘ ⊙ SC

★★**HILTON SUITES-BRENTWOOD.** (9000 Overlook Blvd, Brentwood 37027) S on I-65, exit 74B. 615/370-0111; FAX 615/370-0272. 203 suites, 4 story. S $99; D $109; each addl $10; family rates. Crib free. Pet accepted, some restrictions. TV; cable. Indoor pool. Coffee in rms. Complimentary full bkfst. Restaurant 6–9:30 am, 11:30 am–1:30 pm, 5–10 pm; Sat, Sun 7–11 am, 5–10 pm. Rm serv from 5 pm. Bar 4 pm–midnight. Ck-out noon. Free lndry facilities. Meeting rms. Gift shop. Exercise equipt; weight machine, bicycles, whirlpool. Rec rm. Refrigerators, wet bars. Balconies. Cr cds: A, C, D, DS, ER, MC, V, JCB.

D ⚑ ≈ 🏃 ⊘ ⊙

★★**HOLIDAY INN EXPRESS.** 1111 Airport Center Dr (37214), near International Airport, east of downtown. 615/883-1366; FAX 615/889-6867. 206 rms, 3 story. Apr–Oct: S $58; D $66; each addl $8; under 18 free; lower rates rest of yr. Crib free. TV; cable. Pool. Complimentary continental bkfst, coffee. Restaurant nearby. Ck-out noon. Meeting rms. Bellhops. Free airport transportation. Health club privileges. Some balconies. Cr cds: A, C, D, DS, MC, V, JCB.

D ≈ ✕ ⊘ ⊙ SC

★★**HOLIDAY INN EXPRESS-NORTH.** 2401 Brick Church Pike (37207), I-65 exit 87B, north of downtown. 615/226-4600; FAX 615/228-6412. 172 rms, 6 story. Apr–Oct: S $40–$58; D $52–$68; under 18 free; higher rates special events; some lower rates rest of yr. Crib free. TV; cable. Pool. Restaurant 6 am–10 pm; Fri, Sat to 11 pm. Ck-out noon. Coin lndry. Meeting rms. Valet serv. Sundries. Exercise equipt; weights, bicycles, whirlpool, sauna. Cr cds: A, C, D, DS, MC, V.

D ≈ 🏃 ⊘ ⊙ SC

★**MEDCENTER INN.** 1909 Hayes St (37203), downtown. 615/329-1000; res: 800/777-4904; FAX 615/329-1000, ext 107. 107 rms, 7 story. Mar–June: S, D $48–$69; each addl $7; suites $75–$82; under 18 free; varied lower rates rest of yr. Crib free. TV; cable. Complimentary continental bkfst, coffee. Restaurant nearby. Ck-out noon. Coin lndry. Meeting rm. Refrigerators, wet bars. Cr cds: A, C, D, DS, MC, V.

D ⊘ ⊙ SC

✔ ★★**QUALITY INN EXECUTIVE PLAZA.** 823 Murfreesboro Rd (37013), south of downtown. 615/367-1234. 150 air-cooled rms, 4 story. Mar–mid-Nov: S $37–$47; D $43–$53; each addl $6; under 18 free; lower rates rest of yr. Crib avail. TV; cable. Pool. Restaurant 6 am–2 pm. Bar. Ck-out noon. Coin lndry. Meeting rms. Free airport transportation. Exercise equipt; weight machine, bicycles. Near airport. Cr cds: A, C, D, DS, ER, MC, V, JCB.

D ≈ 🏃 ⊘ ⊙ SC

★★QUALITY INN HALL OF FAME. *1407 Division St (37203), in Music Row.* 615/242-1631; FAX 615/244-9519. 103 rms, 5 story. S, D $55–$65; each addl $6; suites $70–$100; under 16 free. Crib free. TV; cable. Pool. Restaurant 7 am–noon, 5–9 pm. Bar 4 pm–1 am; entertainment, dancing exc Sun. Ck-out noon. Meeting rms. Valet serv. Adj to Country Music Hall of Fame. Cr cds: A, C, D, DS, MC, V, JCB.

D ≅ ⊜ ◎ SC

★★RAMADA INN. *2401 Music Valley Dr (37214), opp Opryland Area.* 615/889-0800; FAX 615/883-1230. 306 rms, 3 story. June–Oct: S, D $82–$98; each addl $8; suites $110–$140; under 18 free; lower rates rest of yr. TV; cable. Heated pool; wading pool, whirlpool, sauna. Restaurant 6 am–10 pm. Rm serv. Bar noon–1 am. Ck-out noon. Meeting rms. Bellhops. Valet serv. Sundries. Gift shop. Airport, Opryland Hotel transportation. Game rm. Cr cds: A, C, D, DS, MC, V.

D ≅ ⊜ ◎ SC

★SHONEY'S INN. *2420 Music Valley Dr (37214), in Opryland Area.* 615/885-4030; res: 800/222-2222; FAX 615/391-0632. 185 rms, 5 story. June–Aug: S $72–$79; D $82–$89; each addl $6; suites $105; under 18 free; higher rates special events; varied rates rest of yr. TV; cable. Indoor pool; whirlpool. Complimentary coffee in rms. Restaurant adj 6–11 am. Bar 4–11 pm. Ck-out 11 am. Meeting rms. Valet serv. Sundries. Gift shop. Free garage parking. Free airport transportation. Cr cds: A, C, D, DS, ER, MC, V.

D ≅ ⊜ ◎ SC

✔★WILSON INN. *600 Ermac Dr (37214), east of downtown.* 615/889-4466; res: 800/333-9457. 110 rms, 5 story, 30 suites. S, D $34.95–$54.95; each addl $5; suites $44.95–$54.95; under 19 free. Crib free. TV; cable. Complimentary continental bkfst, coffee. Restaurant adj open 24 hrs. Ck-out noon. Meeting rms. Refrigerators; wet bar in suites. Cr cds: A, C, D, DS, MC, V.

D ⊜ ◎ SC

Hotels

✔★★CLUBHOUSE INN CONFERENCE CENTER. *920 Broadway (37203), downtown.* 615/244-0150; FAX 615/244-0445. 285 rms, 8 story. S $59–$79; D $69–$89; each addl $10; suites $99–$129; under 12 free; wkend rates. Crib free. TV; cable. Pool. Complimentary full bkfst buffet. Restaurant 5:30–8:30 pm. Ck-out noon. Convention facilities. Gift shop. Free garage parking. Exercise equipt: bicycles, stair machine. Cr cds: A, C, D, DS, MC, V.

D ≅ ✗ ⊜ ◎ SC

★★DOUBLETREE. *315 Fourth Ave N (37219), downtown.* 615/244-8200; FAX 615/747-4815. 337 rms, 9 story. S $99–$129; D $114–$144; each addl $15; suites $125–$550; under 18 free; wkend rates. Crib free. Garage $6. TV; cable. Indoor pool. Restaurant 6:30 am–10:30 pm. Bar 4 pm–1 am. Ck-out noon. Meeting rms. Gift shop. Exercise equipt; weights, bicycles, sauna. *LUXURY LEVEL:* 35 rms, 5 suites. S $124; D $144; suites $250–$525. Private lounge. Wet bar in suites.
Cr cds: A, C, D, DS, ER, MC, V.

D ≅ ✗ ⊜ ◎ SC

★★EMBASSY SUITES. *10 Century Blvd (37214), near International Airport, east of downtown.* 615/871-0033; FAX 615/883-9245. 294 suites, 9 story. Suites $109–$139; each addl $10; under 17 free; wkend plans. Crib free. Pet accepted, some restrictions. TV; cable. Indoor pool. Supervised child's activities. Complimentary full bkfst. Restaurant 6:30–9:30 am, 11 am–2:30 pm, 5–10 pm; Fri, Sat to 11 pm. Rm serv 11:30 am–11 pm. Bar 4 pm–midnight. Ck-out noon. Convention facilities. Concierge. Gift shop. Free airport transportation. Exercise equipt; weights, bicycles, whirlpool, sauna. Game rm. Refrigerators, wet bars. Atrium. Cr cds: A, C, D, DS, MC, V, JCB.

D ≅ ✗ ⊜ ◎ SC

★★GUEST QUARTERS. *2424 Atrium Way (37214), near International Airport, east of downtown.* 615/889-8889; FAX 615/883-7779. 138 suites, 3 story. Mar–Nov: S $119–$175; D $139–$175; each

addl $20; under 18 free; lower rates rest of yr. Crib free. TV; cable. Indoor/outdoor pool; poolside serv. Complimentary coffee in rms. Restaurant 6:30 am–10 pm. Bar 11 am–midnight. Ck-out 11 am. Meeting rms. Free airport transportation. Exercise equipt; weights, bicycles. Game rm. Refrigerators. Some private patios, balconies. Cr cds: A, C, D, DS, MC, V.

D ≅ ✗ ⊜ ◎ SC

★★THE HERMITAGE. *231 6th Ave N (37219), downtown.* 615/244-3121; res: 800/251-1908 (exc TN), 800/342-1816 (TN); FAX 615/254-6909. 112 suites, 9 story. 1-bedrm suites $80–$107; 2-bedrm suites $125–$160; each addl $10; wknd rates. Valet parking $6.50/day. Pet accepted. TV; cable. Complimentary full bkfst. Dining rm 6:30 am–9 pm. Bars 11 am–midnight. Ck-out noon. Meeting rms. Health club privileges. Bathrm phones, refrigerators, wet bars. Hotel built in 1910 as a tribute to Beaux Arts Classicism; fully restored to original elegance. Cr cds: A, C, D, DS, ER, MC, V, JCB.

D ⊘ ⊜ ◎ SC

★★★HOLIDAY INN CROWNE PLAZA. *623 Union St (37219), opp capitol, downtown.* 615/259-2000; FAX 615/742-6056. 476 rms, 28 story. S, D $124–$134; each addl $15; under 18 free; wkend rates. Crib free. Garage $5; valet parking $7. TV; cable. Indoor pool. Restaurant 6:30 am–midnight. Bars 3 pm–2 am. Ck-out noon. Meeting rms. Concierge. Gift shop. Airport transportation. Exercise equipt; bicycle, treadmill. *LUXURY LEVEL: CONCIERGE LEVEL.* 81 rms, 10 suites. S, D $134–$144; suites $250–$650. Private lounge. Complimentary continental bkfst, refreshments.
Cr cds: A, C, D, DS, ER, MC, V, JCB.

D ≅ ✗ ⊜ ◎ SC

★★★LOEWS VANDERBILT PLAZA. *2100 West End Ave (37203), downtown.* 615/320-1700; FAX 615/320-5019. 340 rms, 12 story. S $115–$135; D $130–$155; each addl $20; suites $325–$600; under 18 free. Crib free. Garage $5; valet parking $7. TV; cable. Restaurants 6 am–10 pm. Rm serv to midnight; Fri–Sun to 1 am. Bar 3 pm–1 am; entertainment exc Sun. Ck-out noon. Convention facilities. Concierge. Shopping arcade. Barber, beauty shop. Golf privileges. Minibars. *LUXURY LEVEL: PLAZA LEVEL.* 44 rms, 4 suites, 2 floors. S $140; D $160. Private lounge. Complimentary continental bkfst, refreshments.
Cr cds: A, C, D, DS, MC, V, JCB.

D ⊠ ⊜ ◎

★★★MARRIOTT. *600 Marriott Dr (37214), east of downtown.* 615/889-9300; FAX 615/889-9315. 399 rms, 18 story. S $123–$130; D $145–$132; suites $175–$450; under 17 free; wkend plans. TV; cable. Indoor/outdoor pool; poolside serv, lifeguard. Restaurant 6 am–10:30 pm, snacks to midnight. Bar 11–2 am. Ck-out noon. Lndry facilities. Convention facilities. Free parking. Free airport transportation. Lighted tennis. Exercise equipt; weight machines, bicycles, whirlpool, sauna. Picnic tables, grills. Near Percy Priest Lake. *LUXURY LEVEL: CONCIERGE LEVEL.* 38 rms, 2 floors. S $129; D $149. Concierge. Private lounge, honor bar. Complimentary continental bkfst, refreshments, newspapers.
Cr cds: A, C, D, DS, ER, MC, V, JCB.

D ⊘ ≅ ✗ ⊜ ◎ SC

★★★OPRYLAND HOTEL. *2800 Opryland Dr (37214), 5 mi NE of jct I-40 & Briley Pkwy, in Opryland Area.* 615/889-1000; FAX 615/871-7741. 1,891 rms, 5 story. S, D $169–$199; each addl $15; suites $235–$2,000; under 12 free. Crib free. Valet parking $7. TV; cable. 3 heated pools; wading pools, poolside serv, lifeguard. Supervised child's activities. 7 restaurants 6:30–1 am. Bars 11–2 am; entertainment, dancing. Ck-out 11 am. Convention facilities. Shopping arcades. Barber, beauty shop. Airport, Opryland, Grand Ole Opry transportation. Lighted tennis, pro. 18-hole golf course, greens fee $50. Exercise rm; instructor, weights, bicycles. Some refrigerators. Bathrm phone in suites. Some balconies overlooking garden conservatory and cascades. Showboat cruises avail. Cr cds: A, C, D, DS, MC, V.

D ⊘ ⊠ ≅ ✗ ⊜ ◎

★★★REGAL MAXWELL HOUSE. *2025 Metrocenter Blvd (37228), north of downtown.* 615/259-4343; FAX 615/259-4343, ext

7127. 289 rms, 10 story. S $94–$114; D $104–$124; each addl $10; suites $165–$250; under 17 free; wknd plans. Crib free. Pet accepted, some restrictions; $100. TV; cable. Pool. Restaurants 6:30 am–10 pm. Bar 11 am–midnight. Ck-out noon. Meeting rms. Gift shop. Lighted tennis. Exercise equipt; weight machine, bicycles, whirlpool, sauna, steam rm. *LUXURY LEVEL:* SUMMIT CLUB. 32 rms, 4 suites. S $104–$124; D $114–$134; suites $175–$260. Concierge. Private lounge. Wet bar in suites. Complimentary bkfst, refreshments, newspaper.
Cr cds: A, C, D, DS, ER, MC, V, JCB.

★RODEWAY INN MUSIC CITY. *797 Briley Pkwy (37217), I-40 exit 215, east of downtown.* 615/361-5900; FAX 615/367-0339. 200 rms, 11 story. Apr–Oct: S $48–$56; D $54–$60; each addl $6; suites $97–$173; under 17 free; lower rates rest of yr. Crib free. Pet accepted, some restrictions. TV; cable. Pool. Restaurant 6 am–10 pm. Bars 4 pm–midnight, Fri & Sat to 2 am; entertainment. Ck-out noon. Meeting rms. Free airport transportation. Some steam baths; wet bar in suites. Cr cds: A, C, D, DS, MC, V.

★★SHERATON-MUSIC CITY. *777 McGavock Pike (37214), near International Airport, east of downtown.* 615/885-2200; FAX 615/871-0926. 412 rms, 4 story. S $125–$140; D $135–$150; each addl $15; suites $150–$550; under 17 free; wknd rates. Pet accepted. TV; cable. Indoor/outdoor pools; wading pool, poolside serv. Restaurant 6 am–11 pm. Rm serv 24 hrs. Bar 11–3 am; entertainment, dancing. Ck-out 1 pm. Convention facilities. Concierge. Gift shop. Free airport transportation. Lighted tennis. Golf privileges. Exercise rm; instructor, weight machine, bicycles, whirlpool, sauna. Game rm. Bathrm phones; some refrigerators. Private balconies. On 23 landscaped acres on top of hill. Semiformal decor. Cr cds: A, C, D, DS, ER, MC, V, JCB.

★★STOUFFER. *611 Commerce St (37203), downtown.* 615/255-8400; FAX 615/255-8163. 673 rms, 25 story. S $144–$164; D $164–$184; each addl $20; suites $254–$1,108; under 18 free; wkend packages. Crib free. Garage $4; valet parking $10.54. Pet accepted, some restrictions. TV; cable, in-rm movies avail. Indoor pool; poolside serv. Restaurant 6 am–10 pm; Fri, Sat to 11 pm. Rm serv 24 hrs. Bar 11–2 am; entertainment. Ck-out noon. Convention facilities. Shopping arcade. Concierge. Airport transportation. Exercise rm; instructor, weights, bicycles, whirlpool, sauna. Some bathrm phones, refrigerators. *LUXURY LEVEL:* CLUB FLOOR. 58 rms, 5 suites, 2 floors. S $164–$184; D $184–$204; suites $294–$1,108. Private lounge. Wet bar in suites. Complimentary continental bkfst, refreshments. Cr cds: A, C, D, DS, ER, MC, V, JCB.

★★UNION STATION. *1001 Broadway (37203), downtown.* 615/726-1001; res: 800/331-2123; FAX 615/248-3554. 125 rms, 7 story, 14 suites. S $85–$150; D $105–$170; each addl $10; suites $135–$400; under 13 free; wknd rates. Crib free. Valet parking $7. TV; cable. Pool privileges. Restaurant 6:30 am–11 pm (also see ARTHUR'S). Bar 11 am–11 pm; entertainment. Ck-out noon. Concierge. Gift shop. Airport transportation. Tennis, 18-hole golf privileges. Health club privileges. In renovated historic train station (1897); stained-glass roof. Cr cds: A, C, D, DS, MC, V.

Restaurants

★★★ARTHUR'S. *(See Union Station Hotel)* 615/255-1494. Hrs: 5:30–10:30 pm; Fri & Sat to 11 pm; Sun 5:30–9 pm; Sun brunch 11:45 am–2:30 pm. Closed major hols. Res accepted. Continental menu. Bar 5 pm–1 am. Wine cellar. Table d'hôte: dinner $45. Specializes in seafood, lamb, flaming desserts. Own baking. Menu recited; printed menu avail on request; menu changes wkly. Valet parking. Located in

historic train station (1897) that has been converted into an Old World-style hotel. Elegant dining. Jacket. Cr cds: A, C, D, DS, MC, V.

★★BELLE MEADE BRASSERIE. *101 Page Rd, south of downtown.* 601/356-5450. Hrs: 5:30–10 pm; Fri & Sat to 11 pm. Closed Sun; some major hols. Res accepted. French, Amer menu. Bar. A la carte entrees: dinner $7.95–$22. Specializes in seafood, poultry, pasta. Parking. Outdoor dining. Contemporary decor; original art. Cr cds: A, MC, V.

★CAPTAIN'S TABLE. *313½ Church St, in Printer's Alley, downtown.* 615/256-3353. Hrs: 5:30–11:30 pm. Closed Sun; Jan 1, July 4, Dec 25. Res accepted. Bar 4 pm–12:30 am. Semi-a la carte: dinner $10.95–$17.95. Specializes in steak, lobster. Country singer exc Sun. Atmosphere of ship captain's quarters. Cr cds: A, C, D, MC, V.

✔COCK OF THE WALK. *2624 Music Valley Dr, in Opryland Area.* 615/889-1930. Hrs: 5–9 pm; Fri, Sat to 10 pm. Closed Thanksgiving, Dec 24, 25; also Super Bowl Sun. Res accepted. Bar. Semi-a la carte: dinner $7.75–$11.50. Child's meals. Specializes in catfish, fried dill pickles. Parking. Split level dining in rustic atmosphere. Cr cds: A, MC, V.

★★★F SCOTT'S. *2220 Bandywood Dr, west of downtown.* 615/269-5861. Hrs: 11 am–2:30 pm, 5:30–10 pm; Sun brunch 11:30 am–2:30 pm. Closed most major hols. Res accepted. Bar. Wine list. A la carte entrees: lunch $5–$14, dinner $12–$24. Sun brunch $5–$14. Child's meals. Specializes in seafood, veal, lamb. Pianist Wed–Sat. Parking. Art deco decor. Cr cds: A, D, DS, MC, V.

✔★★GERST HAUS. *228 Woodland St, downtown.* 615/256-9760. Hrs: 11 am–9 pm; Fri & Sat to 10 pm; Sun 3–9 pm. Closed Jan 1, Thanksgiving, Dec 25. Res accepted Mon–Fri. German, Amer menu. Bar. Semi-a la carte: lunch, dinner $4.95–$12.95. Specialties: Wienerschnitzel, pork loin, fresh oyster roll. German band Sat & Sun. Parking. Beer hall atmosphere. Bavarian decor; antiques. Family-owned. No cr cds accepted.

✔★★GOLDEN DRAGON. *81 White Bridge Rd, west of downtown.* 615/356-1110. Hrs: 11 am–10 pm. Chinese menu. Bar. Semi-a la carte: lunch $4.25–$7.50, dinner $6.25–$14.95. Child's meals. Specializes in Hunan, Szechwan and Shanghai dishes. Parking. Chinese decor; lanterns, waterfall. Cr cds: A, MC, V.

★★J ALEXANDER'S. *73 White Bridge Rd, west of downtown.* 615/352-0981. Hrs: 11 am–10 pm; Fri, Sat to midnight. Closed Thanksgiving, Dec 25. Bar. Semi-a la carte: lunch, dinner $5–$15.95. Child's meals. Specializes in prime rib, fresh seafood, salads. Parking. Glass window permits diners to observe salad preparation area. Cr cds: A, DS, MC, V.

✔★JAMAICA. *1901 Broadway, downtown.* 615/321-5191. Hrs: 11 am–11 pm; Sun 5–11 pm. Closed most major hols. Res accepted. Caribbean, Amer menu. Bar to 1 am. Semi-a la carte: lunch, dinner $4.75–$14.75. Child's meals. Specializes in traditional Jamaican dishes, seafood. Parking. Relaxed West Indies atmosphere. Cr cds: A, C, D, DS, MC, V.

★★JIMMY KELLY'S. *217 Louise Ave, west of downtown.* 615/329-4349. Hrs: 5 pm–midnight. Closed Sun; some major hols. Res accepted. Bar. Semi-a la carte: dinner $11–$24. Child's meals. Specializes in hand-cut aged beef. Valet parking. In renovated Victorian mansion (1911). Family-owned. Cr cds: A, C, D, MC, V.

★ ★ ★ MARIO'S. *2005 Broadway, downtown. 615/327-3232.* Hrs: 5:30–10:30 pm. Closed Sun; major hols. Res accepted. Northern Italian, continental menu. Bar. Two wine cellars. A la carte entrees: dinner $19–$27. Specializes in pastas, fresh seafood, veal. Theater dining rm. Parking. Wine display; memorabilia of guests and awards. Family-owned. Cr cds: A, C, D, DS, MC, V.

D

★ ★ ★ THE MERCHANTS. *401 Broadway, downtown. 615/254-1892.* Hrs: 11 am–2 pm, 5–10 pm; Fri to 11 pm; Sat 5–11 pm; Sun 5–10 pm. Closed Jan 1, Thanksgiving, Dec 25. Res accepted. Bar. Wine cellar. A la carte entrees: lunch $4.95–$10.95, dinner $14.95–$19.95. Specializes in fresh grilled meats and seafood. Own baking. Pianist Mon–Sat. Valet parking. Outdoor dining. In historic building; original wood floors; dining on 3 levels. Cr cds: A, C, D, MC, V.

D

★ ★ NEW ORLEANS MANOR. *1400 Murfreesboro Rd, east of downtown. 615/367-2777.* Hrs: 5:30–9 pm. Closed Sun, Mon; Jan 1, Thanksgiving, Dec 24, 25. Res accepted. Serv bar. Dinner buffet $26–$36. Child's meals. Specializes in seafood, lobster, prime rib. Salad bar. Parking. Scenic grounds; colonial-type mansion built in 1930. Cr cds: A, C, D, DS, MC, V.

D

✔ ★ OLD SPAGHETTI FACTORY. *160 2nd Ave N, downtown. 615/254-9010.* Hrs: 11:30 am–2 pm, 5–10 pm; Fri to 11 pm; Sat 4:30–11 pm; Sun 4–10 pm. Closed Thanksgiving, Dec 24–25. Bar. Semi-a la carte: lunch $3.25–$5.25. Complete meals: dinner $4.50–$8.95. Child's meals. Specializes in spaghetti with a variety of sauces. In converted 1869 warehouse; doorway arch from the Bank of London; antiques. Cr cds: DS, MC, V.

D

★ 101ST AIRBORNE. *1362 A Murfreesboro Rd, east of downtown. 615/361-4212.* Hrs: 11 am–2:30 pm, 5–10 pm; Sat 5–11 pm; Sun 5–10 pm; Sun brunch 10:30 am–2:30 pm. Closed Dec 25. Res accepted. Bar from 4 pm. Semi-a la carte: lunch $5.95–$8.95, dinner $13.95–$28.95. Sun brunch $12.95. Child's meals. Specializes in steak, seafood, prime rib. Parking. House dramatizes a headquarters operation for the 101st Airborne Division; World War II memorabilia. Cr cds: A, C, D, DS, MC, V.

D

★ PRIME CUT STEAKHOUSE. *170 2nd Ave N, downtown. 615/242-3083.* Hrs: 5–10 pm; Fri, Sat to 11 pm. Closed Thanksgiving, Dec 25. Res accepted. Bar from 4 pm. Semi-a la carte: dinner $14.95–$19.99. Child's meals. Specializes in steak, marinated chicken, fresh fish. Entertainment Fri, Sat. Option of cooking own steak. Cr cds: A, C, D, DS, MC, V.

D

★ ★ ★ SPERRY'S. *5109 Harding Rd, west of downtown. 615/353-0809.* Hrs: 5–11 pm; Sun, Mon to 10 pm; Fri, Sat to midnight. Closed major hols. Bar to 1 am. A la carte entrees: dinner $10.95–$24.95. Specializes in fresh seafood, steak. Salad bar. Own desserts, soups, sauces. Parking. Nautical and hunting decor. Cr cds: A, C, D, MC, V.

D

★ ★ STOCK-YARD. *901 2nd Ave N, downtown. 615/255-6464.* Hrs: 11 am–2 pm, 5–11 pm; Sat & Sun from 5 pm. Closed most major hols. Bars 7:30 pm–2 am. Semi-a la carte: lunch $5.25–$8.95, dinner $14.50–$29. Child's meals. Specializes in charcoal-grilled steak, fresh seafood, grilled chicken breast. Entertainment. Parking. Cr cds: A, D, DS, MC, V.

D

★ TOUCAN. *26 Music Square E (16th Ave), in Music Row. 615/726-0101.* Hrs: 11 am–8 pm; Fri to 10 pm. Closed Sat & Sun; most major hols. Res accepted. Bar. Semi-a la carte: lunch $5–$12, dinner $8–$18. Child's meals. Specializes in California-style cuisine, fresh

seafood. Valet parking. Veranda, balcony dining. Cr cds: A, C, D, DS, MC, V.

D

✔ ★ TRAPPER'S. *902 Murfreesboro Rd, south of downtown. 615/367-4448.* Hrs: 11 am–10 pm; Fri & Sat to 11 pm; early-bird dinner 4–6 pm. Closed Thanksgiving, Dec 25. Res accepted. Bar to 11 pm, Fri & Sat to midnight. Semi-a la carte: lunch $3.29–$8, dinner $6.95–$14.95. Child's meals. Specializes in steak, chicken. Parking. Informal dining in three areas. Cr cds: A, D, DS, MC, V.

★ ★ VALENTINO'S. *1907 West End Ave, west of downtown. 615/327-0148.* Hrs: 11 am–2 pm, 5–10 pm. Closed Sun; major hols. Res accepted. Northern Italian menu. Bar. Semi-a la carte: lunch $5.95–$9.95, dinner $9.95–$22.95. Specializes in chicken, seafood, pasta. Parking. Cr cds: A, C, D, DS, MC, V.

D

Unrated Dining Spots

APPLEBEE'S. *2400 Elliston Pl, west of downtown. 615/329-2306.* Hrs: 11 am–midnight; Fri, Sat to 1 am; Sun to 10 pm; Sun brunch to 3 pm. Closed Thanksgiving, Dec 25. Bar. Semi-a la carte: lunch, dinner $3.25–$8.50. Sun brunch $3.25–$7.99. Child's meals. Specializes in chicken, steak, hamburgers. Parking. Bar & grill atmosphere; antiques, paintings. Cr cds: A, MC, V.

D

BELLE MEADE BUFFET CAFETERIA. *4534 Harding Rd, in Belle Meade Plaza, west of downtown. 615/298-5571.* Hrs: 11 am–2 pm, 4:30–8 pm; Sun 10:30 am–8 pm. Closed some major hols. Avg ck: lunch $5, dinner $5.50. Child's meals. Specialties: baked squash casserole, fried chicken. No cr cds accepted.

D

MORRISON'S CAFETERIA. *(1000 Two Mile Pkwy, Goodlettsville)* N on I-65, in Rivergate Mall. *615/859-1359.* Hrs: 10:45 am–8:30 pm; Sun to 8 pm. Avg ck: lunch $4.50, dinner $5. Child's meals. Specializes in chicken, roast beef. Cr cds: MC, V.

TOWNE HOUSE TEA ROOM & RESTAURANT. *165 8th Ave N, downtown. 615/254-1277.* Hrs: 8:30 am–2:30 pm; Fri 8:30 am–2:30 pm, 5:30–10 pm; Sat 5:30–10 pm. Closed Sun; major hols. Semi-a la carte: bkfst $3.95–$4.50, lunch $3.45–$5.95, dinner $7.95–$14.95. Buffet: lunch $4.95, dinner $8.95. Salad bar. Own baking, soups. Historic 24-room mansion (1859); fireplaces, oak floors, antiques, paintings. Cr cds: A, C, D, DS, MC, V.

Natchez Trace State Resort Park (D-3)

(40 mi NE of Jackson, off I-40)

Named for the pioneer trail that connected Nashville and Natchez, this 48,000-acre park is the largest recreation area in western Tennessee and the location of a pecan tree that is said to be the world's third largest. Four lakes provide swimming; fishing; boating (launch, rentals). Nature trails, backpacking. Picnicking, playground, grocery, recreation lodge. Tent & trailer sites, cabins, inn. Standard fees. Phone 901/968-8176.

Motels

✔ ★ ★ BEST WESTERN CROSSROADS INN. *(I-40 at TN 22, Wildersville 38388)* 8 mi W of park entrance, on TN 22 at I-40 exit 108. *901/968-2532.* 40 rms. May–Oct: S $34; D $40; each addl $4; family rates; lower rates rest of yr. Crib free. Pet accepted; $6. TV; cable. Pool.

Restaurant nearby. Ck-out 11 am. Picnic tables, grills. Cr cds: A, C, D, DS, ER, MC, V, JCB.

★★★**PIN OAK LODGE.** *(Wildersville 38388)* In park. *901/968-8176.* 20 rms, 2 story, 18 kit. cottages. Mar–Nov: S $43; D $54; each addl $6; kit. cottages $40–$50; under 16 free; lower rates rest of yr. Crib free. TV in motel rms. Pool; wading pool. Playground. Restaurant 7 am–9 pm. Ck-out 11 am. Meeting rms. Lighted tennis. Rec rm. Dock. Balconies. Picnic tables, grills. On lake. State-owned; all facilities of park avail. Cr cds: A, MC, V.

Newport (D-8)

Settled: 1789 **Pop:** 7,123 **Elev:** 1,055 ft **Area code:** 615 **Zip:** 37821

(See Greeneville, Sevierville)

Motels

✔ ★**FAMILY INNS.** *1311 W Highway 2570, 3 mi S on US 411 at I-40 Sevierville exit. 615/623-2626.* 62 rms, 2 story. S $26.75–$79.75; D $29.75–$99.75; each addl $5. TV; cable. Pool; wading pool. Taproom 4 pm–midnight. Ck-out 11 am. Meeting rms. Cr cds: A, C, D, DS, MC, V.

★★**HOLIDAY INN.** *(Box 250) Cosby Hwy, 1 mi S on TN 32, 1 blk S of I-40 Cosby Hwy exit. 615/623-8622; FAX 615/623-8622, ext 292.* 152 rms, 2 story. S, D $39–$84; each addl $6; under 19 free; higher rates special events. Crib free. Pet accepted. TV; cable. Indoor pool; whirlpool, wading pool. Restaurant 6 am–2 pm, 5–10 pm. Rm serv. Taproom. Ck-out noon. Coin lndry. Meeting rms. Holidome. Game rm. Cr cds: A, C, D, DS, MC, V, JCB.

Norris (D-7)

Founded: 1933 **Pop:** 1,303 **Elev:** 1,042 ft **Area code:** 615 **Zip:** 37828

When the TVA started Norris Dam, it built this spacious, permanent planned community. In 1948, it sold the town as a unit for more than $2 million. The new owner, a Philadelphia syndicate, then broke it up into individual properties and resold them. Like the dam, Norris is named for Nebraska Senator George W. Norris (1861–1944), cosponsor of the legislation that founded the authority.

What to See and Do

1. **Museum of Appalachia.** 1 mi E of I-75 exit 122 on TN 61. Log village covering 70 acres has extensive collection of items relating to mountain culture; pioneer, frontier and country items; a working farm with animals; antique & craft shop. (Daily) Phone 494-7680 or -0514. ¢¢¢

2. **Norris Dam and Lake.** 5 mi NW on US 441. This was the first dam built by the TVA. Located on the Clinch River, the dam (265 ft high, 1,860 ft long) impounds a 129-mile-long lake with 800 miles of shoreline. Fishing; boating. Nature trails. Visitor lobby and two overlooks (daily). TVA Forestry-Fisheries Laboratory (Mon–Fri). Phone 632-1875. **Free.**

3. **Norris Dam State Park.** 4 mi NW on US 441. Park covers 4,000 acres overlooking dam and Norris Lake. Gristmill (1795) grinds corn daily in summer. Lenoir Museum has relics of 19th-century American

history (free). Swimming pool; fishing; boating, canoe access. Picnicking, playground, concessions. Camping, tent & trailer sites, cabins. Standard fees. Phone 426-7461.

4. **Big Ridge State Rustic Park.** 12 mi NE on TN 61. Originally developed by TVA, the park covers 3,687 acres along Norris Lake. Swimming; fishing; boating (launch, rentals). Nature programs, hiking trails, game courts. Picnicking, playground. Camping, tent & trailer sites, cabins. Visitor center. Standard fees. Phone 992-5523.

(For further information contact the City of Norris, 20 Chestnut Dr; 494-7645.)

(For accommodations see Knoxville, Oak Ridge)

Oak Ridge (D-7)

Founded: 1943 **Pop:** 27,310 **Elev:** 900 ft **Area code:** 615 **Zip:** 37830

Oak Ridge was built during World War II to house people involved in the production of uranium 235 (the first atomic bomb's explosive element). Once one of the most secret places in the US, Oak Ridge is now host to thousands who come each year, drawn by the mysteries of nuclear energy. Built by the US government, Oak Ridge is now owned by its residents. Although many of the installations are still classified, the area has not been restricted since March, 1949.

What to See and Do

1. **American Museum of Science and Energy.** 300 S Tulane Ave. One of the world's largest energy exhibitions; fossil fuels, energy alternatives, resources and research. Hands-on exhibits, displays, models, films, games and live demonstrations. (Daily; closed Jan 1, Thanksgiving, Dec 25) Phone 576-3200. **Free.**

2. **Children's Museum of Oak Ridge.** 461 W Outer Dr. Participation exhibits and displays include Grandma's Attic, Pioneer Living Area, puppet exhibit, TVA water flume, Space Travel, Coal in Early Appalachia, Native Americans, Nature Room and history of Oak Ridge. Performances, exhibits, seminars, workshops. (Daily; closed some hols) Sr citizen rate. Phone 482-1074. ¢¢

3. **Oak Ridge Art Center.** 201 Badger Ave. Permanent collection of original paintings, drawings and prints; temporary exhibits. (Daily; closed major hols) Phone 482-1441. **Free.**

4. **University Arboretum.** 901 Kerr Hollow Rd. Part of University of Tennessee Forestry Experimental Station. More than 1,000 species of trees, shrubs, flowering plants on 250 acres. Self-guided tours. (Mon–Fri) Phone 483-3571. **Free.**

5. **The Department of Energy's Oak Ridge National Laboratory's Graphite Reactor.** 10 mi SW on Bethel Valley Rd. Nuclear reactor (1943); interpretive exhibits. Visitor overlook with audiovisual presentation. (Daily exc Sun; closed hols) Phone 574-4160. **Free.**

6. **Frozen Head State Park.** Approx 18 mi NW on TN 62, then 4 mi N on Flat Fork Rd, follow signs. More than 12,000 acres in Cumberland Mountains. Trout fishing. Hiking trails (50 mi). Picnicking, playground. Primitive camping. Visitor center. Standard fees. Phone 346-3318.

7. **Bull Run Fossil Plant.** 5 mi SE, on shore of Melton Hill Reservoir. TVA-built with a 800-foot-high chimney, the plant has a roadside overlook. Visitor lobby and tours to powerhouse overlook (daily). Phone 945-2813. **Free.**

8. **Melton Hill Dam and Lake.** 15 mi SW. This TVA dam extends barge travel up the Clinch River to Clinton and provides electric power. Dam (103 ft high, 1,020 ft long) impounds 44-mile-long lake. Fishing; boating. Camping (fee). Visitor overlook. (Daily) **Free.**

(For further information contact the Convention & Visitors Bureau, 302 S Tulane Ave; 482-7821.)

Annual Event

Appalachian Music & Craft Festival. Children's Museum of Oak Ridge (see #2). Mid-Nov.

(See Knoxville, Norris)

Motels

✓★★**ALEXANDER INN.** *210 E Madison. 615/483-3555.* 82 rms, 2 story, 5 kits. S $35–$55; D $40–$65; each addl $5; kit. units $40–$45; under 12 free. Crib free. TV. Pool. Restaurant 11 am–2 pm. Bar 11–1 am. Ck-out noon. Meeting rms. Cr cds: C, D, DS, MC, V.

★**COMFORT INN.** *433 S Rutgers Ave. 615/481-8200; FAX 615/483-6142.* 122 rms, 5 story, 26 suites. S, D $54–$68; each addl $7; suites $64–$68; under 18 free. Crib free. TV; cable. Pool. Complimentary continental bkfst, coffee. Restaurant nearby. Ck-out noon. Coin lndry. Meeting rms. Valet serv. Free local transportation. Exercise equipt; weight machine, bicycles. Health club privileges. Refrigerators in suites. Cr cds: A, C, D, DS, ER, MC, V, JCB.

★**DAYS INN.** *206 S Illinois Ave. 615/483-5615.* 80 rms, 2 story. S $45–$51; D $47–$53; each addl $3; under 12 free. Crib free. TV; cable. Heated pool. Playground. Complimentary coffee in lobby. Restaurant adj 6:30 am–midnight; Fri, Sat to 2 am. Ck-out 11 am. Meeting rms. Valet serv. Some refrigerators. Cr cds: A, C, D, DS, MC, V.

★★**HOLIDAY INN.** *420 S Illinois Ave. 615/483-4371; FAX 615/483-5972.* 149 rms, 2 story. S $48–$61; D $52–$68; each addl $5; under 18 free. Crib free. TV; cable. Pool. Restaurant 6 am–2 pm, 5–10 pm. Rm serv. Bar 4 pm–1 am; dancing exc Sun. Ck-out noon. Coin lndry. Meeting rms. Valet serv. Exercise equipt; weights, treadmill. Cr cds: A, C, D, DS, ER, MC, V, JCB.

Motor Hotel

★★★**GARDEN PLAZA HOTEL.** *215 S Illinois Ave. 615/481-2468; res: 800/342-7336 (exc TN); FAX 615/481-2474.* 168 rms, 5 story. S, D $65–$70; each addl $7; suites $85; under 18 free. Crib free. TV; cable. 2 pools, 1 indoor; poolside serv. Restaurant 6:30 am–2 pm, 5–10 pm. Rm serv. Bar 2 pm–1:30 am; entertainment wkends. Ck-out noon. Meeting rms. Bellhops. Exercise equipt; weight machine, bicycles, whirlpool. Health club privileges. Refrigerator, wet bar in suites. Cr cds: A, C, D, DS, MC, V.

Paris (D-3)

Founded: 1821 **Pop:** 9,332 **Elev:** 519 ft **Area code:** 901 **Zip:** 38242

Only 14 miles from Kentucky Lake, Paris is a growing recreational center. It was named in honor of the Marquis de Lafayette, who was visiting in Nashville when the city was founded. The city is the marketplace for Henry County's cattle, horses, hogs, soybeans, tobacco and small grain. Clay mined in this vicinity is processed in Paris.

What to See and Do

1. **Paris Landing State Park.** 16 mi NE on US 79. An 840-acre park on Kentucky Lake with swimming beach, pools, waterskiing; boating (launch, rentals, marina). Golf, tennis courts. Picnicking, playground, concessions, lodging, restaurant. Camping. Standard fees. Phone 644-7359.

2. **Nathan Bedford Forrest State Park.** 21 mi S on US 641, E on US 70, then 8 mi N on US 191. On the west bank of Kentucky Lake a monument marks the spot where, in 1864, Confederate General Forrest set up artillery. Undetected by Union forces, the hidden batteries detroyed both the Union base on the opposite shore and its protective warships on the Tennessee River. The area is now an 800-acre park offering fishing and canoe access to the lake. Nature trails & programs, backpacking. Picnicking, playground, concession. Camping, group lodge. View from Pilot Knob. Museum (Wed–Sun). Trace Creek Annex, located across Kentucky Lake, interprets a portion of the military history of the area. Standard fees. Phone 584-6356.

(For further information contact the Paris-Henry County Chamber of Commerce, 105 E Wood St, PO Box 8; 642-3431.)

Annual Event

World's Biggest Fish Fry. Henry County Fairgrounds. Celebration includes rodeo, parade, contests, tournaments. Last full wk Apr.

(See Land Between The Lakes, KY)

Motels

★**BEST WESTERN TRAVELER'S INN.** *1297 E Wood St (US 79N). 901/642-8881.* 98 rms, 2 story. S $40–$54; D $42–$57; each addl $4; under 12 free; wkly rates. Crib free. TV; cable. Pool. Complimentary coffee in lobby. Restaurant adj 6 am–midnight. Private club; setups, beer. Ck-out noon. Meeting rms. Cr cds: A, C, D, DS, MC, V.

✓★**TERRACE WOODS LODGE.** *1190 N Market. 901/642-2642.* 19 rms, 1–2 story. S $29–$31; D $33–$35; each addl $4; under 12 free. Crib $4. TV; cable. Complimentary coffee in lobby. Ck-out 11 am. Cr cds: A, C, D, DS, MC, V.

Pigeon Forge (D-8)

Pop: 3,027 **Elev:** 1,031 ft **Area code:** 615 **Zip:** 37863

Located in the shadow of the Smokies, this resort town was named for an old iron foundry on the Little Pigeon River.

What to See and Do

1. **Pigeon Forge Pottery.** 2 blks E on Middle Creek Rd. Visitors can watch craftspeople at work. (Daily; closed Jan 1, Dec 25) For appt phone 453-3883 or -3704. **Free.**

2. **The Old Mill.** 1 blk E off US 441. Water-powered mill, in continuous operation since 1830, grinds cornmeal, grits, whole wheat, rye and buckwheat flours; dam falls are illuminated at night. Site (all yr); guided tours (Apr–Nov, daily exc Sun). Phone 453-4628. **¢¢**

3. **Dollywood.** 1 mi E on US 441, on Dollywood Lane. Dolly Parton's entertainment park. (June–Aug, daily; May & Oct, daily exc Thurs; Sept, Fri–Tues) Phone 428-9488. **¢¢¢¢¢**

4. **Magic World.** On US 441. Family amusement park with dragon coaster, spider ride, magic teacup ride, bumper boats, antique cars, pony cart rides. (June–Oct, daily; May, Wed–Sun; late Mar–Apr, wkends) Phone 453-7941. **¢¢¢¢¢**

5. **Ogle's Water Park.** 2530 Parkway. An eight-acre water amusement park featuring water slides, ocean wave pool, children's water playground; two restaurants. (June–Aug, daily; May & Sept, wkends) Phone 453-8741. **¢¢¢¢**

6. **Smoky Mountain Car Museum.** On US 441. More than 30 gas, electric and steam autos, including Hank Williams Jr's "Silver Dollar" car; James Bond's "007" Aston Martin; Al Capone's bullet-

proof Cadillac; the patrol car of Sheriff Buford Pusser from the movie *Walking Tall*; Elvis Presley's Mercedes. Historic gas pump globe display; *Burma Shave* signs. (May–Oct, daily) ¢¢

7. **Flyaway.** 3106 Parkway. Vertical wind tunnel that simulates skydiving. Instructor assists participants in flight chamber and explains how to maneuver body to soar, turn and descend. Observation gallery (fee). (Mar–Nov, daily; winter schedule varies; closed Dec 25) Phone 453-7777. ¢¢¢¢

(For further information contact the Dept of Tourism, 2450 Parkway, PO Box 1390, 37868; 453-8574 or 800/251-9100.)

Seasonal Events

Country music and comedy shows

Archie Campbell Theatre. Phone 428-3218. Late Apr–Oct.

Bonnie Lou & Buster Country Music Show. US 441. Phone 453-9590. Mid-Mar–Nov.

Memories Theatre. US 441. Phone 428-7852. May–Oct.

Rainbow Country Jamboree. US 441. Phone 428-5600. Mid-Apr–Oct.

Smoky Mountain Jubilee. US 441. Phone 428-1836. Mid-Mar–early Nov.

(See Gatlinburg, Sevierville)

Motels

(Rates may be higher Univ of Tennessee football wkends)

★**AMERICANA INN.** *2825 Parkway (US 441). 615/428-0172.* 173 rms, 4 story. S $40–$50; D $55–$75; higher rates hols, special events. Crib $5. TV. Heated pool; whirlpool. Restaurant 7:30 am–3 pm; Fri–Sat to 8 pm. Rm serv. Ck-out 11 am. Downhill ski 10 mi. Balconies. Cr cds: A, DS, MC, V.

[D] [symbols]

★★**BEST WESTERN PLAZA INN.** *(PO Box 926) 3755 Parkway (US 441). 615/453-5538.* 200 rms, 3–5 story. S, D $69–$89; townhouses $140. Crib $6. TV; cable. Indoor/outdoor pool; whirlpool, sauna. Complimentary coffee in lobby. Restaurant opp 7 am–9 pm. Ck-out 11 am. Meeting rm. Downhill ski 6 mi. Game rm. Some in-rm whirlpools, refrigerators, fireplaces. Cr cds: A, C, D, DS, MC, V.

[D] [symbols]

★★**BILMAR MOTOR INN.** *3786 Parkway (US 441). 615/453-5593; res: 800/343-5610.* 76 rms, 2–3 story. Late May–Labor Day, Oct: D $36–$85; each addl $5; lower rates Mar–late May, after Labor Day–Dec. Closed rest of yr. Crib $5. TV; cable. Heated pool. Restaurant nearby. Ck-out 11 am. Some refrigerators, in-rm whirlpools. Cr cds: DS, MC, V.

[D] [symbols]

✔★★**BRIARSTONE INN.** *3626 Parkway (US 441). 615/453-4225; res: 800/523-3919.* 57 rms, 3 story. No elvtr. May–Oct: S $28–$58; D $36–$92; each addl $5; higher rates special events; lower rates rest of yr. TV; cable. Pool; whirlpools. Restaurant adj 6:30 am–noon. Ck-out 11 am. Refrigerators; some fireplaces. Cr cds: A, DS, MC, V.

[D] [symbols]

★★**COLONIAL HOUSE.** *3545 Parkway (US 441). 615/453-0717; res: 800/662-5444.* 63 rms, 3 story. Mar–Nov: S, D $36.50–$78.50; each addl $5; varied rates wkends & hols; lower rates rest of yr. Crib $5. TV; cable. Heated pool; wading pool. Restaurant adj 7 am–9 pm. Complimentary coffee in lobby. Ck-out 11 am. Downhill ski 10 mi. Some in-rm whirlpools, fireplaces. Some private patios, balconies. On river. Cr cds: A, DS, MC, V.

[symbols]

★★**CREEKSTONE INN.** *4034 River Rd. 615/453-3557; res: 800/523-3919.* 112 rms, 4 story. July–Oct: S $42–$82; D $48–$92; suites $62–$108; family rates; lower rates rest of yr. TV; cable. Pool. Restaurant nearby. Ck-out 11 am. Refrigerators. On Little Pigeon river. Cr cds: A, DS, MC, V.

[D] [symbols]

★★**DAYS INN.** *(Box 1230) 2760 Parkway (US 441). 615/453-4707; FAX 615/428-7928.* 117 rms, 3 story. May–Oct: S $58–$78; D $68–$88; each addl $5; under 17 free; higher rates hols, special events; lower rates rest of yr. Crib free. TV; cable. Heated pool. Complimentary coffee in lobby. Restaurant adj 7 am–10 pm. Ck-out 11 am. Downhill ski 10 mi. Cr cds: A, C, D, DS, MC, V, JCB.

[D] [symbols] [SC]

★★**ECONO LODGE.** *(Box 1337) 2440 Parkway (US 441). 615/428-1231; FAX 615/453-6879.* 202 rms, 3 story. June–Oct: S, D $79; each addl $6; under 12 free; higher rates wkends, hols, special events; lower rates rest of yr. Crib free. TV; cable. Pool; wading pool, whirlpool. Restaurant nearby. Ck-out 11 am. Downhill ski 10 mi. View of river, mountains. Cr cds: A, C, D, DS, MC, V.

[D] [symbols] [SC]

✔★★**GREEN VALLEY.** *4109 Parkway (US 441). 615/453-9091.* 50 rms, 3 story. No elvtr. May–Oct: S, D $38–$78; each addl $5; lower rates rest of yr. Crib $5. TV; cable. Heated pool. Restaurant 7 am–10 pm. Ck-out 11 am. Downhill ski 10 mi. Refrigerators. Cr cds: MC, V.

[D] [symbols] [SC]

★★**HOWARD JOHNSON.** *(Box 1110) 2826 Parkway (US 441). 615/453-9151.* 145 rms, 3 story. May–Oct: S, D $38.80–$88.80; each addl $4; studio rms $36.80–$88.80; kit. units $74.80–$140; under 12 free; higher rates special events; lower rates rest of yr. Crib free. TV; cable. Pool; wading pool. Restaurant 7 am–noon. Ck-out 11 am. Coin lndry. Downhill ski 10 mi. Game rm. Some in-rm whirlpools. Cr cds: A, C, D, DS, MC, V, JCB.

[D] [symbols]

✔★**MAPLES MOTOR INN.** *(Box 112) ½ mi N on US 441. 615/453-8883.* 57 rms, 2 story. Mar–Nov: S $24–$56; D $34–$65; each addl $5; higher rates some hols, special events. Closed rest of yr. Crib $5. TV; cable. Pool. Complimentary coffee in lobby. Restaurant nearby. Ck-out 11 am. Picnic tables, grills. Cr cds: DS, MC, V.

[D] [symbols]

★★**MCAFEE MOTOR INN.** *3756 Parkway (US 441). 615/453-3490; res: 800/925-4443.* 127 rms, 3 story. June–Aug, Oct: S $65; D $65–$89; each addl $5; higher rates: hols, special events; some lower rates rest of yr. Crib $5. TV; cable. Heated pool; wading pool, whirlpool. Restaurant adj 7 am–9 pm. Ck-out 11 am. Downhill ski 10 mi. Refrigerators. Some in-rm whirlpools, wet bars. Some balconies. Picnic tables. Cr cds: A, C, D, DS, MC, V.

[D] [symbols]

★**MOUNTAIN BREEZE.** *2926 Parkway (US 441). 615/453-2659.* 53 rms. June–Oct: D $60–$84; kit. units $108; lower rates Mar–May, Dec. Closed rest of yr. Crib $4. TV; cable. Pool. Complimentary coffee in rms. Restaurant nearby. Ck-out 11 am. Some refrigerators. Cr cds: DS, MC, V.

[D] [symbols] [SC]

✔★★**MOUNTAIN SKY.** *4236 Parkway (US 441). 615/453-3530; res: 800/523-3919.* 116 rms, 2–3 story. No elvtr. May–Oct: S $22–$78; D $22–$86; family rates; higher rates special events; lower rates rest of yr. TV; cable. Pool. Restaurant 6:30 am–noon. Ck-out 11 am. Downhill ski 10 mi. Refrigerators. Cr cds: A, DS, MC, V.

[D] [symbols]

★**PARKVIEW.** *2806 Parkway (US 441). 615/453-5051; res: 800/239-9116.* 38 rms, 1–2 story. June–Oct: S, D $58–$68; each addl $5; higher rates some events; lower rates Mar–May, Nov–late Dec. Closed rest of yr. Crib $5. TV; cable. Heated pool. Complimentary coffee in lobby. Restaurant adj 7 am–10 pm. Ck-out 11 am. Picnic tables, grills. Cr cds: A, DS, MC, V.

★★**RED CARPET INN.** *(Box 989) 3229 Parkway (US 441). 615/453-5568.* 53 rms, 2–3 story. No elvtr. May–Oct: S, D $32–$125; suites $60–$150; under 18 free; lower rates rest of yr. Crib free. TV; cable. Pool; wading pool. Restaurant adj 6:30 am–9:30 pm. Ck-out 11 am. Downhill ski 7 mi. Cr cds: A, C, D, DS, MC, V.

★**RIVERCHASE.** *3709 Parkway (US 441). 615/428-1299; FAX 615/453-1678.* 105 rms, 4 story. June–Oct: D $60–$90; each addl $5; higher rates hol wkends; varied lower rates rest of yr. Crib $5. TV. Heated pool. Restaurant opp 7 am–10 pm. Ck-out 11 am. Downhill ski 10 mi. Miniature golf. Some in-rm whirlpools, fireplaces. Cr cds: A, DS, MC, V.

★**RIVERPLACE INN.** *3223 Parkway (US 441). 615/453-0801; res: 800/428-5590.* 52 rms, 2 story. May–Oct: S, D $38.50–$88.50; each addl $5; under 12 free; higher rates special events; lower rates rest of yr. Closed Mid-Nov–mid-Mar. TV; cable. Pool; wading pool. Restaurant adj 6 am–9 pm. Ck-out 11 am. Meeting rms. Downhill/x-country ski 10 mi. Refrigerators. Balconies. Picnic tables, grills. On river. Cr cds: A, DS, MC, V.

✔ ★**TENNESSEE MOUNTAIN LODGE.** *(Box 105) 3571 Parkway (US 441). 615/453-4784; res: 800/446-1674.* 50 rms, 3 story. May–Oct: S $28–$48; D $32–$60; each addl $5; higher rates special events; lower rates rest of yr. Crib $2. TV; cable. Heated pool; wading pool. Restaurant adj 7 am–9:30 pm. Ck-out 11 am. Downhill ski 10 mi. Refrigerators. On river. Cr cds: A, DS, MC, V.

★★**VALLEY FORGE INN.** *2795 Parkway (US 441). 615/453-7770; res: 800/544-8740.* 130 rms, 4 story. June–Aug, Oct: S, D $52.50–$78.50; suites $10–$20 addl; higher rates wkends, hols, special events; lower rates rest of yr. Crib $4. TV; cable. 2 pools, 1 indoor; wading pool, whirlpool. Complimentary coffee in lobby. Restaurant opp 6 am–9 pm. Ck-out 11 am. Coin lndry. Downhill ski 10 mi. Some refrigerators, in-rm whirlpools. Some balconies. On river. Cr cds: A, DS, MC, V.

Motor Hotels

★★**GRAND HOTEL AND CONVENTION CENTER.** *3171 Parkway (US 441). 615/453-1000; res: 800/362-1188; FAX 615/453-1000, ext 5012.* 425 rms, 5 story. May–Oct: S, D $70–$100; each addl $5; suites $80–$169; under 12 free; higher rates special events; lower rates rest of yr. Crib free. TV; cable. Pool; whirlpool. Restaurant 7 am–10 pm. Rm serv. Ck-out 11 am. Convention facilities. Gift shop. Downhill ski 10 mi. Some fireplaces. Whirlpool in suites. Cr cds: A, C, D, DS, MC, V.

★★**HEARTLAND COUNTRY RESORT.** *2385 Parkway (US 441). 615/453-4106; FAX 615/453-4106, ext 1018.* 160 rms, 5 story. Late May–early Nov: S, D $79–$89; each addl $5; under 18 free; lower rates rest of yr. Crib free. TV; cable. 2 pools, 1 indoor. Continental bkfst. Ck-out 11 am. Meeting rms. Sundries. Exercise equipt; weight machines, bicycles, whirlpool. Game rm. Balconies. Cr cds: A, C, D, DS, ER, MC, V, JCB.

★★★**HOLIDAY INN.** *(Box 1383) 3230 Parkway (US 441). 615/428-2700; FAX 615/428-2700, ext 586.* 208 rms, 5 story, 6 suites. May–Oct: S, D $69–$120; each addl $6; suites $120; under 19 free; lower rates rest of yr. Crib free. TV. Indoor pool; whirlpool, sauna. Restaurant 7 am–10 pm. Ck-out 11 am. Coin lndry. Meeting rms. Down-

hill ski 10 mi. Game rm. Some refrigerators. Cr cds: A, C, D, DS, MC, V, JCB.

★★★**RAMADA INN.** *(Box 220) 4025 Parkway (US 441). 615/453-9081.* 131 rms, 2 story. May–mid-Nov: S, D $59–$95.50; each addl $9; under 18 free; higher rates football wkends, special events; lower rates rest of yr. Crib free. TV; cable. Indoor pool; wading pool, whirlpool, poolside serv. Playground. Restaurant 7 am–11 pm. Rm serv 8 am–8 pm. Ck-out noon. Meeting rms. Sundries. Downhill ski 10 mi. Cr cds: A, C, D, DS, MC, V.

★★**RIVERSIDE MOTOR LODGE.** *3575 Parkway (US 441). 615/453-5555; res: 800/242-8366; FAX 615/453-5555, ext 102.* 56 kit. suites, 5 story. May–Oct: kit. suites $125; each addl after 4, $5; under 16 free; lower rates rest of yr. TV; cable. Indoor pool; whirlpool. Complimentary coffee in lobby. Restaurant nearby. Ck-out 11 am. Cr cds: A, DS, MC, V.

Inns

★**DAY DREAMS COUNTRY INN.** *2720 Colonial Dr. 615/428-0370; res: 800/377-1469.* 6 rms, 2 story. No rm phones. S $69–$89; D $79–$99; each addl $12.50; under 2 free. Crib free. TV avail. Complimentary full bkfst, coffee, refreshments. Restaurant nearby. Ck-out 11 am, ck-in 3 pm. Downhill/x-country ski 10 mi. Antiques. Screened-in porches. Totally nonsmoking. Cr cds: A, MC, V.

★★**HILTON'S BLUFF.** *2654 Valley Heights Dr, US 321S W to Valley Heights Dr. 615/428-9765.* 10 air-cooled rms, 2 story. No rm phones. Apr–Nov: S, D $79–$104; each addl $10–$15; wkly rates; lower rates rest of yr. TV in rec rm. Complimentary full bkfst, coffee and tea. Restaurant nearby. Ck-out 11 am, ck-in 3 pm. Meeting rm. Rec rm. Balconies. Picnic tables, grills. On hill with scenic mountain view; library, deck with rocking chairs. Cr cds: A, MC, V.

Restaurants

✔ ★**APPLE TREE INN.** *3215 Parkway (US 441). 615/453-4961.* Hrs: 6:30 am–10 pm. Closed Dec–Feb. Res accepted. Semi-a la carte: bkfst $1.50–$5.29, lunch $1.50–$6.95, dinner $4.25–$11; family style $8.25. Child's meals. Specializes in spoon bread. Soup, salad bar. Parking. Family-owned. Cr cds: A, MC, V.

★**FARMERS DAUGHTER.** *3509 Parkway (US 441). 615/453-6485.* Hrs: 7 am–1 pm. Closed Dec 25; also Jan–Mar. Semi-a la carte: bkfst $1.99–$7.10. Child's meals. Specializes in biscuits, country ham, low cholesterol dishes. Parking. Country decor; antiques. Cr cds: DS, MC, V.

★★**GREEN VALLEY.** *4125 Parkway (US 441). 615/453-3500.* Hrs: 7 am–10 pm. Closed Dec 24–25. Semi-a la carte: bkfst $2.25–$6.50, lunch $3–$7, dinner $4.50–$15. Child's meals. Specializes in steak, seafood, country ham. Salad bar. Parking. Family-owned. Cr cds: A, MC, V.

✔ ★**MA AND PA'S HOME COOKING.** *3545 Parkway (US 441). 615/429-0558.* Hrs: 7:30 am–10 pm. Semi-a la carte: bkfst $1.50–$7.95, lunch, dinner $2.25–$11.95. Child's meals. Specializes in country cooking. Parking. Cr cds: A, MC, V.

★**SMOKY MOUNTAIN PANCAKE HOUSE.** *301 S Parkway (US 441). 615/453-1827.* Hrs: 6:30 am–1 pm. Closed Thanksgiving, Dec

25. Res accepted. Semi-a la carte: bkfst $1.95–$5.50, lunch $3.40–$4.65. Child's meals. Specializes in pancakes, country ham. Parking. Family-owned. No cr cds accepted.

D

✔ ★**TROTTER'S.** *3716 Parkway (US 441). 615/453-3347.* Hrs: 7 am–9 pm. Closed Dec–Mar. Semi-a la carte: bkfst $1.75–$6, lunch $2.25–$5.95, dinner $6.50–$10.95. Child's meals. Specializes in pan-fried chicken, steak, country ham. Parking. Cr cds: A, DS, MC, V.

D

Savannah (E-3)

Pop: 6,547 **Elev:** 436 ft **Area code:** 901 **Zip:** 38372

What to See and Do

1. **Pickwick Landing Dam, Lock and Lake.** 14 mi S on TN 128. This TVA dam (113 feet high, 7,715 feet long) impounds a 53-mile-long lake with 496 miles of shoreline. Also a 1,000-foot long navigation lock. Powerhouse visitor lobby and tours. Navigation Museum at lock. (Daily). Phone 925-4346. **Free.** Adj is

   Pickwick Landing State Resort Park. 15 mi S on TN 128. Approximately 1,400 acres adj to Pickwick Dam. Swimming pool, beach; fishing; boating (marina, launch, rentals). Nature trails; golf, tennis. Picnicking, playground, concession, cafe. Camping. Lodge (see). Standard fees. Phone 689-3129.

2. **Shiloh National Military Park** (see). 10 mi SW on TN 22.

Lodge

✔ ★★**PICKWICK LANDING.** *(PO Box 15, Pickwick Dam 38365) Just off TN 57, near Pickwick Dam, in state park. 901/689-3135.* 78 rms in 3-story lodge, 10 kit. cabins. Apr–Oct: S $44; D $54; each addl $6; suites $150; kit. cabins (1-wk min) $370/wk; under 16 free; lower rates rest of yr. Crib free. TV; cable. Pool; wading pool. Dining rm 7 am–8 pm. Ck-out 11 am. Meeting rms. Lighted tennis. 18-hole golf, pro, greens fee. Lawn games. Boat rentals. Lodge rms overlook lake; balconies. State-owned; all facilities of state park avail. Cr cds: A, MC, V.

Sevierville (D-8)

Founded: 1795 **Pop:** 7,178 **Elev:** 903 ft **Area code:** 615 **Zip:** 37862

Founded as part of the independent state of Franklin, this seat of Sevier County was named for John Sevier, who later became the first governor of Tennessee. Long a marketing center for a wide belt of farmland, Sevierville is only 16 miles from the Great Smoky Mountains National Park (see).

What to See and Do

1. **Douglas Dam and Lake.** 11 mi NE off TN 66. This TVA dam (202 ft high, 1,705 ft long) on the French Broad River was built on a 24-hour work schedule during World War II to furnish power for national defense. It impounds a lake 43 miles long with 555 miles of shoreline. Swimming; fishing; boating. Camping. Powerhouse visitor lobby and overlook (daily). Phone 475-7964. **Free.**

2. **Smoky Mountain Deer Farm.** 478 Happy Hollow Lane. Petting zoo includes deer, zebra, pygmy goats, llama. Pony rides (fee). (Daily; closed Thanksgiving, Dec 25) Phone 428-3337. ¢¢

3. **Forbidden Caverns.** 13 mi NE on US 411. Natural chimneys, underground streams; stereophonic sound presentations. Temperature in cave is 58°F. (Apr–Nov, daily) Phone 453-5972. ¢¢¢

(For further information contact the Chamber of Commerce, 866 Winfield Dunn Pkwy; 453-6411.)

(See Gatlinburg, Newport, Pigeon Forge)

Motels

★★**COMFORT INN-MOUNTAIN VIEW SUITES.** *860 Winfield Dunn Pkwy. 615/428-5519; FAX 615/428-6700.* 94 air-cooled suites, 3 story. May–Oct: S, D $44–$125; each addl $5; under 18 free; golf plans; higher rates special events; lower rates rest of yr. Crib $7. TV; cable. Indoor/outdoor pool; wading pool, whirlpool. Complimentary continental bkfst. Complimentary coffee in rms. Restaurant nearby. Ck-out 11 am. Meeting rms. Golf privileges. Downhill ski 16 mi. Game rm. Refrigerators, wet bars. Balconies. Cr cds: A, C, D, DS, ER, MC, V.

★**MIZE.** *804 Parkway. 615/453-4684; res: 800/239-9117.* 42 rms, 1–2 story, 4 kits. May–Oct: S, D $38.50–$68.50; each addl $5; kit. units $45–$95; higher rates special events; lower rates rest of yr. Crib free. TV; cable. Pool. Playground. Complimentary coffee. Restaurant nearby. Ck-out 11 am. Picnic tables, grill. Cr cds: A, DS, MC, V.

✔ ★**MOUNTAIN AIRE MOTOR INN.** *1008 Parkway. 615/453-5576; res: 800/332-5576.* 71 rms, 2 story, 23 suites. May–Oct: S $22.50–$68.50; D $28.50–$88.50; each addl $5; suites $28.50–$118.50; wkly rates; higher rates: hols, car shows; lower rates rest of yr. Crib free. TV; cable. Pool; wading pool. Complimentary coffee in lobby. Restaurant nearby. Ck-out 11 am. Refrigerators. Balconies. Picnic tables, grills. Cr cds: DS, MC, V.

★★**OAK TREE LODGE.** *1620 Parkway. 615/428-7500; res: 800/637-7002; FAX 615/429-8603.* 64 rms, 3 story, 16 suites. No A/C. Mid-May–mid-Nov: S, D $39.50–$79.50; each addl $6; suites $59.50–$89.50; under 18 free; higher rates special events; lower rates rest of yr. Crib free. TV; cable. Heated pool. Complimentary coffee in lobby. Restaurant nearby. Ck-out noon. Meeting rms. Tennis. Downhill, x-country ski 10 mi. Lawn games. Refrigerators. Balconies. Picnic tables, grills. Cr cds: A, DS, MC, V.

★★**QUALITY INN.** *(PO Box 250) I-40 exit 407, at TN 66. 615/933-7378; FAX 615/933-9145.* 78 rms, 3 story. No A/C. May–Oct: S $38–$58; D $58–$78; each addl $5; suites $88–$128; under 17 free; higher rates hols, car shows; lower rates rest of yr. Crib free. TV; cable. Indoor pool. Complimentary coffee in lobby. Restaurant adj 6 am–10 pm. Ck-out 11 am. Meeting rms. Downhill/x-country ski 20 mi. Balconies. Cr cds: A, C, D, DS, ER, MC, V.

✔ ★**RIVER VIEW INN.** *423 Forks of the River Pkwy. 615/428-6191; res: 800/447-2601.* 50 rms, 2 story, 12 suites. Apr–Oct: S $24.50–$78.50; D $28–$88; each addl $5; suites $58.50–$118.50; higher rates: car shows, hols; lower rates rest of yr. Crib free. TV; cable. Pool; wading pool. Complimentary coffee in lobby. Restaurant adj 6:30 am–11 pm. Ck-out 11 am. Refrigerators. Balconies. Picnic tables, grills. On river. Cr cds: DS, MC, V.

★**TRAVEL INN.** *400 Park Rd. 615/453-7165.* 50 rms, 2 story, 2 kits. May–Oct: D $45–$75; each addl $5; kit. units $10 addl; family rates; lower rates rest of yr. Crib free. TV; cable. Pool. Coffee in lobby. Restaurant nearby. Ck-out 11 am. Cr cds: A, DS, MC, V.

Restaurants

✔ ★ ★ **APPLEWOOD FARMHOUSE.** *240 Apple Valley Rd. 615/428-1222.* Hrs: 8 am–9 pm; Fri, Sat to 10 pm. Setups. Semi-a la carte: bkfst $4.25–$8.95, lunch $4.95–$7.95, dinner $10.95–$15.95. Child's meals. Specializes in apple fritters, country ham, fried chicken. Parking. Grounds with gazebo, apple trees along river. Cr cds: A, DS, MC, V.

 D **SC**

★ ★ ★ **FIVE OAKS.** *1625 Parkway. 615/453-5994.* Hrs: 11 am–2 pm, 5–10 pm. Res accepted. Continental menu. Semi-a la carte: lunch $2.95–$6.95, dinner $12.95–$22.95. Specialties: châteaubriand, veal, lamb, flambé desserts. Parking. Elegant dining in a restored 1860 private residence; recaptures the charm and grace of former era. Cr cds: A, C, D, MC, V.

 D

★ ★ **JOSEV'S.** *130 W Bruce St, in Crawford's Notch Shopping Center. 615/428-0737.* Hrs: 11 am–4 pm, 5–9:30 pm. Closed Mon; hols. Res accepted. Semi-a la carte: lunch $3.95–$13.95, dinner $8.95–$23.95. Specializes in steak, chicken, seafood. Parking. Cr cds: A, MC, V.

D

Shelbyville (E-5)

Founded: 1809 **Pop:** 14,049 **Elev:** 765 ft **Area code:** 615 **Zip:** 37160

Enshrined in the hearts and thoughts of every true citizen of Shelbyville is the Tennessee walking horse, that most noble of animals whose high-stepping dignity and high-level intelligence is annually celebrated here. There are 50 walking-horse farms and training stables within a 14-mile radius of town; obtain maps at the Chamber of Commerce.

(For further information contact the Shelbyville & Bedford County Chamber of Commerce, 100 N Cannon Blvd; 684-3482.)

Annual Events

Spring Fun Show. Celebration Grounds. Amateur and professional-class walking horses compete. Phone 684-5915. May 26–28.

Tennessee Walking Horse National Celebration. Evans & Calhoun Sts, 1 blk N of US 41A. More than 2,100 horses participate. Events conclude with crowning ceremonies for world grand champion walking horse. For tickets contact PO Box 1010; 684-5915. Late Aug–early Sept.

Motel

★ ★ **QUALITY INN.** *317 N Cannon Blvd. 615/684-6050; FAX 615/684-2714.* 76 rms, 2 story. S $45–$65; D $51–$65; each addl $6; under 12 free; higher rates special events. Crib free. Pet accepted, some restrictions. TV; cable. Pool. Restaurant 6 am–9 pm. Beer, setups 4–11:30 pm. Ck-out noon. Meeting rms. Cr cds: A, C, D, DS, ER, MC, V, JCB.

Shiloh National Military Park (E-3)

(10 mi SW of Savannah on TN 22)

Bitter, bloody Shiloh was the first major Civil War battle in the West and one of the fiercest in history. In two days, April 6 and 7, 1862, nearly 24,000 men were killed, wounded or missing. The South's failure to destroy Grant's army opened the way for the attack on and siege of Vicksburg, Mississippi (see). It was, however, a costly battle for the North as well.

General Grant's Army of the Tennessee, numbering almost 40,000, was camped near Pittsburg Landing and Shiloh Church, waiting for the Army of the Ohio under General Don Carlos Buell to attack the Confederates, who, they thought, were near Corinth, Mississippi, 20 miles south. But the brilliant Southern General Albert Sidney Johnston surprised Grant with an attack at dawn on April 6.

Although General Johnston was mortally wounded on the first day, the Southerners successfully pushed the Union Army back and nearly captured their supply base at Pittsburg Landing. On the second day, however, the Northerners, reinforced by the 20,000-man Army of the Ohio, counterattacked and forced the Confederates to retreat toward Corinth.

At Shiloh one of the first tent field hospitals ever established helped save the lives of many Union and Confederate soldiers. Among the men who fought this dreadful battle were John Wesley Powell, who lost an arm, but later went down the Colorado River by boat and became head of the US Geological Survey, James A. Garfield, 20th president of the United States, Ambrose Bierce, famous satirist and short story writer, and Henry Morton Stanley, who later uttered the famous phrase, "Dr. Livingstone, I presume."

The park is open all year. Guided tours are available from Memorial Day to Labor Day. Contact Superintendent, PO Box 67, Shiloh 38376; 901/689-5696. ¢

What to See and Do

1. **Visitor Center.** 1 mi from park entrance, E off TN 22, near Pittsburg Landing. Museum exhibits and 23-minute historical film; bookstore opp. (Daily; closed Dec 25)
2. **Auto tour.** Self-guided, 10-mile tour begins at the visitor center, where brochures can be obtained. Numbered markers indicate 15 points of interest.
3. **National Cemetery.** 10 acres on a bluff overlooking Pittsburg Landing and the Tennessee River. Buried here are about 3,800 soldiers, two-thirds of whom are unidentified.

(For accommodations see Savannah)

South Fulton

(see Fulton, KY)

Spring City (D-6)

Pop: 2,199 **Elev:** 773 ft **Area code:** 615 **Zip:** 37381

With the creation of Watts Bar Lake in 1942, Spring City has developed a quiet city atmosphere. Lakes, mountains and 200 wooded acres of nature trails make this a lakeside retreat.

What to See and Do

1. **Rhea County Courthouse** (1891). 13 mi S on US 27 in Dayton. Site of the Scopes trial, so-called "monkey trial" in which Clarence Darrow and William Jennings Bryan battled over whether evolution could be taught in the public schools. Restored courthouse includes the courtroom interior as it looked in 1925 and the Scopes trial museum. (Mon–Fri) Phone 775-7801. **Free.**
2. **Watts Bar Dam and Lake.** Dam, 3 mi S on US 27, then 7 mi SE on TN 68. Named for a bar to navigation in the original riverbed, this TVA dam (112 ft high, 2,960 ft long) impounds a 72-mile-long lake with

771 miles of shoreline. Swimming; excellent bass fishing; boating. Camping (fee). Visitor lobby (daily). Phone 365-7505. **Free.**

(For further information contact the Chamber of Commerce, Front St, PO Box 355; 365-5210.)

Cottage Colony

★ ★**WATTS BAR.** *(Dept M.G., Watts Bar Dam 37395) On TN 68, 7 mi E of jct US 27. 615/365-9595; res: 800/365-9598.* 52 cottages, 27 kits. Apr–Oct: S, D $28–$50; kit. units $40–$82. Closed rest of yr. Maid serv avail. Crib free. TV. Pool; wading pool, poolside serv. Playground. Dining rm 7:30 am–8:30 pm. Box lunches, snacks, picnics. Ck-out 1 pm, ck-in 4:30 pm. Gift shop. Meeting rms. Tennis. Dock; boats, pontoon boats, canoes. Hiking trails. Rec rm. Spacious grounds on Watts Bar Lake. Cr cds: A, DS, MC, V.

Stones River National Battlefield

(see Murfreesboro)

Sweetwater (D-7)

Pop: 5,066 **Elev:** 917 ft **Area code:** 615 **Zip:** 37874

What to See and Do

1. **Lost Sea.** 6 mi SE on TN 68. Glass-bottom boats explore the nation's largest underground lake (4½ acres) in the Lost Sea Caverns. Guided tours (1 hr). Temperature is constant at 58°F. (Daily; closed Dec 25) Phone 337-6616. ¢¢¢

2. **McMinn County Living Heritage Museum.** 522 W Madison Ave, 13 mi S on US 11, in Athens. The museum contains 26 exhibit areas with more than 6,000 items that reflect life in this region during the time span from the Cherokees to the Great Depression. (Daily; closed major hols) Phone 745-0329. ¢¢

(For further information contact the Monroe County Chamber of Commerce Visitor Center, 424 New Hwy 68, PO Box 37, Madisonville 37354; 442-4588 or 800/245-5428.)

(See Lenoir City)

Motel

★**COMFORT INN.** *(PO Box 48) 803 S Main St, ½ mi S on US 11. 615/337-6646.* 60 rms, 2 story. S $30–$55; D $36–$55; each addl $4. Crib $5. TV; cable. Pool; wading pool. Complimentary continental bkfst. Restaurant nearby. Ck-out 11 am. Pond, picnic area. Cr cds: A, C, D, DS, ER, MC, V.

Tennessee Valley Authority *

*TVA projects are centered on and around the Tennessee River Valley, primarily in Tennessee, Kentucky and Alabama.

The new prosperity and immense industrial expansion of a large portion of the South is directly linked to the Tennessee Valley Authority, an independent corporate agency of the federal government created by an Act of Congress on May 18, 1933. More than 40,000 square miles in Tennessee, North Carolina, Virginia, Georgia, Alabama, Mississippi and Kentucky continue to benefit directly from its activities. In addition, the entire nation benefits indirectly from TVA research and development in a wide range of fields.

In 1933 most of the Tennessee Valley area was the scene of desperate poverty. Actually, it had never recovered from the Civil War. The depression that began in 1929 had struck another cruel blow. Senator George Norris of Nebraska, President Franklin D. Roosevelt and other national leaders knew that in a river valley of rich potential this was unnecessary and illogical. They proposed that the nation provide the tools the valley's people needed to build a new prosperity through proper use of the Tennessee River, its tributaries and its vast watershed.

Today TVA dams and reservoirs regulate floodwaters on the Tennessee River and help reduce floods downstream on the Ohio and Mississippi rivers. They provide a year-round river channel for modern barges from the Ohio to Knoxville, making the river a busy waterway for industry. The same dams produce power for residents and industries. In the watershed area, TVA helps advance erosion control and vital farming and forestry improvements. It has eliminated malaria from the region by destroying mosquito breeding habitat. It operates a national fertilizer and environmental research center and works through industry and state colleges nationwide to offer better fertilizer materials and methods to America's farmers. Many modern products of the US fertilizer industry are made with processes or equipment developed at this center.

This resource development effort has helped the people of the region strengthen their economy and build an unprecedented prosperity. Per capita income in the TVA area was only 45 percent of the national average in 1933. Today it stands at almost 80 percent of the national average.

Approximately eight million people live in the area served with TVA power. In 1990 they paid an average of 5.7 cents a kilowatt-hour for residential use, compared to the national average of 7.7 cents. TVA power is distributed to local consumers through cooperatives owned by people of each area or by individual cities. Much of the original construction was financed by the federal government, and TVA has always earned appropriate income on this money. Today TVA power facilities are financed with the agency's own power revenues and through bond and note sales. Meanwhile, TVA is repaying the original appropriations invested in its power system, plus dividends on that investment.

TVA operates 39 dams on the Tennessee River and its tributaries; of these, TVA owns 35. Coal-burning power plants, built mostly in the 1950s and 1960s, when power use exceeded the capacity of the dams, provide the primary souce of electricity today. Immense use by atomic and space installations was a main factor in requiring more power supply. Now the TVA system includes 11 coal-fired plants, one hydroelectric pumped-storage plant and two nuclear plants.

For visitors interested in recreation, TVA lakes provide more than 600,000 surface acres of water and 11,000 miles of shoreline. Along these reservoirs, there are more than 100 public parks, 450 access areas and 325 commercial recreation areas. The lakes provide excellent fishing for bass, walleye, crappie and other fish, with no closed season, and many other recreational opportunities. In the 1960s, TVA developed a 40-mile-long recreation and environmental-education area in western Kentucky and Tennessee, called Land Between The Lakes.

Visitors are welcome at TVA dams and steam plants. Public Safety Officers, who conduct tours, are on duty from 9 am–5 pm at most projects. Golden Age and Golden Access Passports (see INTRODUCTION) are honored at all TVA fee recreation areas.

Recreation maps of TVA lakes, with detailed routes to shoreline recreation areas, as well as navigation charts and maps for the major lakes, may be ordered by writing the TVA Map Sales Office, 101 Haney Building, Chattanooga 37401. Specify the lake(s) of interest on each request. A free list of maps and their costs is available. Charts for mainstream lakes of the Tennessee River, showing navigation channels, water depth, buoys, lights, other navigation aids and recreation areas, are also available.

Limited material on the TVA and its diverse programs is available from the Communications Office, TVA, 400 W Summit Hill Dr, Knoxville 37902; 615/632-8000 or -2101.

Tiptonville (D-2)

Pop: 2,149 **Elev:** 301 ft **Area code:** 901 **Zip:** 38079

What to See and Do

Reelfoot Lake. 2 mi E on TN 21. This 13,000-acre lake, 18 miles long and more than 2 miles wide, was created by the New Madrid earthquakes of 1811-12. A bird and game refuge of unusual beauty, the lake has an untamed quality with vast expanses of lily pads and giant cypress trees growing from the water. More than 56 species of fish inhabit these waters, and 260 species of water and land fowl populate the area. On the south shore is

Reelfoot Lake State Park. 5 mi E on TN 21. Approximately 300 acres with a visitor center/museum exhibiting Native American artifacts, natural and cultural displays, earthquake simulator and specimens of local fauna (free). Fishing, duck hunting; boating (launch, rentals). Tennis courts. Picnicking, concession, restaurant, lodge (see). Tent & trailer sites. Boat excursions at park (May-Sept). Bald eagle tours (Dec-mid-Mar). Standard fees. Contact Superintendent, Rte 1, Box 296; 253-7756.

(For further information contact the Northwest Tennessee Tourist Promotion Council, PO Box 963, Martin 38237; 587-4213.)

Lodge

✔ ★**AIR PARK INN.** *(Rte 1, Box 296) 7 mi N on TN 78, 3 mi E on TN 213. 901/253-7756; FAX 901/253-8940.* 20 rms, 1-2 story. S, D $42-$54; each addl $6; suites $62; under 16 free. Closed late Oct-Dec. TV; cable. Pool. Complimentary coffee in rms. Restaurant 7 am-8 pm; closed Mon-Wed. Ck-out 11 am. Meeting rms. Tennis. Private patios. 3,500-ft landing strip. All facilities of Reelfoot Lake State Park avail; overlooks Reelfoot Lake. Cr cds: A, MC, V.

Restaurant

✔ ★**BOYETTE'S DINING ROOM.** *2½ mi E on TN 21. 901/253-7307.* Hrs: 7 am-9 pm. Closed Thanksgiving, Dec 24 & 25. Res accepted. Semi-a la carte: bkfst $2-$5, lunch $2.50-$11, dinner $3.50-$11. Child's meals. Specializes in catfish, country ham, fried chicken, steak. Parking. On Reelfoot Lake. Family-owned. No cr cds accepted.

Ⓓ

Townsend (D-7)

Pop: 329 **Elev:** 1,036 ft **Area code:** 615 **Zip:** 37882

What to See and Do

1. **Tuckaleechee Caverns.** 3 mi S, off US 321. Cathedral-like main chamber is largest cavern room in eastern US; drapery formations, walkway over subterranean streams, flowstone falls; waterfalls tour. Temperature 58°F in caverns. Guided tours every 15-20 minutes (mid-Mar-mid-Nov, daily). Phone 448-2274. ¢¢¢

2. **Cades Cove.** 5 mi SE on TN 73, then 8 mi SW on unnumbered road in Great Smoky Mountains National Park (see).

(For further information contact the Visitors Center, 7906 E Lamar Alexander Pkwy; 448-6134)

(See Gatlinburg, Maryville)

Motels

★★**BEST WESTERN VALLEY VIEW LODGE.** *(PO Box 148) 7726 Lamar Alexander Pkwy. 615/448-2237.* 138 rms, 2 story, 39 suites. May-Oct: S, D $49.50-$89.50; each addl $5; suites $64.50-$125.50; lower rates rest of yr. Crib $5. TV; cable. 3 pools, 1 indoor; whirlpools. Complimentary continental bkfst. Coffee in rms. Restaurant nearby. Ck-out 11 am. Meeting rms. Lawn games. Refrigerators; some fireplaces; minibar in suites. Private patios, balconies. Covered picnic area, grill. Cr cds: A, C, D, DS, MC, V.

★**FAMILY INNS.** *7239 E Lamar Alexander Pkwy. 615/448-9100; res: 800/332-8282; FAX 615/448-6140.* 39 rms, 2 story, 7 suites, 8 kits. May-Oct: S $46-$59; D $48-$80; each addl $5; suites $79-$110; kit. units $54-$89; under 18 free; higher rates hols; lower rates rest of yr. TV; cable. Heated pool. Complimentary continental bkfst, coffee. Restaurant nearby. Ck-out 11 am. Meeting rms. Refrigerator in suites. Picnic tables. On river. Cr cds: A, C, D, DS, MC, V.

Ⓓ ✈ ⊘ Ⓞ SC

✔ ★★**HIGHLAND MANOR.** *(Box 242) 7766 E Lamar Alexander Pkwy. 615/448-2211; res: 800/321-0286.* 50 rms, 2 story, 8 suites. May-Oct: S $39.50-$69.50; D $44.50-$69.50; each addl $5; suites $59.50-$89.50; kit. units $74.50; family, wkly rates; golf plans; lower rates rest of yr. Crib $3. TV; cable. Pool; wading pool. Complimentary continental bkfst, coffee. Restaurant opp 7 am-11 pm. Ck-out 11 am. Meeting rms. National park transportation. 18-hole golf privileges, greens fee $32, pro. Exercise equipt; weight machine, bicycles. Many refrigerators. Balconies. Picnic tables. Opp river. Cr cds: A, C, D, DS, MC, V.

Ⓓ ✈ ⊘ Ⓞ SC

✔ ★**SCENIC.** *8254 TN 73, ¼ mi E. 615/448-2294.* 19 rms. Mid-June-late Aug: S $29.95-$34.95; D $34.95-$44.95; each addl $5; suites $49.95-$59.95; higher rates special events; lower rates rest of yr. TV; cable. Pool. Playground. Complimentary coffee. Restaurant nearby. Ck-out 11 am. Lawn games. Picnic tables, grill. Cr cds: A, DS, MC, V.

⊘ ⊘ Ⓞ SC

★★**TALLEY-HO INN.** *8314 TN 73, ¼ mi off US 321 on TN 73. 615/448-2465; res: 800/448-2465.* 48 rms, 2 story. June-Labor Day & Oct: S, D $37-$62; each addl $5; suites $69-$92; under 6 free; lower rates rest of yr. Crib $5. TV; cable. Heated pool; wading pool. Restaurant 7 am-9 pm. Ck-out 11 am. Meeting rm. Tennis. Many refrigerators. Private patios, balconies. Cr cds: A, D, DS, MC, V.

Ⓓ ✈ ⊘ Ⓞ

Cottage Colony

★**PIONEER CABINS & GUEST FARM.** *(PO Box 207) 253 Boat Gunnel Rd. 615/448-6100; res: 800/621-9751.* 5 kit. cottages, 1 A/C, 2 story. Mid-Mar-Dec (2-day min): cottages $75-$95; wkly rates; lower rates rest of yr. Crib free. TV avail. Restaurant nearby. Ck-out 11 am, ck-in 3 pm. Grocery ¼ mi. Coin lndry, package store ¼ mi. Hiking. Balconies. Picnic tables, grills. On 41 private acres; pond. No cr cds accepted.

Union City (D-3)

Pop: 10,513 **Elev:** 337 ft **Area code:** 901 **Zip:** 38261

What to See and Do

Davy Crockett Cabin. 20 mi S on US 45W, in Rutherford. Frontiersman's cabin is now a museum with period artifacts; grave of Crockett's mother is on grounds. (Late May–Sept, daily exc Mon; rest of yr, by appt) Phone 643-6428. **¢**

(For accommodations see Tiptonville)

Vonore (D-7)

Founded: 1890 **Pop:** 605 **Elev:** 852 ft **Area code:** 615 **Zip:** 37885

What to See and Do

1. **Fort Loudoun** (1756-60). Follow signs from US 411 N of town. Southwestern outpost of England during the French and Indian War, the fort was the first permanent structure erected by the English west of the Appalachians. Besieged by Cherokees in 1760, the starved garrison was forced to surrender. Although promised safe-conduct soldiers and their families were attacked 15 miles outside the fort; 23 people were killed. Restored fort site, enclosed with high palisades, includes rebuilt barracks, blacksmith shop and powder magazine. Ongoing reconstruction. Fort, museum, self-guided tours. (Daily; closed Jan 1, Thanksgiving, Dec 25) Phone 884-6217. **Free.** Also here is

    Tellico Blockhouse (1794–1807). American military outpost, constructed during Tennessee's territorial period, was built as a frontier fort and was later converted to a federally operated trading post. The blockhouse was also the site, in 1798 and 1805, of important treaty negotiations with the Cherokee that affected the growth of Tennessee and the US. Self-guided tours at Fort Loudoun Visitors Center (same days as Fort Loudoun.) **Free.**

2. **Sequoyah Birthplace Museum.** Follow signs from US 411 N of town, on Citico Rd. Displays include archeological artifacts, Cherokee crafts and Cherokee syllabary developed by Sequoyah. Gift shop.

(Mon–Sat & Sun afternoons; closed Jan 1, Thanksgiving, Dec 25) Phone 884-6246. **¢¢**

(For further information contact the Monroe County Chamber of Commerce Visitor Center, 424 New Hwy 68, PO Box 37, Madisonville 37354; 442-4588 or 800/245-5428.)

(For accommodations see Lenoir City, Maryville)

Waverly

(see Hurricane Mills)

Winchester (E-5)

Pop: 6,305 **Elev:** 965 ft **Area code:** 615 **Zip:** 37398

What to See and Do

1. **Tims Ford Dam and Lake.** 10 mi W on TN 50 on the Elk River. A 246-mile shoreline with 10,600 acres of water surface. Visitor overlook (daily). **Free.** On reservoir is

    Tims Ford State Rustic Park. 5 mi W off TN 50W. More than 400 acres with swimming pool; fishing; boating (marina, launch, rentals). Hiking, bicycling. Picnicking, playgrounds, concessions. Tent & trailer camping, cabins. Standard fees. Phone 967-4457.

2. **Franklin County Old Jail Museum** (1897). 400 Dinah Shore Blvd. Restored jail has Native American and early frontier room, Civil War room, World War I & II room, heritage room; also cell area, gallery. (Mid-Mar–late Dec, daily exc Mon) Phone 967-0524. **¢**

3. **Falls Mill** (1873). 12 mi W on US 64. Built as cotton and woolen mill, Falls Mill now produces stone-ground flour and meal products with 32-foot overshot water wheel. Country store, museum. Overnight stays avail. (Daily) Phone 469-7161. **¢¢**

4. **Cowan Railroad Museum.** 6 mi E via US 64 & 41A, in Cowan. Restored turn-of-the-century railroad station and museum. (Thurs–Sun) Donation. Phone 967-7365.

(For further information contact the Franklin County Chamber of Commerce, PO Box 280; 967-6788.)

(For accommodations see Monteagle)

Index

Establishment names are listed in alphabetical order followed by a symbol identifying their classification, and then city, state and page number. Establishments affiliated with a chain appear alphabetically under their chain name, followed by the state, city and page number. The symbols for classification are: (H) for hotels; (I) for inns; (M) for motels; (L) for lodges; (MH) for motor hotels; (R) for restaurants; (RO) for resorts, guest ranches, and cottage colonies; (U) for unrated dining spots. States are arranged alphabetically as are the cities and towns within each state.

Mobil Travel Guide

Order Form

If you would like other editions of MOBIL TRAVEL GUIDES that might not be available at your local bookstore or Mobil dealer, please use the order form below.

Ship to:

Name _____

Address: _____

City _____ State _____ Zip _____

☐ My check is enclosed.

☐ Please charge my credit card

☐ VISA ☐ MasterCard

Credit Card # _____ Expiration _____

Signature _____

Please send me the following Mobil Travel Guides:

☐ B016 **California & the West** (Arizona, California, Nevada, Utah)
$13.95

☐ B017 **Great Lakes Area** (Illinois, Indiana, Michigan, Ohio, Wisconsin, Canada: Major Cities Ontario)
$13.95

☐ B018 **Middle Atlantic States** (Delaware, District of Columbia, Maryland, New Jersey, North Carolina, Pennsylvania, South Carolina, Virginia, West Virginia)
$13.95

☐ B019 **Northeastern States** (Connecticut, Maine, Massachusetts, New Hampshire, New York, Rhode Island, Vermont, Canada: Major Cities Atlantic Provinces, Ontario, Quebec)
$13.95

☐ B020 **Northwest & Great Plains States** (Idaho, Iowa, Minnesota, Montana, Nebraska, North Dakota, Oregon, South Dakota, Washington, Wyoming, Canada: Major Cities Alberta, British Columbia, Manitoba)
$13.95

☐ B021 **Southeastern States** (Alabama, Florida, Georgia, Kentucky, Mississippi, Tennessee)
$13.95

☐ B022 **Southwest & South Central Area** (Arkansas, Colorado, Kansas, Louisiana, Missouri, New Mexico, Oklahoma, Texas)
$13.95

☐ B023 **Frequent Traveler's Guide to Major Cities** (Detailed coverage of 46 major cities, plus airport and street maps)
$14.95

Total cost of book(s) ordered $ _____

Shipping & Handling (please add $2 for first book, $1 each additional book) $ _____

Add applicable sales tax* $ _____

TOTAL AMOUNT ENCLOSED $ _____

Please mail this form to:

Mobil Travel Guides
P.O. Box 493
Mt. Morris, IL 61054
815-734-1104

*To ensure that all orders are processed efficiently, please apply sales tax in Canada and in the following states: CA, CT, FL, IL, NJ, NY, TN and WA.

Mobil Travel Guide

Southeast

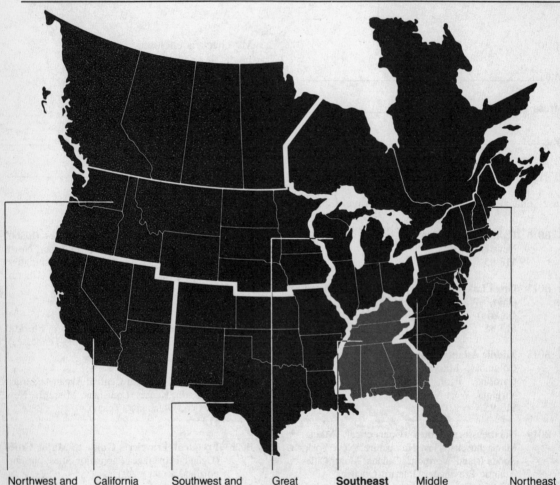

Northwest and Great Plains	California and the West	Southwest and South Central	Great Lakes	**Southeast**	Middle Atlantic	Northeast
Idaho	Arizona	Arkansas	Illinois	**Alabama**	Delaware	Connecticut
Iowa	California	Colorado	Indiana	**Florida**	District of Columbia	Maine
Minnesota	Nevada	Kansas	Michigan	**Georgia**	Maryland	Massachusetts
Montana	Utah	Louisiana	Ohio	**Kentucky**	New Jersey	New Hampshire
Nebraska		Missouri	Wisconsin	**Mississippi**	North Carolina	New York
North Dakota		New Mexico	Canada:	**Tennessee**	Pennsylvania	Rhode Island
Oregon		Oklahoma	Ontario		South Carolina	Vermont
South Dakota		Texas			Virginia	Canada:
Washington					West Virginia	Atlantic Provinces
Wyoming						Ontario
Canada:						Quebec
Alberta						
British Columbia						
Manitoba						

Mobil Travel Guide®

THE GUIDE THAT SAVES YOU MONEY WHEN YOU TRAVEL.

UP TO 10% OFF

5,000 Locations Worldwide. Computerized Driving Directions.

Receive 5% off leisure daily, weekly, weekend, and monthly rates. Compact and larger cars. -OR- Receive 10% off standard daily, weekly, weekend, and monthly rates. On all car classes.

Call **(800)** 654-220 for reservations.
Request CDP **ID# 289259** Taste Publications International.

OFFER EXPIRES DECEMBER 31, 1994

CHOICE HOTELS
INTERNATIONAL

10% OFF

The next time you're traveling, call 1-800-4-CHOICE and request, "The Mobil Travel Guide Discount." You'll save 10% at thousands of participating Choice Hotels around the world!

With your 10% Traveler's Discount, the Choices - and savings - are better. So, call **1-800-4-CHOICE** today!

Advance reservations are required through 1-800-4-CHOICE.
Discounts are based on availability at participating hotels and cannot be used in conjunction with any other discounts or promotions.

OFFER EXPIRES DECEMBER 31, 1994

THEATRE DISCOUNT

Please send _____ tickets at $4.00 each.
(Please add $1.00 to cover handling. Allow 2-3 weeks for delivery.)
Please fill out the form on the reverse side.

Tickets may not be used during the first two weeks of a first-run engagement or for "no-pass shows." Passes have expiration dates, generally one year from purchase.
Valid at all participating theatres. No refunds or exchanges.

OFFER EXPIRES DECEMBER 31, 1994

FREE FANNY PACK

Yours free when you join NPCA Now! Join NPCA and save our national treasures! We are offering a special one-year introductory membership for only $15! Enjoy the many benefits of an NPCA membership and receive: A free National Parks and Conservation Association Fanny Pack. A free PARK-PAK--Travel Information Kit. An annual subscription to the award-winning National Parks Magazine. Access to the NPCA "See the World, Save the Parks" rebate travel program, unforgettable naturalist-led tours, the NPCA discount photo service, car rental discounts and more.
SEE REVERSE FOR ORDER FORM.

OFFER EXPIRES DECEMBER 31, 1994

ONE HOUR MOTOPHOTO®

50% OFF

One Hour MotoPhoto invites you to enjoy 50% off processing and printing.

Valid at all participating locations nationally. Limit one roll per coupon, per family, per visit. Coupon must be presented at time of processing.
May not be used in conjunction with any other discount or special promotion.

OFFER EXPIRES DECEMBER 31, 1994

7007 Sea World Drive
Orlando, FL 32821 • (407) 351-3600

UP TO $15 OFF

Sea World of Florida invites you to enjoy $2.50 off per person. Experience a day of real life adventures at Sea World of Florida, the world's most popular marine life park.

Limit six guests per coupon. Not valid with other discounts or on purchase of multi-park/multi-visit passes or tickets. Present coupon before bill is totaled. Redeemable only on date of attendance. Coupon has no cash value.
Prices subject to change without notice.

OFFER EXPIRES DECEMBER 31, 1994 4242 / 4241

TRAVEL

5% OFF

Save at least 5% and sometimes as much as 40% off the lowest fare you can find to these destinations:
• California • Florida • New York • Europe
1-800-723-8889

SEE REVERSE FOR DETAILS.

OFFER EXPIRES DECEMBER 31, 1994

Sea World
of California   Sea World
of Texas

15% OFF

Sea World of California and Sea World of Texas invite you to enjoy 15% off admission.

Present this coupon at any Sea World ticket window. One coupon is good for your entire group (limit six). Not valid with any other discount, special event, special pricing, senior discount or 12- Month Pass purchase. Not for sale.
An Anheuser-Busch Theme Park. ©1993 Sea World, Inc.

CA
A-3718 C-3717   TX
A-22398 C-22399

OFFER EXPIRES DECEMBER 31, 1994

CHOICE HOTELS
I N T E R N A T I O N A L

Enjoy convenient, relaxing rooms at Sleep, Comfort, Quality, Clarion, Friendship, Econo Lodge and Rodeway hotels and much more! 1,400 Choice hotels will provide a free continental breakfast and children 18 and younger stay free when they share the same room as their parents.

TASTE PUBLICATIONS INTERNATIONAL

TASTE PUBLICATIONS INTERNATIONAL

❑ Yes! I want to preserve and protect our National Parks by becoming a National Parks and Conservation Association Member.
❑ I enclose a check for $15 for my one-year trial membership.
❑ Charge my $15 annual dues to my ❑ Visa ❑ MasterCard

Acct. #: _____ Exp. Date:_____

Signature: _____

Name: _____

Address: _____

City: _____ State: _____ Zip: _____

Phone: _____

Please allow 6-8 weeks for delivery of your first issue of National Parks Magazine.

TASTE PUBLICATIONS INTERNATIONAL   GA94

Make check payable to:
TASTE PUBLICATIONS INTERNATIONAL,
1031 Cromwell Bridge Road, Baltimore, MD 21286.
To process your order, a self-addressed, stamped envelope must be enclosed.

NAME _____

ADDRESS _____

CITY_____STATE_____ZIP_____

TASTE PUBLICATIONS INTERNATIONAL

Orlando, Florida

TASTE PUBLICATIONS INTERNATIONAL

TASTE PUBLICATIONS INTERNATIONAL

---

 of California   of Texas

Sea World of California, the world-renown marine life park, features sharks, penguins, sea lions, dolphins and of course, Shamu.
Pleae call (619) 226-3901 for operating times.

Sea World of Texas is the world's largest (250 acres) marine life park and family entertainment showplace. Don't miss the all new Lost Lagoon, our 5-acre water adventure area featuring surf, sand and sun.
Please call (210) 523-3000 for operating times.

TASTE PUBLICATIONS INTERNATIONAL

 TRAVEL

Just find the lowest available airlane rate for the dates and times you wish to travel, then call the travel hotline; you will be offered two options:
1. Option - will offer your exact same itinerary for 5% off the price.
2. Option - will offer you a travel alternative at a lower price.

TASTE PUBLICATIONS INTERNATIONAL

Mobil Travel Guide®
THE GUIDE THAT SAVES YOU MONEY WHEN YOU TRAVEL.

NATIONAL AMUSEMENTS

THEATRE DISCOUNT

Please send _____ tickets at $4.25 each.

(Please add $1.00 to cover handling. Allow 2-3 weeks for delivery.)

Please fill out the form on the reverse side.

Tickets may not be used during the first two weeks of a first-run engagement or for "no-pass shows." Passes have expiration dates, generally one year from purchase.
Valid at all participating theatres. No refunds or exchanges.

OFFER EXPIRES DECEMBER 31, 1994

GUEST QUARTERS® SUITE HOTELS
WEEKENDER CLUB

FREE WEEKEND NIGHT & DINING DISCOUNT

Join the Guest Quarters Weekender Club and get one free weekend night, plus a 33% dining discount.

And enjoy our special club low weekday and weekend rates.
Call **1-800-258-8826** to join.

OFFER EXPIRES DECEMBER 31, 1994

Denny's

1/2 PRICE ENTREE

Denny's invites you to enjoy any entree on our menu and get a second entree (same or lesser value) for half price.

One coupon per person per visit. No take-out orders. Not valid with any other offer or coupon. Only the lower priced entree will be discounted.

Denny's is committed to providing the best possible service to all customers regardless of race, creed or national origin.

OFFER EXPIRES DECEMBER 31, 1994

FREE CAMPING STAY

Rent a KOA Deal Motor Home from Cruise America and stay free at any participating KOA Kampground.

Call **800-327-7778** for reservations and request a KOA Deal Motor Home rental.

OFFER EXPIRES DECEMBER 31, 1994

$3 OFF

For information, call (818) 622-3794.
100 Universal City Plaza
Universal City, CA 91608

Universal Studios Hollywood invites you to enjoy $3 off the regular admission price per person. Valid for up to 4 people.

This coupon cannot be combined with any other offer or with per capita sight-seeing tours.
Not valid for separately ticketed events.

  01040 18341

 01040 18342

OFFER EXPIRES DECEMBER 31, 1994

National · **Inter rent**

5% - 25% OFF

Receive 5% off weekend, weekly and monthly rates.
or
Receive 25% off select daily business rates.
Call **1-800-CAR RENT**℠ for reservations.
Request Recap **#5708785** Taste Publications International.

Optional Loss Damage is $7.99-$13.99 per day depending on location and subject to change. Rates may include unlimited mileage or 100 miles per day with a per mile charge thereafter.

OFFER EXPIRES DECEMBER 31, 1994

CAMPING WORLD®
RV Accessories and Supplies

SPECIAL OFFER

To receive your free catalog and 10% off certificate, please fill out this form and mail to address on back or call **(800) 626-5944** and mention code number in lower right corner.

Name _____
Address _____ Apt./Lot_____
City_____ State____ Zip_____

OFFER EXPIRES DECEMBER 31, 1994 1006

TASTEE FREEZ

ONE FREE SMALL CONE

Tastee Freez invites you to enjoy one free small cone when a second small cone of equal or greater value is purchased.

Valid at all participating locations nationally.

OFFER EXPIRES DECEMBER 31, 1994

GUEST QUARTERS®
SUITE HOTELS

W

WEEKENDER CLUB®

TASTE PUBLICATIONS INTERNATIONAL

NATIONAL AMUSEMENTS

Make check payable to:
TASTE PUBLICATIONS INTERNATIONAL,
1031 Cromwell Bridge Road, Baltimore, MD 21286.
To process your order, a self-addressed, stamped envelope must be enclosed.

NAME _____

ADDRESS _____

CITY_____STATE_____ZIP_____

TASTE PUBLICATIONS INTERNATIONAL

KOA has over 600 locations
throughout the U.S. and Canada.

Cruise America and Cruise Canada
have over 100 centers.

TASTE PUBLICATIONS INTERNATIONAL

Denny's®

TASTE PUBLICATIONS INTERNATIONAL

 National

1. Valid at participating National locations in the U.S. Program not available on tour packages or certain other promotional rates. Subject to availability of cars and blackout dates. Time parameters, local rental and minimum rental day requirements may apply. Check at time of reservation. 2. Advance reservations are recommended. 3. Rates higher in some cities. 4. Standard rental qualifications apply. Minimum rental age at most locations is 25. 5. In addition to rental charges, renter is responsible for: • Optional Loss Damage Waiver is $7.99-$13.99 per day depending on location and subject to change; per mile charge in excess of mileage allowance. • Taxes; additional charges if car is not returned within prescribed rental period; drop charge and additional driver fee if applicable; optional refueling charge; Personal Accident Insurance/Personal Effects Coverage, Supplemental Liability Insurance (where available). 6. Program subject to change without notice and void where prohibited by law, taxed or otherwise restricted.

TASTE PUBLICATIONS INTERNATIONAL

UNIVERSAL STUDIOS

TASTE PUBLICATIONS INTERNATIONAL

TASTEE FREEZ.

TASTE PUBLICATIONS INTERNATIONAL

CAMPING WORLD®
RV Accessories and Supplies
Camping World
Three Springs Road
P.O. Box 90017
Bowling Green, KY 42102-9017

TASTE PUBLICATIONS INTERNATIONAL

Mobil Travel Guide.
THE GUIDE THAT SAVES YOU MONEY WHEN YOU TRAVEL.

  PREMIER'S BIG RED BOAT America's Travel Agent.

UP TO 25% OFF

The Official Cruise Line of Walt Disney World **and International Tours & Cruises™**

Premier and IT invite you to enjoy up to 25% off a cruise or cruise & Disney resort stay.

Discount is based on two people per cabin. Choose from 3, 4 or 7 day cruise/resort vacation. Offer is not available during holiday dates. Subject to availability. May not be used in conjunction with any other special promotion or discount. For reservations, call International Tours and Cruises at **(800) BUY-TRAVEL (USA)** or **(212) 242-2277 (NYC)**.

OFFER EXPIRES DECEMBER 31, 1994

 Sheraton

CORPORATE RATE

Receive the guaranteed corporate rate at all participating Sheraton Hotels.

Call **(800) 325-7823** for reservations. Request ID# 98251 Taste Publications International.

Please keep a record of your confirmation number.

OFFER EXPIRES DECEMBER 31, 1994

 **I Can't Believe It's Yogurt!** GREAT TASTE-NATURALLY!

ONE FREE REGULAR OR LARGE CUP OR CONE

I Can't Believe It's Yogurt invites you to enjoy one free regular or large cup or cone when a second regular or large cup or cone of equal or greater value is purchased.

Valid at all participating full-sized stores. One coupon per customer, please. May not be used in conjunction with any other offer. Offer good for soft serve frozen yogurt only.

OFFER EXPIRES DECEMBER 31, 1994

 Alamo Rent A Car

ASSOCIATION DISCOUNT

- Guaranteed Low Flat Rate
- Unlimited Free Mileage
- Frequent Flyer Credits with Delta, Pan Am and United Airlines

Call **(800) 732-3232** for reservations. Request ID# **BY 201598** Taste Publications International.

Advance reservations required.

OFFER EXPIRES DECEMBER 31, 1994

 **FOTOMAT**

50% OFF

Coupon valid at all Fotomat locations. Call **1-800-568-FOTO** for a Fotomat near you.

Fotomat invites you to enjoy 50% off any Fotomat film purchase at the regular price.

Present this coupon and receive 50% off your Fotomat film purchase. Valid on Fotomat film only. Not valid with any other coupon or promotional offer.

OFFER EXPIRES DECEMBER 31, 1994

 **QUINTEX CELLULAR**

MOTOROLA DPC 500 FLIP PHONE FOR $199 (Retail value is $349).

To receive your Motorola DPC 500 flip phone for $199 **Call 1-800-550-0600**
Customer will recieve an information kit and credit application. Follow the directions inside and mail completed forms in envelope provided. Offer available to new activations only. Credit approval required. Minimum one year service agreement with carrier of our choice. Customer is responsible for the activation fee and shipping and handling charges. Please allow 2-3 weeks for delivery. Other restrictions apply. Limit 2 phones per customer.

OFFER EXPIRES DECEMBER 31, 1994

 **GENERAL CINEMA THEATRES**

THEATRE DISCOUNT

Please send _____ tickets at $4.50 each.
(Please add $1.00 to cover handling. Allow 2-3 weeks for delivery.)
Please fill out the form on the reverse side.

Tickets may not be used during the first two weeks of a first-run engagement or for "no-pass shows." Passes have expiration dates, generally one year from purchase. Valid at all participating theatres. No refunds or exchanges.

OFFER EXPIRES DECEMBER 31, 1994

AMERICA at 50% Discount®

60 DAY FREE TRIAL OFFER

Enjoy 50% off at over 1,300 hotels and motels coast to coast, valid anytime. Plus 5% instant cash rebate on airline tickets, savings on car rentals, condominiums, cruises and more.

First 60 days are free, then $24.95 annually.

Satisfaction guaranteed or your current year's membership fee will be refunded in full

See reverse for order form.

OFFER EXPIRES DECEMBER 31, 1994

QUINTEX CELLULAR

Quintex Cellular, a national cellular network, wants you to remember us as the superstore in cellular with 72 locations nationwide.
So to get in touch stay in touch with Quintex.
Certificate is valid with phone order or in store purchase.
Cellular service may not be available in all areas.

AMERICA at 50% Discount®
1031 Cromwell Bridge Road, Baltimore, MD 21286.

Yes, I want to start saving now with America at 50% Discount® I understand that if I do not cancel before the end of the sixty (60) day introductory period, the $24.95 annual fee will be charged to the credit card indicated below. To ensure uninterrupted service, my membership will automatically be renewed annually charged to my credit card indicated below. I understand that I am under no obligation to continue my membership beyond the sixty day trial.

Form of payment ☐ VISA ☐ MasterCard

Acct. #:_____ Exp. Date:_____
Signature:_____
Name:_____
Address:_____
City:_____ State:_____ Zip:_____

GENERAL CINEMA THEATRES

Make check payable to:
TASTE PUBLICATIONS INTERNATIONAL,
1031 Cromwell Bridge Road, Baltimore, MD 21286.
To process your order, a self-addressed, stamped envelope must be enclosed.

NAME _____

ADDRESS _____

CITY_____STATE_____ZIP_____

Mobil Travel Guide.

THE GUIDE THAT SAVES YOU MONEY WHEN YOU TRAVEL.

 TWO FREE SHOW TICKETS

Harrah's invites you to enjoy two free show tickets at Harrah's Atlantic City, Lake Tahoe, Las Vegas or Reno locations.

For show schedule and reservations call
1-800-HARRAHS (1-800-427-7247).

Coupon redeemable Sunday thru Friday.

OFFER EXPIRES DECEMBER 31, 1994   MBL

 **CORPORATE RATE**

Receive the guaranteed corporate rate at all participating Days Inns, Hotels and Suites.
Call **(800) 422-1115** for reservations.
Request ID# **990-000-2865** Taste Publications International.

Please keep a record of your confirmation number.

OFFER EXPIRES DECEMBER 31, 1994

AVIS. **ASSOCIATION DISCOUNT**

• Full Line of Fine GM Cars
• Over 3,500 Locations
• Emergency Road Service
Call **(800) 331-1212** for reservations.
Request AWD # **A291800** Taste Publications International.
Advance reservations required.

OFFER EXPIRES DECEMBER 31, 1994

 50% OFF

Sbarro invites you to enjoy 50% off one entree when a second entree of equal or greater value is purchased.

Valid at any of the 600 Sbarro locations nationwide.
This coupon may not be used in conjunction
with any other discounts or promotions.

OFFER EXPIRES DECEMBER 31, 1994

ORVIS® **15% OFF**

Orvis invites you to enjoy 15% off your first order.
Call for free catalog...**1-800-815-5900**.
Ask for Key Offer **#TR101**.

Orvis Travel offers you the finest in accessories, apparel and distinctive luggage for today's active travel lifestyle, whether by car, plane or train. Travel in comfort and style with Orvis.

Orvis...America's Oldest Mail Order Catalog...A New England Tradition Since 1856.

OFFER EXPIRES DECEMBER 31, 1994

 **TRAVEL** **20-60% OFF**

Save up to 60% on 5-7 day Regency Cruises* to the Caribbean, Panama Canal, Can Cun or 2 day cruises to nowhere.

Call 1-800-925-1114.

*Selected sailing dates.

OFFER EXPIRES DECEMBER 31, 1994

---

merry maids. **$10 OFF**

Drop your mop! Enjoy a clean home and save $10 on your first Merry Maids visit. Bonded, trained and insured. Weekly, bi-weekly or one-time services. Satisfaction guaranteed. To arrange for a free written quote, check the Yellow Pages, or call **1-800-WE SERVE** for the Merry Maids nearest you.

Available only at participating offices. New customers only. This coupon may not be used in conjunction with any other discounts or promotions.

 Quality Service Network
ServiceMaster • Terminix • TruGreen
Merry Maids • American Home Shield

OFFER EXPIRES DECEMBER 31, 1994

 UP TO $20 IN FREE CALLING CARD CALLS

When you sign up for the MCI Card®, you'll automatically receive up to $20 in free calling card calls! Just call **1-800-944-9119**. Remember, you don't need to switch your residential long distance service to take advantage of the free MCI Card!

You will receive a credit for up to $20 on your third monthly invoice.
Credit will not exceed invoice usage.

OFFER EXPIRES DECEMBER 31, 1994

DAYS INN

TASTE PUBLICATIONS INTERNATIONAL

Terms and conditions:
- Subject to availability; headliner shows excluded.
- Reservations must be made in advance (except in Las Vegas).
- Offer is valid through December 31, 1994; some dates may be unavailable.
- Must be 21; one coupon per person.
- Offer is not valid with any other promotion.
- Program subject to change or cancellation without notice.
- The following information must be completed prior to redemption.

Harrah's
CASINOS

Name_____

Street Address_____

City_____State_____Zip_____

Date of Birth_____   Gambling Problem? Call 1-800-GAMBLER.

TASTE PUBLICATIONS INTERNATIONAL

MBL

TASTE PUBLICATIONS INTERNATIONAL

AVIS

TASTE PUBLICATIONS INTERNATIONAL

TASTE PUBLICATIONS INTERNATIONAL

ORVIS

Save 15% on your first order.
Choose from any item in our award-winning travel catalog, including:
- Distinctive Sportsman's Luggage
- Travel Accessories and Gadgets
- Classic Clothing Designed Just for the Traveler

Call for your free catalog today: **1-800-815-5900.**
Ask for key offer **#TR101.**
Orvis...Serving America Since 1856

TASTE PUBLICATIONS INTERNATIONAL

MCI

THE MCI CARD IS SIMPLE TO USE.
Unlike AT&T's standard interstate Calling Card, you follow the same simple dialing method to use the MCI Card® from any phone in the U.S., anytime. Easy-to-follow voice instructions then guide you through each step of your call. And your MCI Card lets you make multiple calls without hanging up and redialing.

AND THE MCI CARD NUMBER IS EASIER TO REMEMBER.
Your MCI Card number will most likely be your own home phone number plus a 4-digit number selected by you. That's a lot easier to remember than the scrambled 14-digit authorization numbers AT&T assigns you!

TASTE PUBLICATIONS INTERNATIONAL

---

merry maids

TASTE PUBLICATIONS INTERNATIONAL